Toxicology Principles for the Industrial Hygienist

Edited By
William E. Luttrell, PhD, CIH
Warren W. Jederberg, MS, CIH, RPIH
Kenneth R. Still, PhD, FATS, CIH, CSP, CHMM

Disclaimer

The American Industrial Hygiene Association (AIHA), as publisher, and the authors have been diligent in ensuring that the material and methods addressed in this book reflect prevailing toxicology, and occupational health and safety and industrial hygiene practices. It is possible, however, that certain procedures discussed will require modification because of changing federal, state, and local regulations, or heretofore unknown developments in research.

AIHA and the editors and authors disclaim any liability, loss, or risk resulting directly or indirectly from the use of the practices and/or theories discussed in this book. Moreover, it is the reader's responsibility to stay informed of any changing federal, state, or local regulations that might affect the material contained herein, and the policies adopted specifically in the reader's workplace.

Specific mention of manufacturers and products in this book does not represent an endorsement by AIHA.

Copyright 2008 by the American Industrial Hygiene Association. All rights reserved. No part of this publication may be reproduced in any form, by Photostat, microfilm, retrieval system, or any other means, without prior permission of the publisher.

Stock Number: BTOR08-738
ISBN: 978-1-931504-88-1

American Industrial Hygiene Association
2700 Prosperity Avenue, Suite 250
Fairfax, VA 22031
Tel: (703) 849-8888
E-mail: Infonet@aiha.org
www.aiha.org

Printed in the United States of America

Table of Contents

About the Editors v

Preface vii

List of Reviewers ix

Section 1: Understanding Toxicology

Chapter 1 — The Role of Toxicology in Industrial Hygiene 1
    By Kenneth R. Still, Warren W. Jederberg, and William E. Luttrell
Chapter 2 — Principles of Toxicology 7
    By Randal J. Keller
Chapter 3 — Mechanisms of Toxicity 14
    By William E. Luttrell
Chapter 4 — Disposition of Toxicants 22
    By Susan Shelnutt

Section 2: Sites of Action of Chemicals Found in the Workplace

Chapter 5 — Respiratory Toxicology 38
    By James G. Wagner and Melissa L. Millerick-May
Chapter 6 — Dermal Toxicology 51
    By Warren W. Jederberg
Chapter 7 — Systemic Effects: Cardiovascular and Renal Toxicity 58
    By Lutz W.D. Weber, Janet D. Pierce, and J. Thomas Pierce
Chapter 8 — Toxicology of Sensory Organs 70
    By Lutz W.D. Weber and J. Thomas Pierce
Chapter 9 — Neurotoxicology 82
    By William E. Luttrell
Chapter 10 — Hepatic Toxicology 97
    By Angela J. Harris
Chapter 11 — Reproductive and Developmental Toxicology 114
    By David R. Mattie
Chapter 12 — Immunotoxicology 127
    By Michael G. Holland
Chapter 13 — Genetic Toxicology 138
    By Tao Chen, Robert H. Heflich, Martha M. Moore, and Angela J. Harris
Chapter 14 — Carcinogenesis 155
    By Cody L. Wilson and Karen C. Wilson
Chapter 15 — Teratogenesis 176
    By Cody L. Wilson

Section 3: Chemical Group Toxicology

Chapter 16 — Toxicology of Organic Solvents 186
    By Philip A. Smith
Chapter 17 — Toxicology of Metals 209
    By Gary L. Hook, Peter T. Lapuma, and Gary A. Morris
Chapter 18 — Toxicology of Pesticides 222
    By William E. Luttrell

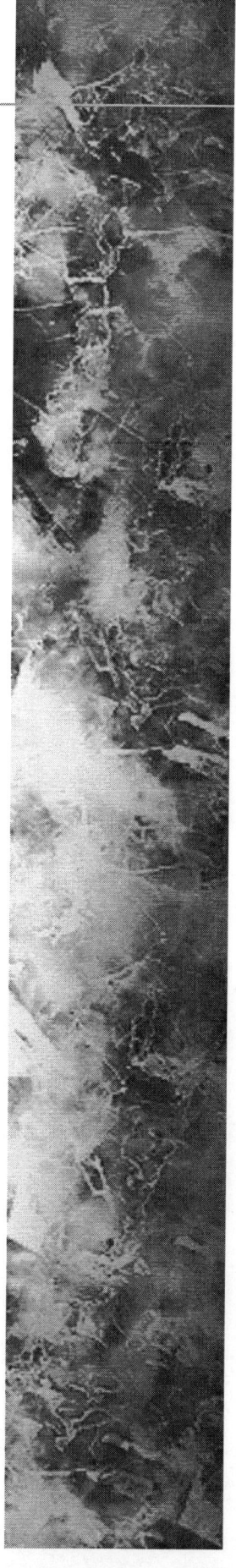

Chapter 19 — Toxicology of Particulate Matter 240
    By William K. Alexander and Kenneth R. Still
Chapter 20 — Toxicology of Gases 254
    By Scott D. Dwyer
Chapter 21 — Toxicology of Radioactive Materials 266
    By William J. Adams, Jr.
Chapter 22 — Toxicology of Complex Chemical Mixtures 275
    By Jonathan Borak, Cheryl A. Fields, and Greg Sirianni

Section 4: Application of Toxicological Information

Chapter 23 — Exposure Assessment 285
    By Coreen A. Robbins, Lonie Swenson, and Susan Arnold
Chapter 24 — Risk Assessment Process for Industrial Hygienists 301
    By Kenneth R. Still and Warren W. Jederberg
Chapter 25 — Military Toxicology for Industrial Hygienists in an Operational Context 308
    By Michael E. Ottlinger, John Cardarelli, and Dino Mattorano
Chapter 26 — Toxicology of Chemical Warfare Agents 317
    By Warren W. Jederberg and Kenneth R. Still
Chapter 27 — Toxicology in Emergency Response Planning 329
    By Warren W. Jederberg
Chapter 28 — Derivation of Occupational Exposure Limits 339
    By Kenneth R. Still, Warren W. Jederberg, and William E. Luttrell
Chapter 29 — Biomonitoring 352
    By Ayodele O. Olabisi, Dean J. Wagner, Gail D. Chapman, Michael Stockelman,
    Timothy Naylor, Erin Wilfong, Nancy Loy, and Bradley B. Phillips
Chapter 30 — Industrial Chemical Hazard Communication 363
    By Warren W. Jederberg
Chapter 31 — Evaluation of Industrial/Commercial Materials 367
    By J. Thomas Pierce, Lutz W.D. Weber, and Jerry Formisano

Section 5: Sources of Toxicological Information

Chapter 32 — Toxicology Test Data 380
    By Brad T. Garber and William E. Luttrell
Chapter 33 — Regulations, Standards, and Guidelines 387
    By Jeffrey A. Church
Chapter 34 — Sources of Chemical Hazard Information 395
    By Warren W. Jederberg
Chapter 35 — Professional Organizations and Publications 399
    By Glenn J. Leach
Chapter 36 — Websites and Electronic Databases 403
    By Amy C. Moscatelli

Glossary 409

Index 425

About the Editors

William E. Luttrell, PhD, CIH

Bill Luttrell is currently an Associate Professor of Chemistry, teaching organic chemistry at Oklahoma Christian University and sponsoring research opportunities in toxicology for undergraduate students. He received his undergraduate training in chemistry at the University of Louisville in Kentucky, and his graduate training in chemistry and toxicology at Old Dominion University and Eastern Virginia Medical School in Norfolk, Virginia. He served on active duty in the U.S. Navy Medical Service Corps as an Industrial Hygiene and Toxicology Officer for twenty years, and then as a civilian toxicologist at the Navy Environmental Health Center for five years. Dr. Luttrell was a member of the faculty of Old Dominion University in the Environmental Health Program for seven years, teaching industrial hygiene and toxicology. He is a full member of the American Industrial Hygiene Association, American Conference of Governmental Industrial Hygienists, Society of Toxicology, and the American Chemical Society. He is a Diplomat of the American Academy of Industrial Hygiene with Certification in Comprehensive Practice. His research interests are primarily in the effects of environmental and workplace exposures to chemical toxins on drug metabolizing enzyme systems. He has published one other book and over fifty research and technical papers, chapters, short articles, and book reviews.

Warren W. Jederberg, MS, CIH, RPIH

Warren W. Jederberg is currently employed as a Senior Analyst for BAI Inc., in Alexandria VA. He earned a Bachelor of Science Degree in Biology from Eastern Oregon College. In 1976, he was awarded a Master of Science Degree in Microbiology from Brigham Young University. From 1974 to 1979, he worked as a Senior Research Specialist for the Department of Dermatology, University of Utah where he conducted and published research relating to the cell-mediated immunity of patients with psoriasis. In 1987, he was awarded a second Master of Science degree in Pharmacology by the University of Utah. During his 28 years as a Medical Service Corps Officer (20 in the Navy and 8 in the Army), Warren filled a wide range of technical, regulatory compliance, and leadership positions in such diverse areas as toxicology research, anti-terrorism & force protections, occupational safety and health, and teaching. In 1997, he became a Diplomat of the American Academy of Industrial Hygiene with Certification in the Comprehensive Practice of Industrial Hygiene. He has served on the AIHA Toxicology and the National Academy of Sciences (NAS) Acute Exposure Guideline Level (AEGL) Committees. He is the author/coauthor of eighteen book chapters, thirty-six peer reviewed articles in professional journals, numerous abstracts and seventeen governmental technical reports.

Kenneth R. Still, PhD, MBA, FATS, CIH, CSP, CHMM, CEA, CHS-III, REM, REPA, REP, Fellow American Industrial Hygiene Association

Kenneth R. Still is Director of Occupational Toxicology Associates, Inc. (OTA, Inc), a private consulting company. Dr. Still received his graduate training at Portland State University and Oklahoma State University in Biology with subsequent training at Johns Hopkins, Harvard, MIT, and University of Cincinnati. Dr. Still served in the U.S. Navy Medical Service Corps as an Industrial Hygiene and Toxicology Officer for 28 years where he held several senior level positions, including Command of the Navy's only toxicology research laboratory for eight years and was Senior Director of Occupational Health and Safety for the Navy's Pacific Fleet. Dr. Still also held leadership positions involving CBRNE, regulatory

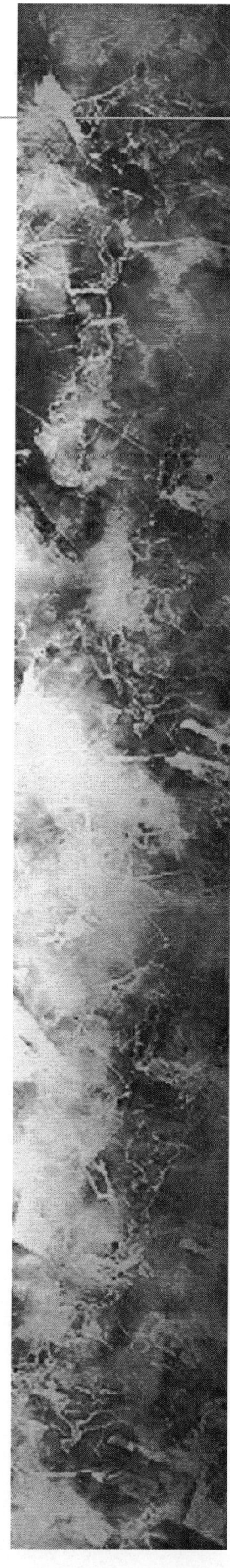

development and maintenance, vulnerability assessment, Occupational Health Program Oversight, and conceptualized, taught, and published the Navy's Workplace Monitor Training Program which is still in use some 25 years after its Navy-wide implementation. Dr. Still has held adjunct Associate Professorships at medical schools including Eastern Virginia Medical, Uniform Services University of Health Sciences, Wright State Medical and the University of Hawaii Medical and has taught graduate/undergraduate courses at Wright State University. Dr. Still has served on numerous national, international and professional committees including the National Academy of Sciences Committee on Toxicology and Institute of Medicine, and the Environmental Protection Agency's Acute Exposure Guidelines. Dr. Still holds full membership in numerous professional societies including AIHA, ACGIH, SOT, ACT, ASSE, ACHMM and NREP. He has published two books and has over 260 research and technical papers, book chapters, and abstracts.

Preface

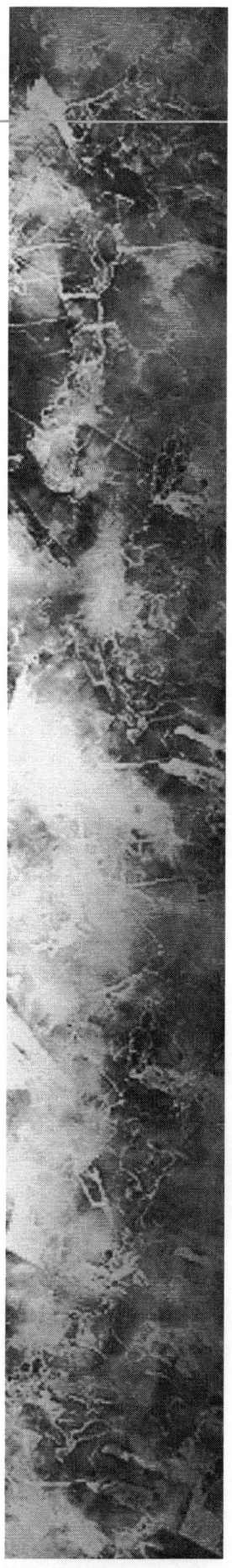

Toxicology Principles for the Industrial Hygienist comes out of our experiences in teaching industrial hygienists and students at all levels about the science of toxicology. Our intent has been for each chapter of this book to cover information that we would want to impart to a practicing industrial hygienist during a one hour conversation. It includes information that is primarily practical, but it also includes basic toxicological knowledge every industrial hygienist should know, especially in preparation for the American Board of Industrial Hygiene (ABIH) Certified Industrial Hygienist (CIH) examination. The information is presented in such a way that it can also be understood by a student of industrial hygiene who has not yet gained workplace experience. We have attempted to focus on the applications of toxicology principles to the practice of industrial hygiene. Whenever possible, case studies have been included, allowing purely theoretical knowledge to be brought into the practical realm. Examples of applications of toxicological principles to the practice of industrial hygiene in real situations are frequent and distinguish this book from other toxicology books.

Certainly, the expertise of the industrial hygienist is in the workplace. However, there are non-workplace environments where toxins originating in the workplace require the attention of the industrial hygienist. Therefore, the expertise of the industrial hygienist is often extended into non-workplace environments; although the focus of this book is on toxins found in workplace environments. This book in intended as an introductory text for industrial hygienists and students of industrial hygiene who require a brief, yet comprehensive coverage of toxicology principles which apply to toxicants of occupational and environmental concerns. It is assumed that users of this book have a basic understanding of chemistry and biology, as well as the fundamentals of human anatomy, physiology, and biochemistry. Therefore, these basic sciences are not covered in great detail, but are often summarized in each chapter.

This book is organized into five sections. The first section describes fundamental information for understanding toxicology. It includes the principles of toxicology that are most frequently needed to fully understand toxicological events, such as the dose-response relationship, mechanisms of toxicology, and the disposition of toxicants. The primary focus of the second section is on the sites of action of chemicals commonly found in the workplace. These sites include: respiratory, dermal, systemic, sensory, neurological, hepatic, reproductive and developmental, immunological, and genetic, including carcinogenesis and teratogenesis. The third section deals with traditional chemical group toxicology, covering organic solvents, metals, pesticides, particulate matter, gases, radioactive materials, and complex chemical mixtures. The fourth section contains the most contemporary information available for applications of toxicological information including: exposure assessment, risk assessment, military toxicology in an operational context, chemical warfare agents, emergency response planning, derivation of occupational exposure limits, biomonitoring, industrial chemical hazard communication, and the evaluation of industrial/commercial materials. The fifth and final section describes sources of toxicological information: toxicology test data; regulations, standards, and guidelines; chemical hazard information, professional organizations and publications, as well as websites and electronic databases. In summary, the contents of this book represent a broad coverage of toxicology as it relates to a growing and changing industrial hygiene profession.

We are indebted to over forty authors who are experts in their respective fields, having expertise most often in both toxicology and industrial hygiene, coming from diverse organizations, including military and federal services (U.S. Navy, U.S. Air Force, U.S. Army, and U.S. Coast Guard). The over fifty technical reviewers made each chapter better and more useful by their recommendations, coming from the AIHA Toxicology Committee and other technical committees of the AIHA, as well as the Occupational and Public Health Specialty Section of the Society of

Toxicology. It was a pleasure working with the AIHA headquarters staff, in particular Katharine Robert, for her professional shepherding of this project. We appreciate AIHA's patience as this project took nearly five years to complete.

Although we have worked very hard to make this book error free, we know that there will be errors of commission and omission, which are our fault and not the authors or reviewers or the AIHA staff. So, as you may read this book and find errors as well as information that you disagree with, we ask that you let us know. We hope to have the opportunity to improve upon this book in the future with your comments and suggestions.

William E. Luttrell, PhD, CIH
Warren W. Jederberg, MS, CIH, RPIH
Kenneth R. Still, PhD, FATS, CIH, CSP, CHMM

March 2008

List of Reviewers

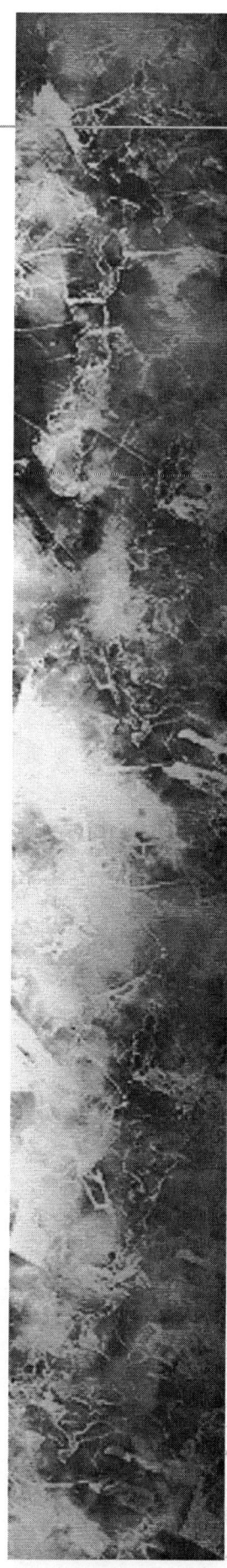

A
Felix Ayala-Fierro, PhD, DABT

B
Anne Baptiste, JD, CIH
Patricia Beattie, PhD, DABT
Linda S. Birnbaum, PhD, DABT
Edward C. Bishop, PhD, PE, CIH
Lee M. Blum, PhD, DABFT
Mark F. Boeniger, CIH
Gregory Bronder, CIH
Thomas Brundshilde, MS

C
Vincet Castranova, PhD

D
David Dahlstrom, CIH
D. Gayle DeBord, PhD
G. Scott Dotson, PhD

E
Karl V. Ebner, PhD, DABT

F
Marvin Faber, PhD, CRSP
Jacqueline A. Fox, MS, DABT

H
Susan D. Harms, PhD, CIH, CSP
Veronique Hauschild
Andrew A. Havics, CHMM, CIH, PE

I
Samuel D. Allen Iske Jr. PhD, CIH, CSP

J
Thomas E. Johnson, PhD, CHP, CLSO, NRRPT

K
Mukund Karanjikar, PhD
Randal Keller, PhD, CIH, CSP, DABT
Carole Kimmel, PhD
Chrysoula Komis, PhD, CIH, CSP, RBP
Marshall Krotenberg, CIH, CSP

L
Rodney R. Larson, PhD, CIH
James LeTexier, M.S.
Thomas A. Lewandowski, PhD, DABT, ERT

M
Silvia Maberti, PhD
Howard Marks, PhD, J.D., MPH.
Melissa McDiarmid, MD, MPH, DABT
Martha Moore, PhD
Michael Moore, PhD
Anuradha Mudipalli, PhD

N
Paul Nony, PhD
Alan F. Nordholm, PhD

P
Douglas Parrish, PhD, CIH, CSP, REH
Mark Pershouse, PhD
Angel L. Plaza, MS
Mark Powley, PhD

R
Trina Y. Redford
Reginald J. Richards, CIH

S
Edward Sargent, MPH, PhD, DABT
Leon Saryan, PhD
Anthony Schatz, PhD, DABT
Allen Silverstone, PhD
Jane Ellen Simmons, PhD, DABT
Raymond Singer, PhD, ABPN
Lakshmi P. Singh
Robert Skoglund, PhD, DABT, CIH
Laurence Smith, MS, CIH, CSP
Bruce Stuart, PhD, ATS

V
Susan M. Viet, PhD, CIH
Leo Vortuni, CIH, CSP, PE

W
R. Dean Wingo, MES, CIH, CSP

Z
John N. Zey, CIH
Michael Ziskin, CHCM, CHMM

Section 1

Understanding Toxicology

Chapter 1

The Role of Toxicology in Industrial Hygiene

*By Kenneth R. Still, PhD, FATS, CIH, CSP, CHMM,
Warren W. Jederberg, MS, CIH, RPIH, and William E. Luttrell, PhD, CIH*

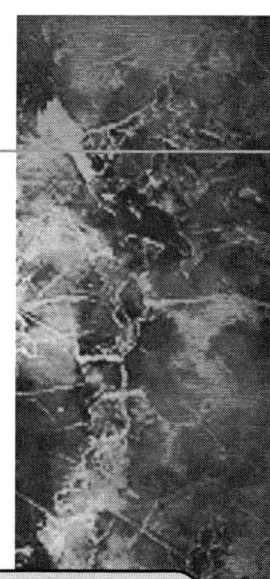

Introduction

In order for the practitioner of industrial hygiene to fulfill the responsibility to "anticipate, recognize, evaluate and control"[1,2] potential exposures to harmful materials, they must be able to apply the principles, methodologies and data from many disciplines within the biological, physical and social sciences. Among the chief disciplines that contribute to the information used to address the full-spectrum of potential impacts on worker health is the discipline of toxicology. Indeed, a brief review of the history of toxicology and industrial hygiene/occupational health reveals that they developed together and are intertwined. It could be said that their futures will continue to be interdependent as many of the incentives for new directions in toxicology research are spawned as a consequence of the addition of new materials and methods in commerce and the workplace. Also, it is now recognized that exposures outside of the workplace (ingestion of contaminants in foods, chemical use in hobbies, environmental contamination) can have a profound impact on worker health and susceptibility to further adverse outcomes.

Toxicology dates to early mankind who used natural products from animals and plants to sustain their existence. These natural products remain in existence today, from animal venoms to plant compounds. The science of toxicology has changed dramatically since the discipline was formally described by Paracelsus (1493–1541). Paracelsus conceived of a key principle of the science of toxicology: "All substances are poisons; there is none which is not a poison. The right dose differentiates a poison from a remedy."[3,4] Whether this axiom is applied in basic acute lethality studies, or is extended to the applied science of chemical risk assessment, Paracelsus' maxim forms a bulwark for all aspects of toxicology. A Renaissance man, Paracelsus formulated other views that remain an integral component of modern toxicology. He promoted the idea that experimentation is essential in understanding the effects of exposure to chemicals and emphasized the distinction between therapeutic and toxic properties of chemicals.

The use of animal models in toxicity testing is still the method of choice for assessing the hazards associated with exposure to

Outcome Competencies

Upon completion of this chapter, the reader should be able to:
- Describe the use of toxicology principles in the practice of industrial hygiene.
- Define toxicology and describe the different types of toxicologists.
- Discuss terminology associated with toxicology.
- Discuss the types of toxicants.
- Be familiar with specifics to consider when studying toxic chemicals.
- Be conversant with terminology associated with toxicity studies.
- Understand the limits to interpreting toxicologic test data.

Prerequisite Knowledge

Basic knowledge of the history and current practice of industrial hygiene

Key Terms

Acute toxicity, chronic toxicity, dose, exposure, hazard, LC_{50}, LD_{50}, LOEL, LOAEL, NOAEL, NOEL, subchronic toxicity, systemic toxicity

Key Topics

1. Routes of Entry
2. Absorption, Distribution, Metabolism, and Excretion (ADME)
3. Types of Toxicology
4. Types of Toxicants
5. Occupational Exposure Limits
6. Human Health and Environmental Risk Assessments
7. Uses of Toxicology Principles
8. Types of Toxicological Tests
9. Uses of Interpretation of Toxicological Data
10. Providing Impetus for Research

chemical compounds. A broad scope of approaches to toxicity testing provides data ranging from acute lethality to organ-specific toxicity to carcinogenicity. Although the use of animal models dominates many toxicology studies, many in vitro alternatives to animal use have been developed over the past two decades. Despite the advent of alternatives, many regulatory agencies still require the use of at least one animal model in safety evaluation studies of chemicals intended for human use.[5] An in-depth historical account of the entire evolution of toxicology can be found in Casarett & Doull's *Toxicology — The Basic Science of Poisons*, 6th edition.[4]

The use and study of poisons for a variety of purposes, has been undertaken since the earliest times. Indigenous peoples have and continue to use naturally occurring toxins to obtain food, in religious rites and against enemies.[4,6–8] Naturally occurring toxins have been implicated in incidents that have affected communities and nations.[4,6–8]

The popular definition of toxicology is "the study of poisons." However, the scientific definition is much more descriptive: toxicology is the study of adverse effects of agents on living organisms and a toxicologist studies the nature of those effects and the probability of their occurrence. The study of toxicology falls into primarily three categories: mechanistic, descriptive and regulatory. When military service is included, a fourth category can possibly be added, that of deployment toxicology. Mechanistic toxicology concerns itself with the identification and characterization of cellular, biochemical, and molecular mechanisms that are utilized by chemicals to exert toxic effects on living organisms. Descriptive toxicology addresses primarily toxicity testing, while regulatory toxicology addresses those areas for decision making that become law or impinge on the safety of humans via the environment or both consumable and non-consumable products. Deployment toxicology, which might be more accurately termed "Deployment Environmental Health", involves both material solutions (hardware/software/information) and the science base to protect U.S. armed forces against threats or vulnerabilities caused by environmental contaminants, as co-ordinated with the Nuclear, Biological and Chemical (NBC) community.[9,10] These primary categories can be further broken down into sub-categories based upon specificity, including environmental, forensic, clinical and ecotoxicology specialties.

Exposure to chemicals is of major concern. The route and site of exposure as well as the duration and frequency of the exposure must be elicited. Routes of entry include primarily pulmonary, dermal, and the gastrointestinal systems. Another route of entry can include injection. As a result of exposure to a chemical, absorption, distribution, metabolism and excretion (ADME) can occur, as exemplified by Figure 1.1.

Toxicants can be classified by system interaction. The most common classifications are:

- *Hepatotoxicants* — cause damage to the liver (Acetaminophen, ethyl alcohol)
- *Nephrotoxicants* — damage to kidneys (Cadmium, Mercury)
- *Neurotoxicants* — damage to the nervous system (Lead)

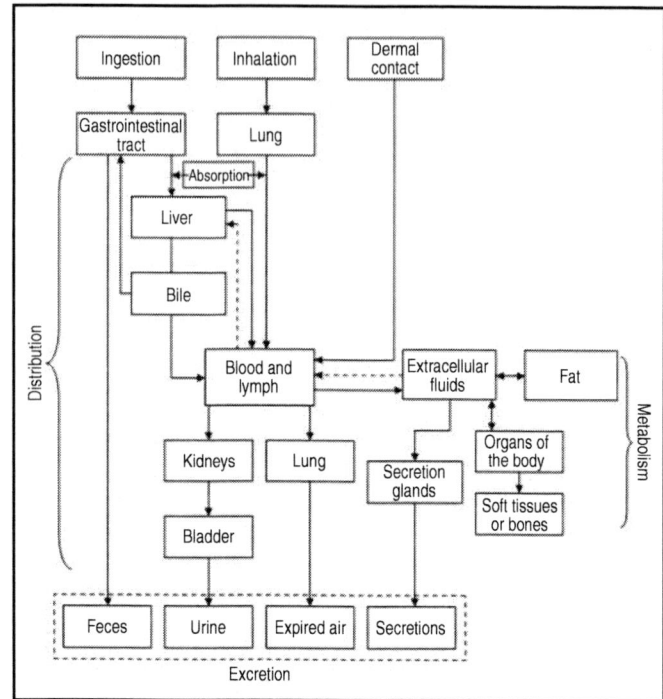

Figure 1.1 — Routes and modes of entry. (Source: C.D. Klaassen, *Cassarett and Doull's Toxicology*, 6th edition (New York: McGraw-Hill, 2001); reprinted with permission).

- *Immunotoxicants* — damage to the immune system (Toluene)
- *Hematoxicants* — damage to the circulatory system (Benzene)
- *Dermatoxicants* — damage to the skin (Magnesium Chromate)
- *Pulmonotoxicants* — damage to the lungs (Asbestos)
- *Carcinogens* — agents that increase cancer risk (Hexavalent chromium)

The "toxicity" of a material is its inherent ability to cause damage to living organisms or tissues. The "hazard" of a material takes into account the probability of biologic organisms being exposed to the toxic material. Terms such as "highly toxic", "moderately toxic", and "nontoxic" are of little value to the worker unless used in relation to common experience. Chapter 24, "Risk Assessment Process for Industrial Hygienists" presents Table 24.1 addressing a common scheme for classification of materials as related to their oral toxicity in humans where the LD_{50} is the concentration of the test material at which 50% of the exposed organisms died. Caution must be exercised in the interpretation of data such as those presented in Table 24.1. Though a compound may be "highly toxic," it may not present a significant hazard, if the probability of exposure is remote. In contrast, material of low toxicity may present a significant hazard under the proper exposure conditions. For example, a small amount of water in the lung can cause severe problems.

Some examples of materials in these toxicity categories are given in Table 1.1.

Table 1.1 — Some Representative Chemical Agents with Various Toxicities[5, modified]

Agent	LD_{50} (mg/kg in Test Animals)	Toxicity Rating
Ethyl alcohol	10,000	Slightly Toxic
Sodium chloride (Table Salt)	4,000	Moderately Toxic
Ferrous sulfate (Iron Tablets)	1,500	Moderately Toxic
Morphine sulfate	900	Moderately Toxic
Phenobarbital sodium	150	Very Toxic
Picrotoxin	5	Extremely Toxic
Strychnine sulfate	2	Supertoxic
Nicotine	1	Supertoxic
Tetrodotoxin	0.1	Supertoxic
Dioxin	0.001	Supertoxic
Botulinum	0.00001	Supertoxic

Toxicity information provided on the Material Safety Data Sheet (MSDS), or other source, should include the test species and conditions under which the data were collected. For example, using the DoD's Hazardous Materials Information System (HMIS)[7], the definition of "Highly Toxic" is:

(1) A chemical that has a median lethal dose (LD_{50}) of 50 milligrams or less per kilogram of body weight when administered orally to albino rats weighing between 200 and 300 grams.

(2) A chemical that has a median lethal dose (LD_{50}) of 200 milligrams or less per kilogram of body weight when administered by continuous contact for 24 hours (or less, if death occurs within 24 hours) with the bare skin of albino rabbits weighing between 2 and 3 kilograms each.

(3) A chemical that has a median lethal concentration (LC_{50}) of gas or vapor in air of 200 parts per million (ppm) or less by volume, or 2 milligrams per liter or less of mist, fume, or dust, when administered by continuous inhalation for 1 hour (or less, if death occurs within 1 hour) to albino rats weighing between 200 and 300 grams each, provided such concentration or condition, or both, are likely to be encountered by man when the chemical is used in any reasonably foreseeable manner.

(4) A chemical that is a liquid having a saturated vapor concentration (ppm) at 68.5°F (20.5°C) equal to or greater than ten times its LC_{50} (ppm), if the LC_{50} value is 1000 ppm or less when administered by continuous inhalation for 1 hour to albino rats weighing between 200 and 300 grams each, provided such concentration, or condition, or both, are likely to be encountered by man when the chemical is used in any reasonably foreseeable manner.

The first three definitions are also used by OSHA (29 CFR 1910.1200, appendix A) to define a "toxic chemical."

The term "hazardous" is used by federal and state agencies to describe substances that are subject to laws and regulations. The Occupational Safety and Health Administration (OSHA) defines a "hazardous chemical" as any chemical which is a physical hazard or a health hazard according to the OSHA Hazard Communications Standard criteria. The Department of Transportation (DOT) describes a "hazardous material" as a substance or material which has been determined by the Secretary of Transportation to be capable of posing an unreasonable risk to health, safety, and property when transported in commerce, and which is so designated. Under DOT a material, including its mixtures and solutions, that (1) is listed in the Appendix to the DOT hazardous materials table; (2) is in a quantity, in one package, which equals or exceeds the reportable quantity (RQ) listed in the appendix to the hazardous materials table; and (3) when in mixture or solution, in a concentration by weight which equals or exceeds the concentration corresponding to the RQ of the material, is hazardous.

Other terms which are used in common sources relate to the cancer causing potential of a material. The American Conference of Governmental Industrial Hygienists (ACGIH) provides definitions of terms in its publication entitled "Threshold Limit Values (TLVs®)[11] and Biological Exposure Indices (BEIs®)."[11] A chemical is listed as a "Confirmed Human Carcinogen" when there is "weight of evidence from epidemiologic studies of, or convincing clinical evidence in, exposed humans." The designation of "Suspected Human Carcinogen" is applied when "the agent is carcinogenic in experimental animals at dose levels, by route(s) of administration, at site(s), of histologic type(s), or by mechanism(s) that are considered relevant to worker exposure. Available epidemiologic studies are conflicting or insufficient to confirm an increased risk of cancer in exposed humans." The term "Animal Carcinogen" is applied when animal studies at high doses resulted in cancers; available epidemiologic data do not reveal increased cancers among exposed individuals; and available evidence suggests that cancer probably will not occur in humans except under "uncommon or unlikely routes of exposure." "Not Classifiable as a Human Carcinogen" means that for a particular agent there is insufficient data to adequately address the issue. "Not Suspected as a Human Carcinogen" means that based on adequate epidemiologic studies there is no evidence that the material will cause cancer in humans. It must be remembered that for substances where no data have been collected, there are no designations.

Uses of Toxicology Principles

One of the most fundamental principles of toxicology is the dose response curve. This curve or relationship displays the fact that a high dose of a xenobiotic has a greater effect than a low dose. The magnitude of the exposure can be expressed as dose, concentration, duration of exposure, or some other expression of exposure, and it is depicted along the x axis. The magnitude of the effect can be expressed as response, number of animals with a certain outcome, or some other expression of effect, and it is depicted along the y axis as a cumulative percent response. Most dose-response curves are sigmoid shape. In the first part of the curve, the flat portion, an increase in dose produces no effect. This is the sub-threshold phase. The lowest dose that produces an observable or measurable effect is the threshold. Beyond the threshold point, the curve rises steeply and enters a linear phase where the increase in response is proportional to the increase in dose. The slope of this linear phase should be of great interest to the industrial hygienist, because if the slope is high, it is an indication that there is a sudden increase in response with a small increase in exposure. In the last part of the curve, the curve flattens out showing a maximal response. At this point, all the exposed individuals or all the susceptible individuals have shown the effect.[12] The relationship between dose and response is discussed throughout this book but in detail in Chapter 2, "Principles of Toxicology", as well as Chapter 32, "Toxicology Test Data."

Another fundamental principle of toxicology involves exposure considerations. The amount of a substance needed to cause an adverse effect varies widely among different materials. For example, botulism toxin can cause death with just a few micrograms being ingested, whereas many other chemicals are essentially harmless following doses in grams. The intrinsic toxicity of a substance is important, but it is the associated degree of risk caused by the exposure circumstances that can be critical in determining if workers become exposed. A very toxic chemical when carefully handled is less hazardous than a relatively nontoxic substance that is improperly handled. A key element in assessing the degree of risk for any chemical is the exposure that can potentially occur. Toxic effects of a chemical are produced only if the chemical or its metabolites reach the appropriate receptors in the body at a concentration and for a length of time sufficient to cause the toxic effects. Exposure considerations such as route of administration, the dose, and the duration and frequency of exposure all will determine if toxic effects actually occur.[13] Exposure circumstances need further study when any of the following conditions exist: (1) uptake routes include both the lung and skin; (2) acute toxicity data from animal studies show extreme toxicity due to very low LD_{50} values; (3) chronic toxicity data shows lethality, carcinogenicity, or embryotoxicity; (4) warning properties of the substance, such as odor or irritation threshold, are at levels substantially higher than typical exposure levels; (5) the substance is a gas, respirable aerosol, or a highly volatile liquid; (6) very large quantities are used over periods of time; (7) there is a large number of workers potentially exposed to the substance (>125); or if any of the following conditions exist: open process, manually operated, frequent intervention in the process during service or maintenance, regular leaks and spills, absence or inadequate ventilation.[14] Exposure considerations are discussed throughout this book but in detail in Chapter 2, "Principles of Toxicology", Chapter 23, "Exposure Assessment", Chapter 24, "Risk Assessment Process for Industrial Hygienists", and Chapter 28, "Derivation of Occupational Exposure Limits."

The principles of toxicology are needed to assess the significance of a toxic effect. When does a toxic effect become significant? When does a pathophysiologic change indicate a disease process? Body defense mechanisms, such as mucociliary clearance and inflammation, normally occur in response to environmental stresses. A disease is likely to occur if the body defense mechanisms become overwhelmed by the environmental stressors. However, some changes that occur in response to chemical exposures do not cause diseases. In these cases, the significance is not completely known. For example, is hyperplasia or hypertrophy considered a normal physiologic adaptation to a stress or should it be considered a pathologic process? Often a worker can be exposed to a toxin and show no sign of illness. Does normal biologic adaptation cause an unacceptable effect on the body? Is there a limit to which the body can compensate for toxic effects? Looking at it from another point of view, is there a certain amount of stress that is beneficial to the body? In other words, can a low-level exposure to a substance ever cause a beneficial effect? Hormesis is an area of study that reports beneficial effects of low-level exposures to a substance, while higher exposures cause disease. Currently, there are no clear cut answers to these questions.[12] In this book, sites of action of chemicals and their effects are discussed in detail in the second section that includes Chapters 5 through 15 which deal with the various tissues and organ systems in the body. Also, Chapter 24—Risk Assessment Process for Industrial Hygienists, discusses issues dealing with the significance of toxic effect.

Types of Toxicological Tests

Toxicology testing has always been important in determining potential toxicity of a chemical. However, because of the Toxic Substances Control Act (TSCA), the Environmental Protection Agency may require data on mutagenic, carcinogenic, teratogenic, synergistic, or behavioral effects by using epidemiologic, in vitro, or laboratory animal methods whenever an unreasonable risk to health or environment may exist and there is not sufficient data to determine the risk. The principles of toxicology have contributed to several fundamental assumptions that underlie all toxicity testing. First, the effects observed in laboratory animals are often the same effects observed in humans. Second, the degree of adverse effect increases as the dose or exposure increases. As a general principle, if the absorption, distribution, metabolism, and excretion of a material are similar in humans and a particular animal species, test results in that species are generally predictive of toxicity of the material in humans. However, since there are usually important differences in these characteristics, toxicology studies must be carefully interpreted.[13] The standard toxicology testing methods that are commonly used to assess chemical toxicity are described in Chapter 32, Toxicity Test Data.

Uses and Interpretation of Toxicological Data

The results of toxicological tests are often used to assess whether exposures may be of any health significance in the workplace, in an emergency situation, and in litigation. Knowledge of how a substance is absorbed, distributed in the body, metabolized, and excreted will help determine if exposure was significant and if it should be evaluated. This information will also determine if biological monitoring is appropriate in a certain situation. For example, in the case of the solvent, trichloroethylene, it is known that it is metabolized into a number of metabolites, including trichloroethanol and trichloroacetic acid, and these are excreted in the urine. If exposure is uncertain, but important, these metabolites can be measured in the urine, giving an indication of the magnitude of exposure. Also, knowing that the half-lives of trichloroethanol and trichloroacetic acid in urine are 10 to 15 hours and 70 to 100 hours, respectively, any biological monitoring after a week from exposure would not be very useful.[13] The entire fourth section of this book, Chapters 23 through 31, describes the application of toxicological information. For example, Chapter 24, "Risk Assessment Process for Industrial Hygienists", presents the application of toxicology data in human health and environmental risk assessment.

In assessing and interpreting toxicological data, the animal model that was used in the study, the route of exposure, the dose levels used, and the time period over which exposure took place, must be considered. The relevance of the animal study to humans is greatly increased if the route of exposure used in the animal study is the same as the route of exposure in humans. An oral feeding study in animals does not have much significance to humans, if there is very little potential for ingestion in humans. The methods used in the animal study must be evaluated by asking specific questions. Did the study use an adequate number of animals? Were control animals used to compare with exposure groups? Was the proper animal model actually used? Was the particular laboratory qualified to conduct the study? Were the results statistically significant? Were potential confounding variables, such as effects of other agents or laboratory procedures considered? Have the results been replicated in other studies? Are the results consistent with any epidemiologic studies with workers having exposure to the substance being studied? Have the limitations of the animal studies been considered? That is, are there wide variations in the susceptibility of individual species and strains of animals?[13]

Providing Impetus for Research

From the industrial hygiene point of view, toxicology is a preventive science. It is to assist us in preventing chemicals from impacting the health of workers and people in the community. In order to accomplish this, a variety of data is needed, including: data about the chemicals being handled; data about the work environment, especially the exposure to the chemicals; and data about the individuals who come into contact with the chemicals.[14] Toxicology helps provide data about the chemicals and data about the individuals who may become exposed to the chemicals. As a result, toxicology provides an impetus for research in these areas. The physico-chemical properties of the chemicals and their toxic properties require research efforts in chemistry, as well as research with experimental animals and in vitro studies. Research in regards to understanding the mechanistic linkages between sources, exposure, dose, and response are necessary before risk assessment can be undertaken. Ultimately, studies must be accomplished that determine how a substance behaves within the body—that is, toxicokinetic parameters are explored. Although this book is not focused upon the research aspects of toxicology, the third section of the book which deals with chemical group toxicology in Chapters 16 through 22, provides a discussion of the most important underlying research that has allowed us to understand the effects of chemicals most commonly found in the workplace. Throughout this book, areas currently needing additional research are highlighted, such as information needed for updating occupational exposure limits (Chapter 28), computational exposure assessment (Chapter 23), and complex chemical mixtures (Chapter 22).

Summary

Toxicology is primarily concerned with assessing toxicological risk involved in handling chemicals. As a result, it is an important part of industrial hygiene. Since this partnership has been successful, cases of serious occupational poisoning involving disease and disability are rare. Now efforts are focused upon insidious types of poisoning, especially in situations where workers are exposed for long periods of time to low concentrations of chemical substances. The approach now is towards health surveillance with exposure monitoring, which includes environmental monitoring and measuring internal exposures to workers by biological monitoring. Based upon these measurements, actions can be taken to minimize exposure and ensure threshold limit values are not exceeded. The setting of such limits depends upon toxicology data.

References

1. **Plog, B.A.:** Overview of Industrial Hygiene. In *Fundamentals of Industrial Hygiene.* Plog, B.A., J. Niland, and P.J. Quinlan (eds.). Itasca IL: National Safety Council, 1996. pp. 3–32.
2. **Rose, V.E.:** History and Philosophy of Industrial Hygiene. In *The Occupational Environment, Its Evaluation, Control, and Management*, 2nd edition. DiNardi, S.R. (ed). Fairfax VA: AIHA Press, 2003. pp. 4–18.
3. **James, R.C.:** General Principles of Toxicology. In *Industrial Toxicology: Safety and Health Applications in the Workplace.* Williams, P.L. and J.L. Burson (eds.). New York: Van Nostrand Reinhold, 1985. pp. 7–26.
4. **Gallo, M.A.:** History and Scope of Toxicology. In *Casarett & Doull's Toxicology — The Basic Science of Poisons*, 6th edition. Klassen, C.D. (ed). New York: McGraw-Hill, 2001. pp. 3-10.
5. **Wilson, C.L:** Introduction. In *Layman's Guide to Toxicology.* Still, K.R. and C.L. Wilson (eds.). CPIA 686 Special Report. 1999. pg 5.
6. **Lewis, W.H.:** *Medical Botany — Plants Affecting Man's Health.* New York: John Wiley & Sons, 1977.

7. **Lu, F.C.:** *Basic Toxicology — Fundamentals, Target Organs, and Risk Assessment*, 3rd edition. Washington, D.C.: Taylor & Francis, 1996.
8. **Smart, J.K.:** History of Chemical and Biological Warfare: An American Perspective. In *Textbook of Military Medicine — Medical Aspects of Chemical and Biological Warfare.* Sidell, F.R, E.T. Takafuji, and D.R. Franz (eds.). Washington, D.C.: The Borden Institute, 1997. pp. 13–16.
9. **Still, K.R., G.B. Briggs, P. Knechtges, W.K. Alexander, and C.L. Wilson:** Risk Assessment in Navy Deployment Toxicology. *Human Ecolog. Risk Assess.* 6:1125–1136 (2000).
10. **Still, K.R., W.W. Jederberg, G.D. Ritchie, and J. Rossi, III:** Exposure Assessment and the Health of Deployed Forces. *Drug Chem. Tox. 25(4)*:383–401 (2002).
11. **American Conference of Governmental Industrial Hygienists (ACGIH):** *TLVs® and BEIs® Based on the Documentation of the Threshold Limit Values for Chemical Substances and Physical Agents & Biological Exposure Indices (2007).* Cincinnati, OH: ACGIH, 2007.
12. **Gochfeld, M.:** Principles of Toxicology. In *Environmental Medicine.* Brooks, S.M., M.G. Gochfeld, J. Herzstein, R.J. Jackson, and M.B. Schenker (eds.). St. Louis, Mo.: Mosby-Year Book, Inc., 1995.
13. **Logan, D.C.:** Toxicology. In *A Practical Approach to Occupational and Environmental Medicine.* McCunney, R.J. (ed.). Boston, Ma.: Little, Brown and Company, 1994.
14. **Niesink, R.J.M.:** Occupational Toxicology. In *Toxicology—Principles and Applications.* Niesink, R.J.M., J. de Vries, and M.A. Hollinger (eds.). Boca Raton, FL: CRC Press, 1996.

Chapter 2

Principles of Toxicology

Randal J. Keller, PhD, CIH

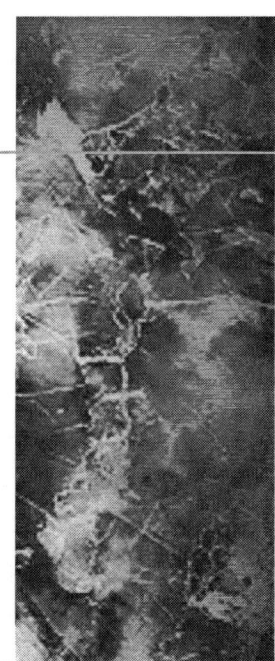

What is Toxicology?

Toxicology is the study of the adverse effects of chemical, physical or biological agents on living organisms and the ecosystem, including the prevention and amelioration of such adverse effects.[1] It has also been described as the "science of poisons."[2] A **toxicologist** is an individual trained to assess those adverse effects.[3] Toxicology is very closely related to the field of pharmacology. Many medical schools in the country contain departments consisting of both pharmacology and toxicology. A pharmacologist looks at the possible beneficial effects of chemicals on living systems. A pharmacologist and toxicologist may be researching the same chemical, with the pharmacologist examining the efficacy or beneficial effects and the toxicologist examining the toxic effects. Generally, these effects are differentiated by dose, since as stated by Paracelsus "All substances are poisons; there is none which is not a poison. The right dose differentiates a poison from a remedy."[3] However, other factors, such as timing of the dose, are involved as well.

There are many types of toxicologists, but industrial hygienists will primarily use information from descriptive, mechanistic and regulatory toxicologists.[2,3] A **descriptive toxicologist** is mainly involved with assessing the safety of chemicals. Any chemical that is introduced into commerce in the U.S. must undergo a safety assessment outlined by federal regulatory agencies. These assessments involve a series of animal testing protocols, such as acute, chronic and reproductive toxicity. Examples of these protocols can be found in the Food and Drug Administration (FDA) Redbook[4] or the Environmental Protection Agency (EPA) Health Effects Test Guidelines.[5] These testing protocols need to be strictly adhered to under Good Laboratory Practices[6] before the manufacturer submits testing results to regulatory agencies such as the FDA. Good laboratory practices are a method of requiring laboratories to carefully document all experimental procedures to assure data quality and integrity. A descriptive toxicologist is the individual responsible for overseeing the study and ensuring that the testing is properly performed. A **mechanistic toxicologist** is usually a researcher

Outcome Competencies
After completing this chapter, the reader should be able to:
- Define the underlined terms used in this chapter.
- Describe the various types of toxicologists.
- Classify toxic agents based upon toxic responses, physical states and usages.
- Describe the types of toxic responses that can occur from chemical exposures.
- Describe the concepts of the dose-response relationship.

Prerequisite Knowledge
Basic understanding of chemistry and biology.

Key Terms
toxicology, toxicologist, descriptive toxicologist, mechanistic toxicologist, regulatory toxicologist, clinical toxicologist, forensic toxicologist, environmental toxicologist, target organ toxicity, poisoning potential, acute toxicity, chronic toxicity, dose-response relationship, lethal dose, lethal concentration, threshold.

Key Topics
1. What is Toxicology?
2. Toxic Agent Classification
3. Exposure
4. Basic Toxicology Principles

employed by a university or a private company. Mechanistic toxicologists try to understand the reasons that chemicals' toxicities occur. This information may be useful in devising antidotes to chemical poisonings, or establishing reasonable levels of exposures to the chemical. A **regulatory toxicologist** generally is employed by the state or federal government. They use data generated by descriptive and mechanistic toxicologists in the risk assessment process to establish exposure levels for various chemicals, such as the establishment of standards for the amount of chemicals permitted in ambient air, in drinking water or in occupational environments.[2,3]

There are other areas of toxicology that an industrial hygienist might interact with.[2,3] If a worker suffers a chemical poisoning, a **clinical toxicologist**, usually a physician trained in emergency care, would medically manage the poisoned patient. **Forensic toxicologists** are experts in the medical and legal aspects of toxicology, and may work with medical examiners in establishing cause of death in situations involving poisonings. An **environmental toxicologist** will look at a wide range of adverse effects that chemicals have on organisms within an ecosystem. These adverse effects include a variety of endpoints, for example, nematode toxicities or behavioral effects on wildlife.[3]

Case Study

Jim was recently employed as an industrial hygienist at a small specialty chemical manufacturing facility. As one of his first duties, Jim decides to develop an air monitoring program to ensure that all chemical exposure levels are below any standards or recommendations. The facility has certain chemicals on site that Jim is unfamiliar with, so he decides to look up what the exposure levels are to these chemicals. He starts by looking at the Permissible Exposure Limits (PELs) set by the Occupational Safety and Health Administration (OSHA).[7] OSHA has established PELs on approximately 500 chemicals, but Jim's chemical is not on that list. Jim next checks the Threshold Limit Values® set by the American Conference of Governmental Industrial Hygienists[8], but he is unable to locate his chemical among the 800 listed. Jim then checks the Workplace Environmental Exposure Levels set by the American Industrial Hygiene Association[9], but his chemical does not appear on their list. After checking The Recommended Exposure Limits (RELs)[10] set by the National Institute for Occupational Safety and Health (NIOSH), and the Toxicological Profiles[11] established by the Agency for Toxic Substances & Disease Registry (ATSDR) and not finding his chemical there, Jim is at a loss.

Unfortunately, the above situation is familiar to many industrial hygienists. With approximately 75,000 chemicals listed in the Toxic Substance Control Act (TSCA) inventory[12], and regulations or recommendations available for only a small percentage of those, it sometimes becomes necessary for industrial hygienists to use general principles of toxicology to make educated decisions on a safe exposure level to a chemical. These principles will help the industrial hygienist in determining how likely it is that the usage of the chemical can pose harm to the worker. For example, understanding the exposure situation (the chemical volatility, amounts used and exposure time), the likely persistence in the body (the water solubility), and structural similarity to known hazardous chemicals are all useful in helping an industrial hygienist minimize the risk of harm to a worker from the chemical. A more complete description of this process can be found in the chapter entitled "Derivation of Occupational Exposure Limits."

Toxic Agent Classification

There are several systems available for the classification of toxic agents that industrial hygienists generally need to be familiar with. These include classifications of target organ, use, effects, physical state, poisoning potential and mechanism of action, as listed in Table 2.1. Most toxicology textbooks, including this one, have a section devoted to the classification of toxic agents based upon **target organ toxicity**.[2,3,13] Section 2 of this book, "Sites of Action of Chemicals Found in the Workplace," examines effects of toxic agents on target organs. Grouping agents by what organs they adversely affect is very common in industrial hygiene. For example, knowing if exposure to this chemical may result in lung damage, liver damage or central nervous system damage may assist in recognizing signs of overexposure. Agents are also commonly classified by use. Pesticides, which are diverse chemicals used to get rid of various pests, whether they are insects, weeds, rats, can be classified together. Solvents can as well, although they too represent a diverse combination of chemicals with markedly differing toxicities. Section 3 of this book, "Chemical Group Toxicology," reviews the toxicity of chemicals by groups, including pesticides and solvents.

Table 2.1 — Toxic Agent Classification

Toxic Agent Classification	Example
Target Organ	Liver toxicant, lung toxicant
Use	Solvent, pesticide
Effects	Carcinogen, teratogen
Physical State	Aerosol, liquid, solid
Poisoning Potential	Highly toxic, virtually nontoxic
Mechanism of Action	Cholinesterase inhibition, P450 Induction

The TLV® booklet[8] includes a column on TLV® Basis — Critical Effects. Effects are another method of toxic agent classification. Some common effects which are listed in the TLV® booklet include irritation, narcosis, cancer, reproductive or genotoxic effects. A relatively high percentage of substances with a TLV® are irritants; and it is important for industrial hygienists to be aware of the critical effects caused by exposure to certain chemicals.

Other methods of classification include physical state, poisoning potential and mechanism of action. The classification by physical state, such as gases, vapors and aerosols, is very important to industrial hygienists because it refers to what they typically measure. Section 3 of this book will further discuss the toxicity of gases and particulate matter. Poisoning potential is a popular method of classification for the layman that addresses the question of how much of a substance can lead to harm. Poisoning potential typically uses a range of exposures and a subjective measure of the associated toxicities, as listed in Table 2.2. For chemicals like botulism toxin where micrograms or few drops of a chemical may lead to death, that chemical might be rated "super toxic." On the other extreme, if a person would only be affected by consuming quarts of a liquid, it might be rated as "practically nontoxic." Mechanism of action is a method of classification usually used among toxicologists. In this method, agents are classified on what they actually do that results in the adverse effect. Some examples of this include cholinesterase inhibitors and chemicals that covalently bind to nucleic acids and cytochrome-P450 inducers. Mechanisms of toxicity will be discussed further in the next chapter.

Table 2.2 — Relative Toxicity.

Category	Lethal Dose for a 70 kg Person (154 lbs)	Relative Amount
Supertoxic	< 5 mg/kg or less	A taste (< 7 drops)
Extremely toxic	5 – 50 mg/kg	7 drops – 1 tsp
Highly toxic	50 – 500 mg/kg	1 tsp – 1 ounce
Moderately toxic	0.5 – 5 g/kg	1 ounce – 1 pint
Slightly toxic	5 – 15 g/kg	1 pint – 1 quart
Practically nontoxic	>15 g/kg	> 1 quart

From the Instructors Guide for The Occupational Environment — Its Evaluation and Control, 1st edition. 1997.

Exposure

An important consideration in assessing the potential toxicity of any toxic agent is to determine the likelihood of exposure to that agent, since as stated in *Casarett & Doull,* "Adverse or toxic effects in a biological system are not produced by a chemical agent unless that agent or its biotransformation products reach appropriate sites in the body at a concentration and for a length of time sufficient to produce the toxic manifestation."[3]

The inherent toxicity of the chemical is unique to the chemical itself, but it presents no hazard to workers unless they have the potential to be exposed to it. Industrial hygienists need to be familiar with not only the toxicity of a chemical, but how workers might be exposed to the chemical since these two factors will ultimately determine the danger the chemical poses.[2] A toxic chemical that is not present in a facility poses no danger to the workers. If the chemical is present, it will not result in toxicity unless workers are exposed to it for an adequate enough duration and at a high enough concentration.

Basic Toxicological Principles

Toxicology is a complex field and requires years of study prior to beginning professional practice. Although it is not the intent of this chapter to train industrial hygienists to become practicing toxicologists, there are a few basic toxicological principles on how chemicals behave in biological systems that are useful for industrial hygienists during their daily work. These include how chemicals enter the body (routes of entry), acute versus chronic toxicity, the types of undesired effects that are caused by chemicals, and the dose response relationship.

Routes of Entry

Most occupational exposures occur by inhalation.[2,13] All exposure standards and recommendations are set for concentrations of airborne contaminants. This is because most workers will be exposed to gases, vapors and aerosols, and may inhale sufficient quantities to be potentially toxic if proper respiratory protection is not used. Once a chemical reaches the alveolar sacs in the pulmonary regions of the lungs, it can readily cross the thin capillary lining found there. The capillary linings of the lungs are among the thinnest membrane barriers in the body, and although their main purpose is to allow gases like carbon dioxide and oxygen to readily cross, other inhaled chemicals can as well. Once a chemical crosses the capillary linings of the lungs, it is in the bloodstream and is capable of causing toxicity to other organs. A further description of the respiratory system will be presented in Chapter 5, "Respiratory Toxicology." The second most common route of entry for occupation chemicals is by skin exposure. The skin consists of three main layers; the epidermis, the dermis and the subcutaneous layer. Once chemicals cross the epidermis, they have access to the blood vessels found in the dermis and subcutaneous layer. The portion of the epidermis which acts as a barrier is called the stratum corneum. Some chemicals, due to their lipophilic properties, can readily cross the stratum corneum. If the stratum corneum is not intact, for example, due to an injury or a skin rash, a chemical can cross into the bloodstream. Although there are no safe levels of skin exposure established, industrial hygienists need to be aware of a chemical's potential to cross the skin. The "TLV® booklet"[8] uses a "Skin" designation to indicate potential skin absorption of a chemical. This tells the industrial hygienists to further consider this chemical, because skin exposure may result in a higher body burden of the chemical than would result from inhalation alone. If the potential for skin absorption exists, workers should be advised to wear proper personal protective clothing. Dermal toxicology will be addressed in detail in its own chapter.

Occupational exposures due to ingestion should not occur but sometimes are found in the following situations. Workers who eat and drink in contaminated areas, or do not adequately wash their hands may ingest chemicals. Workers who smoke may also ingest contaminants that are on their hands. There are also reported cases of workers intentionally ingesting occupational chemicals in suicide attempts, so industrial hygienists should be familiar with the types of emergency treatments that might be required in such cases.

Acute versus Chronic Toxicity

The type of exposure situation can have a great influence on toxicity.[2,3] An acute exposure which generally occurs in a short time frame of 24 hours or less may have a markedly different toxicity than a chronic exposure, which may take place over a period of several years. Most cases of chronic toxicity occur because the toxicant accumulates, or because the organ has insufficient time for repair before a subsequent exposure to the toxicant. Chemicals that accumulate, like lead, are generally associated with chronic toxicity. In some cases, changing the exposure from an acute to chronic one involves changing the target organ toxicity. One well known example of this is ethanol. In an acute exposure, which may involve consuming a large amount of ethanol over a short time period, the target organ is the central nervous system. Tests of impaired drivers involve assessing central nervous system function. If an individual continues to consume large amounts of ethanol over an extended period of time, the target organ shifts to the liver. The reason for this is that ethanol causes a transient effect called steatosis[2], or fatty liver, in which the liver increases its lipid content and turns yellowish in color. Although fatty liver is a reversible condition, if the liver is repeatedly exposed to ethanol before recovery can occur, a scarring of the liver, or cirrhosis will occur. Further examples of liver toxicities will be addressed in Chapter 10, "Hepatic Toxicology."

An occupational example of this same principle involves benzene toxicity. Benzene is an agent capable of causing narcosis, and in an acute exposure the central nervous system is affected. If a low level exposure to benzene occurs over an extended period of time, the target organ shifts to the blood forming tissues, and the result may be anemia or leukemia. The permissible exposure limit of 1 ppm for benzene was established on the basis of the potential for benzene to cause leukemia.[7]

Undesired Effects

There are many types of undesired effects that can occur after exposure to a chemical. One of these effects is allergic reactions, which is a type of immunotoxicity. For an allergic reaction to occur, a person must have prior exposure to the chemical or a structurally similar one at which time antibodies against the chemical are formed. Upon subsequent exposures, the immune system recognizes the chemical as foreign, and causes a sensitization reaction to occur. Immune system toxicities will be covered in Chapter 12, "Immunotoxicology." Chemical exposures might also result in a local or systemic effect. A local effect takes place at the site of exposure to the chemical. An example of a local effect is an acid spill on the skin; the skin will immediately redden at the site of contact with the acid. Systemic effects occur at places other than the site of exposure. Most occupational exposures occur by inhalation, yet many effects other than lung toxicity may occur. For example, inhalation of the vapors from many solvents results in narcosis. Chapter 4, "Disposition of Toxicants" will discuss this concept further.

Some exposures to chemicals result in either reversible or irreversible effects. Reversible effects may heal over time. The example listed above for the inhalation of solvents might be a reversible effect. If a worker inhales a sufficiently high concentration of solvent to produce narcosis, and is subsequently removed from further exposure, they will likely make a complete recovery and not suffer a lifetime of central nervous system impairment. Alternatively, inhalation of mercury vapors over extended periods of time might lead to irreversible nervous tissue damage.[2,3,13] Exposure to agents that are carcinogenic might lead to an irreversible effect. Once a cell has become cancerous, it cannot revert to a non-cancerous cell. Effects to chemicals may also be immediate or delayed. An acid spill on the skin will result in an immediate effect, whereas exposure to a carcinogen may result in the development of cancer decades later. The concepts involved in the carcinogenicity of chemicals will be discussed in Chapters 13–15 on "Mutagenesis, Carcinogenesis, and Teratogenesis."

The Dose Response Relationship

The dose response relationship is of central importance to the study of toxicology. Increasing the dose of a chemical will increase the effect or biological response that the chemical elicits. Dose response curves are typically generated from either the response of an individual organism, or from the study of a population (Figure 2.1).

Individual dose response relationships are useful in industrial hygiene in understanding the effects that increasing levels of chemical exposure causes. For example, if a worker is exposed to a solvent associated with a central nervous system effect like narcosis, as the level of solvent increases, the worker will become increasingly impaired. By measuring some type of impairment (reaction time, etc.) and plotting it against solvent concentration, an individual dose response curve would show increased impairment with increasing solvent exposure.

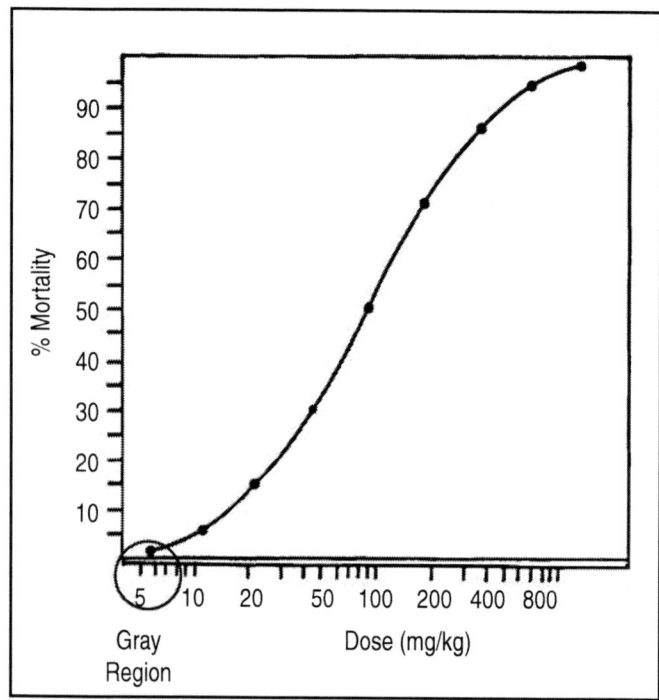

Figure 2.1 — The dose-response relationship (Source: *Casarett and Doull's Toxicology*, 6th edition. Klaassen, C.D. (ed.). New York: McGraw-Hill, 2001; reprinted with permission).

Population dose-response relationships are also used in toxicology (Figure 2.1). In these cases, the response refers to what proportion of the studied population is showing a specific change. Figure 2.1 demonstrates a typical percent mortality curve that shows as the dose of the toxicant increases, mortality increases in the population. Population dose responses are usually a normal frequency distribution. In a population, some individuals exposed to low doses of the toxicant will be adversely affected. These individuals are called hypersensitive. As the dose of the toxicant increases, the majority of the individuals in the population are affected. Some individuals in a population will be resistant to the effects of the toxicant, and will be only adversely affected when the dose is high. Although this example utilizes percent mortality, other endpoints can also be studied with population dose-response relationships, such as the determining the percentage of individuals in a population who exhibit central nervous system impairment at a set concentration of solvent.

There are several sources of information derived from dose response curves that are helpful in the practice of industrial hygiene. If a study is examining lethality, a lethal dose (LD), or lethal concentration (LC) of the chemical might be calculated. An LD_{50} is a statistically derived dose that is expected to cause lethality in 50% of the study population.[2,3,14] This is demonstrated in Figure 2.2 below. Information derived from dose response studies may be used in the establishment of occupational exposure levels. The threshold level, or the lowest of exposure resulting in a measurable response, is important because exposure levels below the threshold cause no detectable response. The NOEL, or no observable effect level and the NOAEL, the no observable adverse effect level, are also determined from the dose-response relationship.[14] The establishment of occupational exposure limits can sometimes utilize the NOEL or the NOAEL. Since the NOEL or NOAEL is determined from laboratory animal testing, a regulatory toxicologists would not directly use this number to set an occupational or environmental exposure level without the application of safety factors. In a simplistic example, if the NOAEL is determined from laboratory animals to be 100 mg/kg, a toxicologist might apply a safety factor of 10 for extrapolation from laboratory animals to humans, and a safety factor of 10 for variations in toxic responses among humans, establishing the occupational exposure limit of (100 mg/kg)/10/10 or 1 mg/kg. This process will be covered more extensively in the chapter entitled "Derivation of Occupational Exposure Limits".

Although dose response curves are used in helping establish safe levels of chemical exposures, they should be used with caution. Several variables may have an influence on the dose response relationship. Some of these variables include route of exposure (inhalation, dermal, ingestion), timing of the dose, sex, age, disease, past exposures, co-exposures, and genetic differences. All of these variables emphasize the complexities in applying information obtained from dose response relationships.

Summary

This chapter has covered the definition of toxicology, which is the study of the adverse effects of chemicals on living systems. Although toxicologists are specifically trained to study these effects, industrial hygienists need to be able to understand and apply some basic principles of toxicology. Not all chemicals that are present in the work environment have established occupational exposure levels, so an industrial hygienist needs to be able to interpret toxicity information on those chemicals and apply it to their specific situation. Knowing the relationship between exposure and toxicity will assist industrial hygienists in developing strategies in minimizing the development of occupational diseases.

References

1. **Society of Toxicology:** "Definition of Toxicology" [Online] Available at http://www.toxicology.org/. [Accessed August 12, 2007].
2. **Schaper, M.M. and M.S. Bisesi:** Environmental and Occupational Toxicology. In *The Occupational Environment: Its Evaluation, Control, and Management*, 2nd edition. DiNardi, S.R. (ed.). Fairfax, VA: AIHA Press, 2003. pp. 21–49.
3. **Klaassen, C.D. (ed.):** *Casarett & Doull's Toxicology — The Basic Science of Poisons*, 6th edition. New York: McGraw-Hill, 2001.
4. **Food and Drug Administration:** "Toxicological Principles for the Safety Assessment of Food Ingredients" [Online] Available at http://www.cfsan.fda.gov/~redbook/red-toca.html. [Accessed August 12, 2007].
5. **U.S. Environmental Protection Agency (EPA):** "OPPTS Harmonized Test Guidelines" [Online] Available at http://www.epa.gov/opptsfrs/publications/OPPTS_Harmonized/870_Health_Effects_Test_Guidelines/index.html. [Accessed August 12, 2007].
6. "Good Laboratory Practice for Non-clinical Laboratory Studies" *Code of Federal Regulations Title 21*, Part 58. 2006.

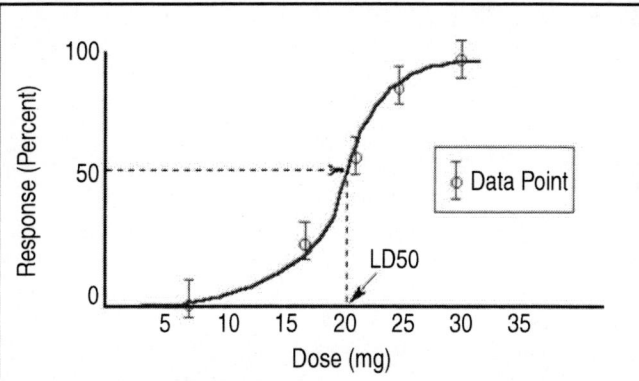

Figure 2.2 — Dose response curve for LD_{50} determination. From Toxicology Tutor, National Library of Medicine.[14]

7. "Toxic and Hazardous Substances," *Code of Federal Regulations Title 29*, Part 1910, Subpart Z. 2006. pp 5-496.
8. **American Conference of Governmental Industrial Hygienists (ACGIH):** TLV®s and BEI®s Based on the Documentation of the Threshold Limit Values for Chemical Substances and Physical Agents & Biological Exposure Indices. Cincinnati, OH: ACGIH, 2006.
9. **American Industrial Hygiene Association (AIHA):** *2006 Emergency Response Planning Guidelines and Workplace Environmental Exposure Level Handbook.* Fairfax, VA: AIHA, 2006.
10. **National Institute for Occupational Safety and Health (NIOSH):** NIOSH Recommendations for Occupational Safety and Health, Compendium of Policy Documents and Statements, DHHS (NIOSH) Publication No. 92-100, 2002.
11. **Agency for Toxic Substance Disease Registry (ATSDR):** "Toxicological Profile Information Sheet." [Online] Available at http://www.atsdr.cdc.gov/toxpro2.html. [Accessed August 12, 2007].
12. **U.S. Environmental Protection Agency (EPA):** 'TSCA Chemical Substances Inventory." [Online] Available at http://www.epa.gov/opptintr/newchems/pubs/invntory.htm. [Accessed August 12, 2007].
13. **Winder, C. and N. Stacey (eds.):** *Occupational Toxicology*, 2nd edition. Boca Raton, FL: CRC Press, 2004.
14. **National Library of Medicine:** "Toxicology Tutor I — Basic Principles." [Online] Available at http://sis.nlm.nih.gov/enviro/toxtutor.html. [Accessed August 12, 2007].

Additional Reading

Klaassen, C.D. and J.B. Watkins (eds.): *Casarett and Doull's Essentials of Toxicology.* New York: McGraw-Hill, 2003.

Lu, F.C.: *Basic Toxicology, Fundamentals, Target Organs, and Risk Assessment*, 3rd edition. Washington, DC: Taylor & Francis, 1996.

Ottoboni, M.A.: *The Dose Makes the Poison: A Plain-Language Guide to Toxicology*, 2nd edition. New York: Van Nostrand Reinhold, 1991.

Stacey, N.H.: *Occupational Toxicology.* London: Taylor & Francis, 1993.

Williams, P.L. and J.L. Burson (eds.): *Industrial Toxicology, Safety and Health Applications in the Workplace.* New York: Van Nostrand Reinhold, 1985.

> *Medicine is not only a science; it is also an art. It does not consist of compounding pills and plasters; it deals with the very processes of life, which must be understood before they may be guided.*
>
> — Paracelsus (1493–1541)

Chapter 3

Mechanisms of Toxicity

Outcome Competencies

- Define underlined terms.
- Identify the physical and chemical properties of a chemical that will influence the degree of effect of exposure to that chemical.
- Discuss the most common chemical interactions that result in adverse effects.
- Differentiate between the effects of toxicants binding to target molecules through covalent and non-covalent reactions.
- Describe the types of toxic actions that can occur when certain xenobiotics enter the body.
- Explain how oxygen transport by hemoglobin can be blocked by certain substances.
- Explain why ethanol can be administered as an antidote for ingestion of methanol.
- Describe how chemicals can pass through cell membranes and how this is a factor in toxicity.
- Differentiate between irritant dermatitis and allergic contact dermatitis.

Prerequisite Knowledge

Basic chemistry, physiology, and biochemistry

Key Terms

xenobiotic, pharmacodynamics, additive and synergistic chemical interactions, potentiation, antagonism, non-covalent and covalent binding, free radicals, enzyme inhibition and induction, uncoupling of biochemical reactions, calcium homeostasis, cytochrome oxidase, carboxyhemoglobin, methemoglobin, sulfhemoglobin, toxic metabolite, bioactivation, neurotransmitters, mutagen, hydrophilic, lipophilic, lipid peroxidation, immunosuppression, hypersensitization, cross-sensitization, dermatitis, cell necrosis, sequestration, pneumoconiosis

Key Topics

1. Introduction
   - Definition of pharmacodynamics
   - Types of chemical interactions
   - Types of reactions between toxicants and target molecules

2. Types of Toxic Actions
   - Interference with the action of enzyme systems
   - Uncoupling of biochemical reactions
   - Inhibition of oxygen transfer
   - Blockade of hemoglobin oxygen transport
   - Synthesis of a toxic metabolite
   - Removal of metallic co-factors
   - Interference with general cellular function
   - Immunosuppression and hypersensitization
   - Direct chemical irritation of tissues
   - Direct cellular toxicity
   - Sequestration of toxic substances

Chapter 3

Mechanisms of Toxicity

By William E. Luttrell, PhD, CIH

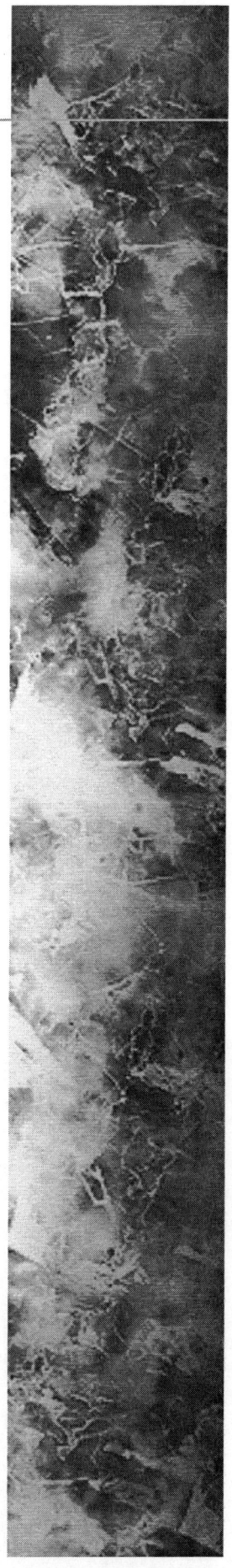

Introduction

The purpose of this chapter is to briefly discuss the most common mechanisms of toxicity. Through these mechanisms, a foreign substance or **xenobiotic**, may act at a specific site of action in the body and have an adverse effect. The following topics are important to this area of toxicology: pharmacodynamics, types of chemical interactions, and types of reactions between toxicants and target molecules.

Pharmacodynamics is the study of the biochemical and physiological effects of chemicals on living systems and the mechanisms of their actions. Some chemicals cause toxicity by their mere presence at a critical site in the body but without interacting with a target molecule. An example is a chemical that precipitates out in the kidney tubules and blocks the flow of urine. Other chemicals may cause toxicity by interaction with the molecules at one or more receptor sites. The initial interaction starts a set of chemical processes that may result in a toxic effect. The degree of effect is directly related to the concentration of the toxic substance at the target site. In addition, toxic effects depend on the physical and chemical properties of the chemical, i.e., solubility, vapor pressure, molecular weights, physical state, etc. However, two chemicals with different properties can initiate a chain of events which lead to similar results. For example, ethanol, a water soluble alcohol, and carbon tetrachloride, a water insoluble chlorinated hydrocarbon, can both cause liver cirrhosis. The specific site of action and the effector organ, where the effect is seen, are not necessarily identical.[1]

Chemicals administered or received simultaneously may act independently of each other. However, in many cases, the presence of one chemical may drastically affect the response of another chemical. The effect that one chemical has on the toxic effect of another chemical is known as interaction. Chemical interactions include **additive and synergistic interactions** as well as potentiation and antagonism. These interactions can result in a reduction or an increase in toxicity of one or both of the chemicals. The interaction is considered additive if the combined effect is equal to the sum of the effect of each chemical given alone. For example, most organophosphates when given simultaneously result in an additive effect on the inhibition of cholinesterase activity. The interaction is considered synergistic if the combined effect is greater than the sum of the effect of each chemical given alone. For example, the effect of asbestos and cigarette smoking on the lung is synergistic.[2] Selikoff et al.[3] found that there was a 5-fold increase in lung cancer incidence among asbestos workers, an 11-fold increase among cigarette smokers, and a 55-fold increase among asbestos workers who were cigarette smokers. **Potentiation** occurs when the toxicity of a substance on a particular tissue is significantly increased by another substance that alone has no toxic effect on that tissue. For example, Borzelleca et al[4] found that trichloroethylene, which has little effect on the liver, increases the hepatotoxicity of carbon tetrachloride significantly. The chemical interaction is considered chemical **antagonism** when two chemicals react to produce a less toxic effect. Antagonism is often desirable and is the basis for most antidotes. There are many examples of chemical antagonism, including the treatment of heavy metal toxicity with dimercaprol which chelates certain heavy metals, such as arsenic and mercury, by making them unable to reach their sites of action. Another example is the use of atropine to reduce the toxicity of an acetylcholinesterase (AChE) inhibitor, ex. organophosphate pesticides. Atropine does not block the receptors on AChE, but blocks the tissue receptors for acetylcholine (ACh) which has accumulated due to the inhibition of AChE.[2]

Toxicants can chemically bind to target molecules through covalent or non-covalent reactions. These chemical reactions can change the target molecules by causing radical formation or electron transfer, or they can change them enzymatically. **Non-covalent binding** can involve nonpolar interactions, and the formation of hydrogen bonds and ionic bonds. This type of binding is seen between toxicants and their targets, such as membrane receptors, intracellular receptors, and ion channels. For example, non-covalent binding occurs between strychnine and its glycine receptor on motor neurons in the spinal cord. This type of binding also allows for the intercalation (insertion between bases) of chemicals such as doxorubicin into the double helix of DNA. Non-covalent binding is usually reversible because of the low bonding energy. In contrast, **covalent binding** is often irreversible, and results in permanent alteration of endogenous molecules because of high bonding energy. For example, neutral **free radicals** such as the hydroxyl radical, HO•, can bind covalently to DNA bases, resulting in the formation of products, such as 8-hydroxypurines. Neutral free radicals can also easily abstract hydrogen atoms from endogenous compounds, converting them into radicals. For example, hydrogen abstraction from deoxyribose in DNA results in the C-4'-radical, the first step to DNA cleavage.[5] Chemicals, such as a nitrite, can oxidize Fe(II) in hemoglobin to Fe(III) by electron transfer, producing methemoglobinemia. Some toxins act enzymatically on specific target proteins. For example, diphtheria toxin blocks the function of elongation factor 2 in protein synthesis and cholera toxin activates a G protein. Snake venom contains hydrolytic enzymes that destroy biomolecules.[2]

Types of Toxic Actions

Interference With the Action of Enzyme Systems

Toxic substances can interfere with the action of enzyme systems by inhibiting the enzyme. Enzymes are large protein molecules that perform essential tasks in the cell through biochemical processes. If certain sites on them are blocked, their biological functions may not be performed. Eventually this can lead to toxic effects. Enzymes can be temporarily or permanently inhibited. For example, many organophosphates specifically bind to acetylcholinesterase (AChE).[6] Some bind reversibly to AChE, resulting in temporary inhibition. However, other organophosphates, such as some nerve agents, are considered to irreversibly bind to AChE, resulting in permanent inhibition until new enzyme can be synthesized. Other examples of **enzyme inhibition** involve many of the heavy metals, such as mercury, arsenic, and lead. They are not as selective as organophosphates, in that they bind to sulfhydryl (SH) groups which are essential to the functioning of many enzymes. There is covalent binding between the metals and the SH groups in the enzyme, inactivating the active site of the enzyme, which can prevent it from performing its cellular function.[1,7]

Toxic substances can also interfere with enzyme systems by inducing or stimulating them. One such enzyme system is the cytochrome P450-dependent monooxygenases, a large group of enzymes involved in the metabolism of certain xenobiotics. P450 enzymes can lead to the detoxification of xenobiotics or activation through the formation of more reactive intermediates. Levels of the various P450 enzymes are sensitive to the presence of xenobiotics. Certain xenobiotics will initiate an increase in the synthesis of specific P450 enzymes through a process known as **enzyme induction**. This process is mediated by receptor binding in the cytoplasm of the cell. For example, 2,3,7,8-tetrachlorodibenzo-p-dioxin (TCDD), benzo[a]pyrene, and other polyaromatic hydrocarbons have the ability to induce certain forms of P450. Once absorbed into the body, these chemicals enter the bloodstream and are distributed to the liver, where most xenobiotics are metabolized; there they can enter the liver cells and bind to a receptor in the cytoplasm forming a receptor-ligand complex. This complex moves into the nucleus, where it interacts with DNA to initiate transcription of genes, including the ones that code for increased manufacture of specific P450 isozymes that can affect the metabolism of other xenobiotics. Chemical inducers of other types of P450 enzymes include phenobarbital and ethanol.[7,8]

Uncoupling of Biochemical Reactions

Some chemicals can **uncouple biochemical reactions** or disrupt specific cellular functions. For example, uncouplers such as dinitroorthocresol, a weed killer, can inhibit the activity of a key enzyme involved in oxidative phosphorylation, a process that produces adenosine triphosphate (ATP) from adenosine diphosphate (ADP). As a result, cellular energy that is normally stored in the high-energy bonds of ATP is lost as heat and unavailable for use in other biochemical processes. Other chemicals can impair ATP synthesis by inhibiting delivery of hydrogen to the electron transport chain, by inhibiting transfer of electrons along the electron transport chain to oxygen, and by interfering with oxygen delivery to cytochrome oxidase. The herbicides, paraquat and diquat, interfere with the transfer of hydrogen to nicotine adenine dinucleotide phosphate (NADP) to form NADPH. If the delivery of hydrogen to the initial electron transport complex is prevented, then the glycolysis and Krebs cycle in cellular oxidation will be inhibited.[1] Toxic substances can also disrupt cellular functions by disturbing **calcium homeostasis**. The body carefully maintains the extracellular level of Ca^{2+} ten-thousand times higher than that in the cytosol of a cell. The body maintains these levels through mechanisms involving the Ca^{2+}-transporting ATPase at the plasma membrane, the calcium stores in the endoplasmic reticulum, mitochondria, and nucleus, as well as the binding of calcium with intracellular calmodulin. Various xenobiotics can cause cytosolic Ca^{2+} to increase and as a result adversely affect calcium dependent cellular structures and functions. Carbon tetrachloride and bromobenzene inhibit Ca^{2+}-transporting ATPase. Acetaminophen and carbon tetrachloride damage the plasma membrane. Cadmium will cause the release of Ca^{2+} from mitochrondria.[8]

Inhibition of Oxygen Transfer

A number of chemicals cause toxicity by interfering with either the use or transport of oxygen in the cell. Chemicals such as hydrocyanic acid and hydrogen sulfide can prevent the use of oxygen in **cytochrome oxidase**, an electron transport system located within the mitochondria of the cell. By binding to iron in cytochrome oxidase, these chemicals prevent the transference of electrons to molecular oxygen in a manner which would allow reaction with hydrogen ions to form water. Since this is the last step in glycolysis, the breakdown of glucose and the production of ATP are stopped. If the cytochrome oxidase system is inhibited in this manner, chemical asphyxiation can occur even though sufficient oxygen is present in the tissues.[1]

Blockade of Hemoglobin Oxygen Transport

Other substances can block hemoglobin oxygen transport through preferential binding. Carbon monoxide (CO) binds to the same site on hemoglobin as oxygen, except it binds with much greater affinity. As a result, CO can block oxygen binding to hemoglobin by forming **carboxyhemoglobin**. At 50 ppm, CO binds to 8 percent of available hemoglobin sites. While nonsmoking human adults normally do not have more than 1 percent of their total blood pigment in the form of carboxyhemoglobin, there is sufficient CO in heavy cigarette smoking to cause 5 to 10 percent saturation. At 30% saturation, throbbing headache, weakness, dizziness, dimness of vision, nausea and vomiting, and collapse can occur. After 60% saturation of hemoglobin with CO, depressed heart function, respiratory failure, and death can occur. Several substances can oxidize iron in hemoglobin to the ferric state to produce **methemoglobin**, which has no oxygen binding ability. When this occurs, hemoglobin is blocked from transporting oxygen. Aromatic amines, aniline, azo compounds, nitro compounds, nitrites, and many other compounds can cause the formation of methemoglobin and as a result decrease the transport of oxygen significantly. Although much less common than methemoglobin, **sulfhemoglobin** can be formed when sulfur binds to the heme moiety in hemoglobin. Sulfhemoglobin too has no oxygen carrying capacity. Unlike methemoglobin, sulfhemoglobin is stable and persists for the life of the red blood cell. Not all sulfur-containing compounds can cause sulfhemoglobin formation and conversely, some chemicals associated with sulfhemoglobinemia do not contain sulfur. In these cases, it is thought that endogenous (natural) sulfhydryl groups may act as sulfur donors during times of oxidative stress induced by the chemicals. Some chemicals, such as surfactants and hydrazine derivatives cause hemolysis, a breakdown in the membranes of red blood cells, resulting in the release of hemoglobin. Free hemoglobin no longer has the ability to transport oxygen.[1,7,8]

Synthesis of a Toxic Metabolite

Biotransformation or metabolism is the process whereby a substance is changed from one chemical to another by a chemical reaction within the body. Metabolism acts as a major defense mechanism within the body by converting toxic chemicals and body wastes into less harmful substances that can be excreted from the body. Unfortunately, biotransformation is not a perfect process and sometimes the metabolite is more toxic than the parent compound. In this case a **toxic metabolite** is synthesized. This process is called **bioactivation**. Many substances have very different toxicities before they are metabolized. Like ethanol, methanol causes central nervous system (CNS) depression. Methanol is broken down by the same enzymes that metabolize ethanol. However, metabolism of methanol results in the formation of formaldehyde which is rapidly metabolized to formic acid which is toxic to the optic nerve and can cause blindness. Because ethanol has a greater affinity for the enzymes responsible for metabolism, it is preferentially metabolized when both alcohols are present. Therefore, using the principle of competitive inhibition of enzymes, ethanol can be administered as an antidote to someone who has ingested methanol.[1]

Removal of Metallic Co-factors

Many enzymes require metal ions as co-factors. That is, they depend upon the presence of specific metal ions for normal function. Iron, copper, and zinc are common metallic co-factors. Chelators are chemicals which tightly bind metal ions and can prevent them from interacting with biological processes. As was previously pointed out in the section on chemical antagonism, this property is useful in the treatment of heavy metal poisoning. However, chelating agents are also potentially toxic because they can bind necessary metal ions making them unavailable to enzymes. For example, dithiocarbamates, used as antioxidants in the rubber industry, are chelating agents. One dithiocarbamate, Dithiocarb, has been used as chelator to treat acute nickel carbonyl poisoning. These compounds will also bind copper ions and as a result inactivate acetaldehyde dehydrogenase, a copper-dependent enzyme. This enzyme is essential for the metabolism of ethanol. If a worker is exposed to dithiocarbamates and then drinks a moderate amount of ethanol, he may experience nausea, violent headaches, and even coma, due to the accumulation of acetaldehyde, a toxic metabolite of ethanol.[1] Interestingly, Antabuse, a drug used to modify behavior in alcoholism, and structurally similar to the dithiocarbamates, also inhibits acetaldehyde dehydrogenase and can cause similar unpleasant symptoms, such as nausea and vomiting, in someone who has ingested ethanol.

Interference with General Cellular Function

Disruption of general cellular function can also occur when chemicals interfere with neurotransmission, affect replication of nucleic acids or protein synthesis, or damage lipids. Within the nervous system, **neurotransmitters**, such as acetylcholine and epinephrine, serve as transmitters of information through the nerves to other nerves, to muscles, and to effector cells throughout the body. Some toxic substances can mimic neurotransmitters, while others can inhibit their transmission. Curare, used by South American tribes as an arrow poison, can block the receptors for acetylcholine in neuromuscular junctions and cause the prolonged relaxation of skeletal muscle. Some chemicals interfere with the synthesis, release, reuptake, or the metabolism of neurotransmitters. For example, the nerve agent, Soman, causes a buildup of acetylcholine by inhibiting the production of acetylcholinesterase. Botulinum toxin causes muscle paralysis by preventing release of acetylcholine from motor neurons. Some chemicals that affect neurotransmission in the central nervous system, such as mescaline and LSD, are hallucinogens.[1,7,8]

Some substances can directly or indirectly interfere with the functioning of cellular nucleic acids. Something that causes a temporary or permanent change in a gene or chromosome or alters chromosome number is known as a **mutagen**. Some chemicals are not themselves mutagenic but can increase the mutagenic potential of other xenobiotics by inducing enzyme systems, such as cytochrome P450. Among the known mutagens are ionizing radiation, certain chemicals, and some viruses. Some mutagens have no apparent effect; others cause a variety of adverse effects, including death. When nucleotides are damaged, the body attempts to repair them with various enzyme systems that exist for that purpose. However, unrepaired damage can lead to mutagenicity or carcinogenicity due to the misreading or incorrect replication of DNA during cell division.[1,7,8] When a chemical, such as an alkylating substance like mustard gas, interferes with the duplication of DNA, the cell cannot divide. Species and individual cell type differences in susceptibility to mutagens have been used to develop treatments for a variety of diseases as well as the development of novel chemotherapeutic agents. Rifampicin, a drug used to treat tuberculosis, can prevent the transcription of RNA from DNA, which can interfere with the use of information stored in DNA by the rest of the cell. An antibiotic, such as streptomycin, can interfere with the translation of information from bacterial RNA to ribosomes so they cannot construct new proteins from amino acids.

Many chemicals are only toxic if they can pass through cell membranes. The ability to pass through a cell membrane depends on the physical properties of the chemical as well as the concentration of the chemical on both sides of the membrane, i.e., the concentration gradient. Cell membranes throughout the body are very similar in structure—basically a layer of fatty acid molecules sandwiched between a bilayer of phospholipid molecules with protein molecules inserted in the bilayer. This bilayer is arranged to create small aqueous pores along the surface. Molecules which are smaller than the diameter of the pores cross the cell membrane by passive diffusion. This is the process by which low molecular weight **hydrophilic** (water soluble) molecules like ethanol are rapidly absorbed through cell membranes of the stomach. Large organic molecules that are **lipophilic** (lipid soluble) dissolve in the cell membrane and diffuse through it. Molecules that are too large to diffuse through aqueous pores or are not lipid soluble enough do not pass through cell membranes unless they are carried through by specialized active transport systems. The lipophilic nature of anesthetic agents, such as ether and cyclopropane, allow them to easily pass into cells of the central nervous system (CNS), causing a depression of cellular activity. Anesthesia includes the depression of the vital centers in the CNS that control respiration and cardiac functions. Lipid solubility is why nonpolar organic solvents, such as gasoline, halogenated organic solvents, and glues, can also act as anesthetics. Lipophilic chemicals can also dissolve in the membranes of the heart and other organs, altering membrane structure and function.

Damage to cell membranes by one xenobiotic can increase the rate of entry of other xenobiotics. Many membranes contain fatty acid chains that are unsaturated. These unsaturated fatty acids can be damaged through **lipid peroxidation**. During this process free radicals formed from halogenated hydrocarbons and other xenobiotics attack the fatty acids, removing hydrogen atoms and converting the fatty acids into free radicals themselves. These free radicals then react with oxygen to form more free radicals and unstable peroxides, which form additional free radicals. As this process spreads, the plasma membrane and other cellular organelles are damaged and it can eventually led to cell death.[1,7,8]

Immunosuppression and Hypersensitization

Some chemicals can cause **immunosuppression** or **hypersensitization** by interacting with the cells of the immune system. Agents that cause the suppression of immune defense mechanisms are known as immunosuppressants. Glucocorticoids, like hydrocortisone, are naturally occurring chemicals that are needed for normal growth and development. Natural glucocorticoids and their synthetic analogues used to treat disease can cause a suppression of the inflammatory response and thereby decrease resistance to other diseases. Antimetabolites used in transplant patients and some chemotherapeutic agents used to treat cancer suppress the production of white blood cells which can lead to susceptibility to bacterial infections. When the immune system is functioning normally, it sometimes becomes sensitized to assaults from foreign substances, including chemicals and microorganisms. This allows it to respond quickly to subsequent exposures to that same agent, even at levels considerably lower than the initial contact. Sometimes the sensitization is very chemical specific; however, it can also be general in nature. Many or all chemicals in a class, such as chromium III and VI salts, nickel and nickel salts, p-phenylene diamines, and small molecular weight aldehydes cause allergic responses in certain sensitive individuals. This can lead to **cross-sensitization**, a condition in which sensitization to a chemically related molecule is acquired after sensitization to the primary allergen. Allergic reactions can range from a mild rash to a life threatening condition called anaphylactic shock. The latter is characterized by symptoms which can include hives, swelling of mucous membranes, shortness of breath, and a drop in blood pressure which can quickly lead to cardiac arrest. The most common causes of anaphylaxis are penicillin, bee stings, foods such as peanuts, seafood and eggs, and latex gloves. While practically any substance can result in an allergic response in certain sensitive individuals, the number of chemicals that cause an actual response of the immune system is limited.[1,7]

Direct Chemical Irritation of Tissues

Unlike sensitizers, chemical irritants react directly with the components of various tissues leading in most cases to immediate local effects. Irritation is most often associated with contact with the skin or eyes, the mucous membranes of the respiratory tract, or the lining of the throat and digestive tract. The response is non-immune mediated and causes a range of symptoms from erythema (redness), edema (swelling) and vesiculation (rash) to corrosion (irreversible changes at the site of contact with scar formation). Prolonged or occluded (covered) contact can increase the potential for irritation or burns to occur. Short periods of contact with strongly alkaline solutions (sodium or potassium hydroxide) or strong acids (hydrochloric, sulfuric, nitric, hydrofluoric) can cause severe burns unless removed promptly. Other chemicals, like phenol and organotins, can also cause burns. Dilute solutions of these same chemicals may lead to a milder reversible inflammatory effect. This reversible effect is often called **dermatitis**, although this is a more generic term that often includes the response caused by dermal sensitizers. Therefore, it is necessary to distinguish between irritant dermatitis and allergic contact dermatitis when describing the mechanism of toxicity of a chemical. Even airborne toxic substances, such as mustard gas, blistering agents, chlorine, and phosgene can cause reddening of exposed skin. When inhaled, chlorine, phosgene, sulfur dioxide, nitrous oxides, and ozone irritate mucus membranes. At extremely low doses, acrolein and chlorpicrine (a warning agent in some methyl bromide formulations) and the tear gases chloracetophenone (MACE) and capsaicin (pepper spray) can cause irritation of the conjunctiva of the eye and lacrimation (tear production).[1,8]

Direct Cellular Toxicity

Toxic substances can cause direct damage to cellular structures. Chlorinated alkanes, chloroform, carbon tetrachloride, and halogenated aromatic compounds, such as bromobenzene, can easily pass into the cells of the liver and kidney and cause direct damage to cell structures. In sufficient concentrations, cell degeneration occurs. This consists of the formation of vacuoles, accumulation of fat, and eventual **cell necrosis** (death).[1]

Sequestration of Toxic Substances

Some toxic substances can undergo **sequestration** by being deposited and stored in certain tissues for long periods of time. Here, they often cause no adverse effects. They can be released into the blood stream later under certain conditions, such as fasting or starvation, and can have adverse effects in tissues far from the site of original deposition. Fat soluble toxic substances, such as DDT and PCBs, are deposited in adipose tissue but they are not highly toxic to adipose tissue. Heavy metals, such as strontium, thorium, and lead, are stored in bone. Some inert chemicals cause toxicity when deposition of particles or fibers exceeds the ability of a tissue or organ to remove them. This type of tissue overload is frequently seen in the lungs. Dusts can be embedded in the lungs, causing an inflammatory response called **pneumoconiosis**. Silica dust can lead to silicosis, and coal dust can induce fibrosis, chronic bronchitis, and emphysema. Asbestos fibers can cause asbestosis and also malignant growths in the lungs.[1,7,8]

Conclusions

Chemicals have a wide variety of interactions with other chemicals and with target molecules within the body. This interaction can be at the chemical, enzymatic, macromolecular, sub-cellular, cellular, and tissue levels. Table 3.1 is a summary of the wide range of mechanisms presented in this chapter.

References

1. **Malachowski, M.J., and A.F. Goldberg:** Action of Toxic Substances: Pharmacodynamics. In *Health Effects of Toxic Substances.* Rockville, Maryland: Government Institutes, Inc., 1995. pp. 55–63.
2. **Lu, F.C.:** Modifying Factors of Toxic Effects. In *Basic Toxicology: Fundamentals, Target Organs, and Risk Assessment,* 3rd edition. Washington, DC: Taylor & Francis, 1996. pp. 57–70.
3. **Selikoff, I.J., E.C. Hammond, and J. Churg:** Asbestos exposure, smoking, and neoplasia. *J. Am. Med. Assoc. 204*:106–112 (1968).
4. **Borzelleca, J.F., T.M. O'Hara, C. Gennings, R.H. Granger, M.A. Sheppard, and L.W. Condie:** Interactions of water contaminants. *Fundam. Appl. Toxicol. 14*:477–490 (1990).
5. **Breen, A.P., and J.A. Murphy:** Reactions of oxyl radicals with DNA. *Free Rad. Biol. Med. 18*:1033–1077 (1995).
6. **Mileson, B.E., et al.:** Common mechanism of toxicity: a case study of organophosphorus pesticides. *Toxicol. Sci. 41*:8–20 (1998).
7. **Stine, K.E., and T.M. Brown:** Cellular Sites of Action. In *Principles of Toxicology*. Boca Raton, Florida: CRC Press, Inc., 1996. pp.37–54.
8. **Lu, F.C.:** Toxic effects. In *Basic Toxicology: Fundamentals, Target Organs, and Risk Assessment*, 3rd edition, pp. 41–56. Washington, DC: Taylor & Francis, 1996.

Additional Reading

Gregus, Z., and C.D. Klaassen: Mechanisms of Toxicity. In *Casarett and Doull's Toxicology: The Basic Science of Poisons*, sixth edition, C.D. Klaassen (ed.). New York: McGraw-Hill, 2001. pp. 35–81.

Table 3.1 — Some Mechanisms of Toxicity

Mechanism of Action	Site of Action/Process	Toxicants
Interference with enzymes by inhibition	Specific enzymes, such as acetylcholinesterase	Organophosphates, nerve agents
	Enzyme sulfhydryl groups	Heavy metals, such as mercury, arsenic, lead
Interference with enzymes by induction	Cytochrome P450-dependent monooxygenases	Dioxin (TCDD), phenobarbital, ethanol
Uncoupling of biochemical reactions	Production of adenosine triphosphate (ATP)	Dinitroorthocresol
	Formation of NADPH from NADP	Paraquat, diquat
	Calcium homeostasis	Carbon tetrachloride, bomobenzene, acetaminophen, cadmium
Inhibition of oxygen transfer	Cytochrome oxidase	Hydrocyanic acid, hydrogen sulfide
Blockage of hemoglobin oxygen transport	Hemoglobin oxygen site	Carbon monoxide
	Oxidation of hemoglobin to methemoglobin	Aromatic amines, aniline, azo compounds, nitro compounds, nitrities
	Formation of sulfhemoglobin	Hydrogen peroxide, sulfur-containing compounds
	Red blood cell membrane breakdown	Surfactants, hydrazine
Synthesis of a toxic metabolite	Optic nerve	Methanol
Removal of metallic co-factors	Enzymes requiring metallic co-factors, such as acetaldehyde dehydrogenase	Chelating agents, dithiocarbamates, Antabuse
Interference with neurotransmission	Receptors for acetylcholine	Chelating agents, dithiocarbamates, Antabuse
	Neurotransmission in CNS	Mescaline, LSD
Interference with nucleic acids	Duplication of DNA	Alkylating agents, like mustard gas
	Transcription of RNA from DNA	Rifampicin
Interference with protein synthesis	Translation of RNA to ribosomes	Streptomycin
Interference with lipids	Cells of the CNS	Anesthetic agents, such as ether and cyclopropane; organic solvents, such as gasoline, halogenated organic compounds
	Lipid peroxidation	Halogenated hydrocarbons
Immunosuppression	Cells of immune system	Glucocorticoids, chemotherapeutic agents
Hypersensitization	Cells of immune system	Chromium III and VI salts, p-phenylene diamines, small molecular weight aldehydes
Direct chemical irritation	Cells of skin	Strong alkaline solutions, strong acids
	Mucus membranes of respiratory tract	Chlorine, phosgene, sulfur dioxide, nitrous oxides, ozone
	Mucus membranes of conjunctiva of eye	Acrolein, chloracetophenone, chlorpicrine
Direct damage to cellular structures	Cells of liver and kidney	Chlorinated alkanes, chloroform, carbon tetrachloride, halogenated aromatic compounds (bromobenzene)
Sequestration	Adipose tissue	DDT, PCBs
	Bone cells	Strontium, thorium, lead
	Alveolar cells	Silica dust, coal dust, asbestos

> *Often the remedy is deemed the highest good because it helps so many.*
>
> Paracelsus (1493–1541)

Chapter 4

Disposition of Toxicants

Outcome Competencies

Upon completion of this chapter, the reader should be able to:

- Define half-life, volume of distribution, toxicokinetics, pharmacokinetics, pharmacodynamics, absorption, distribution, biotransformation, metabolism, half-life, bioavailability, steady-state, active and inactive metabolites.
- List and explain the factors that affect the passage of chemicals through biological membranes.
- List and explain the factors that affect the absorption of chemicals through skin or lungs.
- List and discuss the routes of elimination.
- List the types of biotransformations and give examples.
- Draw a typical graph for a one and two compartment model on Cartesian and log scales. Label the different phases of the curves.
- Calculate a half-life for a chemical given the slope of the line for the elimination phase of blood-concentration versus time curve.
- Determine when approximately 97% of a chemical has been eliminated from the body given the half-life of the chemical.
- State the difference between first-order and zero-order pharmacokinetics and discuss the toxicological implications for chemicals with zero-order elimination.
- Explain why some chemicals accumulate in the body with everyday exposure and why some do not.
- Explain the differences between classic pharmacokinetics and physiologically-based pharmacokinetics.
- Explain why, for some chemicals, blood is drawn at the *end* of a workweek to monitor a worker's exposure to chemicals.
- Explain why urine levels, instead of blood levels, may be suitable for workplace monitoring of chemical exposures in workers.

Prerequisite Knowledge
1. Basic biology and physiology
2. Algebra and beginning calculus

Key Terms
absorption, absorption half-life, active metabolites, Area Under the Curve (AUC), bioavailability, biotransformation, classic pharmacokinetics, distribution, elimination, elimination half-life, excretion, half-life, inactive metabolites, metabolism, pharmacokinetics, Physiologically-Based Pharmacokinetics (PBPK), redistribution, toxicokinetics, volume of distribution

Key Topics
1. Passage of Chemicals through Biological Membranes
   - Passive Diffusion
   - Carrier-mediated Transport
2. Absorption
   - Definition
   - Rate of Absorption
   - Extent of Absorption
   - Skin
   - Lungs
3. Distribution
   - General Principles
   - Redistribution
   - Volume of Distribution
4. Elimination
   - Routes of Elimination
   - Metabolism
5. Mathematical Descriptions
   - First-Order versus Zero-Order Pharmacokinetics
   - First-Order Pharmacokinetics
   - Zero-Order Pharmacokinetics
   - Classic Compartmental Pharmacokinetics
   - Half-life
   - Equations and Calculations
   - Application of Pharmacokinetics to Interpretation of Carboxyhemoglobin Levels
   - Bioavailability
   - Multiple Exposures and Steady-state
   - Physiologically-Based Pharmacokinetics (PBPK)
6. Urine versus Blood Samples in the Workplace

Chapter 4

Disposition of Toxicants

By Susan Shelnutt, RPh, PhD

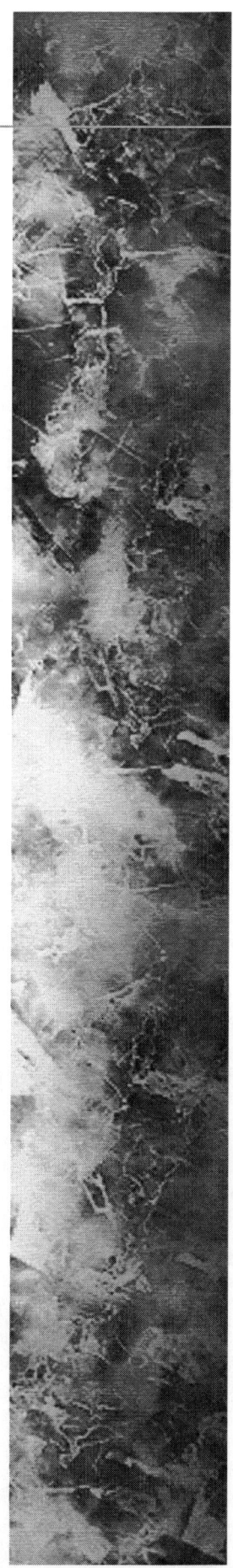

Introduction

Disposition is a broad term that refers to what happens to a chemical once it contacts the body: how well it is absorbed; where in the body the chemical goes (to what organs and tissues is it distributed); how long it stays there; and how it is eliminated. The study of the disposition of toxicants refers to the absorption, distribution, metabolism, and excretion (ADME) of a toxicant, also known as pharmacokinetics or toxicokinetics.

The term "kinetics," as it applies to toxicology, also refers to a mathematical description of the movement of a chemical throughout the body over time. As a chemical is absorbed into the body, the blood level of the chemical increases at a certain rate, which can be described mathematically. As the chemical is metabolized and excreted from the body, the blood level of the chemical decreases at a certain rate, which can also be described mathematically. This is discussed in further detail below.

Technically, "pharmacokinetics" refers to the movement of drugs throughout the body, and "toxicokinetics" refers to the movement of toxicants throughout the body.[1] However, the key principles between the two are the same, and the scientific literature often uses the word pharmacokinetics when referring to toxicants.

Another term "pharmacodynamics" or "toxicodynamics" refers to the biochemical and physiological effects of a drug or toxicant, respectively.[2] An easy way to remember the difference between pharmacokinetics and pharmacodynamics is to notice that pharmacokinetics is "what the body does to the chemical," and pharmacodynamics is "what the chemical does to the body."[3]

The combination of pharmacokinetics and pharmacodynamics (PK-PD) refers to the relationship between blood or tissue concentrations of a chemical and the magnitude of the chemical's effects. For example, peak blood levels of methanol greater than 20 mg/dL are considered toxic, whereas, peak blood levels less than 20 mg/dL are not.[4]

Passage of Chemicals through Biological Membranes

All movement of chemicals throughout the body involves passage through biological membranes.[5] For example, to gain access to the blood stream, a chemical will have to pass through the membranes of the gastrointestinal tract, or the lungs, or the skin. To pass from the blood stream to a body organ, such as the liver, a chemical will have to pass through the membranes of the blood vessels and liver tissue. Thus, it is important to understand the basic principles involved in these processes in order to understand, for example, why some chemicals are better absorbed than others or why some chemicals accumulate in body fat while others do not.

Two processes by which chemicals move through biological membranes are passive diffusion and carrier-mediated transport.

Passive Diffusion

In passive diffusion, no energy is needed for a chemical to pass through a membrane. The rate of passive diffusion through a membrane depends on the surface area of the membrane, the concentration of the chemical, and the chemical's inherent permeability.[5] Since the rate of diffusion is proportional to the surface area of the membrane and to the concentration of the chemical, doubling the surface area or doubling the concentration of the chemical will double the rate of absorption. Doubling both the surface area and the concentration of the chemical will quadruple the rate of absorption. Thus, a worker who spills a 20% solution of a chemical on 200 cm^2 of skin will, in theory, have an absorption rate that is quadruple that of a worker who spills a 10% solution on 100 cm^2 of skin.

In addition, during passive diffusion, chemicals move from an area of high concentration, such as the site of exposure (for example, the skin or lungs), to an area of lower concentration, such as the blood stream. The difference between these two concentrations is referred to as the concentration gradient.

Factors that influence the inherent permeability of a chemical are the size of the molecule, whether it is ionized or non-ionized, and its relative solubility in oil versus water. In general, compounds that are more lipid (oil) soluble diffuse through a biological membrane faster and more easily than those that are less lipid soluble. Molecules that are smaller and non-ionized pass through faster and more easily than those that are larger and ionized.

Most chemicals cross membranes by passive diffusion.[6] Specific examples include solvent absorption through the skin[7], and the absorption of ethanol from the gastrointestinal tract.[6] Generally, a chemical is presumed to cross membranes via passive diffusion unless there is evidence of carrier-mediated transport.

Carrier-mediated Transport

Cells often have specialized transport mechanisms that require energy to facilitate uptake of essential molecules such as nutrients.[5] Chemicals that are structurally similar to these essential molecules can be actively transported or carried into the cell by these mechanisms.[6] Chemicals that are transported into a cell via carrier-mediated transport may become concentrated in that cell. Unlike passive diffusion, cellular-mediated transport can move chemicals against the concentration gradient, from an area of low concentration (such as the blood stream) to an area of high concentration (such as the cell). Chemicals that are ionized or more water-soluble and do not cross membranes well via passive diffusion may cross a biological membrane due to carrier-mediated transport. For example, some metals, such as copper, magnesium, iron, zinc and cobalt that are required for proper function of the central nervous system, are transported into the brain by carrier-mediated transport.[8]

Absorption

Absorption, for the purposes of this chapter, means gaining access to the systemic circulation. While some chemicals are absorbed into the deeper layers of the skin and may cause local skin reactions or allergic reactions, they do not gain appreciable access to the vascular system and the systemic circulation. A chemical gains access to the body following absorption through the skin, lungs, gastrointestinal tract, or the mucous membranes of the mouth, nose and rectum. Absorption can occur via passive diffusion or carrier-mediated transport.

In addition, there are factors that affect the rate and extent of absorption. These factors, such as the chemical properties of the toxicant, and the physiology of the site of absorption, greatly influence the magnitude of the resulting blood levels of a chemical.

Rate of Absorption

The rate of absorption of a chemical has a large effect on the resulting blood levels of that chemical. Given two chemicals that are eliminated from the body at the same rate, the one with the faster rate of absorption will achieve higher blood levels.

The rate of absorption is influenced by the concentration of the chemical. Highly concentrated chemicals are more rapidly absorbed.[9] In addition, the amount of blood flow to an area influences the absorption rate. Application of heat to the skin, which increases blood flow, will result in a faster rate of absorption compared to normal temperature skin.

Extent of Absorption

Extent of absorption refers to the percent of a chemical that reaches the blood circulation. While some chemicals are completely absorbed, it is important to note that many chemicals are only partially absorbed. In addition, the percent absorbed may depend on the route of exposure. For example, elemental mercury is poorly absorbed when swallowed. Less than 0.01% is absorbed in persons with a normal healthy gastrointestinal tract. However, elemental mercury will volatilize, and approximately 75% of an inhaled dose is absorbed into the body.[10]

Skin

The amount of chemical absorbed through the skin depends on the surface area exposed, the concentration of the chemical applied to the skin, and the length of time of the exposure. The integrity of the skin is also a factor. Skin that is abraded or raw is more permeable than healthy skin[6,11], as is skin that is excessively dry or excessively wet.[7]

In addition, compounds that are corrosive or that dissolve the normal oils of the skin ("de-fat" the skin) will damage the skin and may facilitate their own absorption into the body, if not washed off soon after exposure.[6] There are case reports in the literature of people who have spilled concentrated phenol solutions on themselves, developed skin burns, and died within a short period of time, some within minutes. The short time until death is presumably due to the rapid absorption of phenol through burned (damaged) skin.[12]

Occluding the skin will also facilitate the absorption of chemicals.[7] In the workplace, occlusion can occur when chemicals are spilled into a boot or glove. If the boot or glove is not removed and the skin washed, the boot or glove becomes a reservoir that continually bathes the skin with the chemical. There is a case report in the medical literature of a painter who spilled methanol onto his clothes and shoes and continued to wear them for the rest of the day. Although solvents such as methanol usually evaporate from the skin, limiting the amount absorbed from a one-time spill[13], in this case, the methanol had prolonged skin contact. The painter became blind as a result.[14]

For more information on the skin, please refer to Chapter 6, "Dermal Toxicology."

Lungs

The amount of chemical absorbed through the lungs depends on the air concentration, the water solubility of the compound, the size of the particles, and the respiratory rate of the worker.[15] Large particles may be deposited in the oral cavity or pharynx and subsequently swallowed, and thus may not be carried into the lungs. Gas molecules (especially highly reactive or water soluble molecules) may react with the nasal mucosa and thus may not reach the airways.[6] Workers performing heavy labor have a higher respiratory rate and will absorb a greater amount of a chemical than a sedentary office worker with a lower respiratory rate. For more information on the lungs, please refer to Chapter 5, "Respiratory Toxicology."

Distribution

Following absorption, a chemical is distributed via the blood to tissues in the body. Uptake of chemicals by tissues follows the same principles of movement through biological membranes discussed previously.[5] Chemicals may be taken-up into tissues via passive diffusion, following a concentration gradient, or via carrier-mediated transport, moving against a concentration gradient, such that the resulting concentration in the cells is higher than that in the blood. In addition, chemicals that are very lipid soluble tend to be found in higher concentrations in body fat than chemicals that are more water soluble. In the same way, chemicals that are more water soluble may be found in higher concentrations in the blood (which has a high water content) compared to those that are more lipid soluble.

It is important to note that just because a chemical has a high concentration in a particular tissue doesn't mean that the chemical causes an adverse effect in that tissue. Many chemicals have high concentrations in fat, but do not adversely affect fat. Fat often serves as a reservoir (or storage area) for many lipid soluble drugs that ultimately exert their effect on other tissues. Lead is an example of a compound that is stored in bone, but is not toxic to bone.[16]

Redistribution

As a chemical is taken up into tissues from the blood, the blood concentration of the chemical decreases. In addition, some organs, such as liver and kidneys, metabolize and/or excrete the chemical (discussed in detail below) which further decreases the blood concentration of the chemical. At some point in time, the concentration in the tissues becomes greater than the concentration in the blood, and the chemical then moves back into the blood from the tissues, following the concentration gradient. This process is called redistribution. Once back in the blood, the chemical is available to be redistributed to all tissues of the body.

Volume of Distribution

The volume of distribution is the theoretical volume that a chemical occupies in the body. It is best explained using the "swimming pool" example. Suppose someone wished to know the volume of a swimming pool. One way to find out would be to add a known amount of a chemical to the pool, and then analyze a sample of the pool water to determine the concentration of the chemical. The amount of the chemical added to the pool divided by the resulting concentration of the chemical in the sample equals the volume of the pool.

In the same way, the "volume" that a chemical occupies in the body can be determined by administering a known amount of the chemical to a human or laboratory animal, and then measuring the resulting blood concentration. Often, the volume of distribution is reported in units of volume per kg body weight, such as liters/kg (L/kg).

The volume of distribution is a value that is specific for a chemical and varies widely. For example, the volume of distribution for amitriptyline is 15 L/kg[17], while the volume of distribution for ethylene glycol is 0.55 L/kg.[18]

It is important to note that the value for the volume of distribution may not correspond to an actual physiological volume. In the above example, the volume of distribution for amitriptyline (15 L/kg) is 1050 L for a 70 kg person, which is much greater than any physiological volume in the human body. For this reason, the volume of distribution is often referred to as the "apparent" volume of distribution.[19] When a chemical has a volume of distribution that is larger than the physiological volume of the human body, it can be inferred that most of the chemical resides in tissues of the body other than blood, since it is the concentration in the blood that is used to calculate the volume of distribution.

Elimination

Routes of Elimination

Chemicals can be eliminated from the body through metabolism and excretion. All tissues have enzymes that can metabolize chemicals to some extent; however, the liver has the highest concentration of enzymes of any organ in the body and is usually the primary site of metabolism. The kidneys and, to a lesser extent, the lungs, skin and gastrointestinal tract also contribute to metabolism.

Excretion occurs primarily through the kidneys, however, some chemicals are excreted in the feces, breast milk and sweat, and some volatile chemicals are excreted through the lungs via exhaled air.

Metabolism

The body metabolizes chemicals using the same enzymes used to metabolize food, hormones, and other compounds found in the body. The purpose of metabolism is to make chemicals more water-soluble so that they are more readily excreted.[20]

Metabolic transformation of chemicals (also known as biotransformation) can be divided into two types of reactions: Phase I and Phase II.[20] Phase I transformations are oxidation, reduction or hydrolysis reactions that either add or expose a functional group (such as –OH, -NH2, -SH, or -COOH). Cytochrome P450 enzymes (also called microsomal enzymes) are an important family of Phase I enzymes found in the endoplasmic reticulum of the cell. These enzymes catalyze a variety of Phase I biotransformation reactions and are responsible for the metabolism of numerous exogenous compounds.

Phase II transformations are conjugation reactions that result in the formation of a covalent bond between a functional group (either on the parent compound or on the phase I metabolite) and glucuronic acid, sulfate, glutathione, amino acids or acetate. These conjugates are highly polar and easily excreted through the kidneys or through bile, which is then excreted along with feces. Tables 4.1 and 4.2 give examples of Phase I and Phase II reactions.

In many cases, the metabolite does not possess toxicological activity and is referred to as an "inactive" metabolite. Metabolites that still have toxicological activity are referred to as "active" metabolites. Some active metabolites are much more toxic than their parent compound. Methanol is an example of a toxicant that has active metabolites.

Methanol is metabolized by the same enzymes that metabolize ethanol. While ethanol is metabolized to less toxic compounds, first by alcohol dehydrogenase and then by aldehyde dehydrogenase, methanol is metabolized to compounds that are much more toxic (see Figure 4.1). In fact, the characteristic signs and symptoms of methanol toxicity (metabolic acidosis and blindness) are due to the metabolites of methanol, formaldehyde and formic acid. The treatment for methanol poisoning is to give the patient ethanol. Ethanol is preferentially metabolized by alcohol dehydrogenase and aldehyde dehydrogenase, and "occupies" the enzymes, preventing methanol from being metabolized. Methanol is then excreted unchanged by the kidneys and by the lungs.

Table 4.1 — Examples of Phase I Biotransformation Reactions

Reaction	Example
Oxidation	
Aliphatic Hydroxylation	$R-CH_3 \rightarrow R-CH_2-OH$
Aromatic Hydroxylation	Ph-R → R-Ph-OH
N-, O-, or S-dealkylation	$R-(N,O,S)(CH_3)(H) \rightarrow R-(NH_2, OH, SH) + H_2C=O$
Deamination	$R-CH_2-NH_2 \rightarrow R-CHO + NH_3$
N-hydroxylation	$R-NH-CO-CH_3 \rightarrow R-N(OH)-CO-CH_3$
Oxidative dehalogenation, X= halogen, such as Cl⁻, Br⁻, or F⁻	$R-CHX-H \rightarrow R-CHX-OH \rightarrow R-CHO + H-X$
Reduction	
Aromatic nitro Reduction	$R-C_6H_4-NO_2 \rightarrow R-C_6H_4-NH_2$

Table 4.2 — Examples of Phase II Biotransformation Reactions

Reaction	Example
Glucuronidation	R—OH + glucuronide → [glucuronide-R conjugate]
Sulfation	R—OH + sulfate → O⁻—S(=O)(=O)—O—R
Acetylation	C₆H₅—NH₂ + acetate → C₆H₅—NH—C(=O)—CH₃

Mathematical Descriptions

Pharmacokineticists use equations to describe the movement of a chemical through out the body. These equations relate the dose, volume of distribution, bioavailability (defined below), and the absorption and elimination rate constants of the chemical to the blood concentration of the chemical over time. Combined with experimentally determined blood-concentration time data, these equations, allow one to calculate values for the volume of distribution, bioavailability, and absorption and elimination rate constants associated with a specific chemical.

Once the values for these parameters are determined, one can make predictions regarding toxicity. For example, a chemical with slow and incomplete skin absorption, but with fast and complete absorption following ingestion, will be more toxic following ingestion than skin exposure. Chemicals with a slow excretion rate will have longer lasting toxic effects compared to a chemical with a faster excretion rate. In addition, predictions of blood or tissue concentrations can be made for various chemical exposure scenarios.

First-order versus Zero-order Pharmacokinetics

Pharmacokinetic processes, such as absorption and elimination, can be divided into two general types: first-order and zero-order. As will be discussed in detail, in first-order processes, the amount absorbed or eliminated is proportional to the amount of chemical present. In zero-order processes, the amount absorbed or eliminated is a constant amount.

Most drugs and chemicals have first order pharmacokinetics; some, however, have zero-order pharmacokinetics, and others have first-order pharmacokinetics at low doses and zero-order pharmacokinetics at higher doses.

One of the most important characteristics of a chemical with first-order elimination is that the blood concentration increases linearly as the dose of the chemical increases (first-order pharmacokinetics is often referred to as "linear" pharmacokinetics).

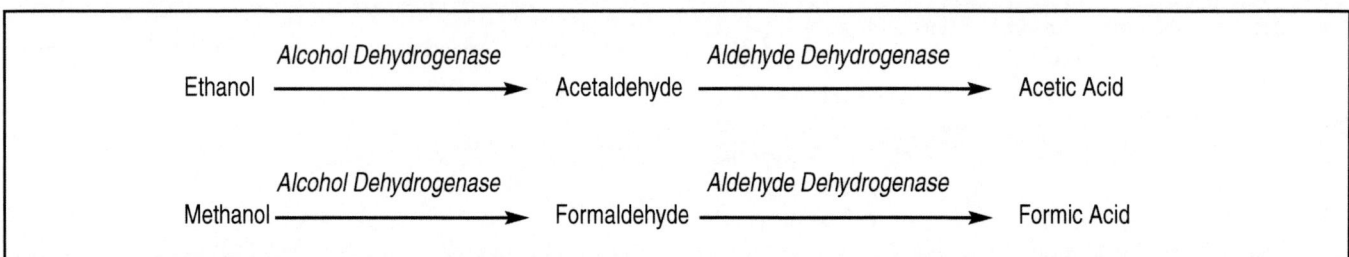

Figure 4.1 — Ethanol and methanol are metabolized by the same enzymes, alcohol dehydrogenase and aldehyde dehydrogenase. Alcohol dehydrogenase converts the alcohol molecule into an aldehyde, and aldehyde dehydrogenase converts the aldehyde into an acid. However, acetaldehyde and acetic acid formed from ethanol are relatively low in toxicity compared to the formaldehyde and formic acid formed from methanol. It is formaldehyde and formic acid that are responsible for the signs and symptoms of methanol toxicity.

Stated differently, when the dose of a chemical with first-order elimination is doubled, the blood concentration doubles; when the dose is tripled, the blood concentration triples. This is not true for zero-order elimination as discussed below.

First-order Pharmacokinetics

In first-order pharmacokinetics, the rate of elimination of a chemical from the body is described by the following equation:

$$\frac{dA}{dt} = -k_{el} A \quad (1)$$

where A is the amount of the chemical in the body, k_{el} is the elimination rate constant, and the negative sign denotes that the chemical is being eliminated from the body. The term "first order" derives from the fact that the rate of elimination is proportional to A to the first power (since $A = A^1$).

Absorption processes can also be first order, and are described by the following equation:

$$\frac{dA}{dt} = k_a A_a \quad (2)$$

where the rate of increase of a chemical in the body is equal to k_a (the absorption rate constant) times A_a (the amount of chemical at the absorption site).

Zero-order pharmacokinetics

In zero-order elimination, a chemical is eliminated from the body at a constant rate, described by the following equation:

$$\frac{dA}{dt} = -k \quad (3)$$

where A is the amount of the chemical in the body, k is the elimination rate, and the negative sign denotes that the chemical is being eliminated from the body. This equation can also be written as

$$\frac{dA}{dt} = -kA^0 \quad (4)$$

since $A^0 = 1$. The term "zero-order" derives from the fact that the rate of elimination is proportional to A to the zero power.

Thus, in zero-order elimination, the amount eliminated is not proportional to the blood concentration, but is a constant rate per unit of time. Table 4.3 shows the elimination of a hypothetical chemical with a constant elimination rate of 25 mg/L/hour.

It is generally accepted that zero-order elimination occurs when metabolism or excretion of the chemical is at maximum capacity. The elimination rate cannot increase (it remains constant) even if the body continues to absorb more of the chemical. In contrast, with first-order elimination, the rate of elimination increases in proportion to the amount of chemical in the body.

Table 4.3 — Example of the elimination of a hypothetical chemical with a constant elimination rate of 25 mg/L/hour (zero-order elimination)

Time (hr)	Blood Concentration (mg/L)	Amount Eliminated (mg/L)	Cumulative Percent Eliminated (%)
0	150	–	–
2	125	25	16.7
3	100	25	20
4	75	25	25
5	50	25	33.3
6	25	25	50
7	0	25	100

A chemical may have first-order elimination at low doses and zero-order elimination at high doses; such is the case with ethanol. At blood concentrations above approximately 20 mg/dL (0.02 g%), ethanol elimination from the body appears to be a zero-order process with a constant elimination rate, which averages 19 mg/dL/hour.[21] At blood concentrations below 20 mg/dL, ethanol elimination is best described as a first order process with an elimination rate that is proportional to the amount of ethanol in the body.[22] Since 20 mg/dL (0.02 g%) is a low blood concentration, well below the current drunk driving limit of 80 mg/dL (0.08 g%), first-order elimination of ethanol is often ignored and sometimes ethanol is referred to as having zero-order elimination.

Zero-order pharmacokinetic processes, also known as non-linear processes, have important implications for toxicity. As mentioned above, when the dose of a chemical with first-order elimination is doubled, the blood concentration of the chemical also doubles; however, when the dose of a chemical with zero-order elimination is doubled, the blood concentration may more-than-double, and the degree to which it increases may not be predictable. The result is that seemingly small changes in dose may result in large increases in blood concentrations that are associated with toxicity. This can be seen with ethanol at the higher doses associated with zero-order elimination; doubling the amount of ethanol ingested more-than-doubles the resulting blood concentration.

Absorption processes can also be zero-order, and are described by the following equation:

$$\frac{dA}{dt} = k_a \quad (5)$$

where the rate of increase of a chemical in the body is equal to k_a, the absorption rate.

Zero-order absorption means that the amount absorbed is not proportional to the amount of the chemical at the absorption site; instead a constant amount is absorbed per unit of time, such as 20 mg/hour.

Classic Compartmental Pharmacokinetics

Classic compartmental pharmacokinetics (as opposed to physiologically-based pharmacokinetics, described below) describes blood-concentration time curves using compartmental models and equations that describe the models.

A typical blood-concentration time curve for a one-compartment model with first-order absorption and elimination is shown in Figure 4.2a. As a chemical is absorbed, distributed and eliminated from the body, its blood concentration increases, peaks, and then decreases over time. The time during which the blood concentration increases is called the absorption phase; the time during which the blood concentration decreases is called the elimination phase. Figure 4.2b shows the same data plotted on a semi-log scale. Notice that plotting the curve on a semi-log scale causes the elimination phase of the curve to be straight (linear).

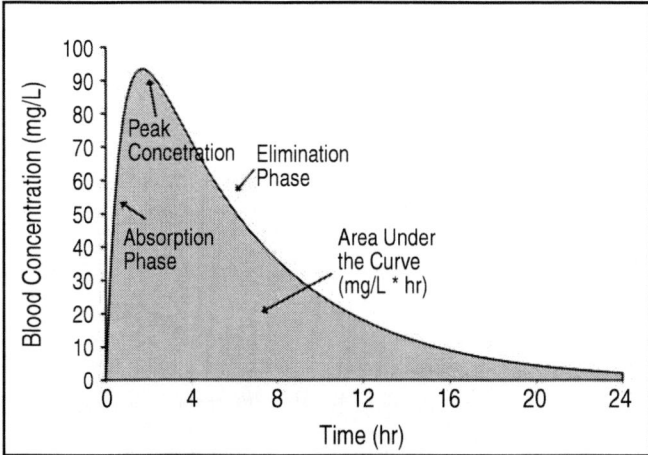

Figure 4.2a — A typical blood concentration versus time plot on a Cartesian (non-log) scale. In this hypothetical example, the absorption half-life is 0.5 hours, and the elimination half-life is 4 hours. After 24 hours (6 elimination half-lives), most, but not all, of the chemical has been eliminated from the blood.

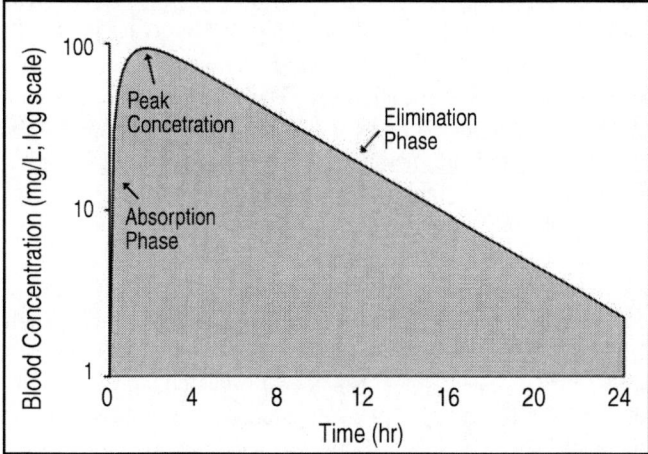

Figure 4.2b — The same blood concentration data from Figure 4.2a plotted on a log scale. Note that only the y-axis is a log scale. Plotting blood concentration data on a log scale causes the elimination phase to be linear.

A schematic of a one compartment model is shown in Figure 4.3. In this model, the chemical is absorbed into the body (represented by the one compartment) at a rate described by the absorption rate constant k_a, and it is eliminated from the body at a rate described by the elimination rate constant k_{el}.

The mathematical equation for a one compartment model is

$$C = \left[\frac{(FDk_a)}{Vd(k_a - k_{el})}\right]\left(e^{-k_{el}*t} - e^{-k_a*t}\right) \quad (6)$$

where C is the blood concentration of the chemical, F is the bioavailability (defined and discussed below), D is the dose, k_a is the absorption rate constant, k_{el} is the elimination rate constant, Vd is the volume of distribution, and e is the natural logarithm base. The reader is referred to the texts in the Additional Reading section of the chapter for derivation of the above equation, if desired.

Figures 4.4a and 4.4b show a blood concentration time curve for a two compartment model plotted on a Cartesian (non-log) and semi-log scale respectively. Figure 4.5 shows a schematic of the model. In a two compartment model, the body is represented by 2 compartments. Compartment 1 represents the blood and tissues into which the chemical is distributed quickly. Compartment 2 represents the tissues into which the chemical is distributed more slowly. k_{1-2} is the rate constant for movement of the chemical from compartment 1 to compartment 2, and k_{2-1} is the rate constant for the movement of the chemical from compartment 2 to compartment 1. The equation for a two compartment model is more complex and will not be reproduced here. The reader is referred to the texts in the Additional Reading section of this chapter if further information is desired.

Notice that for the two compartment model, the shape of the blood concentration time curve after the peak concentration has two distinct phases. The phase immediately following the peak

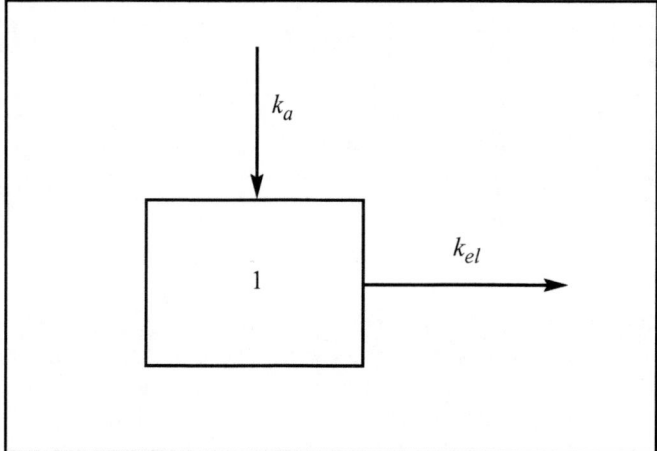

Figure 4.3 — Schematic of one compartment pharmacokinetic model. A chemical is absorbed into the body at a certain rate, described by the absorption rate constant, k_a. It is eliminated from the body at a rate described by the elimination rate constant, k_{el}. The body is represented by one compartment.

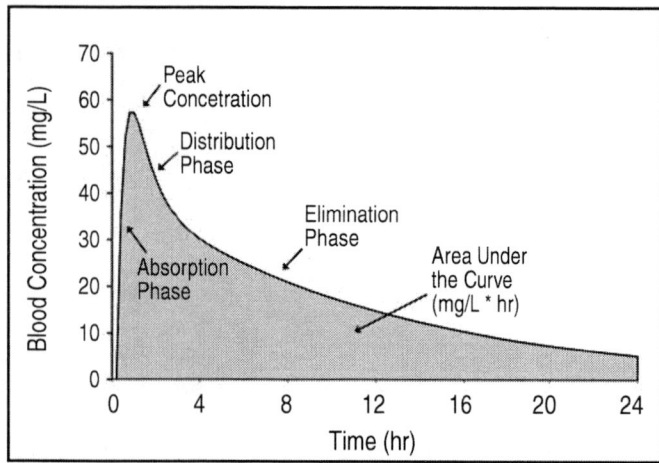

Figure 4.4a — A typical blood concentration versus time for a two-compartment model. In this hypothetical example, the absorption half-life is 0.25 hours, the distribution half-life is 0.5 hours, and the elimination half-life is 8 hours.

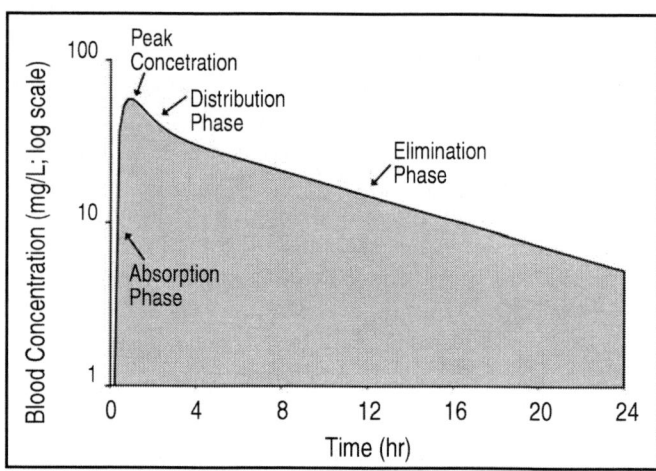

Figure 4.4b — The same blood concentration data from Figure 4.4a plotted on a log scale.

is often termed the distribution phase, referring to the distribution of the chemical into tissues. The part of the curve after the distribution phase is referred to as the elimination phase.

Also note that the compartments do not correspond to specific organs or tissues in the body. The number of compartments a model contains is based solely on the shape of the experimentally determined blood-concentration time curve and a statistical analysis to determine the number of compartments needed to fit the data.

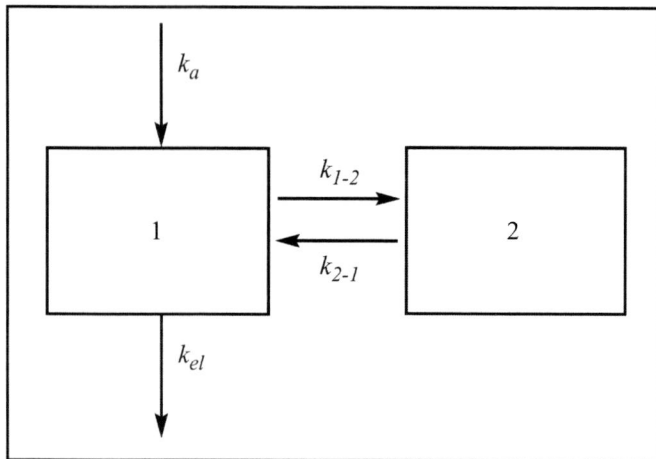

Figure 4.5 — Schematic of two compartment pharmacokinetic model. A chemical is absorbed into the body at a certain rate, described by the absorption rate constant, k_a. It is eliminated from the body at a rate described by the elimination rate constant k_{el}. The body is represented by two compartments. Compartment 1 represents the blood and tissues into which the chemical is distributed quickly. Compartment 2 represents the tissues into which the chemical is distributed more slowly. k_{1-2} is the rate constant for movement of the chemical from compartment 1 to compartment 2, and k_{2-1} is the rate constant for the movement of the chemical from compartment 2 to compartment 1.

Half-life

Half-life is a useful pharmacokinetic parameter commonly calculated for first order absorption and elimination processes. Absorption half-life is defined as the time it takes for one-half of the chemical to be absorbed from the absorption site. For example, an absorption half-life of 0.5 hours means that 50% of the chemical is absorbed from the absorption site every 0.5 hours.

The elimination half-life is the amount of time it takes for the blood concentration of a chemical to decrease by one-half. The symbol $t_{1/2}$ is used to represent half-life, and if no qualifying term such as "absorption" or "elimination" is used, the $t_{1/2}$ is assumed to refer to the elimination half-life.

Table 4.4 shows the elimination of a hypothetical chemical with a half-life of 4 hours. If the starting blood concentration is 150 mg/L, then 4 hours later, the blood concentration will be 75 mg/L (half of 150). After another 4 hours, the blood concentration will be 37.5 mg/L (half of 75), and so on. Note that the *percent* of the chemical eliminated every 4 hours (i.e., 50%) is constant, but the *amount* of chemical eliminated every 4 hours is not constant. The amount eliminated per unit of time is proportional to the amount of chemical in the body. The reader may wish to compare Table 4.4 (showing the elimination of a chemical with first-order pharmacokinetics) with Table 4.3 (showing the elimination of a chemical with zero-order pharmacokinetics) to appreciate the differences.

Table 4.4 also shows the relationship between the number of half-lives and the *cumulative* percent eliminated: after one half-life, 50% of the chemical has been eliminated; after two half-lives, 75% of the chemical has been eliminated, and so on, until after five half-lives, 97% of a chemical has been eliminated from the body. This relationship between the number of half-lives and the cumulative percent eliminated is always true, regardless of the value of the half-life.

Theoretically, the cumulative percent eliminated never reaches 100%, although it is generally accepted in the scientific literature

Table 4.4 — Example of the Elimination of a Hypothetical Chemical with a Half-life of 4 Hours (first-order elimination).

Time (hr)	Number of half-lives	Blood Concentration (mg/L)	Amount Eliminated (mg/L)	Percent Eliminated (%)	Cumulative Percent Eliminated (%)
0	–	150	–	–	–
4	1	75	75	50	50
8	2	37.5	37.5	50	75
12	3	18.8	18.8	50	87.5
16	4	9.4	9.4	50	93.8
20	5	4.7	4.7	50	96.9
24	6	2.3	2.3	50	98.4

that after five half-lives, "all" of a chemical has been eliminated from the body. Thus, to determine the amount of time it takes to eliminate "all" of a chemical from the body, multiply the half-life by five. If a chemical has a half-life of 2 days, it will take 10 days to eliminate it from the body.

Equations and Calculations

There are some simple equations that are useful for calculating blood levels of a chemical following an exposure and for calculating half-life. To derive these equations, one should consider the simplest case, in which a chemical with first–order elimination is injected intravenously. Assume the pharmacokinetics of this chemical is best described by a one-compartment model. Since intravenous injection means that 100% of the chemical reaches the blood stream almost instantaneously, and a one-compartment model means there is no distribution phase, the mathematical terms associated with absorption and distribution can be ignored, and the equations are less complex than, for example, Equation 6 above, which contains an absorption term.

Even though we are deriving these equations for the case of intravenous injection, the equations will apply to the *elimination phase* of a blood concentration-time curve for chemicals with first-order elimination that are absorbed through the skin, lungs or gastrointestinal tract.

Following injection, the blood concentration of the chemical declines over time (see Figure 4.6). The decline shown in Figure 4.6 is a straight line because the data are plotted on a semi-log scale. In practice, there is usually a time lag of at least a few minutes between the end of the injection and the collection of the first blood sample. Thus, the initial blood concentration immediately after injection is usually not known. But the theoretical initial blood concentration (C_0; the y-axis intercept) can be determined by extrapolation from the linear elimination phase (as shown in Figure 4.6).

The equation for the rate of the decline of the blood concentration for a one-compartment model following intravenous injection is

$$\frac{dC}{dt} = -k_{el} \cdot C_0 \qquad (7)$$

where C is the blood concentration, (k_{el}) is the elimination rate constant, and C_0 is the y-intercept. A negative sign is inserted into the equation to show that the blood concentration is decreasing.

Using LaPlace transforms, Equation 7 becomes

$$C = C_0 \cdot e^{-k_{el} \cdot t} \qquad (8)$$

showing that the blood concentration (C) is equal to the initial blood concentration (C_0) times the base of the natural logarithm (e) raised to the power of the negative elimination rate constant (k_{el}) times the time post injection (t). The reader is referred to Gibaldi and Perrier[23] for a discussion of the use of LaPlace transforms in pharmacokinetics, if desired.

Taking the natural logarithm of both sides, Equation 8 becomes

$$\ln C = \ln C_0 - k_{el} \cdot t \qquad (9)$$

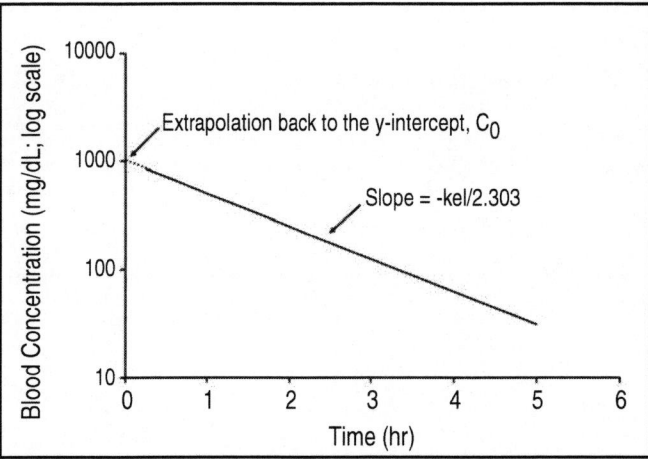

Figure 4.6 — Blood concentration-time curve for intravenous injection of a chemical with first-order elimination kinetics described by a one-compartment model.

Converting the natural log to log base 10, Equation 9 becomes

$$\log C = \log C_0 - \frac{k_{el}}{2.303} \cdot t \qquad (10)$$

Note that Equations 9 and 10 are linear equations following the general form y = mx + b, or more specifically in this case, y = b-mx. Thus, a plot of log C ("y") versus t ("x") yields a declining straight line with a slope ("m") of $-\frac{k_{el}}{2.303}$ and a y intercept ("b") of log C_0. Figure 4.6 shows a graph of Equation 10.

The value of a linear equation is two fold. First, the line best fitting the experimental blood concentration time data can be determined using linear regression, since experimental data has errors associated with it and is never "perfect." Second, once the best-fit line is determined, the slope of the line can be used to calculate k_{el} and, as will be shown, $t_{1/2}$.

Once the best fit line has been determined by linear regression, the value of the slope $\left(-\frac{k_{el}}{2.303}\right)$ can be obtained either from the linear regression computer routine, or from the graph by calculating $\frac{\Delta y}{\Delta x}$. Stated mathematically,

$$\text{Slope} = \frac{\Delta y}{\Delta x} = \left(-\frac{k_{el}}{2.303}\right) \qquad (11)$$

Once the value for the slope is known, the equation can be solved for k_{el}.

$$k_{el} = slope \cdot (-2.303) \qquad (12)$$

Thus, the slope of the line multiplied by -2.303 gives the value for k_{el}.

The half-life of a chemical can be determined from k_{el} in the following way. Equation 10 above shows the following relationship:

$$\log C = \log C_0 - \frac{k_{el}}{2.303} \cdot t \qquad (10)$$

After one half-life ($t_{1/2}$), the concentration (C) is equal to one-half of the initial concentration, or $\frac{C_0}{2}$.

Thus, Equation 10 can be restated as Equation 13 below and then solved for $t_{1/2}$.

$$\log \frac{C_0}{2} = \log C_0 - \frac{k_{el}}{2.303} \cdot t_{1/2} \qquad (13)$$

$$\log \frac{C_0}{2} - \log C_0 = -\frac{k_{el}}{2.303} \cdot t_{1/2} \qquad (14)$$

$$\log \frac{C_0}{2C_0} = -\frac{k_{el}}{2.303} \cdot t_{1/2} \qquad (15)$$

$$\log 2 = \frac{k_{el}}{2.303} \cdot t_{1/2} \qquad (16)$$

$$\frac{(\log 2) \cdot 2.303}{k_{el}} = t_{1/2} \qquad (17)$$

$$t_{1/2} = \frac{0.693}{k_{el}} \qquad (18)$$

Thus, once k_{el} is determined from the slope of the line, the half life of the chemical can be determined using Equation 18.

Application of Pharmacokinetics to Interpretation of Carboxyhemoglobin Levels

Exposure to carbon monoxide results in the formation of carboxyhemoglobin from normal hemoglobin. Carboxyhemoglobin is responsible for some of the toxic effects of carbon monoxide. Emergency physicians often obtain blood carboxyhemoglobin levels in workers exposed to carbon monoxide to help assess the severity of exposure. However, the half-life of carboxyhemoglobin is short (approximately 4–5 hours)[24] and once the exposure to carbon monoxide ceases, such as when a worker is removed from the workplace and taken to the hospital, the carboxyhemoglobin level starts to decrease. In addition, workers are usually administered oxygen by emergency personnel, and the half-life of carboxyhemoglobin in the presence of oxygen is even shorter (approximately 1–2 hours).[24] Thus, the carboxyhemoglobin level obtained in the emergency room after an exposure may be much lower than the carboxyhemoglobin level at the workplace, and it may be of value to estimate the carboxyhemoglobin level of the worker just after his removal from the carbon monoxide source in order to assess the severity of his exposure.

Consider, then, the case of a worker who is over exposed to carbon monoxide. He is removed from the site by emergency personnel who immediately place him on oxygen and transport him to the emergency department. By the time blood is drawn to determine a carboxyhemoglobin level, one hour has elapsed. The laboratory determines that his carboxyhemoglobin level is 20%. What was his carboxyhemoglobin level one hour earlier just after he was removed from the carbon monoxide source?

An estimate of his carboxyhemoglobin level can be easily calculated using the equations above. As stated earlier, the half-life of carboxyhemoglobin in the presence of oxygen ranges from 1–2 hours. For this estimate, one can start by using a carboxyhemoglobin half-life value of 1 hour, and calculate the value for k_{el} by using Equation 18 and solving for k_{el}.

$$t_{1/2} = \frac{0.693}{k_{el}} \qquad (18)$$

$$k_{el} \; \frac{0.693}{1 hr} = 0.693 hr^{-1} \quad (19)$$

Notice that if the unit for half-life is hours, then the unit for k_{el} is hours^{-1}.

Next, Equation 8 can be solved for C_0, the initial carboxyhemoglobin concentration, which, in this example, is the concentration prior to the administration of oxygen (Equation 20). Using Equation 20 and inserting 0.693 for k_{el} and 1 hour for t, since one hour elapsed between when his exposure ended and the blood was drawn, we can determine that C_0 is equal to 40%.

$$C = C_0 \cdot e^{-k_{el} \cdot t} \quad (8)$$

$$C_0 = \frac{C}{e^{-k_{el} \cdot t}} \quad (20)$$

$$C_0 = 40\%$$

When a carboxyhemoglobin half-life value of 2 hours is used, C_0 is 28%. Thus, this worker's carboxyhemoglobin level just after being removed from the exposure, prior to the administration of oxygen, can be estimated to range from 28 to 40%.

Bioavailability

Chemicals may be absorbed into the body more completely when given by one route of exposure versus another route of exposure. For example, a chemical may be better absorbed when ingested than when applied to the skin. The term bioavailability refers to the percent of the chemical that is absorbed into the blood stream (and thus is "available" to the organism) following a specific route of exposure. By definition, the bioavailability of a chemical given by intravenous injection is 100%, since all of the chemical reaches the blood stream.

Scientists determine bioavailability by calculating the area under the blood concentration time curve (Area Under the Curve or AUC) following administration of a chemical via an extravascular (non-intravenous) route of exposure and comparing it to the AUC following intravenous administration[5] (see Figures 4.2a and 4.4a for illustrations of the AUC). If the AUC for a chemical following ingestion is 75% of the AUC following intravenous injection, then the oral bioavailability of the chemical is 75%.

If a chemical cannot be administered intravenously, or if intravenous data are not available, then a relative bioavailability can be determined by comparing the AUCs for two different routes of exposure. For example, the AUC for skin administration could be compared to the AUC following ingestion. If the AUC for skin administration is one-half that of the AUC following ingestion of the chemical, then the bioavailability for skin administration is 50% relative to ingestion. When the AUC following intravenous administration is used to calculate bioavailability, it is termed the absolute bioavailability.

Multiple Exposures and Steady State

When a worker is exposed to a chemical repeatedly through the workweek, the chemical may accumulate in the body over time if some of the chemical still remains in the body when exposure occurs on the following day. Figure 4.7 illustrates the accumulation of a chemical when exposures occur every day to a chemical with an elimination half-life of 24 hours. On the first day, the peak blood level is about 100 mg/dL. On the second day, the exposure occurs when there is still a significant amount of the chemical remaining in the body from day one. The peak blood level on Day 2 is approximately 150 mg/dL. The peak blood level increases each day in an asymptotic manner, until the maximum blood level is obtained, in this case approximately 200 mg/dL. Once at the maximum, the peak blood levels will remain at approximately 200 mg/dL with subsequent exposures every 24 hours. The maximum blood level is referred to as the "steady-state" blood level.

Figure 4.8 illustrates daily exposure to a chemical with an elimination half-life of four hours. Accumulation does not occur in this case, as nearly all of the chemical is excreted prior to the next exposure.

Mercury is an example of a metal that accumulates in workers over the workweek. The American Conference of Governmental Industrial Hygienists (ACGIH) recommends obtaining blood for mercury levels from workers at the end of their last shift of the week to monitor worker's exposures to elemental and inorganic mercury.[25]

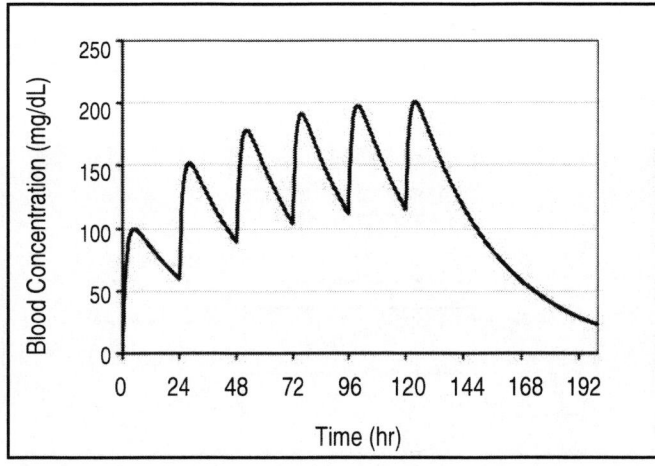

Figure 4.7 — Graph showing the accumulation of a chemical in the body following exposures occurring once every 24 hours to a hypothetical chemical with an absorption half-life of 1 hour and an elimination half-life of 24 hours. The chemical accumulates because another exposure occurs before all of the chemical is eliminated from the previous exposure. Note that the peak blood level increases with each dose until it reaches a maximum, or "steady-state" (approximately 200 mg/dl in this example). Once at steady-state, the peak blood level will remain 200 mg/dL with continued exposures every 24 hours.

Toxicology Principles for the Industrial Hygienist

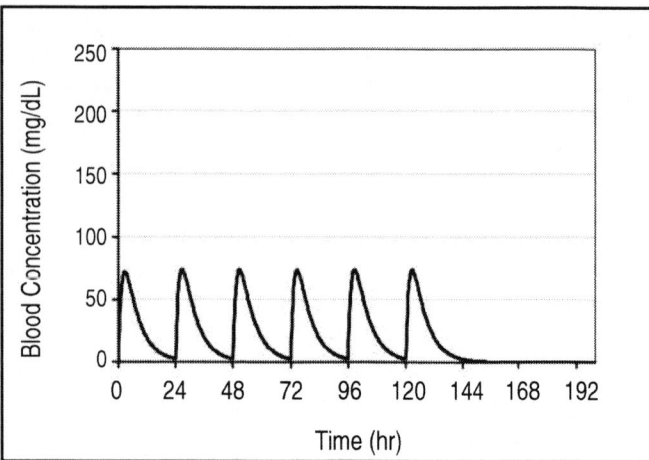

Figure 4.8 — Graph showing the blood levels of a chemical in the body following exposures occurring once every 24 hours to a hypothetical chemical with an absorption half-life of 1 hour but an elimination half-life of only 4 hours. Note that accumulation does not occur as nearly all of the chemical is excreted prior to the next exposure.

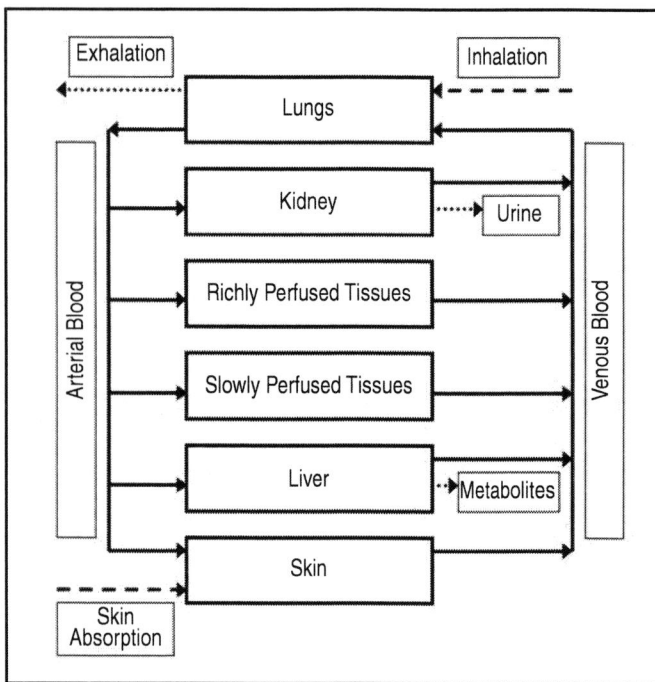

Figure 4.9 — Schematic for a physiologically-based pharmacokinetic model for a chemical absorbed via the lungs and skin, and metabolized primarily by the liver. The solid arrows represent blood routes of blood flow, the long dashes (– – –) represent routes of absorption, and the dotted lines (••••) represent routes of elimination. Each tissue or group of tissues has parameters and constants associated with it, describing the movement of the chemical into and out of the tissue.

Physiologically-Based Pharmacokinetics

In physiologically-based pharmacokinetics (PBPK), the compartments represent specific organs or tissues or groups of organs or tissues that have similar characteristics, such as blood flow rates.[1] A schematic of a typical physiologically-based pharmacokinetic model is shown in Figure 4.9. In this model, some tissues that have high blood flow are grouped together ("Richly Perfused Tissues"), and some tissues that have low blood flow are grouped together ("Slowly Perfused Tissues"). The lungs and kidneys are examples of highly perfused tissues, and fat and bone are examples of slowly perfused tissues.[5]

The advantage to using PBPK is that physiological values used in the model, such as the blood flow to organs, are known. Thus, for example, a model developed for a non-pregnant female could be adapted to a model for a pregnant female by changing the values for blood volume and blood flow and adding a compartment for the fetus. This allows the modeler to predict tissue concentrations of a chemical without having to do an experiment. PBPK modeling can also be used to predict tissue concentrations in humans based on animal data. Dennison et al.[3] recently used a PBPK model to predict blood concentrations of toluene, ethylbenzene and xylene in workers who are exercising compared to those at rest, by increasing the respiratory rate in exercising workers.

Urine Versus Blood Samples in the Workplace

In the workplace, it is preferable to collect urine samples rather than blood samples to monitor an employee's exposure to chemicals, due to the ease of urine collection. This can be done for chemicals that are excreted in urine (or have a metabolite that is excreted in urine) if a correlation exists between the urine level and the effects of the chemical.

For example, ACGIH recommends that workers exposed to arsenic be monitored by analyzing their urine for inorganic arsenic plus methylated arsenic metabolites. Since arsenic can accumulate in the body, the urine sample is collected at the end of the workweek, and the concentration is compared to the Biological Exposure Index (BEI®) of 35 µg/L. ACGIH set the BEI® for inorganic arsenic plus methylated metabolites based on PBPK modeling indicating that inhalation of arsenic at an air concentration of 0.01mg/m³ (the current threshold limit value set by the ACGIH as a time-weighted average) results in urine levels of approximately 35 µg/L.[26] In addition, epidemiological studies conducted in workers show that a urine level of 35 µg/L is not associated with an increased risk of lung cancer.[26]

Sometimes urine concentrations of chemicals are expressed as mg of chemical per gram of creatinine (mg/g). Creatinine is a breakdown product from muscle that is excreted in urine at a reasonably constant rate. Since urine concentrations of a chemical can vary widely depending on the fluid intake of the worker during the day, expression of the chemical concentration as mg per gram of creatinine, which has much less variability, may be preferred.

Summary

There are fundamental biological and physiological principles that influence the absorption, distribution, metabolism and excretion of chemicals, and allow one to understand their fate and toxicity. Mathematical modeling allows one to make predictions of the blood or tissue concentrations following a chemical exposure and the severity of health effects.

References

1. **Medinsky, M.A. and J.L. Valentine:** Toxicokinetics. In *Cassarett and Doull's Toxicology: the Basic Science of Poisons,* 6th edition. Klaassen, C.D. (ed.). New York: McGraw-Hill, 2001. pp. 225–237.
2. **Benet, L.Z., D.L. Kroetz, and L.B. Sheiner:** Pharmacokinetics: the dynamics of drug absorption, distribution, and elimination. In *Goodman & Gilman's The Pharmacological Basis of Therapeutics*, 9th edition. Hardman, J.G. and L.E. Limbird (eds.). New York: McGraw-Hill, 1996. pp. 3–27.
3. **Dennison, J.E., P.L. Bigelow, M.M. Mumtaz, M.E. Andersen, I.D. Dobrev, and R.S. Yang:** Evaluation of potential toxicity from co-exposure to three CNS depressants (toluene, ethylbenzene, and xylene) under resting and working conditions using PBPK modeling. *J. Occup. Env. Hyg. 2(3)*:127–135 (2005).
4. **Ford, M.D., and K. McMartin:** Ethylene glycol and methanol. In *Clinical Toxicology.* Ford, M.D., K.A. Delaney, L.J. Ling, and T. Erickson (eds.). Philadelphia: W.B. Saunders Company, 2001. pp. 757–767.
5. **Rowland, M. and T.N. Tozer:** *Clinical pharmacokinetics: concepts and applications,* 3rd edition. Baltimore, MD: Williams & Wilkins, 1995.
6. **Rozman, K.K., and C.D. Klaassen:** Absorption, distribution, and excretion of toxicants. In *Cassarett and Doull's Toxicology: the Basic Science of Poisons*, 6th edition. Klaassen, C.D. (ed.). New York: McGraw-Hill, 2001. pp. 107–132.
7. **Rowse, D.H. and E.A. Emmett:** Solvents and the skin. *Clin. Occ. Env. Med. 4(4)*:657–730 (2004).
8. **Zheng, W., M. Aschner, and J. F. Ghersi-Egea:** Brain barrier systems: a new frontier in metal neurotoxicological research. *Toxicol. Appl. Pharmacol. 192(1)*:1–11 (2003).
9. **Hardman, J.G. and L.E. Limbird:** *Goodman & Gilman's the Pharmacological Basis of Therapeutics*, 9th edition. New York: McGraw-Hill, 1996.
10. **Yip, L., R.C. Dart, and J.B. Sullivan, Jr.:** Mercury. In *Clinical Environmental Health and Toxic Exposures*, 2nd edition. Sullivan, Jr., J.R. and G.R. Krieger (eds.).. Philadelphia: Lippincott Williams & Wilkins, 2001. pp. 867–879
11. **Korinth, G., T. Weiss, J. Angerer, and H. Drexler:** Dermal absorption of aromatic amines in workers with different skin lesions: a report on 4 cases. *J. Occ. Med. Tox. 1*:17 (2006).
12. **Gottlieb, J. and E. Storey:** Death due to phenol absorption through open skin. *Maine Med. J. 27(8)*:1161–1164 (1936).
13. **Boman, A. and H.I. Maibach:** Influence of evaporation and repeated exposure on the percutaneous absorption of organic solvents. *Curr. Problems Dermatol. 25*:47–56 (1996).
14. **Dutkiewicz, B., J. Konczalik, and W. Karwacki:** Skin absorption and per os administration of methanol in men. *Internatl. Arch. Occ. Env. Health 47(1)*:81–88 (1980).
15. **Newman, L.S.:** Clinical pulmonary toxicology. In *Clinical Environmental Health and Toxic Exposures*, 2nd edition. Sullivan, Jr., J.R. and G.R. Krieger (eds.). Philadelphia: Lippincott Williams & Wilkins; 2001. pp. 206–223.
16. **Kosnett, M.J.:** Lead. In *Clinical Toxicology.* Ford, M.D., K.A. Delaney, L.J. Ling, and T. Erickson (eds.). Philadelphia: W.B. Saunders Company; 2001. pp. 723–736.
17. **Benet, L. Z., S. Øie, and J.B. Schwartz:** Appendix II. Design and optimization of dosage regimens: pharmacokinetic data. In *Goodman & Gilman's The Pharmacological Basis of Therapeutics*, 9th edition. Hardman, J.G. and L.E. Limbird (eds.). New York: McGraw-Hill, 1996. pp. 1707–1792.
18. **Agency for Toxic Substances and Disease Registry (ATSDR):** *Toxicological profile for ethylene glycol and propylene glycol*. Atlanta, GA: Agency for Toxic Substances and Disease Registry, 1997.
19. **Shargel, L. and A. Yu:** *Applied biopharmaceutics and pharmacokinetics,* 4th edition. Stamford, CT: Appleton & Lange, 1999.
20. **Parkinson, A.:** Biotransformation of xenobiotics. In *Cassarett and Doull's Toxicology: the Basic Science of Poisons*, 6th edition. Klaassen, C.D. (ed.). New York: McGraw-Hill, 2001. pp. 133–224.
21. **Jones, A.W., and L. Andersson:** Influence of age, gender, and blood-alcohol concentration on the disappearance rate of alcohol from blood in drinking drivers. *J. Forensic Sci. 41(6)*:922–926 (1996).
22. **Wagner, J.G., P.K. Wilkinson, A.J. Sedman, D.R. Kay, and D.J. Weidler:** Elimination of alcohol from human blood. *J. Pharm. Sci. 65(1)*:152–154 (1976).
23. **Gibaldi, M. and D. Perrier:** *Pharmacokinetics*. New York: Marcel Dekker, Inc., 1982.
24. **Tomaszewski, C.:** Carbon monoxide. In *Clinical Toxicology.* Ford, M.D., K.A. Delaney, L.J. Ling, and T. Erickson (eds.). Philadelphia: W.B. Saunders Company; 2001. pp. 657–667.
25. **American Conference of Governmental Industrial Hygienists (ACGIH):** Mercury, elemental and inorganic: recommended BEI. In: Documentation of the TLV®s and BEI®s with Other Worldwide Occupational Exposure Values. CD-ROM 2007. Cincinnati, OH: ACGIH, 2007.

26. **American Conference of Governmental Industrial Hygienists (ACGIH):** Arsenic and soluble inorganic compounds: recommended BEI. In: Documentation of the TLV®s and BEI®s with Other Worldwide Occupational Exposure Values. CD-ROM 2007. Cincinnati, OH: ACGIH, 2007.

Additional Reading

Gibaldi, M. and D. Perrier: *Pharmacokinetics.* New York: Marcel Dekker, Inc., 1982.

Klaassen, C.D.(ed.).: *Casarett and Doull's Toxicology: The Basic Science of Poisons*, 6th edition. New York: McGraw-Hill, 2001.

Rowland, M. and T.N. Tozer: *Clinical Pharmacokinetics: Concepts and Applications,* 3rd edition. Baltimore, MD: Williams & Wilkins, 1995.

Shargel, L. and A. Yu: *Applied Biopharmaceutics and Pharmacokinetics*, 4th edition. Stamford, CT: Appleton & Lange, 1999.

Section 2

Sites of Action of Chemicals Found in the Workplace

Chapter 5

Respiratory Toxicology

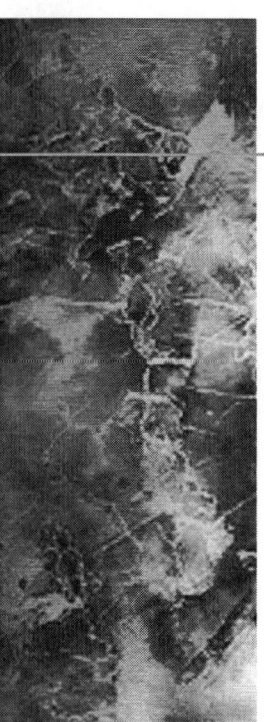

Outcome Competencies

Upon completion of this chapter the reader should be able to:

- Describe the basic attributes of the respiratory system.
- Describe the defense mechanisms of the respiratory system.
- Explain how behavioral, genetic, and environmental factors contribute to an individual's susceptibility to airway exposures.
- Understand the difference between sensory and pulmonary irritants.
- Give examples of common workplace irritants.
- Define respiratory sensitizer, and describe the problems with isocyantes in the workplace.
- Provide examples of workplace exposures that cause pneumoconiosis.
- Describe the biological process that leads to pulmonary fibrosis.
- Describe the history and exposure hazards of artificial flavorings.
- Understand the putative causes of sick building syndrome and provide examples of toxicants believed to underlie the adverse health effects.
- Describe the role of mold in damp building syndrome.

Prerequisite Knowledge

A basic understanding of biochemistry, human physiology and anatomy.

Key Terms

aerodynamic diameter, airway remodeling, antibody, antigen, antioxidants, bronchoconstriction, conducting airways, cytokine, endotoxin, epidemiology, fibrosis, gene-environment interaction, glutathione, irritants (respiratory), macrophage, malodorant, Material Safety Data Sheet (MSDS), mucus, mycotoxin, neutrophil, occupational asthma, Occupational Exposure Limit (OEL), oxygen radical, physicochemical properties, pneumoconiosis, polymorphism (genetic), prevalence, reactive oxygen species, respiratory airways, sensitizer, solubility, vanilloid receptor

Key Topics

1. Airway Structure and Function
   - Defense Mechanisms
   - Susceptibility
   - Susceptibility: Behavior-environment interactions
   - Susceptibility: Gene-environment interaction
2. Occupational Respiratory Toxicants
   - Irritants
   - Sensitizers
   - Others Sensitizers
3. Pneumoconiosis
   - Flavorings
4. Sick Building Syndrome
5. Damp Building Syndrome

Chapter 5

Respiratory Toxicology

By James G. Wagner, PhD, and Melissa L. Millerick-May, MSc

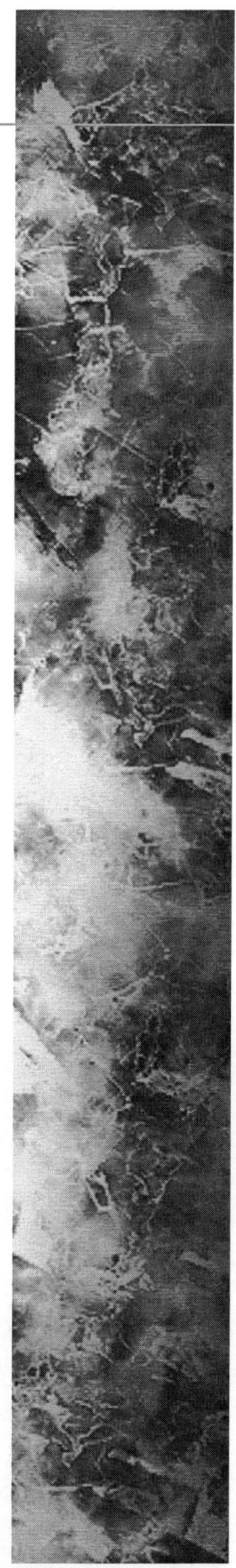

Introduction

Together with the skin and eyes, the respiratory tract is one of the most common routes of exposure to hazardous materials in the workplace. Unique features of mammalian airways make them exquisitely sensitive to the effects of airborne toxicants. From the tip of the nose to the alveolus of deep lung, a mucosal surface area equal to half a tennis court is exposed to a variety of gases and particulate matter, concentrations of which are replenished with every breath. Furthermore only two cells layers (epithelial and endothelial) that together measure less than 1 μm provide a tenuous barrier between inhaled air and circulating blood. As such the lung presents a vulnerable portal of entry for toxicants that not only injure airway cells, but can then affect extrapulmonary sites such as cardiovascular and central nervous systems. Toxic responses of airways range from acute irritation to more chronic remodeling in the forms of asthma, fibrosis, and cancer. The pulmonary toxicity of a chemical material depends upon the concentration of the chemical in the air, the length of time (duration) an individual is exposed, and the volume of inhaled air which increases with increasingly heavy workloads. This chapter begins with a brief overview of anatomical and cellular features of the respiratory tract that contributes to its unique susceptibility to inhaled toxicants. Some of the more common occupational toxicants are then reviewed with regard to the current understanding of their occupational hazard, primary health outcome and mechanism of toxicity.

Airway Structure and Function

Put simply the primary function of the respiratory tract is to deliver air to the deep lung where the trafficking of inbound oxygen and outbound carbon dioxide takes place between the airways and circulating blood. In reality the complexity of this process involves over 40 different cell types and the cooperative efforts of neural, cardiovascular, and immune systems. Airways can be generally divided into the functions of **conduction**, or movement of air, and **respiration**, the actual exchange of gases to and from circulating blood. These functions are achieved by the conducting and respiratory airways, respectively.

Conducting airways begin with the nasal cavity, which serves to warm and humidify air, as well as remove particles greater than 5 μm. Inspired air continues through the pharynx, larynx, trachea and finally the extrapulmonary bronchi, where it meets the first of approximately 60,000 branch points that distribute airways exponentially throughout the lung tissue. Moving down the branching tree of the intrapulmonary conducting airways, the number of branches increases, while airway diameter decreases. From the trachea airways diverge into the bronchus, bronchioles and then terminal bronchioles, which represent the junction between conducting and respiratory airways. (Figure 5.1)

Respiratory airways branch further into respiratory bronchioles, alveolar ducts, and the finally the alveolar sacs. Instead of a viscous layer of mucus, these airways are lined with a thinner layer consisting of surfactant lipids and proteins, which facilitate the distension of alveolar airways

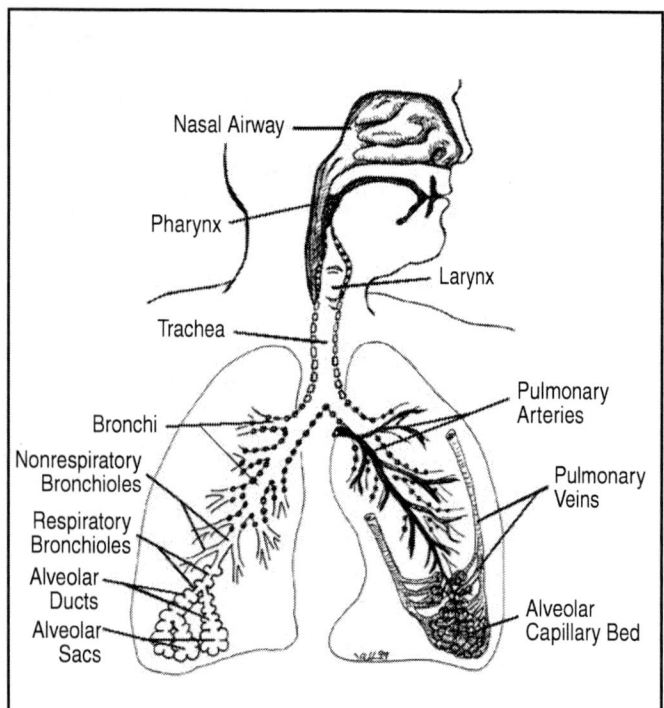

Figure 5.1 — Anatomy of the Human Respiratory Tract. Conducting airways begin at the entry to the nasal cavity and branch geometrically until they terminate at the terminal bronchioles. Respiratory airways include the respiratory bronchioles, alveolar ducts and alveolar sacs. (Illustration courtesy of Dr. Jack R. Harkema).

and allows for gas exchange. However this relatively thinner fluid layer provides less protection for alveolar cells.

Defense Mechanisms

Initial protection from inspired toxic substances is to **limit entry** to the more sensitive tissues in deeper airways. Physical or mechanical barriers include nasal hairs, the mucus layer, and impaction of particles at bends and bifurcations of airways. Bronchoconstriction and shallow respiration are acute, physiological responses to restrict airflow to the deep lung and occur after exposure to common pulmonary irritants such as ozone and oxidant gases, sulfides, acids (bleaches) and surfactants.

Clearance of inhaled materials that might deposit onto the surface of conducting airway walls can be accomplished by the action of the mucociliary escalator. Mucus and serous fluids are constantly secreted into airway lining fluid which is moved by the action of ciliated cells up and out of the lung and into the glottis where it can be swallowed. Movement of the nasal mucus layer is in the opposite direction, to the distal nasal cavity and toward the glottis. Rates of mucociliary transport are estimated at 5–8 mm/min in the nose, and a range of 4–21 mm/min in different branches of conducting airways.

Particulate matter that reaches the deeper lung tissues is cleared by alveolar macrophages via the internalization process of phagocytosis. Particle-containing macrophages themselves leaves the lung airspaces either up the mucociliary escalator or via lymphatic vessels. Ingestion of some types of particles can activate macrophages to secrete inflammatory mediators that can lead to chronic inflammation and tissue scarring. An example of macrophage-mediated injury is fibrosis induced from silica or asbestos inhalation.

Molecular and cellular defenses in the lung are too numerous to discuss in detail beyond a few key examples. With a higher oxygen content than other body tissues, the airways have a variety of antioxidant molecules and enzymes designed to neutralize oxygen radicals or repair cellular macromolecules injured during oxidative stress. Ascorbic acid (vitamin C), uric acid, and the sulfur-containing tripeptide glutathione, are three critical antioxidants found in the airway lining fluid that form the first line of defense to directly detoxify oxidant or reactive gases and their intermediate products. Antioxidants protect cellular macromolecules (e.g, lipids, proteins and DNA) from oxidative injury. Intracellular glutathione is also important for the repair of oxidized proteins and lipids, as well as recycling oxidized vitamin C back into an active form. A pair of critical cellular antioxidant enzymes is superoxide dismutase and catalase (see discussion in Chapter 3, "Mechanisms of Toxicity"), which convert the superoxide radical to first hydrogen peroxide and then to water (Figure 5.2).

Susceptibility

Site-specific injury in the respiratory tract can often be predicted by the **physicochemical properties** of the inhaled materials. For example water soluble gases deposit more readily in nasal and upper airways compared to less soluble gases. Nasal airways also scrub larger particles (greater than 10 μm) via impaction onto airway walls and bends. The aerodynamic size of particles is also a determinant of site deposition. For example, physical dimensions of fibers may be greater than 10 μm in length but with a radius 2 μm or less, their aerodynamic shape allows them to move with the flow of inspired air to deeper lung tissue. By comparison as particles size gets less than 0.1 μm (nanoparticles, see Chapter 19, "Toxicology of Particulate Matter") they begin to behave like gases and deposit both in deep lung and upper airways.

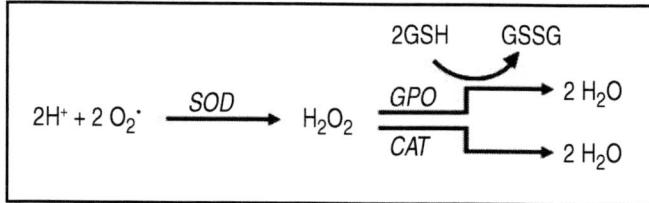

Figure 5.2 — Detoxification of superoxide radicals. Superoxide dismutase (SOD) converts superoxide ions to hydrogen peroxide, which is then neutralized to water by the action of either catalase (CAT) or glutathione peroxidase (GPO). The latter reaction consumes reduced glutathione (GSH) to its oxidized form, or GSSG.

Antioxidants are more concentrated in airway lining fluid of conducting airways, which is also comparatively thick and consists of mucous and serous fluids. By necessity the deeper respiratory airways lack mucous, and instead have a thin layer of surfactant with lower concentrations of antioxidants. As such, oxidative injury rarely occurs in conducting airways and is more common in alveolar regions. A common response to repeated exposure to oxidant gases and depletion of airway oxidants is the mobilization of ascorbate, uric acid and glutathione to airway lining fluid where concentrations reach 2–6 fold compared to normal levels.

Different airway cell populations possess different concentrations of antioxidant molecules and enzymes, as well as **drug-metabolizing systems**. For example Type I alveolar cells have little oxidant buffering capacity and die readily during oxidative stress, whereas neighboring Type II alveolar epithelial cells with significant antioxidant ability are relatively insensitive. While P450 enzymes found in Clara cells (pulmonary conducting airways) and the olfactory epithelium (nasal airways) can help detoxify inhaled chemicals, they can also bio-activate certain materials into more toxic forms.[1,2] For example the toxicity of formaldehyde, one of the few nasal carcinogens, is promoted by P450 pathways in the nose, and Clara cells are involved in the bio-activation of a number of key occupational toxicants, including trichloroethylene[3], naphthalene[4] and styrene[5], to name a few.

Susceptibility: Behavior - Environment Interactions

The prevalence and severity of adverse response to inhaled materials can be exacerbated by pre-existing airway conditions. A critical factor for increasing an individual's risk for occupational lung disease is **cigarette smoke**. Both primary and second-hand smoke can predispose individuals for enhanced response to occupational exposures. After declining in the 1990s, cigarette smoking has remained the same or slightly increased in high school students since 2003.[6] People with **pre-existing asthma** also have enhanced responses to common occupational irritants.[7] Reports of asthma prevalence in the United States have increased by 74% between 1980 and 1996[8], and many of these new cases are in children. Thus as more people enter the workforce as cigarette smokers or with preexisting airway hypersensitivities, the potential for more complications from occupational exposures may grow in the future. These demographics may or may not carry over to the future workplace.

Susceptibility: Gene-environment Interaction

Independent from behavioral confounders such as smoking, certain individuals demonstrate heightened susceptibility to diseases, adverse drug reactions, allergy, or response to toxic exposures. It has become more appreciated that genetic differences contribute to this variability of responses. Single genes or gene families can exist in multiple forms, or polymorphisms which, when expressed, would code for slightly different protein structures. As such, critical proteins involved in host inflammation and immune processes can vary from individual to individual, and render them more or less sensitive for a specific disease or adverse response to drugs or toxicants.

Recent case studies have demonstrated the prevalence of specific genetic polymorphisms in patients with certain forms of pneumoconiosis. Molecular pathways involved in fibrotic pneumoconiosis are well described, and include several inflammatory proteins including most importantly tumor necrosis factor (TNFα), and growth stimulating proteins such as transforming growth factor (TGFβ). Individuals with certain genetic variants of TNFα and TGFβ proteins appear to be predisposed for contracting chronic beryllium disease, coal workers' pneumoconiosis, farmer's lung disease or forms of silicosis.[9] The mechanisms by which these altered proteins might promote disease are not understood, but it is hypothesized that changes in their structure make them non-responsive to normal regulatory or antiinflammatory signals that are critical to control inflammation and repair of tissues. Furthermore it is not clear if both protein variants for TNFα and TGFβ are required to sensitize individuals for the development of pneumoconiosis.

Both animal and epidemiological studies demonstrate that genetic polymorphisms in proteins that regulate key antioxidant defense proteins (e.g., glutathione) can lead to exaggerated responses to ozone exposure.[10,11] It is possible that responses to other oxidant gases that are neutralized by endogenous antioxidants may be similarly enhanced. Asthma-like reaction to isocyanate, a growing occupational airway disease (see discussion below), may also be linked to polymorphisms in glutathione metabolism[12], as well as to genetic variants of important cytokine and receptors involved in allergic responses.[13] As is the case with pneumoconiosis, it is not clear if more than one genetic variant per individual is sufficient to increase sensitivity for a given occupational or environmental disease. Gene-environment interactions are an emerging focus for research both at the National Institutes of Health (NIH) and National Institutes for Environmental Health Sciences.[14,15] A goal for these research efforts is to understand how genetic variations can be applied to the management of health risks in the workplace.

Occupational Respiratory Toxicants

Irritants

Primary irritants exert their effect on the respiratory tract via direct contact (mechanical or chemical reaction), while **secondary irritants** give rise to systemic effects. An example of a primary irritant is ammonia which is highly water soluble, and overexposure results in nasal/throat irritation due to chemical reactions taking place at the epithelium. Secondary irritants indeed may cause a local response upon acute exposure; however, their effects may appear to be trivial in contrast to the presence of systemic effects resulting from absorption of the toxicant. Examples of secondary irritants include hydrogen sulfide gas, certain aromatic hydrocarbons, alcohols, esters, and ketones.

Irritants are also classified as either engendering sensory irritation or pulmonary irritation.[16] Responses to **sensory irritants** are initiated in the nose, and include burning and painful sensations, nasal inflammation and hypersecretion, and vasodilation and obstruction. Pulmonary responses to sensory irritants also result in decreased breathing frequency. In occupational settings, odorants can also be perceived as sensory irritants, although they stimulate different neurons (olfaction) and do not result in pain, inflammation or any actual responses engendered by sensory irritants.[17] The perception to inhalation of malodorants is a concern in the workplace to distinguish the perceived versus actual health risks.[18] Recent studies suggest however that odorant-stimulated neuron activation can cross-talk and enhance the neuronal pathways of sensory irritants.[19]

By comparison **pulmonary irritants** stimulate receptors in the pulmonary conducting airways and alveoli, and induce inflammation, bronchoconstriction, edema, cough, and mucus hypersecretion. Rather than decrease breathing frequency however, they increase breathing rate (rapid shallow breaths). Some agents such as isocyantes and machining fluid mixtures elicit both sensory and pulmonary irritant-type responses.[20] In addition to differences in their effect on breathing frequency, other descriptive factors used to classify irritants include the types of neurons and receptors activated by exposure. More studies that compare the neurogenic pathways of inflammation and changes in airway physiology are needed to better classify the differences and health risks of irritants.

As a group, irritants are extremely broad and commonly found occupationally, and include bleaching agents, ammonia, sulfuric and hydrochloric acids, isocyanates, volatile organics and oxides of nitrogen and sulfur. Many airborne irritants will also cause ocular responses of excessive tearing and pain. Removing from or limiting exposures usually resolves symptoms with no long-term consequences. Capsaicin, the key ingredient in pepper spray, is used as a model irritant in the research laboratory to study the neurological and respiratory effects of irritant exposure, believed to be mediated predominately via vanilloid receptors in both nasal and pulmonary airways.[21]

Nitrogen Dioxide

Nitrogen dioxide (NO_2) is produced as a result of combustion (vehicle exhaust, burning of oil, coal), and is produced commercially for use as an oxidizing agent, as well as an intermediate in the production of nitric acid. Occupational exposures may occur during welding, mining/blasting, heat treat, electroplating, and petroleum refining operations to name a few.

Increases in indoor NO_2 are associated with sore throat, colds, cough and wheeze in domestic[22] and school settings.[23] A notable case of NO_2-associated respiratory toxicosis occurred at an indoor ice arena in the early 1990s, when more than 50 people were affected with upper airways symptoms that persisted for at least 5 years.[24,25] Characterized by low solubility in aqueous media, NO_2 reaches pulmonary airways to form reactive oxygen species in airway lining fluid that are neutralized by soluble antioxidants such as ascorbate and uric acid.[26,27] In controlled exposures with 2 ppm NO_2, neutrophilic inflammation persisted with repeated daily exposure 94 h/day for 4 consecutive days). However, exposure-related deficits in pulmonary function after the first day returned to normal by the second day, despite continued exposures.[28]

Other Irritants

Cleaning solutions are a rich source of sensory and pulmonary irritants, and while custodial and cleaning workers are at highest risk, exposures to other workers often occur. Bleach contains varying concentrations of hypochlorous acid, aerosols from which engender acute irritant and avoidance responses. The formation of chloramines generated during heavy use of chlorine-based disinfectants has been blamed for acute eye and respiratory effects in disparate occupations including lifeguards and indoor pools[29] poultry processing[30] and food catering.[31] Chlorinated disinfectant products are generally more reactive and have extra-pulmonary toxicity associated with them.

A review of the chemical Material Safety Data Sheet (MSDS) for ingredients and vapor pressure, along with knowledge of the chemical's intended use (e.g. process parameters) will assist in the determination of potential exposures that may result in respiratory irritation. Because adherence to occupational exposure limits may not be sufficient to prevent irritation, it is frequently necessary to completely enclose processes, and/or provide additional local exhaust ventilation to remove noxious odors from the work area.

Sensitizers

Initial exposure to a sensitizer usually does not result in an adverse reaction, especially if concentrations are low. However with repeated and intermittent exposures, some individuals will begin to develop severe responses to exposure concentrations to which they previously had no responses. Sensitization usually requires repeated exposures over days to weeks. Development of respiratory sensitization to biogenic substances, metals, cutting oils, machining fluids, and low molecular weight proteins can induce asthma-like inflammation, bronchoconstriction and mucus hypersecretion.[32] Depending on the specific agent, hypersensitivity reactions generally involves antigen (hapten) formation, antibody production, and an antigen/antibody reaction that occurs following subsequent exposure(s).

Isocyanates

Isocyanates are low molecular weight compounds used in a wide range of industrial and non-industrial applications. These compounds are used in molding applications, flexible and rigid foaming systems, resin applications, and coating processes. Exposures may occur as a result of inhalation during operations such as spraying (e.g. urethane paints) and curing after heating (e.g. foaming), as well as at room temperatures. Over-exposures to these compounds are known to result in occupational asthma in some individuals, thus many employers require that bronchial provocation testing be performed prior to placing workers in areas where isocyanate exposures may occur.

Understanding the etiology and mechanisms of airway hypersensitivity induced by isocyanates and other low molecular-weight compounds has been problematic. Isocyanates are classified as haptens, which are compounds too small to directly stimulate specific antibody responses. Although antigens, haptens must conjugate to host proteins to become immunogenic and stimulate production of antibodies. Antibodies to several isocyanates: protein conjugates have been identified, including the conjugates with serum albumin and the matrix protein keratin.[33,34] However not all people with positive antibody responses have asthma symptoms, and symptoms of isocyanate-induced asthma do not always correlate with the antibody concentrations.[35,36] Another controversial risk factor is dermal exposure. In animal models airway reactivity to isocyanates can occur by either previous sensitization by either inhalation or dermal exposure.[37] Although direct evidence that skin exposure in humans can lead to airway responses is lacking, exposure to isocyanates during non-aerosolization tasks can still result in internal doses of isocyanates only 8–10 fold less than what results from aerosol operations.[38] As such, the contribution of dermal exposure to isocyanate-induced asthma is becoming a factor for evaluating the risks of workplace exposures.

Others Sensitizers

The increasing prevalence of respiratory hypersensitivity and asthma in the workplace has made it the most common form of occupational lung disease.[39] Every occupation has its specific sensitizer and unique disease description, from mushroom worker's lung[40] and yachtmaker's lung[41], to asthma and rhinitis in laboratory rodent handlers[42] and hairdressers.[43] Other examples include sensitivity to styrene, metals (aluminum, chrome, platinum, zinc fume), and oil mist, and the numbers continue to grow. Asthma in the general population has grown dramatically in the last 20 years[8], and workers with pre-existing asthma already display enhanced responses to irritants. It is possible that asthmatics may also develop new hypersensitivities to occupational asthmogens.

Individuals with preexisting asthma or with histories of hypersensitivities may exhibit adverse respiratory symptoms to exposure levels much lower than regulated limits. Incorporating employee health data (e.g. absenteeism, visits to the medical dept.) in conjunction with industrial hygiene monitoring data in areas of sensitizer use will help to identify and manage exposure risks. Sentinel event notification systems that allow medical, epidemiology, and industrial hygiene staffs to work together to identify processes and chemicals used by employees exhibiting symptoms consistent with chemical sensitization (e.g. rhinitis, cough, wheeze) can help distinguish exposure related effects from typical seasonal ailments (e.g. cold, flu, seasonal allergy).

A recent case study involving latex allergy in health care workers demonstrated that even when sensitized individuals stopped using latex gloves, respiratory symptoms persisted while remaining in the work environment, due to elevated airborne concentrations of latex allergen as a result of continued use in the area by others, entrapment of the powder in ventilation systems, and further dispersion throughout the rest of the building.[44] Thus, although sensitized individuals may be removed from unhealthy work environments to alternate work activities (e.g. moved from the hospital floor to administrative offices), risk for continued exposure and adverse responses may continue.

Pneumoconiosis

Pneumoconiosis is a classic example of development of disease as a result of chronic inhalation overexposures to dusts with disease latency spanning years to decades. Common pneumoconioses include **coal workers' pneumoconiosis** (coal dust), **siderosis** (iron), **stannosis** (tin), and **baritosis** (barium). Overexposure to dusts of antimony, Portland cement, talc, and kaolite are examples of other materials that may result in pneumoconioses. Occupations at greatest risk include those that involve blasting, drilling, loading/dumping, and crushing.[45] Mortality due to all-cause pneumoconiosis (including asbestosis) has decreased between the years of 1968–2000.[46] Comparison of the death rates between the years of 1968–1981 and 1982–2000 shows a declines of 36% among males for coal workers' pneumoconiosis (CWP), and 70% for other forms of silicosis.[46] Methods to control exposures to dusts in mining operations have been published and disseminated.[47] Federal surveillance programs for coal mine workers which offer regular physical examinations, routine x-rays and placing affected individual in a 'low dust' environment have likely contributed to the improvement in pneumoconiosis-related mortality.[48]

Pneumoconiosis diseases are typified by pulmonary fibrosis. Fibrosis, or interstitial lung disease, is a result of overproduction of extracellular proteins that are either enmeshed in the airway walls make them stiff and less flexible during breathing, or are deposited into airspaces where they occlude airflow. Mechanisms for particulate-induced fibrosis have been well described and involve a central role for the alveolar macrophage, which normally clears particles from the lung without adverse consequences. However due to the shape, chemistry, or quantity of particles during some occupational exposures, engulfment by macrophages can lead to hypersecretion of inflammatory mediators and growth factors, which ultimately progresses to activation of fibroblasts and their overproduction of extracellular matrix proteins. Human and animal studies also demonstrate an immune component to **chronic beryllium disease** and more recently for forms of **silicosis**.[49,50] Lymphocytes and cytokines normally associated with autoimmune or allergic response play a critical role in these pneumoconioses, though their contribution to the fibrotic process is not understood.

Newer technologies in manufacturing and processing are creating new forms of metal-induced fibrosis and interstitial lung diseases. **Hard metal lung** disease occurs from chronic exposures to aerosolized tungsten carbide and cobalt from tools as a result from cutting and grinding operations. This unique disease is characterized by both fibrosis and immune-mediated features similar to that induced by exposure to beryllium.[51] Another emerging fibrotic disease is from exposure to **indium** and indium/tin, which occurs in workers manufacturing liquid-crystal screens.[52,53] Exposures are greatest during surface grinding operations which can generate metal aerosols. Other metal-induced interstitial lung diseases have been associated with nickel, chromium and iron where chronic exposures to aerosols or dusts are common.[54]

Case Study

Occupational asthma (OA) or work-related asthma (WRA) has been reported to account for up to 15 percent of adult asthma "and includes 1) immunologic OA, characterized by a latency period before the onset of symptoms; 2) non-immunologic OA, which occurs after single or multiple exposures to high concentrations of irritant materials; 3) work-aggravated asthma, which is preexisting or concurrent asthma aggravated by workplace exposures; and 4) variant syndromes."[1] Isocyanates are low molecular weight compounds widely used in industry, including the automobile industry, and have been reported to be the "leading cause of occupational asthma in the industrialized world."[2] As a result, health and safety professionals are acutely aware of the potential hazards of using these materials, and routinely implement extensive testing, education, and control programs accordingly. Many times, however, businesses that utilize these materials do not employ or consult health and safety professionals to assist with hazard recognition, evaluation, and control in their facilities, and employees may not be fully aware of the hazards that come with working with these materials. The following case-study illustrates such a scenario.

Chester, D.A., et al.: Asthma Death after Spraying Polyurethane Truck Bedliner. *Am. J. Ind. Med.* 48:78–84 (2005).

Truck bedliners have become a popular accessory, as they provide protective properties including scratch resistance and rust prevention. They may be factory installed as pre-formed injection-molded plastic inserts that are bolted into the truck-bed prior-to or at the time-of vehicle purchase, or they may be sprayed-on in an aftermarket automotive customization installation/repair facility. Spray-on polyurethane bedliners are a product of the spraying of a 2-part isocyanate/polyol 'system', where isocyanate and polyol components are kept separate until mixing immediately prior to spray application. Due to the nature of the application process, all spraying and curing must take place indoors to prevent moisture contamination. Spray-on bedliner application typically takes place in small aftermarket vehicle accessory facilities.

In 2003, an employee of an after-market facility that performed spray-on bedliner installations, died approximately one hour after completing an installation inside a van. The employee was a man in his mid-forties, and had a history of asthma but had never been hospitalized for it. Three other individuals worked in this facility, a receptionist, and two other individuals that assisted in preparing vehicles for bed-liner application, as well as installation of other aftermarket products including rust preventatives and undercoating. Bedliner application took place in the 'general shop' area and not during normal business hours due to the strong odor generated during applications. An exhaust system was not used, and air exchange was limited through a vehicle doorway that was left raised a few-feet from the ground. A small box-fan was placed in an open pedestrian door entrance to help facilitate air-movement.

On the morning the employee died, he sent his assistant out of the area to perform alternate tasks while the spraying was taking place. The victim was outfitted with a positive pressure half-mask (tight-fitting) supplied air respirator, cap, disposable painting hood, and latex gloves. The pump supplying ambient air to the respirator had a HEPA filter, and was designed for use with a 40-foot air hose. However it was fitted with an 80-foot air hose in this case. The employee sprayed the bedliner into the bed floor and partially up the sides of the inside of the van. It was not known *how* the spraying was conducted: whether it was from outside or from inside the cargo area of the van.

Approximately 20 minutes after the initiation of the spray process, a coworker returned to find the job completed, the equipment turned off, and the individual gasping for air outside of the building. The coworker rushed the individual to an urgent care facility where CPR was initiated. He was then transported via ambulance to a nearby hospital where he was later pronounced dead. Autopsy findings included "mucus in the airways and eosinophils in the bronchial walls and mucosa." Autopsy results also included other findings (e.g. diffuse pulmonary emphysema) suggestive of COPD, possibly resulting in the self-diagnosis by the deceased of having asthma. The cause of death was consistent with two possibilities "1) the isocyanates aggravated his previous medical condition (whether it was COPD or asthma), or 2) he became sensitized to the isocyanate in addition to his previous condition". The impression noted by the medical examiner was "Asthmatic reaction due to inhalation of chemicals."[3]

Investigators documented multiple items that may have contributed to this incident. These factors included 1) vehicle type – spraying inside of a van results in more of a confined environment potentially resulting in increased concentrations than what would normally be encountered, 2) lack of dedicated spray-room and local exhaust ventilation, 3) lack of a comprehensive respiratory protection program, 4) inadequate owner/employee knowledge, 5) non-identification of potential work-related illness by medical personnel, 6) lack of medical monitoring of employees exposed to sensitizers or other asthma causing agents, and 7) lack of a workplace hazard assessment to identify health and safety issues, personal protective equipment to be used, and safe work procedures."[3] They conclude that many business owners do not have the knowledge necessary or staff available to evaluate and address health and safety in their workplace, thus putting themselves and their employees at an increased risk for becoming injured or developing a work-related illness.

References
1. **Mapp, C.E., et al.:** Occupational Asthma. *Am. J. Respir. Crit. Care Med.* 172:280–305 (2005).
2. **Bonauto, D.K., et al.:** Work-Related Asthma in the Spray-On Truck Bed Lining Industry. *J. Occup. Environ. Med.* 47:514–517 (2005).
3. **Chester, D.A., et al.:** Asthma Death after Spraying Polyurethane Truck Bedliner. *Am. J. Ind. Med.* 48:78–84 (2005).

Flavorings

Bronchiolitis obliterans is a pulmonary disease that involves the plugging of bronchiole airways with fibrous tissue, and is usually associated with improper resolution of infections or after lung transplantation. In 2000, several workers in a microwave popcorn production plant were diagnosed with bronchiolitis obliterans that was later attributed to inhalation exposure to diacetyl, which is a ketone used for artificial flavoring.[55] At NIOSH research laboratories, inhalation studies of laboratory animals exposed to butter flavoring vapors caused acute cell death in nasal and bronchiole airways[56], but how this initial injury progresses to chronic fibrotic responses is not clear. Overall, employees at the affected popcorn production plant had increased prevalence of cough, shortness of breath and asthma-like symptoms.[55,57] Exposure assessments demonstrate high airborne concentrations of diacetyl during mixing operations, but also significant (albeit 20-fold less) concentrations during packing procedures.[58] Furthermore diacetyl emissions are greater for liquids and pastes compared to powdered preparations, yet respirable particles from powders can also pose a hazard.[59] Exposure-effect relationships in workers are still undefined. Volatile emissions from ketone flavorings are not limited to popcorn production plants, but can occur from other artificial flavoring operations. At least two other non-popcorn cases of bronchiolitis obliterans have been reported in plants using diacetyl-based flavorings.[60]

Sick Building Syndrome

Chronic exposures to volatile organic hydrocarbons (VOCs), molds, and bacteria that arise from specific structural elements and routine building operations can lead to a variety of exposure-related illnesses defined loosely as sick building syndrome (SBS). Health problems ranging from neurological to respiratory symptoms are attributed to a variety of factors such as off-gassing of building materials, operation of office equipment, ventilation and air conditioning contamination, and mold associated with high humidity or water damage. Acute exposures that occur during remediation and assessment efforts can also elicit adverse health effects. SBS and damp-building syndromes are more commonly reported in non-industrial settings including offices, schools and public buildings.

Generation of **VOCs** indoors can arise from the operation of office equipment including computers and copy machines, off-gassing of carpeting, woods and laminates, and from biogenic sources such as, mold, fungi or bacteria. Exposures increase during the first year after new building construction, after refurbishment or purchase of new equipment, and with heavy traffic. Depending on building materials, **formaldehyde** and **terpenes** that are slowly released from construction woods and carpeting account for a majority of VOCs in office buildings. Terpene-based cleaning products and air fresheners that contain limonene and pinene (citrus and pine oils, respectively) have contributed to indoor VOC exposures in the last decade. The health risk for indoor terpenes and other VOCs may be enhanced by reactions with indoor ozone, which results in production of several secondary oxidative products, many of unknown toxicity. For example in controlled studies, coexposures to terpenes and ozone caused airway irritation in laboratory mice[61] and perceived airway symptoms in human volunteers[62] that were greater than what is elicited by either agent alone. Furthermore these chemical reactions can cause formation of submicron particulates, which may contribute to the enhanced airway responses.[63] Indoor ozone is typically 20–70% of outdoor levels, concentrations of which can increase along with NO_2 and formaldehyde emissions with heavy use of photocopiers.[64]

Indoor air concentrations of VOCs are typically below 10 µg/m^3, and animal models generally require doses > 1 mg/m^3 to induce significant respiratory injury. Most animal and clinical studies are also of short durations, and do not replicate the chronic nature of workplace exposures. As such the toxicity of workplace-specific mixtures and reaction chemistry and frequency of exposures may be more important determinants of health risk assessment than exposure to single agents. Furthermore adverse airway responses to VOCs usually are not serious, but are rather elicit of irritation or sensory stimulation. Whether as a perceived annoyance or with actual airway pathology, VOC exposures can contribute to deficits in worker performance.[65–67] As with sensory irritants, the challenge for the industrial hygienist is help determine when inhaled materials present a real risk to human health versus perceptions of a adverse health effects.

Damp Building Syndrome

A related phenomenon to sick building syndrome are the multiple symptoms associated with the presence of mold and fungi in water damaged buildings. Especially with the media coverage of flood damage from Hurricane Katrina and morbidity attributed to black molds, the need for sound risk assessment for both building inhabitants and remediation workers is necessary. Reported health effects attributed to indoor mold exposures have included headaches, neurocognitive deficits, airway irritation, loss of olfactory senses, nose bleeds and pulmonary hemorrhage, among others.[68–70]

Inhalation of mold contaminants in agricultural settings has been studied since the 1950s with the description of "farmer's lung", which is associated with molds in hay, cotton and sugar cane.[71] This disease is characterized by common mechanisms, namely airway hypersensitivity and production of IgG antibodies against specific antigens found in molds. Similar immune-mediated mechanisms have been proposed for asthma-like symptoms in inhabitants or workers in buildings with water damage and mold. Based on the nature of agricultural work, the generation of airborne dusts and their exposures are more obvious than what might occur indoors. Indeed indoor spore concentrations are on average 10–100 fold less than that found outdoors (indoor average 800 spores/m^3).[72] But concentrations of specific spore species are indeed greater indoors, especially when water damage is evident, reaching levels as much as 10,000–50,000 spores/m^3.[72,73] Concentrations may also spike during the removal of damaged materials or by high velocity drying fans during remediation and cleanup efforts.

Systemic or airway infection of molds and fungi are not proposed as the primary cause of damp building syndromes. Rather, hypersensitivity and immune processes similar to the etiology of farmer's lung, and reactions to certain mold-derived toxins, or mycotoxins, likely mediated the reported effects. Mold and bacterial growth on water damaged gypsum, drywall and wood are also a source of VOCs.[74] Visible identification and odor of molds does not necessarily correlate with airborne exposure or toxicity. Furthermore isolates of the same species can produce qualitatively different toxins. The toxic principle to explain non-allergic type symptoms in people from mold exposures remains elusive.

Recent controversy has focused on contaminations of Stachybotrys species that produce among other mycotoxins a number of tricothecenes, which have been characterized as food toxins but with unknown airway effects in humans.[75] In laboratory animals, airway exposure to spores or extracts from Stachybotrys can elicit inflammation and allergic-type responses in mouse lungs.[76] In the mid 1990s, an outbreak of pediatric pulmonary hemorrhage was attributed to water damaged dwellings and ultimately associated with the presence of Stachybotrys, though a definitive mechanistic link has been debated.[77-79] Analytical tools for evaluating the concentrations of airborne spores and potential toxins have developed rapidly in the last 5 years, and will significantly improve the risk assessment and management of mold exposures.

Other biogenic toxins that contribute to buildings syndromes, as well as to agricultural exposures are glucans and endotoxins from fungi and bacteria, respectively. Both are highly inflammagenic to airways and activate non-immune pathways, but also exacerbate asthma.[80] Indoor concentrations of endotoxins and glucans are directly associated with asthma and airway symptoms.[81,82] Furthermore common factors such as humidity and temperature favor both mold and bacterial contaminations, and both airborne spores and endotoxin are commonly found together indoors.[83,84] As such, indoor air in the context of sick and damp building syndromes is a complex mixture of airway irritants and inflammagens, that when inhaled may elicit synergistic effects in airways. (Refer to Chapter 19, "Toxicology of Particulate Matter").

Summary

The respiratory tract is a vulnerable surface for interactions with workplace toxicants. Behavioral and genetic factors can further increase susceptibility to contracting occupational airway diseases. Thousands of airborne chemicals and biogenic substances exist in the workplace and can elicit irritant, hypersensitivity and airway remodeling responses. The intersection of host susceptibility, the airborne concentration of materials, and the length of exposure will determine the health outcome. Workers are rarely exposed to a single toxicant, and often airborne materials are unidentified or of unknown toxicity. With new materials introduced into the workplace each year, it is a growing challenge for the industrial hygienist to best determine the health risk from complex exposure scenarios to protect the health of the worker.

References

1. **Dahl, A.R. and W.M. Hadley:** Nasal cavity enzymes involved in xenobiotic metabolism: effects on the toxicity of inhalants. *Crit Rev Toxicol. 21(5)*:345–372 (1991).
2. **Hukkanen, J., O. Pelkonen, J. Hakkola, and H. Raunio:** Expression and regulation of xenobiotic-metabolizing cytochrome P450 (CYP) enzymes in human lung. *Crit. Rev. Toxicol. 32(5)*:391–411 (2002).
3. **Green, T.:** Pulmonary toxicity and carcinogenicity of trichloroethylene: species differences and modes of action. *Environ. Health Perspect. 108(2)*:261–264 (2000).
4. **Boland, B., C.Y. Lin, D. Morin, L. Miller, C. Plopper, and A. Buckpitt:** Site-specific metabolism of naphthalene and 1-nitronaphthalene in dissected airways of rhesus macaques. *J. Pharmacol Exp. Ther. 310(2)*:546–554 (2004).
5. **Sarangapani, R., J.G. Teeguarden, G. Cruzan, H.J. Clewell, and M.E. Andersen:** Physiological based parmacokinetic modeling of styrene and styrene oxide respiratory-tract dosimetry in rodents and humans. *Inhal. Toxicol. 14(8)*:789–834 (2002).
6. **U.S. Centers for Disease Control and Prevention (CDC):** Cigarette use among high school students—United States, 1991–2005. *MMWR 55(26)*:724–726 (2006).
7. **Chatkin, J.M., S.M. Tarlo, G. Liss, D. Banks, and I. Broder:** The outcome of asthma related to workplace irritant exposures: a comparison of irritant-induced asthma and irritant aggravation of asthma. *Chest. 116(6)*:1780–1785 (1999).
8. **Mannino, D.M., D.M. Homa, L.J. Akinbami, J.E. Moorman, C. Gwynn, and S.C. Redd:** Surveillance for asthma—United States, 1980–1999. *MMWR Surveill. Summ. 51(1)*;1–13 (2002).
9. **Yucesoy, B. and M.I. Luster:** Genetic susceptibility in pneumoconiosis. *Toxicol. Lett. 168(3)*:249–254 (2007).
10. **Romieu, I., et al.:** Genetic polymorphism of GSTM1 and antioxidant supplementation influence lung function in relation to ozone exposure in asthmatic children in Mexico City. *Thorax. 59(1)*:8–10 (2004).
11. **Yang, I.A., et al.:** Association of tumor necrosis factor-alpha polymorphisms and ozone-induced change in lung function. *Am. J. Respir. Crit. Care Med. 171(2)*:171–176 (2005).
12. **Mapp, C.E., et al.:** Glutathione S-transferase GSTP1 is a susceptibility gene for occupational asthma induced by isocyanates. *J. Allergy Clin. Immunol. 109(5)*:867–872 (2002).
13. **Bernstein, D.I., et al.:** Diisocyanate asthma and gene-environment interactions with IL4RA, CD-14, and IL-13 genes. *Ann. Allergy Asthma Immunol. 97(6)*:800–806 (2006).
14. **National Institutes of Health (NIH):** Genes Environment and Health Initiative. http://genesandenvironment.nih.gov/. [Accessed on October 19, 2007].
15. **National Institute of Environmental Health Sciences:** The Environmental Genome Project http://www.niehs.nih.gov/envgenom/home.htm. [Accessed on October 19, 2007].

16. **Alarie, Y., G.D. Nielsen, and M.M. Schaper:** Animal bioassays for evaluation of indoor air quality. In *Indoor Air Quality Handbook*. Spengler, J.D., J.M. Samet and J.F. McCarthy (eds.). New York: McGraw-Hill, 2001. pp 23.21–23.49.
17. **Schiffman, S.S. and C.M. Williams:** Science of odor as a potential health issue. *J. Environ. Qual. 34(1)*:129–138 (2005).
18. **Dalton, P.:** Upper airway irritation, odor perception and health risk due to airborne chemicals. *Toxicol. Lett. 140–141*:239–248 (2003).
19. **Hummel, T. and A. Livermore:** Intranasal chemosensory function of the trigeminal nerve and aspects of its relation to olfaction. *Int. Arch. Occup. Environ. Health 75(5)*: 305–313 (2002).
20. **Castranova, V., D.G. Frazer, L.K. Manley, and R.D. Dey:** Pulmonary alterations associated with inhalation of occupational and environmental irritants. *Int. Immunopharmacol. 2(2–3)*:163–172 (2002).
21. **Geppetti, P., S. Materazzi, and P. Nicoletti:** The transient receptor potential vanilloid 1: role in airway inflammation and disease. *Eur. J. Pharmacol. 533(1–3)*:207–214 (2006).
22. **Belanger, K., J.F. Gent, E.W. Triche, M.B. Bracken, and B.P. Leaderer:** Association of indoor nitrogen dioxide exposure with respiratory symptoms in children with asthma. *Am. J. Respir. Crit. Care Med. 173(3)*:297–303 (2006).
23. **Pilotto, L.S., R.M. Douglas, R.G. Attewell, and S.R. Wilson:** Respiratory effects associated with indoor nitrogen dioxide exposure in children. *Int. J. Epidemiol. 26(4)*: 788–796 (1997).
24. **Rosenlund, M. and G. Bluhm:** Health effects resulting from nitrogen dioxide exposure in an indoor ice arena. *Arch. Environ. Health. 54(1)*:52–57 (1999).
25. **Rosenlund, M., S. Jungnelius, G. Bluhm, and M. Svartengren:** A 5-year follow-up of airway symptoms after nitrogen dioxide exposure in an indoor ice arena. *Arch. Environ. Health 59(4)*:213–217 (2004).
26. **Kelly, F.J., A. Blomberg, A. Frew, S.T. Holgate, and T. Sandstrom:** Antioxidant kinetics in lung lavage fluid following exposure of humans to nitrogen dioxide. *Am. J. Respir. Crit. Care Med. 154(6 Pt 1)*:1700–1705 (1996).
27. **Velsor, L.W. and E.M. Postlethwait:** NO2-induced generation of extracellular reactive oxygen is mediated by epithelial lining layer antioxidants. *Am. J. Physiol. 273(6 Pt 1)*:L1265–1275 (1997).
28. **Blomberg, A., et al.:** Persistent airway inflammation but accommodated antioxidant and lung function responses after repeated daily exposure to nitrogen dioxide. *Am. J. Respir. Crit. Care Med. 159(2)*:36–543 (1999).
29. **Massin, N., A.B. Bohadana, P. Wild, M. Hery, J.P. Toamain, and G. Hubert:** Respiratory symptoms and bronchial responsiveness in lifeguards exposed to nitrogen trichloride in indoor swimming pools. *Occup. Environ. Med. 55(4)*:258–263 (1998).
30. **King, B.S., Page, E.H., Mueller, C.A., Dollberg, D.D., Gomez, K.E. and Warren, A.M.:** Eye and respiratory symptoms in poultry processing workers exposed to chlorine by-products. *Am. J. Ind. Med. 49(2)*:119–126 (2006).
31. **Massin, N., et al.:** Respiratory symptoms and bronchial responsiveness among cleaning and disinfecting workers in the food industry. *Occup. Environ. Med. 64(2)*:75–81 (2007).
32. **Petsonk, E.L.:** Work-related asthma and implications for the general public. *Environ Health Perspect. 110(4)*: 569–572 (2002).
33. **Choi, J.H., et al.:** Increased levels of IgG to cytokeratin 19 in sera of patients with toluene diisocyanate-induced asthma. *Ann. Allergy Asthma Immunol. 93(3)*:293–298 (2004).
34. **Wisnewski, A.V.:** Developments in laboratory diagnostics for isocyanate asthma. *Curr. Opin. Allergy Clin. Immunol. 7(2)*:138–145 (2007).
35. **Park, H.S., S.K. Lee, H.Y. Kim, D.H. Nahm, and S.S. Kim:** Specific immunoglobulin E and immunoglobulin G antibodies to toluene diisocyanate-human serum albumin conjugate: useful markers for predicting long-term prognosis in toluene diisocyanate-induced asthma. *Clin. Exp. Allergy 32(4)*:551–555 (2002).
36. **Bernstein, D.I., Ott, M.G., Woolhiser, M., Lummus, Z. and Graham, C.:** Evaluation of antibody binding to diisocyanate protein conjugates in a general population. *Ann Allergy Asthma Immunol. 97(3)*:357–364 (2006).
37. **Johnson, V.J., J.M. Matheson, and M.I. Luster:** Animal models for diisocyanate asthma: answers for lingering questions. *Curr. Opin. Allergy Clin. Immunol. 4(2)*:105–110 (2004).
38. **Pronk, A., et al.:** Dermal, inhalation, and internal exposure to 1,6-HDI and its oligomers in car body repair shop workers and industrial spray painters. *Occup. Environ. Med. 63(9)*:624–631 (2006).
39. **American Lung Association:** Occupational Lung Disease Fact Sheet. http://www.lungusa.org. [Accessed on October 19, 2007].
40. **Moore, J.E., R.P. Convery, B.C. Millar, J.R. Rao, and J.S. Elborn:** Hypersensitivity pneumonitis associated with mushroom worker's lung: an update on the clinical significance of the importation of exotic mushroom varieties. *Int. Arch. Allergy Immunol. 136(1)*:98–102 (2005).
41. **Volkman, K.K., J.G. Merrick, and M.C. Zacharisen:** Yacht-maker's lung: A case of hypersensitivity pneumonitis in yacht manufacturing. *Wisc. Med. J. 105(7)*:47–50 (2006).
42. **Fisher, R., W.B. Saunders, S.J. Murray, and G.M. Stave:** Prevention of laboratory animal allergy. *J. Occup. Environ. Med. 40(7)*:609–613 (1998).
43. **Moscato, G., P. Pignatti, M.R. Yacoub, C. Romano, S. Spezia, and L. Perfetti:** Occupational asthma and occupational rhinitis in hairdressers. *Chest. 128(5)*:3590–3598 (2005).

44. **Amr, S. and M.E. Bollinger:** Latex Allergy and Occupational Asthma in Health Care Workers: Adverse Outcomes. *Environ. Health Perspect. 112*:378–381 (2004).
45. **Brown, J.A.:** Haz-Map, National Library of Medicine. http://hazmap.nlm.nih.gov/index.html. [Accessed on October 19, 2007].
46. **Attfield, M.D., J.M. Wood, V.C. Antao, and G.A. Pinheiro:** Changing Patterns of Pneumoconiosis Mortality — United States, 1968–2000. *MMWR. 53(28)*:627–632 (2004).
47. **Kissell, F.N.:** Handbook for Dust Control in Mining. *IC 9465 Information Circular, United States Department of Health and Human Services.* 1–132 (2003).
48. **U.S. Centers for Disease Control and Prevention (CDC):** Coal Workers' Health Surveillance Program. http://www.cdc.gov/niosh/topics/surveillance/ords/CoalWorkersHealthSurvProgram.html. [Accessed on October 19, 2007].
49. **Amicosante, M. and A.P. Fontenot:** T cell recognition in chronic beryllium disease. *Clin. Immunol. 121(2)*:134–143 (2006).
50. **Huaux, F.:** New developments in the understanding of immunology in silicosis. *Curr. Opin. Allergy Clin. Immunol. 7(2)*:168–173 (2007).
51. **Moriyama, H., et al.:** Two-dimensional Analysis of Elements and Mononuclear Cells in Hard Metal Lung Disease. *Am. J. Respir. Crit. Care Med. 176(1)*:70–77 (2007).
52. **Chonan, T., O. Taguchi, and K. Omae:** Interstitial pulmonary disorders in indium-processing workers. *Eur. Respir. J. 29(2)*:317–324 (2007).
53. **Homma, S., et al.:** Pulmonary fibrosis in an individual occupationally exposed to inhaled indium-tin oxide. *Eur. Respir. J. 25(1)*:200–204 (2005).
54. **Nemery, B.:** Metal toxicity and the respiratory tract. *Eur. Respir. J. 3(2)*:202–219 (1990).
55. **Kreiss, K., et al.:** Clinical bronchiolitis obliterans in workers at a microwave-popcorn plant. *N. Engl. J. Med. 347(5)*:330–338 (2002).
56. **Hubbs, A.F., et al.:** Necrosis of nasal and airway epithelium in rats inhaling vapors of artificial butter flavoring. *Toxicol. Appl. Pharmacol. 185(2)*:128–135 (2002).
57. **Kanwal, R., et al.:** Evaluation of flavorings-related lung disease risk at six microwave popcorn plants. *J. Occup. Environ. Med. 48(2)*:149–157 (2006).
58. **Kullman, G., et al.:** Characterization of respiratory exposures at a microwave popcorn plant with cases of bronchiolitis obliterans. *J. Occup. Environ. Hyg. 2(3)*:169–178 (2005).
59. **Boylstein, R., et al.:** Diacetyl emissions and airborne dust from butter flavorings used in microwave popcorn production. *J. Occup. Environ. Hyg. 3(10)*:530–535 (2006).
60. **U.S. Centers for Disease Control and Prevention (CDC):** Fixed obstructive lung disease among workers in the flavor-manufacturing industry — California, 2004–2007. *MMWR 56(16)*:389–393 (2007).
61. **Wilkins, C.K., et al.:** Formation of strong airway irritants in mixtures of isoprene/ozone and isoprene/ozone/nitrogen dioxide. *Environ. Health Perspect. 109(9)*:937–941 (2001).
62. **Tamas, G., C.J. Weschler, J. Toftum, and P.O. Fanger:** Influence of ozone-limonene reactions on perceived air quality. *Indoor Air 16(3)*:168–178 (2006).
63. **Wainman, T., Zhang, J., Weschler, C.J. and Lioy, P.J.:** Ozone and limonene in indoor air: a source of submicron particle exposure. *Environ Health Perspect. 108(12)*:1139–1145 (2000).
64. **Brown, S.K.:** Assessment of pollutant emissions from dry-process photocopiers. *Indoor Air 9(4)*:259–267 (1999).
65. **Sunesson, A.L., I. Rosen, B. Stenberg, and M. Sjostrom:** Multivariate evaluation of VOCs in buildings where people with non-specific building-related symptoms perceive health problems and in buildings where they do not. *Indoor Air 16(5)*:383–391 (2006).
66. **Takigawa, T., et al.:** Were volatile organic compounds the inducing factors for subjective symptoms of employees working in newly constructed hospitals? *Environ. Toxicol. 19(4)*:280–290 (2004).
67. **Wolkoff, P., Wilkins, C.K., Clausen, P.A. and Nielsen, G.D.:** Organic compounds in office environments — sensory irritation, odor, measurements and the role of reactive chemistry. *Indoor Air 16(1)*:7–19 (2006).
68. **Rea, W.J., et al.:** Effects of toxic exposure to molds and mycotoxins in building-related illnesses. *Arch. Environ. Health 58(7)*:399–405 (2003).
69. **Lee, T.G.:** Health symptoms caused by molds in a courthouse. *Arch. Environ. Health 58(7)*:442–446 (2003).
70. **Etzel, R.A., et al.:** Acute pulmonary hemorrhage in infants associated with exposure to Stachybotrys atra and other fungi. *Arch. Pediatr. Adolesc. Med. 152(8)*:757–762 (1998).
71. **Sweeney, P.J.:** Farmer's lung; a clinical account of a disease probably caused by fungi. *Ulster Med. J. 21(2)*:150–154 (1952).
72. **MacIntosh, D.L., et al.:** Airborne fungal spores in a cross-sectional study of office buildings. *J. Occup. Environ. Hyg. 3(7)*:379–389 (2006).
73. **Santilli, J. and W. Rockwell:** Fungal contamination of elementary schools: a new environmental hazard. *Ann. Allergy Asthma Immunol. 90(2)*:203–208 (2003).
74. **Claeson, A.S., M. Sandstrom, and A.L. Sunesson:** Volatile organic compounds (VOCs) emitted from materials collected from buildings affected by microorganisms. *J. Environ. Monit. 9(3)*:240–245 (2007).
75. **Pestka, J.J. and A.T. Smolinski:** Deoxynivalenol: toxicology and potential effects on humans. *J. Toxicol Environ Health B Crit Rev. 8(1):*39–69 (2005).
76. **Leino, M., et al.:** Intranasal exposure to a damp building mould, Stachybotrys chartarum, induces lung inflammation in mice by satratoxin-independent mechanisms. *Clin. Exp. Allergy 33(11)*:1603–1610 (2003).

77. **Dearborn, D.G., I. Yike, W.G. Sorenson, M.J. Miller, and R.A. Etzel:** Overview of investigations into pulmonary hemorrhage among infants in Cleveland, Ohio. *Environ. Health Perspect. 107(3)*:495–499 (1999).
78. **U.S. Centers for Disease Control and Prevention (CDC):** Update: pulmonary hemorrhage/hemosiderosis among infants — Cleveland, Ohio, 1993–1996. *MMWR 46(2)*:33–35 (1997).
79. **U.S. Centers for Disease Control and Prevention (CDC):** Update: Pulmonary hemorrhage/hemosiderosis among infants — Cleveland, Ohio, 1993–1996. *MMWR 49(9)*: 180–184 (2000).
80. **Boehlecke, B., et al.:** Low-dose airborne endotoxin exposure enhances bronchial responsiveness to inhaled allergen in atopic asthmatics. *J. Allergy Clin. Immunol. 112(6)*: 1241–1243 (2003).
81. **Blanc, P.D., et al.:** Impact of the home indoor environment on adult asthma and rhinitis. *J. Occup. Environ. Med. 47(4)*:362–372 (2005).
82. **Michel, O., et al.:** Severity of asthma is related to endotoxin in house dust. *Am. J. Respir. Crit. Care Med. 154(6 Pt 1)*:1641–1646 (1996).
83. **Solomon, G.M., M. Hjelmroos-Koski, M. Rotkin-Ellman, and S.K. Hammond:** Airborne mold and endotoxin concentrations in New Orleans, Louisiana, after flooding, October through November 2005. *Environ. Health Perspect. 114(9)*:1381–1386 (2006).
84. **Park, J.H., J. Cox-Ganser, C. Rao, and K. Kreiss:** Fungal and endotoxin measurements in dust associated with respiratory symptoms in a water-damaged office building. *Indoor Air 16(3)*:192–203 (2006).

Chapter 6

Dermal Toxicology

By Warren W. Jederberg, MS, CIH, RPIH

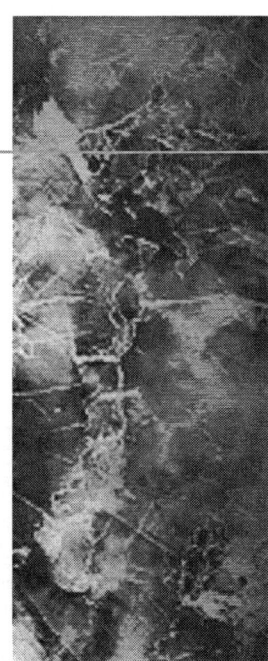

Introduction

The skin is second only to inhalation as the most common exposure route for industrial chemicals. According to Bureau of Labor Statistics (BLS), the injury rate for recordable skin disease was 4.4 per 10,000 workers in 2005. Though the rate has decreased from 8.2 in 1992, the number of occupational illnesses caused by skin absorption of chemicals is not known.[1–3] However, occupational skin problems have potential impact on the health and welfare of millions of workers and are one of the leading causes of lost days as a result of work-related illnesses.[4–6] Many activities outside of the workplace may compromise the integrity of the barrier function of the skin and contribute to topical and systemic disorders. There are a number of possible agents that can injure the skin: chemical, mechanical, physical, and botanical. The concurrent exposure to chemicals and other agents can significantly modify the potential for damage to the skin.

Structure and Function of the Skin

The average surface area of human skin for adults is 1.96 m^2 (male) and 1.69 m^2 (female) and weighs between 2.38 Kg and 2.74 Kg.[7,8] It ranges in thickness from 0.5 mm in the eyelids to 4.0 mm on the palms and soles. Though the number of adnexal structures (hair follicles, sweat glands, pain receptors, etc.) varies across anatomical locations, the basic structure of the skin is consistent.[8,9]

Skin is classically described as having two major components, the epidermis and the dermis (Figure 6.1). The outer most layer of epidermis (the stratum corneum) is made of mature keratinocytes that are now 80% keratin in content and is often called "the horny layer".[3,10] This layer provides the most important barrier function of the skin. It is resistant to water and water-soluble polar chemicals.[3,8,10,11] This layer normally renews itself approximately every 4 weeks.[3,6,11] The rate of diffusion of materials through the stratum corneum varies across anatomical

Outcome Competencies

After completion of this chapter, the reader should be able to:

- Describe the basic structure and functions of the skin.
- Describe the differences between irritant contact dermatitis and allergic contact dermatitis.
- Describe the purpose and limitations of skin notations in various criteria documents.
- Describe and use knowledge of the structure and functions of the skin in assessing risk and establishing exposure mitigation strategies in the work place.

Prerequisite Knowledge

1. Fundamentals of industrial hygiene workplace evaluation processes.
2. College level biology and chemistry.
3. Basic immunology.

Key Terms

skin notation, skin designation, stratum corneum, dermis, epidermis, contact dermatitis, photosensitization, occupational acne

Key Topics

1. Function of Skin
2. Irritant Contact Dermatitis
3. Allergic Contact Dermatitis
4. Photosensitization

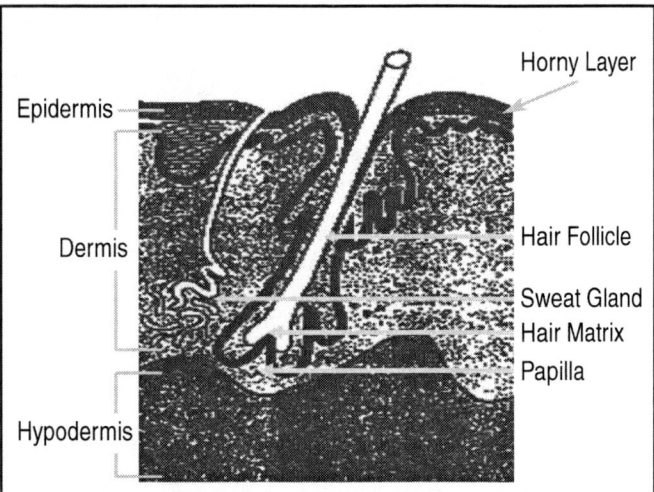

Figure 6.1 — Basic Structure of the Skin
From: **Jederberg, W.W. and K. Still (eds.):** Introduction to Dermatotoxicology. *The Layman's Guide to Toxicology.* CPIA Publication 686. Columbia, MD: The Johns Hopkins University, 1999. pp. 69–76. (Used with permission).

sites (foot sole > scrotum > palm > forehead > abdomen).[3] Any physical, chemical or biological disruption of the stratum corneum will allow greater penetration of substances into the circulation.

The keratinocytes in the epidermis are capable of a wide range of metabolic functions and have been compared with the liver, though at a much lower level, in ability to detoxify chemicals.[3,8,12,13] Other components of the epidermis include melanocytes which are responsible for pigmentation and Langerhans' cells which play important roles in contact dermatitis.[10–12,14,15]

The dermis is much thicker than the epidermis and contains connective tissue composed of collagen elastic fibers. It is rich in blood vessels and nerve fibers. Muscular elements, hair follicles, oil and sweat glands, and receptor organs for touch, pain, heat, and cold are also in the dermis.[8,11,13,14]

Occupational Skin Disorders

There are several major skin reactions of importance in occupational environments: (1) contact dermatitis (including irritant and allergic contact dermatitis) (2) photosensitization, (3) urticarial reactions, and (4) acne.[3,8,10,11,15]

Contact Dermatitis

Contact dermatitis is generally found in the area of actual exposure. It accounts for the largest percentage of occupational skin disease.

Irritant contact dermatitis reactions include corrosion, acute irritation and cumulative irritation. The reactions do not involve any immune cell function but are a result of the direct physical and chemical properties of the agent.[8,10,12,14–17] Occupations where irritant contact dermatitis is common are machinists, magazine printers/workers, agricultural workers, artists, automobile and aircraft industry workers, bakers and confectioners, bookbinders, butchers, cooks and caterers, electroplaters, hairdressers, jewelers, mechanics, plastics workers, shoemakers, tannery workers and others.[16–18] Natural and synthetic products associated with irritant contact dermatitis include: pesticides, oils, greases, phenol, alkalis and acids, soaps, tomatoes, parsnip, parsley, foxglove, turnips, caster bean milkweed, poison sumac, mango, gingko, nickel, chromates, mercury, gold, among many others.[3,12–15,16,19]

Allergic contact dermatitis is the result of a type IV cell-mediated hypersensitivity reaction and can usually be distinguished from simple contact dermatitis by its appearance well beyond the area of direct contact and that it occurs 12–24 hours after exposure.[3,11,13–15] Occupations where allergic contact dermatitis is frequently seen are those involved with metal workers, plastics and rubbers, pharmaceuticals, building/construction, beautician products, and those working in the health care, landscaping and gardening, woodworking, jewelry, explosives and manufacturing trades.[8,11,15,16] Among some 2,800 compounds that cause allergic contact dermatitis, only 250 are associated with asthma.[20]

Photosensitization

Contact photosensitization is the most common occupational phototoxic reaction and is caused mainly by plants. A toxic reaction occurs when the photoactive chemical contacts and is absorbed into the skin. Sunlight (usually ultraviolet A) then activates the chemical. Some materials which may cause contact photosensitization include: St. Johnswort, horsebrushes, tetracycline, nalidixic acid, eosin and acridine dyes, anthracene, psoralen containing plants (e.g. lime, celery and parsnip), and pitch (coal tar derivatives).[3,8,10,11,16,19] These kinds of reactions are seen among farmers, asphalt workers, miners and others. In contrast to contact photosensitization, there is photoallergy which is not very common but is also a true type IV hypersensitivity reaction. Exposure to halogenated salicylanilides (used in soaps), hexachlorobenzene (an insecticide), musk ambrette (a fragrance), ketoprofen (nonsteriodal anti-inflammatory drugs), photothiazines (topical drugs), and a variety of plants.[3,8,10,11,14,16] Medical personnel may be exposed to photosensitizing drugs while field workers are exposed to photosensitizers in plants and chemicals. Machinists may be exposed to these agents through some of the antimicrobials contained in metal-working fluids. Oil field and road construction workers are exposed to the photosensitizing components of coal tar, pitch and other hydrocarbons.

Urticarial Reactions

Urticaria is a vascular reaction of the skin resulting in the appearance of smooth, slightly elevated patches (wheals) that are redder or paler than the surrounding skin and often accompanied by severe itching.[21] Urticarial reactions may result from direct reactions or be type I hypersensitivity reactions and are the result of the release of substances that act on the vascular system.[3,8,11,14,15] Materials that can cause this reaction through non-immunologic mechanisms include curare, aspirin, azo dyes, benzoates, plant and animal toxins, cobalt chloride, nicotinic acid, cinnamic aldehyde and many others.[3,14,22,23] Some materials suspected of causing contact urticaria through the immunologic process are chloro-2,4-dinitrobenzene, diethyltoluamide, tetanus antitoxin, penicillin, streptomycin, potatoes, tulips, silk, wool, moths, insect stings, beer, and some plants and animal toxins.[11,15,22–24]

Occupational Acne

The clinical manifestations of acne are comedones (blackheads or whiteheads) and inflammatory folliculitis.[3,8,12,14] In the industrial environment acne may be caused by coal-tar pitch, creosote, greases, and oils.[3,11,14,15] A less frequent but particularly difficult to treat form is chloracne. Some materials that cause this condition include and may be caused by a wide variety of halogenated aromatic hydrocarbons (polyhalogenated dibenzofurans, polychlorodibenzofurans, polychloronaphthalenes, polychlorinated biphenyls (PCBs), dioxins and chlorobenzenes).[3,8,10,12,14] One hundred and ninety-three cases of chloracne were the result of a dioxin industrial accident in Seveso, Italy, in 1976. Long-term studies illustrate the effects of dioxin exposure on other systems than the skin.[25–28]

Sampling for Skin Exposures

When considering strategies for sampling of potential exposure to the skin and quantitating the relative potential contribution that dermal exposure may make to overall dose, there are a number of problems to overcome. First, there are no uniform good models for differentiating between the systemic toxicity caused via inhalation and dermal exposure with agents where both routes are available.[29,30] Second, the total amount of exposed skin will vary depending upon the anthropomorphic and work habits of the worker. Third, physical work conditions and underlying medical conditions may greatly influence the barrier function of the skin and consequently, the dose absorbed through the skin.[30–34] When sampling large groups of workers, it may be acceptable to use the standard exposure values recommended by the U.S. EPA for Human Health Risk Assessments.[7] Suggested direct sampling include: skin swabs and liquid rinses, the use of surrogate skin (skin pads and whole-body dosimeters, tracer and other in situ techniques, and wipe sampling.[29,35,36] In order to assess the contribution of dermal exposure to overall toxicity, a comprehensive knowledge of the processes and chemicals involved in the occupational setting are required. Professional judgment must be used in applying standards and interpreting monitoring results.[29,37]

Skin Notation Issues

In assessing the potential dermal toxicity of materials in the workplace, caution must be exercised in interpreting what various "skin notations" in the literature mean. Chemical agents not only alter the structural and functional character of the skin, but also may penetrate in sufficient amounts to cause systemic problems. This is the meaning of the "Skin Notation" in the Threshold Limit Values (TLV®s) published by the American Conference of Governmental Industrial Hygienists.[38] Other criteria are used in other countries to affix a "skin notation" to a compound.[39] These materials require additional attention, particularly when involved in operations characterized by high airborne concentration under conditions where dermal exposure may occur for extended periods of time. Under such circumstances, biological monitoring may be required to get a complete picture of exposure. As biological monitoring is covered elsewhere in Chapter 29, "Biomonitoring," a detailed discussion is not presented here. Table 6.1 contains a partial list of these compounds and demonstrates the diversity of compounds that might be found in the occupational environment. Note that federal regulations and the TLV® booklet do not give the skin notation/designation because the material is irritative or

Table 6.1 — Some Compounds with "Skin" Notation

Acetone cyanohydrin	Acrolein	Acrylamide	Acrylic Acid
Acrylonitrile	Aldrin	Allyl Alcohol	Aniline
Ammonium perfluorooctanoate	Benzene	Benzidine	o-sec-Butylphenol
Carbon disulfide	Carbon tetrachloride	Chlordane	Chlorinated camphene
Chlorodiphenyl	2-Chloroprionic acid	Chloropyrifos	Cresol (all isomers)
Cyclohexanol	Cyclohexanone	Cyclonite	Decaborane
Diazinon	Dichlorvos	Dieldrin	Diethylene triamine
Diisopropylamine	Dimethylformamide	Dinitrobenzene (all isomers)	Diquat
Endrin	Epichlorohydrin	Ethyl bromide	Ehtylene dibromide
Ethylene glycol dinitrate	Formamide	Furfuryl alchohol	Heptachlor
n-Hexane	Hydrazine	Hydrogen cyanide	Isooctyl alcohol
Lindane	Malathion	Mercury compounds	
(alkyl, aryl compounds)	Methanol	Methyl acrylate	Methyl bromide
Methy chloride	Methyl hydrazine	Methyl iodide	Methyl isocyanate
Methyl n-butyl ketone	Methyl parathion	Nicotine	p-Nitoraniline
Nitrotoluene	Parathion	Pentachlorophenol	Phenol Sodium
fluoroacetate	Tetraethyl lead	Thioglycolic acid	o-Toliudine
Toluene	1,1,2-Trichloroethane	2,4,6-Trinitrotoluene	Xylidine

corrosive, but because there is potential for systemic toxicity from cutaneous exposure.

Therefore, some chemicals that are irritative or corrosive are not given the skin notation/designation in the absence of systemic toxicity.[37–41]

Case Studies

Two nurses employed at the same community hospital, developed severe latex allergy manifested with dermatologic and respiratory symptoms. They also were sensitized to various chemical and other environmental and food allergens. They continued to experience respiratory symptoms that became severe despite the discontinued use of latex. Once diagnosis of latex allergy was established, efforts were made to minimize direct contact with latex, but little attention was given to their work environment.[42]

A 30-year-old woman has a two and one-half year history of generalized, pruritic, diffuse and erythematous skin eruption that began suddenly. All patch tests were negative. There was a partial response to oral glucocorticoids, with prompt recurrence of the eruption after discontinuation of medication. There was also a history of pustular eruptions on both upper and lower extremities that were unresponsive to therapy. The diagnosis was allergic contact dermatitis to textile dyes. The patient was advised to avoid dye sources (i.e. hair dyes and orange, red and blue clothing), pants with liners, elastic underwear, and tight clothing. It was recommended that she wear loose-fitting clothing made from 100 percent natural based fabrics. All clothing was washed with an extra rinse cycle. Management included topical and systemic glucocorticoids, and avoidance of exposure. The incidence of allergic contact dermatitis to textile dyes is estimated to be between 0.05 and 15.9%.[43]

Summary and Conclusion

The skin is the primary barrier against toxicants in the environment. Though its main function is that of a physical barrier, it has many other functions. Any compromise of the skin enhances the potential toxicity of environmental stressors, whether they are physical, biological or chemical. In assessing the relative contribution to overall toxicity of materials in the occupational setting, all aspects of exposure must be considered including the contribution made through dermal exposure. Research is on-going to determine the relationship between dermal and inhalation exposure when both routes are possible. The practicing industrial hygienist or occupational health professional must be cautious in interpreting dermal toxicology data that are readily available but may need to seek further guidance to determine its applicability in any given exposure scenario.

Additional Reading

- **Marzulli, F.N. and H.I. Maibach (eds.):** *Dermatotoxicology.* Washington, DC: Taylor & Francis, 1995.

- **Kanerva, L.P., P. Elsner, and H.I. Maibach (eds.):** *Handbook of Occupational Dermatology.* New York, NY: Springer, 2000.

References

1. "Safety and Health Topics — Dermal Exposure." Available at: www.osha.gov/SLTC/dermalexposure/exposure.html. [Accessed April 26, 2007].
2. Bureau of Labor statistics [Online] Available at: www.bls.gov/iif/oshwc/osh/os/ostb1613.pdf. [Accessed and compiled April 26, 2007]
3. **Rice, R.H., and D.E. Cohen:** Toxic Responses of the Skin. In *Casarett & Doull's Toxicology — The Basic Science of Poisons* (6th Edition), C.D. Klaasen (ed.). New York: McGraw-Hill, 2001. pp. 653-671.
4. **Rycroft, R.J.:** Clinical Assessment in the workplace: Dermatitis. *Occup. Med.* 46:364–366 (1996).
5. **Hogan, D.J.:** *Skin Lesions and Environmental Exposures* (ATSDR Case Studies in Environmental Medicine). Agency for Toxic Substances and Disease Registry, 1993.
6. **Percival, L., S.B. Tucker, S.H. Lamm, M.M. Key, B. Wilds, and K.S. Grumski:** A case study of dermatitis, based on collaborative approach between occupational physicians and industrial hygienists. *Am. Ind. Hyg. Assoc. J.* 56(2):184–188 (1995).
7. **U.S. Environmental Protection Agency (EPA):** *Exposure Factors Handbook* (EPA 600/P95/002Fa). Washington, D.C.: EPA, 1997.
8. **Weber, L.W., and J.T. Pierce:** Development of Occupational Skin Disease. In *The Occupational Environment: Its Evaluation, Control and Management,* 2nd Edition, DiNardi, S.R. (ed.). Fairfax, VA: AIHA Press, 2003. pp. 348–360.
9. **Montagna, W.:** *The Structure and Function of Skin.* New York: Academic Press, 1962.
10. **Emmett, E.A.:** Occupational Skin Disease. In *Occupational Toxicology.* N.H. Stacey (ed.). London: Taylor & Francis Ltd., 1993. pp. 89–105.
11. **Niesink, R.J.M.:** Dermatotoxicology: Toxicological Pathology and Methodological Aspects. In *Toxicology: Principles and Applications.* Niesink, R.J.M., de Vries, J. and M.A. Hollinger (eds.). New York: CRC Press, 1996. pp. 503–529.
12. **Reitschel, R.L.:** Dermatotoxicity: Toxic Effects in the Skin. In *Industrial Toxicology: Safety and Health Applications in the Workplace.* Williams, P.L., and J.L. Burson (eds.). New York: Van Nostrand Reinhold, 1985. pp. 138–161.
13. **Tucker, S.B., and M.K. Marcus:** Occupational Skin Disease. In *Environmental and Occupational Medicine,* 2nd edition. W.N. Rom (ed.). Boston: Little, Brown and Company, 1992. pp. 551–560.
14. **Taylor, J.S.:** The Skin and Occupational Dermatoses. In *Fundamentals of Industrial Hygiene,* 4th edition. Plog, B.A., Niland, J. and P.J. Quinlan (eds.). Itasca: National Safety Council, 1996. pp. 53–82.

15. "Acne." [Online] Available at: www.ccohs.ca/oshanswers/diseases/acne.html [Accessed November 24, 2006].
16. **Crowe, M.A. and W.D. James:** Allergic and Irritant Contact Dermatitis. In *Textbook of Military Medicine — Military Dermatology.* James, W.D. (ed.). Washington DC: Borden Institute, 1998. pp. 111–142.
17. **Burgess, W.A. (ed.):** Metal Machining. In *Recognition of Health Hazards in Industry — A Review of Materials and Processes,* 2nd edition. New York: John Wiley & Sons, Inc., 1995. pp. 140–166.
18. **Cook, C., and E. Page.:** Case Studies — Exposures of Workers at a Magazine Printing Company. *Appl. Occu. And Envir. Hyg. 16(6)*:639–644 (2001).
19. "OSH Answers: Dermatitis, Irritant Contact." [Online] Available at www.ccohs.ca/oshanswers/diseases/dermatitis.html. [Accessed November 24, 2006].
20. **De Groot, A.C.:** *Patch Testing: Test Concentrations and Vehicles for 2800 Allergens.* Elsevier, 1986.
21. "Cutaneous Toxicity: Toxic Effects on Skin." [Online] Available at: http://extoxnet.orst.edu/tibs/cutaneou.htm. [Accessed May 10, 2007].
22. Urticaria. In *Dorland's Illustrated Medical Dictionary*, 26th edition. Philadelphia, PA: W.B. Saunders Company, 1981. p. 1429.
23. **Meir, J. and J. White (eds.):** *Handbook of Clinical Toxicology of Animal Venoms and Poisons.* New York: CRC Press, 1995.
24. **Lewis, W.H. and M.P.F. Elvin-Lewis (eds.):** Allergy. In *Medical Botany — Plants Affecting Man's Health.* New York: John Wiley & Sons, 1977. pp. 64–89.
25. **Bertazzi, P.A., et al.:** Health Effects of Dioxin Exposure: A 20-Year Mortality Study. *Am. J. Epi. 153(11)*:1031–1044 (2001).
26. **Bertazzi, P.A., et al.:** The Seveso Studies on Early and Long-Term Effects of Dioxin Exposure: A Review. *Environ. Health Perspect. 106(2)*:625–633 (1998).
27. **Landi, M.R., et al.:** 2,3,7,8-Tetrachlorodibenzo-p-Dioxin Plasma Levels in Seveso 20 Years after the Accident. *Environ. Health Perspect. 106(5)*:273–277 (1998).
28. **Guo, Y.L., M.L. Yu, C.C. Hsu, and W.J. Rogan:** Chloracne, Goiter, Arthritis, and Anemia after Polychlorinated Biphenyl Poisoning: 14-Year Follow-Up of the Taiwan Yucheng Chohort. *Environ. Health Perspect. 107(9)*: 715–719 (1999).
29. **Fahrenbacher, M.C., F. Arnold, H. Marquart, and P. Evans:** Approaches for Occupational Dermal Exposure Assessment and Management. In *The Occupational Environment: Its Evaluation, Control and Management,* 2nd edition. DiNardi, S.R. (ed.). Fairfax, VA: AIHA Press, 2003. pp. 328–345.
30. **Doran, E.M., R.A. Fenske, J.C. Kissel, C.L. Curl, and N.J. Simcox:** Impact of Dermal Absorption Factors in Occupational Exposure Assessment: Comparison of Two Models for Agricultural Re-entry Workers Exposed to Azinphosmethyl. *Appl. Occ. Environ. Hyg. 18*:669–677 (2003).
31. **Hebisch, R., and J. Auffarth:** Dermal Exposure: How to Get Information. *Appl. Occ. Environ. Hyg. 16(2)*:169–173 (2001).
32. **Kezic, S., et al:** Dermal Absorption of Neat Liquid Solvents on Brief Exposures in Volunteers. *Am. Ind. Hyg. Assoc. J. 62*:12–18 (2001).
33. **Sinclair, G.C., R.C. Wester, and H.I. Maibach:** Partition Coefficients for Benzene in Human Skin. *Am. Ind. Hyg. Assoc. J. 63*:685–688 (2002).
34. **Sun, C.C., et al.:** Percutaneous Absorption of Inorganic Lead Compounds. *Am. Ind. Hyg. Assoc. J. 63*:641–646 (2002).
35. **Marquart, H., S. Maidment, J.L. McClaflin, and M.C. Fehrenbacher:** Harmonization of Future Needs for Dermal Exposure Assessment and Modeling: A Workshop Report. *Appl. Occ. Environ. Hyg. 16(2)*:218–227 (2001).
36. **Brouwer, D.H., R.J. Aitken, R. Oppl, and J.W. Cherrie:** Concepts of Skin Protection: Considerations for the Evaluation and Terminology of the Performance of Skin Protection Equipment. *J. Occ. Env. Hyg. 2*:425–434 (2005).
37. **Goldberg, A.M., and H.I. Maibach:** Dermal Toxicity: Alternative Methods for Risk Assessment. *Environ. Health Perspect. 106(2)*:493–496 (1998).
38. **American Conference of Governmental Hygienists (ACGIH):** 2007 TLV®s and BEI®s — *Threshold Limit Values for Chemical Substances and Physical Substances and Physical Agents, Biological Exposure Indices.* Cincinnati, OH: ACGIH. 2007. (published yearly).
39. **Nielsen, J.B., and P. Grandjean:** Criteria for Skin notation in different countries. *Am. J. Ind. Med. 45(3)*:275–280 (2004).
40. **U.S. Department of Labor: Safety and Health Topics:** Surface Contamination. [On line] Available at: www.osha.gov/SLTC/surfacecontamination/index.html. [Accessed May 11, 2007].
41. **Chen C.P., M.F. Boeniger, and H.W. Ahlers:** Use of Dermal LD50 as a Criterion for Skin Notation — Letter to the Editor. *Appl. Occ. Env. Hyg. 18(3)*:154–155 (2003).
42. **Amr, S. and M.E. Bollinger:** Latex Allergy and Occupational Asthma in Health Care Workers: Adverse Outcomes. *Environ. Health Perspect. 112(3)*:378–381 (2004).
43. **Joe, E.K.:** "Allergic Contact Dermatitis to Textile Dyes", Dermatology Online Journal (1): 9 [Online] Available at: Dermatology.cdlib.org/DOJvol7num1/NYUcases/contact/joe.html. [Accessed May 11, 2007].

"What sense would it make or what would it benefit a physician if he discovered the origin of the diseases but could not cure or alleviate them?"

Paracelsus (1493– 1541)

Chapter 7

Systemic Effects: Cardiovascular and Renal Toxicity

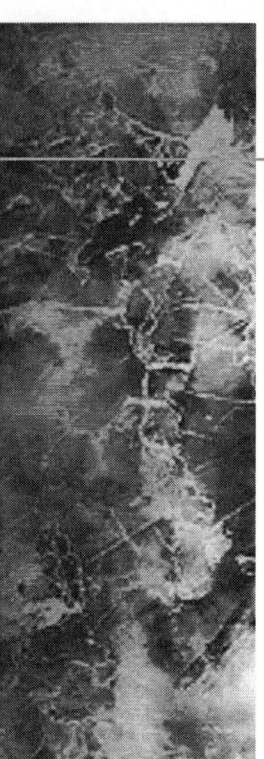

Outcome Competencies

Upon completion of this chapter, the reader should be able to:
- Understand basic functions of the heart, the vascular system, and the kidneys.
- Describe the interactions of various chemicals within the cardiovascular and renal systems.
- Assess different responses of the cardiovascular system to toxic insult.
- Identify the effects that may result from the action of cardiotoxic chemicals.
- Distinguish between the various leading nephrotoxicants in an occupational setting.
- Specify various heavy metals that are toxic to the kidneys.

Key Topics

1. A Brief Survey of the Cardiovascular System
2. Anatomy and Function of Blood Vessels and Circulatory Regulation
3. Important Cardiotoxic Substances
4. Response of the Cardiovascular System to Toxic Insult
5. Toxic Changes in the Blood Vessels
6. A Brief Survey of Kidney Structure and Function
7. Kidney Function
8. Kidney Toxicity
9. A Synopsis of Toxic Insults Affecting both the Cardiovascular System and the Kidney

Key Terms

actin/myosin, Adenosine triphosphatase (ATPase), aldosterone, aliphatics, arrhythmogenic, autocrine, baroreceptor, bathmotropic, cardiomyopathy, chemoreceptor, chronotropic, cytokines, cytotoxic, diastole, depolarization, dromotropic, dysrhythmias, endocytotic, endothelin, glomerulus, glycoprotein, homocysteine, inotropic, inulin, juxtaglomerular apparatus, Loop of Henle, mechanoreceptor, membrane potential, myocyte, nephron, nociception, oxidative phosphorylation, paracrine, pharmacodynamics, pharmacokinetics, proprioception, renin/angiotensin, repolarization, sinoatrial node, symport, tachycardia, vasa recta, vasoconstriction, vasomotor, xenobiotic

Chapter 7

Systemic Effects: Cardiovascular and Renal Toxicity

By Lutz W.D. Weber, PhD, DABT, Janet D. Pierce, RN, DSN, and J. Thomas Pierce, PhD

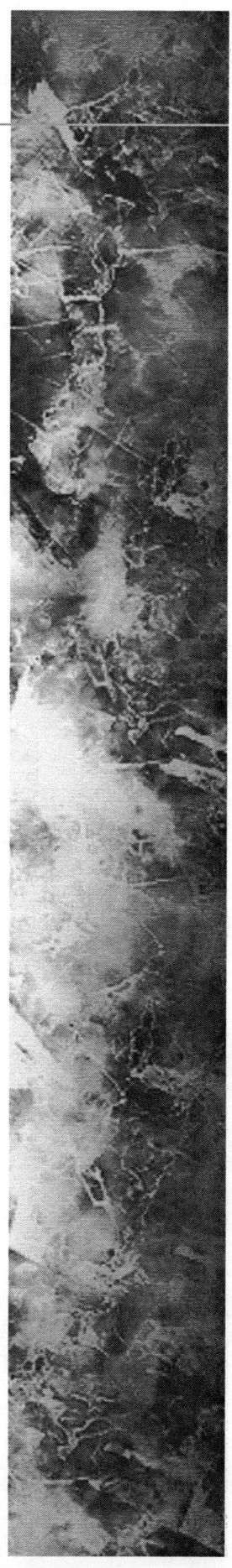

Introduction

This chapter will allow the reader to appreciate the interaction of various chemicals with two major organ systems. Its emphasis is in areas of cardiovascular, renal and systemic toxicity, which is derived by integrating two or more systems.

In order to understand the action of toxic materials one must have some idea of the normal structure and function of the heart, the vascular system, and the kidney. This chapter attempts to integrate effects occurring across multiple systems such as the cardiovascular system (heart, major and minor arteries and veins, including the microarchitecture of arterioles, capillaries and venules), and the renal system (afferent and efferent arterioles, glomerulus, loop of Henle, and collecting duct). In the context of this chapter it will be inevitable to distill a few basics. References to these systems can often be shortened to heart or kidney, realizing that the other elements of either system may be involved.

The major function of the vascular system is to supply blood, oxygen, nutrients, and regulatory substances such as hormones or cytokines, to the tissues, and to transport metabolic wastes from the tissues of production to the organs of removal. The kidney is a dynamic system that filters impurities and metabolic end products from the blood, for which purpose a constant, vigorous blood flow at physiologic hydrostatic pressure is necessary. This is so important for the kidney that it maintains its own mechanism of blood pressure regulation, the renin/angiotensin system. This system has the ability of affecting the whole cardiovascular system, thus the functional link between the cardiovascular and kidney systems is established. A second issue exists in that for proper function, the cardiovascular system is very much dependent on the balance of the minerals sodium, potassium, calcium, and magnesium, plus the range of anions that complement these cations electrochemically. Homeostasis involving all of these is maintained by the kidney. The situation is complicated by the fact that many drugs that are widely used in treating cardiovascular or kidney diseases affect the ion balance and/or sensitize these organs to the actions of toxicants.

A Brief Survey of the Cardiovascular System

The cardiovascular system (CV) can be visualized as a continuous, fluid-filled system of elastic pipes (the vasculature) driven by a pump (the heart). Components of the vasculature include arteries, arterioles, capillaries and veins. The contraction of the heart is brought about by the myocard (heart muscle), composed of striated muscle fibers. The cells that make up the heart muscle, called myocytes, are specialized cells that are connected to one another by specialized intercellular junctions that allow the rapid propagation of the electrical impulses that regulate heart rate.[1]

There are 4 major properties of heart cells: 1) automaticity (heart cells can trigger recurrent action potentials — see below — without nerve stimulation), 2) excitability (the cells are able to change the electrostatic charge that exists across their membrane), 3) conductivity (the cells are able to propagate an incoming electrical impulse to neighboring cells), and 4) contractility (the heart cells contain muscle fibers that can contract). The electrical activity of the heart

· · · 59

originates at the level of the individual myocardial cells. An electrical field or potential exists across the membrane of heart cells based on concentration gradients of ions that are maintained at the expense of metabolic energy. When a suitable electrical impulse arrives, ion channels in the membrane are transiently opened and ions move along concentration gradients, resulting in depolarization (the electrical field across the cell membrane collapses), plateau (the cell membrane remains without electrical charge for a short time), and repolarization of the heart cell membrane (ion pumps reestablish the ion gradients and thus the electrical field). This sequence of events is also known as the action potential. The phases of the action potential cause contraction and relaxation of the heart.[2] The period during which the heart muscle relaxes and the ventricle fills with blood is called diastole; the period of contraction is called systole.[2]

There are various types of ion channels that affect the permeability of the heart cell membrane. For instance, one type allows fast passage of Na^+, establishing the depolarization part of the action potential, while other channels sustain slow inward currents of Ca^{2+} and Na^+ that are responsible for the depolarization plateau of heart muscle cells. These processes are critically linked to the action of a class of drug widely used to fight high blood pressure, the β-adrenergic blockers.[3] Both contractile and electrical functions of the heart are critical.

The electrical stimuli controlling heart activity originate in the sinoatrial (SA) node, a group of modified heart cells located in the right atrium (pre-chamber) of the heart whose rhythmic discharge can be modulated by autonomic innervation or circulating catecholamines. This is the natural pacemaker of the heart because it propagates the strongest electrical signal and has a rate, normally between 60–100 beats per minute in an adult, that is faster than the proper rate of the other heart cells. The SA node's spontaneous discharge means that even a completely isolated heart continues to beat as long as it metabolism remains intact.[4] The frequency with which cells of the SA node discharge is influenced externally by the autonomic nervous system (the part of the nervous system that is not controlled by will), which ultimately determines the heart rate. The cardiac output in turn is determined as the product of the heart rate multiplied by the volume of blood pumped.[5]

Xenobiotics can affect heart function by causing changes in heart rate (chronotropism), conduction of impulses (dromotropism), excitability of heart cells (bathmotropism), or force of contraction (inotropism). The most common functional abnormalities are dysrhythmias (changes from normal heart rhythm) and contractility disturbances.[2] Regulation of heart function is achieved by both intrinsic (originating within the heart) and extrinsic factors (originating outside the heart). Intrinsic control of the heart via the SA node relates primarily to cardiac output. The extrinsic controls of the heart are multiple: the autonomic nervous system, chemoreceptors that respond to changes in ionic environment of the blood, stretch receptors that respond to changes in blood volume, and respiratory reflexes.

Blood pressure is the product of cardiac output and systemic vascular resistance. Blood pressure is regulated by the autonomic nervous system, the renin/angiotensin-aldosterone system, and other local control mechanisms. By maintaining adequate blood pressure, the body is assured of adequate oxygen delivery. An important and widely used new class of anti-hypertensive agents, the angiotensin-converting enzyme (ACE) inhibitors, target this system.[6] Significantly, these drugs have been recognized to sensitize the kidney to the action of other drugs, such as diuretics or non-steroidal anti-inflammatory drugs (NSAIDs), with the result of exaggerated pharmacological effects and possibly kidney failure.[3] Endothelin, a substance released by the kidney, appears to exert an important local effect on blood pressure, but also affects the CV system.[7] Many additional factors affect arterial blood pressure such as age, body size, fluid volumes, and electrolyte levels.

The diagnostic elements used for cardiovascular function assessments include heart rate (or pulse) and rhythm (as visualized in an electrocardiogram). Other parameters of heart function can also provide clues useful in identifying exposure to foreign substances such as drugs, toxicants, environmental pollutants, or even excessive alcohol intake. For example, ethanol reduces the force of contraction of the heart when plasma levels exceed 75 mg per 100 mL (0.075%). Thus, by lowering the force of contraction, alcohol could potentially lower the threshold for ventricular fibrillation.[5]

Anatomy and Function of Blood Vessels and Circulatory Regulation

The vessels of the CV system are divided into arteries and veins. A cross-section of a vessel wall shows three layers: the endothelium, the inner layer that usually consists of only one cell layer; a center layer that is composed of smooth muscle cells surrounding the vessel together with elastic fibers such as collagen; and an external connective tissue layer. The muscular layer in arteries is thicker than that in veins. Unlike arteries, veins contain membranous valves that prevent blood from flowing backwards during diastole. There are several variables that affect arterial vessels, such as local control mechanisms, the autonomic nervous system, baroreceptors (responding to hydrostatic pressure), and the vasomotor center in the medulla of the brain. All these factors can influence the oxygen delivery to the tissues.[8]

Normal functioning of the CV system requires at least two important parameters to be accurately regulated: the mean arterial blood pressure and the cardiac output. The mean arterial blood pressure is normally kept within fairly narrow limits. The cardiac output is controlled by the oxygen consumption of the organism as a whole and can show considerable variation. In the short term, the blood pressure is controlled by arterial baroreceptors located close to the heart. Baroreceptors signal to the brain, where the information is either relayed back to affect the heart directly, or to affect the tone of the vascular smooth muscles. In the long term, regulation is achieved by adjustment of blood volume. This adjustment is achieved through an interaction between hormonal systems located in the kidney (renin/angiotensin system, antidiuretic hormone, and aldosterone).[4]

Important Cardiotoxic Substances

Toxic effects can result from the interaction of a cardiotoxic chemical with a receptor. The study of bodily exposure to chemicals is often times separated into the aspects of pharmacokinetics ("body changes the chemical") and pharmacodynamics ("chemical changes the body"). These effects need not necessarily be detrimental; in case they are adverse, the terms toxicokinetic and toxicodynamic may be used. Both the persistence in the host (as in -kinetic) and the occurrence of an (adverse) effect (as in -dynamic) account for the level of effect. Paracelsus' famous quote, "The right dose differentiates a poison and a remedy", may today be extended by Haber's rule, which states that biological effects are the product of an agent's concentration and its exposure time, or c × t = constant.

Many chemicals cause cardiotoxicity in the occupational setting. There are the heavy metals, mostly causing dysrhythmias with the long-term outcome of chronic degenerative changes: the aliphatic alcohols (including ethanol), glycols, and aldehydes, and a number of aromatic solvents, that are bathmotropic and/or arrhythmogenic (producing irregular heart beat) and cause heart disease with chronic exposure; and finally the halogenated aliphatic hydrocarbons, including fluorohydrocarbon refrigerants and anesthetic gases, that are bathmotropic and arrhythmogenic like the alcohols, but with long-term exposure eliciting degenerative changes similar to the heavy metals.[9]

The halogenated alkanes, including common solvents such as 1,1,1-trichloroethane, can depress heart rate, contractility, and conduction. Some of these compounds also sensitize the heart to the arrhythmogenic effects of β-agonists such as endogenous epinephrine and its synthetic analogs, primarily the β-adrenergic receptor agonists such as isoproterenol that have positive chronotropic and inotropic effects. A normal drug dose combined with halogenated hydrocarbon exposure can lead to changes in the electrocardiogram that resemble those caused by hypoxia (lack of oxygen) or necrosis (cell death) of the endocard (the cell layer lining the inside of the heart).[10] The presence of significant concentrations of 1,1,1-trichloroethane can affect an exposed worker who is taking a common heart medicine, a β-blocker, in different ways than an otherwise healthy worker. Fluorocarbons (freons) have also been reported to have a similar sensitizing effect on the myocardium.[11] The pesticide lindane (γ hexachlorocyclohexane) has been known to cause CV toxicity. It appears to affect membrane permeability, resulting in symptoms that resemble hyperkalemia (elevated potassium concentrations in serum). Among the most commonly used drugs, and thus of interest due to their potential synergism with industrial toxicants, are non-sedating H1-antihistamines[12], known for causing dysrhythmias.

A more recent discovery relates to exposure to particulate matter. Multiple studies suggest that workers experience disturbances in heart function after environmental or occupational exposure to particulate matter with a median mass diameter of 2.5 μm (PM 2.5).[13–15] The biochemical responses to this exposure suggests two possible modes of action: 1) a long-acting (several hours) and a short-acting (several minutes) component, possibly related to the production of cytokines (a class of protein-like substances that act as vital signaling molecules inside and between cells) and the sympathetic stress response, or 2) a cumulative effect that begins shortly after exposure begins. Prospective cohort studies indicate that mean lifespan shortening is on the order of 2 years when exposures to extant ambient fine particles at concentrations of 25–125 micrograms per cubic meter of air extend across life.[13–15] These prospective cohort studies are complemented by pathological data attesting to the long-term contribution of cytokine-induced inflammatory changes. Professional judgment becomes necessary to distinguish cases where occupational exposure to, e.g., a halogenated compound might have triggered an adverse effect, from those cases where environmental particulate matter was the causative agent.

Response of the Cardiovascular System to Toxic Insult

Adverse effects of most industrial chemicals are by definition systemic. Any structural change in the heart or even the vasculature from toxic agents may have detrimental health effects. Chemicals specifically toxic to the heart may change or alter one or more of the "tropisms" mentioned before. A wide variety of agents, including pharmaceuticals (i.e., nicotine, ethanol, caffeine, and certain antibiotics), industrial chemicals (i.e., heavy metals, carbon monoxide, and solvents such as halogenated aliphatics and carbon disulfide) and physical conditions (i.e., hypothermia and hypoxia) can cause functional and/or structural changes. However, many agents affect more than one of these aspects simultaneously, and it should be noted that that the evident symptom is generally a dysrhythmia.[5]

Chronotropic and/or dromotropic changes typically manifest themselves as dysrhythmias. Many conditions or substances may be responsible for dysrhythmias. The major causes most likely of interest include chemical toxicity, hypoxia, and hyperthermia. The list may be extended to stimulants such as caffeine, tobacco, and amphetamines. Industrial substances that cause heart tachydysrhythmias (abnormal increase in heart rate) include a variety of solvents, most notably chlorinated hydrocarbons such as trichloroethylene (TCE), but also aromatic solvents (xylene, toluene), aliphatic hydrocarbons (naphthas, gasoline), and halofluorocarbon refrigerants. The toxicity of these solvents is thought to involve a change in the permeability of the excitable membrane of the heart cell. Deficiencies in calcium, potassium, or magnesium have a negative effect on heart function. The intricate process of depolarization and repolarization also can be altered by "look-alike" ions that mimic or antagonize the action of physiological ions. For example, thallium competes with potassium for membrane transport mechanisms, as does possibly barium.[3]

The heart cell contains an adenosine triphosphatase (ATPase) that is essential for heart muscle contraction/relaxation and is activated by increasing the intracellular free calcium concentration (as occurs during heart cell depolarization).[1] Substances that interfere with this ATPase affect the contractility of the heart muscle, which is also known as inotropic effect. The cardiotoxicity of halogenated solvents appears to be due at least in part to an inhibition of ATPase. Bathmotropism affects the conductivity of the heart cell. Typical bathmotropic CV toxicants include the already mentioned haloalkanes and ethanol, possibly through effects on membrane permeability.

Certain heavy metals pose a significant risk for CV disease. The toxic action(s) of cadmium, lead and cobalt are thought to involve binding to and blockade of essential sulfhydryl groups on functional proteins such as calcium channels. Lead appears to exert a negative inotropic effect on the heart by inhibiting oxidative phosphorylation in heart cell mitochondria, thus depriving the heart of energy required for contraction. Long-term exposure to lead causes CV disease by reducing the elasticity of the arteries, thus contributing to sclerotic hardening.[10] Cadmium and mercury appear to affect the CV system mostly by way of their nephrotoxicity, which will be discussed below. In contrast, chromium (in physiological concentrations) has a positive effect on the CV system; its deficiency is associated with an increased risk for atherosclerosis (build up of plaque inside large and medium-sized arteries).

Carbon monoxide is a significant CV toxicant. Studies suggest that it may damage vessels, resulting in an increased risk of atherosclerosis over time.[16] Two other gases, arsine and stibine, exert toxicity primarily in the lung producing pulmonary edema. Arsenic trioxide may also produce cardiotoxicity by blocking cellular production of ATP. Consequently, the lack of metabolic energy in the form of ATP can alter the crucial balance of cellular ions, especially calcium.

Cardiomyopathy (damage to the heart muscle) can be caused by a variety of factors including overexposure to toxicants such as lead, arsenic, and cobalt, but also alcohol. Dilated (formerly called congestive) cardiomyopathy is related to the above mentioned toxicants lead, arsenic, cobalt, and alcohol. The tendency of cobalt, formerly used as a foam stabilizer in beer, to induce endemic cardiomyopathy in chronic alcoholics reflects the combined effects of nutritional deficiencies often accompanying alcoholism.[5]

As with morphological injury to the liver and kidney, cellular injury to the heart may result in the release of intracellular enzymes into the blood where they can be identified by using biochemical tests of heart injury. Soon after a myocardial infarction (heart attack) increased levels of aspartate aminotransferase (AST), lactate dehydrogenase (LDH), creatine phosphokinase (CPK), and troponin can be observed. Blood tests for these heart enzymes are of particular diagnostic value when combined with other techniques for assessment of cardiotoxicity.[17]

Toxic Changes in Blood Vessels

Exposure to sufficient doses of toxicants that result in dramatic effects on blood pressure may cause death, while minor effects may go unnoticed for a long time. Lead and other heavy metals may block calcium channels causing difficulties for the CV system to maintain normal blood pressure, such as hypertension that develops only with long-term, subacute exposures.

Many common solvents are central nervous system depressants that may precipitate circulatory collapse and shock. Insufficient cardiac output with the potential outcome of shock also may be the result of decreased heart contraction, cardiomyopathies, or agents that cause severe peripheral vasodilatation (widening of blood vessels). An example of industrial agents that may produce circulatory depression are nitrated aliphatics. Some of these, such as trinitroglycerin or pentaerythritol tetranitrate, serve as explosives but also as medications because of their specific and powerful vasodilator action. Mononitrated compounds such as amylnitrite, used as a solvent or process intermediate, have similar effects, as does sodium nitroprusside[1]. All of these agents have in common that they lead to the production of nitric oxide (NO), a potent physiological signal transducer molecule.

Carbon monoxide (CO) is the leading cause of toxic deaths among workers. Although CO is now recognized as an important regulating agent in the CV system, chronic exposure can damage the vascular endothelium and accelerate atherogenesis, exposing the underlying connective tissue.[18] The subsequent coagulation phenomenon with which the system tries to repair the damage may lead to thrombosis (blood clot) and even embolism (obstruction of a blood vessel by a foreign substance or a blood clot).[18] Acute exposures to high concentrations of CO can induce myocardial infarction, vasospasm and sudden death. Another way of looking at these phenomena is to note that exposure to CO may uncover a potentially fatal heart arrhythmia.[19]

Carbon disulfide is another classic industrial toxin associated with accelerated atherosclerotic disease in workers.[20] This effect has been known for more than 100 years and is well described in the occupational literature. Its mechanism is poorly understood but may be mediated by the propensity of carbon disulfide to react with essential sulfhydryl groups, inhibiting enzymes. Workers exposed to carbon disulfide may have five times the incidence of coronary disease compared with non-exposed workers.[21] Carbon disulfide can also cause peripheral neuropathies and neurobehavioral abnormalities. Carbon disulfide exposure in the occupational and environmental survey is often overlooked as a potential cause of atherosclerotic disease that is more typically attributed to dietary and genetic factors.[22]

A more direct toxic effect has been observed with the industrial substance allyl amine whose active metabolite acrolein may produce damage to vessels walls.[23] Caffeine intoxication can lead to prolonged arterial constriction and subsequent damage to the endothelium. Other substances that may obstruct blood flow or damage blood vessels are the oral steroid contraceptives. They have long been known to predispose for possibly life-threatening embolisms due to the venostasis (lack of blood flow) and subsequent endothelial damage they can cause.[24] Homocysteine, an endogenous substance that attains hazardous levels in the blood particularly as a result of kidney failure, damages the vascular endothelium and is significantly associated with serious CV disease.[25]

A Brief Survey of Kidney Structure and Function

The major excretory functions of the kidney are to eliminate wastes formed during normal metabolism and excrete xenobiotics and their metabolites. This occurs through a complex series of steps involving the filtration of blood and the reabsorption of water and essential nutrients and minerals. The following paragraphs will focus on the kidney because ureters, bladder and urethra serve mostly transfer and storage purposes.

The smallest functional unit in the kidney is the nephron (there are about 1.25 million in each kidney), which along with a series of arterioles and capillaries, has six major subunits: Bowman's capsule, proximal convoluted tubule, loop of Henle, distal convoluted tubule, vasa recta, and collecting duct. The loop of Henle and the convoluted tubules are tightly wrapped in a net of capillaries, but there are also arterioles that run parallel to the hairpin structure of the loops of Henle; these arterioles are called vasa recta (= straight vessels). The blood in the vasa recta flows in the same direction as the urine flows in the loop of Henle; this structure constitutes an important part of the counter-current system that makes the kidney function. Several collecting tubes converge into a collecting duct equipped with ion and water channels that contribute to the composition of final urine.[26,27]

The arteriole entering Bowman's capsule is called afferent, the one leaving the capsule is called efferent arteriole. Inside Bowman's capsule the arteriole splits up into a mesh of capillaries called the glomerulus, which is a filtration unit. Through these filtration units the kidney filters approximately 20% of the blood pumped by the heart into Bowman's space (the space between capsule and glomerulus) by means of the blood's hydrostatic pressure. The total volume of urine is about 200 liters/day and about 99% of that volume is reabsorbed as it passes through the nephron before final urine is formed.[26] The walls of the glomerular vessels are porous. The cells of the glomerulus are secured to a structure called the basement membrane that, along with the glomerulus cells, serves to allow or restrict the passage of certain ions and solutes into the proximal convoluted tubule. The basement membrane contains negatively charged groups, establishing an ionic barrier that repels negatively charged molecules, yet lets uncharged or positively charged molecules pass through with ease.[26]

The primary urine leaves Bowman's capsule via a proximal convoluted tubule that is tightly surrounded by a capillary net from the efferent arteriole. Primary urine has basically the same composition as plasma without proteins. The cell walls in the convoluted tubule are highly permeable to water; two-thirds of the primary urine fluid and ions are reabsorbed here, along with most of the filtered glucose. This is achieved by two mechanisms: active transport, mostly powered by Na^+,K^+-ATPase in the descending loop of Henle, and osmotic pressure created by serum proteins and ionic charges associated with them, called colloid-osmotic pressure. The action of Na^+,K^+-ATPase removes sodium from the primary urine, creating an osmotic gradient that causes a passive flow of water and counter ions from the urine back into the blood.[26]

There are also other energy-dependent transport mechanisms located in the wall of the convoluted tubule, some of which reabsorb molecules such as glucose, while others expel organic acids and bases from blood into the urine. Altogether, the proximal tubule achieves the major portion of volume reduction of primary urine, yet does not create major changes in the ionic composition of primary urine.[2]

The descending loop of Henle employs no active transport systems yet accomplishes most of the remaining concentration of primary to final urine. This part of the loop of Henle is tightly enveloped by a network of capillaries formed by the efferent arteriole. Thus, the fluid that has followed the solutes expelled from the convoluted tubule is rapidly taken up by these water-permeable capillaries by means of the colloid-osmotic pressure (40–60 mm Hg). The ascending part of the loop of Henle, on the other hand, is impermeable to water, thus preventing a backflow of fluid from the vasa recta into the tubule. This structure also contains a powerful Na^+, K^+-ATPase that moves Na^+ out of the tubule into the intracellular space. However, because in this part of the loop water cannot follow the ions, the developing concentration gradient draws water from the close-by, highly permeable descending loop of Henle or the collecting duct, and the extra fluid is removed by the capillaries and the vasa recta. Thus, the nephron accomplishes, at the expense of energy, reduction of primary urine volume and preservation of minerals. The final concentration of urine takes place in the collecting duct as water is removed from the urine.

Because the nephron is not freely permeable to substances other than water and inorganic ions, urine concentrates everything that is actively transported into it or not reabsorbed from it. The whole system works because of an intricately controlled dynamic dis-equilibrium: the moment blood flow in the nephron ceases, fluid cannot be removed and urine formation comes to a halt. The excretion of urea along this path is not well understood. It is possible that there is active secretion of urea along the pars recta, and the net removal of urea consists of the portion that leaves the collecting duct with urine flow.[8]

The collecting tubule, as discussed above, plays itself an active role in the final composition of urine. Its walls are made of two types of cells, both of which respond to antidiuretic hormone (ADH) that regulates how water passes through the cells of the collecting tubule wall. Absence of ADH results in diuresis (or water loss). The distal and collecting tubules are also sensitive to the mineralocorticoid aldosterone. Taken together, this responsiveness to hormones gives the distal and collecting tubules ultimate control over the ratio of water to solute in urine.[4]

Close to Bowman's capsule is a structure known as the juxtaglomerular apparatus. It receives input from the sympathetic and parasympathetic nervous systems and has the ability to increase or shut down blood flow to the glomerulus. This constitutes one system by which the kidney affects blood pressure and flow, albeit locally. The granular cells of the juxtaglomerular apparatus produce and release renin, an enzyme that is crucial in the release of angiotensin II, a potent vasoconstrictor.[26] The

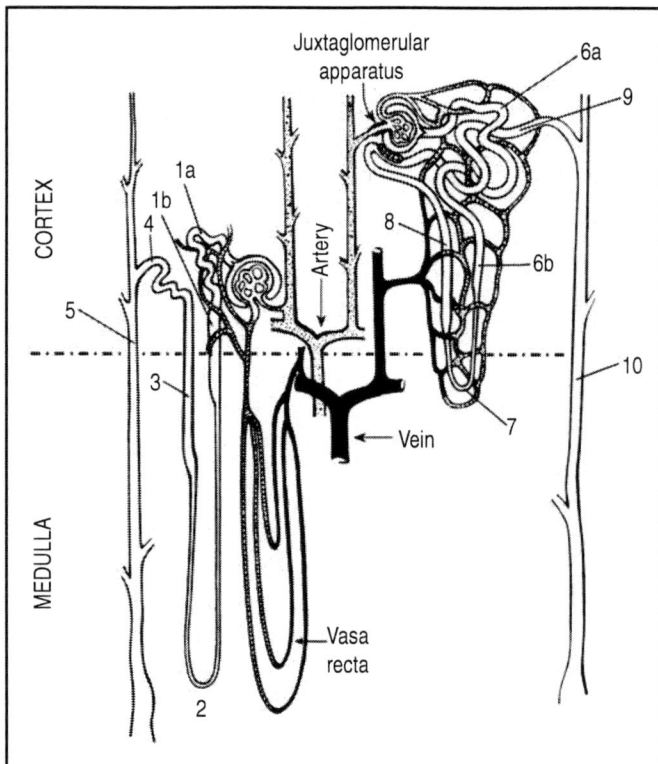

Figure 7.1 — 1 and 6: proximal tubulus; a: convoluted, b: straight; 2 and 7: loop of Henle, thin part; 3 and 8: thick, ascending part; 4 and 9: distal, convoluted part; 5 and 10: collecting tubule (numbers 1–5 refer to a medullary, 6–10 to a cortical nephron).

juxtaglomerular apparatus also responds to the vasodilator prostaglandin E2 produced within the kidney, and may represent a point of attack for the nephrotoxicity of nonsteroidal anti-inflammatory drugs (NSAIDs).[28] Thus, the juxtaglomerular apparatus holds a key position in the control of kidney function because it controls the hydrostatic pressure across the glomerulus, regulating both kidney blood flow and glomerular filtration rate. This affects the water balance of the organism, the extracellular fluid volume, mineral homeostasis, and ultimately blood pressure.[2]

Kidney Function

The kidney, with some assistance from the lung, maintains the acid-base balance of the organism. This is accomplished by active proton pumps along the proximal, distal, and collecting tubules, and by two crucial enzyme activities. One of the two enzymes affects NH_3/NH_4^+ balance, while the other, the ubiquitous carbonic anhydrase, takes care of rapid adjustment of the equilibrium between CO_2, HCO_3^- and H^+.[1]

Despite their small size, about 150 grams apiece, the kidneys receive about 20% of cardiac output. Thus, the kidneys are a likely target for pharmaceuticals as well as toxic substances. Given the high energy demand of the kidney to keep all the active transport systems at go, any sudden drop in blood flow (serious water loss by sweating or vomiting; shock; hemorrhage) could gravely impair kidney function.[5] However, the kidney has an amazing ability to adapt to increasing workload. An extreme example would be loss of one kidney, where the other kidney assumes full function in a short time.

A few parameters commonly used to assess kidney function are glomerular filtration rate (GFR; the total volume of primary urine formed per minute) and clearance. GFR is commonly assessed by excretion of the polysaccharide inulin, which is freely filtered in the glomerulus, but due to its molecular size cannot be taken up again or diffuse back; thus, its appearance in urine over time provides a reasonable measure of GFR. GFR in humans is normally around 125 mL/min. Clearance is a virtual blood volume that is freed completely of a given substance per unit time. In the case of inulin, clearance pretty much equals GFR. For substances that are reabsorbed, clearance is less than GFR: the clearance for glucose is essentially zero, and substances that are strongly bound to serum protein also have low clearance because only the unbound fraction is available for filtration. For substances that are actively secreted in the nephron, clearance may be much higher than GFR; para-aminohippurate (PAH), a normal metabolite, is an example of a substance that is practically 100% eliminated by the kidney. In the latter case, the clearance equals kidney plasma flow, or about 660 mL/min for humans. Another commonly used measure of kidney function is creatinine clearance. Creatinine is a major metabolic waste product from muscle function that is eliminated via kidney by an active transport system; its clearance is affected by certain drugs, such as cimetidine or trimethoprime, that compete with it for the same transporter.[26]

Both re-absorption and secretion are active processes. The renal glucose transporter, for example, becomes saturated at a glucose concentration of about 15 mM (270 mg/100 mL). Thus, saturation of the glucose transporter is the reason for the appearance of glucose in the urine of diabetics.[8] The action of these energy-driven transporters can be beneficial or detrimental. The older cephalosporin antibiotics are moved by an anion transporter from the blood into the tubular cell. These compounds do not diffuse effectively out of the cell into the urine, and the high concentrations that are built up damage the tubular cells. The β-lactam antibiotics, the important cytostatic compound cisplatin, and many plant toxins (e.g., aflatoxins, ochratoxin) act through the same pathway.[29] A somewhat similar situation exists with the aminoglycoside antibiotics. Following filtration they are reabsorbed from the tubular lumen by an endocytotic system (transport of large molecules across the cell membrane inside a membrane-coated vesicle) that normally recovers peptides but traps the antibiotic on the inside, thus causing damage to the tubular cell.[29]

Kidney Toxicity

One of the most important nephrotoxicants in the occupational setting are heavy metals, halogenated aliphatic solvents, and several other organic solvents, as described in more detail below. Differentiating between occupational exposure and synergistic or undesired effects from many commonly used drugs may be difficult when it comes to solving workplace problems. While some toxicants may destroy the complete nephron, most nephrotoxicants preferentially affect specific parts of the nephron.[30] Conditions such as old age are also associated with a marked decrease in the number of nephrons. Chronic kidney disease causes irreversible loss of nephrons, negating the regenerative ability of the kidney. As a result, nephrons that are still functional are overburdened by increased glomerular filtration volume, resulting in hyperfiltration, yet decreased clearance.[19] In contrast, acute kidney failure is different from the chronic disease in that it obliterates this organ's ability to form urine without immediate damage to anatomical structures.

The only typical diuretic toxicants with some occupational relevance are organomercurials. The first available diuretics were generally based on mercury, and it may well be assumed that they worked by damaging the ion conservation system of the nephron, which in turn rendered it incapable of conserving water.[29] Because of their overt kidney toxicity, any effort is being made to avoid human exposure completely.

Despite its ability to adjust to increased work load, the kidney does not effectively adjust to increased drug and/or chemical loads. The kidney possesses numerous metabolizing enzymes that can form toxic metabolites from otherwise innocuous substances before or after filtration. Many of these are commonly used drugs, such as antibiotics, or analgesics, such as aspirin, ibuprofen, or acetaminophen.[28] Their use as medication must always be considered as a an additional burden to the kidney when assessing potential kidney damage from occupational exposure to industrial chemicals.

Halogenated hydrocarbons can be metabolized into toxicants by the kidney. Carbon tetrachloride and chloroform are metabolized to phosgene which damages the nephron, primarily the proximal tubule. Pre-exposure to agents, such as alcohol in this example, that induce the metabolizing enzymes, exacerbates the effect, yet the increased amount of phosgene is likely not generated in the kidney, but in the liver. Other occupationally relevant nephrotoxicants are hexachlorobutadiene and trichloroethylene. After being conjugated with glutathione in the liver, these compounds are eliminated in the kidney by the cation transporter.[26] Inside the tubular cell these conjugates are cleaved by β-lyase with the formation of a sulfur derivative of the parent compound that is cytotoxic.[26] Bromobenzene causes nephrotoxicity with very similar symptoms, but by an unknown mechanism.[31]

Toluene, metabolized to hippuric acid, can induce an elevated anion gap and metabolic acidosis after significant intoxication, but this is seen more often with intentional abuse than with workplace exposures. Neurological toxicity would likely predominate at low level exposure, e.g., in the ppm range above the TLV® setting, while kidney failure has occurred secondary to tubular necrosis after acute toluene exposure.[32]

Heavy metals are potentially nephrotoxic in part by their kidney vasoconstrictive action, and in part by their ability to block functional sulfhydryl groups, causing cytotoxicity. Early symptoms of metals toxicity include excretion of substances otherwise reabsorbed in the kidney, such as glucose and amino acids, with accompanying increased urine production. With progressive damage to the nephron there will be necrosis, urine volume will decline steeply, blood urea nitrogen (BUN) will increase, and death may ensue. The classical example is mercury. It affects the kidney at several levels. First, it reduces kidney blood flow, then it disturbs sodium balance severely. Presumably this involves inhibition of the Na^+,K^+-ATPase, either by blocking sulfhydryl groups or by inhibiting mitochondrial ATP synthesis.[33]

It appears that among the many toxic heavy metals, lead is the one considered most damaging to both the CV system and the kidney, presumably by inhibiting ATP synthesis and altering calcium homeostasis. Cadmium acts in a more complicated fashion. The zinc-transporting metallothioneins bind cadmium effectively in the liver, from where they are transported to the kidney. Here, the complex is degraded inside the tubular cell, probably following receptor-mediated endocytosis. Large amounts of cadmium are set free locally, where they inactivate sulfhydryl groups and impede enzyme function.[29] Chromium VI, in particular as the chromate, is also a nephrotoxicant. It causes severe damage to the proximal tubule, and although its oxidative capabilities may be involved, a precise mechanism is not known.[29]

Ethylene glycol (antifreeze) is metabolized by alcohol and aldehyde dehydrogenases to oxalic acid, filtered in the glomerulus, and reabsorbed by a transporter for small organic cations. Inside the tubular cells, increasing concentrations of oxalic acid combine with calcium ions and precipitate as the insoluble calcium oxalate, possibly causing cell death.[29] A similar mechanism may apply to the toxicity of fluoride ions, viz., via precipitation as insoluble calcium fluoride.

A Synopsis of Toxic Insults Affecting both the Cardiovascular System and the Kidney

A sizeable number of toxicants affect both the cardiovascular system and the kidneys, though not all are industrial toxicants with relevance in the workplace setting. Of the three major classes of CV toxicity — immune system-mediated hypersensitivity, exaggerated response to medication, and adverse response to chemical exposure — only the last is of true interest to the industrial hygienist, yet the professional must not lose sight of the other two because of the multiple ways these three mechanisms can cross-interact.

The most likely class of substances that may cause both CV and kidney toxicity is that of the halogenated aliphatic hydrocarbons. Very commonly used as solvents, degreasers, or process intermediates, but also as anesthetic gases and refrigerants, all these substances are central nervous system depressants at acute exposure levels. In this capacity they may affect the CV system (but not the kidney) via the autonomic nervous system. However, it is conceivable that at low exposure levels they share one mechanism of action that accounts for their toxicity at the cellular level across the tissues. Metabolism of these agents commonly involves the formation of reactive oxygen species and lipid peroxidation. Both effects efficiently upset calcium homeostasis, initially inhibiting mitochondrial ATP synthesis, enzyme function, and cellular protein synthesis.[34] With higher and/or continued exposure they may cause cell death. Due to their high dependence on ATP supply, both the heart and the kidney are especially sensitive to this type of toxicity.

A second, less significant class of potential nephrotoxicants from the occupational arena comprises many solvents such as aliphatic alcohols, aromatic solvents such as xylene and toluene, gasoline, and glycols that can be degraded to oxalic acid. Solvents with nitro groups and explosives based on nitroorganics may be added.

A third, and major, class of toxic agents the industrial hygienist needs to monitor comprises the heavy metals. Their interference mostly with reactive or functional sulfhydryl groups on proteins or with ionic balance appears to have outcomes not entirely different from the halogenated hydrocarbons: interference with cellular energy synthesis that may ultimately result in cell death. In many cases the kidney may be the more sensitive organ. Once kidney failure develops, increased homocysteine levels in the blood could possibly cause significant CV problems.[25]

Finally, the industrial hygienist confronted with a case, or cases, of occupational cardiovascular and kidney toxicity will need to establish a thorough work history and remain cognizant of the medical history for each case to find out about the numerous common medications that may have contributed to the condition. In addition, pre-existing infections may have exacerbated the situation, and abuse of substances such as ethanol, coffee, tobacco, or analgesics may have heightened the sensitivity of the patient.

References

1. **Boron, W.F, and E.L. Boulpaep:** *Medical Physiology: A Cellular and Molecular Approach.* Philadelphia, PA, W.B. Saunders. 2005.
2. **Guyton, A.:** (2006). Textbook of Medical Physiology, 11th edition. Philadelphia, PA: W.B. Saunders. 2006.
3. **McPhee, S.J., V.R. Lingappa, W.F. Ganong, and J.D. Lange:** *Pathophysiology of Disease: An Introduction to Clinical Medicine,* 4th edition. New York, NY: Lange Medical Books/McGraw Hill. 2006.
4. **O'Connell Smeltzer, S.C., and B.G. Bare:** *Brunner & Suddarth's Textbook of Medical-Surgical Nursing*, 10th edition. Philadelphia, PA: Lippincott Williams & Wilkins. 2005.
5. **Porth, C.M.:** *Pathophysiology: Concepts of Altered Health States*, 7th edition. Philadelphia, PA: Lippincott Williams & Wilkins. 2005.
6. **Mignat, C., and T. Ungert:** ACE inhibitors. Drug interactions of clinical significance. *Drug Saf. 12*:334–347 (1995).
7. **Hocher, B., Thone-Reineke, C., Bauer, C., Raschack, M., and Neumeyer, H.H.:** The paracrine endothelin system: pathophysiology and implications in clinical medicine. *Eur. J. Clin. Chem. Clin. Biochem. 35*:175–189 (1997).
8. **Gangong, W.F.:** *Review of Medical Physiology*, 22nd edition. New York, NY: McGraw-Hill Publishing. 2005.
9. **Ramos, K.S., R.B. Melchert, E. Chacon, and Acosta, D. Jr.:** Toxic responses of the heart and vascular system. In *Casarett and Doull's Toxicology: The Basic Science of Poisons*, 6th edition. Klaassen, C.D. (ed.). New York, NY: McGraw-Hill Companies, Inc. 2001. pp. 597–652.
10. **Needleman, H.L.:** The persistent threat of lead: medical and sociological issues. *Curr. Probl. Pediatr. 18*:697–744 (1988).
11. **Taylor, A.E.:** Cardiovascular effects of environmental chemicals. *Otolaryngol. Head Neck Surg. 114*:209–211 (1996).
12. **Yap, Y.G., and A.J. Camm:** Potential cardiotoxicity of H1-antihistamines. *Clin. All. Immunol. 17*:389–419 (2002).
13. **Dockery, D.W., et al.:** An association between air pollution and mortality in six U.S. cities. *N. Engl. J. Med. 329*:1753–1759 (1993).
14. **Pope, C.A. 3rd, et al.:** Particulate air pollution as a predictor of mortality in a prospective study of U.S. adults. *Am. J. Resp. Crit. Care Med. 151*:669–674 (1995).
15. **Dockery, D.W., et al.:** Health effects of acid aerosols on North American children: respiratory symptoms. *Environ. Health Perspect. 104*:500–505 (1996).
16. **Gandini, C., et al.:** Carbon monoxide cardiotoxicity. *J. Toxicol. Clin. Toxicol. 39*:35–44 (2001).
17. **Babuin, L., and A.S. Jaffe:** Troponin: the biomarker of choice for the detection of cardiac injury. *Can. Med. Assn. J. 173*:1191–1202 (2005).
18. **Durante, W., Johnson, F.K., and Johnson, R.A.:** Role of carbon monoxide in cardiovascular function. *J. Cell Mol. Med. 10*:672–686 (2006).
19. **Kumar, V., Abbas, A.K., and Fausto, N.:** *Pathologic Basis of Disease*, 7th edition. Philadelphia, PA: W.B. Saunders, Co. 2005.
20. **Kristensen, T.S.:** Cardiovascular diseases and the work environment. A critical review of the epidemiologic literature on chemical factors. *Scand. J. Work Environ. Health 15*:245–264 (1989).
21. **Sulsky, S.I., Hooven, F.H., Burch, M.T., and Mundt, K.A.:** Critical review of the epidemiological literature on the potential cardiovascular effects of occupational carbon disulfide exposure. *Int. Arch. Occup. Environ. Health 75*:365–380 (2002).
22. **Hennig, B., Oesterling, E., and Toborek, M.:** Environmental toxicity, nutrition, and gene interactions in the development of atherosclerosis. *Nutr. Metab. Cardiovasc. Dis. 17*:162–169 (2007).
23. **Yousefipour, Z., Ranganna, K., Newaz, M.A., and Milton, S.G.:** Mechanism of acrolein-induced vascular toxicity. *J. Physiol. Pharmacol. 56*:337–353 (2005).
24. **Tierney, L., McPhee, S., and Papadakis, M.:** *Current Medical Diagnosis & Treatment*, 45th edition. McGraw-Hill Medical. 2006.
25. **Perna, A.F., Castaldo, P., De Santo, N.G., Galletti, P., and Ingrosso, D.:** Homocysteine and chronic renal failure. *Miner. Electr. Metab. 25*:279–285 (1999).

26. **Sullivan, L.P., and Grantham, J.J.:** *Physiology of the Kidney*, 2nd edition. Philadelphia, PA: Lea & Fiebiger. 1982.
27. **Caughey, A.V., del Castillo, C., Palmer, N., Spizer, K., and Tuttle, D.N.:** *Blueprints, Pathophysiology: Renal and Hematology and Oncology.* Malden, MA: Blackwell Publishing. 2004.
28. **Kenny, G.N.:** Potential renal, haematological and allergic adverse effects associated with nonsteroidal anti-inflammatory drugs. *Drug 44*:31–36 (1992).
29. **Schnellmann, R.:** Toxic responses of the kidney. In: *Casarett and Doull's Toxicology: The Basic Science of Poisons*, 6th edition. Klaassen, C.D. (ed.). New York, NY: McGraw-Hill Companies, Inc. 2001. pp. 491–514.
30. **Bernard, A., and Hermans, C.:** Biomonitoring of early effects on the kidney or the lung. *Sci. Total Environ. 199*: 205–211 (1997).
31. **Van Vleet, T.R., and Schnellmann, R.G.:** Toxic nephropathy: environmental chemicals. *Semin. Nephrol. 23*:500–508 (2003).
32. **Lauwerys, R., Bernard, A., Viau, C., and Buchet, J.P.:** Kidney disorders and hematotoxicity from organic solvent exposure. *Scand. J. Work Environ. Health 11 Suppl 1*:83–90 (1985).
33. **Kone, B.C., Brenner, R.M., and Gullans, S.R.:** Sulfhydryl-reactive heavy metals increase cell membrane K+ and Ca2+ transport in renal proximal tubule. *J. Memb. Biol. 113*:1–12 (1990).
34. **Siems, W., et al.:** Oxidative stress in chronic renal failure as a cardiovascular risk factor. *Clin. Nephrol. 58(Suppl 1)*: S12–S19 (2002).

> *The physician must give heed to the region in which the patient lives, that is to say, to its type and peculiarities.*
>
> Paracelsus (1493–1541)

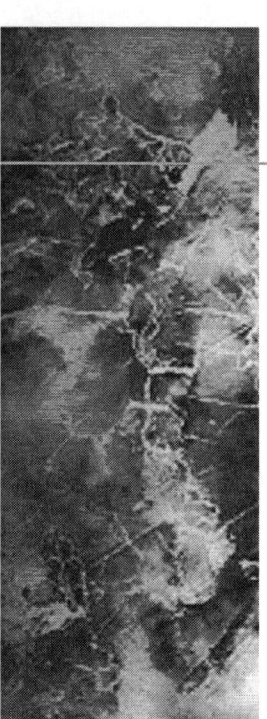

Chapter 8

Toxicology of Sensory Organs

Outcome Competencies

After completing this chapter, the reader should be able to:

- Define the sensory system and its components.
- Explain the basic functions of the sensory system.
- Distinguish between sensory toxicity and neurotoxicity.
- Predict possible interaction of the sensory system with other systems of the organism.
- Separate pre-existing conditions from work-related exposure.
- Evaluate how toxic agents affect functions of the sensory system.

Prerequisite Knowledge

Basic anatomy and physiology, specifically, basics of nerve and neuron function.

Key Terms

action potential, adaptation, anosmia, apical, asphyxiant, asthenia, auditory, autosomal, axonopathy, chemoreceptor, cochlea, cutaneous, depolarization, desensitization, dysesthesia, dysfunction, dystrophy, EEG, endocochlear, gustatory, habituation, hypoesthesia, mechanoreceptor, miotic, mydriatic, myelin, nausea, neuropathy, nociception, nociceptor, nystagmus, olfactory, ototoxicity, paresthesia, presbycusis, proprioception, receptor, retrograde axonopathy, sensory, somatosensory, stimulus, synapse, thermoreceptor, threshold, tinnitus, vertigo, vestibular, visual, xenobiotic

Key Topics

1. An Overview of the Sensory System
2. Receptors
3. Stimuli
4. Seeing (Vision; the Visual System)
5. Hearing and Balance (The Auditory and Vestibular Systems)
6. Touch and Temperature (The Somatosensory System)
7. Smell (The Olfactory System)
8. Taste (The Gustatory System)
9. Proprioception (Perception of Self)
10. Nociception, Irritation
11. The Internal Sensory System
12. Hereditary diseases affecting the sensory system
13. Case Study: Impaired color vision following exposure to an industrial solvent

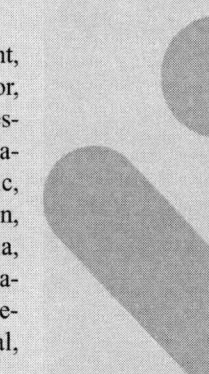

Chapter 8

Toxicology of Sensory Organs

By Lutz W.D. Weber, PhD, DABT, and J. Thomas Pierce, MBBS, PhD

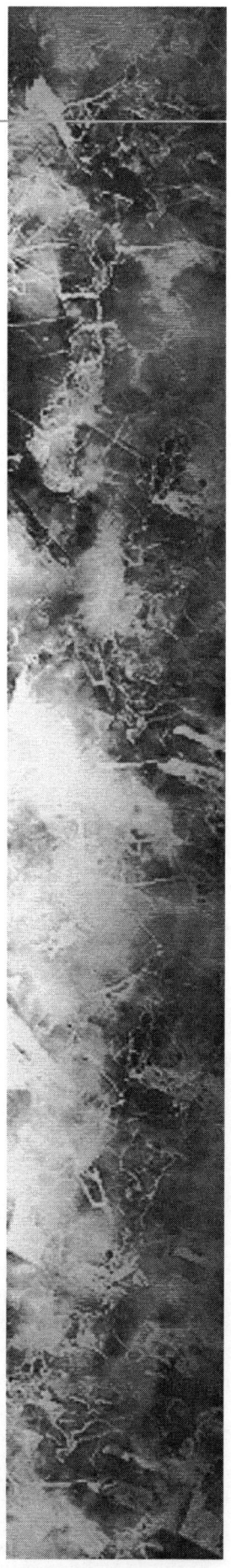

Introduction

The sensory system is the part of the nervous system that connects an organism to the outside world. That places it into a very special category because it means that adversity to this system is most likely to represent point-of-entry, rather than systemic, effects. By the same token, the sensory system could act as a sentinel regarding more systemic effects that would likely occur at higher concentrations. As the interface between a higher organism and its environment, the sensory system has a lot to do with learning (using the visual, auditory, and proprioceptive [perception of self] systems), behavior (influenced by the visual, auditory, gustatory, and somatosensory systems), and avoidance (mostly involving nociception [perception of noxious stimuli]). Many cognitive disorders such as attention deficit hyperactivity disorder (ADHD) and autism are thought to be the result of sensory dysfunction.[1]

In simplest terms, sensory pathways consist of a receptor, a nervous pathway to relate input from the outside world, and an area in the brain that processes this information. Sensory receptors are highly specialized nerve cells where the receptor portion frequently is located at the nerve ending. Sensory toxicity and neurotoxicity should not be confused, although in both cases nerves are involved. Neurotoxicity refers to adversity to the function of peripheral nerve fibers as well as the central nervous system, while sensory toxicity deals only with the nerve cells and receptors of the sensory system. This chapter targets the receptor portion of the pathway and how the receptor portion of the pathway responds to toxic insults. The pathways that relate sensory input to the central nervous system, i.e., damage to the conducting nerve fibers (axonopathy) and CNS toxicity, although frequently the origin of sensory impediment, will be mentioned when necessary, yet are of secondary relevance to this overview. However, because non-invasive methods of diagnosis in humans commonly do not allow a precise distinction between sensory toxicity and neurotoxicity, the contents of this chapter will unavoidably be far more descriptive than explanatory or mechanistic. The toxicological implication is subtle in that only a fine, largely undefined line separates perception of effect from objective sensation of a noxious stimulus.

An Overview of the Sensory System

Higher organisms generally have 5 senses: vision, hearing (or auditory), taste (or gustatory), smell (or olfactory), and touch and temperature (or somatosensory). Sometimes, balance is also considered part of the sensory system because of its close association with the auditory system of the inner ear. Proprioception may be added here as a special entity that integrates input from the somatosensory, vision, and balance systems. Finally, nociception also uses various types of receptors. On a different scale, there are four main classes of receptors in the sensory system: mechanoreceptors (auditory, touch, balance), photoreceptors (vision), chemoreceptors (smell and taste) and thermoreceptors (temperature). These receptors are sometimes also called -ceptors, with an appropriate prefix. In functional terms one can differentiate two principal types of receptors, one type that relates "normal" input from the environment, and another one that relates potentially dangerous input from the outside. The latter type of receptors can be chemo- mechano-, or thermoreceptors and are known as nociceptors; their message is normally perceived as pain.[2]

Receptors

Whether by sight, hearing, smell, taste touch, or temperature, sensory transduction begins with the action of sensory receptors that interface with our world. Each sensory receptor uses energy from the environment to trigger electrochemical signals that are transmitted to the brain. Further processing takes place within specific regions of the cerebral cortex, hence names and mapped locations exist for the visual and olfactory cortex. Interestingly, over-stimulation by noxious or otherwise toxic responses may lead to impaired ability to process subsequent signals.

Chemoreceptors operate in a stepwise manner:

1. A chemical binds to a specific receptor protein in the cell membrane of a cilium on a receptor cell;
2. Receptor activation stimulates a G-protein;
3. The alpha subunit of the G-protein activates adenylyl cyclase, producing cAMP;
4. cAMP binds to a cAMP-gated cation channel;
5. Opening of the channel increases permeability to sodium, potassium and calcium ions;
6. Net inward current leads to membrane depolarization and increase in calcium ion concentration;
7. Increased calcium ion concentration opens Ca-activated chloride channels;
8. Action potential is conducted to the central nervous system (CNS).

Much less is known about mechanoreceptors. The most distal part of mechanoreceptors, the so-called end organ, is a highly specialized structure that responds to mechanical stress or strain. A stimulus to the end organ will trigger an action potential, or firing, of the nerve cell, the frequency of which initially reflects the intensity of the stimulus. These mechanoreceptors respond in two basic ways: upon continued stimulation, the so-called phasic type will decrease its firing rate quickly, while the tonic type upholds a constant firing rate for a longer time.

The hair cell of the auditory and vestibular systems, the most sensitive of all mechanoreceptors, is not a true nerve cell because it neither projects an axon, nor does it normally generate action potentials. Hair cells are specialized to detect minuscule movements along one particular axis. The cells are polarized, with the hair bundle projecting from the apical end and synaptic contacts made at their basal end.[3]

Stimuli

In order to relate a message, a sensory receptor needs a stimulus. In the first place, the stimulus has to be of the appropriate type (e.g., photons for a photoreceptor, pressure or stretch for a mechanoreceptor, a chemical for a chemoreceptor, temperature for a thermoreceptor). Next, the stimulus has to surpass a certain threshold to trigger the transduction of action potentials through the attached nerve pathway. The intensity of a stimulus is usually reflected in the firing rate of the neurons within the pathway. The duration of a stimulus also plays a role: continuous or repeated stimulation of a sensory receptor will result in a decrease in firing rate, known as adaptation, desensitization, or habituation. This can work both ways: the higher light sensitivity of the eye after "getting used to the dark" would be an example of reverse habituation (adaptation). By the same token, training can be used to lower sensory thresholds or improve proprioception (e.g., manual dexterity).

As mentioned above, there is an appropriate stimulus for each receptor. However, sensory receptors can also be triggered by inappropriate stimuli. Two typical examples would be the perception of lights when one rubs the eyes with some degree of force, or the ringing sound one perceives after a hard blow on an ear. In these cases, the energy required to stimulate the receptor exceeds the energy from an appropriate stimulus by many orders of magnitude (in the case of eye rubbing, mechanical pressure in the ounces per square inch range as compared with the energy of a few photons). Thermoreceptors in the skin can be stimulated by chemicals, for example capsaicin to mimic heat or menthol to mimic cold. The taste buds of the tongue can be stimulated by the minimal current from a flashlight battery to the perception of an odd taste.

Seeing (Vision; The Visual System)

The anatomy and physiology of the eye are admittedly complex, each the subject of entire volumes. Selectively, some of the structures and fluids of interest are presently considered. Tears are surprisingly complex, and are based on a plasma ultra-filtrate. They bathe the cornea in a layer that is less than 10 microns thick, keep it wet and allow oxygen to diffuse from the air to the corneal cells. Tears are very important in that they help flush away foreign substances and provide a renewable first line of defense against many chemical or physical agents. Secretions of the eye (and the nose) can be used as biomarkers for occupational or environmental exposures.[4]

The visible aspect of the eye can be simply described in terms of eyelid, sclera (the white portion of the eye), cornea, and conjunctiva (the mucous membrane that is opposed to the sclera). Chemical splash injuries or even trauma to the face may involve one or more of these structures. Topical and/or systemic exposure to noxious agents may affect the inner parts of the eye, such as the lens, iris, pupil, retina, vitreous body, or optic nerve.

The integrated visual system consists of peripheral receptors in the retina along with central pathways and cortical centers. An understanding of these interrelated elements is important in the sense that a loss of sight may occur for a variety of reasons from structures other than what is termed the eye.

Each eye has two major components: an optical part to gather and focus light and form an image (cornea, lens, and vitreous body) and a neural part (the retina) that converts the optical image into a neural code. Vertebrates have two types of photoreceptors, rods and cones. In terms of the energy of the stimulus, photoreceptors are supposedly the most sensitive receptors because they can respond to the energy of a single photon. The three different types of cones in the vertebrate eye respond to different colors (maximum sensitivities at 420, 534, and 564 nm), while the rods respond to light intensity, with little sensitivity for color (maximum sensitivity at 498 nm). The human eye can detect light between approximately 370 and 700 nm wavelength (the visible spectrum).[5]

Little is known concerning specific effects of toxic agents on color perception or light sensitivity, i.e., on the rods and/or cones in the retina. Jaundice can induce yellow vision (xanthopsia), as can treatment with digitalis glycosides.[6] Erythropsia is a common consequence of elevated exposure of the eye to ultraviolet radiation, occasionally observed in patients who had the lens(es) of their eye(s) replaced.[7] Solvents are known to induce changes in color vision.[5] A loss in sensitivity towards light and dark, or night blindness, is one of the symptoms of retinitis pigmentosa and other hereditary forms of retinal dystrophies[8] simply because of pigment deposition in the retina. This side effect has also been observed in connection with phenothiazine drug treatment. In otherwise healthy humans vitamin A deficiency has long been known to cause night blindness, and this may be related to zinc deficiency.[9] There is also a number of genetic diseases where the organism's ability to form retinal pigment from vitamin A is compromised.[10] Certain forms of cancer precipitate an autoimmune retinopathy that goes along with reduced light sensitivity.[11] X-linked stationary night blindness is a congenital disease in which voltage-gated calcium channels of the retina do not work properly.[12]

Eye movements and pupillary responses provide clues to systemic effects of CNS-active substances. More typically associated with drug overdose, but also within the context of cholinergic responses, are miotic and mydriatic changes (narrowing and widening of the pupil) that provide clues to the nature of offending substances. Thus, coma itself (with no eye opening response) is a sign of acute poisoning. Nystagmus, the involuntary rhythmic movements of the eyes, can also serve as a useful indicator of central nervous system effects of poisons. Smooth pursuit eye movement is crucial to maintain clear vision of a moving visual target. Nystagmus is closely tied to the function of the balance organ in the inner ear. Aside of being a fairly frequent occurrence in healthy people and being a symptom in numerous diseases, nystagmus is caused by many CNS-active drugs and by alcohol consumption.

A number of chemicals are known to cause damage to the visual system. Inorganic lead, organophosphates, and certain organic solvents are known to damage the rods and cones in the retina. Methanol, through its metabolite, formic acid, damages the optical nerve. Other chemicals and/or drugs, such as acrylamide, carbon disulfide, ethambutol, and certain cytostatics damage the optic nerve and tract, while lead and methyl mercury exert their toxic action in the central visual system.[13] Although the outcome is a change in function of the sensory system, the origin of such effects is damage to nerve conduction or the CNS, which are considered neurotoxicity, not sensory toxicity. Lack of B vitamins can cause neuropathy of the optic nerve, potentially mimicking a chemically induced adverse effect.

The cornea and lens of the eye are essential parts of the visual system, although they constitute neither mechano-, nor chemoreceptors. However, the cornea can be damaged easily by chemical burns from contact with liquids and solids, immediate caustic injuries, immediate solvent splash, surfactant or detergent injuries and those with delayed or latent action. As a protective measure, it is rich in nociceptors (see below). Chemical splash injuries require copious irrigation with clean water on a pre-hospital basis whereas puncture wounds require immediate patching. While both types of injuries require ophthalmology consults, a proper understanding of the mechanism of injury is critical to treatment and may not be available or accurate if left entirely to the patient.

Hearing and Balance (The Auditory and Vestibular Systems)

Sensation in both the auditory and vestibular systems begins in the inner ear. Both systems use a highly specialized mechanoreceptor, the so-called hair cell, in a physical system that is fine-tuned to respond either to sound frequency and intensity (the eardrum, hammer, anvil, staple, and the cochlea) or to changes of position detected in a three-dimensional system using the inertia of the inner-ear fluid.[5,14]

Adversity can result from damage along any portion of the auditory pathway, sometimes at the peripheral auditory system and, specifically, at the cochlea or inner ear. The cochlea consists of the sensory epithelium with hair cells (the organ of Corti) and specific ganglion cells and neuronal cell bodies connected via synapses to the hair cells. All this, plus the supporting tissue and fluid to maintain structural integrity, are enclosed in the bony capsule of the cochlea.[15] The term cochlea is Greek for housed snail, a perfect metaphor for the shape of this organ, spiraled and tapering to resonate at ever increasing sound frequencies.

These systems are the two sensory systems most likely to be affected by chemicals, frequently medication. In case of the auditory system, typical symptoms of toxicity include increased threshold for sound perception; tinnitus, a perceived sound ("ringing") in the ears in the absence of external sound stimulation, and a reduction of the dynamic range between sound detection and the pain threshold for sound. In case of the balance system, vertigo and nausea are the most typical symptoms of adversity. Yet both systems are not necessarily affected jointly by the same agent, as evidenced by the fact that excessive alcohol intake affects balance, but not hearing.

A remarkable number of chemicals are known to elicit ototoxicity after short-term, high-level or after long-term, low-level exposure. Commonly used drugs that cause ototoxicity include salicylates, aminoglycoside antibiotics, cytostatics, quinine, ethacrynic acid, furosemide, and loop diuretics.[16] Salicylate and quinine ototoxicity typically proceeds with the development of tinnitus that includes significant outer hair cell dysfunction. While not definitive, these hair cells changes are generally reversible whereas those from long-term noise exposure are not. Aminoglycoside antibiotic and platinum-containing cytostatics cause permanent high frequency hearing impairment with loss of outer hair cells, especially in the high-frequency portion of the cochlea. Loop diuretics inhibit Na^+,K^+-ATPase activity, leading to a loss of the endocochlear potential, a transitory effect because the enzyme inhibition is reversible.[16]

Among the environmental agents causing ototoxicity are solvents, such as toluene, which damages the cochlea and outer hair cells, affecting both hearing ability and equilibrium. Its higher homologues xylene and ethyl benzene, respectively, as well as styrene are also suspected of being ototoxic.[15] Styrene, in addition to damaging outer hair cells, is also known to adversely affect olfaction and vision.[17] Trichloroethylene and carbon disulfide both have been shown to damage the cochlea in exposed humans. Trichloroethylene, supposedly via its metabolite, dichloroacetic acid, additionally affects several other sensory nerves, viz., trigeminus, facialis, the optic nerve, and oculomotor nerves.[18] Carbon disulfide and xylene cause hearing impairment mostly by an adverse effect on peripheral nerves (i.e., neurotoxicity). The ototoxic actions of styrene and trichloroethylene have been observed in experimental animals only; at this point it is not clear whether or not humans are also affected.

Several heavy metals cause ototoxicity, such as mercury, which destroys hair cells, or arsenic, which causes damage to the organ of Corti. Trialkyltins damage hair cells and/or spiral ganglion cells. Manganese is also ototoxic, but by an as yet unknown mechanism. Lead and methylmercury, but also organotins, cause demyelination of nerves in the auditory system; this type of damage is not considered sensory toxicity.[15] Olfactory or auditory toxicity caused by heavy metals generally affects the central and peripheral innervation more than the sensory neuron or receptor.[15] In addition, agents that hinder oxygen availability to the inner ear, such as asphyxiants (carbon monoxide, cyanide) and agents that lead to the formation of methemoglobin (organonitrites).

Noise, or persistent overstimulation, damages the auditory system by increasing the threshold of perception or causing loss of perception of certain frequencies. However, no less important is the fact that exposure to noise and organic solvent will do more damage to the auditory system than either agent alone. Epidemiological studies have revealed that in industries with significant noise levels and exposure to chemicals, a much larger percentage of workers was diagnosed with hearing loss, compared with industries that have noise exposure only.[19]

Typical damage to the auditory system, specifically, the hair cells, can be caused by mechanical overstimulation or chemical lesion. All this must be considered in light of the fact that loss of auditory capability with age (presbycusis) is very common, and that exposure to noise exacerbates the effects of chemical exposure. In either case, the result is loss of hair cells. Tinnitus with hearing loss specifically at high frequencies is a common side effect of many drugs (high doses of salicylates; aminoglycoside antibiotics; diuretics).[20] However, this is typically a central nervous, not a sensory effect.[21]

Touch and Temperature (The Somatosensory System)

The qualities of the somatosensory system that are of interest within the limits of this chapter extend to cutaneous (or superficial) light touch, pressure, vibration, superficial pain, and temperature. The "deep" qualities comprise visceral sensation, visceral pain, deep pain, and deep pressure. Visceral sensations, such as hunger, thirst, are not at focus here.

The mechanoreceptors for touch are generally located in the outer skin or epithelia of the upper digestive tract and are primary neurons. At least four different types of mechanoreceptors are currently known. Their density varies greatly with body region, fingertips and lips being highly innervated while, e.g., the back of the hand or the sole of the foot have comparatively sparse innervation. The surface area from which one given end organ receives input is known as a receptive field. The denser the innervation, the smaller the receptive field, and the higher is the receptive sensitivity.[22]

On a different level, different cutaneous sensory qualities use several types of nerve fibers and end-organ receptors. Pressure and vibration are transduced by large-diameter, heavily myelinated fibers. Pain and temperature, on the other hand, are propagated by barely or not at all myelinated fibers. Light touch uses a variety of fiber sizes. Understandably, a given agent is likely to affect one fiber type more than another. Moreover, some agents preferentially produce motor or sensory impairment, while others impair both functions to a similar degree.

The typical symptoms of somatosensory dysfunction are paresthesia (tingling, prickling sensation or numbness of the skin), and/or dysesthesia (abnormal skin sensations in absence of a stimulus). A critical problem in their evaluation, however, is the difficulty in controlling the characteristics of stimulus presentation or the existence of not measurable or inconsistent psychological parameters, such as suggestibility, cooperativeness, and responsiveness of the patient.[23]

There are a remarkable number of chemicals that affect the somatosensory system, although, as in other cases of sensory dysfunction, it is often times not clear whether the agent affects the sensory receptor itself or the peripheral and central nervous pathways. Lead, arsenic, thallium, mercury vapor, and methylmercury are somatosensory toxicants via a neurotoxic mode of action. PCBs and 2,3,7,8-tetrachlorodibenzo-p-dioxin have been shown to cause paresthesia and hypoesthesia (reduced sense of touch) in exposed humans.[24]

Several small, reactive organic molecules, e.g. carbon disulfide, methyl bromide, allyl chloride, and acrylamide, cause somatosensory symptoms, such as paresthesia (tingling and/or impaired sense of touch, pinprick, and vibration). N-hexane, by way of its metabolite, 2 hexanone (methyl n-butyl ketone), and n-heptane cause a specific disease of peripheral nerve fibers known as retrograde axonopathy (destruction of the axon beginning at the distal end and proceeding towards the nerve cell body). Although all solvents, at high enough concentrations, cause paresthesia, some organohalogens solvents are specifically associated with adverse somatosensory effects: trichloroethylene causes paresthesia as well as impaired pinprick and vibration sense, while 1,1,1-trichloroethane elicits paresthesia and impairs the senses for touch, pain, and vibration. Organophosphates and synthetic pyrethroid insecticides also cause somatosensory toxicity.[23]

A careful diagnosis of the modalities of somatosensory adversity may assist in identifying the causative agent. For example, Rice[23] points out that the cytostatics taxol and cisplatin affect vibration and proprioception, while hardly affecting the senses of pain and temperature. Acrylamide, on the other hand, affects the sense of vibration, but not pain. n-Hexane elicits somatosensory deficits first, then affects the motor system (muscle weakness). Lead is said to elicit a similar sequence of sensory toxicity. Acrylamide affects both systems to a similar extent. The senses for vibration and proprioception have been known to be impaired before those for pain and temperature.[23]

Thermoreception works mainly with just two receptor types, for warm and cold, respectively. These receptors take part in the maintenance of a constant body temperature. Generally, they operate closely to the range of physiologically acceptable temperatures. Certain chemicals, such as menthol and capsaicin, can trigger the sensations of cold and hot, respectively, in these receptors. The thermoreceptors that alert the organism to extremes of hot or cold are part of the nociceptive system (see below). Arsenic, carbon disulfide, methyl n-butyl ketone, or overdoses of the B vitamin pyridoxine are known to impair the sense of temperature.[23] The diseases diabetes and leprosy cause a skin paresthesia that severely affects patients' ability to properly perceive adverse mechanical impacts.[25]

Smell (The Olfactory System)

The olfactory epithelium of an adult human contains 6 cell types. The first type, about 6 million sensory receptor neurons, provides olfactory sensation; these are bipolar neurons with a short apical dendrite and a long, thin unmyelinated axon of approximately 0.2 µm diameter. It is thought that odorants are not directly recognized by olfactory neuronal receptors, but by olfactory binding proteins that transport them to odorant receptors. Olfactory binding proteins are carriers for small lipophilic molecules; they make up more than 1% of soluble protein in the olfactory epithelium. Information on the olfactory receptors is still rather incomplete. It has been said that humans have about 2000 different olfactory receptors that allow them to recognize about 150,000 different scents[26], and each sensory neuron expresses but one receptor.[27] Evidently, this opens a plethora of possibilities for hereditary forms of specific types of anosmia (loss of the sense of smell).

The second cell type are the supporting (or sustenacular) cells of the olfactory epithelium; they are rich in Phase I and II enzymes, with catalytic capacities approximating those in liver. These enzymes can inactivate odorants or activate olfactory toxicants. Exhaustion of this metabolic capacity by excessive chemical exposure can result in toxicity, as occurs with formaldehyde when the detoxifying coenzyme, glutathione, becomes depleted. The third type are the cells in Bowman's glands that produce mucus providing some protection to the epithelium. The fourth and fifth cell types, the light basal and dark basal cells, constitute multipotent stem cells from which the olfactory epithelium regenerates continuously. In contrast to many other types of neural tissue, olfactory receptors are steadily regenerated in a 2–8 week cycle in humans. The sixth cell type, the microvillar cells, have no currently known function.[28]

Olfactory toxicity in humans has not received thorough attention, possibly due to the fact that humans rely far less on their sense of smell than many animals do. Indeed, the anatomy of the human olfactory system is rather simple compared with that of many animals. Still, in an occupational setting an impaired sense of smell can result in dangerous exposures when a worker is not able to smell a toxic volatile substance.[29]

There are a sizeable number of chemical agents that can affect olfaction. Corrosive or chemically reactive agents rank prominently (fluorine, chlorine, sulfur dioxide, nitrogen dioxide, carbon monoxide, carbon disulfide, hydrogen sulfide, formaldehyde, ammonia, hydrazine). Exposure to heavy metals and their compounds (lead, cadmium, chromium VI salts, mercury, nickel, zinc) as well as dusts (wood, lime, silica, cement, cotton, paper, grain) can lead to anosmia (loss of the sense of smell), usually based on destruction of the olfactory epithelium. Hydrogen sulfide inactivates many enzymes, prominently cytochrome oxidase, affecting the ability of the sustenacular cells to inactivate odorants. Air concentrations in excess of 200 ppm hydrogen sulfide ablate the function of the olfactory nerve.[29]

Workers exposed to reactive chemicals, such as acrylic or methacrylic acids or esters, were found to have a decreased ability for odor identification. Exposure to solvents, such as toluene, xylene, methyl ethyl ketone, and 2-hexanone also diminished the ability of workers to identify odors. The adverse action of these solvents was found to be cumulative.[29]

Many more industrial solvents and chemicals (trichloroethylene, halomethanes, acetone, ethyl acetate, butyl acetate, gasoline, benzene, acetophenone, pentachlorophenol) adversely affect the olfactory system. In industries using such chemicals, high percentages of long-term exposed workers (up to 50% and more) develop anosmia.[26] A less adverse effect on olfaction is an increased threshold for the perception of certain odors. Understandably, the chemically reactive substances quoted above, and including some heavy metal compounds, such as chromium VI and cadmium salts as well as mercury salts and organomercurials, and the dusts, are the most likely to damage sensory receptor neurons directly, while other compounds are more likely to cause damage to the conductive nerves or the CNS itself, among them mercury and its compounds. It is beyond the scope of this chapter to give a more detailed account of the known or presumed modes of action of these various chemicals.

Two thirds of all cases of olfactory dysfunction are due to prior upper respiratory tract infections, paranasal sinus disease, or head trauma.[30] When confronted with a case of anosmia, it is important to obtain sufficient background information because there are numerous non-occupational factors that can cause this condition: there is a congenital form of anosmia; intranasal and intracranial tumors can be the cause, but also endocrine disorders such as hypogonadotropic hypogonadism (including the congenital Kallmann syndrome), Addison's disease, Turner's syndrome, Cushing's syndrome, hypothyroidism. Certain states of mental disease, e.g., schizophrenia, chronic hallucinatory psychoses, and seasonal affective disorder, are also known to affect the ability to perceive odors.

Taste (The Gustatory System)

The gustatory or taste system has 5 basic receptors (taste buds): sweet, salty, sour, bitter, and umami. The latter is the Japanese term for flavorful or meaty taste; this receptor responds to glutamate, which is found in protein-rich foods. This receptor is thus responsible for the flavor-enhancing properties of monosodium glutamate (MSG).[28] The fact that humans (and likely many other species) can differentiate many types of "taste" although they have only five basic qualities of taste perception has to do with the sense of smell. Food does not "taste" when the olfactory nerve endings are incapacitated by a congestion: much of what we consider gustatory is actually olfactory. Different from the mechano- and thermoreceptors, the term receptor in the gustatory and olfactory systems is likely to mean a protein molecule that responds in a specific way (conformational change) to a given substance, type of substance, or portion of a molecule (such as an SH- or S-S-group). The fact that one perceives two up to six hydroxyl groups on an equal number of carbon atoms as sweet, but also chemically totally unrelated molecules (saccharin, cyclamate, aspartame), gives testimony to the functional latitude of gustatory receptors. In the case of extremely spicy food, nociception (pain) also plays a role in gustation.

Despite the fact that there are only five basic tastes, there is a wide degree of variability in the genetic coding of taste receptors manifesting itself in significant differences how humans perceive certain qualities of taste.[31] Thus, comparatively little is known about toxic damage to the sense of taste.[29] It is clear that extremely spicy food will dull the perception of other, more subtle taste qualities, but there is also the likelihood of desensitization, or habituation, greatly raising the threshold for this type of perception. It is also clear that oral intake of chemically reactive or corrosive materials can impede taste sensation permanently or transiently by destroying the taste buds.

Proprioception (Perception of Self)

Proprioception is the sensory function that tells the central nervous system of the relative positions of movable body parts (joints, tendons, muscles) to each other, whether they move or not, and how fast they move. Although not part of the classical five senses, proprioception is a special subsystem of the sensory system that uses predominantly mechanoreceptors. Propriocep-

tion is also closely linked to balance. Because this system is rather sensitive to alcohol, police use it as a sobriety test (move finger to nose with eyes shut). In this connection one can think also of spatial vision, eye-hand coordination, all sorts of manual skills, and language. It is evident that this system is of major importance in an occupational setting, and that any malfunction could have grave consequences. An overdose of vitamin B6 (pyridoxine) is known to temporarily impair proprioception. A classical case of a proprioceptive poison is the organophosphate triorthocresyl phosphate ("ginger Jake" syndrome, where the proprioceptive sensors for coordinated walking are impaired). Acrylamide, allyl chloride, and n-hexane also affect proprioception.[23]

Nociception, Irritation

Nociceptors are receptors that warn of two types of noxious influence, extreme heat/cold (outside the physiological range, i.e., <5°C or >45°C), or excessive mechanical stress, commonly perceived as pain.[32] The hot or cold nociceptors are part of the sensory system only, while pain receptors can also be part of proprioception (e.g., overextension of joints) and other internal systems (e.g., overextension of gut, bladder, muscles).[33] This may also include damage to the organism caused by aggressive chemicals.

Irritation can be considered a special form of nociception, warning of adverse agents. Many chemicals, e.g., chloromethanes, produce irritation. Two different parts of the sensory system can work together to produce nociception: an odor, e.g., acetic acid, is related to the CNS via the olfactory nerve, while irritation of the upper respiratory system by the same chemical is conducted by nociceptive nerves such as the vagus, trigeminus, or glossopharyngeus.[34] In this example, irritation of the olfactory system, at appropriately high concentrations, is joined by irritation of the eyes and the respiratory tract. Immediate lacrimation, delayed corneal epithelial edema, corneal epithelial vacuoles, delayed corneal epithelial injury, corneal and conjunctival discoloration can be the result if the warnings of the nociceptive system are disregarded. Highly unpleasant odors are also considered a form of irritation (e.g., organic sulfur compounds, decaying organic matter).

The Internal Sensory System

There are a considerable number of mechano- and chemoreceptors in the human body that relate internal messages of homeostasis, or a lack thereof, to the central nervous system. Such receptors may register oxygen saturation, pH, electrolytes, blood pressure, etc. However, these receptors are not at the focus of this chapter.

Hereditary Diseases Affecting the Sensory System

The influence of normal genetic variability has been addressed above, specifically in the sections on olfactory and gustatory perceptions. However, there is also a variety of heritable conditions that may affect or obscure adverse effects on the sensory system brought forth by occupational or environmental exposure. Hereditary neuropathies constitute a field of numerous, yet altogether rare diseases that cover a very wide spectrum of gene abnormalities. They may comprise hereditary sensory neuropathies (HSN), hereditary motor and sensory neuropathies (HMSN), or hereditary sensory and autonomic neuropathies (HSAN). These conditions generally manifest themselves during adult life, starting between ages 20 and 40. As far as sensory disturbances are involved, loss of sensation begins in toes, then moves up the feet and lower limbs with time. In progressed state, hands become affected. Reflexes are reduced or absent, possibly affecting proprioception. Commonly observed symptoms are severe pain and poorly healing foot ulcers that get infected (diagnosis may be obscured by this plus peripheral neuropathy plus pain from diabetes). Hearing loss and muscle wasting may occur, resulting in gait disturbances and weakness. Frequently these conditions go along with either excessive, or minimal to no sweating. The symptoms overlap between various forms of the diseases. Pathological findings associated with these diseases are abnormal or absent myelin in nerve fibers of all sizes. The most common type of these diseases is hereditary motor and sensory neuropathy, also called Charcot-Marie-Tooth (CMT) syndrome, that exists in at least 4 subforms. These heritable diseases appear in several genotypes (autosomal dominant, autosomal recessive, X-linked) as well as phenotypes (demyelinating form with greatly reduced nerve conduction velocity, axonal form with mildly reduced nerve conduction velocity, intermediate forms, etc.).[35] Several of the typical symptoms of this type of disease, viz., loss of sensation in the legs, poorly healing ulcers, and pain, are also observed in diabetics, making a clear distinction between genetic disease, metabolic disease, or environmental/occupational exposure quite difficult.

There are several genetically very heterogeneous hereditary motor diseases that go without sensory loss, such as distal hereditary motor neuropathy and other congenital motor neuropathies such as amyotrophic lateral sclerosis (ALS, Lou Gehrig's Disease, which also has a familial variant). However, because these diseases lack the sensory component, they will not be considered further in the context of this chapter. Other conditions, such as dystonia, dysautonomia, or retinitis pigmentosa in its various manifestations, and congenital deafness and blindness, are congenital and of such a severe nature that affected persons are very unlikely to ever come under the care of an industrial hygienist.

About 1 in 1000 newborns suffers from hearing loss, about half of them in a hereditary fashion. Other mutations lead to progressive hearing loss, including the age-related presbycusis. The autosomal recessive types are associated with congenital, prelingual (before learning to talk) deafness, while the autosomal dominant ones lead to postlingual progressive hearing loss.[36] This needs to be kept in mind when encountering a possible case of chemical-related hearing loss.

Several forms of hereditary vision deficit exist, of whom retinitis pigmentosa was already mentioned.[37] Others include macular dystrophies that have been known to manifest themselves at an adult age. Age-related macular degeneration is also thought to possibly involve a genetic component.[38] Elevated blood pressure may result in hypertensive retinopathy that has also been observed in connection with diabetes. There is also a familial form of the already mentioned sensitivity to aminoglycoside-induced ototoxicity.[15] Aside from the age-related forms of sensory deficits, these hereditary diseases are too rare to be of major concern for the practicing industrial hygienist.

Case Study: Impaired color vision following exposure to an industrial solvent

Imagine yourself working for an Agency comparable to the Occupational Safety and Health Administration (OSHA). You are called to a hospital specializing in occupational diseases where physicians have seen over time an increasing number of workers presenting with very similar symptoms that they can't quite fathom. By the time you get involved, a total of 26 workers have been identified who uniformly present with upper and lower limb weakness, asthenia (a feeling of weakness without actual loss of strength), leg pain, walking difficulty, and paresthesias in hands and arms. Other symptoms that point to involvement of the nervous system, such as nausea, headache, general somatic pain, and nervousness, are less frequent, only in about one of four exposed workers or less. Because the attending physicians weren't entirely sure about a diagnosis, they took EEGs from the 26 patients. Four workers show abnormalities in their EEGs (bilateral synchronal symmetric sharp spike wave discharge).

Question 1: What is your diagnosis?

If you diagnosed "peripheral neuropathy", you're head-on. These symptoms are characteristic of peripheral neuropathy. As a logical next step you look for a causative agent. There are quite a few chemicals that cause peripheral neuropathies. Therefore,

Question 2: How do you go about finding the causative agent?

If you decided to look for and study any questionnaires that the attending physicians filled when they first saw the individual patients, you are right again. And indeed, you find that all workers have one thing in common: they work in small leather industries of less than 100 employees, mostly shoe manufacturers, about 5 to 30 miles away from the hospital. The good doctors were prescient enough to make sure that most of the patients are at the hospital when you are there, too, and so you ask the workers whether they have experienced any specific exposures, odors, contact with liquids, etc. Again you discover a common denominator: they all work with a glue that has a characteristic odor that the workers liken to gasoline or lighter fluid.

Question 3: What do the terms leather industry, glue, and gasoline-like odor tell you?

This is not an easy one, and you really earned your spurs when you answered: n-hexane. Leather industries commonly use glues that contain n-hexane, which causes a peripheral neuropathy. To make sure, you order urine tests. All workers' urines prove positive for 2,5-hexanedione and its pyrrole derivatives. Biomarkers for other common solvents, such as phenol (for benzene) or trichloroacetic acid (for trichloroethylene) are negative. You conclude that the cause of the neuropathy is n-hexane exposure.

Question 4: What do you do next?

To make sure that you are not on a wild-goose-chase, perform air sampling in key locations. The measurements at several work sites confirm the exposure scenario because n hexane air levels range from 44 to 320 ppm. Most measurements exceed the Threshold Limit Value® (TLV®) of 50 ppm by far. Ventilation in the workplaces is essentially non-existent. Now you have a case.

n-Hexane is a solvent commonly used to extract fats, as a cleaning agent in the textile, furniture, and printing industries, or as a solvent for rubber cement used in the leather industry. The industrially used material is typically a mixture that contains about 52% n-hexane, with the remainder being structural isomers, such as methylpentane, methylcyclopentane, etc. Because the other components of technical hexane do not elicit neuropathies, they are very unlikely to have contributed to the symptoms. The peripheral neuropathy commonly associated with n-hexane exposure is the result of the organism's attempt to detoxify the xenobiotic, forming the ultimate toxicant, 2,5-hexanedione. This diketone reacts with lysine residues in neurofilaments, forming cross-links that lead to axonal swelling and eventually destruction of the peripheral nerve fiber. The condition migrates from the periphery towards the nerve cell body and hence is called retrograde axonopathy.

Both diagnoses, "peripheral neuropathy" and "n-hexane-induced retrograde axonopathy," fall squarely into the realm of neurotoxicity. Only the numbness in extremities qualifies as sensory toxicity. Because you are the scientific type, you wonder if the workers might have other neurological problems. None of the workers had complained about visual problems, but you have read in an article that changes in color vision have been observed in n-hexane-exposed persons. However, your means are limited, so all you can do is use a simple test for color vision disturbances.

Question 5: What is a simple test for color vision disturbances?

A very simple color vision test is the FM-100 hue test. It is based on 85 colored discs of the same saturation and brightness that are used to detect a person's ability to differentiate color tones. The test can be carried out under normal sunlight, and is administered separately for the right and the left eye, respectively. You don't need any fancy equipment; a pocket calculator with basic statistic functions will do. All you do is to write down if a patient is able to tell the difference between two close hues of a color. There is no bias on your side because you see the numbers on the backs of the color discs; the patient doesn't.

So, you decide to administer the FM 100 hue test to these 26 patients (25.1 ± 10.3 years of age, having worked for 7.4 ± 5.1 years) and to 50 non-exposed healthy controls (30.7 ± 7.3 years of age, having worked for 7.6 ± 3.5 years). However, first you administer another questionnaire to control for possible confounders, such as smoking, alcohol use, and pre-existing or congenital conditions. As a result you have to exclude four exposed workers from the study, two because of genetic conditions (color blindness), and two because of substance abuse. The test indicates highly significant ($p < 0.001$) increases in the error scores, in both eyes, for the blue-yellow and red-green chromatic localizations in the remaining 24 exposed workers. The total error scores for both chromatic localizations in exposed workers are 168.3 ± 70.5 and 181.5 ± 103.0 for the right and left eye, respectively, 4–5 times higher than in controls (36.0 ± 19.8 and 35.6 ± 18.2 for the right and left eye, respectively).

This case study is not fictional. It is based on an occurrence in Istanbul, Turkey, that has been described by Issever et al.[39] It should be added that workplace exposure limits in Turkey may differ from the one quoted here, which is the ACGIH TLV®. The authors of the study point out that in similar studies changes in color vision had not involved damage to ocular structures, but likely reflect neural alterations.[39] The presence of blue-yellow loss, prevalent in the present case, reflects alterations to the external retinal layers, while red-green loss is associated with changes to internal layers of the retina or the optical nerve. Issever et al.[39] also refer to a hypothesis that solvent-related chromatopsias might involve direct solvent effects on lipophilic constituents of the cones in the retina. This would represent a case of true sensory toxicity. For you, however, there is one more thing to do.

Question 6: How do you address this workplace problem in the local leather industries?

At this point you know what to do: the affected workers have to be removed from the workplace exposure immediately, although those who have had symptoms for a long time may never fully recover. The second step is to convince the owners of the small leather industries to install ventilation systems that protect the workers from further exposure. Looking for a glue that does not contain n-hexane as the solvent would be even better.

Summary

Three factors are important for the industrial hygienist when it comes to assessing occupational exposure: duration of exposure, level of exposure (dose), and individual susceptibility for a given agent. With respect to the first two factors, Shusterman et al.[40] investigated the important question of whether or not Haber's rule (the product of dose and time is constant, or, in other terms, a short exposure to a high dose has the same effect as a long exposure to a low dose) applies to sensory irritation in humans. This question is important for the assessment of cumulative effects as they may occur, among others, in the case report above. Shusterman et al.[40] concluded from a review of various studies in humans that, for irritant agents, a better description was provided by "product of dose/concentration squared and time equals constant." The situation was confounded by the observation that numerous sensory irritants showed a time response that displayed either a plateau (habituation), or even a drop-off (desensitization). However, they also found that irritant dusts (e.g., calcium oxide) act in ways more consistent with Haber's law, even with a tendency towards exposure time playing a greater role than dose.

With respect to the third factor, individual susceptibility, it is difficult to set clear standards for irritation or perception thresholds in an occupational setting because they are subject to a variety of modifying influences, e.g., habituation or adaptation, individual sensitivity, psychological predisposition, and input from other parts of the sensory system, all together establishing an individual bias. The situation is further complicated by the existence of a multitude of genetic variations among sensory receptors, above all in the olfactory system. In consequence, threshold values for a given substance may be overprotective for one person in a given situation, but not protective for another person, or the same person under a different set of circumstances.[41] The connection between psychological state and response to an irritant is also known as psychophysics. Psychophysics is the scientific study of the relationship between the physical dimension(s) of a stimulus and the behavioral response it generates. This may be of considerable importance for the evaluation of adverse occupational or environmental exposures, but goes beyond the limits of this toxicity-oriented overview.

Multiple chemical sensitivity (MCS) can be considered a form of adverse effect to the sensory system. Cullen[42] defined this syndrome as patients who have:

1. One or more documented instances of environmental exposure, illness, or insult;
2. The symptoms appear in more than one organ (system);
3. The symptoms recur and abate in response to predictable stimuli;
4. The symptoms are elicited by chemicals from chemically diverse classes with different modes of action;
5. The symptoms are elicited by exposures that are demonstrable, albeit of low level;
6. The symptoms cannot be explained by a single, widely available test of organ function;
7. Exposure levels are much lower than "average" exposure levels (i.e., less than 1%) known to cause adverse effects in humans. This condition may complicate a precise evaluation of sensory adversity in the occupational or environmental arena.

References

1. **Emmons, P.G., and L.M. Anderson:** *Understanding Sensory Dysfunction: Learning, Development And Sensory Dysfunction In Autism Spectrum Disorders, ADHD, Learning Disabilities and Bipolar Disorder.* London, UK: Jessica Kingsley Publishers, 2005.
2. **Purves, D., G.J. Augustine, D. Fitzpatrick, et al.:** *Neuroscience,* 3rd edition. Sunderland, MA: Sinauer Associates Inc., 2004.
3. **Purves, D., G.J. Augustine, D. Fitzpatrick, et al.:** Chapter 12, The Auditory System. In *Neuroscience,* 3rd edition. Sunderland, MA: Sinauer Associates Inc., 2004.
4. **Norbäck, D., and G. Wieslander:** Biomarkers and chemosensory irritations. *Int. Arch. Occup. Environ. Health 75*:298–304 (2002).
5. **Purves, D., G.J. Augustine, D. Fitzpatrick, et al.:** Chapter 10, Vision: The Eye. In *Neuroscience,* 3rd edition. Sunderland, MA: Sinauer Associates Inc., 2004.
6. **Butler, V.P., J.G. Odel, E. Rath, et al.:** Digitalis-induced visual disturbance with therapeutic digitalis concentrations. *Ann. Intern. Med. 123*:676–680 (1995).
7. **Bennett, L.W.:** Pseudophakic erythropsia. *J. Am. Optom. Assoc. 65*:273–276 (1994).
8. **Inglehearn, C.F.:** Molecular genetics of human retinal dystrophies. *Eye 12(Part 3b)*:571–579 (1998).
9. **Smith, J.C.:** The vitamin A-zinc connection: a review. *Ann. N. Y. Acad. Sci. 355*:62–75 (1980)
10. **Thompson, D.A., and A. Gal:** Vitamin A metabolism in the retinal pigment epithelium: genes, mutations, and diseases. *Prog. Retin. Eye Res. 22*:683–703 (2003).
11. **Mansour, A.M.:** Ocular manifestations of various systemic disorders. *Curr. Opin. Ophthalmol. 5*:105–109 (1994).
12. **Doering, C.J., and G.W. Zamponi:** Molecular pharmacology of non-L-type calcium channels. *Curr. Pharm. Des. 11*:1887–1898 (2005).
13. **Grant, W.M., and J.S. Shuman:** *Toxicology of the Eye,* 4th edition. Springfield, IL: Charles C. Thomas Publisher, 1993.
14. **Purves, D., G.J. Augustine, D. Fitzpatrick, et al.:** Chapter 13, The Vestibular System. In *Neuroscience,* 3rd edition. Sunderland, MA: Sinauer Associates Inc., 2004.
15. **Fechter, L.D., and Y. Liu:** Auditory Toxicology. In: *Comprehensive Toxicology, Vol. 11: Nervous System and Behavioral Toxicology.* Lowndes, H.E., and K.R. Reuhl (eds.). New York: Pergamon Press/ Elsevier Science, 1997. pp. 265–280.
16. **Ikeda, K.:** Gene-based deafness research: Ion transport and hearing. *Tohoku J. Exp. Med. 202*:1–11 (2004).
17. **Gobba, F.:** Occupational exposure to chemicals and sensory organs: a neglected research field. *Neurotox. 24*: 675–691 (2003).
18. **Feldman, R.G.:** Trichloroethylene. In *Handbook of Clinical Neurology, Vol. 36: Intoxications of the Nervous System.* Vinken, P.J., and G.W. Bruyn (eds.). Amsterdam: North-Holland, 1979. pp. 457–464.
19. **Morata, T.C., D.E. Dunn, and W.K. Sieber:** Occupational exposure to noise and ototoxic organic solvents. *Arch. Environ. Health. 49*:359–365 (1994).
20. **Cazals Y.:** Auditory sensori-neural alterations induced by salicylate. *Prog. Neurobiol. 62*:583–631 (2000).
21. **Syka, J.:** Plastic changes in the central auditory system after hearing loss, restoration of function, and during learning. *Physiol. Rev. 82*:601–636 (2002).
22. **Purves, D., G.J. Augustine, D. Fitzpatrick, et al.:** Chapter 8, The Somatic Sensory System. In *Neuroscience,* 3rd edition. Sunderland, MA: Sinauer Associates Inc., 2004.

23. **Rice, D.C.:** Somatosensory Neurotoxicity: Agents and Assessment Methodology. In *Comprehensive Toxicology, Vol. 11: Nervous System and Behavioral Toxicology.* Lowndes, H.E., and K.R. Reuhl (eds.). New York: Pergamon Press/Elsevier Science, 1997. pp. 333–350.
24. **Spencer, P.S., H.H. Schaumburg, and A.C. Ludolph:** *Experimental and Clinical Neurotoxicology.* New York: Oxford University Press, 2000.
25. **Hughes, RA.:** Epidemiology of peripheral neuropathy. *Curr. Opin. Neurol. 8:*335–338 (1995).
26. **Doty, R.L., and L. Hastings:** Neurotoxic exposure and olfactory impairment. *Clin. Occup. Environ. Med. 1:*547–575 (2001).
27. **Shykind, B.M.:** Regulation of odorant receptors: one allele at a time. *Hum. Mol. Genet. 14:*R33–R39 (2005).
28. **Purves, D., G.J. Augustine, D. Fitzpatrick, et al.:** Chapter 14, The Chemical Senses. In *Neuroscience,* 3rd edition. Sunderland, MA: Sinauer Associates Inc., 2004.
29. **Dorman, D.C., J.G. Owens, and K.T. Morgan:** Olfactory System. In *Comprehensive Toxicology, Vol. 11: Nervous System and Behavioral Toxicology.* Lowndes, H.E., and K.R. Reuhl (eds.). New York: Pergamon Press/ Elsevier Science, 1997. pp. 281–294.
30. **Holbrook, E.H., and D.A. Leopold:** An updated review of clinical olfaction. *Curr. Opin. Otolaryngol. Head Neck Surg. 14:*23–28 (2006).
31. **Drayna, D.:** Human taste genetics. *Annu. Rev. Genomics Hum. Genet. 6:*217–235 (2005).
32. **Purves, D., G.J. Augustine, D. Fitzpatrick, et al.:** Chapter 9, Pain. In *Neuroscience,* 3rd edition. Sunderland, MA: Sinauer Associates Inc., 2004.
33. **Kandel, E.R., J.H. Schwarz, and T.M. Jessell:** *Principles of Neural Science,* 4th edition. Part V: Perception. New York: McGraw-Hill, 2001.
34. **Dalton, P.:** Evaluating the human response to sensory irritation: Implications for setting occupational exposure limits. *Am. Ind. Hyg. Assoc. J. 62:*723–729 (2001).
35. **Auer-Grumbach, M., B. Mauko, P. Auer-Grumbach, and T.R. Pieber:** Molecular genetics of hereditary sensory neuropathies. *Neuromolec. Med. 8:*147–158 (2006).
36. **Morton, C.C.:** Genetics, genomics, and gene discovery in the auditory system. *Hum. Molec. Genet. 11:*1229–1240 (2002).
37. **Huber, A.:** Genetic diseases of vision. *Curr. Opin. Neurol. 7:*65–68 (1994).
38. **Musarella, M.A.:** Molecular genetics of macular degeneration. *Doc. Ophthalmol. 102:*165–177 (2001).
39. **Issever, H., G. Malat, H.H. Sabuncu, and N. Yuksel:** Impairment of colour vision in patients with n-hexane exposure-dependent toxic polyneuropathy. *Occup. Med. 52:*183–186 (2002).
40. **Shusterman, D., E. Matovinovic, and A. Salmon:** Does Haber's law apply to humans sensory irritation? *Inhal. Toxicol. 18:*457–471 (2006).
41. **Maurissen, J.P.:** Quantitative sensory assessment in toxicology and occupational medicine. *Toxicol. Lett. 43:* 321–343 (1988).
42. **Cullen, M.R.:** The worker with multiple chemical hypersensitivities: An overview. *Occup. Med. 2:*655–661 (1987).

Additional Reading

Any of the pertinent chapters in:

Grant, W.M., and J.S. Shuman: *Toxicology of the Eye,* 4th edition. Springfield, IL: Charles C. Thomas Publisher, 1993.

Lowndes, H.E., and K.R. Reuhl (eds.): *Comprehensive Toxicology, Vol. 11: Nervous System and Behavioral Toxicology.* New York: Pergamon Press/Elsevier Science, 1997.

Purves, D., G.J. Augustine, D. Fitzpatrick, et al.: *Neuroscience,* 3rd edition. Sunderland, MA: Sinauer Associates Inc., 2004.

Spencer, P.S., H.H. Schaumburg, and A.C. Ludolph: *Experimental and Clinical Neurotoxicology.* New York: Oxford University Press, 2000.

Vinken, P.J., and G.W. Bruyn (eds.): *Handbook of Clinical Neurology, Vol. 36: Intoxications of the Nervous System.* Amsterdam: North-Holland, 1979.

> *All things are poison and nothing is without poison, only the dose permits something not to be poisonous.*
>
> Paracelsus (1493–1541)

Chapter 9

Neurotoxicology

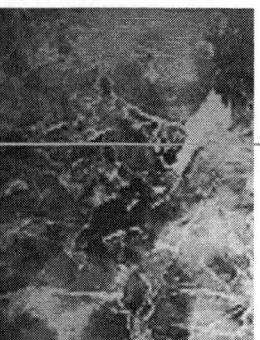

Outcome Competencies

Upon completion of this chapter, the reader should be able to:

- Define terms in bold text.
- Describe the organization of the nervous system.
- Explain the cells and major anatomical structures of the nervous system.
- Describe how an action potential is generated.
- Explain the process of chemical neurotransmission and understand the role of the major neurotransmitters, such as acetylcholine, biogenic amines, amino acids, and neuroactive peptides.
- List the major mechanisms of neurotoxic effects and common neurotoxins in each category.
- Differentiate the mechanisms of toxicity of organic, inorganic, and elemental mercury.
- Differentiate between proximal and distal axonopathies and list toxicants that will produce each.
- Describe the neurotoxic effects of lead.
- Discuss how blocking agents, depolarizing agents, stimulants, depressants, and anticholinesterase agents adversely affect neurotransmission.
- Discuss the neurologic disorders due to exposure to carbon monoxide or dioxins.

Prerequisite Knowledge

Basic anatomy, physiology, and biochemistry of the human nervous system

Key Terms

acetylcholine, acetylcholinesterase, action potential, adrenergic receptor antagonist, afferent nerves, anticholinesterase, astrocyte, ataxia, axon, axonopathy, biogenic amine, blood-brain barrier, central nervous system, delayed neuropathy, dentrite, demyelination, distal axonopathy, efferent nerves, erethism, gamma-aminobutyric acid, ganglion, hippocampus, latency period, muscarinic blocker, myelin, myelinopathy, myelin sheath, narcosis, neurasthenic, neuroglia, neuron, neuronopathy, neuropeptide, neurotransmitter, neurotoxic esterase, neurotoxic syndrome, nicotinic receptor, oligodendrocyte, paresthesia, parasympathetic nervous system, peripheral nervous system, peripheral neuropathy, peristalsis, pralidoxime, presynaptic terminal, proximal axonopathy, postsynaptic membrane, resting membrane potential, Schwann cell, solvent neurotoxic syndrome, sympathetic nervous system, synapse

Key Topics

1. Anatomy and Physiology of the Nervous System
    - Organization of the nervous system
    - Cells of the nervous system
    - Physiology of the nervous system
2. Mechanisms of Neurotoxic Effects
    - Neuronopathy
        - Methylmercury
        - Case Study: Dimethylmercury
        - Inorganic mercury
        - Elemental mercury
        - Trimethyltin
        - Aluminum
        - Manganese
        - Methanol
        - Carbon monoxide
        - Hydrogen cyanide
    - Axonopathy
        - Acrylamide
        - Carbon disulfide
        - n-Hexane
        - Organophosphate insecticides
        - Case Study: Tri-o-cresyl phosphate
    - Myelinopathy
        - Triethyltin
        - Hexachlorophene
        - Lead
    - Neurotransmission Toxicity
        - Blocking agents
        - Depolarizing agents
        - Stimulants
        - Depressants
        - Anticholinesterase agents
3. Selected Neurologic Disorders Due to Neurotoxins
    - Carbon monoxide
    - Dioxins and related compounds

Chapter 9

Neurotoxicology

By William E. Luttrell, PhD, CIH

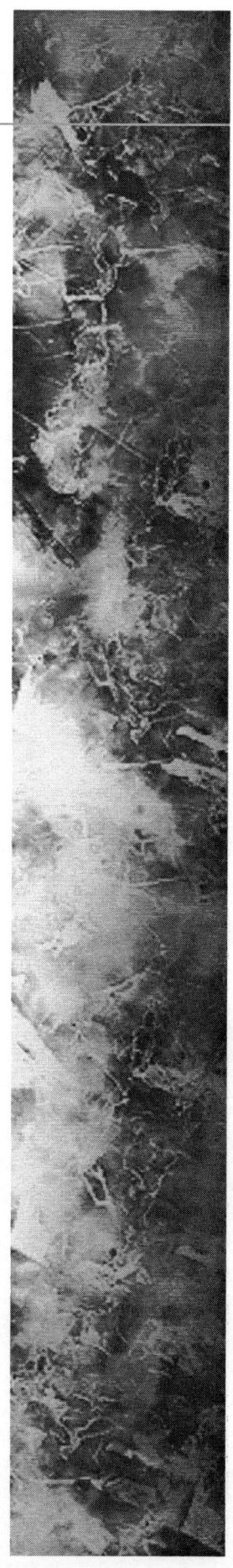

Introduction

This chapter will first provide a brief overview of the organization of the nervous system by describing its anatomy and physiology. The basic mechanisms of neurotoxic effects will also be explained by describing how the normal anatomy and physiology are altered by toxins through neuronopathy, axonopathy, myelinopathy, and neurotransmission toxicity. In each of these categories of toxicity, specific neurotoxins will be presented. The chapter will conclude by providing a detailed discussion of selected neurologic disorders that can be caused with exposure to neurotoxins commonly found in the workplace and/or environment, namely carbon monoxide and dioxins. Examples of worker exposures to neurotoxins and actual case studies showing how neurotoxicology can impact the practice of industrial hygiene are included throughout the chapter.

Anatomy and Physiology of the Nervous System

Organization of the Nervous System

The nervous system consists of the central nervous system (CNS) and the peripheral nervous system (PNS). The structure and function of the CNS and the PNS are unique to each system and they are integrated to regulate organ and body functions. The organization of the nervous system is shown in Figure 9.1.

Central Nervous System (CNS)

The central nervous system includes the brain and spinal cord.

Peripheral Nervous System (PNS)

All of the nerves outside the CNS are in the PNS. The PNS consists of the **afferent nerves** that transmit sensory information to the CNS and **efferent nerves** that carry information from the CNS to glands or muscles. Afferent transmission includes information about touch and pain, as well as general sensory perceptions. Efferent transmission is divided into somatic motor and autonomic information. The skeletal muscles of the body are stimulated through the somatic motor nervous system. The **autonomic nervous system** is divided into the **sympathetic** and **parasympathetic nervous systems**. The heart, and smooth muscle in the digestive tract, blood vessels, and glands, such as the salivary and adrenal glands, and the pancreas, receive integrated stimuli from the sympathetic and parasympathetic nervous systems. In both the sympathetic and parasympathetic nervous systems, the central nervous system communicates with the muscle or gland through two different neurons. The first neuron, known as the preganglionic neuron, connects the CNS with a group of nerve cells called **ganglion**. The second neuron, known as the postganglionic neuron, connects the ganglion with the muscle or gland cell it is controlling.

Cells of the Nervous System

Neuron

The **neuron** is the most fundamental component of the nervous system. It carries stimuli to and from the CNS. Neurons serve as receptors for stimuli internal and external to the body. They carry external information to the CNS and carry nerve impulses from the CNS to muscles and glands. As depicted in Figure 9.2, the structure of

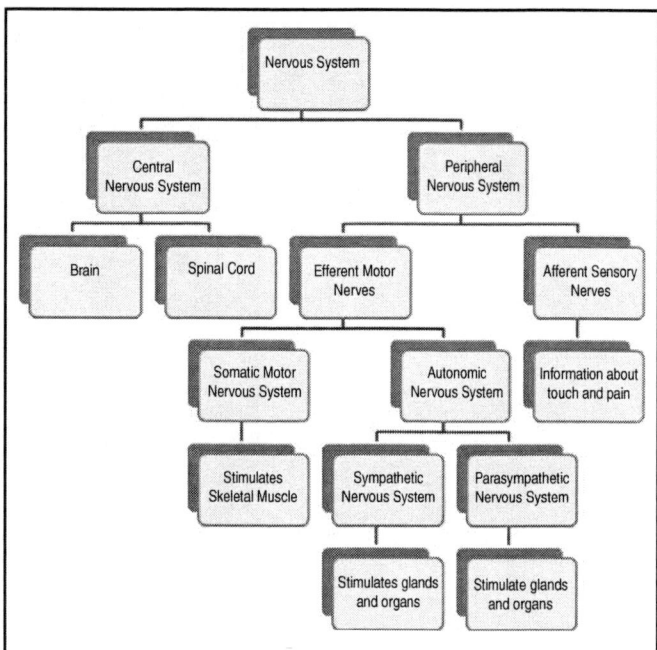

Figure 9.1 — Organization of the Nervous System.

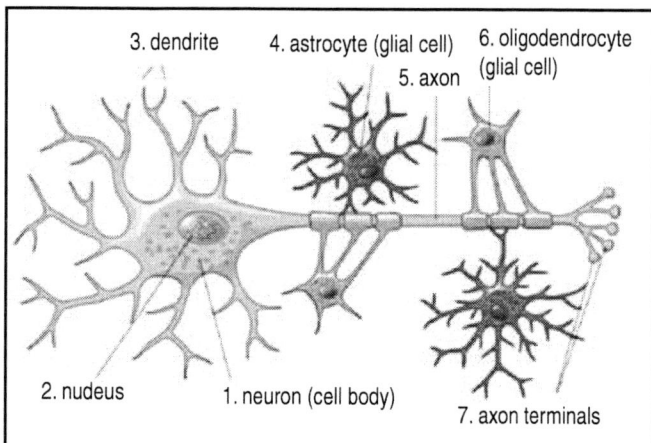

Figure 9.2 — The Cells of the Nervous System.[1] (Source: Cool School, 2008. http://www.coolschool.ca/lor/BI12/unitla/ U12L04.htm)

the neuron consists of the (1) cell body, the (5) **axon**, and the (3) **dendrite**. The cell body, sometimes known as the soma, contains the (2) nucleus, an endoplasmic reticulum, and a Golgi complex, as well as mitochondria. The relatively short and branching processes from the cell body are the (3) dendrites. They are primarily responsible for carrying impulses toward the cell body of the neuron. The dendrites receive stimuli from touch, pain, smell, and other neurons. The dendrites are important for the integration of impulses that reach the neuron. The very long and single process from the cell body is the axon. It carries nerve impulses away from the cell body of the neuron. The axons of sensory nerves carry information to the CNS. The axons of the motor nerves carries information to muscles and glands.

Neuroglia

The supporting cells of the nervous system are known as **neuroglia** or glia cells. Oligodendrocytes, Schwann cells, and astrocytes are three types of neuroglia.

Oligodendrocytes in the Central Nervous System

The cell processes of (6) **oligodendrocytes** surround the nerve cell axons in the central nervous system, as depicted in Figure 9.2. The cell processes wrap around the axon forming concentric layers of cell membrane known as a **myelin sheath**. These axons are myelinated nerves. The myelin sheath is a good insulator and as result it allows easy movement of ions, such as sodium and potassium, into and out of the axon. This is important in maintaining the membrane potential and the formation and propagation of an action potential. Therefore, the cell processes of the oligodendrocyte facilitate the transmission of nerve impulses along the axon.

Schwann Cells in the Peripheral Nervous System

Schwann cells surround the nerve cell axons in the peripheral nervous system. In a similar manner as the oligodendrocytes, they also facilitate nerve transmission along the axon by forming a myelin shealth. The myelin sheath facilitates rapid ion movement and nerve conduction in axons by focusing depolarization specifically at restricted neural areas known as nodes of Ranvier, which minimize the area of membrane depolarization and expended energy for repolarization.

Astrocytes

The cell processes of **astrocytes** can form close association with capillary endothelial cells thereby forming an effective barrier that can decrease the rate of absorption of many substances into brain tissue. This is known as the **blood-brain barrier.**

Physiology of the Nervous System

Overall, the nervous system detects stimuli and initiates responses through the use of electro-chemical events. When a stimulus is received, such as from the sensation of pain or heat, the cell membrane of the neuron undergoes a change in permeability with a movement of sodium and potassium ions across the cell membrane. This results in the generation of an electrical charge known as an action potential. The **action potential** travels along the nerve cell and eventually reaches the end of the axon. Here it causes the release of a **neurotransmitter**. This chemical messenger causes the initiation of a response in another nerve cell or a tissue cell, such as a muscle or gland cell. The generation of an action potential requires energy.

Action Potential

Information is carried from the source of the stimulus to the central nervous system through the propagation of action potentials along the axons of afferent nerves. The central nervous system sends signals to muscles and glands by originating action potentials that travel along the axons of efferent nerves.

For an action potential to be generated, the ion distribution across the cell membrane must be changed. When a net positive charge is on the outside and a net negative charge is on the inside of the nerve cell membrane, the resting phase exists. The charge difference that exists across the cell membrane during the resting phase is called the **resting membrane potential**. It is the result of uneven distribution of sodium and potassium ions on each side of the cell membrane. The resting membrane potential is generated and maintained by sodium-potassium ATP-ase dependent pumps. A higher sodium ion concentration exists on the outside of the cell membrane than inside, and the opposite is true for potassium ion concentration. Negatively charged ions and protein molecules are in higher concentration on the inside of the cell. The overall effect of the distribution of these substances is a positive charge on the outside of the cell and a negative charge on the inside of the cell. The resting membrane potential is primarily sustained by the uneven distribution of sodium and potassium ions.

When stimulated, a nerve cell membrane becomes more permeable to sodium ions at the localized point of stimulation. Since a higher concentration of sodium exists on the outside of the membrane, sodium ions rapidly diffuse into the membrane. The inside of the membrane becomes positive, while the outside of the membrane becomes negative temporarily. Potassium ions then diffuse out of the cell membrane in response to the sodium ions coming into the cell membrane, generating an action potential. The electric field of the action potential causes the adjacent portion of the cell membrane to become depolarized specifically at the node of Ranvier, and a wave of depolarization skips to the next node. This action potential travels down to the end of the nerve, resulting in the release of chemical neurotransmitter, which stimulates the affected tissue cell.[2]

Chemical Neurotransmitters

There are numerous chemical neurotransmitters in the nervous system, including acetylcholine, biogenic amines, amino acids, and neuroactive peptides. These chemical substances are released from the axon terminal into the **synapse**. The end of the axon in the synapse is called the **presynaptic terminal** (or presynaptic membrane). The cell membrane of the stimulated tissue is called the **postsynaptic membrane** (or postsynaptic terminal). The space between the pre-synaptic terminal and postsynaptic membrane is the synaptic cleft. The synaptic vesicles, containing the neurotransmitter, come into contact with the presynaptic membrane, which releases the neurotransmitter substance into the synaptic cleft. It diffuses across the synaptic cleft and binds to receptors on the postsynaptic cell membrane. Binding of the neurotransmitter to the postsynaptic cell membrane causes a response in the affected tissue. The neurotransmitter is rapidly broken down by enzymes or reabsorbed by the presynaptic terminal to prevent constant stimulation. Figure 9.3 depicts the basic structure of the synapse and the release of neurotransmitter into the synaptic cleft.

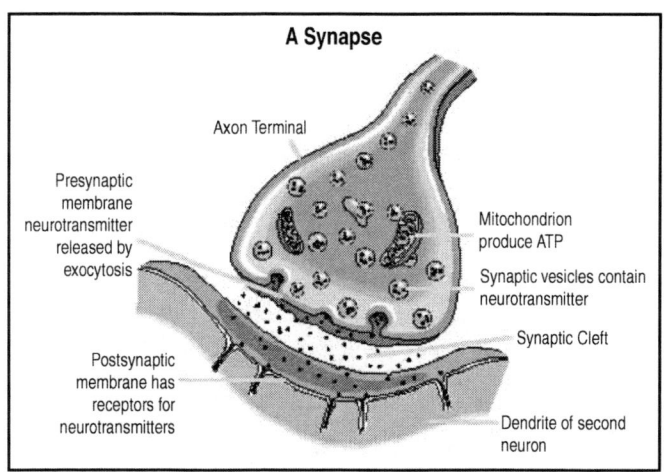

Figure 9.3 — A Synapse. (Source: Cool School, 2008.)

Acetylcholine

Acetylcholine (ACh) is a major neurotransmitter in the autonomic nervous system. This system controls primarily involuntary muscles and glands through its sympathetic and parasympathetic branches. When stimulated, the sympathetic branch causes the "fight or flight" response, which includes tachycardia (increase in heart rate), dilation of lung bronchioles, dilation of the pupil, constriction of peripheral blood vessels, and a decrease in digestive system activity. When stimulated, the parasympathetic branch causes many of the opposite effects, including bradycardia (decrease in heart rate), constriction of bronchioles, constriction of the pupil, increase in the activity of digestive smooth muscle, and an increase in secretions from glands. Acetylcholine is the neurotransmitter released by the preganglionic neuron in both the sympathetic and parasympathetic branches, and by the postganglionic neurons of the parasympathetic branch. Acetylcholine is also the neurotransmitter released by the neurons that control voluntary muscles, and it is released by the neurons in certain areas of the central nervous system. Acetylcholine is synthesized in the neuron from molecules of acetyl CoA and choline. It is stored in the neuron and its release is triggered by an influx of calcium that occurs during an action potential reaching its membrane. Acetylcholine is hydrolyzed by the enzyme acetylcholinesterase, breaking it down and ending its neurotransmitter function.

Biogenic Amines: Norepinephrine, Epinephrine, Dopamine, Serotonin, and Histamine

The biogenic amines include the following neurotransmitters: norepinephrine, epinephrine, dopamine, serotonin, and histamine. Norepinephrine is released by the postganglionic neurons of the sympathetic nervous system. It is also released by certain neurons in the central nervous system. The medulla, pons, or nerve cells in the midbrain (also called brain stem) release norepinephrine, epinephrine, dopamine, and serotonin, connecting with many other areas of the brain. Many of the neurons in the hypothalamus release histamine. The group of neurotransmitters known as catecholamine includes norepinephrine, epinephrine, and dopamine.

Amino acids: Gamma-aminobutyric Acid (GABA), Glycine, Glutamate, Aspartate

Gamma-aminobutyric acid (GABA) is synthesized in neurons throughout the nervous system. It is an inhibitory neurotransmitter. It acts only at the inhibitory GABA receptor and the chloride ion membrane channel. GABA is found in higher concentrations in the cells of the cerebellum, spinal cord, and in cells originating in the hippocampus and leading to the midbrain. It is synthesized and stored in the presynaptic neuron. Following its release, it binds to a postsynaptic receptor. GABA binding causes an increase in chloride permeability, allowing chloride to enter the neuron, making the membrane potential more negative. GABA is taken back up by cells in the pre-synaptic neuron and glial cells. GABA seems to be involved in nerve pathways that control emotions.

Neuroactive Peptides: Opioid Peptides (Enkephalines and Endorphins)

These substances act as neurotransmitters, but they act at much lower concentrations and their actions last much longer. **Neuropeptides** affect membrane potential or they may be released along with another neurotransmitter, and act by altering the release or binding of the neurotransmitter. There are many neuropeptide groups in the nervous system, but one of the better known groups is the opioid peptides. This group includes the enkephalins and endorphins. Several different opioid receptors occur in the CNS. They may have inhibitory effects on pathways that cause the transmission of pain impulses. Opium and related substances, such as morphine and codeine and heroin exert their narcotic effect by interacting with the opioid receptor. Tolerance to these substances develops quickly.[3]

Mechanisms of Neurotoxic Effects

Toxic substances can damage the structure of the neuron. The damage can be classified as neuronopathy, axonopathy, or myelinopathy, all of which can result in disruption of neurotransmission and toxicity. They can also affect neurotransmission between the pre-synaptic terminal and the postsynaptic membrane by disrupting normal events.

Neuronopathy

Toxic substances can interact with the nerve cell body which will cause the entire nerve cell, including the dendrites and axons, to degenerate. Ultimately, the entire neuron is destroyed (neuronopathy). Low concentrations of specific toxic substances can cause localized neuronopathy in specific parts of the nervous system. High concentrations of toxic substances can cause neuronopathy throughout the nervous system.

Methylmercury

Mercury-containing waste from various industries, such as paper production, and from its use as a fungicide, can find its way into lakes, rivers, and the oceans. There it is converted to an organic mercury compound, methylmercury, which bioaccumulates in the food chain, concentrating in fish and shellfish. Organic mercury compounds are easily absorbed through the gastrointestinal tract. Absorption of methylmercury is 90% to 95% efficient through this route. A major case of human poisoning as a result of exposure to methylmercury occurred in Minamata, Japan, after the bay became contaminated with mercury-containing waste. Since organomercurials are lipid-soluble compounds, they will easily pass through the blood-brain barrier into the CNS.[4] At low doses methylmercury will have effects in parts of the CNS that can disrupt muscle coordination, resulting in **ataxia**, the loss of muscle coordination and control. In developing fetuses and young children methylmercury can cause generalized neuronopathy leading to mental retardation and paralysis. At high doses it can cause generalized neuronopathy. This xenobiotic, a foreign chemical to the body, causes inhibition of protein synthesis in the rough endoplasmic reticulum. It also damages the endothelial cells of the blood-brain barrier by breaking down the capillary endothelial cell membrane.[3]

Case Study: Dimethylmercury

A tragic case of delayed cerebellar disease and death was reported in a research chemist following accidental exposure to dimethylmercury.[5] This compound is more lipid soluble and therefore more dangerous than methylmercury. It can undergo transdermal absorption, and its volatility permits inhalation. Dimethylmercury is lethal at a dose of about 400 milligrams of mercury, which is equivalent to just a few drops or about 5 mg per kg of body weight. The research chemist was exposed to the toxin on only one day, with a small spill of several drops onto the dorsum of a latex-gloved hand. Apparently, lethal tissue concentrations resulted from transdermal absorption through the permeable latex glove. There was possible inhalation, although a fume hood was in use. The first symptoms of poisoning did not occur until 150 days later, indicating a **latency period**. The exposure took place in the month of August. It was not until the end of December that the first symptoms appeared. During this time, the individual did not experience any ill effects and she pursued her normal duties as a professor of chemistry at Dartmouth College. After symptoms began to appear, the full neurological syndrome of severe dimethylmercury poisoning rapidly developed. After two weeks the individual was severely affected and remained in serious condition until her death a few months later. Therefore, there was a 150-day latency period followed by a sudden onset of symptoms of severe dimethylmercury poisoning. It was concluded that the latency period was due to the slow production and accumulation of a toxic metabolite. It is known that dimethylmercury is converted to divalent inorganic mercury in the brain over months. It is likely that the accumulation of this metabolite was the critical toxic event in this particular case of dimethylmercury poisoning. Recently, possible mechanisms for this latency period have been discussed for both acute and chronic exposures to dimethylmercury.[6]

Inorganic Mercury

The monovalent (mercurous) and divalent (mercuric) inorganic salts of mercury have neurologic toxicity. Divalent compounds are more toxic than monovalent compounds.[4] Severe cases of poisoning occur through accidental and intentional ingestion, since inorganic mercury salts are principally absorbed through the gastrointestinal tract. The phrase "mad as a hatter" originated from workers in the hat industry being exposed to inorganic mercury, leading to symptoms of mercury poisoning. It also inspired the character of the Mad Hatter in Lewis Carroll's *Alice's Adventures in Wonderland*. The symptoms displayed by these workers included depression, moodiness, insomnia, confusion, and tremors.[3] Neuropsychologic effects that include behavioral and cognitive disturbances are the earliest effects associated with mercury exposure.[3] After ingestion of inorganic mercury salts in large quantities, abdominal pain and diarrhea can occur quickly, with renal effects, including oliguria and proteinuria becoming apparent later.

Elemental Mercury

The elemental form of mercury also has neurologic toxicity. Elemental mercury is easily absorbed through the lungs as a vapor. Absorption of elemental mercury is about 80% efficient after inhalation exposure. Less than 0.01% of elemental mercury is absorbed from the gastrointestinal tract making ingestion an unimportant exposure route for elemental mercury. Acute inhalation of high concentrations of mercury vapor has a corrosive effect on lung tissue, causing bronchitis and interstitial pneumonitis, as well as nervous system effects of tremor and excitability. Chronic inhalation of lower concentrations of mercury vapor leads to **neurasthenic** symptoms that include headache, fatigue, dizziness, memory loss, and depression. Other clinical findings can also be present in the exposed person: tremor, thyromegaly or increased thyroid uptake of radio-iodine, tachycardia or pulse irregularity, gingivitis, dermatographism, hematologic changes, and elevated urine mercury levels. As intoxication becomes more severe, **erethism** (withdrawal, memory loss, excitability, and depression), tremor, and gingivitis are predominant symptoms along with diffuse polyneuropathy.[4]

Residual effects of long term exposure to mercury vapor were reported in former mercury miners about eighteen years after the end of mercury exposure.[7] Seventy six male ex-mercury miners who had been exposed to high concentrations of mercury vapor and had a history of mercury intoxication were compared with controls matched for age, sex, and education. As expected, the symptoms caused by mercury poisoning decreased after the end of exposure. However, matched paired comparison showed that performances of motor coordination, simple reaction time, and short term memory had declined significantly in the exposed group. There were positive correlations between poorer neurological performance and variables related to mercury exposure. The duration of exposure correlated with poorer performance of hand-eye coordination, tapping, and a color card reading test. It was concluded that there are slight but persistent effects on neurobehavioral function, especially on motor coordination, among mercury miners even more than ten years after the end of exposure.

Trimethyltin

This compound is sometimes known as organotin and it has been used as a plasticizer and in antifungal agents. It is able to pass through the blood-brain barrier and enter the brain where it leads to diffuse neuronal injury. Many of the exposed neurons show cytoplasmic bodies followed by cellular swelling and necrosis.[8] This organometal compound most easily damages neurons in a very specific area of the brain, the **hippocampus** and surrounding areas. The hippocampus is involved in acquiring memories and it is a part of the limbic system, which has a role in emotions. Animals exposed to trimethyltin show behavioral changes, such as aggression, and disruption of memory-related processes.[3]

Aluminum

Aluminum has been associated with Alzheimer's Disease, since elevated concentrations have been found in the brains of people suffering with the disease. However, there is no definitive scientific evidence that aluminum causes this disease. Some believe that it may interfere with ion uptake, ATP metabolism, or protein synthesis. Aluminum may have an adverse affect on cell membrane integrity, causing a lack of proper ion distribution and disrupting normal nerve cell function.[3]

Neurobehavioral performance was studied in aluminum welders.[9] Twenty aluminum welders, who had been exposed to aluminum for an average of 8.1 years, were tested for tremor and reaction time and screened for neuropsychiatric symptoms. The welder's urinary aluminum concentration was determined and the aluminum in air was measured inside the respiratory protection worn by the welder. Each welder was compared with a construction worker matched for age. Welders reported more neuropsychiatric symptoms. Years of aluminum exposure was predictive of poorer performance on the tests. There was a statistically significant relation between longer reaction times and aluminum concentrations in air.

Manganese

This toxicant can also be found in industrial waste that is released into air emissions and into bodies of water. This substance is an essential element for several enzymes, especially those involved in cholesterol and fatty acid synthesis. High concentrations of manganese can cause damage in the CNS, especially the brain. Neuropsychiatric symptoms can occur that include irritability, difficulty in walking, and speech abnormalities that can occur following exposure to manganese. If exposure is continuous and prolonged, Parkinson-like symptoms similar to Parkinson's syndrome, such as tremors and spastic contractions of skeletal muscles, can occur.[3]

Methanol

Exposure to this chemical can result in nerve damage causing blindness or death. At first the individual experiences mild inebriation and depression. An asymptomatic period follows for twelve to fourteen hours. During this time, the blood pH can decrease causing acidosis. Eye pain, blurred vision, and constriction of the visual fields will begin to occur. Depending on the level of exposure, symptoms may progress to temporary or permanent blindness. Cessation of breathing and death can occur, if not treated.

Carbon Monoxide and Hydrogen Cyanide

Exposure to both of these toxicants can result in similar adverse effects. By interfering with aerobic metabolism, they will cause nerve cells to be deprived of oxygen that maintains normal cell function and integrity. Metabolic processes in the nerve cells are disrupted, which leads to cell death. Acute exposure to carbon monoxide or hydrogen cyanide in sufficient concentrations can lead to death.[3]

Axonopathy

Damage to axons is axonopathy and is most often in the peripheral nervous system with resulting sensory and motor dysfunction. Axonopathies are usually categorized as either proximal or distal. **Proximal axonopathies** result in the swelling of proximal axons with the formation of giant axonal swellings. This occurs because the transport of proteins from the cell body to the axon is blocked. As a result, neurofilaments accumulate, forming the giant axonal swelling. The distal part of the axon, deprived of proteins, eventually degenerates. Degeneration of myelin around the swelling can also occur in proximal axonopathies. The synthetic aminonitrile compound, β,β-iminodiproprionitrile (IDPN), produces a proximal axonopathy. 3,4-dimethyl-2,5-hexanedione, a metabolite of 2,5-hexanedione, will also produce proximal axonopathy.

Abnormal changes in distal portions of axons can result in **distal axonopathies**. The damage that has occurred depends on the toxicant producing the change. It may include swelling, damage to mitochondria, and accumulation of neurofilaments. It often includes the degeneration of myelin. Since the damage often appears first in the axon terminal, distal axonopathies are sometimes called "dying-back neuropathies." They can occur following a single exposure to some toxicants, or following chronic exposure. The onset of symptoms are often weeks after exposure.[3]

Axons that innervate the hands and feet are usually affected first by chemicals that cause axonopathies, resulting in loss of feeling and motion. Cases in which the exposure continues result in axons associated with the central nervous system, especially in the spinal cord, being affected, resulting in serious impairment of motor functions with progressive weakening of skeletal muscle. Acrylamide, carbon disulfide, n-hexane, and organophosphates can cause such axonopathies.[2]

Acrylamide

This compound is a vinyl monomer used in paper products, water treatment, and it is a waterproofing agent. There have been cases of factory and construction workers being exposed to high doses of acrylamide.[8] It produces distal axonopathies primarily by inhibiting axonal transport.[3] The neuropathy begins with degeneration of the nerve terminal. If intoxication continues, the more proximal axon also degenerates. The depression of fast axonal transport has been observed in peripheral nerve axons from animals lacking neurofilaments when exposed to acrylamide *in vitro*.[8]

Carbon Disulfide

Workers have been exposed to this compound in the vulcan rubber and viscose rayon industries.[8] In prolonged low doses this compound can induce psychiatric disturbances. At higher exposures it can result in a toxic encephalopathy that can include a toxic psychosis with hallucinations, delirium and manic-depressive derangements.[10] In addition to CNS effects, exposure to carbon disulfide can cause a distal axonopathy that is identical to that caused by hexane. The carbon disulfide molecule reacts with protein amino groups to form dithiocarbamate adducts. The dithiocarbamate adducts of lysyl amino groups decompose to isothiocyanate adducts, electrophiles that then react with protein nucleophiles to yield covalent cross-linking in neurofilaments of distal axons. Thiourea cross-links are irreversible and result in biologically significant changes leading to axonal neurofilamentous swellings. These modifications on peripheral proteins can be used as biomarkers of the effect of carbon disulfide exposure. If exposure continues, sensory and motor symptoms will develop as a result of chronic axonopathy. Also, carbon disulfide can lead to changes in mood and signs of diffuse encephalopathic disease. It can accelerate the process of atherosclerosis, which may be an indication that the effects of carbon disulfide on the CNS may be partially vascular in nature.[8]

n-Hexane

When exposed to high concentrations of n-hexane repeatedly in the workplace or by intentional inhalation of hexane-containing glues, individuals develop a progressive sensorimotor distal axonopathy. Interestingly, it was observed that methyl n-butyl ketone (2-hexanone) causes the same neuropathy, since they both form the same ultimate toxic metabolite, 2,5-hexanedione. Other γ-diketones or γ-diketone precursors are similarly neurotoxic, while α-diketones and β-diketones are not.[10] The cytoskeleton of the axon, especially the neurofilament, is the target of γ-diketones. Neurofilament proteins are cross-linked by this interaction with the toxic metabolite of n-hexane. As a result, neurofilament transport becomes impaired and neurofilament-filled axonal swellings occur. With continued exposure to n-hexane, swellings are more proximal and there is degeneration of the distal axon with its myelin. Neurofilament accumulation and axon degeneration are followed by clinical peripheral neuropathy. In the case of experimental animals, weakness begins in the hind limbs. As exposure continues, successive weakness in more proximal muscle groups occurs.[8] Sensory nerves are involved late with n-hexane induced axonopathy, while motor nerves early in the progression of the axonopathy.[11] When animals are exposed to n-hexane and methyl n-butyl ketone at the same time, there is synergistic interaction between these two compounds. Animals exposed to both of these compounds will show earlier onset and greater severity of neurotoxic signs. There is greater production of 2,5-hexanedione in animals exposed to both n-hexane and methyl n-butyl ketone than in animals exposed to only one of the compounds.[10]

Organophosphate Insecticides

Some organophosphate compounds can cause distal axonopathies that result in **delayed neuropathy**. This is in addition to acute inhibition of **acetylcholinesterase** throughout the body, especially in synapses. These compounds include tri-o-cresyl phosphate (TOCP) and leptophos.[11] During the 1920s and 1930s, "Ginger Jake" paralysis was linked with ingestion of ginger extract contaminated with trace amounts of TOCP. Another outbreak of distal axonopathy occurred in Morocco when olive oil contaminated with TOCP was consumed.[8] The neuropathy occurred following either acute exposure to high levels or chronic exposure to lower levels of the organophosphates. One to two weeks after acute exposure, symptoms of weakness and even paralysis of the lower limbs would begin. Recovery was slow and usually not complete. Species sensitive to the delayed neuropathy include humans, cats, sheep, and birds (chickens). It can be readily reproduced in hens, usually with a delay of eight to ten days after exposure.[11] The axonopathy in the peripheral nervous system can be repaired; however, when axonal degeneration is in the long axons in the spinal cord, it is progressive and may resemble multiple sclerosis.[8] It is likely that the organophosphate axonopathy is due to the inhibition of an esterase enzyme different from acetylcholinesterase known as the "neurotoxic esterase" or the "neuropathy target esterase" (NTE). Although binding to this molecule appears to be correlated with toxicity, the normal function of the **neurotoxic esterase** and the consequences of its inhibition are not completely clear at this time.[3] Due to the association of NTE with the development of delayed neuropathy, it has diagnostic importance for this toxic effect of particular organophosphate compounds.

Case Study: Tri-o-cresyl phosphate

Since fire poses a catastrophic threat, all ships use hydraulic systems in elevators with fluids that contain fire-retardants. For many years phosphate ester-based hydraulic fluids were used in Navy ships in aircraft elevators, weapons handling systems, weapons elevators, ballast valve operating systems, and replenishment at sea systems. Fluids that were once marketed with brand names such as Cellulube, Fyrquel, and Houghto-Safe, contained a small amount of tri-o-cresyl phosphate (TOCP). Being under pressure, hydraulic systems leaked, and at times, large spills of hydraulic fluid occurred. If there was a small leak, as in a flange joint, a fine spray created a mist that would fill a space. If the wrong valve was activated, an entire pump room could flood with thousands of gallons of hydraulic fluid. For example, an inexperienced pump room operator opened an exhaust drain valve, which resulted in releasing Cellulube under high pressure (about 1200 psi) into a sump tank. The sump tank was deformed by the pressure overload, and the cover seals failed. Approximately 1500 gallons of Cellulube overflowed into the pump room. Acting in haste, the pump room personnel took no precautions to avoid breathing the oil mist or to avoid skin contact with it. They scooped up most of the fluid in buckets, walking around ankle-deep in Cellulube. After about two hours of work, their shoes and clothes became soaked and their skin contaminated with Cellulube. The proper use of adequate respiratory, eye, and skin protection would have prevented exposure of personnel to the hydraulic fluid, and in particular TOCP. Obviously, in this situation the potential existed for inhalation of mist, exposure of eyes, and direct skin contact. Skin contact may have been sufficient to produce contact dermatitis. Eye exposure could have produced conjunctivitis. If prolonged exposure of the skin occurred, absorption through the skin of TOCP may have produced mild peripheral axonopathy.[12]

Myelinopathy

Normal function of the nervous system can be disrupted if there is damage to **myelin**. Damage to myelin can result in blockage of an action potential completely, or it may delay or reduce the amplitude of an action potential. When this occurs, symptoms can include numbness, weakness, and paralysis. Also, action potentials may arise spontaneously in demyelinated neurons, causing **paresthesias**.[3] Toxicants exist that cause the separation of the myelin lamellae, called intramyelinic edema, and cause the loss of myelin, called **demyelination**. Intramyelinic edema can progress to demyelination with the loss of myelin from the axon. Demyelination can also occur due to the direct toxicity to the myelinating cell. Remyelination can occur in the CNS but only to a limited extent. In the peripheral nervous system Schwann cells can remyelinate axons after a demyelination injury.[8] Triethyltin, hexachlorophene, and lead are demyelinating agents.

Triethyltin

An incident occurred in France in 1954, in which over 1000 people were exposed to triethyltin in a contaminated antibacterial preparation. Since this compound is highly lipid soluble, it was able to bind directly to sites within myelin, resulting in intramyelinic edema. The myelin sheath was split and large fluid-filled vacuoles were formed within the myelin. The effects of triethyltin were reversible.[3]

Hexachlorophene

An antimicrobial agent very similar to triethyltin, hexachlorophene, is also highly lipid soluble and has similar effects upon myelin. It was at one time widely used to wash the skin of newborn infants to avoid staphylococcal skin infections.[13] It is still used today in germicidal soaps and detergents.[2] After being easily absorbed through the skin, hexachlorophene enters myelin and results in intramyelinic edema. Studies showed that some of the infants received damage to myelin in both the central and peripheral nervous systems. As with triethyltin, the effects of hexachlorophene were also reversible in the early stages of exposure.[3] However, with continued and increasing exposure, hexachlorophene causes segmental demyelination. With high doses, axonal degeneration is seen, along with degeneration of photoreceptors in the retina. Humans exposed to acute and large doses may show weakness, confusion, and seizures. Progression can result in coma and death.[8] See Chapter 8, "Toxicology of Sensory Organs" for discussion of other chemicals that adversely affect the cells of the retina.

Lead

Lead exposure can result in **peripheral neuropathy** because of segmental demyelination in the peripheral nervous system. Swelling and other morphological changes are seen in Schwann cells. In addition to the nervous system, lead toxicity exists in other organ systems. Adults are exposed to lead in the workplace through lead smelting and soldering and in the home through drinking water from lead pipes and consuming food contaminated with lead. Levels of lead in the ambient air, surface water, and soil can affect blood lead levels in adults and children. Primary exposure in children is through ingestion of soil and lead paint residues. Chronic lead exposure in adults causes peripheral neuropathy, along with toxic effects outside the nervous system, including gastritis, colicky abdominal pain, anemia, and deposition of lead in the gums and epiphyses of long bones in children. In humans, electrophysiologic studies have shown a slowing of nerve conduction, axonopathy, and a predominant involvement of motor axons.[8] An effect of lead on the membrane structure of myelin and myelin membrane fluidity has been shown in rats.[14]

Cumulative exposure to inorganic lead was found to be related to performance on neuropsychological tests.[15] Four hundred sixty seven Canadian male lead smelter workers were given a neuropsychological screening battery. Time integrated blood levels were developed from blood lead concentration records obtained through regular medical monitoring. Integrated blood level groups differed significantly on digit symbol and logical memory tests. Researchers concluded that a dose-effect relation was found between cumulative exposure and neuropsychological performance at a time when current blood lead concentrations were low and showed no association with performance. In another study, effects of low level exposure to lead on neurophysiological functions among lead battery workers was reported.[16] The exposure of sixty workers from a lead battery factory was estimated from historical blood lead measurements and from analysis of lead in the tibial and calcaneal bones using X-ray fluorescence. Peripheral and central nervous system functions were evaluated by measuring conduction velocities, sensory distal latencies, sensory amplitudes, and vibration thresholds as well as by quantitative measurement of the absolute and relative powers and mean frequencies of different electroencephalograph (EEG) channels. Sensory amplitudes showed a negative correlation with long term exposure to lead. Vibration thresholds measured in the arm were related to recent exposure to lead. Vibration thresholds measured in the leg were related to long term exposure. Alpha and beta activities of the EEG were more common in subjects with higher long term exposure to lead. Researchers concluded that vibratory thresholds, quantitative EEG, and sensory amplitude provide sensitive measures of effects of lead in occupationally exposed adults. Another study reported cognitive effects of chronic exposure to lead and solvents in construction workers.[17] Exposures were estimated using X-ray fluorescence of tibial bone lead and occupational history of solvent exposure. Workers were classified into four exposure groups: lead, solvent, lead/solvent, and control. There were at least thirty three workers in each group. The construction workers completed tests to evaluate concentration, motor skills, memory, and mood. Compared to controls, the lead, solvent, and lead/solvent groups performed significantly more poorly on a test of verbal memory, while the lead and lead/solvent groups were slower than the solvent and control groups on a task of processing speed. Bone lead was a significant predictor of information processing speed and latency of response. Solvent exposure was a significant predictor of verbal learning and memory.

Children under the age of five years have higher blood lead levels than adults in the same environment, because of mouthing of objects and the consumption of substances other than food. The most common acute exposure in children is through the consumption of paint chips containing lead pigments. This has led to the use of lead free paints in homes. Acute high level exposures to lead in children will result in severe cerebral edema, likely due to lead causing damage to endothelial cells. Recently, it has been shown that extremely low levels of exposure to lead in normal children may have an effect on their intelligence.[8] Studies have shown correlations between elevated lead levels in deciduous teeth and performance on tests of verbal abilities, attention, and behavior.[18] Lead exposure is known to have an adverse effect on the intellectual abilities of children.[19]

Neurotransmission Toxicity

Toxic substances can disrupt normal events during neurotransmission between the presynaptic terminal and the postsynaptic membrane. These toxic substances can be categorized according to their mechanisms of action, including: blocking agents, depolarizing agents, stimulants, depressants, or anticholinesterase agents.

Blocking Agents

A toxin can bind to the presynaptic terminal and prevent the release of neurotransmitter. In the case of botulism, the bacterium *Clostridium botulinum* toxin binds to the presynaptic terminal and prevents the release of acetylcholine at the neuromuscular and the peripheral nervous system synapses. A toxin can also bind to the postsynaptic membrane and prevent the binding of the neurotransmitter. Curare is a competitive postsynaptic acetylcholine antagonist at the neuromuscular junction.[20] Atropine, a substance found in the plant *Atropa belladonna*, is a **muscarinic blocker**, since it binds to muscarinic receptors, blocking the binding of acetylcholine. Atropine is, therefore, an anticholinergic compound that competitively binds with cholinergic postsynaptic receptors. Blocking muscarinic receptors blocks the effect of parasympathetic neurons on muscles and glands and causes the autonomic nervous system to become imbalanced with the sympathetic branch being predominant. Atropine exposure can cause tachycardia, dilation of the pupils, dilation of bronchioles, decrease in **peristalsis**, and decrease in saliva and other secretions. Scopolamine is another muscarinic blocker and it is found in the plant *Hyoscamus niger*.[3] Phenoxybenzamine, phentolamine, propranolol, and tolazoline are antiadrenergic compounds, since they bind with the adrenergic postsynaptic receptors preventing response when adrenergic compounds attempt to bind. They are, therefore, **adrenergic receptor antagonists**.[20]

Depolarizing Agents

The resting membrane potential that normally exists across the cell membrane is maintained by an energy-dependent (ATP) sodium-potassium pump, which transports sodium ions out of the cell and potassium into the cell. Toxins can eliminate the resting membrane potential by altering the permeability of the cell membrane towards sodium and potassium ions. The organochlorine insecticide dichlorodiphenyl trichloroethane (DDT) depolarizes the presynaptic neuron membrane partially, causing it to be in an almost continuous state of excitation with the release of neurotransmitter in response to weak stimuli. Individuals with exposure may develop persistent tremors, irritability, hypersensitivity to external stimuli, and dizziness. DDT increases the cell membrane permeability to sodium and decreases it to potassium. DDT also inhibits the sodium-potassium ATPase enzyme, which is involved in the production of energy for the sodium-potassium pump. All of these effects lower the resting membrane potential, making the nerve more sensitive to stimuli. Pyrethroid insecticides are less toxic and less persistent than the organochlorine insecticides. Exposure to the skin can cause burning, itching, or tingling sensation. Pyrethroids also affect sodium and potassium permeability, resulting in increased sensitivity of the nerve to stimuli with continuous release of neurotransmitter. Succinylcholine, a skeletal muscle relaxant used in surgery, persistently depolarizes the muscle cell membrane, effectively blocking the effect of the neurotransmitter.[20]

Stimulants

Stimulants can exert an effect by increasing the sensitivity of neurons to stimuli or by inhibiting the re-absorption of neurotransmitters. Nicotine is a stimulant that increases the excitability of neurons. It binds to and stimulates a subset of receptors that normally bind acetylcholine, called **nicotinic receptors**. These receptors are found in the central nervous system and the neuromuscular junction. In the central nervous system nicotine causes an addictive effect. Nicotine stimulates neurons in the sympathetic nervous system, resulting in increased heart rate and elevated blood pressure, which may contribute to the onset of myocardial ischemia.[21] Workers exposed to wet tobacco leaves, or exposure to nicotine-containing pesticides can have heart and respiratory rates increase, nausea, and perspiration. This can be followed by a slowing of the heart rate and a drop in blood pressure. Death can occur if respiratory paralysis occurs.[2,8] In the case of strychnine, the inhibitory neuronal activity of glycine, a competitive antagonist at post synaptic sites, is prevented from occurring. This also results in excitability in the CNS.[20]

Caffeine (1, 2, 7-trimethylxanthine) is a stimulant of the central nervous system. By preventing the breakdown of cyclic AMP, it affects the active transport system that maintains the sodium/potassium concentration gradient across the cell membrane.[20] Intoxication with caffeine is characterized by nervousness, insomnia, flushed face, gastrointestinal disturbance, muscle twitching, rambling speech and thoughts, increased heart rate, and periods of inexhaustibility.[2]

Cocaine is a strong stimulant of the central nervous system causing euphoric and addictive effects. The base form of cocaine can easily cross the blood-brain barrier and enter the brain, especially when it is smoked. In this form it reaches higher brain concentrations faster than the salt form (cocaine hydrochloride) given intravenously. It inhibits the reabsorption of catecholamine neurotransmitters, which include epinephrine, norepinephrine, and dopamine.[22] Under normal conditions, neurotransmitters are reabsorbed and broken down in the presynaptic neuron. Inhibition of this process allows the neurotransmitters to remain in the synaptic cleft. This results in continuous stimulation of the postsynaptic membrane of the affected tissue. For example, during an overdose of cocaine, there can be constant stimulation of the heart with increased heart rate that can lead to heart failure and death.[2] Chronic abuse of cocaine is associated with increased risk of cerebrovascular disease, cerebral perfusion defects, and cerebral atrophy in adults.[23] It is also associated with neurodegenerative changes in the striatum of the brain. These changes may be the underlying cause of some of the neurologic and psychiatric effects of chronic cocaine abuse.[24]

Depressants

Depressants of neurotransmission cause adverse effects mainly by interfering with the maintenance of the resting membrane potential and the generation of the action potential. Volatile organic toxicants, aromatic organic solvents, and alcohols all impair neurotransmission and are strong central nervous system depressants.

Volatile organic solvents commonly found in the workplace, such as carbon tetrachloride, chloroform, and methylene chloride, are very lipophilic and easily absorbed through the myelin sheath and cell membrane of neurons. Normal excitability is altered in the neuron and conduction of nerve impulses becomes impaired. These substances prevent normal ion exchange of sodium, potassium, and calcium cations (Na^+, K^+, and Ca^{2+}) across the cell membrane, which affects the resting membrane and action potentials. As a result, the central nervous system becomes depressed and can lead to a general anesthetic effect. At low exposures, a feeling of being light-headed, dizziness, and loss of coordination may occur. If exposure continues, unconsciousness can progress to respiratory or cardiac arrest.[2]

Most volatile organic solvents have been shown to produce central nervous system disturbance. Short-term effects include headaches, tiredness, sense of intoxication, drowsiness, dizziness that progresses to unconsciousness. If high exposures persist, convulsions and death can occur. Most of these symptoms are reversible following cessation of short-term exposure to moderate or high doses.[25] Chronic exposure to low concentrations of volatile organic solvents can be much more serious. Usually the first symptoms are nonspecific and difficult to evaluate. Often psychological techniques are used to study long-term effects of solvents on nerve function. Language comprehension, logical and spatial thinking, power of observation, coordination and memory are measured. Some solvents will affect certain functions more than others.[26] See Chapter 16, "Toxicology of Organic Solvents" for a discussion of volatile organic solvents in more detail.

The term, **solvent neurotoxic syndrome**, describes the major symptoms of the central nervous system when affected by exposure to a mixture of volatile organic solvents. They include difficulties in concentration, forgetfulness, headaches, irritability, insensitivity, personality disorders, mental disabilities and suicidal tendencies.[10] This syndrome has also been called painters' syndrome, chronic toxic encephalopathy, or psycho-organic syndrome. Typically, these workers are exposed to a mixture of several solvents at concentrations below currently accepted occupational standards. The threshold limit value (TLV®) applies to exposure involving a single solvent, whereas adverse effects to a mixture of solvents can occur at a level much lower than the individual TLVs®.[4] Neuropsychologic testing in exposed workers has shown a diffuse pattern of performance impairment.[27,28] Chronic toxic encephalopathy, known as "chronic painters' syndrome," was studied in seventy house painters, who were suspected to be suffering from dementia due to organic solvent intoxication.[29] In fifty of the seventy cases no contributing etiological factors could be identified except exposure to organic solvents. Neuropsychological examination showed signs of intellectual impairment in thirty nine painters and neuroradiological examination demonstrated the presence of cerebral atrophy in thirty one painters. The authors of this study concluded that long-term exposure to organic solvents with acute intoxication symptoms may gradually lead to the development of a chronic brain syndrome, which they have called "chronic painters' syndrome." In another study, five former shipyard painters were described who had worked between sixteen and forty five years as industrial painters inside ships.[30] Each individual underwent structured neurological examination, color vision testing, and detailed psychometric testing. An estimation of past organic solvent exposure was completed by obtaining an occupational history. All the painters gave a history of exposure to high concentrations of solvents at work, and several reported episodes of acute **narcosis**. Each individual showed neurological deficits and some had overt neurological disease. The following symptoms constituted a syndrome — acquired blue-yellow color vision deficits, coarse tremor, impaired vibration sensation in the legs and cognitive impairment. Their estimated cumulative exposures to organic solvents ranged between thirteen and thirty-seven years. The authors of this study concluded that chronic exposure to organic solvents can lead to serious neurological diseases in humans.

Compounds that have one or more benzene rings in their structure are aromatic organic solvents and they also have depressant effects on the central nervous system. This group of compounds includes benzene, toluene, and xylene. Toluene slows the speed of perception and reaction time. When toluene or xylene vapors are enhaled in sufficient concentrations, fatigue, mental confusion, headaches, nausea, and dizziness can occur.[2] Toluene is a significant hazard as a drug of abuse. It is used as a solvent in paints, glues, and other household products, and may be abused by "glue sniffers."[3] A study was completed in over seven hundred male printing workers to assess the effects of exposure to mixtures of n-hexane, toluene, isopropyl alcohol, and benzene on neurological symptoms.[31] After controlling for age, smoking, alcohol drinking, past exposure history, working hours and shift work, current exposure to solvent mixtures was significantly associated with the total number of neurological symptoms. Memory loss, abnormal or reduced smell, among other symptoms were increased in the exposed group.

The other group of organic solvents that strongly depress the normal function of the central nervous system is alcohols. Methanol and ethanol are most commonly encountered. Ingestion of fifteen mL of methanol can cause blindness, while ingestion of seventy to one hundred mL may cause death. Initial symptoms include headache, vomiting, abdominal pain, shortness of breath, restlessness, and delirium. Ethanol is the most widely used drug in the U.S. It affects the central nervous system centers that control heart rate and blood pressure, resulting in bradycardia and dilation of the blood vessels. In large acute doses, ethanol can cause cardiac arrest. Symptoms begin with excitation, intoxication, and progress to stupor, hypoglycemia, and coma. Before loss of consciousness, there is a decrease in visual acuity and muscular coordination.

Anticholinesterase Agents

These agents bind directly to the enzyme, acetylcholinesterase, and inhibit it from breaking down acetylcholine. This affects nerves, ganglion, and muscles throughout the body that are stimulated by the neurotransmitter acetylcholine. This results in an increased and prolonged stimulation of the postsynaptic membranes due to the increased amount of acetylcholine. Adbominal cramps, blurred vision, miosis, and increased salivation and sweating are indications of cholinergic excess and are easily reversed by atropine which blocks muscarinic receptors.[4] Also, a compound called **pralidoxime** (2-PAM) helps accelerate the reversal of acetylcholinesterase inhibition.[3] Organophosphate pesticides and carbamate insecticides are the most common anticholinesterase agents.

Organophosphate compounds, which include parathion, malathion, diazinon, soman, sarin, etc., bind tightly to the enzyme.

In the case of parathion, the binding is prolonged, but eventually is reversible. With the nerve gas agents, soman and sarin, the binding is irreversible. The effects continue until new anticholinesterase can be synthesized. See Chapter 26, "Toxicology of Chemical Warfare Agents" for a more detailed discussion of nerve gas agents. Acute and severe organophosphate poisoning is characterized by an increase in secretions—four classic symptoms including salivation, lacrimation, urination, and defecation. These symptoms can progress to muscular twitching, extreme weakness, and paralysis. Paralysis of the diaphragm and chest muscles can cause respiratory arrest and death. As discussed earlier, chronic exposure to organophosphates can cause distal axonopathies that can result in delayed neuropathy. Individuals develop paralysis primarily in the lower legs, and also loss of overall strength. There can also be damage to the spinal cord, leading to symptoms similar to amyotrophic lateral sclerosis (ALS). Chronic exposure to organophosphates can also result in psychiatric changes that may include depression, impaired memory, decreased concentration, nightmares, sleepwalking, and emotional instability.[2]

Carbamate insecticides, which include carbaryl, aldicarb, and sevin, also bind to acetylcholinesterase and inhibit the breakdown of acetylcholine. In this case, the carbamate-enzyme complex is not stable and readily disassociates, resulting in reversible inhibition of acetylcholinesterase. Acute exposure can result in lightheadedness, nausea, vomiting, blurred vision, and muscular weakness. In high exposures convulsions can occur.[2] Although the toxic effects of carbamates are similar to those following organophosphate exposures, the onset of symptoms and the recovery are more rapid, due to the more rapid association and disassociation of the carbamate-enzyme complex.[10]

Adrophonium, neostigmine, and physostigmine competitively inhibit acetylcholinesterase.[20] Chapter 18, "Toxicology of Pesticides" provides additional discussion of organophosphates and carbamates used as pesticides.

Selected Neurologic Disorders Due to Neurotoxins

Carbon Monoxide

This compound is emitted from all sources of incomplete combustion of carbon-containing fuel and is of primary concern as an indoor air pollutant. The neurologic symptoms of carbon monoxide poisoning have been well described[32] and they are related to the levels of carboxyhemoglobin in the blood. Chapter 3, "Mechanisms of Toxicity", provides a detailed discussion of the significance of carboxyhemoglobin formation and its role in adversely affecting highly oxygen dependent tissues, such as the nervous system. At low levels, headache is commonly experienced. There is progression to giddiness, malaise, nausea, weakness, and dyspnea as levels increase. Alertness and consciousness become altered at carboxyhemoglobin levels above 40% to 45%.[33]

In regards to neurotoxicity, there is evidence of behavioral effects at low levels of carboxyhemoglobin (less than 10%), which may occur from tobacco smoking and outdoor air pollution. Experimental studies at less than 5% have inconsistent results. At 5% carboxyhemoglobin level, rapid performance of complex dual tasks are impaired.[34] After acute high level exposure, delayed neuropsychiatric syndromes occur presumably due to delayed demyelination.[35] The clinical characteristics of 86 patients with carbon monoxide-induced delayed neurotoxicity suggested major impairments, with apathy, amnesia, disorientation, irritability, distractibility, and memory deficits.[33,36]

Effects of a single exposure of carbon monoxide on sensory and psychomotor response were measured in two groups of volunteers. Twenty young, healthy male subjects were exposed to a single exposure of 650 ppm carbon monoxide for 45 minutes. Mean carboxyhemoglobin was increased by 7.61%. In another twenty subjects exposed to 950 ppm for 45 minutes, carboxyhemoglobin was increased by 11.22%. Before and after exposures, all subjects were given tests for depth perception, visual discrimination for brightness, reaction time to a visual stimulus, and flicker fusion discrimination. The reaction time test showed a significant mean reduction in both exposure groups.[37]

Dioxins and Related Compounds

There is limited evidence of neurotoxicity from exposures to dioxin and related compounds. However, there are concerns about this possible effect in addition to potential carcinogenesis, immunotoxicity, and developmental and reproductive effects. These toxic effects of exposure to halogenated aromatic hydrocarbons, including polychlorinated dibenzo-p-dioxins (PCDDs), polychlorinated biphenyls (PCBs), and the polychlorinated dibenzofurans (PCDFs) have been summarized.[33,38]

An uncontrolled reaction during the manufacture of 2,3,5-trichloroacetic acid in a chemical manufacturing plant in Seveso, Italy, released large amounts of 2,3,7,8-tetrachlorodibenzo-p-dioxin (TCDD) (dioxin) into the environment. Effects, such as chloracne and hepatomegaly, as well as peripheral and central nervous system symptoms were more common in individuals living near the plant than those living further away.[39] Abnormal nerve conduction studies were documented, but they did not correlate with the occurrence of chloracne. Exposure of the populations in Yusho, Japan, and YuCheng, Taiwan, to PCBs and PCDFs and polychlorinated quaterphenyls (PCQs) resulted in severe multiorgan-system disease. Consumption of food cooked in contaminated rice oil was the source of the PCBs, PCDFs, and PCQs. Sensory polyneuropathy, along with extremity numbness and abnormal nerve conduction velocity testing, were described in exposed individuals.[40]

Studies have shown the potential for occupational dioxin exposure. Concentrations of PCDDs and PCDFs in exhaust gas of an infectious waste incineration plant in Japan, were found to be above the Japanese legal limit value. Blood samples of five workers were collected at one and sixteen months after the end of occupational dioxin exposure. Blood samples were also collected from control subjects. One month after the end of occupational dioxin exposure, the mean toxic equivalents for the workers was 2.7 times as high as that for the controls. At sixteen months, the mean toxic equivalents for the workers decreased and was 1.6 times that for the controls. This study showed that the serum dioxin levels for infectious waste incinerator workers were higher than for the controls.[41] Another study concluded that diverse worker groups were exposed to TCDD during the synthesis of the herbicide 2,4,5-trichlorophenoxyacetic acid (2,4,5-T) from trichlorophenol (TCP).[42]

Dioxins and related compounds are primarily absorbed through the gastrointestinal tract, although absorption through inhalation and percutaneous absorption are possible, especially when the compounds are suspended in a lipophilic vehicle. These compounds are highly fat soluble and are easily stored in body fat and organs with high lipid content, such as the bone marrow, brain, peripheral nerves, liver, and kidneys. The presumed mechanism of action of dioxins and related compounds is related to their common ability to induce hepatic cytochrome P-450 microsomal enzymes, especially aryl hydrocarbon hydroxylase.[33,43]

Summary

The human nervous system has unique structures and functions. It is among the most sensitive anatomical and physiological systems to toxic insult in the body. Toxins that have sufficient lipid solubility to pass through the skin can adversely affect the peripheral and central nervous systems. Airborne toxins that are easily absorbed through the respiratory tract can enter into the bloodstream quickly and have an adverse effect on the central and peripheral nervous systems. Many toxins that are ingested and are absorbed easily through the GI tract get into the blood and gain entry into the nervous system quickly as well. Almost all neurotoxic effects are easily detected because of the primary importance of the nervous system in body functions and in behavior. Chemical exposures at low concentrations can affect the nervous system before the same concentrations have noticeable effects in other systems. Small changes in body functions and behavior controlled by the nervous system can be changed by very small exposures to neurotoxins.

Exposures in the workplace that result in neurotoxicological outcomes continue to be identified. In this chapter, representative toxins have been included in the discussion — acrylamide, carbon disulfide, n-hexane, lead, manganese, mercury, volatile organic solvents, organophosphates, carbon monoxide, dioxins, and several other common compounds.

In general, since nervous tissue does not regenerate readily after injury and certainly not after death, the primary prevention of neurotoxicological effects must be considered essential by the industrial hygienist. Once significant symptoms are produced due to toxic insult to the nervous tissue, treatment options become extremely limited. Additional research is needed to further explain normal neurologic and neuropsychologic functions at the cellular and subcellular levels to provide a better understanding of neuronal function under stressed and diseased states.

This will assist in identifying neurotoxins in the workplace earlier and also provide insight into the development of additional treatment options.

References

1. **The ALS (Amyotrophic Lateral Sclerosis) Association:** The Cells of the Nervous System. http://www.alsa.org/research/article.cfm?print=1&id=823. [Accessed on October 15, 2007].
2. **Kent, C.:** Neurotoxicity. In *Basics of Toxicology*. New York: John Wiley & Sons, Inc., 1998.
3. **Stine, K.E. and T.M. Brown:** Neurotoxicology. In *Principles of Toxicology*. New York: CRC, Lewis Publishers, 1996.
4. **So, Y.T.:** Nervous system. In *Environmental Medicine*. Brooks, S.M., M. Gochfeld, J. Herzstein, R.J. Jackson, and M.B. Schenker (eds.). St. Louis, MO: Mosby-Year Book, Inc., 1995.
5. **Nierenberg, D.W., et al.:** Delayed cerebellar disease and death after accidental exposure to dimethylmercury. *New Eng. J. Med. 338(23)*:1672–1676 (1998).
6. **Weiss, B., T.W. Clarkson, and W. Simon:** Silent latency periods in methylmercury poisoning and in neurodegenerative disease. *Environ. Health Persp. 110(suppl 5)*:851–854 (2002).
7. **Kishi, R., et al.:** Residual neurobehavioural effects associated with chronic exposure to mercury vapour. *Occup. Environ. Med. 51*:35–41 (1994).
8. **Anthony, D.C., T.J. Montine, W.M. Vanentine, and D.G. Graham:** Toxic responses of the nervous system. In *Casarett and Doull's Toxicology—The Basic Science of Poisons*. Klaassen, C.D. (ed.). New York: McGraw-Hill, 2001.
9. **Bast-Pettersen, R., V. Skaug, D. Ellingsen, and Y. Thomassen:** Neurobehavioral performance in aluminum welders. *Am. J. Ind. Med. 37(2)*:184–192 (1999).
10. **Winder, C.:** Occupational toxicology of the nervous system. In *Occupational Toxicology*, 2nd edition. Winder, C., and N. Stacey (eds.). Boca Raton, FL: CRC Press, 2004.
11. **Lu, F.C. and S. Kacew:** Toxicology of the nervous system. In *Lu's Basic Toxicology—Fundamentals, Target Organs, and Risk Assessment*, 4th edition. New York: Taylor & Francis, 2002.
12. **Fouch, D.W.:** Cellulube update. In *Fathom*. Norfolk, VA: Naval Safety Center, 1979. pp. 18–21.
13. **Mullick, F.G.:** Hexachlorophene toxicity: Human experience at the AFIP. *Pediatrics 51*:395–399 (1973).
14. **Dabrowska-Bouta, G., et al.:** Chronic lead intoxication affects the myelin membrane status in the central nervous system of adult rats. *J. Mol. Neurosci. 13*:127–139 (1999).
15. **Lindgren, K.N., V.L. Masten, D.P. Ford, and M.L. Bleecker:** Relation of cumulative exposure to inorganic lead and neuropsychological test performance. *Occup. Environ. Med. 53*:472–477 (1996).

16. **Kovala, T., et al.:** Effects of low level exposure to lead on neurophysiological functions among lead battery workers. *Occup. Environ. Med.* 54:487–493 (1997).
17. **Fiedler, N., et al.:** Cognitive effects of chronic exposure to lead and solvents. *Am. J. Ind. Med.* 44(4):413–423 (2003).
18. **Needleman, H.L, and C.A. Gatsonis:** Low level lead exposure and the IQ of children. A meta analysis of modern studies. *JAMA* 263:673–678 (1990).
19. **Needleman, H.L.:** Childhood lead poisoning. *Curr. Opin. Neurol.* 7:187–190 (1994).
20. **Malachowski, M.J. and A.F. Goldberg:** Target Organ Effects. In *Health Effects of Toxic Substances*. Rockville, MD: Government Institutes, Inc., 1995.
21. **Benowitz, N.L.:** Clinical pharmacology of nicotine. *Annu. Rev. Med.* 37:21–32 (1986).
22. **Giros, B., et al.:** Hyperlocomotion and indifference to cocaine and amphetamine in mice lacking the dopamine transporter. *Nature* 379:606–612 (1996).
23. **Filley, C.M. and J.P. Kelly:** Alcohol- and drug-related neurotoxicity. *Curr. Opin. Neurol. Neurosurg.* 6:443–447 (1993).
24. **Wison, J.M., et al.:** Striatal dopamine, dopamine transporter, and vesicular monoamine transporter in chronic cocaine users. *Ann. Neurol.* 40:428–439 (1996).
25. **U.S. Environmental Protection Agency (EPA):** *Indoor Air Health: Neurotoxic Effects of a Controlled Exposure to a Complex Mixture of Volatile Organic Compounds*. Research Triangle Park, NC: EPA, 1990.
26. **World Health Organization (WHO):** *Organic Solvents and the Central Nervous System*. Environmental Health 5. Copenhagen, Denmark: WHO, 1985.
27. **Grasso, P., et al.:** Neurophysiological and psychological disorders and occupational exposure to organic solvents. *Food Chem. Toxicol.* 10:819–852 (1984).
28. **Lindstrom, K.:** Behavioral effects of long-term exposure to organic solvents. *Acta. Neurol. Scand.* 66(suppl 92):131–141 (1982).
29. **Arlien-Soborg, P., P. Bruhn, C. Gyldensted, and B. Melgaard:** Chronic painters' syndrome. Chronic toxic encephalopathy in house painters. *Acta. Neurol. Scand.* 60(3):149–156 (1979).
30. **Dick, F., S. Semple, R. Chen, and A. Seaton:** Neurological deficits in solvent-exposed painters: a syndrome including impaired colour vision, cognitive defects, tremor and loss of vibration sensation. *Q. J. Med.* 93:655–661 (2000).
31. **Yu, I.T., et al.:** Occupational exposure to mixtures of organic solvents increases the risk of neurological symptoms among printing workers in Hong Kong. *Journal of Occupational & Environmental Medicine* 46(4):323–330, 2004.
32. **Dinman, B.D.:** The management of carbon monoxide intoxication. *J. Occup. Med.* 16:662 (1974).
33. **Linz, D.H. and D.H. Garling:** Toxicology of selected neurotoxic agents. In *Environmental Medicine*. Brooks, S.M., M. Gochfeld, J. Herzstein, R.J. Jackson, and M.B. Schenker (eds). St. Louis, MO: Mosby-Year Book, Inc., 1995.
34. **Anger, W.K. and B.L. Johnson:** Chemicals affect behavior. In *Neurotoxicity of Industrial Chemicals*, Volume 1. O'Donoghue, J.L. (ed.). Boca Raton, FL: CRC Press, 1985.
35. **Remick, R.A. and J.E. Miles:** Carbon monoxide poisoning: neurologic and psychiatric sequelae. *Can. Med. Assoc. J.* 117:654 (1977).
36. **Min, S.K.:** A brain syndrome associated with delayed neuropsychiatric sequelae following acute carbon monoxide intoxication. *Acta. Psychiatr. Scand.* 73:80 (1986).
37. **Ramsey, J.M.:** Effects of single exposures of carbon monoxide on sensory and psychomotor response. *Am. Ind. Hyg. Assoc. J.* 34(5):212–216 (1973).
38. **Rosenman, K.D.:** Dioxin, polychlorinated biphenyls, and dibenzofurans. In *Environmental and Occupational Medicine,* 2nd edition. Rom, W.N. (ed.). Boston, MA: Little & Brown, 1992.
39. **Pocchiari, F., V. Silano, and A. Zampieri:** Human health effects from accidental release of tetrachlorodibenzo-p-dioxin (TCDD) at Seveso, Italy. *Ann. NY Acad. Sci. 320*:311 (1979).
40. **Chen, R.C., et al.:** Polychlorinated biphenyl poisoning: correlation of sensory and motor nerve conduction, neurologic symptoms, and blood levels of polychlorinated biphenyls, quaterphenyls and dibenzofurans. *Environ. Res.* 37:340 (1985).
41. **Kumagai, S. and S. Koda:** Polychlorinated dibenzo-p-dioxin and dibenzofuran concentrations in serum samples of workers at an infectious waste incineration plant in Japan. *J. Occup. Environ. Hyg.* 2(2):120–125 (2005).
42. **Moody, L., W.E. Halperin, M.A. Fingerhut, and P.J. Landrigan:** The chronic health effects of occupational exposure to dioxin: Unanswered questions. *Am. J. Ind. Med.* 5(3):57–160 (1984).
43. **Nessel, C.S., and M.A. Gallo:** Dioxins and related compounds. In *Environmental Toxicants: Human Exposures and Their Health Effects*. M. Lippmann, M. (ed.). New York: Van Nostrand Reinhold, 1992.

Chapter 10

Hepatic Toxicology

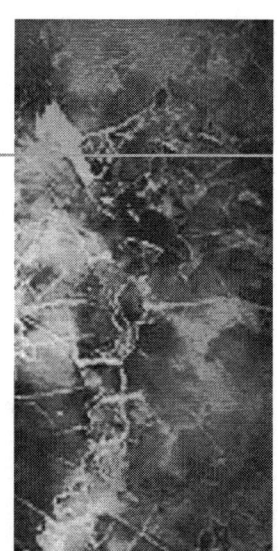

By Angela J. Harris, PhD, DABT

Introduction

The potential for some chemicals to cause liver toxicity in workers was originally recognized in those employees who used these chemicals more frequently or at higher concentrations than other workers. Industrial hygienists and other workplace safety professionals were often the first to link reports of employee illness with a specific work assignment or chemical exposure. The subsequent institution of workplace practices that reduced or eliminated such exposures led to a decrease in occupational liver toxicity. Timely intervention in the workplace has even been known to reduce wartime casualties.

For instance, shortly before the beginning of WWI, eight German workers in an airplane factory were employed to waterproof the linen on airplane wings by applying a varnish of cellulose acetate dissolved in 1,1,2,2-tetrachloroethane (1,1,2,2-TCA). The solution, called "dope", contained 30–50% 1,1,2,2-TCA[1] and was used to increase tautness, resilience, and water resistance of the wing fabric. Four of the eight workers applying dope developed jaundice and one died.[2] As a result, Germany banned the use of 1,1,2,2-TCA shortly before war broke out. However, in England, the first cases of liver damage due to airplane "doping" were not reported until the Fall of 1914 when 19 workers developed jaundice in an airplane manufacturing facility in Hendon.[1] Four workers died. One became ill and died after being employed as a doper for only 11 weeks. Upon autopsy, the coroner found "a shrunken liver" and the Medical Inspector of Factories, Dr. T.M. Legge, opined "that the condition of the liver might be connected with the action of some poison to which the deceased was exposed during life."[1] A total of 70 cases of liver toxicity including 12 deaths associated with airplane doping were reported in England by 1917.[3] 1,1,2,2-TCA was soon banned from airplane dope in England, as well as in several other countries. In an address to the Medical Society of London, Dr. Willcox stated:

> "The outbreak of war naturally caused greatly increased activity in these factories, and the workers were employed overtime, so that any toxic influences to which they might be exposed in their work would be greatly increased."[1]

Outcome Competencies

Upon completion of reading this chapter the reader should be able to:
- Understand basic liver structure and function.
- Know the primary types of liver injury that may occur due to occupational exposure to hepatotoxicants.
- Know examples of specific occupational hepatotoxicants discovered due to workplace exposures.

Prerequisite Knowledge

The reader should have an understanding of basic anatomy and physiology, chemistry, cell biology and industrial hygiene practices.

Key Terms

Antigen, apoptosis, bile, bile duct, bilirubin, bioactivation, canaliculi, cholestasis, cirrhosis, direct bilirubin, endothelial cell, extracellular matrix, fibrosis, free radical, hepatic, hepatitis, hepatocytes, hepatomegaly, hepatotoxicant, hypoxic, Ito cells, Kupffer cells, microhepatica, necrosis, oncosis, parenchyma, phagocytose, reactive metabolite, reactive oxygen species (ROS), sinusoid, stellate, total bilirubin, toxicant, toxin, xenobiotics

Key Topics

1. Basic Liver Structure and Function
   - Key Liver Cell Types
   - Major Liver Functions
2. Major Types of Liver Injury Caused by Workplace Chemicals
   - Liver Cell Death and Fatty Liver
   - Immune Mediated Damage
   - Cirrhosis/Fibrosis
   - Biliary Damage
   - Cancer
   - Complexity of Liver Damage

This is a classic example of recognition of chemical toxicity due to a substantial increase in chemical exposure because of the nature of the job (application of dope to the wing) and/or increased time on the job (longer working hours, increased production of planes).

Basic Liver Structure and Function

The liver is located in the upper right quadrant of the abdomen, beneath the diaphragm and weighs about three pounds in most humans. It is the second largest organ of the human body and performs a myriad of metabolic and cellular functions that affect nearly every other organ system. Life is not possible without a functioning liver. Unlike many other major organs, the liver is capable of regenerating itself even after significant loss of tissue. The phenomenon of liver regeneration has been known for centuries and is even recognized in Greek mythology. In this classic story, Prometheus was punished for stealing fire and giving it to man by being chained to a mountain. There, an eagle came and ate Promethius' liver, however, each day his liver grew back, only to be eaten again by the eagle.

The liver is basically a chemical and biological filter between what a person eats and what circulates throughout the body. All of the blood from the intestinal tract, spleen and pancreas is delivered to the liver by the portal vein (Figure 10.1). Xenobiotics may also enter the blood stream via inhalation and dermal absorption (See Chapter 4, "Disposition of Toxicants"). Venous blood from the gut percolates through the liver before exiting through the hepatic (central) vein. Almost one third of the total body volume of blood is filtered through the liver every minute, and about 75% of that is venous blood from the portal vein. The liver is therefore able to extract and process absorbed nutrients and xenobiotics from the blood. Xenobiotics are foreign substances not produced by the body (i.e. drugs, some chemicals). These compounds are metabolized by enzymes that are particularly abundant in the liver into substances that are more water soluble and therefore more easily eliminated. Xenobiotics may also be metabolized into much more toxic compounds by these enzymes. This makes the liver particularly susceptible to toxicity from xenobiotics.

Key Liver Cell Types
Hepatocytes

Hepatocytes are the major cell type found in the liver and make up about 70–80% of liver cellular mass. Hepatocytes perform many of the liver functions discussed later in this chapter and hence are called liver parenchymal cells. By definition, the parenchymal cell is one that has the characteristics of the tissue or organ. Hepatocyte functions include protein synthesis and storage; synthesis of bile salts, cholesterol and phospholipids; and metabolism and elimination of endogenous and exogenous substrates (xenobiotics). Hepatocytes have some rather unusual cellular features. Since hepatocytes are extremely active in protein synthesis and secretion, they have an extensive network of both rough and smooth endoplasmic reticulum. In addition, a large percentage of hepatocytes are binucleate (have two nuclei) or contain multiple copies of nuclear DNA in one nucleus (polyploidy). This plays a critical role in rapid regeneration of liver mass.

Organization of Hepatocytes

Hepatocytes in the liver are arranged in long cords with tight junctions between adjacent cells to prevent substances in the blood from leaking into extracellular space. Two concepts, the lobule and the acinus, have been proposed to describe the arrangement of hepatocytes as a functional unit (Figure 10.2). The acinus is considered superior to the lobule concept as a functional model, however lobule terminology will be used mainly in this chapter since it has been used in some of the historical examples of occupational exposure to hepatoxicants discussed in the following sections. Where possible the corresponding acinar terminology is also included.

A lobule consists of cords of hepatocytes interspersed with blood filled sinusoids. Poorly oxygenated blood from a branch of the portal vein is mixed with oxygenated blood from the hepatic artery as it enters the lobule. Together, the branch of the portal vein, the hepatic artery and a nearby bile duct are called the portal triad. The blood flows from the portal triad, percolates past the hepatocytes and eventually exits the lobule via the hepatic vein, sometimes called the central vein (Figure 10.3).

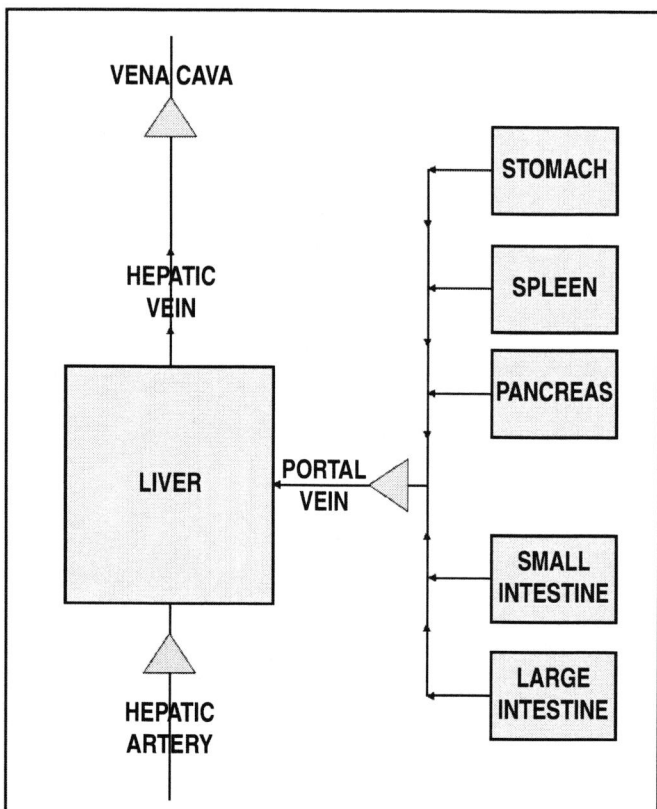

Figure 10.1 — The liver as a filter. Schematic of blood flow from the gut into the liver before entry into systemic circulation via the vena cava.

Hepatocytes nearest the portal triad are more oxygenated and nutrient-rich than most distal hepatocytes since they lie nearer the oxygen-rich arterial blood supply of the hepatic arteriole and the nutrient-rich blood from the hepatic vein. Oxygen and nutrients are increasingly depleted by the metabolically active hepatocytes as blood moves through the sinusoid. Therefore, there is less oxygen available for hepatocytes located near the hepatic vein. These hepatocytes are more hypoxic (lacking oxygen) than those located near the hepatic artery. Gradients in oxygenation have important implications physiologically and hepatocytes are often described based on their location (lobule concept) or zone (acinar concept) to specify hepatocytes in particular cellular environments. Hepatocytes nearest the portal triad are known as periportal (Zone 1) hepatocytes, those near the center of the cord are called midzonal (Zone 2) hepatocytes, and hepatocytes nearest the hepatic vein are referred to as centrilobular (Zone 3).

Differential Hepatocyte Function

Functional gradients in hepatocytes based on their location in the lobule have also been reported. For instance, centrilobular hepatocytes contain more cytochrome P450 (CYP450) enzymes which play an important role in the metabolism and elimination of xenobiotics. In some cases, metabolism of a xenobiotic may produce a metabolite that is more reactive and therefore more toxic than the parent molecule. This is called bioactivation. Centrilobular hepatocytes are often most vulnerable to the toxic effect of chemicals activated by CYP450 enzymes since they have the greatest capacity to produce the toxic metabolite. For instance, the highest levels of CYP2E1, a CYP450 enzyme that bioactivates carbon tetrachloride (CC_{l4}), are found in centrilobular hepatocytes.[4] Indeed, CC_{l4} toxicity is characterized by massive cell death of centrilobular hepatocytes.

Endothelial Cells

Sinusoids are blood vessels that are interspersed between cords of hepatocytes. (Figure 10.3). Sinusoids are lined with a discontinuous layer of endothelial cells such that large fenestrae, or pores, are present. Fenestrae facilitate the movement of certain substances (smaller than 250 Kda) and fluids between blood and hepatocytes. The area between endothelial cells and hepatocytes is called the space of Disse (Figure 10.3). Endothelial cells play an important role as scavengers and have been shown to efficiently extract lipoproteins, connective tissue components, glycoproteins and denatured proteins from blood.[5] There is also evidence that endothelial cells play an important role in control of immune responses.[6]

Kupffer Cells

Also present in the sinusoids are resident macrophages, the Kupffer cells. About 80% of the total resident macrophages in the body are present in the liver. The primary function of macrophages is to ingest (phagocytose) and degrade foreign microorganisms and particulate. Therefore, their role is protective.

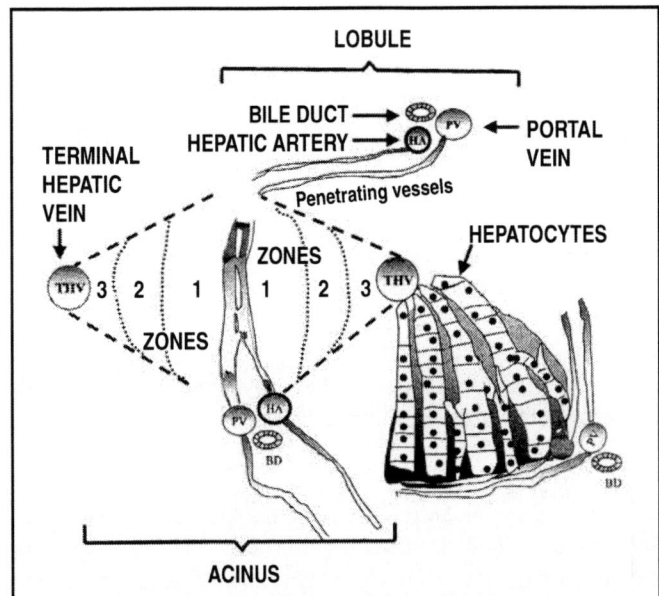

Figure 10.2 — The acinus and lobule, functional units of the liver. In the lobule concept, venous and arterial blood enters the lobule from the portal triad located at the corners of the lobule, and flows past hepatocytes to the terminal hepatic vein (central vein) at the center of the lobule. The most oxygenated hepatocytes are the periportal hepatocytes near the portal triad. In the acinus, blood from the portal vein and hepatic artery flows along the midline of the acinus before exiting through the terminal hepatic vein. The most heavily oxygenated hepatocytes in the acinus are those in Zone 1. (Reprinted from Casarett and Doull: Toxicology, the Basic Science of Poisons, Vol. 6: Toxic Responses of the Liver. New York, McGraw-Hill Medical Publishing Division, 2001.)

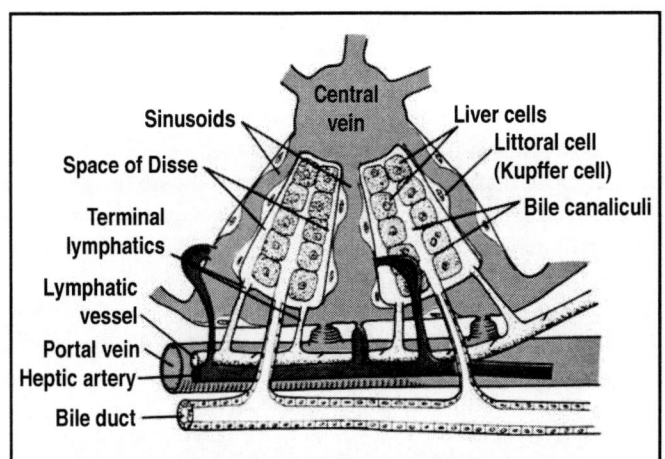

Figure 10.3 — Major organization of the lobule. This schematic shows the structural relationship of the portal vein, hepatic artery and bile duct (portal triad) to hepatocyte cords in the lobule. Also shown are the bile canaliculi, where bile is excreted by hepatocytes and moved toward the bile duct. The sinusoids are blood vessels though which blood flows toward the central vein located at the top of the figure. (Reprinted from Guyton, Taylor, and Granger [as modified from Elias]: Circulatory Physiology, Vol. 2: Dynamics and Control of the Body Fluids. Philadelphia, W.B. Saunders Company, 1975.)

However, Kupffer cells, once activated (e.g. by vitamin A, endotoxin etc.) can actually increase the extent of liver damage caused by some industrial hepatotoxicants by releasing high levels of reactive oxygen species (ROS).[7] Activated Kupffer cells also secrete cytokines which can stimulate or exacerbate an inflammatory response.

Ito Cells

Ito cells reside in the sinusoid, and are generally located in the Space of Disse. Also called "stellate" or "fat-storing" cells, Ito cells are the major site of vitamin A storage in the body. When significant liver toxicity occurs, Ito cells may be transformed to a more "fibroblast-like" cell and begin synthesizing massive amounts of extracellular matrix (ECM) components including collagens and proteoglycan.[8] Replacement of damaged hepatocytes with ECM by activated Ito cells can ultimately lead to fibrosis.

Major Liver Functions

The normal physiological functions performed by the liver make it a primary target organ for chemically induced toxicity. It is therefore important that industrial hygienists have an understanding of basic liver function as well as the major mechanisms by which chemicals in the workplace can disrupt normal hepatic processes.

Bile Formation

Bile is a greenish yellow alkaline fluid composed primarily of bile salts (e.g. deoxycholate, taurocholate), cholesterol and phospholipids. The human liver can produce up to one liter of bile per day. Bile may either flow into the intestine or be stored in the gallbladder where it can be concentrated up to five-fold. Bile plays a critical role in efficient digestion and uptake of lipids from the intestine. If bile is absent, fat cannot be digested and is excreted in the feces. Individuals with significant hepatotoxicity may therefore experience diarrhea due to the presence of excreted fat. Bile also plays a role in the excretion and elimination of many endogenous and xenobiotic substances. An important example is bilirubin. Bilirubin is a by-product of hemoglobin degradation that occurs during the normal turnover of red blood cells. The bilirubin released from this process is transported to the blood where it is carried to the liver bound to serum albumin. Bilirubin is then absorbed by hepatocytes where it is dissociated from albumin and conjugated with glutathione. Conjugated bilirubin is excreted by hepatocytes into the bile canaliculi and transported to the intestine in bile. There some bilirubin is excreted in feces, which gives feces the characteristic brown color and some bilirubin is reabsorbed and transported back to the liver. About 5% is excreted in urine. Hepatotoxicity that results in decreased excretion of bilirubin from hepatocytes or impairs transport of bilirubin from the liver may lead to the accumulation of excess bilirubin in extracellular fluids. This is the cause of jaundice seen with significant liver toxicity.

Synthesis and Secretion

Bile acids are synthesized from cholesterol by hepatocytes and then excreted into enlarged spaces called bile caniculi (Figure 10.3). Caniculi contents are prevented from entering the sinusoid by tight junctions between adjacent hepatocytes. The flow of bile in the lobule is opposite to that of blood flow. Bile from the caniculi moves toward the portal triad enters the common bile duct and empties into the duodenum to assist with digestion or is stored in the gall bladder.

Enterohepatic Circulation

About 95% of bile deposited in the intestine is reabsorbed via the portal vein and transported back to liver where it is efficiently extracted by hepatocytes, transported back into the caniculi and then re-deposited in the intestine. This process is called enterohepatic circulation. Bile is re-used very efficiently and as a consequence very little bile is detected in systemic circulation in healthy humans. As discussed above, bilirubin is efficiently recovered and reused via enterohepatic recycling. Enterohepatic recycling also plays an important role in the toxicity of some metals. For instance, methylmercury absorbed from the intestinal tract is transported to the liver where it is secreted into the bile and released back in the intestinal tract. At sufficiently high concentrations, the cycle can be repeated many times, increasing the half-life of methylmercury in the body.

Metabolism

The liver is the primary site for metabolism of endogenous substances and xenobiotics in the body. Hepatocytes carry out a large number of chemical reactions that involve multiple metabolic pathways and play a key role in biotransformation of xenobiotics. Biotransformation pathways are categorized as Phase I or Phase II reactions. Absorbed xenobiotics are transported to the liver through the portal vein, however the most easily absorbed molecules are lipophilic or water-insoluble. These properties make them difficult for the body to eliminate so lipophilic xenobiotics must first be metabolized to more water-soluble substances in order to favor elimination.

Phase I Metabolism

Phase I reactions introduce a functional group such as a hydroxyl group (-OH), a carboxyl group (-COOH), an amine group ($-NH_2$) or a thiol (-SH) onto the molecule. Although these reactions often result in only a marginal increase in water solubility, they may expose or create functional groups that can then be acted upon by Phase II enzymes. The major enzymes in Phase I biotransformation reactions are members of the CYP450 superfamily. Although these enzymes are present in tissues throughout the body, they are present at particularly high levels in the liver. These enzymes are further sub-classified based on genetic similarity. Examples important in hepatotoxicity include those in the sub-families of CYP2E (CYP2E1) and CYP3A.

Phase II Metabolism

Metabolism by Phase II enzymes usually results in a large increase in the water solubility of a xenobiotic, greatly facilitating elimination in the urine or the feces. These reactions include sulfation, glucuronidation, methylation, and acetylation as well as conjugation reactions with glutathione or amino acids (glutamic acid, glycine and taurine). For instance, as mentioned previously in this chapter, the excretion of bilirubin is enhanced by conjugation with glutathione. Phase II reactions are not always preceded by Phase I.

Nutrient Homeostasis

It is not surprising that the liver plays a pivotal role in maintaining nutrient homeostasis given its location between absorbed nutrients from the gut and systemic circulation. Among those roles is storage of certain vitamins and minerals, and integrated metabolism of carbohydrates, lipids and amino acids. Toxicity may occur when nutrient homeostasis is altered to the extent that critical cellular needs are not met.

Storage

Several important substances are stored in the liver until needed, including blood, certain vitamins and iron. Iron is actively scavenged by Kupffer cells. When excess iron is present, it binds with apoferritin, an iron binding protein present in high levels in hepatic cells. When blood iron levels drop, iron is released from storage in the liver into the system circulation. Therefore, the liver acts both to maintain homeostasis of circulating iron as well as to store excess iron. When iron is present at levels that exceed the storage capacity of the liver, liver toxicity may occur. Iron toxicity is first seen in periportal (Zone 1) hepatocytes since they are nearest the site of iron uptake and have the highest level of oxygenation. Iron in the presence of oxygen releases ROS which initiate destructive processes in cellular lipids leading to toxicity.

The liver also stores vitamins A, D and B_{12}. Ito cells are the primary storage site for vitamin A. This property also makes Ito cells the first liver cell type to be adversely affected by vitamin A toxicity.

The liver has an incredible storage capacity for blood. Under normal conditions, the liver contains about 10% of the body's total blood volume in the sinusoids and hepatic veins. However, the liver is a tremendous reservoir and can store an additional 500–1000 mL if necessary.

Metabolism
  Carbohydrates

Blood glucose levels are tightly regulated within a relatively narrow range. The liver plays a pivotal role in maintaining normal serum glucose over both short and long periods of time. Immediately after eating a meal, serum glucose levels dramatically increase. Excess glucose is taken up by the liver and stored as glycogen in a process called glycogenesis. When serum glucose levels drop, glucose is mobilized from stored hepatic glycogen (glycogenolysis) and exported back into the blood for systemic circulation. If glycogen stores are depleted through fasting or starvation, the liver is capable of synthesizing glucose from other nutrient sources like amino acids and glycerol from triglycerides (gluconeogenesis) or conversion from other carbohydrate molecules such as fructose or galactose.

  Lipids

Most lipoproteins are synthesized in the liver. The primary function of lipoproteins is to transport other lipids or fats in the bloodstream. Examples are low density lipoproteins (LDL) that transport cholesterol out of the liver to other cells and high density lipoproteins (HDL) that sequester cholesterol from the cells in other tissues and transport it back to the liver. In addition to lipoproteins, the liver synthesizes cholesterol. These molecules are important structural components of cell and intercellular membranes, and are also precursors for the synthesis of other molecules. For instance, about 80% of synthesized cholesterol is used in the production of bile acids by hepatocytes. The liver is also the primary site where excess carbohydrates and proteins are converted to fat which is transported to adipose cells and stored. Lastly, oxidation of triglycerides to acetylcoenzyme A (acetyl-CoA) for energy production occurs at a very high rate. Acetyl-CoA that is not needed by the liver is converted into acetoacetic acid which is released by hepatic cells into the extracellular fluid and absorbed by other tissues for use.

  Amino Acids

Amino acids must be deaminated before being converted to fat and most deamination occurs in hepatic cells. In addition, the liver uses deaminated amino acids for synthesis of the non-essential amino acids, lipids and glucose.

Synthesis of Macromolecules
  Protein Synthesis

Hepatocytes synthesize about 90% of plasma proteins. An example is albumin which acts as a transport molecule for many substances carried in the blood. Most of the major clotting proteins, such as Factor VII, fibrinogen and prothrombin are also synthesized in the liver. Therefore, massive loss of functional liver tissue can cause uncontrolled hemorrhage due to lack of the necessary clotting factors. Interestingly, depletion of clotting factors has been shown to be a signal for liver growth and regeneration.[9] Significant liver toxicity can result in reduction of circulating plasma proteins due to loss of functioning hepatocytes. Therefore, some liver function tests are based on measurement of serum proteins.

  Urea Synthesis

Large amounts of ammonia are produced in the body due to normal biological processes such as deamination of amino acids mentioned above. In addition, some ammonia is formed in the gut by resident bacteria. The liver converts ammonia to urea which is excreted in urine. Individuals with liver failure can accumulate high levels of ammonia in the brain due to disruption of hepatic function. This has been hypothesized to contribute to development of hepatic encephalopathy in patients with liver failure.

Table 10.1 — Normal values for commonly used serum liver enzyme tests.

Test	Normal Values	End Point
Alanine aminotransferase (ALT)	10 – 55 U/L	Hepatocellular necrosis
Aspartate aminotransferase (AST)	10 – 40 U/L	Hepatocellular necrosis
Alkaline phosphatase (AP)	45 – 115 U/L	Cholestasis
5-Nucleotidase (5'-NUC)	0 – 11 U/L	Cholestasis
Bilirubin	0.0 – 1.0 mg/dL	Cholestasis
Gamma glutamyl transpeptidase (GGTP)	0 – 30 U/L	Cholestasis

Evaluating Liver Damage

Liver function tests (LFTs) are a panel of blood tests used clinically and in research to evaluate or monitor liver function. As a rule, LFTs are not performed routinely in an occupational setting, but may be appropriate under certain circumstances such as an accidental release of a liver toxicant or the presence of symptoms of liver toxicity in several workers working in the same environment. Symptoms suggesting liver toxicity may include jaundice, nausea, fatigue and upper abdominal pain.

Liver Function Tests

Measurement of liver enzymes and other proteins in the serum are commonly used tests to assess liver function. The most frequently used tests are alanine transaminase (ALT), aspartate transaminase (AST), albumin (Alb), alkaline phosphatase (AP), total bilirubin (TBIL) and gamma glutamyl transpeptidase (GGTP). ALT and AST were formerly known as serum glutamic pyruvic transaminase (SGPT) and serum glutamic oxaloacetic transaminase (SGOT), respectively. Normal serum levels are shown in Table 10.1.

Hepatocyte Cell Death

ALT and AST are intracellular enzymes that are produced by hepatocytes. Thus, elevated levels of ALT and AST in the serum indicate hepatocellular damage sufficient to cause leakage of intracellular enzymes into the blood. Unfortunately serum aminotransferases levels do not correlate well with the degree of liver damage and may not be increased even in individuals with significant liver damage. AST is produced by cardiac and skeletal muscle cells as well as hepatocytes, so serum AST levels may be elevated after vigorous physical activity in the absence of liver damage or toxicity.

Total bilirubin (TBIL) is also used to evaluate liver function. High total bilirubin levels in combination with normal direct (conjugated) bilirubin is indicative of a deficiency in bilirubin metabolism by hepatocytes. This could be a result of any toxic effects that reduce the uptake, conjugation and/or secretion of bilirubin by damaged hepatocytes.

Altered Biliary Function

AP has widespread tissue distribution, although serum levels are thought to be primarily from bone and liver. GGTP, an enzyme synthesized in both hepatocytes and biliary epithelial cells, is often used in conjunction with AP to differentiate between elevated bone AP and liver AP. Increased hepatic AP is usually associated with biliary system damage. Elevated serum AP can be caused by increased synthesis and release of AP or by accumulation of bile acids because of biliary obstruction. Bile acids can also damage cellular membranes, releasing intracellular AP. Hepatic 5'-nucleotidase is found in canalicular and sinusoidal plasma membranes. Like AP, elevated serum 5'-nucleotidase is indicative of biliary damage.

Elevated direct bilirubin suggests biliary obstruction of some type since bilirubin is being conjugated by the liver but is not being excreted.

Protein Synthesis

As mentioned previously, the liver synthesizes and secretes about 90% of serum proteins. Decreased levels of serum proteins may therefore be indicative of chronic and/or massive liver failure. For instance, serum albumin is a highly abundant protein produced by the liver which can be used as a marker of the liver's ability to synthesize proteins. Similarly, measuring prothrombin time (the time for blood to clot) can also be used to assess protein synthesis capacity. Prolonged prothrombin time suggests that insufficient clotting factors are present in the serum for the blood to clot normally.

Dye Clearance Measurement

Dye clearance tests are used to quantify liver toxicity based on clearance of the dye from the circulation. Hepatocytes preferentially absorb these dyes which are then excreted unchanged in the bile. As they are absorbed by hepatocytes, the dyes are removed from systemic blood circulation. Therefore, decreased dye clearance indicates loss of functioning hepatocytes and as a consequence, reduced bile formation (cholestasis). The two most commonly used dyes are sulfobromophthalein (BSP) and indocyanin green (ICG). To perform the test, a measured quantity of dye is administered by intravenous injection. Blood samples are removed at timed intervals, the quantity of dye remaining is measured and the clearance rate is calculated.

Major Types of Liver Injury Caused by Workplace Chemicals

Introduction

The mechanisms of liver toxicity described in the following sections are focused on workplace exposures to industrial chemicals. However, the industrial hygienist should be aware that many classic hepatotoxicants are not in fact industrial chemicals, but drugs or natural toxins. For example, acetaminophen and alcohol are two of the best characterized liver toxicants. Liver toxicity is the most common reason for drug recall in the United States. So there is considerable literature describing the mechanism of liver toxicity from certain drugs, including acetaminophen. Drug-induced liver toxicity should always be considered when evaluating potential cases of hepatic damage in the workplace. Nonetheless, a number of industrial chemicals also have the potential to cause some degree of liver toxicity in workers. The ACGIH TLV®-TWA for 107 chemicals is based at least in part on avoiding liver toxicity. Unlike exposure to drugs, most occupational exposures to hepatotoxicants occur mainly by skin absorption or inhalation. Therefore discussion of chemical toxicity in this chapter will be focused primarily on dermal and inhalation exposure routes.

Liver Cell Death and Fatty Liver
Cell Death (Apoptosis and Necrosis)

There are two types of cell death, apoptosis and necrosis. Apoptosis, also called programmed cell death, occurs in response to cellular signals that initiate specific death pathways. Apoptosis is basically cellular suicide. Apoptotic cells have a very different appearance than necrotic cells. Apoptotic cells shrink, the nucleus condenses and then fragments. Small bud-like "apoptotic bodies" pinch off the cells and are ingested by Kupffer cells. There is very little if any cellular debris and no leaking of intracellular contents. As a result, there is no inflammatory response associated with apoptosis. The role of apoptosis in liver toxicity is a growing area of research, although its relevance for most hepatotoxicants is not yet known.[10]

In contrast to apoptotic cells, necrotic cells swell. Plasma membranes lose integrity allowing leakage of intracellular liver enzymes which may become detectable in serum (ALT etc). Necrotic cells release chemical signals that attract an influx of inflammatory cells. Hepatitis is the general term used for an influx of inflammatory cells associated with cellular necrosis. There are three main patterns of necrotic death; focal, zonal and panacinar. Focal death is the death of just a few cells in a defined area. Zonal suggests that centrilobular, midzonal or periportal cells are preferentially targeted. Zonal death usually occurs when toxicity is a consequence of zonal gradients in metabolic activity. A good example of zonal death is the centrilolobular (Zone 3) necrosis seen in the livers of animals and humans exposed to toxic levels of CCl_4. Panacinar cell death is massive cell death affecting large numbers of hepatocytes as well as other liver cells. Very few if any live cells are apparent in panacinar death.

Fatty Liver (Steatosis)

Steatosis is characterized by an increase in hepatic lipid content and is often seen in conjunction with hepatocellular necrosis. Steatosis is readily visible as round vesicles of fat that fill the cytoplasm of hepatocytes, often displacing the nucleus to the periphery of the cell (Figure 10.4). Steatosis, although not necrosis, is frequently reversible once exposure stops. It is not known if steatosis directly causes hepatocyte injury, however steatosis is clearly a marker of potential hepatotoxicity.

Carbon Tetrachloride

Carbon tetrachloride (CCl_4) is a heavy, non-flammable liquid with a sweet odor that most people can smell at about 10–21 ppm. Historically, CCl_4 has been widely used in the dry-cleaning industry, in the manufacture of refrigerants and as a degreaser. CCl_4 was also used in some fire extinguishers, particularly those made by Pyrene for use on electrical fires, or in automobiles, airplanes and ships (Figure 10.5). Current uses of CCl_4 still include the manufacture of refrigerants and plastic-foam blowing agents although its use is being gradually phased out as suitable replacements are found.

Case Study

Admittedly, finding a way to clean your greasy, oily clothes when working on a military ship could be difficult. In 1943, a group of French sailors on a Fighting French submarine depot ship found that the contents of the 'Pyrene' fire extinguishers on board did an excellent job cleaning their clothes.[11] This was not surprising since the extinguishers contained almost pure CCl_4. The sailors used about 4 pints in a relatively small room over the space of 3 months. Several individuals reported headache, malaise and vomiting which at the time was thought to be flu. One man had to be hospitalized due to sudden onset of seizures. The man later died from complications of renal toxicity that was later attributed to his use of CCl_4 to clean his clothes. Although

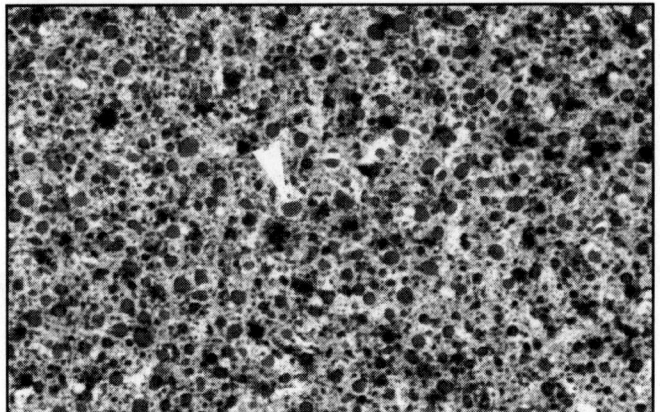

Figure 10.4 — Steatosis of the liver. The fat globules in this section of rat liver can be seen as prominent dark round spheres within the hepatocytes (Photo courtesy of Dr. Martin Ronis and Dr. January Schultz, Arkansas Children's Hospital Research Institute, Little Rock, AR. 72202).

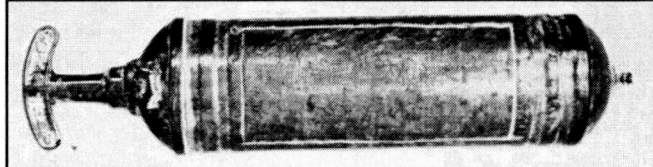

Figure 10.5 — Pyrene fire extinguisher. (Reprinted from Hunter: The Diseases of Occupations, Vol 6: The Aliphatic Carbon Compounds. London, Hodder and Stoughton, 1978.)

there had been no clinical evidence of liver toxicity, extensive centrilobular necrosis of the liver was found upon autopsy.

As early as 1939, it was reported that the most common symptoms following acute or chronic carbon tetrachloride exposure in humans was gastrointestinal disturbance (nausea, diarrhea, vomiting) with tenderness over the liver and jaundice.[12–13] Symptoms following acute exposures usually occurred after about 24 hours but always within a few days of exposure. Fortunately, human cases of liver toxicity due to occupational CCl_4 exposure have been quite rare. Isolated case reports detail liver toxicity in workers using CCl_4.[14–18] However, epidemiological studies of worker populations have been equivocal in establishing an association between occupational exposure to CCl_4 and increased risk of liver disease.[19–21]

Mechanism of Toxicity

Most studies evaluating the mechanism of CCl_4 induced liver toxicity have been conducted in animals. Animals exposed to CCl_4 have a similar pattern of liver damage as has been found in humans who died from over-exposure to CCl_4.[22] Inhalation of high levels of CCl_4 has been shown to cause elevated serum enzyme levels[17,18,23], steatosis and centrilobular (zone 3) necrosis.[15,24,25] Increased liver weight has been reported.[14] Liver fibrosis or cirrhosis can develop after acute and chronic exposure[24–26], although a certain degree of liver regeneration by hepatocyte proliferation has been shown to occur.

The metabolism of CCl_4 is a classic example of bioactivation of a parent compound to a more reactive metabolite (free radical) by phase I enzymes. CYP2E1 is the predominant CCl_4 metabolizing enzyme in humans exposed to low levels of CCl_4. However, other CYP450 enzymes, including those of the CYP3A sub-family also metabolize CCl_4.[27] Alcohol consumption increases the levels of CYP2E1 in hepatocytes, so individuals who drink alcohol are much more likely to develop liver toxicity following exposure to CCl_4 than those who don't drink.[15–17,28] Therefore, simultaneous occupational exposure to CCl_4 and alcohol may potentiate liver toxicity.[18]

CYP2E1 bioactivates CCl_4 to the reactive trichloromethyl radical ($\cdot CCl_3$) by removal of a chlorine molecule (de-halogenation).[29] In the presence of molecular oxygen the trichloromethyl radical quickly forms another reactive metabolite, the trichloromethylperoxy radical ($CCl_3OO\cdot$).[30] A free radical is any molecule that contains an unpaired electron. Free radicals are inherently destructive since they abstract or "steal" electrons from surrounding molecules in order to stabilize their own molecular structure. CYP450s are located in the endoplasmic reticulum of cells and the polyunsaturated fatty acid of phospholipids in the endoplasmic reticulum membranes are especially vulnerable to attack from free radicals. The peroxy radicals from bioactivated CCl_4 can cause significant cellular toxicity through destruction of intracellular membranes. This destructive process is called lipid peroxidation. Lipid peroxidation of membranes in the endoplasmic reticulum and Golgi apparatus ultimately disrupts the synthesis and elimination of triglyceride-rich lipoproteins and liver proteins.[31–33] Steatosis is the result of blocked transport of lipids due, at least in part, to lipid peroxidation.

As the cellular structure deteriorates, soluble liver enzymes begin to appear in the plasma, and necrosis is seen in the centrilobular (Zone 3) hepatocytes where the highest levels of the activating enzyme (CYP2E1) are found. Ito cells, activated by either CCl_4 metabolites or the presence of massive necrosis, begin producing large amounts of type-I collagen[34] leading to liver fibrosis in the affected regions of the liver. Hepatocyte regeneration begins soon after hepatocyte loss. Chronic exposure to CCl_4 has been shown to increase the incidence of liver cancer in rats and mice. Since CCl_4 does not appear to be mutagenic it is thought that carcinogenesis only occurs after CCl_4 exposures that induce hepatocyte proliferation due to massive toxicity.[35] CCl_4 has been designated an A2 Suspected Human Carcinogen by the ACGIH.

Basis for the ACGIH TLV®

The current ACGIH TLV®-TWA for CCl_4 of 5 ppm was developed using a physiologically based pharmacokinetic (PBPK) model. In this case, the lowest observed effect level (LOEL) identified for hepatotoxic effects was 10 mg/kg in rats.[36–37] Adjustments in the LOEL were made by application of uncertainty factors to account for using animal data to estimate human exposure and to account for possible individual differences in response to CCl_4 exposure.[38] The resulting NOEL dose estimate for humans was used to calculate an airborne concentration that a worker could breathe over a 40 hour work-week without undue risk of liver toxicity.[39]

1,1,2,2-Tetrachloroethane

1,1,2,2-Tetrachloroethane (1,1,2,2-TCA) is a colorless non-flammable liquid with the sweet, aromatic odor found in other chlorinated solvents. The odor is readily detected at about 1.5 ppm.[40] As mentioned at the beginning of this chapter, liver toxicity associated with the use of 1,1,2,2-TCA before and during World War I resulted in a significant decline in its use as a solvent. Currently, there is very limited manufacture and use of 1,1,2,2,-TCA in the U.S.

Case Study

1,1,2,2-TCA is thought to be one of the most toxic of the chlorinated hydrocarbon solvents.[12] A review of the literature up to 1939 showed 124 cases of 1,1,2,2-TCA poisoning of which about 20% were fatal. Toxicity was attributed primarily to effects on the liver, not the narcotic effect commonly observed after over-exposure to chlorinated solvents. Workers with high occupational exposure to 1,1,2,2-TCA from doping airplanes usually presented with jaundice, pale stools and tenderness over the upper abdomen.[1] Upon autopsy, the livers were found to be markedly reduced in size. Microscopic examination showed extensive necrosis centrilobular (zone 3) necrosis.

Mechanism of Toxicity

The primary route of occupational exposure to 1,1,2,2-TCA is through inhalation of vapors, although some absorption through the skin occurs. The mechanism by which 1,1,2,2-TCA causes toxicity has not been well established. There is evidence that the primary pathway may be similar to that of CCl_4-lipid peroxidation due to free radical formation. The formation of free radicals, presumably from de-halogenation has been demonstrated in vivo and in vitro[41,42] and lipid peroxidation has been reported in mice exposed to 1,1,2,2-TCA.[41] Also, 1,1,2,2-TCA or 1,1,2,2-TCA reactive metabolites have been shown to bind to molecules in liver tissue.[43,44]

As with CCl_4, animals exposed to 1,1,2,2-TCA develop liver steatosis.[1,45–47] Changes in serum liver enzymes have typically not been reported except after very high exposures, although serum triglycerides were decreased in animals treated with 1,1,2,2-TCA.[46,47]

Basis for the ACGIH TLV®

The current ACGIH TLV®-TWA for 1,1,2,2-TCA is 1 ppm. Results from animal studies and human volunteers indicate that mild liver effects become apparent at air levels about 10 ppm.[39] An adjustment factor of 10 was applied to the LOEL to minimize the potential for health effects in workers exposed to 1,1,2,2-TCA.

Immune-Mediated Damage

Immune mediated toxicity is not directly caused by a toxicant. Instead, the toxicity is due to an attack by the body's own immune system as a result of chemically induced changes in endogenous proteins. The general mechanism is thought to occur as follows. First, exposure to a new chemical occurs. The chemical is bioactivated in the liver to a reactive metabolite that binds to a specific protein in hepatocytes. The immune system does not recognize the modified protein and treats it as a foreign entity by forming antibodies against the metabolite-protein complex (protein adduct). No immediate toxicity is apparent. However if a second exposure occurs, the reactive metabolite again binds to the protein forming more of the initial protein adduct. This time, cells containing the protein adduct are attacked by the new antibodies formed after the first exposure. Considerable liver toxicity then occurs as hepatocytes are destroyed by the body's own immune system.

Halothane

Halothane is a clear, nonflammable, highly volatile gas with a pleasant odor that is apparent at about 33 ppm.[40] The only use for halothane is as an anesthetic, therefore worker exposure is limited to halothane manufacture or workers in a clinical setting where halothane is used.

Case Study

Liver failure with a fatality rate of about 50% has been found in some patients given halothane as an anesthetic.[48] The incidence of "halothane hepatitis" has been estimated as 1/1000–1/30,000 cases. It has been found to occur most often in patients who had previously been given halothane as an anesthetic and particularly in those with short intervals between exposures.[48–50] Although it is not known why some individuals develop halothane hepatitis, possible risk factors include genetic susceptibility, being female, and obesity.[51] Halothane hepatitis is characterized by severe hepatocellular necrosis, jaundice and substantial elevations of serum transaminase levels. There have been case reports of occupational halothane hepatitis in medical[51-53] and research[54] personnel however, there is no epidemiological literature indicating that workers with occupational exposure to halothane have increased risk of immune-mediated hepatotoxicity.

Mechanism of Toxicity

Like CCl_4 and 1,1,2,2-TCA, halothane is metabolized by CYP2E1 to reactive metabolites capable of binding to cellular macromolecules. In the presence of oxygen, halothane is converted to trifluoroacetyl chloride (TFAC)[55] which is highly localized to the endoplasmic reticulum.[49] TFA then binds to proteins, including CYP450 enzymes, producing modified cellular proteins called TFA-antigens. An antigen is simply any molecule that stimulates an immune response. In some people, the body forms antibodies against the TFA-antigens. It is not known why some individuals form antibodies and some do not. When the person is next exposed to halothane, the immune system mounts a defense against the newly forming TFAC-antigens. The precise mechanism of the response is unknown, since some workers have circulating antibodies to TFA-antigens, but no toxicity.[56] Possible pathways include targeting of TFA-antigens by antibodies or by antigen-specific cytotoxic T cells.[56]

Basis for the ACGIH TLV®

It is difficult to develop an occupational standard based on an immune response, because of the nature of the toxicity. The current ACGIH TLV®-TWA of 50 ppm is based on reported health effects in humans and consideration of use of halothane as a 50:1 mixture with nitrous oxide (nitrous oxide: halothane).[39]

Cirrhosis/Fibrosis

Cirrhosis is the replacement of functioning hepatocytes with fibrotic tissue. Chronic, repeated exposure to hepatotoxicants causes hepatocyte death which stimulates the deposition of collagen by activated Ito cells. This drastically alters the liver architecture. At some point there is a permanent loss of liver function because fibrous tissue cannot perform the work of hepatocytes, and cirrhosis is not a reversible process.

Trinitrotoluene

Trinitrotoluene (TNT) is produced commercially as a pale yellow flammable crystalline solid. It is highly explosive and can be detonated either through concussion or by heating to explosion temperature. TNT is used to make explosives such as bombs and grenades. Occupational exposure to TNT occurs during manufacture of TNT, the manufacture of munitions containing TNT and demilitarization of existing munitions. TNT is primarily absorbed through the skin; however, inhalation of dusts and fumes also occurs.

Case Study

Obviously, there is increased potential for exposure to TNT during times of war when more munitions are required. When the manufacture of TNT is substantially increased, there is often a concurrent increase in overtime work for employees. Thus, the highest levels of exposure to TNT have occurred during wartime, especially during World War I and World War II. "Toxic jaundice" was described as a rare side effect of TNT exposure in the early 1900s.[2] Although rare, about 25% of workers who developed toxic jaundice died. There were 475 cases of TNT poisoning reported in Great Britain between 1916 and 1941, of which 125 were fatal. In one munitions factory, 62 cases of toxic jaundice with 16 deaths were reported.[3] Six cases with four deaths were in workers under the age of 18 years. Presenting symptoms varied from non-existent to some combination of giddiness, drowsiness and dark urine. There was often a latency period of several weeks between the exposure to onset of jaundice. Elevated serum bilirubin levels were sometimes found. Liver toxicity was associated with a substantial reduction in the size and weight of the liver (Figure 10.6). Portal cirrhosis was found upon autopsy in the livers of seven individuals who died of toxic jaundice.[3] In 1917, Dr. T.M Legge, the first medical inspector of factories in England studied the work practices of TNT workers and concluded that dermal exposure was the primary route of exposure for those developing liver toxicity.[2] This was tested by Benjamin Moore in 1918-*personally*. Moore left the factory and went to a nearby orchard, distant from any other source of TNT, to perform his experiment. He rubbed a small pellet containing 20% TNT in his palm. Two hours later his urine tested positive for a urinary marker of TNT. By the next day, the level of TNT biomarker present in the urine was similar to that seen in the factory workers. He also had all of the symptoms associated with exposure to TNT including headache, nausea, malaise and drowsiness. Moore repeated the experiment about two weeks later with similar results. This is not a recommended practice in industrial hygiene today, but it was an important experiment at the time.

By the time World War II began, better industrial hygiene practices were in place to reduce both dermal and inhalation exposure to TNT. In 1942, Bridge reported the following to the Royal Society of Medicine[57]:

> "Finally, as regards the prevention of illness from TNT, I would summarize this as cleanliness of the air breathed, secured by effective ventilation or, failing the practicability of that, filtration through an effective respirator, cleanliness of the implements used and the cleanliness of the person, secured by protective clothing and by personal attention to the care of the skin."[57]

In many cases, the application of barrier creams to prevent exposure to TNT was done under strict supervision (Figure 10.7).

Mechanism of Toxicity

The mechanism of TNT toxicity is not well characterized. It has been shown that TNT is absorbed by inhalation, ingestion and dermal exposure in a number of different species, including man. The current hypothesis is that TNT is metabolized by enzymes present in the endoplasmic reticulum to reactive metabolites

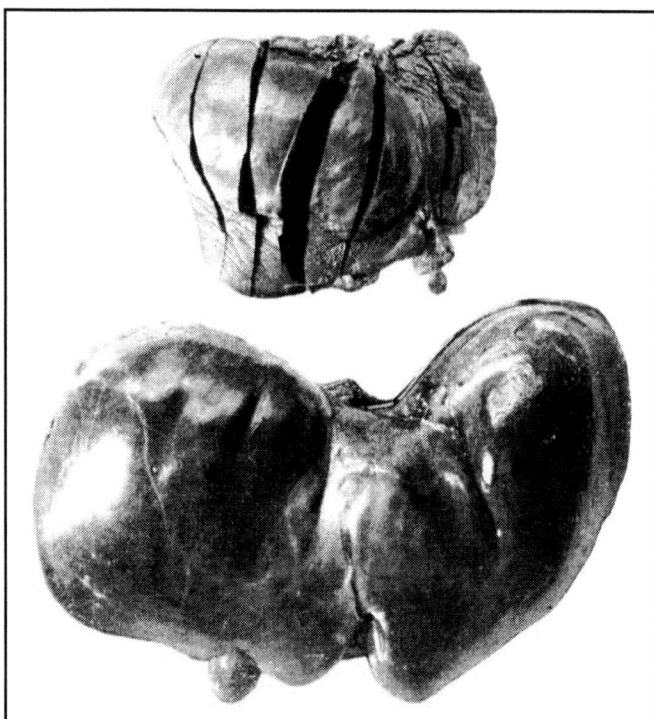

Figure 10.6 — Liver necrosis due to TNT. The liver at the top is that of a 14 year old boy who worked filling bags with TNT for 5 weeks before he became jaundiced. He died of hepatic failure 2 months later. The bottom liver is a normally sized liver. (Reprinted from Hunter: The Diseases of Occupations, Vol 6: The Aromatic Carbon Compounds. London, Hodder and Stoughton, 1978.)

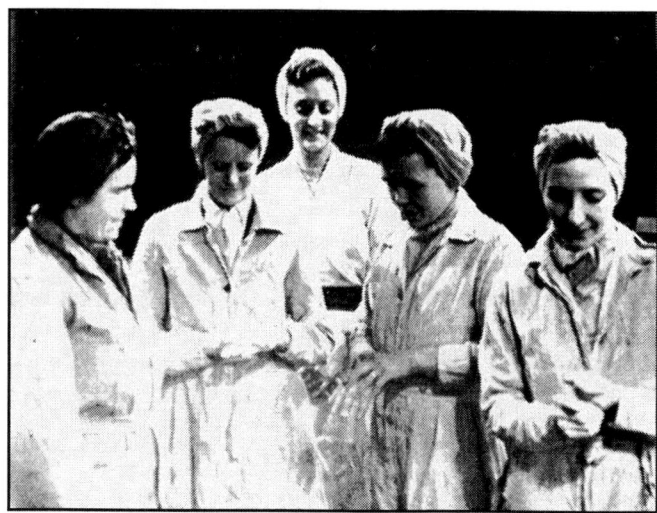

Figure 10.7 — Application of barrier cream and protective clothing under supervision in a shell-filling factory in 1944. (Reprinted from Hunter: The Diseases of Occupations, Vol 6: The Aromatic Carbon Compounds. London, Hodder and Stoughton, 1978.)

capable of binding to liver proteins[58-59] and producing oxidative stress.[60,61] The production of ROS, including superoxide radical, may be the mechanism by which activation of Ito cells occurs.[61] Ito cell activation leads to increased production and deposition of ECM, with concomitant disruption of the liver architecture.

Basis for the ACGIH TLV®
The ACGIH TLV®-TWA was based on the reported health effects in employees at facilities with available industrial hygiene data. Some changes in liver enzymes were found in workers exposed to 0.3–0.8 mg/m^3 TNT at a munitions factory.[62] Therefore, a TLV®-TWA of 0.1 mg/m^3 was recommended to add a margin of safety for munitions workers.[39] A skin notation was added since dermal absorption was shown to be an important route of exposure.

Biliary Damage
Canalicular Cholestasis
Cholestasis is a reduction in bile volume or reduced secretion of certain bile components, such as bilirubin, into bile. For instance, some toxicants can cause blockage of the caniculi (bile ducts), causing bilirubin to accumulate in blood or urine, jaundice. Excess bilirubin may also appear in the urine and cause it to turn a dark orange or brown color. Deposition of some bile products in the skin can also cause profound itching, which can be a sign of liver disease.

Bile Duct Damage
Some hepatotoxicants cause direct damage to the bile ducts. This can lead to loss of bile ducts, called vanishing bile duct syndrome. Chronic exposure to bile duct toxicants can also lead to cellular proliferation and fibrosis and eventually bile duct cirrhosis.

Methylene Dianiline
Methylene dianiline (MDA) is a crystalline solid that is colorless to pale yellow or brown with a faint fishy odor. The odor can be detected at 0.5–1.0 ppm with minimal irritant effects. However, at 4.0 ppm, there can be significant eye irritation.[39] Most MDA is used in the production of polymeric isocyanates which are used to manufacture polyurethane foam, elastomers like "Spandex" and other resins. MDA has also been used in epoxy hardening agents and as an antioxidant in rubber.

Case Study
A total of 13 workers developed symptoms of liver toxicity after working as mill helpers in a plant that used powdered MDA to manufacture a hard plastic insulating material.[63] During the process, the mill helpers kneaded a hot, doughy mixture of the resin mixed with MDA that had been sprinkled in by a mill operator. The mixture reached temperatures of 180°F and contained about 10% MDA. Mixing was performed with a metal blade and cloth gloved hands over several hours.. Between 1966 and 1972, all mill workers at one facility reported jaundice and dark urine. Most also reported some combination of abdominal pain, nausea, anorexia and fever. Four had high serum AP values.

It was quickly noted that only the helpers who physically manipulated the MDA product developed symptoms of liver toxicity. The mill operator, who stood across from the helper during the process but did not manually handle the mixture, was not affected. Therefore, dermal exposure was thought to be the most significant route of exposure. Inhalation was thought to play a minor role in exposure, if any.

Mechanism of Toxicity
The symptoms reported by the mill helpers were similar to those found in individuals in an English community who had eaten bread made from flour inadvertently contaminated with MDA.[64] All liver biopsies from affected persons showed cholestasis and damage to the biliary tree. Animals fed MDA show bile duct damage and cholestasis.[65-69]

Although the exact mechanism of toxicity is not known, it is thought that MDA is metabolized to a reactive metabolite that is primarily excreted through the bile.[69] Reactive metabolites concentrated in biliary ducts would explain the early necrosis of biliary epithelial cells in treated animals.[67] In vitro studies show that MDA can be metabolized by N-acetyl transferases to N-hydroxylamine, an intermediate that may be able to bind to cellular macromolecules and cause toxicity.[70]

Basis for the ACGIH TLV®
The current ACGIH TLV®-TWA of 0.1 ppm is based in part on the McGill and Moto study[63] described in the case study introduction. Industrial hygiene data at the affected factory showed an air concentration of 0.1 ppm where the mill helpers and mill operators worked; however, only the mill helpers who manually handled the hot MDA mixture were affected. The mill operators who did not handle the mixture, but breathed the same air were not. Therefore, inhalation of 0.1 ppm MDA would not be expected to cause liver toxicity. Other industrial hygiene and animal studies yielded similar data.[39]

Cancer
Cancers in the liver can arise from hepatocytes (hepatocellular carcinoma), bile duct cells (cholangiosarcomas) or from sinusoidal cells (angiosarcomas). Liver angiosarcomas are extremely rare cancers that have been shown to be increased by occupational exposure to high levels of vinyl chloride.

Vinyl Chloride
Vinyl chloride (VC) is a colorless, extremely flammable gas that has a pleasant, mildly sweet odor at high concentrations. The process of polymerizing VC into polyvinyl chloride (PVC) was discovered in Germany in the 1930s.[71] About 500–1500 molecules of VC are used to form one molecule of PVC. PVC is used in multiple products, including pipes, wire coatings, furniture and various automotive parts.

Case Study
On January 5, 1970, a 36-year old employee at a PVC production facility was hospitalized in Kentucky for tarry stools.[72]

He had no other complaints and was discharged with a tentative diagnosis of bleeding duodenal ulcers. Four months later, he was readmitted with tarry stools, visible pallor and an enlarged liver. In addition, he had slightly elevated serum levels of total bilirubin, ALT and AST; suggesting liver toxicity. A liver biopsy showed that the man had angiosarcoma, an extremely rare form of liver cancer. The man died on September 27, 1971. He had worked for approximately 14 years as a helper and operator in a PVC production facility. The significance of this finding was not fully appreciated at the time of the man's diagnosis and death. It was not until Dr. Creech, the physician at the PVC plant discovered that a second employee died due to liver angiosarcoma in May 1973, followed by a third employee in December of the same year, that suspicion of a possible association between occupational exposure to VC and angiosarcoma was published. The total number of angiosarcoma cases reported in the entire U.S. for a year was only about 27[73], and three had occurred at this one PVC plant. A complete review of medical histories at the plant ultimately identified an additional two workers who had died more than 5 years previously of angiosarcoma.[74] Medical screening of all employees was immediately initiated which resulted in diagnosis of angiosarcoma in two additional employees.

NIOSH reported in 1974[75] that 26 cases of angiosarcoma from six countries had been found. Sixteen of those were from four plants in the U.S. Most cases, about 81%, were identified in helpers who had cleaned the reactors in the PVC facilities. Polymerization of VC was performed in large pressurized containers called "autoclaves," "polypots," or "polykettles".[71] Before the late 1960s to early 1970s, residual PVC encrusted on the autoclaves was cleaned by personnel actually lowered into the autoclave. The cleaning consisted largely of scraping and chipping by hand, and could occur twice a day.[71,74] Residual VC was released from the autoclave when opened, and was also trapped in the caked PVC. Autoclave workers are thought to have had the highest exposure to VC of any other workers in the industry. Air levels of VC up to 3,000 ppm have been estimated for autoclave cleaners during the early days of PVC manufacture.[71] Although exposure declined gradually, it was still significant in the 1970s. For instance, the VC air concentration for autoclave workers has been estimated at 1,000 ppm for 1945–55, about 500 ppm for 1955–60; about 300–400 ppm for 1960–1970 and around 150 ppm by 1973. Compare this to the current ACGIH TLV® of 1 ppm.[39]

Mechanism of Toxicity

Vinyl chloride is absorbed very efficiently into the bloodstream once it is inhaled, and is then rapidly distributed to primarily the liver and kidney.[76] There is no indication that VC is carcinogenic. However, once in the liver, VC is bioactivated by CYP2E1 to 2-chloroethylene oxide, a reactive metabolite capable of binding to DNA and RNA.[76] This can cause mutations that eventually lead to cancer (See Chapter 13, "Carcinogenesis"). 2-Chloroethylene oxide is converted to 2-chloroacetaldehyde by an apparently spontaneous rearrangement. 2-Chloroacetaldehyde binds readily to proteins. Binding to proteins can cause toxicity by preventing proper functioning or by initiating cellular pathways leading to cell death due. Research has found that up to 70% of VC metabolites were able to migrate out of hepatocytes.[76] Migration of VC metabolites into the sinusoid may explain why the primary tumor associated with VC overexposure is not derived from hepatocytes, but from the endothelial cells that line the blood vessels or sinusoids (angiosarcoma).

Workers with angiosarcoma were also found to have varying degrees of liver fibrosis.[77,78] Fibrosis was also apparent in some individuals exposed to VC but without angiosarcoma. It has been postulated that this may be an immune-mediate response or that reactive metabolites activate Ito cells, leading to overproduction of ECM and fibrosis. Activated sinusoidal cells may also be the cause of sinusoidal dilatation observed in VC exposed workers and the ultimate pathway to development of angiosarcoma.

VC metabolites are conjugated with glutathione and excreted primarily in the urine, as thiodiglycolic acid.[79] In fact, most of an inhaled dose of VC is excreted in the urine within one day. Very little un-metabolized VC is exhaled at fairly low exposures ($\leq$ 10 ppm), although it may be as much as 12% at exposures approaching 1000 ppm.[79] These data explain in part the rationale in establishing a TLV for a known carcinogen (see following section). At lower doses, the VC metabolites are conjugated with glutathione and quickly eliminated. However, at some point, the concentration of VC conjugates may overwhelm the amount of conjugating enzyme, glutathione S-transferase, available to perform the reaction. Once the concentration of VC metabolites reaches the point where cellular detoxification resources are saturated, unconjugated VC metabolites are available to interact with DNA and proteins. At that point, liver toxicity and DNA damage begins to occur. Vinyl chloride has been designated an A1 Confirmed Human Carcinogen by ACGIH.

Basis for the ACGIH TLV®

The TLV®-TWA of 1 ppm was based on the liver angiosarcoma endpoint although health effects other than angiosarcoma have been reported in humans exposed to VC. At very high concentrations, VC has a narcotic effect. These effects are fairly well characterized from human studies conducted well before it was known that VC caused cancer. Two humans exposed to 2.5% (25,000 ppm) for 3 minutes reported dizziness and disorientation, as well as a burning sensation on the soles of the feet.[80] In another study, humans were exposed for 5 minutes to concentrations of VC ranging from 0, 0.4% (4,000 ppm), 0.8% (8,000 ppm), 1.2% (12,000 ppm), 1.6% (16,000 ppm) and 2.0% (20,000 ppm).[81] A slightly heady feeling was reported by one in six volunteers at 8,000 ppm. Five of six reported intoxication with dizziness, lightheadedness and some nausea at 16,000 ppm. All volunteers reported symptoms at 20,000 ppm. However, it is apparent that these exposures are high even for autoclave workers.

Simonato[82] reported on a large cohort of VC exposed workers. Of 14,351 workers, 24 developed angiosarcoma. This study evaluated several exposure variables including job title, and duration and extent of exposure and found a strong association between cumulative exposure and development of angiosarcoma.[82] The lowest cumulative exposure in an employee diagnosed with angiosarcoma was 288 ppm-years, resulting from exposure to about 28.8 ppm VC for 10 years. An air concentration of 6.5 ppm would result in the same cumulative exposure if spread over a 45 year working career. Therefore, 6.5 ppm could be regarded as the lowest concentration to which a person could be exposed for 45 years and develop angiosarcoma. This value is similar to the lowest VC airborne level shown to cause any cancer in animals.[83] Based on the lowest-observed-effect levels (LOEL) determined from human epidemiological studies and animal studies, and the observation that no occupational cases of liver angiosarcoma have been reported since 1974, when industry compliance of the OSHA PEL of 1 ppm began, the ACGIH recommended a TLV®-TWA for VC of 1 ppm.[39] No STEL was recommended because of the strong association of increasing exposure with increased risk of liver angiosarcoma.[82]

Complexity of Liver Damage

Multiple liver injuries may be present depending on the chemical, the duration and concentration of the exposure, the genetic susceptibilities of the individual and the extent of liver injury. For instance, the previous section described liver angiosarcoma in workers with high occupational exposures to VC. Exposure to VC may also cause fibrosis, without angiosarcoma. In addition, VC metabolites can migrate out of the hepatocytes and cause damage to the sinusoid (sinusoidal dilatation) and endothelial cells.

This chapter began with a discussion of 1,1,2,2-TCA which is known to cause centrilobular necrosis, however autopsy results from workers describe a number of effects.

> *"The characteristic features are a very extreme degree of destruction of liver tissue; large tracts of liver have entirely disappeared, and their place is taken by an organizing fibrous tissue, a fibrous replacement. Such liver tissue as remains, however, shows very little evidence of degenerative changes. In fact we have, in this case, clear evidence of active regeneration of liver tissue....And I am inclined to attribute the late stages of the disease in this patient to the effects of the replacement fibrosis, the contraction of the scar tissue reducing the function of the liver still further, and leading, finally to the fatal result."*[1]

In summary, there was little necrosis, but extensive fibrosis despite some indications of liver regeneration. Compare this to an autopsy of two other individuals who also died as a result of 1,1,2,2-TCA overexposure.

> *"In both there was very extensive destruction, necrosis of the liver cells over large areas in the organ; very little liver tissue persisted, its place being occupied by broke-down debris of the cells, together with dilated blood capillaries. These two cases differ from the previous one, firstly in that there is no replacement-fibrosis; the cases, apparently, terminated fatally before there was time for these other changes to occur. Secondly, they differ essentially in that there is no evidence of regeneration in those portions of the liver tissue which persist...the most intense changes had occurred in the centers of the lobules."*[1]

In this case, there was centrilobular necrosis and some sinusoidal damage, but no fibrosis or regeneration.

Conclusion

Liver toxicity is certainly a concern for the industrial hygienist. Many chemicals used in industry are known to cause liver toxicity or cancer, and a number of occupational standards and guidelines are determined to minimize adverse effects on the liver. Liver function tests are useful to assess liver function; however, many are non-specific and not particularly sensitive since a great deal of liver damage can occur before it is detected by altered serum liver enzymes. In addition, non-occupational factors, such as prescribed or over the counter drugs and alcohol use, can cause liver toxicity or substantially increase liver toxicity from workplace exposures. These factors need to be considered when a potential concern about liver toxicity is raised in the workplace. Liver toxicity due to occupational exposure has historically been found in worker populations with high exposures to a chemical or in areas that have had unexpected increases in production due to war or other reasons. Therefore, a greater degree of vigilance is necessary during such times to ensure the welfare of employees. As usual, determination of workplace practices that need to be modified to reduce workplace exposure is the key to prevention of liver toxicity on the job. Historically, occupational health and safety workers have played the key role in identification of industrial hepatotoxicants.

References

1. **Willcox, W.H., B.H. Spilsbury, T.M. Legge:** An outbreak of toxic jaundice of a new type amongst aeroplane workers-Its clinical and toxicological aspect. *Trans. Med. Soc. London* 38:129–156 (1915).
2. **Hunter, D.:** *The Diseases of Occupations.* Kent, UK: Hodder and Stoughton, Kent, UK. 1978.
3. **Legge, T.M., et al.:** Toxic jaundice in munition workers and troops. *Br. Med. J.* 1:155–158 (1917).
4. **Tsutsumi, M., J.M. Lasker, M. Shimizu, A.S. Rosman, C.S. Lieber.:** The intralobular distribution of ethanol-inducible P450IIE1 in rat and human liver. *Hepatology* 10:437–446 (1989).
5. **Smedsrød, B., H. Pertoft, S. Gustafson, and T.C. Laurent.:** Scavenger functions of the liver endothelial cell. *Biochem. J.* 266:313–327 (1990).
6. **Knolle, P.A., and A. Limmer.:** Control of immune responses by scavenger liver endothelial cells. *Swiss Med. Wkly.* 133:501–506 (2003).

7. **elSisi, A.E., D.L. Earnest, and I.G. Sipes.:** Vitamin A potentiation of carbon tetrachloride hepatotoxicity: role of liver macrophages and active oxygen species. *Toxicol. Appl. Pharmacol.* 119:295–301 (1993).
8. **Senoo, H.:** Structure and function of hepatic stellate cells. *Med. Electron. Microsc.* 37:3-15 (2004).
9. **Hemingway, J.T.:** Influence of plasma proteins in the control of mitosis-rates in regenerating liver. *Nature* 191: 706–707 (1961).
10. **Copple, B.L., C.M. Rondelli, J.F. Maddox, N.C. Hoglen, P.E. Ganey, and R.A. Roth:** Modes of cell death in rat liver after monocrotaline exposure. *Toxicol Sci.* 77:172–182 (2004).
11. **Forbes, J.R:** Carbon tetrachloride nephrosis. *Lancet* 247:590–592 (1944).
12. **McClurkin, T.:** The physiological effects of toxic gases and vapors. *J. Inst. Petrol.* 25:382–391 (1939).
13. **von Oettingen, W.F.:** The halogenated aliphatic, olefinic, cyclic, aromatic, and aliphatic-aromatic hydrocarbons including the halogenated insecticides, their toxicity and potential dangers. *Public Health Service Publication* No. 414. 75-112 (1955).
14. **McGuire, L.W.:** Carbon tetrachloride poisoning. *JAMA* 99:988–989 (1932).
15. **Norwood, W.D., P.A. Fuqua, and B.C. Scudder:** Carbon tetrachloride poisoning. *Arch. Ind. Hyg. Occup. Med.* 1: 90–100 (1950).
16. **Jennings, R.B.:** Fatal fulminate acute carbon tetrachloride poisoning. *AMA Arch. Pathol.* 59:269–284 (1955).
17. **New, P.S., G.D. Lubash, L. Scherr, and A.L. Rubin AL:** Acute renal failure associated with carbon tetrachloride intoxication. *JAMA* 181:903–906 (1962).
18. **Deng, J-F., J-D. Wang, T-S. Shih, and F-L. Lan:** Outbreak of carbon tetrachloride poisoning in a color printing factory related to the use of isopropyl alcohol and an air conditioning system in Taiwan. *Am. J. Ind. Med.* 12:11–19 (1987).
19. **Tomenson, J.A., C.E. Baron, J. O'Sullivan, J.C. Edwards, M.D. Stonard, and R.J. Walker:** Hepatic function in workers occupationally exposed to carbon tetrachloride. *Occup. Environ. Med.* 52:508–514 (1995).
20. **Stewart A and L.J. Witts.:** Chronic carbon tetrachloride intoxication. *Br J Ind. Med.* 1:11–19 (1944).
21. **Heimann, H. and C.B. Ford CB:** Low concentrations of carbon tetrachloride capable of causing mild narcosis. *Industrial Bulletin* 20:209–210 (1941).
22. **Kanetaka, T. and T. Oda:** Toxic liver injuries. *Acta. Path. Jap.* 23:617-627 (1973).
23. **Jaeger, R.J., R.B. Conolly, and S.D. Murphy:** Short-term inhalation toxicity of halogenated hydrocarbons. *Arch Environ Health* 30:26–31 (1975).
24. **Belyaev, N.D., V.C. Budker, L.V. Deriy, I.A. Smolenskaya, and V.M. Subbotin:** Liver plasma membrane-associated fibroblast growth: Stimulatory and inhibitory activities during experimental cirrhosis. *Hepatology* 15: 525–531 (1992).
25. **Sakata, T., A. Watanabe, N. Hobara, and H. Nagashima:** Chronic liver injury in rats by carbon tetrachloride inhalation. *Bull. Environ. Contam. Toxicol.* 38:959–961 (1987).
26. **McDermott, W.V. and H.L. Hardy:** Cirrhosis of the liver following chronic exposure to carbon tetrachloride. *J. Occup. Med.* 5:249–251 (1963).
27. **Zangar, R.C., J.M. Benson, V.L. Burnett, and D.L. Springer.:** Cytochrome P450 2E1 is the primary enzyme responsible for low-dose carbon tetrachloride metabolism in human liver microsomes. *Chem. Biol. Interac.* 125: 233–243 (2000).
28. **Manno, M., M. Rezzadore, M. Grossi, and C. Sbrana:** Potentiation of occupational carbon tetrachloride toxicity by ethanol abuse. *Hum. Exp. Toxicol.* 15:294–300 (1996).
29. **McCay, P.B., E.K. Lai, J.L. Poyer, C.M. DuBose, and E.G. Janzen:** Oxygen and carbon-centered free radical formation during carbon tetrachloride metabolism. *J. Biol. Chem.* 259:2135–2143 (1984).
30. **Mico, B.A. and L.R. Pohl:** Reductive oxygenation of carbon tetrachloride: trichloromethyl peroxy radical as a possible intermediate in the conversion of carbon tetrachloride to electrophilic chlorine. *Arch. Biochem. Biophys.* 225: 596–609 (1983).
31. **Boll, M., L.W.D. Weber, E. Becker, and A. Stampfl:** Hepatocyte damage induced by carbon tetrachloride: Inhibited lipoprotein secretion and changed lipoprotein composition. *Z. Naturforsch.* 56:283–290 (2001).
32. **Dianzani, M.U. and G. Poli:** Carbon tetrachloride-induced block of hepatic lipoprotein secretion: Studies of the pathogenesis using isolated hepatocytes. *Front. Gastrointest. Res.* 8:1–15 (1984).
33. **Smuckler, E.A. and E.P. Benditt:** Studies on carbon tetrachloride intoxication. III. A subcellular defect in protein synthesis. *Biochemistry* 4:671–679 (1963).
34. **Nieto, N., et al.:** Rat hepatic stellate cells contribute to the acute-phase response with increased expression of alpha 1(I) and alpha 1(IV) collagens, tissue inhibitors of metalloproteinase-1, and matrix-metalloproteinase-2 messenger RNAs. *Hepatology* 33:597–607 (2001).
35. **Mirsalis, J.C., et al.:** Induction of hepatic cell proliferation and unscheduled DNA synthesis in mouse hepatocytes following in vivo treatment. *Carcinogenesis* 10:1521–1524 (1985).
36. **Kim, H.J., S. Odend'hal, and J.V. Bruckner:** Effect of dosing vehicles on the acute hepatotoxicity of carbon tetrachloride in rats. *Toxicol. Appl. Pharmacol.* 102:34–49 (1990).
37. **Kim, H.J., J.V. Bruckner, C.E. Dallas, and J.M. Gallo:** Effect of dosing vehicles on the pharmacokinetics of orally administered carbon tetrachloride in rats. *Toxicol. Appl. Pharmacol.* 102:50–60. (1990).
38. **Paustenbach, D.J., H.J. Clewell III, M.L. Gargas, and M.E. Anderson:** A physiologically based pharmacokinetic model for inhaled carbon tetrachloride. *Toxicol. Appl. Pharmacol.* 96:191–211 (1990).

39. **American Conference of Governmental Industrial Hygienists (ACGIH):** Threshold limit values for chemical substances and physical agents and biological exposure indices. Cincinnati, OH: ACGIH, 2006.
40. **Amoore, J.E. and E. Hautala:** Odor as an aid to chemical safety: Odor thresholds compared with threshold limit values and volatilities for 214 industrial chemicals in air and water dilution. *J. Appl. Toxicol. 3*:272–290 (1983).
41. **Paolini, M., et al.:** On the hepatotoxicity of 1,1,2,2-tetrachloroethane. Toxicology 73:101-115 (1992).
42. **Tomasi, A., E. Albano, A. Bini, B. Botti, T.F. Slater, and V. Vannini:** Free radical intermediates under hypoxic conditions in the metabolism of halogenated carcinogens. *Toxicol. Pathol. 12*:240–246 (1984).
43. **Eriksson, C. and E.B. Brittebo:** Epithelial binding of 1,1,2,2-tetrachloroethane in the respiratory and upper alimentary tract. *Arch. Toxicol. 65*:10–14 (1991).
44. **Hanley, T.R., J.F. Quast, and A.M. Schumann:** The metabolism and hepatic macromolecular interactions of 1,1,2,2-tetrachloroethane (TCE) in mice and rats. Dow Chemical Company. Submitted to the U.S. Environmental Protection Agency under TSCA Section 8D. OTS0514187 (1988).
45. **Horiuchi, K., S. Horiguchi, K. Hashimoto, K. Kadowaki, and K. Aratake:** Studies on the industrial tetrachloroethane poisoning. *Osaka City Med. J. 8*:29–38 (1962).
46. **Tomokuni, K.:** Studies on hepatotoxicity induced by chlorinated hydrocarbons. Lipid and ATP metabolisms in the liver of mice exposed to 1,1,2,2-tetrachloroethane. *Acta. Med. Okayama. 23*:273–282 (1969).
47. **Tomokuni, K.:** Hepatotoxicity induced by chlorinated hydrocarbons. II. Lipid metabolism and absorption spectrum of microsomal lipids in the mice exposed to 1,1,2,2-tetrachloroethane. *Acta. Med. Okayama 24*:315–322 (1970).
48. **Jurdi-Nuwayhid, F.:** Untoward side effects and toxicities of inhalational anesthetics. *Middle East J. Anaesthesiol. 7*:283–289 (1984).
49. **Kenna, J.G., and R.M. Jones:** The organ toxicity of inhaled anesthetics. *Anesth. Analg. 81*:551–566 (1995).
50. **Plummer, J.L., M.J. Cousins, P.M. Hall:** Volatile anesthetic metabolism and acute toxicity. *Rev. Drug. Metab. Drug Interact. 4*:49–98 (1982).
51. **Otedo, A.E.:** Halothane induced hepatitis: case report. *East Afr.Med. J. 81*:538–539 (2004).
52. **Keiding, S., M. Dossing, and F. Hardt:** A nurse with liver injury associated with occupational exposure to halothane in medical personnel. *Br. J. Anaesth. 53*:1173–1177 (1984).
53. **Klatskin, G. and D.V. Kimberg:** Recurrent hepatitis attributable to halothane sensitization in an anesthetist. *N. Engl. J. Med. 280*:515–522 (1969).
54. **Sutherland, D.E. and W.A. Smith:** Chemical hepatitis associated with occupational exposure to halothane in a research laboratory. *Vet. Hum. Toxicol. 34*:423–424 (1992).
55. **Kenna, J.G., J.L. Martin, H. Satoh, and L.R. Pohl:** Factors affecting the expression of trifluoroacetylated liver microsomal protein neoantigens in rats treated with halothane. *Drug Metab. Dispos. 18*:788–793 (1990).
56. **Njoku, D.B., et al.:** Autoantibodies associated with volatile anesthetic hepatitis found in the sera of a large cohort of pediatric anesthesiologists. *Anesth. Analg. 94*:243–249 (2002).
57. **Bridge, J.C:** Discussion on trinitrotoluene poisoning. *Proc. R. Soc. Med. 35*:553 (1942).
58. **Leung, K.H., M. Yao, R. Stearns, and S.H. Chiu:** Mechanism of bioactivation and covalent binding of 2,4,6-trinitrotoluene. *Chem. Biol. Interact. 97*:35–51 (1995).
59. **Liu, Y.Y., A.Y. Lu, R.A. Stearns, and S.H. Chiu:** In vivo covalent binding of [14C]trinitrotoluene to proteins in the rat. *Chem. Biol. Interact. 82*:1–19 (1992).
60. **Glass, K.Y., C.R. Newsome, and P.B. Tchounwou:** Cytotoxicity and expression of c-fox, HSP70, and GADD45/153 proteins in human liver carcinoma (HepG2) cells exposed to dinitrotoluenes. *Int. J. Environ. Res. Public Health. 2*: 355–361 (2005).
61. **Kong, L.Y., Q.G. Jiang, and Q.S. Qu:** Formation of superoxide radical and hydrogen peroxide enhanced by trinitrotoluene in rat liver, brain, kidney, and testicle in vitro and monkey liver in vivo. *Biomed. Environ. Sci. 2*:72–77 (1989).
62. **Morton, A.R., M.V. Ranadive, J.A. Hathaway:** Biological effects of trinitrotoluene from exposure below the threshold limit value. *Am. Ind. Hyg. Assoc. J. 37*:56–60. (1976).
63. **McGill, D.B. and J.D. Motto:** An industrial outbreak of toxic hepatitis due to methylenedianiline. *N. Engl. J. Med. 291*:278–282 (1974).
64. **Kopelman, H., M.H. Robertson, P.G. Sanders, and I. Ash:** The Epping jaundice. *Brit. Med. J. 1*:514–516 (1966).
65. **Cruz, V.S., H. Liu, L. Kaphalia, and M.F. Kanz:** Effects of methylenedianiline on tight junction permeability of biliary epithelial cells in vivo and in vitro. *Toxicol. Lett. 169*:13–25 (2007).
66. **Kanz, M.F., G.H. Gunasena, L. Kaphalia, D.K.J. Hammond, and Y.A. Syed:** A minimally toxic dose of ethylene dianiline injures biliary epithelial cells in rats. *Toxicol. Appl. Pharmacol. 150*:414–426 (1998).
67. **Bailie, M.B., T.P. Mullaney, and R.A. Roth:** Characterization of acute 4,4'-methylene dianiline hepatotoxicity in the rat. *Environ. Health. Perspect. 2*:130–133 (1993).
68. **Kanz, M.F., L. Kaphalia, B.S. Kaphalia, E. Romagnoli, and G.A. Ansari:** Methylene dianiline: acute toxicity and effects on biliary function. *Toxicol. Appl. Pharmacol. 117*:88–97 (1992).
69. **Kanz, M.F., A. Wang, and G.A. Campbell:** Infusion of bile from methylene dianiline-treated rats into the common bile duct injures biliary epithelial cells of recipient rats. *Toxicol. Lett. 78*:165–171 (1995).
70. **Kajbaf, M., O. Sepai, J.H. Lamb, and S. Naylor:** Identification of metabolites of 4,4-diaminodiphenylmethane (methylene dianiline) using liquid chromatographic and mass spectrometric techniques. *J. Chromatogr. 583*:63–76 (1992).

71. **Binns, C.H.B.:** Vinyl chloride: A review. *J. Soc. Occup. Med. 29*:134–141 (1979).
72. **Creech, J.L. and M.N. Johnson:** Angiosarcoma of liver in the manufacture of polyvinyl chloride. *J. Occup. Med. 16*:150–151 (1974).
73. **Falk, H.:** Vinyl chloride-induced hepatic angiosarcoma. In *Unusual Occurrences as Clues to Cancer Etiology*. R.W. Miller, et al. (eds.). Tokyo: Japan Sci. Soc. Press, 1988. pp. 39–46.
74. **Falk, H., J.L. Creech, C.W. Heath, M.N. Johnson, and M.M. Key:** Hepatic diseases among workers at a vinyl chloride polymerization plant. *JAMA 230*:59–63 (1974).
75. **National Institute for Occupational Safety and Health (NIOSH) and U.S. Centers for Disease Control and Prevention (CDC):** Angiosarcoma of the liver in vinyl chloride/polyvinyl chloride workers. *J. Occup. Med. 16*:809 (1974).
76. **Bolt, H.M., H. Kappus, R. Kaufmann, K.E. Appel, A. Buchter, W. Bolt:** Metabolism of 14 C-vinyl chloride in vitro and in vivo. *IARC Sci Publ. 976*:151–163 (1976).
77. **Jones, D.B. and P.M. Smith:** Progression of vinyl chloride induced hepatic fibrosis to angiosarcoma of the liver. *Br. J. Ind. Med. 39*:306–307 (1982).
78. **Popper, H. and L.B. Thomas:** Alterations of liver and spleen among workers exposed to vinyl chloride. *Ann. N.Y. Acad. Sci. 246*:172–194 (1975).
79. **Watanabe, P.G. and P.J. Gehring.:** Dose-dependent fate of vinyl chloride and its possible relationship to oncogenicity in rats. *Environ. Health. Perspec. 17*:145–152 (1976).
80. **Patty, F.A., W.P. Yant, and C.P. Waite:** Acute response of guinea pigs to vapors of some new commercial organic compounds. *Public Health Rep. 45*:A63–71 (1930).
81. **Lester, D., L.A. Greenberg, and W.R. Adams:** Effects of single and repeated exposures of humans and rats to vinyl chloride. *Am. Ind. Hyg. Assoc. J. 24*:265–275 (1963).
82. **Simonato, L., et al.:** A collaborative study of cancer incidence and mortality among vinyl chloride workers. *Scand. J. Work Environ. Health 17*:159–169 (1991).
83. **Maltoni, C., G. Lefemine, A. Biliberti, G. Cottil, and D. Carretti:** Carcinogenicity bioassays of vinyl chloride monomer: A model of risk assessment on an experimental basis. *Environ. Health. Perspect. 41*:3–29 (1981).

Additional Reading

Bolt, H.M.: Vinyl chloride-a classical industrial toxicant of new interest. *Crit. Rev. Toxicol. 35*:307–23 (2005).

Brodkin, C.A., S. Lee, and C.A. Redlich: Liver diseases. In *Textbook of Clinical Occupational and Environmental Medicine*, 2nd Edition. Rosenstock., L., M.R. Cullen, C. A. Brodkin, and C.A. Redlich (eds.). Philadelphia: Elsevier Saunders, 2005. pp 587–602.

Bruatbar N, and J. Williams: Industrial solvents and liver toxicity: risk assessment, risk factors and mechanisms. *Int. J. Hyg. Environ. Health 205*:479–491 (2002).

Kaplowitz, N., and L.D. DeLeve: *Drug-induced liver disease*. New York: Marcel Dekker, Inc., 2003.

Klaassen, C.D. (ed.): *Casarett and Doull's Toxicology: The basic science of poisons*. 6th edition. New York: McGraw-Hill, 2001.

Roberts, R.A., P.E. Ganey, C. Ju, L.M. Kamendulis, I. Rusyn, and J.E. Klaunig: Role of the Kupffer cell in mediating hepatic toxicity and carcinogenesis. *Toxicol. Sci. 96*:2–15 (2007).

Zimmerman, H.J.: *Hepatotoxicity: The adverse effects of drugs and other chemicals on the liver*. 2nd edition. Philadelphia: Lippincott Williams & Wilkins, 1999.

> *Place no suspicion against another, rather allow the end of everything to display.*
>
> Paracelsus (1493–1541)

Chapter 11

Reproductive and Developmental Toxicology

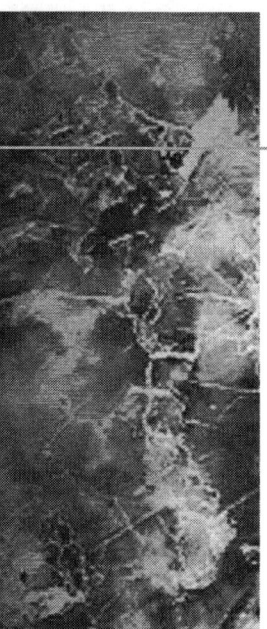

Outcome Competencies

Upon completion of this chapter, the reader should be able to:
- Define basic reproductive and developmental toxicity, recognize key occupational chemicals and their potential adverse effects.
- Classify chemicals by their type of reproductive toxicity and determine the impact of measuring the reproductive and developmental toxicity for a given occupational chemical.
- Begin a comparison of chemicals based on reproductive and developmental endpoints.
- Begin to evaluate the potential reproductive and developmental toxicity of an occupational chemical by looking for available data and consider if sufficient studies have been performed to ascertain reproductive effects.

Prequisite Knowledge

A basic knowledge of biology is required and a background in anatomy and physiology would be beneficial. Knowledge of chemistry with an understanding of concentration units is essential. An understanding of the chemical risk assessment process is helpful as basic knowledge of the risk assessment process is needed in order to interpret toxicological data or understand how exposure limits based on these types of effects are derived.

Key Terms

azoospermia, developmental toxicology, follicle stimulating hormone, interstital cell stimulating hormone, infertility, luteinizing hormone, NOAEL, oligospermia, progesterone, reproductive toxicology, subfertility, thalidomide, xenobiotics, spermatogenesis, spermiogenesis

Key Topics

1. Introduction
   - definitions
   - concern
   - principles
   - assumptions
2. General Reproductive Outcomes
   - 2-Bromopropane
   - Fuels and Solvents
   - Ethanol
3. Gender Differences
   - DBP
   - TCDD
4. Fertility Effects
   - DCBP
   - Glycol Ethers
   - Welding Exposures
   - Styrene
   - Lead
   - Military Exposures
5. Animal Studies with Reproductive Toxicants
   - Types of Animal Studies
   - Trimethyltin
   - Inorganic Arsenic
   - Gasoline
   - Vinyl Chloride
   - Beta-chloroprene
   - Perfluoroalkyl Acids
   - Fire Retardants
   - Mixtures

Chapter 11

Reproductive and Developmental Toxicology

By David R. Mattie, PhD, DABT

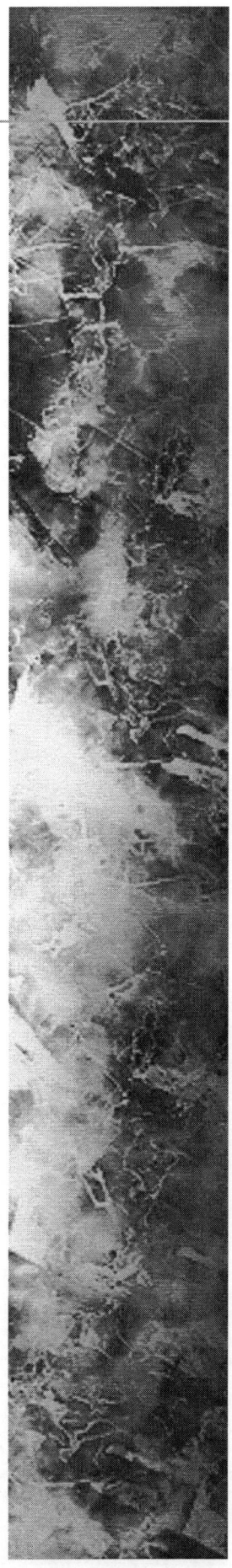

Introduction

Reproductive toxicology concerns the potential hazards of chemicals on reproductive processes. Toxic effects can occur in sexual organs and their functions, endocrine regulation, fertilization, transport of the fertilized ovum, implantation, and development. Developmental toxicology, a subset of reproductive toxicology, focuses on agents that could cause abnormal development of the fertilized egg through the embryo, fetus and the offspring all the way to maturity. Development can be divided into prenatal (embryonic and fetal) and postnatal (development following birth until the end-differentiation of organs is achieved) events and developmental toxicology is the study of effects of exposures on those events. Depending on when exposure occurs during development, the effect may be immediate or not become evident for weeks, months, or years after exposure. Reproductive and developmental toxicity are not always clearly distinguished temporally as a number of reproductive endpoints (e.g., nursing) extend into the developmental period.

The toxic effects of drugs and industrial and environmental chemicals on the human reproductive system have become a major health concern. Reproduction of a species requires proper development and function of the reproductive systems in both the parents and the offspring. In humans, reproductive disorders include reduced fertility or infertility, impotence, menstrual disorders, spontaneous abortion, low birth weight and other developmental (including heritable) defects, premature reproductive senescence, and various genetic diseases affecting the reproductive system and offspring. For example, fertility issues can involve either or both parents. An estimate of male infertility in the United States was 8.4%.[1] The causes of human sterility problems are reported to be associated with the female 39% of the time, 20% of the time with the male and, in 26% of the cases, the reason involves both potential parents.[2,3] In addition to infertility, a variety of pregnancy outcomes are possible endpoints in reproductive toxicology. For example, spontaneous abortions occur in approximately 10–20% of clinically identified pregnancies. As for live births, approximately 7% involve low birth weights, 3% suffer from significant birth defects and 12–15% may be affected by developmental disabilities, including cerebral palsy, mental retardation, autism and a variety of learning disabilities.[4]

There are several basic principles of developmental toxicology. A primary principle is that embryo or fetal effects are expressed as death, malformation, growth disorder or abnormal function. Other principles involve the interaction of genetics and environment for the organism; the impact of the dose at the target tissue; and the importance of the developmental stage at the time of exposure on the outcome(s). The final principle is that the disorder observed is based on molecular mechanisms of action that prevent recovery and repair of cells.[5]

Reproductive and developmental toxicity may be discovered in animals before being recognized in humans, or it may be uncovered in humans, triggering animal research.[5] The classic case of a developmentally toxic chemical is thalidomide. Affected newborns had a rare absence of limbs or various degrees of decreased length of limbs. Thalidomide, used as a sleep aid or for nausea

115

and vomiting, had no apparent toxicity or addictive properties in adults at therapeutic doses.[6] It was removed from the market in 1961 but lead to the development of animal testing of drugs for potential effects during pregnancy.

The U.S. Environmental Protection Agency (EPA) published guidelines for developmental toxicity in risk assessment in 1991.[7] The guidelines are based on a number of assumptions. A chemical or agent producing an adverse developmental effect in experimental animal studies has the potential to pose a hazard to humans following sufficient exposure during development. The four manifestations of developmental toxicity (death, structural abnormalities, growth alterations, and functional deficits) are all concerns. The types of developmental effects seen in animal studies are not necessarily the same as those that may be produced in humans. It is assumed that the most sensitive laboratory species is appropriate for use to estimate human risk. A threshold generally is assumed for the dose-response curve for chemical agents that produce developmental toxicity.[8]

In 1996, the U.S. EPA published *Guidelines for Reproductive Toxicity Risk Assessment*.[9] The guidelines for reproductive toxicity risk assessment have a similar set of basic assumptions. An adverse reproductive effect in experimental animals is assumed to pose a potential threat to humans. In general, the effects of xenobiotics on male and female reproductive processes are assumed to be similar unless shown otherwise. The specific effects in humans are not necessarily the same as those seen in the experimental species. In the absence of information, data from the most sensitive species should be used to determine the most appropriate experimental species. Without information to the contrary, a chemical agent affecting reproductive function in one sex is assumed to adversely affect reproductive function in the other sex. A nonlinear dose-response curve should be assumed for reproductive toxicity.[9]

Identification and characterization of reproductive hazards can be based on data from either experimental animal or human studies. Such data can result from experimental animals using controlled experimental exposures or from routine or accidental occupational or environmental exposures. This chapter will focus on occupational exposures that have potential to affect reproduction in humans.

General Reproductive Outcomes

Only a few chemicals can be incriminated as being reproductive toxic agents after conception in humans, but in experimental studies in animals, a large number of chemicals have been shown to have an adverse effect on reproduction and many more have not yet been examined.[10] A number of relevant studies are described here. Baranski summarized studies on the association between reproductive outcomes and various occupational exposures or occupations for both females and males.[10]

2-Bromopropane

Multiple reproductive effects in males and females have been seen following exposure to the chemical 2-bromopropane (2BP), used occupationally in the electronics industry.[11] In the early 1990s, an occupational health manager reported that a cluster of women performing small-sized tactile switch assembly in a South Korean electronics factory were experiencing amenorrhea (lack of menstruation).[12] 2BP had been introduced into the electronics plant in early 1994 as a substitute solvent for chlorofluorocarbons, which deplete atmospheric ozone. Because there were little or no toxicity data available at that time, the solvent was presumed to be non-toxic, and no personal protective equipment was worn. Evaluation of workers in this environment uncovered a high incidence of bone marrow effects as well as secondary amenorrhea accompanied by increased circulating FSH and LH levels and hot flashes in 16 of 25 exposed women. Additionally, 6 of 8 exposed men displayed effects, two with azoospermia (no measurable sperm) and four with oligospermia (low sperm count) and reduced sperm motility. Subsequent rat studies have determined that 2BP causes destruction of ovarian follicles in all stages of development, substantiating the cause of amenorrhea and increased hormone levels in the female workers.[13] In male rats, spermatogonia have been identified as targets[14], thus explaining the reduced sperm production seen in the male workers.

Fuels and Solvents

Fuels and solvents containing hydrocarbons (HCs) are common exposures in the environment, yet little is known about their effects on the endocrine system. Many women are now potentially exposed to fuels and solvents in the workplace. A study of female U.S. Air Force personnel was conducted to examine the potential effects on menstrual cycle function by low-dose fuel (primarily JP-8 jet fuel) and solvent exposures. The internal dose of HCs in fuels and solvents was estimated by measuring levels in exhaled breath in 63 women. Toluene was the most frequently found analyte in the breath, with values up to 52.0 ppb. Benzene breath levels were up to 97.5 ppb. A number of urinary endocrine markers associated with non-conceptive (vs. conceptive) menstrual cycles in ovulatory women were measured in 100 women; non-conceptive urinary markers included lower pre-ovulatory luteinizing hormone (LH), lower mid-luteal phase pregnanediol 3-glucuronide (Pd3G) and estrone 3-glucuronide, and higher follicle phase Pd3G. Regression analysis revealed that pre-ovulatory LH levels were significantly lower among women whose total aliphatic HC levels were above the median. The relationship between elevated aliphatic HC exposure and lowered pre-ovulatory LH levels suggested that compounds in fuels and some solvents may act as reproductive endocrine disruptors but confirmation is still needed. Also undetermined is the potential effects of fuels and solvents on conception.[15]

Ethanol

Ethanol has been shown to be a developmental toxicant (fetal alcohol syndrome) when consumed during pregnancy at levels that produce a blood alcohol concentration of 150 to 200 mg/dL.[16–18] For reference, the legal blood alcohol content limit for driving in the U.S. is <0.08 g/dL, equating to 80 mg/dL.[19]

However, occupational exposure to ethanol is typically by the inhalation route. A physiologically-based model was developed for rats and mice for inhalation exposures up to 600 ppm ethanol. Based on the rat and mouse data and human literature values, the model predicted blood alcohol levels would be less than 1 mg/dL.[20] Using the model to predict blood alcohol concentration for the maximum permitted human occupational exposure level in the United Kingdom and the U.S. of 1000 ppm, the predicted blood levels were still less than 1 mg/dL.[21] When the data for ethanol as an industrial chemical were reviewed, there was no evidence that industrial exposure to ethanol is a developmental toxicity hazard.[21]

Gender Differences

Although the effects of xenobiotics on male and female reproductive processes are assumed to be similar unless shown otherwise[9], it is important to consider whether gender differences occur. In some cases, one sex may be susceptible and the other not. That is, chemicals that produce a selective reduction in gonadotropin secretion from the pituitary may affect 17B-estradiol versus testosterone production in a selective manner. As a result, ovary-dependent endpoints could be impaired, while testes-dependent endpoints are unaffected. Additionally, the impact may be reversible in one gender, and irreversible in the other. For example, in the case of chemicals that destroy germ cells in the early stages of meiotic division, extensive damage may cause irreversible ovarian failure in females, and reversible reductions in spermatogenesis in males. This is because within the ovary, the oocyte is arrested in prophase of the first meiotic division, and once destroyed, no more are formed. Within the testis, spermatogonia, the germ cells undergoing spermatogenesis to produce sperm, can divide by mitosis to maintain a continuously renewable source of these cells. It is important to investigate the effects of reproductive toxicants in both genders for these reasons and to determine the targeted site(s) in order to evaluate and predict potentially different levels of risk between women and men.[11]

DBP

Di-n-butyl phthalate (DBP) is a plasticizer and solvent used in industry and is a low level contaminant found in a wide variety of different media ranging from drinking water to infant formula.[22] Exposure to DBP during gestation and lactation specifically impaired the androgen-dependent development of the male reproductive tract, suggesting that DBP is not estrogenic but antiandrogenic in the rat.[23] This was also shown by DBP exposure during a critical window of development, gestation days 12 to 21, when the male reproductive tract is undergoing major differentiation.[24] As for female rats, effects of DBP have been reported in pregnant and pseudo-pregnant rats. Effects included impaired implantation in mated females and decreased decidualization in the pseudopregnant animals (the decidua is a cellular matrix formed in the uterine endometrial stroma during the menstrual cycle).[25] For DBP, it appears that different effects are produced between male and female rats but it is not known if this relationship occurs in humans.

TCDD

The epidemiological data for reproductive and developmental effects in humans exposed to TCDD are very limited, which is why animal data must be relied upon more heavily for risk assessment. Data suggest that TCDD influences the sex ratio in children with more females born than males, but more research is needed.[26] Human exposure has not been shown to produce birth defects (spontaneous abortions, stillbirths, infant deaths or congenital malformations) and no association has been shown for TCDD exposure and changes in FSH and LH sex hormones. A number of studies have reported adverse effects on the development of the reproductive system in male and female rat offspring exposed to TCDD *in utero* and via lactation at low maternal doses during gestation.[27] These effects, particularly in male rat offspring, appear to be the most sensitive endpoints. A reference dose (RfD or lifetime exposure level established by the U.S. EPA to protect the public rather than just workers) of 1–10 pg/kg-d was set based on chloracne in children and developmental effects in fetal rats. The RfD is expected to be a highly protective exposure limit for human reproductive health, especially since reproductive and developmental effects were absent among humans at a level of 440 ng/kg.[27]

Fertility Effects

A major subset of reproductive effects involves fertility. Infertility in humans is the inability to produce a clinically recognizable pregnancy after 1 year of unprotected intercourse.[10] A couple finally achieving a pregnancy after one year is considered to be subfertile. Fertility disorders, especially those due to toxic chemical exposure, are not easy to diagnose as there are a number of inaccuracies associated with measuring the endpoints.[3] Time to pregnancy is a sensitive measure of fertility in either sex although there are potential problems in study design, statistical analysis and interpretation of time to pregnancy studies.[28] Other issues with infertility studies are confounders such as drugs, alcohol, smoking, hormonal imbalances unrelated to exposure, diseases, structural issues, ovulation problems in women, socioeconomic status, age and education. Infertility has many causes, and only a portion of these are related to occupational factors. There are few substances proven to influence fertility in occupational medicine. These are lead, organic mercury compounds, manganese, carbon disulfide, 2-bromopropane and dibromochloropropane (DBCP).[3,10,29]

The impact of occupational agents on the fertility of male workers has been explored only to a limited extent. Infertility or unsuccessful pregnancy outcome traditionally has been assumed to be linked with female health problems.[10] However, evidence, substantiated by animal studies, indicates that spermatogenesis (production of round spermatids) and spermiogenesis (cellular differentiation of spermatids into spermatozoa, the motile reproductive cells) are highly susceptible to many toxic substances.[10] A number of cases involving occupational exposure to a chemical that produced infertility are presented as examples.

DBCP

Infertility was discovered among men working in a California pesticide factory.[30] The cause was shown to be exposure to the chemical 1,2-dibromo-3-chloropropane (DBCP) used as a nematocide. Starting in 1962, the company formulated DBCP in a special agricultural chemical division. Workers in that division became aware that very few of them had recently fathered children. A preliminary examination of 5 men revealed oligospermia or azoospermia, which were later found to be the major effects of this chemical. All 39 employees in the division were then tested by medical history questionnaire with interview, medical examination, semen analysis, urinalysis, complete blood count (CBC), blood chemistry, serum levels of thyroid hormones, testosterone, follicle stimulating hormone (FSH, promotes sperm production) and interstitial cell stimulating hormone (ICSH, controls testosterone production). After eliminating 11 vasectomized men and 3 men with intermediate sperm count levels, the remaining 11 men with low sperm counts (≤1 million) were compared with the men with normal sperm counts (≥ 40 million) for age and time worked in the division. Bilateral open testicular biopsies were performed on 9 volunteers with different exposure times and sperm counts. Airborne concentrations of DBCP in the factory were believed to be lower than 1 ppm, a value recommended in 1961 based on eye and respiratory irritation.[31] Actual measurements made with personal air samplers in 1977 averaged 0.4 ppm for an eight-hour day.

None of the men had loss of libido or sexual function or any other sexual characteristics. There was a significant relationship between length of exposure to DBCP and sperm counts. Workers with sperm counts less than 1 million had been exposed at least 3 years while workers exposed for only 3 months had normal sperm counts. Sperm motility in workers exposed longer was also reduced and there was an increase in abnormal morphology of sperm. Although testosterone levels were not different, FSH and ICSH levels were significantly elevated among the workers exposed for longer durations. Testicular biopsy results showed the severely affected men with loss of spermatogonia presented no evidence of inflammation or severe fibrosis.[30]

Animal exposures to 12 ppm DBCP for 72–90 days produced severe atrophy of the testes with degenerative changes in the semi-niferous tubules and reduction in number of sperm cells.[31] Additional testing in rats demonstrated that DBCP is directly toxic to sperm.[32] Based on the human and animal data, it appears that very low levels of DBCP can, over time, still produce testicular effects in humans.

Glycol Ethers

Glycol ethers are useful solvents with widespread applications in industrial and commercial uses. A study of men was conducted in 1984 at a large shipbuilding facility with measured levels of ethylene glycol ethers. Workers expressed concern after an evaluation by NIOSH; the study was in response to their concern.[33] The occupational exposure limits were 200 ppm for 2-ethoxyethanol (2-EE) and 25 for 2-methoxyethanol (2-ME) based on 1970 regulations, but the TLVs® were only 5 ppm for both in 1986.[34] The potential for developmental and reproductive effects was not clear at the time. Paints containing ethylene glycol ethers were used by 75% of the sampled interior painting crew members.[33] A participation rate of 50% was achieved for the 159 painters invited to take part in the study while the participation rate was only 32% for the controls consisting of clerks and draftsmen. A follow-up survey was conducted that ensured there was no bias associated with the low participation rates.[35] Each worker was given a questionnaire, a physical exam and had blood, urine and semen collected. Blood was measured for complete blood count (CBC) with white blood cell differential count, serum FSH and luteinizing hormones, and serum testosterone. Urine was tested for the metabolites of 2-EE and 2-ME, ethoxyacetic acid and methoxyacetic acid, respectively, to confirm exposure to ethylene glycol ethers. Semen was analyzed for volume and pH, and for sperm count, concentration, motility, velocity, viability and morphology. Industrial hygiene surveys measured exposures as 8-hour time weighted averages; 2-EE concentrations ranged from 0–80.5 mg/m^3 with a mean of 9.9 mg/m^3 (TLV® of 19 mg/m^3; 5ppm) and 2-ME concentrations ranged from 0–17.7 mg/m^3 with a mean of 2.6 mg/m^3 (TLV® of 16 mg/m^3; 5 ppm). Lead was also measured because it is known to cause a depression of sperm count; the metal was not shown to be a confounder in this study.[35]

The results of the semen analysis suggested that there was an effect of ethylene glycol ethers on sperm count. The proportion of exposed painters with a sperm count of ≤20 million/cc was 13%, with 5% as expected based on control values. The proportion of exposed workers with azoospermia was 5%, with only 1% as the expected value.[35] Testicular atrophy was seen in mice exposed to 2-ME at concentrations equal to or greater than 250 mg/kg after 5 weeks.[34]

A retrospective cohort study was conducted for exposures to ethylene glycol ethers (EGE) among workers at two semiconductor manufacturing plants in the eastern United States in 1980-1989 as part of a larger evaluation of reproductive health.[36] Semiconductor manufacturing workers and their spouses were interviewed to obtain reproductive and occupational histories. Exposure to mixtures containing EGE (none, low, medium, and high) was assessed based on reported processes and company records. Of the 1,150 pregnancies recorded, 561 were in female employees and 589 in wives of male employees. Potential exposure among female workers to mixtures containing EGE was associated with increased risks of spontaneous abortion (relative risk in the high exposure group = 2.8; 95% confidence interval (CI) 1.4–5.6) and subfertility (i.e., a successful pregnancy but more than 1 year of unprotected intercourse was required to achieve the pregnancy; odds ratio in the high exposure group = 4.6; 95% CI 1.6–13.3). Both of these risks exhibited a significant trend for dose-response relationship with potential EGE exposure (p=0.02). There was no increased risk of spontaneous abortion among spouses of male workers potentially exposed to mixtures containing EGE, but there was an insignificant increase (odds ratio in the high exposure group = 1.7; 95% CI 0.7–4.3) in subfertility risk.[36]

Welding Exposures

A number of studies have been conducted to examine the potential for welding to affect fertility because of the metals involved, as well as exposure to heat and low doses of ultraviolet radiation. A cross sectional study of the reproductive system was conducted in male metal workers at three plants involving welders producing mild steel constructions for industry or stainless steel equipment for the food industry and stainless steel pumps. Mild steel is a carbon steel that may not be covered by a standard specification and is easier to weld. The participation rate was 37.1% in welders and 36.7% in non-welding subjects. Moderate deterioration was found in several semen parameters, as well as an increase in FSH in mild steel welders and less than reliable changes of semen quality in stainless steel welders who, on average, were exposed to lower concentrations of welding fumes for fewer years.[37] A follow up study using a longitudinal design was conducted on the same categories of welders. Three semen samples were collected one month apart prior to 3 weeks of vacation and then again at 3, 5 and 8 weeks following the end of the vacation period. Semen was analyzed for sperm concentration, morphology, sperm count, volume, linear penetration rate, motility and immature sperm forms. No consistent improvements in any semen parameter in the follow up period were found in either the mild steel or stainless steel welders. The major components of welding fumes are iron, zinc and manganese, while other metals like chromium, nickel, copper, cadmium and lead are present in trace quantities.[38] Although they were not identified in this study, the metals in the welding fumes appear to be producing testicular damage and decreased semen quality that cannot recover in only a three week non-exposure period. There may also be a non-causal nature of reported associations between welding exposure and poor semen quality.[39]

Based on preliminary data, another study was conducted to investigate sperm quality and reproductive hormones among workers performing arc and gas welding in a workshop. Although sperm concentration was in the normal range in all seventeen welders, motility, morphology and the Hypo Osmotic Swelling test (HOS) suggested that welding might have had some adverse effects. Hormonal levels were normal in all but two welders.[38] Welding has the potential to produce reproductive effects but a more comprehensive study is still needed.

Styrene

Styrene is used as a monomer to make plastics that are also used in rubber, insulation, fiberglass, pipes, automobile parts, food containers, and carpet backing. Because of its widespread use, it has been investigated for potential reproductive effects. A study on male reproductive toxicity in reinforced plastics workers was reported by Kolstad et al.[40] This longitudinal study provided suggestive evidence that low-level styrene exposure may deteriorate spermatogenesis. Efforts to repeat the study in other countries failed and the preliminary findings of international time-to-pregnancy studies within the reinforced plastics industry do not indicate a relationship between exposure to styrene and male fecundity.[40]

However, the presumed metabolite of styrene, styrene oxide, has been shown to produce reproductive and developmental toxicity as well as maternal toxicity in laboratory animals. Sikov and co-workers[41] conducted experiments to evaluate the reproductive and developmental toxicology in rats and rabbits exposed to styrene oxide by inhalation. Female rats were exposed to 100 or 300 ppm styrene oxide or to filtered air for 7 h/day, 5 days/week for 3 weeks. Mortality occurred in rats that received prolonged exposure to 100 ppm styrene oxide while 300 ppm was acutely lethal. The rats of the 0 and 100 ppm groups were then mated and exposed to 0 or 100 ppm styrene oxide daily through 18 days of gestation (dg). Female rabbits were artificially inseminated and exposed for 7 hours daily to 0, 15, or 50 ppm styrene oxide through 24 dg. Both concentrations used for rabbit exposures produced mortality. The rats were euthanized at 20 dg and the rabbits at 30 dg. Exposure during gestation appeared to increase pre-implantation loss in rats, and tended to increase the incidence of resorptions in rabbits. In both species, fetal weights and crown-rump lengths were reduced by gestational exposure. Incidences of ossification defects of the sternebrae and occipital bones were increased by gestational exposure of rats to styrene oxide.[41] Species differences in styrene metabolism to styrene oxide could explain the differences between humans and animals. When the rate of formation of styrene glycol, a measurable metabolite of styrene, was compared in human, rat and mouse liver microsomes, the rate of metabolism for humans was slower than in rats and mice. Although discrepancies between humans and animals may exist, developmental and reproductive toxicity testing is necessary to help prevent human effects.[42]

Lead

Environmental exposures to lead are known to result in developmental issues among children.[43] Occupational exposures to lead typically involve higher exposure concentrations than in the general environment.[44] A cross sectional survey to examine the sperm count of 503 men employed by 10 companies (two smelters, three battery companies, three copper alloy foundries, a university hospital and a private security company) was conducted in the U.K., Italy, and Belgium.[45] The mean blood lead concentration was 31.0 µg/dL (range 4.6–64.5) in 362 workers exposed to lead and 4.4 µg/dL in 141 reference workers. Semen volume and sperm concentration were determined in fresh semen samples. Period of sexual abstinence and age were adjusted in the statistical analysis. The median sperm concentration was reduced by 49% in men with blood lead concentration above 50 µg/dL, although there was no indication of a linear trend of lower sperm concentration with increasing blood lead values. A threshold slope least square regression identified a blood lead concentration of 44 µg/dL as a potential threshold for sperm reduction. Abnormal sperm chromatin structure was not related to blood lead concentration, but some indications of deterioration of sperm chromatin were found in men with the highest concentrations of lead within spermatozoa. Adverse effects on total sperm count, sperm concentration, and chromatin structure appear unlikely below the threshold for blood lead concentration of 44 µg/dL, but this concentration may not protect all workers. Reduced semen quantity or quality was not associated with longer term exposure.[45] The current action level of the OSHA lead standard in the U.S. is 40 µg/dL, which is consistent with this threshold.

Concerns for exposure to lead involve not only male and female adults but potential effects on the growth and development of children.[43] Most prospective studies of lead exposure confirm the main outcome of cross sectional studies, namely an inverse association between environmental lead exposure during development and cognitive ability in children.[46] Cognitive impairment involving IQ-decrements between 1 to 3 points were shown to be associated with increasing lead from 10 to 20 µg/dL,46 but changes in IQ can occur at blood lead levels below 10 µg/dL.[47,48]

Military Exposures

The military has men and women working in occupations involving exposure to industrial chemicals and materials such as solvents. Limited information is available on the reproductive effects of solvents and fuels. In a prospective study at a military base, 50 aircraft maintenance workers were evaluated prior to jet fuel and solvent exposure and at 15 and 30 weeks after exposures began to examine the potential reproductive effect of exposure to solvents and fuels. The solvents studied included 1,1,1-trichloroethane (TCA), toluene, methyl ethyl ketone (MEK), xylene and methylene chloride, while the fuel studied was JP-4 jet fuel. Workers were evaluated for sperm production, structure and function. Industrial hygiene and expired breath samples were analyzed for exposure by measuring benzene, total naphthas (surrogate for jet fuel), and total solvents by summing trichloroethane, methyl ethyl ketone, xylenes, toluene and methylene chloride. Exposure levels were below 10% of the OSHA standard for all chemicals except benzene, which was still below permissible exposure limits. Among maintenance crews, sheet metal workers had the highest mean breath levels for both total solvents and fuels. For most sperm measures, mean values remained in the normal range throughout the 30 weeks of the study. When jobs were analyzed by groups, paint shop workers had a significant decline in sperm motility of 19.5% at 30 weeks. Exposure to jet fuel did not show an apparent effect on semen quality for aircraft maintenance workers.[49]

Infertility risk factors were investigated in a military population associated with a naval base in France. Sixty couples with infertility for more than 12 months were compared with 165 couples who had conceived a child. All of the men in these couples had been employed in the military, 67 of them as submariners, and many as submarine maintenance workers. Exposures were to one or more of the following: heat, solvents, nuclear radiation, radar waves and electromagnetic fields. Although no radiation exposure measurements were available, the results of the study suggested that the greater risk factors for fertility were associated with working in very hot conditions.[50] Several articles review the complex effects of occupational stressors (including heat) and their effects on human reproduction.[51,52]

Animal Studies with Reproductive Toxicants

Toxicity studies in animals can identify potential hazards to development or reproductive function. For several chemicals discussed above, effects in humans have been linked to chemical exposures before animal studies were conducted to predict a potential hazard. However, animal studies play an important part in reproductive toxicology and can be predictive for humans by examining dose–response patterns, routes of exposure and cellular/molecular mechanisms before sufficient human information is available.

Examples presented earlier in the chapter involved occupational exposures to humans prior to studies being conducted in animals. Ideally, animal developmental and reproductive studies are conducted prior to human exposure.

Types of Animal Studies

Designing the study correctly is just as important as conducting the study. Animal reproductive studies should be designed to closely mimic human exposures in order to reveal realistic risk.[11] Conducting studies using the route of exposure in the occupational setting is important to consider. A number of studies have been identified by the U.S. EPA for use in the testing of pesticides and toxic substances by the Office of Prevention, Pesticides and Toxic Substances (OPPTS) for reproductive and developmental effects. The studies are identified by an OPPTS guideline number. The reproduction/developmental toxicity screening test (OPPTS 870.3550) involves dosing male and female rats two weeks prior to mating, throughout mating and during gestation. The pups are examined on Day 4 after birth when the study ends. This test does not provide complete information on all aspects of reproduction and development. In particular, it offers only limited means of detecting postnatal effects of prenatal exposure, or effects that may be induced during postnatal exposure. The combined repeated dose toxicity study with the reproduction/developmental toxicity screening test (OPPTS 870.3650) has the same dosing schedule and endpoints as the reproduction/developmental toxicity screening test but involves more general toxicity endpoints. The prenatal developmental toxicity study (OPPTS 870.3700) involves exposing animals throughout gestation and examining the fetuses on the day before they are scheduled to be born. The reproduction and fertility effects study (OPPTS 870.3800) involves exposure and mating of animals from two generations, both the parents and their offspring. Dosing starts 10 weeks prior to mating of the parents and ends when the second generation is weaned. The two-generation reproduction test is designed to provide information concerning the effects of a chemical on the integrity and performance of the male and female reproductive systems, including gonadal function, the estrous cycle, mating behavior, conception, gestation, parturition, lactation and weaning, and on the growth and development of the offspring.

Many chemicals have not been tested for reproductive and developmental toxicity. It cannot be assumed that if there are no positive data for a chemical that it is not a reproductive or developmental toxicant because it may never have been tested. For a list of chemicals which have been tested and found to be reproductive toxicants, the State of California Environmental Protection Agency Office of Environmental Health Hazard Assessment, under the Safe Drinking Water And Toxic Enforcement Act of 1986, lists chemicals known to the state to cause cancer or reproductive toxicity.[53]

The Screening Information Data Set (SIDS) is a series of toxicological tests developed by the Organization for Economic Cooperation and Development (OECD) in 1999 to screen high production volume (HPV) chemicals. The following tests are part of the SIDS: acute toxicity, repeat-dose toxicity (28-day or 90-day), developmental/reproductive toxicity, genotoxicity/mutagenicity, ecotoxicity and environmental fate. For reproductive toxicity, measurements of sperm motility and morphology were considered ready for addition to the SIDS.[54] A number of individual chemicals have been identified through animal studies to be developmental or reproductive toxicants through studies such as those identified above. A selection of chemicals whose reproductive effects are defined by animal studies follow.

Trimethyltin

Trimethyltin (TMT) appears to be the most toxic of the organotins and acts on the central nervous system in both adults and neonates. Pregnant rats exposed to single doses of 5, 7 or 9 mg/kg TMT during gestation experienced decreased maternal weight from controls that became more pronounced with increasing dose. Litter sizes were decreased for groups treated with the TMT highest dose. Pup weights were also decreased with differences seen based on dose and exposure time during gestation. There was minimal neuropathology in the hippocampus of exposed pups. Although exposure to TMT during gestation in this study resulted in toxicity in exposed pups, there was maternal toxicity as evidenced by the decreased body weights.[55] These animal studies suggest that adequate protection of the human mother should protect the developing fetus and neonate from TMT, although it may not always be the case.

Inorganic Arsenic

Inorganic arsenic has been used in agriculture as an insecticide, herbicide, rodenticide and fungicide, as well as a component of glass, alloys, electronic components (semiconductors) and pigments. The As^{+3} and As^{+5} oxidation states of arsenic have toxicologic significance.[56] A variety of species, have shown embryotoxic effects after exposure to inorganic arsenic. Changes seen in animals after exposure to trivalent or pentavalent arsenic include malformations of the skeleton, neural tube (developing brain), eyes and genitourinary systems; prenatal deaths have also been seen.[57] However, a more recent review points out that the repeated dose studies carried out following EPA OPPTS Guidelines for assessing developmental toxicity did not support inorganic arsenic as being a developmental toxicant.[56]

Gasoline

Reproductive animal studies may have the effect of reducing uncertainty for chemicals to which humans are frequently exposed. A two-generation reproductive toxicity study in rats was conducted for vapor recovery unit gasoline. A two-generation study exposes both the parents, their offspring (F1) and ends after the birth of the second generation of offspring (F2). Inhalation exposures were at concentrations of 5000, 10,000 and 20,000 mg/m³ gasoline vapors. No reproductive toxicity was seen for this volatile fraction of formulated gasoline with which humans are most likely to come in contact.[58]

Vinyl Chloride

The current ACGIH TLV® for vinyl chloride (VC) is 1 ppm.[59] However, the potential effects of VC exposure on the human reproductive system is not known as epidemiological studies involving workers have not been conclusive.[60] To assess potential maternal, embryo-fetal developmental and reproductive toxicity of inhaled VC exposures were conducted in rats at 0, 10, 100, and 1100 ppm. Female rats were exposed to VC daily from gestation day 6 through 19 in the embryo-fetal/developmental study and the parental generation male and female rats were exposed to VC for 10 weeks prior to mating and during the three-week mating periods in the two-generation reproductive study. In addition, the F1 generation female rats were exposed from conception through gestation and lactation Day 4 through 25. No developmental or reproductive effects were seen in rats up to 1100 ppm VC suggesting that VC is not an occupational hazard at the TLV®.[60]

Beta-chloroprene

Beta-chloroprene, the 2-chloro analog of 1,3-butadiene, is used in the manufacture of polychloroprene rubber. This synthetic rubber is used in automotive applications (belts, hoses and gaskets), adhesives, wire and cable insulation, structural shock absorbers and other load-bearing products. Beta-chloroprene has been in commercial production since 1932. A number of inhalation toxicity studies were conducted as inhalation is the primary route for potential occupational exposure of this chemical. One study in mice and two studies in rats found the no observable adverse effect level (NOAEL) to be 32 ppb based on nasal injury in rats. Overall, the data from reproductive and developmental studies suggest that beta-chloroprene does not impact male or female reproduction or developmental parameters in pregnant female rats, except possibly when levels approach lethality (greater than 161 ppm repeated exposure; 280 ppm acutely).[61] Beta-chloroprene is an example of a chemical that has been tested for male and female reproduction/developmental parameters and was found to be negative.

Perfluoroalkyl Acids

Perfluoroalkyl acids such as perfluorooctane sulfonate (PFOS) and perfluorooctanoic acid (PFOA) have applications in numerous industrial and consumer products. PFOS is converted into other intermediates such as acids, alcohols, and sulfonamides for further polymerization and esterification. PFOA, primarily as the ammonium salt, can be used as a surfactant and an emulsifier in the production of polytetrafluoroethylene as well as other fluoropolymers and fluoroelastomers. The toxicology of several of these compounds has been investigated in the past, but there is renewed interest in this class of chemicals because PFOS and PFOA have been found in human serum at ppb levels. Although this class of chemicals has not shown any evidence of birth defects or malformations, reproductive studies have found various adverse effects, such as pre- and post-weaning mortality, delays in eye opening and pubertal onset, reduced body weight at weaning and subsequent weight gain, that raise human health risk issues.[62]

Fire Retardants

By volume, approximately 25% of flame retardants in use are brominated compounds in which the bromine component is responsible for the flame retardant activity. The three commercial poly-brominated diphenyl oxide flame retardants manufactured are: decabromodiphenyl oxide (DBDPO), octabromodiphenyl oxide (OBDPO) and pentabromodiphenyl oxide (PeBDPO). DBDPO's main application is in high impact polystyrene for electronic enclosures. OBDPO is used to flame retard business equipment constructed of acrylonitrile–butadiene–styrene plastic while PeBDPO is used to flame retard polyurethane foam used as cushioning in upholstery. DBDPO is relatively non toxic (NOAEL in repeated dose studies was greater than or equal to 1000 mg/kg body weight.) and does not affect development or reproduction in rats. OBDPO is toxic (NOAEL in a 90-day study was equal to 15 mg/m^3 or about 100 mg/kg), caused developmental effects but was not tested for reproductive toxicity. PeBDPO is more toxic (NOAEL<2 mg/kg/d in a 90-day study), but did not cause developmental effects. PeBDPO was not tested for reproductive toxicity but was shown to decrease serum thyroxin (T4) levels, which could lead to developmental effects if exposure occurs during pregnancy. Within this class of chemicals, the developmental and reproductive effects vary by chemical.[63]

Mixtures

Exposure to mixtures of chemicals or metals is also a concern. Workers are rarely exposed to just one chemical; occupational exposures typically include complex mixtures of chemicals.(64) Toxic interaction can result in additive, greater-than-additive (potentiation, synergistic), or less-than-additive (antagonistic) response. Few studies have examined mixture effects on reproductive endpoints. Three studies are discussed below. To be realistic, more studies need to be conducted on exposures to chemical mixtures (see chapter on Toxicology of Complex Chemical Mixtures).

To examine the developmental toxicity of three metals, lead nitrate (Pb, 25 mg/kg, subcutaneous (SC) dosing), methylmercury chloride (Hg, 12.5 mg/kg, oral dosing) and sodium arsenite (As, 6 mg/kg, SC) were administered to CD1 mice on gestation day 10 either separately or in binary or ternary combinations. Fetuses were examined for malformations and variations on day 18 of gestation. Exposure of pregnant mice to Pb and As at doses that were practically nontoxic to dams, concurrently with organic Hg at a toxic dose, caused supra-additive interactions in maternal toxicity. With regard to developmental toxicity, the most relevant effects (decreased fetal weight, cleft palate) corresponded to the Hg-treated groups. At the doses in this study, the interactive effects of Pb and As on Hg-induced developmental toxicity were not greater than the effect of adding or combining the effects of the three metals.[65]

Another study of mixtures looked at the effects of selenium and methylmercury on development, as selenium has been shown to reverse the neurotoxic effects of methylmercury under certain conditions. Exposure to levels 0, 40 and 400 mg/kg/day methylmercury during gestation produced changes in spatial discrimination in offspring. However, rats on a low selenium diet (0.06 ppm) also showed changes in spatial discrimination. Based on the results of exposure to the low or high (0.6 ppm) selenium diets in combination with methylmercury, there was no interaction between methylmercury and selenium. The higher level of selenium did not provide protection from methylmercury in this study.[66]

In rats, n-butyl acetate (BA) produces maternal toxicity by significant decreases in body weight gain at 2000 and 3000 ppm, and by reduced food consumption at concentrations 1000 ppm following whole body inhalation exposure, 6 h/day, from day 6 to 20 of gestation, at concentrations of 0, 500, 1000, 2000 and 3000 ppm. BA was not a developmental toxicant because the only effect seen was significant decrease in fetal weight at 3000 ppm. When simultaneous exposures to ethylbenzene (EB; 0, 250 or 1000 ppm) and BA (0, 500 or 1500 ppm), or to toluene (TOL; 0, 500 or 1500 ppm) and BA (0, 500, 1500 ppm) were evaluated, the maternal weight gain was reduced after exposure to 1000 ppm EB, to 1500 ppm BA, or to 1500 ppm TOL, either alone or in binary combinations. A significant reduction of fetal weight was associated with exposure to 1000 ppm EB alone, to the mixture of EB and BA (both concentrations), or to 1500 ppm TOL alone or combined with BA at either concentration. No embryolethal or developmental effects were observed at any exposure. Although combinations of chemical exposure produced toxicity seen as reduced body weight, there was no evidence of interaction between the chemicals to produce maternal or developmental effects.

Case Study[68]

In a California pesticide factory, a number of cases of infertility were discovered. The effects seen in 14 of 25 non-vasectomized men were azoospermia and oligospermia. Serum levels of FSH and luteinizing hormone were elevated. Testosterone levels were normal. The company employing these men manufactured fertilizers and ammonia. It also formulated pesticides for agricultural and household use. The workers mixed, diluted, and repackaged technical-grade pesticides. Some 100 different chemicals were used in the production of 200 products. These included organophosphorus compounds, halogenated hydrocarbons and carbamates. For several years before this study, the men working in the plant had become increasingly aware that few of them had recently fathered children. The agricultural chemical division (ACD) of the plant was identified early in the study as the area where the infertility problems were seen. A relationship between the time working with the nematocide, 1,2-dibromo-3-chloropropane (DBCP) was seen. After this study, communications with other plants producing DBCP evidenced the extent of the infertility problem.

Summary

Reproductive toxicology focuses on reproductive processes and structures while developmental toxicology on normal development starting at the fertilized egg. A number of chemicals have been shown to cause reproductive or developmental toxicity. However, the greatest effect by chemical exposure in the workplace is infertility, the inability to produce pregnancy following a year or more of unprotected intercourse. There are fewer studies identifying reproductive outcomes other that fertility. A few chemicals have different effects in one gender than the other.

Animal toxicity studies can be used to identify the potential for reproductive and developmental toxicity or they can be used to identify the mechanism of action and safe exposure limit when an occupational exposure reveals the toxicity of a chemical. The animal studies need to be designed to represent the occupational exposure as closely as possible. Much more data are needed to address the potential reproductive and developmental toxicities of occupational exposure.

Additional Reading

The Navy Environmental Health Center has published a technical manual on *Reproductive and Developmental Hazards: A Guide for Occupational Health Professionals*.[69] The manual provides guidance to Navy occupational health professionals in the evaluation and management of reproductive and developmental hazards in the workplace. The manual may be found on the Navy Environmental Health Center, Occupational and Environmental Medicine Directorate Web site at the following Internet address: http://www-nehc.med.navy.mil/occmed/ index.htm.

The National Toxicology Program (NTP) Center for the Evaluation of Risks to Human Reproduction (CERHR) was established by the NTP and the National Institute of Environmental Health Sciences (NIEHS) in 1998 to address the impact of chemical exposures on human reproductive and developmental health and to serve as an environmental and reproductive health resource for government agencies and the general public[70] CERHR evaluations involve the critical review of reproductive, developmental, and other relevant toxicity data by independent panels of scientists. The products of these evaluations are expert panel reports. Over the last five years, CERHR conducted expert panel evaluations on 14 chemicals. Panel reports have been published for 13 chemicals and 12 NTP-CERHR monographs (available on the internet) have been issued on the following chemicals: butyl benzyl phthalate (BBP), di-n-butyl phthalate (DBP), di-n-hexyl phthalate (DHP), di-isodecyl phthalate (DIDP), di-isononyl phthalate (DINP), di-n-octyl phthalate (DnOP), methanol, 1-bromopropane, 2-bromopropane, ethylene glycol, propylene glycol and fluoxetine. NTP conclusions for acrylamide and di(2-ethylhexyl) phthalate (DEHP) have not been finalized.[69]

TOXNET contains Developmental and Reproductive Toxicology Database (DART) citations since 1989 on birth defects and other aspects of reproductive and developmental toxicology[71] TOXNET is managed by the National Library of Medicine's Division of Specialized Information Services and is co-funded by EPA, National Library of Medicine and NIEHS. The Environmental Teratogen Information Center Back File (ETICBACK) contains citations from pre-1950 through 1989.

The Reproductive Effects of Chemical, Physical and Biologic Agents (REPROTOX) Database is a computerized repository for literature on reproductive and developmental toxicology.[72] This resource was developed to provide summary information to health care providers on the effects of chemical and physical agents on fertility, pregnancy and lactation. Agents include industrial and environmental chemicals, as well as over-the-counter, prescription and recreational drugs. There are summaries for more than 4,000 agents, along with references for the data included.

Textbooks are:

- **Timbrell, J. A.:** *Principles of Biochemical Toxicology*, 3rd edition. London: Taylor and Francis, London, 2000. pp. 394. ISBN 0-7484-0736-7. A highly readable introductory text.
- **Klaassen, C.D. (ed.):** *Casarett & Doull's Toxicology: The Basic Science of Poisons*, 6th edition. New York: McGraw-Hill, 2001. pp. 1236. ISBN 0-07-134721-6. A more detailed text. See Chapters 10 and 19.
- **Hayes, A.W. (ed.):** *Principles and Methods of Toxicology*, 4th edition. Philadelphia: Taylor and Francis. pp. 1887. ISBN 1-56032-814-2. A good general toxicology text. See Chapters 28, 29 and 30.
- **Koren, G. (ed.):** *Maternal-Fetal Toxicology: A Clinician's Guide*, 3rd edition. New York: Marcel Dekker, Inc., 2001. pp. 830. ISBN 0-8247-0378-2. A little more specific.
- **Hood, R.D. (ed.):** *Developmental and Reproductive Toxicology: A Practical Approach*, 2nd edition. Boca Raton, FL: CRC Press, Taylor & Francis Group, 2006. pp. 1149. ISBN 978-0-8493-1254-0. A good reference.
- **California Environmental Protection Agency, Office of Environmental Health Hazard Assessment:** Chemicals known to the state to cause cancer or reproductive toxicity. http://www.oehha.ca.gov/prop65/prop65_list/files/060107LST.pdf [Accessed June 1, 2007].

References

1. **Mosher, W.D. and W.F. Pratt:** Fecundity and infertility in the United States: Incidence and trends. *Fertil. Steril.* 56:192–193 (1991).

2. **WHO:** Towards more objectivity in diagnosis and management of male infertility. *Int. J. Androl.* Suppl 7 (1987).
3. **Winker, R. and H.W. Rudiger:** Reproductive toxicology in occupational settings: an update. *Int. Arch. Occup. Environ. Health 79*:1–10 (2006).
4. **Sheiner, E.K., E. Sheiner, R.D. Hammel, G. Potashnik, R. Carel:** Effect of occupational exposures on male fertility: literature review. *Ind. Health 41*:55–62 (2003).
5. **Vorhees, C.V.:** Concepts in teratology and developmental toxicology derived from animal research. *Ann. N. Y. Acad. Sci. 562*:31–41 (1989).
6. **Rogers, J.M. and R.J. Kavlock:** Developmental Toxicology. Chapter 10 in *Casarett & Doull's Toxicology: The Basic Science of Poisons*. McGraw-Hill, New York, 2001, Sixth Edition, pp. 1236. Edited by Curtis D. Klaassen. ISBN 0-07-134721-6 (2001).
7. **U.S.EPA.** Guidelines for developmental toxicity risk assessment. Office of Research and Development, Washington, D.C. EPA/600/FR-91/001 (1991).
8. **Kimmel, C.A., W.M. Generoso, R.D. Thomas, and K.S. Bakshi:** A new frontier in understanding the mechanisms of developmental abnormalities. *Toxicol. Appl. Pharmacol. 119*:159–165 (1993).
9. **U.S. EPA:** Guidelines for Reproductive Toxicity Risk Assessment. U.S. Environmental Protection Agency, Risk Assessment Forum, Washington, DC, 630/R-96/009 (1996).
10. **Baranski, B.:** Effects of the workplace on fertility and related reproductive outcomes. *Environ. Health Perspect. 101(Suppl 2)*:81–90 (1993).
11. **Hoyer, P.B.:** Reproductive toxicology: current and future directions. *Biochem. Pharmacol. 62*:1557–1564 (2001).
12. **Kim, Y., K. Jung, T. Hwang, G. Jung, J. Kim, H. Kim, et al.:** Hematopoietic and reproductive hazards of Korean electronic workers exposed to solvents containing 2-bromopropane. *Scand. J. Work Environ. Health 22*:387–391 (1996).
13. **Yu, X., M. Kamijima, G. Ichihara, W. Li, J. Kitoh, Z. Xie, et al.:** 2-Bromopropane causes ovarian dysfunction by damaging primordial follicles and their oocytes in female rats. *Toxicol. Appl. Pharmacol. 159*:185–193 (1999).
14. **Omura, M., Y. Romero, M. Zhao, and N. Inoue:** Histopathological evidence that spermatogonia are the target cells of 2-bromopropane. *Toxicol. Lett. 104*:19–26 (1999).
15. **Reutman, S.R., G.K. LeMasters, E.A. Knecht, R. Shukla, J.E. Lockey, G.E. Burroughs, et al.:** Evidence of reproductive endocrine effects in women with occupational fuel and solvent exposures. *Environ. Health Perspect. 110*:805–811 (2002).
16. **ILSI (International Life Sciences Institute):** Health Issues Related to Alcohol Consumption. 2nd edition), McDonald I. (ed.). Blackwell Science: Oxford (1999).
17. **Barr H. and A. Streissguth:** Identifying maternal self-reported alcohol use associated with fetal alcohol spectrum disorders. *Alcohol. Clin. Exp. Res. 25*:283–287 (2001).
18. **Driscoll C., A. Streissguth, and E. Riley:** Prenatal alcohol exposure: comparability of effects in humans and animal models. *Neurotoxicol. Teratol. 12*:231–237 (1990).
19. **Heng, K., S. Hargarten, P. Layde, A. Craven, and S. Zhu:** Moderate alcohol intake and motor vehicle crashes: the conflict between health advantage and at-risk use. *Alcohol. 41*:451–454 (2006).
20. **Pastino, G., B. Asgharian, K. Roberts, M. Medinsky, and J. Bond:** A comparison of physiologically based pharmacokinetic model predictions and experimental data for inhaled ethanol in male and female B6C3F1 mice, F344 rats and humans. *Toxicol. Appl. Pharmacol. 145*:147–157 (1997).
21. **Irvine, L.F.:** Relevance of the developmental toxicity of ethanol in the occupational setting: a review. *J. Appl. Toxicol. 23*:289–299 (2003).
22. **Foster, P.M.D., R.C. Cattley, and E. Mylchreest:** Effects of di-n-butyl phthalate (DBP) on male reproductive development in the rat: implications for human risk assessment. *Food Chem. Toxicol. 38(Suppl 1)*:S97–99 (2000).
23. **Mylchreest, E., R.C. Cattley, and P.M.D. Foster:** Male reproductive tract malformations in rats following gestational and lactational exposure to di(n-butyl) phthalate: an antiandrogenic mechanism? *Toxicol. Sci. 43*:47–60 (1998).
24. **Mylchreest, E., D.G. Wallace, R.C. Cattley, and P.M.D. Foster:** Dose-dependent alterations in androgen-regulated male reproductive development in rats exposed to di(n-butyl) phthalate during late gestation. *Toxicol. Sci. 55*:143–151 (2000).
25. **Ema, M., E.M. Miyawaki, and K. Kawashima:** Effects of dibutyl phthalate on reproductive function in pregnant and pseudopregnant rats. *Reprod. Toxicol. 14*:13–19 (2000).
26. **Mocarelli, P., P.M. Gerthoux, E. Ferrari, D.G. Patterson, S.M. Kieszak, P. Brambilla, N. Vincoli, S. Signorini, P. Tramacere, V. Carreri, E.J. Sampson, W.E. Turner, and L.L. Needham:** Paternal concentrations of dioxin and sex ration of offspring. *Lancet 355*:1858–1863 (2000).
27. **Greene, J.F., S. Hays, and D. Paustenbach:** Basis for a proposed reference dose (RfD) for dioxin of 1-10 pg/kg-day: a weight of evidence evaluation of the human and animal studies. *J. Toxicol. Environ. Health B Crit. Rev. 6*: 115–159 (2003).
28. **Joffe, M.:** Time to pregnancy: a measure of reproductive function in either sex. Asclepios Project. *Occup. Environ. Med. 54*:289–295 (1997).
29. **Koren, G (ed.):** Maternal-Fetal Toxicology, A Clinician's Guide. Marcel Dekker, Inc., New York, 2001, Third Edition, pp. 830.
30. **Whorton D., R.M. Krauss, S. Marshall, and T.H. Milby:** Infertility in male pesticide workers. *Lancet 2*:1259–1261 (1977).
31. **Torkelson, T.R., S.E. Sadek, V.K. Rowe, J.K. Kodama, H.H. Anderson, G.S. Loquvam and C.H. Hine:** Toxicologic Investigations of 1,2-Dibromo-3-Chloropropane. *Toxicol. Appl. Pharmacol. 3*:545–559 (1961).

32. **Kluwe, W.M., J.C. Lamb IV, A.E. Greenwell, and F.W. Harrington:** 1,2-Dibromo-3-chloropropane (DBCP)-induced infertility in male rats mediated by a post-testicular effect. *Toxicol. Appl. Pharmacol.* 71:294–298 (1983).

33. **Sparer, J., L.S. Welch, K. McManus, and M.R. Cullen:** Effects of exposure to ethylene glycol ethers on shipyard painters. I. Evaluation of exposure. *Am. J. Ind. Med. 14*: 497–507 (1988).

34. **Paustenbach, D.J.:** Assessment of the developmental risks resulting from occupational exposure to select glycol ethers within the semiconductor industry. *J. Toxicol. Environ. Health.* 23:29–75 (1988).

35. **Welch, L.S., S.M. Schrader, T.W. Turner, and M.R. Cullen:** Effects of exposure to ethylene glycol ethers on shipyard painters. II. Male reproduction. *Am. J. Ind. Med. 14*:509–526 (1988).

36. **Correa, A., R.H. Gray, R. Cohen, N. Rothman, F. Shah, H. Seacat, et al.:** Ethylene glycol ethers and risks of spontaneous abortion and subfertility. *Am. J. Epidemiol. 143*: 707–717 (1996).

37. **Bonde, J.P.:** Semen quality and sex hormone among mild steel and stainless steel welders: a cross sectional study. *Br. J. Ind. Med 47*:508–514 (1990a).

38. **Kumar, S., S.S.A. Zaidi, A.K. Gautam, L.M. Dave, and H.N. Saiyed:** Short communication: Semen quality and reproductive hormones among welders — a preliminary study. *Environ. Health Prevent. Med.* 8:64–67 (2003).

39. **Bonde, J.P.:** Semen quality in welders before and after three weeks of non-exposure. *Br. J. Ind. Med 47*:515–518 (1990b).

40. **Kolstad, H.A., J.P. Bonde, M. Spano, A. Giwercman, W. Zschiesche, D. Kaae, et al.:** Change in semen quality and sperm chromatin structure following occupational styrene exposure. ASCLEOPIOS. *Int. Arch. Occup. Environ. Health* 72:135–141 (1999).

41. **Sikov, M.R., W.C. Cannon, D.B. Carr, R.A. Miller, R.W. Niemeier, and B.D. Hardin:** Reproductive toxicology of inhaled styrene oxide in rats and rabbits. *J. Appl. Toxicol.* 6:155–164 (1986).

42. **Nakajima, T., E. Elovaara, F.J. Gonzalez, HV Gelboin, H. Vainio, T. Aoyama:** Characterization of the human cytochrome P450 isozymes responsible for styrene metabolism. *IARC Sci Publ.(127)*:101–108 (1993).

43. **Zelikoff, J.T., J.E. Bertin, T.M. Burbacher, E.S. Hunter, R.K. Miller, E.K. Silbergeld, et al.:** Health risks associated with prenatal metal exposure. *Fundam. Appl. Toxicol.* 25:161–170 (1995).

44. **Matte, T.D., P.J. Lanrigan, and E.L. Baker:** Occupational lead exposure. In *Human Lead Exposure*, H.L. Needleman (ed.), pp. 155–168. Boca Raton, FL: CRC Press, 1991. As cited in **Zelikoff, J.T., J.E. Bertin, T.M. Burbacher, E.S. Hunter, R.K. Miller, E.K. Silbergeld, et al.:** Health risks associated with prenatal metal exposure. *Fundam. Appl. Toxicol.* 25:161–170 (1995).

45. **Bonde, J.P., M, Joffe, P Apostoli, A Dale, P Kiss, M Spano, et al.:** Sperm count and chromatin structure in men exposed to inorganic lead: lowest adverse effect levels. *Occup. Environ. Med.* 59:234–242 (2002).

46. **Winneke, G., H. Lilienthal, and U. Kramer:** The neurobehavioural toxicology and teratology of lead. *Arch. Toxicol. Suppl.* 18:57–70 (1996).

47. **Toscano, C.T. and T.R. Guilarte:** Lead neurotoxicity: From exposure to molecular effects. *Brain Research Reviews 49*:529–554 (2005).

48. **Canfield, R. L., C.R. Henderson, Jr., D.A. Cory-Slechta, C. Cox, T.A. Jusko, and B.P. Lanphear:** Intellectual impairment in children with blood lead concentrations below 10 microg per deciliter. *N. Engl. J. Med.* 348:1517–1526 (2003).

49. **Lemasters, G.K., D.M. Olsen, J.H. Yiin, J.E. Lockey, R. Shukla, S.G. Selevan, S.M. Schrader, G.P. Toth, D.P. Evenson, G.B. Huszar:** Male reproductive effects of solvent and fuel exposure during aircraft maintenance. *Reprod Toxicol.* 13:155–166 (1999).

50. **Velez de la Calle, J.F., E. Rachou, M.T. le Martelot, B. Ducot, L. Multigner, and P.F. Thonneau:** Male infertility risk factors in a French military population. *Hum. Reprod.* 16:481–486 (2001).

51. **Oliva, A., A. Spra, and L. Multigner:** Contribution of environmental factors to the risk of make infertility. *Hum. Reprod. 16(8)*:1768–1776 (2001)

52. **Kumar, S.:** Occupational Exposure Associated with Reproductive Dysfunction. *J. Occup. Health 46*:1–19 (2004)

53. **California Environmental Protection Agency, Office of Environmental Health Hazard Assessment:** Chemicals known to the state to cause cancer or reproductive toxicity. Http://www.oehha.ca.gov/prop65/prop65_list/files/060107LST.pdf. [Accessed June 1, 2007).

54. **Green, S, A. Goldberg, and J. Zurlo:** TestSmart–high production volume chemicals: an approach to implementing alternatives into regulatory toxicology. *Toxicol. Sci.* 63:6–14 (2001).

55. **Paule, M.G., K. Reuhl, J.J. Chen, S.F. Ali and W. Slikker, Jr.:** Developmental toxicology of trimethyltin in the rat. *Toxicol. Appl. Pharmacol.* 84:412–417 (1986).

56. **DeSesso, J.M., C.F. Jacobson, A.R. Scialli, C.H. Farr and J.F. Holson:** An assessment of the developmental toxicity of inorganic arsenic. *Reproductive Toxicology, 12(4)*: 385-433 1998).

57. **Willhite, C.C. and V.H. Ferm:** Prenatal and developmental toxicology of arsenicals. *Adv. Exp. Med. Biol.* 177: 205–228 (1984).

58. **McKee, R.H., G.W. Trimmer, F.T. Whitman, C.S. Nessel, C.R. Mackerer, R. Hagemann, et al.:** Assessment in rats of the reproductive toxicity of gasoline from a gasoline vapor recovery unit. *Reprod. Toxicol.* 14:337–353 (2000).

59. **ACGIH (American Conference of Governmental Hygienists):** Threshold Limit Values and Biological Exposure Indices. American Conference of Governmental Hygienists, Cincinnati, OH (2007).

60. **Thornton, S.R., R.E. Schroeder, R.L. Robison, D.E. Rodwell, D.A. Penney, K.D. Nitschke,** *et al.***:** Embryo-fetal developmental and reproductive toxicology of vinyl chloride in rats. Toxicol. Sci. 68:207-219 (2002).
61. **Valentine, R. and M.W. Himmelstein:** Overview of the acute, subchronic, reproductive, developmental and genetic toxicology of beta-chloroprene. *Chem. Biol. Interact. 135–136*:81–100 (2001).
62. **Lau, C., J.L. Butenhoff, and J.M. Rogers:** The developmental toxicity of perfluoroalkyl acids and their derivatives. *Toxicol. Appl. Pharmacol. 198*:231–241 (2004).
63. **Hardy, M.L.:** The toxicology of the three commercial polybrominated diphenyl oxide (ether) flame retardants. *Chemosphere 46*:757–777 (2002).
64. **Viau, C.:** Biological monitoring of exposure to mixtures. *Toxicol. Lett. 134*:9–16 (2002).
65. **Belles, M., M.L. Albina, D.J. Sanchez, J. Corbella, and J.L. Domingo:** Interactions in developmental toxicology: effects of concurrent exposure to lead, organic mercury, and arsenic in pregnant mice. *Arch. Environ. Contam. Toxicol. 42*:93–98 (2002).
66. **Reed, M.N., E.M. Paletz , M.C. Newland:** Gestational exposure to methylmercury and selenium: Effects on a spatial discrimination reversal in adulthood. *NeuroToxicology 27*:721–732 (2006).
67. **Saillenfait, A.-M., F. Gallissot, J.-P. Sabaté, N. Bourges-Abella and S. Muller:** Developmental toxic effects of ethylbenzene or toluene alone and in combination with butyl acetate in rats after inhalation exposure. *J. Appl. Toxicol. 27*: 32–42 (2007).
68. **Whorton, D., R.M. Krauss, S. Marshall, T.H. Miley:** Infertility in male pesticide workers. *Lancet 2(8051)*: 1259–1261, 1977.
69. **Navy Environmental Health Center (NEHC):** Reproductive and developmental hazards: a guide for occupational health professionals, *Technical Manual* NEHC-TM-OEM 6260.01A, NEHC, Portsmouth, VA, http://www-nehc.med.navy.mil/occmed/index.htm. [Accessed April 2006].
70. **Jahnke, G.D., A.R. Iannucci, A.R. Scialli, and M.D. Shelby:** Center for the evaluation of risks to human reproduction--the first five years. *Birth Defects Res. B Dev. Reprod. Toxicol. 74*:1–8 (2005).
71. **Fonger, G.C., D. Stroup, P.L. Thomas, and P. Wexler:** TOXNET: A computerized collection of toxicological and environmental health information. *Toxicol. Ind. Health 16*:4–6 (2000).
72. **Scialli, A.R.:** Data availability in reproductive and developmental toxicology. *Obstet. Gynecol. 83*:652–656 (1994).

Chapter 12

Immunotoxicology

By Michael G. Holland, MD, FACMT, FACOEM, FACEP

Immunotoxicology

This chapter will introduce the industrial hygiene student to the normal functioning human immune system, and occupational exposures associated with immune suppression. This chapter will not cover autoimmune disorders (such as systemic lupus erythematosus), and will not discuss in detail any immune-stimulatory disorders such as allergy or hypersensitivity pneumonitis.

Human Immune System

A basic understanding of the immune system is necessary before the student of toxicology can understand the way certain toxicants act as immuno-suppressants. When functioning normally, the human immune system protects the body from infections and cancers by the ability to recognize self from non-self (foreign), and then destroy these non-self entities (microorganisms, protein antigens, tumor cells, etc), while protecting the body's own tissues from harm. An improperly functioning immune system predisposes a patient to certain infections or cancers, depending on the type of immune defect. When the ability to recognize self is lost, autoimmune diseases can result, such as type 1 diabetes mellitus (antibodies against insulin-producing pancreatic cells), myasthenia gravis (antibodies against nicotinic acetylcholine receptors), and multiple sclerosis (antibodies against myelin basic protein).

Innate Immunity

The immune system functions via two ongoing, complimentary mechanisms: innate or non-specific immunity, and acquired or specific immunity (also referred to as adaptive immunity). Innate immunity is present at birth, and requires no prior exposure to foreign proteins or microorganisms to function. Included in the innate system are barriers to foreign invasion such as skin (prevents entry into tissues and blood), gastric acid (kills in-

Outcome Competencies

Key Terms
- adaptive immunity, alkylating agents, antibody, antigen, antineoplastic drugs, alkylating agents, B-lymphocytes, basophils, chemokines, Cluster of Differentiation (CD), C-reactive protein (CRP), Colony-Stimulating Factors (CSF), complement, cytokines, eosinophils, erythrocytes, erythropoietin, granulocytes, Granulocyte CSF (G-CSF), Granulocyte-macrophage CSF (GM-CSF), Grey, Hematopoietic Stem Cell (HSC), immunoglobulin, innate immunity, Interleukins (IL), Interpherons (IFN), leukotriene, lymphocytes, lymphoid progenitor cell, macrophages, Macrophage CSF (M-CSF), Major Histocompatibility Complex (MHC), mast cells, myeloid progenitor cell, monocytes, NK cells (natural Killer cells), neoplasia, neutrophils, phagocytosis, progenitor cell, Radiation Absorbed Dose (RAD), Roentgen Equivalent Man (REM), Seivert, T-lymphocytes, Th cells, Tumor Necrosis Factors (TNF)

Key Topics
1. Immune System
   - Innate Immunity
   - Adaptive Immunity
   - Helper T-Cell Lines
   - Major Histocompatibility Complex and Antigen-presenting Cells
   - Cytokines
   - Blood Cell Development
2. Toxic Exposures Associated with Immune System Suppression
   - Benzene
   - Perchlorate
   - Ionizing Radiation
   - Anti-neoplastic drugs
   - Ethylene oxide

gested microorganisms), and respiratory mucous (traps inhaled particles and organisms). Also included in the non-specific, innate immunity are the phagocytic cells (ie., monocytes, macrophages, and neutrophils; and the natural killer cells (NK). Neutrophils and monocytes circulate in the blood stream, whereas tissue macrophages exist in areas where entry of foreign proteins and organisms may occur, such as in the lung alveoli. These phagocytic cells ingest and destroy microorganisms. The NK cells are a type of lymphocyte that can kill tumor cells, microorganisms, and virally-infected cells.[1]

In addition, innate immunity includes soluble **complement** proteins (named because they *complement* the action of antibodies), cytokines, and acute phase reactants. The activation of the complement cascade occurs as a result of various stimuli, such as exposure to bacterial carbohydrates or cell wall components. Complement proteins help kill microbes by various processes. Some enhance phagocytosis (C3b), whereas others perforate microbial cell membranes (C5b, C6, C7, C8, C9), stimulate release of inflammatory mediators (C3a, C4a, C5a), or attract inflammatory cells (C5a). Monocytes and lymphocytes interact with foreign antigens (Ag) and secrete soluble proteins known as cytokines (interferon, interleukin, many others). Cytokines can also be secreted in response to other cytokines, and they modulate the intensity of the inflammatory or immune reaction by either enhancing or inhibiting various processes, depending on the cytokine involved (see below). Mast cells, basophils and eosinophils release inflammatory mediators such as histamine, leukotrienes (formerly known as slow reacting substance of anaphylaxis), and cytokines that amplify the inflammatory response. Medications directed against the actions of these chemical mediators (antihistamines like diphenhydramine, loratidine, many others; leukotriene inhibitors: zafirlukast, montelukast) are the mainstays of allergy and asthma treatments. Acute phase reactants, like C-reactive protein (CRP), augment the body's ability to resist infection, and help promote tissue repair. Levels of these proteins vary widely in the serum in response to inflammation, infection, and tissue injury. This has led to using CRP as a marker of inflammation in certain inflammatory diseases such as rheumatoid arthritis.[2]

Adaptive Immunity[1,2]

Adaptive immunity (also known as acquired or specific immunity) evolved more recently phylogenetically. These immune responses react to specific antigens, and memory plays an important role, hence the term adaptive immunity: foreign antigens are recognized from prior exposures, leading to a more vigorous immune response. The adaptive immune response is the reason why vaccinations and immunizations are effective in providing long-lasting immunity. The cells involved in the adaptive immune reactions are lymphocytes, and the soluble components are the immunoglobulins. **T-lymphocytes** (thymus-derived) are responsible for the cell-mediated immunity, where-as **B-lymphocytes** (bursal-equivalent in man; develop in **B**ursa of Fabricius in birds) are responsible for humoral immunity via secretion of immunoglobulins. Both types of lymphocytes respond to foreign proteins and antigens, and through gene activation, form clones of cells which react to that specific antigen, and which persist, thereby promoting memory and increased response upon re-exposure to these antigens.

B-lymphocytes can respond directly to soluble antigen via the surface immunoglobulins on their cell membrane. Immunoglobulins are antibodies that can respond directly to soluble foreign antigens. Because the genes that code for the immunoglobulins are located at multiple non-adjacent chromosomal sites, the number of possible combinations is nearly limitless, allowing specific recognition of and response to an equally vast number of possible foreign antigens. There are five types of immunoglobulins: IgM, IgG, IgA, IgE, and IgD. IgM is the first circulating antibody produced by B-cells in response to initial antigen exposure. Later in an exposure or infection, and upon acquiring a lasting immune response, the primary circulating antibodies produced are IgG. In some instances, by testing for the predominant type of antibody to a particular antigen that is present in the host, one can determine if the infection is in the acute phase (IgM predominates) or if the presence of the antibody represents prior exposure with long-term immunity (IgG predominates). IgA is a secretory antibody present in tears, mucus, intestinal secretions and breast milk. It acts as first line of defense, and in breast-fed infants is crucial for the baby's resistance to gastrointestinal infections. IgE is a circulating immunoglobulin involved primarily in inflammatory and allergic responses. In this regard, basophils and tissue mast cells are important, because they have receptors with a high affinity for IgE. In atopic diseases such as allergy and asthma, allergens bound to the IgE then cross-link with the cell surface IgE receptor, causing release of the inflammatory mediators causing edema, inflammation, bronchospasms, and other manifestations of those disease processes.

T-lymphocytes recognize antigens through their surface T-cell receptor protein. As T-lymphocytes develop in the thymus, they express a large number of these surface receptors at various stages of development. These receptor proteins are coded by multiple disparate genes similar to those coding for the immunoglobulins, allowing a virtually limitless possible number of clones which can recognize foreign antigens. The T-cell receptor is complexed with the CD3 molecule, and T-lymphocytes are further differentiated into subsets by their surface protein molecules. Flow cytometry can separate these lymphocyte subsets into Clusters of Differentiation, identified as CD subtypes. New CD groups are frequently being identified, and there are currently over 300 CD types known. The National Library of Medicine chronicles the full registry of CD groups: http://www.ncbi.nlm.nih.gov/prow. Lymphocytes with CD4 and CD8 surface molecules are especially important, since they react directly with membrane polypeptides and glycoproteins on antigen-presenting cells. CD4 helper T-cells interact with the MHC Class II molecules (see below under Major Histocompatibility Complex), thereby causing the CD4 cells to secrete cytokines that augment the immune response. These CD4 cells then stimulate B-cell production as well as the development of CD8 cytotoxic killer cells. The Human Immunodeficiency Virus (HIV) responsible for Acquired Immune Deficiency Syndrome (AIDS) binds to the CD4 molecule and markedly reduces the numbers of CD4 helper T-cells. This reduction in the number of helper T-cells drastically weakens the immune system and makes HIV-infected individuals susceptible to many opportunistic infections and cancers.

Helper T-Cell Lines

Naïve T helper lymphocytes (Th), known as CD4+ cells, develop into two populations of cells, designated Th1 and Th2, depending on the inciting stimulus. If the naïve T cells are exposed to the cytokine interferon-gamma (IFN-γ), they will develop into Th1 cells, whereas if interleukin-4 (IL-4) is prevalent, they become Th2 cells. Once these cell lines acquire these properties, they are maintained over time, causing a persistent response. Th1 cell lines produce the cytokines IL-2, interferon-γ (IFN-γ), and tumor necrosis factor-β (TNF-β). Th1 cell predominance favors development of cell-mediated immunity. Th2 cell lines produce IL-4, IL-5, IL-6, and IL-13, and favors the development of humoral immunity.

Individuals whose antibody-producing B-lymphocytes develop under the Th2 influence of IL-4 will produce IgE, and therefore will have exaggerated eosinophilic inflammatory responses. These individuals have increased incidence of atopic manifestations such as asthma and allergies. Individuals with Th1 cell predominance are more likely to have cell-mediated immune responses and are therefore less likely to suffer from allergic diseases. There is some evidence that the current epidemic of asthma and atopic diseases in more highly developed Western countries may be related to the relatively recent reduction in childhood antigen exposures. Exposure early in life to infectious diseases (such as daycare attendees), to pets in the home, and to an agricultural environment (such as growing up on a farm) exposed children to bacterial endotoxins and antigens, which have been shown to favor Th1 cell line development, cell-mediated immune response predominance, and therefore a lower incidence and prevalence of atopic disease. Children who do not experience these antigen exposures are subject to enhanced Th2 cell line development, and therefore more likely to develop allergic disorders, including asthma. This has observed phenomenon has been termed the **hygiene theory of asthma**, whereby the children in modern societies are raised in environments that may be 'too clean" (or at least relatively antigen-free), resulting in an excess of asthma and other atopic disorders.[3–6] There is evidence that some chemical exposures modulate the immune response in other immunologic diseases. For instance, 95% of hypersensitivity pneumonitis cases occur in non-smokers. It has been theorized that the immunosuppressive effects of tobacco smoke causes reduced production of specific antibodies to inhaled organic antigens, as an explanation for the decreased incidence of this disease in smokers, given the same antigen exposure levels as non-smokers.[7,8]

Major Histocompatibility Complex and Antigen-Presenting Cells

A class of proteins exists on the surface of most cells of the human body, and is the primary way the body can distinguish self from non-self. These protein cell membrane molecules are called the Major Histocompatibility Complex (MHC), and are divided into two classes. MHC Class I molecules are present on all nucleated cells and platelets, and are designated Human Leukocyte Antigen (HLA)-A, -B, and –C. The MHC Class I HLA genes play an integral role in the immune response to intracellular infections, tumors, and grafts and transplants. The MHC Class II molecules are designated as HLA-D, -DR, -DP, and -DQ; they are located on the surface of antigen presenting cells, which include B cells, macrophages, dendritic cells (present in spleen, lymph nodes), activated T cells, and others. Most T lymphocytes cannot recognize the foreign antigen until the antigen-presenting cells deliver it bound to the MHC protein. This highly complex interaction not only requires binding of the antigen-MHC unit with the T cell receptor, but also requires involvement of CD4 or CD8, as well as CD28 and CD80 or CD86 surface molecules.[1,2,9,10]

Cytokines

Cytokines, as mentioned above, are a large group of protein molecules produced by T cells and monocytes, and consist of Interleukins (IL), Tumor Necrosis Factors (TNF), Interferons (IFN), Colony Stimulating Factors (CSF), and chemokines. These act as chemical messengers which can act locally or remotely to influence the immune response. Interaction of a lymphocyte with its specific Ag will trigger secretion of cytokines. This secretion can also be triggered by other influences that are not Ag-specific; thus, they are involved in both innate and adaptive immune processes. When secreted, they have various actions on the immune response, such as recruiting other immune cells, or suppressing or augmenting various cell responses depending on the cytokine involved. As an example, virally-infected cells release interferon, which confers viral resistance to surrounding cells.[2] Several diseases have been shown to be mediated by various cytokines. Newer treatments have become available which consists of administering monoclonal antibodies (ie., infliximab) directed against certain cytokines like TNF-α to treat inflammatory diseases such as rheumatoid arthritis and Crohn's disease, among others.[11] In other cases, the cytokine itself is used as treatment of disease: interferon-beta-1a for multiple sclerosis[12] and interferon-alpha-2b for chronic Hepatitis C.[13]

Blood Cell Development[14]

The white blood cells (WBC) discussed in the previous section develop primarily in the bone marrow in adults, but in the fetus, they also develop in extra-medullary sites such as the liver and spleen. In diseases where the marrow is damaged, extramedullary hematapoeisis (blood cell development outside the marrow) also occurs in adults. The most important cells in the marrow are the **hematopoietic stem cells** (HSC). These cells are pleuripotent, meaning they can develop into any of the blood cell types by first differentiating into a progenitor cell, which is a stem cell committed to developing into any of the various types of blood cells. The pleuripotent HSC matures first to become either a committed lymphoid or myeloid precursor. The lymphoid progenitor cell develops into the various types of lymphocytes (B, T, NK), whereas the myeloid precursor cell gives rise to monocytes, neutrophils, eosinophils and basophils, erythrocytes and platelets. Also, these HSC stem cells give rise to mast cells, dendritic cells, and other cells. When a bone marrow transplant is performed, it is these HSC that migrate to the marrow and regenerate the bone marrow of the transplant recipient.

The most abundant white blood cells (WBC) are the polymorphonuclear (PMN) white cells, so-called because their nucleus is segmented into multiple lobes. These cells are also commonly known as polys or segs, because of their nucleus morphology; or granulocytes because of the granular nature of their cytoplasm. The staining pattern of these granules further differentiates the PMNs into neutrophils, eosinophils, and basophils. The granules in neutrophils contain active chemicals and enzymes that help destroy bacteria and other foreign antigens. The normal WBC count is 4,000 to 11,000 cells per mL of blood, and 50–75% of these are PMNs. The total WBC count, and the percentage of PMNs, increases in the face of acute infections. The other circulating WBCs are the lymphocytes and monocytes, which are discussed below.

Since the half-life of a neutrophil is the shortest of all blood cells, at about six hours, these have the fastest turnover. Eosinophils are also short-lived, and are plentiful in the mucosa of the gastrointestinal tract (where they are active in defense against parasites), as well as the respiratory and urinary tracts. Increases in eosinophil counts are seen in parasitic diseases as well as in allergic/atopic diseases. Basophils have granules that contain histamine and heparin. They, like the tissue mast cells, degranulate in response to IgE, releasing these inflammatory mediators into the area. These cells are especially active in the allergic responses, including anaphylaxis. Monocytes circulate in the bloodstream for 3 days, and then migrate to the tissues and are known there as macrophages, where they have a postulated half-life of 120 days. Macrophages engulf (phagocytize) bacteria and other foreign invaders, and also function as antigen-presenting cells. In various tissues, they have different nomenclature: microglial cells in the brain, Kuppfer cells in the liver, and alveolar macrophages in the lung: These are all monocytes which migrated from the circulation. The multinucleated giant cells seen in granulomatous diseases such as tuberculosis are also macrophages that arise from monocytes. Lymphocytes account usually for between 20–40% of circulating WBC. This only represents about 2% of the total lymphocytes; most of the rest are in the lymphoid organs. Estimates are that about 3.5×10^{10} lymphocytes enter the circulation per day, many of them having re-entered the circulation via the lymphatic system.

All the blood cell production is stimulated by various cytokines. The red blood cell production is stimulated by **erythropoietin** (EPO), which is predominantly produced by the kidney (hence the anemia seen in chronic kidney failure). WBC production is stimulated by **colony-stimulating factors** (CSFs). These factors stimulate the committed stem cells to proliferate and mature into the various WBCs. Depending on the type of WBC they promote, they are known as: **granulocyte-macrophage CSF** (GM-CSF), **granulocyte** CSF (G-CSF), and **macrophage CSF** (M-CSF). Recombinant DNA technology has allowed artificial production of many of these growth factors, which has revolutionized the treatment of leukopenic states after cancer chemotherapy (ie., Nupogen®), as well treatment of patients exposed to other immunotoxic drugs such as colchicine and podophyllin. In the case of EPO, blood-doping for performance enhancement in athletic competitions represents a recent controversial use of this product.

Toxic Exposures and the Immune System

The bone marrow is the most mitotically active tissue in the body, producing hundreds of billions of new WBCs daily. It is the ability to produce these billions of WBCs that allows a person to mount an effective immune response. This production of blood cells involves rapid cell division of the various cell lines, and any toxicant exposure or physical problem that affects the ability of the marrow to produce blood cells will adversely affect the immune response and the body's ability to fight infection or tumors. This rapid cell division makes the bone marrow very sensitive to chemicals, drugs, or physical agents that interfere with cell division.

Oxygen and any absorbed toxicants are carried by the vascular supply to the bone marrow. Since the developing myeloid precursors contain the enzyme myeloperoxidase, the generation of reactive oxygen species and a resultant oxidant stress can develop.[15] This has implications for activation of xenobiotics such as benzene into its immunotoxic metabolite (see below). The small number of agents relevant to the occupational setting that have been demonstrated, or are suspected to be toxic to the immune system in a suppressive manner are discussed in the following section.

Benzene

Benzene is a volatile aromatic hydrocarbon with a molecular formula of C6-H6, and a molecular weight of 78.1 daltons. It has a vapor density of 2.8 (air =1), a vapor pressure of 95 mmHg @ 25°C, and is measured in air concentrations with the conversion factor of 1 ppm= 3.26 mg/m^3, and 1 mg/m^3 = 0.306 ppm. Benzene is found naturally in the environment at low concentrations, and is formed during incomplete combustion of fossil fuels (petroleum products, coal, and even wood). It was once widely used as a solvent, in inks and dyes, and in the rubber and shoe industries. It is still commonly used as a chemical intermediate. It is present naturally in crude oil, and therefore in gasoline formulations in most countries, which is the major source of environmental exposures.(16)

Benzene was suspected to be an occupational carcinogen as far back as the 1920s. In the 1960's and 1970's, studies of Italian and Turkish shoe workers exposed to benzene in glues showed increased risk for hematopoetic cancers.(17) Numerous subsequent epidemiologic studies since then have confirmed the link between benzene and acute myeloid leukemia (AML), also known as acute non-lymphoid leukemia (ANLL). It is classified as a Group I carcinogen by IARC (International Agency for Research on Cancer), on the basis of having sufficient evidence for carcinogenicity in humans. Benzene is also strongly linked to other blood disorders and cancers, such as aplastic anemia and myelodysplastic syndrome (MDS), but no consistent link has been shown between benzene exposure and development of the other types of leukemia (lymphocytic leukemias [CLL, ALL] and chronic myeloid leukemia [CML]). The incidence of AML appears to have a dose–response relationship, occurring more frequently in the more heavily exposed groups. Some genetic susceptibility or enzyme polymorphism(18) is likely to be a determinant as well, since only a small minority of workers develop leukemia or the MDS, even in heavily–exposed groups. Dose-response relationships are evident from studies of long-term exposures in workers exposed occupationally for many years, and these exposure cohorts have been extensively studied over the past several decades. These studies reveal that the risks for AML are not only dose-dependent, but there is a threshold, below which there probably is no risk. The most highly studied group is the Pliofilm cohort, since these workers exclusively used benzene as a solvent, and had high exposures prior to 1950. Analysis of this cohort reveals no AML risks in anyone who began work after 1950, when exposure levels were greatly reduced form the pre-1950 levels. In a study of 18,000 petroleum workers exposed to gasoline, there was no excess AML in those exposed to less than 128 ppm-years, and concluded that the threshold for AML is likely between 370–530 ppm-years.(19) Similarly, comprehensive reviews of the Pliofilm workers as well as other exposure settings have estimated that the AML threshold is between 50–500ppm-years.(20) Thresholds for other hematologic effects reveal that the Lowest Observed Adverse Effect Levels (LOAEL) after years of benzene exposure were: 100 ppm (320 mg/m^3) for pancytopenia and aplastic anemia; and 30–35 ppm (96–112 mg/m^3) for MDS.(21) Aplastic anemia, AML, and MDS all affect the bone marrow's ability to produce cells to mount an immune response and to fight infection; therefore benzene is a prototypical immune toxicant. However, even though hypothesized as a risk factor for multiple myeloma and non-Hodgkin's lymphoma, the epidemiological evidence is lacking for benzene as a causative agent for these relatively rare hematologic cancers.(22,23)

Benzene is well-absorbed by the inhalation route, and therefore most published studies of exposures pertain to benzene vapors. Benzene is also absorbed by the dermal route, but the significance of occupational exposures by this route has been the subject of much debate in the literature. Older studies felt the dermal exposures were probably insignificant compared to inhalation exposures at the time, and primarily involved exposure to pure benzene, especially in the high amounts seen in the pre-1950 cohorts. Quantification of this exposure is difficult, however, since in any skin exposure scenario, the evaporation of benzene will cause inhalational absorption to occur simultaneously. However, as occupational inhalational exposure limits have decreased, it is theorized that the relative contribution of dermal exposure may have some increased importance. Additionally, exposures now are primarily to benzene as a small component of other mixtures. If benzene is mixed with other liquids with similar volatilities (such as gasoline or toluene), the cutaneous retention will be negligible, and inhalation exposure will predominate. However, when benzene is contained in less volatile mixtures such as oil or water, skin contact time may be longer, and benzene absorption may be possible. However, in all animal species studied, percutaneous absorption of benzene averages less than 0.2% of an applied dose. When viewed in light of the amount of benzene exposure from environmental sources (gasoline, traffic, passive and active smoking, etc.), benzene entering the body from skin exposure is probably trivial.(24) Since benzene is not found in significant amounts in water, food, or consumer products, the contribution by the gastrointestinal route to the total exposure is probably negligible.

Benzene is highly lipid soluble, and therefore would be expected to have a large volume of distribution (Vd), but precise data is lacking. Benzene is metabolized by the hepatic microsomal enzyme mixed function oxidase system. Specifically, the isoenzyme CYP 2E1 metabolizes benzene to the very reactive intermediate benzene oxide (BO). This compound is metabolized via four different pathways to various other metabolites: 1) BO is in equilibrium with the seven sided ring structure oxepin, which can be metabolized by microsomal enzymes, breaking the ring structure and producing *trans, trans*-muconic acid (*t,t-* muconic acid, or TTMA). 2) BO can also be conjugated with glutathione into the measurable metabolite s-phenyl mercapturic acid (SPMA). 3) BO can be metabolized by epoxide hydrolase and other enzymes into catechol, or 4) BO can undergo non-enzymatic rearrangement into phenol. It is phenol that then undergoes further metabolism by CYP 2E1 into hydroquinone.(25) Free hydroquinone is metabolized by myeloperoxidase in the marrow to the genotoxic compound 1,4 benzoquinone.(26) It is believed that these toxic quinone metabolites are largely responsible for benzene's immunotoxic properties.

Benzene workplace exposure standards have steadily decreased over the last century as evidence of its toxicity appeared in the scientific literature. The ACGIH TLV® was 100 ppm in 1946; it was then lowered to 50 ppm in 1947, to 25 ppm in 1957, to 10 ppm in 1976, and finally to 0.5 ppm in 1996.(27) The current OSHA PEL for benzene is 1 ppm (lowered from 10 ppm in 1987). Workers exposed to benzene at levels above the OSHA action level of 0.5 ppm 8hr TWA are required to be in a medical monitoring program, including pre-placement and annual physical examinations, as well as blood tests monitoring the red blood cells, white blood cells, and platelet counts. Accidental over-exposures are monitored by measuring end-of-shift urine phenol concentrations. Specific standards and requirements of the program are available on the OSHA website.[28]

Monitoring urinary phenol levels after excessive benzene exposure is only valid after respiratory exposures to levels greater than 5 ppm (16 mg/m^3), which are higher than the current occupational exposure limits. A significant amount of phenol is present in food, so that at the current lower workplace air concentrations, there is too much interference from the dietary contributions to distinguish it from that attributable to occupational exposures. More useful biomarkers for monitoring those exposed to lower levels, such as that from non-occupational environmental sources, are routinely used in research studies. These include *trans, trans*-muconic acid (TTMA), s-phenylmercapturic acid (SPMA), and urinary benzene. TTMA is not toxic, but its metabolic precursor, muconaldehyde is possibly leukemogenic; thus TTMA measurements are a marker of both benzene exposure as well as some of its possible toxic activity. Urinary TTMA represents approximately 7–58% of an inhaled dose after exposures to air concentrations below 0.1ppm. Its half life is approximately 5 hours. SPMA represents the end product of benzene oxide when it is conjugated with glutathione, and is very specific for benzene exposure. It represents approximately 0.11% of an absorbed dose after benzene inhalation exposure, and its half-life is 9 hours. Unfortunately it is useful only for exposures to benzene air concentrations above 0.5ppm.[29] Urinary benzene has been found to be one of the best biomarkers for benzene exposures at levels less than 0.15 ppm (<478ug/m^3). Since cigarette smoke has considerable benzene content, all of these biomarkers can be up to five times higher in cigarette smokers than non-smokers exposed to comparable ambient environmental benzene levels.[30]

Perchlorate[31,32]

Perchlorate is an anion composed of one chlorine atom and four oxygen atoms (ClO_4^-). It forms a weak association with its cation (Na^+, K^+, $NH4^+$), making it very water soluble, as well as soluble in polar organic solvents. Sodium perchlorate is the most soluble of the common perchlorate salts, followed by ammonium and potassium. Regardless of the salt, whenever perchlorate compounds enter water, they dissociate and free perchlorate ions (ClO4) are released. These free perchlorate ions are chemically the same regardless of the primary compound from which it may have been derived.

Perchlorates are well absorbed orally, and this represents the predominant route of exposure. They are rapidly distributed in total body water, with an approximate Vd of 0.34 L/kg. Perchlorate ions are not metabolized, and are excreted unchanged in the urine, with a serum half-life of approximately 6–8 hours.[33]

Perchlorate-containing compounds are excellent oxidizing agents, which led to their early use as propellants and explosive agents. These compounds are used today in various aspects of the automotive, aerospace and munitions industries as well as in the formulation of commercial fireworks. Specifically, potassium perchlorate is used in the manufacture of motor vehicle airbags, sodium perchlorate in the explosives and fireworks industries, and ammonium perchlorate (the most widely used perchlorate) as a propellant oxidant in military rockets and munitions.

In the early 1950s, high doses of potassium perchlorate were used as a therapeutic modality in the treatment of Grave's disease, a form of hyperthyroidism. Most current knowledge regarding the potential adverse health effects of perchlorates in humans stems from this now-abandoned pharmacologic use of perchlorate salts. Over the course of high dose treatments with potassium perchlorates, patients treated with >400 mg/d of potassium perchlorate were at risk for developing agranulocytosis and fatal aplastic anemia. Because of this complication as well as the development of safer drugs, the therapeutic use of perchlorates in the treatment of hyperthyroidism fell out of favor in the 1960's. The exact mechanism of perchlorate's bone marrow toxicity remains unknown, but there are no reports of bone marrow toxicity in patients receiving less than 400 mg/d of potassium perchlorate. In fact, this dosage level has been proposed to be a safe upper dose limit for perchlorate exposure. Occupational studies have never revealed any bone marrow toxicity at the much lower perchlorate exposure levels in that setting.[32]

A major public health question currently surrounds the issue of perchlorates in public drinking water systems and their effects on human thyroid health. In the U.S., perchlorates have been found in ground water and soil near a variety of locations where these compounds were produced, utilized or stored. Ammonium perchlorate is quite hygroscopic, so most manufacturing facilities for its U.S. military applications are located in the desert southwest. In 2001, the U.S. Environmental Protection Agency (EPA) began surveying all large public water supplies, as well as a sample of smaller water supplies for the presence of perchlorate. The EPA found perchlorate contamination of drinking water supplies in several areas in Nevada and California. However, epidemiological evidence reveals that at the highest perchlorate drinking water levels, the total daily dose would be 50 μg per day, a level that is without effects on the thyroid or on bone marrow.[32]

Anti-neoplastic Drugs

Cancer cells divide and grow rapidly, as they are abnormal cell lines that lack the usual controls on growth and cell division. Chemotherapeutic drugs for cancer treatments take advantage of this fact, and interfere with mitotic cell division or the protein synthesis necessary for normal metabolic activities of growing cells. This is accomplished by causing breaks in DNA, interfering with mitotic spindle formation, or disrupting protein synthesis thereby preferentially killing these rapidly dividing cancer cells. However, these drugs will have the same effect on other cells in the body that are also rapidly dividing, most notably the bone marrow. This is why a cancer patient undergoing a course of chemotherapy may experience a rapid drop in the

WBC count, and may be prone to infections; or develop anemia due to reduced red blood cell counts. The treatment with Granulocyte colony stimulating factor (G-CSF) and erythropoietin (EPO), to boost WBC's and RBC's respectively, has simplified this treatment problem, allowing more regular use of chemotherapeutic regimens. In addition to immediate effects on the bone marrow, many chemotherapeutic agents place the patient at future risk for other cancers due to the genotoxic effect of these drugs.[34] Specifically, many alkylating agents are known to increase the risk of subsequent leukemia and MDS in the treated patient.[35]

Exposure to anti-neoplastic drugs is not limited to the cancer patient. There is a growing concern among healthcare workers, most notably nurses and pharmacists, over possible health effects of those who work with these compounds. These compounds can be absorbed both via inhalation, and through dermal contact. Pharmacy employees are exposed when mixing specific doses of these antineoplastic agents, and nurses are exposed when administering these medications, as well as handling patients' body fluids which may contain excreted drugs. Housekeeping and other hospital personnel may be exposed to anti-neoplastic drugs when disposing of materials such as IV bags/bottles, tubing, medication vials; and patient care items contaminated with patients' body fluids (bedpans, urine bags, etc). The Occupational Safety and Health Administration (OSHA) published guidelines for worker protection in 1986, and the National Institute for Occupational Safety and Health (NIOSH) published a NIOSH Alert in 2004 for this same purpose[36], and helpful guidelines are available at the NIOSH website.[37] These guidelines advocate worker evaluation protection to include medical monitoring exams, biomonitoring for effects (CBC, urinalysis), use of personal protective equipment (gowns, gloves, etc) as well as engineering controls (exhaust hoods for pharmaceutical preparation and mixing).

Several epidemiologic studies have been performed investigating possible effects of healthcare workers exposed to antineoplastic drugs. Studies have documented workplace exposures in pharmacies following OSHA protocols[38]; and urinary excretion of drugs, confirming that workers exposed by mixing or administering these drugs do absorb and excrete them, despite use of laminar flow hoods and personal protective equipment.[39,40] Studies have found effects in these healthcare workers, including urinary mutagenic effects (sister chromatid exchanges) in pharmacists not using properly ventilated hoods for admixing[41]; and increased amounts of dicentric chromosomes and acentric chromosome fragments in peripheral blood lymphocytes in nurses handling chemotherapeutic drugs.[42] Some epidemiologic studies have shown an increased risk of leukemia among nurses[43,44], but the authors did not study nurses by type of nursing, and the amount of antineoplastic drug exposures (if any) were unknown. One study of physicians handling these drugs claimed an increased risk ratio, but the lower boundary of the corresponding confidence interval was less than 1.0. One study showing increased leukemia risk among nurses handling alkylating agents was based on only two leukemia cases, therefore no firm conclusions could be drawn.[45] Nevertheless, common sense would dictate that engineering controls and PPE be used to minimize exposure to these agents.

Ionizing Radiation

Ionizing radiation is a high energy form of electromagnetic radiation, in the form of: a) x-rays and gamma rays, which penetrate deeply into body tissues, or; b) charged alpha, beta, or neutron particles, which cause internal damage only if inhaled, ingested, or otherwise gain entry through a wound. When the radiation waves pass through the body, or when particles are systemically absorbed, the energy is transferred to biologic molecules, causing atoms to become energized or excited and bonds to break, thereby leading to the formation of highly reactive ions and radicals. These highly reactive entities can interact with cellular components and cause damage (ie., DNA breaks). The most radiosensitive normal (non-malignant) tissues are those with high cellular turnover (high mitotic activity), most notably the bone marrow and the GI mucosal lining cells. Since cancer cells are rapidly growing and dividing, this is the basis for radiation therapy to a tumor to reduce its size, or adjuvant radiotherapy to an area of the body after tumor resection.

The common units used to measure radiation internal doses are the rad (Radiation Absorbed Dose), and the rem (Roentgen Equivalent Man). The newer SI unit for a rad is a Grey, abbreviated Gy, where one Gy = 100 rad; and the new unit for rem is the Seivert, abbreviated Sv, where one Sv = 100 rem. Although the SI units are preferred scientifically, the conventional rad and rem are still widely used. One Gy or 100 rad is defined as 1 Joule of initial energy (of charged particles released by the ionization events) per kg of tissue. The rem is a measure of the biological effect that a certain rad dose amount will have on the tissues. The relationship between the two is a multiplier known as the quality factor. For penetrating gamma and x-ray radiation, as well as beta particle radiation, the quality factor is one, so the rad and the rem are equivalent for these types of radiation exposures. Internally absorbed alpha particles will have a much higher biological effect per rad, and the quality factor is 20, meaning the rem will be 20 times the rad for an absorbed alpha particle. The relationship for SI units is the same as that with rad and rem, (ie. for penetrating radiation waves), one Gy is equivalent to one Sv.[46]

Radiation effects are dependent on dose, which can be influenced by time (exposure duration), distance (from the source), and shielding. Exposures to known sources should be for the minimal time duration necessary. Shielding with lead or concrete barriers can minimize exposures, and every effort should be made to increase the distance away from the exposure, since the dose decreases by the square of the distance from the source. Thus, in practical terms, the dose 4 meters away from a source will be 1/16 of the dose at one meter away from that same source ($1/4^2 = 1/16$).

It is well-known that high doses of ionizing radiation can cause bone marrow failure. The acute radiation syndrome occurs generally after a total body dose of > 100 rads (1 Grey), and the LD50 is approximately 400–500 rads (4–5 Gy). After doses as low as 25 rads, a depression of peripheral blood cell counts will be evident, and clinical immunosuppression can occur after 100 rads of total body dose. At doses of 2 Gy (200 rads), a radiation-induced hematologic syndrome ensues, with significant risk of infection and bleeding due to suppression of the ability of bone marrow to produce WBCs and platelets. The most imminent danger of immunosuppression is septicemia (overwhelming bacterial infection in the bloodstream), and reduced numbers of the polymorphonuclear neutrophils (PMNs) is the major risk factor for this complication. The earliest cause of reduced PMN counts after radiation exposure is margination of neutrophils (i.e., leaving the circulating blood and sequestering in tissues or attaching to blood vessel walls). However, the nadir of the neutrophil count resulting from radiation-induced bone marrow suppression will occur at about 30 days post-exposure (sooner after very high exposures), and the risk of septicemia will be greatest at this point. Although circulating lymphocytes are mature, non-replicating cells, they are unique in that they are very sensitive to radiation. The total lymphocyte count deteriorates predictably after a known dose of radiation exposure, as has been extensively studied. Therefore, the total lymphocyte count has great prognostic value, since the change in lymphocyte count over the first 48 hours can be used to back extrapolate and estimate what total radiation dose was received, and prognostic predictions made. Estimation of survivability can be determined, as well as triage and treatment decisions made regarding need for hospital admission, aggressive treatment, or palliative care.[47]

Subsequent leukemia risk is significant in survivors of the acute radiation syndrome, which again causes an immunocompromised state. Leukemia can develop as early as 2 years after exposure, whereas the latency for development of solid tumors is longer, on the order of 5 years to several decades. The Life Span Study of atomic bomb survivors in Hiroshima and Nagasaki showed increased risks for leukemia and other cancers, especially in those exposed at a young age.[48]

Less intense exposures than those resulting in acute radiation sickness were experienced in the Chernobyl nuclear accident. These moderate doses are theorized to place workers at increased risk for hematopoeitic cancers, but studies thus far are inconclusive.[49,50] Similarly, x-ray technicians are theorized to have an increased risk of hematopoeitic cancers, and studies show increased risks for Chinese radiological technologists working prior to 1970[51], and U.S. technologists working prior to 1970[52], when work practices allowed higher exposures than current standards. However, no increased risks are seen with those exposed at current workplace exposure levels. Patients undergoing large doses of therapeutic radiation for medical purposes (ie., spinal irradiation for ankylosing spondylitis) show similar increased leukemia risks. Nuclear weapons industry workers from the former Soviet Union received high doses (avg. 1 Sv) from 1948–1951 in a hurried effort to develop the technology, and showed increased risks for hematopoeitic cancers.[53]

The OSHA standard for nuclear power industry workers limits the annual radiation dose to 5 rem per year (0.05 Sv), and also 1.25 rem (0.0125 Sv) per quarter. The standard requires pre-placement and periodic examinations, biomonitoring of hematologic effects (CBC), as well as film badge or thermoluminescent dosimeter (TLD) monitoring of workers' exposures. The full OSHA standard is available electronically on the OSHA website.[54]

Ethylene Oxide

Ethylene oxide (EtO) is a widely used gas sterilizing agents in the health care industry for materials and products that cannot withstand heat/steam sterilization (rubber and plastic products). It is also used as a fumigant for food products, as well as a highly reactive chemical intermediate for the manufacturing of diethylene glycol and other glycol ethers. It has a highly reactive ring-like structure that readily produces DNA and protein adducts. It is a colorless gas with an ethereal odor, with a molecular wt of 44 daltons, and an empiric formula of C_2H_4O.[55]

EtO readily forms bonds with DNA, and has been shown to be mutagenic in animal studies. A long-term EtO inhalation study in rats showed an increase in leukemia, among other cancers.[56] In 1994, IARC classified EtO as a Group 1 carcinogen (limited evidence in humans, sufficient evidence in animals). A non-human primate study showed increased sister chromatid exchanges and chromosomal aberrations after EtO inhalation exposure.[57] Other animal studies confirmed that EtO was mutagenic and carcinogenic. Human epidemiologic studies have suggested an association with leukemia in EtO sterilization workers and with EtO production workers.[58,59] A later meta-analysis of ten different studies of health effects from EtO showed there was no increased risk of leukemia by intensity or frequency of exposure; nor was there a quantitative association (two studies that had shown increased risks were confounded by worker exposures to other carcinogens).[60] Current data therefore suggest that EtO exposure is not a risk for leukemia or other hematologic cancers.

OSHA published an occupational standard for EtO in 1984, with a PEL of 1 ppm, and an action level of 0.5 ppm. The standard requires biological monitoring and physical examinations for workers at or above the action level. Many hospital central sterile supply workers involved in gas sterilization of medical equipment are covered by this standard. The increasing use of disposable, single use sterile devices has reduced the need for this type of sterilization, and engineering controls which have implemented a closed sterilization system have eliminated exposures in many workers. Therefore worker monitoring and exams are no longer required in facilities without EtO exposures.

References

1. **Beers, M.H. and R. Berkow (eds.):** Biology of the Immune System (Chapter 146). In *The Merck Manual of Diagnosis and Therapy,* 17th edition. New York: John Wiley & Sons, Inc., 1999.

2. **Delves, P.J. and I.M. Roitt:** Advances in Immunology: The Immune System. *N. Engl. J. Med. 343*:37–49 & 108–117 (2000).
3. **McGeady, S.J.:** Immunocompetence and Allergy. *Pediatrics 113(4)*:1107–1113 (2004).
4. **Marks. G.B.:** Environmental factors and gene-environment interactions in the aetiology of asthma. *Clin. Exp. Pharmacol. Physiol. 33(3)*:285–289 (2006).
5. **Rautava, S., O. Ruuskanen, A. Ouwehand, S. Salminen, and E. Isolauri:** The hygiene hypothesis of atopic disease — an extended version. *J. Pediatr. Gastroenterol. Nutr. 38(4)*:378–388 (2004).
6. **Matricardi, P.M., G.R. Bouygue, and S. Tripodi:** Inner-city asthma and the hygiene hypothesis. *Ann. Allergy Asthma Immunol. 89(6 Suppl 1)*:69–74 (2002).
7. **Mohr, L.C.:** Hypersensitivity pneumonitis. *Curr. Op. Pulm. Med. 10(5)*:401–411 (2004).
8. **Girard, M., E. Israel-Assayag, and Y. Cormier:** Pathogenesis of hypersensitivity pneumonitis. *Curr. Op. Aller. Clin. Immunol. 4(2)*:93–98 (2004).
9. **Kasper, D.L., et al.:** Introduction to the Immune System (Chapter 295). In *Harrison's Principles of Internal Medicine*, 16th edition. New York: The McGraw-Hill Companies, Inc., 2005.
10. **Kasper, D.L., et al.:** The Major Histocompatibility Gene Complex (Chapter 296). In *Harrison's Principles of Internal Medicine*, 16th edition. New York: The McGraw-Hill Companies, Inc., 2005.
11. **Olsen, N.J. and C.M. Stein:** New Drugs for Rheumatoid Arthritis. *N. Eng. J. Med. 350*:2167–2179 (2004).
12. **Noseworthy, J.H. et al.:** Multiple Sclerosis. *N. Eng. J. Med. 343*:938–952 (2000).
13. **McHutchison, J.G., et al.:** Interferon alfa-2b alone or in combination with ribavirin as initial treatment for chronic hepatitis C. *N. Eng. J. Med. 339*:1485–1492 (1998).
14. **Ganong, W.F. (ed.):** SECTION VI: Circulation, CHAPTER 27: Circulating Body Fluids, in *Review of Medical Physiology*, 22nd edition. New York: Lange Medical Books/McGraw-Hill, 2005.
15. **Morgan, G.J. and C.L. Alvares:** Benzene and the Hemopoeitic stem cell. *Chem.-Bio. Inter. 153–154*:217–222 (2005).
16. **Toxnet:** Benzene. Available at: http://toxnet.nlm.nih.gov/cgi-bin/sis/search/f?./temp/~9F567m:1 [Accessed 5/9/2006].
17. **Savitz, D.A. and K.W. Andrews:** Review of Epidemiologic Evidence on Benzene and Lymphatic and Hematopoietic Cancers. *Am. J. Ind. Med. 31*:287–295 (1997).
18. **Moran, J.L., D. Siegel, and D. Ross:** A potential mechanism underlying the increased susceptibility of individuals with a polymorphism in NAD(P)H:quinone oxidoreductase 1 (NQO1) to benzene toxicity. *Proc. Natl. Acad. Sci. USA 96(14)*:8150–8155 (1999).
19. **Wong, O.:** Risk of acute myeloid leukaemia and multiple myeloma in workers exposed to benzene. *Occup. Environ. Med. 52(6)*:380–384 (1995).
20. **Pyatt, D.:** Benzene and hematopoetic malignancies. *Clin. Occ. Environ. Med. 4*:529–555 (2004).
21. **Duarte-Davidson, R., et al.:** Benzene in the environment: an assessment of the potential risks to the health of the population. *Occup. Environ. Med. 58(1)*:2–13 (2001).
22. **Bergsagel, D.E., et al.:** Benzene and Multiple Myeloma: Appraisal of the Scientific Evidence. *Blood 94(4)*:1174–1182 (1999).
23. **Wong, O. and H. Fu:** Exposure to benzene and non-Hodgkin lymphoma, an epidemiologic overview and an ongoing case-control study in Shanghai. *Chem.-Bio. Interact. 153–154*:33–41 (2005).
24. **Wester, R.C. and H.I. Maibach:** Benzene percutaneous absorption: dermal exposure relative to other benzene sources. *Int. J. Occup. Environ. Health. 6(2)*:122–126 (2000).
25. **Kim, S., et al.:** Using urinary biomarkers to elucidate dose-related patterns of human benzene metabolism. *Carcinogen. 27(4)*:772–781 (2006).
26. **Lebailly, P., et al.:** Genetic polymorphisms in microsomal epoxide hydrolase and susceptibility to adult acute myeloid leukaemia with defined cytogenetic abnormalities. *Br. J. Haem. 116*:587–594 (2002).
27. **Pyatt, D.:** Benzene and hematopoetic malignancies. *Clin. Occ. Environ. Med. 4*:529–555 (2004).
28. **Occupational Safety and Health Administration (OSHA):** OSHA benzene standard. http://www.osha.gov/pls/oshaweb/owadisp.show_document?p_table=STANDARDS&p_id=10042. [Accessed 4/08/2006].
29. **Dor, F., W. Dab, P. Empereur-Bissonnet and D. Zmirou:** Validity of biomarkers in environmental health studies: the case of PAHs and benzene. *Crit. Rev. Toxicol. 29*:129–168 (1999).
30. **Fustinoni, S., et al.:** Urinary t,t-muconic acid, S-phenylmercapturic acid and benzene as biomarkers of low benzene exposure. Proceedings of the International Symposium on Recent Advances in Benzene Toxicity. Chem.-Biologic. Interact. 153-154:253-256 (2005).
31. **National Research Council:** *Health Implications of Perchlorate Ingestion.* Committee to Assess the Health Implications of Perchlorate Ingestion. Washington D.C.: National Research Council, 2005.
32. **Soldin, O.P., L.E. Braverman, S.H. Lamm:** Perchlorate Clinical Pharmacology and Human Health: A Review. *Therap. Drug Monit. 23*:316–331 (2001).
33. **Crump, K.S. and J.P. Gibbs:** Benchmark Calculations for Perchlorate from Three Human Cohorts. *Environ. Health Perspect. 113(8)*:1001–1008 (2005).
34. **Ng, A., G.M. Taylor, and O.B. Eden:** Treatment-related leukaemia–a clinical and scientific challenge. *Ca. Treat. Rev. 26(5)*:377–391 (2000).
35. **Levine, E.G. and C.D. Bloomfield:** Leukemias and myelodysplastic syndromes secondary to drug, radiation, and environmental exposure. *Semin. Oncol. 19(1)*:47–84 (1992).

36. **National Institute for Occupational Safety and Health (NIOSH):** NIOSH Publication No. 2004-165: Preventing Occupational Exposure to Antineoplastic and Other Hazardous Drugs in Health Care Settings, September 2004. Available at: http://www.cdc.gov/niosh/docs/2004-165/. [Accessed 9/4/2007].

37. **National Institute for Occupational Safety and Health (NIOSH):** NIOSH safety and Health Topic: Occupational Exposure to Antineoplastic Agents. Available at: http://www.cdc.gov/niosh/topics/antineoplastic/. [Accessed 4/8/2007].

38. **McDevitt, J.J., P.S. Lees, and M.A. McDiarmid:** Exposure of hospital pharmacists and nurses to antineoplastic agents. *J. Occup. Med. 35(1)*:57–60 (1993).

39. **Ensslin, A.S., et al.:** Biological monitoring of cyclophosphamide and ifosfamide in urine of hospital personnel occupationally exposed to cytostatic drugs. *Occup. Environ. Med. 51(4)*:229–233 (1994).

40. **Ensslin, A.S., et al.:** Biological monitoring of hospital pharmacy personnel occupationally exposed to cytostatic drugs: urinary excretion and cytogenetics studies. *Int. Arch. Occup. Environ. Health 70(3)*:205–208 (1997).

41. **Kolmodin-Hedman, B., et al.:** Occupational handling of cytostatic drugs. *Arch. Toxicol. 54(1)*:25–33 (1983).

42. **Oestreicher, U., G. Stephan, and M. Glatzel:** Chromosome and SCE analysis in peripheral lymphocytes of persons occupationally exposed to cytostatic drugs handled with and without use of safety covers. *Mutat Res. 242(4)*:271–277 (1990).

43. **Lie, J.A. and K. Kjaerheim:** Cancer risk among female nurses: a literature review. *Euro. J. Ca. Preven. 12(6)*:517–526 (2003).

44. **Morton, W. and D. Marjanovic:** Leukemia incidence by occupation in the Portland-Vancouver metropolitan area. *Amer. J. Ind. Med. 1984;6(3)*:185–205.

45. **Skov, T. and B. Maarup:** Leukaemia and reproductive outcome among nurses handling antineoplastic drugs. *Br. J. Ind. Med. 49(12)*:855–861 (1992).

46. **Little, M.P.:** Risks associated with ionizing radiation. *Br. Med. Bull. 68*:259–275 (2003).

47. **Mettler, F.A. Jr. and G.L. Voelz:** Major radiation exposure--what to expect and how to respond. *N. Eng. J. Med. 346(20)*:1554–1561 (2002).

48. **Wakeford, R.:** The cancer epidemiology of radiation. *Oncogene. 63*:6404–6428 (2004).

49. **Gluzman, D., et al.:** Patterns of hematological malignancies in Chernobyl clean-up workers (1996–2005). *Exper. Oncol. 28(1)*:60–63 (2006).

50. **Moysich, K.B., R.J. Menezes and A.M. Michalek:** Chernobyl-related ionising radiation exposure and cancer risk: an epidemiological review. *Lancet Oncol. 3(5)*:269–279 (2002).

51. **Wang, J.X., et al.:** Cancer incidence among medical diagnostic X-ray workers in China, 1950 to 1985. *Int. J. Cancer 45(5)*:889–895 (1985).

52. **Linet, M.S., et al.:** Incidence of haematopoietic malignancies in U.S. radiologic technologists. *Occup. Environ. Med. 62(12)*:861–867 (2005).

53. **Cardis, E., D. Richardson, and A. Kesminiene:** Radiation risk estimates in the beginning of the 21st century. *Health Phys. 80(4)*:349–361 (2001).

54. **Occupational Safety and Health Administration (OSHA):** Ionizing radiation – 1910.1096 http://www.osha.gov/pls/oshaweb/owadisp.show_document?p_table=STANDARDS&p_id=10098 [Accessed 9/4/2007].

55. **Toxnet:** Ethylene Oxide, available at: http://toxnet.nlm.nih.gov/cgi-bin/sis/search/f?./temp/~O3Pi28:1 [Accessed 5/30/2006].

56. **Lynch DW, et al.:** Carcinogenic and toxicologic effects of inhaled ethylene oxide and propylene oxide in F344 rats. *Toxicol. Appl. Pharmacol. 76(1)*:69–84 (1984).

57. **Lynch, D.W., et al.:** Sister-chromatid exchanges and chromosome aberrations in lymphocytes from monkeys exposed to ethylene oxide and propylene oxide by inhalation. *Toxicol. Appl. Pharmacol. 76(1)*:85–95 (1984).

58. **Hogstedt, C., N. Malmqvist, and B. Wadman:** Leukemia in workers exposed to ethylene oxide. *J. Am. Med. Assoc. 241(11)*:1132–1133 (1979).

59. **Hogstedt, C., et al.:** A cohort study of mortality and cancer incidence in ethylene oxide production workers. *Brit. J. Ind. Med. 36(4)*:276–280 (1979).

60. **Shore, R.E., M.J. Gardner, and B. Pannett:** Ethylene oxide: an assessment of the epidemiological evidence on carcinogenicity. *Brit. J. Ind. Med. 50(11)*:971–997 (1993).

> *The eyes do not become used, the foot still less.*
>
> Paracelsus (1493– 1541)

Chapter 13

Genetic Toxicology

Outcome Competencies
Upon completion of this chapter, the reader should be able to:
- Have a basic knowledge of genetic toxicology and an overview of assays for detecting genotoxicity and mutagenicity.

Prerequisite Knowledge
It is assumed that readers of this chapter have a basic understanding of biochemistry, genetics, physiology, and cell biology.

Key Terms
Ames test, alkylating agent, allele, aneuploidy, apoptosis, atherosclerosis, base excision repair, basepair substitution, *BRCA* genes, carcinogen, carcinogenesis, centromere, chromosomal aberrations, chromosomal nondisjunction, chromosomal translocation, clastogen, codon, deamination, depurination, depyrimidination, deletion, DNA adduct, DNA glycosylase, exon, frameshift, gene amplification, genotoxicity, genotoxin, haemangiosarcoma, homologous recombination repair, *Hprt* gene, insertion, inversion, intron, kinetochore, loss of heterozygosity, Lesch-Nyhan syndrome, methylation, micronucleus, missense mutation, monosomy, mutagen, mutagenesis, mutagenicity, mutant, mutation, nonhomologous end-joining repair, nonsense mutation, nucleotide excision repair, oncogene, *P53* gene, reactive oxidative species, polyploidy, S9 mix, Schiff base, senescence, silent mutation, sister chromatid exchange, SOS chromotest, trisomy, V(D)J recombination

Key Topics
1. Introduction
   - Genetic toxicology
   - Types of mutations
   - Health impact of mutations
2. DNA Damage
   - Hydrolysis of DNA bases
   - DNA adducts
   - Crosslinking of DNA strands
   - Single-strand breaks
   - Double-strand breaks
3. DNA Repair
   - Direct reversal of base damage
   - Base excision repair
   - Nucleotide excision repair
   - Mismatch repair
   - Nonhomologous end-joining
   - Homologous recombination repair
   - Translesion synthesis
4. Mechanisms of Mutation Induction
   - Mutation from deamination of cytosine
   - Spontaneous mutation at CpG sites
   - Mutation caused by 8-oxguanine
   - Mutation resulting from O^6-alkylguanine
   - Mutation resulting from bulky DNA adducts
   - Deletions and insertions
   - Loss of heterozygosity (LOH)
   - Chromosomal translocation
   - Aneuploidy and polyploidy
5. Regulatory Applications of Genotoxicity Assays
6. Assays for Detecting Genotoxicity
   - *In vitro* genotoxicity assays
   - *In vivo* genotoxicity assays
   - Short-term genotoxicity assays used in regulatory batteries
   - Germ cell genotoxicity/mutation assays
7. How Short-term Genetic Toxicology Assay Data are Used in Industrial Hygiene
   - Use in setting Threshold Limit Values
   - Use by international regulatory bodies
8. Use of Genotoxicity Endpoints in Biomonitoring Studies

Chapter 13

Genetic Toxicology

*By Tao Chen, PhD, DABT, Robert H. Heflich, PhD,
Martha M. Moore, PhD, and Angela J. Harris, PhD, DABT*

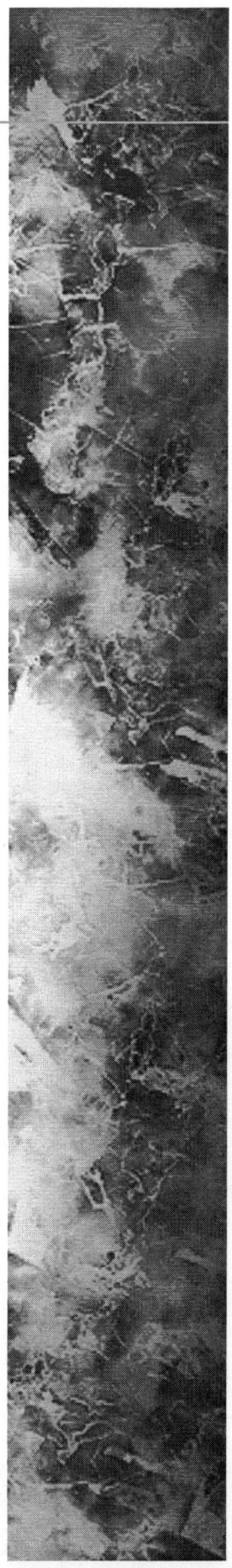

Introduction

Genetic Toxicology

Genetic toxicology is the study of harmful changes to the DNA of living cells. Although the focus of genetic toxicology is on the induction of mutations, which are heritable changes in DNA sequence, genetic toxicology is broader in scope than mutation. Genetic toxicology includes not only the induction of mutations but also the DNA damage that may or may not lead to mutations and the non-heritable changes associated with mutagenesis, such as micronuclei formation. Chemical and physical agents that produce changes in DNA are classified as genotoxic. Most genotoxic agents either interact directly with DNA or are metabolized by cells to derivatives that can interact with DNA. Thus, genetic toxicology includes the production of DNA damage, the processing of that damage by DNA repair, the conversion of DNA damage into mutations and other genetic alterations, and the ultimate effects of these genetic alterations on the phenotype of the cell. From a practical standpoint, genetic toxicologists use a number of standardized assays for detecting the genotoxicity of test agents.

Types of Mutations

Nuclear DNA consists of two antiparallel strands of complementary nucleotides whose sugar-phosphate moieties are linked together to form the backbones of the two polymers. The two strands in turn are linked together by hydrogen bonds formed between the purines (G for guanine and A for adenine) and pyrimidines (T for thymine and C for cytosine) of the nucleotides to form a double helix. A nucleotide pair consists of one purine and one pyrimidine, and A always pairs with T (forming two hydrogen bonds) and G with C (forming three hydrogen bonds). The order of bases in the DNA defines the function of the molecule. Areas of the DNA that code for proteins (i.e. genes) are decoded in groups of 3 bases (codons), each codon specifying a single amino acid in the protein. A remarkable property of DNA is its ability to replicate itself by separating its two strands, each strand serving as a template for the synthesis of a new complementary strand.

As indicated above, mutations are heritable changes in the nucleotide sequence of DNA. An agent that can induce mutations is a mutagen. A mutagen that can directly bind to DNA and cause mutations is called a direct-acting mutagen, whereas an agent that needs metabolic activation (i.e., to a DNA-reactive derivative) to induce mutations is called an indirect mutagen or promutagen. Mutagenicity is the ability of chemicals to cause mutations. Mutagenesis refers to the process involved in producing a mutation. A mutant is a cell or organism possessing one or more genes that have undergone mutation.

Mutations can be classified as gene mutations or chromosome mutations. Gene mutations are relatively small-scale alterations that are recognized by their effects on a single gene. They include basepair substitutions, frameshifts, and intragenic deletions and insertions. Basepair substitutions exchange a single nucleotide for another. If a purine is exchanged for a purine (A ↔ G) or a pyrimidine for a pyrimidine (C ↔ T), the basepair substitution is called a transition. If a purine is exchanged for a pyrimidine or a pyrimidine for a purine (C/T ↔ A/G), the mutation is referred to as a transversion. Basepair substitutions that occur in the protein coding regions of a gene may be classified according to the effect of the mutation on the protein, i.e., as silent mutations, missense mutations, or nonsense mutations. Silent mutations code for the same amino acid as the normal sequence (more than one codon sequence can code for each amino acid) so that the amino acid sequence of the protein is not changed. Missense mutations alter the codon to code for a different amino acid, which can change the functional properties of the protein. Nonsense mutations code for a stop codon, which leads to a truncated (and usually nonfunctional) protein.

Frameshifts involve the insertion or deletion of a small number of nucleotides (i.e., 1 or 2) in the DNA protein coding sequence, thereby altering the reading frame and the types of amino acids coded by the gene. Frameshifts usually generate a premature stop codon and truncated gene product, and generally result in the abolition of gene function. Basepair substitutions, frameshifts, and small deletions and insertions collectively are known as point mutations.

Intragenic deletions and insertions are much larger than point mutations, removing or adding up to tens of thousands of nucleotides within a gene. A large intragenic deletion may result in the loss of several introns and exons from the gene. In addition, deletions may lead to loss of heterozygosity (LOH), which is the loss of one allele (a sequence variant of a gene) from a pair of chromosomes that previously had two different alleles. LOH also can occur through a recombinational process (also considered to be mutagenic) that replaces the allele on one chromosome with the allele found on the chromosome's homolog.

Chromosome mutations are large-scale changes in chromosomal structure. They mainly result from chromosomal breaks and from changes in the number of chromosomes. A substance that causes DNA breaks is a clastogen while a substance that causes a change in the number of chromosomes is an aneugen. Chromosome mutations include multigene deletion, gene amplification, chromosomal translocation, inversions, chromosomal nondisjunction, aneuploidy, and polyploidy. Deletions of large chromosomal regions generally lead to loss of several genes. Gene amplification (or gene duplication) can lead to multiple copies of chromosomal regions, increasing the dosage of the genes located within them. Chromosomal translocation is the relocation of a section of a chromosome to another chromosome or the interchange of sections of nonhomologous chromosomes (reciprocal translocation), and can result in the loss of function or alteration in the function of the genes at the break points. Aneuploidy is a change in chromosome number while polyploidy is an increase in the number of chromosome sets. The microscopically visible broken chromosomes that are characteristic of clastogens are an indication of genotoxicity, but they usually are not mutations because the overwhelming majority are not heritable.

Health Impact of Mutations

Mutations that confer an advantage to the cell or organism in which they occur are rare. The majority of mutations are either silent or are deleterious. Silent mutations produce no phenotype, whereas deleterious mutations can result in either the loss of gene function, such as occurs with cancer-associated mutations in the *P53* tumor suppressor gene, or a gain of function, such as occurs with tumor-specific mutations that activate the *RAS* oncogene. When a mutation eliminates or alters the function of a protein that plays a critical role in the body, it may result in disease. It has been estimated that over 60% of human disease involves mutations as a contributing if not causative factor. Many chemicals that potentially can contaminate industrial environments have been identified as human genotoxins and mutagens, including aminobiphenyl, asbestos, benzene, and benzidine. The mutations induced by such chemicals have the potential to contribute to the disease burden.

Mutations can be induced in either germ cells (germline mutations) or somatic cells (somatic mutations). Germline mutations occur in the eggs or sperm of animals and humans, and they can be passed on to their descendants, who will carry the mutation in every cell of their bodies. Somatic mutations occur in the other cells (non-germ cells) of the body and cannot be transmitted to subsequent generations of the organism. Mutations in germ cells are responsible for inherited diseases (i.e., sickle cell anemia and Lesch-Nyhan syndrome) and predispositions to diseases, including cancer. Mutations that occur in somatic cells can cause cancer, atherosclerosis, and possibly contribute to the aging process (Figure 13.1).

Mutations are thought to be involved in the etiology of cancer because multiple genetic events are involved in the different stages of carcinogenesis.[1] Cancer is viewed as the result of accumulated mutations to a cell's DNA.[2] Research in molecular cancer genetics has identified inherited and somatic cell mutations associated with cancer in oncogenes, tumor suppressor genes, DNA repair genes, and other genes responsible for genomic stability.[3–5] A recently published study shows that the number of mutated genes that drive the development of cancer is greater than previously thought.[6] These results are consistent with a model of colorectal tumorigenesis in which the steps required for the development of cancer often involve mutations conferring a growth advantage to cells.[7]

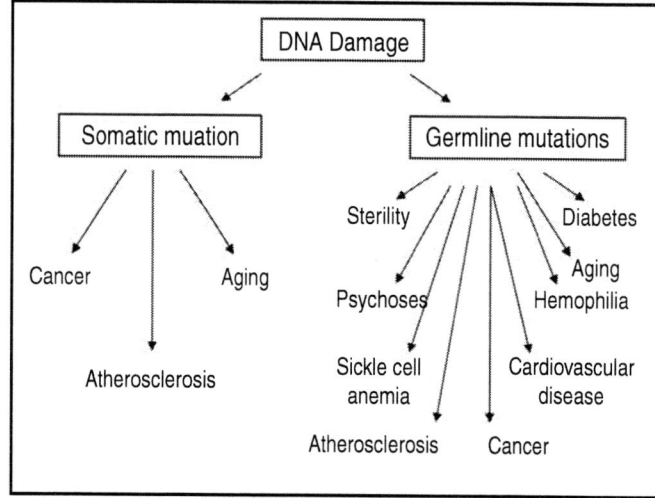

Figure 13.1 — Health consequences of mutations.

Vinyl chloride is an example of an industrial genotoxin that induces cancer. A number of cases of hepatic haemangiosarcoma have been diagnosed in workers exposed to vinyl chloride.[8] Vinyl chloride forms ethano-adducts in DNA and induces chromosomal aberrations, sister chromatid exchanges, and micronuclei in rodents exposed *in vivo*. It is also causes mutations in various short-term test systems. The *P53* gene is often mutated in haemangiosarcomas that develop in humans exposed to vinyl chloride, with A:T → T:A transversion the main type of mutation. These mutations are consistent with the formation of DNA ethano-adducts by vinyl chloride in the liver. Because of these observations, the International Agency for Research on Cancer (IARC) classified vinyl chloride as a Group 1 carcinogen, meaning that there is adequate evidence that it is carcinogenic to humans.[8]

DNA Damage

In the following three sections, we will describe the events leading to mutation: the production of DNA damage, processing damage by DNA repair, and the conversion of the damage into mutations. Table 13.1 summarizes the major types of DNA damage, examples of the genotoxic agents that cause these types of damage, the DNA repair systems that process the different types of DNA damage, and the mutations that can be induced by the damage.

When a genotoxic agent binds to DNA, DNA adducts, a type of DNA damage, are formed. Adducts and other forms of DNA damage can cause abnormal cell functions and cell death or mutations. In human cells, endogenous and exogenous genotoxic agents produce as many as one million molecular lesions per cell per day.[9] Endogenous DNA damage is caused by normal cellular processes that generate reactive oxidative species, methylation of bases for gene regulation, and mis-incorporated bases due to DNA replication errors. Exogenous DNA damage can be caused by environmental agents such as ultraviolet light, x-irradiation, plant toxins, and chemicals. Generally speaking, endogenous DNA damage is responsible for spontaneous mutations, whereas exogenous DNA damage results in induced mutations. Although it is often difficult to differentiate low levels of induced mutation from true spontaneous mutation, the different types of endogenous and exogenous DNA damage may be discerned by specific patterns of mutation, often referred to as a mutational fingerprint or spectrum.

Table 13.1 — Types of DNA damage induced by particular genotoxic agents, the DNA repair pathways that respond to the damage, and the mutations that result from the unrepaired damage.

Type of DNA damage	Agents that can cause DNA damage	Mechanisms for repairing DNA damage	Major mutations induced by DNA damage
DNA hydrolysis products			
Deaminated bases	Spontaneous deamination of 5-methylcytosine	BER, MMR	G:C → A:T transition
Apurinatic lesions	Alkylating agents, thermal disruption	BER	G:C → T:A transversion, deletion
Apyrimidinic lesions	Alkylating agents, thermal disruption	BER	A:T → T:A transversion, deletion
DNA monoadducts			
8-oxoguanine	Reactive oxygen species	BER	G:C → T:A transversion
Alkyl adducts	Alkylating agents like ENU, spontaneous methylation	MGMT, BER	Basepair substitution
Bulky adducts	Benzo[a]pyrene, N-2-actylaminofluorene	NER	Basepair substitution, frameshift
Crosslinks			
Thymine dimer	UV light, mitomycin C	NER	Tandem mutation, basepair substitution
Interstrand crosslinks	bifunctional alkylating agents like carmustine		Frameshift, deletion, chromosome mutation
Intrastrand crosslinks	Cisplatin	NER, MMR	Basepair substitution
DNA and protein crosslinks	Aldehydes	NER, BER	Chromosome mutation
Single-strand breaks	Free radicals, ionizing radiation, UV, alkylating agents	MMR	Deletion, insertion, basepair substitution
Double-strand breaks	Ionizing radiation	NHEJ and HRR	LOH, deletion, translocation

BER, base excision repair; MGMT, methylguanine methyltransferase; NER, nucleotide excision repair; MMR, mismatch repair; NHEJ, nonhomologous end a joining repair; HRR, homologous recombination repair.

Hydrolysis of DNA Bases

Hydrolysis of DNA bases includes deamination, depurination, and depyrimidination. Deamination occurs spontaneously, such as the deamination of cytosine to uracil and the deamination of 5-methylcytosine to thymine. Depurination and depyrimidation are the loss of purine and pyrimidine residues in DNA due to cleavage at the nucleotide glycosidic bond, producing apurinic or apyrimidinic (AP) sites. AP sites can subsequently undergo opening of the ribose ring and single-strand breaks. Many alkylating agents can induce AP sites by forming adducts that destabilize the glycosidic bond.

DNA Adducts

Electrophilic chemicals can bind covalently to DNA and form addition products known as DNA adducts. Since DNA adducts generally contain a portion of the mutagenic species, they are chemical-specific, and DNA adducts have been used as biomarkers of genotoxic exposure to particular chemicals. For example, bulky DNA adducts are formed by relatively large molecules, such as polycyclic aromatic hydrocarbons and heterocyclic amines, binding to DNA. N7-methylguanine is a major adduct induced by many simple alkylating agents, while 8-oxoguanine is a DNA adduct produced by reactive oxygen species and is a major component of endogenous DNA damage.[10,11] Not all DNA adducts produced by an agent are the direct result of the physical interaction between the agent or its metabolites and DNA. A case in point is the 8-hydroxyguanine DNA adduct, which is produced by the reactive oxygen species generated as a consequence of exposure to radiation and some chemicals.

Crosslinking of DNA Strands

Crosslinks are produced by chemicals that contain two reactive moieties, and thus are capable of forming crosslinks within DNA strands (intrastrand crosslinks), between DNA strands (interstrand crosslinks), and between DNA and protein (DNA-protein crosslinks). Crosslinks may block DNA replication and lead to cell death or mutations. Alkylating agents used in cancer chemotherapy, such as carmustine and nitrogen mustard, can form interstrand crosslinks in double-stranded DNA. Carmustine is particularly cytotoxic because it creates a replication-blocking DNA interstrand crosslink between the N1 of guanine and the N3 of the opposing cytosine. Cisplatin frequently acts on adjacent N-7 guanines, forming 1,2-intrastrand crosslinks. Aldehydes such as acrolein and crotonaldehyde found in tobacco smoke or automotive exhaust can form DNA-protein crosslinks through the formation of a Schiff base between a free amino group in a protein and the aldehyde.

Single-Strand Breaks

Breaks in one strand of the DNA double helix are called single-strand breaks. They are among the most common lesions arising in cells. Single-strand breaks mainly result from DNA attack by endogenous free radicals and alkylating agents. In addition, single-strand breaks are induced directly by exposure to ionizing radiation and as a secondary consequence of the repair of a variety of genotoxins.

Double-Strand Breaks

Double-strand breaks are generated in DNA when the two complementary strands of the DNA double helix are broken simultaneously at sites that are sufficiently close to one another that base-pairing and chromatin structure are insufficient to keep the two DNA ends together. As a consequence, the two DNA ends generated by a double-strand break can become physically dissociated from one another. DNA double-strand breaks are probably the most dangerous type of DNA damage as they are potent inducers of mutations and cell death. One such break can kill a cell if it leads to the inactivation of an essential gene or, more commonly, triggers apoptosis.[12]

Ionizing radiation and certain chemicals such as bifunctional alkylating agents can produce double-strand breaks. Also, double-strand breaks can occur when DNA polymerase encounters an unrepaired single-strand break in the DNA. In addition, cells break their DNA on purpose for special functions. The best characterized example of this is V(D)J recombination, which occurs in developing B- and T-lymphocytes to provide the antigen-binding diversity of the immunoglobulin and T-cell receptor proteins. Although these processes are under tight control, they can sometimes go awry, with potentially devastating consequences for the cell and for the organism.

DNA Repair

Cells have three mechanisms that protect them from the consequences of DNA damage: apoptosis, senescence, and DNA repair. DNA repair generally preserves the viability of the cell; however, if DNA damage cannot be repaired, the cell may undergo apoptosis, also known as programmed cell death. Apoptosis is a vital component of organism development and maintenance, but it also removes cells with heavily damaged DNA, thus protecting the organism from the mutations potentially induced by the damage. Senescence is an irreversible state of cellular dormancy. It serves as a functional alternative to apoptosis in cases where the physical presence of a cell is required for spatial reasons. If DNA base damage is repairable, cells will directly reverse the damage, or use the unmodified complementary strand of the DNA or the sister chromatid as a template to recover the original information (error-free base or nucleotide repair). Alternatively, cells may employ an error-prone recovery mechanism known as translesion synthesis to replicate damaged DNA. Double-strand breaks in DNA are repaired by two separate processes, homologous recombination repair and non-homologous end-joining repair.

Direct Reversal of Base Damage

DNA repair by direct reversal includes photolyase repair, reversal repair of cytosine and adenine methylation, and O^6-methylguanine-DNA methyltransferase (MGMT) repair. Photolyase repair uses the photolyase enzyme to directly reverse cyclobutane pyrimidine dimers generated from exposure to UV light. For the direct reversal of cytosine and adenine methylation, DNA dioxygenases enzymatically convert methyladenine and methycytosine in DNA to adenine and cytosine by oxidative demethylation.[13] Dioxygenases also can repair ethyladenine residues in DNA with the release of acetaldehyde.

MGMT repair involves transfer of the methyl group from O^6-methylguanine to a cysteine residue in the protein, restoring the adducted base to a guanine. The MGMT protein, however, is inactivated by this reaction, so that removal of each methyl group requires one molecule of the protein. Therefore, this mechanism of DNA repair is expensive for the cell and MGMT repair can be overwhelmed by high levels of DNA damage. MGMT repair also can remove ethyl, chloroethyl, and benzyl groups from guanine.

Base Excision Repair

Base excision repair (BER) corrects damage to single nucleotides produced by oxidation, alkylation, or hydrolysis. After the damaged base is flipped out of the DNA helix, a damage-specific DNA glycosylase is used to break its β-N glycosidic bond and create an AP site. An AP endonuclease recognizes the site, nicking the damaged DNA on the 5' side (upstream) of the AP site and creating a free 3'-OH. Finally, a DNA polymerase extends the DNA from the free 3'-OH to replace the nucleotide of the damaged base with the correct one; the break in the DNA strand then is sealed using DNA ligase. BER has two subpathways, known as short-patch BER and long-patch BER. The short-patch pathway removes only the damaged nucleotide while the long-patch pathway excises 2–10 nucleotides along with the damaged base.

Nucleotide Excision Repair

Nucleotide excision repair (NER) corrects ethylation products, bulky DNA adducts, helix-distorting changes such as thymine dimers, and single-strand breaks. It does not require an adduct-specific glycosylase, so it operates on a greater variety of lesions than BER. Also unlike BER, NER removes the damaged base along with up to 30 adjacent nucleotides, even when only a single damaged base needs to be removed. Therefore, NER creates a large "patch" around the damage. NER begins with recognizing the damage, followed by unwinding the DNA in the vicinity of the damage to produce a "bubble", cutting the damaged area with an endonuclease, using the opposite strand as a template to synthesize the correct nucleotides by DNA polymerases, and sealing the breaks by DNA ligase.

There are two subtypes of NER: global-genome repair and transcription-coupled repair. While global-genome NER gradually removes damaged nucleotides from the entire genome, transcription-coupled NER specifically repairs those portions of DNA that serve as a template for transcription.

Mismatch Repair

Mismatch repair (MMR) deals with correcting mismatched bases in double-stranded DNA (e.g., A:C or G:T), as well as mispaired nucleotides resulting from recombination. In MMR, several different proteins recognize the mismatch and cut the mismatched base from the DNA. There are two types of mismatch repair; long patch and short patch. Long patch repair can excise tracts up-to a few kilobases long. Short patch repair removes lengths of around 10 nucleotides. After the bases are removed, a DNA polymerase fills the repair patch with correct bases and a DNA ligase seals the break. Unlike BER, which recognizes and removes defective bases, MMR recognizes and removes normal (or modified) bases that are mispaired. MMR corrects not only single base mispairs, but also insertion/deletion loops that result from strand misalignments. Repairing these later mispairs can produce frameshift mutations.

Non-homologous End-Joining

Non-homologous end-joining (NHEJ) is a relatively simple and efficient means of DNA double-strand repair, but it is error-prone. NHEJ rejoins two broken ends without regard to correcting any deletions or rearrangements of DNA. The Ku protein heterodimer initiates NHEJ by binding to broken DNA ends and bringing them together. A DNA-dependent protein kinase complex and WRN protein are attracted to Ku. WRN unwinds the DNA strands and stimulates endonuclease activity in preparation for ligation. In human cells, DNA ligase IV joins the two ends.[14] The tumor-suppressor protein BRCA1 also plays a critical role in NHEJ.[15]

Homologous Recombination Repair

In contrast to NHEJ, homologous recombination repair (HRR) exactly reconstitutes the original sequence using the sister chromatid as a template. HRR is the dominant method used in the S and G2 phases of the cell-cycle when a sister chromatid has been created. Homologous pairing of the sister chromatids is often mediated by the Rad51 protein. Rad52 protein recognizes double-strand breaks and adheres to the free ends of the break while Rad51 searches the undamaged sister chromatid for a homologous repair template. The tumor-suppressor protein BRCA2 colocalizes with Rad51 during HRR, and contributes significantly to its activity.[16,17]

Translesion Synthesis

Translesion synthesis allows the DNA replication machinery to replicate past damaged DNA by using specialized DNA polymerases that are able to use damaged strands of DNA as the template for synthesis. Although this is an error-prone process, translesion synthesis reduces the danger of creating double-strand breaks.[18]

Mechanisms of Mutation Induction

Mutation induction is influenced by cell proliferation, DNA sequence context, mutagen characteristics, and other factors. DNA replication is necessary for many types of DNA repair and for mutations.[19] In general, mutations result from an imbalance between repair and damage to DNA during DNA replication. Unrepaired or misrepaired DNA damage that enters replication may result in incorrect synthesis on the new strand, and further DNA replication that fixes normal bases on both strands can produce a mutation. DNA context, the area surrounding the damaged/

mutated base, can influence the modification, replication, and repair of DNA. DNA has so-called hotspots where mutations occur many times more frequently than on average. A hotspot can be an unusual base (5-methylcytosines in CpG sites) or a special structure of the DNA (repeated sequence of cytosines).

Mutations induced by particular mutagens are not just an increase in random genetic changes, but occur in a pattern specific to the inducing agent. This specific pattern is called a mutation spectrum, defined as the types and locations of changes in DNA sequence brought about spontaneously or by exposure to a mutagen. Mutation spectra have been referred to as the fingerprints of mutagens and can be used for associating exposure to particular agents with their ultimate consequences (e.g., cancer or germ cell mutation).[20] Therefore, the mechanisms for mutation induction are frequently different from one mutagen to another. In this section, we will introduce some of the better-understood mechanisms of mutation induction.

Mutation from Deamination of Cytosine

Deamination of cytosine occurs spontaneously or as a result of exposure to genotoxins. This reaction converts cytosine to uracil in DNA. Although uracil is a "normal" base in RNA, a specific glycosylase exists for its removal from DNA; it can also be removed through mismatch repair. Unrepaired uracils in DNA can lead to G:C→A:T transition.

Spontaneous Mutation at CpG Sites

Many eukaryotic organisms methylate the cytosines in CpG dinucleotides to 5-methylcytosines. While this methylation is believed to be important for cellular function, it also creates a hotspot for mutation. Spontaneous deamination of a 5-methylcytosine results in thymine and ammonia. Thymine, being a normal base, is not removed by excision repair. If not corrected by mismatch repair, DNA replication of this thymine will result in the insertion of adenine in the new strand, with the ultimate induction of a G:C→A:T transition.

Mutation Caused by 8-oxoguanine

The mutagenicity of 8-oxoguanine, a major oxidative lesion, is mediated by its ability to basepair with adenosine rather than cytosine during DNA replication. The 'correct' pairing of 8-oxoguanine with cytosine distorts the DNA and behaves as a mismatch, whereas an 8-oxoguanine-adenine mismatch has no distortion and mimics a normal basepair. This base pairing, however, results in G:C→T:A transversion.[21]

Mutation Resulting From O^6-alkylguanine

Guanine alkylated on the O^6 position by agents like ethylnitrosourea or endogenous methylating agents forms basepairs with thymine. The consequence of this mispairing is G:C→A:T transition.

Mutation Resulting from Bulky DNA Adducts

While bulky DNA adducts, like the adducts formed by polycyclic aromatic hydrocarbons, can block DNA replication and cause cell death, some of them also can cause mutations by mispairing. For example, the bulky DNA adduct, N-(deoxyguanosin-8-yl)-2-aminofluorene (dG-C8-AF), induces G:C→T:A transversion. Several mechanisms have been suggested for mutation induction by this lesion.[22] dG-C8-AF adducts can directly pair with adenine or the adducts can degrade to produce AP sites. The AP sites or the adducts themselves become non-informational lesions that can be replicated by error-prone translesion polymerases, generally inserting an adenosine.

Deletions and Insertions

Frameshifts are caused by small deletions and insertions. A major fraction of such mutations arise in DNA contexts having short local repeats. Such repeats are comparatively prone to mutation by slippage of the replication fork in which the DNA polymerase misaligns complementary DNA strands within the locally repeated sequence during DNA replication. As a result, the number of basepair repeats changes, introducing a deletion or an insertion of one or more of the basepair repeat units. Some crosslinking agents like 9-aminoacridine are potent inducers of frameshifts. These chemicals intercalate between the basepairs of DNA and cause physical distortion of DNA that can lead to addition or deletion of basepairs through strand slippage. Several other mechanisms like rearrangement of a mismatch loop and mispairing during NHEJ repair also have been suggested for induction of small deletions and insertions. Large deletions, like chromosome deletions, can be produced by the misrepair of base damage or by the incorrect rejoining of double-strand breaks.

Loss of Heterozygosity (LOH)

Apart from the X and Y chromosomes, there are normally two copies of each chromosome in mammalian cells (referred to as dipoidy), with cells containing at least two copies of each gene, one on each set of chromosomes. Many of the gene copies are not identical, being inherited from different parents and being subject to spontaneous mutation. A cell containing two different copies of a particular gene is called a heterozygote for that gene (e.g., $P53^{+/-}$, where the 'plus' refers to the wild-type copy (or allele) and the 'minus' a mutant copy). The loss of one of the two alleles is called LOH. LOH can result in either a homozygous (two copies of the mutant allele, $P53^{-/-}$) or hemizygous (one copy of the mutant allele, $P53^{0/-}$) status for the previously heterozygous allele ($P53^{+/-}$). Mitotic recombination will result in homozygosity, while large deletions or whole chromosome loss results in hemizygosity. LOH is an important mutational event in tumorigenesis and it is an efficient mechanism for the loss of a normal allele in heterozygous tumor suppressor genes. LOH leaves only the mutant allele in the cell, which eliminates the tumor suppressor function of the gene.

Chromosomal Translocation

Translocation is a chromosomal mutation that results from the rearrangement of segments of DNA between non-homologous chromosomes. Large translocations are generally detected microscopically. Unlike simple chromosome breakage, translocations often are heritable and can result in a wide range of medical problems, such as leukemia, breast cancer, and Down syndrome. The mechanisms responsible for translocation are not understood well. However, ionizing radiation and some genotoxins are efficient inducers of the process.

Aneuploidy and Polyploidy

Cells that have extra chromosomes or are missing chromosomes are aneuploid. When one chromosome of the pair is missing, the condition is called monosomy (e.g., monosomy X: a female with only one X chromosome). An extra chromosome is trisomy (e.g., trisomy 21, causing Down syndrome). Aneuploidy usually results from non-disjunction during meiosis but also can occur in mitosis. Polyploidy is a condition in which there are more than 2 sets of chromosomes. Unlike other kinds of mutations, aneuploidy and polyploidy usually do not result from direct DNA damage but from the disruption of spindle formation. For example, the anticancer drugs paclitaxel and vinblastine induce aneuploidy by affecting tubulin polymerization or spindle microtubule stability during cell division.

Regulatory Applications of Genotoxicity Assays

Short-term assays for detecting genotoxicity have become a prominent part of toxicology testing, and have been widely used for regulatory purposes. Mutagenicity, particularly germ cell mutagenicity, is an important endpoint in and of itself, and assays have been developed to specifically measure mutation in germ cells. The major use of genotoxicity assays, however, is either for predicting the carcinogenic potential of test agents or for assessing the mode-of-action (MOA) for chemicals already known to be carcinogens. Since mutation is involved in carcinogenesis and evaluating genotoxic potential with short-term tests is considerably less expensive and time consuming than directly testing for carcinogenic potential, analyzing for genotoxicity has practical value in identifying agents that are potentially carcinogenic. These assays have provided invaluable information from their use as screens for potential carcinogens and their application to understanding the mechanisms of carcinogenesis. The most commonly used assays have been extensively validated, and their ability to predict the rodent, if not the human, carcinogenicity of test agents has been established.

The new U.S. EPA Cancer Risk Assessment Guidelines[23] provide for the use of the chemical's MOA in selecting the extrapolation model that will be used for quantitative risk assessment to establish allowable exposure limits for chemicals in the environment. The MOA is defined as the sequence of key events that are required for the chemical to induce tumors. If mutation is the key event (somewhat equivalent to the rate limiting key first event), or if the MOA is uncertain, the EPA Guidelines provide for the use of a linear low-dose extrapolation from the observable cancer dose-response curve. If there are sufficient data to determine that the chemical acts via a mutagenic MOA, there is a provision for applying age-dependent adjustment factors (ADAFs), in the absence of a specific susceptibility for early life risk. If there is sufficient information to determine that the MOA is something other than mutation induction, then the Guidelines

Table 13.2 — Some common assays for detecting genotoxicity.

Assay name	Endpoint	Reference
In vitro assays (all somatic cell assays)		
DNA adduct analysis	DNA adducts	(24)
Comet assay	DNA strand breakage	(25)
Alkaline elution assay	DNA strand breakage	(26)
Micronucleus assay in mammalian cells	Clastogenicity; aneugenicity	(27)
Unscheduled DNA synthesis in cells	DNA repair	(28)
Sister chromatid exchange in mammalian cells	DNA damage	(29)
Ames assay	Gene mutation	(30)
CHO *Hprt* mutation assay	Gene mutation	(31,32)
Mouse lymphoma assay	Gene and chromosome mutation	(33)
Chromosomal aberration in mammalian cells	Clastogenicity, aneugenicity	(34)
In vivo assays		
Rodent micronucleus assay	Clastogenicity, aneugenicity (somatic cell)	(35,36)
Sister chromatid exchange in rodents	DNA damage (somatic cell)	(29)
Unscheduled DNA synthesis in rodent liver	DNA repair (somatic cell)	(28)
Hprt mutation assay	Gene mutation (somatic cell)	(37-39)
Tk mutation assay	Gene and chromosome mutation (somatic cell)	(40)
Transgenic rodent mutation assays	Gene mutation (somatic and germ cell)	(41)
Dominant lethal assays	Clastogenicity (germ cell)	(42)
Mouse heritable translocation test	Chromosome mutation (germ cell)	(43)
Mouse spot test	Gene mutation (germ cell)	(44)
Mouse specific locus test	Gene mutation (germ cell)	(45)

allow for the use of nonlinear models. Generally the cancer data used in the risk assessment will be from a rodent cancer bioassay. However, if human cancer data are available, as is the case with inorganic arsenic, the human data are used. The EPA Guidelines provide a general framework for the use of genetic toxicology data as a part of the MOA assessment.

Assays for Detecting Genotoxicity

Genotoxicity testing is the evaluation of agents for their ability to induce alterations in DNA, including mutations. More than 200 assays have been developed for detecting genotoxicity, studying genetics, exploring mechanisms of mutagenesis, and predicting the carcinogenic potential of environmental agents. Table 13.2 lists some of these assays. Although they differ from each other because they detect different genotoxic endpoints (e.g., DNA damage, gene mutation, chromosomal damage), an agent that causes a reliable positive result in any of these tests is considered genotoxic.

In vitro Genotoxicity Assays

In vitro genetic toxicity tests offer certain advantages. The time required for performing these assays is relatively short (from a few days to a few weeks). The more common assays are inexpensive, do not involve live animals, and have large data bases. Because these assays are mechanism-based, they are widely accepted by the scientific and regulatory communities. A major problem with *in vitro* assays is that they do not accurately integrate *in vivo* biotransformation, DNA repair, and tissue susceptibility into the responses. Many promutagens are modified by enzymes within the body, creating metabolites that are the ultimate mutagenic form of the parent chemical. In an effort to duplicate *in vivo* biotransformation, many in vitro assays use a crude rat liver enzyme preparation, called S9 mix, that contains many of the enzymes necessary to perform this metabolism.

In vivo Genotoxicity Assays

It is widely accepted that *in vivo* assays are more relevant for modeling responses in humans than are *in vitro* assays because they integrate the effects of *in vivo* biological processes. It also is commonly held that many agents that are positive in highly sensitive *in vitro* assays do not produce sufficient damage to be genotoxic *in vivo*, and thus do not represent a hazard to humans. On the other hand, some mutagens induce mutations in a tissue-specific manner that cannot be detected by an *in vitro* assay. As an example, the non-steroidal anti estrogen tamoxifen induces endometrial cancer in women, and liver and endometrial tumors in rats. Tamoxifen is inactive in the Ames *Salmonella typhimurium* gene mutation assay and many other *in vitro* tests because of deficiencies in the metabolic activation systems in these assays. In contrast, tamoxifen induces mutations in rat liver using a transgenic rat mutation assay.[46,47]

Short-term Genotoxicity Assays Used in Regulatory Batteries

Although a number of genotoxicity assays have been developed over the years, only a handful are recommended by regulatory agencies for evaluating genotoxicity.[48] Generally, a complete evaluation of the genotoxicity of a test agent involves the use of a battery that includes a bacterial gene mutation assay (generally the Ames test), an *in vitro* cytogenetic assay in mammalian cells and/or the mouse lymphoma/$Tk^{+/-}$ mammalian cell mutation assay, and an *in vivo* cytogenetic assay (generally the rat micronucleus assay). Although germ-cell assays are used far less frequently than the above-listed tests, they are used when information about germ-cell effects is desired. Other 'follow-up' assays are used for confirmation, when necessary, such as to confirm that the genotoxicity detected *in vitro* is manifested *in vivo*. Several of the common genotoxicity assays used for regulatory assessment are described below.

Ames Test

The Ames test is formally called the *Salmonella typhimurium* reversion assay, or more commonly, the *Salmonella* test. This test is used worldwide as an initial screen to determine the mutagenic potential of agents. International guidelines have been developed for its use by laboratories to ensure the uniformity of testing procedures. The assay's development, detailed procedures, test design, and results interpretation have been reviewed.[30,49]

The test is a short-term bacterial assay for identifying point mutagens. It uses several different *Salmonella* strains (tester strains) that have preexisting mutations in genes necessary for the synthesis of the required amino acid, histidine. The tester strains are mutants and are unable to grow and form colonies on a medium without histidine. Mutations that restore a functional sequence (i.e., 'reverts' the mutation) will enable the bacteria to synthesize histidine. The *Salmonella* strains used in the test have different preexisting mutations, and each of these mutations is designed to respond to mutagens that act via different mechanisms, such as basepair substitutions at A:T and G:C and frameshifts in different sequence contexts. When a mutagen produces mutations at these sites and reverts the tester strains, the reverted bacteria can form colonies on a plate containing a minimal agar medium containing only trace amounts of histidine. The particular tester strain reverted gives information on the types of mutations induced by the test agent, and the magnitude of the responses is an indication of mutagenic potency. A similar test in *E. coli* measures mutation in the tryptophane biosynthetic pathway. The assay is conducted both with and without S9 exogenous activation. The S9 fraction is a mixture of microsomes and cytosol often taken from the rat liver. It contains a wide variety of Phase I and Phase II enzymes, including cytochrome P450 enzymes, carboxylesterases, acetyltransferases, and other drug metabolizing enzymes. Before collection, the rat is sometimes treated with Phenobarbital or other compounds that will cause an induction of these enzymes. When used with the Ames test, the S9 fraction can cause the *in vitro* metabolic activation or inactivation of a promutagen, just as may happen *in vivo*. Therefore, the use of the S9 fraction can help create assay conditions that more closely resemble the exposure of an animal to a promutagen under real conditions.

CHO/Hprt Mutation Assay

The CHO/*Hprt* mutation assay uses the *hypoxanthine-guanine phosphoribosyl-transferase* gene (*Hprt*) as a reporter of mutation in Chinese hamster ovary (CHO) cells.[31,32] The *Hprt* gene codes for an enzyme that participates in the purine salvage pathway. *Hprt* mutants can be detected by their resistance to the toxic purine analog, 6-thioguanine (6-TG). The purine salvage pathway is not essential for cells in culture and a mutation in the *Hprt* gene will disable the pathway and prevent 6-TG from killing the cells. Therefore, wild-type cells will be poisoned by 6-TG via the purine salvage pathway while mutant cells will survive and form colonies.

In the CHO/*Hprt* assay, cells are exposed to the test substance, both with and without exogenous metabolic activation (S9). The treated cells then are grown for one week to allow expression of the mutant phenotype prior to treatment with 6-TG. Mutant frequency is determined by seeding a large number of cells (millions) in medium containing 6-TG to detect mutant cells, and a lesser number (hundreds) in medium without 6-TG to determine the cloning efficiency of the cells (viability). After a suitable incubation time, colonies are counted and the mutant frequency is derived from the number of mutant colonies detected in 6-TG-containing medium as a function of the number of viable cells plated.

Mouse Lymphoma Assay

The mouse lymphoma assay (MLA), using the *thymidine kinase* gene (*Tk*) as the mutational target, detects a broad spectrum of genetic damage, including both point and chromosomal mutations. Unlike the X-linked, hemizygous *Hprt* gene, the *Tk* gene can undergo mitotic recombination and *Tk* mutant cells can survive when the wild-type allele of the $Tk^{+/-}$ cell is inactivated by large deletions or chromosomal rearrangements. This assay is widely used for regulatory purposes and is included in the core battery of genotoxicity tests. Detailed procedures and current guidance for the conduct of the MLA are given elsewhere.[33,50-55]

The MLA is conducted using the L5178Y/$Tk^{+/-}$-3.7.2C mouse lymphoma cell line and it detects mutations that inactivate the gene product of the wild-type *Tk* allele (*Tk*1b). In this assay, *Tk*-deficient ($Tk^{-/-}$ or $Tk^{0/-}$) mutants are selected with the pyrimidine analog trifluorothymindine (TFT). TFT inhibits the growth of $Tk^{+/+}$ or $Tk^{+/-}$ cells but not $Tk^{-/-}$ or $Tk^{0/-}$ mutant cells that have a nonfunctional pyrimidine salvage pathway. A striking feature of the *Tk* mutant colonies recovered in TFT selective medium is the induction of large colonies growing at normal growth rates and small colonies growing at slower rates. The relative frequency of the two colony classes is mutagen-dependent, with chemicals that are mainly clastogens primarily inducing small colony mutants and chemicals that mainly induce point mutations primarily producing large colony mutants. There are currently two equally acceptable protocols for conducting the MLA, the soft agar method[56] and a method using liquid medium and limiting-dilution cloning in 96-well plates.[57] The assay is performed both with and without S9 exogenous metabolic activation.

In vitro Chromosome Aberration Assay

This assay measures the clastogenicity of test agents, detecting microscopically visible aberrations in both chromosomes (breakage, or breakage and reunion of both chromatids at an identical site) and in chromatids (breakage of single chromatids or breakage and reunion between chromatids). Because it also can identify polyploidy, this assay can identify chemicals that cause changes in chromosome number.

The test employs cultures of established mammalian cell lines, cell strains, or primary cell cultures (human lymphocytes), with CHO cells probably being most frequently used for testing purposes. Cell cultures are exposed to the test substance with and without S9 metabolic activation. After a period of culture optimized to maximize the recovery of first division metaphases, the cells are treated with colcemid, harvested, and slides prepared. After staining, metaphase cells are analyzed microscopically for the presence of chromosome aberrations. Standard forms are used to score and record gaps, breaks, fragments, and reunion figures, as well as numerical aberrations. Data from treated cultures are compared with those of negative and positive controls. The type of aberration, its frequency, and dose trends within a given time period are all considered when evaluating a test agent as positive or negative. Detailed guidelines for the assay can be found on the Organization for Economic Cooperation and Development (OECD) and Food and Drug Administration (FDA) websites.[34,58]

Rodent Micronucleus Assay

The rodent micronucleus test is an *in vivo* assay that measures damage to the chromosomes and mitotic apparatus of blood-forming cells in the bone marrow. DNA fragments or whole chromosomes that are not included in the main nuclei during cell division form cytoplasmic DNA bodies, termed micronuclei. A unique feature of erythropoeisis in mammals is that the main nucleus is extruded during the early development of erythrocytes and any DNA not included in the main nucleus remains behind in the otherwise enucleated cell, making micronuclei particularly easy to identify in these cells. An increase in the frequency of micronucleated bone marrow cells or peripheral blood erythrocytes in treated animals is an indication of induced chromosome damage. Micronuclei are distinguished by the presence or absence of a kinetochore or centromeric DNA in the micronuclei: micronuclei lacking a centromere are assumed to have been produced by chromosome breakage while centromere-positive micronuclei indicate aneugenicity.

The bone marrow of rodents is routinely used in this test since erythrocytes are produced in that tissue. Micronucleated erythrocytes also are measured in the peripheral blood of mice and rats. Micronucleus data usually are expressed as the percent of micronucleated bone marrow cells or peripheral blood erythrocytes. Animals typically are exposed to the test agent on two or three consecutive days by either intraperitoneal injection to maximize the detection of a response or by a route appropriate to the agent. If bone marrow is sampled, the animals are sacrificed 24 to 72 hr after treatment, and the bone marrow recovered from the femurs or tibias, spread on slides, and stained. When peripheral blood is used, the blood is collected 24 to 72 hr after treatment, and slides prepared and stained. Blood can be obtained from the tail vein or other appropriate blood vessel, so that multiple sampling of animals is possible. Micronuclei are usually scored manually using a microscope. However, automated systems have been developed using image analysis and flow cytometry. The data should be interpreted by considering the dose-related change in the frequency of micronucleated cells, the statistical significance of the test results, and other factors. For details of the assay, readers are encouraged to consult published guidelines.[35,36,58]

Transgenic Rodent Mutation Assay

Transgenic rodent mutation assays measure gene mutations in tissues and organs of mice and rats. The assays are suitable for testing chemical compounds for regulatory purposes and are capable of measuring both somatic and germ cell mutation. The World Health Organization (WHO)/International Program on Chemical Safety (IPCS) has published an Environmental Health Criteria document on transgenic rodent mutation assays and their use in toxicity assessment.[59] Also, OECD is developing guidelines for the use of transgenic rodent mutation assays.[41] It is anticipated that transgenic rodent mutation assays will fill a gap in regulatory testing strategies and complement *in vivo* chromosomal aberration and micronucleus assays that detect mainly clastogenic agents.

The cells in the transgenic animals used in these assays contain foreign target genes (reporter transgenes of bacterial or viral origin) that are used for detecting *in vivo* mutations. The Big Blue mouse and rat and Muta mouse are widely used for these assays and the Big Blue mouse and rat are commercially available. The Big Blue models use the *lacI* (1080 bp) and *cII* (294 bp) genes as mutational targets, while the Muta mouse uses *lacZ* (3100 bp) and *cII* as reporter genes. In these *in vivo* models, reporter genes are located in so-called shuttle vectors that are derivatives of bacteriophages. The vectors can be recovered from the rodents and the mutants detected in an appropriate bacterial host. After exposure of transgenic animals to a test substance, DNA is isolated from individual organs or tissues and single copies of the vector DNA are excised from the high molecular weight rodent DNA and 'packaged' into infectious virus particles. If appropriate *E. coli* host cells are infected, plated, and incubated, plaques (or colonies, depending on the assay) containing individual transgene vectors become visible on the plates. Mutant frequencies are determined by comparing the number of mutant plaques/colonies to the total number of plaques/colonies.

Germ Cell Genotoxicity/Mutation Assays

Tests for Chromosomal Translocations

Male mice are treated with the test compound (see Leonard, 1977 for details.)[60] Chromosomal translocations can be evaluated in the spermatocytes of the treated males and also in the spermatocytes of the male offspring of the treated males. The first test provides information as to whether the chemical causes chromosomal damage in the spermatocytes of the exposed animal. This is evidence of potential heritable mutation and also of potential negative impacts on fertility. The second test (the F_1 translocation test) provides information as to whether the chemical can induce permanent chromosomal damage that can be passed to the first generation (the F_1) and presumably subsequent generations of offspring. For the spermatocyte translocation test, the spermatocytes of treated males are analyzed 50–100 days following treatment. Microscope slides are prepared and spermatocytes undergoing cell division are evaluated for the presence of chromosomal translocations. Most of the spermatocytes containing chromosomal translocations will be unsuccessful in fertilizing an egg and creating a viable offspring. For the F_1 translocation test, the treated males are mated and the test is performed using the testis from the F_1 offspring and by evaluating cells undergoing cell division using microscope slides. Damage induced in the various germ cell stages of the parent male (spermatozoa, mature spermatid, young spermatid, spermatocyte, and spermatogonia) are assessed by mating the exposed male at various times post-treatment and evaluating the testis of the F_1 offspring for these various times post-mating. Chemicals that can cause translocations in the F_1 offspring are of particular concern because these events are heritable and can impact subsequent generations.

The Mouse Specific Locus Test

The specific locus test is a mutagenicity test developed and extensively used by William and Liane Russell at the Oak Ridge National Laboratories.[61] The test involves the mating of wild-type exposed or unexposed mice with mice that are homozygotes for a particular set of recessive genes. The offspring of this mating are then evaluated for the various mutant phenotypes. The reporter genes require two copies of the mutant allele to express the mutant phenotype. The offspring of the mating between the wild-type and the mutant mice will be heterozygous for these alleles and will have a normal phenotype unless there is a new mutation in the wild type allele. This test provides for the detection of newly induced recessive mutations at the specific loci and also any newly induced visible dominant mutations at any locus.

The Dominant Lethal Assay in Male Mice

A newly induced dominant lethal mutation in a gamete (egg or sperm) will be lethal to the zygote produced by that gamete, thus reducing the litter size. This provides the basis for the dominant lethal assay.[62] Any normal strain of mice can be used for this assay. Because large normal litter sizes provide the most information per mated pair, it is recommended that F1 hybrids or outbred strains be used. While either males or females may be treated, generally males are treated and then mated to a number of untreated females. A treated male is caged for one week with 3 virgin females that are 8–10 weeks of age. The females are sacrificed and the uterus is dissected 17 days after the introduction to the male. One can also use the presence of vaginal plugs to determine the time of pregnancy and the analysis can be done at a standard time after the initiation of pregnancy. The uterus is examined for the presence of normally developing fetuses and for fetuses that have died and have not developed. An increase in dead implants in the litters from treated males above that seen from litters from the untreated control male is an indication that the chemical is inducing an increase in dominant lethal events. In addition to providing genetic toxicology information, the dominant lethal assay also provides information as to the potential for the test chemical to negatively impact fertility.

How Short-Term Genetic Toxicology Assay Data Is Used in Industrial Hygiene

Why should occupational safety, health and environmental professionals be interested in genetic toxicology testing? Although the data from these tests are not often used directly in setting occupational exposure standards and guidelines, genotoxicity data are considered when setting these values, particularly in the case of carcinogens and chemicals that can cause mutations capable of being inherited.

Use in Setting Threshold Limit Values®

The American Conference of Governmental Industrial Hygienists (ACGIH) includes a section in the Threshold Limit Value (TLV®) documentation on all chemicals in which a TLV® is recommended.[63] In two cases the TLV® has been set based principally on genotoxicity data. The TLV® for two cyanohydrin isomers, 1-chloro-2-propanol and 2-chloro-1-propanol, was set at 1 ppm primarily because of positive responses in multiple *in vitro* and *in vivo* tests, including the Ames assay, MLA, rat bone marrow cytogenetics, the sister chromatid exchange and chromosome aberration assays in CHO cells, the SOS chromotest (a bacterial DNA damage assay), and the Syrian hamster embryo (SHE) cell clonal transformation and *in vitro* micronucleus assays.

In most cases, genotoxicity data are one component of a complete assessment of available scientific data that are used to identify airborne chemical concentrations below which adverse health effects are not expected in humans exposed for a working lifetime.

Use by International Regulatory Bodies

Several countries, including Germany, Ireland, the Netherlands, Norway, Spain, and the United Kingdom, have classification schemes for industrial chemicals shown to be mutagens. These classifications are shown in Table 13.3. In Germany, for instance, the Maximum Concentration at the Workplace (MAK) Commission for the Investigation of Health Hazards of Chemical Compounds in the Work Area reviews the available scientific research and proposes workplace values; the MAK Commission also classifies substances that are carcinogens or germ cell mutagens. Five categories of germ cell mutagens have been established by the German MAK[64] (Table 13.3).

There are no Category 1 mutagens listed under MAK (Table IV). This is because there have been no epidemiological studies to date that have unambiguously shown an increase in heritable mutations after exposure.[64] However, 11 chemicals have been classified as Category 2 mutagens (Table 13.4) and 34 others have been otherwise classified as somatic cell mutagens under MAK.

Genetic Toxicity Endpoints as Biomarkers in Human Biomonitoring Studies

Some of the endpoints measured by the short-term tests listed in Table 13.2 can also be measured in samples taken from exposed human populations. Thus, genotoxicity-related endpoints can be used as biomarkers of exposure (e.g., DNA adducts, DNA damage measured with the Comet assay), susceptibility (e.g., functional polymorphisms in genes/proteins involved in DNA repair and chemical metabolism), and effect (e.g., mutations in

Table 13.3 — Mutagen Classification Schemes.

Country		Classification
Germany	1	Germ cell mutagens shown to increase the mutant frequency in the progeny of exposed humans.
	2	Germ cell mutagens that have been shown to increase the mutant frequency in the progeny of exposed mammals.
	3A	Substances that have been shown to induce genetic damage in germ cells of humans or animals, or which produce mutagenic effects in somatic cells and have been shown to reach the germ cells in their active forms.
	3B	Substances suspected of being germ cell mutagens because of their genotoxic effects in mammalian somatic cells *in vivo*. Includes those clearly mutagenic *in vitro* and structurally related to known *in vivo* mutagens.
	4	Not applicable
	5	Germ cells mutagens of low potency and are not expected to contribute significant genetic risk in humans.
Ireland	M1	Substances known to be mutagenic in humans
	M2	Substances that should be regarded as reproductive toxins in humans.
Netherlands	M	Mutagenic
Norway	M	Mutagenic
Spain	M2	Can be considered mutagenic in humans
United Kingdom	R60	May impair fertility
	R62	Possible risk of impaired fertility

Table 13.4 — MAK Germ Cell Classification.

Chemical MAK	Classification
Acrylamide	2
Benzo[a]pyrene	2
1,3-Butadiene	2
1,2-Dibromo-3-chloropropane	2
Diepoxybutane	2
Diethyl sulfate	2
Ethylene oxide	2
Ethylenimine	2
Nitrogen mustard	2
Olaquindox	2
Trimethyl phosphate	2
Antimony (elemental)	3A
Antimony (inorganic)	3A
Arsenic (elemental)	3A
Arsenic (inorganic)	3A
Arsenic acid (salts also)	3A
Arsenic pentoxide	3A
Arsenic trioxide	3A
Arsenous acid	3A
Benomyl	3A
Benzene	3A
Cadmium (metal and inorganic)	3A
Calcium arsenate	3A
Carbendazim	3A
4-Chloro-o-toluidine	3A
Cobalt (elemental and metal)	3A
Cobalt (compounds as Co)	3A
1,4-Dichloro-2-butene	3A
Hard metal (containing tungsten carbide and cobalt)	3A
Hydroquinone	3A
Lead Arsenate (As$_2$O$_8$Pb$_3$)	3A
Sodium arsenite	3A
Urethane	3A
0-Aminoazotoluene	3B
p-Dichlorobenzene	3B
Epichlorohydrin	3B
Ethidium bromide	3B
Naphthalene	3B
Nitrotoluene-o-isomer	3B
Ochratoxin A	3B
Propylene imine	3B
Quinone	3B
Trichloroethylene	3B
Ethanol	5
Formaldehyde	5

the *HPRT* gene and chromosome aberrations). Genotoxicity biomarkers can be used for exposure assessments, to identify susceptible populations, and to predict disease before the clinical occurrence of symptoms (and potentially to apply preventive measures). Experimentally, genotoxicity biomarkers can be used to gain insight into biological processes involved in a disease and in enhancing etiological studies of disease.

Perhaps the most useful genotoxicity biomarker at present is chromosome aberrations measured in peripheral blood lymphocytes. In a large collaborative cohort study that began in the 1980s, chromosome aberrations have been validated as a predictor of cancer risk, with a doubling of aberration frequency associated with a 20–25% increase in the incidence of cancer.[65] An additional collaborative study is underway to validate micronucleus frequency as a biomarker of cancer, and recent results indicate that there is a positive association between the biomarker and disease outcome.[66] These efforts have led to a large increase in human biomonitoring studies employing micronuclei and chromosome aberration, including a large number of studies evaluating the effects of work-place exposures.[67,68]

Summary

Genetic toxicology is the study of harmful changes to the DNA of living cells, focusing on the mutagenicity of chemicals. Many chemicals found in industrial environments have been identified as potential human mutagens. Mutagenesis is a process that involves damage to DNA, followed by DNA repair and the induction of heritable alterations in DNA sequence. A number of genotoxins can damage DNA through directly binding to DNA to cause DNA adducts, hydrolysis of nucleotides, breaking of DNA strands, or crosslinking of DNA. If the damage has not resulted in cell death, the damaged DNA can be repaired in that cell using several damage-specific and more general mechanisms. The main mechanisms for the repair of DNA adducts, hydrolyzed nucleotides, single-strand breaks, and DNA crosslinking involve excision repair (including BER, NER and MMR), while HRR and NHEJ repair double-strand breaks in DNA. Mutations are induced by the replication of DNA containing un-repaired or mis-repaired DNA damage. The induction of mutations is not just an increase in random genetic changes, but occurs in a pattern specific to the inducing agent. It has been estimated that over 60% of human disease involves mutations, including mutations in germ cells and in somatic cells. Cancer is believed to be the result of an accumulation of mutations in cellular DNA. Therefore, genetic toxicology has become an important part of cancer research. Genotoxicity assays have been widely used for regulatory purposes. They are used to identify germ cell mutagens, for predicting the potential carcinogenicity of test chemicals (prior to the completion of a cancer bioassay) and also as a part of the weight of the evidence evaluation of the MOA for chemicals known to be carcinogens. Genotoxicity data are considered when setting occupational exposure standards and guidelines, particularly in the case of carcinogens and chemicals that can cause mutations capable of being inherited in offspring.

References

1. **Hennings, H., et al.:** Critical aspects of initiation, promotion, and progression in multistage epidermal carcinogenesis. *Proc. Soc. Exp. Biol. Med. 202*:1–8 (1993).
2. **Knudson, A.G., Jr.:** Mutation and cancer: statistical study of retinoblastoma. *Proc. Natl. Acad. Sci. USA 68*:820–823 (1971).
3. **Knudson, A.G., Jr.:** Antioncogenes and human cancer. *Proc. Natl. Acad. Sci. USA 90*:10914–10921 (1993).
4. **Loeb, L.A.:** A mutator phenotype in cancer. *Cancer Res. 61*:3230–3239 (2001).
5. **Moolgavkar, S.H. and A.G. Knudson, Jr.:** Mutation and cancer: a model for human carcinogenesis. *J. Natl. Cancer Inst. 66*:1037–1052 (1981).
6. **Greenman, C., et al:** Patterns of somatic mutation in human cancer genomes. *Nature 446*:153–158 (2007).
7. **Vogelstein, B., et al.:** Genetic alterations during colorectal-tumor development. *N. Engl. J. Med. 319*:525–532 (1988).
8. **International Agency for Research on Cancer (IARC):** Vinyl chloride, polyvinyl chloride and vinyl chloride-vinyl acetate copolymers. *IARC Monogr. Eval. Carcinog. Risk Chem. Hum. 19*:377–438 (1979).
9. **Lodish, H., et al.:** *Molecular Biology of the Cell.* New York: W.H. Freeman, 2004.
10. **Beckman, K.B. and B.N. Ames:** Endogenous oxidative damage of mtDNA. *Mutat. Res. 424*:51–58 (1999).
11. **Dizdaroglu, M.:** Oxidative damage to DNA in mammalian chromatin. *Mutat. Res. 275*:331–342 (1992).
12. **Rich, T., R.L. Allen, and A.H. Wyllie:** Defying death after DNA damage. *Nature 407*:777–783 (2000).
13. **Duncan, T, et al.:** Reversal of DNA alkylation damage by two human dioxygenases. *Proc. Natl. Acad. Sci. USA 99*:16660–16665 (2002).
14. **Critchlow, S.E. and S.P. Jackson:** DNA end-joining: from yeast to man. *Trends Biochem. Sci. 23*:394–398 (1998).
15. **Deng, C.X. and R.H. Wang:** Roles of BRCA1 in DNA damage repair: a link between development and cancer. *Hum. Mol. Genet. 12(1)*:R113–123 (2003).
16. **Haber, J.E.:** Partners and pathways repairing a double-strand break. *Trends Genet. 16*:259–264 (2000).
17. **Orelli, B.J. and D.K. Bishop:** BRCA2 and homologous recombination. *Breast Cancer Res. 3*:294–298 (2001).
18. **Prakash, S. and L. Prakash:** Translesion DNA synthesis in eukaryotes: a one- or two-polymerase affair. *Genes Dev. 16*:1872–1883 (2002).
19. **Bielas, J.H. and J.A. Heddle:** From the cover: proliferation is necessary for both repair and mutation in transgenic mouse cells [In Process Citation]. *Proc. Natl. Acad. Sci. USA 97*:11391–11396 (2000).
20. **Vogelstein, B. and K.W. Kinzler:** Carcinogens leave fingerprints. *Nature 355*:209–210 (1992).
21. **Hsu, G.W., M. Ober, T. Carell, and L.S. Beese:** Error-prone replication of oxidatively damaged DNA by a high-fidelity DNA polymerase. *Nature 431*:217–221 (2004).
22. **Chen, T., et al:** Gene- and tissue-specificity of mutation in Big Blue rats treated with the hepatocarcinogen N-hydroxy-2-acetylaminofluorene. *Environ. Mol. Mutagen. 37*:203–214 (2001).
23. **U.S. Environmental Protection Agency (EPA):** Guidelines for Cancer Risk Assessment. http://cfpub.epa.gov/ncea/cfm/recordisplay.cfm?deid=116283. 2005. [Accessed on September 20, 2007].
24. **Phillips, D.H., et al.:** Methods of DNA adduct determination and their application to testing compounds for genotoxicity. *Environ. Mol. Mutagen. 35*:222–233 (2000).
25. **Tice, R.R., et al.:** Single cell gel/comet assay: guidelines for in vitro and in vivo genetic toxicology testing. *Environ. Mol. Mutagen. 35*:206–221 (2000).
26. **Elia, M.C., et al.:** Rapid DNA degradation in primary rat hepatocytes treated with diverse cytotoxic chemicals: analysis by pulsed field gel electrophoresis and implications for alkaline elution assays. *Environ. Mol. Mutagen. 24*:181–191 (1994).
27. **Miller, B., et al:** Evaluation of the in vitro micronucleus test as an alternative to the in vitro chromosomal aberration assay: position of the GUM Working Group on the in vitro micronucleus test. Gesellschaft fur Umwelt-Mutationsforschung. *Mutat. Res. 410*:81–116 (1998).
28. **Madle, S., et al.:** Recommendations for the performance of UDS tests *in vitro* and *in vivo*. *Mutat. Res. 312*:263–285 (1994).
29. **Tucker, J.D., et al.:** Sister-chromatid exchange: second report of the Gene-Tox Program. *Mutat. Res. 297*:101–180 (1993).
30. **Mortelmans, K. and E. Zeiger:** The Ames Salmonella/microsome mutagenicity assay. *Mutat. Res. 455*:29–60 (2000).
31. **Hsie, A.W., P.A. Brimer, T.J. Mitchell, and D.G. Gosslee:** The dose-response relationship for ethyl methanesulfonate-induced mutations at the hypoxanthine-guanine phosphoribosyl transferase locus in Chinese hamster ovary cells. *Somatic Cell Genet. 1*:247–261 (1975).
32. **Li, A.P., et al.:** A guide for the performance of the Chinese hamster ovary cell/hypoxanthine-guanine phosphoribosyl transferase gene mutation assay. *Mutat. Res. 189*:135–141 (1987).
33. **Chen, T. and M.M. Moore:** Screening for chemical mutagens using the mouse lymphoma assay. In: *Optimization in Drug Discovery: In-vitro Methods.* Yan, Z. and G.W. Caldwell (eds.). Totowa, NJ: Humana Press, 2004. p. 337–352.
34. **Organization for Economic Cooperation and Development (OECD):** OECD Guideline for the Testing of Chemicals: *In Vitro* Mammalian Chromosome Aberration Test. http://www.oecd.org/dataoecd/18/33/1948434.pdf. 1997. [Accessed on September 20, 2007].
35. **Hayashi, M., et al.:** In vivo rodent erythrocyte micronucleus assay. *Mutat. Res. 312*:293–304 (1994).

36. **Organization for Economic Cooperation and Development (OECD):** OECD Guideline for the Testing of Chemicals: Mammalian Erythrocyte Micronucleus Test. http://www.oecd.org/dataoecd/18/34/1948442.pdf. 1997. [Accessed on September 20, 2007].
37. **Aidoo, A., S.M. Morris, and D.A. Casciano:** Development and utilization of the rat lymphocyte hprt mutation assay. *Mutat. Res. 387*:69–88 (1997).
38. **Albertini, R.J.:** Somatic gene mutations in vivo as indicated by the 6-thioguanine- resistant T-lymphocytes in human blood. *Mutat. Res. 150*:411–422 (1985).
39. **Jones, I.M., K. Burkhart-Schultz, and A.V. Carrano:** A method to quantify spontaneous and *in vivo* induced thioguanine-resistant mouse lymphocytes. *Mutat. Res. 147*:97–105 (1985).
40. **Dobrovolsky, V.N., D.A. Casciano, and R.H. Heflich:** $Tk^{+/-}$ mouse model for detecting *in vivo* mutation in an endogenous, autosomal gene. *Mutat. Res. 423*:125–136 (1999).
41. **Lambert, I.B., T.M. Singer, S.E. Boucher, and G.R. Douglas:** Detailed review of transgenic rodent mutation assays. *Mutat. Res. 590*:1–280 (2005).
42. **Adler, I.D., et al.:** Recommendations for the categorization of germ cell mutagens. Arbeitsmedizin, Sozialmedizin, Umseltmedizin 34:400-403. *In English:* http://www.swan.ac.uk/cget/ejgt/mak.htm. 1999. [Accessed on September 20, 2007].
43. **Russell, L.B. and M.D. Shelby:** Tests for heritable genetic damage and for evidence of gonadal exposure in mammals. *Mutat. Res. 154*:69–84 (1985).
44. **Styles, J.A. and M.G. Penman:** The mouse spot test. Evaluation of its performance in identifying chemical mutagens and carcinogens. *Mutat. Res. 154*:183–204 (1985).
45. **Russell, L.B. and W.L. Russell:** Frequency and nature of specific-locus mutations induced in female mice by radiations and chemicals: a review. *Mutat. Res. 296*:107–127 (1992).
46. **Chen, T., et al.:** Mutations induced by alpha-hydroxytamoxifen in the lacI and cII genes of Big Blue transgenic rats. *Carcinogen. 23*:1751–1757 (2002).
47. **Davies, R., et al.:** Mutational spectra of tamoxifen-induced mutations in the livers of lacI transgenic rats. *Environ. Mol. Mutagen. 28*:430–433 (1996).
48. **Cimino, M.C.:** Comparative overview of current international strategies and guidelines for genetic toxicology testing for regulatory purposes. *Environ. Mol. Mutagen. 47*:362–390 (2006).
49. **U.S. Food and Drug Administration (FDA):** Bacterial Reverse Mutation Test. http://www.cfsan.fda.gov/~redbook/redivc1a.html. 2000. [Accessed on September 20, 2007].
50. **U.S. Food and Drug Administration (FDA):** Redbook 2000, Toxicological Principles for the Safety of Food Ingredients: IV.C.1.c. Mouse Lymphoma Thymidine Kinase Gene Mutation Assay. http://www.cfsan.fda.gov/~redbook/redivc1c.html. 2001. [Accessed on September 20, 2007].
51. **Moore, M.M., et al.:** Mouse lymphoma thymidine kinase locus gene mutation assay: International Workshop on Genotoxicity Test Procedures Workgroup Report. *Environ. Mol. Mutagen. 35*:185–190 (2000).
52. **Moore, M.M., et al.:** Mouse lymphoma thymidine kinase gene mutation assay: meeting of the International Workshop on Genotoxicity Testing, San Francisco, 2005, recommendations for 24-h treatment. *Mutat. Res. 627*:36–40 (2007).
53. **Moore, M.M., et al.:** Mouse lymphoma thymidine kinase gene mutation assay: follow-up meeting of the International Workshop on Genotoxicity Testing—Aberdeen, Scotland, 2003—Assay acceptance criteria, positive controls, and data evaluation. *Environ. Mol. Mutagen. 47*:1–5 (2006).
54. **Moore, M.M., et al.:** Mouse lymphoma thymidine kinase gene mutation assay: International Workshop on Genotoxicity Tests Workgroup report—Plymouth, UK 2002. *Mutat. Res. 540*:127–140 (2003).
55. **Moore, M.M., et al.:** Mouse lymphoma thymidine kinase gene mutation assay: follow-up International Workshop on Genotoxicity Test Procedures, New Orleans, Louisiana, April 2000. *Environ. Mol. Mutagen. 40*:292–299 (2002).
56. **Turner, N.T., A.G. Batson, and D. Clive:** Procedures for the L5178/$Tk^{+/-}$ - $Tk^{-/-}$ mouse lytmphoma assay. In: *Handbook of Mutagenecity Test Procedures.* Kilbey, B., M. Legator and C. Ramel (eds.). Amsterdam, The Netherlands: Elsevier, 1984. pp. 239–268.
57. **Cole, J., C.F. Arlett, M.H. Green, J. Lowe, and W. Muriel:** A comparison of the agar cloning and microtitration techniques for assaying cell survival and mutation frequency in L5178Y mouse lymphoma cells. *Mutat. Res. 111*:371–386 (1983).
58. **U.S. Food and Drug Administration (FDA):** In vitro mammalian chromosomal aberration test. http://www.cfsan.fda.gov/~redbook/redivc1b.html. 2003. [Accessed on September 20, 2007].
59. **International Programme on Chemical Safety (IPCS):** Transgenic Animal Mutagenicity Assays. http://www.who.int/ipcs/publications/ehc/ehc233.pdf. 2006. [Accessed on September 20, 2007].
60. **Leonard, A.:** Tests for heritable translocations in male mammals. In *Handbook of Mutagenicity Test Procedures.* Kilbey B.J., M. Legator, W. Nichols, and C. Ramel (eds.). Amsterdam, The Netherlands: Elsevier Scientific Publishing Company, 1977. pp. 293–299.
61. **Searle, A.G.:** The specific locus test in the mouse. In *Handbook of Mutagenicity Test Procedures.* Kilbey, B.J., M. Legator, W. Nichols, and C. Ramel (eds.). Amsterdam, The Netherlands: Elsevier Scientific Publishing Company, 1977. pp. 311–324.
62. **Batman, A.J.:** The dominant lethal assay in the male mouse. In *Handbook of Mutagenicity Test.* Kilbey, B.J., M. Legator, W. Nichols, and C. Ramel (eds.). Amsterdam, The Netherlands: Elsevier Scientific Publishing Company, 1977. pp. 325–334.

63. **American Conference of Governmental Industrial Hygienists (ACGIH):** *Threshold Limit Values for Chemical Substances and Physical Agents and Biological Exposure Indices.* Cincinnati, OH: ACGIH, 2006.
64. **Adler, I.D., et al.:** Summary report of the Working Group on Mammalian Germ Cell Tests. *Mutat. Res. 312*:313–318 (1994).
65. **Bonassi, S.:** Combining environmental exposure and genetic effect measurements in health outcome assessment. *Mutat. Res. 428*:177–185 (1999).
66. **Bonassi, S., et al.:** An increased micronucleus frequency in peripheral blood lymphocytes predicts the risk of cancer in humans. *Carcinogen. 28*:625–631 (2007).
67. **Albertini, R., et al.:** The use of non-tumor data in cancer risk assessment: reflections on butadiene, vinyl chloride, and benzene. *Regul. Toxicol. Pharmacol. 37*:105–132 (2003).
68. **Bonassi, S., et al.:** Human population studies with cytogenetic biomarkers: review of the literature and future prospectives. *Environ. Mol. Mutagen 45*:258–270 (2005).

Additional Reading

Li, A.P. and R.H. Heflich: *Genetic Toxicology.* Boca Raton, FL: CRC Press, 1991.

Preston, R.J. and G.R. Hoffmann (eds.): *Genetic Toxicology.* New York, NY: McGraw-Hill, 2001.

Brusick, D. (ed.): *Methods for Genetic Risk Assessment.* Boca Raton, FL: CRC Press, 1994.

Frieberg, E.C., G.C. Walker, and W. Siede: *DNA Repair and Mutagenesis.* Washington, DC: ASM Press, 1995.

Chapter 14

Carcinogenesis

Outcome Competencies
Upon completing this chapter, the reader will be able to:

1. **Knowledge**
   - Define carcinogenesis, mutagenesis, neoplasia, benign, malignant, tumor, bioactivation, electrophilic, epigenetic, cross-sectional study, cohort study, case-control study.
   - Describe mutagenesis as a mode of action in carcinogenesis.
   - List factors causally related to cancer in humans.
   - Describe the key mechanisms and features of initiation, promotion, and progression.
2. **Comprehension**
   - Explain the historical aspects of chemical carcinogenesis.
   - Summarize the basis for tumor nomenclature conventions, including differentiating between benign and malignant tumors.
   - Explain the role of metabolism in chemical carcinogenesis.
   - Distinguish between oncogenes and tumor suppressor genes.
3. **Application**
   - Describe the role of lifestyle and dietary factors in chemical carcinogenesis.
   - Interpret carcinogen hazard characterization data generated by international and U.S. federal agencies.
   - Interpret simple cancer epidemiology data.
4. **Analysis**
   - Diagram the relationship between DNA repair and cell replication in chemical carcinogenesis.
   - Compare and contrast the role of tumor suppressor genes and oncogenes in chemical carcinogenesis.
   - Distinguish between genetic and epigenetic mechanisms of carcinogenesis.
   - Compare and contrast the carcinogen hazard characterization ranking schemes developed by International Agency for Research on Cancer, U.S. Environmental Protection Agency, and the National Toxicology Program.
   - Compare and contrast the three major types of epidemiological observational studies.
5. **Synthesis**
   - Integrate concepts of mechanisms of carcinogenesis with the nature of multistage carcinogenesis.
6. **Evaluation**
   - Evaluate chemical, occupational exposure, mechanistic toxicology, and epidemiologic data to qualitatively appraise whether a chemical, biological, or physical agent is a potential carcinogen in the occupational environment.

Prerequisite Knowledge
1. Mechanisms of toxicity
2. Basic human genetics (gene structure, function, basic concepts in polymorphisms)
3. Cellular physiology and biology
4. Basic biochemistry
5. Xenobiotic metabolism
6. Genetic toxicology
7. Human physiology

Key Terms
Neoplasia, Benign, Malignant, Tumor, Carcinogenesis, Bioactivation, Electrophilic, Mutagenesis, Epigenetic

Key Topics
1. Historical Aspects of Chemical Carcinogenesis
2. Carcinogenesis and Tumor Nomenclature
3. Mechanisms of Carcinogenesis
   - Metabolism of Proximate Carcinogens to Ultimate Carcinogens
   - The Role of DNA Repair and Cell Replication in Chemical Carcinogenesis
   - Epigenetic Mechanisms of Carcinogenesis
   - Key Targets of Carcinogens: Oncogenes and Tumor Suppressor Genes
4. Nature of Chemical Carcinogenesis
   - Multistage Carcinogenesis
5. Factors Causally Related to Cancer in Humans
   - Epidemiology Principles
   - Lifestyle and Dietary Factors
   - Biological Factors: Chronic Infections and Hormones
   - Chemical and Physical Factors: Occupational Exposures
6. Hazard Characterization of Carcinogens by International and U.S. Federal Agencies

Chapter 14

Carcinogenesis

By Cody L. Wilson, PhD, DABT, CHMM, and Karen C. Wilson, DVM

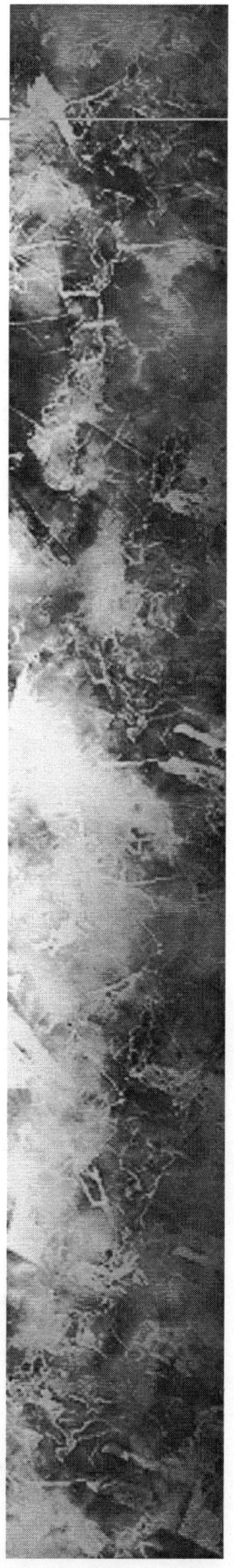

Introduction

Recent headlines report an overall decline in cancer-related deaths in the United States.[1] Whether this decline is a result of decreased exposure to carcinogens, earlier detection using new screening techniques, or a combination of these or other factors, discerning the reasons is difficult. An even greater challenge to unravel is which of numerous factors are involved in cancer causation: a person exposed to a carcinogen or that has a family history or other genetic predisposition may not necessarily have or get cancer. At the same time, spontaneous cases of cancer arise that can have any number of potential causes, including susceptibility of individuals to develop cancer. A disease characterized by uncontrolled, abnormal proliferation of cells, most cancers start as a single cell, normal with regard to structure and function, that undergoes multiple genetic mutations that begin as lesions at DNA targets. Many of these lesions escape the cell's protective mechanisms, pass as mutations to the next generation of cells, which continue to replicate, passing increasingly altered genetic material to each subsequent generation of cells. Continued expansion of this group of cells through multiple, complex mechanisms highlighted by further genomic damage and instability leads to production of a tumor, which then recruits its own blood supply and may begin to spread to other parts of the body. Cancer is an insidious disease, but is marked by fascinating biological changes. This chapter highlights some of those processes and the chemical, physical, and biological agents implicated in causation.

Historical Aspects of Chemical Carcinogenesis

One of the first recorded links between cancer and an occupation appeared in 1778, by Sir Percival Pott, a London surgeon. Pott linked a scrotal cancer, known at that time as "soot-wart", to the occupation of chimney sweep. Sliding down soot-covered ropes day in and day out, along with poor hygiene, allowed for continuous contact with carcinogenic material found in the soot. The culprit was a group of carcinogens known today as polycyclic aromatic hydrocarbons (PAHs), by-products of incomplete combustion. As with cancer hazards of the present, physicians at the time were challenged by the great time lapse between cancer hazard exposure and onset of the disease. Dr. Pott's observation of the link between adult scrotal cancer and employment as a chimney sweep was historical. As a preventive measure, Dr. Pott recommended daily baths for chimney sweeps, which was seen as successful over 100 years later in an 1892 publication in the *British Medical Journal*, "Why foreign sweeps do not suffer from scrotal cancer."[2] Unfortunately, the sweeps of Britain did not adhere to the recommendations of bathing as the Northern European chimney sweeps had, and consequently had a much higher incidence of adverse occupational health effects, including scrotal cancer.[3]

Despite the pioneering work of Pott and others, it was not until the mid-20th century that the majority of the studies linking increased risk of cancer and a particular work environment were published.[4] Better capabilities in carcinogen screening and testing, along with continued epidemiologic studies and observations and cancer screening for at-risk workers, have likely

155

contributed to a decline in the incidence of occupationally-related cancers.

Carcinogenesis and Tumor Nomenclature

As with most technical topics, the study of carcinogenesis and tumor biology have specialized vocabularies. *Neoplasia* means "new growth," but may not necessarily be cancer. Another term often used is *tumor*, which at its basis refers to a swelling of any kind (benign, noncancerous), not just that associated with cancer or malignancy. The Latin *cancer* is a literal translation of the Greek word *karkinos*, or crab. Early observers of cancer chose the image of the crab to describe the appearance of tumors invading surrounding tissue.[5]

Since around 1885, tumor nomenclature has followed a set of loose rules that describes the tumor by tissue of origin — epithelial, connective, muscular, and nervous — and that each tissue has both benign and malignant tumors. As a general rule, the suffix "-*oma*" is applied as part of the nomenclature for nearly all tumors types, regardless of histologic origin or whether benign or malignant; however, exceptions can and do occur (see Table 14.1). About 80% of all tumors are of epithelial origin and these tumors can arise from glands or surface linings.[5] The remaining 20% of tumors are accounted for by the other three tissue types, along with tumors of mixed cell types, including those arising from one or more embryonal germ layers. Examples of these interesting tumors include pleiomorphic adenomas, nephroblastomas, teratomas, and teratocarcinomas.

At the basis of these naming conventions is what distinguishes a benign tumor from a malignant tumor. Table 14.2 compares some features of benign and malignant tumors, and pathologists consider many general and specific guidelines when diagnosing tumors. In general, the major distinction between benign and malignant tumors is the ability of the tumor to invade surrounding tissues and subsequently metastasize, or establish a secondary tumor(s), to distant sites. Mechanisms of metastasis for many tumors are becoming increasingly clearer; however, many unanswered questions about metastasis still plague the study of tumor biology. Importantly, there are other stages that exist between benign and malignant states. Among these are other lesions such as some metaplasias, dysplasias, and carcinomas *in situ*.

Mechanisms of Carcinogenesis

Metabolism of Proximate Carcinogens to Ultimate Carcinogens

In early work on elucidating the mechanistic role of chemicals in tumor development, structural similarities between chemical classes were investigated. A group of "direct acting carcinogens" — those that require no metabolic activation for their activity — are sufficiently electrophilic to react covalently with biological nucleophiles. Only a few chemicals belong to this class of carcinogens: ethylene oxide, dimethylsulfate, bis-2-(chloromethyl) ether, and dimethylcarbamyl chloride are examples.[6]

Table 14.1 — Tumor nomenclature.

Cell/Tissue of Origin	Benign Tumor	Malignant Tumor
Epithelial tissues		
Surface Linings	Polyp; papilloma	Carcinoma
Glands	Adenoma	Adenocarcinoma
Connective tissues		Sarcoma
	Examples:	Examples:
	osteoblasts → osteoma	osteosarcoma
	fibroblasts → fibroma	fibrosarcoma
		Exceptions:
		myelomas,
		lymphomas,
		leukemias
Muscle tissues		
Smooth muscle	Leiomyoma	Leiomyosarcoma
Striated muscle	Rhabdomyoma	habdomyosarcoma
Nervous tissues		Apply word "malignant" to name of benign tumor:
	Examples:	Examples:
	Schwann Cells → Schwannoma	Malignant Schwannoma
	Ependymal cells → Ependymoma	
	Exceptions:	Exceptions:
	Melanocytes → Nevus	Astrocyte → Glioblastoma
		Neuroblast → Neuroblastoma
		Melanocytes → Melanoma

Table 14.2 — Features in benign and malignant tumors.[5]

Feature	Benign	Malignant
Growth Rate	Slow	Fast
Mode of Growth	Expansile	Infiltrative
Metastases	No	Common
Recurrence after removal	Rare	Common
Gross features:		
Capsule	Common	Pseudocapsule
Necrosis	Rare	Common
Microscopic features:		
Atypia	Mild	Severe
Nuclear/cytoplasmic ratio	Normal	Increased
Mitoses	Few	Many

By the mid-20th century, however, it became evident that most chemical carcinogens — aromatic and heterocyclic amines, aminoazo dyes, PAHs, N-nitrosamines, and others — are nucleophilic in nature and require metabolic activation (or bioactivation) to what were termed "ultimate carcinogens."[7] That is, proximate carcinogens give rise to ultimate carcinogens via bioactivation by the cytochrome P-450 (P450, CYP) Phase I drug metabolizing enzymes (DMEs). The purpose of the CYP enzymes is to catalyze conversion of organic xenobiotics into electrophilic derivatives that may then react with hydrophilic molecules and be readily excreted in the urine. CYP families 1, 2, and 3 are the most important with regard to carcinogen metabolism, and all show tissue-specific expression patterns.[8,9] For example, *CYP1A1* is expressed primarily in lung and liver, *CYP1A2* primarily in liver, and *CYP2E1* and *3A4* predominately in liver.[9]

Once formed, these intermediates are reactive with nucleophiles and can follow at least two major pathways. First, many of the reactive intermediates formed via Phase I enzyme-catalyzed reactions can react with polar molecules such as glutathione, glucuronic acid, acetic acid, and sulfate residues. Glutathione-*S*-transferases, glucuronosyltransferases, *N*-acetyltransferases, and sulfotransferases, respectively, catalyze these reactions and function to attach the reactive intermediate to a polar compound so that it can be readily excreted in the urine. It is important to note that completion of the bioactivation and conjugation processes does not completely render a chemical harmless until it is excreted. This concept is exemplified by metabolism of the bladder carcinogen 2-naphthylamine. Following P450-mediated *N*-hydroxylation and conjugation via glucuronosyltransferase in the liver, the glucuronide conjugate is reactivated to a nitrenium ion in the acidic environment of the urinary bladder, making it highly reactive with deoxyadenosine DNA residues.[10]

A second major pathway ensues from dysfunction of the DME pathway and can lead to mutagenesis. Like the direct acting carcinogens, these reactive intermediates which we will now term ultimate carcinogens, have the property of being strong electrophilic reactants and, under ideal conditions, are rapidly conjugated and excreted via the Phase II system. However, there are at least three caveats to this general rule: (1) if the concentration of the intermediate exceeds the catalytic capacity of the phase II enzymes or if the polar molecule (e.g., glutathione) is limited with respect to concentration, the reactive intermediate can escape the Phase II system and react with nucleophilic moieties, such as DNA, RNA, and proteins; (2) the Phase II enzymes — like the Phase I enzymes — are highly polymorphic in humans. These gene polymorphisms can have significant impact on the metabolic capacity of the enzymes they express, in some cases increasing the potential for carcinogenesis,[11] while other polymorphisms confer a protective effect[12], and in some cases have no effect[13,14]; and (3) Phase II enzymes involved in protection can also activate chemical carcinogens, exemplified by glutathione-*S*-transferase activation of 1, 2-dihaloethanes.[15] Likewise, CYP-mediated N-hydroxylation derivatives of procarcinogenic heterocyclic amines, aminoazo dyes, or arylamines are converted by *N*-acetyltransferases or sulfotransferases into highly reactive ester intermediates that bind to DNA.[16]

Reactive intermediates that evade or escape conjugation via Phase II metabolism — or procarcinogens that are activated by Phase II metabolism — become available to react with biological nucleophiles: DNA, RNA, and proteins. The stability of reactive intermediates has been studied extensively both in vitro and *in vivo* and, while these molecules do have finite stability and can travel only limited distances to alkylate DNA and RNA, they can diffuse outside the cells in which they were bioactivated and, in some cases, distribute readily between anatomical compartments in animal models.[17,18]

The Role of DNA Repair and Cell Replication in Chemical Carcinogenesis

The spectrum of mutations in cancer cells is diverse, and ranges from point mutations that involve only a few DNA nucleotides to chromosomal alterations that encompass millions of nucleotides. Many tumors, if not most, exhibit increasing genomic instability and more diverse mutation types as progression to and beyond a malignant phenotype occurs. Although some distinct mutational events and sequences are common to cancers of the same histological origin, the genetic heterogeneity among tumors and cancer cells can be extensive.[19,20]

As discussed in Chapter 13, mutagenesis is the process of chemicals causing transmissible changes in the genetic material. DNA-damaging events can arise from two major sources: exogenous agents such as viruses, radiation, and chemicals (both industrial and natural); and, endogenous agents, such as generation of reactive oxygen and nitrogen species and chemical changes to DNA that arise from normal cellular processes.[21] With regard to the latter, Lindahl[22] estimates that approximately 10^4 mutagenic events in the form of depurinated sites are generated daily per cell and that reactive oxygen species may generate even more damage.[23] Regardless of the source, repair of DNA damage is clearly essential for life. The complexities of DNA repair are beyond the scope of this chapter, but a brief overview of these processes is warranted in a study of chemical carcinogenesis.

The extensive implications of DNA damage are limited by a broad array of DNA repair systems.[24] Base-excision repair, nucleotide-excision repair (NER) (including two major pathways: transcription coupled repair and global genomic repair), and double strand break repair for broken chromosomes and mismatch repair, constitute the major mechanisms of DNA repair, the details of which are left to Chapter 13, "Genetic Toxicology." Factors common to most repair processes include damage recognition, damage removal, DNA synthesis to fill in missing sequences, and ligation back to the parental DNA. Importantly, genes involved in DNA repair are themselves subject to mutation, and many familial disorders that predispose individuals to cancer find their basis in germline mutations of DNA repair genes. For example, xeroderma pigmentosum is an autosomal recessively-inherited condition in which individuals are hypersensitive to ultraviolet light and are predisposed to skin cancer. The mutations important in xeroderma pigmentosum are those found in genes involved in nucleotide excision repair, resulting in dysfunctional repair of UV-induced DNA damage.[25] Likewise, DNA repair genes are often targets of epigenetic carcinogens, and this is exemplified by inhibition of nucleotide excision repair processes by the carcinogenic metals, Ni, As, and Cr.[26]

Cell cycle control is also a critical feature of DNA repair. The purpose of the link between replication and repair is clear: repair mechanisms frequently need time to repair DNA damage and halting cellular replication can allow for additional time for these processes. For this reason, repair mechanisms are tightly linked to cell cycle control genes, such as *TP53* (also known as *p53*). For example, the *TP53* protein modulates DNA repair processes that include nucleotide and base excision repair and double-strand break repair[27], but this molecule is also critical in modulating expression of cell cycle related genes that mediate replication arrest at one of two major cell cycle checkpoints: at the G_1-S interface or at the G_2-M interface. Cell cycle arrest at either of these interfaces — DNA replication or mitosis — in theory allows for additional time for DNA repair. Similarly, *TP53* modulates at least two major apoptotic (programmed cell death) pathways, one of which is triggered in response to DNA damage.[28] This pathway leads to a cascade of enzyme activation, ultimately causing apoptosis. A related pathway, also largely regulated by *TP53*, is cellular senescence, which confers a permanent withdrawal from the cell cycle and is also inducible by DNA damage. Such activities, whether apoptosis or senescence, have the obvious effect of permanently removing a cell from the dividing population and preventing transmission of mutations to the next generation of cells. Like the factors directly involved in DNA repair, genes involved in cell cycle regulation also exhibit a range of mutations in both germline (mutations that are transmissible from parent to progeny) and somatic (mutations in all other body cells) cells. Li-Fraumeni syndrome, is a rare familial autosomal disorder characterized by a high incidence of multiple cancers early in life and is caused, at least partially, by inheritance of a *TP53* mutant allele. Importantly, *TP53* can also be mutated in somatic cells, such as that induced by aflatoxin B1. Such mutations render the molecule — and pathways of which it is a component — dysfunctional.[29] As will be discussed further below, *TP53* mutations are the most common genetic alterations in human cancer, with over 50% of cancers exhibiting at least one mutation causing loss of activity of this critical protein.[30]

Epigenetic Mechanisms of Carcinogenesis

Our extensive discussion of bioactivation of procarcinogens to mutagenic ultimate carcinogens is critical to an understanding of chemical carcinogenesis. However, not all carcinogens are genotoxic or mutagenic. Many chemical carcinogens work through epigenetic mechanisms. This does not mean they are *non*-genetic, but that their mechanism of carcinogenicity involves alteration of gene activity without direct structural changes to DNA. Another major feature that distinguishes epigenetic from genotoxic carcinogens is that production of tumors by these compounds generally requires very high doses given over time without interruption. For many (but not all) genotoxic carcinogens, one-time treatment is sufficient to induce tumorigenesis in experimental models. Cytotoxic compounds, peroxisome proliferators, hormones, fibrous materials, promotion agents of two-stage carcinogenesis (discussed below) and others of a multitude of diverse compounds are representative of epigenetic carcinogens.

Mechanisms of epigenetic carcinogens can be divided into several major, sometimes overlapping, categories.[31] As a general principle, with the possible exception of induction of oxidative stress, each of these mechanisms is related to cell growth and differentiation. Some agents confer a selective growth advantage, allowing clonal expansion of spontaneously initiated cells. Indeed, increased cell division can be caused by diverse agents such as high levels of some hormones, excess calories, and chronic inflammation.[23] Cytotoxicity with subsequent sustained cell proliferation results in an increased chance of spontaneous mutation being incorporated into DNA, a risk factor for carcinogenesis. For example, tumor development by the nongenotoxic fungicide chlorothalonil is preceded by pronounced hyperplastic changes in renal proximal tubules in experimental models.[32]

Interruption of gap junction intercellular communication (GJIC) is another epigenetic mechanism of carcinogenesis. GJIC is important for cell-cell communication in regulating cellular homeostasis, cell proliferation, differentiation, and death. Many tumor promoters inhibit GJIC, including phenobarbital and 12-O-tetradecanoyl-phorbol-13-acetate (TPA).[33] Almost all cancer cells seem to have some alteration in GJIC, as maintenance of the transformed or cancerous phenotype depends on a lack of communication between cells.

The role of steroid hormones as epigenetic carcinogens is exemplified by estradiol, although some evidence suggests estradiol has both genotoxic and epigenetic activity.[34] Purported epigenetic mechanisms of carcinogenesis involve hormone-dependent receptor-mediated proliferation of mammary epithelial cells carrying spontaneous mutations or stimulation of growth factor receptors from neighboring cells, resulting in proliferation of exposed cells. Given the complexity of breast cancer as a disease, it is possible, perhaps even probable, that both epigenetic and genotoxic mutagenic mechanisms are at play.

Cellular oxidative stress is another potential epigenetic mechanism of carcinogenesis.[35–38] Reactive oxygen and reactive nitrogen species are a major source of DNA damage and chemical agents, whether endogenous or exogenous, can induce production of reactive species. For example, many, if not all, metals have the capacity to produce multiple radical species, and in most cases produce radical oxygen species (ROS). For example, ROS production by arsenic is considered one of the possible mechanisms of carcinogenesis induced by this metal.[39] Similarly, chromium and nickel are capable of generating ROS through several different mechanisms. As discussed, several metals also adversely affect DNA repair processes, another possible epigenetic carcinogenic effect of metals.

Similarly, mechanisms of peroxisome proliferator action are through oxidative damage. The peroxisome proliferators are a large group of carcinogens that includes plasticizers, solvents, food flavors, some herbicides, and hypolipidemic and other drugs.[31] As peroxisomes are sources of a variety of peroxidative enzymes, including catalase and hydrogen peroxide-generating oxidases, their proliferation results in increased potential for oxidative DNA damage and decreased GJIC. In addition to the more direct-acting mechanisms of generating oxidative species, peroxisome proliferators can also alter regulation of key genes through interaction with the Peroxisome Proliferator Activated Receptor α (PPAR-α).[40] Importantly, peroxisome proliferation and liver tumors from the group of peroxisome proliferators is observed only in rodents. As such, the carcinogenicity of peroxisome proliferators in humans is questionable except at very high doses and extreme conditions of exposure.[41]

Perturbation of biochemical DNA modifications are also examples of epigenetic mechanisms of carcinogenesis. DNA hypermethylation generally causes downregulation of gene expression, while hypomethylation results in increased expression. Several metals, including nickel and arsenic, and to a lesser extent, chromium and cadmium, can produce extensive alterations in DNA methylation.[26] For example, arsenic has been shown to hypermethylate the promoter region of *TP53* in cells in culture and has been observed in basal cell carcinomas of arsenic exposed individuals.[42,43] Global hypomethylation leading to malignant transformation in arsenic-exposed rat liver cells has also been demonstrated[44], suggesting that arsenic-induced changes in genomic methylation status may be species specific. Importantly, whether in cells in culture, animal models, or humans, changes to methylation patterns have the potential to promote aberrant expression of genes involved in growth regulation. Similarly, histone deacetylation is another mechanism of controlling gene expression by limiting access of transcriptional machinery to DNA and this mechanism has been observed in studies of nickel carcinogenicity.[45]

While many carcinogens fit neatly into either the epigenetic or genotoxic categories, long term application of low doses of some genotoxic agents can contribute to epigenetic alterations that promote clonal expansion of exposed cells (see Figure 14.1).[46] For example, the classic genotoxic carcinogen 2-acetylaminofluorene (AAF), a suspected human carcinogen, induces liver, lung, and mammary tumors in rodent models because of a relatively high rate of *N*-hydroxylation in rodent liver.[47] As discussed above, in humans and dogs, *N*-glucuronides are formed in the liver and subsequently transported to the urinary bladder where the amines are released to form reactive nitrenium ions.[48] The genotoxic nature of 2-AAF has been clearly established. However, some reports suggest that 2-AAF can also function as a complete carcinogen (i.e., has both initiating and promoting activities, described further below) in some animal models.[49] Epigenetic effects such as changes in mitochondrial permeabil-

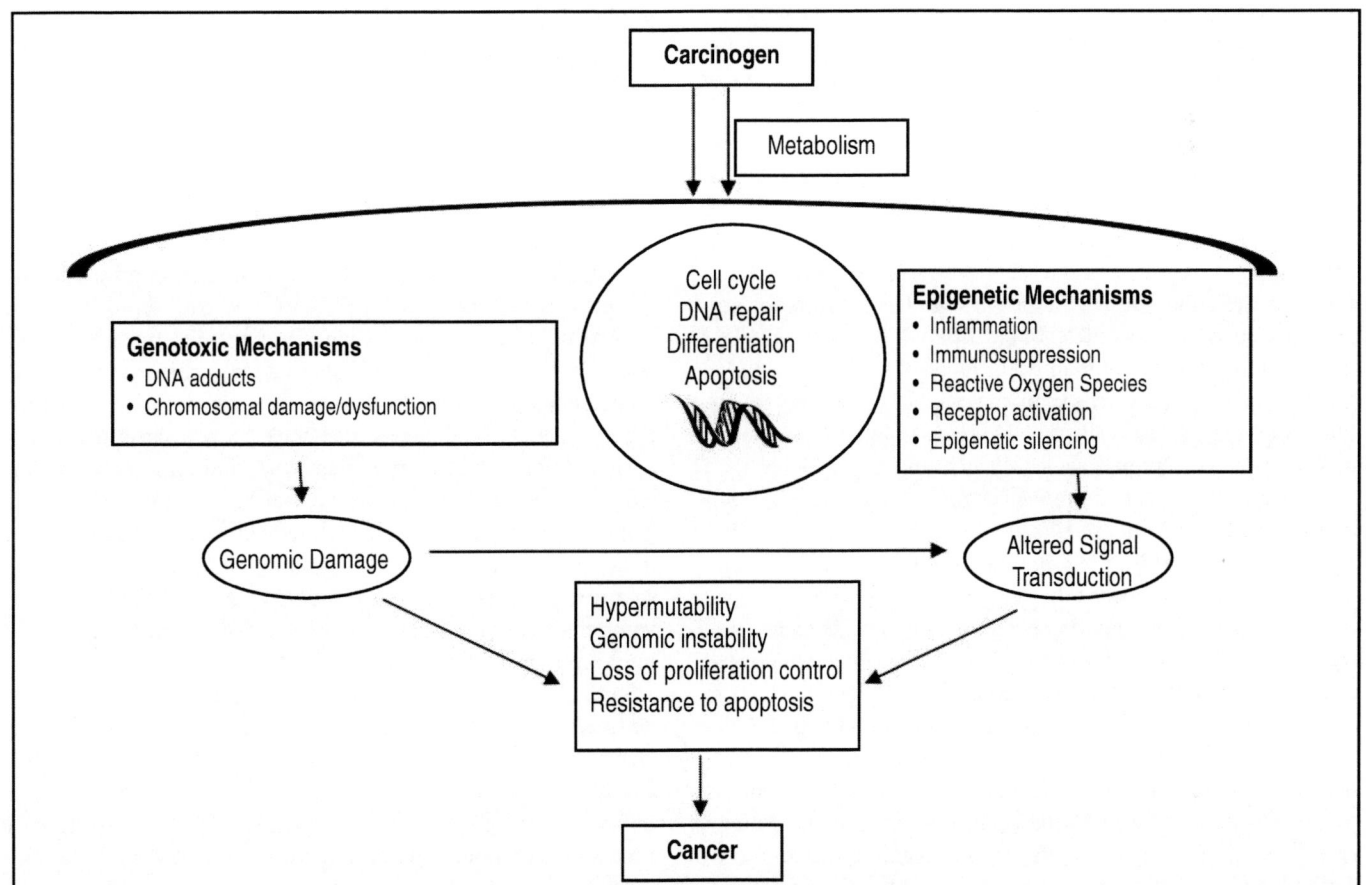

Figure 14.1 — Genotoxic and non-genotoxic mechanisms in chemical carcinogenesis.[46]

ity and gene alterations that increase resistance to apoptosis in the liver may also contribute to selection and clonal outgrowth of resistant cells.[50] In conclusion, it is important to recognize that a carcinogen may have a major mode of action (e.g., genotoxic carcinogen), but may also induce epigenetic effects that enhance the growth of damaged cells (see Figure 14.1).

Key Targets of Carcinogens: Oncogenes and Tumor Suppressor Genes

While chemical carcinogens can and do mutate many, many genes, some genes are more critical targets than others. This chapter has discussed the role of DNA repair and the fact that DNA repair genes themselves are subject to mutagenesis. Likewise, the capacity of the drug metabolizing enzymes involved in bioactivation of procarcinogens is affected by mutagenic action. However, as discussed, cancer is a disease caused by unrestricted proliferation and autonomous growth brought about by multiple genetic and epigenetic mechanisms. Hence, the genes and proteins regulating the processes of growth, differentiation, proliferation, and death are arguably the most critical targets in neoplasia. Three different classes of genes have been described that are critical to the neoplastic process: proto-oncogenes, cellular oncogenes, and tumor suppressor genes.

The term oncogene literally means "gene that produces cancer" and oncogenes were initially discovered as transforming DNA or RNA sequences of viral genomes.[5] These viruses, at some point in their evolution, acquired normal cellular genes, which were termed proto-oncogenes. Proto-oncogenes are the cellular counterparts of these viral oncogenes and play a critical role in growth-related processes. Cellular oncogenes have no known analogs in oncogenic viruses. Cells regulate their growth and differentiation by positive and negative pathways, and these pathways have multiple regulatory steps, many of which have components that are cellular and proto-oncogenes. Cellular and proto-oncogenes are classified into one or more of several functions and are either growth factors, growth factor receptors, signal transduction molecules, intracellular kinases, or nuclear transcription factors. Importantly, the range of functions imparted by oncogenes to tumor cells spans that which is necessary for autonomous growth: the cells are able to stimulate themselves to produce their own growth factors in an autocrine fashion.[51]

Activation of oncogenes, whether proto-oncogenes or cellular oncogenes, generally results in production of a defective, hyperactive protein and/or overproduction of the normal protein. These two pathways occur through several major mechanisms: 1) a deletion or point mutation in the DNA coding sequence will result in a new protein with altered activity produced in normal quantities; 2) a deletion in non-coding DNA sequences results in altered regulation of a normal protein; 3) through the phenomenon of gene amplification, a normal protein can be overproduced; 4) a chromosome rearrangement causes a gene to overproduce a normal protein; 5) chromosome rearrangement results in a portion of a gene fusing with another actively transcribed gene, resulting in overproduction of the fusion protein, which is sometimes hyperactive; and, 6) hypomethylation of a

Table 14.3 — Properties of oncogenes and tumor suppressor genes.[51]

Property	Proto-oncogene	Tumor Suppressor Gene
# of mutational events required to contribute to cancer	1	2
Function of the mutant allele	Gain of function; dominant	Loss of function; recessive
Mutant allele may be inherited?	No examples	Yes, frequently
Somatic mutation contributes to cancer	Yes	Yes
Tissue specificity of mutational event	Sometimes	Inherited form has tissue preference

cellular oncogene results in altered regulation of gene expression of a normal protein.[52] In short, oncogenes are involved in cellular growth control, which means they are responsible, in part, for transmitting growth signals (peptide hormones, growth factors, xenobiotics, etc.) from the cell surface to the nucleus, ultimately affecting gene expression.

While oncogene activation results in a *gain of function*, modification or mutation of a tumor suppressor gene results in a *loss of function* (see Table 14.3). Tumor suppressor genes are normal cellular genes that, when inactivated, cause dysregulation of growth and differentiation pathways, enhancing the probability of neoplastic transformation. Examples of functions of tumor suppressor genes include: induction of terminal differentiation, triggering cellular senescence, induction of apoptosis, cell growth regulation, and facilitating cell-cell communication. In contrast to oncogenes which, for activation must lose only one wild-type allele to contribute to a malignantly transformed (cancerous) phenotype, tumor suppressor genes must lose both alleles by mutation in cancerous cells.[53] As discussed with inherited defects in DNA repair enzymes and drug metabolizing enzymes, this is a characteristic that gives tumor suppressor genes special significance, in that these changes can be inherited in germ cells. Inheritance of a germline mutation in the tumor suppressor genes *TP53* or *Rb* predisposes an individual to development of cancers, such as Li-Fraumeni syndrome and familial retinoblastoma, respectively.[54,55]

Retinoblastoma is among the best known examples of inherited neoplastic conditions. This tumor develops from the outer layer of the retina and usually grows within the eye in young children. In hereditary cases, a child inherits one mutated retinoblastoma gene (*Rb*) allele and one wild-type (functional) *Rb* allele. Upon mutation of the remaining wild-type Rb allele, excessive cell proliferation ensues, leading to retinoblastoma.[56] In sporadic (non-heritable) cases, both *Rb* alleles are lost to mutational events in somatic cells. This model, pioneered by Alfred Knudson, developed into what is now known as the "Two Hit Hypothesis" — two distinct mutational events must occur for a tumor suppressor gene to lose function and contribute to cancer. We have already alluded to the mechanism by which a mutant tumor suppressor gene might contribute to cancer: through dysfunction in the normal role of regulating the cell cycle, a theme common to all tumor suppressor genes.

Nature of Chemical Carcinogenesis

The natural course of tissue development and sustainment is characterized by several basic processes that include cell proliferation, differentiation, and death (see Figure 14.2). An understanding of the balance between cellular life and death and the factors that regulate both is critical to understanding the natural history of tumorigenesis. Cancer is much more than just a condition of increased proliferation of cells: proliferation is necessary, but not sufficient. The loss of control mechanisms balancing cell proliferation and cell death and the loss of restraint from invading other tissues are two heritable traits of cancer cells that form the basis of neoplasia. When these control mechanisms are damaged by endogenous factors or environmental agents, the balance can be shifted to result in increased or decreased proliferation or death. With regard to cancer, we are concerned with damaged cells escaping the pathway to apoptosis or senescence and surviving to proliferate, thus passing the damaged mechanisms to the next generation of cells. Importantly, this process nearly always occurs in distinct steps,

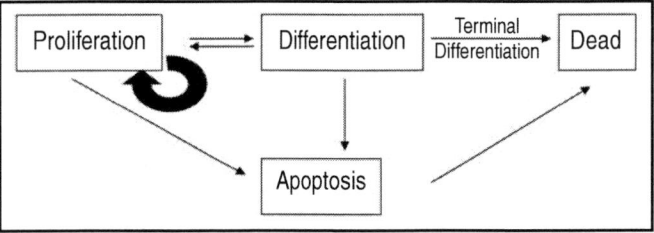

Figure 14.2 — The relationship between cellular proliferation, differentiation, and death. A characteristic of malignantly transformed (i.e., cancerous) cells is that they have escaped mechanisms that would force movement to the Differentiation or Apoptosis compartments. Hence, they continue to produce more and more cancer cells.

moving from a reversible hyperplasia to a benign tumor to a malignant tumor of increasing aggressiveness. The major stages describing carcinogenesis first observed over sixty years ago—initiation, promotion, and progression—have become axiomatic in the field of cancer biology.

Multistage carcinogenesis

Initiation and promotion as distinct events in experimental tumor production were recognized as early as the 1940s. Indeed, the classic system for demonstration of these two stages is induction of tumors in mouse skin[57,58], with a two-stage model of tumor induction demonstrated in rat liver nearly three decades later.[59] Key mechanisms, features and prototypical agents associated with these three stages are summarized in Table 14.4.

Table 14.4 — Key features of Initiation, Promotion, and Progression.

Stage	Key Mechanisms	Key Features	Examples
Initiation	• Mutations at critical targets, such as oncogenes and tumor suppressor genes	• Occurs rapidly • Does not require repeated application of agent; implications for non-threshold chemicals • Irreversible upon "fixation" by cell replication	• 7,12-dimethylbenz-[a]-anthracene (DMBA) • N-methyl-N-nitrosurea • Benzo[a]pyrene (B[a]P)
Promotion	• Enhancement or repression of gene expression • Inhibition of apoptosis • Functional alterations only — not a directly mutagenic event • Clonal expansion of initiated cells	• Occurs slowly • Requires repeated application of promoter • Reversible, at least early in the process • Measurable dose-response threshold	• Tetradecanoyl-phorbol acetate (TPA; phorbol ester) • 2, 3, 7, 8-tetrachlorodibenzo-p-dioxin (TCDD)
Progression	• Increasingly complex genomic instability (chromosomal alterations, gene amplification, etc.) • Continued selection of cells with genotypes/phenotypes conferring a growth advantage in the in the conditions of the extracellular environment	• Irreversible • Tumor becomes polyclonal as a result of genomic instability • Survival of the most aggressive cells occurs by evolutionary pressures exerted by the cellular environment (host immune system, chemotherapy, etc.) • Increased rate of growth, invasiveness, metastasis	• Arsenic salts, asbestos fibers, benzene

Initiation

The process of initiation involves a permanent change(s) to critical gene targets (see Figure 14.3). This can occur through mutations induced by biological, physical, or chemical agents. There are several key determinants in initiation, the most critical being that one or more mutations occur at one or more critical DNA targets (e.g., tumor suppressor gene(s), oncogene(s)). A classical example of initiation by a chemical is that of the PAH, benzo[a]pyrene (B[a]P). The potency of B[a]P as an initiator of carcinogenesis is virtually non-existent unless the compound is metabolized by both Phase I and Phase II drug metabolizing enzymes to its ultimate carcinogen, the benzpyrene diol-epoxide metabolite, (+) *anti*-7,8-dihydrodiol-9,10-epoxide (BPDE).[60] Importantly, alterations in genes that code for the cytochromes P-450 responsible for PAH metabolism — CYP1A1, 1B1, 3A4 — and microsomal epoxide hydrolase (EH), may render an experimental model (or a human) more resistant or susceptible to damage by toxicants of this or other classes tied to this family of drug metabolizing enzymes. While several different DNA adducts may arise through the four stereoisomers generated by metabolism of B[a]P, the predominant metabolite forms a covalent adduct with deoxyguanosine as the (+)-*trans-anti*-BPDE-N2-deoxyguanosine.[61]

A mutation is necessary for initiation, but it is not sufficient. DNA damage surveillance and repair mechanisms are active in normal cells, with activity tied to the cell cycle and DNA replication. Thus, for initiation to occur, it is critical that a mutation escape the DNA repair process. Bulky adducts, such as those formed by B[a]P and other PAH diol-epoxides, are subject to the nucleotide excision repair (NER) pathway, with repair efficiency dependent on the stereochemistry and conformation of the adduct.[62] For example, the (+)-*cis-anti*-BPDE-N²-deoxyguanosine adduct adopts a conformation resulting in a severe DNA distortion, making it easier to detect and repair via the NER pathway. In contrast, the major adduct, (+)-*trans-anti*-BPDE-N²-deoxyguanosine, displays a conformation with the major part of the molecule tucked into the minor DNA groove.[63] The latter event results in DNA distortion that is much less severe compared to that induced by the (+)-*cis* isomer and repair proceeds at a rate about 10 times lower than that observed for this minor adduct. As such, the (+)-*trans-anti*-BPDE-N²-dG adduct is repaired at very low efficiency, potentially allowing the lesion to persist through DNA replication.

Anti-BPDE-induced mutations at specific genes have consistently been found both in experimental systems and in human tumors. For example, in human bronchial epithelial cells in culture, *anti*-BPDE binds preferentially to dG residues within codon 12 of *K-RAS*, an oncogene. This 'hot spot' characteristic at codon 12 is the result of preferential binding to the site and the inefficient repair of resulting adducts.[64] As discussed, ras is a protein involved in signal transduction and mutations can impair this activity.[65] Likewise, mutational "hot spots" are also found on codons 157, 248, and 273 of the tumor suppressor *TP53*.[66]

Under ideal conditions, the cell cycle has a series of checkpoints in which DNA repair can take place prior to mitosis. Failure of cell cycle arrest in the presence of DNA damage greatly increases the likelihood that any DNA lesions will result in the DNA replication machinery misreading the sequence, producing a mutated copy of the gene. In the present example, the (+)-*trans-anti*-BPDE-N²-dG adduct is stealthy and can elude detection and subsequent cell cycle arrest.[67,68] DNA replication proceeds and reads the dG adduct as a dT, resulting in a G→T transversion, which is then passed to the daughter cells through mitosis. Initiation at the cellular level is irreversible and, unless the cell is eliminated through other tissue or immunological processes, the change is fixed in the genome and will continue to pass to subsequent generations of cells.

Promotion

Tumor promotion results in proliferation and/or survival of these initiated cells to a greater extent than the normal, surrounding cells and enhances the probability of additional genetic damage, including endogenous mutations accumulating in the expanding population of these cells (see Figure 14.4). The key event is proliferation of a single, initiated cell to an expanded focus of cells via provision of a selective growth advantage or survival of these cells. In general, all chemical tumor promoters cause inflammation, changes in gene expression, and hyperplasia. Promotion is a much slower event than initiation, occurring over a period of weeks and months in experimental models and is, at least in early stages, a largely reversible event. This stage requires repeated application or exposure to the promoter.[7] Tumor promoters have very weak or no carcinogenic activity when tested alone but, upon application to initiated cells, markedly enhance tumor yield when applied repeatedly.[69] Other important characteristics of promotion include the notion that the efficiency of a promoter is sensitive to aging[70], hormonal[71], and dietary factors[72]), and that endogenous promoters (e.g., steroid hormones) may affect spontaneous initiated cells.[73] Prototypical promoters used in experimental models include 12-O-tetradecanoylphorbol-13-acetate (TPA), the most active ingredient of croton oil found in the seeds of *Croton tiglium* [74], and phenobarbital. Saccharin, estradiol, peroxisome proliferators, and 2, 3, 7, 8-TCDD, as discussed, are also potent promoters in various animal models.

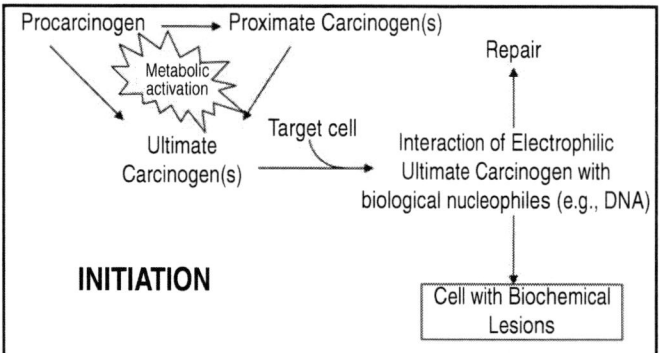

Figure 14.3 — Schematic view of the process of initiation of chemical carcinogenesis in the rat liver model.[59]

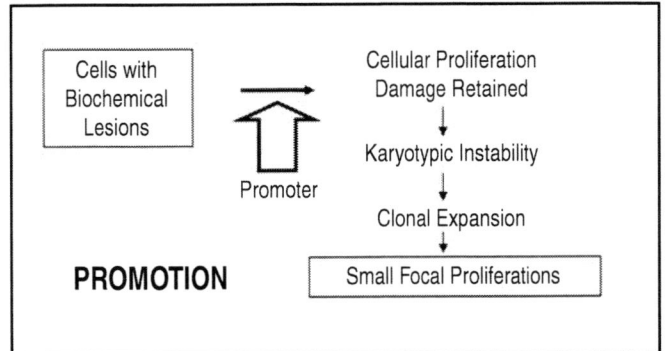

Figure 14.4 — Schematic view of key events in the promotion stage of multi-stage carcinogenesis in the rat liver model.[59]

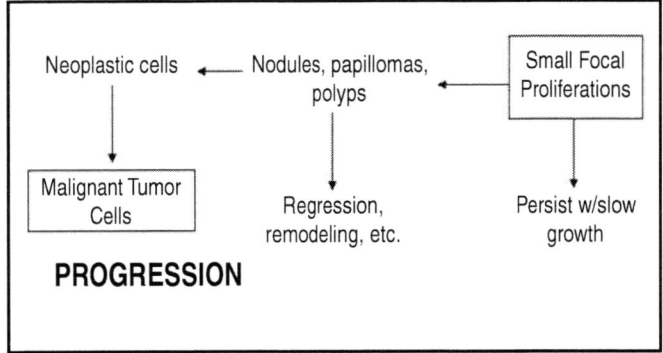

Figure 14.5 — Major biological events in tumor progression.

Progression

If initiation and promotion are characterized by relatively simple genetic alterations and subsequent outgrowth of cells containing these alterations, progression can be characterized as the continuing evolution of a multi-focal group of cells to a state of malignancy (see Figure 14.5). The hallmark of progression — increasing karyotypic instability — leads to a capacity for growth independent of environmental stimuli, such as hormones.[75] Karyotypic instability is the molecular basis for the evolution of characteristics such as invasion, metastasis, and the rate of growth and responses to hormonal influences to higher and higher degrees of malignancy.[76] In contrast to the promotion stage, the changes that occur in progression are irreversible. As with the two previous stages discussed, there are known progressor agents that act to induce chromosomal aberrations, but may not be capable of initiation.[52] Examples of these agents — all clastogenic — are arsenic salts, asbestos fibers, benzene, benzoyl peroxide, hydroxyurea, and the polychlorinated biphenyl (PCB), 2, 5, 2', 5'-tetrachlorobiphenyl.[52]

Why are multiple stages necessary in cancer development? First, cells have several redundant regulatory mechanisms that need to be altered to allow unrestricted proliferation. Therefore, multiple genetic events are needed to eliminate these regulatory mechanisms on a permanent basis. Further, cancer is not only a result of cell proliferation, but also of multiple abnormal behaviors. Loss of unrestricted proliferation, loss of balance between proliferation and differentiation, autonomous growth, induction of angiogenesis, invasion to adjacent tissues, and finally metastasis to distant sites are all biologically abnormal behaviors characteristic of cancers. Finally, it is important to remember that the multi-stage dogma was developed through experimental studies and that exceptions to the model have been noted, although it is likely that nearly all tumor development occurs through processes that can be described by a multi-stage model.

Factors Causally Related to Cancer in Humans

Historically, as seen in Percival Pott's link between "soot wart" and the chimney sweep profession, initial investigations into cancer causation were through epidemiologic studies. By determining a positive association between individuals with cancers and their exposure to certain environmental factors, potential cancer causing agents among occupational environments could be identified and further investigated. By the 1960s, most epidemiologists agreed that 60% to 90% of cancers owed their conception, in part, to an individual's exposure to an environmental factor, and therefore are potentially preventable.[77] In 1995, Ames reviewed major risk factors — those factors having the greatest contribution to cancer incidence — as diet, tobacco use, chronic infections, such as Hepatitis B and C, and hormones. Less important risk factors, those factors contributing much less to overall global cancer burden, were occupational exposures, sun exposure, medical interventions, such as chemotherapeutics, pollution, and hereditary factors.[23] Today, major risk factors can be broadly classified into lifestyle and dietary factors and biological, chemical, and physical agents.

Epidemiology Principles

It is important to note that the observed associations between cancer and environmental factors are dynamic. In many cases, like that discussed for fruit and vegetable consumption, a factor may be strongly defined protective through epidemiological evidence but found to not be protective by the next study. Understanding different observational study types can allow the industrial hygienist to stay current in this ever changing field. Examples of analytical observational studies that researchers rely upon include cross-sectional, cohort, and case control. The importance of these analytical studies lies in their attempt to establish cause through association. Cohort studies examine subjects based upon whether they were exposed or not exposed to a factor, while case-control studies look at individuals as "diseased" and "not diseased." Cross-sectional studies examine disease and exposure at a particular time. Using asbestos as an example, a cohort study would group individuals according to whether they had exposure to asbestos or not and rates of diseases such as mesothelioma can be compared. Cohort studies are most commonly prospective, in which individuals are followed over time to assess outcome. Cohort studies have the disadvantage of being time consuming and costly, requiring a large number of subjects and cases have to follow up. A case-control study is always retrospective, looking at diseased individuals (cases) and comparing exposure or other factors with the incidence of that disease in a control group. In the asbestos example, a history of asbestos exposure would be compared between cases of mesothelioma and a control group without mesothelioma. Case-control studies are much less expensive and time consuming, but can be susceptible to bias. Examples of such bias include selection of individuals for the study and their ability to recall exposure. In cross-sectional studies, subjects are chosen without regard to their exposure or disease status. For example, a population might be surveyed for history of asbestos exposure and particular diagnoses, such as mesothelioma. Exposure rates and disease rates can still be compared. The difficulty in establishing association lies in which came first, the exposure or the disease. Data obtained from the occupational venue lends itself easily to cross-sectional studies using questionnaires or preemployment medical exams.[78] While epidemiologic evidence is critical in uncovering associations between exposure and cancers, evidence from investigations into the mechanisms of disease gives biological credibility to the epidemiologic study.

Lifestyle and Dietary Factors

Of the major causes of cancer involving lifestyle, tobacco smoking is estimated by some to contribute to up to one third of cancers in developed countries.[79] Despite the epidemiologic evidence linking smoking to several diseases, the mechanism by which smoking causes cancer in some individuals and not others is not well understood, but multiple hypotheses have been advanced. Smoking-related cancers are reported as 60% lung, 20% upper airway/digestive tract and, others to lesser extents, including pancreas, bladder, kidney, and liver.[80]

Of lifestyle factors, associations between dietary factors and disease are among the most difficult to ascertain. In 1981, Doll estimated dietary factors may contribute to one third of cancers.[81] Differences in rates among cancers between Eastern and Western cultures is most likely a result of differences in dietary factors. The typical Western diet is calorie rich, promoting obesity, and is associated with higher incidences of breast, prostate, colon, and endometrial cancers. Obesity appears to increase insulin-like growth factors, involved in stimulating cell proliferation of the breast, prostate, colon and lung, and, if elevated, is associated with higher cancer rates of these target tissues.[82]

As reported in 1997, the gastric cancer rate in Japan was six times higher than that in the U.S. The breast cancer rate was three times lower, and prostate was seven times lower than in the U.S.[83] The typical Japanese diet, while on average is less calorie dense, is higher in salt- and nitrate- preserved foods. This high salt content appears to promote *Helicobacter pylori* infection by altering the mucous environment in the stomach.[84] Smoking can also potentiate *H. pylori* infection by increasing gastric acid secretion.[85] Epidemiologic data on *H. pylori* infection in Asian populations draws a link between the incidence of gastric cancer (the most frequently occurring cancer in parts of Asia) and the high rate of *H. pylori* infection relative to Western populations.[86,87] The gastric cancer rate for Japan has dropped in recent years, some of which has been attributed to education efforts in prevention.[88]

In 2003, consumption of fruits and vegetables were considered strongly associated with decreased rates of breast, colorectal, prostate, and bronchogenic cancers. However, in 2006, the evidence that consumption of fruits and vegetables prevents colorectal and bronchogenic cancers was determined to be somewhat limited, and even inadequate in the case of breast and prostate cancers.[89] Regardless, fruits and vegetables provide nutrients necessary for a healthy lifestyle, and have been shown in numerous other studies to contain compounds known as anticarcinogens that may reduce the incidence of certain cancers.[90]

Food contaminants include both natural and synthetic carcinogenic factors. Mycotoxins, such as Aflatoxin B_1 produced by *Aspergillus flavus*, are among the many natural carcinogens found as contaminants in food. Aflatoxin B_1 is strongly associated with liver cancers, and is of greatest concern in Asia and Africa, where the predominant diet of peanuts and maize are often highly contaminated with the toxin. As discussed above, aflatoxin B_1 metabolites directly target DNA in liver cells, and are thought to cause a G→T transversion in the TP53 gene.[91] When present in populations with a high incidence of Hepatitis B virus (HBV) infection, the rates of aflatoxin-induced liver cancer are profound. HBV works by directly inserting itself into host DNA, and elicits indirect action through invoking inflammatory processes. The risk of hepatocellular carcinoma is nearly 37 times higher in an HBV positive carrier, regardless of aflatoxin exposure.[92] Together, chronic HBV infection and dietary aflatoxin B_1 play a major role in the incidence of liver cancer in Africa and Asia, where 80% of the world liver cancer cases are diagnosed and exposure to these agents begins early in life.[93]

Some synthetic food contaminants, such as lipid-soluble pesticides, can accumulate in tissues of animals and people. Perhaps the most famous example of these is the organochlorine pesticide dichlorodiphenyltrichloroethane (DDT), which is thought to be an endocrine disruptor, and has been associated with an increased risk of breast and other cancers. It is important to note that the actual contribution of these pesticides to cancer incidence is controversial.[94] DDT was banned in the United States in 1972, but its use continues in some parts of the world, particularly in developing countries, to control vectors of highly important diseases such as malaria. Although a relationship between tissue burden and cancer incidence is tenuous, as a population, Africa, Asia, and Latin America have greater DDT tissue burdens than the US and Europe.[95] and farmers, in particular, have greater opportunity for exposure.

Biological Factors: Chronic Infection and Hormones

Another major factor, chronic infections, accounts for 18% of cancers worldwide and are mostly a problem for developing countries.[93] Examples of infectious agents associated with cancer include Human Papilloma Virus (HPV) in cervical cancer, Hepatitis B and C in liver cancer, Epstein-Barr virus in lymphomas, and *Helicobacter pylori* in stomach cancer.[93] Of the viral agents, it is estimated that the retroviruses (RNA) and DNA tumor viruses account for about 20% of the human tumor burden. For example, the Hepatitis B DNA virus, commonly transmitted by close personal contact, from mother to infant, and by blood transfusions and intravenous injections, is causally associated with primary hepatocellular carcinoma. Likewise, human papilloma virus (HPV) is associated with nearly all squamous carcinomas of the cervix, penis, vulva, and anus.[5]

There are several possible mechanisms by which viruses might be carcinogenic. First, transient expression of viral gene products in a cell might initiate a cascade of events, including altered cellular gene expression. Second, a virus might cause mutations in cellular genes in the process of integrating into the genome. Viral genes may also become permanently associated with the cell either as independently replicating plasmids or as integrated genes and with their proteins being required to maintain the cancerous phenotype of the cell. A fourth potential mechanism of carcinogenesis by chronic infection lies in the inflammatory process wherein DNA damage can occur from chemical inflammatory mediators. Finally, another potential mechanism involves functional modification of normal cellular proteins by viral proteins, as in the case of DNA viruses.

Hormonal factors may also contribute to about 30% of cancers in the United States.[96] A potential mechanism of hormonal carcinogensis, as discussed above, is stimulation of cellular proliferation.[97] Breast cancer, prostate, endometrial, and ovarian cancers are the most common hormonally associated cancers. Breast cancer is one of the most common cancers worldwide, with an incidence of 10.4% in 2003, second only to lung cancer which had a 2003 worldwide incidence of 12.3%.[93] Hormone related cancers, at least in part, have been controversially associated with oral contraceptives and hormone replacement, but may be greatly influenced by obesity factors.

Chemical and Physical Factors: Occupational Exposures

Importantly, occupational related cancers likely do not contribute much to the overall global cancer burden. However, incidences of certain cancers are highly concentrated among small groups exposed to certain occupational hazards, including chemical, biological, and physical agents. Additionally, many occupational exposures are confounded by other exposures, for example, the purported synergistic association between cigarette smoking and asbestos in lung cancer.[93] Of historical occupational hazards, the association of asbestos exposure to human malignant mesothelioma is probably one of the most prominent and is discussed in greater detail below.

A discussion of potential physical causes of tumors herein is restricted to carcinogenic fibers and ultraviolet (UV) and ionizing radiation. It should be noted, however, that other physical agents, such as physical trauma to tissue predisposed to tumor development and chronic inflammatory processes (arguably both chemical and physical processes) have been demonstrated.[98] Likewise is the phenomenon of the so-called "plastic sheet sarcoma," wherein synthetic implants of specific textures and dimensions induce fibrosarcomas in experimental animals.[99]

UV light, a nonionizing radiation, is known to induce skin cancer in experimental models[100], causes specific types of DNA damage, i.e., cyclobutane pyrimidine (thymidine) dimers and photoproducts[101], and is causally linked to human skin cancer. These lesions, if not repaired, will be fixed as mutations and transferred to the next generation of cells upon DNA and cellular replication. In addition to these mutagenic events, UV irradiation also triggers posttranslational modifications in the nuclear, cytosolic, and membrane compartments of the cell.[102]

Ionizing radiations transfer energy by producing ion pairs through interaction with free and atomic electrons when passing through matter. Sources of ionizing radiation are part of the natural environment, but are also anthropogenic. For example, most of the radiation background in the United States is attributable to natural sources, with about 18% owed to medical and industrial sources.[103] Although occupational radiation-induced cancers were reported long before the discovery of ionizing radiation, Majno and Joris suggest that the true role of radiation in carcinogenesis was not perceived until less than thirty years ago.[5]

In contrast to many chemical carcinogens, radiation produces no unique forms of cancer.[104] Evidence for carcinogenicity of radiation at high dose levels is most obviously pointed out by studies of survivors of the atomic bomb release in August 1945.[105] However, at low dose levels, such as those encountered in medical diagnostics, the magnitude of the effect is more difficult to quantify.[104] Several reasons for this challenge include the fact that the effects of radiation in the human population are small compared to the natural incidence of cancer in the same populations; the latency period between exposure and effect increases the complexity of population studies; and, there is some difficulty in extrapolation from animal studies.[104] In spite of these difficulties, studies of occupational exposures have focused on several groups. Radiologists prior to about 1940 had an increased incidence of leukemia when compared with physicians who did not work with radiation. In contrast to exposures of less than one rem per year among today's radiologists, some estimates suggest that radiologists in the mid-20th century accumulated thousands of rem over a lifetime.[104] Similar effects were observed in x-ray technologists of that era.[106] Among nuclear power facility workers, a lower incidence of cancer and lower death rate than the general population are observed. This so-called "healthy worker effect" has been observed in several studies and reflects the possibility that workers at such facilities may actually be healthier than a similar age and sex distribution of the general population.[107]

The mechanistic underpinning of ionizing radiation-induced cellular damage involves interaction directly with DNA (direct effect) and indirectly with DNA through ionization of water molecules in the cytoplasm. This latter, indirect effect generates ROS that causes subsequent damage to DNA, lipid peroxidation, and enzyme inactivation. The relative proportions and types of DNA damage also vary with the type of radiation.[108] Some of the same mutagenic events observed following exposure to ionizing radiation also arise from endogenous production of ROS from processes within the cell. For example, single-

and double-stranded breaks and base damage result from both endogenous and exogenous sources. However, if repaired, such damage is largely inconsequential. As has already been demonstrated, when damage overwhelms repair mechanisms or escapes DNA repair surveillance lesions may become "fixed" upon cell replication.

Fibrous particles constitute another class of potentially carcinogenic physical agents. Occupational exposures include asbestos mining, construction, demolition, shipbuilding, and insulation and brake workers.[93] The man-made vitreous fibers (MMVFs) and the several classes of asbestos are among the best studied fibers with regard to carcinogenesis. In both groups of fibers, fiber size, deposition, retention, and biopersistence are critical determinants of carcinogenicity.

Significant commercial production of the MMVFs began over 100 years ago and they can be divided into two major categories: filaments and wools. Within each of these categories are products that represent a range of compositions and durabilities. However, the major epidemiological evidence for potential risk for respiratory and other cancers induced by occupational exposure to MMVFs focuses on exposure to glass wool, continuous glass filament, and rock/slag wool during manufacture. None of these studies have reported consistent evidence that exposure to fibers is associated with an increased risk of lung cancer or mesothelioma.[109] Animal studies evaluated by IARC (2002) found that incidence of mesotheliomas and lung cancers were highly dependent on the route of exposure (intra-tracheal instillation vs. intraperitoneal injection vs. inhalation), with intra-tracheal instillation and intraperitoneal injection producing a greater number of tumors in most studies (see Table 14.5).[109] Deposition and retention and biopersistence, particularly with respect to long fibers (>20 μm) are also determinants of pathogenicity.[109]

While the MMVF family is clearly of importance, the asbestos group of fibers may be the most notorious with regard to adverse health effects. The term "asbestos" describes at least six types of hydrated fibrous silicate minerals, each with unique chemical and physical properties and frequently admixed in exposures. These six types are divided further under two mineral groups based on their crystalline characteristics: serpentine and amphibole. All forms of asbestos are rated as Known Human Carcinogens (Group 1) by IARC.[93] As with the MMVFs, fiber length is highly associated with carcinogenic potential.[110] Many of the same mechanisms discussed for MMVFs are also hypothesized to play a role in development of some asbestos related diseases, discussed further below. The link between asbestos dust and fiber inhalation and cancer has been recognized since the 1950s[93], and inhalation of asbestos fibers has been associated with two major malignancies in humans. Bronchogenic carcinoma arises from the lung epithelium and generally develops over a latency period of 10 to 20 years following exposure.[110] Malignant mesothelioma, a second major malignancy related to asbestos exposure, arises from the body cavity lining. The latency period for malignant mesothelioma can exceed 50 years, the longest of all the asbestos-related diseases.[110] Interestingly, these tumors display a range of histological subtypes, sometimes resembling carcinomas and others resembling fibroblastic sarcomas, or a mixture of both. Malignant mesothelioma incidence has been increasing since the discovery of the association with asbestos exposure in the 1960s.[79] Asbestos use in most European countries was banned in 1990s, with an anticipated peak in mesothelioma incidence in 2020.[93] Globally, asbestos is not completely out of the picture as a risk. Asia still imports and utilizes asbestos and questions are arising as to potential under-diagnosis or under-reporting of asbestos related cancers on that continent.[111]

Table 14.5 — Summary of evidence of carcinogenicity for Man-Made Vitreous Fibers. i.t.i.- intratracheal instillation. i.p.- intraperitoneal.[109]

	Continuous Glass Filament	Insulation Glass Wool	Special-purpose Glass fibers	Rock wool	Slag Wool	Refractory Ceramic Fibers
Human Epidemiologic Studies	No evidence for excess risk	No evidence for excess risk	—	No evidence for excess risk	No evidence for excess risk	Insufficient data to permit evaluation
Animal Carcinogenicity Data	No significant increase in tumor response	No increase in tumors via inhalation route, but tumors via i.p. injection	('475' and E-glass) increases in mesotheliomas and lung tumors	No increase in tumors via inhalation route or i.t.i., but tumors via i.p. injection	No increase in tumors via inhalation route, but tumors via i.p. injection	Significant increase in mesotheliomas and lung tumors via inhalation; no tumors after i.t.i.; tumors via i.p. injection
IARC Classification	3	3	2B	3	3	2B

With regard to potential mechanisms of toxicity and carcinogenicity, fibers are phagocytosed by macrophages upon deposition in the lung. Depending on fiber length, phagocytosis may or may not be complete. Incomplete phagocytosis induces an inflammatory cascade, resulting in release of ROS and RNS, potentially leading to DNA damage in and hyperproliferation of lung cells. In addition to mutations induced by ROS, once inside lung cells fibers can directly interfere with chromosomal function, potentially leading to cell transformation and proliferation. Yet another hypothesized mechanism for carcinogenesis involves fibers acting as co-carcinogens or carriers of chemical carcinogens to target tissues.[110] Regardless of the mechanism of carcinogenesis, the fiber biopersistence in the lungs can dictate the severity and persistence of inflammation and, at least in animal models, is related to fibrosis and tumor development.[109]

There is also evidence to suggest that environmental exposure to the mineral fiber erionite, possibly more potent as a carcinogen than crocidolite asbestos, may contribute to bronchogenic carcinoma and background incidence of non-occupationally related mesothelioma[112,113] With regard to other malignant diseases, no strong relationship has been demonstrated between cancers of the gastrointestinal tract and consumption of asbestos contaminated food or beverages.[114]

Chemical carcinogens can nominally be grouped into several classes, and chemicals representative of these classes that are associated with cancer incidence in the workplace have been discussed throughout this chapter. These major classes, along with examples, are: alkylating agents (e.g., ethyl carbamate, bis-2-(chloromethyl)ether); PAHs (e.g, benzo[a]-pyrene); the aromatic amines (e.g., 2-naphthylamine); N-nitrosamines (e.g., 4-(methylnitrosamino)-1-(3-pyridyl)-1-butanone (NNK), a tobacco-specific nitrosamine (TSNA)); heterocyclic aromatic amines (e.g., 2-amino-1-methyl-6-phenyl-imidazo-[4,5-b]pyridine (PhIP)); naturally occurring carcinogens (e.g., aflatoxin B1); metals (e.g., Ni, Cd, As); hormones (e.g., estrogens); and, alkyl halides (e.g., vinyl chloride).

As discussed, the relationship between occupational chemical exposure and cancer has been observed at least since the days of Percival Pott. While not considered a major risk factor in the calculation of overall worldwide cancer burden, occupational exposures to chemical carcinogenic agents nonetheless constitutes an important cause of cancer. An organized, intensive process establishing the carcinogenic risk of specific chemicals and chemical processes in industry was not undertaken until after 1970. Table 14.6 lists some of the processes and occupations for which sufficient data exists to implicate these processes directly in human cancer. Although the list accounts for exposures to chemical, physical, and biological exposures, it is surprisingly small given the extraordinary number of chemicals in commerce worldwide. Importantly, better methods with which to identify chemical carcinogens prior to entering production, trained occupational and public health professionals and professional societies, and adequate but reasonable regulation has likely contributed to the decline in the number of occupations and specific chemicals strongly related to cancer causation. The chemicals, sites of action, and industrial uses classified as human carcinogens or as probably carcinogenic to humans for which exposures are mostly occupational are found in Tables 14.7 and 14.8.

Hazard Characterization of Carcinogens by International and U.S. Federal Agencies

Multiple ranking schemes have been developed and implemented, whether through international cooperative efforts such as the International Agency for Research on Cancer (IARC), or through national programs and organizations such as the U.S.

Table 14.6 — Industries and occupations classified as carcinogenic to humans (IARC Group 1), probably carcinogenic to humans (IARC Group 2A), or possibly carcinogenic to humans (Group 2B).[93]

Industry, occupation	Cancer site/cancer (suspected cancer sites in parentheses)
IARC Group 1	
Aluminum production	Lung, bladder
Auramine, manufacture of	Bladder
Boot and shoe manufacture/repair	Nasal cavity, leukemia
Coal gasification	Skin, lung, bladder
Coke production	Skin, lung, kidney
Furniture and cabinet making	Nasal cavity
Hematite mining (underground) with exposure to radon	Lung
Iron and steel founding	Lung
Isopropanol manufacturing (strong-acid process)	Nasal cavity
Magenta, manufacture of	Bladder
Painter (mainly in the construction industry)	Lung
Rubber industry (certain occupations)	Bladder, leukemia
IARC Group 2A	
Art glass, glass containers and pressed ware (manufacture of)	(Lung, stomach)
Hairdresser or barber (occupational exposure as a)	(Bladder, lung)
Non-arsenical insecticides (occupational exposures in spraying and application of)	(Lung, myeloma)
Petroleum refining (occupational exposures in)	(Leukemia, skin)
IARC Group 2B	
Carpentry and joinery	(Nasal cavity)
Dry cleaning (occupational exposures in)	(Bladder, esophagus)
Textile manufacturing industry (work in)	(Nasal cavity, bladder)

Reprinted with permission from the *Annual Review of Biochemistry*, Volume 62 © 1993 by Annual reviews. www.annualreviews.org.

Table 14.7 — IARC Group 1 chemicals for which exposures are mostly occupational.(93)

Agent	Cancer site/cancer	Main industry/use	NTP Class	US EPA Class	ACGIH Class
4-Aminobiphenyl [92-67-1]	Bladder	Rubber manufacture	KHC[A]	--	A1
Arsenic and As compounds [7440-38-2]	Lung, skin	Glass, metals, pesticides	KHC	A	A1
Asbestos [1332-21-4]	Lung, pleura, peritoneum	Insulation, filter material, textiles	KHC	A	A1
Benzene [71-43-2]	Leukemia	Solvent, fuel	KHC	A; K/L[B]	A1
Benzidine [92-87-5]	Bladder	Dye/pigment manufacture	KHC	A	A1
Beryllium and Be compounds [7440-41-7]	Lung	Aerospace industry/metals	KHC	CBD[C] (o)[D] K/L(i) [E]	A1
Bis(chloromethyl) ether [542-88-1]	Lung	Chemical intermediate/by-product	KHC	A	A1
Cadmium and Cd compounds [7440-43-9]	Lung	Dye/pigment manufacture	KHC	B1	A2
Chloromethyl methyl ether [107-30-2]	Lung	Chemical intermediate/by-product	KHC	A	A2
Chromium[VI] compounds [18540-29-2]	Nasal cavity, lung	Metal plating, dye/pigment manufacturing	KHC	A; K/L(i); CBD(o)	A1
Coal-tar pitches [65996-93-2]	Skin, lung, bladder	Building material, electrodes	KHC	A	A1
Coal-tars [8007-45-2]	Skin, lung	Fuels	KHC	A	A1
Ethylene oxide [75-21-8]	Leukemia	Chemical intermediate, sterilizing agent	KHC	--	A2
Mineral Oils, untreated and mildly-treated	Skin	Lubricants	KHC	--	--
Mustard gas (sulfur mustard) [505-60-2]	Pharynx, lung	Chemical warfare agent	KHC	--	--
2-Naphthylamine [91-59-8]	Bladder	Dye/pigment manufacture	KHC	--	A1
Nickel compounds	Nasal cavity, lung	Metallurgy, alloys, catalyst	KHC	A	A1
Shale-oils [68308-34-9]	Skin	Lubricants, fuels	--	--	--
Silica, crystalline [14808-60-7]	Lung	Stone cutting, mining, foundries	KHC	--	A2
Soots	Skin, lung	Pigments	KHC	L[F](i)	--
Strong inorganic acid mists containing sulfuric acid	Larynx, lung	Metal, batteries	KHC	--	--
Talc containing asbestiform fibers	Lung	Paper, paints	--	--	--
2, 3, 7, 8-Tetrachlorodibenzo-p-dioxin [1746-01-6]	Several organs	Contaminant	KHC	--	--
Vinyl chloride [75-01-4]	Liver	Plastics monomer	KHC	A; K/L	A1
Wood dust	Nasal cavity	Wood industry	KHC	--	--

NTP Class: [A]-Known Human Carcinogen. USEPA Classes: [B]-Known/Likely Human Carcinogen; [C]-Cannot Be Determined; [D]-(o), Oral Route; [E]-(i), Inhalation Route; [F]-Likely Human Carcinogen. ACGIH Classes: A1-Confirmed Human Carcinogen ; A2-Suspected Human Carcinogen.

Environmental Protection Agency (EPA) carcinogen classification system and the Report on Carcinogens (RoC) published by the National Toxicology Program (NTP), an interagency program headquartered at the National Institute of Environmental Health Sciences (NIEHS). Each of these programs provides slightly different information in its reports and carcinogen ranking schema.

The IARC approach is broad in scope and includes complex mixtures, occupational exposures, physical and biological agents, lifestyle factors and other potentially carcinogenic exposures.(115) Through a complex process beyond the scope of the current discussion, a large body of evidence is considered as a whole in order to reach an overall evaluation of the carcinogenicity of an agent to humans and places the agent in one of five categories: Group 1 (carcinogenic to humans); Group 2A (probably carcinogenic to humans); Group 2B (possibly carcinogenic to humans); Group 3 (not classifiable as to its carcinogenicity to humans); or, Group 4 (probably not carcinogenic to humans). This categorization is derived from scientific judgment based on the strength of the evidence presented in studies in humans and experimental animals, including mechanistic and other relevant data.(115)

The process used by the U.S. EPA for carcinogen risk assessment has evolved since the initial Guidelines for Carcinogen Risk Assessment was published in 1986; however, the approach of the agency is still to characterize the weight of evidence for human carcinogenicity.(116) This process assesses weight of evidence for carcinogenicity in humans and experimental animals, then categorizes an agent, substance, or mixture into one of several groups based on the combined evidence. The criteria for assessment of potential carcinogenicity for both humans and experimental animals are detailed, and beyond the scope of this discussion; however, any evidence of carcinogenicity in humans or experimental animals is represented in one of these categories.

Table 14.8 — IARC Group 2 chemicals for which exposures are mostly occupational.[93]

Agent	Cancer site/cancer	Main industry/use	NTP Class	US EPA Class	ACGIH CLASS
Acrylonitrile [107-13-1]	Lung, prostate, lymphoma	Plastics, rubber, textiles, monomer	RA[A]	B1	A3
Benz[a]anthracene [56-55-3]	Lung, skin	Combustion fumes	RA	B2	A2
Benzidine-based dyes	Bladder	Paper, leather, textile dyes	KHC[B]	A	A1
Benzo[a]pyrene [50-32-8]	Lung, skin	Combustion fumes	RA	B2	A2
1,3-Butadiene [106-99-0]	Leukemia, lymphoma	Plastics, rubber, monomer	KHC	HC[C](i)[D]	A2
Captafol [2425-06-1]	—	Pesticide	—	—	A4
Chlorinated toluenes	Lung	Chemical intermediates	—	—	—
4-Chloro-ortho-toluidine [95-69-2]	Bladder	Dye/pigment manufacture, insecticides	RA	—	—
Creosotes [8001-58-9]	Skin	Wood preservation	—	B1	—
Dibenz[a,h]anthracene [53-70-3]	Lung, skin	Combustion fumes	RA	B2	—
Diethyl sulfate [77-78-1]	—	Chemical intermediate	RA	B2	A3
Dimethylcarbamoyl chloride [79-44-7]	—	Chemical intermediate	RA	B2	A2
Dimethyl sulfate [77-78-1]	—	Chemical intermediate	RA	B2	A3
Epichlorohydrin [106-89-8]	—	Plastics/resins monomer	RA	B2	A3
Ethylene dibromide [106-93-4]	—	Chemical intermediate, fumigants, fuels	RA	LC[E]	A3
Formaldehyde [50-00-0]	Nasopharynx	Plastics, textiles, laboratory agent	RA	B1	A2
Glycidol [556-52-5]	—	Chemical intermediate, sterilizing agent	RA	—	A3
4,4'-methylenebis(2-chloroaniline) [101-14-4]	Bladder	Rubber manufacture	RA	—	A2
Methyl methansulfonate [66-27-3]	—	Laboratory research	RA	—	—
ortho-Toluidine [95-53-4]	Bladder	Dye/pigment manufacture	RA	B2	A3
Polychlorinated biphenyls [1336-36-3]	Liver, bile ducts, leukemia, lymphoma	Electrical components	RA	B2	—
Styrene oxide [96-09-3]	—	Plastics, chemical intermediate	RA	—	—
Tetrachloroethylene [127-18-4]	Esophagus, lymphoma	Solvent, dry cleaning	RA	—	A3
Trichloroethylene [79-01-6]	Liver, lymphoma	Solvent, dry cleaning, metal	RA	—	A5
Tris(2,3-dibromopropyl) phosphate [126-72-7]	—	Plastics, textiles, flame retardant	RA	—	—
Vinyl bromide [593-60-2]	—	Plastics, textiles, monomer	RA	—	A2

NTP Class: [A]-Reasonably Anticipated to be a Human Carcinogen. USEPA Class: [B]-Known Human Carcinogen; [C]-Human Carcinogen; [D]-(i), Inhalation Route; [E]-Likely Carcinogen. ACGIH Class: A1-Confirmed Human Carcinogen; A2-Suspected Human Carcinogen; A3-Confirmed animal carcinogen with unknown relevance to humans; A4-Not classifiable as a human carcinogen; A5-Not suspected as a human carcinogen.

The 1986 Guidance for Carcinogen Risk Assessment spelled out five groups, designated by letter codes: Group A—Human Carcinogen, Group B—Probable Human Carcinogen, Group C—Possible Human Carcinogen, Group D—Not Classifiable as to Human Carcinogenicity, and Group E—Evidence of Non-Carcinogenicity for Humans. These classifications are still in use by many in the public and environmental health fields, but it is important to note that the 1996 Guidance document replaced these five "letter" categories with three descriptors: "Known/Likely" human carcinogen, carcinogenic potential "Cannot be Determined," and "Not Likely" to be carcinogenic to humans.[117] Guidance again shifted with the interim 1999 Guidelines wherein these descriptors were expanded and, with additional changes, was modified in the 2005 Guidelines.[118,119] The 2005 Guidelines focus heavily on the use of data from studies of mode of action—a sequence of key events and processes, starting with interaction of an agent with a cell, proceeding through operational and anatomical changes, and resulting in cancer formation—in carcinogen risk assessment.[119] The current set of five standard descriptors includes: "Carcinogenic to Humans," "Likely to Be Carcinogenic to Humans," "Suggestive Evidence of Carcinogenic Potential," "Inadequate Information to Assess Carcinogenic Potential," and "Not Likely to Be Carcinogenic to Humans." Importantly, the use of these descriptors in cancer risk assessment should be in conjunction with the entire range of information available rather than simply focusing on the descriptor. The categories/descriptors, as well as the current number of agents classified under each, presented in all four versions of the Guidelines, are summarized in Table 14.9.

The National Toxicology Program is responsible for publishing the RoC, which contains a list of substances 1) which are either known to be carcinogens or may reasonably anticipated to be human carcinogens; and 2) to which a significant number of people in the United States may be exposed. The RoC is a compilation of scientific and public health data on carcinogenic agents and exposure circumstances that may pose a carcinogenic hazard to human health. The document is also a useful source of federal regulations to exposure limits, carcinogenic mechanisms of action, and the potential for human exposure to the listed substances. Importantly, listing in the RoC only designates a potential hazard, but does not establish exposure conditions under which excessive cancer risk would be present for individuals on a daily basis. The criteria for listing an agent, substance, mixture, or exposure circumstance in the RoC as a "Known To Be a Human Carcinogen," must include sufficient evidence of carcinogenicity from studies in humans indicating a causal relationship between exposure to the agent, substance, or mixture, and human cancer.[120] If there is limited evidence of carcinogenicity from studies in humans which indicates that causal interpretation is credible, but that alternative explanations could not be excluded, an agent, substance, or mixture may be listed as "Reasonably Anticipated to be a Human Carcinogen," although several other criteria and forms of evidence (e.g., experimental animal data) may also be evaluated in this determination.[120] The most recent publication, the 11th RoC, was released in January 2005 and lists 58 "Known" carcinogens and 188 agents that are reasonably anticipated to be human carcinogens ("Reasonably Anticipated").[120]

Conclusions

There are many potential causes of cancer in humans, most of which are associated with the environment in which we live and to which exposure can be at least partially controlled. Lifestyle and dietary factors, biological factors such as chronic infections and hormones, and chemical and physical factors associated with the occupational environment all contribute to the global cancer burden, although some factors more than others. In efforts focused on public and worker health protection, both international and U.S. federal agencies have developed and implemented multiple ranking schemes to assist public, environmental, and occupational health professionals in carcinogen risk assessment.

A disease characterized by uncontrolled, abnormal proliferation of cells, most cancers start as a single, normal cell that undergoes multiple genetic mutations beginning as lesions at DNA targets. Many of these lesions escape cellular protective mechanisms (i.e., DNA repair) and pass as mutations to the next generation of cells. Survival of these aberrant cells leads to replication, passing increasingly altered genetic material to each subsequent generation of cells. Continued expansion of this group of cells through multiple, complex mechanisms highlighted by further genomic damage and instability leads to production of a tumor, which then recruits its own blood supply and may begin to spread to other parts of the body.

While carcinogens can and do mutate many genes, some genes are more critical to normal cell function than others. We discussed the critical role of DNA repair and the fact that DNA repair genes themselves are subject to mutagenesis. Likewise,

Table 14.9 — U.S. EPA classification system for categorizing weight of evidence for carcinogenicity from human and animal studies.[116–119]

Guidelines and Criteria	Number of Agents
1986 Guidelines	
• Group A (Human carcinogen)	11
• Group B1 (Probable human carcinogen — based on limited evidence of carcinogenicity in humans)	5
• Group B2 (Probable human carcinogen — based on sufficient evidence of carcinogenicity in animals)	66
• Group C (Possible human carcinogen)	40
• Group D (Not classifiable as to human carcinogenicity)	106
• Group E (Evidence of non-carcinogenicity for humans)	3
1996 Guidelines	
• Known/likely human carcinogen	8
• Carcinogenic potential cannot be determined	15
• Not likely to be carcinogenic to humans	4
1999 Guidelines	
• Carcinogenic to humans	1
• Likely to be carcinogenic to humans	4
• Suggestive evidence of carcinogenicity, but not sufficient to assess human carcinogenic potential	1
• Data are inadequate for an assessment of human carcinogenic potential	12
• Not likely to be carcinogenic to humans	2
2005 Guidelines	
• Inadequate information to assess carcinogenic potential	4

the capacity of the drug metabolizing enzymes involved in bioactivation of procarcinogens is affected by mutagenic action. However, as discussed, cancer is a disease caused by unrestricted proliferation and autonomous growth brought on by multiple genetic and epigenetic mechanisms. Hence, the genes and gene products regulating the processes of growth, differentiation, proliferation, and death — oncogenes and tumor suppressor genes — are arguably the most critical targets in neoplasia.

References

1. **Jemal, A, R. Siegel, E. Ward, T. Murray, J. Xu, and M. Thun:** Cancer statistics 2007. *CA Cancer J. Clin. 57*: 43–66 (2007).
2. **Butlin, H.T.:** Cancer of the scrotum in chimney sweeps and others: Why foreign sweeps do not suffer from scrotal cancer." *Br. Med. J. 2*:1–6 (1892).
3. **Legge R.T.:** Industrial medicine's hall of fame: Percival Pott, F.R.S. surgeon, St. Bartholomews Hospital, London; a short biography, with a reproduced chapter from his classic work, chimney sweeps' cancer. *Ind. Med. Surg. 24*: 419–420 (1955).
4. **Monson, R.:** *Occupational Epidemiology* 2nd ed. Boca Raton: CRC Press, 1990.
5. **Majno, G, and I. Joris:** *Cells Tissues and Disease: Principles of General Pathology.* Cambridge, Ma: Blackwell Science, 1996.
6. **Miller, E.C. and J. Miller:** Mechanisms of chemical carcinogenesis. *Cancer 47*:1055–1064 (1981).
7. **Miller, E.C.:** Some current perspectives on chemical carcinogenesis in humans and experimental animals: Presidential address. *Cancer Res. 38*:1479–1496 (1978).
8. **Guengerich, F.P. and T. Shimada:** Oxidation of toxic and carcinogenic chemicals by human cytochrome P-450 enzymes. *Chem. Res. Toxicol. 4*:391–407 (1991).
9. **Nishimura, M., H. Yaguti, H. Yoshitsugu, S. Naito, and T. Sato:** Tissue distribution of mRNA expression of human cytochrome P450 isoforms assessed by high-sensitivity real-time reverse transcription PCR. *Yakugaku Zasshi 123*: 369–375 (2003).
10. **Garrod, J.W., and D. Manson:** The metabolism of aromatic amines. *Xenobiotica 16*:933–955 (1986).
11. **Miller, D.P., K. Asomaning, G. Liu et al:** An association between glutathione-S-transferase P1 gene polymorphism and younger age at onset of lung carcinoma. *Cancer 107*: 1570–1577 (2006).
12. **Cascorbi, I., I. Roots, and J. Brockmoller:** Association of NAT1 and NAT2 polymorphisms to urinary bladder cancer: significantly reduced risk in subjects with NAT*10. *Cancer Res. 61*: 5051–5056 (2001).
13. **Persson, I., I. Johansson, and M. Ingelman-Sundberg:** *in vitro* kinetics of two human CYP1A1 variant enzymes suggested to be associated with interindividual differences in cancer susceptibility. *Biochem. Biophys. Res. Commun. 231*: 227–230 (1997).
14. **Nebert, D.W.:** Inter-individual susceptibility to environmental toxicants — A current assessment. *Toxicol. Appl. Pharmacol. 207*: S34–S42 (2005).
15. **Ozawa, N. and F. Guengerich:** Evidence for formation of an S-[2-(N7-guanyl)ethyl]glutathione adduct in glutathione-mediated binding of 1, 2-dibromoethane to DNA. *Proc. Natl. Acad. Sci. USA 80*: 5266–5270 (1983).
16. **Dipple, A.:** DNA adducts of chemical carcinogens. *Carcinogenesis 16*: 437–441 (1995).
17. **Shen, A.L., W. Fahl, and C. Jefcoate:** Metabolism of benzo[a]pyrene by isolated hepatocytes and factors affecting covalent binding of benzo[a]pyrene metabolites to DNA in hepatocyte and microsomal systems. *Arch. Biochem. Biophys. 204*: 511–523 (1980).
18. **Kapitulnik, J., P. Wislocki, W. Levin, H. Yagi, D. Jerina, and A. Conney:** Tumorigenicity studies with diol-epoxides of benzo[a]pyrene which indicate that ($\pm$)-*trans*-7β,8α-dihydroxy-9α,10α-epoxy-7,8,9,10-tetrahydrobenzo[a]pyrene is an ultimate carcinogen in newborn mice. *Cancer Res. 38*: 354–358 (1978).
19. **Vogelstein, B., E.R. Fearon, and S.E. Kern et al.:** Genetic alterations during colorectal-tumor development. *N. Engl. J. Med. 319*: 325–332 (1988).
20. **Kallioniemi. A., O-P. Kallioniemi, J. Piper et al.:** Detection and mapping of amplified DNA sequences in breast cancer by comparative genomic hybridization. *Proc. Natl. Acad. Sci. USA 91*:2156–2160 (1994).
21. **Loeb, L.A.:** Endogenous carcinogenesis: molecular oncology into the twenty-first century — presidential address. *Cancer Res. 49*:5489–5496 (1989).
22. **Lindahl, T.:** Instability and decay of the primary structure of DNA. *Nature 362*:709–715 (1993).
23. **Ames, B.N., L. Gold, and W. Willet:** The causes and prevention of cancer. *Proc. Natl. Acad. Sci. USA. 92*: 5258–5265 (1995).
24. **Wood, R.D., M. Mitchell, J. Sgouros, and T. Lindahl:** Human DNA repair genes. *Science 29*:1284–1289 (2001).
25. **Cleaver, J.E.:** Do we know the cause of xeroderma pigmentosum? *Carcinogenesis 11*:875–882 (1990).
26. **Durham, T.R. and E. Snow:** Metal ions and carcinogenesis. Cancer: Cell structures, carcinogens, and genomic instability. *Experientia. Supplementum. 96*:97–130 (2006).
27. **Sengupta, S. and C. Harris:** p53: traffic cop at the crossroads of DNA repair and recombination. *Nat. Rev. Mol. Cell. Biol. 6*:44–55 (2005).
28. **Lacroix, M., R.-A. Toillon, and G. Leclerq:** p53 and breast cancer, an update. *Endocr. Relat. Cancer. 13*:293–325 (2006).
29. **Hsu, I.C., R. Metcalf, T. Sun et al.:** Mutational hotspot in the p53 gene in human hepatocellular carcinomas. *Nature 350*:427–428 (1991).
30. **Levine, A.J., J. Momand, and C. Finlay:** The p53 tumor suppressor gene. *Nature 351*:453–456 (1991).

31. **Rakitsky, V.N., V. Koblyakov, and V. Turusov:** Nongenotoxic (epigenetic) carcinogens: pesticides as an example. A critical review. *Teratog., Carcinog. Mutagen.* 20:229–240 (2000).

32. **Wilkinson, C.F. and J. Killeen:** A mechanistic interpretation of the oncogenicity of chlorothalonil in rodents and an assessment of human relevance. *Regul. Toxicol. Pharmacol.* 24:69–84 (1996).

33. **Ren, P., P. Mehta, and R. Ruch:** Inhibition of gap junctional intercellular communication by tumor promoters in connexin43 and connexin32-expressing liver cells: cell specificity and role of protein kinase C. *Carcinogenesis* 19: 169–175 (1998)

34. **Liehr, J.G.:** Is estradiol a genotoxic mutagenic carcinogen? *Endocr. Rev.* 21: 40–54 (2000).

35. **Schilter, B., Marin-Kuan, M., and Delatour, T. et al.:** Ochratoxin A: Potential epigenetic mechanisms of toxicity and carcinogenicity. *Food Addit. Contam.* 22 Suppl 1:88–93 (2005).

36. **Fukushima, S., Kinoshita, A., and Puatanachokchai, R., et al.:** Hormesis and dose-response-mediated mechanisms in carcinogenesis: evidence for a threshold in carcinogenicity of non-genotoxic carcinogens. *Carcinogenesis.* 26: 1835–1845 (2005).

37. **Giminez-Conti, I.B., Binder, R.L., Johnston, D., and Slaga, T.J.:** Comparison of the skin tumor-promoting potential of different organic peroxides in SENCAR mice. *Toxicol. Appl. Pharmacol.* 149:73–79 (1998).

38. **Trosko, J.E. and Upham, B.L.:** The emperor wears no clothes in the field of carcinogen risk assessment: ignored concepts in cancer risk assessment. *Mutagenesis.* 20:81–92 (2005).

39. **Shi, H., X. Shi, and K. Liu:** Oxidative mechanism of arsenic toxicity and carcinogenesis. *Mol. Cell. Biochem.* 225: 67–78 (2004).

40. **Green, S.:** Nuclear receptors and chemical carcinogenesis. *Trend. Pharmacol. Sci.* 13:251–255 (1992).

41. **Cattley, R.C., J. De Luca, and C. Elcombe et al.:** Do peroxisome proliferating compounds pose a hepatocarcinogenic hazard to humans? *Regul. Toxicol. Pharmacol.* 27: 47–60 (1998).

42. **Mass, M.J. and L. Wang:** Arsenic alters cytosine methylation patterns of the promoter of the tumor suppressor gene p53 in human lung cells: a model for a mechanism of carcinogenesis. *Mutat. Res.* 386:263–277 (1997).

43. **Boonchai, W., M. Walsh, M. Cummings, and G. Chenevix-Trench:** Expression of p53 in arsenic-related and sporadic basal cell carcinoma. *Arch. Dermatol. 136*: 195–198 (2000).

44. **Zhao, C.Q., M. Young, B. Diwan, T. Coogan, and M. Waalkes:** Association of arsenic-induced malignant transformation with DNA hypomethylation and aberrant gene expression. *Proc. Natl. Acad. Sci. USA* 94:10907–10912 (1997).

45. **Zhang, Q., K. Salnikow, T. Kluz, L. Chen, W. Su, and M. Costa:** Inhibition and reversal of nickel-induced transformation by the histone deacetylase inhibitor trichostatin A. *Toxicol. Appl. Pharmacol.* 192:201–211 (2003).

46. **Luch, A.:** Nature and nurture — lessons from chemical carcinogenesis. *Nature Rev Cancer* 5:113–125 (2005).

47. **U.S. Department of Health and Human Services:** *Report on Carcinogens, 10th ed.* Public Health Service, National Toxicology Program, 2004.

48. **Freudenthal, R.I., E. Stephens, and D. Anderson:** Determining the potential of aromatic amines to induce cancer in the urinary bladder. *Int. J. Toxicol.* 18:353–359 (1999).

49. **Neumann, H.G., A. Ambs, S., and A. Bitsch:** The role of nongenotoxic mechanisms in arylamine carcinogenesis. *Environ. Health Perspect.* 102:S173–S176 (1994).

50. **Klöhn, P.C., M. Soriano, W. Irwin et al.:** Early resistance to cell death and to onset of the mitochondrial permeability transition during hepatocarcinogenesis with 2-acetylaminofluorene. *Proc. Natl. Acad. Sci. USA* 100: 10014–10019 (2003).

51. **Wong, R.S. and E. Passaro, Jr.:** Growth factors, oncogenes, and the autocrine hypothesis. *Surg. Gynecol. Obstet.* 168:468–473 (1989).

52. **Pitot, H.C. III and Y. Dragan:** Chemical Carcinogenesis. In *Casarett and Doull's Toxicology: The Basic Science of Poisons*, 6th ed., C.D. Klaassen, (ed.), pp. 241–320. New York: McGraw-Hill, 2001.

53. **Levine, A.J.:** The tumor suppressor genes. *Annu. Rev. Biochem.* 62:623–651 (1993).

54. **Malkin, D., F. Li, and L. Strong et al.:** Germ line p53 mutations in a familial syndrome of breast cancer, sarcomas, and other neoplasms. *Science* 250:1233–1238 (1990).

55. **Sanders, B.M., M. Jay, G. Draper, and E. Roberts:** Non-ocular cancer in relatives of retinoblastoma patients. *Br. J. Cancer* 60:358–365 (1989).

56. **Knudson, A.G., Jr.:** Mutation and cancer: statistical study of retinoblastoma. *Proc. Natl. Acad. Sci. USA* 68:820–823 (1971).

57. **Friedwald, W.F. and P. Rous:** The initiating and promoting elements in tumor production. An analysis of the effects of tar, benzpyrene, and methylcholanthrene on rabbit skin. *J. Exp. Med.* 80:101–126 (1944).

58. **Berenblum, I. and P. Shubik:** A new, quantitative approach to the study of the stages of chemical carcinogensis in the mouse's skin. *Br. J. Cancer* 1:383–391 (1947).

59. **Peraino, C., R. Fry, and E. Staffeldt:** Reduction and enhancement by phenobarbital of hepatocarcinogenesis induced in the rat by 2-acetylaminofluorene. *Cancer Res.* 31: 1506–1512 (1971).

60. **Sims, P., P. Grover, A. Swaisland, K. Pal, and A. Hewer:** Metabolic activation of benzo[a]pyrene proceeds by a diol-epoxide. *Nature* 252:326–328 (1974).

61. **Cheng, S.C., B. Hilton, J. Roman, and A. Dipple:** DNA adducts from carcinogenic and noncarcinogenic enantiomers of benzo[a]pyrene dihydrodiol epoxides. *Chem. Res. Toxicol.* 2:334–340 (1989).

62. **Hess, M.T., D. Gunz, N. Luneva, N. Geacintov, and H. Naegeli:** Base pair conformation-dependent excision of benzo[a]pyrene diol epoxide-guanine adducts by human nucleotide excision repair enzymes. *Mol. Cell. Biol.* 17: 7069–7076 (1997).
63. **Geactinov, N.E., M. Cosman, B. Hingerty, S. Amin, S. Broyde, and D. Patel:** NMR solution structures of stereoisomeric covalent polycyclic aromatic carcinogen-DNA adducts: principles, patterns, and diversity. *Chem. Res. Toxicol.* 10:111–146 (1997).
64. **Feng, Z., W. Hu, and J. Chen et al.:** Preferential DNA damage and poor repair determine ras gene mutational hotspots in human cancer. *J. Natl. Cancer Inst.* 94: 1527–1536 (2002).
65. **Ross, J.A. and S. Nesnow:** Polycyclic aromatic hydrocarbons: correlation between DNA adducts and ras oncogene mutations. *Mutat. Res.* 424:155–166 (1999).
66. **Denissenko, M.F., A. Pao, M. Tang, and G. Pfieffer:** Preferential formation of benzo[a]pyrene adducts at lung cancer mutational hotspots in p53. *Science* 274:430–432 (1996).
67. **Khan, Q.A. and A. Dipple:** Diverse chemical carcinogens fail to induce G1 arrest in MCF-7 cells. *Carcinogenesis* 21: 1611–1618 (2000).
68. **Lehmann, A.R.:** Replication of damaged DNA in mammalian cells; new solutions to an old problem. *Mutat. Res.* 509:23–34 (2002).
69. **Weinstein, I.B.:** The origins of human cancer: molecular mechanisms of carcinogenesis and their implications for cancer prevention and treatment — Twenty-seventh G.H.A. Clowes Memorial Award Lecture. *Cancer Res.* 48: 4135–4143 (1988).
70. **Van Duuren, B.L., A. Sivak, C. Katz, I. Seidman and S. Melchionne:** The effect of aging and interval between primary and secondary treatment in two-stage carcinogenesis on mouse skin. *Cancer Res.* 35:502–505 (1975).
71. **Carter, J.H., H. Carter, and J. Meade:** Adrenal regulation of mammary tumorigenesis in female Sprague-Dawley rats: incidence, latency, and yield of mammary tumors. *Cancer Res.* 48:3801–3807 (1988).
72. **Cohen, L.A., M. Kendall, E. Zang, C. Meschter, and D. Rose:** Modulation of N-nitrosomethylurea-induced mammary tumor promotion by dietary fiber and fat. *J. Natl. Cancer Inst.* 83:496–501 (1991).
73. **Pitot, HC:** Endogenous carcinogenesis: the role of tumor promotion. *Proc. Soc. Exp. Biol. Med.* 198:661–666 (1991).
74. **Berenblum, I:** The cocarcinogenic action of croton resin. *Cancer Res.* 1:44–48 (1941).
75. **Noble, R.L.:** Hormonal control of growth and progression in tumors of Nb rats and a theory of action. *Cancer Res.* 37: 82–94 (1977).
76. **Foulds, L:** The experimental study of tumor progression: a review. *Cancer Res.* 14:327–339 (1954).
77. **Higginson, J.:** Present trends in cancer epidemiology. *Proc. Can. Cancer Conf.* 8:40–75 (1969).
78. **Monson, R.:** Occupation. In *Cancer Epidemiology and Prevention*, D. Schottenfeld and J.F. Fraumeni (eds.), pp. 373–405. New York: Oxford Univeristy Press, 2006.
79. **Peto, J.:** Cancer epidemiology in the last century and the next decade. *Nature 411:* 390–395 (2001).
80. **Ezzati, M., S. Henley, A. Lopez, and M. Thun:** Role of smoking in global and regional cancer epidemiology: current patterns and data needs. *Int. J. Cancer.* 116:963–971 (2005).
81. **Doll, R. and R. Peto:** The causes of cancer: quantitative estimates of avoidable risks of cancer in the United States today. *J. Natl. Cancer Inst.* 66:1191–1208 (1981).
82. **Yu, H and T. Rohan:** Role of insulin-like growth factor family in cancer development and progression. *J. Natl. Cancer Inst.* 92:1472–1489 (2000).
83. **Kakizoe, T.:** Cancer statistics in Japan. *FPCR Publication Tokyo Japan.* 10–18 (1997).
84. **Kato, S., T. Tsukamoto, T. Mizoshita et al.:** High salt dose-dependently promote gastric chemical carcinogenesis in Helicobacter pylori-infected Mongolian gerbils associated with a shift in mucin production from glandular to surface mucous cell. *Int. J. Cancer* 119:1558–1566 (2006).
85. **Maity, P., K. Biswas, S. Roy, R. Banjerjee, and U. Bandyopadhyay:** Smoking and the pathogenesis of gastroduodenal ulcer –recent mechanistic update. *Mol. Cell. Biochem.* 253:329–238 (2003).
86. **Kuipers, E.J., A. Uyterlinde, A. Pena et al.:** Long-term effect of Helicobacter pylori gastritis. *Lancet* 345: 1525–1528 (1995).
87. **Marchetti, M., B. Arico, D. Burroni et al.:** Development of a mouse model of Helicobacter pylori infection that mimics human disease. *Science* 267:1655–1658 (1995).
88. **Inoue, M., and S. Tsugane:** Epidemiology of gastric cancer in Japan. *Postgrad. Med. J.* 81:419–424 (2005).
89. **Vainio, H. and E. Weiderpass:** Fruit and Vegetables in cancer prevention. *Nutr. Cancer* 54:111–142 (2006).
90. **National Research Council:** *Carcinogens and Anticarcinogens in the Human Diet: A Comparison on Naturally Occurring and Synthetic Substances.* Washington, D.C.: National Academy Press, 1996.
91. **Smela, M.E., M. Hamm, P. Henderson, C. Harris, T. Harris, and J. Essignmann:** The aflatoxin B(1) formidopyrimidine adduct plays a major role in causing mutations observed in human hepatocellular carcinoma. *Proc. Natl. Acad. Sci. USA.* 99:6655–6660 (2002).
92. **Lupberger, J. and E. Hildt:** Hepatitis B virus-induced oncogenesis. *World J. Gastroenterol.* 13:74–81 (2007).
93. **Stewart, B.W. and P. Kleihues (eds):** *World Cancer Report.* Lyon: IARC Press, 2003.
94. **Ames, B.N. and L. Gold:** Environmental Pollution, Pesticides, and the Prevention of Cancer: Misconceptions. *FASEB Journal* 11:1041–1051 (1997).
95. **Jaga, K. and C. Dharmani:** Global surveillance of DDT and DDE levels in human tissues. *Int. J. Occup. Med. Environ. Health* 16:7–20 (2003).

96. **Henderson, B.E., R. Ross, M. Pike, and J. Casagrande:** Endogenous hormones as a major factor in human cancer. *Cancer Res. 42*:3232–3239 (1982).
97. **Henderson, B.E. and H. Fiegelson:** Hormonal carcinogenesis. *Carcinogenesis 21*:427–433 (2000).
98. **Lifeso, R.M., R. Rooney, and M. El-Shaker:** Post-traumatic squamous cell carcinoma. *J. Bone Joint Surg. Am. 72*: 12–18 (1990).
99. **Bischoff, F. and G. Bryson:** Carcinogenesis through solid-state surfaces. *Prog. Exp. Tumor Res. 5*:85–133 (1964).
100. **Mondal, S. and C. Heidelberger:** Transformation of C3H/10T1/2 CL8 mouse embryo fibroblasts by ultraviolet irradiation and a phorbol ester. *Nature 260*:710–711 (1976).
101. **Beukers, R. and W. Berends:** Isolation and identification of the irradiation product of thymine. *Biochim. Biophys. Acta 41*:550–551 (1960).
102. **Minamoto, T., M. Mai, and Z. Ronai:** Environmental factors as regulators and effectors of multistep carcinogenesis. *Carcinogenesis 20*:519–527 (1999).
103. **National Council on Radiation Protection and Measurements:** *Ionizing Radiation Exposure of the Population of the United States.* Report No. 93. Bethesda, MD, 1987.
104. **Ritenour, E.R.:** Health effects of low level radiation: carcinogenesis, teratogenesis, and mutagenesis. *Semin. Nucl. Med. 16*:106–117 (1986).
105. **Beebe, G.W., H. Kato, and C. Land:** Studies of the mortality of A-bomb survivors. 6. Mortality and radiation dose, 1950–1974. *Radiat. Res. 75*:138–201 (1978).
106. **Miller, R. and S. Jablon:** A search for late radiation effects among men who served as x-ray technologists in the U.S. Army during World War II. *Radiology 96*:269–274 (1970).
107. **Loken, M.K.:** Low level radiation: biological effects. *CRC Crit. Rev. Diagn. Imaging 19*:175–202 (1980).
108. **Preston, R.J. and G. Hoffman:** Genetic toxicology. In *Casarett and Doull's Toxicology: The Basic Science of Poisons* 6th ed, C.D. Klaassen (ed.), pp. 321–350. New York: McGraw-Hill, 2001.
109. **International Agency for Research on Cancer:** Man-made Vitreous Fibres. *IARC Monographs on the Evaluation of Carcinogenic Risks to Humans* 81. Lyon, France: IARC Press, 2002.
110. **Kane, A.B., Boffetta, P., Saracci, R., and Wilbourn, J.D., Eds.:** *Mechanisms of Fiber Carcinogenesis. IARC Scientific Publications* 140. Lyon, France: IARC Press, 1996.
111. **Takahashi, K. and A. Karjalainen:** A cross country comparative overview of the asbestos situation in 10 Asian Countries. *Int. J. Occup. Env. Health. 9*:244–248 (2003).
112. **Baris, Y.I., M. Artvinli, A. Sahin:** Environmental mesothelioma in Turkey. *Ann. NY Acad. Sci. 30*:423–432 (1979).
113. **McDonald, J.C., and A. McDonald:** Mesotheliomas: is there a background? *Eur. Respir. Rev. 11*:71–73 (1993).
114. **Bignon, J.:** Mineral fibres in the non-occupational environment. *IARC Sci. Publ. 90*:3–29 (1989).
115. **International Agency for Research on Cancer:** Preamble. *IARC Monographs on the Evaluation of Carcinogenic Risks to Humans* Lyon, France: IARC Press, 2006.
116. "Guidelines for Carcinogen Risk Assessment," *Federal Register* 51: (1986). pp. 33992-34003.
117. **U.S. Environmental Protection Agency:** Guidelines for Carcinogen Risk Assessment. EPA/600/P-92/003C, 1996.
118. **U.S. Environmental Protection Agency:** Guidelines for Carcinogen Risk Assessment. NCEA-F-0644, 1999.
119. **U.S. Environmental Protection Agency:** Guidelines for Carcinogen Risk Assessment. EPA/630/P-03/001B, 2005.
120. **U.S. Department of Health and Human Services:** *Report on Carcinogens,* 11th ed. Public Health Service, National Toxicology Program, 2005.

> *Misery makes the quarrel and wretchedness in this world.*
>
> Paracelsus (1493–1541)

Chapter 15

Teratogenesis

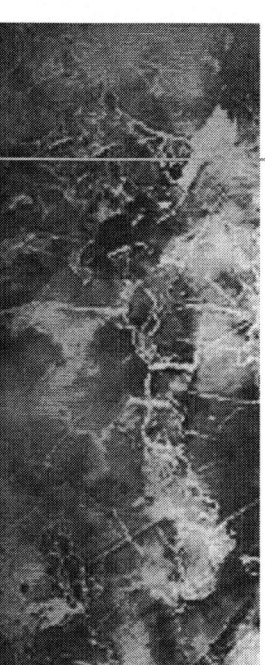

Outcome Competencies
Upon completing this chapter, the reader will be able to:

1. **Knowledge**
   - Define blastocyst, congenital, embryonic stage, epigenetic, fetal programming, fetal stage, gastrulation, organogenesis, placenta, teratogenesis, teratogen, zygote.
   - Describe key events in human prenatal development.
   - Describe the basic principles of teratology.
   - List the major mechanisms of teratogenesis and provide examples of each.

2. **Comprehension**
   - Explain the relationship between embryonic/fetal exposure to teratogens at specific developmental stages (e.g., embryonic and fetal periods) and teratogenic outcomes observed at those stages.
   - Explain the concept of fetal programming.
   - Explain the key features of interpreting teratogenic dose information in the context of industrial hygiene practice.

3. **Application**
   - Describe the roles of exposure timing and dose-response in teratology.
   - Predict the potential teratogenic outcomes of exposure to a known teratogen given exposure timing and information on the dose-response relationship.

4. **Analysis**
   - Compare and contrast mechanisms of carcinogenesis and teratogenesis.
   - Distinguish between genetic, epigenetic, and physiologic mechanisms of teratogenesis.

5. **Synthesis**
   - Integrate concepts of exposure timing and the dose-response relationship with mechanisms of teratogenesis.

6. **Evaluation**
   - Evaluate chemical, occupational exposure, mechanistic teratology, and epidemiologic data to qualitatively appraise whether a chemical agent is a potential teratogen in the occupational environment.

Prerequisite Knowledge
1. Mechanisms of toxicity
2. Basic human genetics (gene structure, function)
3. Cellular physiology and biology
4. Basic concepts in developmental biology
5. Basic biochemistry
6. Genetic toxicology
7. Human physiology

Key Terms
Blastocyst, congenital, embryonic stage, epigenetic, fetal programming, fetal stage, gastrulation, organogenesis, placenta, teratogenesis, teratogen, zygote

Key Topics
1. Introduction and Background
2. Key Points in Prenatal Human Development
3. Basic Principles of Teratology
   - Exposure Timing and Stage of Developmental Susceptibility Dose-Response
4. General Mechanisms of Teratogenesis
5. Environmental Chemicals Known to be Teratogenic
6. Conclusions

Chapter 15

Teratogenesis

By Cody L. Wilson, PhD, DABT, CHMM

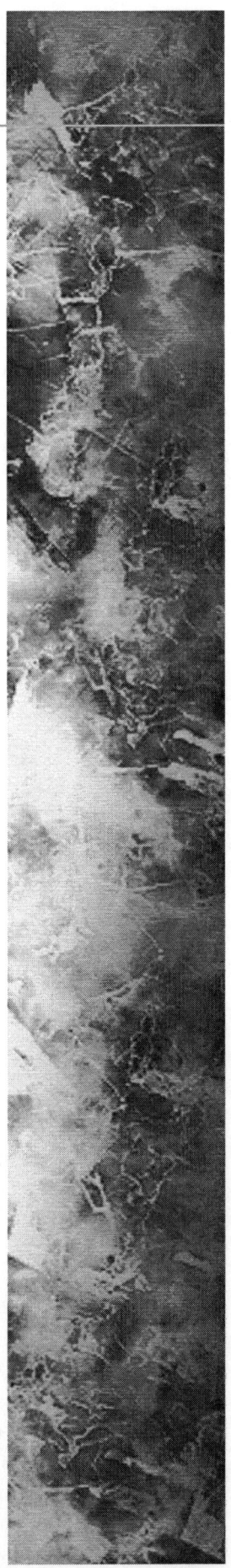

Introduction and Background

Teratology, from the Greek word teratos, meaning monster, is the study of abnormal development and congenital malformations. The systematic study of teratogenesis began in the early nineteenth century with some early theories of congenital malformations suggesting that interbreeding between animals and humans were the source of such anomalies. While these beliefs were rooted in the mythology of a much earlier age, they were held even in seventeenth century Puritanical New England, when George Spencer, afflicted with cataracts, was accused of fathering a cyclopean pig.[1] Fortunately, a systematic study of human prenatal development in the nineteenth and twentieth centuries laid the groundwork for further discovery of some of the environmental agents and maternal and fetal conditions that adversely impact normal development.

Despite the considerable work that has ensued since the days of poor nearsighted George Spencer, the reasons for adverse pregnancy outcomes are still largely unknown. Fewer than half of all human conceptions results in the birth of a normal, healthy infant.[2] Most of these losses are spontaneous abortions attributed to largely unknown causes. Of the successful births annually, it is estimated that 3% are born with severe congenital malformations.[3] It is important to note that the vast majority — 65 to 75% — of congenital malformations are still of unknown etiology.[3,4] Fifteen to twenty-five percent of the known causes are attributed to genetic diseases, including spontaneous mutations that arose during development. Environmental causes constitute approximately 10%, with most of those attributed to maternal conditions and behaviors (e.g., alcoholism, nutritional deficits, smoking). Less than 1% is attributed to chemicals, prescription drugs, high-dose ionizing radiation, and hyperthermia. The focus of this chapter is to highlight some key developmental processes, the mechanisms and agents by which they are interrupted, and the general rules important in risk assessment of potential teratogens in the occupational environment.

Key Points in Prenatal Human Development

A review of the key events in normal human prenatal development is necessary for an understanding of the conditions and agents that disrupt it (see Figure 15.1 and Table 15.1). Development is characterized by rapid change driven by regulation of key genes at specific time points, intercellular communication, and interaction between embryonic cells and other factors in the maternal environment. Although we have a fairly intricate knowledge about the processes by which a fertilized egg divides and proceeds through development of an embryo into a fetus, little is known about the specific genes and other signals that regulate these early events or how interactions among cells with each other and with other factors in a three-dimensional environment affect development.

After fertilization, maternal factors present in the ovum before fertilization jump start zygote development. Within several days after fertilization, the zygote genome becomes activated and takes control of the embryonic development process.[5,6] Over the span of five to seven days after fertilization, the zygote migrates to the uterus, dividing

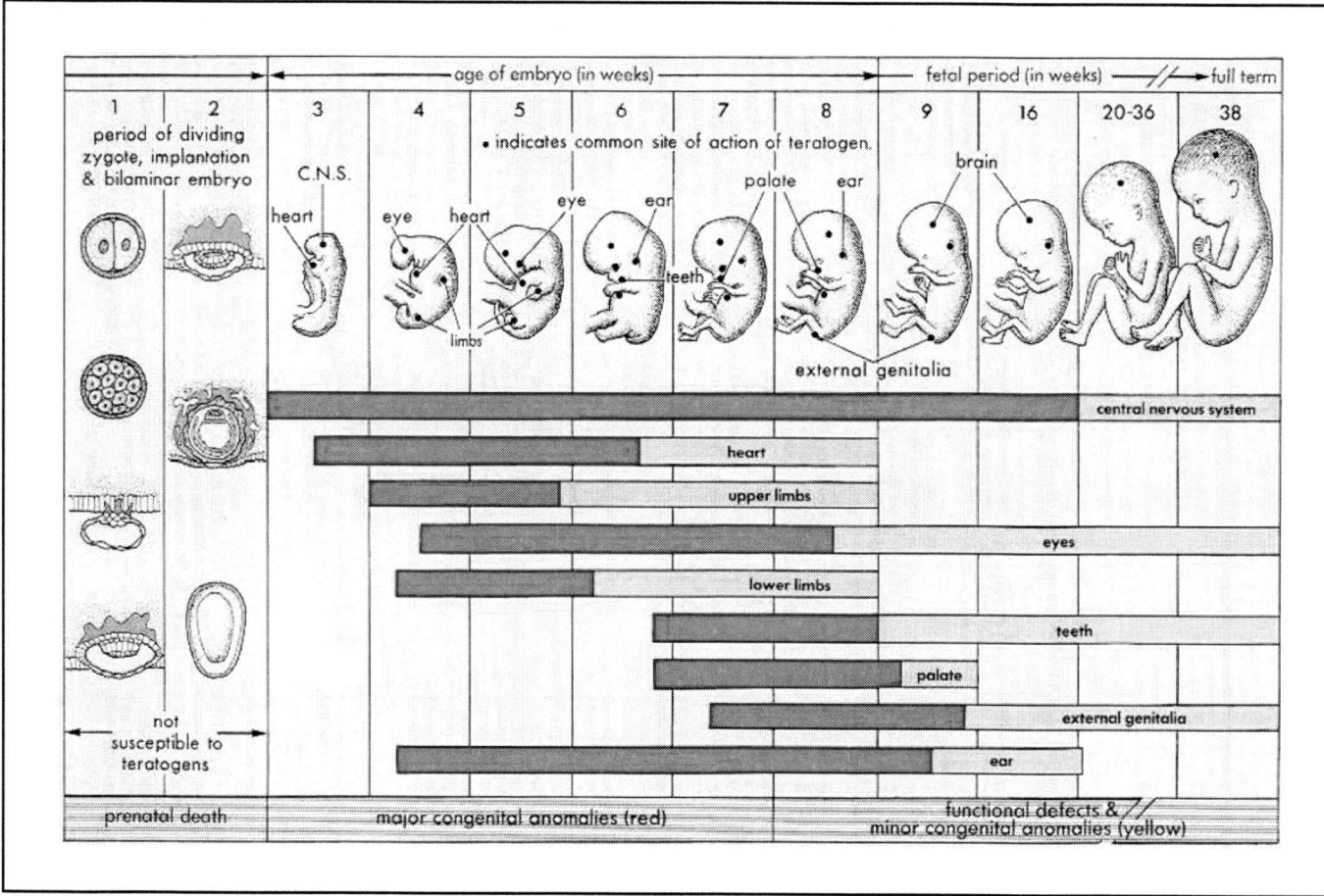

Figure 15.1 — Critical periods of human development. Dark bars indicate highly sensitive periods when teratogens may induce major anomalies, while lighter bars represent susceptible periods of lower sensitivity to teratogens.[7]

Table 15.1 — Key events in human development.[8]

Developmental Event	Gestation Day	Comment
Blastula formation	4–6	Fertilization and Predifferentiation
Implantation	6–7	"
Primitive Streak	16–18	Embryonic Stage (8-56)
Neural Plate	18–20	"
First Somite	20–21	Period of Organogenesis
Heart-first beats	22	"
Lower Limb Bud	29–30	"
Heart septation	46–47	"
Palate closure	56–58	"
Total Gestational Time	**267 days**	

several times *en route*. By post fertilization day 7, the embryo has reached the uterus and has developed a cavity called the blastocele and is now termed a blastocyst. On or about days 8 to 9, the blastocyst has implanted into the uterine wall.[9]

Formation of the placenta occurs by post fertilization day 10 or 11 and is a critical process in human development. The placenta anchors the developing embryo to the uterine wall and connects it to the maternal blood supply, now providing nutrients in the form of ions and metabolites and functioning as a mechanism for waste removal from the embryo. Important in toxicology, the maternal and fetal blood usually do not mix directly, but soluble molecules pass through a series of tissues embedded in the uterine wall that have arisen both from the mother and the embryo.[9]

By the end of the third week, the next major phase of development — gastrulation — has occurred. Gastrulation is the process by which cells of the embryo differentiate into the three primary germ cell layers: endoderm, mesoderm, and ectoderm.[9] During this phase, in a specific region along the posterior axis of the embryo, the primitive streak forms, a structure through which cells migrate to set up regions and fields where cells will continue to differentiate during gastrulation. Endoderm will give rise to the epithelium of the entire digestive tract, thyroid, and structures associated with the digestive tract. Mesoderm will give rise to cardiac, smooth, and skeletal muscle, fat, bone, and structures of the urogenital system. Ectoderm is the origin of, among other tissues, the central and peripheral nervous systems, skin, cornea and lens of the eye, epithelium that lines the mouth and the nasal cavities, epithelium of the pituitary and pineal gland, and several nerve clusters. The level of intricacy required for the control mechanisms regulating gastrulation and all phases of development cannot be overstated: the events are highly regulated by specific genes turned on and off at specific times, highly integrated intercellular interactions, and interactions between cells and the extracellular milieu.[9] Importantly, the signaling mechanisms regulating growth and death are the least understood elements of embryonic development in any organism.

The period of organogenesis begins with formation of the neural plate from ectoderm, around Post Fertilization Day 21 and continues through Day 56. The teratological consequences are great during this phase, as disruptions to the normal process may not be lethal to the conceptus, but could result in functional and structural impairment. Even within the phase of organogenesis, each developing structure has windows of susceptibility to teratogenic insult whereby exposure to a particular agent outside that window does not result in an adverse effect at any dose. For example, the limb reduction defects observed in humans exposed *in utero* to the sedative drug thalidomide are restricted to a 14 day period between the 21st and 33rd day of pregnancy. Within this window, administration of the drug from the 21st through the 31st days is associated most frequently with the arms affected, while later in the window of susceptibility development of the legs was primarily affected.[10]

While organs become present and recognizable over the period of organogenesis, the fine structure morphogenesis conferring organ functionality proceeds during the fetal period (Post Fertilization Days 56 through 267). Branching of the bronchial tree, neural outgrowth and synaptogenesis, and induction of tissue-specific enzymes are among the events of structural and biochemical maturation observed during the fetal period. In contrast to the period of organogenesis, exposure to potential teratogens during the fetal period generally results in impaired growth and functionality, some of which may not be apparent until much later in life.[11]

Much recent work has focused on the phenomenon of fetal programming. The concept of programming relates fetal adjustments made in response to adverse changes in the biological environment. While such adjustments may have been advantageous during fetal life, they have permanent consequences that may confer disease after birth.[12] Importantly, adverse or unfavorable changes in the fetal biological environment may be a result of maternal lifestyle, or may be a consequence of hormonal and nutritional conditions experienced by the fetus during key developmental periods. For example, in the "thrifty phenotype" hypothesis, genetic changes favoring the storage of metabolic energy become predominant in the fetus in response to episodes of maternal food restriction. These genetic changes may become fixed and, after birth, the expression pattern of these genes can alter insulin sensitivity and otherwise alter metabolic regulation.[13] Recent experiments and observations suggest that changes to the biological environment may even occur well before or after fetal life.[12] The key point is that even subtle adverse conditions, whether exogenous (i.e., exposure to xenobiotics through lifestyle or occupation) or endogenous (i.e., maternal food restriction or abundance) experienced by the fetus may have lasting functional consequences.

Basic Principles of Teratology

As discussed in the context of carcinogenesis, alterations in gene structure and expression sometimes result in altered function, and this is especially important in rapidly dividing cells where such changes can become fixed, potentially altering subsequent cellular, tissue, and organ functionality. The processes regulating development — both genetic and epigenetic — are susceptible to toxicant-induced alterations. Just as in carcinogenesis, cells may recover from such alterations with no net effect. Also, like the process of chemical carcinogenesis, exposure timing, dose, and interaction of xenobiotics with spatially and temporally susceptible targets are central principles of teratogenesis.

Exposure Timing and Stage of Developmental Susceptibility

The stage of embryogenesis during which exposure occurs is critical in determining which, if any, adverse effects will be observed (see Table 15.2). As discussed, teratogenic effects of administration of the drug thalidomide has a relatively narrow (i.e., approximately two weeks) window of temporal susceptibility. In contrast, the window of susceptibility for induction of mental retardation from ionizing radiation is about seven weeks (from the 8th to the 15th week).[3] During pre-implantation, toxicity generally results in embryolethality or has a minimal effect on growth, although some evidence suggests that structural and functional malformations may arise from exposures during this period.[3]

Directly related to the stage of structural susceptibility is a temporal window during which maternal, fetal, and placental physiological changes can influence pharmacokinetics and subsequent teratogenic effects of xenobiotics (see Table 15.3). In addition to pharmacokinetic processes altered by physiological

Table 15.2 — Susceptibility and effects vary with the stage of embryogenesis.

GD	Event	Potential Effects
0–8	Fertilization and predifferentiation	Death or no apparent effect
8–56	Embryonic stage; intensive differentiation, mobilization, organization and majority of organogenesis	Susceptibility to teratogenesis highest at this stage
56–267	Fetal stage; period of growth and functional maturation	Growth retardation and functional anomalies (vs. functional morphologic anomalies)

GD: Gestation Day

Table 15.3 — The effect of maternal physiologic alterations on pharmacokinetic parameters.[2]

Physiological Parameter	Pharmacokinetic Change
Gastrointestinal System	
Motility	↓ results in delayed absorption
Transit Time	↑ absorption of slowly absorbed xenobiotics
Respiratory System	
Tidal Volume	↑ Absorption, Elimination
Cardiovascular System	
Plasma Albumin Concentration	↑ concentration of unbound xenobiotic
Output	↑ Distribution
Peripheral Blood Flow	↑ Absorption
Uterine/Placental Blood Flow	↑ Distribution, Placental Transfer
Mammary Blood Flow	↑ Distribution, Excretion in Milk
Renal System	
Renal Blood Flow	↑ Excretion
Glomerular Filtration Rate	↑ Excretion

changes, expression of drug metabolizing enzymes has been demonstrated in the placenta, but the major site of bioactivation of xenobiotics is the maternal liver.[3] Likewise, transcripts of several P450s have been detected as early as Week 11 in human fetal liver.[14]

Transport of xenobiotics between the embryo and mother is controlled by the placenta. Differences in placental structure and function, both with regard to stage of development and between species, makes difficult the task of extrapolating from experimental animal exposures to drawing conclusions about exposure and teratogenesis in humans. However, most chemicals and drugs cross the placental barrier and, in general, crossing the placenta in one species results in the same capability in other species.[14]

Dose-Response

The dose-response relationship is also a critical feature of teratogenesis. With the possible exception of some mutagenic teratogens, teratogenic agents generally follow an s-shaped dose-response curve typical of other threshold toxicological phenomena.[3] The implication is that there is a threshold below which no teratogenic effect is observed and that both frequency and degree of deviant development increase as the dose increases from no effect to lethality. The basis for the threshold—as observed in other threshold phenomena in toxicology—includes mechanisms such as the restorative growth potential of the embryo, cellular mechanisms capable of accommodating toxicant insult, and maternal metabolic defenses (i.e., drug metabolizing enzymes). Generally, with regard to the severity and incidence of malformations, all exogenous teratogens studied appropriately exhibit a dose threshold during organogenesis.[3] Stated another way, for all exogenous teratogens studied thus far, there is some dose at which no effect will occur. As an example, a 1 mg dose of thalidomide administered anytime during any phase of pregnancy will not adversely affect the embryo, but higher doses during the critical windows of susceptibility will induce adverse effects.[3]

In the context of industrial hygiene practice, there are several important features to mention concerning the interpretation of teratogenic dose information from the scientific literature. First, it is important to note the differences between experimental teratogenesis studies in animals, where dose-response information may be reported in the context of maternal dose and/or fetal dose, and observational studies in humans, where the maternal dose-response relationship is nearly always reported. As such, consideration of the context of the reported teratogenic doses is highly warranted. Similarly, the question of interspecies extrapolation — a common challenge in the toxicological sciences — also exists in the case of teratogenic phenomenon. When comparing effects among different species, the temptation is to extrapolate from animal to human directly using some dose, usually reported in units of mg/kg body weight. Interspecies extrapolation of dose is most correctly performed in conjunction with pharmacokinetic profiles and studies of susceptibility. The history of the study of thalidomide provides an excellent example of the importance of considering variability in species susceptibility, in that rat and mouse embryos were found to be relatively insensitive to the teratogenic effects of thalidomide, while the rabbit, monkey, and human models were sensitive.[15] So, experimental models and humans exposed in the same relative developmental windows exhibited very different dose-response data. In contrast, exposures to ionizing radiation reported in rads or Sieverts (Sv) are comparable in most mammalian species.[16]

General Mechanisms of Teratogenesis

Mechanisms of teratogenesis can be divided generally into genetic (e.g., altered nucleic acid integrity or function, mutations), physiologic (e.g., diminished supplies of precursors or substrates, decreased energy supply, altered membrane characteristics), and epigenetic (e.g., cell cycle dysregulation, DNA methylation, intercellular communication, apoptosis) mechanisms. These categories arguably have both semantic and biological overlap, but in general convey the relationship between the extracellular environment and the epigenetic linkages between these extracellular signals and gene regulation, whether transcriptional, translational, or post-translational. Despite these potential mechanisms and an ever-growing understanding of the events regulating human development, specific molecular targets for all human teratogens remain elusive, including those for the most thoroughly studied of teratogens, thalidomide and ethanol.[15,17]

Mutagenic events and consequent genetic toxicities can also induce teratogenesis in experimental animal models and in humans. As discussed in Chapter 13, ("Genetic Toxicology"), mutagenesis is the process of producing heritable changes in the genetic material that involves alterations in the message, structure, or quantity of DNA. Structural changes include events such as base substitutions, deletions, and additions; and chromosomal rearrangements like deletions, translocations, and inversions. Like the process of teratogenesis itself, mutagenesis also must occur through windows of susceptibility, which are limited to specific DNA-associated processes like replication, repair, and other features that otherwise leave DNA vulnerable to attack by exogenous or endogenous chemical or physical factors. An excellent compilation of the genetic toxicities of known human teratogens was written by Bishop in 1997.[15]

Epigenetic mechanisms may include direct regulation of gene function (e.g., DNA methylation, activity of transcription factors), regulation of cellular differentiation through alteration of post-transcriptional, translational, or post-translational events, and regulation of the distribution and function of proteins. The lines distinguishing genetic from epigenetic events in teratogenesis become blurred, as agents can contribute to the incidence of mutations through epigenetic activity. For example, the nonsteroidal synthetic estrogen diethylstilbestrol (DES) shows some evidence of both mutagenic and epigenetic activity.[15]

Interestingly, embryogenesis and carcinogenesis share many molecular links, with at least some of the genes, intercellular interactions, and regulatory factors critical for normal embryogenesis also playing a role in tumor development, either as properly functioning genes or as factors modified by interaction with chemical and physical agents. In addition to signals for cells to divide or differentiate, equally important are signaling events that drive specific cells to die at specific times. The importance of apoptosis in carcinogenesis is discussed in Chapter 14, "Carcinogenesis", and the process, regulated largely by the same set of genes, is equally important in human development. For example, apoptosis helps shape the developing embryo by controlling the spacing in the middle ear and is responsible for the death of skin cells between fingers and toes. At least one model of teratogenesis by ethanol involves dysregulated apoptosis.[18]

Environmental Chemicals Known to be Teratogenic

Tables 15.4 and 15.5 list physical and chemical agents known to be teratogenic or potentially teratogenic in humans. Shepard lists more than 3,000 agents in his catalog, and fewer than half produce congenital anomalies in experimental animal models. However, only about 40 are known to cause developmental defects in humans.[8] The important point is that far more is known about experimental teratology than about the impact of chemical and physical agents on human development. While many chemical, physical, and biological agents and events are known as *potential* teratogens, the basic principles discussed above — timing of exposure with regard to developmental stage, dose, and pharmacokinetic factors — as well as maternal and fetal genetic predisposition, must be considered when evaluating whether an agent or condition is teratogenic.

Table 15.4 — Teratogenic agents in human beings.[8]

Radiation	*Drugs*
Atomic weapons	Aminopterin and
Radioiodine	methylaminopterin
Therapeutic	Androgenic hormones
	Busulfan
Infections	Captopril
Cytomegalovirus	Cocaine
Herpes simplex virus 1 and 2	Coumarin anticoagulants
Parvovirus B-19	Diethylstilbestrol
Rubella virus	Diphenylhydantoin
Syphilis	Enalapril
Toxoplasmosis	Etretinate
Varicella virus	Fluconazole, high doses
Venezuelan equine	Iodides and goiter
encephalitis virus	Lithium
	Methylene blue via intraamniotic
Maternal and Metabolic Imbalance	injection
Alcoholism	Methimazole
Amniocentesis, early	Misoprostol
Chorionic villus sampling	Penicillamine
(before day 60)	1, 3-cis-Retinoic acid
Cretenism, endemic	Tetracyclines
Diabetes	Thalidomide
Folic acid deficiency	Trimethadione
Hyperthermia	Valproic Acid
Myasthenia gravis	
Phenylketonuria	*Environmental Chemicals*
Rheumatic disease and	Toluene abuse
congenital heart	Mercury, organic
block	Cigarette smoking
Sjorgren's syndrome	Polychlorinated biphenyls
Virilizing tumors	

Table 15.5 — Possible and unlikely teratogens.[8]

Possible Teratogens	*Unlikely Teratogens*
Binge drinking	Agent Orange
Carbamazepine	Anesthetics
Colchicine	Aspartame
Disulfiram	Aspirin
Ergotamine	Bendectin
Glucocorticoids	Illicit drugs (marijuana, LSD)
High Vitamin A	Metronidazole (Flagyl)
Lead	Oral contraceptives
Primidone	Progesterone (Hydroxy- and
Quinine, suicidal doses	Medroxy-)
Streptomycin	Rubella vaccine
Zidivudine (AZT)	Spermicides
Zinc deficiency	Video display terminals and
	electromagnetic waves
	Ultrasound

Teratogenesis Case Study: Toluene

The organic solvent toluene (methylbenzene) is a benzene derivative widely used in industrial environments and is also found in many household products. While dermal and ingestion exposure is possible, inhalation is the most common route of human exposure. Occupational environments in which chronic low-level or high-level (in the case of industrial accidents) exposure might occur include those involved in the production and manufacture of various industrial chemicals like benzene, toluene diisocyanate, phenol, benzoic acid, toluene sulfates, nitrotoluene, saccharine, and styrene. In addition, intentional exposure to vapors through sniffing or "huffing" paints, adhesives, and fuels is a popular form of substance abuse. The current OSHA Permissible Exposure Limit (PEL), NIOSH Recommended Exposure Limit (REL), and ACGIH Threshold Limit Value (TLV®) are set at 100 ppm. The OSHA limit is based on hepatotoxic and nervous system effects, and the NIOSH limit is based on CNS depression associated with toluene exposure.[19] A sense of euphoria is not achieved until exposures reach around 500 ppm.[20]

Toluene is a lipid soluble compound and readily crosses the placenta, having been recovered in the fetal compartment of documented exposed humans and experimental animal models. Studies of the teratogenic effects of toluene in rodent models (mouse, rat) ranging in concentration from 100 to 2,000 ppm for multiple exposure times and covering the period of skeletal formation and organogenesis resulted in growth and skeletal retardation (even at lower doses) and other anomalies at the high end of the dose regimen.[21] Intermittent exposures that might mimic occupational conditions produced growth and skeletal retardation only at the highest levels, comparable to those experienced by chronic abusers (>2000 ppm).[22]

Studies linking human occupational exposures to teratogenesis are confounded by concomitant exposure to other substances, making teratogenic outcomes difficult to clearly interpret. As such, much of the information on toluene teratogenesis comes from studies in chronic solvent abusers. Even among this group, co-exposure, especially to alcohol, is often a confounding factor. In both groups, a lack of information concerning the exposure levels, gestational timing, and exposure durations make interpretation even more complex and uncertain. Among those studies that have managed to reduce confounding factors or in which exposure parameters are clear, an increase in non-specific malformations has been observed in offspring of chronic solvent abusers (exposures up to 12,000 ppm).[23] In addition to the intrauterine growth retardation observed in animals, a recognizable pattern of craniofacial anomalies has been described among the offspring of this group of exposed individuals.[21]

As exemplified in other toxicological processes, gene polymorphisms in xenobiotic metabolism are a determinant of susceptibility to toxicant induced injury and play a significant role in teratogenic processes. Toluene is metabolized by alcohol dehydrogenase and aldehyde dehydrogenase (ALDH) to benzoic acid and subsequently to the hydrophilic compound, hippuric acid.[23] The prevalence of *ALDH2* polymorphisms among certain subgroups of Japanese and North Americans can be as high as fifty percent. *ALDH2* deficiency results in alcohol intolerance and in lower rates of toluene metabolism, increasing the risk of toluene teratogenicity even at lower levels of exposure in at-risk individuals.[24]

Conclusions

Multiple factors determine whether exposure to a potential teratogen will result in an adverse outcome. For an agent to be teratogenic, exposure must occur during periods of development when the target for that agent is most susceptible to insult. Likewise, an adequate dose of the agent must reach the target during this window of susceptibility. Upon reaching the target, potential teratogens can induce damage through genetic, physiologic, and/or epigenetic mechanisms. Teratogenesis and carcinogenesis share many molecular links, including the fact that many teratogens and carcinogens target some of the same molecular targets, whether through epigenetic or mutagenic (or both) mechanisms. Whereas many of the agents causally associated with cancer are known, the cause of most teratogenic events are not known, although dose, exposure timing, and stage of developmental susceptibility during pregnancy are critical determinants of teratogenesis. Of the more than 3000 agents that have been investigated for teratogenic potential, fewer than 50 are known to cause developmental defects in humans. Despite considerable work in understanding the details underlying key events in human development, reasons for adverse pregnancy outcomes are still largely unknown.

References

1. **Brent, R.L.:** Medicolegal aspects of teratology. *J. Pediatr.* 71:288–298 (1967).
2. **Rogers, J.M. and R. Kavlock:** Developmental Toxicology. In *Casarett and Doull's Toxicology: The Basic Science of Poisons,* 6th ed., C.D. Klaassen, (ed.). New York: McGraw-Hill, 2001.
3. **Brent, R.L.:** Environmental causes of human congenital malformations: The pediatrician's role in dealing with these complex clinical problems caused by a multiplicity of environmental and genetic factors. *Pediatrics* 113:957–968 (2004).
4. **Brent, R.L. and D. Beckman:** Environmental teratogens. *Bull. N.Y. Acad. Med.* 66:123–163 (1990).
5. **Jones, J.M. and J. Thomson:** Human embryonic stem cell technology. *Semin. Reprod. Med.* 18:219–223 (2000).
6. **Edwards, R.G.:** Genetics, epigenetics and gene silencing in differentiating mammalian embryos. *Reprod. Biomed.Online* 13:732–753 (2006).
7. **Moore, K.L. and T.V.N Persaud:** *The Developing Human: Clinically Oriented Embryology,* 6th ed. Philadelphia: W.B. Saunders, 1998.

8. **Shepard, T.H.:** *Catalog of Teratogenic Agents*, 10th ed. Baltimore: The Johns Hopkins University Press, 2001.
9. **Gilbert, S.F.:** *Developmental Biology.* Sunderland, MA: Sinauer Associates, 2000.
10. **Brent, R.L. and L. Holmes:** Clinical and basic science lessons from the thalidomide tragedy: what have we learned about the causes of limb defects? *Teratology 38*:241–251 (1988).
11. **Auroux, M.:** Behavioral Teratogenesis: An extension to the teratogenesis of functions. *Biol. Neonate 71*:137–147 (1997).
12. **Schwartz, J. and J. Morrison:** Impact and mechanisms of fetal physiological programming. *Am. J. Physiol. Regul. Integr. Comp. Physiol. 288*:R11–R15 (2005).
13. **Hales, C.N., and D. Barker:** The thrifty phenotype hypothesis. *Br. Med. Bull. 60*:5–20 (2001).
14. **Hakkola, J., O. Pelkonen, M. Pasanen, and H. Raunio:** Xenobiotic-metabolizing cytochrome P450 enzymes in the human feto-placental unit: role in intrauterine toxicity. *Crit. Rev. Toxicol. 28*:35–72 (1998).
15. **Bishop, J.B., K. Witt, and R. Sloane, R.A.:** Genetic toxicities of human teratogens. *Mutat. Res. 396*:9–43 (1997).
16. **Brent, R.L.:** Utilization of developmental basic science principles in the evaluation of reproductive risks from pre- and post-conception environmental radiation exposures. *Teratology 59*:182–204 (1999).
17. **Stephens, T.D., C. Bunde, and B. Fillmore:** Mechanism of action in thalidomide teratogenesis. *Biochem. Pharmacol. 59*:1489–1499 (2000).
18. **Sulik, K.:** Genesis of alcohol-induced craniofacial dysmorphism. *Exp. Biol. Med. 230*:366–375 (2005).
19. **Occupational Safety and Health Administration (OSHA):** *Occupational Safety and Health Guideline for Toluene.* [Standard] Washington, D.C.: OSHA, 1996.
20. **Ron, M.A.:** Volatile substance abuse: a review of possible long-term neurological, intellectual, and psychiatric sequelae. *Br. J. Psychiatry 148*:235–246 (1986).
21. **Wilkins-Haug, L.:** Teratogen update: toluene. *Teratology 55*:145–151 (1997).
22. **Ono, A.K., K. Sekita, A. Ohno et al:** Reproductive and developmental toxicity studies of toluene. I. Teratogenicity study of inhalation exposure in pregnant rats. *J. Toxicol. Sci. 20*:109–134 (1995).
23. **Toutant, C. and S. Lippman:** Fetal solvents syndrome. *Lancet 1*:1356 (1979).
24. **Kawamoto, T., K. Matsuno, Y. Kodama, K. Murata, and S. Matsuda:** ALDH2 polymorphism and biological monitoring of toluene. *Arch. Environ. Health 49*:332–336 (1994).

Section 3

Chemical Group Toxicology

Chapter 16

Toxicology of Organic Solvents

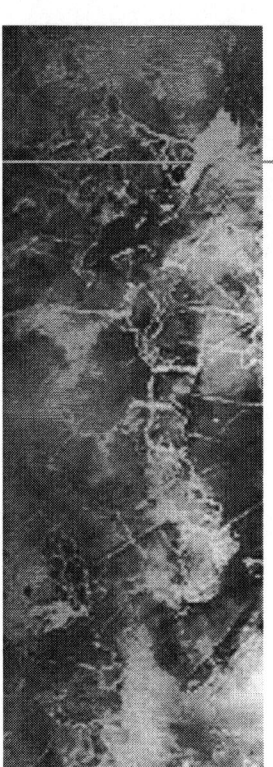

Outcome Competencies

Mastery of the material in this chapter will provide the industrial hygienist with a working knowledge of toxicologically relevant solvent exposure routes, the relationship between occupational exposure limits and toxicology, the importance of biotransformation in uneventful elimination of foreign compounds from the body, as well as in production of problematic metabolites.

The reader will have an understanding of the scope of generally expected toxicological responses to organic solvents, and will have detailed knowledge on specific and unique responses from exposure to methyl-*n*-butyl ketone, n-hexane, benzene, and carbon disulfide. In the cases of these specific toxicological responses, the reader will have a general understanding of the underlying biochemical mechanisms that lead to the unique negative outcomes discussed.

Prerequisite Knowledge

The reader should have solid experience as a practicing industrial hygienist, and a basic understanding of biology and chemistry.

Key Terms

Aerosol, alkane, alkene, aplastic anemia, aromaticity, axonal neuropathy, erythema, gas, hepatomegaly radical, ketone, K_{ow}, leukemia, lipid peroxidation, lipophilic, lymphoma, metaplasia, narcosis, Painter's Disease, partition coefficient, solvent, $t_{1/2}$, vapor, vapor hazard index, vapor hazard ratio, viscose rayon

Key Topics

1. Identification of Xenobiotic & Exposure Route
2. Dose (or Concentration)
3. Distribution, Local, and Systemic Toxicity
4. The Dose-Response Relationship
   – Responses to Organic Solvent Exposure
5. Biotransformation and Elimination
   – Biotransformation as a pathway to increased xenobiotic elimination
   – Biotransformation gone awry
   – Elimination
6. Biological Monitoring as a Surrogate for Measurement of Absorbed Dose
7. Use of the Vapor Hazard Ratio for Preliminary Evaluation of Vapor Exposure Hazards
8. Unique Solvent Exposure Effects
   – Benzene
   – N-Hexane and Methyl n-Butyl Ketone
   – Carbon Disulfide

Chapter 16

Toxicology of Organic Solvents

By Philip A. Smith, PhD, MPH, CIH

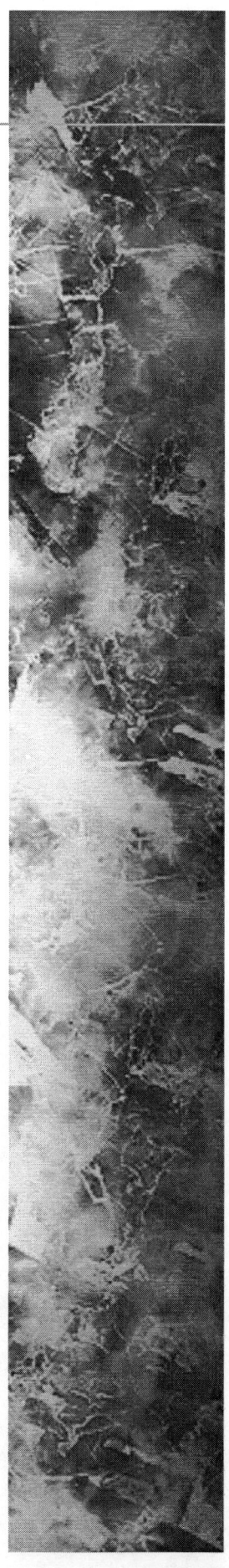

Introduction

A solvent has been defined as "a substance capable of dissolving another substance (solute) to form a uniformly dispersed mixture (solution) at the molecular or ionic size level."[1] Among the important characteristics of a solvent, one of the more fundamental is whether or not it can appreciably mix with water. To the life scientist, water is probably the most important solvent, with unique properties that make it essential to life. Among its other notable properties, water, due to its ability to participate in hydrogen bonding, will readily dissolve a wide range of ions and polar compounds important to biological systems, and will also absorb and release large amounts of heat with relatively little change in temperature.

The saying "like dissolves like" is well understood to anyone who has observed the behavior of salad dressing composed of oil and water fractions, and applies equally to organic (carbon-containing) solvents. Many organic solvent compounds are miscible only in other organic solvents, and give two distinct phases when added to water, while "small molecule" organic solvents capable of participation in hydrogen bonding, such as acetone, and methanol, are miscible in water as well. Representative classes of organic solvents and physical property information, including water solubility, are provided for representative members of each class in Table 16.1.

In general, organic solvents are used where the solvating properties of a selected liquid or mixture of liquids are needed. It is because of their low cost, ready availability, and the variety of properties found among the range of available organic solvents that they are useful in many applications and are heavily used in worldwide industry. Organic solvents are commonly used in simple dip tanks of various sizes (Figure 16.1), or vapor phase degreaser systems for parts cleaning. Organic solvent exposures can arise during many other work-related processes or operations, including the manufacture, mixing, and application of paints and other coatings (Figure 16.2), dry cleaning of clothing, refinery operations, work related to transportation of solvent products by various means, electronics manufacturing and repair, gluing of various articles, stripping of paint and other coatings, surface or spot cleaning, and the delivery of dissolved materials such as pesticides. A frequently useful characteristic of the lighter solvents is that they readily vaporize following use which is beneficial when the presence of the solvent would be undesirable in a finished product.

As described elsewhere in this volume, the discipline of toxicology describes the potential for xenobiotic (foreign) compounds to cause harm or adverse health effects to biological systems. With reference to a given organism, the term "xenobiotic" includes all compounds which are foreign, and these can include both man-made and naturally-occurring chemicals. In addition to understanding the intricacies of exposure, and evaluation and control of exposures, an industrial hygienist's effectiveness also depends upon having a working understanding of the potential for specific xenobiotic compounds or mixtures to cause harm. The regulatory and non-regulatory standards against which occupational exposures are measured are, or should be, based upon the potential for harm that such exposures can produce to a worker exposed to those levels for periods of a full workday, day after day. This

Table 16.1 — Important physical properties for a variety of organic solvents.

Solvent	molecular weight (g/mol)	density (g/mL)	boiling point (°C)	dipole moment (debye)	k_{OW}	water solubility (g/L)	vapor pressure (kPa)	saturation vapor concentration (ppm, v/v)
CS_2	76.14	a,e1.263	a46	a0	d1.94	h,f1.18	a,f48.2	475,697
Benzene	78.11	a,e0.877	a80.0	a0	c2.13	b,f1.78	a,f12.7	125,339
Toluene	92.14	a,e0.867	a110.6	a0.375	c2.73	b,f0.515	a,f3.79	37,404
g o-Xylene	106.17	a,h0.880	a144.5	a0.64	c3.12	b,f0.175	a,f0.880	8,685
n-Pentane	72.15	a,e0.626	a36.0	a0	c3.39	b,f0.0385	a,f68.3	674,069
n-Hexane	86.18	a,f0.655	a68.7	a0	c3.90	b,f0.0095	a,f20.2	199,358
n-Heptane	100.20	a,e0.684	a98.5	a0	c4.66	b,f0.00293	a,f6.09	60,104
n-Octane	86.18	a,f0.699	a125.6	a0	c5.18	b,f0.00066	a,f1.86	18,357
n-Nonane	128.26	a,e0.718	a150.8	a0	c5.45		a,f0.570	5,625
cyclohexane	120.19	a,e0.862	a80.7	a0	c3.44	b,f0.0055	a,f13.0	128,300
CCl_2	84.93	a,e1.327	a40	a1.60	c1.25	h,f0.793	a,f58.2	574,389
CCl_4	153.82	a,e1.594	a76.8	a0	c2.83	h,f0.0130	a,f15.2	150,012
Acetone	58.08	a,e0.790	a56.0	a2.88			a,f30.8	303,972
Methyl isobutyl ketone	100.16	a,e0.798	a116.5	a3.11			a,f2.64	26,055
Methyl n-butyl ketone	100.16	a,e0.811	a127.6	a,i2.7			a,f1.54	15,131

a reference 69
b reference 70
c reference 71, experimentally measured
d reference 72, experimentally measured
e measured at 20 °C
f measured at 25 °C
g two additional xylene isomers exist
h measured at 10 °C
i non-gas phase measurement

Figure 16.1 — Dip tank used for part cleaning. This tank is equipped with hinged cover and local exhaust ventilation for contaminant control.

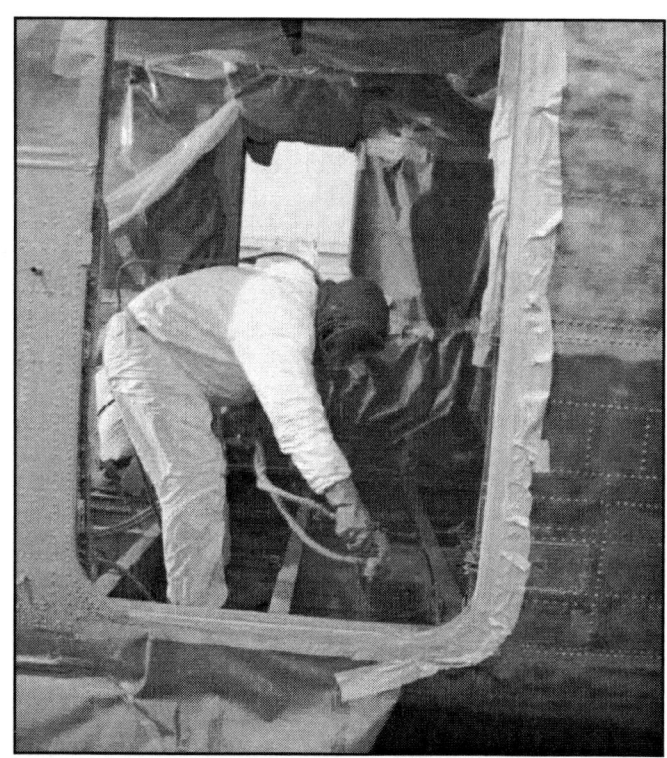

Figure 16.2 — Spray painting rotary wing aircraft.

concept is clearly stated in the introduction section of the Threshold Limit Values (TLV®) for Chemical Substances in the Work Environment, published by the American Conference of Governmental Industrial Hygienists: "Threshold Limit Values® refer to airborne concentrations of chemical substances and represent conditions under which it is believed that *nearly* all workers may be repeatedly exposed, day after day, over a working lifetime, without adverse health effects."[2] Simply stated, well thought out workplace exposure standards for chemicals must account for known adverse health effects that could result from chemical exposures, and thus are based upon knowledge derived from the field of toxicology.

As opposed to occupational toxicology, which focuses on worker exposures and health effects, the environmental toxicologist works in a separate but closely related discipline. The environmental toxicologist is typically concerned with anthropogenic (man-made or synthetic) xenobiotics as contaminants of air, soil, water, and food, and their corresponding health effects upon members of the general population, often exposed to such foreign chemicals at vanishingly low levels. These concerns will not be addressed here, but this chapter will instead focus specifically on discussing the toxicology of organic solvents as encountered with industrial or workplace exposures, and within the context of the fundamental assessment that a toxicologist must address. This assessment involves

1. Identification of the xenobiotic in question and its exposure route,
2. The absorbed dose, or the exposure concentration that will produce an absorbed dose,
3. The distribution and local or systemic toxicity of the xenobiotic,
4. The relationship between the observed toxicity (response) and dose, usually called "the dose-response relationship", and
5. the metabolism (biotransformation) and elimination of the xenobiotic and its metabolites.

In this chapter, these areas will be examined as they relate to organic solvents. Also, the interface between the toxicology of organic solvents and other industrial hygiene concepts such as biological exposure indices, and the idea of the vapor hazard ratio will be touched upon. Finally, compound-specific toxicological responses will be discussed for four organic solvents with fairly unique and substantially negative occupational health effects. Due to the unusual nature of the underlying toxicology for these compounds, occupational health professionals should pay special attention to them. The large number of unique organic solvents used in occupational settings, the range of their physical properties, and the possibility that exposure to each may produce unique health effects guarantees that this discussion will just scratch the surface of the topic. In spite of the special focus on several organic solvent compounds with "unique" responses, the industrial hygienist should not lose sight of the more typical responses observed with exposure to the vast number of other organic solvent compounds for which

potential occupational exposures exist. The hygienist is well-advised to continually follow developments as additional health effects or new solvent compounds of concern are uncovered.

Toxicology-Identification of Xenobiotic & Exposure Route

When distilled to simplicity, the study of toxicology is a search for knowledge that both describes and explains harmful effects to biological systems caused by exposures to foreign compounds or agents. The toxicologist must understand several variables when dealing with the effect of any xenobiotic compound on human health. The first fundamental question that must be answered in dealing with a chemical exposure by both the toxicologist and by the industrial hygienist is "what is the chemical?" We often assume that we know the answer to this question, yet in many instances poorly-defined mixtures of organic solvents may be present in the workplace. Hook et al. provide an example where ethylbenzene, propylbenzene, and at least three additional substituted benzene solvents were present at high proportions in a widely used marine paint mixture. The material safety data sheet (MSDS) for this paint did not mention the presence of the specific compounds, nor even their general class (substituted benzene compounds), but identified them only by the trade name "solvent 100." Analysis by gas chromatography with mass spectrometry detection (GC-MS) was used to identify the actual compounds present.[3] In this case, without further work to answer the question "what is the chemical?" an industrial hygienist relying only on MSDS data would not know to assess worker exposures to the substituted benzene compounds, and an incomplete exposure assessment would result. With the widespread availability of GC-MS instrumentation in most industrial hygiene laboratories, this need not be the case.

The presence of unsuspected or unknown organic solvent compounds can be readily explored from samples of either bulk liquids or vapors captured during a sampling event. Organic solvents thus sampled are good subjects for GC-MS analysis, owing to their general inherent volatility (a helpful characteristic for any GC analysis). Other spectrometric methods can also prove useful for samples that are relatively pure, including nuclear magnetic resonance and infrared spectrometry. While the full range of tools available to the analytical chemist can be brought to bear in identifying xenobiotics to which exposures may occur, the ability of the GC-MS system to separate and identify a large number of even trace level compounds in a sample (down to about nanogram levels in a single GC-MS analysis run), and the widespread availability of reliable GC-MS instruments in industrial hygiene laboratories make this method the most likely to be used. Over the years, a trend has emerged towards less expensive yet more capable bench top MS instrumentation and improved capillary column technology which have made this identification method cheaper and easier to use, and it is now rather commonplace. In industrial settings where large amounts of a solvent or solvent mixture are used, or where frequent human exposures are expected to a given solvent, GC-MS analysis of bulk material or headspace samples of vapors should be carefully considered to obtain important identity information about the actual solvents present.

As this tool should be considered for use in situations where an industrial hygienist must correctly assess exposures to complicated organic solvent mixtures and can also be very helpful to the toxicologist, a brief description of electron impact GC-MS (EI-GC-MS) analysis is provided. In EI-GC-MS, a mixture of chemicals is introduced into a heated injector port on the GC-MS instrument, and the mixture components move with a carrier gas flow along the capillary GC column for separation into discrete bands as different molecules interact uniquely with the thin film coating the inside of the column. It is desired that by the time analytes elute into the MS detector, discrete bands of molecules that physically occupy different sections of the column at a given time will contain only molecules of a single compound. The mass spectrometer (MS) accepts the GC column effluent, ionizes the intact molecules (which then tend to fragment), separates the ions of various masses thus produced according to mass/charge (m/z) ratio, and provides two pieces of information: a trace of total ion current at the MS detector over time, and a mass spectrum at any given time on the trace that is based upon the m/z ratios and the relative abundances of the various ions observed in the mass range scanned. The trace of total ion current gives a two-dimensional chromatogram with signal intensity plotted with the y-axis against column retention time on the x-axis. In a chromatogram, the individual compounds that were separated into discrete bands on the GC column are graphically represented as peaks with a characteristic and reproducible retention time. When available alone, the mass spectrum for a peak provides some information on the structure of the compound analyzed, but the combined mass spectrum for a peak, along with its GC retention time can be used to make a definitive identification based on comparison of both these characteristics to those of known standards. The relative certainty of the resulting identifications produced by EI-GC-MS can greatly lessen the natural skepticism that ought to exist in the mind of the industrial hygienist, and guide industrial hygiene sampling and exposure assessment efforts.

Assuming that the identity of the xenobiotic compound, or compounds (in the frequent cases where mixtures are present) is known, the question of exposure route should next be asked by both the toxicologist and the industrial hygienist. It is the solvent's physical properties, and how it is used in the workplace that will determine its potential exposure routes, and the exposure routes combined with the physical characteristics of a xenobiotic then determine whether, and to what degree it is absorbed across membranes such as are present in skin, or the membranes lining the respiratory and gastrointestinal (GI) tracts.

The experienced industrial hygienist has likely encountered the three distinct physical classes of air contaminants in the workplace: aerosols, gases, and vapors. Many heavily used organic solvents give rise to vapors, which constitute one of the more interesting and diverse classes of air contaminants. Vapors are produced when molecules from a liquid or solid that exists as such at normal pressure and temperature conditions, escape to the gas phase. In cases where a solvent is sprayed or agitated with enough energy to disperse liquid droplets into the air, a solvent aerosol may be produced. The liquid solvent aerosol may be deposited on external surfaces of skin and clothing, and also may be inhaled and deposited in airway passages. Also, the relatively large surface area of finely divided solvent aerosol droplets can lead to an increased rate of evaporation and higher vapor concentrations compared to situations where an equal volume of undisturbed liquid solvent with much less combined surface area evaporates from a vessel.

Two primary occupational exposure routes thus routinely exist for the organic solvents: direct exposure from contact of the liquid with skin or other body surfaces, and exposure of the external body and pulmonary surface area to the same compounds dispersed into the gas phase. The more obviously visible form is that of a liquid, but the corresponding vapors resulting from evaporation of a liquid solvent can result in airborne concentrations that are quite high, theoretically up to the concentration of the saturation vapor pressure for the compound in question. Vapor pressures and corresponding saturation air concentrations for some typical solvents are provided in Table 16.1. The relatively large surface area of the lungs, the constant dynamic introduction of contaminated air through the process of breathing, the thin layer of highly perfused cells lining the alveolar regions of the lungs (facilitating rapid transfer of O_2 and CO_2 between blood and the gas phase) make the pulmonary exposure route highly significant for absorption of the various additional gases and vapors that happen to be present in the air. Typical comparisons discussed in various toxicology texts between skin and pulmonary surface areas give rise to values such as 140 m^2 for the gas exchange regions of the lung[4] (about twice the area as that of a tennis court), and 1.5 to 2 m^2 for the external dermal surfaces.[5]

A simple example of "exposure route" factors that must be considered during an industrial hygiene evaluation is often found in small repair shops where a scaled down variation of the industrial dip tank is used for intermittent brush cleaning of parts (Figure 16.3). Assuming the use of the same solvent in a large parts-cleaning system (Figure 16.1) the scale of the potential vapor exposure hazard might be expected to be correspondingly greater in a room filled with bigger dip tanks having a much larger combined liquid surface area from which evaporation may occur. However, the actual exposure profile is unlikely to scale up in the same way because if present, a well-designed and operational local exhaust ventilation system can be expected to control the vapor hazard from a large batch process where baskets of parts are mechanically lowered and raised into and out of dip tanks. In contrast, manual cleaning in the small scale operation by definition will involve a worker close to, or even in contact with the liquid being used to clean the parts. Skin contact with liquid solvent allows for the possibility of dermatitis -referred to as "the most frequently reported occupational disease."[6] In the smaller scale setting, pulmonary exposure to solvent vapors would also be relatively uncontrolled, an important

Figure 16.3 — Small-scale solvent part washer used for hand cleaning.

factor for solvents with high vapor pressure and/or low airborne occupational exposure limits (OELs). This example demonstrates the inherent connection between principles of toxicology for organic solvents in general and common industrial hygiene practice. A correct exposure evaluation must consider a xenobiotic compound's exposure route, which by itself is also a fundamental question that a toxicologist must address in predicting or studying health effects from chemical exposures.

Toxicology–Dose (or Concentration)

The absorbed dose is of critical importance to the toxicologist, so much so that the concept of dose has come to define the central tenet of toxicology as stated by Paracelsus, a sixteenth century physician credited with the following insight[7]:

> "All substances are poisons; there is none which is not a poison. The right dose differentiates a poison from a remedy."

In other words, the dose makes the poison.

Absorbed dose is defined as the amount (usually mass) of xenobiotic that crosses a biological membrane at some point and thus enters the internal compartments of a biological system. Besides the pulmonary and dermal exposure routes that are important for organic solvents under usual workplace conditions, toxicologists understand that exposures may occur via oral, ocular, and other routes as well. Even in the case of oral ingestion, a xenobiotic compound is not actually absorbed across biological membranes unless and until it encounters favorable conditions at some point in the GI tract. Numerous examples may be found of compounds that are not significantly absorbed via this exposure route, and these may be essentially passed through the tract with little or no significant effect on the biological organism.

As will be described in greater detail, following exposure via a given route, a xenobiotic solvent may distribute into various internal compartments according to its physical properties. The time course and proportionality of this distribution can be described by mathematical models, and predictable levels of the compound or its metabolites will accumulate at target sites within the body where interference with normal physiological properties can occur if the target site concentration is sufficient. The result is described as a toxic response, or simply as "toxicity."

Along with knowledge of the exposure route, knowledge of the target tissue and absorbed dose are the important variables in studying and predicting toxicity, and not merely the amount of chemical compound to which one is exposed: dose is not equivalent to exposure. Up to this point in our brief review of toxicological principles, the questions asked by the industrial hygienist and the toxicologist have closely mirrored one another, but on the question of dose they diverge somewhat. This is because a traditional OEL for an organic solvent will be founded upon an acceptable xenobiotic airborne exposure concentration, and not on dose. In animal toxicology studies the amount of compound administered can be carefully controlled, and the process of absorption can be bypassed using injection techniques to allow a robust dose estimate. The industrial hygienist has no way to directly measure absorbed dose of an organic solvent. Nevertheless, through knowledge of likely occupational exposure routes, typical rates of xenobiotic uptake, distribution kinetics within the body, and metabolism and elimination rates of xenobiotic material, measurable air concentrations can be related to undesirable health effects that could more easily be predicted if we could actually measure absorbed dose.

Toxicology-Distribution, Local, and Systemic Toxicity

Once entry is gained to an organism's internal environment, the travels of xenobiotic molecules inside the body are collectively termed "distribution." Distribution of a xenobiotic is dictated by physical properties such as fugacity, lipid solubility, and perfusion and blood flow characteristics of specific tissues. The term "fugacity" refers to the flux or movement tendency of a compound in a multiphase system, and the k_{ow} is a fundamentally important physical property constant that provides an estimate of a compound's lipid solubility. The k_{ow} term is defined as the *n*-octanol/water partition coefficient which is a simple ratio of the amounts of a compound present in the respective phases when the chemical of interest is mixed in a 2-phase octanol/water system and agitated until equilibrium is established. The relative amounts of a compound that end up in each of these phases allows the toxicologist and other health scientists to predict where in the body a compound will tend to accumulate. This in turn affects the general mechanism followed, and the overall duration of xenobiotic elimination. The more lipid soluble compounds partition into the octanol phase, and thus compounds with larger k_{ow} values will tend to partition to fatty tissues in the body, and in general are eliminated less rapidly compared to more water soluble compounds (Table 16.1). Since the k_{ow} values for solvents can range over many orders of magnitude, it is common practice to list or report log k_{ow} values.

When discussing the distribution of absorbed xenobiotic compounds, the idea of systemic toxicity should also be discussed. The term "systemic toxicity" refers to undesirable effects at target sites remote from the point of exposure. In contrast, "local toxicity" refers to undesirable changes to the physiology of an organism that occur at or near the site of initial xenobiotic exposure. Systemic toxicity can only occur after absorption of xenobiotic across a biological membrane and distribution of the compound throughout the various internal compartments (dependant upon the physical properties of the specific compound). The elicitation of subsequent undesirable effects is based upon the concentration of the xenobiotic or its metabolites attained in the susceptible remote target tissue, or organ. As briefly stated earlier, when a sufficient concentration of a specific xenobiotic (and/or metabolite) is attained to interfere with normal physiological processes in some way, a toxic response is said to occur.

Toxicology-the Dose-Response Relationship

As discussed to this point, systemic toxicity can occur when absorption, distribution, and subsequent presence of a xenobiotic or its metabolite at a susceptible target site combine to elicit interference with normal physiological processes. If this produces a measurable change, it can be called a "response" and can be quantified. In classifying types of dosing and responses, some compounds elicit harmful responses with chronic (long duration) exposures where either a slowly eliminated compound or metabolite accumulates with repeated dosing until a harmful level is attained in the body. It is also possible that even though a xenobiotic may not accumulate over the long term, an accumulation of physiological changes that are not quickly reversed could lead to a chronic response. For xenobiotic compounds that elicit effects with only a single, or few exposure(s) placed closely together in time, both the exposure and elicited responses are classified as "acute."

A wide range of possible responses exist, from a subtle quantifiable change of physiology, to death of the organism. A response can be described by variables with a range of quantitative outcomes, such as increased blood pressure, whereas death of the organism would be an example of a discrete ("all or none") response. Regarding chemicals in general, the expectation is that responses are usually benign at best, as by definition a response represents a shift away from the prevailing physiological conditions, which are nearly constant and within a "normal" range in a healthy organism. Whatever the relevant response, once it has been specified, the toxicologist can gather data about the distribution of responses observed in a population from which observations were made. This is done to allow prediction of the probability for the response with a given dose administered to a single organism. Knowledge regarding the consequences resulting from human exposures is typically desired from animal studies. In such a study, a very large number of possible responses could be examined but the toxicologist attempts to select the most relevant. To standardize reporting of acute study results the toxicologist will quantify the predicted dose at which 50% of an idealized test population would experience the specified response.

The statistical nature of the dose-response relationship and how it relates to risk assessment is more fully discussed in the classical toxicology text, *Cassarrett and Doull's Toxicology*.[8] For those with a basic understanding of statistics and mathematical modeling, the concept of the dose-response curve offers an opportunity to combine knowledge of probability, biological processes, and factors affecting variability of these processes between individual organisms to arrive at a concept of risk. An example of the types of questions that may be asked by various regulatory agencies is "at what dose will a single organism out of 1 million so dosed respond?" An answer to such a question may be easily estimated, usually by extrapolating from available high dose-response information and using any one of numerous mathematical models based upon different assumptions regarding the shape of the dose-response curve in the low dose region. No response data are usually available from low dose exposures when reasonable numbers of test subjects are studied. Thus, when examining such estimates of risk one should always keep in mind that the study producing such information is based upon high-dose extrapolation from an animal cohort much smaller than the size needed to statistically observe such a low response rate at the low dose estimated to produce the "1-in-a-million" response, as it is very impractical to dose and observe millions of rats in a single study.

The industrial hygienist should strive to understand the known and suspected responses associated with the various exposures he or she evaluates. New chemicals with potential for adverse health effects among exposed workers are continually introduced into commerce, with neither exposure standards nor much information available regarding health effects in many cases. The observant industrial hygienist who communicates regularly with the supporting occupational medicine team and toxicologists can play a positive role in developing knowledge about important fundamentals of toxicology (exposure route, airborne exposure concentrations associated with negative health effects, etc.) that must eventually be understood. Diagnosis and treatment of medical issues should rightly be left to the realm of occupational medicine, and objective observations and anecdotal information obtained during workplace evaluations should be communicated to the occupational medicine physician and toxicologist. Advances in our understanding of occupational diseases have historically involved workplace observations that correlated with medical diagnoses. Examples include the work of Percival Pott who linked scrotal cancer in 18th century chimney sweeps to prolonged contact with soot and poor hygienic practices.[9] Pott's well-founded idea has been shown to be correct, and has been further refined; it is now well understood that soot from the incomplete combustion of wood and coal contains numerous polycyclic aromatic hydrocarbons, some of which are known carcinogens upon chronic exposure. Kennaway and coworkers spent more than 33 years searching for the carcinogenically active components of coal tar through a combination of fluorescence spectroscopy, fractionation of the numerous components of the complex coal tar mixture, and murine skin painting studies. In the biological studies, a fraction of the coal tar (in some cases relatively pure single compounds) with a characteristic fluorescence spectrum was repeatedly painted on the skin of laboratory mice which were meticulously followed for a considerable period of time, as long as 800 days or more, to detect the possible production of cancer. The end result of this work was the discovery of a number of individual polycyclic aromatic hydrocarbon carcinogens, including the powerful carcinogenic compound benzo[a]pyrene.[10]

Responses to Organic Solvent Exposure

Organic solvent compounds are typically lipophilic and thus tend to extract fat components from skin upon contact. Thus the nearly universal biological responses to organic solvents as a class include irritation and de-fatting of skin at the primary exposure site (local toxicity). It has been noted that skin exposure to several of the chlorinated organic solvents can produce "erythema, blistering, and burns"[11] (erythema being redness of skin). In the case of skin exposure to virtually all organic solvents, dermatitis can eventually result, and as stated earlier, this is known as "the most frequently reported occupational disease."[6] Most industrial hygienists who have experience with the solvent methylene chloride understand its capacity to produce severe irritation with skin exposure to the liquid, or a noticeable burning sensation with exposure of unprotected skin to elevated vapor levels. The author has vivid memories of completing industrial hygiene work in a large indoor hangar where methylene chloride-containing paint stripper was being used to remove paint from aircraft surfaces. To approach the work area where this material was being sprayed onto aircraft surfaces within less than about 30 feet quickly produced a very noticeable burning sensation to exposed skin surfaces, forcing those without adequate skin protection to leave the area without delay.

The common systemic effects produced with absorption of most organic solvent compounds into the body are acute and in most cases transitory, resulting from interference with the nervous system of the exposed organism. Graded responses can range from dizziness, lightheadedness, sensory disturbances, headache, drowsiness, nausea, narcosis, or even death from a single large exposure.[11,12] It is thought that the physical properties of lipophilic solvents provide for concentration of solvent molecules directly in nerves and cells having high lipid content that support the nervous system[11], interfering with their normal functions.

In contrast to the near universal localized and systemic acute responses to organic solvent exposure noted above, risks of specific chronic type responses are also well-known with exposures to individual solvents. Some notable examples include acute myelogenous leukemia (a type of cancer linked to chronic benzene exposure)[13], atherosclerosis (linked to chronic carbon disulfide exposure)[14], and axonal neuropathy (linked to chronic exposure to n-hexane and methyl-n-butyl ketone).[15,16] These individual solvents and their associated unique responses will be discussed later in further detail.

Some controversy exists in the medical community regarding whether or not a constellation of responses known by some as "painter's disease" can result from chronic exposures to organic solvents as a general class. There are medical researchers who believe that such exposures over time can produce "persistent symptoms such as headache, fatigue, irritability, memory impairment, depression, emotional instability, sleep disturbance, alcohol intolerance, loss of libido or potency, and loss of interest in daily activities."[11] The subjective nature of many of these types of symptoms, and their numerous associated confounding variables ensure that a lively debate will exist for some time as to whether or not this syndrome can be attributed to chronic exposure to organic solvents.

Toxicology–Biotransformation and Elimination

Biotransformation as a Pathway to Increased Xenobiotic Elimination

Numerous detoxifying metabolic (biotransformation) mechanisms exist where xenobiotic compounds may be altered through action of enzymes that typically make such compounds more water soluble, and thus more easily mobilized and excreted or eliminated from the body. Many biotransformation enzyme processes occur in the liver, although other types of tissues (i.e, lungs, skin, kidneys, and GI tract) are also known to contain relatively lower amounts of such enzymes. In most instances such biotransformation leads to increased elimination of many types of absorbed xenobiotic compounds and thus lessens the potential for negative responses.

Biotransformation Gone Awry

Well-known examples exist where biotransformation can actually lead to production of intermediates that cause disruption to physiological processes, and such metabolites can thus be more harmful than the parent compound originally absorbed. It is a biotransformation pathway for the organic solvents n-hexane and methyl n-butyl ketone that has been shown to lead to production of 2,5-hexanedione. With administration of all three compounds individually, the same neuropathy is produced in an animal model[15], similar to the neuropathy observed in workers from repeated occupational exposure to both n-hexane[16] and methyl-n-butyl ketone.[17,18] The hexanedione biotransformation product is thought to be the causative agent for the observed neuropathy.

Metabolism of the solvent methanol can lead to production of formic acid which can dramatically lower physiological pH. Endogenous metabolism of methanol to formic acid within the retina itself is thought to occur, resulting in selective retinal toxicity, producing the characteristic effects of methanol consumption on vision, including blindness in some cases.[19]

In the case of the solvent carbon tetrachloride, its characteristic hepatic (liver) toxicity is directly related to metabolism in the liver by an important and heterogeneous class of enzymes (cytochrome P-450, or CYP-450) found there in great abundance. The CYP-450 enzymes were named as such due to the ability of the iron-containing heme site of the enzyme to absorb light of 450 nm wavelength when bound to carbon monoxide. Numerous CYP-450 isozymes exist, capable of metabolizing a vast array of xenobiotic compounds.[20] Biotransformation by very specific CYP-450 isozymes located in the endoplasmic reticulum of certain hepatic cells convert CCl_4 to a $\cdot CCl_3$ free radical compound as discussed in a thorough review completed by Recknagel.[21] The radical is thought to react further within the hepatic cells near the location where the metabolic conversion occurs, leading to lipid peroxidation and the characteristic toxicity patterns observed in individuals heavily exposed to the solvent. The evidence listed by Recknagel for this includes "morphological alteration of the hepatic endoplasmic reticulum, loss of drug-metabolizing activity, ...the resultants of a primary attack by the split products of carbon tetrachloride metabolism on the lipoidal elements of the endoplasmic reticulum."[21]

Complicating the work of the toxicologist attempting to predict a response based upon exposure route and dose alone, biotransformation enzyme systems are inducible. With exposure to certain compounds (often substrates for the specific enzyme or enzyme class), elevated enzyme levels and correspondingly elevated biotransformation activities occur. Evidence exists that the specific CYP-450 isozyme class induced by heavy ethanol consumption is also responsible for the conversion of CCl_4 to the free radical species mentioned above. Manno et al.[22] showed that among two groups of workers similarly exposed to CCl_4, in both cases workers with abnormally high ethanol consumption developed severe hepatotoxicity (liver toxicity), nephrotoxicity (kidney toxicity) and hepatomegaly (enlarged liver). Similarly exposed workers in both groups who did not report excessive alcohol intake suffered no observable ill effects. The induction of the specific CYP-450 enzyme class 2E1 by ethanol thus puts heavy drinkers of this solvent at increased risk of hepatotoxicity from exposure to the solvent carbon tetrachloride. Numerous other examples of specific CYP-450 enzyme induction can be cited, with inducing compounds known to occur in particular foods, liquids, and specific environmental contaminants.

Elimination

In similar fashion as for absorption, elimination of a xenobiotic can occur via multiple routes. For volatile compounds, exhalation of the unchanged compound can be thought of as the reverse of the pulmonary absorption process, where the net diffusion of the gas phase xenobiotic will always be towards lower concentrations.

In a highly complex overall biotransformation system, following initial Phase I activity by enzymes such as members of the CYP-450 class, Phase II biotransformation adds a polar group such as a sulfate moiety, a simple amino acid, a glucose molecule, or an important thiol compound called glutathione to a reactive site created during Phase I biotransformation. The important compound glutathione contains a reactive thiol group and is found in high cellular concentrations. It serves as a pool of reducing equivalent within cells, replenished by reduced cellular nicotinamide adenine dinucleotide phosphate (NADPH) which continually reduces the oxidized disulfide bonds that tend to form between two glutathione molecules. Glutathione's ability to scavenge oxygen free radicals and tie up potentially harmful reactive sites on xenobiotic molecules is important to moderating the effects such reactive species would otherwise elicit. Conjugation of glutathione is facilitated by glutathione S-transferase isozymes, which speed up the overall rates of reaction.

With attainment of further water solubility from Phase II biotransformation, excretion can then be favored in the urine or from the liver as a component of bile that is passed into the GI tract for elimination in the feces.

In mathematically describing elimination kinetics, the exponential "first order" elimination equation is the norm, although in situations where saturable metabolic pathways play an important role in elimination of a xenobiotic (and are thus rate-limiting), a zero order curve is possible (a straight line on an arithmetic or non-logarithmic plot). A frequently used example of a xenobiotic compound with a zero order elimination curve is ethanol.[23] In an exponential decay model the elimination rate constant corresponds to a fraction of the body burden eliminated in a given unit of time, and in the simplest static case where dosing does not continue, the characteristic exponential decay curve results that is mathematically identical to a curve that describes radioactive decay (Figure 16.4). In a dynamic one-compartment model situation where uniform dosing occurs on a regular basis that is relatively frequent compared to the compound's half-life ($t_{1/2}$), a "sawtooth" graph results when theoretical body burden is plotted against time (Figure 16.5). This results from only partial elimination after each successive dose that follows the exponential 1st order equation. In the case of a theoretical compound with elimination kinetics as per Figure 16.5, an elimination $t_{1/2}$ much longer than the dosing periodicity produces a steadily increasing body burden. Where dosing is continuous and constant, a steady state body burden (mass of xenobiotic) will exist that is defined as the dose per unit time, divided by the elimination rate constant which has units of reciprocal time. Figure 16.6 shows repeated dosing for a compound more representative of typical solvents, with relatively short elimination $t_{1/2}$ values which are often measured in hours.

Biological Monitoring as a Surrogate for Measurement of Absorbed Dose

When a method for biological monitoring is available it should be considered especially appropriate and useful if skin exposure and absorption are significant. Unlike air sampling which is generally recognized as a valid estimate of airborne exposures, standard methods to reproducibly measure skin deposition and absorption are not available. With biological monitoring, measurement of the xenobiotic or its metabolites in body tissues,

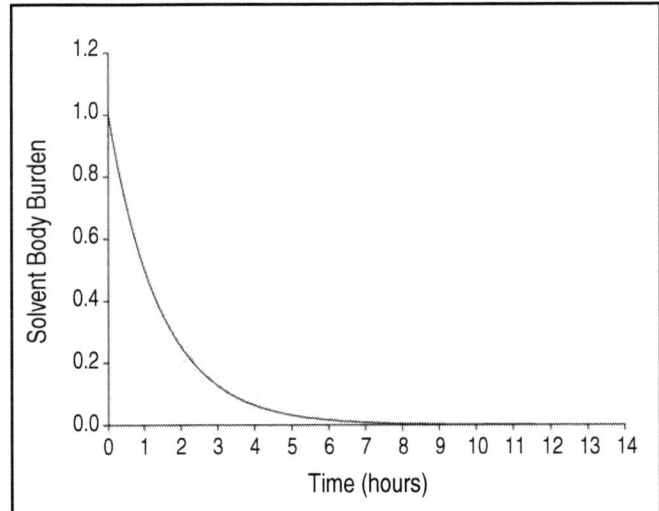

Figure 16.4 — First order elimination curve for a hypothetical solvent with biological half life of 1.0 hour. At time "0" amount of xenobiotic present in the biological organism is arbitrarily set to 1.0; in all situations where first order kinetics and a given biological half life pertain the actual mass or amount of the xenobiotic present in the biological system will be proportional.

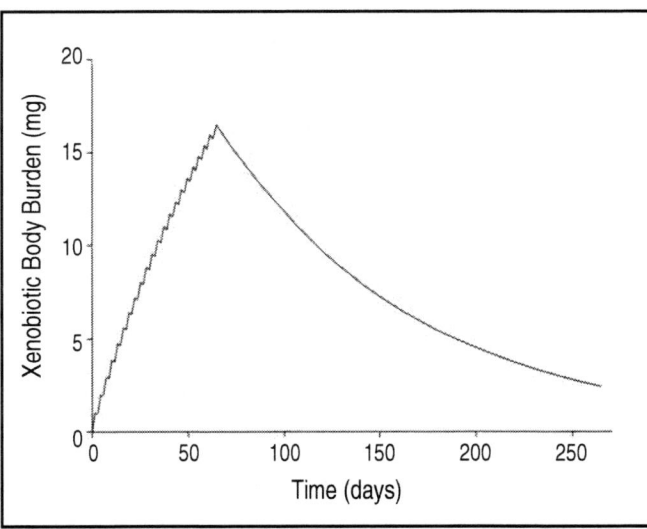

Figure 16.5 — Theoretical body burden over time for a xenobiotic compound having a $t_{1/2}$ of 72 days; 1 mg absorbed daily through Day 63. Exponential decay curve based on that $t_{1/2}$ observed from that point assumes no further dosing. Compare to Figure 16.6 where a relatively shorter elimination $t_{1/2}$ does not allow increasing body burden accumulation as opposed to the case here with a longer elimination $t_{1/2}$.

fluids, or exhaled air can account for both dermal and pulmonary exposure and subsequent absorption into biologically relevant tissues.

Although not an organic solvent, the element lead provides an extreme example of biological monitoring for a xenobiotic with a long biological $t_{1/2}$ (years). Due to the very slow elimination of lead, a blood lead measurement does not tell the occupational health professional anything about a single received dose, as it represents essentially a lifetime cumulative exposure.[24] In contrast, the more volatile organic solvents absorbed into the body are often eliminated within hours, and an end-of-shift biological sample requirement is typical. Such a biological sample for a xenobiotic eliminated within hours, in contrast to those taken to evaluate lead exposure, provides information relevant only to the immediate short-duration exposure, and would not represent a longer-term exposure average or trend.

To accomplish biological monitoring, the occupational medicine team supporting exposed workers usually monitors for either the unchanged xenobiotic or its metabolites in body tissues, fluids (blood or urine), or in exhaled air. As the relatively small acetone molecule is miscible in aqueous systems, it provides a prime example of an organic solvent compound that can be found unchanged in urine following absorption.[25] In the case of less water-soluble solvent compounds, the unchanged compounds are not typically sought from aqueous body matrices as a biological measure of exposure, even though they can be present there at very low concentrations. Their low water solubility would require careful handling to ensure that the parent compounds would not be volatilized, introducing large amounts of error in the quantitative

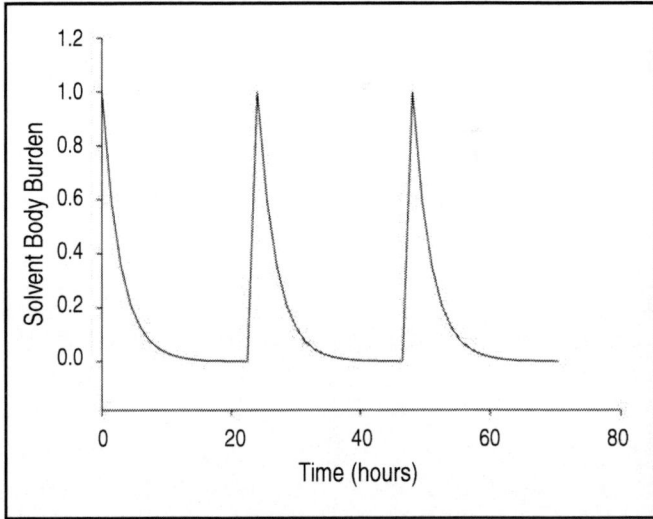

Figure 16.6 — Theoretical body burden of a xenobiotic solvent compound having a $t_{1/2}$ of 2 hours; 1 mg absorbed at the same time of day, daily for three days. Exponential decay curve based on that $t_{1/2}$ observed after final dose on Day 3 assumes no further dosing. Compare to Figure 16.5 where the relatively longer elimination $t_{1/2}$ allows increasing body burden accumulation with continued dosing as opposed to the case here with a shorter elimination $t_{1/2}$.

measurements. Instead, applicable biological exposure indices for these types of solvent compounds are often based on the presence of their respective water-soluble metabolites in a relevant body fluid. In the cases of *n*-hexane, carbon disulfide, and benzene, the relevant water soluble metabolites are respectively 2,5-hexanedione[26], 2-thiothiazolidine-4-carboxylic acid[27], and s-phenylmercapturic acid[28] in urine at workshift end (Figure 16.7). Measurement of an unchanged solvent compound in exhaled air is typified by the biological exposure index for the volatile solvent 1,1,1-trichlorethane. Recommended biological measurements for exposure to this compound include sampling and analysis for the unchanged compound in exhaled air, as well as measurement of its water-soluble metabolites trichloracetic acid (in urine) and trichlorethanol (in either blood or urine).[29]

Use of the Vapor Hazard Ratio for Preliminary Evaluation of Vapor Exposure Hazards

The idea that toxicology information is accounted for in an airborne exposure occupational exposure limit (OEL) assumes that the magnitude of an OEL relates to a discrete inhalation exposure level that can lead to unacceptable risk. Repeating from the introduction section, the discipline of toxicology describes the potential for xenobiotic compounds to cause adverse health effects to biological systems, and "Threshold Limit Values® refer to airborne concentrations of substances and represent conditions under which it is believed that nearly all workers may be repeatedly exposed day after day without adverse health effects."[2] Thus when properly set, an OEL for chemical exposure

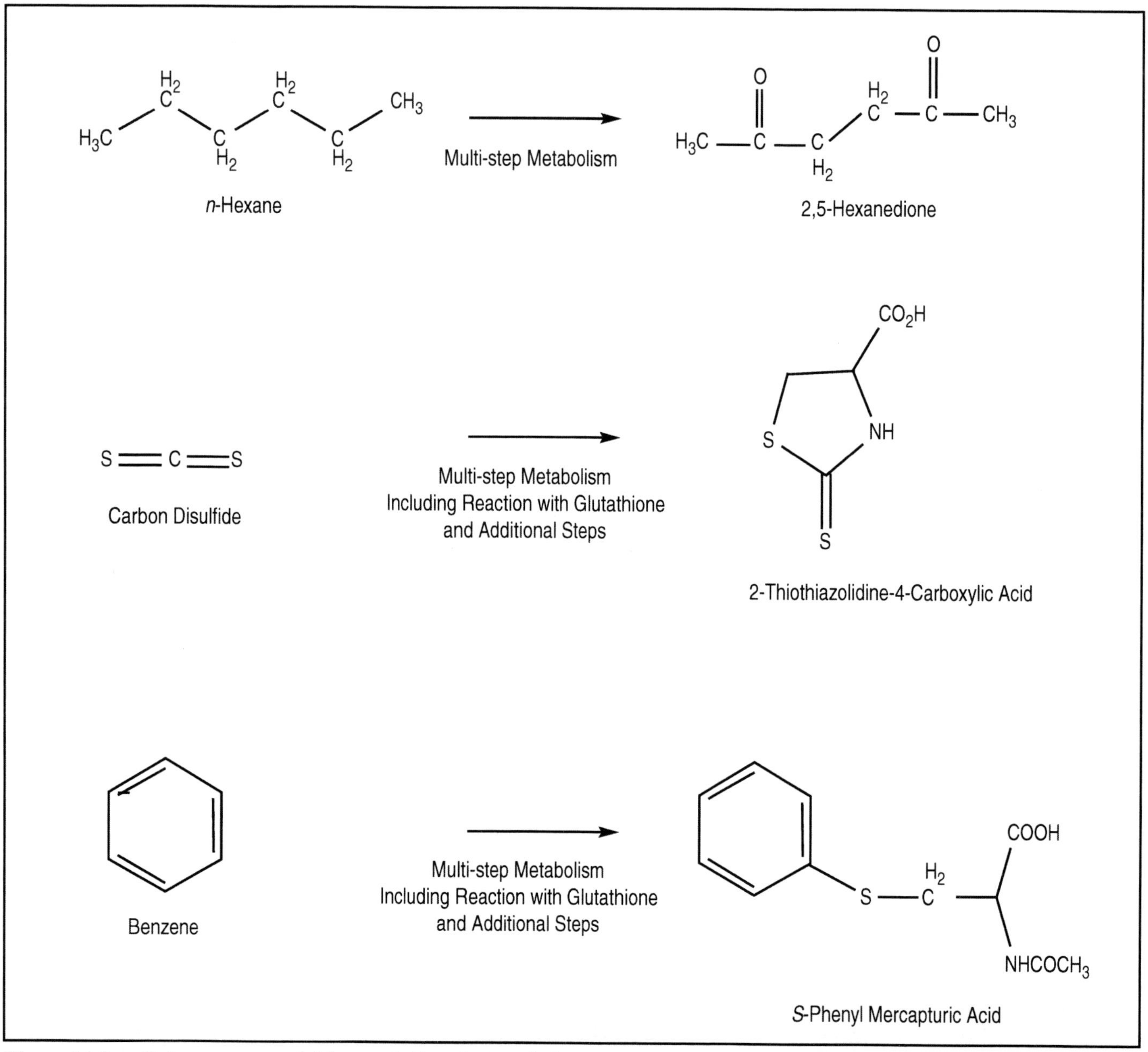

Figure 16.7 — Relevant water soluble metabolites that result from exposure to *n*-hexane, carbon disulfide, and benzene; the presence of a water-soluble metabolite is necessary if biological exposure monitoring of workers' urine is to be of any use.

is based upon toxicology. Whether acute or chronic toxicological responses are understood to exist for a given organic solvent, a standardized measure is desirable to account for the potential of inhalation exposure to cause adverse health effects, as well as for the potential of the solvent to be present as an air contaminant in the first place. If dealing solely with exposure to solvent vapors (the simplest exposure case) a simple prioritization system exists that allows the industrial hygienist to do this.

Popendorf[30] first proposed simultaneous consideration of the vapor pressure and toxicology for a compound with a single term that incorporates both factors. The vapor hazard ratio (VHR) is calculated by dividing the vapor pressure concentration of a pure solvent compound by its corresponding OEL in the denominator, using the same units for both (i.e., parts per million). While the magnitude of the vapor pressure term in the VHR accounts for the tendency of a solvent compound to vaporize, the magnitude of the OEL term accounts as simply as possible for its toxicology. The VHR of a given chemical allows a quick and simple observation regarding the potential for a vapor-only exposure to exist above the relevant OEL. In all cases where the VHR is <1, creation of a vapor-only airborne concentration above the OEL is not possible under typical conditions.

The examples provided in Table 16.2 illustrate how this concept can be employed to aid the industrial hygienist in recommending substitutes for high-hazard solvents, or in examining where limited resources should first be used to assess exposures. A compound such as carbon tetrachloride carries a VHR of 30,263 due to its relatively high saturation vapor pressure concentration and relatively low (more restrictive) OEL. As a comparison, the VHR calculated for n-pentane is 1,127 due to a more than 100-fold greater (less restrictive) OEL, even though the saturation vapor pressure concentration for the latter compound is about five times larger. In cases where a compound's vapor pressure is extremely low the VHR calculation produces a relatively small number, even when the OEL may also be low (more restrictive).

Figure 16.8 provides a graphic presentation of the VHR concept. Excluding the compound n-hexane, the straight chain aliphatic hydrocarbon compounds containing six through nine carbon atoms have progressively and predictably lower VHR values due mostly to the successively lower vapor pressure concentrations as hydrocarbon molecular size increases. In the figure, the VHR for hexane isomers other than n-hexane falls predictably in line with the other aliphatic compounds, while the VHR for the compound n-hexane appears out of line (higher than expected). This can be explained by the relatively low OEL for the specific 6 carbon straight chain alkane, which as shall be discussed further in the next section is related to its special toxicology in comparison to the other aliphatic hydrocarbons shown in the figure.

A recent book on control of airborne chemical hazards by Popendorf contains an extensive listing of VHRs[31] allowing a systematic approach in evaluation of the potential for specific compounds to produce vapor-only overexposures. As a final word concerning the VHR and its limitations, it should be used cautiously or not at all in examining exposure scenarios where skin exposure to solvent liquids or inhalation exposure to liquid solvent aerosol could exist, as discussed already, the VHR does not take any exposure potential except for airborne vapor into account.

Unique Solvent Exposure Effects

Beyond the nearly universal local and systemic types of toxicity from exposure to solvents in general, solvent-unique effects are also possible. Such solvent-unique effects have been identified and confirmed from the observations of astute medical practitioners, followed by epidemiological and workplace studies, as well as animal studies in the laboratory to define dose-response relationships and the biochemical mechanisms involved in producing relevant responses.

Table 16.2 — Vapor Hazard Ratio Data for Selected Organic Solvents

Solvent Compound	SVC[a]	OEL[b]	VHR[c]	VHI[d]
Benzene	125,339	0.5	250,678	5.4
Carbon disulfide	475,697	10	47,570	4.7
Methyl n-butyl ketone	15,131	5	3,026	3.5
Carbon tetrachloride	150,012	5	30,002	4.5
Cyclohexane	128,300	100	1,283	3.1
n-Pentane	674,069	600	1,123	3.1
n-Hexane	199,358	50	3,987	3.6
n-Heptane	60,104	400	150	2.2
n-Octane	18,357	300	61	1.8
n-Nonane	5,625	200	28	1.4

[a]SVC = Saturation vapor concentration (ppm, v/v)
[b]OEL = Occupational exposure limit, 2007 ACGIH TLV (ppm, v/v)
[c]VHR = Vapor hazard ratio (SVC/OEL)
[d]VHI = Vapor hazard index (log VHR)

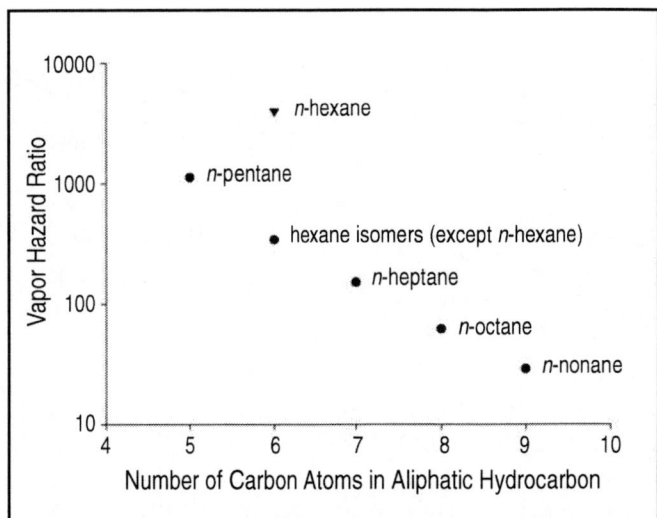

Figure 16.8 — Vapor hazard ratios (VHRs) for the straight chain aliphatic hydrocarbon series C_5-C_9, and for all hexane isomers excluding n-hexane. It should be noted that the Threshold Limit Values for all the other members of the straight chain series except n-hexane are identical for all isomeric forms of each specific alkane. VHR data from Popendorf.[31]

The fairly well known solvent-unique exposure effects for benzene, *n*-hexane, methyl *n*-butyl ketone, and carbon disulfide are discussed below. This group of solvents with unique undesirable responses should not be considered exhaustive, as additional examples could also be mentioned, including carbon tetrachloride and some other halogenated hydrocarbon solvents that are known to produce unique liver toxicity[10], and the unique response of the human eye to methanol metabolites[19] discussed above under "metabolism gone awry."

In addition to the relatively well-understood solvent-unique health effects from occupational exposures to the four select solvents listed above, continued observation of workers exposed to organic solvent compounds is likely to uncover additional solvent-unique effects, especially subtle ones that could be caused by a number of non-occupational factors. The current controversy surrounding what has been called "painter's disease" from chronic exposures to organic solvents may ultimately be proved, with mechanisms identified to explain the connection between the observed responses and the exposures that are believed by some to cause them. If and when available, such mechanistic studies could show that unique solvents or solvent classes may reasonably be concluded to produce the responses in question, or it may be demonstrated that exposure to virtually all organic solvents could contribute to the observed responses. The need to understand mechanisms by which biological responses to xenobiotics occur explains the usefulness of animal studies to the mechanistic toxicologist, although *in vitro* testing systems also have an important role in elucidating an understanding of the connection between dose and observed response.

Benzene

The physical properties of benzene are found in Table 16.1. Benzene is the simplest member of a series of cyclic aromatic hydrocarbons (Figure 16.9), and is the only member of the series that is a liquid solvent at standard temperature and pressure, with the next member of the series (naphthalene) and all successively larger polycyclic aromatic hydrocarbon compounds being solids. Benzene is an important starting material in numerous chemical manufacturing processes, is commonly found in chemistry laboratories, and is a naturally-occurring component of gasoline. Since the discovery of its cancer causing potential, benzene has been removed from a host of consumer and industrial products in developed countries, and thus exposures to benzene today are expected primarily among laboratory, manufacturing, refinery, and petroleum transportation workers. Benzene was formerly used routinely as a solvent for cleaning and was actually added to gasoline for improved internal combustion engine performance, but it has since fallen out of favor for these types of uses where less problematic compounds can replace it. Not only is benzene no longer considered a viable gasoline additive, but additional refining during gasoline production has greatly reduced the magnitude of benzene content in U.S. gasoline, even below levels that were otherwise routinely encountered in gasoline where benzene had not been purposefully added. Benzene remains as a significant compound in worldwide commerce, especially as a starting material for further synthesis of numerous useful chemical products.

In discussing benzene, the concept of aromaticity should be addressed, as the characteristics of aromaticity greatly affect the

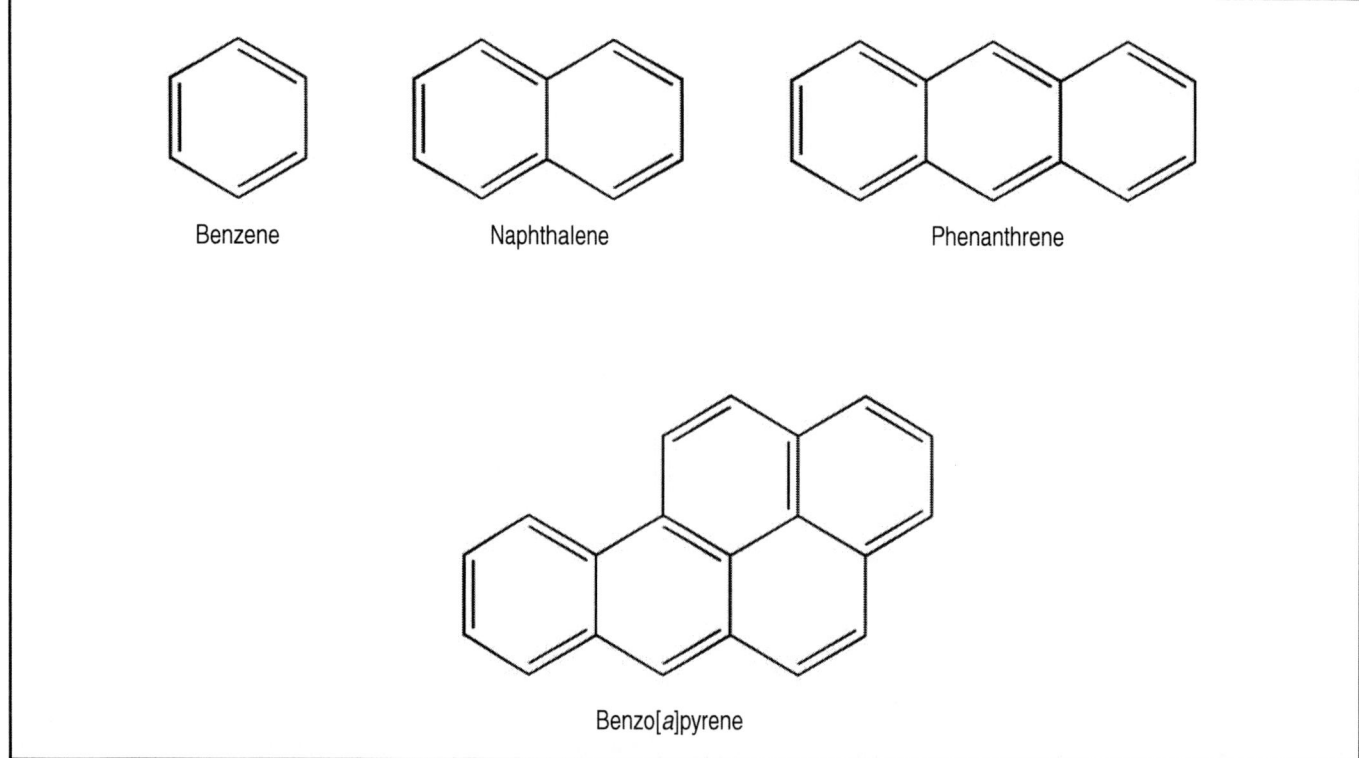

Figure 16.9 — A small number of representative cyclic aromatic hydrocarbons; benzene is the only solvent among these, as all of the polycyclic aromatics are solids at standard temperature and pressure.

geometry, physical properties, and stability of the benzene molecule. Benzene is the simplest cyclic aromatic compound, and contains only carbon and hydrogen atoms with each carbon atom covalently bound to two neighboring carbon atoms in its ring structure, and to one hydrogen atom oriented towards the outside of the ring structure. Initially certain physical properties of benzene were puzzling. It was well known that an unsaturated hydrocarbon compound would have fewer than the possible maximum number of non-carbon atoms due to the presence of double (or even triple) bonds between carbon atoms. In the case of a cyclic saturated six-carbon compound, up to twelve non-carbon atoms can be bonded covalently to the molecule (two each per carbon atom found in the molecule) as in the case of cyclohexane (Figure 16.10). The benzene molecule (also with six carbon atoms forming its ring structure) has only six hydrogen atoms attached, and thus would appear to fit in with unsaturated compounds, including straight and branched chain alkene compounds having double bonds found at fixed locations in a molecule, and with the bond lengths of those double bonds shorter than those of single bonds. However, this is not what is actually found in the cyclic aromatic compounds, including benzene. The carbon-carbon bond lengths of the cyclic aromatic compound benzene are all of equal length, and this length is intermediate between that of either a typical single or double bond. Based on these two observations, it appears as though the carbon-carbon bonds present in an aromatic compound represent a type of bond different than those found in alkanes, alkenes, and alkynes. Such an explanation actually approximates what is known about aromaticity: the six carbon ring of benzene differs from that of the cyclic six carbon alkane compound cyclohexane, primarily due to the presence not only of the unusual carbon-carbon bonds lengths, but also of bonding electrons that exist above and below the flat plane of the ring structure and that are not fixed to a given location on the molecule.

The most stable configuration of an aromatic compound is that of one or more flat 6-membered rings, with (in the case of benzene) a single hydrogen atom radiating outward from each carbon atom in the ring in the same plane as that of the flat six-membered carbon ring. This is in contrast to the bonds found in the non-aromatic compound cyclohexane. In the non-aromatic cyclic compound bond angles are dictated by the repulsive forces that exist between bonding electrons, and no delocalized bonding electrons exist to force a planar structure as is found in benzene. Specifically, because of the delocalized bonding electrons found in a simple aromatic compound that contains only carbon and hydrogen, all of the carbon-to-carbon bonds in the molecule are of intermediate length between that expected of strictly single bonds, or of strictly double bonds. The bonding with delocalized electrons and the geometry of the planar benzene molecule provide unusual stability to the compound, as well as altered water solubility relative to its fully saturated alkane analog, cyclohexane (Table 16.1). The delocalized bonding electrons found in an aromatic molecule such as benzene provide a capability for a highly polar compound such as water to induce a momentary dipole in the benzene molecule when polar functional groups closely approach the aromatic compound. This allows the benzene molecule to have relatively more (but still limited) interaction with the highly polar water molecule, increasing the solubility of benzene in water relative to that of its cyclic alkane analog (Table 16.1).

The non-polar benzene molecule is readily absorbed across biological membranes, and its high vapor pressure relative to its OEL yields a VHR for benzene of over 250,000. Concerning disposition of absorbed benzene, Bergman completed a study where ^{14}C-benzene was administered to mice, with nearly 40% of a benzene dose eliminated as a vapor during breathing one hour after exposure, while the total amount excreted via this route was greater than 40% after several more hours.[32] In the same study, about 30% of the radioactivity from the ^{14}C-benzene administered was found in the animals' urine. Andrews et al. used similar methods and found that less than 1% of radioactivity from ^{14}C-benzene administered was recovered in the feces, while

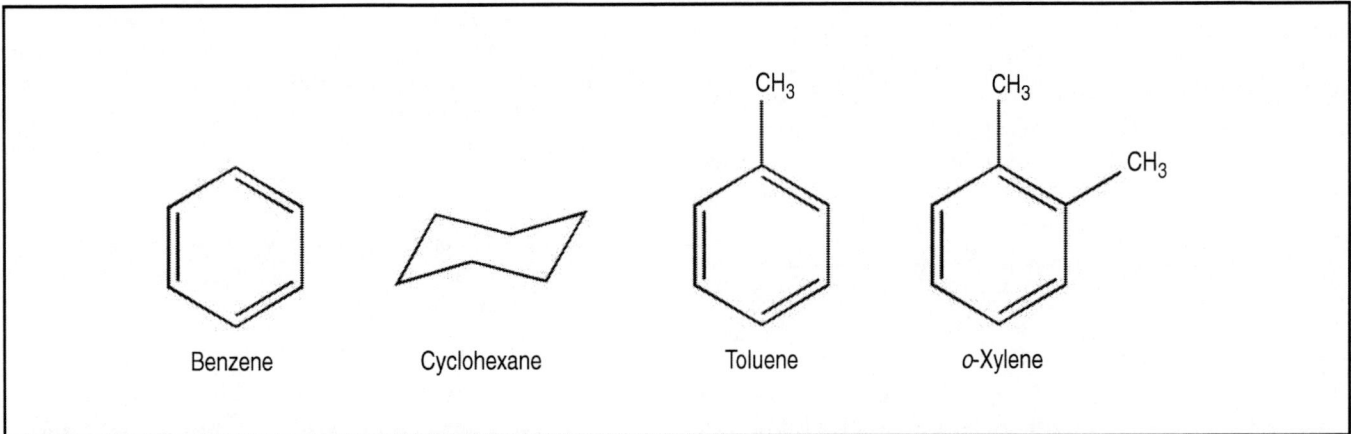

Figure 16.10 — Comparison of structures for benzene, cyclohexane, and the methylated aromatic compounds toluene and o-xylene; hydrogen atoms are not shown except as noted in methyl group substituents. The geometry of benzene ring is planar, while that of the saturated alkane cyclohexane is three-dimensional due to repulsive forces between electrons forming the carbon-carbon and carbon-to-hydrogen covalent bonds in the molecule.

22.6% was recovered in the urine after 24 hours and 71.5% was recovered in exhaled air after 4–6 hours.[33]

The target of primary toxicological importance for the unique chronic exposure effects of benzene is the blood-forming system in humans and animal systems studied. In examining benzene toxicity, the pioneering occupational health physician Alice Hamilton communicated the idea that benzene exposure is correlated with leukemia as early as 1931.[34] Landrigan, in briefly reviewing studies that point to the distinct health effects from benzene exposure notes "in the century that has passed since the seminal observation that benzene is toxic to blood, a steadily accumulating body of data has shown to an ever-higher degree of certainty that benzene can cause a broad range of hematologic dysfunction, including all types of leukemia, lymphomas, myeloid metaplasia, and aplastic anemia."[35] Of great interest and as the subject of some curiosity to both the toxicologist and the industrial hygienist, the blood responses seen with benzene exposure are not observed with exposure to seemingly very similar compounds such as the aromatic compounds toluene and the three xylene isomers, which differ from benzene in that simple methyl groups replace one or more of the benzene molecule's Hydrogen atoms in these four molecules (Figure 16.10).

Considering currently prevailing benzene exposure patterns, it is clear that the single unique, serious, and undisputed health effect that causes benzene to stand out from all other solvents is its ability to cause the cancer leukemia. Evidence for this has been seen during the course of numerous studies, including work by Infante et al. who provide evidence of a strong association between benzene exposure and leukemia among rubber manufacturing workers exposed to benzene (and no other solvents) at fairly substantial levels between 1940 and 1949.[36] Aksoy describes increased risk of leukemia in Turkish shoe manufacturing and repair workers using solvents (including benzene) in their work.[37] Most recently, Hayes et al. report an increased risk for leukemia among Chinese workers with total benzene exposure levels estimated to be "below 200 ppm-years."[38]

It is generally accepted that metabolites of benzene, and not the parent compound itself, are directly responsible for its carcinogenicity[39,40] and probably also for the other blood effects seen with repeated benzene exposure. In animal models, partial removal of the liver before exposure to benzene has been shown to decrease production of benzene metabolites, and to also protect against expected benzene toxicity.[41] Co-administration of the aromatic solvent toluene with benzene lessened the hematotoxicity of benzene as measured by uptake of ^{59}Fe during synthesis of red blood cells; in mice exposed to benzene alone ^{59}Fe uptake into newly formed red blood cells was inhibited, showing disruption of erythropoiesis (formation of new red blood cells).[33] However, in the case where toluene was administered at the same time as benzene the expected diminution of ^{59}Fe uptake was lessened. A likely explanation for this result would be that the enzyme systems that would otherwise toxify benzene were engaged metabolizing the toluene which is very similar chemically to benzene in terms of molecular size, aromaticity, and polarity.

As alluded to previously, non-cancer blood effects from benzene exposure are also well-documented in the literature. Aksoy et al. noted variable responses among various blood components within a group of "217 apparently healthy workers manufacturing shoes under unhygienic conditions with solvents containing benzene."[42] Effects associated with chronic benzene exposure were observed in 51 out of the 217 individuals studied, and these included in some cases elevated levels of leucocytes, and abnormally low levels in others. Elevated basophils and/or eosinophils were observed, in other cases abnormally low levels of platelets were seen. In six of the workers, a decrease in all cellular blood components (pancytopenia) was observed.

Hamilton mentions that benzene was, at the time of her writing, being used therapeutically to attempt to counteract the overabundance of the specific type of blood component found in leukemia, as its toxicity to formation of blood components was by then well recognized. The irony of this was obvious to Dr. Hamilton, whose reasoning demonstrates an understanding of Paracelsus' central tenet of modern toxicology: "this paradoxical phenomenon — leukemia produced by an agent that is used in the treatment of leukemia — is to be explained by an inverse action of benzene when given in small doses as compared with what is seen when larger doses are given."[34] Those who have followed in her footsteps have a different perspective, benefitting from more than 70 years of additional study, and it appears ironic to us now that this compound would have ever been considered for use as a therapy.

Rappaport et al.[43] summarize the current thinking and knowledge regarding the mechanistic link between benzene metabolites produced by CYP-450 mixed function oxidase enzymes (Figure 16.11) and the now familiar toxic responses that result from exposure to this solvent:

> Although benzene is the simplest aromatic compound, its metabolism is surprisingly complex. Following CYP2E1 oxidation of benzene to benzene oxide (BO)[44,45], a series of enzymatic and nonenzymatic steps lead to many other metabolites, notably phenol, catechol, hydroquinone, and the ring-opened muconaldehydes (ultimately transformed to t,t-muconic acid). Portions of catechol and hydroquinone are oxidized to 1,2- and 1,4-benzoquinone, respectively, which are electrophilic and capable of reacting with DNA and other critical macromolecules, as are BO and the muconaldehydes. The toxicity of benzene is thought to involve one or more of these electrophilic metabolites (most notably 1,4-benzoquinone) and/or reactive oxygen species produced by redox cycling of catechol, hydroquinone and the respective benzoquinones.[39,40]

The evidence linking benzene exposure to leukemia is discussed by Snyder et al.[46]:

> There is unequivocal evidence that benzene is a cause of acute myelogenous leukemia (AML), the adult form of acute leukemia. Individual cases in benzene-exposed individuals began to be reported in the 1920s, but the causal relationship was not fully accepted until less than two decades ago.

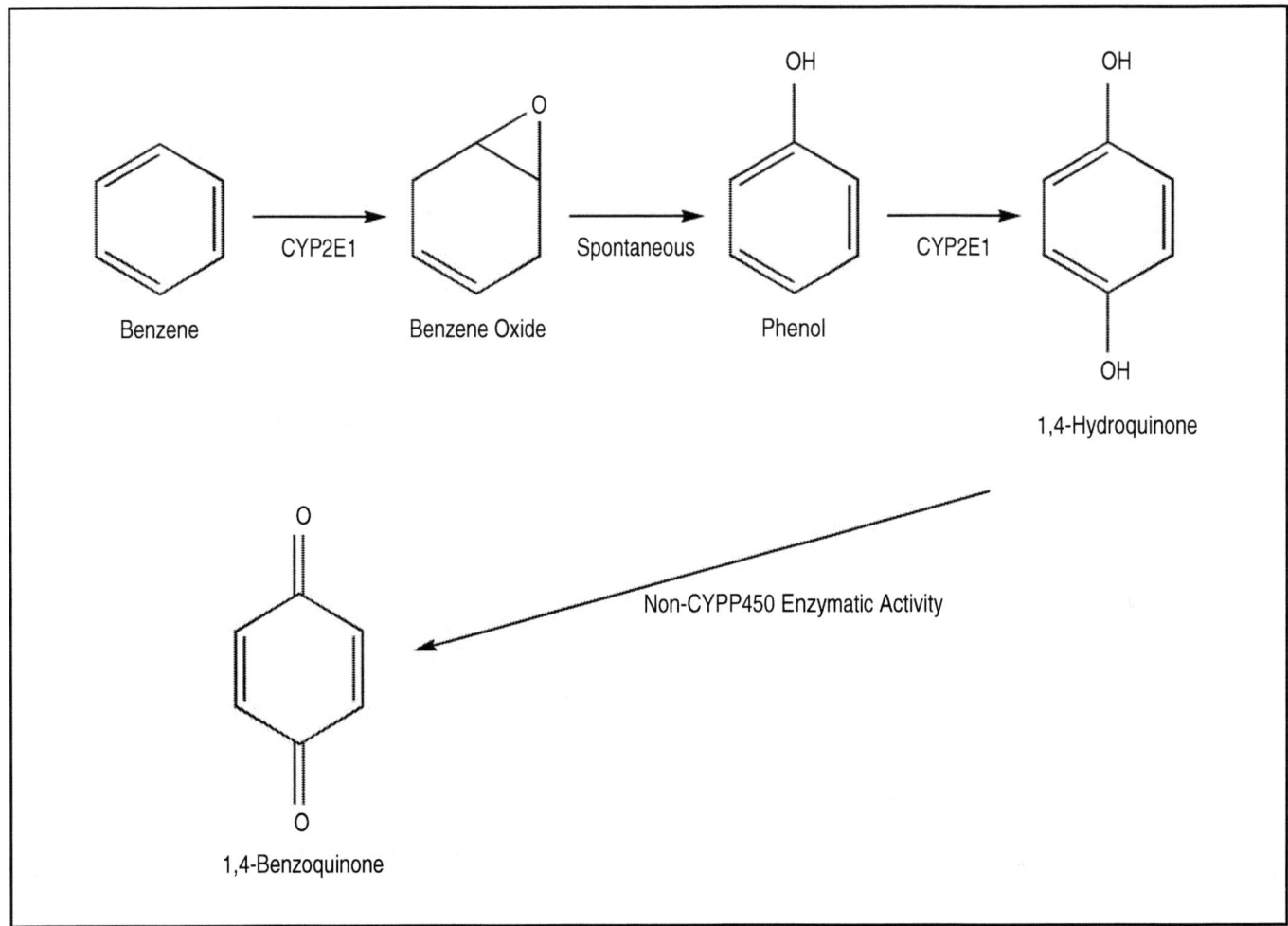

Figure 16.11 — Important benzene metabolites.

This relationship was first accepted by hematologists who have long recognized that anyone with aplastic anemia from apparently any cause has an increased risk of AML. For example, AML as a second tumor is, unfortunately, common in cancer patients whose bone marrow is affected by radiation and alkylating agents used in chemotherapy.[47] ...in Turkey, a glue used in the fashioning of leather goods which had relatively low levels of benzene as a solvent was replaced in the 1960s with one containing much higher levels. Soon thereafter, Aksoy and his colleagues reported a wave of patients with aplastic anemia followed by identification of numerous individuals with AML, many of whom had previously been identified as having aplastic anemia.[42,48]

Carcinogenesis is a complicated multi-step process, and the exact role of benzene metabolites in the production of leukemia and other blood effects remains somewhat elusive, but Snyder provides a useful hypothesis regarding a possible mechanism which is generalized as follows: after metabolism of benzene to multiple reactive metabolites, one or several of these disrupt the formation of blood cells and related processes that normally occur in the bone marrow. This may be the result of more than one mechanism, although a plausible link could be based on the known ability of benzene metabolites to covalently bind to DNA and other important macromolecules, in this case in hematopoietic stem cells. The initial damage to the hematopoietic stem cell population in the bone marrow from chronic benzene exposure would produce the commonly observed non-cancer blood effects, and account for biochemical mechanisms that lead to accumulation of immature white blood cells. The presence of a cell line among this pool that had undergone leukogenic transformation through DNA damage or incorrect repair would "serve as the parent of an expanding clone of leukemia cells."[40] Due to the role of the blood forming system in production of immune cells, and the disruptions benzene causes to normal conditions among these target cells, Snyder notes that when death from chronic benzene exposure occurs either due to leukemia or to other blood abnormalities, it is manifested through a lessened immune system capability.[40]

n-Hexane and Methyl n-Butyl Ketone

n-Hexane is a six carbon straight chain saturated alkane found in many products. The physical properties of the n-alkane series C_5 (n-heptane) through C_9 (n-nonane) are provided in Table 16.1. The simple nature of this series, the lack of relatively reactive heteroatoms (atoms other than C and H), and the relatively high exposure limits that have come to exist for mixtures of similar straight-chain hydrocarbons (and other typical aliphatic compounds) could lead the uninformed occupational health professional to the inaccurate conclusion that the six-carbon straight chain member of this series is relatively benign. Another compound that contains 6 linearly arranged carbon atoms is the solvent methyl-*n*-butyl ketone. This compound belongs to a class of ketones that are widely used in industry, with the simplest being acetone (Figure 16.12). Although virtually all of the ketone solvent compounds shown in this figure are capable of acute nervous system effects, along with *n*-hexane the methyl-*n*-butyl member of the ketone series carries the potential to elicit a unique and debilitating neuropathic response when workers are chronically exposed.

Because of its apparent similarity to other relatively innocuous aliphatic hydrocarbons, the solvent *n*-hexane was for many years considered a relatively benign compound, capable of causing local contact irritation, and acute central nervous system effects that apply to organic solvents as a general class. It was first discovered to have serious health effects by Japanese researchers who observed axonal neuropathy associated with exposure to the compound among workers in poorly ventilated spaces where air concentrations of the compound exceeded 500 ppm (v/v).[49] Shortly thereafter, researchers in the U.S. discovered cases of axonal neuropathy among workers using *n*-hexane from open drums in a poorly ventilated workspace.[16] Workers dipped rags in the liquid solvent to dissolve and clean excess glue from finished cabinets, and industrial hygiene air samples collected on sorbent tubes with subsequent analysis by gas chromatography revealed stated average *n*-hexane concentrations in this workplace of 650 ppm (v/v). Chang et al.[50] attributed similar health effects to *n*-hexane exposure among workers using the solvent in an offset printing process.

In the early 1970s, Billmaier et al. reported similar neuropathy among printing machine operators at a plant where printed fabric was manufactured.[17] A thorough investigation showed neuropathy cases to be present among a select group of workers, with the onset of problems coinciding to a change of solvent used in the printing process from methyl isobutyl ketone to methyl *n*-butyl ketone. Later, Mallov reported 3 cases of neuropathy in a group of painters who spray painted structural components of a dam. The observed neuropathy coincided with replacement of methyl isobutyl ketone and methyl isoamyl ketone (22% by weight each) in the paint used with methyl *n*-butyl ketone present at 44% (by weight) of the reformulated paint.[18] Mallov also noted that the spray painters were likely exposed by both the dermal and inhalation routes, as thinner containing methyl n-butyl ketone was used by these workers for hand cleaning.

Although methyl *n*-butyl ketone currently has a relatively low OEL, of 5 ppm (v/v)[2], it also has a low vapor pressure and a relatively low VHR of 31. Thus, while there is a possibility for vapor exposures that will exceed the OEL, under identical conditions of use the potential would be much lower than for n-hexane, which has a VHR of 3,987 owing entirely to its much greater vapor pressure. In the manuscript by Billmaier's group, measured levels of methyl-*n*-butyl ketone in workplace air where their neuropathy cases were observed ranged from around 2 to over 150 ppm (v/v), depending upon sampling location. In addition to exposure via inhalation, these researchers noted that: "poor work practices, such as eating in work areas, washing hands with solvent, and using solvent soaked rags to clean equipment and machinery were observed. No respirators were worn, and gloves were rarely used."[17]

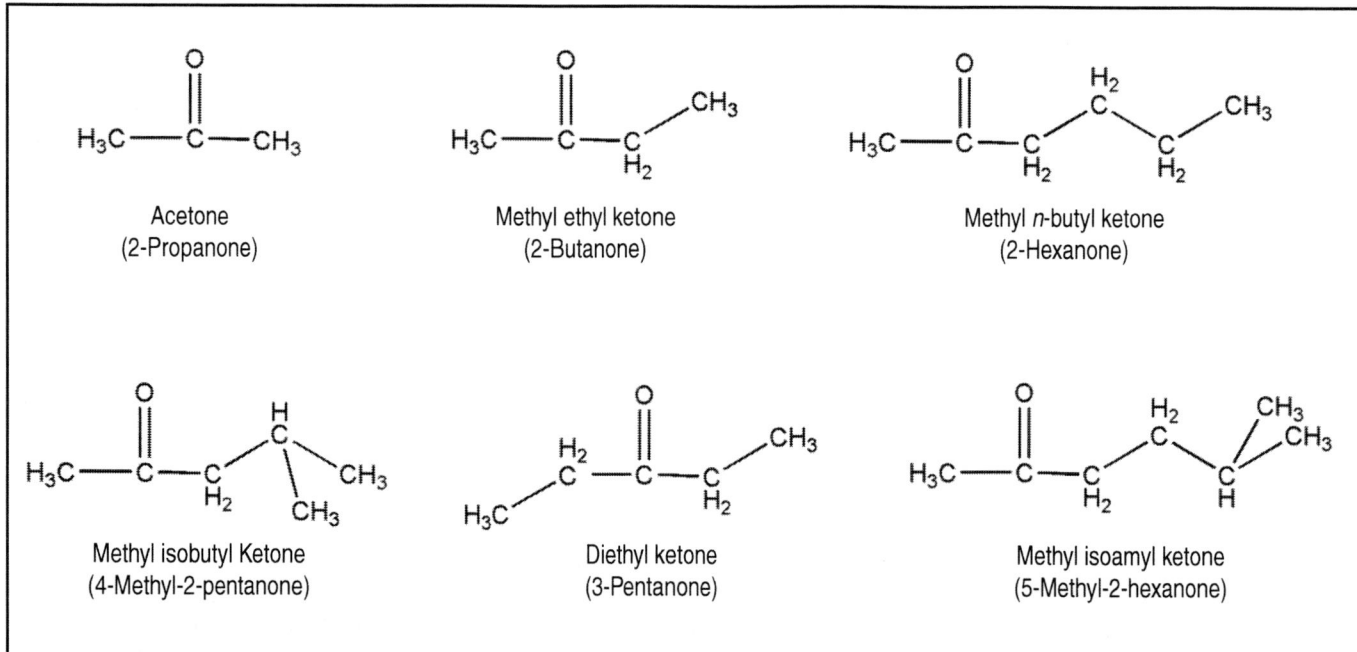

Figure 16.12 — Some common ketone solvents.

It is now known that biotransformation of both solvents leads to production of 2,5-hexanedione (Figure 16.13), a compound that has been shown to be capable of inducing similar neuropathies in animal models.[17,51] Governa et al. demonstrated the presence of 2,5-hexanedione in the urine of workers exposed to *n*-hexane[52], and the work of several research groups has confirmed a metabolic pathway for both *n*-hexane and methyl-*n*-butyl ketone that culminates in production of the hexanedione compound.[53-55] Animal studies show that absorbed *n*-hexane predictably distributes to tissues with high lipid content.[56] Elimination is rapid, with a blood clearance $t_{1/2}$ of around 100 min in a group of 6 human volunteers exposed to n-hexane vapors at different concentrations, and with and without physical exertion.[57] DiVincenzo et al.[54] showed that methyl-*n*-butyl ketone can be absorbed to an appreciable extent via the intact skin of human volunteers. In the same paper, retention of >75% of the compound was described following inhalation exposure, with 2,5-hexanedione observed in the plasma. Based on this work these researchers state that "methyl n-butyl ketone is readily absorbed by the lungs, the gastrointestinal tract, and through the skin, is not eliminated extensively unchanged in breath or urine, and is metabolized to CO_2 and 2,5-hexanedione" and that "...repeated daily exposure to high concentrations of methyl n-butyl ketone may lead to a prolonged exposure to neurotoxic metabolites."

Effects following chronic exposure to n-hexane[16,50,58] and methyl-n-butyl ketone[16,18], can include atrophy of affected muscles, weakness in the extremeties, distal parasthesia (perception of tingling), and "stocking-glove" numbness. A biological mechanism for the initially puzzling neurotoxicity of n-hexane and methyl-*n*-butyl ketone was identified in 1975 when Spencer and Schaumburg reported that the compound 2,5-hexanedione produces similar effects in rats to those observed in humans exposed to both methyl n-butyl ketone and to *n*-hexane.[51] The mechanism through which the 2,5-hexanedione metabolite of both *n*-hexane and methyl-*n*-butyl ketone produces damage to nerve tissues is understood to involve formation of a covalently bonded

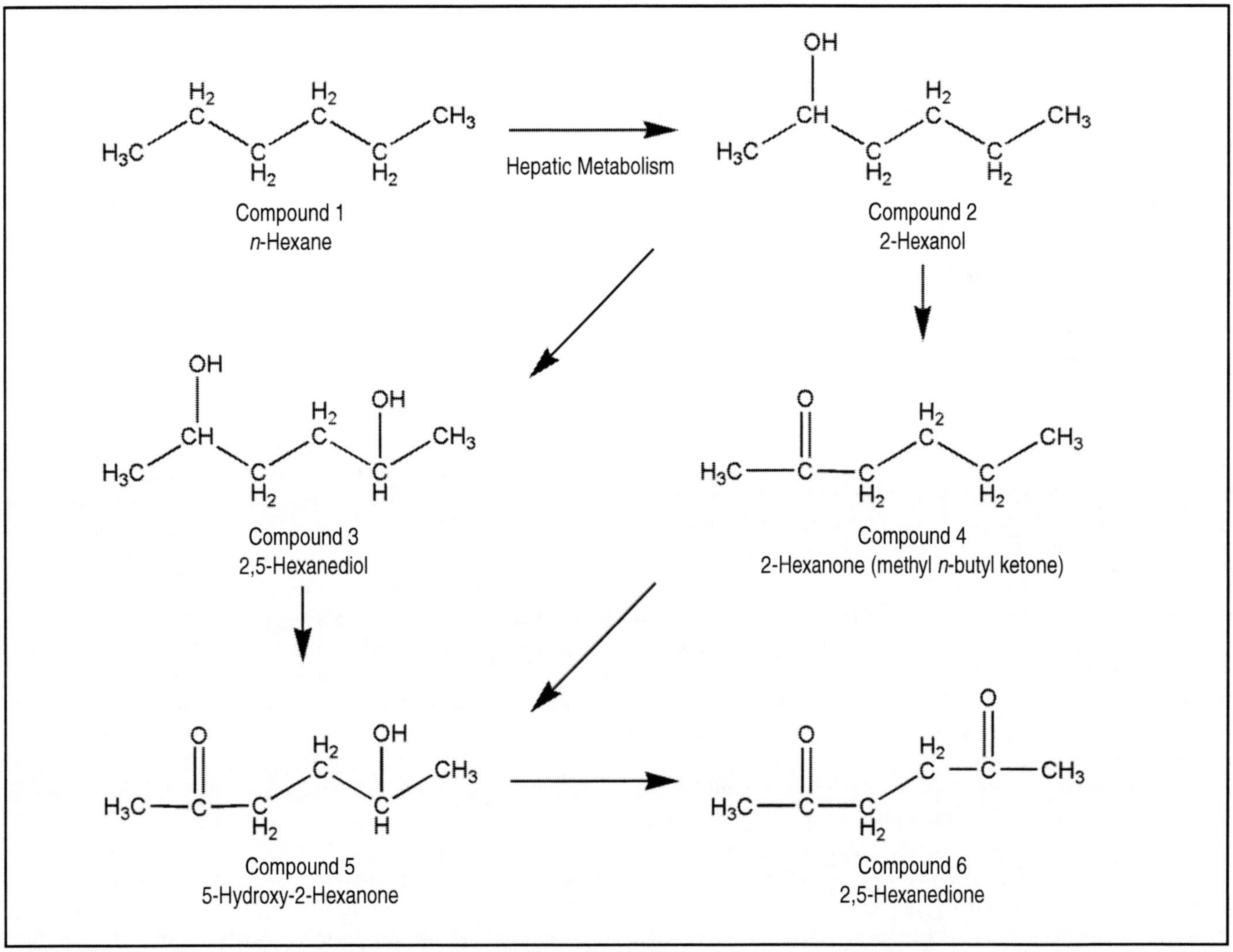

Figure 16.13 — Metabolism of *n*-hexane (Compound 1) and associated compounds to the γ-diketone 2,5-hexanedione. The distinct peripheral neuropathy caused by both *n*-hexane (Compound 1) and methyl *n*-butyl ketone (compound 4) was observed in several occupational populations exposed to these compounds independently of each other; the production of the same distinct type of neurotoxicity was later shown to occur in laboratory animals with dosing of all the compounds shown.

adduct of 2,5-hexanedione with amino groups, such as those that can be found on the side chain or "R-group" of the amino acid lysine.[59] Figure 16.14 shows the formation of a cyclic pyrrole compound following bonding of the hexanedione compound with a lysine residue. It is thought that the pyrrole so formed undergoes additional reactions leading to cross-linking of proteins in the axon[59], producing the microscopically observed axonal swelling[16,50,58], with peculiar neurofilament accumulations[16,58] observed in the affected peripheral nerves of symptomatic workers. Spencer et al.[51] showed similar findings of axonal swelling composed of abnormal masses of neurofilaments present in rats chronically dosed directly with 2,5-hexanedione.

Carbon Disulfide

Carbon disulfide (CS_2) is a clear liquid with a distinctive odor comparable to flatus. Its physical properties are found in Table 16.1. The toxicological effects unique to this compound are complex and are distinctly unique compared to those of other solvents used in industry. This solvent is commonly used in small amounts to dissolve analytes for gas chromatographic analysis with flame ionization detection, as the CS_2 molecule produces a very weak background response with this detector. By far the largest potential for occupational exposure exists in the manufacturing process of viscose rayon. During this process, cellulose is chemically modified, including a step where sodium hydroxide is added to wood pulp and the reaction mass is treated with CS_2, leading to the covalent addition of the solvent molecule to alcohol groups present on cellulose polymers. Nascent synthetic polymer is extruded into a continuous filament, and following acidification, the solvent is liberated from the newly formed filament and is removed through evaporation. Early exposures to workers in the viscose rayon industry were heavy, as adequate ventilation controls were essentially non-existent. The specific rayon manufacturing tasks listed by Gordy and Trumper as producing elevated CS_2 exposures included working near incompletely dried spools of newly formed rayon, and installation and repair of ventilation systems to control CS_2 vapors in a rayon plant.[60] The debilitation and suffering due to the wide range of neuropathies caused by heavy exposure to CS_2 are documented by Vigliani, who provides details of forty three cases from the Italian viscose rayon industry with exposure during roughly 20 years prior to the early 1950s.[61]

Gordy and Trumper's series of cases due to CS_2 exposure in the viscose rayon industry demonstrated symptoms that ranged from frequent headaches to loss of weight.[60] A common theme among these early high-exposure patients was visual difficulties (e.g., blindness or altered perception) and abnormal emotional expressions (e.g., inappropriate weeping or laughter). Among the numerous categories of responses upon chronic exposure to this compound, it has been shown to produce the effects of peripheral neuropathology (as does n-hexane and methyl n-butyl ketone).[62] The evidence for neuropsychic effects such as psychosis[60,61] being associated with high exposures to CS_2 is strong. Several epidemiology papers have also shown significant coronary heart disease increases among workers exposed to CS_2[63,64], and strong evidence is found in a study by Egaland et. al. that exposure is associated with elevated low-density lipoprotein cholesterol and increased blood pressure.[65]

Thus chronic carbon disulfide exposure can produce a wide ranging constellation of numerous responses, the most obvious of which are manifested in various decrements of nervous system performance. The range of the different responses is so extensive that a sense of confusion can easily develop in the student attempting to catalog them. One of the many responses that could almost be overlooked amongst the heavily exposed due to its relative subtlety is the peripheral sensory and motor neuropathy mentioned in the previous paragraph.[62] This neuropathy is similar in many ways to that produced by n-hexane and methyl n-butyl ketone, as it is also manifested by production of distal axonal swellings, with an unusual and disorganized accumulation of neurofilaments in the affected axons.[66] Even the mechanism believed responsible for these effects closely resembles that thought to be involved in the case of neuropathy produced by hexacarbon neuropathy: covalent modification of axonal proteins. In the case of CS_2 this is thought to occur by formation of protein adducts with the reactive sulfur atoms present on the CS_2 molecule.[67] Cohen et al. attributed CS_2 toxicity to formation of covalent protein adducts as early as 1959.[68]

Conclusion

Organic solvents are used in many workplace settings mainly for cleaning and controlled delivery of dissolved materials, and solvent compounds are found as components of many bulk materials including fuels. Due to the large number of uses for organic solvents and the numerous occasions where solvents are encountered, exposures to organic solvents are fairly common for large numbers of workers.

The central tenet of toxicology, that "the dose makes the poison" is a foundation upon which modern occupational exposure limits are based, and it is important that industrial hygienists understand the concept of exposure route and absorbed dose in correctly assessing potentially harmful exposures. Both the industrial hygienist and the toxicologist must identify the specific chemical to which workers are exposed, and it is the toxicologist that takes such information and then seeks to fully understand the associated biological events that occur following dosing, and their significance. We have discussed the general principle that toxicity involves the disruption of homeostasis (physiological balance) in a biological organism, producing an adverse health effect. To the industrial hygienist, the organisms of concern are human workers with direct exposures to hazardous chemicals, and other people in the general population that could be exposed incidentally. As the magnitude of existing standards for airborne exposure to chemical substances (including organic solvents) is related to the likelihood that adverse health effects can result, it is shown that our exposure standards are or should be based upon toxicology.

The physical properties of most organic solvents, and the availability of OELs for evaluating their airborne exposures tend

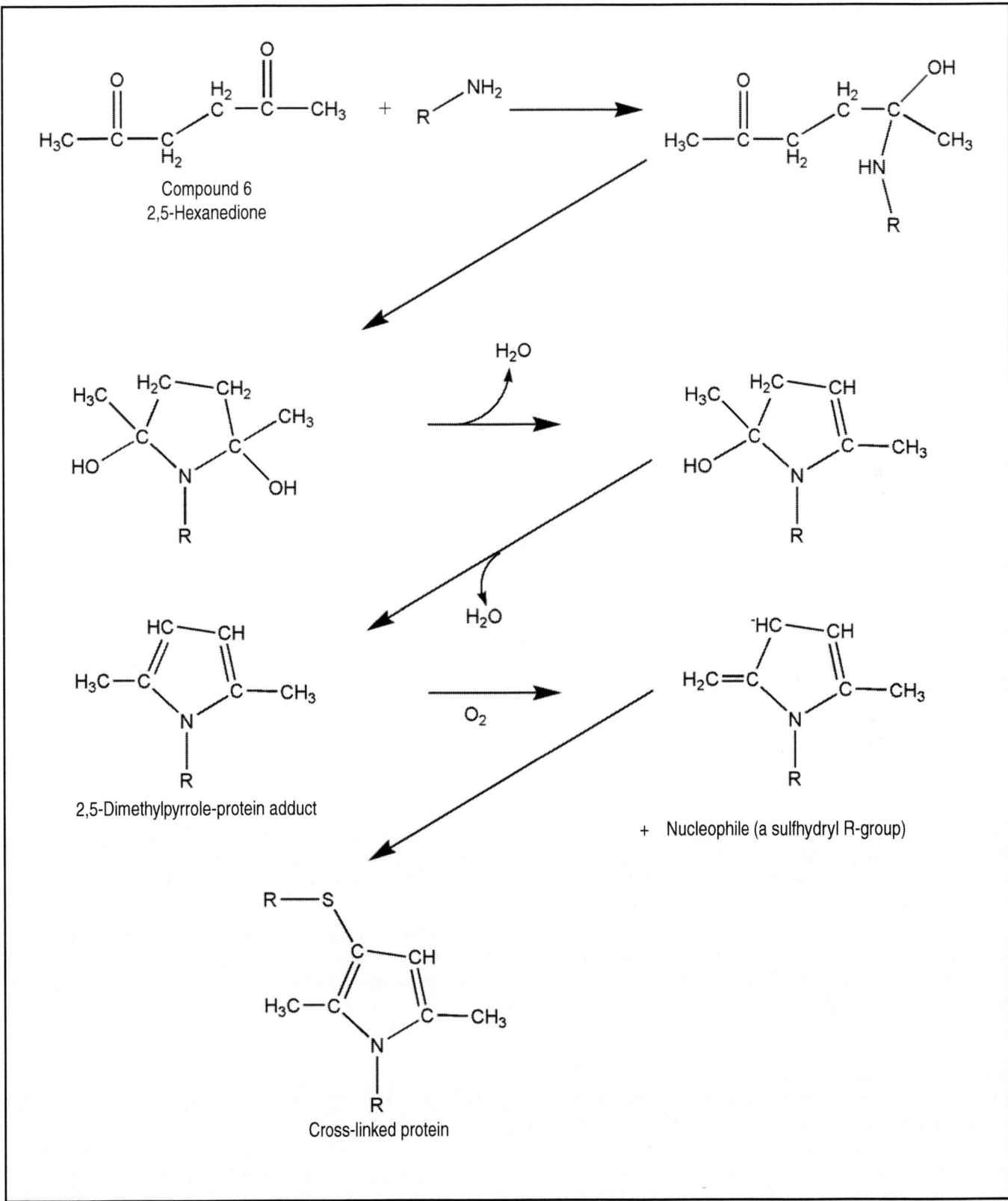

Figure 16.14 — Hypothesized mechanism for protein crosslinking by 2,5-hexanedione, compound 6 from Figure 16.18.[66] Initial reaction of 2,5-hexanedione is with an amino side chain (R-NH$_2$) such as that found on the amino acid lysine. After formation of the 2,5-dimethylpyrrole-protein adduct, oxidation of the adduct produces a reactive intermediate that can bind with a nucleophile such as the sulfhydryl group (R-SH) found on the amino acid cystiene. The result can be cross-linking of two separate proteins that contain these residues in locations where they are available to react.

to accentuate our focus on inhalation of organic solvent vapors, although skin exposures to solvent liquids and inhalation of liquid solvent aerosols are also possible. In situations where exposure is frequently or always to vapors alone, the work of the industrial hygienist can be assisted through the use of Poppendorf's vapor hazard ratio tool which can be used to prioritize further evaluation efforts, and where possible select candidates for substitution by a less hazardous solvent for one of greater hazard. In cases where skin exposure is unavoidable, or frequently occurs, biological exposure indices that help us to account for the absorption, distribution, and in many cases the metabolism of solvent (and other) chemical compounds need to be considered. The industrial hygienist must communicate on workplace conditions and work practices with the toxicologists and allied occupational health professionals in cases where a biological exposure index may prove useful, and should do so regardless when unusual health effects are observed among workers, to help establish or rule out causality.

The general neurological effects from organic solvent exposure contrasts with the specific effects of several individual organic solvent compounds. The interplay of absorption, distribution and metabolism to produce general and very specific responses was examined, with specific attention to the leukemogen and blood poison benzene, the peripheral neurotoxins n-hexane and methyl n-butyl ketone, and to CS_2, the very broad spectrum nervous system poison that also can produce elevated risk for cardiovascular disease among those exposed. The study of benzene's toxicology shows that it is a poison of the blood forming elements that requires metabolism to exert its selective effects on the hematopoeitic system. Both n-hexane and methyl n-butyl ketone are metabolized to 2,5-hexanedione, which has been shown to bind to proteins with crosslinking of very specific proteins thought to produce axonopathy and the neurological effects now observed repeatedly in both workers as well as in animal models. The solvent carbon disulfide has been shown to be capable of eliciting the same types of axonopathies as the two hexacarbon compounds just discussed, apparently through a similar mechanism of protein crosslinking.

Each industrial hygienist should understand the general and near-universal responses that are possible with acute exposure to virtually all organic solvents, but should also understand that in addition to instances where unique effects are known from prior experience that in unpredictable circumstances we are likely to see solvent-unique effects that today are unknown. Whether general or specific unique responses, each response from chemical exposure represents an imbalance or disruption to normal physiology, and the toxicologist's understanding of the fundamental biology and biochemical mechanisms for such disruptions should be translated into better understanding among industrial hygiene and safety professionals regarding the feasibility of different control strategies such as elimination or substitution of hazardous compounds, and the implementation of protective measures against the various routes of exposure. Proper risk assessment in the workplace regarding exposure to organic solvents and all other xenobiotics can benefit greatly from a cross-functional, multi-disciplinary effort and communication between the industrial hygienist, occupational toxicologist, and medical health professionals.

References

1. **Sax, N.I., and R.J. Lewis Sr.:** *Hawley's Condensed Chemical Dictionary*, 11th edition. New York: Van Nostrand Reinhold Company, 1987. p. 1080.
2. **American Conference of Governmental Industrial Hygienists (ACGIH):** 2006 TLVs® and BEIs®, Threshold Limit Values for Chemical Substances and Physical Agents, Biological Exposure Indices. Cincinnati, OH: ACGIH, 2006.
3. **Hook, G., G. Kimm, T. Hall, and P. Smith:** Solid phase microextraction for rapid field sampling and analysis by gas chromatography-mass spectrometry. *Trends Anal. Chem. 21*:534–543 (2002).
4. **Witschi, H.R. and J.A. Last:** Toxic Responses of the Respiratory System. In *Casarett and Doull's Toxicology, the Basic Science of Poisons*, 6th edition. New York: McGraw-Hill Medical Publishing Division, 2001. p. 519.
5. **Cohen, D.E. and R.H. Rice:** Toxic Responses of the Skin. In *Casarett and Doull's Toxicology, the Basic Science of Poisons,* 6th edition. New York: McGraw-Hill Medical Publishing Division, 2001. p. 653.
6. **Stevenson, C.J.:** Occupational Diseases of the Skin. In *Hunter's Diseases of Occupations*, 8th edition. Raffle, P.A.B., P.H. Adams, P.J. Baxter, and W.R. Lee (eds.). London: Edward Arnold Publishers, 1994. pp 691–719.
7. **Gallo, M.:** History and Scope of Toxicology. In *Casarett and Doull's Toxicology, The Basic Science of Poisons*, 6th edition. New York: McGraw-Hill Medical Publishing Division, 2001. p. 4.
8. **Eaton, D.L., and Klaassen, C.D.:** "Principles of Toxicology" in *Casarett and Doull's Toxicology, The Basic Science of Poisons*, 6th edition. New York: McGraw-Hill Medical Publishing Division, 2001. p. 11–34.
9. **Lawley, P.D.:** Historical origins of current concepts of carcinogenesis. *Adv. Cancer Res. 65*:17–111 (1994).
10. **Kennaway, E.:** The identification of a carcinogenic compound in coal-tar. Br. Med. J. 2:749-752 (1955).
11. **Xiao, J.Q., and S.M. Levin:** The diagnosis and management of solvent-related disorders. *Am. J. Ind. Med. 37*: 44–61 (2000).
12. **Dick, F.D.:** Solvent neurotoxicity. *Occup. Environ. Med. 63*:221–226 (2006).
13. **Landrigan, P.J.:** Benzene and blood: one hundred years of evidence. *Am. J. Ind. Med. 29*:225–226 (1996).
14. **Davidson, M., and M. Feinleib:** Carbon disulfide poisoning: a review. *Am. Heart J. 83*:100–114 (1972).
15. **Krasavage, K.I., I.L. O'Donoghue, and G.D. Divicenzo:** The relative neurotoxicity of methyl-n-butyl ketone, n-hexane, and their metabolites. *Toxicol Appl. Pharmacol 52*:433–441 (1980).

16. **Herskowitz, A., I. Nobuyoshi, and H. Schaumburg:** n-Hexane Neuropathy, a syndrome occurring as a result of industrial exposure. *New Engl. J. Med. 285*:82–85 (1971).
17. **Billmaier, D., H.T. Yee, N. Allen, B. Craft, N. Williams, S. Epstein, and R. Fontaine:** Peripheral neuropathy in a coated fabrics plant. *JOM 16*:665–671 (1974).
18. **Mallov, J.S.:** (1976) MBK neuropathy among spray painters. *JAMA 235*:1455–1457.
19. **Bruckner, J.V. and D.A. Warren:** "Toxic Effects of Solvents and Vapors" in *Casarett and Doull's Toxicology, the Basic Science of Poisons*, 6th ed. New York: McGraw-Hill Medical Publishing Division, 2001. p. 894–895.
20. **Parkinson, A.:** "Biotransformation of Xenobiotics" in *Casarett and Doull's Toxicology, the Basic Science of Poisons*, 6th ed. New York: McGraw-Hill Medical Publishing Division, 2001. p. 172.
21. **Recknagel, R.O.:** Carbon Tetrachloride Hepatotoxicity. *Pharmacol. Rev. 19*:145–208 (1967).
22. **Manno, M., M. Rezzadore, M. Grossi, and C. Sbrana:** Potentiation of Occupational Carbon Tetrachloride Toxicity by Ethanol Abuse. *Hum. Exp. Toxicol. 15*:294–300 (1996).
23. **Medinsky, M.A. and J.L. Valentine:** "Toxicokinetics" in *Casarett and Doull's Toxicology, the Basic Science of Poisons*, 6th ed. New York: McGraw-Hill Medical Publishing Division, 2001. p. 229.
24. **American Conference of Governmental industrial Hygienists (ACGIH):** "Lead, Recommended BEI®" in *Documentation of the TLVs® and BEIs® with other Worldwide Occupational Exposure Values*. Cincinnati, OH: ACGIH, 2004.
25. **American Conference of Governmental industrial Hygienists (ACGIH):** "Acetone, Recommended BEI®" in *Documentation of the TLVs® and BEIs® with other Worldwide Occupational Exposure Values*. Cincinnati, OH: ACGIH, 2004.
26. **American Conference of Governmental industrial Hygienists (ACGIH):** "n-Hexane, Recommended BEI®" in *Documentation of the TLVs® and BEIs® with other Worldwide Occupational Exposure Values*. Cincinnati, OH: ACGIH, 2004.
27. **American Conference of Governmental industrial Hygienists (ACGIH):** "Carbon disulfide, Recommended BEI®" in *Documentation of the TLVs® and BEIs® with other Worldwide Occupational Exposure Values*. Cincinnati, OH: ACGIH, 2004.
28. **American Conference of Governmental industrial Hygienists (ACGIH):** "Benzene, Recommended BEI®" in *Documentation of the TLVs® and BEIs® with other Worldwide Occupational Exposure Values*. Cincinnati, OH: ACGIH, 2004.
29. **American Conference of Governmental industrial Hygienists (ACGIH):** "Methyl Chloroform, Recommended BEI®" in *Documentation of the TLVs® and BEIs® with other Worldwide Occupational Exposure Values*. Cincinnati, OH: ACGIH, 2004.
30. **Popendorf, W.:** Vapor pressure and solvent vapor hazards, *Am. Ind. Hyg. Assoc. J. 45*:719–726 (1984).
31. **Popendorf, W.:** *Industrial Hygiene Control of Airborne Chemical Hazards*, 2006, CRC Press, Boca Raton, FL, pp 663–680.
32. **Bergman, K.:** Whole Body Autoradiography and Allied Tracer Techniques in Distribution and Elimination Studies of some Organic Solvents. *Scand. J. Work Environ. Health 5(1)*:29–92 (1979).
33. **Andrews, L.S., E.W. Lee, C.M. Witmer, J.J. Kocsis, and R. Snyder:** Effects of Toluene on the Metabolism, Disposition and Hemopoietic Toxicity of [3H]benzene. *Biochem. Pharmacol. 26*:293–300 (1977).
34. **Hamilton, A.:** General Review: Benzene (benzol) Poisoning. *Arch. Path/ Lab. Med. 11*:434–454, 601–632 (1931).
35. **Landrigan, P.J.:** Benzene and Blood: One Hundred Years of Evidence. *Am. J. Ind. Med. 29*:225–226 (1996).
36. **Infante, P.F., R.A. Rinsky, J.K. Wagoner, and R.J. Young:** Leukaemia in Benzene Workers. *The Lancet 2*: 76–78 (1977).
37. **Aksoy, M., S. Erdem, and S. Dincol:** Leukemia in Shoe Workers Exposed Chronically to Benzene. *Blood 44*: 837–841 (1974).
38. **Hayes, R.B., Y. Songnian, M. Dosemici, and M. Linet:** Benzene and Lymphohematopoietic Malignancies in Humans. *Am. J. Ind. Med. 40*:117–126 (2001).
39. **Snyder, R.:** Benzene and Leukemia. *Crit. Rev. Toxicol. 32*:155–210 (2002).
40. **Snyder, R.:** Overview of the Toxicology of Benzene. *J. Toxicol. Environ. Health A, 61*:339–446 (2000).
41. **Sammett, D., E.W. Lee, J.J. Kocsis, and R. Snyder:** Partial Hepatectomy Reduces Both Metabolism and Toxicity of Benzene. *J. Toxicol. Environ. Health 5*:785–792 (1979).
42. **Aksoy, M., K. Dincol, T. Akgun, S. Erdem, and G. Dincol:** Haematalogical Effects of Chronic Benzene Poisoning in 217 Workers. *Br. J. Ind. Med. 28*:296–302 (1971).
43. **Rappaport, S.M., S. Waidyanatha, K. Yeowell-O'Connell, N. Rothman, M.T. Smith, L. Zhang, Q. Qu, R. Shore, G. Li, and S. Yin:** Protein Adducts as Biomarkers of Human Benzene Metabolism. *Chemical-Biological Interaction 153–154*:103–109 (2005).
44. **Lindstrom, A.B., K. Yeowell-O'Connell, S. Waidyanatha, B.T. Golding, R. Torneo-Velez, S.M. Rappaport:** Measurement of Benzene Oxide in the Blood of Rats Following Administration of Benzene. *Carcinogenesis 18*:1637–1641 (1997).
45. **Lovern, M.R., M.J. Turner, M. Myer, G.I. Kedderis, W.E. Bechtold, P.M. Schlosser:** Identification of Benzene Oxide as a Product of Benzene Metabolism by Mouse, Rat, and Human Liver Microsomes. *Carcinogenesis 18*: 1695–1700 (1997).
46. **Snyder, R., G. Witz, B.D. Goldstein:** The Toxicology of Benzene. *Env. Hlth. Perspectives. 100*:293–306 (1993).

47. **Goldstein, B.D. and H. Kipen:** "Lessons on the Second Cancers Resulting from Cancer Chemotherapy" In *Biological Reactive Intermediates IV.* Witmer, C.M. (ed.). New York: Plenum Press, 1990. pp. 619–625.
48. **Aksoy, M. and S. Erdem:** Follow-Up Study on the Mortality and the Development of Leukemia in 44 Pancytopenic Patients with Chronic Benzene Exposure. *Blood, 52:* 285–292 (1978).
49. **Yamamura, Y.:** n-Hexane Polyneuropathy. *Folia Psychiatr Neurol Jap 23:*45–57 (1969).
50. **Chang, C.M., et al.:** n-Hexane Neuropathy in Offset Printers. *J. Neurol. Neurosurg. Psych.* 56:538–542 (1993).
51. **Spencer, P.S. and H.H. Schaumburg:** Experimental Neuropathy Produced by 2,5-Hexanedione — A Major Metabolite of the Neurotoxic Industrial Solvent Methyl n-Butyl Ketone. *J. Neurol. Neurosurg. Psychiatry* 38:771–775 (1975).
52. **Governa, M., et al.:** Urinary Excretion of 2,5-Hexanedione and Peripheral polyneuropathies in workers exposed to hexane, *J. Toxicol. Environ. Health,* 20:219–228 (1987).
53. **Abdel-Rahman, M.S., L.B. Hetland, and D. Couri:** Toxicity and Metabolism of Methyl n-Butyl Ketone. *Am. Ind. Hyg. J.* 37:95–102 (1976).
54. **DiVincenzo, G.D., M.L. Hamilton, C.J. Kaplan, W.J. Krasavage, and J.L. O'Donoghue:** Studies on the Respiratory Uptake and Excretion and the Skin Absorption of Methyl n-Butyl Ketone in Humans and Dogs. *Toxicol. Appl. Pharmacol.* 44:593–604 (1978).
55. **Couri, D., M.S. Abdel-Rahman, and L.B. Hetland:** Biotransformation of n-Hexane and Methyl n-Butyl Ketone in Guinea Pigs and Mice. *Am Ind. Hyg. Assoc. J.* 39:295–300 (1978).
56. **Böhlen, P., U.P. Schlunegger, and E. Lauppi:** Uptake and Distribution of Hexane in Rat Tissues. *Toxicol. Appl. Pharmacol.* 25:242–249 (1973).
57. **Veulemans, H., E. Van Vlem, H. Janssens, et al.:** Experimental Human Exposure to n-Hexane. *Int. Arch. Occup. Environ. Health* 49:251–263 (1982).
58. **Ruff, R.L., C.K. Petito, and L.S. Acheson:** Neuropathy Associated with Chronic Low Level Exposure to n-Hexane. *Clin. Toxicol.* 18:515–519 (1981).
59. **St. Clair, M.B.G., et al.:** Pyrrole Oxidation and Protein Cross-Linking as Necessary Steps in the Development of γ-Diketone Neuropathy. *Chem. Res. Toxicol.* 1:179–185 (1988).
60. **Gordy S.T. and M. Trumper:** Carbon Disulfide Poisoning with a Report of Six Cases. *JAMA 110:*1543–1549 (1938).
61. **Vigliani, E.C.:** Carbon Disulphide Poisoning in Viscose Rayon Factories. *Br. J. Ind. Med.* 11:235–244 (1954).
62. **Corsi, G., P. Maestrelli, G. Picotti, S. Manzoni, and P. Negrin:** Chronic Neuropathy in Workers with Previous Exposure to Carbon Disulphide. *Br. J. Ind. Med.* 40:209–211 (1983).
63. **Tiller, B.M., R.S.F. Schilling, and J.N. Morris:** Occupational Toxic Factor in Mortality from Coronary Heart Disease. *Br. Med. J.* 4:407–411 (1968).
64. **Hernberg, S., T. Partanen, C-H. Nordman, and P. Sumari:** Coronary Heart Disease among Workers Exposed to Carbon Disulfide. *Br. J. Ind. Med.* 27:313–325 (1970).
65. **Egaland, G.M., et al.:** Effects of Exposure to Carbon Disulphide in Low Density Lipoprotein Cholesterol Concentration and Diastolic Blood Pressure. *Br. J. Ind. Med.* 49:287–293 (1992).
66. **Graham, D.G., V. Amaranth, W.M. Valentine, S.J. Pyle, and D.C. Anthony:** Pathogenic Studies of Hexane and Carbon Disulfide Neurotoxicity. *Crit. Rev. Toxicol.* 25:91–112 (1995).
67. **Valentine, W.M., et al.:** CS_2-Mediated Cross-Linking of Erythrocyte Spectrin and Heurofilament Protein: Dose Response and Temporal Relationship to the Formation of Axonal Swellings. *Toxicol. Appl. Pharmacol.* 142:95–105 (1997).
68. **Cohen, A.E., L.D. Scheel, J.F. Kopp, et al.:** Biochemical Mechanisms in Chronic Carbon Disulfide Poisoning. *Ind. Hyg. J.* 20:303–323 (1959).
69. **Lide, D.R.:** *Handbook of Organic Solvents.* Boca Raton, FL: CRC Press, 1995.
70. **McAuliffe, C.:** Solubility in Water of Paraffin, Cycloparrafin, Olefin, Acetylene, Cycloolefin, and Aromatic Hydrocarbons. *J. Phys. Chem.* 70:1267–1275 (1965).
71. **Ran, Y., Y.H. Gang Yang, J.L.H. Johnson, and S.H. Yalkowski:** Estimation of aqueous solubility of organic compounds by using the general solubility equation, *Chemosphere* 48:487–509 (2002).
72. **Meylan, W.M. and P.H. Howard:** Table from Estimating Octanol-Air Partition Coefficients with Octanol-Water Partition Coefficients and Henry's Law Constants. http://esc.syrres.com/interkow/KoaData.htm. [Accessed October 5, 2007].

Chapter 17

Toxicology of Metals

*By Gary L. Hook, PhD, MPH, CIH,
Peter T. LaPuma, Ltc, PhD, CIH, PE, and Gary A. Morris, PhD, CSP*

Introduction

The definition of a metal is somewhat broad and imprecise. One definition is *"any of a category of electropositive elements that are usually whitish, lustrous, and, in the transition metals, typically ductile and malleable with high tensile strength. Typically metals form salts with nonmetals, basic oxides with oxygen, and alloys with one another…"*.[1] However, there are plenty of exceptions to this definition of a metal. The definition of a "heavy metal" is even more imprecise and has little to do with toxicity. In general, a heavy metal is described by density and is generally regarded as a metal with an atomic number greater than 20 (calcium is 20).[2] Humans and all living things have been absorbing and excreting metals since long before the industrial age. Water contains minerals and trace amounts of metals. Plants take up metals in the soil and when we ingest plants, some fraction of the metals are absorbed in the digestive tract. We also inhale fugitive dust from soil that contains metals and some metals are taken in through the lungs. Inhaled dust particles can also be brought up the respiratory tract with mucocilliary action, swallowed and enter into the digestive system. In the digestive system, metals can either be excreted through the feces or absorbed into the body.[3–5]

The fate and transport of metals in the human body vary but in general the amount of metals taken up from routine non-occupational exposures are not high enough to be toxicologically significant. Interestingly, some well known toxic industrial metals are actually nutrients in the right valence state such as arsenic and trivalent chromium, which will be discussed later. If the metal is absorbed into the body, the metal can be stored in the bone where it could remain for many years. Many metals are stored in the bone and slowly released into the blood over long periods of time. Once in the blood, metals can be excreted by the kidneys into the urine or interact with the body in some other way. Most metals can also be excreted through the hair or nails. Metal toxicity and the location of injury is often determined by the valence state of the metal, the other types of atoms bonded to the metal, the solubility of the metal and the dose of the metal.

Outcome Competencies

Upon completion of this chapter, the reader should be able to:
- Understand general tendencies of metal fate and transport in living things
- Appreciate the influence of the physical state and valence of a metal on toxicity
- Know uses and toxicity of the following occupationally significant metals: arsenic, beryllium, cadmium, chromium, cobalt, lead, manganese, mercury, nickel, tin
- Be familiar with the major case studies linked to each metal
- Understand the role of chelating agents

Prerequisite Knowledge

This chapter is designed to provide general information about metal toxicity for a beginning industrial hygienist. It is assumed that the reader has little prior knowledge of metal toxicity. A basic science background such as human biology, chemistry, physics, environmental science, engineering or other related sciences would help in understanding most of the concepts in this chapter.

Key Terms

Metal toxicity, chelating, arsenic, beryllium, cadmium, chromium, cobalt, lead, manganese, mercury, nickel, tin

Key Topics

1. **Introduction** — biological interaction with metals, valence and physical states, general fate and transport of metals
2. **Occupationally Significant Metal Uses, Toxicokinetics, Toxicity, Case Studies** — arsenic, beryllium, cadmium, chromium, cobalt, lead, manganese, mercury, nickel, tin
3. **Chelating Agents** — how they may be used to treat metal toxicity

Factors that Affect Metal Toxicity

The physical state of the metal can affect the biological uptake and distribution. Most metals are solid at room temperature with the notable exception of elemental mercury. Even though metals are predominantly solids, industrial manipulation of metals can result in significant inhalation hazards. Heating metals (e.g. smelting, welding) can produce oxide fumes of the metal. Mechanical handling (crushing, grinding, machining) results in metal particulates that may pose an inhalation hazard. Some metals are dissolved into acidic baths for electroplating, which can generate mist droplets containing dissolved metal. In the workplace, inhalation exposures to metals tend to be the dominant route of entry, but dermal absorption can occur with many metals. Other direct dermal effects such as ulcerations or chemical burns are possible.

The valence state of a metal can influence absorption and other biological interactions. There are no clear generalities with regard to valence state and biological response because every metal is unique. Discussions about valence states will be addressed in the following sections when individual metals are covered.

In this chapter only a selection of metals with significant occupational interest will be discussed. Metals that pose a radiological hazard will not be included. The metals to be addressed are: arsenic, beryllium, cadmium, chromium, cobalt, lead, manganese, mercury, nickel, and tin.

Arsenic (Symbol = As, MW = 74.9 g/mol, TLV®-TWA = 0.01 mg/m^3, BEI = 35 µg AS/L urine)

Like most metals, arsenic is found naturally in soil and water. Inorganic arsenic (combined with O, Cl, or S) is more prevalent in the environment and organic arsenic (combined with C and H) is more prevalent in living organisms. Arsenic exists in four valence states: -3, 0, +3, and +5. Toxicity of arsenic is complicated because arsenic can form many compounds with different valence states and all have a wide variety of toxicological effects. In general, trivalent "arsenites" tend to be more toxic than pentavalent "arsenates".[6–8] Also, inorganic arsenicals are generally more toxic than organics. However, these generalities cannot be taken as absolute because there are many exceptions. Also, living organisms and the environment regularly alter the chemical structure so exposure would often involve a mix of arsenic compounds.

Arsenic and its compounds are easily absorbed from the gastrointestinal tract. Skin can also be a route of exposure and systemic toxicity can occur after dermal contact. It is primarily excreted in the urine, but it can also be excreted by desquamation of skin and in the sweat.[9]

Since 1985, all arsenic in the United States is imported.[10] Arsenic is obtained as a byproduct of smelting copper, cobalt, gold and in particular, lead. Approximately 95% of arsenic is transported and consumed as arsenic trioxide (As$_2$O$_3$) dust.[10–12] Therefore, workplace air exposures would most commonly involve As$_2$O$_3$ dust. Inhalation of As$_2$O$_3$ dust can cause irritation to the mucous membranes, which can lead to laryngitis, bronchitis, or rhinitis.[13,14] Higher exposures can cause perforation of the nasal septum.[15] The International Agency for Research on Cancer (IARC) lists arsenic and arsenic compounds as Group 1, human carcinogens. This does not mean all arsenic compounds are included in the group. The IARC determination is heavily based on evidence with inorganic arsenic as they relate to lung and skin cancer. Bladder, liver and kidney cancer are implicated as well. Skin contact can cause redness and swelling and chronic skin exposures can lead to hyperpigmentation, folliculitis, ulcerations and warts.[16]

Ingesting high doses of arsenic can cause nausea, vomiting and diarrhea, decreased production of red and white blood cells (anemia), abnormal heart rhythm, damage to blood vessels and damage to the peripheral nervous system. Ingestion effects have occurred from inhaling high doses of arsenic. It is thought that mucocilliary transport of arsenic dust from the lungs to the digestive system is responsible for these effects. Ingesting very high levels of inorganic arsenic can result in death. Like most metals, arsenic is eliminated in hair and nails. High levels of arsenic exposure can manifest as pale bands across the fingernails, known as Mees Lines.[17]

Any brief summary of occupational case studies would be difficult due to the number of arsenic compounds and the diversity of their health effects. However, a brief discussion of arsine gas and arsenic in pressure treated lumber is noteworthy. Arsine gas (AsH$_3$) is used heavily in semiconductor production and is a highly toxic form of arsenic. It destroys red blood cells and its Immediately Dangerous to Life and Health (IDLH) exposure level is only 6 ppm. Arsine was even used in warfare by the Germans in WWI. Numerous deaths have occurred from accidental formation of arsine. Acid and arsenic will form arsine especially in the presence of zinc. Because arsenic is a common impurity in many metals, arsine could be formed when acid contacts most any metal. Two workers died from arsine gas exposure from using phosphoric acid to clean the inside of an aluminum tanker that was used to transport sodium arsenite (weed killer) 6 months prior. Five died while washing aluminum slag contaminated with arsenic. Two died when an aluminum ladder reacted with a few inches of sodium arsenite in the bottom of a tank.[18]

Arsenic was used heavily in agriculture as pesticides and herbicides. Though its use is very much curtailed today, some pesticides contain arsenicals, such as cacodylic acid used on cotton plants. Arsenic is also added to other metals, lead ammunition, automotive body solder and brass to improve corrosion resistance.[11] Since the mid 70s, arsenic has been used as a wood preservative in "pressure treated lumber" primarily as chrome copper arsenate (CCA). CCA had accounted for more than 90% of the US consumption of arsenic trioxide.[10] However, due to concerns over dermal absorption of arsenic, a voluntary phase out of CCA as a wood preservative started as of Jan 2004. Exposure can still occur with occupations that handle existing or allowable exceptions involving pressure treated lumber. Pressure treated lumber should never be burned as the fly ash contains arsenic.[17]

Beryllium (Symbol = Be, MW = 9.0 g/mol, TLV®-TWA = 0.002 mg/m³)

Beryllium is an alkaline earth metal and is unique in that it's not a heavy metal, but it is quite toxic. Beryllium is a brittle, steel-gray metal. Approximately 65% of the known beryllium resources are in the U.S. The U.S. is one of only three countries that process beryllium ore.[19] The physical and mechanical properties of beryllium are very unique. Beryllium is six times stronger than steel, 66% of the weight of aluminum, and has one of the highest melting points of any metal, making it valuable for a wide variety of industrial uses. However, it is not used as extensively as other metals in part due to its cost and toxicity. Beryllium metal is used primarily in aerospace and defense applications because it is strong, lightweight, and dimensionally stable across a wide temperature range.[20]

When inhaled, half of the beryllium is cleared in two weeks, with the remainder being removed very slowly. Some is never cleared and becomes fibrotic granulomata in the tissues. When ingested, beryllium can be absorbed through the stomach. It is distributed to all tissues, but most goes to the bones and the liver. It has a short half-life in tissues, except for the lungs. A variable amount of beryllium is excreted in the urine.[9]

Beryllium containing compounds are highly toxic to the lungs and can cause skin disorders. OSHA reports that beryllium causes lung and skin disease in 2–10% of exposed workers.[21] In a case control study, it was concluded that there were increased lung cancer rates for workers exposed to beryllium.[22] Skin contact can cause contact dermatitis involving inflammation, itching, redness, rashes, swelling, and blisters. Contact dermatitis usually improves a few weeks after exposure ends.

Two lung disorders caused by beryllium are referred to as acute beryllium disease (ABD) and chronic beryllium disease (CBD), or berylliosis. ABD is caused by breathing high levels of beryllium dust or fumes, which results in an allergic type inflammatory reaction in the lungs. ABD can lead to death but, due in part to good industrial hygiene practices, it is relatively rare. CBD is more common in industries working with beryllium. CBD causes granulomas (nodules) that develop in the lungs, which interfere with normal lung function. Approximately 20% of CBD cases are fatal.[23] Onset of CBD can occur within months or up to 30 years after exposure to beryllium. Individuals who get CBD are highly sensitized to beryllium causing allergic reactions with subsequent exposures. Occupational exposure can occur in mining, extraction, and in processing of metal alloys containing beryllium.[21] Only trained professionals in well-controlled environments should handle beryllium containing compounds. IARC classifies beryllium as a Group 1 human carcinogen.[24]

Cadmium (Symbol = Cd, MW = 112.4 g/mol, TLV®-TWA = 0.01 mg/m³, TLV®-TWA = 0.002 mg/m³ respirable fraction, BEI = 5 µg/g creatinine urine, BEI = 5 µg/L blood)

Most cadmium used in the U.S. is extracted during the production of other metals like zinc, lead, and copper. Cadmium does not corrode easily. Approximately 70% of cadmium is used in nickel-cadmium batteries, 12% as pigments in plastics, ceramics, and glass, 17% as stabilizer for polyvinyl chloride (PVC), 8% as metal coatings and the remainder in special alloys.[25,26]

About 5 to 8 percent of cadmium that is ingested is absorbed through the gastrointestinal tract. Inhalation usually results in 15 to 30 percent respiratory absorption. 50 percent of cadmium fumes may be absorbed through the lungs. Cadmium is distributed primarily to the liver and kidney by binding to red blood cells and proteins in the serum, such as albumin. There tends to be progressive accumulation in the soft tissues, such as the kidneys. Cadmium is excreted in the urine.[9]

The kidney is the primary target organ with chronic cadmium exposure. Kidney damage can lead to increased frequency of kidney stone formation. Softening of the bones can also occur with long-term exposure.[27] With high-level inhalation exposure, severe pulmonary edema can lead to death from respiratory failure. Symptoms may be delayed for days.[28] High levels of cadmium ingestion from food or beverages can cause severe irritation to the gastrointestinal epithelium as well as nausea, vomiting, salivation, abdominal pain, cramps, and diarrhea.[29–31] Categorization of cadmium as a lung carcinogen is conflicting. At the time of this writing, American Conference of Governmental Industrial Hygienists (ACGIH®) lists cadmium as A2, suspected human carcinogen. The U.S. EPA lists cadmium as a probable human carcinogen and the IARC classifies cadmium as a Group 1, human carcinogen.

The most infamous case study involving cadmium is the environmental release of cadmium in a Japanese river, which lead to a disease known as "Itai Itai" (translated in Japanese as "ouch-ouch"). Mining activities along the Jinzu River for zinc, copper and lead from 1910–1945 released significant quantities of cadmium into the river. The river was used for rice irrigation, drinking and cooking. Cadmium accumulated in the fish, rice and the human populations along the river. The cadmium exposure caused bone softening, increased bone breaks and severe pain in the joints and back. The exposure also caused irreversible kidney damage. The disease often limited the victim's movements, caused severe pain and sometimes death.[32]

Chromium (Symbol = Cr, MW = 52g/mol, TLV®-TWA = 0.5 mg/m³ (Cr^0 and Cr^{3+}), TLV®-TWA = 0.05 mg/m³ (water-soluble Cr^{6+}), TLV®-TWA = 0.01 mg/m³ (Insoluble Cr^{6+}), BEI = 25 µg/L total Cr in urine at end of workweek, BEI = 10 µg/L total Cr in urine as increase during shift)

The most stable and biologically significant valence states of chromium are metallic chromium (Cr^0), trivalent chromium (Cr^{3+}) and hexavalent chromium (Cr^{6+}). Cr^0 and Cr^{6+} are predominantly man-made substances, while Cr^{3+} is the valence state found naturally in the environment.[33] Cr^{3+} is also found to a lesser extent dissolved in water and, at trace amounts, it is found in living things such as plants, animals, and humans. Cr^0 is the metal, which is not naturally found in the environment and is considered biologically inert. Cr^{3+} is an essential nutrient, which helps insulin function properly in the body. Cr^{3+} supplements have even shown some success in research to treat Type II diabetes. While Cr^{3+} is generally regarded as safe, people can overdose with dietary supplements and some people can develop allergic skin reactions with dermal exposure to Cr^{3+}. Cr^{6+} is listed as a Group 1 human carcinogen. When Cr^{6+} reduces to Cr^{3+}, it binds to DNA causing genetic alteration that can increase the risk of cancer. With repeated contact, Cr^{6+} can also cause perforations or ulcerations on the skin or mucus membranes. Most notably, it can cause perforations in the nasal septum when Cr^{6+} containing aerosols are routinely inhaled.[34]

Chromium and chromates easily cross through the cell membranes of the respiratory and gastrointestinal tracts on anion carriers since they are structurally similar with sulfate and phosphate anions. They are distributed throughout the body, including the lungs, liver, kidney, and blood. They are excreted in the urine independent of oxidation state.[9]

Chromite ore has not been mined in the U.S. since 1961.[35] Chromium ores are imported to the U.S. predominantly from South Africa, Turkey and Russia.[36], but then undergo further processing in refineries in the U.S. Various processing techniques determine the valence state and form of the chromium. Most Cr^0 is used as a corrosion inhibitor with other metals. It is added to steel to produce stainless steel and it is in alloy cast iron. It is also used for surface treatments like "chrome" plated surfaces. The base metal is placed into an acidic bath containing dissolved salts of Cr^{6+} and through an anode-cathode reaction, the chromium is plated onto the base metal as Cr^0. Occupational exposures to Cr^{6+} can occur from the acid bath or inhalation of mist particles, but the resulting chrome plated surface is not hazardous. Cr^{6+} containing particles can be liberated if welding a metal that contains any form of chromium.[34]

Until recently, pressure treated lumber in the U.S. had been impregnated with chromated copper arsenate (CCA), which contains Cr^{6+} (see arsenic for more information). Chromium is also used in the leather tanning industry. Cr^{3+} is the only form of chromium with leather tanning properties; therefore, any Cr^{6+} that might be present would be as an impurity.[37] Chromate salts (with Cr^{6+}) are added to primer paints as a corrosion inhibitor, but Cr^{3+} may be added to paint as a pigment. Cr^{6+} is found in cements and a range of products containing cement such as mortars, grouts, and tile adhesives. Many applications involving chromium will often contain a mix of Cr^{3+} and Cr^{6+}, so some research may be prudent to fully evaluate worker exposure to Cr^{6+}. Chromium is also an additive for photography, pyrotechnics, dyes, paints, inks, and plastics.

There are numerous case studies mostly involving the inhalation of Cr^{6+}. In general, most studies demonstrate a wide variety of respiratory disorders, loss of lung function, perforated nasal septum and lung cancer.[38] Most studies conclude that in workers exposed to Cr^{6+}, there is a high prevalence of lung cancer. In studies involving stainless steel work and leather tanning where the exposure is predominantly Cr^{3+}, the correlation to lung cancer is mixed. In many chromium plating studies, where Cr^{6+} is more prevalent, the link to lung cancer is clear.[34]

Cobalt (Symbol = Co, MW = 58.9 g/mol, TLV®-TWA = 0.02 mg/m³, BEI = 15 μg/L urine, BEI = 1 μg/L blood)

Cobalt is a hard, brittle metal with a shiny bluish hue and magnetic properties similar to iron. Zaire produces the majority of the world's cobalt.[39] Cobalt is produced as a by-product from copper, nickel, and lead mining. Cobalt has numerous characteristics that make it a valuable resource in industry. Vitamin B-12 contains cobalt and it is beneficial in treating anemia because it promotes red blood cell generation. In the 1960s, some breweries added cobalt salts to beer to stabilize the foam. However, this practice is discontinued because of a link to cardiomyopathy (heart damage).[40] Cobalt –60 is an artificially produced radiological isotope used as a high-energy radiation source. Cobalt is alloyed with iron and nickel to make alnico, an alloy with strong magnetic properties used in turbine engines. Cobalt exposure in the workplace can occur when grinding with tungsten carbide cutting tools, which sometimes contain cobalt. Because of its physical appearance, hardness, and resistance to oxidation, cobalt is used in electroplating and as a pigment in porcelain, glass, pottery, tiles, and enamels.[41]

Cobalt salts are well absorbed in the gastrointestinal tract. As much as 80% of the ingested cobalt is excreted in the urine in the human. It is also found in the feces, milk, and sweat. It is widely distributed throughout the body—muscle, fat, liver, heart, and hair.[9]

Inhalation exposure to high levels of cobalt can cause asthma, pneumonia, and wheezing.[41] Inhalation of cobalt metal dust and fume can cause irritation of the skin and eyes.[42] It has also been linked to intestinal fibrosis, interstitial pneumontis, heart disorders, thyroid disorders and sensitization of the respiratory tract. In sensitized individuals, exposure can trigger asthma-like attacks, with wheezing, bronchospasm, and dyspnea.[43] Chronic respiratory exposure may result in reduced lung function and a fibrosing lung disorder sometimes refered to as "hard metal disease".[44] In a case study of an individual with a 36 year history of cobalt exposure, chronic skin exposure to cobalt dust and fume was shown to cause dermatitis in skin folds and on the arms, legs, and neck.[45] The IARC lists cobalt and cobalt compounds as group 2B, possible human carcinogens.[24]

Lead (Symbol = Pb, MW = 207.2, TLV®-TWA = 0.05 mg/m³, BEI = 30 μg/100 mL blood)

Lead is prevalent in the environment and serves no known use biologically. It is a soft, malleable metal with very high density and strength, low melting point and resistance to corrosion. These characteristics have proven to be useful in many industries. In its elemental form, lead is predominantly used in the production of car batteries. For the most part, lead is recycled from car batteries though mining is still necessary. Lead is also used for radiation shielding and for reduction of sound and vibration. Lead compounds have been widely used in paints, plastics and in glazes for ceramics. Alloys of lead have been used in pipes and solders, which are often in older buildings. While the use of lead in paint and gasoline has been restricted, occupational exposure to lead dust and fumes can occur in battery manufacturing, lead smelting, and refining operations.

Adults absorb 5 to 15 percent of lead that is ingested with less than 5 percent being retained. About 90 percent of lead particles in ambient air that are inhaled and deposited in the lungs are small enough (less than 0.5 μm in diameter) to be absorbed through the alveoli. Once absorbed through ingestion or respiration, lead and its compounds are distributed throughout the body. The largest pool of lead is in the skeleton, with a half-life of more than 20 years. The bones contribute as much as 50 percent of blood lead. Lead also accumulates in liver and kidney, as well as the central nervous system. About 90 percent of blood lead is associated with the red blood cell membrane and hemoglobin. Lead is primarily excreted by the kidney into the urine. It is also excreted with other body fluids, including milk.[9]

Lead is often categorized as inorganic (e.g. lead sulfide) and organic lead (e.g. tetraethyl lead added to gasoline). Inorganic and organic lead toxicity are similar so they will be discussed together. The differences have more to do with severity of effects and biological uptake. Exposure to lead is most closely associated with neurological effects, but liver, kidney, blood, reproductive and developmental effects can occur as well.[46] Early neurological symptoms may be as mild as a headache and irritability. With continued exposure, the symptoms can lead to muscle tremors, memory loss, confusion, impairment of mental and visual functions, seizures, coma and even death.[47–51] Ingestion can cause gastrointestinal symptoms similar to colic and generally include cramping, nausea, vomiting, weight loss, and constipation.[47,49,52] Lead is hematotoxic because it inhibits heme synthesis required for hemoglobin in red blood cells. Lead exposure may be linked to reproductive effects in both males and females; however, studies on fertility, and spontaneous abortions are conflicting.[53–56] Lead is also a teratogen. The transplacental transport of lead to a developing fetus has been well documented. The developing fetus is highly susceptible to neural damage from lead.[57] One distinction between inorganic and organic lead is that inorganic lead often involves muscle pain, which is not associated with organic lead. Another difference is that tetraethyl lead (formerly found in leaded gasoline) is easily absorbed through skin and severe exposures include lead toxicity effects plus hallucinations, hyperactivity and loud shouting.

Due to lead's almost ubiquitous nature, there are numerous occupational case studies describing lead exposure and its hematologic, neurologic and renal effects. However, there is now growing evidence demonstrating the potential for and association between cancer and lead exposure. This evidence stems from case studies of workers in battery and smelting operations as well as workers exposed to lead in other industries. One study of over 27,000 cases and 108,000 controls used a job-exposure matrix comparing lead exposure to occupation and industry codes.[58] This study found an increased risk for brain cancer in workers with an increased risk of lead exposure based upon their occupation/industry code. A cohort study of almost 4,000 primary smelter workers demonstrated an elevated risk of lung cancer for all workers with the highest risk in workers exposed to lead.[59] A meta-analysis of case control and cohort studies evaluated occupational exposure to inorganic lead and the risk of cancer. This analysis found significantly elevated excess risk for stomach, lung and bladder cancers among exposed workers. As noted by the authors, information concerning confounders such as smoking and other potential lead exposures could not be identified in this meta-analysis and could possibly contribute to the elevated cancer risk.[61] Even with the growing number of case studies indicating the potential for an association between lead exposure and cancer, the human cancer evidence is still considered inadequate. Therefore the IARC has classified inorganic lead as a Group 2B and organic lead as a Group 3 carcinogens.[60]

Manganese (Symbol = Mn, MW = 54.94g/mol, TLV®-TWA = 0.2 mg/m^3)

Manganese can be found in rock, soil, water and to some degree air. It does not occur naturally as a metal but is a component in over 100 types of minerals. Manganese is an essential micronutrient needed for bone mineralization as well as protein and energy metabolism.[62] Humans generally obtain their essential manganese through food and water.

Manganese is no longer mined in the United States. The import of manganese is closely linked to U.S. steel production because 85–90% of manganese is used to harden and strengthen steel.[63,64] There are approximately 2,060 U.S. facilities that process manganese. Although the facilities are found throughout the country, many are in Ohio, Indiana and Pennsylvania.[65] Manganese is also used as a fungicide and pesticide. Some water and wastewater treatment plants use potassium permanganate as a fungicide. Manganese is found in dry-cell batteries, matches and glass-bonding. Manganese may also be used as an additive in fuel to boost octane. Canada has been using manganese as a gasoline additive since 1990 and its use as an additive is increasing in the U.S.[66,67]

Manganese is distributed throughout the body after absorption through the small intestine and from inhalation of dusts. It easily passes through the blood-brain barrier. It is secreted in the bile and eliminated from the body in the feces.[9]

Manganese miners exposed to high levels of manganese dust in the air have developed permanent neurological disorders to include poor motor coordination, which can lead to tremors. Symptoms can also include psychological disturbances. These symptoms are collectively referred to as "manganism." The neurological effects have been referred to as a "Parkinsonism-like disease."[68,69] In men, symptoms can also include impotence and loss of libido.[70,71] The mechanism of manganese neurotoxicity is not well understood. Suggested theories include inhibited mitochondrial enzyme activity and increased production of free radicals causing oxidative injury.[72–74]

An epidemiologic study of 115 male workers from a ferromanganese and silicomanganese alloy factory were exposed to manganese oxide dusts and fumes. Total manganese dust concentrations were between 0.014–11.48 mg/m^3 and the mean duration of exposure was 16.7 years. The workers had significantly higher blood manganese levels and showed decreased motor function performance as compared to matched control workers with no manganese exposure.[75] Other studies on manganese workers show similar results.[76,77] A more recent 8-year prospective cohort study on 92 workers in a dry alkaline battery plant was conducted. Tests for hand eye coordination and hand steadiness showed that the group with higher manganese exposure performed significantly worse than low exposure groups.[78] Neurological disorders and emotional disturbances appear to become more pronounced with older workers.[79]

Mercury (Symbol = Hg, MW = 200.59, TLV®-TWA = 0.01 mg/m^3 (alkyls), TLV®-TWA = 0.1 mg/m^3 (aryls), TLV®-TWA = 0.025 mg/m^3 (elemental and inorganic), BEI® = 35 µg/g creatinine in urine, BEI® = 15 µg/L blood)

Mercury is found in the environment in elemental (also known as metallic), inorganic and organic forms. Elemental mercury is a dense material that is a silver-white liquid at room temperature. Being a liquid, elemental mercury can become airborne as a vapor. Although its volatility is very low, evaporation can become a significant exposure if heated. Inorganic mercury, commonly called mercury salts, is solid at room temperature. Organic mercury compounds, referred to as organomercury, are typically solids but some forms are liquids (e.g. dimethylmercury).

Mercury for industrial purposes is obtained through mining cinnabar ore (HgS) and through the secondary processing of scrapped mercury containing materials. Mercury is used to produce batteries, switches, thermostats, and dental amalgam. Mercury is used in plating operations, tanning operations, production of chlorine and caustic soda and as a catalyst in polymer reactions. Mercury was at one time used in many products as a fungicide. However, many of these uses have been restricted due to the toxicity associated with mercury.[80] Of historical interest was the use of mercury in the felt industry. During the 19th century, numerous cases of poisoning from ingesting mercury during the production of hats gave birth to the phrase "mad as a hatter". This phrase came about as a result of the psychiatric syndrome known as "erythism" or Mad Hatter's disease.[81]

Elemental mercury (vapor) is lipophilic and is rapidly absorbed after inhalation.[82,83] There is limited evidence of absorption of inorganic mercury from inhalation exposures. Ingestion of inorganic mercury does exhibit limited absorption into the body, but there is negligible absorption of elemental mercury.[84,85] Once absorbed, mercury is distributed to many tissues with the kidneys and the central nervous system being the primary target organs. Renal effects can range from various levels of renal dysfunction to acute renal failure.[86,87] Central nervous system effects can range from headache, insomnia, irritability, nervousness, memory loss, tremors, weakness and polyneuropathy (several peripheral nerves throughout the body malfunction simultaneously).[88,89] Mercury is excreted in the urine and feces. After inhalation of mercury vapor, a small amount is exhaled. Fecal excretion is the major route of elimination for inorganic mercury. After exposure to methyl mercury, 90 percent is excreted in feces. Renal excretion increases as time increases after exposure.[9]

Depending on the route of exposure, organomercury compounds can be absorbed to varying degrees. Absorption from oral exposure is very high with up to 95% being absorbed.[90] Similar to other forms of mercury, once absorbed, organomercury is distributed to many tissues but the kidneys and CNS are primary target organs. Reported CNS effects include irritability, numbness and tingling limbs, memory loss, slurred speech, unsteady gait, and fine movement degradation.[91,92]

The most significant cases of mercury exposure have occurred as a result of ingestion of organic mercury. Compounds such as methyl mercury are more toxic than elemental mercury and are more readily absorbed due to their high solubility. The most prominent case of methyl mercury poisoning occurred in Minamata Japan from 1953 to 1961.[93] In this instance, Chisso Corporation had been discharging inorganic and organic mercury waste into the waters of Minamata Bay. Under anaerobic conditions, inorganic mercury can undergo biotransformation to organic mercury. Organic mercury is known to be far more toxic than the inorganic form, is extremely soluble and is biomagnified in the food chain. This resulted in thousands of people being affected with dysfunctions of the central nervous system, birth defects and death in numerous cases. Another classic methylmercurcy case includes the poisoning of Iraqi farmers and their families after ingesting homemade bread made from seeds treated with a methylmercury fungicide.[94] As with Minamata, thousands in Iraq demonstrated a wide range of central nervous system abnormalities with some instances resulting in death.

Nickel (Symbol = Ni, MW = 59.7 g/mol, TLV®-TWA = 1.5 mg/m^3 (elemental), TLV-TWA = 0.1 mg/m^3 (soluble inorganics), TLV®-TWA = 0.2 mg/m^3 (insoluble inorganics), TLV®-TWA = 0.1 mg/m^3 (nickel subsulfide)

Nickel has both ferrous and non-ferrous properties.[95] Nickel is not mined in the United States. The majority of the world's nickel is found in Ontario, Canada.[19] Nickel has many physical properties that make it commercially valuable such as its strength, corrosion resistance, high ductility, good thermal and electrical conductivity, magnetic characteristics, and catalytic properties.[96] About 65% of the nickel consumed in the Western World is used in the production of stainless steel. Approximately 12 % of nickel is used in "super alloys," which are used in high stress components like turbine blades and other jet engine parts.[19]

About 35% of inhaled nickel is absorbed through the lungs into the blood. Particles larger than 30 µm are inhalable 50 percent of the time, while particles less than 10 µm may be deposited in the lower respiratory tract. Nickel is excreted into the urine and it correlates well with airborne concentrations of insoluble nickel compounds. Nickel compounds will penetrate the skin, but different chemical species of nickel have various rates of dermal absorption. After absorption nickel is rapidly distributed throughout the body — kidneys, lungs, adrenals, ovaries, testes. In addition to the urine, nickel is excreted in the bile.[9]

Allergic reactions are the most common health effect of nickel exposure in humans. Skin reactions are sometimes referred to as "nickel itch." It is estimated that approximately 10–15% of the population is sensitive to nickel.[97] Some jewelry contains nickel, which can cause local skin reactions. In more severe cases, nickel can trigger asthma. Welding stainless steel or nickel containing alloys will produce nickel fumes. One study concluded that nickel electroplating is a potential cause of occupational asthma.[98] Chronic occupational exposure to certain forms of nickel can cause bronchitis, reduced lung function, lung cancer, and cancer of the nasal sinus.[97] Nickel carbonyl (nickel combined with carbon monoxide) is an extremely toxic form of nickel. Exposure may occur with nickel coatings, plating glass and as a catalyst in chemical reactions. The NIOSH IDLH (Immediately Dangerous to Life and Health) exposure limit for nickel carbonyl is 2 ppm and the LC_{50} (lethal concentration in 50 percent) is 30 ppm.[96] The IARC (International Agency for Research on Cancer) has reported that some nickel compounds are carcinogenic to humans, group 1. Metallic nickel is listed as a possible human carcinogen, group 2B.[24]

Tin (Symbol = Sn, MW = 118.71, TLV®-TWA = 2 mg/m³ (metal, oxide and inorganics, except tin hydride), TLV®-TWA = 0.1 mg/m³ (organics)

Tin, one of the earliest known metals, is predominately obtained through the mining of Cassitertite (SnO_2). Tin is naturally present in the environment in the organic form. Inorganic tin is in the environment but is rapidly transformed into organic tin, which can accumulate in the food chain.

Tin has not been mined in the U.S. since the early 1990s. The major sources for tin are foreign imports and secondary production through recycling. While inorganic and organic tin have numerous industrial uses, tin, as a pure metal, has few uses. Inorganic tin is used in solders and in alloys that tend to be strong and easily molded. Bronze is a popular alloy containing tin and copper. Inorganic tin, in the Sn^{2+} and Sn^{4+} oxidation states is used in ceramic, glass and electroplating industries. Tinplate is used in the production of cans for food storage and for the preservation of the food's appearance and taste.[99]

Organic tin is referred to as organotin due to its tin-carbon bonds. Tetraorganotin has four carbon bonds and is typically used as a precursor for production of other organotin compounds. Mono- and diorganotin compounds are frequently used as heat stabilizers. Triorganotin compounds such as tributyltin (TBT) are the most well know forms of organotin compounds because of their use as biocides. These biocides are used as antifouling agents in marine paints, agricultural products and as a wood preservative. The use of tin in paints has been significantly reduced as a result of the Organotin Antifouling Paints Control Act (June 16, 1988), and the 1989 decision by the US Navy to discontinue the use of organotin coatings.[100]

About 90 percent of ingested tin is found in the feces. The small amount absorbed through the GI tract will concentrate in the liver and kidneys. This will be excreted by the kidneys primarily with a smaller amount in the bile. If inhaled, tin remains in the lungs, most extracellularly with some in macrophages. Organic tins are better absorbed than inorganic species of tin with highest concentrations in blood and liver.[9]

In general, inorganic tin is less toxic than organic tin. There is no known toxicity associated with metallic tin; however, excessive inhalation of tin may lead to respiratory tract irritation.[101] Cases of nausea, vomiting, diarrhea, stomach cramps, fatigue, and headache have resulted from ingestion of food contaminated with tin.[99] Mild eye, skin and mucous membrane irritation has resulted from exposure to tin oxide.[42] The occupational lung disease stannosis, a non-fibroid benign pneumoconiosis, is the result of exposure to tin fumes.[102–104]

For organic tin, the toxicity is greatest in the trimethyl and triethyl tin compounds. Toxicity tends to decrease as the number of carbon atoms increase. One study reported neurobehavioral changes following methyltin chloride exposure to include headaches, deafness, disorientation, aggressiveness and coma.[105] One of the six exposed subjects died. The survivors had delayed recovery with some neurological effects remaining after six years of follow-up. Another study reports the occurrence of dermal effects such as skin irritation and inflammation from exposure to tributyltin and dibutyltin compounds.[106]

Case studies demonstrating biological effects from organotin compounds date back as far as the mid 1800s. The most tragic incident of tin exposure occurred in 1954. More than 100 deaths and numerous injuries occurred when a French medication containing an organotin compound was used for treating skin infections. NIOSH[107] has evaluated a number of published studies regarding occupational exposures resulting from the handling or application of fungicides containing organotin. These studies reveal a wide range of effects including skin irritation and mucus membranes, malaise, headaches, nausea, vomiting, loss of consciousness and liver damage.

Chelating Agents

Chelating agents are often discussed in relation to metals. They are chemical structures that bind to metals to make the metal more soluble in water. If a metal is more soluble, it is more likely to go into the blood where the kidneys will have a chance to eliminate the metal. It's worth mentioning chelating agents in relation to metal toxicity as it is a potential treatment option with severe metal poisoning. However, chelating therapy is not commonly used because chelating agents are often very toxic themselves and are not very useful for cases of chronic or subacute toxicity.

Ideal chelating agents are water-soluble, not easily biotransformed, make nontoxic complexes with toxic metals, and are easily excreted. BAL (2,3-dimercaptopropanol) forms chelates in vivo with several toxic metals, including inorganic mercury, cadmium, chromium, cobalt, and nickel. Ethylene diamine

Table 17.1 — Metal Toxicity Guide

	Lung* Cancer	Lung Disorder	Kidney	PNS	CNS	Cardio	Skin	Reminders
Arsenic	1	x				anemia		Nail band
Arsine Gas						RBC**		Highly lethal
Beryllium	1	edema					x	Lung granuloma
Cadmium	1	edema	x					Itai Itai
Chromium (Cr^{6+})	1	x						Nasal perforations
Cobalt	2B					heart		Was added to beer
Lead			x	x	x	Heme***		Adds muscle pain
Tetraethyl Lead			x	x	x			Skin abs, hallucinate
Manganese					x			Parkinsonism-like
Methyl mercury				x	x			GI absorbed
Metallic mercury					x			Not as GI absorbed
Nickel	1	x					x	Nickel itch
Metallic Nickel	2B	x					x	
Organic Tin		edema			x		x	
Dimethyl Tin		edema			x		x	More skin abs

* Lung Cancer groups from IARC Monographs Volumes 1-88 where:
Group 1 – Carcinogenic to Humans
Group 2A – Probably carcinogenic to humans
Group 2B – Possibly carcinogenic to humans
Group 3 – Not Classifiable
** Destroys red blood cells
*** Interferes with heme synthesis

tetraacetic acid (EDTA) is the chelating agent of choice for treating lead toxicity. Penicillamine, a hydrolytic product of penicillin, removes copper in people suffering from Wilson's disease, and it will also remove lead, mercury, and iron.[9]

The body also has natural "chelating" proteins that are metal-binding. Metallothioneins bind essential and nonessential metals such as Cd, Cu, Hg, Ag, and Zn. Transferrin is a plasma protein that binds most of the ferric iron, as well as Al^{3+} and Mn^{2+} ions.[9]

Summary

Table 17.1 is provided as a guide for some occupationally significant metals. This table is not an exhaustive list and some more minor health effects are not shown. For further toxicity information on these and many other metals, a good source for general information on chemical toxicity is the Agency for Toxic Substance Disease Registry (ATSDR) ToxFAQs™. The ToxFAQs™ products are a free web based resource designed for the general public with links to more detailed documents. The web address for ToxFAQs™ is www.atsdr.cdc.gov/toxfaq.html.

References

1. **Morris, W.:** *The American Heritage Dictionary of the English Language*, 2nd edition. Boston, MA: Houghton Mifflin Company, 1982.
2. **Duffus, J.H.:** "Heavy Metals — A Meaningless Term?", International Union of Pure and Applied Chemistry (IUPAC) Technical Report, *Pure Appl. Chem.* 74:793–807 (2002).
3. **Stahlhofen, W., J. Gebhart, and J. Heyder:** Experimental Determination of the Regional Deposition of Aerosol Particles in the Human Respiratory Tract. *Am. Ind. Hyg. Assoc. J. 41*, 385–398 (1980).
4. **Brain, J. D., Godleski, J., and W. Kreyling, W.:** In Vivo Evaluation of Chemical Biopersistence of Nonfibrous Inorganic Particles. *Environ. Health Perspect. 102*, 119–125 (1994).
5. **Lippmann, M., and R.B. Schlesinger:** Interspecies Comparisons of Particle Deposition and Mucociliary Clearance in Tracheobronchial Airways. *J. Toxicol. Environ. Health. 13*:441–469 (1984).
6. **Maitani, T., N. Saito, M. Abe, S. Uchiyama, and Y. Saito:** Chemical form-dependent induction of hepatic zinc-thionein by arsenic administration and effect of co-administered selenium in mice. *Toxicol. Lett.* 39:63–70 (1987).
7. **Sardana, M.K., G.S. Drummond, S. Sassa, and A. Kappas:** The potent heme oxygenase inducing action of arsenic in parasiticidal arsenicals. *Pharmacology* 23:247–253 (1981).
8. **Willhite, C.C.:** Arsenic-induced axial skeletal (dysraphic) disorders. *Exp Mol Pathol* 34:145–158 (1981).

9. **Goyer, R. A., and Clarkson, T. W.:** Toxic effects of metals. In *Casarett and Doull's Toxicology — The Basic Science of Poisons,* Klaassen, C. D. (ed.). New York, NY: McGraw-Hill, 2001, pp. 811–867.

10. **United States Geological Survey (USGS):** "Arsenic. U. S. Geological Survey — Mineral Information." [Online] Available at http://minerals.usgs.gov/minerals/pubs/commodity/arsenic/160498.pdf. (1998). [Accessed on: 4/19/06].

11. **Carapella, S.C.:** Arsenic and arsenic alloys. In *Kirk-Othmer Encyclopedia of Chemical Technology.* Kroschwitz, J.I. and M. Howe-Grant (eds.). New York, NY: John Wiley and Sons, vol 3:624–633 (1992).

12. **Hanusch, K., H. Grossmann, K-A. Herbst, et al.:** Arsenic and arsenic compounds. In *Ullman's Encyclopedia of Industrial Chemistry.* Gerhartz, W., et al. (eds.). Weinham, Germany: VCH Verlagsgesellschaft, 113–141 (1985).

13. **Morton, W.E., G.A. Caron:** Encephalopathy: An uncommon manifestation of workplace arsenic poisoning? *Am. J. Ind. Med. 15*:1–5 (1989).

14. **Pinto, S.S., C.M. McGill:** Arsenic trioxide exposure in industry. *Ind. Med. Surg. 22(7)*:281–287 (1953).

15. **Sandstrom, A.I.M., S.G.I Wall, and A. Taube:** Cancer incidence and mortality among Swedish smelter workers. *Br. J. Ind. Med. 46*:82–89 (1989).

16. **Perry, K., R.G. Bowler, H.M. Buckell, H.A. Druett, and R.S. Scilling:** Studies in the incidence of cancer in a factory handling inorganic compounds of arsenic — II: Clinical and environmental investigations. *Br. J. Ind. Med. 5*:6–15 (1948).

17. **Agency for Toxic Substances and Disease Registry (ATSDR):** Toxicological Profile for Arsenic, Sept 2000. [Online] Available at http://www.atsdr.cdc.gov/toxprofiles/tp2.html [Accessed Jan 6, 2006].

18. **National Institute for Occupational Safety and Health (NIOSH):** Current Intelligence Bulletin 32, Arsine (Arsenic Hydride) Poisoning In The Workplace; U.S. Department of Health and Human Services, Public Health Service, National Institute of Occupation Safety and Health, Publication 79-142. [Online] Available at http://www.cdc.gov/niosh/79142_32.html (1979). [Accessed 4/19/06].

19. **United States Geological Survey (USGS):** "Beryllium Statistics and Information." [Online] Available at http://minerals.usgs.gov/minerals/pubs/commodity/beryllium/. [Accessed March 20, 2005].

20. **Mroz, M.M., R. Balkissoon, and L.S. Newman:** Beryllium. In *Patty's Toxicology,* 5th ed., Vol. 2. Bingham, B., C.H. Cohrssen, and E. Powell (eds.). New York: John Wiley & Sons, Inc., 2001. pp 177–211.

21. **Occupational Safety and Health (OSHA):** Beryllium. [Online] Available at http://www.osha.gov/SLTC/beryllium/. [Accessed March 21, 2005].

22. **Sanderson, W.T., E.M. Ward, K. Steenland, M. R. Peterson.:** Lung cancer case-control study of beryllium workers. *Am. J. Ind. Med. 39*:133–144 (2001).

23. **Lenntech Technologies:** "Beryllium." [Online] Available at http://www.lenntech.com/Periodic-chart-elements/be-en.htm. [Accessed March 22, 2005].

24. **International Agency for Research on Cancer (IARC):** "List of IARC Evaluations, 2005." [Online] Available at http://www-cie.iarc.fr/htdocs/monographs/vol52/11-cobaltandcobaltcomp.htm. [Accessed March 22, 2005].

25. **International Agency for Research on Cancer (IARC):** Cadmium and certain cadmium compounds. In: *IARC monographs on the evaluation of the carcinogenic risk of chemicals to humans. Beryllium, cadmium, mercury and exposures in the glass manufacturing industry.* IARC monographs, Vol. 58. Lyon, France: World Health Organization. International Agency for Research on Cancer, 119–146, 210–236. (1993).

26. **United States Geological Survey (USGS):** Minerals yearbook: Cadmium. Reston, VA: U.S. Geological Survey. 1997.

27. **Thun, M.J., A.M. Osorio, S. Schober, W.H. Hannon, B. Lewis, and W. Halperin:** Nephropathy in cadmium workers: Assessment of risk from airborne occupational exposure to cadmium. *Br. J. Ind. Med. 46*:689–697 (1989).

28. **Seidal, K., N. Jorgensen, and C.-G. Elinder:** Fatal cadmium induced pneumonitis. *Stand. J. Work Environ. Health 19*:429–431 (1993).

29. **Andersen, O., J.B. Nielsen, and P. Svendsen:** Oral cadmium chloride intoxication in mice: Effects of dose on tissue damage, intestinal absorption and relative organ distribution. *Tox. 48*:225–236 (1988).

30. **Buckler, H.M., W.D. Smith, and W.D. Rees:** Self poisoning with oral cadmium chloride. *Br. Med. J. 292*:1559–1560 (1986).

31. **Shipman, D.L.:** Cadmium food poisoning in a Missouri school. *J. Environ. Health 49*:89 (1986).

32. **Shigematsu, I.:** The epidemiological approach to cadmium pollution in Japan. *Ann. Acad. Med. Singapore. 13*:231–236 (1984).

33. **U.S. Environmental Protection Agency (EPA):** Health Assessment Document for Chromium. Research Triangle Park, NC: Environmental Assessment and Criteria Office, U.S. Environmental Protection Agency. EPA 600/8-83-014F (1984).

34. **Agency for Toxic Substances and Disease Registry (ATSDR):** Toxicological Profile for Chromium, Sept 2000. [Online] Available at http://www.atsdr.cdc.gov/toxprofiles/tp7.html [Accessed Jan 6, 2006].

35. **Stokinger, H.E.:** Chromium, Cr. In *Patty's Industrial Hygiene and Toxicology,* 3rd edition, Vol. IIA. Clayton, G.D. and F.E. Clayton (eds.). New York, NY: John Wiley & Sons, 1589–1605 (1981).

36. **United States Geological Survey (USGS):** "Chromium. U.S.G.S minerals information: 1998. Mineral Commodities Summaries." [Online] Available at http://minerals.usgs.gov/minerals/pubs/mcs/1998. [Accessed on April 19, 2006].

37. **Hemminki, K., and Vainio, H.:** Human exposure to potentially carcinogenic compounds. *IARC Scientific Publication* No. 59, 37–45 (1984).
38. **Cohen, S.R., D.M. David, and R.S. Kramkowski:** Clinical manifestations of chromic acid toxicity: Nasal lesions in electroplate workers. *Cutis.* 13:558–568 (1974).
39. **Grimsley, L. F.:** Iron and Cobalt. In *Patty's Toxicology,* 5th ed., Vol. 3. Bingham, E., B. Cohrssen, and C.H. Powell (eds.) New York: John Wiley & Sons, Inc., 2001. pp 179–181.
40. **Alexander, C.S.:** Cobalt-beer cardiomyopathy: A clinical and pathologic study of twenty-eight cases. *Am. J. Med.* 53(4):395–417 (1972).
41. **Agency for Toxic Substances and Disease Registry (ATSDR):** "Toxicological Profile for Cobalt." [Online] Available at http://www.atsdr.cdc.gov/toxprofiles/tp33.html. [Accessed March 22, 2005].
42. **Sittig, M.:** *Handbook of Toxic and Hazardous Chemicals,* 3rd edition. New Jersey: Noyes Publication, 1991.
43. **Hathaway, G.L., N.H. Proctor, J.P. Hughes, and M.L. Fischman:** Proctor and Hughes' *Chemical Hazards of the Workplace,* 3rd edition. New York: Van Nostrand Reinhold, 1991.
44. **National Library of Medicine:** Hazardous Substances Data Bank: Cobalt Metal. Bethesda, MD. 1995.
45. **Genium Publishing Corp.:** "Material Safety Data Sheet No. 82." Schenectady, NY: Genium Publishing Corp., 1988.
46. **Hansen, K.S., and F.R. Sharp:** Gasoline sniffing, lead poisoning, and myoclonus. *J. Am. Med. Assoc.* 240(13):1375–1376 (1978).
47. **el Awad, K.M.A., A.S. Hamed, Y.A. Elhaimi, and Y. Osman:** Effects of exposure to lead among lead-acid battery factory workers in Sudan. *Arch. Env. Health* 41(4):261–265 (1986).
48. **Hogstedt, C., M. Hane, A. Agrell, and L. Bodin:** Neuropsychological test results and symptoms among workers with well-defined long-term exposure to lead. *Br. J. Ind. Med.* 40(1):99–105 (1983).
49. **Schneitzer, L., H.H. Osborn, A. Bierman, and B. Kaul:** Lead poisoning in adults from renovation of an older home. *Ann. Emer. Med.* 19(4):415–420 (1990).
50. **Stollery, B.T.:** Reaction time changes in workers exposed to lead. *Neurotox. Terat.* 18(4):477–483 (1996).
51. **Williamson, A.M., and R.K.C. Teo:** Neurobehavioral effects of occupational exposure to lead. *Br. J. Ind. Med.* 43(6):374–380 (1986).
52. **Kumar, S., S. Jain, and C.S. Aggarwal:** Encephalopathy due to inorganic lead exposure in an adult. *Jap. J. Med.* 26(2):253–254 (1987).
53. **Nordstrom, S., L. Beckman, and I. Nordensen:** Occupational and environmental risks in and around a smelter in northern Sweden: V. Spontaneous abortion among female employees and decreased birth weight in their offspring. *Hereditas.* 90(2):291–296 (1979).
54. **Lerda, D.:** Study of sperm characteristics in persons occupationally exposed to lead. *Am. J. Ind. Med.* 22(4):567–571 (1992).
55. **Coste, J., L. Mandereau, F. Pessione, M. Bregu, C. Faye, D. Hemon, and A. Spira:** Lead-exposed workmen and fertility: A cohort study on 354 subjects. *Eur. J. Epidem.* 7(2):154–158 (1991).
56. **Bonde, J.P.E., and H. Kolstad:** Fertility of Danish battery workers exposed to lead. *Internatl. J. Epidem.* 26(6):1281–1288 (1997).
57. **Goyer, R.A.:** Transplacental transport of lead. *Environ. Health Persp.* 89:101–105 (1990).
58. **Cocco, P., M. Dosemeci, and E.F. Heineman:** Brain Cancer and Occupational Exposure to Lead. *J. Occ. Environ. Med.* 40(11):937–942 (1998).
59. **Lundstrom, N.G., et al.:** Cumulative lead exposure in relation to mortality and lung cancer morbidity in a cohort of primary smelter workers. *Scand. J. Work, Environ. Health* 23(1):24–30 (1997).
60. **Fu, H., and P. Boffetta:** Cancer and occupational exposure to inorganic lead compounds: a meta- analysis of published data. *Occ. Environ. Med.* 52:73–81 (1995).
61. **International Agency for Research on Cancer (IARC):** List of IARC Evaluations, 2005. [Online] Available at http://monographs.iarc.fr/htdocs/monographs/suppl7/leadandleadcompounds.html. [Accessed February 7, 2006].
62. **Wedler, F.C.:** Biochemical and nutritional role of manganese: an Overview. In Manganese in Health and Disease. Klimis-Tavantzis, D.J. (ed.) Boca Raton, FL: CRC Press, 1994. pp. 1–36.
63. **United States Geological Survey (USGS):** Mineral Industry Surveys: Manganese: 1997 Annual review. U.S. Geological Survey, U.S. Department of the Interior (1998).
64. **U.S. Environmental Protection Agency (EPA):** Health assessment document for manganese. Final draft. Cincinnati, OH: U.S. EPA, Office of Research and Development. EPA-600/8-83-013F (1984).
65. **U.S. Environmental Protection Agency (EPA):** Toxic Release Inventory (TRI96). Washington, D.C.: Office of Toxic Substances. (1998).
66. **Davis, J.M., A.M. Jarabek, D.T. Mage, and J.A. Graham:** The EPA health risk assessment of methylcyclopentadienyl manganese tricarbonyl (MMT). *Risk Analysis* 18:57–70 (1998).
67. **Zayed, J., A. Vyskocil, and G. Kennedy:** Environmental contamination and human exposure to manganese: Contribution of methylcyclopentadienyl manganese tricarbonyl in unleaded gasoline. *Int. Arch. Occup. Environ. Health* 72:7–13. (1999).
68. **Calne, D.B., N.S. Chu, C.C. Huang, C.S. Lu, and W. Olanow:** Manganism and idiopathic parkinsonism: similarities and differences. *Neurol.* 44:1583–1586 (1994).

69. **Chu, N.S., F.H. Hochberg, D.B. Calne, and C.W. Olanow:** Neurotoxicity of manganese. In *Handbook of Neurotoxicology*. Chang, L. and R. Dyyer (eds.). New York, NY: Marcel Dekker, Inc., 91–103 (1995).
70. **Emara, A.M., S.H. el-Ghawabi, O.I. Madkour, and G.H. el-Samra:** Chronic manganese poisoning in the dry battery industry. *Br. J. Ind. Med.* 28:78–82 (1971).
71. **Mena, I., O. Marin, S. Fuenzalida, and G.C. Cotzias:** Chronic manganese poisoning: Clinical picture and manganese turnover. *Neurol.* 17:128–136 (1967).
72. **Suarez, N., E. Walum, and H. Eriksson:** Cellular neurotoxicity of trivalent manganese bound to transferring or pyrophosphate studied in human neuroblastoma (SH-SY5Y) cell cultures. *Toxicol. in Vitro 9*:717–721 (1995).
73. **Barbeau, A.:** Manganese and extrapyramidal disorders (a critical review and tribute to Dr. George C. Cotzias). *Neurotox.* 5:13–35 (1984).
74. **Donaldson, J.:** The physiopathologic significance of manganese in brain: Its relation to schizophrenia and neurodegenerative disorders. *Neurotox.* 8:451–462 (1987).
75. **Mergler, D., et al.:** Manganese neurotoxicity, a continuum of dysfunction: Results from a community based study. *Neurotox.* 20:327–342 (1999).
76. **Crump, K.S. and P. Rousseau:** Results from eleven years of neurological health surveillance at a manganese oxide and salt producing plant. *Neurotox.* 20:273–286 (1999).
77. **Lucchini R., et al.:** Neurobehavioral effects of manganese in workers from a ferroalloy plant after temporary cessation of exposure. *Scand. J. Work Environ. Health* 21:143–149 (1995).
78. **Roels, H.A., et al.:** Prospective study on the reversibility of neurobehavioral effects in workers exposed to manganese dioxide. *Neurotox.* 20:255–272 (1999).
79. **Bowler, R.M., D. Mergler, M.P. Sassine, F. Larribe, and K. Hudnell:** Neuropsychiatric effects of manganese on mood. *Neurotox.* 20:367–378 (1999).
80. **Hefflin, B.J. et al.:** Mercury exposure from exterior latex paint. *Appl. Occ. Environ. Hyg.* 8(10):886-870 (1993).
81. **O'Carroll, R.E., G. Masterson, N. Dougall, K.P. Ebmeier, and G.M. Goodwin:** The neuropsychiatric sequelae of mercury poisoning. The Mad Hatter's disease revisited. *Br. J. Psych.* 167:95–98 (1995).
82. **Hursh, J.B., T.W. Clarkson, M.G. Cherian, J.J. Vastal, and R.V. Mallie:** Clearance of mercury (Hg-197, Hg-203) vapor inhaled by human subjects. *Arch. Environ. Health.* 31(6):302–309 (1976).
83. **Barregard, L., et al.:** Kinetics of mercury in blood and urine after brief occupational exposure. *Arch. Environ. Health.* 47(3):176–184 (1992).
84. **Rahola T., T. Hattula, A. Korolainen, J.K. Miettmen:** Elimination of free and protein-bound ionic mercury 203Hg2+ in man. *Ann. Clin. Res.* 5:214–219 (1973).
85. **Suzuki T., et al.:** An acute mercuric mercury poisoning: Chemical speciation of hair mercury shows a peak of inorganic mercury value. *Hum. Exper. Tox.*11(1):53–57 (1992).
86. **Langworth, S, C.G. Elinder, K.G. Sundquist, and O. Vesterberg:** Renal and immunological effects of occupational exposure to inorganic mercury. *Br. J. Ind. Med.* 49(12):873–874 (1992).
87. **Rowens, B., D. Guerrero-Betancourt, C.A. Gottlieb, R.J. Boyes and M.S. Eichenhorn:** Respiratory failure and death following acute inhalation of mercury vapor: A clinical and histologic perspective. *Chest.* 99(1):185–190 (1991).
88. **Karpathios T., et al.:** Mercury vapor poisoning associated with hyperthyroidism in a child. *Acta. Paed. Scand.* 80(5):551–552 (1991).
89. **Lilis, R., A. Miller, and Y. Lerman:** Acute mercury poisoning with sever chronic pulmonary manifestations. *Chest.* 88:306–309 (1985).
90. **Aberg, B., et al.:** Metabolism of methyl mercury (203 Hg) compounds in man. *Arch. Env. Health 19(4)*:478–484 (1969).
91. **Hook, O., K.D. Lundgren, and A. Swensson:** On alkyl mercury poisoning. *Acta. Med. Scand. 150(2)*:131–137 (1954).
92. **Hunter, D., R.R. Bomford, and D.S. Russell:** Poisoning by methyl mercury compounds. *Quart. J. Med.* 9:93–213 (1940).
93. **Goldwater, L.J.:** Mercury: A History of Quicksilver. Baltimore, MD: York Press. 1972. pp 8–9.
94. **Bakir, F., et al.:** Methylmercury poisoning in Iraq. *Sci. 181(96)*:230–241 (1973).
95. **Czerczak, S. and J.P. Gromiec:** Nickel, Ruthenium, Rhodium, Palladium, Osmium, and Platinum. In *Patty's Toxicology*, 5th ed., Vol. 3. Bingham, E., B. Cohrssen, and C.H. Powell (eds.). New York: John Wiley & Sons, Inc., 2001. pp 195–219.
96. **Nickel Producers Environmental Research Association (NiPERA):** The Nickel Page. [Online] Available at http://www.nipera.org (Accessed March 21, 2005).
97. **Agency for Toxic Substances and Disease Registry (ATSDR):** Toxicological Profile for Nickel. [Online] Available at http://www.atsdr.cdc.gov/toxprofiles/tp15.html. [Accessed March 22, 2005].
98. **Bright, P., et al.:** Occupational asthma due to chrome and nickel electroplating. *Thorax.* 52:28–32 (1997).
99. **Blunden, S. and T. Wallace:** Tin in canned food: a review and understanding of occurrence and effect. *Food Chem. Tox. 41(12)*:1651–1662 (2003).
100. **Champ, M.A.:** A review of organotin regulatory strategies, pending actions, related costs and benefits. *Sci. Total Environ.* 258:21–71 (2000).
101. **Graf, G.G.:** Tin, tin alloys, and tin compounds. In *Ullmann's Encyclopedia of Industrial Chemistry*, Vol. A27. Arpe, H.H. (ed.). Weinheim: Wiley-VCH, 1996. pp. 49–81.
102. **Cutter, H.C., W.W. Faller, J.B. Stocklen, W.L. Wilson:** Benign pneumoconiosis in a tin oxide recovery plant. *J. Ind. Hyg.* 31:139–141 (1949).
103. **Dundon, C.C. and J.P. Hughes:** Stannic oxide pneumoconiosis. *Am. J. Roentgenol. Rad. Ther.* 63:797–812 (1950).

104. **Pendergrass, E.P. and A.W. Pryde:** Benign pneumoconiosis due to tin oxide: A case report with experimental investigation of the radiographic density of the tin oxide dust. *J. Ind. Hyg. Tox. 30*:119–123 (1948).
105. **Rey, C., H.J. Reinecke, and R. Besser:** Methyltin intoxication in six men: Toxicologic and clinical aspects. *Vet. Human Tox. 26(2)*:121–122 (1984).
106. **Lyle, W.:** Lesions of the skin in process workers caused by contact with butyltin compounds. *Br. J. Ind. Med. 15*:193–196 (1958).
107. **National Institute for Occupational Safety and Health (NIOSH):** NIOSH Criteria Documents: Criteria for a Recommended Standard: Occupational Exposure to Organotin Compounds; U.S. Department of Health and Human Services, Public Health Service, National Institute of Occupation Safety and Health, Publication 77-115. [Online] Available at http://www.cdc.gov/niosh/77-115.html (1976).

> *In the meantime, I benefit the sick, and have sought to serve each and everyone of them truly.*
>
> Paracelsus (1493– 1541)

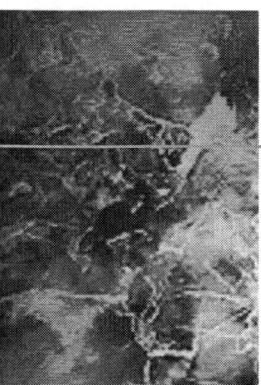

Chapter 18

Toxicology of Pesticides

Outcome Competencies

Upon completion of this chapter, the reader should be able to:
- Define terms in bold text.
- List the major categories of pesticides.
- Discuss the value of pesticides vs. human and environmental poisoning caused by pesticides.
- Describe the significance of bioaccumulation and biomagnification of pesticides.
- Give examples of worker exposures to pesticides through inhalation and dermal absorption.
- Describe biological monitoring for workers exposed to pesticides.
- Describe how organophosphates bind to and inactivate acetylcholinesterase.
- List the signs and symptoms of organophosphate poisoning.
- Describe the antidotes available for treatment of organophosphate poisoning.
- Describe the "T syndrome" and "CS syndrome" that can be caused by exposure to pyrethrums.
- Differentiate between the mechanisms of toxic action of organochlorines, organophosphates, carbamates, and pyrethroids.
- List the possible chemical interactions that may have contributed to the Gulf War illnesses.
- Describe the trace contaminates in chlorophenoxy compounds that are linked with chronic adverse effects.
- Recognize chemical structures of the major categories of pesticides.
- Describe the basis for the World Health Organization recommended classification of pesticides by hazard.

Prerequisite Knowledge

Basic human anatomy and physiology, organic chemistry, biochemistry

Key Terms

acaricides, algicides, alopecia, antidotes, arthralgia, actericides, ataxia, azoospermic, bioaccumulation, biological exposure indices (BEI), biomagnification, bradykinesia, chloracne, cholinergic syndrome, choreoathetosis, citric acid cycle, cytochrome P450 enzymes, defoliants, dicumarol, dioxin, environmental persistence, enzymes, exfoliation, free radicals, fungicides, hepatomas, hepatomegaly, herbicides, hypoxemia, insecticides, larvicides, miticides, molluscides, nematocides, neuropathy target esterase (NTE), oligospermic, organophosphate-induced delayed polyneuropahty (OPIDP), oximes, oxons, paresthesia, pediculicides, pesticides, phase I and II detoxification, prothrombin, pyridostigmine bromide pheromones, physostigmine, rodenticides, scabicides, selectivity, slimicides, specificity, splenomegaly, thyroxine,

Key Topics

1. Introduction to Pesticides
   - Definition of pesticide
   - Brief history of development and use of pesticides
   - Value of pesticides
   - Worker exposure and incidence of poisoning with pesticides
2. Insecticides
   - Organochlorines
   - Anticholinesterases
   - Pyrethroids
3. Herbicides
   - Chlorophenoxy compounds
   - Bipyridyl compounds
   - Triazines
   - Arsenical herbicides
   - Dinitrophenols
   - Case studies involving herbicides
4. Rodenticides
   - Anticoagulant rodenticides
   - Fluoroacetic acid and its derivatives
   - ANTU (alpha-naphtylthiourea)
5. Fumigants
   - DBCP (1,2-dibromo-3-chloropropane)
   - Hydrogen cyanide
6. Fungicides
   - Pentachlorophenol
   - Dithiocarbamates

Chapter 18

Toxicology of Pesticides

By William E. Luttrell, PhD, CIH

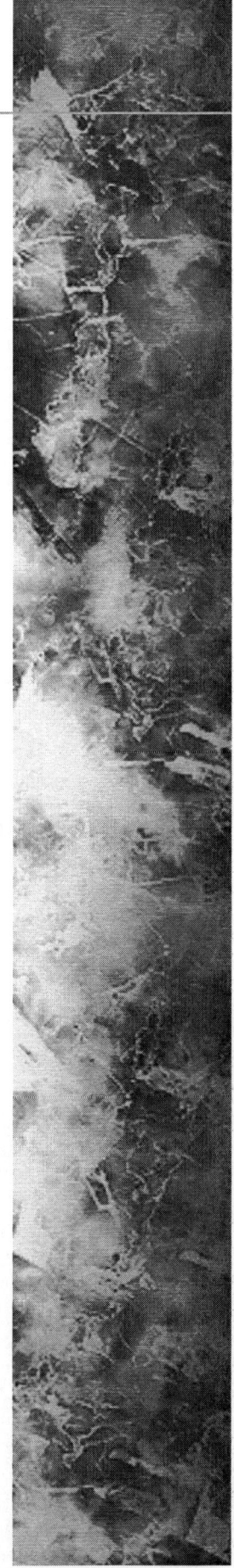

Introduction to Pesticides

Definition of Pesticide

Pesticides are used in a wide variety of places—in industry, business, and in the home. Depending on the biological organisms to be killed, they include **algicides, acaricides, bactericides, fungicides, herbicides, insecticides, larvicides, miticides, nematocides, molluscides, pediculicides, rodencides, scabicides,** and **slimicides**, as well as **pheromones** (attractants), **defoliants**, dessicants, plant growth regulators, and repellants. They are designed to kill specific forms of life and they are applied in very large quantities to the environment.[1] According to the U.S. EPA, a **pesticide** is any substance or mixture of substances intended for preventing, destroying, repelling, or mitigating any pest. A pesticide is also any physical, chemical, or biological agent that will kill an undesirable plant or animal pest. In general, a pest is any harmful, destructive, or troublesome animal, plant, or microorganism. Pesticide is a general term for a variety of agents that are specifically classified on the basis of the pattern of use and organisms killed. Major agricultural classes of pesticides include insecticides, herbicides, and fungicides.[2]

A Brief History of Development and Use of Pesticides

Throughout history, man has taken measures to control pests that have threatened the food supply as well as the health of the public. Sulfur was used as a fungicide in Europe in the 1800s to control mildew on fruit plants. Centuries ago, water extracts of tobacco leaves were sprayed on plants as insecticides. Pyrethrum extracted from chrysanthemum flowers was used as an insecticide in the mid 1800s. Arsenic trioxide was used as weed killer in the late 1800s. Copper arsenite was used to control the Colorado beetle in the late 1800s. The widespread use of arsenical pesticides in the early 1900s caused concern because some treated fruits and vegetables were found to have toxic residues. Before World War II, modern chemistry allowed the development of several insecticides and fungicides. Much of the work with pesticides during World War II was kept secret, including experimental work with dichlorodiphenyltrichloroethane (DDT). After the war, there was rapid development of chemical agents as insecticides, fungicides, herbicides. Substantial progress was made in developing agents with **selectivity** and **specificity** toward certain pests while reducing the toxicity to other life.[2]

Value of Pesticides

Insecticides have contributed to the control of some important vector-borne diseases—malaria, onchocerciasis ("river blindness"), filariasis, yellow fever, rickettsial pox, viral encephalitis, typhus, and bubonic plague. Countless millions of people have been saved from these diseases by the proper use and application of these chemical compounds. Insecticides have also been widely used to protect the agricultural products, since some insects are detrimental to plants and their products. Up to 50% of harvested crops can be damaged by post-harvest infestation by pests. The protection of crops has resulted in a dramatic increase in abundant and inexpensive fruits and vegetables all over the world. Herbicides have been developed to kill weeds; and other pesticides have been developed to control other pests such as fungi and rodents. Because of the carelessness, misuse, and abuse of pesticides by particular corporations and by a few individuals in a limited number of incidents, some environmental and consumer advocacy groups are calling for a total ban on pesticide use. There needs to be a balance found between over-use and total ban so careful and appropriate use of beneficial chemicals can continue.[2]

Worker Exposure and Incidence of Poisoning with Pesticides

Even though much work has been done to develop second and third-generation derivatives of the original pesticides, all pesticides today have a certain degree of toxicity. A completely safe pesticide does not exist. In the future, pesticides will continue to cause accidental and/or intentional poisoning of wildlife, farm animals, and humans. However, pesticides can be used safely and present a low level of risk to humans and wildlife, if they are handled and applied properly. Occupational exposure to pesticides can occur when workers are involved in manufacturing, formulating, and applying pesticides.[3] In highly industrialized countries, the handling of pesticides has become progressively safer due to technological improvements, increasing awareness, and training of professional applicators. In developing countries, pesticides are often applied by farmers who may have poorly maintained equipment, inefficient hand-sprayers, inadequate personal protective equipment, and insufficient training.[4] The incidence of poisoning is at least thirteen times higher in developing countries than in highly industrialized countries.[2]

In this chapter each major pesticide category is presented. The following topics are summarized for each category using representative agents, especially those toxic to humans: sources and uses, pertinent chemical and physical properties and chemical structures, sites and mechanisms of toxic action, signs and symptoms of poisoning, absorption, distribution, biotransformation, excretion, bioaccumulation and biomagnification, standards of exposure, and standards of treatment. Case studies linking the pesticide to the workplace are presented in several categories.

Insecticides

Organochlorines

Pertinent Chemical and Physical Properties

These synthetic insecticides[1] are often divided into groups according to their chemical structure, which seems to play a role in determining which portion of the nervous system is adversely affected by exposure. For example, dichlorodiphenylethanes (DDT) primarily affect the peripheral nervous system. Cyclodienes, such as aldrin and endrin, primarily affect the central nervous system.[5]

Sites and mechanisms of toxic action

Organochlorine pesticides are considered less acutely toxic, but more chronically toxic than organophosphates.[1] Since there is a variety of organochlorines, there are different acute toxicities and toxicokinetics displayed by individual compounds.[4] In general, they are central nervous system stimulants that can produce neuronal disruptions that lead to convulsions, coma, and death. The exact mechanism of toxic action is not known. However, some organochlorines, such as aldrin, dieldrin and lindane, are known to induce hyperexcitation at synaptic and neuromuscular junctions that cause repetitive discharges in central, sensory, and motor neurons.[3]

Signs and Symptoms of Poisoning

Since chlorinated insecticides increase the sensitivity of neurons to stimuli, symptoms caused by exposure to organochlorine compounds can include tremors, hyperexcitability, muscular weakness, and convulsions. Depression of the respiratory system, cardiac arrhythmia, liver and kidney damage can occur with high exposures.[5] They are known heptatoxins, inducing liver enlargement and centrolobular necrosis. Organochlorine compounds can also induce microsomal monoxygenases, and as a result, affect the toxicity of other chemicals.[3]

Absorption

Since these compounds are only slightly soluble in water, they are usually mixed with a petroleum solvent, such as kerosene or toluene. Due to this, they readily penetrate the skin and cause systemic effects. Organochlorine compounds are also easily absorbed through inhalation and ingestion.[5]

Excretion

Many organochlorine compounds are excreted in the bile, and then rapidly reabsorbed from the digestive tract and sent to the liver. These compounds or their metabolites, which can include free radicals, have targets in the liver when activated or inhibited may produce liver cancer in laboratory animals. Some of these compounds have been found to have hormone qualities and they may have a role in promoting hormone-induced cancers, including breast cancer.[1]

Bioaccumulation

Organochlorine insecticides, including lindane, dieldrin, endrin, and chlordane, are quite persistent in the environment, and as a result undergo **bioaccumulation**. Since they are very fat soluble, they bioaccumulate in fatty tissues of the body and are retained there for years.[5] Due to their capability to bioaccumulate, the EPA has implemented tight regulations that have phased them out of use. Methoxychlor has gained favor due to its low toxicity to mammals and its low persistence in the environment.[1]

Dichlorodiphenylethanes
DDT

After its development in the 1940s, DDT was widely used in agricultural and health programs, because of its low toxicity to mammals and its persistence environmentally, which reduced the need for repeated applications.[3] Unfortunately, it was found to disturb the metabolism of estrogens in birds, adversely affecting reproduction and survival of their young.[6] Although initially DDT was considered safe to humans, it was later banned in the U.S. in 1973, due to its **environmental persistence** and ecological adverse effects. Be that as it may, it is still used as a vector control agent in many tropical countries.[1] Being very lipophilic, it was found to accumulate in the fat portion of body fluids, including milk, presenting a **biomagnification** problem. Another chlorinated ethane derivative, methoxychlor, proved to be less toxic and less persistent. DDT may cause its toxic effect in the mammalian nervous system by adversely affecting the axon membrane.[7] Although many of the organochlorine compounds have been shown to induce hepatomas in mice, studies with DDT have shown no carcinogenicity in rats or hamsters. Epidemiological studies in humans have been negative for cancer, and DDT has shown negative results in short-term mutagenesis assays.[8] 2,2-bis(4-chlorophenol)acetic acid (DDA) is the primary urinary metabolite of DDT, while 1,1-dichloro-2,2-bis(4-chlorophenyl)ethylene (DDE) is the metabolite preferentially stored in fat tissue.[4] Low DDE as compared to total stored DDT residues in fatty tissue indicates a high and recent exposure to DDT. Occupational exposures to DDT can be monitored by measuring DDT and/or DDE in blood plasma or by measuring DDA urinary excretion.[9] DDT has been labeled a probable human carcinogen by the EPA. DDE has been found to have either anti-androgenic or estrogenic properties in a number of mammalian species. The chemical structure of DDT is given in Table 18.1.

Cyclodienes

Many of these insecticides are now banned or restricted in most countries—including aldrin, dieldrin, and endrin.[4] They were widely used in the control of mosquitoes, flies, and other insects. Chlordane has had limited use in the control of termites. Thermal degradation of chlorinated cyclodienes produces hydrogen chloride, phosgene, and chlorine gases. Since they are fat soluble and water insoluble, they persist in the environment after application. Their primary route of exposure is through dermal absorption. They tend to bioaccumulate in fatty tissue and target the central nervous system. Symptoms of exposure include excitability, dizziness, headache, weakness, **paresthesia**, muscle twitching, convulsions, and unconsciousness. Death in a worker who spilled a 25 percent mixture of chlordane and did not remove contaminated clothing has been reported.[5] The chemical structure of chlordane is given in Table 18.1.

Chlorinated Benzenes
Hexachlorobenzene

This compound is still in use as a fungicide for seed treatment in some countries.[4] Since it is fat soluble, it bioaccumulates in fatty tissues and metabolizes slowly. Chronic exposure can cause **hepatomegaly, alopecia**, itching, **ataxia**, irritability, and tremors. Teratogenic effects have been demonstrated in rats.[5] The chemical structure of hexachlorobenzene is given in Table 18.1.

Cyclohexanes
Hexachlorocyclohexane

Lindane (γ - 1,2,3,4,5,6 hexachlorocyclohexane)
Lindane is the γ-isomer of hexachlorocyclohexane. Lindane has been used as an agricultural insecticide, as well as residentially to kill lice, fleas, ticks, flies, mosquitoes, and carpet beetles. It has been used as a component of a pediculicide shampoo for head lice.[2] It can be used as a fumigant because of its volatile nature. Occupational exposures occur by inhalation and dermal absorption. High exposure can result in symptoms within one to six hours with vomiting and diarrhea occurring first and then convulsions and tremors.[5] The chemical structure of lindane is given in Table 18.1.

Chlordecone (kepone)

This is an organochlorine compound used to control fire ants[1] that was discovered to be toxic when 76 of 148 workers in a factory in Hopewell, Virginia, developed a neurological syndrome, known as "Kepone shakes."[10] Symptoms appeared about thirty days after the beginning of exposure, which included tremors, altered gait, behavioral changes, ocular flutter, **arthralgia**, headache, chest pains, weight loss, hepatomegaly, **splenomegaly**, and impotence. Reduced sperm count and motility were also demonstrated in exposed workers. Central nervous system involvement may be due to kepone interfering with metabolic processes in Schwann cells. These toxic effects were also demonstrated in animal studies, with the central nervous system, liver, adrenals, and testes as major target organs.[11] As other organochlorines do, kepone induces hepatic microsomal monooxygenase enzymes. It is also associated with the formation of hepatomas and malignant tumors in organs other than the liver in rats and mice.[10] The chemical structure of kepone is given in Table 18.1.

Case Study involving Lindane and other Organochlorines

The levels of organochlorine insecticides were monitored in the air, blood, and urine of mango orchard pesticide applicators over a two year period.[12] The purpose of this study was to determine the distribution pattern of organochlorine insecticides in peripheral blood and their excretion in urine of exposed workers. Fifty-two pesticide applicators in Malihabad, India, were selected for serum and urine pesticide measurements. Twenty-four unexposed workers were selected as a comparison group. The pesticide applicators did not use any personal protective respiratory equipment, gloves, or coveralls during the handling of the pesticides. They collected forty-five air samples in the working environment of the exposed workers during the study. The following mean/highest concentrations (ng/m^3) of organochlorine compounds were reported: lindane (512/2897), aldrin (27/240), endosulfan (8/216), and DDT (31/528). In the case of lindane, the mean concentration exceeded the current American Conference of Governmental Industrial Hygienists (ACGIH) threshold limit value-8-hour time weighted average (TLV®-TWA) of 500 ng/m^3.[13] The highest concentrations of aldrin and endosulfan exceeded the current TLV®-TWAs of 50 and 100 ng/m^3, respectively. In the case of DDT, the highest concentration measured did not exceed the TLV®-TWA of 1000 ng/m^3. They reported that the mean concentrations of these four organochlorine compounds were significantly higher ($p < 0.05$) than the ambient background levels. In addition, they measured each of these

Table 18.1 — Chemical Structures of Insecticides

A. Organochlorines
  1. Dichlorodiphenylethanes
     DDT (1,1,1-trichloro-2,2-bis(4-chlorophenyl)ethane)

  2. Cyclodienes
     Chlordane (octachloro-4,7-methanohydroindane)

  3. Chlorinated benzenes
     Hexachlorobenzene

  4. Cyclohexanes
     Lindane (γ -1,2,3,4,5,6-hexachlorocyclohexane)

  5. Chlordecone (kepone)

B. Anticholinesterases
  1. Organophosphates
     Chlorpyrifos (O,O-diethyl O-3,5,6-trichloro-2-pyridyl phosphorothioate)

  2. Carbamates
     Baygon (2-isopropoxyphenyl N-methylcarbamate)

C. Pyrethroids
   Pyrethrin I ((Z)-(S)-2-methyl-4-oxo-3-(penta-2,4-dienyl) cyclo pent-2-enyl (1R)-trans-2,2-dimethyl-3-(2-methyl prop-1-enyl)cyclo-propane carboxylate)

compounds in the serum of exposed workers and unexposed workers. In each case, the mean concentration of the organochlorine compound in the sera was significantly higher ($p < 0.05$) in the exposed workers than in the unexposed workers. In regards to excretion in urine, they measured each organochlorine compound in the urine of the exposed and unexposed workers. Lindane and DDT levels in the urine of exposed workers were significantly higher ($p < 0.05$) than those in unexposed workers. Aldrin and endosulfan levels were similar in exposed and unexposed workers. Overall, they found that the excretion of organochlorine compounds in the urine increased as the years of exposure increased. Workers exposed for less than twenty years showed higher serum levels than workers exposed for greater than twenty years. They concluded that the body has a certain capacity for organochlorine compounds to be in the serum, and beyond that, it excretes them in the urine.

Anticholinesterases
Organophosphates
Sources and Uses
The organophosphate insecticides were first synthesized in 1937, by a group of German chemists lead by Gerhard Schrader. Sadly, many of their preliminary compounds that were found to be extremely toxic were further developed as chemical warfare agents by the Nazis in World War II, such as the nerve agents, soman, sarin, and tabun.[14] Sarin (*O*-isopropylmethylphosphonofluoridate) was used against the people of a Kurdish village in northern Iraq in 1988.[15] These agents have been used by terrorists in two attacks in Japan, Matsumoto on June 27, 1994, and in Tokyo on March 20, 1995.[16] Chapter 26, "Toxicology of Chemical Warfare Agents," includes a detailed discussion of the nerve agents. Although all organophosphorus esters used today were derived from the "nerve gases," they are at least four generations of development away from those initial highly toxic compounds.[2]

Currently, there are hundreds of different organophosphate compounds used in thousands of different products. Due to their common use as insecticides, thousands of cases of acute poisoning have been reported, especially in rural areas and in developing countries.[5] Organophosphorus poisoning represents about 30% of all systemic pesticide poisoning cases in California and about 77% in China.[4]

Pertinent Chemical and Physical Properties
Organophosphate compounds have the following general chemical structure:

$$\begin{matrix} & O\text{ or }S \\ R_1 & \| \\ & P-O-X \\ R_2 & \end{matrix}$$

R_1 and R_2 are side chains that can contain oxygen, carbon, and hydrogen atoms, while X represents a leaving group that is important in the metabolism and excretion of these compounds.

As indicated, the atom double-bonded to the phosphorus atom can be an oxygen or sulfur. If it's an oxygen atom, then the compound is a "phosphate." If it is a sulfur atom, then the compound is a "phosphorothioate." In order for phosphorothioates to inhibit esterase enzymes, they must undergo oxidative desulfuration. Since compounds containing phosphorus double-bonded to sulfur are more stable and lipid soluble, most commercial organophosphorus insecticides are phosphorothioates. When these compounds undergo oxidation, their oxidized forms contain phosphorus double-bonded to oxygen. These forms are known as **oxons**. The oxidized form of parathion is paraoxon. The oxidized form of chlorpyrifos is chlorpyrifos-oxon.[4] The chemical structure of chlorpyrifos is shown in Table 18.1. Keep in mind that many organophosphate applications may use xylene and toluene as solvents and so these compounds may also be responsible for some of the toxic effects seen in exposed individuals.[5]

Sites and Mechanisms of Toxic Action
The basic mechanism of action of organophosphates is the binding to and inactivation of acetylcholinesterase (AChE) in the insect, resulting in disruption of its nervous system. Since this enzyme is also found throughout the mammalian body, including the brain, the autonomic nervous system, and neuromuscular junctions, symptoms of organophosphate poisoning are systemic in nature. As depicted in the following interaction, the organophosphate binds to a serine hydroxyl group in the active site of the AChE protein (E-OH)[2]:

$$E-OH + \begin{matrix}R_1\\ \\R_2\end{matrix}\!\!\!\searrow\!\!\!\underset{}{\overset{\overset{O\text{ or }S}{\|}}{P}}-O-X \rightarrow E-O-\underset{R_2}{\overset{\overset{O}{\|}}{P}}\!\!\!\nearrow\!\!\!^{R_1} + HO-X$$

$$\downarrow$$

$$E-OH + \begin{matrix}R_1\\ \\R_2\end{matrix}\!\!\!\searrow\!\!\!\underset{}{\overset{\overset{O}{\|}}{P}}-OH$$

This interaction results in a stable, phosphorylated, and for the most part, unreactive inhibited enzyme that has the organophosphate bound to its active center. At the same time, the organophosphate releases its leaving group, forming HO-X. Under normal circumstances, the unreactive inhibited enzyme is reactivated at a very slow rate with the release of the organophosphate from the active center and the recreation of the active enzyme (E-OH). Therefore, exposed humans, such as handlers and applicators of organophosphate insecticides, and mammals that are present in the environment where these insecticides are applied are susceptible to the toxic effects of these compounds.[1] As described in detail in Chapter 9, "Neurotoxicology," as AChE is inhibited, acetylcholine (ACh) begins to accumulate at nerve endings throughout the body, leading to the

cholinergic syndrome. The severity of signs and symptoms of poisoning is correlated with the degree of inhibition of AChE in blood, but the exact relationship depends upon the particular organophosphate compound.[3]

Signs and Symptoms of Poisoning

Acute organophosphate poisoning can lead to cholinergic symptoms that include diarrhea, excessive salivation, constriction of the pupils, fluid in the respiratory tract causing extreme or fatal difficulty in breathing, and loss of bladder control. Effects on skeletal muscles can include twitching, weakness, and paralysis. Smooth muscle contraction can cause cramping in the GI tract and retention of fluid in the lungs. Effects on the central nervous system can include tremors, delirium, confusion, slurred speech, disequilibrium, loss of coordination, and convulsions.[1]

There is also a non-cholinergic intermediate syndrome that can occur in individuals who are acutely intoxicated with organophosphate compounds. After the cholinergic phase, paralysis can occur in proximal limb muscles, neck flexors, motor cranial nerves, and in respiratory muscles. This syndrome can occur in cases of exposure to compounds that cause profound and prolonged inhibition of AChE. This can lead to death if artificial respiration is not used.[4]

Some organophosphorus compounds, such as chlorpyrifos, cause a sensorimotor polyneuropathy known as **organophosphate-induced delayed polyneuropathy (OPIDP)**. This is characterized by flaccid paralysis of the lower limbs with involvement of the upper limbs in severe cases. The sensory peripheral nervous system is also affected, but to a smaller degree. There is degeneration of long and large-diameter axons in peripheral nerves and the spinal cord. These symptoms of poisoning are not related to the inhibition of AChE. It appears that the molecular target in OPIDP is a nervous system protein called **neuropathy target esterase (NTE)**. This esterase is also present in peripheral lymphocytes and its inhibition can be used to predict the development of OPIDP.[4] This delayed polyneuropathy is also discussed in Chapter 9, "Neurotoxicology."

If industrial workers are repeatedly exposed to organophosphorus compounds, such as sarin nerve agent, persistent electroencephalogram (EEG) changes can occur. These exposures cause cholinergic symptoms and inhibit red blood cell (RBC) AChE activity.[4]

Absorption

Organophosphates are easily absorbed through the skin, lungs, and GI tract.[1] Symptoms are dependent upon the route of absorption. Inhalation results in a rapid onset of symptoms within one to two hours. If the neat liquid form of an organophosphate is accidentally inhaled as a fine mist, death can occur. The particle size distribution of the mist droplets will determine the pulmonary absorption of the compound. Dermal absorption usually results in symptoms occurring as long as twelve hours after the exposure began. However, dermal absorption of a few milliliters of a potent organophosphate liquid spilled into a worker's boot could also be fatal. Repeated, moderate skin exposure may not cause symptoms until one to two weeks after exposure.[5] Dermal absorption is significant in most cases of occupational poisoning with organophosphates.[4]

Biotransformation

Organophosphorus ester insecticides are readily biotransformed by plants, invertebrates, and vertebrate species. **Phase I detoxification enzymes** form reactive metabolites, while **Phase II enzymes** conjugate the polar phase I metabolites with natural substituents to form products that have water solubility and excretability. Phase I and II enzyme systems are discussed in detail in Chapter 4, "Disposition of Toxicants." Organophosphorus esters easily undergo oxidation at several different sites in the molecule by the action of **cytochrome P450 enzymes**. Oxidative desulfuration of phosphorothioate (parathion) and phosphorodithioate (malathion) esters, produces an increase in the toxicity of the oxygen analogs that are formed. This reaction is a major detoxification pathway in mammals having tissue aryl and aliphatic hydrolases. Since insects are deficient in these enzymes, they are more susceptible to organophosphorus esters. Dealkylation with the formation of an aldehyde also easily occurs. Dearylation occurs with phenol and either a dialkylphosphoric or dialkylphosphorothioic acid being formed. The cytochrome P450 system can also catalyze aromatic ring hydroxylation, thioether oxidation, deamination, alkyl and N-hydroxylation, N-oxide formation, and N-dealkylation.[2]

Excretion

Urinary dimethyl(thio)phosphates and diethyl(thio)phosphates, the metabolites of dimethoxy and diethoxy organophosphorus compounds, can be easily measured. However, since organophosphorus compounds with different toxicity may give similar levels of urinary dialkyl(thio)phosphates, the hazard can only be determined if the levels are calibrated against AChE inhibition. The leaving group (X), which can be specific for a particular organophosphate compound, is also excreted and can be measured in the urine.[4] For example, the American Conference of Governmental Industrial Hygienists (ACGIH) has specified a **biological exposure indice (BEI)**, p-nitrophenol, specifically for parathion. It is to be measured in the urine at the end of a work shift and should be less than 0.5 mg/g creatinine. The BEI indicates a concentration below which almost all workers do not experience adverse health effects.[13]

Standards of Exposure

Exposed individuals can have blood tests performed for AChE activity for comparison to baseline activity values.[1] High RBC AChE inhibition is considered diagnostic of acute organophosphorus poisoning. Baseline activity values or pre-shift measurements are necessary due to high interindividual variability in RBC AChE activity levels with a coefficient of variation as high as 13–16%. The minimal differences for statistical recognition of inhibited RBC AChE is about 15% when compared to one pre-exposure value. It is about 12% when compared to five pre-exposure values. 20–25% reduction in RBC AChE is diagnostic of exposure; 30–50% reduction indicates overexposure; greater than 50% reduction is associated with symptoms of intoxication. At this level of inhibition, the worker must be removed from exposure until RBC AChE activity returns to normal.[4]

Standards of Treatment

All cases of organophosphate poisoning should be considered a medical emergency and the exposed individual should be hospitalized as quickly as possible. If exposure is sufficient to cause **hypoxemia** due to respiratory depression, bronchospasm, bronchial secretions, pulmonary edema, and muscular weakness, immediate artificial respiration and suctioning through an endotracheal tube may be necessary to sustain life. Specific **antidotes** are available for acute organophosphate poisoning. Atropine, a highly toxic antidote, has been successfully used to block the initial muscarinic effects of accumulating acetylcholine. Subsequent treatment with one of the specific antidotal chemicals, the **oximes** (pralidoxime chloride or 2-PAM, pralidoxime methanesulfonate or P2S) can be used to treat moderate to severe nicotinic and CNS signs and symptoms. Aggressive treatment of acute organophosphate poisoning does not offer protection against the development of delayed-onset neurotoxicity or persistent sensory, cognitive, and motor defects that may occur after the exposed individual has survived the acute poisoning.[2]

Case Studies Involving Organophosphates

As reported by the Texas Department of Health and the Surveillance Branch of NIOSH[17], a patient was seen in an emergency medical facility with symptoms of acute pesticide poisoning. The patient was a greenhouse pesticide applicator who had applied Sulfotepp fumigants (Plantfume 103 and Fulex) about twelve hours before he was seen. Sulfotepp (tetraethylthiodiphosphate) is an organophosphate pesticide. The 32-year-old male pesticide applicator became ill after igniting Plantfume 103 and Fulex fumigant canisters in the first of four interconnected greenhouses. He reported feeling ill and smelling the chemical in the first greenhouse, but he and three other applicators completed the fumigation job in all four greenhouses before stopping work. His symptoms included headache, nausea, diarrhea, vomiting, cough, slight dizziness, sweating, fatigue, abdominal pain, anxiety, muscle aches, chest tightness, drowsiness, restlessness, shortness of breath, and excessive salivation, the classical symptoms of acute organophosphate poisoning. He did not seek medical care until about twelve hours after exposure. At that time, his red blood cell acetylcholinesterase level was 14,730 IU/L, which was within the normal range of 7,700 to 17,500 IU/L. He did not have any previously measured baseline acetylcholinesterase level for comparison. He was not given any treatment and was released from the emergency department. The applicator denied any direct contact with the pesticide product. He reported wearing personal protective equipment indicated by the product label instructions, including a full body suit, boots, gloves, and a full-face air-purifying respirator equipped with a pesticide pre-filter. Following an onsite investigation, it was concluded that the applicator was exposed by inhalation due to inadequate respiratory protection. Also, since Sulfotepp is classified as a "toxicity category I" (highly poisonous) pesticide, just a small dose was sufficient to cause adverse symptoms. The Texas Department of Health and NIOSH now recommend that Plantfume 103 and Fulex labels be amended to indicate that supplied air respiratory protection be used. In order for respiratory protection to be effective, periodic respirator fit testing should be required for every worker potentially exposed.

The Veterinary Medicines Directorate (VMD) of the U.K. Department of Health has investigated the possible relationship between chronic fatigue and exposure to organophosphate pesticides in sheep farming.[18] They were interested in knowing if repeated exposure to organophosphates pesticides in sheep dip increased the probability of developing chronic fatigue in sheep farmers. Using a questionnaire, a group of mostly sheep farmers was asked questions that would provide their history of exposure to organophosphate pesticides. A second questionnaire was used to collect information to determine if the subjects had chronic fatigue when first making contact with the Veterinary Medicine Directorate and at the time of the survey. They reported a high prevalence of chronic fatigue among those who completed the questionnaires. Chronic fatigue was also found to persist since the subjects first reported to the VMD. Higher chronic fatigue scores were associated with higher estimates of exposure to organophosphate pesticides. They concluded that further research is needed to determine the specific cause of chronic fatigue among sheep farmers exposed to pesticides.

Carbamates

Sources and Uses

There are far fewer carbamic acid ester insecticides in the marketplace than organophosphate insecticides. In the 1950s, there was interest in developing insecticides with anticholinesterase activity but reduced mammalian toxicity. As a result, several aryl esters of methylcarbamic acid were synthesized. These carbamate insecticides were synthesized as analogs of **physostigmine**, an anticholinesterase alkaloid extracted from the Calabar bean.[2] Commonly used carbamates include carbaryl (Sevin), aldicarb (Temik), carbofuran, and propoxur (Baygon).[3] They are active ingredients in household products, such as flea collars and pet shampoos.[1] They are often used as dusts or sprays in mosquito control programs.[5]

Pertinent Chemical and Physical Properties

Carbamates have the following general chemical structure:

$$R_1 - O - \overset{\overset{\displaystyle O}{\|}}{C} - \overset{\overset{\displaystyle H}{|}}{N} - R_2$$

If R_2 is a methyl group, then the carbamate is an insecticide or nematocide. If R_2 is an aromatic group, then the carbamate is a herbicide. In this case, it is not an inhibitor of AChE because a bulky R_2 group is attached to the nitrogen atom. If R_2 is a benzimidazole, the carbamate is a fungicide.[4] The chemical structure of Baygon is shown in Table 18.1. Carbamate insecticides are esters of N-methylcarbamic acid.[3]

Sites and Mechanisms of Toxic Action

Carbamate insecticides inhibit AChE, but herbicides and fungicides do not. The mechanism of action of carbamates is similar to that of organophosphates, except they tend to bind reversibly to cholinesterase. That is, carbamylation of AChE is short-lasting and the regeneration of enzyme activity is rapid.[4] As a result, in general, they are considered less toxic than organophosphates. Aldicarb is an exception since it is considered to be highly toxic.[1]

Signs and Symptoms of Poisoning

Just as with organophosphate compounds, acute exposures to high concentrations of carbamates can result in lightheadedness, nausea, vomiting, sweating, blurred vision, salivation, muscular weakness, and convulsions.[1] However, with carbamates, signs of toxicity appear quicker than they do with organophosphates. In addition, for many signs and symptoms resulting from carbamate poisoning, there is a greater dose range from that which causes minor effects to those that are lethal. Due to this, carbamates are considered safer than organophosphate insecticides.[3] Symptoms due to poisoning usually subside within a few hours after the end of exposure and at the same time RBC AChE activity reappears.[19]

Biotransformation

Carbamates are often metabolized quickly, which contributes to their lower toxicity to humans than organophosphates.(5) Depending upon the substituents attached to the basic structure, carbamate ester insecticides can undergo attack at several different locations in their structure simultaneously. First, the carbamate ester group can be hydrolyzed by tissue carboxylesterases (carboxylic acid ester hydrolases) with the release of a substituted phenol, carbon dioxide, and methylamine. Several oxidative and reductive reactions involving cytochrome P450 enzymes can occur, resulting in metabolites that are more polar than the parent insecticide. The hydrolysis of carbamate ester insecticides can occur by direct ring hydroxylation or by oxidation of a side chain, resulting in the hydroxylation of N-methyl groups, N-demethylation of secondary and tertiary amines, O-dealkylation of alkoxy side chains, and thioether oxidation. Subsequent to these Phase I reactions, Phase II conjugation reactions can occur at any free reactive grouping with glucuronide and sulfate derivatives. GSH conjugates can also be formed.[20]

Excretion

Urinary metabolites of carbamates have been measured in humans. Workers exposed to carbaryl have 1-naphthol in their urine 4–8 hours after the end of exposure. After an 8-hour shift with exposures to 5 mg/m³ carbaryl, levels of 30 mg/L urinary 1-naphthol were measured. Following exposure to propoxur, urinary 2-isopropoxyphenol was measured.[21]

Standards of Exposure

Exposures to carbamates can be monitored by measuring RBC AChE.[4]

Standards of Treatment

Treatment for carbamate toxicity is similar to that for organophosphate ester insecticide intoxication. Although atropine administration is effective for severe poisonings with carbamates[1], the use of oxime antidotes is contraindicated with carbamate toxicity. When pralidoxime was used in treating carbaryl intoxications, it enhanced the toxicity.[22] Diazepam was found to relieve mental anxiety associated with exposure and it also counteracted some aspects of the CNS and neuromuscular signs that were not affected by atropine.[2]

Pyrethroids

Sources and Uses

Pyrethrum comes from the flowers of *Chrysanthemum cinerariaefolium*.[3] Pyrethroids are synthetic derivatives of the active components of pyrethrum. They entered the marketplace in 1980, and by 1982, were used worldwide.[23] Chemists synthesized new compounds with better stability in light and air than organophosphates and carbamates, better persistence in the environment than organochlorines, more selectivity in target species, and lower mammalian toxicity.[4] The pyrethroids have extensive use in agriculture and are components of household sprays, flea products for pets, and plant sprays for home and greenhouse use.[2]

Pertinent Chemical and Physical Properties

The synthetic pyrethroid ester insecticides have two basic chemical structures.[2] As shown below, the first has an intact cyclopropane ring and is known as a type I ester. R_1 and R_2 can be methyl, bromine, or chlorine groups. R_3 can be hydrogens or a cyano substituent. R_4 can be 3-phenoxybenzoate or other substitutents.

Pyrethroid ester insecticides can also have the following basic chemical structure:

As shown above, this is the "open" structure of type II esters. R_4 can be 3-phenoxybenzoate or other substituents. R_5 can be substituted phenyl substituents. Pyrethrin I, which is a type I ester, is shown in Table 18.1.

Sites and Mechanisms of Toxic Action

The active components of pyrethrum are pyrethrin I and pyrethrin II. Pyrethrin I acts primarily on the central nervous system and pyrethrin II acts primarily on the peripheral nervous system.[3] Both pyrethrins, type I and II esters, modify the gating kinetics of sodium channels in membranes of nervous tissues. Type I esters hold sodium channels open for a shorter period of time (milliseconds), while type II esters hold the channels open for a longer period of time (seconds).[24] Insect sodium channels have been found to be 100 times more sensitive to pyrethrins than mammalian channels.[25] Type II esters at high concentrations affect GABA-gated chloride channels in mammalian brain, which may be responsible for seizures seen with type II ester poisoning.[26]

Signs and Symptoms of Poisoning

Compared to organophosphates and carbamates, pyrethrums have lower toxicity in mammals. However, they are known neurotoxicants.[3] With sufficient exposure, acute poisoning is characterized by dizziness, headache, nausea, muscular fasciculation, convulsive attacks, and coma.[27] Depending upon the presence or absence of an α-cyano substituent in its chemical structure, there are two patterns of symptoms described in rats.[28] The "T (tremor) syndrome" is characterized by aggressive sparring, sensitivity to external stimuli and tremors, if rats are exposed to a pyrethrum lacking the α-cyano substituent. If it is present, the "CS syndrome" occurs, which is characterized by burrowing behavior, coarse tremors, clonic seizures, sinous writhing (**choreoathetosis**), and profuse salivation; therefore, the term "CS (choreoathetosis/salivation) syndrome." It has not been possible to distinguish the two syndromes in humans.[29] In the occupational setting, workers have reported abnormal skin sensations primarily on the face that are burning and tingling.[30] The sensations begin right after beginning work and disappear within 24 hours of onset. Only unprotected parts of the skin are affected by this neurotoxicity. Pyrethroids have been found to cause repetitive firing of sensory nerve endings of the skin by acting on sodium channels.[28] They have also been found to be allergens, causing contact dermatitis in sensitive individuals. Asthma has also been reported in some individuals exposed to pyrethroids.[3]

Biotransformation

Pyrethroids cause little if any chronic toxicity in animals or humans, as shown by chronic animal feeding studies. As a result, it has been concluded that there is very little storage or accumulation of pyrethroid esters in the body. It is also a very good possibility that the detoxification of these compounds is very efficient. The two ester linkages in pyrethroid esters, the terminal methyl ester in type II esters and the centrally located ester adjacent to the cyclopropane moiety in type I esters, are susceptible to hydrolysis by nonspecific carboxylesterases and tissue esterases throughout the body.[2] Organophosphorus esters that inhibit tissue esterases have been found to potentiate pyrethroid ester toxicity in several different species.[31] This emphasizes the importance of knowing all components of mixtures of pesticides in order to anticipate the consequences of worker exposure.

Excretion

Urinary levels of parent pyrethroids as well as metabolites have been measured after occupational exposure.[29] There was no correlation between their concentrations and the degree of cutaneous sensations reported by exposed workers.

Standards of Treatment

Removal from exposure and treatment of symptoms are most commonly used. Lavage with creams will help dermal paresthesia by binding to the lipophilic pyrethroids. Topical steroids have been used for contact dermatitis. Inhaled steroids have been used for persistent asthma, but in the case of labored breathing that occurs shortly after or during acute exposure, rapid acting beta-agonists are recommended instead of inhaled steroids. In the case of type II ester poisonings, the chloride channel agonists, ivermectin and pentobarbitone, have been successfully employed.[2]

Case Studies Involving Pyrethroids

Permethrin, a synthetic pyrethroid, is an approved insecticide by the EPA. It has been extensively used to impregnate Army battle-dress uniforms in the field. Aerosol spray cans were used in the impregnation method by soldiers prior to and during the Gulf War. Excessive exposures to permethrin is known to cause hyperactivity, tremor, ataxia, convulsion, and eventually paralysis.[3] Along with this insecticide, hundreds of thousands of military personnel were exposed between August 1990 and April 1991, to a variety of other chemicals, including **pyridostigmine bromide**, used prophylactically for possible exposure to nerve gases, and N,N-diethyl-m-toluamide (DEET), an insect repellent against mosquitoes, biting flies and ticks. DEET has been used in almost all effective insect repellents, having widespread dermal application with little evidence of toxicity. During this period, military personnel were also exposed to airborne contaminants from oil well fires, diesel exhaust, toxic paints, pesticides, depleted uranium, as well as multiple immunizations. Among the veterans of the Gulf War, there was an increased frequency of reporting the following chronic symptoms—headache, loss of memory, fatigue, muscle and joint pain, ataxia, skin rash, respiratory difficulties, and gastrointestinal disturbances. One report suggests that chemical interactions between permethrin, pyridostigmine bromide, and DEET may have contributed to the symptoms of the Gulf War illnesses.[32]

A study was completed to evaluate the influence of exposure to pyrethroids on birth weight among women in an agricultural district in Central Poland.[33] One hundred and four women who delivered a single, live infant between January 1, 1994 and December 31, 2000, were involved in this study. It was found that maternal exposure to synthetic pyrethroids in the first or second trimester through involvement in field work was associated with a small but statistically significant decrease in birth weight. It was concluded that this observed effect of pyrethroids may be due to a slower pace of fetal development corresponding to the small-for-gestational-age (SGA) birth.

Herbicides

An herbicide is any chemical compound that can either kill or severely injure plants. It is used for eliminating plant growth or killing off of plant parts.[34] A great deal of effort has gone into developing numerous chemical compounds that can be used selectively in eliminating unwanted plant species and at the same time protecting desirable crops. In this section, herbicides are classified according to their ability to interfere with specific biochemical phyto-processes essential for normal growth and development in plants. Since there are no counterparts in mammalian biochemical systems, very little risk of toxicity is associated with most of these chemicals. With a few significant exceptions, the herbicides have been shown to have low toxicity in mammals. There is current concern with these chemicals in that there has been demonstrated or suspected mutagenicity, teratogenicity, and/or carcinogenicity associated with the agent(s) themselves or with contaminants and by-products of their manufacture.[2] It is no surprise that the major route of exposure to herbicides is dermal and they cause skin rashes and contact dermatitis in many exposed workers.

Chlorophenoxy Compounds

These herbicides have been used to kill broadleaf plants by acting as plant growth hormones.[3] They can be absorbed through the skin of workers and are primarily excreted unchanged in the urine.[35] With exposures that may occur from normal use, toxic effects have been very rare in humans. They are generally considered to be weakly toxic to mammals. Trace contamination with dioxins, 2,4-D (2,4-dichlorophenoxyacetic acid) and 2,4,5-T (2,4,5-trichlorophenoxyacetic acid), has linked these herbicides with possible chronic adverse effects, including liver disorders and neurological damage.[5] The chemical structure of 2,4-D is given in Table 18.2. **Chloracne**, the primary toxic effect of 2,4,5-T in humans, has been attributed to the contaminant 2,3,7,8-tetrachlorobenzo-p-dioxin (TCDD), which is generally known as **dioxin**.[3] Chloracne is an acne-like skin disorder that can occur after dermal exposure to dioxin.[5] Due to this possible contamination with TCDD, the use of 2,4,5-T has been restricted in several countries.[4] Be that as it may, TCDD contamination has been reduced over the years due to improved industrial technology.[36] A cancer mortality study using an international cohort of workers exposed to chlorophenoxy herbicides showed a significant excess of mortality for soft-tissue sarcomas, but not for non-Hodgkin's lymphomas occurring 10 to 19 years after the beginning of exposure.[37] A mixture of 2,4,5-T and 2,4-D, known as Agent Orange, was used during the Vietnam War as a defoliant.[5] Thousands of military personnel were exposed to Agent Orange, which was contaminated with TCDD. Studies of these exposed personnel as well as other studies of workers involved in the manufacture or application of these compounds have been inconclusive.

Bipyridyl Compounds

Paraquat (1,1'-dimethyl-4,4'-biphyridylium salts) and diquat (6,7-dihydrodipyrido-1,1'-ethylene-2,2'-bipyridylium salts), broad spectrum weed killers, are among the bipyridyl compounds. They are considered more toxic than most of the insecticides and are known to cause toxicity through the formation of free radicals. A **free radical** is a chemical species containing an atom with a single unpaired electron. It is highly reactive, because acquiring an electron will complete its octet. Due to its chemical bond breaking potential, it can disrupt biochemically important molecules in biological systems, resulting in cellular damage. Paraquat is known to cause delayed-onset damage to the respiratory system. An emphysema-like illness, which is often fatal, can result from acute exposure. Within a day of exposure, acute symptoms can include gastrointestinal distress with nausea, vomiting, and malaise. These symptoms may subside, but then the exposed individual can develop progressive failure of the respiratory system within one or two weeks from the time of exposure. Pulmonary effects can occur after exposure from inhalation but also following exposure by the oral route.[3] Pulmonary involvement is related to selective paraquat accumulation in the lungs due to active transport into the alveolar cell.[5,38] Once in the alveolar cell, paraquat alters cellular metabolism and damages the cell membrane, adversely affecting gas exchange and the overall respiratory process.[5,38] Adverse effects can also be seen in the liver and kidney from paraquat exposure.[1] Most cases of occupational poisonings include skin absorption.[39] Chronic exposure to paraquat from aerial spraying can cause irritation and inflammation of mucous membranes, headaches, coughing, and skin irritation. The fingernails can change in color, an indicator of exposure to paraquat. They may show discoloration or ridging. Diquat is less toxic than paraquat. The primary target tissues of acute exposure to diquat are the gastrointestinal tract, the liver, and kidneys. Unlike paraquat, diquat does not accumulate in lung tissue.[5] The chemical structure of paraquat is given in Table 18.2.

Triazines

These herbicides have low acute toxicity and there have never been any cases of systemic poisoning reported in humans. Exposed individuals excrete unchanged compound as well as dealkylated metabolites.[40] Atrazine is one of the more commonly used triazines.[4] It is undergoing review for cancer risk by the EPA. Based upon available scientific studies, EPA believes that atrazine is not likely to cause cancer in humans. Its chemical structure is given in Table 18.2.

Aresenical Herbicides

Dimethylarsenic acid and methylarsenic acid are in use as herbicides. They have low toxicity and neither acute nor long-term effects have been reported in workers. Although these two

Table 18.2 — Chemical Structures of Herbicides

A. Chlorophenoxy compounds
   2,4-Dichlorophenoxyacetic acid (2,4-D)

B. Bipyridyl compounds
   Paraquat (1,1'-dimethyl-4,4'-bipyridylium)

C. Triazines
   Atrazine (2-chloro-4-ethylamine-6-isopropylamino-S-triazine)

D. Arsenical herbicides
   Dimethylarsenic acid

E. Dinitrophenols
   2,4-Dinitrophenol

compounds are not carcinogens, they may contain traces of inorganic arsenic, which is a recognized human carcinogen.[4] The chemical structure of dimethylarsenic acid is given in Table 18.2.

Dinitrophenols

Derivatives of 2,4-dinitrophenol are used in weed control. The most used compound is 2,4-dinitrophenol as a wood preservative and woodworm insecticide. Its chemical structure is given in Table 18.2. They act by uncoupling oxidative phosphorylation in the mitochondrial cytochrome oxidase system. This results in acute toxicity symptoms that include fatigue, restlessness, nausea, hot flashes, excessive sweating, rapid breathing, tachycardia, and coma.[1] Fatal hyperthermia can occur.[4]

Case Studies Involving Herbicides

A study was conducted in which data from previously published studies were used to evaluate the urinary excretion of 2,4-dichlorophenoxyacetic acid (2,4-D), following a single dermal application to human volunteers.[41] These studies were evaluated with the objective of determining the best method of predicting the total absorbed dose following multiple and varied exposures in occupational settings. Data from a biological monitoring study on six professional pesticide applicators over a two week period were used to generate estimates of the urinary excretion of the pesticide 2,4-D that would result from a single dose. The estimates that were generated for the 24 hour urinary excretion of 2,4-D over a six day period were very close to those obtained in controlled studies. From this, a method was developed to use the generated estimates to determine total absorbed dose of pesticides for a group of 95 professional pesticide applicators. The method developed requires information on the amount of pesticide used for six days prior to the collection of two, 24 hour urine samples. Therefore, urinary excretion of 2,4-D can be used to estimate total daily dose of this herbicide in the occupational setting.

A cancer mortality study was conducted in a cohort of licensed herbicide applicators in the Netherlands.[42] The objective was to determine the long-term health effects of exposure to herbicides. Early in the study, they reported that there might be an increased risk for multiple myeloma in their cohort of 1,341 licensed herbicide applicators. However, this result was based upon a small number of cases. They expanded the follow-up of their cohort by 13 years; now having to report on the causes of death of 196 exposed workers. They report that the herbicide applicators in their study were at an increased risk for skin cancer mortality. This study was unable to definitely attribute the excess skin cancer to herbicide exposure or to excess exposure to sunlight.

Rodenticides

Rats, mice, rabbits, gophers, and other species are often the target for eradication because of their potential to damage crops, to serve as vectors that spread disease, and to present dangers to livestock as a result of their holes. Several rodenticides can be harmful to a variety of species of animals because they are non-biodegradable and non-specific in their effects. Therefore, the use of these compounds is often under strict control.[2,5] Occupational exposures to rodenticides are rare, but accidental or intentional ingestion of most rodenticides poses an acute toxicologic problem.[2]

Anticoagulant Rodenticides

These compounds are antimetabolites of vitamin K and inhibit the liver synthesis of **prothrombin** and other clotting factors, preventing blood clotting.[2] Warfarin is the principal anticoagulant rodenticide. It is a colorless, odorless solid that has been used to kill rats and mice by being dispensed in grain-based baits.[2,5] It has been used extensively because it is toxic in humans only if ingested repeatedly.[3] It has little effect if only a single dose is given.[2] Warfarin contains the anticoagulant, **dicumarol**. Due to the prevention of blood clotting, an animal exposed to warfarin will show bleeding gums, bleeding around the eyes, easy bruising, and life-threatening bleeding in the gastrointestinal tract and brain. These symptoms may not become apparent for two to four days after ingestion or dermal exposure.[5] Since it is a blood thinner, large doses of vitamin K can be used as an antidote.[1] The chemical structure of warfarin is given in Table 18.3.

Fluoroacetic Acid and its Derivatives

Sodium fluoroacetate ("1080") has been used to control ground squirrels, coyotes, and other mammalian pests. This compound disrupts cellular respiration through the blockage of the **citric acid cycle**, and so is extremely toxic to any oxygen-using organism.[3] It specifically causes the incorporation of fluoroacetate into fluoroacetyl-coenzyme A, which condenses with oxaloacetate to form fluorocitrate, which inhibits the enzyme aconitase and prevents the conversion of citrate to isocitrate in the citric acid (Krebs) cycle.[2] Tissues that are energy dependent, such as the heart and central nervous system, are targets of this rodenticide. Symptoms of severe poisoning include cyanosis, convulsions and alterations in heart rate. Cause of death is usually ventricular fibrillation or respiratory failure.[4] Rodenticide applicators can be exposed through inhalation, ingestion, or skin absorption. Symptoms may not appear for up to two hours after exposure. Workers may experience nausea, weakness, fatigue, vomiting, and minor electrocardiogram changes at lower doses. At higher doses, humans can suffer from renal failure, seizures, coma, respiratory arrest, and arrhythmia.[4,5] There are no known antidotes for fluoroacetate poisoning. Due to its effects on many organisms in the environment, its use has been curtailed by the EPA.[1] The chemical structure of sodium fluoroacetate is given in Table 18.3.

ANTU (alpha-naphtylthiourea)

This compound has wide variability in species sensitivity—the rat being the most sensitive and the human being relatively resistant.[4] It is suspected that ANTU is biotransformed in vivo into a reactive intermediate.[2] In sensitive animals, it causes extensive pulmonary edema and pleural effusion as a result of its action on the pulmonary capillaries. Although neither death nor permanent sequelae have been reported in humans from exposure to this rodenticide, poisonings have occurred with tracheobronchial hypersecretions, pulmonary edema, and respiratory difficulty.[2,4,43] The presence of carcinogenic impurities, such as β-naphthylamines, has been noted in some formulations of ANTU and has been the reason for some countries to withdraw it from use.[44] The chemical structure of ANTU is given in Table 18.3.

Fumigants

These compounds are used to kill insects, nematodes, weed seeds, bacteria, and fungi in soil and in consumables like grains, fruits and vegetables, and clothes, and in ships, freight cars, and buildings. Due to the volatility of these substances, the treatment is carried out in enclosed spaces. There is a wide range of fumigants—from acrylonitrile to ethylene oxide; many having other uses. We have focused on two in this section: DBCP and hydrogen cyanide. Fumigants can be liquids (DBCP) that easily vaporize at room temperature; solids that release a gas when reacting with water (aluminum phosphide releases phosphine gas); and gases (hydrogen cyanide). Fumigants are generally nonselective, highly reactive, and cytotoxic.[2] Occasionally occupational exposures may occur, but since the vapors and gases of fumigants readily escape when the enclosed space is opened, these agents can be safely handled by trained applicators.[5]

DBCP (1, 2-dibromo-3-chloropropane)

DBCP is a soil fumigant and a nematocide. It is easily absorbed through the skin.[4] DBCP has been found to cause squamous cell carcinoma in the stomach of rats and mice.[45] This fumigant has also been found to cause sterility in male rats.[46] A study of male workers involved in the production of DBCP found that 13% were **azoospermic**; 17% were **oligospermic**; and 16% had low normal sperm counts.[47] Seven years later a study showed that

Table 18.3 — Chemical Structures of Rodenticides, Fumigants, and Fungicides

Rodenticides

A. Anticoagulant rodenticides
   Warfarin (2-hydroxy-3-(3-oxo-1-phenyl-butyl)-chromen-4-one))

B. Fluoroacetic acid and its derivatives
   Sodium fluoroacetate

C. ANTU (alpha-naphtylthiourea)

Fumigants

A. DBCP (1,2-dibromo-3-chloropropane)

B. Hydrogen cyanide

Fungicides

A. Pentachlorophenol

B. Dithiocarbamates
   Thiram (bis(dimethylthiocarbamolyl)disulfide)

---

the azoospermic and oligospermic workers had no major improvements in testicular function.[48] Because of these adverse effects, DBCP use has been banned in several countries. The chemical structure of DBCP is given in Table 18.3.

Hydrogen Cyanide

This compound is an insecticidal fumigant. It blocks cellular respiration. Occupational exposure occurs through inhalation, while accidental or intentional poisoning is most often through ingestion of a cyanide salt. When exposure begins or the dose is low, respiration and heart rate are stimulated; the exposed individual still has oxygenated venous blood and is not cyanotic. As exposure continues and the dose becomes higher, respiration slows and gasping occurs until respiration completely stops.[4] When used by trained fumigant applicators, this compound can be safely handled. Workers can be biomonitored by measuring urinary excretion of thiocyanates.[49] The chemical structure of hydrogen cyanide is given in Table 18.3.

Fungicides

Most fungicides have low toxicity in mammals. However, all fungicides are cytotoxic and most of these compounds produce positive results in the usual in vitro microbial mutagenicity assays.[2] This is not surprising since the microorganisms used in these assays are similar to the microbes that the fungicides were designed to kill through cytotoxicity or through lethal genetic mutations.[50] Due to these positive mutagenicity tests and the possibility of teratogenic and carcinogenic potential in many of these compounds, a number of fungicides have been banned in many countries. Although one group of extremely toxic fungicides, organomercurials, have been banned from use in many countries, they were used extensively before 1970, and may still be found in developing countries. There are many chemically different fungicides with diverse structures. Pentachlorophenol and dithiocarbamates, which are discussed below, are among this diverse group of pesticides.

Pentachlorophenol

This is a fungicide that is commonly used as a wood preservative[3], but also has been used as an algicide, bactericide, herbicide, insecticide, and molluscide. When first produced, this fungicide was actually a mixture of pentachlorophenol, tetrachlorophenol and traces of chlorinated dibenzo-p-dioxins, polychlorinated dibenzofurans and polychlorobenzenes.[51] There has been a decreasing concentration of impurities in recent years due to improved production technologies.[4] Be that as it may, the use of this fungicide has been phased out of use in many applications because of the contaminants.[2] Its mechanism of action is to interfere with the production of ATP by mitochondria. As a result, in exposed humans, this compound causes the decoupling of the phosphorylation of ADP, resulting in the release of heat. This can cause a fever, sweating and dehydration[5], which can be easily confused with the onset of flu. Several cases of human poisoning have been described, mainly after skin exposure, with 30–100% of the dose deposited on the skin being absorbed.[52] Survivors of poisoning often show dermal irritation and **exfoliation**, as well as irritation of the upper respiratory tract.[2] Since pentacholorophenol is eliminated from the body slowly, chronic exposures to this compound may result in its accumulation in the body with the onset of symptoms slowly.[1] Monitoring of exposure can be accomplished by measuring urinary excretion of pentachlorophenol.[4] The chemical structure of this substituted aromatic compound is given in Table 18.3.

Dithiocarbamates

These environmentally stable compounds are used as fungicides mainly, but have also been used as slimicides, insecticides, and herbicides.[2,4] They have low acute toxicity in humans, although there have been cases of poisoning reported in humans that are questionable. Dithiocarbamates interfere with ethyl alcohol metabolism and cause alcohol intolerance. High doses cause anti-thyroid effects in animals, most likely by interfering with iodination of **thyroxine** precursors. However, with workers exposed to dithiocarbamates, neither alterations of thyroid function nor an increased incidence of thyroid tumors were detected.[53] Two fungicide sprayers from Brazil, who were suffering from an apparent Parkinson-like illness, had occupational histories of annual exposure to diothiocarbamates over four to five years. Both workers showed symptoms that included inability to walk, difficulty in talking, tremors in hands and feet, a short-stepped gait and **bradykinesia**.[54] One of the more commonly used dithiocarbamates is thiram. Its chemical structure is given in Table 18.3.

Summary

As discussed in this chapter, pesticides have a broad range of characteristics, including chemical structures and biological activities. Having such variability of biological effects, it is very difficult to establish a classification system that is suitable for such a broad range of compounds.[2] One classification system recommended by the World Health Organization (WHO) Expert Committee on Insecticides in the early 1970s[55,56], for use by developing countries, has proven to be useful. The WHO recommended classification of pesticides is based upon the LD_{50} value that is the lower confidence limit value for the most sensitive sex, which provides a large safety factor being built into the classification scheme. The terms "solids" and "liquids" refer to the physical state of the pesticide product or formulation.[4] It appears that acute toxicity is the best parameter to use to estimate the hazard to humans. Table 18.4 shows the WHO recommended classification of pesticides by hazard.

As noted in Table 18.4, the WHO Recommended Classification of Pesticides by Hazard, addresses those hazards by the oral or dermal penetration routes. Be that as it may, severe risks come from the sudden or persistent inhalation of pesticides in the forms of liquid spray/mists or solid particle dusts, resulting in acute intoxication and chronic disease. In many occupational cases, inhalation may be the most likely form of accidental or chronic exposure. Measuring airborne concentration (mg/m^3) alone is not sufficient for estimating the potential hazard of an

Table 18.4 — The WHO Recommended Classification of Pesticides by Hazard[2]

Class		LD_{50} for the Rat (mg/kg body weight)			
		Oral		Dermal	
		Solids	Liquids	Solids	Liquids
Ia	Extremely hazardous	≤ 5	≤ 20	≤ 10	≤ 40
Ib	Highly hazardous	5–50	20–200	10–100	40–400
II	Moderately hazardous	50–500	200–2000	100–1000	400–4000
III	Slightly hazardous	> 500	> 2000	> 1000	> 4000
III+	Unlikely to present hazard in normal use	> 2000	> 3000	—	—

airborne pesticide, because the fraction of the material reaching the alveolar region of the respiratory tract and its persistence there determine the nature and severity of the resultant pulmonary or systemic disease. Therefore, the time-weighted average concentration as well as the associated particle (liquid droplet or solid dust) size distribution of an aerosolized pesticide must be determined to evaluate the potential hazard and to determine recommended protective measures.

References

1. **Malachowski, M.J. and A.F. Goldberg:** *Health Effects of Toxic Substances.* Rockville, MD: Government Institutes, Inc., 1995. pp. 98–99.
2. **Ecobichon, D.J.:** Toxic effects of pesticides (Chapter 22). In *Casarett and Doull's Toxicology—The Basic Science of Poisons*, 6th edition. Klaassen, C.D. (ed.). New York: McGraw Hill Medical Publishing Division, 2001. pp. 763–810.
3. **Lu, F.C. and S. Kacew:** *Lu's Basic Toxicology—Fundamentals, Target Organs and Risk Assessment*, 4th edition. New York: Taylor & Francis, 2002. pp 285–301.
4. **Moretto, A. and M. Lotti:** Toxicity of Pesticides (Chapter 13). In *Occupational Toxicology*, 2nd edition. Winder, C. and N. Stacey (eds.). Boca Raton, FL: CRC Press, 2004. pp. 344–371.
5. **Kent, C.:** *Basics of Toxicology.* New York: John Wiley & Sons, Inc., 1998. pp. 215–227.
6. **Blomqvist, A., Berg, C., Holm, L., Brandt, I., Ridderstrale, Y. and B. Brunstrom:** Defective reproductive organ morphology and function in domestic rooster embryonically exposed to o,p'-DDT or ethynylestradiol. *Biol. of Reprod.* 74:481–486 (2006).
7. **Coats, J. R.:** Mechanisms of toxic action and structure-activity relationships for organochlorine and synthetic pyrethroid insecticides. *Enviro. Health Perspect.* 87: 255–262 (1990).
8. **Kendall, R. J. and T. E. Lacher:** *Wildlife Toxicology and Population Modeling: Integrated Studies of Agroecosystems.* Boca Raton, FL: CRC Press, 1994.
9. **Anwar. W. A.:** Biomarkers of human exposure to pesticides. *Environ. Health Perspect. 105 (Suppl 4)*:801–806 (1997).
10. **Hartman, D. E.:** *Neuropsychological Toxicology: Identification and Assessment of Human Neurotoxic Syndromes.* New York, NY: Plenum Press, 1995.
11. **Joy, R.M.:** Chlorinated Hydrocarbon Insecticides. In *Pesticides and Neurological Diseases*, 2nd edition. Ecobichon, D.J. and R. M. Joy (eds.). Boca Raton, FL: CRC Press, 1994.
12. **Chandra, H., B.S. Pangtey, D.P. Modak, K.P. Singh, B.N. Gupta, R.S. Bharti, and S.P. Srivastava:** Biological monitoring of chlorinated pesticides among exposed workers of mango orchards: A case study in tropical climate. *Bulletin Env. Contam. Tox. 48*:295–301 (1992).
13. **American Conference of Governmental Industrial Hygienists (ACGIH):** *2007 TLVs® and BEIs® Based on the Documentation of the Threshold Limit Values & Biological Exposure Indices.* Cincinnati, OH: ACGIH, 2007.
14. **Clement, J.G.:** Toxicity of the combined nerve agents GB/GF in mice: Efficacy of atropine and various oximes as antidotes. *Arch. Tox. 68*:64–66 (1994).
15. **Webb, J.:** Iraq caught out over nerve gas attack. *New Scientist 138*:4 (1993).
16. **Masuda, N., et al.:** Sarin poisoning in Tokyo subway. *Lancet 345*:1446 (1995).
17. **Tharr, D.:** Acute pesticide poisoning associated with use of a Sulfotepp fumigant in a greenhouse. *Applied Occup. Env. Hyg. 11(9)*:1105–1107 (1996).
18. **Tahmaz, N., A. Soutar, and J.W. Cherrie:** Chronic fatigue and organophosphate pesticides in sheep farming: A retrospective study amongst people reporting to a UK pharmacovigilance scheme. *Ann. Occup. Hyg. 47(4)*:261–267 (2003).
19. **Weinbroum, A. A.:** Pathophysiological and clinical aspects of combat anticholinesterase poisoning. *Brit. Med. Bull. 72(1)*:119–133 (2005).
20. **Kassahun, K., Jochheim, C. M., and T. A. Baillie:** Effect of carbamate thioester derivatives of methy- and 2-chloroethyl isocyanate on glutathione levels and glutathione reductase activity in isolated rat hepatocytes. *Biochem. Pharmacol. 48(3)*:587–594 (1994).
21. **Brouwer, R., van Maarleveld, K., Ravensberg, L., Meuling, W., de Kort, W., and J. J. van Hemmen:** Skin contamination, airborne concentrations, and urinary metabolite excretion of proposur during harvesting of flowers in greenhouses. *Am. J. Ind. Med. 24(5)*:593–603 (1993).
22. **Ecobichon, D.J., and R.M. Joy:** *Pesticides and Neurological Diseases*, 2nd edition. Boca Raton, FL: CRC Press, 1994.
23. **Van den Bercken, J., and H.P.M. Vijverberg:** Interaction of pyrethroids and DDT-like compounds with the sodium channels in the nerve membrane. In *Pesticide Chemistry. Human Welfare and the Environment. Mode of Action, Metabolism and Toxicology*, Volume 3. Miyamoto, J. and P. C. Kearney (eds.). Oxford, England: Pergamon Press, 1983. pp. 115–121.
24. **Joy, R.M.:** Pyrethrins and pyrethroid insecticides. In *Pesticides and Neurological Diseases*, 2nd edition. Ecobichon, D.J. and R. M. Joy (eds.). Boca Raton, FL: CRC Press, 1994. pp. 291–312.
25. **Warmke, J.W., et al.:** Functional expression of Drosophila para sodium channels. Modulation by the membrane protein TipE and toxin pharmacology. *J. Gen. Physiol. 110*:119–138 (1997).
26. **Bradberry, S. M., Cage, S. A., and J. A. Vale:** Poisoning due to pyrethroids. *Toxicol. Rev. 24(2)*:93–106 (2005).
27. **Chen, S., et al.:** An epidemiological study on occupational acute pyrethroid poisoning in cotton farmers. *Brit. J. Ind. Med. 48*:77–81 (1991).

28. **Aldridge, W.N.:** An assessment of the toxicological properties of pyrethroids and their neurotoxicity. *Crit. Rev. Tox. 21*:89–104 (1990).
29. **Soderlund, D. M., Clark, J. M. Sheets, L. P., Mullin, L. S., Piccirillo, V. J., Sargent, D., Stevens, J. T., and M. L. Weiner:** Mechanism of pyrethroid neurotoxicity: Implications for cumulative risk assessment. *Toxicology 171(1)*: 3–59 (2002).
30. **Zhang, Z., J. Sun, S. Chen, Y. Wu, and F. He:** Levels of exposure and biological monitoring of pyrethroid in spraymen. *Brit. J. Ind. Med. 48(2)*:82–86 (1991).
31. **Ahmad, M.:** Potentiation/antagonism of pyrethroids with organophosphate insecticides in Bemisia tabaci (Homoptera: Aleyrodidae). *J. Econ. Entomol. 100(3)*:886–893 (2007).
32. **Institute of Medicine (IOM):** *Health Consequences of Service During the Persian Gulf War: Initial Findings and Recommendations for Immediate Action.* Washington, D.C.: National Academy Press, 1995.
33. **Hanke, W., P. Romitti, L. Fuortes, W. Sobala, and M. Mikulski:** The use of pesticides in a Polish rural population and its effect on birth weight. *Internatl. Arch. Occup. Env. Health 76(8)*:614–620 (2003).
34. **Jager, G.:** Herbicides. In *Chemistry of Pesticides*. Buchel, K.H. (ed.). New York: Wiley Publishing Co., 1983. pp. 322–392.
35. **Roberts, D. M., and N. A. Buckley:** Urinary alkalinisation for acute chlorophenoxy herbicide poisoning. *Cochrane Database Syst. Rev. 1*:CD005488 (2007).
36. **Shibamoto, T., Yasuhara, A., and T. Katami:** Dioxin formation from waste incineration. *Rev. Environ. Contam. Toxicol. 190*:1–41 (2007).
37. **Saracci, R., et al.:** Cancer mortality in workers exposed to chlorophenoxy herbicides and chlorophenols. *Lancet 338*:1027–1032 (1991).
38. **Smith, L.L., M.S. Rose, and I. Wyatt:** The pathology and biochemistry of paraquat. In *Oxygen Free Radicals and Tissue Damage*, Ciba Foundation Series 65 (New Series). Amsterdam, The Netherlands: Excerpta Medica, 1979. pp. 321–347.
39. **Smith, J.G.:** Paraquat poisoning by skin absorption: a review. *Human Tox. 7*:15–19 (1988).
40. **Catenacci, G., F. Barbieri, M. Bersani, A. Ferioli, and D. Cottica:** Biological monitoring of human exposure to atrazine. *Tox. Letters 69*:217–222 (1993).
41. **Harris, S.A., P.N. Corey, A.M. Sass-Kortsak, and J.T. Purdham:** The development of a new method to estimate total daily dose of pesticides in professional turf applicators following multiple and varied exposures in occupational settings. *Internatl. Arch. Occup. Env. Health 74(5)*:345–358 (2001).
42. **Swaen, G.M.H., L.G.P.M. Van Amelsvoort, J.J.M. Slangen, and D.C.L. Mohren:** Cancer mortality in a cohort of licensed herbicide applicators. *Internatl. Arch. Occup. Env. Health 77(4)*:293–295 (2004).
43. **Hayes, Jr., W.J.:** *Pesticides Studied in Man.* Baltimore, MD: Williams & Wilkins, 1982.
44. **Tomlin, C.:** *The Pesticide Manual. A World Compendium*, 11th edition. Surrey, U.K.: The British Crop Protection Council, 1997.
45. **Ghanayem, B. I., Maronpot, R. R., and H. B. Matthews:** Association of chemically induced forestomach cell proliferation and carcinogenesis. *Cancer Lett. 32(3)*:271–278 (1986).
46. **Meistrich, M. L., Wilson, G., Shuttlesworth, G. A., and K. L. Porter:** Dibromochloropropane inhibits spermatogonial development in rats. *Reprod. Toxicol. 17(3)*:263–271 (2003).
47. **Slutsky, M., Levin, J. L., and B. S. Levy:** Azoospermia and oligospermia among a large cohort of DBCP applicators in 12 countries. *Int. J. Occup. Environ. Health 5(2)*: 116–122 (1999).
48. **Eaton, M., M. Schenker, M.D. Whorton, S. Samuels, C. Perkins, and J. Overstreet:** Seven-year follow-up of workers exposed to 1,2-dibromo-3-chloropropane. *J. Occup. Med. 28*:1145–1150 (1986).
49. **Adewusi, S. R., and A. A. Akindahunsi:** Cassava processing, consumption, and cyanide toxicity. *J. toxicol. Environ. Health 43(1)*:13–23 (1994).
50. **Knight, A. W., Keenan, P. O., Goddard, N. J., Fielden, P. R., and R. M. Walmsley:** A yeast-based cytotoxicity and genotoxicity assay for environmental monitoring using novel portable instrumentation. *J. Environ. Monit. 6(1)*: 71–79 (2004).
51. **Masunaga, S., Takasuga, T., and J. Nakanishi:** Dioxin and dioxin-like PCB impurities in some Japanese agrochemical formulations. *Chemosphere 44(4)*:873–885 (2001).
52. **Fenske, R.A., S.W. Horstman, and R.K. Bentley:** Assessment of dermal exposure to chlorophenols in timber mills. *Appl. Ind. Hyg. 2*:143–147 (1987).
53. **Steenland, K., Dedillo, L., Tucker, J., Hines, C., Sorensen, K., Deddens, J., and V. Cruz:** Thyroid hormones and cytogenetic outcomes in backpack sprayers using ethylenebis(dithiocarbamate) (EBDC) fungicides in Mexico. *Environ. Health Perspect. 105(10)*:1126–1130 (1997).
54. **Ferraz, H.B., et al.:** Chronic exposure to the fungicide maneb may produce symptoms and signs of CNS manganese intoxication. *Neurol. 38*:550–553 (1988).
55. **World Health Organization (WHO):** *WHO Technical Report Series 513 (Safe Use of Pesticides): Twentieth Report of the WHO Expert Committee on Insecticides.* Geneva, Switzerland: WHO, 1973.
56. **World Health Organization (WHO):** *The WHO Recommended Classification of Pesticides by Hazard and Guidelines to the Classification 1996–1997, WHO/PCS/96.3*, Geneva, Switzerland: WHO, 1996.

Additional Reading

Hayes, Jr., W.J. and E.R. Laws, Jr. (eds.): *The Handbook of Pesticide Toxicology.* San Diego, CA: Academic Press, 1991.

Tomlin, C. (ed.): *The Pesticide Manual*, 14th edition. Surrey, U.K.: British Crop Protection Council, 2006.

Chapter 19

Toxicology of Particulate Matter

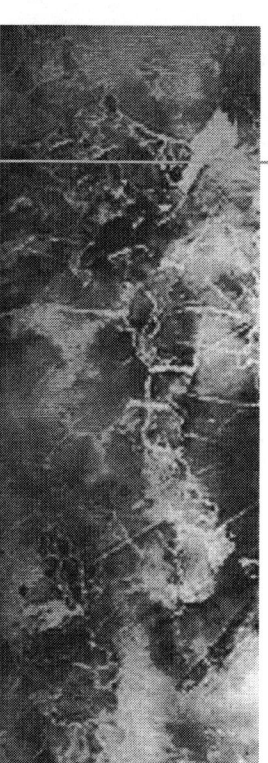

Outcome Competencies

Upon completion of this chapter, the reader should be able to:

- Discuss the toxicity of particulate maters associated with the physical attributes of the particles with limited consideration for their chemical make-up.
- Discuss the history of aerosol science.
- Discuss instrumentation and methodologies used to determine particle size.
- Discuss the exposure/dose relationship with regard to particles.
- Increase awareness of the key elements in aerosol particle size analysis.
- Be more knowledgeable regarding enhanced toxicity associated with particles size, compared to the chemical composition of the bulk material specifically for nanoparticles.

Key Terms

accepted shapes, biological factors, chemical properties, concentration, Cunningham Slip Correction Factor, curvilinear motion, deposition mechanisms, density (difference between bulk and particle density), dose, Dynamic Shape Factor, equivalent diameters, Fick's Laws of Diffusion, fractal dimension, Hatch-Choate Equations, Knudsen Number, Mean Free Path, mobility, monodisperse, morphology, Newton's Law, opsonization, particle, Particle Clearance and Translocation, particulate motion/deposition, physical properties, polydisperse, Reynolds Number, Stokes' Law, ultrafine particles, uniform motion

Key Topics

1. Aerosol Characterization
   - General Microscopy
   - Aerodynamic Particle Sizing
   - Inertial Separators
   - Electrostatic and Thermal Precipitators
   - Direct Reading Instruments
2. Particles as a Chemical Class
   - Mechanisms of Action
   - Examples
     - Non Specific Granular Dusts
     - Nanoparticles
     - Endotoxins

Chapter 19

Toxicology of Particulate Matter

*By William K. Alexander PhD, CIH
and Kenneth R. Still, PhD, FATS, CIH, CSP, CHMM*

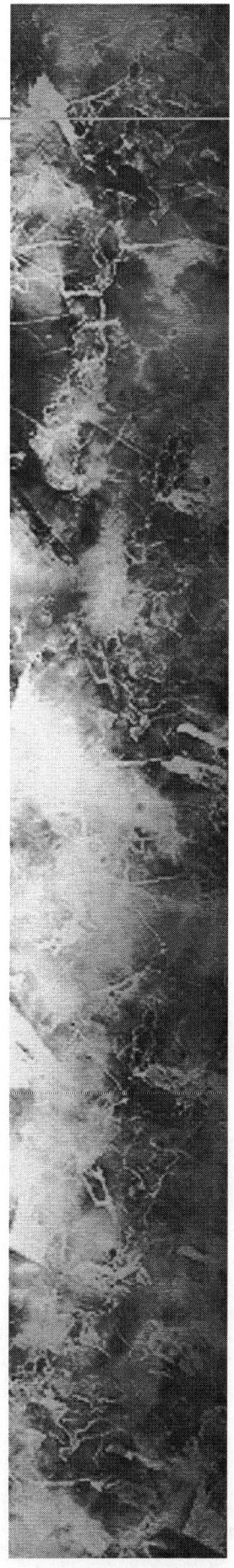

Introduction

Retrospectively, exposure dose relationships were linked to mass. Very small particles, with diameters in the nanometer range, were thought to provide insignificant mass of material delivered to the target organ or system and were generally ignored. Today, concerns are rising regarding enhanced toxicity related to particle size and number delivered to the respiratory system and from there to other organs and systems. This chapter will provide brief information on the history of particle size analysis, key terms, constants, factors, instrumentation, and other items associated with evaluation of particle exposure concentrations, dose, and toxicity. In general, and unless otherwise indicated, the context of discussions in this chapter are in the industrial environment with the particles suspended in air. The intent of the chapter is to provide the reader with the basic vocabulary, concepts, and information on aerosol characterization, particle size distribution analysis, current technology to determine the particle size distribution, and information on new findings regarding enhanced toxicity that may be associated with a particle's size or particulates as a class.

Background

It would not be possible to determine when scientists began to collect data on particle motion and their physical and physiological impact on human health. Much of the work done providing the underlying basis for today's current state of knowledge was derived from larger materials moving through the air, such as cannon balls. Certainly Galileo was interested in these larger "particles" during his work on gravity in the late 1600s. Sir Isaac Newton and others followed Galileo's work adding and refining assumptions and collecting data to provide improved predictive models of the particle's motion. This process continued with Stokes, Einstein, and continues today. Few areas of science have such a diverse and colorful history as the study of particle motion. From the flight of cannon balls to the movement of nanoparticles, the ability to quantify parameters of an aerosol in order to predict its movement continues to be refined.

Aerosol particle characterization has its own vocabulary, procedures, and instrumentation. Aerosol particle size distributions are generally accepted to be lognormal. Particle size distributions are generally described by a measure of central tendency (median or mean) and a standard deviation (geometric). Distributions may be based on the number, the surface area, the volume, the mass or other parameters of the particles and the aerosol. With regard to the number of particles in the aerosol, the largest numbers of particles are contributed by those with the smallest diameters. Limitations of technology can impact our ability to accurately identify the mean/median particle diameter and the standard deviation introducing potential error in predictive models of the aerosol. Some limitations of the aerosol, the instruments and the methodologies are intuitive. Particles cannot have a diameter of zero imposing a lower limit. Particles much larger than a few hundred microns settle very quickly and are lost from the aerosol posing an upper size limit. Limitations of the instrumentation to entrain and capture or accurately resolve large and small aerosol particles may prevent accurately identifying the size of all the particles in the sample and the distribution. Similarly, all of the different technologies and methodologies have weaknesses that can introduce variation and error into the characterization of the aerosol or the description of individual particles. As technology improves with regard to identification of smaller particle diameters, a lower limitation regarding the material will become its atomic or molecular size. Endotoxins may be a variant of this premise as their molecular size and particle size, linked to their biological origins and activities, may play a role in toxicity but that role is yet to be clarified. Improvements in instrumentation and technologies are allowing researchers to resolve smaller diameter particles in larger numbers. Particles having diameters of 2.5 to ten microns (PM 2.5 and PM 10, respectively) have received great interest regarding their potential for deposition in the respiratory system. A great deal of research continues in developing improved ways to discern and quantify the smallest of particles in the aerosol.

There are a number of procedures and technologies available to characterize aerosolized materials. They include sieves, optical instruments, light and electron microscopy, light scattering, inertial and gravitational samplers, and others. Particles are categorized by number, surface area, mass, volume, and other parameters based on the means of determination. It is possible to determine other parameters of an aerosol (mass data from count data) in some cases using complex mathematical tools. This ability to determine higher moments in a particle distribution is linked to the lognormal distribution. Care must also be taken to recognize the difference between a particle's physical diameter and its aerodynamic diameter. Particle diameter, density and shape factors are of concern in determining aerodynamic properties to estimate the locations of deposition and the probable timeframe between absorption and elimination to assist in quantifying the potential dose.

Exposure/dose models of the past have been predicated on the mass of material delivered to the target organ or system leading to the toxic effect, the dose. Recent research indicates that particulate materials may pose additional health impacts beyond those anticipated based on the dose of the bulk material. These differences may be attributed to inaccuracies in the exposure/dose relationship, an area of intensive and continuing research. The ability to capture the aerosolized particulates and draw them into the respiratory system is characterized by very complex processes including fluid mechanics, deposition mechanisms, and other processes all of which continue to be the center of on going research. Elevated toxicity may be associated with changes in the particles from the generation process or from materials they may capture in the intervening air, absorbing or allowing them to adsorb on the surface, carrying them to the target. The differences may be brought on by properties of the particles as they are deposited in the respiratory system and undergo the ADBE processes. ADBE processes are similarly complex and existing models help to predict the toxic effects of the exposure but are limited by assumptions. Particulates may pose contact hazards to the skin, eyes, and other surface regions. They may also be re-aerosolized from these surfaces providing a second exposure potential. The particle size distribution of a second aerosolization may differ from the primary characterization. Particles may show enhanced ability to cross physiological barriers to carry the toxic materials to the target organs/systems. Research continues to clarify all these areas of question regarding particulate exposures with specific interest in the relationship between particle size and toxicity.

Continuing research indicates that previous assumptions and models, with regard to toxicity of particulates may be inadequate. The idea that the smallest particles did not contribute to toxicity since their mass was insignificant is no longer considered realistic specifically with the rise of nanotechnology. Further research and newer technologies will continue to improve the information on particles that can be captured, entrained, and deposited in the respiratory system and their relationship to the overall adverse health outcome associated with the exposure.

Key Concepts and Definitions

(The items listed below are important in aerosol science but, because of the intended depth of information provided in this chapter, their derivation may beyond the scope of this work. They may not be discussed further in the text. They, with their brief definition, are listed here to help the reader develop a basic vocabulary.)

Accepted Shapes: Accepted shapes for particles include spheres, aggregates, irregular (fractal) and fibers (rods, tubes, wires, etc.). Voids or uneven surfaces may exist in all shapes and alter the volume and density calculations used to determine size of the particles. Spheres may join together to form chains or networks. The particles, spheres and irregulars, may have rough surfaces with void spaces. Aggregated networks may have internal void spaces. Elongated chains may appear as fibers. Inability to define these void spaces can impact the determination of particle volume.

Biological Factors: The ADBE processes, pre-existing conditions, and other variables that can be associated with differences in the exposure/dose relationship and adverse health outcomes between individuals. (See Chapter 12, "Immunotoxicology").

Chemical Properties: Characteristics of a substance that determine how it will react with other substances. Chemical properties of the aerosol and the individual particles may differ from those of the bulk material. Chemical properties of the particles may differ from those of the bulk material if the particles are altered in the production process or if materials in the air are captured and either absorbed into or adsorbed on the particles.[1]

Concentration: Particle concentration can be derived in number of particles, surface area, mass, volume, or other aspects per unit volume of air (i.e. milligrams per cubic meter). Concentration factors, linked to particle size information, begin to define the limits of exposure and dose. Further, linked to clearance mechanisms, and ADBE process factors, researchers can refine estimates of the mass of material actually absorbed and delivered to the target organ when evaluating dose response characteristics of a toxic material.

Cunningham Slip Correction Factor: During the early 1900s it was noted that the settling of some particles was different than predicted when using Stokes Law. Stokes had assumed that the velocity of the gas at the surface interface of the particle was zero. In 1910, Cunningham recognized that the assumption of zero velocity at the particle's surface could be incorrect for smaller particles (diameter < 1.0 micrometer). Cunningham developed a correction factor to improve the predictive ability and extend the useful range of Stokes Law.[2]

Curvilinear Motion: Models developed within this frame of reference attempt to capture non-linear motion, acceleration, and other dynamic factors impacting particle motion. Models developed to predict particle motion in this environment are considerably more complex but more accurately reflect the industrial environment.

Deposition Mechanisms: Currently there are five accepted means in which particulates are deposited in the respiratory system. These means are impaction, sedimentation, diffusion, interception, and electrostatic attraction. Impaction occurs when the particle's mass and velocity are too great to make the turns in the airway, the particle departs the streamline path, strikes the surface and is deposited. Sedimentation occurs when the particle's mass is sufficient to overcome its buoyant forces in the airway and the particle settles and is captured on the surface. The diffusion process reflects Brownian motion of the small particles (sub-micron) entering small airways with low flow velocity and long residence time. Interception occurs when a particle or fiber does not deviate from its air streamline path but strikes a surface, due to its size, and is captured. Electrostatic capture is based on the attraction derived from the differences in the charge of the particle and that of the surface. For a more refined explanation of particle deposition in the respiratory tract, see Chapter 12, "Immunotoxicology."

Density (difference between bulk and particle density): Particle aerodynamic properties are generally derived using an estimate of the density of the particle. Particle mass may not be difficult to discern but determining the actual volume of the particle is often a major undertaking. Errors in volume impact the calculation of the particle's density and impact the determination of the aerodynamic equivalent diameter. Density values of the bulk material do not always predict the density of the particles generated in a process. While it would seem counter intuitive, research is finding that there may be differences in the density of the particle compared to the density of the parent material. In general the differences are attributed to errors in the determination of the particle's volume.

Dose: The mass of material delivered to the target organ or organ system.

Dynamic Shape Factor: Theoretical models, such as Stokes, are based on a number of assumptions. Among them, arguably the most common is that the particle is spherical. Few particles truly fit this requirement and it was found that particle shape influenced parameters such as settling time.[3] Dynamic shape factors then seek to explain the difference in the predicted motion compared to the actual motion, such as settling time, associated with the shape of the particle.

Equivalent Diameters: Diameter of a sphere with which the instrument of choice would yield the same size measurement as the particle under consideration. Examples include physical, volume, surface, mass, and other equivalent diameters.[4]

Physical: A particle's physical diameter is derived from the geometry and physical structure of the particle generally discerned by microscopy or another means that visualizes the particle. If the particle is spherical this diameter has significant meaning. If the particle is not spherical, the significance of this diameter deteriorates. There are a number of different conventions of measurements of a particle's diameter in use today. Among them are Martin's Diameter, Projected Area Diameter, and Feret's Diameter. Martin's Diameter is the length of a line that divides the particle into two equal size areas. The Projected Area Diameter is the diameter of a circle with the same area as the particle's silhouette. Feret's Diameter is the length of a reference line that is perpendicular to left and right tangential lines on the particle. These diameters have the hierarchy of relative size:

Martin's < Projected Area < Feret's

Aerodynamic: Aerodynamic diameters are based on the aerodynamic properties of the particles. The Stokes, or equivalent sphere diameter, is the diameter of a spherical particle with the same density as the parent material that has the same settling time as the particle being considered. It is different from the Aerodynamic Equivalent Sphere in that the density of the material for the latter is given as 1.0 g/cm^3. These diameters are not derived directly by optical means. Based on the instrument and the process used to develop these diameters an aerodynamic equivalent diameter has the greatest potential to predict the behavior of the particles in the atmosphere and in the respiratory system.

Fick's Laws of Diffusion: The mass transfer of one material (gas) through another in the absence of a flow is diffusion. Fick, in the early 1800s, developed two equations to predict this diffusion; (1) in a steady state and (2) in a non steady-state. Steady-state indicates that the mass of material released into a contained volume (concentration) does not change with time. The non steady-state equation, Fick's Second Law of Diffusion, allows for changes in concentration with time. Diffusion is always from an area of more concentration to one of less and is thus always down the gradient.

Fractal Dimension: When measuring a distance, a contour appearing to be straight at one magnification may show convolutions at greater magnification. The inability to resolve inclusions, voids, and other differences contribute to errors in the determination of the volume and surface area of a particle.

Hatch-Choate Equations: In 1929, Hatch and Choate developed mathematical tools to derive higher moments (mass, surface area, volume) based on the count median diameter (weighted distributions). The premise of the equations is that the distribution is perfectly log-normal. Any deviation from log-normal will induce error. Derivation of the Hatch-Choate equations can be found in many aerosol textbooks.

Knudsen Number: A dimensionless number, which represents the ratio between the mean free path and the particle radius. Knudsen numbers divide motion into four flow regimes, which are: continuum, slip, transition, and free-molecular.

Mean Free Path: The average distance that an object (usually an atom or molecule) can move before colliding with something.

Mobility: The ability of particles and substances to move, either by random motion or under the influence of fields or forces. It is the ratio of the particle velocity to the applied force. The force can be provided by gravity, electrical fields, diffusion, or other means.[5]

Monodisperse: Within the limitations of measurement, all particles in the aerosol have the same diameter.

Morphology: The shape of a particle. The shape may have significance in determining a particle's aerodynamic properties and toxicity factors. The foundational equations for determining properties of particulates are based in spheres. Fumes and products of heating processes may have this form. Particles derived by attrition processes are generally not spherical. Even the products of combustion processes cannot be assumed to be spherical. Particle morphology is important when diameters are developed by optical means. They become less important when aerodynamic factors are used to determine the equivalent particle size.

Newton's Law: This law was derived from experiments on the range of cannon balls. Derivation of the equations he developed is beyond this text but the key issue was that air provided resistance (drag) to the cannonball as it moved. Newton was able to estimate the force of that resistance as he visualized the column of air that the cannonball would displace as it flew to the target. Drag was the energy required to accelerate the air in that column as the cannonball flew. Newton made a number of assumptions in deriving his model. Primary among his assumptions was that the inertial forces of the cannonball accelerated in the firing process greatly exceeded the viscous properties of the intervening air column.

Opsonization: A means to enhance the susceptibility of bacterial cells to phagocytosis.

Particle: A very small piece or part, a tiny portion, or speck. The bulk material may be solid or liquid. Particles are considered to have mass but their dimensions are negligible for most purposes. Particles are sufficiently small to become aerosolized by natural air currents in nonspecific environments.

Particle Clearance and Translocation: Clearance is the time required to remove the particle from the body after deposition. In the broadest sense particles can be divided into a number of size categories. Divisions include sub-micron and super-micron or inhalable and respirable, or they can be divided by specific diameter measurements such as $PM_{2.5}$ or PM_{10}. The respiratory system provides a number of protection mechanisms to clean incoming air of particles. Although still the subject of continuing research, it is predicted that particles with aerodynamic diameters of 10 micrometers (μm) or greater are captured in the head and neck (HN) region including the naso-pharanx, mouth and larynx. Particles with aerodynamic diameters less than 10 μm but greater that 2.5 μm are deposited in the tracheobronchial (TB) region while those with smaller diameters may enter the lower (alveolar) regions of the lung. Particles may be sufficiently small that their entry into the lung still does not lead to deposition and they may remain for some time in the lung to be exhaled in subsequent inhalation/exhalation cycles. A great deal of research continues in the development of models to predict deposition by aerodynamic diameter of the particle. The values for the diameters cited and the area of deposition are not absolute. Current models relate a probability of deposition in a location based on particle aerodynamic properties. Estimates of the clearance time are then predicated on the location of deposition. As an example, the mucociliary escalator is designed to clear particles deposited in the HN and TB regions. The time required for an insoluble particle at the lower limit of the mucociliary escalator to reach the mouth and be removed from the respiratory system is expected to be approximately 24 hours. Translocation is the movement of the particles within the body, out of the respiratory system and into other organs systems. Solubility of the particle plays a significant role in the removal or absorption processes. Similarly, a relatively insoluble particle may be inhaled, deposited, carried to the mouth by the mucociliary escalator and swallowed entering the gastro-intestinal system providing a second opportunity for ADBE processes. A great deal of research is currently in progress regarding submicron particles to clarify their deposition and translocation mechanisms, times and sites.

Particulate Motion/Deposition: Foundational models and the premise for particle deposition are based on linear motion in controlled environments. Settling times are based on particle diameter and are independent of the gas or particle density. Particles released in air are assumed to instantaneously reach their maximum settling velocity. Curvi-linear motion and more realistic models of particle deposition require a number of assumptions, constants, and qualifiers to improve predictions. The derivation of these values is beyond the scope of this work but it is important to recognize that particle deposition modeling is complex, there is a great body of literature existing in the step-by-step improvement of predictive applications. Research continues today to improve deposition models. The key thrust has been that toxicity is linked to the mass of material delivered to the target organ or system, the dose. Dose is linked to deposition location and the ADBE processes that follow.

Physical Properties: Particle size, shape and other factors that contribute to capture, entrainment, deposition, ADBE processes and a physiological response. Probably the most important properties relating to particle deposition and subsequent toxicity are particle size, number concentration, surface area, mass concentration, shape, and electrical charge. Integration of these factors provides information on the movement of the aerosol as a whole as well as the individual particles. Particle size, the aerodynamic diameter specifically, is arguably the most important parameter in that it allows for prediction of where in the respiratory system, or in other systems, the particle will be deposited. The physical interface of particles with cells may lead to physiological responses whether from simple friction, by providing a location for chemical activities or through other, as yet unrecognized mechanisms.

Polydisperse: Particles of more than one diametric size are contained within the aerosol.

Reynolds Number: A dimensionless parameter relating the inertial forces to the frictional forces (viscosity) of the medium.[6] The inertial forces are in the numerator. Re > 1000 is in the Newton range while an Re < 1 is in the Stokes range. A great deal of research continues on particle motion in the transition range where 1 < Re < 1000.

Stokes' Law: In the middle 1800s Stokes found that the motion of smaller particles was not accurately described by Newton's equations. Smaller particles, with what were then considered to be insignificant mass, had little inertia therefore the viscous properties of the air column they displaced played a more significant role in their motion. Again the derivation of the Navier-Stokes equations are beyond this text but the key issue was the shift from the importance of inertial forces based on the mass of the particle to the viscous forces of the air as the primary source of resistance. Stokes made a number of assumptions in the derivation of his model for particle motion. Many of these assumptions have been the basis for much continuing research. For a listing of the assumptions and more information on Stokes Law, the reader should consult any of the currently available texts on aerosols.

Ultrafine Particles: Particles with a diameter less then 100 nanometers.

Uniform Motion: Generally the easiest motion to predict as there are only two forces recognized, a constant external force such as gravity or an electrical field and the resistance imparted by the gas medium. Uniform motion provided the foundation for much of the early development of the laws of motion. Differences between the predicted and observed values for particle motion, as well as improvements in technology, allowed researchers to identify errors and seek correction factors. The probability of simple uniform motion in an industrial environment is very small.

Aerosol Characterization

The key parameter in predicting the motion of an aerosol is the size of the particles, indicated by a measure of central tendency. Often a median diameter is selected due to the lognormal distribution and the potential impact of extreme values. A second important measure is the determination of the spread of the distribution of particle diameters or the standard deviation. There are a number of methods to determine particle size including sieving, microscopy, and direct reading instruments. The technique used to determine the particle size is also important and care must be taken to understand what is being measured, how it is measured, and what the outcome value means. The count or number median diameter derived from microscopy is different from the count or number median aerodynamic diameter determined using an aerosol particle sizer.

General Process (Microscopy)

It is to some extent easier to determine the diameter of spherical particles than those with irregular shapes. When using microscopy to determine the diameter of irregular particles, a number of different conventions may be used. Among them the three most often chosen are Martin's, Feret's, and the Projected Area diameters. Some advantages of microscopy in sizing particles include the ability to see if the particles show signs of agglomeration. The shape of the particles can be seen and accounted for. The equipment can be relatively inexpensive and easy to maintain. Fractal dimension evaluation, visual acuity, resolution, and other factors can be drawbacks to microscopy. Consistency and deliberate actions are key in minimizing the introduction of variation during microscopic analysis.

Having selected the diameter convention for sizing the particles, the initial step in the characterization process is to measure the diameter of the particles and to construct a histogram. Statistical considerations are required to determine the total number of particles to be counted in the sample. The histogram constructed will indicate the number of particles counted in pre-determined size bins. Particle sizes in an aerosol are not normally distributed. As discussed earlier, it is generally considered that they are log-normally distributed. As seen in Figure 19.1, the histogram will be skewed to the right showing more particles in the smaller size ranges given the limitation of the sampling procedure and instrumentation discussed earlier. Making a log transformation should develop a more normal distribution as seen in Figure 19.2. Using the data from the histogram, another distribution is developed comparing the frequency of a particle size as a percentage of all the particles counted (measured). This latter data is a summation of percentage so that for any given particle size, it is possible to discern the percentage of particles in the sample greater or smaller than that identified diameter. Plotting this data, comparing cumulative percentage to particle diameter, provides a sigmoidal curve. Re-plotting this data on log-probability paper straightens the center portion of the line as seen in Figure 19.3. From this log-probability plot it is possible to read directly the particle diameter at which 50% of the particles are equal to or smaller than the stated diameter. This value is the number (or count) median particle diameter of the

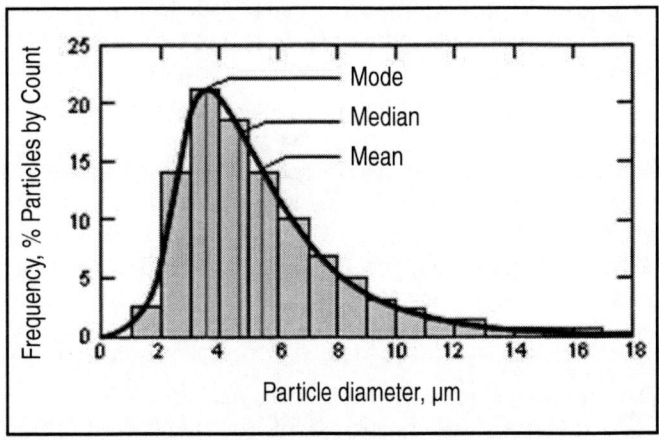

Figure 19.1 — Histogram of a Particle Size Distribution.

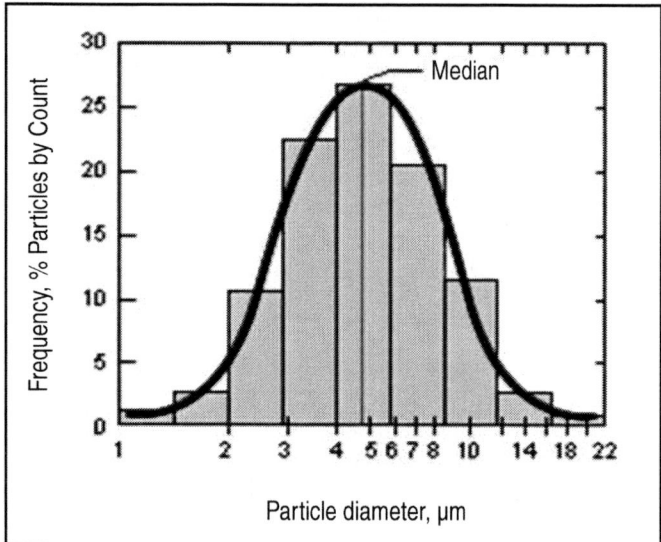

Figure 19.2 — Histogram of a Lognormal Particle Size Distribution.

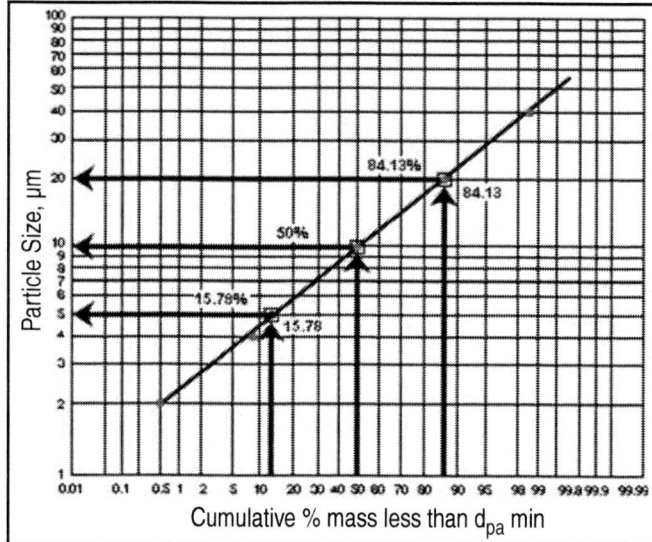

Figure 19.3 — Log-probability Plot.

sample. The geometric standard deviation (GSD) is then determined by dividing the identified 50% diameter by the 15.87% diameter value. It is also possible to divide the 84.13% diameter value by the 50% value. Finally, the GSD can be determined by taking the square root of the 84.13% diameter value divided by the 15.87% diameter value. The GSD represents the slope of the line and its value cannot be less than one. It is a dimensionless number. If the aerosol was monodisperse the GSD would be equal to one. Plots of higher moments for the particles (i.e. surface area or mass) should yield lines parallel to the count line. The GSD, slope of these lines, for all of the moments will be the same, based on a true lognormal distribution. In this example, the diameter identified would be the number, or count, median diameter. From the count median diameter, other parameters (i.e. the mass median diameter or surface area median diameter) can be determined using the equations of Hatch and Choate. It is important for the reader to understand that these are not aerodynamic diameter values. Particle deposition, and the subsequent dose and toxicity, is based on aerodynamic particle sizes but to derive those values from these requires the summation of all of the aerosol characterization knowledge gathered from Galileo to the present including dynamic shape factors, slip correction factors, and others.

This has been a simplified discussion of the general process for determining the median diameter and the GSD of an aerosol particle size distribution. The overall process is not simple and great care must be exercised if the data derived is to be accurate and reproducible. For a more in depth discussion of aerosol particle size characterization techniques and procedures the reader should consult one of the many textbooks on the subject currently available, such as Hinds, Aerosol Technology, 1999.

Aerodynamic Particle Sizing Instruments

As discussed earlier, microscopy (including electron microscopy) can be used to determine particle size. Microscopy is not the only means to determine particle size. New and refined instruments are constantly being introduced to the consumer. Particle sizing technologies work on a number of different principles including inertia, time-of-flight, light scattering, fluorescence, and others. Not all instruments are best for the application intended. Before selecting the instrument to be used researchers should consider a number of issues including the particle size range that can be identified by the instrument (resolution), ease of use, calibration procedures and the availability of standards, format for data presentation, sample volume required, whether the sample must be preserved for further analysis, and reliability of the instrument in its environment.

Aerodynamic diameters are generally given in one of two forms, the Stokes Equivalent Sphere (SES) or the Aerodynamic Equivalent Sphere (AES). Based on an irregular (non-spherical) particle, the SES is the diameter of a sphere that would have similar aerodynamic properties to the particle and the same density as the bulk material. The AES is the diameter of a sphere of unit density (1.0 g/cm^3) with aerodynamic properties similar to the particle. Equations are provided to convert between SES and AES if necessary.

Inertial Separators

Inertial instruments include cyclones, impactors, elutriators, aerosol centrifuges, and impingers. These instruments may be used to pre-select a cut-off particle diameter for other analytical instruments downstream. Similarly they may be used to fractionate the aerosol into portions with particles sizes greater than a specified diameter, such as PM 10. Impactors, cyclones, and aerosol centrifuges may be cascaded to provide more than two fractions of the aerosol. Simple inertial instruments function on the aerodynamic properties of the particle providing an SES diameter.

There are areas of concern for all types of inertial samplers. Particles may strike the impaction plate and bounce in impactors, changing their location of collection and distorting the final result. Particles impacting the collection surface may fracture. Constant air flow must be provided for cyclones and there are considerations for electrostatic issues with nylon units. High air flow rates in centrifuges can alter flow patterns and adversely impact sizing capability. High air flow rates can similarly impact elutriator sizing capability. Efficiency of inertial methods diminishes when particles become smaller than approximately 0.2 micrometers. Care must be taken to operate the instrument of choice in accordance with the manufacturer's specifications to minimize the potential for errors.

Electrostatic and Thermal Precipitators

Electrostatic precipitators function using electrostatic forces to separate particles from the gas stream in which they are moving. Particles passing through the instrument are charged by some means (i.e. corona discharge, flame, absorption of ionizing radiation, or friction). Charged particles are separated from the gas stream and collected on a surface for further analysis. Thermal precipitators remove particles from a gas stream by moving them through a narrow channel in which a thermal gradient is provided. Particles move from the area of higher temperature to lower and are collected on an appropriate surface for further analysis. Smaller particles are collected earlier in the process than larger particles requiring consideration in the further analysis. At low gas flow rates collection efficiency is very high for both electrostatic and thermal instruments. Volatile materials should not be sampled using these instruments. Post collection analysis is usually conducted by microscopy (light or electron). The researcher should be aware of the advantages and limitations of these instruments and plan accordingly.

Direct-Reading Instruments

These instrument types arguably represent the cutting edge in particle technologies. They function on a number of different principles. Instruments in this category include condensation nucleus counters, quartz microbalance, beta-attenuation, light scattering, light attenuating, electrical detectors, optical particle counters, particle relaxation size analyzers, differential mobility particle sizers, and others. Each instrument functions best within a range of particle sizes. Each has issues of calibration, standards, maintenance, reliability, cost, and ease of use. Each instrument has strengths and weaknesses that must be evaluated as part of the overall sampling plan. The instruments may provide information on the mass/number concentration, or the particle size distribution or both.

Overall, instrumentation for determining particle size distributions can be very expensive and complex. The descriptions provided are cursory and are intended only to give the reader an idea of the capabilities available. Further research into the instrumentation is highly recommended and can be found through the manufacturers of the instruments or a number of textbooks currently in publication.

Particulates as a Chemical Class

Chemical composition of the aerosolized particles may be significantly different from the bulk material (e.g. combustion products compared to fuel vapor).[7] Even among attrition processes, the particles may undergo heating and cooling that could alter their chemical properties (solubility, volatility, etc.). Beyond the chemical make-up, particle shape and size (fibers, agglomerates, etc.) may play a role in the overall physiological impact and the exposure/dose relationship. The toxic effects may be brought on by materials that absorbed into the particles or adsorbed onto their surface during the generation process or while transiting in the intervening air.[8] Finally, the physical presence of the particles, independent of chemical make-up or size/shape may have an influence on physiological responses and eventual health outcomes.

Mechanism of Action

Research into the mechanisms of action for particles, as a class, continues and is extremely complex. Materials used as surrogate particles include, but are not limited to, polystyrene latex (PSL), titanium dioxide (TiO_2), and carbon black. Production of these materials can be tightly controlled as can the particle diameter. Factors associated with the particle's physical properties (shape, number, surface area, mass, etc.), chemical make-up, solubility, the differences that may exist between the particles' core and the materials on its surface and other, as yet unrecognized factors, all contribute to the complexity of discerning the relationship between particle exposure concentration and the adverse health outcome it produces. Pre-existing conditions can exacerbate the health impact of particle exposure and deposition within the respiratory system. Problems with the body defense mechanisms such as the mucociliary escalator or macrophages may extend the time that particles are available to pose a physical impact or to undergo ADBE. Within this chapter we will restrict our discussion to the impact of the particle's physical characteristics, without its chemical or carrier aspects, to reflect the current knowledge about particles as a class of toxic materials attempting to provide information on the relationship between particle size and toxicity.

The literature for determining the impact of particles, per se, on the immune or respiratory systems is limited but growing.[9] Kobzik et al., reported an increase in tumor necrosis factor (TNF) production following uptake of opsonized particles (particles which have been made more susceptible to phagocytosis) in vitro.[10] Similar findings were made in an intranasal or intratracheal instillation study, in mice, using *Aspergillus fumigants* allergen and PSL.[11] Certainly a key cell type involved in the immediate physiological response to particle exposures is the airway myocyte.[12] This research found that particle exposures led to elevated cytosolic calcium (Ca^{+2}), which activates the airway contractile structures, increasing resistance to air flow, and reducing ventilation. In reviews of the existing literature in 1997, both Driscoll and Finkelstein, independently, concluded that particles induce elevated macrophage production and mobility.[13,14] They reported that epithelial cells are also activated and the production of cytokines is elevated. Guthrie et al. in a 1997 study, evaluated the mineralogical and geochemical properties of particles and their capacity to induce cancer.[15] His findings indicated links between particle size, shape, dissolution behavior, ion exchange, sorptive properties and surface reactivity to cancer risk. Churg reported a direct relationship between the number of particles entering the lung (interstitial space) and the total number of particles applied in the exposure concentration.[16] Granum et al. found that IgE increased in mice dosed with ovalbumin (OVA) and two sizes (diameters) of PSL.[17] The study found that IgE increased with the number of particles delivered and the surface area of the particles but not the mass of the delivered allergen. The study did not specify a relationship between the particle diameter and the increase in IgE. In a 2000 study, Castillejos et al. evaluated coarse and fine particle fractions with regard to increased mortality. The results of this project indicated that a stronger relationship was found with the mass concentration of the coarse fraction of the ambient exposure concentration and morbidity but could not tease out the issues of fine and ultrafine particle numbers, the mass to mass relationship between the coarse, fine and ultrafine fractions, the potential for adsorbed materials on the surface of the particles, the surface shape and structure of the particles, and other issues.[18] The log-normal distribution of aerosolized materials would indicate larger particle number concentrations for the fine and ultrafine fractions (limited by the atomic or molecular size) with increases in the overall number concentration of the coarse particles. That a relationship exists between airborne particulate concentrations and localized mortality seems clear in the literature. Gehr et al. found that smaller particles might not be efficiently removed by the mucociliary escalator, increasing their retention time and potential to induce an inflammatory response in the body.[19] Working again with mice, Granum et al. found that IgE response was elevated in mice when non-soluble particles and an allergen, chicken OVA, were introduced to the respiratory system (i.p.) as compared to those that received only the OVA.[20] Increased eosinophils were also found as well as increased cytokine production in the lung and spleen. The study used polystyrene latex particles as a surrogate for natural particles, but the evidence tended to support an adjuvant capability for particles with regard to airway reactivity and inflammation. Latex as an allergen could be a confounder in the analysis. In general these antigen-specific mediators enhance recruitment of lymphocytes and other inflammatory cell types to the location of the particles. Devouassoux et al. also reported a link between IgE and diesel particle exposures.[21] The process reportedly included effects on T2 helper cells, mast cells, and basophils. The study could not discern the means of toxicity based on particle size or number concentration. Genotoxic effects were reported for particles and fibers by Schins in a 2002 study. Results of this study indicated reactive oxygen species (ROS) played a key role in lipid peroxidation and overall toxicity.[22] While the report cited the chemical make-up of the particles as a key factor it also indicated links to particle size, shape, solubility, crystallinity, and the potential for mutagens to be carried on the surface as additional contributors to overall toxicity. Meta analysis of data collected in Italian studies of the short-term effects of air pollution reported a direct association between mortality from natural causes, including heart disease, and increased air pollution concentrations of PM 10 and other materials.[23] Last et al. reported no difference in airway reactivity or fibrosis in mice exposed to OVA and PM 2.5 or OVA alone. They noted that goblet cell hyperplasia was associated with the PM 2.5 exposures.[24] Some studies have attempted to elucidate the physical characteristics of the particle with regard to the physiological response of the body. Characteristics include diameter, number, surface area, mass, shape and other features. Hetland et al. reported that the coarse fraction of ambient PM in several European cities contributed more to elevated interleukin 6 and Tumor Necrosis Factor (TNF) levels than did the fine fraction.[25] Barlow et al. reported that particles in the lung activate type II alveolar cells to release chemo-attractants for alveolar macrophages.[26] They found that carbon black nanoparticles significantly increased the release of chemo-attractant over fine fraction carbon black particles. This may be a property of nanoparticles but the overall work seemed to lead to the conclusion that particle size contributes to macrophage response to particles in the lung. Barlow called the alveolar macrophages the "key cell" type in dealing with particles and any degradation of their capabilities would be important.

The literature would seem to indicate that many factors contribute to the ability of particles to impact the respiratory and immunologic systems. While most laws and regulations are predicated on a mass basis, the particles' diameter (aerodynamic) contributes significantly to its deposition location within the respiratory system and hence its retention time allowing it to be dissolved and taken up by the body, transported to another body system (i.e. the gastrointestinal tract) or be removed by the body's defense mechanisms. Overall, the number of particles seems to be important when they are of sufficient size to cross the body's natural barriers to elicit a response. Their surface area likewise would appear to be significant if it either allows the particle to carry adsorbed materials into the body and across the defensive barriers or if the surface provides some kind of interaction point more directly with the alveolar cells (physical abrasion or sites for follow-on chemical reactions). It is clear that while the number of fine and ultrafine particles, in the exposure atmosphere, contribute little to the mass delivered to the body, they can still have a significant impact on the physiological responses. A great deal more work is required to tease out the specific physical characteristics that make this true and to determine the role of particle size in toxicity. A generic issue with these studies is that the particles are synthetic vice natural. Great care is required to attempt to minimize, if not preclude, the adsorption of materials on the surface either in production or in transfer to the subject's respiratory system. The probability of no contamination from the environment is subject to interpretation. Overall, these studies indicate that particles induce inflammatory responses in the lung, without regard to their chemical make-up. Several different cytokines and chemokines as well as antigen-specific mediators are involved. ROS, lipid peroxidation, and the development of antioxidants are also involved. The exact mechanisms of damage and respiratory system reactivity have not been determined but the evidence supports an adjuvant role for particles in regard to toxicity.

Examples
Not Specifically Toxic Granular Dusts

It has been recognized for some time that seeming inert materials can bring on adverse health impacts. Heppleston evaluated exposures to three seemingly inert materials, silica, coal, and asbestos, all with known and significant adverse health impacts.[27] His findings indicated that particle size and shape played a role in toxicity. In a 1994 study Oberdoster evaluated the relationship between particle size and retention time in the lung using titanium dioxide particles. Their results indicated a correlation between particle surface area and the physiological effect.[28] Soutar evaluated dusts from several inert materials and found they caused physiological changes through three mechanisms; (1) overloading the clearance mechanisms, (2) increased toxicity due to ultrafine particles, and (3) increasing the toxicity of other materials in a mixture.[29] Roller continued this work evaluating what they called not specific granular dusts, which included quartz.[30] They found that particle volume and diameter were the best indicators of a dose metric. These studies indicated several different potential mechanisms of action for these dust particles from irritation caused by their interface with the cells of the lung or the macrophages to the adjuvant effect and the potential to carry other toxic materials into the body. While there were differences in the findings and proposed mechanisms of action for the dusts, these studies and others indicated that particles could bring on physiological changes simply by their presence in the respiratory system. Their retention and ability to translocate within the body was predicated on the particle diameter. Although these finest of particles contributed little mass of material and the materials were considered relatively inert, they could still elicit toxic effects. Increased surface area might indicate transport of other materials on the surface or a large area for irritation at the cellular interface. While the exact mechanisms of action are incompletely defined and remain the subject of ongoing research, particle size was viewed to be critical. These studies and others contribute to the body of knowledge and the recognition that particle size selective sampling and changes in the current laws based on the mass of material in the exposure atmosphere may be required.

Nanoparticles

Classical thought indicated that the dose made the poison. Dose was the mass of the product delivered to the target organ or system. The development of nanoparticles and nanotechnologies may require that fundamental premise be reevaluated.

Nanotechnologies are on the rise. They have impact in electronics, pharmaceuticals, coatings, and other sectors of industry. Evidence is mounting that nanoparticles, particles with aerodynamic diameters in the nanometer range, pose potential health hazards beyond that expected from the mass (dose) they can deliver.[31] Nanoparticles may be found in the form of spheres, tubes, wires, rods, dots, irregular, agglomerations, and aggregates. They are produced by a number of different processes including pyrolysis, combustion, vaporization, colloidal and attrition. They pose potential uptake venues through inhalation, dermal contact, and ingestion. Nanoparticles contain a core and may have coatings and other materials to enhance their desired effects on their surface, which must be considered when determining their diameter and toxicity.

Johnston et al. showed that polytetrafluoroethylene (PTFE) particles could overload the lung in rats and could lead to fatality even though the particles were considered to be inert, insoluble, and presented very little mass ($<50\ \mu g/m^3$).[32] Tran et al. found that particle surface area was more efficiently correlated to toxicity than mass with regard to the ultrafine fraction of an aerosol.[33] A good body of work has been developed since that study indicating an inverse relationship between toxic effects of insoluble particles and particle diameter, on a mass to mass basis.[34] From the body of knowledge developed by these and other studies it was accepted that the means of particle toxicity was through oxidative stress. Donaldson reported a three-step process, which started with a $Ca+2$ ion modulation signaling event.[35] In the sensory portion, glutathione and other products are oxidized and their cellular concentrations increase. These products lead to a response by the cell releasing transcription factors such as Necrosis Factor (NF)-kb and AP-1, to initiate pro-inflammatory genes to produce mediators, which are proteins (cytokines including a number of interleukins (IL) such as IL 2, IL 6, and IL 8, Tumor Necrosis Factor (TNF) α and other products) that are produced to reduce the oxidative stress (antioxidants). The work could not separate the effects caused by the particle, its inherent chemistry, or the materials that the particle adsorbed onto its surface with regard to the initiation of the signaling event. Still, working with carbon black, Donaldson reported that the surface area and features of the particle, in close proximity to and/or in direct contact with the alveolar cells, played a key role in the inflammatory process. They also reported that ultrafine particles (diameter < 100 nanometers) inhibit phagocytosis more than the same mass of fine particles. Warheit reported in a 2004 study that nanoparticles and other ultrafines, may evade the body's defense mechanisms and translocate from the airspace into the interstitial space, what Warheit called the "vulnerable compartment".[36] Inoue et al. found an inverse relationship between particle size and the ability to produce antigen-related airway inflammation and immunological responses.[37] The cytokines IL-5, IL-13 and antibody based IgG were included in the list of products modulated in the process. In 2005, Oberdorster followed this work with a report that indicated that translocation (transcytosis) of ultrafine particles moved across physiological barriers (epithelial and endothelial cells) into the blood and lymphatic systems to attack sensitive targets including the liver, spleen, bone marrow, and heart.[38] Kaiser, in the 2005 study cited earlier, indicated that ultrafine particles could cross other physiological barriers, such as the blood brain barrier, to attack sensitive sites. In a 2006 study, Warheit et al. reported that surface area was not a major factor in pulmonary toxicity for nanoparticles.[39] However, Hardman reported the finding in 2006 that quantum dot toxicity was based on a number of things including size, charge, concentration, outer coating bioactivity, and oxidative, photolytic and mechanical stability.[40]

A great deal of work continues with regard to ultrafine and nanoparticle toxicity. What is clear is that particle size and number rather than mass may be the key to their toxic effects. The issue of the role of surface area is less clear and requires further research. Whether the toxic effect is caused by the particle and physical contact with sensitive targets, or the chemistry of the particle—either inherent from the parent material or from adsorbed materials on the surface—remains unclear. There is evidence that particles thought to be insoluble and non-toxic can elicit a response. The mechanism of response (inflammatory) includes the production of a number of cytokines, chemokines, and antibody related agents. The ability to escape the body's primary defense mechanisms, including macrophages and cellular barriers, is significant in the overall toxicity of these particles. The need for the desirable qualities of nanoparticles across the industries will ensure their continued development and use for the future. Additional work to discern the mechanisms of their toxic effects will also have to follow.

Endotoxins

Endotoxins may pose a different problem than the issues of mass transfer for particulates or the ability to move within the body associated with nanoparticles. Some of the issues related to the toxicity of endotoxins and an association with particle size may be related to their biological origin. A good deal of research has been undertaken to explain the toxicity, mechanisms of action of endotoxins, and the relationship with those factors and particle size.

Endotoxins are part of the outer membrane of the cell wall in Gram negative bacteria. The biological activity of endotoxins is related to their lipopolysaccharide (LPS) makeup. Toxicity is related to the lipid component while immunogenicity is related to the polysaccharide components. Lipopolysaccharides elicit inflammatory responses and may be a part of the overall pathology of Gram-negative bacterial infections. In the bacterial organism, the LPS serves as a permeability barrier restricting passage to low molecular weight hydrophilic compounds. They provide support to defense systems against lysozymes, serum components, and other antibacterial agents. They also play a role in the colonization and surface structure defensive mechanisms against phagocytosis.

Early work suggested a relationship between endotoxin particle size and toxicity. In a 1965 study, Beer et al. reported finding the highest lethal activity was associated with particles of intermediate size.[41] Beer than treated the LPS with sodium dodecyl sulfate (SDS) to break it down into smaller subunits. They reported the LPS broke down into monodisperse subunits but the toxic activity was not changed. From this they reported that toxicity was not related to particle size. Ribi et al. in 1966 also reported that endotoxin disaggregated using with sodium deoxycholate broke into subunits of a single size (molecular weight between 9,000 and 20,000).[42] Somewhat in contrast, Hejna found in a 1978 study that triethylamine (TEA) — bovine serum albumin (BSA), solubilization of wild type LPS disaggregated into a number of size classes.[43] Their results indicated the O-antigenic side chain length determined aggregate particle size. They reported un-disaggregated LPS to have a particle size of 300 nanometers. In 1983, Olenchock et al. evaluated endotoxins in cotton.[44] Using a cascade impactor they found endotoxin contamination in all of the aerosol size fractions with the highest concentrations in the range from 2.9 to 5.9 micrometers. They did not provide an explanation for the relationship between the size fraction and the mass concentration. In a 1986 study, Perkins et al. attempted to discern the relationship between endotoxin particle size and toxicity but their findings were mixed and they reported the need to continue the research.[45] Kujundzic et al. in 2006, reported the results of a novel collection method for determining endotoxin particle size and mass concentration.[46] They reported the greatest mass concentration of endotoxin was associated with particle sizes less than one micrometer. In a 2007 study, Wang et al. evaluated the size distribution of airborne mist and endotoxin containing materials in metal working fluids. They reported the highest mass concentrations of endotoxin in the particle size fraction less than 0.39 micrometers, which they reported was smaller than the diameter of the intact bacterial cell. They could not clarify the relationship between endotoxin particle size and toxicity nor did they explain why the highest endotoxin concentration occurred in this size range.[47]

The literature supports a relationship between endotoxin exposure and the production of cytokines, most often TNF-α. In 2001, Long et al. reported this relationship but also noted, as did others, that several other confounders (including the presence of volatile organic compounds and trace metals) existed in the sampling and analysis and could not discern the relationship between particle size and endotoxin toxicity.[48] The literature remains unclear with regard to the LPS breakdown into a single particle size that enters the respiratory system as an independent unit or attaches itself to other particles for future deposition. Similarly, beyond these confounders, and in the context of the submicron particle sizes in which the highest endotoxin concentrations appear to be present, the current literature seems to be unclear regarding whether the endotoxin, by virtue of its biological make-up or the physical presence of the particles, leads to the triggering mechanism for cytokine production and any elevated toxicity. Research continues in this area.

Conclusions

The study of particulate materials has a diverse and colorful history. Some of the greatest names in science worked in the projects to evaluate how particles moved through air and to develop predictive models. From cannon balls to quantum dots, the work continues today. New correction factors are being developed and predictive models for settling times or deposition within the respiratory system are being reviewed and improved. Particle size distribution analysis is complex. Many things are accepted as givens now in particle research. The particle size distribution is accepted to be log normal. The key parameters for characterization of an aerosol are the particle size and the geometric standard deviation. The aerodynamic properties of the particle are critical in determining its movement through the air. New instruments are being developed and older ones improved to aid the researcher in characterizing an aerosol. Particulate materials have long been viewed as a means to deliver materials into the respiratory system. Models have demonstrated that particle size and aerodynamic properties impact the location of deposition and the ADBE processes that follow. In general it has been believed that the toxicity associated with the exposure was based on the chemical make-up of the material or by biotransformation processes. It was believed that submicron diameter particles, ultrafine particles, and those with diameters in the nanometer range made up the largest number of particles in an aerosol exposure but that their toxicity was insignificant because their mass was minimal. The basic assumption that the mass delivered to the target organ, or dose, determines the toxicity is under critical review as toxic effects are being associated with these smallest of particles. Dose remains the correct term but further consideration may be required to expressing the dose in different terms for particulates (i.e. by surface area or volume). The true mechanisms of action for these ultrafine particles are not well characterized at this time and a great deal of research continues to determine how particles of what are considered to be inert materials can bring on adverse health responses. Growth in the nanotechnology field will continue based on economic and social needs. In the past, we have based decisions on those needs and found that in the longer term they were bad investments (i.e. asbestos, PCBs, lead based paints, and others). Endotoxin toxicity may be related to particle size but may also be related to other as yet undiscovered factors. Continuing research will be required in this area to determine the association between particle size and toxicity. Overall particles as a class will continue to receive great interest as researchers attempt to discern the importance of particle size in toxicity.

References

1. **Kaiser, J.:** Mounting Evidence Indicts Fine-Particle Pollution. *Sci.* 25:307,5717, 1858–1861, (2005).
2. **Kim, J.H., G.W. Mulholland, and D.Y.H. Pui:** Slip Correction Measurement of certified PSL Nanoparticles Using a Nanometer Differential Mobility Analyzer (Nano-DMA) for Knudsen Number from 0.5 to 83, *J. Res. Natl. Stand. Technol.* 110:31–54 (2005).
3. **Dressler, M.:** Dynamic Shape Factors for Particle Shape Characterization, Particle and Particle Systems Characterization, Vol. 2, Issue 1–4, p. 62–66, 2004.
4. **DeCarlo, P.F., J.G. Slowik, D.R. Worsnop, P. Davidovits, and J.L. Jimenez:** Particle Morphology and Density Characterization by Combined Mobility and Aerodynamic Diameter Measurements. Part 1: Theory. *Aerosol Sci. Tech.* 38:1185–1205 (2004).
5. **Hinds, W.C.:** *Aerosol Technology: Properties, Behavior, and Measurement of Airborne Particles.* New York: John Wiley and Sons. 1999.
6. **Peters, R. D. and L. Sumner:** Intuitive Derivation of Reynold's Number, arXiv:physics/0306193, Vol 1., 27. June 2003.
7. **Park, K., D. Kittelson, and P. McMurry:** Structural Properties of Diesel Exhaust Particles Measured by Transmission Electron Microscopy (TEM): Relationships to Particle Mass Mobility. *Aerosol Sci. Tech.* 38(9):881–889 (2004).
8. **Katrib, Y., S.T. Martin, Y. Rudich, P. Davidovits, J.T. Jayne, and D.R. Worsnop:** Density changes of aerosol particles as a result of chemical reaction. *Atmos. Chem. Phys. Discuss.* 4:6431–6472 (2004).
9. **Granum, B. and M. Lovik:** The effect of particles on allergic immune responses. *Toxicol. Sci.* 65:7–17 (2002).
10. **Kobzik, L., S. Huang, J.D. Paulauskis, J.J. Godleski:** Particle opsonization and lung macrophage cytokine response. In vitro and in vivo analysis. *J. Immunol.* 151:2753–2759 (1993).
11. **Kurup, V.P., B.W.P. Seymour, H. Choi, and R.L. Coffman:** Particulate Aspergillus fumigants antigens elicit a Th2 response in BALB/c mice. *J. Allergy Clin. Immunol.* 93:1013–1020 (1994).
12. **Roux, E., P.J. Noble, D. Noble, M. Marhl:** Modeling of calcium handling in airway myocytes. *Prog. Biophys. Mol. Biol.* 90(1–3):64–87 (2006).
13. **Driscoll, K.E., J.M. Carter, D.G. Hassenbein, and B. Howard:** Cytokines and particle-induced inflammatory cell recruitment. *Environ. Health Perspect.* 105(Suppl):1159–1164 (1997).
14. **Finkelstein, J. N., C. Johnston, T. Barrett, and G. Oberdorster:** Particulate-cell interactions and pulmonary cytokine expression. *Environ. Health Perspect.* 105(Suppl):1170–1182 (1997).
15. **Guthrie, G.D. Jr.:** Mineral properties and their contribution to particle toxicity, *Environ. Health Perspect.* 105(5):1003–1011 (1997).
16. **Churg, A., B. Stevens, and J.L. Wright:** Comparison of the uptake of fine and ultrafine TiO2 in a tracheal explant system. *Am. J. Physiol.* 274:L81–L86 (1998).
17. **Granum, B., P.I. Gaarder, E.C. Groeng, R.B. Leikvold, E. Namork, and M. Lovik:** Fine particles of widely different composition have an adjuvant effect on the production of allergen specific antibodies. *Toxicol. Lett.* 118:171–181 (2000).
18. **Castillejos, M., V.H. Borja-Alberto, D. Dockery, D.R. Gold, and D. Loomis:** Airborne coarse particles and mortality. *Inhal. Toxicol.* 12:61–72 (2000).

19. **Gehr, P., M. Geiser, H.L. Hof, and S. Schurch:** Surfactant-ultrafine particle interactions: what we learn from PM10 studies. *Phil. Trans. R. Soc. Lond. A(358)*:2707–2718 (2000).

20. **Granum, B., P.I. Gaarder, and M. Lovik:** IgE adjuvant activity of particles-what physical characteristics are important?. *Inhal. Toxicol. 12(3)*:365–372 (2001).

21. **Devouassoux, G. and C. Brambilla:** Effects of diesel particles on allergic inflammatory response: cellular targets and molecular mechanisms. *Rev. Mal. Respir. 19(4)*:467–479 (2002).

22. **Schins, R.P.:** Mechanisms of genotoxicity of particles and fibers. *Inhal. Toxicol. 14(1)*:57–78 (2002).

23. **Biggeri, A., P. Bellini, and B. Terrcini:** Meta-analysis of the Italian studies on short-term effects of air pollution. *Epidemiol. Prev. 28(4–5)*:4–100 (2004).

24. **Last, J.A., R. Ward, L. Temple, K.E. Pinkerton, and N.J. Kenyon:** Ovalbumin-induced airway inflammation and fibrosis in mice exposed to ultrafine particles. *Inhal. Toxicol. 16(2)*:93–102, 2004.

25. **Hetland, R.B., F.R. Cassee, M. Lag, M. Refnes, E. Dybing, and P.E. Schwarze:** Cytokine release from alveolar macrophages exposed to ambient particulate matter: Heterogeneity in relation to size, city, and season, Particle Fiber *Toxicol. 2*:4 (2005).

26. **Barlow, P.G. A. Clouter-Baker, K. Donaldson, J. Mac-Callum, and V. Stone:** Carbon black nanoparticles induce type II epithelial cells to release chemotoxins for alveolar macrophages. *Part. Fiber Toxicol. 2*:11 (2005).

27. **Heppleston, A.G.:** Pulmonary Toxicology of Silica, Coal, and Asbestos. *Environ. Health Perspect. 55*:111–127 (1984).

28. **Oberdorster, G., J. Ferin, and B. Lehnert:** Correlation Between Particle Size, in vivo Particle Persistence, and Lung Injury. *Environ. Health Perspect. 102(5)*: (1994).

29. **Soutar, C.A., B.G. Miller, N. Gregg, A.D. Jones, R.T. Cullen, R.E. Bolton:** Assessment of Human Risks from Exposure to Low Toxicity Dusts. *Ann. Occup. Hyg. 41(2)*:123–133, 1997.

30. **Roller, M. and F. Pott:** Lung Tumor Risk Estimates from Rat Studies with Not Specifically Toxic Granular Dusts. *Ann. N.Y. Acad. Sci. 1076*:266–280 (2006).

31. **Aitken, R.J., K.S. Creely, C.L. Tran:** Nanoparticles: An occupational hygiene review, Report prepared by the Institute of Occupational Health for the Health and Safety Executive Committee, Research Report 274. 2004.

32. **Johnston, C.J., J.N. Finkelstein, P. Mercer, N. Corson, R. Gelein, G. Oberdorster:** Pulmonary effects induced by ultrafine Polytetrafluoroethylene (PTFE) particles. *Toxicol. Appl. Pharmacol. 1(168)*:208–215 (2000).

33. **Tran, C.L., D. Buchanan, R.T. Cullen, A. Searl, A.D. Jones, and K. Donaldson:** Inhalation of poorly soluble particles II. Influence of particle surface area on inflammation and clearance. *Inhal. Toxicol. 12*:1113–1126 (2000).

34. **Faux, S.P., C.L. Tran, B.G. Miller, A.D. Jones, C. Montellier, and K. Donaldson:** In vitro determinants of particulate toxicity: the dose metric for poorly soluble dust, Health and Safety Executive Research Report 154. 2003.

35. **Donaldson, K., and V. Stone:** Current hypothesis on the mechanisms of toxicity of ultrafine particles, *Ann 1st Super. Sanita, 39(3)*:405–410 (2003).

36. **Warheit, D.B.:** Nanoparticles: Health impacts?, Materials Today, The Dupont Company, Newark, DE, USA, published by Elsevier Ltd. Feb, 2004.

37. **Inoue, K., H. Takano, R. Yanagisawa, M. Sakura, T. Ichinose, K. Sadakane, and T. Yoshikawa:** Effects of nanoparticles on antigen-related airway inflammation in mice. *Respir. Res. 6(1)*:106 (2005).

38. **Oberdorster, G., E. Oberdorster, and J. Oberdorster:** Nanotoxicology: an emerging discipline evolving from studies of ultrafine particles. *Environ. Health Perspect. 113(7)*:823–839, 2005.

39. **Warheit, D.B., T.R. Webb, C.M. Sayes, V.L. Colvin, and K.L. Reed:** Pulmonary instillation studies with nanoscale TiO2 rods and dots in rats: toxicity is not dependent upon particle size and surface area. *Toxicol. Sci. 91(1)*:227–236 (2006).

40. **Hardman, R.:** A Toxicological Review of Quantum Dots: Toxicity Depends on Physiochemical and Environmental Factors. *Environ. Health Perspect. 114(2)*: (2006).

41. **Beer, H., T. Stahelin, H. Douglas, and A. Braude:** Relationship Between Particle Size and Biological Activity of E. Coli Bovine Endotoxin. *J. Clin. Invest. 44(4)*: (1965).

42. **Ribi, E., R.L. Anacker, R. Brown, W.T. Haskins, B. Malmgren, K.C. Milner, and J.A. Rudbach:** Reaction of Endotoxins and Surfactants, I. Physical and biological properties of endotoxin treated with sodium deoxycholate. *J. Bacteriol. 92*:1493–1509 (1966).

43. **Hejna, J. and J.A. Cameron:** Effect of Particle Size of Solubilization of Wild-Type and Re Chemotype Lipopolysaccharides Solubilized with Bovine Serum Albumin and Triethylamine. *Infect. Immunity Jan.*:187–193 (1978).

44. **Olenchock, S.A., J.C. Mull, and W.G. Jones:** Endotoxins In Cotton: Washing Effects and Size Distribution. *Am. J. Ind. Med. 4*:515–521 (1983).

45. **Perkins, H.H., S.A. Olenchock, P.D. Milner, and M. Kinoshits:** Relationship Between Bacteria and Endotoxin in Cotton Lint and in Card Generated Cotton Dust, Proceedings of the Tenth Cotton Dust Research Conference, Las Vegas, NV, Jan, 1986.

46. **Kunjundzic, E., M. Hernandez, and S.L. Miller:** Particle size distributions and concentration of airborne endotoxin using novel collection methods in homes during the winter and summer seasons. *Indoor Air 16(3)*:216 (2006).

47. **Wang, H., T. Reponen, S. Lee, E. White, S. Grinshpun:** Size distribution of airborne mist and endotoxin-containing particles in metalworking fluid environments. *J. Occup. Envrion. Hyg. 4(3)*:157–165 (2007).

48. **Long, C.M., H.H. Suh, L. Kobizk, P.J. Catalano, Y.Y. Ning, and P. Koutrakis:** A Pilot Investigation of the Relative Toxicity of Indoor and Outdoor Fine Particles: In Vitro Effects of Endotoxin and Other Particulate Properties. *Environ. Health Perspect. 109(10)*: 1019–1026(2001).

> *The art of healing comes from nature, not from the physician. Therefore the physician must start from nature, with an open mind.*
>
> Paracelsus (1493– 1541)

Chapter 20

Toxicology of Gases

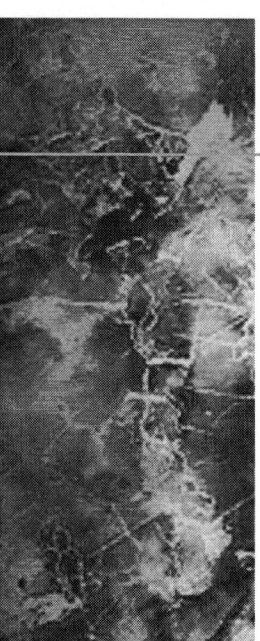

Outcome Competencies

Upon completion of this chapter, the reader should be able to:

- Describe the anatomy of the human respiratory system and explain the significance of each part on exposure to occupationally-significant gases.
- Define blood-gas partition coefficient and explain the importance of this characteristic in the absorption of occupationally-significant gases.
- Identify the sources and uses of the occupationally-significant gases.
- Identify jobs or tasks that might involve exposure to the occupationally-significant gases.
- Describe the characteristic toxic effects of each of the occupationally-significant gases.
- Identify agencies, public and private, that publish recommended exposure limits and promulgated standards for occupational exposures to gases.

Key Terms

arrhythmia, ataxia, atelectasis, carboxyhemoglobin, cooperativity, dysmetria, dyspnea, edema, erythema, Forced Expiratory Volume (FEV), Forced Vital Capacity (FVC), hemoglobin, hypoxia, inspiratory capacity, lacrimation, Lhermitte's Sign, methemoglobin, microatelectasis, myocardial infarction, myoglobin, necrosis, nystagmus, pre-ventricular contraction, rhinorrhea, Romberg's Sign, Silo filler's disease (SFD), tachycardia, tidal volume, Total Lung Capacity (TLC)

Key Topics

1. Absorption of Gases through the Lungs
2. Blood-to-Gas Partition Coefficient (Gas Solubility in Blood)
3. Occupationally Significant Gases
   - Carbon Monoxide
     - Sources
     - Uses
     - Toxicokinetics
     - Toxicity
     - Case Studies
   - Nitrogen Oxides
     - Sources
     - Uses
     - Toxicokinetics
     - Toxicity
     - Case Studies
   - Sulfur Dioxide
     - Sources
     - Uses
     - Toxicokinetics
     - Toxicity
     - Case Studies
   - Ozone
     - Sources
     - Uses
     - Toxicokinetics
     - Toxicity
     - Case Studies
   - Ethylene Oxide
     - Sources
     - Uses
     - Toxicokinetics
     - Toxicity
     - Case Studies

Chapter 20

Toxicology of Gases

By Scott D. Dwyer, PhD, DABT

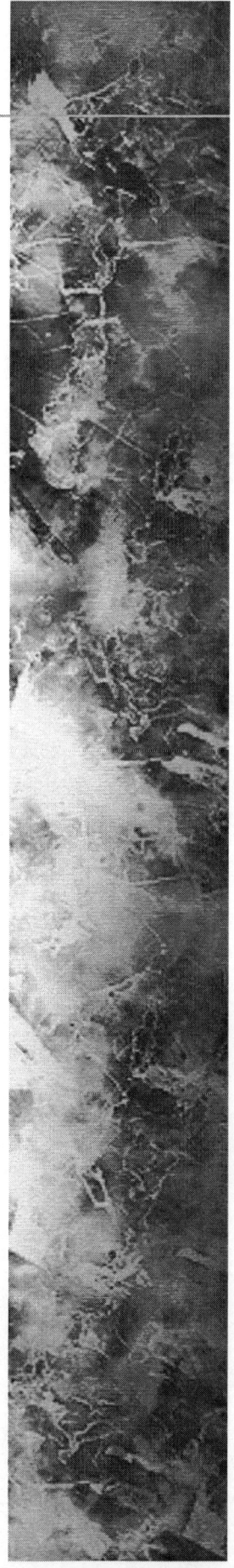

Introduction

As one would expect, the respiratory system is uniquely suited to the intake and absorption of gases. The respiratory system is comprised of three regions: the nasal passages, the conducting airways, and the gas exchange region. Each region performs an important function in respiration. The nasal passages warm and humidify the inhaled air, direct the inhaled air from the atmosphere into the conducting airways, and via the trigeminal (fifth cranial) nerve in the olfactory epithelium, provide our sense of smell. Nasal tissues also metabolize foreign substances by cytochrome p-450 dependent monooxygenases, other oxidative (Phase I) enzymes, conjugative (Phase II) enzymes, proteases, and peptidases.[1] The conducting airways, comprised of the pharynx, larynx, and trachea, direct inhaled air from the nasal passages to the gas exchange region of the lung, secrete mucus to capture particulate matter, and transport the particulate matter trapped in mucus to the pharynx where it can be swallowed or expectorated. The mucus secreted by cells in the trachea and bronchi may also have anti-oxidant, acid-neutralizing, and free radical scavenging properties. The trachea bifurcates into the two bronchi, which direct inhaled air into the lungs. The bronchi then branch into bronchioles, which terminate in acini. Each acinus is comprised of a terminal bronchiole, alveolar ducts, and alveolar sacs. An alveolar sac, or alveolus, is the site where gas exchange occurs. The wall of each alveolus is only one or two cells thick to facilitate gas exchange between capillaries of the pulmonary blood supply and the air spaces within the lung.

Absorption of Gases through the Lungs

Once fresh inspired air has reached the alveoli, simple diffusion drives oxygen from the alveoli into the pulmonary blood supply for transport and distribution throughout the body. Concurrently, simple diffusion also drives carbon dioxide from the pulmonary blood supply into the alveoli to be exhaled. To deliver sufficient oxygen to the body and to remove sufficient carbon dioxide from the body, the lungs must provide:

- An exceedingly large surface area for gaseous exchange relative to the volume of blood in contact with that area,
- A short diffusion path between alveolar air and the pulmonary blood supply, and
- Favorable concentration gradients for oxygen and carbon dioxide between alveolar air and blood.

Estimates of the total alveolar surface area available for gas exchange in an adult range from 70 to 140 m^2, which is an area as large as a singles tennis court. The volume of blood in contact with this surface area is only 60 to 140 mL (less than one-half cup). This ratio of surface area to blood volume, and the narrow distance between alveolar air and blood in the alveolar capillaries of approximately 0.0006 mL, encourages the rapid diffusion of oxygen and carbon dioxide. Favorable concentration gradients are maintained by:

- Ventilation which continuously renews alveolar air, maintaining oxygen concentration close to that of atmospheric air and preventing the accumulation of carbon dioxide, and
- The flow of pulmonary arterial blood into the alveolar capillaries, which continuously

brings blood with low oxygen concentration and high carbon dioxide concentration.

Oxygen that has diffused into the blood then diffuses into red blood cells and binds with hemoglobin.

Blood-to-Gas Partition Coefficient (Gas Solubility in Blood)

Inhaled gases diffuse primarily from the alveolar space into the blood and dissolve until equilibrium is reached between gas molecules diffusing from the alveoli into the blood and gas molecules diffusing from the blood into the alveoli. At equilibrium, the ratio of gas in the alveoli to the gas dissolved in blood is constant and the ratio is known as the blood-gas partition coefficient. Each gas has a unique blood-gas partition coefficient, which can vary between gases by orders of magnitude. For example, the blood-gas partition coefficient of chloroform is 15, indicating that a significantly higher concentration of chloroform is dissolved in blood compared to the concentration in alveolar air. In contrast, the blood-gas partition coefficient of ethylene is 0.14, indicating that a much higher concentration of ethylene remains in the alveoli compared to that quantity dissolved in blood. Gases with low blood-gas partition coefficients more rapidly reach equilibrium in the lungs and uptake depends on perfusion rate. Gases with high blood-gas partition coefficients reach equilibrium more slowly and uptake depends on the ventilation rate.

A more detailed discussion of the respiratory system appears in Chapter 5, "Respiratory Toxicology."

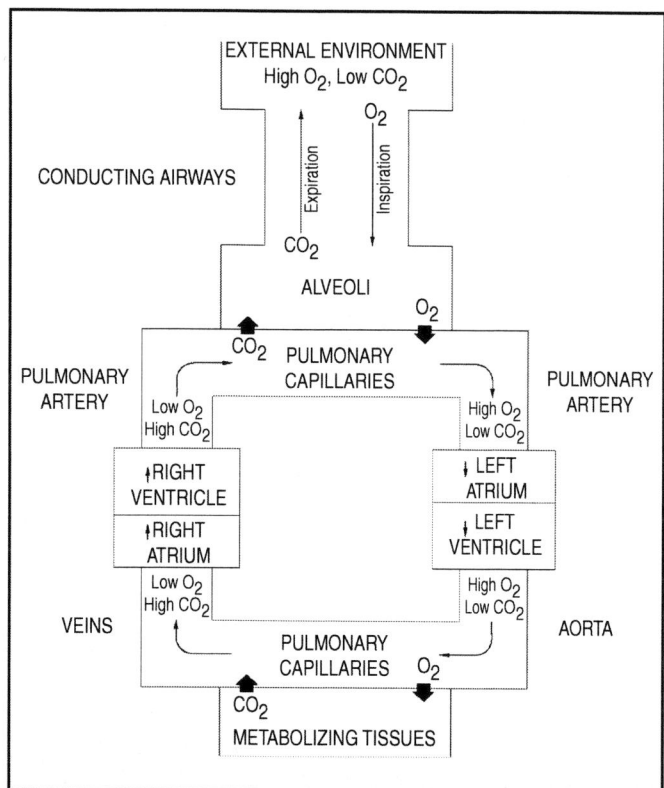

Figure 20.1 — Source: Levitzky, M.G Pulmonary Physiology. New York: McGraw Hill Medical, 7th edition (2007).

Occupationally Significant Gases
Carbon Monoxide

Sources

The list of carbon monoxide sources is extensive because so many sources of this odorless, colorless, and non-irritating gas exist. Essentially, the combustion of any carbonaceous material (petroleum fuels, coal, natural gas, wood, plastics) generates carbon monoxide. Thus internal combustion engines, cooking and heating appliances, and many industrial processes are sources.

Uses

Carbon monoxide is an important component in the production of methanol, ethylene, aldehydes, isocyanates, acrylates, acetic acid, and phosgene. It is used in blast furnaces to extract metals from ores as carbon monoxide reduces the ore. Synthesis gas, a combination of carbon monoxide and hydrogen, can be an important energy source in the chemical industry.

Toxicokinetics

Carbon monoxide diffuses rapidly from inhaled air across the gas exchange portions of the respiratory tract and is absorbed into the pulmonary circulation. Diffusion and absorption into blood is driven by the concentration gradient, which also represents the driving force for elimination of carbon monoxide during exhalation if an exposed individual is moved to an atmosphere free of carbon monoxide. Only a small fraction of carbon monoxide is oxidized to carbon dioxide and is excreted as such during exhalation.

Once absorbed, most of the inhaled carbon monoxide strongly but reversibly binds to hemoglobin within red blood cells. The binding strength of carbon monoxide to hemoglobin is approximately 200 times greater than that of oxygen and this characteristic is generally considered to cause most of the adverse health effects ascribed to carbon monoxide. Under normal conditions, hemoglobin molecules exhibit cooperativity in the binding of oxygen; that is, the binding of an oxygen molecule by a hemoglobin molecule increases the affinity of that hemoglobin molecule for oxygen. Carbon monoxide upsets the normal cooperative binding of oxygen by not only displacing oxygen from hemoglobin, but also causing hemoglobin to bind the remaining oxygen molecules more tightly, impairing the release of oxygen to tissues. Thus, carbon monoxide induces hypoxia by two mechanisms: displacement of oxygen from hemoglobin and impairing the release of oxygen from hemoglobin to tissues.

Some inhaled and absorbed carbon monoxide remains in blood plasma or in extracellular fluid bound to other proteins that contain heme molecules, including myoglobin and cytochromes.

Toxicity

The symptoms of carbon monoxide intoxication appear first in the central nervous system as headache, lightheadedness and dizziness, and can progress to fatigue, seizures, and coma.[2,3] As the body burden of carbon monoxide increases, compensatory physiological mechanisms intervene which both reduce and exacerbate the effects of carbon monoxide: vasodilation enhances blood flow to tissues but also produces flushing, tachycardia, and decreased systemic blood pressure. With higher concentrations of carboxyhemoglobin, the Central Nervous System (CNS) effects worsen as the headache and lightheadedness give way to decreased coordination, nausea, vomiting, fainting, convulsions, coma, and death. When death does not occur, severe intoxication may produce other latent but serious CNS effects including personality and memory problems, peripheral neuropathies, psychiatric disturbances, blindness, and deafness.

The early CNS effects of carbon monoxide poisoning partly mimic those of the flu, especially at low to moderate levels of intoxication.[2] Therefore, the health care professional treating a poisoning victim must be alert to the conditions that caused the CNS effects to avoid a misdiagnosis. Special attention should be paid to the conditions under which exposure and intoxication occurred and to whether co-workers or family members also exhibit symptoms. Hyperbaric oxygen has been shown to be an effective treatment for carbon monoxide poisoning.[4]

Carbon monoxide also produces cardiovascular effects.[3,5] High levels of intoxication can cause myocardial infarction (MI) in subjects with normal coronary arteries and more moderate levels of intoxication can cause MI in patients with coronary artery disease. Carbon monoxide may also exacerbate pre-existing cardiovascular disturbances, including pre-ventricular contractions (PVCs), which can lead to sometimes fatal arrhythmias.

Exposure to other chemicals, for example among firefighters responding to a structural fire, may be additive or synergistic with the toxicity of carbon monoxide. Studies of animals exposed to hydrogen cyanide (HCN), a by-product of plastics combustion, have revealed synergistic lethality with carbon monoxide. Carbon dioxide is additive with carbon monoxide in its action as a simple asphyxiant. Methylene chloride, and possibly other chlorinated and non-chlorinated hydrocarbon solvents, also produces CNS effects, which are additive with those of carbon monoxide. Mammals also partly metabolize methylene chloride to carbon monoxide.

Case Studies

The medical literature is replete with case studies of carbon monoxide poisonings in both occupational and non-occupational settings. Most unintentional deaths occur in poorly ventilated spaces where combustion appliances (e.g., space heaters or water heaters) are operated.[6–8] A 21-year old woman died from carbon monoxide exposure after lethal levels accumulated in a small building used as a laundry and lavatory on her family's farm. The woman collapsed while showering and was discovered in the shower stall with the water still running 45 to 50 minutes after she had entered the building. The building and the unvented water heater that produced the carbon monoxide had been used by the family for more than 10 years without incident although the family reported an occasional "bad smell." On the day of her death, several factors coincided to create the lethal atmosphere. These factors were recreated during the prosecuting attorney's investigation of the death. The weather had been cold and the single window, which was ordinarily open, had been closed to maintain warmth. The victim had ignited the heater to warm the building about 10 to 15 minutes before entering to take a shower. The exhaust pipe of the heater, which was later determined to be too small by legal standards, exited the building through the wall adjacent to the heater and shower stall, and the wind on this particular day was blowing directly into the exhaust pipe preventing the efficient removal of exhaust fumes. The combined effects of the closed window, the inability of the exhaust system to effectively remove combustion products from the heater and building, the wind direction, and the length of time the woman allowed for the water and room to warm resulted in a lethal accumulation of carbon monoxide in the building and her subsequent death.

Nitrogen Oxides (Nitrogen Dioxide, Nitric Oxide, Nitrous Oxide)

Nitrogen dioxide (NO_2) and nitric oxide (NO) are addressed together because they exist in equilibrium; NO is oxidized in the atmosphere to form NO_2. Nitrogen tetroxide (N_2O_4) is the common liquid form of NO_2 although the fraction of NO_2 increases with increasing temperature. These three compounds (NO_2, NO, and N_2O_4) are collectively referred to as NO_x and of these, NO_2 is the most acutely toxic.

Nitrous oxide (N_2O), commonly known as "laughing gas," was discovered in 1772 and has been in use since that time as an analgesic and anesthetic for surgical procedures.

Sources

NO and NO_2 are produced naturally during the metabolism of nitrogenous compounds by bacteria, and by fires, volcanic activity, and atmospheric fixation of nitrogen by lightning. The most significant source is anthropogenic: combustion of fossil fuels for transportation and industry. Silo gas, which contains high concentrations of NO_2, is an important source in agricultural settings.[9] NO is generally produced commercially by passing air through an electric arc or by oxidation of ammonia over platinum gauze. NO_2 is produced commercially by oxidation of NO. Nitrous oxide (N_2O) is commercially produced by the heating of ammonium nitrate to produce N_2O and water.

Uses

The primary industrial uses of NO are in the production of nitric acid, bleaching of rayon, and as a chemical stabilizer for propylene, methyl ether, and other compounds.

NO_2 has been used to bleach flour; in nitration of organic compounds and explosives; and in the manufacture of oxidized cellulose compounds for hemostatic cotton. NO_2 is also a chemical intermediate in the production of nitric acid. It is used as a catalyst for production of sulfuric acid, and as an oxidizing agent for rocket fuels.

N_2O has few industrial uses but is widely used as an analgesic and anesthetic in human and veterinary medicine.

Toxicokinetics

After inhalation, NO_2 is rapidly absorbed in the lower respiratory tract because of its low water solubility. The extent of absorption is significant and in experimental studies can exceed 90%. Once absorbed, NO_2 apparently binds to respiratory tract tissue. Experiments in rhesus monkeys that compared the disposition of radio-labeled nitrogen and xenon revealed that ^{13}N concentrations in the thorax remained stable, while the concentration of ^{125}Xe declined almost to baseline levels indicating that NO_2 was bound to respiratory tract tissue, whereas xenon was exhaled or was absorbed and transported away from the respiratory tract.

NO is also poorly soluble in water and absorbed to an extent similar to NO_2 (90% or more). Once absorbed into the blood, NO binds to hemoglobin with an affinity about 1,000 times greater than carbon monoxide. The methemoglobin that is thus produced is rapidly restored to hemoglobin by methemoglobin reductase and oxygen releasing nitrate and nitrite. Some inhaled NO also combines with oxygen to form NO_2. Within 48 hours of exposure, most inhaled NO is excreted as nitrate in the urine.

N_2O is rapidly absorbed and distributed throughout the body especially in highly vascularized organs, including the brain, heart, and kidney. N_2O is minimally soluble in blood, which allows rapid onset of, and recovery from, anesthesia. N_2O is not metabolized to an appreciable extent and is largely exhaled unchanged.

Toxicity

NO_2 is the most toxic of the nitrogen oxides and the magnitude of adverse health effects depends largely on the exposure concentration and to a lesser extent on the duration of exposure. While NO_2 is known to produce irritation and burns on contact with the skin or mucous membranes, the respiratory effects are more serious. Short term exposures to relatively low concentrations will generally cause non-specific symptoms, including cough, dyspnea, headache, nausea, vertigo, fatigue, and somnolence and these symptoms may persist for two weeks or more without discernable clinical signs. Acute exposure to substantial concentrations of nitrogen oxides can trigger spasms of the airways or larynx and can result in death. Silo filler's disease (SFD), which occurs as a result of exposure to the high concentrations of NO_2 in silo gases, is a well-documented occupational hazard among otherwise healthy agricultural workers. Dyspnea is often the most common symptom of SFD.[10]

Nitrogen dioxide also produces a characteristic syndrome most often observed in industrial settings. Various symptoms may be observed, including cough, dyspnea, wheezing, chest pain, heart palpitations, weakness, sweating, nausea, vomiting, headache, and eye irritation. Moving the exposed individual to fresh air can alleviate symptoms for several hours, however, acute respiratory distress will develop, which includes pulmonary edema accompanied by rapid and shallow breathing, cyanosis, and productive coughing, which progresses to anoxia. Acute respiratory distress syndrome (ARDS) can have several causes, including septic shock, trauma, aspiration of gastric material, barbiturates and other drugs, pancreatitis, as well as NO_2, however the clinical picture regardless of cause is similar.[11] Two phases characterize this progressive syndrome: an exudative phase of 1 to 7 days duration characterized by pulmonary capillary congestion, endothelial swelling and microatelectasis. This phase is also associated with pulmonary edema, fibrin deposition, and formation of hyaline membranes in the lungs. Hypoxemic respiratory failure follows but is unaffected by treatment with supplemental oxygen and patients may require a ventilator. After seven days, the fibroproliferative phase begins that results in stiffened lungs, increased blood carbon dioxide levels, and diffuse alveolar damage. Treatment of ARDS is supportive and generally involves oxygenation and ventilation. Most individuals survive NO_2-induced ARDS but historically the fatality rate is high.

By contrast, nitric oxide (NO) is relatively nontoxic[12] and is frequently used in clinical medicine to treat pulmonary hypertension, pulmonary embolism, acute respiratory distress, and various cardiovascular disturbances.[13–15] NO is synthesized by several cell types (neutrophils, macrophages, neurons, and endothelial cells) and mediates normal physiological actions, including vasorelaxation, inhibition of platelet adhesion and aggregation, neurotransmission, and the bactericidal activity of immune cells. Exposure to high levels, however, has produced cyanosis and death in animals and the Threshold Limit Value® (TLV®) for NO is based on the formation of methemoglobin.

Nitrous oxide (N_2O) toxicity appears to be mediated largely through the inactivation of vitamin B_{12}, which is an essential mammalian enzyme co-factor.[16] The enzymes affected are involved in folate metabolism and normal myelin formation, thus N_2O toxicity produces neurological effects similar to a vitamin B_{12} deficiency, including neurological damage that manifests as numbness and tingling in the trunk and extremities, limb weakness, impaired balance and an unsteady gait, loss of finger dexterity, impotence, Lhermitte's sign (a sudden, transient feeling like an electric shock through the back and legs when flexing the neck), spastic paralysis of the bladder and bowel, personality change, depression, and memory loss.[17,18] N_2O has also been linked to an increase in spontaneous abortions among women exposed occupationally.[19]

Case Studies

Chronic abuse of N_2O affected several levels of the CNS in a 41-year-old male who inhaled up to 10,000 mL/day for more than ten years.[20] The man complained of motor clumsiness and distal parasthesia in all four limbs. An MRI revealed degeneration of the spinal cord at the cervical (C2-C7) level, electrophysiological tests revealed somatosensory abnormalities, and blood chemistry revealed a significantly decreased serum vitamin B_{12} concentration.

A 31-year old male sought medical attention after developing complete numbness from nipples to toes.[17] The man had abused nitrous oxide approximately once per month since age 15 and in the months preceding the development of complete numbness had a history of "imbalance, limb weakness, and numbness and tingling from the toes to the waist and in the hands and forearms."[17] He had a ten-year history of heavy drinking but had been abstinent for two years and was being treated with diazepam for anxiety. During the two years preceding his clinic visit, the man had inhaled approximately 500 to 750 cartridges of nitrous oxide during 5–6 hour sessions that occurred 2 to 3 times per week. Upon physical examination, the man showed decreased pinprick and light touch from waist to toes and in his hands. He had a diminished vibration sensation in his feet and ankles, mild finger-to-nose and heel-to-shin dysmetria, and mild foot drop. He also showed Lhermitte's sign and Romberg's sign, both of which indicate neurological disorders. Magnetic resonance (MR) images revealed effects on the cervical spinal cord but not the thoracic or lumbar regions. These symptoms and the MR results are consistent with classic vitamin B_{12} deficiency. Nitrous oxide interrupts normal B_{12} metabolism and in doing so impairs normal production of myelin. The patient was treated with injections of B_{12} and abstained from nitrous oxide abuse. After seven months, the adverse neurological effects of nitrous oxide were reduced and although a subsequent bout of abuse followed this improvement, a second period of abstinence resulted in normal MR images of the cervical spine.

Accidental exposure to nitrogen dioxide fumes in a young laborer caused acute respiratory distress, severe hypoxemia, and pulmonary edema within a few hours.[21] The man recovered after seven days of mechanical ventilation and corticosteroid therapy. Three weeks after hospital discharge, his lung function had returned to normal.

Sulfur Oxides — Sulfur Dioxide

Sources

Natural sources of sulfur dioxide (SO_2) include volcanoes, biological decay, oceans, and forest fires. Sulfur dioxide is also a by-product of the combustion of sulfur-containing compounds, including coal and petroleum products, and of smelter operations and paper mills. Sulfur dioxide is produced for use in refrigeration, bleaching, fumigation, food and beverage preservation, and as an intermediate in the manufacture of many chemicals.

Uses

Sulfur dioxide is widely used in the food industry because of its antimicrobial properties. The application of sulfur dioxide to fruits and vegetables increases the storage life, preserves color and flavor, and enhances the retention of ascorbic acid and carotene in the food product. Sulfur dioxide is used as a disinfectant in breweries and prevents the formation of nitrosamines in beer. Sulfur dioxide is also used in the manufacture of wine to destroy bacteria, mold, and unwanted yeasts.

In the chemical manufacturing industry, sulfur dioxide is used in the production of chlorine dioxide, acetyl chloride, and other chemicals, as a component of wood pulping liquors, as a reducing agent in mineral processing, as an oxygen scavenger in oil refining, and as a solvent, bleaching agent, and cleaning agent. Sulfur dioxide is used as an alkali neutralizer in the production of glass.

Toxicokinetics

Sulfur dioxide is a highly water soluble gas and as such is readily absorbed across the mucosa of the nasal passages and the upper respiratory tract.[22–24] The rate of absorption appears to be concentration dependent. Transport to the lower respiratory tract is minimal, thus less is absorbed in this region, except during exercise or periods of increased physical activity due to the increased ventilatory demand of exercise. Transport of sulfur dioxide to the lower respiratory tract is also more significant during mouth breathing as compared to nose breathing.

Once inhaled, approximately 12–15% of the sulfur dioxide absorbed in the nasal passages desorbs and is exhaled. Most of the remainder dissolves within the moist tissue of the nasal and upper respiratory tract to form sulfite, bisulfite, and hydrogen ions or is transported to the lower respiratory tract by continuous absorption and desorption from the respiratory tract tissues. These metabolites are then absorbed into the systemic circulation from the lower respiratory tract. Based on studies of dogs, systemic absorption is more significant from the lower respiratory tract than the upper region.

Metabolites of sulfur dioxide are readily absorbed into the systemic circulation and distributed to tissues throughout the body. Radio-labeled sulfur dioxide has been detected in many tissues of the body, including the trachea, lungs, kidney, esophagus, heart muscle, liver, spleen, striated muscle, brain, ovaries, testes, stomach, pancreas, eye, skin, and submaxillary gland.

Once sulfur dioxide is converted to sulfite in the respiratory tract mucosa, it may be oxidized to sulfate by sulfite oxidase. Sulfites may also form S-sulfonates in the blood by producing disulfide bonds with plasma proteins, but the fate of S-sulfonates is not known although glutathione binding may be involved.

Sulfur dioxide is primarily excreted in the urine as sulfate although up to 15% may be exhaled unchanged after desorption from the respiratory tract mucosa.

Toxicity

Sulfur dioxide is an irritating gas and triggers bronchoconstriction and mucus secretion upon inhalation. Asthmatics appear to be more sensitive to sulfur dioxide exposures than non-asthmatics, although significant decrements in pulmonary function may follow exposure in the latter group.[25,26] Exercise appears to exacerbate sulfur dioxide-induced bronchoconstriction.[27]

Reactive airway dysfunction syndrome (RADS) may follow even a single exposure to high airborne concentrations of sulfur dioxide. Cellular injury in the respiratory tract followed by the proliferation of mucus-secreting goblet cells, airway mucosal edema, inflammation, and airway smooth muscle bronchospasm comprise the symptoms of RADS. Bronchoconstriction is mediated by cholinergic and non-cholinergic mechanisms and is most likely due to the production of bisulfite that occurs when sulfur dioxide dissolves in the moist airway mucosa. The primary health effects of sulfur dioxide exposure are summarized in Table 20.1.[24]

Table 20.1 — Primary health effects of sulfur dioxide exposure

Sulfur Dioxide Concentration (ppm)	Primary Health Effect
≥ 0.1	Bronchoconstriction in sensitive exercising asthmatics
0.3–1	Possibly detected by taste or smell
1–2	Lung function changes in healthy non-asthmatic individuals
2	ACGIH recommended TLV®-TWA
3	Easily detected odor
5	NIOSH recommended STEL
6–12	May cause nasal and throat irritation
10	Upper respiratory irritation, some nosebleeds
20	Definitely irritating to eyes; chronic respiratory symptoms develop at this level; respiratory protection is necessary
50–100	Maximum tolerable exposures for 30–60 minutes
≥ 100	NIOSH recommended immediate danger to life

Source: Reference 24 ppm, parts per million
ACGIH, American Conference of Governmental Industrial Hygienists
TLV®-TWA, Threshold Limit Value® – Time-weighted Average
NIOSH, National Institute for Occupational Safety and Health
STEL, Short-term Exposure Limit

Case Studies

Workers in a refrigeration plant reported irritation and shortness of breath after exposure to sulfur dioxide at concentrations of five to 100 ppm.[24] A significant incidence of respiratory symptoms was also reported in pulp mill workers exposed to 10 to 20 ppm of sulfur dioxide.[24] Respiratory disease or declines in pulmonary function, however, were not observed in a 10-year follow-up of a worker exposed to 4 to 33 ppm.[24] Similarly, no effects on pulmonary function were observed in smelter workers exposed to more than five ppm of sulfur dioxide for up to 20 years.[24]

Ozone

Sources

Ozone (O_3) is created naturally primarily from the reaction of ultraviolet light from the sun and oxygen molecules in the stratosphere and secondarily by the reaction of lightning and oxygen molecules in the troposphere. Anthropogenic sources include the reaction of ultraviolet rays on the nitrogen oxides and hydrocarbons that comprise, in part, the photochemical smog produced by motor vehicles and various industrial processes. Smaller amounts of ozone are produced by photocopiers, mercury vapor lamps, electrostatic air cleaners, high-voltage electrical equipment and transmission lines, and electric arc welding. Ozone is also manufactured for industrial uses by the electric irradiation of air.

Uses

Ozone is most useful for its oxidizing properties which find application in disinfection, bleaching processes, deodorization, and in chemical manufacturing.

Toxicokinetics

Because of its low water solubility, a large percentage of ozone is captured in the mucosa of the nasopharynx; as much as 40 to 50% of an inhaled dose is removed from inspired air in this way, but a significant portion also travels deep into the lung where it too is captured in the mucosa for an overall removal efficiency of approximately 95%. Removal efficiency appears to be directly related to concentration and inversely related to respiration rate.[12] Only a small percentage of inhaled ozone is absorbed into the blood. The most significant area of deposition is the acinar region from the terminal bronchioles to the alveoli. Once captured in the mucosa of the respiratory tract, ozone reacts with several types of biological materials and tissues to produce peroxides, aldehydes, and various free radical species.

Toxicity

The toxicity of ozone is manifest in morphological cell alterations, and functional, immunological, and biochemical changes in exposed individuals.

Biochemical Changes

Free radical reactions between ozone and the proteins and lipids of cell membranes might be the primary toxic effect. The free radical reactions result in the denaturation of unsaturated fatty acid side chains of lipoproteins, which creates additional organic free radicals. The adverse effects of these reactions include increased airway permeability secondary to destruction of intracellular organelles, and disruption of cellular metabolism. Exposure to high concentrations of ozone can produce cell destruction and the fatal pulmonary edema and hemorrhage observed in experimental animals.[12]

Respiratory symptoms of ozone toxicity include cough, substernal pain, shortness of breath, chest tightness, dry throat, wheezing, and dyspnea. Non-respiratory symptoms can include somnolence and fatigue, dizziness, insomnia, reduced ability to concentrate, cyanosis, pulmonary edema, and eye irritation.

Functional Changes

Acute exposures to ozone can trigger increased airway reactivity that manifest in the exposed individual as decrements in lung function. Specific functional parameters decline due to ozone exposure, including inspiratory capacity, tidal volume, forced vital capacity (FVC), total lung capacity (TLC), and forced expiratory volume (FEV), while airway resistance and respiration rate increase.[28,29] Some studies suggest that the pulmonary function of women may be more sensitive to ozone than men, and younger individuals may be more sensitive than older individuals.[29]

Cell Morphology Changes

The principal site of ozone toxicity is the acinar region, the junction of the conducting airways and the alveoli. Type I alveolar cells and ciliated cells appear to be the most susceptible to ozone toxicity. Over several days of exposure, Type I cells are replaced by their precursor stem cells, the Type II cells, and hypertrophy and hyperplasia of ciliated cuboidal cells also is observed.[30,31] These effects are manifest as inflammation but are reversible after acute exposure to ozone ceases.

Chronic exposures to ozone can produce fibrotic changes that stiffen lung tissue. Emphysematous changes may also be observed. In various studies of animals, several pathological changes in lung structure and function have been observed, including inflammation, bronchiolitis, abnormal lung growth, changes in nasal secretions, and the development of nodules.[32–35] These pathological changes appear to be irreversible.

Immunological Changes

Studies of animals have shown a decreased resistance to bacterial infection after ozone exposure and ozone has been shown to impair the functional capacity of human macrophages and other cells involved in the immune response.[36,37]

Table 20.2 — Significant concentrations of ozone

Ozone Exposure Standard	Exposure Concentration (ppm)	(mg/m³)
OSHA PEL TWA	0.1	0.2
NIOSH REL	0.1	0.2
ACGIH TLV®	0.05	0.1
EPA NAAQS 1-hr	0.12	0.23

Sources: References 38–40
OSHA, Occupational Safety and Health Administration
PEL, Permissible Exposure Limit
TWA, Time-weighted Average
NIOSH, National Institute for Occupational Safety and Health
REL, Recommended Exposure Limit
IDLH, Immediately Dangerous to Life or Health
ACGIH, American Conference of Governmental Industrial Hygienists
TLV®, Threshold Limit Value®
EPA, Environmental Protection Agency
NAAQS, National Ambient Air Quality Standard

Case Studies

Evidence of sinusitis, mucus membrane irritation, sleep disturbance and shortness of breath was observed in a 45-year-old man occupationally exposed to ozone.[42] Occupational asthma has also been linked to ozone exposures in the workplace at levels as low as 0.04 ppm.[43]

Ethylene Oxide

Sources

Ethylene oxide (C_2H_4O) is produced commercially by the direct oxidation of ethylene by air or oxygen in the presence of a silver oxide catalyst.

Uses

Nearly all of the ethylene oxide produced in the United States is used as an intermediate in the manufacture of other chemicals, such as ethylene glycol, various surfactants, glycol ethers, higher glycols, and ethanolamines. The chemicals produced from ethylene oxide include automotive antifreeze, textiles, detergents, solvents, polyurethane foam, various medications, and adhesives. Less than 1% is used in sterilization processes or as a fumigant. Ethylene oxide is especially well known in the sterilization of medical equipment and devices that are incompatible with steam sterilization, for example, various plastic devices.

Toxicokinetics

Based on studies of animals, ethylene oxide is rapidly absorbed from the lungs after inhalation exposure and distributed throughout the body based on studies of animals. Although data on metabolism are limited, ethylene oxide appears to be hydrolyzed to ethylene glycol or conjugated with glutathione and excreted primarily in urine, with lesser amounts excreted in expired air and feces.[44]

Toxicity

Ethylene oxide is a relatively unstable, highly reactive molecule, which accounts, in part, for its toxicity. At room temperature, ethylene oxide exists as a colorless gas that is noticeable only at relatively high concentrations (260 ppm for perception, 500–700 ppm for recognition). Initial signs of inhalation exposures are respiratory and eye irritation.[44] The physiological responses to acute exposures will include rhinorrhea, lacrimation, and salivation. Respiration may become labored due to lung congestion and lung infections and pneumonia may occur which may cause death some time after exposure. Workers exposed to ethylene oxide at 700 ppm for two months developed cataracts. Subcapsular lens opacity has also been observed in workplace settings where sterilization equipment has malfunctioned, safety precautions are not enforced, or protective equipment has not been used.[45]

CNS effects, including ataxia, prostration, convulsions, nausea and vomiting, seizures, weakness in the limbs, and gait disturbances have been observed in studies of animals (rat, mouse, rabbit, monkey, and dog) after acute exposures to concentrations greater than 200 ppm. Similar effects may occur after longer term exposures (10–11 weeks) to lower concentrations (50 ppm). In humans, high concentrations (in the range of several hundred parts per million) may produce nystagmus, ataxia, incoordination, weakness, and slurred speech. At air concentrations as low as 3 ppm, the upper and lower limbs may develop a sensorimotor neuropathy resulting in increased tolerance to pain and impaired motor coordination. Neurotoxicity is generally partially or completely reversible. At the current occupational exposure levels, including the Occupational Safety and Health Administration Permissible Exposure Limit (OSHA PEL) 1 ppm over an eight hour time weighted average (TWA) or 5 ppm over a 15 minute TWA, neurotoxic effects are not likely to occur.

Exposure of the skin to dilute solutions containing ethylene oxide can cause significant irritation, edema, burns, and necrosis. These effects occur with increasing severity as the concentration of ethylene oxide in liquid increases up to a 50% solution at which point evaporation limits further damage. Dermal exposures in humans may occur if the ethylene oxide solution or ethylene oxide gas is absorbed into clothing and the clothing is worn for some time.

Reproductive effects including testicular damage and abnormal sperm have been observed in studies of rats and guinea pigs exposed to ethylene oxide at concentrations greater than 200 ppm for six months. At a concentration of 100 ppm, a reduction in fertility index and litter sizes was observed in a study of rats. Fetal malformations and death have also been observed in studies of rats exposed to high concentrations of ethylene oxide (~1,000 ppm) during gestation.

Ethylene oxide is known to readily react with proteins, RNA, and DNA. Mutagenicity has been observed in cultured mammalian (including human) cells. Mutagenic effects on germ cells in treated animals can produce heritable changes that can damage or cause the death of a fetus. These effects have not been observed in humans. However, concentrations of 10 ppm or more have produced other mutagenic effects, such as sister chromatid exchanges (SCEs) in cultured human lymphocytes. At the current occupational exposure levels, the risk of heritable genetic defects is considered to be low.

According to the National Toxicology Program, ethylene oxide is "known to be a human carcinogen" based on sufficient evidence of carcinogenicity from studies in humans, including a combination of epidemiological and mechanistic investigations, which indicate a causal relationship between exposure to ethylene oxide and human cancer.[46]

No deaths in humans are known to have occurred after exposure to high concentrations of ethylene oxide.

Case Studies

Most case studies of ethylene oxide toxicity involve occupational exposures.[46] Four sterilizer workers exposed to ethylene oxide that leaked from a sterilization unit developed neurological defects.[47,48] The workers reported intermittent ethylene oxide odors indicating that the exposure level could have reached 700 ppm. Workers 1 and 2 had been exposed to the leaking sterilization unit for three weeks; Worker 3 had been exposed for two weeks, and Worker 4 had been exposed for two months. Worker 1 was new at the job and presumably required more time to complete sterilization tasks, whereas Worker 4 had been a sterilization operator for eight years, was the most efficient of the four operators, and was the only one of the four who was asymptomatic. Worker 1 presented with marked CNS effects, including headaches, nausea, vomiting, lethargy, and seizures described as an acute cerebral syndrome. Workers 2 and 3 were reported to have numbness, limb weakness, clumsy hand movements, and decreased muscle stretch reflexes. Worker 3 also presented with slurred speech and mental confusion. Nerve conduction studies in Workers 2 and 3 revealed sensorimotor neuropathies. Worker 4 was asymptomatic but also demonstrated a sensorimotor neuropathy in nerve conduction studies. After termination of ethylene oxide exposure, Workers 1, 2, and 3

Table 20.3 — Exposure levels for gases discussed in this chapter

Standard	Carbon Monoxide (ppm)	(mg/m³)	Nitrogen dioxide (ppm)	(mg/m³)	Sulfur dioxide (ppm)	(mg/m³)	Ozone (ppm)	(mg/m³)	Ethylene oxide (ppm)	(mg/m³)
OSHA PEL	50	55	5[a]	9[a]	5	13	0.1	0.2	0.05[b], 1.0[c]	0.09[b], 1.8[c]
NIOSH REL	35, 200[a]	40, 229[a]	1[d]	1.8[d]	2, 5[d]	5, 13[d]	0.1[a]	0.2[a]	<0.1, 5[a]	0.18, 9[a]
ACGIH TLV	25	29	3, 5[d]	5.6, 9.4[d]	2, 5[d]	5.2, 13[d]	0.05	0.1	1	1.8
NAAQS 1-hour	35	40	NA	NA	NA	NA	0.12	0.23	NA	NA
NAAQS 8-hour	9	10	NA	NA	NA	NA	0.08	NA	NA	NA
NAAQS 24-hour	NA	NA	NA	NA	0.14[e]	NA	NA	NA	NA	NA
NAAQS Annual[f]	NA	NA	0.053	100	0.03[e]	NA	NA	NA	NA	NA

Sources: References 38–41
[a] Ceiling value not to be exceeded at any time.
[b] Ethylene oxide action level based on 8-hour time-weighted average.
[c] Ethylene oxide permissible exposure limit based on 8-hour time-weighted average.
[d] Short-term Exposure Limit (STEL), a 15-minute time-weighted average that should not be exceeded at any time during a workday.
[e] Based on sulfur oxides
[f] Annual arithmetic mean concentration.
OSHA, Occupational Safety and Health Administration
NIOSH, National Institute for Occupational Safety and Health
ACGIH, American Conference of Governmental Industrial Hygienists
NAAQS, National Ambient Air Quality Standard
PEL, permissible exposure limit
REL, recommended exposure limit
TLV®, Threshold Limit Value®, 8-hour workday, 40-hour workweek
NA, not available

demonstrated significant subjective improvement but nerve conduction studies in Workers 3 and 4 had not improved ten months after the initial study.[48]

Unintentional releases of ethylene oxide in a factory caused nausea, vomiting, chest tightness, shortness of breath, dizziness, cough, and ocular irritation in exposed workers.[49] One worker temporarily lost consciousness. Oxygen therapy and supportive care were used to treat the workers and all were discharged in stable condition.

Case studies have also reported dermal effects if ethylene oxide has been inadequately rinsed from garments, bed sheets, bandages, or medical supplies or equipment.[47,50] Dermal effects include erythema, ulcerations, blisters, and burns.

Summary

The occupationally significant gases present various mechanisms of action from impairment of oxygen transport to inhibition of enzymes to peroxidative damage to neurological damage. In an occupational setting, the likelihood of these toxic effects can be reduced by limiting exposure to levels at or below the recommended levels of private and government agencies and promulgated standards. Table 20.3 summarizes some of these exposure levels for the gases discussed in this chapter.

The list of values in this table is not exhaustive and other agencies, both domestic and foreign, have developed similar kinds of exposure standards. This table also does not provide the supporting documentation that accompanies the publication of these values by the various agencies. The interested reader should consult the primary sources of these exposure values before applying them in a professional setting.

References

1. **Illum, L. and A.N. Fisher:** Intranasal delivery of peptides and proteins, In: *Inhalation Delivery of Therapeutic Peptides and Proteins*. Adjei A. and P Gupta (eds.). New York: Marcel Dekker, Inc., 1997.
2. **Kao, L.W. and K.A. Nanagas:** Carbon monoxide poisoning. *Emerg. Med. Clin. North Am. 22(4)*:985–1018 (2004).
3. **Kao, L.W. and K.A. Nanagas:** Toxicity associated with carbon onoxide. *Clin. Lab. Med. 26(1)*:99–125 (2006).
4. **Stoller, K.P.:** Hyperbaric oxygen and carbon monoxide poisoning: a critical review. *Neurol. Res. 29(2)*:146–155 (2007).
5. **Johnson, C.D.:** Carbon monoxide toxicity with neurological and cardiac complications. *Bol. Assoc. Med. PR. 97(4)*:315–322 (2005).
6. **Sedda, A.F. and G. Rossi:** Death scene evaluation in a case of fatal accidental carbon monoxide toxicity. *For. Sci Int. 164(2–3)*:164–167 (2006).
7. **Risser, D. and B. Schneider:** Carbon monoxide-related deaths from 1984 to 1993 in Vienna, Austria. *J. For. Sci. 40(3)*:368–371 (1995).
8. **Girman, J.R., Y.L. Chang, S.B. Hayward, and K.S. Liu:** Causes of unintentional deaths from carbon monoxide poisonings in California. *West J. Med. 168(3)*:158–165 (1998).
9. **Pavelchak, N., L. Church, S. Roerig, M. London, W. Welles, and G. Casey:** Silo gas exposure in New York State following the dry growing season of 1995. *Appl. Occup. Environ. Hyg. 14(1)*:34–38 (1999).
10. **Zwemer, F.L. Jr., D.S. Pratt, and J.J. May:** Silo filler's disease in New York State. *Am. Rev. Respir. Dis. 146(3)*:650–653 (1992).
11. **Nadeem, R., Abdelkarim, T., and G.A. Salzman:** Acute respiratory distress syndrome. *Hospital Physician 38(11)*:51–58 (2002).
12. **Clayton, G.D. and F.E. Clayton (eds.):** *Patty's Industrial Hygiene and Toxicology*, 4th edition. New York: John Wiley & Sons, 1994.
13. **Fernandez-Perez, E.R., M.T. Keegan, and B.A. Harrison:** Inhaled nitric oxide for acute right-ventricular dysfunction after extrapleural pneumonectomy. *Respir. Care 51*:1172–1176 (2006).
14. **Mojoli, F., M. Zanierato, C. Campana, and A. Braschi:** Inhaled nitric oxide test in a pregnant patient with severe pulmonary hypertension. *Anaesthesia 61*:912 (2006).
15. **Szold, O., W. Khoury, P. Biderman, J.M. Klausner, P. Halpern, and A.A. Weinbroum:** Inhaled nitric oxide improves pulmonary functions following massive pulmonary embolism: a report of four patients and review of the literature. *Lung 184*:1–5 (2006).
16. **Weimann, J.:** Toxicity of nitrous oxide. *Best Pract. Res. Clin. Anaesthesiol. 17(1)*:47–61 (2003).
17. **Pema, P.J., H.A. Horak, and R.H. Wyatt:** Myelopathy caused by nitrous oxide toxicity. *AJNR Am. J. Neuroradiol. 19(5)*:894–896 (1998).
18. **Layzer, R.B.:** Myeloneuropathy after prolonged exposure to nitrous oxide. *Lancet. 2(8102)*:1227–1230 (1978).
19. **Rowland, A.S., D.D. Baird, D.L. Shore, C.R. Weinberg, D.A. Savitz, and A.J. Wilcox:** Nitrous oxide and spontaneous abortion in female dental assistants. *Am. J. Epidemiol. 141(6)*:531–538 (1995).
20. **Lin, C.Y., W.Y. Guo, S.P. Chen, J.T. Chen, K.P. Kao, Z.A. Wu, and K.K. Liao:** Neurotoxicity of nitrous oxide: multimodal evoked potentials in an abuser. *Clin. Toxicol. 45*:67–71 (2007).
21. **Aggarwal, A.N., R.M. Ramanathan, and S.K. Jindal:** Acute respiratory distress syndrome following nitrogen dioxide exposure. *Indian J. Chest. Dis. Allied Sci. 40*:275–279 (1998).
22. **Kleinman, M.T.:** Sulfur dioxide and exercise: Relationships between response and absorption in upper airways. *J. Air Pollut. Control Assoc. 34*:32–37 (1984)
23. **Speizer, F.E., and N.R. Frank:** The uptake and release of SO_2 by the human nose. *Arch. Environ. Health 12(6)*: 725–728 (1966).

24. **Agency for Toxic Substances and Disease Registry (ATSDR):** Toxicological Profile for Sulfur Dioxide. Atlanta, Georgia. December. Available on-line at http://www.atsdr.cdc.gov/toxprofiles/tp116.html. 1998. [Accessed on June 20, 2007].

25. **Horstman, D.H., E. Seal Jr., L.J. Folinsbee, P. Ives, and L.J. Roger:** The relationship between exposure duration and sulfur dioxide-induced bronchoconstriction in asthmatic subjects. *Am. Ind. Hyg. Assoc J. 49(1)*:38–47 (1988).

26. **Rondinelli, R.C., J.Q. Koenig, and S.G. Marshall:** The effects of sulfur dioxide on pulmonary function in healthy nonsmoking male subjects aged 55 years and older. *Am. Ind. Hyg. Assoc. J. 48(4)*:299–303 (1987).

27. **Sheppard, D., A. Saisho, J.A. Nadel, and H.A. Boushey:** Exercise increases sulfur dioxide-induced bronchoconstriction in asthmatic subjects. *Am. Rev. Respir. Dis. 123(5)*: 486–491 (1981).

28. **Bedi, J.F., D.M. Drechsler-Parks, and S.M. Horvath:** Duration of increased pulmonary function sensitivity to an initial ozone exposure. *Am. Ind. Hyg. Assoc. J. 46(12)*: 731–734 (1985).

29. **Drechsler-Parks, D.M., J.F. Bedi, and S.M. Horvath:** Pulmonary function responses of older men and women to ozone exposure. *Exp. Gerontol. 22(2)*:91–101 (1987).

30. **Chow, C.K., M.Z. Hussain, C.E. Cross, D.L. Dungworth, and M.G. Mustafa:** Effect of low levels of ozone on rat lungs. I. Biochemical responses during recovery and reexposure. *Exp. Mol. Pathol. 25(2)*:182–188 (1976).

31. **Plopper, C.G., C.K. Chow, D.L. Dungworth, M. Brummer, and T.J. Nemeth:** Effect of low level of ozone on rat lungs. II. Morphological responses during recovery and reexposure. *Exp. Mol. Pathol. 29(3)*:400–411 (1978).

32. **Barry, B.E., F.J. Miller, and J.D. Crapo:** Effects of inhalation of 0.12 and 0.25 parts per million ozone on the proximal alveolar region of juvenile and adult rats. *Lab Invest. 53(6)*:692–704 (1985).

33. **Crapo, J.D., B.E. Barry, L.Y. Chang, and R.R. Mercer:** Alterations in lung structure caused by inhalation of oxidants. J. Toxicol. Env. Health. 13(2-3):301-21 (1984).

34. **Eustis, S.L., L.W. Schwartz, P.C. Kosch, and D.L. Dungworth:** Chronic bronchiolitis in nonhuman primates after prolonged ozone exposure. *Am. J. Pathol. 105(2)*:121–137 (1981).

35. **Fujinaka, L.E., D.M. Hyde, C.G. Plopper, W.S. Tyler, D.L. Dungworth, and L.O. Lollini:** Respiratory bronchiolitis following long-term ozone exposure in bonnet monkeys: a morphometric study. *Exp. Lung Res. 8(2–3)*: 167–190 (1985).

36. **Gilmour, M.I., P. Park, D. Doerfler, and M.K. Selgrade:** Factors that influence the suppression of pulmonary antibacterial defenses in mice exposed to ozone. *Exp. Lung Res. 19(3)*:299–314 (1993).

37. **Becker, S., M.C. Madden, S.L. Newman, R.B. Devlin, and H.S. Koren:** Modulation of human alveolar macrophage properties by ozone exposure in vitro. *Toxicol. Appl. Pharmacol. 110(3)*:403–415 (1991).

38. **Doull, J.:** Recommended Limits for Occupational Exposure to Chemicals, In: *Casarett & Doull's Toxicology: The Basic Science of Poisons*, 6th edition. Klaasen, C. D. (ed.). New York: McGraw-Hill, 2001.

39. **National Ambient Air Quality Standards (NAAQS).** Available on-line at http://www.epa.gov/air/criteria.html [Accessed on October 16, 2007].

40. **National Institute for Occupational Safety and Health (NIOSH):** NIOSH Pocket Guide to Chemical Hazards. Available on-line at http://www.cdc.gov/niosh/npg/ [Accessed on October 16, 2007].

41. **Occupational Safety and Health Administration (OSHA):** Table Z-1 Limits for Air Contaminants (29 CFR 1910.1000, Table Z-1). Available on-line at http://www.osha.gov/pls/oshaweb/owadisp.show_document?p_table=STANDARDS&p_id=9992 [Accessed on October 16, 2007].

42. **Parks, S., and D.W. Paul:** Ozone exposure: a case report and discussion. *J. Okla. State Med. Assoc. 93(2)*:48–51 (2000).

43. **Lee, H.S., Wang, Y.T., and K.T. Tan:** Occupational asthma due to ozone. *Singapore Med. J. 30(5)*:485–487 (1989).

44. **Gardiner, T.H., J.M. Waechter, and D.E. Stevenson:** Epoxy Compounds, In: *Patty's Industrial Hygiene and Toxicology*, 4th edition. Clayton, G.D. and F.E. Clayton (eds.). New York: John Wiley & Sons, 1993.

45. **Sobaszek, A., J.C. Hache, P. Frimat, V. Akakpo, G. Victoire, and D. Furon:** Working conditions and health effects of ethylene oxide exposure at hospital sterilization sites. *J. Occup. Environ. Med. 41(6)*:492–499 (1999).

46. **National Toxicology Program:** 11th Report on Carcinogens (RoC). Available on-line at http://ntp.niehs.nih.gov/index.cfm?objectid=72016262-BDB7-CEBA-FA60E922B18C2540. [Accessed on June 20, 2007].

47. **Agency for Toxic Substances and Disease Registry (ATSDR):** Toxicological Profile for Ethylene Oxide. Atlanta, Georgia. December. Available on-line at http://www.atsdr.cdc.gov/toxprofiles/tp137.html. 1990. [Accessed on October 18, 2007].

48. **Gross, J.A., Haas, M.L., and T.R. Swift:** Ethylene oxide neurotoxicity: Report of four cases and review of the literature. *Neurology 29*:978–983 (1979).

49. **Lin, T.J., C.K. Ho, C.Y. Chen, J.L. Tsai, and M.S. Tsai:** Two episodes of ethylene oxide poisoning—a case report. *Kaohsiung J. Med. Sci. 17(7)*:372–376 (2001).

50. **Karacalar, A. and S.A. Karacalar:** Chemical burns due to blood pressure cuff sterilized with ethylene oxide. *Burns. 26(8)*:760–763 (2000).

Additional Reading

Levitzky, M.G.: *Pulmonary Physiology*, 7th Edition. New York: McGraw Hill Medical, 2007.

Gardner, D.E. (ed.): *Toxicology of the Lung*, 4th Edition. Boca Raton: CRC Press, 2006.

Klaassen, C.D. (ed.): *Toxicology: The Basic Science of Poisons*, 7th Edition. New York: McGraw Hill Professional, 2007.

> *Thoughts are free and are subject to no rule. On them rests the freedom of man, and they tower above the light of nature.*
>
> Paracelsus (1493– 1541)

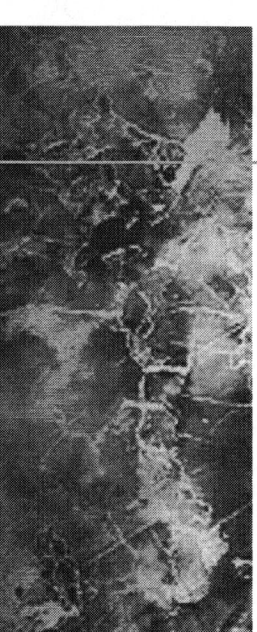

Chapter 21

Toxicology of Radioactive Materials

Outcome Competencies

Upon completion of this chapter, the reader should be able to:

- Predict the nature and severity of health effects from ionizing radiation based on absorbed dose.
- Explain the concept of naturally occurring radioactivity.
- Explain the differences between internal and external irradiation.
- Explain the nature and time course of acute and chronic health effects caused by exposure to ionizing radiation.
- Describe the health effects of low dose radiation.
- Discuss the four types of radiation and describe how and why they are harmful to humans.
- Understand the biochemical mechanism of ionizing radiation injury (free radical damage to DNA).
- Summarize the actual health effects caused by the Chernobyl reactor accident of 1986.
- Predict the health consequences of exposure to depleted uranium.
- Discuss the radiation toxicity of plutonium compared to other elements.

Prerequisite Knowledge

- Basic knowledge of chemistry and physics
- Knowledge of basic biology: cells, tissues, organs, subcellular organelles, etc.
- Knowledge of the atom and its parts: protons, neutrons, electrons
- Basic knowledge of cell, tissue, organ and organism response to damage by physical and chemical agents.

Key Terms[1,2]

alpha particle, beta particle, curie, deterministic effects, dose, gamma ray, gray, isotope, neutron, proton, quality factor, rad, rem, radiation, radioactivity, radionuclide, radioactive half-life, sievert, stochastic effects, x-rays

Key Topics

1. Basic radiation concepts: alpha, beta, gamma, x-ray, proton, neutron, electron
   - Basic Radiation Concepts
   - Sources of Radioactivity

2. Mechanisms of damage: DNA double strand breaks, cell death, mutation
   - Risks and Benefits of Radiation
   - Radiation Detection
   - Biological Effects of Radiation
   - Health Effects of Ionizing Radiation
   - Acute Effects
   - Stochastic and Delayed Effects
   - Chronic Effects of Radiation Exposure

3. Toxicology of Ra, U, Radon, DU, Pu
   - Environmental Contamination

4. Human Exposures:
   - Risks to humans from a radiological accident
   - Types of Radiological Accidents
   - The Impact of a Nuclear Reactor Accident: Chernobyl Revisited

Chapter 21

Toxicology of Radioactive Materials

By William J. Adams, Jr., PhD

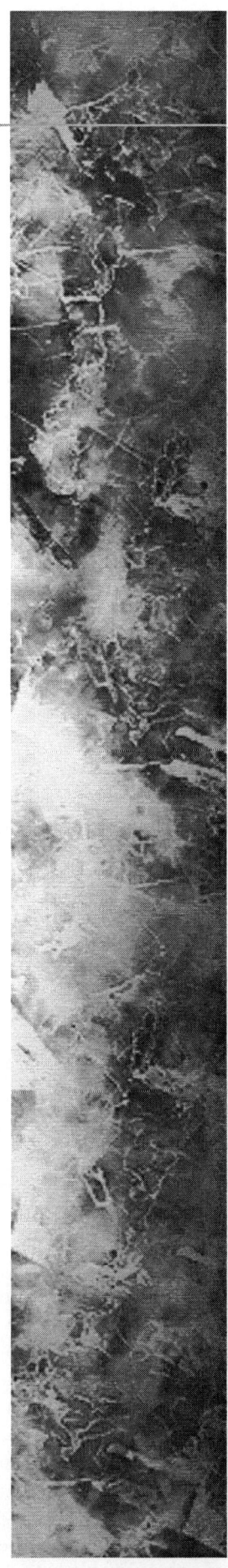

Introduction

Over 100 years after the "Radiation Age" began with Roentgen's description of X-rays in 1895, virtually every nation in the world uses radioisotopes and radio-pharmaceuticals for medical purposes. The bombing of Hiroshima and Nagasaki in 1945 with nuclear weapons changed the face of warfare. Nuclear reactors produce electricity commercially in 30 nations and propel the naval ships of five others. All nations possess some form of medical and industrial radiographic equipment. Because of the ubiquitous nature of radiation and radioactive objects or tools, the danger posed by radiation is widespread.

Basic Radiation Concepts

The health hazards associated with radiation are due to the physical nature of radioactivity and radiation. **Radiation** is the emission and propagation of energy through space. **Ionizing radiation** is any radiation capable of producing ion pairs, directly or indirectly, in its passage through matter. **Radioactivity** is the property of certain nuclides of spontaneously emitting particles or gamma radiation or emitting x irradiation. The word is also used as a synonym for radioactive material. A **radionuclide** is a species of atom characterized by instability, which emits radiation to achieve a more stable state.

Radiation comes in two forms: particles comprising alpha particles, beta particles and neutrons; and waves or photons, comprising gamma and x-rays. Photons travel in straight lines at the speed of light, but can be scattered, reflected or absorbed. Gamma and x-ray photons penetrate deeply into tissues. Alpha and beta particles, which are charged, do not penetrate deeply into tissues. Alpha particles do not travel far in air, usually less than 10 cm, and are stopped by a sheet of paper or by the outer layer of the skin if less than 7MeV. Beta particles can travel up to 15 meters in air, but are easily stopped by the skin or overlying clothing. Alpha and beta particles are dangerous when introduced into the body, and beta particles can also damage skin. Neutrons are deeply penetrating and can cause damage to tissue at depth.[3,4]

Sources of Radioactivity

The earth contains radioactive material as a result of its formation. Radiation from the sun also bathes the earth, and the sun is the only natural producer of new radioactivity near Earth. Humans have possessed the knowledge to make radiation for just over 100 years, and the knowledge and ability to create radioactive materials *de novo* since the late 1930s. As a result, naturally-occurring radioactivity is found everywhere, and every human being contains small amounts of radioactive material. Man-made, or non-naturally occurring radiation, is used in medicine, in the form of diagnostic and therapeutic radiation, radio-pharmaceuticals and nuclides. Other forms of non-naturally occurring radiation are industrial radiography sources and nuclear reactor fuel. Nuclear reactors use the fission process to generate heat, making steam which can turn turbines to generate electricity. Radiation therapy uses several types of radionuclides such as cobalt-60, iodine-131 and cesium-137 to kill cancer cells, while diagnostic radiation sources are used to image the human body. Diagnostic x-rays are produced by x-ray machines that produce x-rays but do not contain radionuclides. Radio-pharmaceuticals are used in human diagnosis and therapy. Isotopes such as gallium-67, iodine-125, thallium-204 and technetium-99 are used most frequently. Industrial Radiography is the process of using photons to detect faults in industrial items such as concrete floors, large pipes and valves. Isotopes used for this include cobalt-60 and iridium-192.[1,3–6]

Risks and Benefits of Radiation

While there is no question that radiation exposure poses a health risk to human beings, the benefits of radiation are also well known: medical diagnosis and treatment, many industrial uses such as industrial radiography and use in various measurement devices, and nuclear electricity generation. Risk is a measured quantity, with an uncertainty derived from the data used and assumptions used to model the risk. Safety, on the other hand, is a value judgment made by individuals. Scientists may agree on the statistical risks of an activity, yet disagree on whether the activity is considered safe. This is particularly true regarding the health effects associated with radiation exposure. While the effects due to high dose exposure are well documented in the scientific literature, the effects due to low dose exposure, especially if protracted over many years, are a matter of scientific controversy.[2,7–9]

Radiation Detection

Because ionizing radiation cannot be sensed, knowledge of its existence depended on the development of instruments capable of detecting it. That technology has existed for just over 100 years. Compared to other toxic hazards, radiation is relatively easy to detect, although it is difficult to measure accurately. A variety of instruments exist that detect and measure radioactivity. Radionuclides which cannot be identified and quantified in real time can be identified and quantified in a laboratory using equipment that is commonly available and fairly easy to use.

Most portable survey meters measure the rate of radioactive transformation of a radionuclide; they are used for gross measurement and are not designed to provide identification of specific radionuclides, but rather detect the amount and rate of radiation emitted from radionuclides. Other portable survey meters are designed to identify specific radiation types, such as alpha particles, beta particles, neutrons or gamma/x-rays rays. While not designed to provide quantitative or isotopic analysis, they are invaluable as means to identify the presence and relative hazard from radionuclides. Personal dosimeters are small instruments designed to measure the radiation dose to an individual, and come in many forms, from pencil shaped self-reading dosimeters to sophisticated electronic dosimeters with remote telemetry. They are used to measure and track individual exposures to radiation and allow employers to maintain worker exposures within established regulatory limits. A useful table describing the advantages and disadvantages of various radiation detection devices has been produced by the Health Physics Society.[10] For further information, see references 4, 6, and 10.

Mechanisms of Damage
Biological Effects of Radiation

Ionizing radiation is a well-recognized cause of human death and injury, and like every other cause of death and injury, "the dose makes the poison" to quote Paracelsus. The effects of ionizing radiation on living cells and tissues are among the most studied and best-understood areas in biology. The discovery of x-rays in 1895 by Roentgen resulted in great strides in the diagnosis and treatment of human disease. Four months after Roentgen's paper was published, J. Daniels published a paper describing radiation-induced hair loss following irradiation of the skull. Studies of radiologists and radiology technicians showed that radiation could induce skin ulceration as well as cancers, while studies of radium dial painters, uranium miners, atomic bomb survivors, and radiation therapy patients provided knowledge about the mechanisms of human radiation injury. The biochemical target of radiation in the cell is the cellular DNA, although the radiochemical mechanisms for biological responses and actual human illness are still uncertain.

Exposure to ionizing radiation can result from direct radiation, exposure to radioactive materials released into air, or from radioactive material deposited on the ground. Since living cells are predominantly made up of water, exposure results in the ionization of water molecules leading to the production of free radicals, which are extremely reactive. Damage to the DNA is thought to cause all of the biological effects seen in radiation poisoning, from cell death to mutation leading to cancer formation.

As a general rule, the severity of the effect is proportional to the dose of radiation received; the greater the dose, or radiation exposure, the more serious the effect. Cellular damage can result in damage to specific organs, such as the bone marrow which produces blood cells. Bone marrow damage may manifest itself in an inability to fight infection, leading to the death of the exposed person.

Other factors which influence the effects of radiation include dose rate, type of radiation, and uniformity of dose. Generally, the higher the dose rate, the faster the dose is received, and the more severe the effect. If radioactive material enters the body, the exposure is said to be internal; alpha and beta emitting radionuclides are much more hazardous when they enter the body and can release energy directly to the body's cells. Internally deposited radioactivity can deliver dose as long as it remains in the body and is radioactive. A small amount of internally deposited radioactivity could thus cause a greater absorbed dose over a period of time than a short dose from a larger external source of radiation.

The three key concepts in radiation protection are time, distance, and shielding. By reducing the time of exposure, less dose is accumulated. Radiation dose occurs over time; dose is received in dose unit per unit time, such as rem/min. In addition, radiation intensity declines by an inverse square function. That means that radiation dose declines by the reciprocal or inverse of the distance from the source to the person squared. For example, a source reading 100 rem/hr at 1 foot will give a dose rate of 1 rem/hr at 10 feet. Simply put, as you get farther away from the source, the dose rate drops off by an inverse function, which means it drops off rapidly. Finally, radiation can be stopped by appropriate shielding. A piece of paper will stop alpha particles; normal clothing will shield the skin from most beta particles. Gamma and x-rays are stopped by various thicknesses of lead, concrete or steel. Neutrons can be blocked by water or polyethylene. All reactors are surrounded by shielding of some sort. Medical radiographers wear lead aprons and gloves to reduce exposure. Radiography sources, such as iridium-192, are stored in heavy lead containers that shield the radiation.

Health Effects of Ionizing Radiation

Health effects from ionizing radiation exposure are classified by the time it takes for the disease to manifest itself. Effects that occur soon after exposure are called acute effects, while those that take months to years to manifest are referred to as chronic effects. Acute effects such as nausea are observed within minutes to weeks after high dose radiation exposure; delayed effects such as cancer or cataracts are observed months to years after the radiation exposure. Another critical distinction is that between whole body exposure and partial body exposure: whole body exposure subjects every cell of the body to radiation, and results in the generalized syndromes described below. Partial body exposure may result in serious local effects without threatening survival. For a given dose of radiation, the more body exposed, the greater the threat to the person's health.

Deterministic Effects

At doses above 100 rads, effects are directly proportional to the dose. These effects are called deterministic, since the dose determines the severity of the effect. Deterministic effects are grouped into the three components of the acute radiation syndrome (ARS); these components are the hemopoietic, the gastrointestinal, and the neurovascular syndromes. The hemopoietic system, which is the blood forming organ system, is the most sensitive and sustains severe damage at doses above 100 rads. It is characterized by loss of white blood cells and anemia, resulting in disordered blood clotting and the inability to combat infection. As the radiation dose increases to about 400 rads, the gastrointestinal system is damaged, resulting in diarrhea, fluid loss into the bowel, and systemic infection due to invasion by bowel flora. Above 700 rads cardiovascular damage occurs due to damage to endothelial cells which line blood vessels, leading to generalized bleeding into organs and vascular collapse. At doses above 1000 rads the nervous system itself is damaged.

As dose increases, injury is caused by cell death. At some point, enough cells are killed that the individual shows a physiological effect such as vomiting. Cells that divide rapidly are the most sensitive, and it is that sensitivity that determines the subtypes of the acute radiation syndrome: the hemopoietic syndrome, the gastrointestinal syndrome, and so on.

Acute effects may include severe physiological injury or death, which can occur within hours for very high doses or after several months at lower doses. Human health effects caused by high-dose acute exposures to ionizing radiation are listed in Table 21.1. Acute doses of radiation begin to cause death at doses of approximately 150 rad to the whole body. Acute radiation syndrome is well understood but difficult to treat successfully, and caused 28 deaths during the first few months after the 1986 Chernobyl accident.

Table 21.1 — Health Effects Due to Acute Exposure to Ionizing Radiation

Effect	Acute dose in Rad	Gray*
Changes in peripheral blood count	50	0.5
Vomiting (threshold)	100	1.0
Death (threshold)	150	1.5
LD 50/60** with minimal medical treatment	320-360	3.2-3.6
LD 50/60 with supportive medical treatment	480-540	4.8-5.4

* The System Internationale (SI) unit for absorbed dose is the Gray; 1 Gray (Gy) equals 100 rads. The Sievert is the SI unit for equivalent dose. 1 Sievert equals 100 rems. Rads and Rems are the dose units used by the United States.
**LD 50/60 is the dose of radiation which would be expected to kill 50 percent of the target population in 60 days.
Modified from NCRP Report 98, "Guidance on Radiation Received in Space Activities" NCRP, Bethesda, MD, 1989[17]

Chronic Effects

Chronic effects, also called delayed effects, occur months to years after exposure, and may also be observed in survivors of high-dose acute radiation syndrome or in people who have received low doses of radiation over an extended time. Cataract formation is a deterministic delayed effect caused by acute doses of 60–150 rads of mixed gamma and neutron radiation, or by fractionated doses above 800 rads total dose. At doses below 10 rads there are no demonstrated adverse health effects; biological effects such as chromosomal abnormalities may be seen, but these have not yet been shown to result in a health decrement. At doses below 100 rads, the principal health effect seen is an increase in cancer incidence beginning several years after the exposure. Increased incidence of leukemia was found in atomic bomb survivors beginning 2 years after the bombing, with a peak incidence occurring 6 to 7 years after the event. The increase in cancer incidence observed in human populations exposed to radiation doses in the 10 to 100 rad range is termed a stochastic effect, since the probability but not the severity of effect increases with dose. While the overall incidence of cancer within the exposed group rises, it is not possible to predict which individuals will be affected.

At radiation doses below 10 rad, cancer induction has not been proven. It is possible that there is little or even no risk associated with low dose exposure, but epidemiological methods are not sensitive enough to answer the question. Low dose radiation is a weak carcinogen, and characterizing the risk from low dose radiation is critical to understanding the long-term health effects. The Health Physics Society has urged caution in the estimation of radiation-induced health risks at low doses of radiation.[7] For more information on Mechanism of Action and Biological Effects, see references 2, 5, 7, 8, 11-20, and 29-31.

Toxicology of Radium, Radon, Uranium, Depleted Uranium and Plutonium

Environmental Contamination

Naturally-occurring radioactivity is present as a result of the processes that created the universe. Naturally-occurring radioactive materials include uranium, thorium, radium and many other radionuclides with atomic numbers of 92 and lower. There is also some naturally-occurring radioactivity as a result of cosmic radiation from the sun that strikes the earth continuously. The entire earth is radioactive to some extent, and some areas have higher background levels of radiation than others. Some naturally-occurring radioactivity in the environment is released from the burning of fossil fuels such as coal or natural gas. Naturally occurring radioactivity accounts for about 80% of annual radiation exposure. The average annual dose to Americans is estimated to be 300 mrem/year.[29]

Once radioactive material is released into the environment, it may migrate through the air or in soil and water, exposing people by ingesting radioactively contaminated foods or water, by breathing radioactively-contaminated air, or by direct radiation exposure from radionuclides in the air or on the ground. However, it must be noted that the presence of radioactivity in the environment does not mean that a health hazard exists. For radiation to injure humans, the dose must be great enough to overcome body defenses and repair mechanisms. If the dose is not large enough, there will be no biological harm done by the exposure. For an injury to occur, the exposure must be large enough to reach the threshold for injury. The specific nature of that threshold is subject to many influences, and may even vary within a single individual over time.[3,4,13]

Radium Toxicity

Radium (Ra) is a naturally-occurring metal formed from the radioactive decay of uranium and thorium. The two principal isotopes found are Radium-226 and Radium-228, both of which emit energetic alpha particles and the International Labor Office has classified Radium (Ra) as being a Very High Radiotoxicity substance. Radium has been used extensively in the past in a variety of medical and industrial products. It has been used as a therapeutic agent against cancers, as a source for the radiographic examination of metals, and as a component in luminous paints used on watch dials and other instruments used in darkness. By the late 1920s the toxicity of radium was well-recognized. For many years radium was used in a wide variety of consumer preparations such as candies and sodas which were touted as miracle cures for many illnesses. Radium is known to cause tumors of the lung, bone, nasal passages and mastoid cells.[21]

Radon Toxicity

Radon (Rn) is a colorless, odorless, inert gaseous radionuclide that results from the natural decay of uranium. It is found naturally in soil, and the classical studies in Radon toxicity were performed in uranium miners, who demonstrated elevated levels of lung cancer. Radon-222 emits an energetic alpha particle, and the International Labor Office considers it to be of moderate radiotoxicity. The U.S. Environmental Protection Agency alleges that Radon-222 is the leading cause of lung cancer in U.S. non-smokers, and estimates that radon causes over 21,000 lung cancer deaths every year due mainly to inhalation exposures in dwellings. This has been a controversial position since it is based on extrapolation of effects from uranium miners, who experienced high levels of exposure over long periods of time, to home dwellers experiencing relatively low exposures.[22]

Uranium: Toxicological and Radiological Effects

Natural uranium (U) is a dense, reactive, silver colored metal that is moderately radioactive and almost twice as dense as lead. Uranium is found naturally throughout the environment. Naturally occurring uranium can be found in the air that is breathed and in the foods and water that are ingested. In some areas of the world, such as the Colorado Plateau, concentrations of uranium are high enough to allow mining. Natural uranium is composed of three radioisotopes: U-238, which comprises 99.27 % of naturally occurring uranium, and U-234 (0.01%) and U-235 (0.72%), which together make up less than 1% of naturally occurring uranium. Depleted uranium (DU) is naturally occurring uranium which has been processed to remove U-235 and U-234; as a result, DU has an even higher concentration of U-238 (typically 99.75% or higher) than naturally occurring uranium, making it even less radioactive.[23]

Health Hazards of Expended DU Munitions

There is no medical evidence to date to suggest that exposure to environmental levels of DU resulting from munitions use adversely affects health. Studies by the U.S. National Academy of Sciences and the RAND Corporation have concluded that DU exposure at levels found in the Persian Gulf War does not constitute a health risk. The International Labor Office considers depleted uranium to be in Radioisotope Toxicity Group 4, a substance with low radiotoxicity. The Agency for Toxic Substances and Disease Registry, U.S. Department of Health and Human Services, in its 1999 publication *Toxicological Profiles for Uranium* (Updated), states there are no known human health effects due to irradiation by DU. Kidney disease, associated primarily with the chemical (heavy metal) toxicity of uranium, has been diagnosed in uranium miners exposed to relatively high levels of uranium for extended periods. The risk of equivalent exposures to even unprotected personnel entering a general area where DU munitions have been used is extremely low. There are, however, two situations which may lead to exposures in excess of peacetime safety standards and thus may result in some health risk. The first situation with a possible health risk is being in physical proximity, that is, being in or within 50 meters, to a vehicle struck by a DU munition. This can result in inhalation of DU dust particles as well as the imbedding of DU fragments in wounds. The second situation is spending long periods of time working inside a vehicle struck by a DU munition, or working inside a vehicle which carried DU munitions and which had an onboard fire. The precautionary measures found in current policies and procedures are effective in preventing exposures caused by the second situation. Furthermore, the simple precautions mandated by the U.S. Army Medical Command (dust mask and gloves) for personnel working in the immediate vicinity of vehicles struck by DU munitions virtually eliminate any potential risk to these individuals.[24,25]

Plutonium Toxicity

Plutonium is a metal that is found in trace amounts in nature, but is made in large amounts in nuclear reactors. Plutonium found in the environment may be naturally-occurring in trace amounts in uranium ores[26] or the result of past atmospheric nuclear weapon detonations. The most common isotopes found are Pu-238, Pu-239, and Pu-240. Pu-238 and Pu-239 decay primarily by the emission of alpha particles. There is a small group of former nuclear weapons workers who have body burdens of plutonium and have been medically evaluated for several decades. To date no excess cancers have been found, but the group is statistically quite small, containing only 26 subjects. Animal studies have demonstrated numerous health effects following high dose exposure to plutonium isotopes; however, these studies were performed at levels several orders of magnitude greater than the human occupational exposures. Both Pu-238 and Pu-239 are rated as very highly radiotoxic by the International Labor Office, although the commonly held notion that plutonium is one of the most toxic substances to humans is not supported by any data.[26]

Human Exposures

Risks to Humans from a Radiological Accident

The health risks to humans depend on many factors, including the type of accident, the amount of radiation dose absorbed, the specific nuclides causing the exposure, whether the exposure is internal to the body or external to it, age, gender, and general health.

Calculating the risk from an exposure below 10 rad requires modeling, since there is no human data to support a risk estimate. The numbers that are used are derived from studies of human groups exposed to radiation unintentionally, such as the Atomic Bomb survivors, the radium dial painters, or ankylosing spondylitits patients. Since these exposures were not intentional, they were not measured at the time they were received. All doses were estimated using other models. When all the sources of error are tabulated, the risk estimates are found to have a large amount of variation. The risks derived from modeling are much better than unscientific estimates based on anecdotes.

A good model provides a rational boundary on potential health effects. But the model used matters: many models use data from the Atomic bomb survivors, but it must be kept in mind that the number of cancers in Atomic bomb survivors at doses below 0.2 Gy (20 rads) may not be significantly different from zero. All of the models for estimating the human health effects of radiation exposure utilize assumptions and simplifications which distort what is a highly complex, multi-factorial situation. While these simple models may produce a level of understanding adequate for a non-technical audience, they may not be very useful when applied to complicated policy choices.

It is remarkably difficult to determine if exposure to a hazard causes a specific disease in a specific individual unless the hazard is rare and the accompanying disease is also rare. If the hazard is common, such as radiation, and the alleged affect, such as leukemia, is also common, little more can be done than to perform a calculation of "probability of causation", which is a statistical calculation, not a statement of certainty.

Sources of uncertainty include the following:

- Which part of the body is exposed;
- Dose of radiation to the various body parts;
- Which types of cells are exposed: resistant cells or sensitive cells;
- Which part of the cell is exposed: nucleus or cytoplasm;
- Whether the exposure causes cell death or neoplastic transformation;
- Whether the cancer that develops is really due to the radiation or to failures of the body's defense mechanisms such as the immune surveillance system;
- Reliability of dosimetry, since accidental exposures are rarely controlled;
- Dose calculations for estimated doses may be inaccurate, and
- Often it is difficult to prove that an exposure even occurred, let alone estimating the dose.[14–16,19]

Types of Radiological Accidents

The types of radiological accidents are as varied as the number of radioactive sources themselves. (See Table 21.2). The most obvious accidents occur at nuclear reactors, and the 1986 Chernobyl accident and its consequences will be discussed below. Nuclear weapons accidents also can result in the spread of radioactivity, but actual nuclear detonations are not properly thought of as radiological accidents. Intentional attacks on nuclear facilities may result in the spread of radioactive material. Accidents may also occur at fuel production facilities, such as the September 1999 accident at a nuclear fuel fabrication plant in Tokaimura, Japan which resulted in 2 deaths and hundreds of people being exposed to radiation levels higher than normal background. Radioactive sources may be used as weapons themselves, such as radiological dispersal devices or isotopic weapons. In these situations the radioactive material is not used to create an explosion as in a nuclear bomb, instead the idea is to simply expose humans to the radiation from the source. Finally, there is the most common type of radiological accident, the truly unintentional exposure of humans to a source that has been lost, stolen, or otherwise abandoned and is not stored safely. Often referred to as "orphan" sources, these types of accidents result in several deaths every year.[3,9,19,27,28] Table 21.2 below shows the author's assessment of the probability and severity of a number of radiological and nuclear events.

Table 21.2 — Types of Radiological Accidents

Type of Accident	Probability of Occurrence	Number of deaths	Number of injuries
Nuclear Weapon Detonation	Low	High: 1000's of deaths	High: 1000's to 10's of 1000's
Serious Nuclear Reactor Accident	Low	Medium: 0–100 deaths	Medium: 0–1000
Nuclear Criticality Accident	Medium	Low: 0–5 deaths	Low: 0– 0?
Non-serious Nuclear Reactor Accident	High	Low: 0–5 deaths	Low: 0–100
Radioactive Source Accident, e.g. Goiana, Thailand, Egypt	High	Low: 0–10 deaths	Low: 0–100
Radiological Dispersal Device	Low	Low: 0–5 deaths	Low: 0–?
Environmental Contamination	High	Low: 0–5 deaths	Low: 0–?
Attack on a nuclear reactor	Low–Medium	Low: 0–10 deaths	Low: 0–100

Orphan Source Accidents

Accidental exposures to what are known as "orphan" radioactive sources and resulting in fatalities occur periodically. In February 2000, at least 30 people in Bangkok, Thailand were exposed to radiation from a cobalt-60 source that had been removed from an obsolete radiation therapy device stored in an open area. The source was sold to a junk dealer. Seven people were seriously injured and 3 died from acute radiation syndrome. In June 2000, U.S. Navy personnel were asked to assist Egyptian authorities in diagnosing what was thought to be an unusual infectious disease. The American personnel identified the sickness as acute radiation syndrome and also discovered a large radiation source in a private home. The owner of the home and his nine-year old son died of acute radiation syndrome. The source was later found to be an iridium-192 source used to perform industrial radiography of large pipes and valves, and was lost by an Egyptian radiography firm. In 1987, a similar accident occurred in Goiana, Brazil which resulted in 4 deaths and widespread local contamination due to cesium-137 from an abandoned radiotherapy device.

There have been only two instances of radiation release from nuclear reactors capable of causing immediate or long-term health effects to nearby populations—Windscale, now Sellafield, in the United Kingdom in 1957 and Chernobyl in Ukraine in 1986. Chernobyl was the largest nuclear reactor accident in history, and the model for subsequent "worst-case accident" scenarios. The Chernobyl accident resulted in:

- Approximately 56 fatalities as of December 2005;
- Permanent relocation of more than 100,000 people;
- Mobilization of almost 1 million people to contain and clean up the accident;
- Long-term contamination of over 150,000 square kilometers of farmland in Belarus, Ukraine and Russia;
- Chronic diseases, albeit at lower than projected incidence, among those exposed to radioactive material, and
- A global effort by the nuclear power industry to improve safety systems and operator training that has resulted in a significant increase in the safety level of the industry, and has greatly reduced the threat of a second "Chernobyl" type accident.

The Impact of a Nuclear Reactor Accident: Chernobyl Revisited

The 1986 accident at Chernobyl resulted in 30 deaths within the first 4 months: 2 immediate deaths due to burns, and 28 deaths caused by acute radiation syndrome. Longer-term health impacts were characterized by the early biological effects due to I-131 in the form of an increase in thyroid tumors in exposed children. Long-term environmental contamination by Cs-137 and Sr-90 also occurred, resulting in the evacuation and permanent resettlement of many of the inhabitants near the plant, and eliminating farming in some affected areas. These areas likely will be excluded from unrestricted use for upwards of 600 years, after which most radioactivity will have decayed.[28] Also released at Chernobyl were very small amounts of plutonium-239 and -240, which were measurable with sensitive analytical apparatus but which presented no known health risk. Because plutonium is not volatile, very little is able to leave the immediate area of the reactor. Since the amount of plutonium released at Chernobyl was very small compared to the large amounts of cesium and strontium, plutonium is not a significant contributor to dose and thus is not a health hazard. By comparison, the amount of plutonium released at Chernobyl is far less than the estimated 350,000 Curies released to date by global atmospheric testing of nuclear weapons. The health impacts seen are the same as for all radiation exposure, acute radiation syndrome at high doses and cancer induction for low doses.

The immediate health impacts from a reactor accident such as Chernobyl depend on the nature of the accident. Explosions and fires can cause blast and thermal injuries. Release of radioactive material can result in direct exposure to humans at the nuclear power facility and in the surrounding area to ionizing radiation and radioactive contamination. A small number of people on the facility, such as emergency workers and clean-up personnel, are likely to receive high radiation exposures in a short time. If the area is not temporarily or permanently evacuated, large numbers of people may receive low dose radiation exposure from radioactively contaminated air, soil, and water. The evacuation and quarantine of radioactively contaminated areas after the Chernobyl accident contributed to reducing short- and long-term health hazards by preventing human contact with radioactively contaminated materials.

Ingestion of contaminated animals, plants, and dairy products also poses a health hazard to humans. Some of the highest radiation doses experienced after Chernobyl by the general public resulted from ingesting contaminated food such as milk, mushrooms, and vegetables. It has been known for many years that radioactive iodine can enter cow's milk within 2 days of a cow eating contaminated fodder, making cow's milk a source of I-131. Because iodine is an essential trace mineral, it is readily absorbed by cows and humans alike. This was the case in Belarus, Russia, and Ukraine, where milk was contaminated with radioactive iodine within two days of the accident. The contaminated milk was the major source of radioactive iodine ingestion by people in the affected area. Contaminated milk and foodstuffs were ingested in the immediate aftermath of the accident before authorities had time to test for contamination and warn the population not to eat the contaminated items. Cow's milk also concentrates Cs-137. The Cs-137 released during the Chernobyl accident is still found in fruit, grain products, meat, milk, and vegetables produced in Russia, Belarus and Ukraine. Measures to reduce the contamination in foodstuffs have been implemented, resulting in radiation levels in food that are much lower than before; many foodstuffs are considered safe for consumption.

The long-term health impact of the Chernobyl accident has not been as great as originally anticipated. Nevertheless, the ultimate cost of Chernobyl has not been fully realized, as the morbidity and mortality it caused may not be manifested for another 25 years or more. It is also unlikely that the exact number of deaths that can be attributable to the accident will ever be determined. Shortly after the accident occurred, scientists predicted an occurrence of thousands of cases of cancer, especially leukemias; however, recent epidemiological evidence indicates that there have been no known cases of leukemia or solid cancers in Ukraine, Belarus, or Russia that are directly attributable to radiation. These effects could change as the exposed adult population ages, since many radiation-induced cancers may not become apparent for several decades after the accident. However, children who inhaled or ingested radioactive iodine released from Chernobyl are at increased risk of thyroid cancer. To date, 1,800 cases of thyroid cancer have been diagnosed, representing an increase of over 400 percent from pre-accident rates, and many more cases are expected to occur during the next 2 decades. No increase in thyroid cancer has been observed in children born after May 1986. Similarly, adults exposed to radioactive iodine have not shown an increased risk for thyroid cancer. By contrast, no health effects have ever been demonstrated in Americans potentially exposed to radiation after the 1979 Three Mile Island reactor accident. The average dose from that accident was calculated as 1 mrem to the 2 million people in the area. As a comparison, a complete chest x-ray results in 6 to 10 mrem exposure.[2,3,8,9,11,12,18,19,27,28]

References

1. **Shleien, B., L.A. Slaback, and B.K. Birkey (eds.):** *Handbook of Health Physics and Radiological Health*, 3rd Edition. Baltimore, MD: Williams and Wilkins, 1998.
2. **National Academy of Sciences:** *Health Effects of Exposure to Low Levels of Ionizing Radiation: BEIR VII Phase 2.* National Research Council. Washington, DC: National Academy Press, 2006.
3. **Eisenbud, M. and T Gesell:** *Environmental Radioactivity*, 4th Edition, San Diego, CA: Academic Press, 1997.
4. **Cember, H.:** *Introduction to Health Physics*, 3rd Edition, New York: McGraw-Hill, 1996.
5. **Mettler, F.A., and A.C. Upton:** *Medical Effects of Ionizing Radiation*, 2nd Edition, Philadelphia, PA: W.B. Saunders Company, 1995.
6. **Shapiro, J.:** *Radiation Protection*, 4th Edition, Cambridge, MA: Harvard University Press, 2002.
7. **Health Physics Society:** *Risk Assessment, and Radiation Risk in Perspective:* Position Statements of the Health Physics Society. Health Physics Society Membership Directory 1999–2000.
8. **Meister, K.:** *The Health Effects of Low-Level Radiation*, American Council on Science and Health, September 2005, http://www.acsh.org/publications/pubID.1186/pub_detail.asp [Accessed on July 12, 2006].
9. **U.S. Nuclear Regulatory Commission:** *NRC Fact Sheet on the Accident at Three Mile Island*, last revised March 27, 2006 http://www.nrc.gov/reading-rm/doc-collections/fact-sheets/3mile-isle.html.
10. **Health Physics Society:** *What Radiation Detecting Device Should I Use?* Table found on the Health Physics Society Webpage, updated November 2004 http://hps.org/publicinformation/ate/faqs/devices.html [Accessed on July 12, 2006].
11. **Hall, E.J. and A.J. Giaccia:** *Radiobiology for the Radiologist*, 6th Edition. Philadelphia, PA: Lippincott, Williams and Wilkins, 2006.
12. **Cigna, A.A.:** *Interactions with human nutrition and other indices of population health, in 1997 Health Impacts of large releases of radionuclides.* Wiley, Chichester (CIBA Foundation Symposium 203) p 141–154.
13. **Modan, B.:** *Low Dose Radiation Epidemiological Studies: An Assessment of Methodological Problems*, Ann. ICRP 22(1-E):59-73 (1999).
14. **National Council on Radiation Protection and Measurements:** *NCRP Report No. 116: Limitation of Exposure to Ionizing Radiation.* Bethesda, MD: National Council on Radiation Protection and Measurements, 1993
15. **National Council on Radiation Protection and Measurements:** *NCRP Report No. 115: Risk Estimates for Radiation Protection.* Bethesda, MD: National Council on Radiation Protection and Measurements, 1993.
16. **National Council on Radiation Protection and Measurements:** *NCRP Report No. 126: Uncertainties in Fatal Cancer Risk Estimates Used in Radiation Protection.* Bethesda, MD: National Council on Radiation Protection and Measurements, 1997.

17. **National Council on Radiation Protection and Measurements:** *NCRP Report No. 98: Guidance on Radiation Received in Space Activities.* Bethesda, MD: National Council on Radiation Protection and Measurements, 1989.
18. **National Council on Radiation Protection and Measurements:** *NCRP Report No. 96: Comparative Carcinogenicity of Ionizing Radiation and Chemicals.* Bethesda, MD: National Council on Radiation Protection and Measurements, 1989.
19. **International Atomic Energy Agency:** *Safety Reports Series No. 2: Diagnosis and Treatment of Radiation Injuries,* Jointly sponsored by the International Atomic Energy Agency and the World Health Organization. IAEA, Vienna, 1998.
20. **Casarett, A.:** *Radiation Biology.* Upper Saddle River, NJ: Prentice-Hall, 1968.
21. **Agency for Toxic Substances and Disease Registry (ATSDR):** *Toxicological Profile for Radium,* Agency for Toxic Substances and Disease Registry, U.S. Public Health Service, in collaboration with U.S. Environmental Protection Agency, December 1990.
22. **Agency for Toxic Substances and Disease Registry (ATSDR):** *Toxicological Profile for Radon,* Agency for Toxic Substances and Disease Registry, U.S. Public Health Service, in collaboration with U.S. Environmental Protection Agency, December 1990.
23. **Agency for Toxic Substances and Disease Registry (ATSDR):** *Toxicological Profile for Uranium,* U.S. Department of Health and Human Services, Public Health Service, Agency for Toxic Substances and Disease Registry, September 1999.
24. **Raabe, O.G.:** *A Short Review of Depleted Uranium Toxicity.* Jane's Defense Weekly, January 12, 2001.
25. **World Health Organization (WHO):** *Depleted Uranium Factsheet,* World Health Organization, revised January 2003 http://www.who.int/mediacentre/factsheets/fs257/en/ [Accessed on July 12, 2006].
26. **Agency for Toxic Substances and Disease Registry (ATSDR):** *Toxicological Profile for Plutonium,* Agency for Toxic Substances and Disease Registry, U.S. Public Health Service, in collaboration with U.S. Environmental Protection Agency, December 1990.
27. **International Atomic Energy Agency:** *Ten Years after Chernobyl: What do we really know?* (Pamphlet). Vienna, Austria: International Atomic Energy Agency, 1996.
28. **World Health Organization (WHO):** *Health Effects if the Chernobyl Accident and Special Health Care Programmes* Report of the UN Chernobyl Forum Expert Group, World Health Organization, 2005. www.who.int/entity/ionizing_radiation/a_e/chernobyl/-EGH%20Master%20file%202005.08.24.pdf [Accessed on July 12, 2006].
29. **National Council on Radiation Protection and Measurements:** *NCRP Report No. 93: Ionizing Radiation Exposure of the Population of the United States*, Bethesda, MD: National Council on Radiation Protection and Measurements, 1987)
30. **United Nations (UN):** United Nations Scientific Committee on the Effects of Atomic Radiation, *UNSCEAR 2000 report Volumes 1and 2: Sources and Effects of Ionizing Radiation* [Accessed on July 12, 2006]. http://www.unscear.org/unscear/en/publications/2000_1.html and http:// ww.unscear.org/unscear/en/publications/2000_2.html
31. **United Nations (UN):** United Nations Scientific Committee on the Effects of Atomic Radiation, *UNSCEAR 2001 report: Hereditary Effects of Radiation* [Accessed on July 12, 2006]. http://www.unscear.org/unscear/en/publications/2001.html

Chapter 22

Toxicology of Complex Chemical Mixtures

By Jonathan Borak, MD, DABT, Cheryl A. Fields, MPH, and Greg Sirianni, MS, CIH

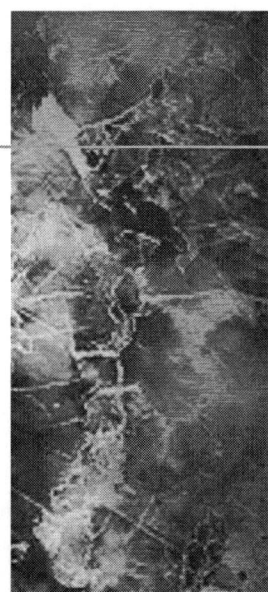

Introduction

An important informational challenge confronts industrial hygienists who undertake the development and implementation of programs aimed at protecting workers from harmful exposures to toxic chemicals. The great majority of toxicology data have been derived from studies of individual agents exposed at fixed doses by single routes of exposure. By contrast, most exposures actually involve multiple chemicals occurring in mixtures of varying composition, and often involving multiple exposure routes and media. Common examples of such exposure mixtures include ambient air pollution, second-hand tobacco smoke, liquid gasoline and its vapors, and welding fume. Moreover, there are few industrial work sites where only a single chemical is used; thus most industrial workplaces are also examples of exposure to mixtures of varying composition.

Establishing a workplace chemical safety program generally requires predicting the likely effects of exposure to such mixtures under various exposure conditions (i.e., exposure level and durations), but empirical data are only rarely sufficient to rigorously support such predictions. Stated simply, an almost infinite number of combinations of chemicals can exist, but only a few have been subject to rigorous testing. As a result, even in an era of seemingly unlimited internet searching capacity, it is rarely possible to "look up" the specific toxicity profiles of a particular mixture. On the other hand, by relying on certain basic principles of toxicology, it is often possible to formulate an initial qualitative assessment of a toxic mixture. Moreover, as described below, that approach coupled with a series of assumptions adopted by the American Conference of Governmental Industrial Hygienists (ACGIH)[1] can lead to useful quantitative assessments of a mixture's toxicity.

About Mixtures

Combinations of chemicals are referred to as "mixtures." The actual composition of mixtures, in terms of both the components (e.g., individual chemicals) and their relative proportions, may be relatively constant or may vary in uncertain and almost

Outcome Competencies

Upon completion of this chapter the reader should be able to:

- Distinguish between simple and complex mixtures.
- Define four general categories of interactions.
- Identify the potential for interaction using a simple, multi-step approach.
- Explain why knowledge of the metabolic pathways and/or mechanisms of action is essential in predicting interactions.
- Predict the toxicity of a mixture based on the potential interactions of that mixture.
- Demonstrate an appreciation for the complexity involved in predicting toxicity associated with exposures to mixtures.

Prerequisite Knowledge

Students should possess an introductory understanding of the following toxicological concepts:

- Dose and dose-response
- Mechanisms of toxicology
- Metabolic pathways (activation/detoxication; induction/inhibition)

Key Terms

additivity, antagonism, complex mixture, dispositional antagonism, dose additivity, functional antagonism, potentiation, receptor antagonism, response additivity, simple mixture, synergism

Key Topics

1. Definition of mixtures
2. An approach to predicting toxicity of mixtures
3. Identifying the major types and subtypes of interactions

275

unlimited ways. **Simple mixtures** are comprised of a relatively small number of chemicals, generally less than ten. The composition of a simple mixture can often be known both qualitatively (i.e., its specific components) and quantitatively (i.e., the relative proportions of those components). For example, various cleaning products, solvent mixtures, and pesticides cocktails may be encountered and used as mixtures of relatively fixed proportions. By contrast, **complex mixtures** comprise many chemicals, sometimes hundreds or thousands, and their compositions are only rarely known with precision. Examples of complex mixtures include welding fume, metal-working fluids, gasoline, tobacco smoke, and drinking water. In most cases, the air we breathe (especially in industrial settings) also represents a complex mixture.

The composition of a mixture may vary from sample to sample, such as when the mixture is manufactured by a variety of sources or for a variety of purposes or applications. In such cases, although the various mixtures share the same name, they may not have the same composition. Consider, for example, a complex mixture such as gasoline. The composition of gasoline depends on the crude oil from which it is derived, the particular processes by which it is produced, and the presence of foreign additives. There is a large range of gasoline types and blends: leaded vs. unleaded; high octane 'premium' vs. low octane 'regular'; high vapor pressure 'winter' blends vs. low vapor pressure 'summer' blends, and so forth. Each may be comprised of more than 250 organic components, each of which has its own physical properties, chemical properties, and toxic potential.

In addition, the composition of a given mixture may vary according to the medium in which it is encountered. For example, the numerous organic components that comprise gasoline have unique vapor pressures and volatility. As a result, the specific composition of liquid gasoline can be expected to differ from the composition of its vapors; those vapors will contain greater proportions of the more volatile components and smaller proportions of the less volatile ones, as illustrated in Table 22.1.

Moreover, its vapor composition will vary according to ambient temperature and atmospheric pressure. Accordingly, workers exposed to gasoline can experience significantly different internal exposures depending on whether they had inhalation exposure of vapors, or skin exposure to splashed liquid, or accidental ingestion.

Prior to 2004, ACGIH had adopted a relatively simplified approach, assuming that the vapor phase composition of a mixture is similar to that of the corresponding liquid phase.[7] More recently, ACGIH has determined that its guidance for mixtures does not apply to substances in mixed phases, e.g., simultaneous exposure to both liquid and vapor.[1] Thus, vapor compositions should not be directly inferred from the composition of the corresponding liquid; they should be directly determined.

Predicting the Toxicity of Mixtures

In an ideal world, the hazards of individual mixtures would be determined by subjecting the mixture itself to standard toxicological testing. In practice, such an approach is rarely practicable.

Table 22.1 — Representative composition of primary components in gasoline liquid vs. gasoline vapor

Primary Components in Gasoline	Liquid Gasoline (% volume)*	Gasoline Vapor (% volume)*
Hydrocarbons categorized by type		
Alkanes	60–70%	90%
Straight chain	4–8%	47%
Branched	25–40%	34%
Cyclic	3–7%	2%
Alkenes	5–10%	11%
Straight chain	4–8%	3%
Branched	25–40%	3%
Aromatics	25–30%	2%
Benzene	1–2%	<1%
Toluene	11 (3–21)%w/w	1.6 (0–7)%w/w
Ethylbenzene	3 (1–5)%w/w	0.009 (0–0.1)%w/w
Xylene	11 (6–16)%w/w	0.5 (0–21)%w/w

* unless otherwise specified
Adapted from: [2–6]

There is an almost infinite number of unique mixtures, but only a few have been studied systematically. Instead, hazard assessments and toxicity predictions are usually based on the toxicological data available for the mixture components deemed most important based on their relative proportions in the mixture or their known toxicity. Information describing the toxicity of those individual components is then combined to predict the likely toxicity of the entire mixture.

However, the relationships and interactions between individual mixture components can be complex. One important set of concerns is whether the different components of a mixture cause similar toxic effects and if so, whether they have the same or different modes of action. Such concerns are often referred to as examples of pharmacodynamic interactions (i.e., the effects of chemicals on the target tissue: receptors, individual cells, or organ as a whole). Another set of concerns involves the possibility that one component may influence the metabolic transformation of another component, thereby either increasing or decreasing its toxicity. This is an example of pharmacokinetic interactions (i.e., the absorption, distribution, metabolism and excretion of chemicals). A third type of concern is that the various components may directly compete, for example for cellular binding sites.

It can thus be difficult to predict the effects of a mixture on the basis of the effects known for each of its components singly. In some cases, the mixture components may have similar and additive effects, while in other cases there may be off-setting, opposite effects. In some cases, mixture components compete for metabolic binding sites, thus reducing their combined effects, while in other cases one component may induce the enzymes that activate a second component, thereby potentiating its effects. Because a multiplicity of mechanisms may explain these various interactions, there is no single best approach to combining toxicity information about a mixture's components.

Fortunately, as noted above, it is often possible to make useful predictions by applying basic toxicological principles to data available for the most important of the components in a given mixture. First, of course, it is necessary to identify those most important components. It is also necessary to determine whether there is sufficient toxicological information about each one. Then, if sufficient information is available, the major concern becomes whether and how those components interact. The types of interactions between mixture components can be grouped into four general categories: **additivity, synergism**, **potentiation**, and, **antagonism**. Although actual mixtures may contain numerous components that simultaneously interact in various ways, the following discussion illustrates those four categories by reference to simple, two-component mixtures.

Types of Interactions
Additivity

When the components of a mixture have a combined effect that is equal to the sum of their individual effects (response additivity) or of their individual dose levels (dose additivity), they are said to show additivity. This is illustrated simplistically in the table below which considers hypothetical 'toxic effect units'.

Additivity	
Component(s)	Toxic Effect Units
A	3
B	3
(A + B)	6

Implicit in the concept of additivity is that the individual components do not actually interact with each other, but independently contribute to similar toxicity — either by noncompetitively acting through the *same mechanism of action* (dose additivity) or by causing similar toxic effects through *different mechanisms of action* (response additivity).

The method used to estimate a mixture's toxicity differs depending upon whether the components interact via the same or similar mechanisms of action (dose additivity) or through dissimilar mechanisms of actions (response additivity). In general, the approach for dose additivity involves scaling the doses of individual chemicals by their relative toxic potencies and then summing the scaled doses to estimate their combined effect. In estimating response additivity, the effects of individual components are considered independent (i.e., they cause harm in different ways), thus the combined effect of the mixture is obtained by simply summing the effects caused by each component alone. Specific examples of each approach are provided below.

The toxic equivalency approach is a special case of the Relative Potency Factor (RPF) approach that can be applied in situations of dose additivity. A classic example involves the important group of 29 organochlorine compounds, comprised of dibenzodioxins, dibenzofurans, and PCBs, that bind to the aryl hydrocarbon (Ah) receptor and thereby initiate a cascade of biochemical processes that lead to increased gene expression (increased transcription and increased translation) which in turn can cause toxicity. The potency of each of those 29 compounds is related to its binding affinity for the Ah receptor, and has been empirically quantified, relative to the most potent of the compounds (2,3,7,8-tetrachlrorodibenzo-p-dioxin, TCDD), and expressed as its Toxic Equivalency Factor (TEF).[8,9] In turn, for any given mixture of those compounds, the mixture's potency can be expressed as the sum of the TEFs of its components weighted by the proportion that each compound contributes to the mass of the mixture. By means of this toxic equivalence (TEQ) approach, the toxicity of a mixture can be predicted and described as though it contained only TCDD in an amount sufficient to cause an equivalent toxicological effect. In other words, the toxic potency of a mixture can be regarded as equal to the weighted sum of the toxicity factors of its components. For chemicals that do not act as carcinogens, the Hazard Index (HI) approach is another useful method for estimating dose additivity.[10] This approach involves summing the hazard indices (the ratio between the estimated dose and the reference dose) across components of a mixture and across anticipated routes of exposure to provide a total hazard index.[11] A detailed outline of this approach as used by ACGIH is provided in the sidebar.

The alternative type of additivity (i.e., response (or effect) additivity) occurs when a person is exposed to a mixture comprised of components with the same or similar toxic effects, but *different mechanisms of action*. Consider, for example, exposure to mixtures of respiratory irritants, such as acid aerosols, ozone, and fine particulate matter, each associated with a different mechanism of action. Such exposures are a common concern of air pollution scientists, and they are also encountered in a wide variety of workplaces. One might predict that the effects of such exposures (e.g., wheezing, shortness of breath) would be about the same as the sum of the effects caused by each irritant alone. Or consider a different example, the likely effects of a mixture of medications. One might predict that by taking one aspirin tablet and one ibuprofen tablet (medications with similar analgesic effects, but different mechanisms of action), it would achieve a therapeutic effect about the same as the sum of those obtained by taking either one alone.

Although **dose additivity** and **response additivity** are logically similar, they can lead to contradictory predictions when dealing with chemicals that have toxic thresholds, i.e., dose levels below which toxic effects do not occur. Suppose a mixture contains two or more toxic components, each at levels below its toxicity threshold. In that case, each component alone would be expected to have no toxic effect and, therefore, the sum of those effects (i.e., response additivity) would predict that the mixture was also without toxicity. But if the individual components exert their toxicity via the same or similar mechanisms, it might well be that the sum of the individual doses (i.e., dose additivity) might result in an effective dose sufficient to pose a substantial toxic hazard. Accordingly, predictions that a mixture will not be toxic should be viewed with caution when they are based solely on response additivity, especially for chemicals with well regarded toxicity thresholds.

Synergism: "Greater than Additive"

When the components of a mixture have a combined effect that is greater than the sum of their individual effects, they are said to show **synergism**. This is illustrated simplistically in the following table which considers hypothetical 'toxic effect units.'

Synergism	
Component(s)	Toxic Effect Units
A	3
B	3
(A + B)	7

Unlike additivity discussed above, synergism indicates that there is interaction between the mixture components or between their individual biological effects such that the combination produces more toxicity than would be predicted by simply adding their effects.

Synergism has been well demonstrated for pharmaceutical agents, but much less so for industrial and workplace exposures. There are numerous synergistic drug interactions with important positive therapeutic implications. For example, combining an opiate analgesic (e.g., codeine) with a non-opiate analgesic (e.g., acetaminophen) generally results in greater pain relief than would be expected from their individual activities. Likewise, the administration of certain antibiotic combinations (e.g., Vacomycin and β-lactams) produces greater that expected antibacterial activity against some microbial strains, and are therefore favored for the treatment of particular types of infection.[12]

Potentially harmful synergistic effects can also occur. Unexpectedly severe central nervous system (CNS) depression can result when individuals taking certain sedative-type medications also consume ethanol. Out of concern for such synergism, patients prescribed sedatives, tranquilizers or antihistamines are often warned to avoid ethanol. Such adverse synergism is the pharmacological basis for the effects of a 'Mickey Finn', an alcoholic beverage to which a sedative has been added in order to incapacitate the drinker.

One reason that synergistic effects may be seen more often in therapeutic, rather than workplace contexts, is that synergism is mathematically more likely to occur in the midrange of chemicals' dose-response curves.[13,14] It is common to administer such high doses to patients in whom specific pharmacological effects are the goal, but they are almost always avoided in workplace settings where such effects are generally regarded as signs of toxicity. Thus, at the generally lower levels of exposure occurring in contemporary worksites, it may not be possible to document synergism, as opposed to additivity.

Potentiation: "Greater than Additive"

Potentiation is said to occur if a chemical that lacks a specific toxicity increases that specific toxicity of a second chemical, when they are administered together. This is illustrated simplistically in the following table which considers hypothetical 'toxic effect units.'

Potentiation	
Component(s)	Toxic Effect Units
A	0
B	3
(A + B)	5

The presence of potentiation is indicative of often complex pharmacokinetic or pharmacodynamic interactions that predispose those who are exposed to greater toxicity than would be predicted by simply adding the activities of the individual components. Such interactions are a common concern in industrial worksites.

Potentiation can occur if chemical A upregulates the enzymatic process by which chemical B is metabolically transformed to its toxic metabolite, thus leading to greater quantities or higher peak levels of the ultimate toxicant than would otherwise be expected. Such metabolic potentiation has been well demonstrated for mixtures containing ketones such as acetone, an industrial solvent of generally low toxicity that also occurs naturally as a result of fat metabolism. Acetone is normally metabolized by cytochrome P450 isoenzymes and rapidly excreted. As acetone body burdens rise, synthesis of those isoenzymes is induced, thereby providing an endogenous mechanism for eliminating increased acetone loads. But such upregulated enzymatic activity can also result in enhanced metabolism of other substances that are substrates for those isoenzymes.

The relevance of acetone potentiation has been shown for a variety of workplace exposures. For example, acetone alone does not cause peripheral neuropathy, but it potentiates the neuropathic effects of n-hexane, a solvent oxidized by cytochrome P450 to form 2,5-hexadione, a neurotoxic metabolite that causes peripheral polyneuropathy. Progressive neuropathy has been reported in workers exposed to *n*-hexane in the printing, automotive, shoe, laboratory, and other industries.[15] Human and animal studies document increased neuropathy, along with increased formation of 2,5-hexadione, in those exposed to combinations of *n*-hexane and acetone, as compared to exposure to comparable doses of *n*-hexane alone.[16–18]

Similar potentiation has been shown for the combinations of acetone and a variety of other industrial chemicals. One example is carbon tetrachloride, a solvent that is metabolized to a highly reactive carbon-centered radical (•CCl$_3$) by reductive dehalogenation, a metabolic process catalyzed by cytochrome P450. Although acetone alone does not cause hepatotoxicity, mixtures of acetone and carbon tetrachloride caused greater liver damage than did comparable exposures to carbon tetrachloride alone.[19,20] Similarly, potentiation of carbon tetrachloride hepatotoxicity has been shown for isopropanol, which is metabolized to acetone.[21]

Potentiation can also occur if chemical A disrupts or downregulates the metabolic detoxication or elimination of chemical B or its toxic metabolite. Many electrophilic chemicals, including the toxic metabolites of numerous workplace chemicals, undergo detoxication by conjugation with glutathione, a sulfur-containing tri-peptide which is an important scavenger of such activated toxic molecules. If the body's glutathione levels are depleted, then its capacity to detoxify electrophiles is reduced, thus enhancing their capacity to cause toxicity. For example, naphthalene, a common aromatic hydrocarbon, is oxidized by cytochrome P450 to form a reactive electrophilic epoxide intermediate, 1,2-naphthalene oxide, which can undergo detoxication by conjugation with glutathione. Depletion of glutathione causes no direct toxic effects on the lung, but the combination of naphthalene plus agents that deplete lung glutathione, such as chronic ethanol exposure[22], increases pulmonary toxicity of naphthalene.[23,24]

Predicting likely potentiation between chemicals requires understanding of their individual mechanisms of action, knowledge of the metabolic pathways leading to the formation of toxic metabolites and their detoxication, and the ways that those pathways are likely to be up- or downregulated. This requires much specific information about the individual components of the mixture. Fortunately, it is often possible to make qualitative predictions based on knowledge of the types of chemicals and their respective properties. For example, if a particular mixture contains a known enzyme inducer, then it is likely that its actions will potentiate the toxicity of other components normally activated by that enzyme.

Antagonism: "Less than Additive"

When the components of a mixture have a combined effect that is less than the sum of their individual effects, they are said to show **antagonism**. This is illustrated simplistically in the following table which considers hypothetical 'toxic effect units.'

Antagonism

Component(s)	Toxic Effect Units
A	3
B	3
(A + B)	4

Antagonism indicates that there are interactions between the mixture components or between their individual biological effects which lead to interference in or inhibition of the toxicological activity of one or more of the components. Examples of antagonism are often grouped according to their underlying modes of action: **functional antagonism, dispositional antagonism**, and **receptor antagonism**.

Functional antagonism is said to occur when the biological effects of mixture components are offsetting, tending to counterbalance each other. Most well documented examples reflect the interactions of primary and secondary messengers on the control of physiological functions such as vascular permeability and bronchial constriction.[25,26] A crude example, by contrast, involves drinking strong coffee in an effort to offset the depressants effects of consuming too much ethanol. Accordingly, functional antagonism is the opposite of response additivity.

Dispositional antagonism occurs when one component of a mixture alters the absorption, distribution, metabolism or excretion of other components so that effective levels of the toxicants are reduced. For example, dispositional antagonism can be expected if chemical A upregulates the enzymes that catalyze detoxication of chemical B, or if chemical A downregulates the enzymes that transform chemical B to its toxic metabolite. Accordingly, dispositional antagonism is the opposite of potentiation.

Most well documented examples of dispositional antagonism are derived from studies of pharmacological agents, but some are specifically relevant to industrial chemicals. One therapeutically important example involves the interaction between two common aliphatic alcohols, methanol (CH_3OH) and ethanol (C_2H_5OH). Methanol is primarily metabolized by alcohol dehydrogenase and aldehyde dehydrogenase, yielding formic acid which can accumulate and cause severe acidosis and neurological injury. Ethanol is metabolized by those same enzymes, with which it has much greater affinity than does methanol: the affinity constant (K_m) of ethanol for alcohol dehydrogenase is about 15-times greater than that of methanol.[27-29] As a result, if a person is exposed to a mixture of those two alcohols, ethanol is preferentially metabolized, while methanol may be excreted untransformed. Thus, co-exposure to ethanol prevents by dispositional antagonism the formation of the metabolite that causes methanol toxicity. Until very recently, victims of methanol exposure were routinely administered ethanol at doses sufficient to block formic acid accumulation, thus preventing methanol-associated neurological damage.

Similar, albeit sometimes more subtle dispositional antagonism has been demonstrated for exposures to a variety of industrial solvents. Co-exposure to benzene and toluene reduced the formation of benzene metabolites, and thereby reduced the formation of benzene-albumin adducts, a biomarker of benzene toxicity.[30,31] Likewise, metabolic interactions have been shown for mixtures of toluene and xylene, toluene and isopropyl alcohol, and toluene and methyl ethyl ketone, but generally at levels that exceed permissible exposure limits.[32,33]

Receptor antagonism describes situations in which two or more chemicals compete for cellular receptor sites, thereby altering physiological response. The proposed toxicity of ammonium perchlorate, an oxidizer found in rocket fuel and munitions, involves competition with iodine for the sodium iodide transporter, a membrane protein receptor that facilitates iodine uptake into the thyroid. In addition to perchlorate, a variety of environmental and industrial anions including nitrate, thiocyanate and chlorate competitively block iodine uptake.[34] Accordingly, ammonium perchlorate has been used therapeutically to block the thyroid toxicity of excessive iodine exposures.

Industrial hygienists should be more cautious in evaluating settings in which the effects of mixtures are expected to be greater than or less than additive. There are no simple rules for determining appropriate exposure limits in such situations, unlike those where additivity is reasonably expected. It is likely that simple additivity models will lead to insufficiently protective exposure limits for synergistic mixtures and overly protective limits for antagonistic mixtures, but the extent of such over- or under-protection can only be determined by a toxicological assessment of the individual mixture components.

Summary

The interactive effects of mixture components can pose important concerns for workplace safety. In particular, there is the possibility that even when each alone is without significant risk, their combined effects might pose significant toxicological hazard. A relatively simple first step for evaluating such situations relies on the Additive Mixture Formula developed by ACGIH.[1]

First, determine the toxicological effects of each of the major components in the mixture by referring to its listing in the "TLV® Basis" section of the ACGIH Table of Adopted Values. When two or more substances have similar toxicological effects, their additive effects should be regarded as an important concern. Whether the mixture exceeds its appropriate threshold limit, assuming none of its component exposures exceeds their TLV®s, can be determined by adding the ratios of each component's air concentration to its TLV® (e.g., [$CA_A \div T_A$], where C_A is time-weighted exposure level of chemical A and T_A is its TLV®). If the sum of the ratios exceeds 1, then the exposure exceeds the mixture's threshold limit and should be reduced.

It must be recognized that this approach does not apply for chemical mixtures that demonstrate potentiation. In addition, there are numerous chemicals for which there are no established threshold values. For such situations, it is necessary to learn more about the specific chemicals, their toxic effects and mechanisms of action. Finally, note that such an additive approach

---

Occupational Exposure Limits for Mixtures: An Example

Industrial hygienists must often determine whether workers simultaneously exposed to multiple chemicals are at risk of harmful effects. Such evaluations require a practical approach to the interactive effects of mixtures. One popular approach is provided by the ACGIH in its *Threshold Limit Values® for Mixtures*, which is useful for simple mixtures, which contain only a few components that cause similar toxic effects. This approach assumes that the combined effects of those components, rather than their individual effects, deserve primary consideration.

1. First identify the mixture components of concern, based upon their concentrations in the work environment and their known toxicities. Identify those with similar toxic effects.
2. Determine the appropriate occupational exposure limits for each. Depending on the conditions of exposure, it may be appropriate to consider full-shift exposure limits, short-term exposure limits or both.
3. For each set of chemicals with similar toxic effects, determine the ratios of each chemical's concentration (C) to its relevant exposure limit (T). Then, sum those ratios.

$$\frac{C_1}{T_1} + \frac{C_2}{T_2} + ... + \frac{C_n}{T_n} = ?$$

If the sum of the ratios exceeds 1, then the exposure exceeds the mixture's threshold limit and should be reduced.

Example: An industrial hygienist is asked to evaluate a worksite where workers are routinely exposed simultaneously to three aromatic solvents (styrene; toluene; and xylene) which can cause similar toxic effects. The following table summarizes the 8-hour time weighted average exposures documented in that worksite along with the occupational exposure limits (ACGIH TLV® values) for the three solvents.

Chemical	Exposure Level TWA (*C*)	ACGIH TLV® (*T*)
Styrene	4 ppm	20 ppm
Toluene	8 ppm	20 ppm
Xylenes	50 ppm	100 ppm

Review of these data indicates that each of the three solvents is found at a level no greater than 20-50% of its occupational exposure limit. Thus, if these agents are considered individually, the workplace apparently poses no excessive risks of harm.

But consideration of the three solvents simultaneously leads to a different conclusion. The following equation applies the ACGIH Mixtures formula to the worksite example:

$$\frac{4}{20} + \frac{8}{20} + \frac{50}{100} = 0.2 + 0.4 + 0.5 = 1.1$$

Even though each of the individual solvents was present at levels well below its respective occupational exposure limit, the sum of those three exposures would exceed the corresponding occupational exposure limit for the mixture as estimated using the ACGIH formula. Accordingly, the industrial hygienist should conclude that the workplace does pose an excessive risk of harmful effects and the exposures must be reduced.

Note that this approach relies on a number of assumptions about the similarity of dose-response relationships for each of the mixture components; such assumptions are not necessarily valid. It also does not apply to substances in mixed phases (i.e., both liquid and gas). It also is not valid for carcinogenic effects.

has not been universally adopted. The German DFG, for example, "decidedly refrains" from calculating exposure limits for mixtures until the toxicological actions of each particular mixture has been studied.[35]

Applying basic toxicological principles to predict toxicity of mixtures

Steps to follow:	Consider:
1) IDENTIFY important components in the mixture	Highest volume; greatest toxic potency
2) COLLECT toxicological information about each one; if sufficient information is available, proceed to step 3	If no direct information: consider structure-activity relationships, similar mixtures
3) DETERMINE whether these components interact	Pharmacodynamics; Pharmacokinetics
4) PREDICT type(s) of interactions	Additive; Synergistic; Potentiation; Antagonism

References

1. **American Conference of Governmental Industrial Hygienists (ACGIH):** *2006 Threshold Limit Values® (TLV®s) for Chemical Substances and Physical Agents and Biological Exposure Indices (BEI®s)*. Cincinnati: American Conference of Governmental Industrial Hygienists, 2006.
2. **Pope, A.M., D.P. Rall:** *Environmental Medicine. Integrating a missing element into medical education*. Washington, DC: National Academy Press, 1995.
3. **McDermott, H.J. and S.E. Killiany:** Quest for a gasoline TLV®. *Am. Ind. Hyg. Assoc. J. 39*:110–117 (1978).
4. **Runion, H.E.:** Benzene in gasoline. *Am Ind. Hyg. Assoc. J. 36*:338–350 (1975).
5. **UK Health Protection Agency:** Petrol-Toxicological overview. 2006. Ref Type: Report.
6. **Agency for Toxic Substances and Disease Registry (ATSDR):** Chemical and Physical Information. In *Toxicological Profile for Gasoline*, Agency for Toxic Substances and Disease Registry. Washington, DC: U.S. Department of Health & Human Services, 1995. p. 107.
7. **American Conference of Governmental Industrial Hygienists (ACGIH):** *2003 Threshold Limit Values® (TLV®s) for Chemical Substances and Physical Agents and Biological Exposure Indices (BEIs)* Cincinnati: American Conference of Governmental Industrial Hygienists, 2003.
8. **van den Berg, M., et al.:** Toxic equivalency factors (TEFs) for PCBs, PCDDs, PCDFs for humans and wildlife. *Environ. Health Perspect. 106*:775–792 (1998).
9. **van den Berg, M., et al.:** The 2005 World Health Organization reevaluation of human and mammalian toxic equivalency factors for dioxins and dioxin-like compounds. *Toxicol. Sci. 93*:223–241 (2006).
10. **Agency for Toxic Substances and Disease Registry (ATSDR):** *Guidance Manual for the Assessment of Joint Toxic Action of Chemical Mixtures*. Atlanta: U.S. Department of Health and Human Services, 2004.
11. **Beck, B.D., E.J. Calabrese, T.M. Slayton, and R. Rudel:** The Use of Toxicology in the Regulatory Process. In *Principles and Methods of Toxicology*. Hayes, A.W. (ed.). Boca Raton: CRC Press, 2008. pp. 45–102.
12. **Rochon-Edouard, S., M. Pestel-Caron, J.F. Lemeland, and F. Caron:** In vitro synergistic effects of double and triple combinations of β-lactams, vancomycin, and netilmicin against methicillin-resistant Staphylococcus aureus strains. *Antimicrob. Agents Chemother. 44*:3055–3060 (2000).
13. **Borgert, C.J.:** Chemical mixtures: an unsolvable riddle? *Hum. Ecol. Risk Assessment 10*:619–629 (2004).
14. **American Conference of Governmental Industrial Hygienists (ACGIH):** *2007 Threshold Limit Values® (TLV®s) for Chemical Substances and Physical Agents and Biological Exposure Indices (BEIs)*. Cincinnati: American Conference of Governmental Industrial Hygienists, 2007.
15. **Centers for Disease Control and Prevention (CDC):** n-Hexane-related peripheral neuropathy among automotive technicians — California, 1999–2000. *MMWR 50*: 1011–1013 (2001).
16. **Ladefoged O. and L. Perbellini:** Acetone induced changes in the toxicokinetics of 2,5-hexanedione in rabbits. *Scand. J. Work Environ. Health 12*:627–629 (1986).
17. **Ladefoged, O., K. Roswall, and J.J. Larsen:** Acetone potentiation and influence on the reversibility of 2,5-hexanedione-induced neurotoxicity studied with behavioural and morphometric methods in rats. *Pharm. Toxicol. 74*:294–299 (1994).
18. **Luisa Mateus, M., A.P. dos Santos, and M.C.C. Batoreu:** Acetone-induced changes in the formation of n-hexane neurotoxic derivatives in rats. *Toxicol. Lett. 88*:25 (1996).
19. **Raymond, P. and G.L. Plaa:** Ketone potentiation of haloalkane-induced hepato- and nephrotoxicity. I. Dose-response relationships. *J. Toxicol Environ Health 45*:465–480 (1995).
20. **Charbonneau, M., S. Oleskevich, J. Brodeur, and G.L. Plaa:** Acetone potentiation of rat liver injury induced by trichloroethylene-carbon tetrachloride mixtures. *Fund. Appl. Toxicol. 6*:654–661 (1986).
21. **Plaa, G.L., W.R. Hewitt, P. Du Souich, G. Caille, and S. Lock:** Isopropanol and acetone potentiation of carbon tetrachloride-induced hepatotoxicity: single versus repetitive pretreatments in rats. *J. Toxicol. Environ. Health 9*:235–250 (1982).
22. **Moss, M., D.M. Guidot, M. Wong-Lambertina, T. Ten Hoor, R.L. Perez, and L.A.S. Brown:** The effects of chronic alcohol abuse on pulmonary glutathione homeostasis. *Am. J. Respir. Crit. Care Med. 161*:414–419 (2000).

23. **Phimister, A.J., M.G. Lee, D. Morin, A.R. Buckpitt, and C.G. Plopper:** Glutathione depletion is a major determinant of inhaled naphthalene respiratory toxicity and naphthalene metabolism in mice. *Toxicol. Sci. 82*:268–278 (2004).
24. **Warren, D.L., D.L. Brown, Jr., and A.R. Buckpitt:** Evidence for cytochrome P-450 mediated metabolism in the bronchiolar damage of naphthalene. *Chem. Biol. Interact. 40*:287–303 (1982).
25. **Jenne, J.W., T.K. Shaughnessy, W.S. Druz, C.J. Manfredi, and R.E. Vestal:** In vivo functional antagonism between isoproterenol and bronchoconstrictants in the dog. *J. Appl. Physiol. 63*:812–819 (1987).
26. **Hempel, A., T. Noll, A. Muhs, and H.M. Piper:** Functional antagonism between cAMP and cGMP on permeability of coronary endothelial monolayers. *Am. J. Physiol. Heart Circ. Physiol. 270*:H1264–H1271 (1996).
27. **Bouchard, M., R.C. Brunet, D. Pierre-Olivier, and G. Carrier:** A biologically based dynamic model for predicting the disposition of methanol and its metabolites in animals and humans. *Toxicol. Sci. 64*:169–184 (2001).
28. **Howland, M.A.:** Antidotes in depth: Ethanol. In *Goldfrank's Toxicologic Emergencies.* Goldfrank, L.R., N.E. Flomenbaum, N.A. Lewin, R.S. Weisman, M.A. Howland, and R.S. Hoffman (eds.). Norwalk, CT: Appleton & Lange, 2002. pp. 995–998.
29. **Jacobsen, D. and M.E. McMartin:** Antidotes for methanol and ethylene glycol poisoning. *Clin. Toxicol. 35*:127–143 (1997).
30. **Inoue, O., et al.:** Urinary t,t-muconic acid as an indicator of exposure to benzene. *Br. J. Ind. Med. 46*:122–127 (1989).
31. **Lin, Y.S., et al.:** Albumin adducts of electrophilic benzene metabolites in benzene-exposed and control workers. *Environ. Health Perspect. 115*:28–34 (2007).
32. **Tardif, R., S. Lapare, G.L. Plaa, and J. Brodeur:** Effect of simultaneous exposure to toluene and xylene on their respective biological exposure indices in humans. *Int. Arch. Occup. Environ. Health 63*:279–284 (1991).
33. **Uaki, H., et al.:** Dose-dependent suppression of toluene metabolism by isopropyl alcohol and methyl ethyl ketone after experimental exposure of rats. *Toxicol. Lett. 81*:229–234 (1995).
34. **Tonacchera, M., et al.:** Relative potencies and additivity of perchlorate, thiocyanate, nitrate, and iodide on the inhibition of radioactive iodide uptake by the human sodium iodide symporter. *Thyroid 14*:1012–1019 (2004).
35. **Deutsche Forschungsgemeinschaft:** *List of MAK and BAT values 2006: Commission for the Investigation of Health Hazards of Chemical Compounds in the Work Area.* New York: Wiley-VCH, 2006.

Section 4

Application of Toxicological Information

Chapter 23

Exposure Assessment

By Coreen A. Robbins, PhD, CIH, Lonie J. Swenson, CIH, and Susan Arnold, CIH

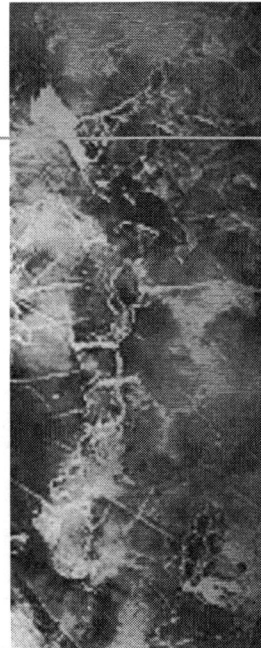

Introduction

Exposure assessment has been defined generally as "identification and evaluation of the human population exposed to a toxic agent, describing its composition and size, as well as the type, magnitude, frequency, route and duration of exposure."[1] Exposure can be defined as the occurrence of a 'receptor' in the presence of an 'agent' of interest, with direct contact of the outer boundary or the receptor (*e.g.*, skin) by the agent in some manner. That is, exposure occurs when the receptor is in contact with an environmental media (air, water, etc.) containing the agent. It is therefore possible for an agent to be *present* in the environment with no exposure occurring because the receptor and agent are not in contact (*e.g.*, liquid chemicals stored in a sealed container). *Exposure* is distinct from *dose*, the latter defined as the amount of the agent actually absorbed by the receptor, or receptor target tissue or organ. It is therefore possible for *exposure* to an agent to occur without any subsequent *dose*. *Assessment* is generally the evaluation and measurement of the potential for, or actual exposure. Note that exposure assessments are also used to estimate dose by extrapolation from environmental measurements; and measures of receptor dose (*e.g.*, via biological exposure indices) are used to estimate exposure.

Exposure assessment (EA) is at the heart of industrial hygiene and is critical to the recognition, evaluation and control of hazardous exposures in the workplace, but is also applicable to exposures in the general environment, including homes and outdoors.[2,3] Recognizing hazards is a first approximation of exposure. Evaluating hazards is the act of quantifying and qualifying potential exposures now recognized. Control of hazards is impossible without some assessment of exposure. A discussion of EA is appropriate in a toxicology text for industrial hygienists because the two are inextricably linked: "Understanding the underlying toxicological relationships — such as between workplace exposure and internal dose, target-organ dose, pre-clinical effects, and clinical effects — is fundamental to exposure assessment."[4] In practice, this means that the industrial hygienist must appreciate the potential for adverse health effects for likely

Outcome Competencies

- After completion of this chapter, the reader should be able to:
- Define exposure assessment
- Describe the processes involved in exposure assessment in industrial hygiene.
- Identify fundamental types of exposure assessment and when they are used.
- Discuss the significance of toxicology and exposure routes in exposure assessment.
- Explain the importance of integrating toxicology data and principals with exposure assessment in industrial hygiene.
- Identify at least two reference sources for information about sampling and analytical methods used to measure exposures.

Key Terms

area sample, biomonitoring, Biological Exposure Indices (BEI®), ceiling limit, exposure assessment, modeling, personal sample, physical-chemical models, risk assessment, short-term exposure limit, Threshold Limit Values® (TLV®)

Key Topics

1. Process of Exposure Assessment
2. Dermal Exposure Assessment
3. Inhalation Exposure Assessment
4. Computational Modeling Exposure Assessment
5. Measurement of Exposure
6. Sample Duration
7. Exposure Assessment Research Needs

exposure scenarios in order to know when and if they should monitor exposures or take some other action.

Exposure assessment is considered by some to be a profession in its own right, with its origin credited to industrial hygiene.[5] Expanding from its use by industrial hygienists in the occupational setting, it is now used to examine human contact with toxicants found in the personal or community environments. Although the science to conduct EAs is within the continuum that follows the movement of a toxicant from its source through to an ultimate health effects, industrial hygiene takes this a step further to devise and implement reduction or elimination of exposure.

Exposure assessments are also used in the fields of risk assessment, epidemiology, and toxicology.[3] The activities and goals of EA vary in these different disciplines. In the field of risk assessment, EA may include estimates of exposures from sources in all environments, home, work and school. The main objective of EA in a risk assessment is to determine the source, type, magnitude, and duration of contact with the agent of interest.[6] In epidemiology, the goal is typically to define exposures for jobs, tasks, or job categories in order to compare effects among workers experiencing different levels of exposures. Toxicologists use EA data to estimate doses, and to elucidate the relationship between exposures and health effects. Exposure assessment in industrial hygiene (IH) encompasses many activities, but the measurement of exposure is often the central activity. Industrial hygienists use EA data typically for risk assessment and management in the occupational environment. The ultimate goal of IH exposure assessment is to prevent or stop exposures that could result in adverse health effects.

Occupational Exposure Assessment

Occupational exposure assessment (OEA) is a process which includes identifying and characterizing workplace exposures; evaluating their significance; and developing exposure estimates for individuals or groups of workers.[4] The assessment process is based on measurement and evaluation of characteristics of the work environment and may involve hypothesis testing. Occupational exposure has been defined as "the act or the condition of being subjected (as a result of work) to a chemical, physical, or biological agent, or to a specific process, practice, behavior, or work organization."[4] Exposure refers to the presence of an agent that contacts the body or is experienced by the worker, and dose refers to the amount of the agent absorbed or retained by the body.

Occupational exposure assessment (OEA) is defined as: "the application of a body of knowledge to determine the relevant characteristics of one or more environmental factors that pose health and safety risks to workers."[4] Although safety-related factors are important aspects of EAs, since this chapter is within a toxicology context, safety-related factors will not be addressed.

Occupational Exposure Assessment and Toxicology

Fundamental to OEA is an understanding of the underlying toxicological relationships between workplace exposure and internal dose, and target-organ dose, pre-clinical and clinical effects.[4] Exposure assessment data for substances must be combined with toxicity information to determine the potential for health risk. This is because health risks from exposure are directly related to the exposure level and the toxicity of the substance. For example, exposure to high concentrations of a substance of low inherent toxicity may not pose any risk; conversely, exposure to low concentrations of a substance of high toxicity may pose a risk of adverse health effects.

Exposure Assessment and Risk Assessment

The interaction between the toxicity and the exposure is key to determining health risk. In this way, EA and risk assessment (RA) are overlapping and inseparable for the industrial hygienist.[2]

Exposure assessment is considered to be one step in the process of risk assessment. It includes[7]:

- hazard identification,
- dose-response analysis,
- exposure assessment, and
- risk characterization and management

However, it is also the case that EA for the industrial hygienist involves hazard identification, dose-response analysis, and risk characterization. The IH goal of preventing or stopping potentially harmful exposures is a risk management activity. Risk management is predicated on RAs, which are in turn driven by the quality of the industrial hygienist's EA. Historically, RA has been associated with federal agencies and environmental RA for the general population. Comprehensive industrial hygiene EA is essentially an RA in the occupational environment for individual workers or groups of workers, or occupational risk assessments.

Although the classical industrial hygiene OEA involves agents in the industrial workplace, the scope of OEA has become much broader over the last fifteen to twenty years because of changes in technology and increased attention to non-industrial work environments.[7] Beyond the industrial environment, EA skills and other IH knowledge and concepts have been transported to also address problems in "indoor, non-industrial environments" such as commercial buildings, homes and schools.

Process of Exposure Assessment

Exposure assessment in industrial hygiene is a large topic and the subject of entire books. It is central to the IH program and supports all of its elements. (See Figure 23.1)[2] The AIHA has published a "Generic Exposure Assessment Standard" which calls on OSHA to adopt such a standard.[8] The details of the

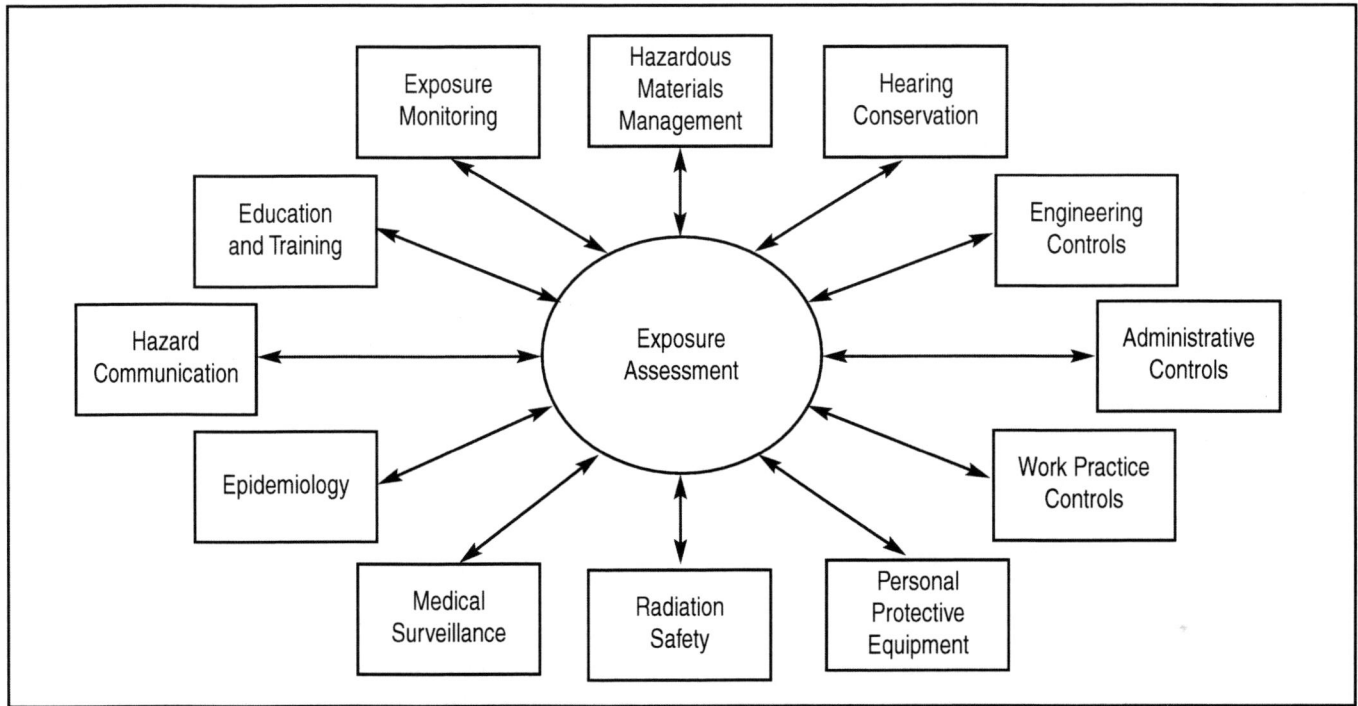

Figure 23.1 — Exposure assessment's central role in industrial hygiene.[2]

steps in an OEA vary among authors and authorities; however, all versions include the same essential elements.[2,8,9] The steps include establishing an EA strategy, basic characterization of the workplace and hazards present, exposure measurement prioritization and monitoring, interpretation of EA data and institution of health hazard controls, reporting, and reassessment or re-evaluation. (See Figure 23.2)[4] In reality, these steps do not necessarily occur in order in the tidy boxes that are assigned to them. The steps overlap and intertwine, and iterations between the steps occur. The following is adapted from these sources and others as noted.[2,8]

Start

An EA strategy is established. The initial EA strategy defines and documents the role of the industrial hygienist, and the exposure assessment program and goals.[2]

Basic Characterization

This is essentially an inventory of workplace, including the worker population, and physical, chemical and biological hazards present.[8] Basic characterization and qualitative assessment and prioritization are needed to narrow the range of possible substances and workers to monitor. It is rarely feasible to monitor all compounds in the workplace. Basic data gathered include information about the jobs and tasks performed, materials used, processes, and controls in place.[2]

This step usually includes developing groups of worker who are thought to be similarly exposed.[9] These homogeneous exposure groups (HEGs) are " a group of employees who experienced agent exposure similar enough that monitoring agent exposure of any worker in the group provides data useful for predicting exposure of the remaining workers."[10]

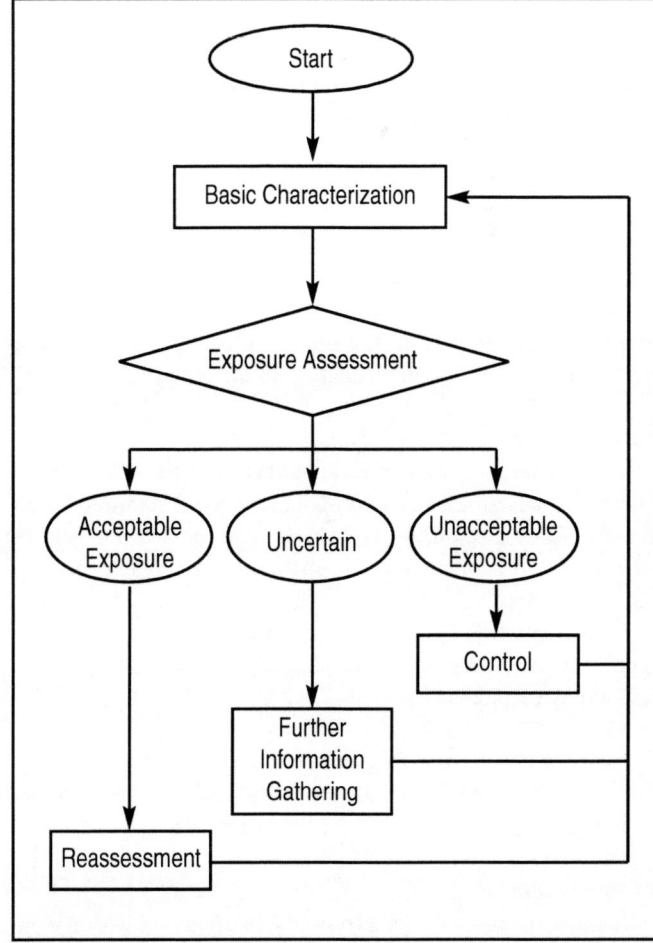

Figure 23.2 — Exposure assessment: the overall process (adapted from[4]).

Exposure Assessment

<u>Qualitative Exposure Assessment and Prioritization.</u> Information collected through basic characterization is used to determine where EA is not needed, where it is needed, and the priority for assessing the areas that require attention.[8]

<u>Exposure Monitoring.</u> Measurements are carried out to characterize the magnitude and variability of worker exposures that cannot be assessed with qualitative information. Exposure monitoring is conducted to provide baseline data, but is also used to evaluate workplace controls, ensure regulatory compliance, and inform management and workers.

Exposure monitoring may be conducted for compliance with occupational exposure limits (OELs), implementation of an IH program, epidemiologic studies, complaint or problem investigation, worker compensation/toxic tort cases, task/source investigations, risk assessment and management, and evaluation of changes in the workplace.[9] Although the reasons for exposure monitoring appear to be different, the questions in most cases is the same: what is the exposure, what is the potential dose, and can it have an adverse affect at exposure conditions found in the workplace. The complexity increases as more substances are present in the workplace. See Chapter 22, "Toxicology of Complex Chemical Mixtures" for more information.

Exposure monitoring is at the center of EA and is the main focus of this chapter. Although methods exist to estimate exposures using agent information and models, exposure monitoring provides input data for these models and is needed to validate the models and calculated exposures.

Interpretation and Decision Making, Health Hazard Control

All of the information from the first three steps is used to determine the acceptability of worker exposures. Prioritized control strategies are implemented for unacceptable exposures. Industrial hygiene control programs are changed and adjusted based on the information gleaned from the previous EA steps.

Further Information Gathering

Additional exposure monitoring or health effects data are collected to resolve uncertain exposures. Exposure monitoring may include personal monitoring or biological monitoring. Mathematical modeling technique may be used to estimate exposures for new processes and products. It may be necessary to research and collect toxicological and epidemiological data for some agents. Consultation with occupational physicians and toxicologists may be indicated.

Recommendations and Reporting

Recommendations are made based on all information and interpretation, and documented for future reference.

Re-evaluation

Reassessments may need to be made after process or work practice changes, or introduction of new hazards. Similar exposure groups may need to be updated after changes that cause rearrangement of these exposure groups that alter their exposure profile.

Exposure Monitoring

Exposure is defined as "an event consisting of contact at a boundary between a human and the environment at a specific contaminant concentration for a specified interval of time."[11] Contact occurs at an exposure surface and over an exposure period. Exposure monitoring is intended to measure this event in a way that informs about potential dose. Exposure can be illustrated mathematically as:

$$E = \int_{t^1}^{t^2} C(t)\, dt$$

where E is exposure, C(t) is a concentration that varies with time, integrated from the start to the end of exposure. Exposure has dimension of mass times time, divided by volume. For example, min•mg/m^3, could represent a 60 minutes exposure to a chemical vapor in air. The amount is related to the potential dose by multiplying exposure by the contact rate, such as breathing rate, food intake rate, etc. Industrial hygiene exposure measurements are usually expressed as concentration per volume, averaged for a standard period of time, such as eight hours for an 8-hour, time-weighted average (TWA) or 15 minutes for a short-term exposure limit (STEL).

In the context of human toxicology, the assessment is a measurement of the potential dose to the human body. While the toxicologist ideally desires a measurement of how much of substance "A" is reaches the target organ, the industrial hygienist most often measures the amount of substance "A" only in the environment. The toxicologist must then extrapolate that measurement to an estimate of delivered dose. Industrial hygiene related biological exposure indices (BEI®s) are available for some compounds, whereby the dose is estimated from toxicants or byproducts found in exhaled air or bodily fluids or tissues. In many cases, the exposure concentration is inferred from the BEI measurement. However, BEI®s are less common than environmental measures and are less useful to the IH in preventing exposure and determining the environmental source and means to control it because BEI®s generally do not provide information about the source(s) of exposure.

In order for environmental monitoring to represent human exposure, the assessment method must be designed to measure substances in a way that mimics human exposure, e.g., air samples are collected to evaluate inhalation exposures and surface samples are collected to evaluate dermal exposure. If exposures are measured this way, they are not a measure of dose, but they can sometimes be used to estimate the dose received. The dose calculation takes into account exposure level and duration, and includes factors such as breathing rate and fraction retained for inhalation exposure, or absorption rate and skin area exposed for dermal exposure.

In keeping with the goal to measure agents in a way that is representative of human exposure, samples are collected on or near the individual worker rather than in the general area of the worker. The preference for personal versus general area samples comes from the need to collect samples that mimic exposure for a person performing a particular job or task. Air samples collected in the "breathing zone" are thought to more accurately reflect individual exposure than "general area" samples. Skin patches collected from areas of exposed skin better represent exposure than environmental surface samples. As sample methods are less reflective of exposure routes, for example, as with general area or source sampling, these measurements are usually less accurate representatives of exposure or dose. General area measurements can be used to estimate the exposure of bystanders or co-workers who have no direct contact with the substance but work in the area of those working with it directly.

Measured environmental exposure levels are not always correlated with dose. For example, total dust measurements likely include non-respirable particles that in some cases do not add to dose, but contribute significant mass to the sample. Many particle methods require the collection of respirable dust to account for this.

Exposure assessment should be framed with the following questions:

- Does exposure to the substance have the potential to affect employee health?
- What is the substance of interest and where does it occur? Is it a particle, gas or vapor?
- What are the routes of exposure? Can it be inhaled, ingested and/or absorbed through the skin, or some combination?
- What assessment methods exist for the substance? Is there a NIOSH or other validated method available?
- What exposure standard or guideline will be used to interpret results? Is there a health-risk based OSHA PEL, AIHA WEEL, or ACGIH TLV®? If not, what criteria will be used to interpret the results of assessment?

Exposure measurement methods can be generally grouped into the categories of inhalation, dermal, and biological exposure assessment. However, there are substances for which more than one route of exposure is possible. For example, exposure to benzene can occur through inhalation and dermal exposure routes. There are no sampling methods to directly measure exposure by ingestion; measures of surface contamination are used to estimate the possible exposure via hand-to-mouth, and ingestion exposure would be included in biological exposure indices.

Exposures can also be assessed using computational programs that "model" or estimate exposures using existing exposure data, or source strength and related data. Exposure modeling techniques use data from all assessment methods and can be applied to all routes of exposures.

Measurement of Exposure via Inhalation

Assessment of potential inhalation exposure is probably the most common and important measurement activity for the IH. It is the primary route of exposure for a vast array of agents in particulate and vapor form. So inhalation exposure assessment often includes measurements of aerosols of particles or gases and vapors.

Aerosols are generally categorized by the physical form of the substance and the method of generation.[12] Particles that may be aerosolized may be in the form of dusts, fumes, or mists. Dusts may be comprised of particles or fibers. Although there is no strict classification of aerosols, the following list of terms corresponds to common usage; adapted from Hinds[12]:

- Aerosols: A suspension of solid or liquid particles in a gas. Particle size ranges from 0.001 to over 100 μm.
- Dust: A solid particle aerosol formed by mechanical disintegration of a parent material, such as by crushing or grinding.
- Fume: A solid-particle aerosol produced by the condensation of vapors or gaseous combustion products. Particle size is generally less than 1 μm. Note that this definition is different from the popular use of the term to refer to any noxious contaminant in the atmosphere.
- Smoke: A visible aerosol resulting from incomplete combustion. Particles may be solid or liquid and are usually less than 1 μm in diameter.
- Mist: A liquid-particle aerosol formed by condensation or atomization. Particle size ranges from sub-micrometer to about 20 μm.
- Fog: A visible mist.
- Smog Photochemical reaction products: usually combined with water vapor. Particles are generally less than 1 or 2 μm. The term is derived from the words smoke and fog.
- Cloud: A visible aerosol with defined boundaries.

Particles, non-Fibrous

Dust particles may be comprised of minerals (asbestos, quartz), and other elements (magnesium, lead), organic/biological material (fungal spores, bacteria, pollen, grain dust). The toxicological effect of the particle is determined by its size and physical/chemical properties. Particles are often described in terms of their aerodynamic equivalent diameter (AED). This is the diameter of a sphere that would have the same value of a particular physical property as that of the irregular particle. The shape is usually ignored, although long, thin fibers are treated as simplified non-spherical shapes in different orientations.[12] The size and shape of the particle determines if it can be inhaled, and where and how in the respiratory system deposition will occur. Larger particles (>10 μm) deposit in the nose, mouth, and upper respiratory tract by the processes of impaction, sedimentation and diffusion. Particles <5 μm AED deposit mainly in the tracheobronchial region. Smaller particles (<2.5 μm AED) can be deposited in the lower airways including the alveoli. Once deposited, the physical/chemical properties of the particle determine whether it will dissolve or be vulnerable to clearance mechanisms (e.g., macrophages). Any mechanical irritation or deposition of chemicals into the respiratory system will be dependent on these properties of the particles.

Exposure assessment of particles involves measurement of mass concentration (mg/m^3) or particle number (usually, number /cm^3). Whether the particle mass or number is measured depends ideally on the toxicological mechanism of action. The number of particles may be of interest for small insoluble particles such as asbestos fibers that are found in great number for relatively low mass; or for extremely small particles with low mass and large surface areas such as nanoparticles. The mass of particles may be of more interest if the particles contain or are made of agents that are soluble in the tracheal-bronchial region and lung, since few large particles will contribute greater total mass than numerous small particles.

Measurement of mass concentration is usually done by collecting particles on sample media and weighing the amount collected. To determine particle numbers, particles are collected on media, such as micropore filters, and counting the particles using light or electronic microscopy. Often, particles are counted depending on some type of size selection criteria. For example, the NIOSH Method 7400 asbestos fiber counting method "A" rules specifies counting only fibers longer than 5 μm.[13] Real time particle-counts are measured indirectly using electronic particle counters that employ techniques such as light-scattering technology.

Assessment of exposure to particles, whether by mass or number, often needs to be tailored to measure particles that preferentially deposit in the part of the respiratory tract that is important for the site of action for that particular dust. Methods are available for dusts take into account the need for size-selective sampling. For example, use of the TLV® for silica requires the use of a cyclone collection device because the guideline is specific for respirable particulate mass (0.25 mg/m^3).[14] The cyclone allows collection of dust that is in the respirable size range. For some dusts the total mass of inhalable dust is more important because deposition and health effect occurs in all parts of the respiratory tree. Or, exposure standards have been developed using total dust measurements. For example, some wood dusts have been implicated in nasal cancer, so an estimate of inhalable particles is needed.[15]

The combination of particle size and chemical composition is measured in some cases. This is done when sampling for silica under the OSHA Standard for silica.[16] The OSHA standard requires adherence to an exposure limit that takes into account the mass of respirable dust and the proportion of certain types of silica (cristobalite, tridymite) in the dust. Note that the current TLV® for crystalline silica (0.025 mg/m^3) is based simply on the mass of respirable dust.[14]

Fibers

Fibers are generally defined as particles with a diameter to length ratio of greater than 3 to 1. Respirable fibers have AEDs in the range of 5 to 10 μm, with diameters less than 3 μm.

The lung deposition, retention and health effects of fiber exposure are dependent on fiber characteristics including fiber size and durability.[17] Small fibers (< 2 μm long) are considered to be nuisance dusts, whereas respirable fibers longer than 5 μm have the potential to cause disease.[18] Size-selective sampling methods for fibers were introduced in the 1960's. Prior to the development of these methods, all sizes and shapes of particles, fibers or not, were counted as particles. Results were reported in terms of "mmpcf" million particles per cubic foot. Methods for selectively sampling fibers evolved as the realization that health effects of fibers are different from other particles. These methods generally involve counting particles that meet the criteria for a fiber. Typically, fibers are collected on filters and the filter contents are examined using optical microscopes. These methods do not distinguish between fiber types. SEM and TEM methods are used when there is need to know the identity of the fiber (asbestos or fiberglass) and/or the chemical composition of the fibers present. A common method for collecting and analyzing asbestos fibers in the NIOSH Method 7400.[13] Counting rules dictate that only those fibers greater than 5 μm are counted. If the "B" rules of the method are used, then fibers with diameters over 3.5 μm are not counted.

Biological Particles

Many sampling methods exist for collecting airborne bacteria and fungi. The most commonly employed method is the Andersen sampler. This device uses impaction to collect bacterial and fungal spores on nutrient agar. The six-stage Andersen bioaerosol sampler allows size-selective sampling of particles in the size ranges of 0.65–1.1, 1.1–2.1, 2.1–3.3, 3.3–4.7, 4.7–7.0 and >7.0 micrometers, AED.[19] Collected spores are grown to visible colony size, and the colonies are identified and counted. Other methods for collecting fungal spores, "spore trap" samplers, are impaction method collection devices. The collection media is usually a sticky surface, upon which spores are trapped from the moving air stream. The sample is examined for the presence of spores. Since spores don't need to be viable to be counted, this method will detect both viable (culturable) and non-viable (non-culturable) spores. However, there is no currently validated NIOSH method for this type of sampler and the analytical variability is unknown.

Gases & Vapors

A vapor is defined as a gas derived from evaporation or sublimation of a substance that is a liquid or solid at "room temperature." A gas is simply a substance found only in the gaseous state at "room temperature." For simplicity, the term "gas" will be used instead of "gases and vapors." Unlike particle samples, sampling methods for gases are not selective for the likelihood of deposition at the target organ. The sample is collected to determine the concentration of the gas in the environment. Although the concentration measured can be used as a surrogate for dose, the dose in different organs and tissues is dependent on the bioactive properties of the substance and human factors such as breathing rate. Although most methods are designed to collect a single substance, often the sampled environment contains numerous compounds. The chapter on complex mixtures includes discussion of these situations. Some issues involved with mixtures include synergistic health effects, and sample interference or augmentation.

Many methods are available for assessing the concentration of vapors and gases. From the standpoint of the toxicology of the materials being sampled, the sampling method often depends on the time it takes for adverse effects of the substance to appear. Sampling methods are generally one of two types, one that provides instantaneous analysis or display of gas concentration, or one that integrates gas concentration of a period of time. The first type is called a "real time," "direct reading" instrument. Direct reading instruments measure exposure as it occurs, or in "real time." These are useful with substances that require continuous monitoring and/or produce toxicity in a short time frame such, as carbon monoxide; or for capturing peak exposures that may be harmful, such as a high solvent exposure during a short duration task. For example, real-time, direct-reading instruments are usually used to measure carbon monoxide (CO) exposure since instruments can specifically detect CO, and immediate adverse effects are possible. Real-time instruments are also used to measure compounds that are potentially explosive, since the level of these compounds is something you need to know immediately if their presence is anticipated. Explosions are not a problem from the standpoint of toxicity, but they can result in adverse health effects.

Although some real-time instruments have probes that are specific to certain chemicals, some are non-specific and respond to a large number of substances. For many compounds, direct reading instruments are not available that allow identification and quantification of individual compounds. For example, it is not possible to isolate perchlorethylene concentration using an instrument that responds to chlorinated solvents. A substance that is present at potentially toxic levels can be missed if it cannot be distinguished from other substances in the environment. Typically, the user has to assume that entire concentration measured is that of the substance of interest.

To accurately identify and quantify airborne concentration typically requires that they be collected in or on some sample media, and the sample is later analyzed with an instrument in a laboratory. Gas samples can be collected in a container, such as a Tedlar bag or Suma canister, or chemicals present are captured from the air passing through an adsorbent or chemical-reactive material in a tube (e.g., activated charcoal, silica gel). These samplers are often compound-specific, and can be selected to measure the substance of interest. For examples, solvent vapors or mixtures of solvent vapors are often collected on adsorbent charcoal tubes; the sample is later processed using a gas chromatograph (GC) or GC with a mass spectrophotometer (MS). This technique can often provide identification and quantification of the solvents vapors present in the tested environment. For example, air samples for benzene are collected on charcoal tubes and are later subjected to analysis with the GC. If the exposure to benzene is associated with gasoline, other related compounds, such at toluene, ethyl-benzene and xylene, "BTEX" can be quantified in this analysis. These types of sample integrate the concentration of the substance during the sample interval, so some data about short-term high and low exposure are lost.

A wide array of methods and instruments are available for use is assessing exposures to gases and vapors. The method or instrument selected will be dependent on the type of gas or vapor expected. For detailed information on available methods and sampling instruments, the reader should consult available resources such as the ACGIH *Air Sampling Instruments* text[20] and the *NIOSH Manual of Analytical Methods*.[21]

Sample Duration and Toxicology

Many exposure standards and guidelines are based on an 8-hour workday exposure. Comparisons to such standards and guidelines using samples that reflects the 8-hr, time-weighted average (TWA) is usually the most desirable. Sometimes sample data are limited to short-term samples, and the industrial hygienist has to estimate the intervening exposure based on work practices. For example, if a worker uses benzene-containing solvents to clean metal engine parts for only a total of one hour per day, the exposure during the remaining seven hours is assumed to be zero (in the absence of other data). Computation of 8-hour TWA is described in the ACGIH TLV® booklet.[22]

ACGIH includes Short-Term Exposure Limits (STELs) along with the TLV® for some substances. The STEL is a 15-minute TWA exposure level that should not be exceeded at any time during a workday. These limits are designed to limit short-term excursions for substances that could be harmful due to a short-term exposure, even though averaging out the short exposure over eight hours would be below the 8-hr TWA. Ceiling limits (CL) are levels that should not be exceeded at any time during the workday due to the potential for adverse effects even if the exposure is very brief. For example, glutaraldehyde has only a relatively low ceiling limit (0.05 ppm) because it is an irritant at low levels, and is a also sensitizer.[23] Thus, it follows that toxicological effects determine the guideline or standard exposure interval, which in turn will determine the sample duration.

In some cases, both short term samples and full-shift samples are indicated by exposure standards/guidelines that have both short term and 8-hour TWA exposure values. For example, benzene standard has both an 8-hr TWA TLV® (0.5ppm), and a STEL (2.5 ppm). In the example of the cleaning metal parts with benzene-containing solvents, it may be necessary to collect 15-minute samples during the actual cleaning activity. Longer duration samples may need to determine the 8-hour time-weighted exposure if, for example, the worker is also near others using benzene-containing solvents.[24] In all cases, it is critical to consult the applicable exposure guideline or standard to determine the sample duration.

Dermal Exposure Assessment

Exposure to chemicals in the workplace can occur through the skin. This is one of the most common ways of contacting chemicals, yet it is a frequently overlooked exposure route when assessing workplace exposures. There is a general lack of knowledge and understanding of how dermal exposures occur and how to quantify these exposures.

Chemicals that come in contact with the skin may remain on the skin's surface or they can be absorbed into the body. Once a chemical penetrates the skin, it can be carried to other parts of the body by the blood and lymph systems. Other organs in the body can be the target for chemicals absorbed through the skin. For example, organophosphate pesticides are readily absorbed through the skin and the target organ is the nervous system. See Chapter 6, "Dermal Toxicology" for a detailed discussion.

The type of chemical and the form it is in will influence whether a chemical will be absorbed. Generally, inorganic chemicals in a dry or powder form are poorly absorbed through intact skin. Organic chemicals in a powder form are less likely to be absorbed than the same chemical in an aqueous solution or suspension. Organic chemicals in an oily solution or solvent form are more likely to be absorbed than aqueous solutions of the same chemicals. Similarly, ionized solutes are less well absorbed than non-ionized substances and lower molecular weight chemicals are less well absorbed than higher molecular weight chemicals. Chemicals with a higher affinity for the lipid phase (fat soluble chemicals) will be absorbed through the skin more readily.

Dermal Exposure Assessment Methods

Dermal exposure assessment is a complex issue. Various models have been proposed for quantifying dermal exposures but validation of the models is limited. At best, many of the models realistically provide only a qualitative or semi-quantitative assessment of the exposure and dose because of the data gaps that exist and assumptions that are required. Currently, there is no general agreement on how to measure skin contamination, limited data on absorption of chemicals across the skin (percutaneous absorption), limited data on the potential for skin contamination based on workers' activities and behaviors, and no recognized metric for interpreting dermal exposures.

The practicing industrial hygienist does have some tools to use in evaluating dermal exposures and conducting dermal exposure assessments. Recognition of the potential for dermal exposure is the first step in the dermal exposure assessment. The industrial hygienist should have knowledge of the types and forms of chemicals present and their potential for dermal exposure. The "skin" notation on the threshold limit values (TLVs®) identifies chemicals with the potential for absorption or toxicity via the skin route of exposure. However, this notation does not include the potential for chemicals to cause skin damage and dermatitis. The OSHA Technical Links internet site includes "Chemical Sampling Information" which lists substances that have a potential for ingestion toxicity, skin absorption, and/or a hazardous effect on skin (see "Health Factors," OSHA, 2007). Material safety data sheets (MSDSs) may provide useful information to assess the importance of the dermal exposure pathway. Other resources include ACGIH's Biological Exposure Index® (BEI®) and supporting data.

The type of exposure, the degree of contact, and the work activities that can contribute to a dermal exposure should be evaluated. Is the potential dermal exposure episodic such as from occasional mixing or splashes? Is the potential for dermal exposure ongoing from immersion of hands or arms in the chemical? Can the chemical be deposited on the skin from mist or transferred from work or other surfaces to the worker's skin? Can chemicals soak through clothing or gloves or be trapped on the skin by the worker's clothing? What is the form of the chemical? How much body surface is potentially affected? How frequent is the exposure? What is the duration of contact? What type or personal protective equipment (PPE) is used? Worker-specific factors such as condition of the skin should also be assessed.

Rating schemes for estimating dermal exposures are available that incorporate the qualitative considerations discussed above.[25] The ranking factors include the dermal contact area, dermal concentration of the chemical, dermal contact frequency, dermal retention time, and the dermal penetration potential.

There are also methods for measuring chemicals in the work environment that have the potential to be absorbed through the skin. Before instituting any sampling program, the industrial hygienist should have developed a hypothesis regarding the potential exposure, develop a sampling plan that will answer that hypothesis, and understand how the resultant data are to be used.

One of the simplest sampling techniques is source sampling of surfaces in the work area. Wipe sampling (also called swipe sampling or smear sampling) can be used to identify potentially hazardous conditions and to evaluate the effectiveness of housekeeping, work practices, decontamination programs, and the use of PPE. There is limited guidance on acceptable surface contamination amounts. Wipe samples do not assess health risk. However, they can identify areas where special cleaning practices are needed or not needed, how effective PPE use is (for example wipe sampling inside gloves or coveralls), or to assess how work practices may transport chemicals in the work environment. The OSHA Technical Manual available on the OSHA web site provides information on media and techniques for wipe sampling including wiping surfaces with filters, gauze squares, charcoal-impregnated pads, or direct-reading colorimetric sampling on surfaces.[26] Wipe sampling techniques can also be used to obtain wipe samples directly from skin surfaces.

A second type of sampling for dermal exposures is the use of patches. This is a passive form of sampling. The purpose of patch sampling is to estimate the amount of a specific chemical deposited on the skin or clothing. Absorbent patches are attached to the worker's skin or clothing prior to exposure. They are then removed at the completion of exposure and analyzed for the chemical of interest. The amount of chemical detected can then be used to estimate the exposure to the surface area of the corresponding body part. The method can have errors associated with it. For example, if a single splash hits the patch directly the exposure may be overestimated; whereas if splashes miss the patch entirely, then the exposure may be underestimated. Similar to patch sampling, whole body sampling can be conducted with workers wearing a suit that is then analyzed for the chemical of interest. The whole body suit sampling technique has largely been used in evaluating pesticide exposures. Soutar et al.

provide a discussion on the use of patches and whole body suits in assessing dermal exposure.[27]

A third method of evaluating dermal exposure is the use of fluorescent tracers that are added to the chemical of interest. The deposition and retention of the chemical on skin surfaces is then measured directly using ultraviolet fluorescence imaging detection equipment.

Dermal exposures can also be measured indirectly using biological monitoring methods. Although these methods can be used to detect compounds absorbed through the skin, they cannot distinguish the amount due to skin versus inhalation exposure. For example, benzene is absorbed through the skin, and the TLV® for benzene has a "skin" notation; however, the BEI® for benzene can be used only to estimate total benzene exposure, not just that exposure due to dermal contact.[28] In situations where inhalation exposure potential is known, or is limited by respiratory protection, the BEI® could be used to estimate absorption due to dermal exposure.

The methods and limitations of some of the methods and models for assessing risks of dermal exposures in the workplace have been recently critically reviewed,[29] and extensive discussions of dermal exposure assessment methods and models are available in the exposure assessment chapter of the U.S. EPA document, *Dermal Exposure Assessment: Principles and Applications*;[30] and in Warren et al.[31] Practical information sources for assessing dermal exposure have been compiled by Hebisch.[32]

Biological Exposure Assessment (eg., BEI®s)

Biological exposure measurements are one step closer to measuring absorbed dose. Biological monitoring has been defined as "the measurement and assessment of agents or their metabolites either in tissues, secreta, excreta, expired air or any combination of these to evaluate exposure and health risk compared to an appropriate reference."[33] Thus, these measurements may be of substances or their byproducts in exhaled air, urine and blood, etc., and allow an estimate of absorbed dose to the worker.[34] Biological "effects monitoring" is included in the general category of biologic monitoring. This can include such measures such as pulmonary function, etc. Biological monitoring has been used to successfully to assess the renal effects of cadmium, lead effects on hemoglobin synthesis, and organophosphate effects on cholinesterase activity.[33] These are well-validated and widely used.

Biomonitoring is useful in determining exposed groups and estimating delivered dose. Biomonitoring has also been used in the diagnosis of diseases that are exposure-related. This method requires that there is specificity for the substance in the analysis methods, metabolism, and source. Analytical specificity requires that the method used to measure the substance is specific for that substance. Metabolic specificity means that the substance measured is derived from the parent compound, and does not have contributions from other substances. Since biological monitoring cannot identify the source of a substance, source specificity means that the majority of the substance of interest is derived from the occupational source (or other expected source). Often exposures occur outside of the workplace, from the ambient air and from food and water. Thus, the comparison is made between individual levels and some reference level from the 'unexposed' population. For highly exposed workers, the differences from the population will be large and easily detected, but if the difference is small, than this method is not useful in distinguishing occupational exposure.

Quantitative exposure assessment using biomarkers is possible for a number of compounds for which the main route of exposure is inhalation. The accuracy of the exposure estimate varies among different chemicals. For example, exposure to styrene is well-described and results are uniform. But for other compounds, the relationship is less clear. For example, the relationship between demethylformamide exposure and the concentrations of its metabolite, methylhydroxymethylformamide in urine, have provided widely different results.[33] This may be due to dermal exposure or other causes. This is a major drawback of biomonitoring, in that it does not provide information about the route of exposure, but represents the total amount absorbed.

The half-life of the substance in the body largely determines the utility and frequency required for biomonitoring. The half-lives of substances varies widely, the half-life for mercury is about 60 days,[33] but the half-life for CO is about four hours in room air. For substance with half-lives shorter than two hours, biomonitoring is not often feasible. For half-lives of two to ten hours, a sample at the end of the work shift reflects exposure over the day. The shorter the half-life, the more frequent sampling must be to accurately represent exposure.

Biological monitoring is also a method used to measures effects of substances. For example, the cholinesterase activity in plasma and erythrocytes can be measured in cases where organophosphate insecticide exposure is suspected.[33] Effect biomarkers are not typically used to identify exposed populations. However, in some occupational settings, it may be possible to exclude other exposures that affect the biomarker, and exposures can be determined. Biomarkers have also been used to diagnosis exposure-related disease in individuals. For example, the presence of asbestos bodies is a biomarker of exposure to asbestos that is used to diagnose asbestosis and mesothelioma.[35]

Although biological exposure monitoring can be used to determine exposed individuals or populations, and to measure dose and effect, alone it cannot be used to identify the sources, routes, and duration of exposures.[36] For example, a BEI® is available for benzene, which could be used to estimate the benzene exposure for the worker using benzene-containing solvents to clean metal parts; however, the BEI® results would not allow the industrial hygienist to determine whether other jobs, tasks or processes contributed to the total exposure.[28] Therefore, biomarkers or biological exposure indices should be used to complement traditional industrial hygiene exposure assessment.[34]

Computational Methods of Exposure Assessment

Where comprehensive and scientifically valid exposure and risk assessments are required, the inclusion of modeling is a critical element of the EA process. Historically, the comprehensive assessment of exposures in a systematic framework has not occurred, and risks due to most personal chemical exposures have not been estimated.[37] Therefore, conclusions about the acceptability of exposure are often made without a formal assessment or collection of data.[38,39]

Modeling: An Integral Part of Exposure Assessment

Models are at the very core of the science of exposure assessment. Consider the four steps in the scientific process:

1. Define the hypothesis
2. Conduct experiments to test the hypothesis
3. Analyze the results
4. Draw conclusions and possibly form new hypotheses

An EA is initiated by the formation of a hypothesis about exposure, however consciously or subconsciously formulated. The hypothesis is in fact a model; it is a qualitative and quantitative expression of what the assessor believes to be taking place. Typically, to test the hypothesis, the industrial hygienist observes the tasks or activities related to the exposure and conducts experiments – taking physical measurements or monitoring exposures. The analytical results are then compared to the OEL. The comparison lets the assessor accept or reject the hypothesis and perhaps form new hypotheses. It also allows the assessor to calibrate their professional judgment about this kind of exposure scenario. Clearly there was some model applied when the hypothesis was formed. However, in many cases these hypotheses are never tested with experiments (exposure monitoring) due to lack of resources or because the industrial hygienist is confident of the outcome.[38,39]

Physical-Chemical Models

Physical-chemical models are used to predict contaminant concentrations in the environment using first principals (e.g., heat and mass transfer) and empirical observations. These models describe the concentration due to a source such as a leak or an open tank or mixing in an enclosed space.[40] These models need to be validated with measurements over a wide array of conditions.

Physical-chemical models allow the assessor to estimate historical exposures that cannot be readily be recreated. By adjusting the values for room dimensions, air exchange rates, emission rates and other determinants of exposure, the assessor can explore the effects on the airborne concentration in any hypothetical situation. Accordingly, physical-chemical models also lend themselves to estimating possible future exposure scenarios.

The models can be used deterministically; using single, point values for the variables in the algorithm and producing a single value for the airborne concentration. They can also be used probabilistically, in which ranges or distributions of values are used in place of single point values. For example, a single ventilation rate is used in a deterministic model, whereas a range of possible ventilation rates is used in the probabilistic model. The resulting output is a distribution of values of predicted airborne concentrations. The models presented here are neither elegant nor complete. They should be interpreted with careful consideration of the assumptions and inherent limitations.

The discussion of exposure modeling in this chapter is centered on inhalation. While models exist for assessing dermal and incidental oral exposures, they will not be discussed here.

Assumptions in Concentration Exposure Modeling

The models considered here do not estimate human exposure directly; rather, they estimate an airborne concentration. The link to human exposure is made through the association with the time spent in the environment. The use of this and other assumptions are important and necessary in exposure assessment. These assumptions must be understood and acceptable to the assessor before any conclusions can be drawn based on the model under consideration.

Modeling as a Tiered, Iterative Approach

In accordance with the precautionary principle, models are typically applied in a tiered, iterative manner. Conservative assumptions that are expected to over-estimate the true exposure are used in lieu of data; as more information becomes available, more complex and accurate models are applied. Tier I models include very simple screening level tools that require little data, time and expertise. Accordingly, the exposure estimate can be orders of magnitude greater than the 'true' exposure. Their utility lies in screening out *de minimis* exposures; for example, where the predicted exposure; albeit conservative, is less than the occupational exposure limit, the assessor can quickly conclude the exposure to be acceptable. (And document the basis for such a conclusion.)

<u>Tier I: Saturation or Zero Ventilation Model</u>

This model estimates the atmospheric concentration of an evaporating chemical in the gas or vapor phase, excluding misting. The model ignores any ventilation that may be in place and estimates a worst-case concentration. This algorithm predicts a worst-case airborne concentration that is less than the OEL so the hygienist is able to classify the exposure as acceptable based on a simple, very conservative model.

The equilibrium saturation concentration (C_{sat}) in volume parts of contaminant per million volume parts of air (ppm, v/v) will be

$$C_{sat} = \frac{(10^6)(\text{vapor Pressure})}{(\text{atmospheric pressure})} \quad (1)$$

Units: Vapor pressure and atmospheric pressure can be in expresses as mm Hg, atmospheres, Pascals, etc. as long as both are expressed in the same units.

Vapor pressure at any ambient temperature is an experimentally determined quantity; however, it can also be estimated from any class of liquids from boiling point data either atmospheric pressure or under vacuum.[41] The vapor pressure of the components within mixtures can also be estimated using established procedures[42] such as Henry's law constant (ratio of vapor to solution concentration) or Raoult's law (portion of a substance's pure vapor pressure in the headspace is the same as its mole fraction (in solution).

Tier 2: General Ventilation Model

One of the oldest and most used models in inhalation exposure modeling is the "box" or general ventilation model. It relies very simply on the concept of the conservation of mass. Imagine a box of air, any box of air. Now imagine it is a black box; that is, you cannot go into it and you cannot look into it. Now consider that as you begin to put an airborne contaminant into the box you will constantly measure any contaminant that subsequently comes out. We know that the average concentration in the box can be described as:

$$\text{Concentration} = \frac{(\text{Amount going into the Box}) - (\text{Amount coming out of Box})}{\text{Volume of the Box}} \quad (2)$$

If the contaminant is going into the box at a steady rate and leaving with the outgoing air at the same rate, then we know that the system is at "steady-state" and that the average concentration in the box is constant. This is actually a relatively simple and very useful relationship given by Equation 3 below.

If we are to believe that the concentration in the box is the same or homogeneous throughout the volume of the box then we need to make the assumptions that the contaminant:

- remains airborne (does not absorb onto surfaces)
- does not change chemically within the box and
- upon entering the box is instantly and completely mixed with the air in the box.

This is the so-called Well-Mixed Box construct.

Using this simple steady-state model and assumptions a general ventilation equation for this situation is:

$$C_{eq} = \frac{G}{Q} \quad (3)$$

C_{eq} = steady state concentration, mg/m^3
G = rate going into the box, mg/hr.
Q = ventilation rate of air leaving the box, m^3/hr.

Of course, the real world is often much more complicated. The mixing of airborne contaminants is often not at equilibrium nor is it complete and instantaneous. Also, some substances of interest are removed by non-ventilatory mechanisms such as adsorption or chemical reaction. Also, the non steady-state situation is significantly more complicated to describe mathematically. A differential equation that attempts to take all of these factors into account can be written for the pollutant concentration within the box for any time:[43]

$$VdC = Gdt - (C)(Q)(m) \, dt - (C)(k) \, dt \quad (4)$$

In equation 4, V is the assumed volume of the box (m^3), t is the time variable (hr), C is the concentration in the box at any given time (mg/m^3), G is the rate of generation of pollutant within the box (mg/hr), Q is the volume flow rate of air exchange in the box (m^3/hr), m is the dimensionless mixing efficiency of ventilation in the assumed box,[41] and k has units of m^3/hr and is the removal rate by mechanisms other than ventilation and filtration.

Typically, we do not have specific information on non-ventilatory loss rate (k), the mixing efficiency (m) or on the time course of exposure. Thus, we assume values for these factors and for the ventilation (Q) and generation rate (G) that render a reasonable upper bound estimate of C. Indeed, we often default to the steady-state condition for our analysis.

Using these assumptions, our general ventilation model that incorporates the mixing factor and ignore "k" (i.e., set k =0) is:

$$C_{eq} = \frac{G}{(Q)(m) + k} = \frac{G}{(Q)(m)} \quad (5)$$

Tier IIa: Dispersion Model

The general ventilation model avoids the question of contaminant mixing in the volume. It also ignores near field exposure or sharp gradients of concentration for workers close to the source. A diffusion model has been developed for heat flow[43] and applied to indoor air modeling.[44,45] The equation for a continuous point source is presented in the references to predict concentration at position r and time t.

$$C = \frac{G}{240\pi Dr} \left[1 - \text{erf} \left(\frac{r}{\sqrt{4tD}} \right) \right] \quad (6)$$

where "erf" means the error function

C is concentration, mass/volume (mg/m^3)
G is steady-state emission rate, mass/time (mg/hour)
r is the distance from the source to the worker (meter)
D is the effective or eddy diffusivity, area/time (m^2/hour)
t is elapsed time (hour)

Diffusion of contaminants in workroom air occurs principally because of the turbulent motion of the air.[46] In most industrial environments, molecular diffusion is not significant between the emission source and the worker's breathing zone. Instead, the normal "turbulence" of typical indoor air cause eddies (or packet-like motions) that have the effect of breaking up the contaminant cloud and hastening its mixing with the workroom air. Therefore, applications of diffusion models in industrial environments use experimentally determined diffusion coefficients (D) called eddy or effective diffusivities. These eddy diffusivity coefficients are 3–5 orders of magnitude larger than molecular diffusivity.

The eddy diffusivity term (D) can be based on experimental measurements at the site being modeled. Some eddy diffusivity values are also available in the literature.[45,47] Measurements of D in indoor industrial environments have ranged from 3 to 690 m^2/hour with 12 m^2/hour being a typical value.

Plotting the predicted airborne concentration (C) at one position, r, for many values of time, t, gives an increasing curve of concentration that approaches a steady-state level.

For sources (emitting into a hemisphere) on a surface and at equilibrium, the equation[15] simplifies to:

$$C_{eq} = \frac{G}{120\pi Dr} \qquad (7)$$

These sources are not readily available in the literature, so the burden is placed on the user to empirically derive these data or accept very wide bands of uncertainty associated with estimated values.

There is little doubt that the Eddy Diffusivity model could be a very valuable tool that can potentially provide near and far field exposure estimations; however, this approach in general suffers because it lacks the reasonable characterization of the primary predictor variable, eddy diffusivity (adapted from Jayjock, et al.)[48]

Modeling and Uncertainty

There are generally two types of uncertainty impacting exposure assessment; one is the natural variability associated with a given process or task, and the other is lack of knowledge, or ignorance. It is the latter that drives the predicted output of these models. Recognizing and documenting the uncertainty in any assessment is crucial to the integrity of the process, and this is no less true with modeling.

When using the models deterministically; where the output is a single value, uncertainty can be incorporated and the results communicated as not less than half the predicted value and not more than twice the predicted value. The degree of confidence with which the assessor can place on the result of a deterministic model application is appropriately displayed with this approach.

Probabilistic techniques allows for the degree of uncertainty to be quantified. Working with a distribution of outputs, the assessor can quantitatively express the level of confidence for a given predicted concentration. Conversely, the assessor can communicate what fraction of a given population of exposures would be expected to be above or below a given value.

Probabilistic tools can also help the assessor identify the parameters that have the greatest impact on the predicted concentration, and would therefore produce the greatest change in the output when refined. This is valuable information when resources for testing are limited, as they almost always are.

Exposure Assessment Research Needs

NIOSH has identified priorities in research related to the field of exposure assessment.[49] They recommend research be focused in the areas of study design, on monitoring methods, applied toxicology, and education and communication. Advancing the science of exposure assessment can result in improved, identification of at-risk workers, cost-effective control and intervention strategies, and improved baseline data for standard setting and risk assessment.

<u>Study Design</u>

The success of any exposure assessment rests on the study design and sampling strategy. Research is needed to refine job exposure matrices, and a national occupational exposure survey of current conditions with continuous updates is called for. Continued research on statistical analysis of exposure data is also a priority.

<u>Monitoring Methods</u>

The first priority is the development of guidelines to evaluate monitoring methods. Development is needed in the areas of dermal exposure assessment, biomonitoring methods, and rapidly deployable field methods.

<u>Applied Toxicology</u>

The first priority is mechanistic research on chemical physical, and biological agents. The next priority is the need for a toxicity assessment protocol. The third priority is for development and evaluation of pharmacokinetic and predictive models. The final need is a call for more research on a general toxicology approach to assess exposures to mixtures.

<u>Education and Communication</u>

Research is needed to evaluate the curricula of occupational safety and health programs relative to exposure assessment; and to address the effect of external requirements (i.e., Accreditation Board for Engineering and Technology, ABET) on these curricula. Lastly, research is needed to determine the best means of communicating exposure assessment issues and results.

Computational Exposure Assessment Research Needs

In the past, exposure and risk assessments have been limited to situations in which either a substance had been implicated in some adverse health effect, or new toxicological findings indicate that a substance has new and potentially dreaded adverse health effects. This approach addresses risks after the fact; after some untoward effect has occurred. The reactive approach to exposure and risk assessment did not require the explicit use of modeling thus model development and refinement was not at the forefront of scientific research. However, pressure to embrace a more proactive approach has resulted in recent enactment of regulations in the EU and Canada that require a proactive and comprehensive approach to assessing risk to chemicals which may impact consumer as well as occupational exposures. These new regulations will require increased use of computational EA and this will likely result in improvement and expansion of existing methods of computational EA.

There are many opportunities for improving the nescient science of exposure modeling including developing peer reviewed, publicly available parameter data and establishing standardized methods for collecting the data. These data will also facilitate the much needed critical evaluation of the existing models, helping researchers better understand the bounds of their applicability, and promote the refinement of these and development of new models.

Summary

Exposure assessment is at the heart of industrial hygiene and is critical to the recognition, evaluation and control of hazardous exposures in the workplace, but is also applicable to exposures in the general environment, including homes and outdoors. Fundamental to OEA is an understanding of the underlying toxicological relationships between workplace exposure and internal dose, and target-organ dose, pre-clinical and clinical effects. Since the interaction between the toxicity and the exposure is key to determining health risk, EA and RA are overlapping and inseparable for the industrial hygienist.

Although the classical industrial hygiene OEA involves agents in the industrial workplace, the scope of OEA has become much broader over the last fifteen to twenty years because of changes in technology and increased attention to non-industrial work environments.

The process or steps in an EA include: establishing an EA strategy, basic characterization of the workplace and hazards present, exposure measurement prioritization and monitoring, interpretation of EA data and institution of health hazard controls, reporting, and reassessment or re-evaluation.

Monitoring, or actual measurement of potential exposure is often the central activity for exposure assessment in industrial hygiene. In order for environmental monitoring to represent human exposure, the assessment method must be designed to measure substances in a way that mimics human exposure, e.g., air samples are collected to evaluate inhalation exposures and surface samples are collected to evaluate dermal exposure.

Exposure measurement methods can be generally grouped into the categories of inhalation, dermal, and biological exposure assessment. However, there are substances for which more than one route of exposure is possible. Exposures can also be assessed using computational programs that "model" or estimate exposures using existing exposure data, or source strength and related data.

NIOSH has identified priorities in research related to the field of exposure assessment, which include the areas of study design, monitoring methods, applied toxicology, and education and communication. Future opportunities for improving the nescient science of exposure modeling including developing peer reviewed, publicly available parameter data and establishing standardized methods for collecting the data.

References

1. **U.S. Environmental Protection Agency (EPA):** Glossary of IRIS Terms. U.S. Environmental Protection Agency http://www.epa.gov/iris/gloss8.htm. [Accessed on July 30, 2007].
2. **Ignacio, J.S. and W.H. Bullock (eds.):** *A Strategy for Assessing and Managing Occupational Exposures*, 3rd edition. Fairfax, VA: American Industrial Hygiene Association, 2006.
3. **Berglund, M., C.-G. Elinder, and L. Jarup:** Human Exposure Assessment: An Introduction. Geneva, Switzerland: World Health Organization (WHO), 2001.
4. **National Institute for Occupational Safety and Health (NIOSH):** Health Effects of Occupational Exposure to Respirable Crystalline Silica. National Institute for Occupational Safety and Health, Centers for Disease Control. http://www.cdc.gov/niosh/02-129A.html. [Accessed on July 28, 2007].
5. **Ott, W.R.:** Human exposure assessment: the birth of a new science. *Expo. Anal. Environ. Epidemiol. 5(4)*:449–472 (1995).
6. **Klaassen, C.D. (ed.):** *Casarett & Doull's Toxicology: The Basic Science of Poisons.* New York: McGraw-Hill, 2001.
7. **National Research Council (NRC):** *Risk Assessment in the Federal Government: Managing the Process.* Washington, DC: National Academy Press, 1983.
8. **American Industrial Hygiene Association (AIHA):** AIHA White Paper: A Generic Exposure Assessment Standard. *Am. Ind. Hyg. Assoc. J. 55(11)*:1009–1012 (1994).
9. **Stewart, P.A. and M. Stenzel:** Exposure assessment in the occupational setting. *Appl. Occup. Environ. Hyg. 15(5)*: 435–444 (2000).
10. **Hawkins, N.C., S.K. Norwood, and J.C. Rock:** *A Strategy for Occupational Exposure Assessment.* Akron, OH: AIHA, 1991.
11. **National Research Council (NRC):** *Human Exposure Assessment for Airborne Pollutants: Advances and Opportunities.* Washington, DC: National Academy Press, 1994.
12. **Hinds, W.C.:** *Aerosol Technology: Property, Behavior, and Measurement of Airborne Particles.* New York: John Wiley & Sons, 1982.
13. **National Institute for Occupational Safety and Health (NIOSH):** Asbestos and other Fibers by PCM. National Institute for Occupational Safety and Health, Centers for Disease Control http://www.cdc.gov/niosh/nmam/pdfs/7400.pdf. [Accessed on July 28, 2007].
14. **American Conference of Governmental Hygienists (ACGIH):** Documentation of the TLV®: Silica, crystalline: alpha-quartz and cristobalite. Cincinnati, OH: American Conference of Governmental Industrial Hygienists, 2005.
15. **American Conference of Governmental Industrial Hygienists (ACGIH):** Documentation of the TLV®: Wood Dusts (draft). Cincinnati, OH: American Conference of Governmental Industrial Hygienists, 2003.

16. **Occupational Safety and Health Administration (OSHA):** Table Z-3 Mineral Dusts - 1910.1000 Table Z-3. U.S.Department of Labor, Occupational Health and Safety Administration http://www.osha.gov/pls/oshaweb/owadisp.show_document?p_table=STANDARDS&p_id=9994. [Accessed on December 14, 2007].

17. **Lippmann, M.:** Pathways and measuring exposure to toxic substances. In *Patty's Toxicology*. Bingham, E., C. Cohrssen, and C.H. Powell (eds.). New York: John Wiley & Sons, 2001. pp 17–51.

18. **Berman, D.W. and K. Crump:** Technical Support Document for a Protocol to Assess Asbestos-Related Risk. Washington, D.C.: U.S. Environmental Protection Agency, # 9345.4-06:(2003).

19. **Andersen, A.A.:** New Sampler for the Collection, sizing and enumeration of viable airborne particles. *J. Bact.* 76:472–484 (1958).

20. **American Conference of Governmental Industrial Hygienists (ACGIH):** *Air Sampling Instruments for Evaluation of Atmospheric Contaminants*, 9th edition. Cincinnati, OH: ACGIH, 2001.

21. **National Institute for Occupational Safety and Health (NIOSH):** NIOSH Manual of Analytical Methods (NMAM). Cincinnati, OH: National Institute for Occupational Safety and Health, Centers for Disease Control. http://www.cdc.gov/niosh/nmam/. [Accessed on July 28, 2007].

22. **American Conference of Governmental Industrial Hygienists (ACGIH):** Threshold Limit Values®. Cincinnati, OH: ACGIH, 2007.

23. **American Conference of Governmental Industrial Hygienists (ACGIH):** Documentation of the TLV®: Glutaraldehyde. Cincinnati, OH: ACGIH, 2001.

24. **American Conference of Governmental Industrial Hygienists (ACGIH):** Documentation of the TLV®: Benzene. Cincinnati, OH: ACGIH, 2001.

25. **Sahmel, J. and M. F. Boeniger:** Dermal Exposure Assessments. In *A Strategy for Assessing and Managing Occupational Exposures*, 3rd edition. Ignacio, J.S. and W.H. Bullock (eds.). Fairfax, VA: AIHA, 2006. pp. 133–157.

26. **Occupational Safety and Health Administration (OSHA):** OSHA Technical Manual: Sampling for Surface Contamination. U.S.Department of Labor, Occupational Health and Safety Administration http://www.osha.gov/dts/osta/otm/otm_ii/otm_ii_2.html. [Accessed on December 14, 2007].

27. **Soutar, A., S. Semple, R.J. Aitken, and A. Robertson:** Use of patches and whole body sampling for the assessment of dermal exposure. *Ann. Occup. Hyg. 44(7)*:511–518 (2000).

28. **American Conference of Governmental Industrial Hygienists (ACGIH):** Documentation of the TLV®: Recommended BEI®: benzene, phenyl hydride. Cincinnati, OH: ACGIH, 2001.

29. **McDougal, J.N. and M.F. Boeniger:** Methods for assessing risks of dermal exposures in the workplace. *Crit. Rev. Toxicol. 32(4)*:291–327 (2002).

30. **U.S. Environmental Protection Agency (EPA):** Dermal Exposure Assessment: Principles and Applications — Part 2, Applications of dermal exposure assessment. U.S. Environmental Protection Agency http://www.epa.gov/NCEA/pdfs/derexp.pdf. [Accessed on July 30, 2007].

31. **Warren, N.D., H. Marquart, Y. Christopher, J. Laitinen, and J.J. VAN Hemmen:** Task-based dermal exposure models for regulatory risk assessment. *Ann. Occup. Hyg. 50(5)*:491–503 (2006).

32. **Hebisch, R. and J. Auffarth:** Dermal exposure: how to get information. *Appl. Occup. Environ. Hyg. 16(2)*:169–173 (2001).

33. **Aitio, A. and A. Kallio:** Exposure and effect monitoring: a critical appraisal of their practical application. *Toxicol. Lett. 108(2–3)*:137–147 (1999).

34. **Lowry, L.K.:** Role of biomarkers of exposure in the assessment of health risks. *Toxicol. Lett. 77(1–3)*:31–38 (1995).

35. **Roggli, V.L. and A. Sharma:** Analysis of Tissue Mineral Fiber Content. In *Pathology of Asbestos-Related Diseases*. Roggli, V.L., T.D. Oury, and T.A. Sporn (eds.). New York: Springer, 2004. pp. 309–354.

36. **Lioy, P.J.:** Assessing total human exposure to contaminants — A multidisciplinary approach. *Environ. Sci. Tech. 24*: 938–945 (1990).

37. **U.S. Environmental Protection Agency (EPA):** Human Health Research Program Review: Final Report of the Subcommittee on Human Health, May 18, 2005; Revised July 27, 2005. U.S. EPA http://www.epa.gov/osp/bosc/pdf/hh0507rpt.pdf. [Accessed on July 30, 2007].

38. **Mulhausen, J.R.:** Interpreting Monitoring Data: Are We Making the Right Judgments? presented at Professional Conference on Industrial Hygiene, Denver, CO: (2005).

39. **Mulhausen, J.R.:** Exposure Judgments: Continuously Improving Accuracy Using the AIHA Strategy with its Exposure Control Banding Approach. Presented at RT 233, AIHce, Chicago, IL: (2006).

40. **Lynch, J.:** Theory and rational of exposure assessment. In *Patty's Toxicology*. Bingham, E., B. Cohrssen, and C.H. Powell (eds.). New York: John Wiley & Sons, 1990. pp. 17–51.

41. **Haas, H. B. and R. F. Newton:** Correction of Boiling Points to Standard Pressure. In *CRC Handbook of Chemistry and Physics*. Boca Raton, FL: CRC Press, 1978. p. D-228.

42. **Lyman, W. J., Reehl, W. F., and Rosenblat, D. H. (eds.):** *Handbook of Chemical Property Estimation Methods*. New York: McGraw-Hill, 2007.

43. **Carslaw, H.S. and J.C. Jaeger:** *Conduction of Heat in Solids*, 2nd edition. London: Oxford University Press, 1959.

44. **Roach, S.A.:** On the role of turbulent diffusion in ventilation. *Ann. Occup. Hyg. 24(1)*:105–132 (1981).

45. **Wadden, R.A., P.A. Scheff, and J.E. Franke:** Emission factors for trichloroethylene vapor degreasers. *Am. Ind. Hyg. Assoc. J. 50(9)*:496–500 (1989).
46. **Keil, C.B.:** Diffusivity in Modeling. In *Mathematical Models for Estimating Occupational Exposure to Chemicals*, Keil, C.B. (ed.). Fairfax, VA: AIHA Press, 2000.
47. **Scheff, P.A., R.L. Friedman, J.E. Franke, L.M. Conroy, and R.A. Wadden:** Source activity modeling of Freon emissions form open-top vapor degreasers. *Appl. Occup. Environ. Hyg. 7*:124–134 (1992).
48. **Jayjock, M.A., C.F. Chaisson, S. Arnold, and E.J. Dederick:** Modeling framework for human exposure assessment. *J. Expo. Sci. Environ. Epidemiol. 17*:S81–S89 (2007).
49. **National Institute for Occupational Safety and Health (NIOSH):** Exposure Assessments Methods: Research Needs and Priorities. National Institute for Occupational Safety and Health, Centers for Disease Control http://www.cdc.gov/niosh/docs/2002-126/2002-126.html#Contents. [Accessed on July 28, 2007].

Chapter 24

Risk Assessment Process for Industrial Hygienists

*By Kenneth R. Still, PhD, FATS, CIH, CSP, CHMM
and Warren W. Jederberg, MS, CIH, RPIH*

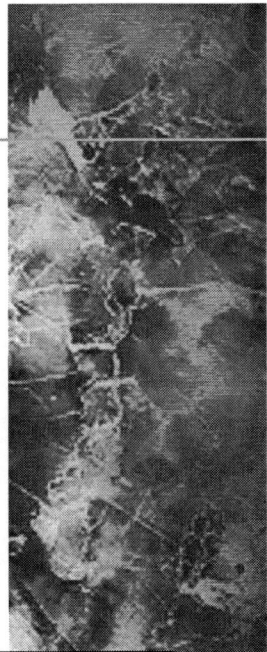

Introduction

Does an Industrial Hygienist need to know about risk assessment? Is risk assessment part of the position description of an Industrial Hygienist? Does risk assessment belong strictly under the aegis of the professional risk assessor? The answer to the first two questions is of course yes and to the third question, no. Risk assessment is an integral part of the work that industrial hygienists perform as an intimate part of their position description. And, there is a dire need for professional risk assessors.[1,2] Risk assessment is not confined to the realm of industrial hygiene but is woven through all industries and activities that involve human beings.

After the passage of the OSHAct in 1970 many organizations and activities were concerned about how they could determine if a worker health risk existed at their location. The government turned to the National Academy of Sciences for a resolution. In 1983 the National Research Council published the renowned "Red Book" on risk assessment in the government.[3] This protocol of risk assessment principles is still used today in industry and academic programs. In 1994 the "Red Book" was updated to include basic risk assessment tenets and updated methodological techniques and was published as Science and Judgment in Risk Assessment.[4] The basic elements of risk analysis and risk assessment are presented in this chapter. Detailed coverage of other aspects of risk assessment can be found in other chapters of this book (see Chapters 23,: "Exposure Assessment," 28, "Derivation of Occupational Exposure Limits," and 30, "Industrial Chemical Hazard Communication"). Additionally, the reader is directed to the references and additional reading list provided at the end of the chapter.

The risk assessment process is only one aspect of risk analysis. Risk analysis is a science that is used in numerous industries and is comprised of four primary elements: risk assessment, risk evaluation, risk management and risk communication.[5] Each of the four elements of risk analysis stand alone and are usually conducted by specialists in those areas. The analysis of the four areas is conducted separately and then

Outcome Competencies

Upon completion of this chapter, the reader should be able to:

- Be familiar with the basic elements of the formal health risk assessment process and how they overlap with the principles of the practice of industrial hygiene.
- Achieve elemental understanding of the role that toxicological data play in the process will be reviewed.

Prerequisite Knowledge

Basic principles of hazard identification and control.

Key Terms

absorbed dose, effective dose, hazard, low-dose extrapolation, modifying factor, risk, slope factor, uncertainty factor

Key Topics

1. Risk assessment
2. Risk evaluation
3. Risk management
4. Risk evaluation
5. Risk communications
6. Hazard identification
7. Dose response assessment
8. Exposure assessment
9. Risk characterization
10. Low-dose extrapolation

utilized jointly to address a risk issue. The entire spectrum of risk analysis may be addressed in more depth in one element than another because each element can, and in many cases does, stand-alone. Risk analysis is the application of qualitative and quantitative analytical techniques to potential risks, as well as methods to use the resulting information from those analytical techniques.[5,6]

The risk assessment process is a critical function essential for making decisions relative to establishing risk reduction procedures and for formulating appropriate exposure levels from potentially hazardous chemicals.[7,8,9] These decisions are based on quality science that guides sound judgments, which result in effective risk characterization and risk management.[5,7] Risk assessment is the process of characterizing the resultant risk from chemical releases, which may affect human health or the environment. More expressly stated, risk assessment is using science to quantify individual risk, i.e., the technical assessment of the nature and magnitude of risk. The modern day use of the risk assessment process has its roots in the insurance industry.[7,10] The use of actuarial processes for determination of insurance premiums gave rise to the use of comparable processes to determine the amount of personal risk in numerous scenarios, but especially in human health concerns from occupational and environmental settings. The currently used risk assessment process has only been defined in the last 25 years.[3,4,6] In comparison to other sciences, risk assessment is a neophyte.

To best understand the risk analysis and risk assessment processes, understanding the risk analysis terminology is paramount. The process of risk analysis has four distinct purposes: (1) to determine environmental and health problems associated with a variety of activities and substances, for example hazardous waste disposal or the use of specific chemicals or mixtures; (2) to compare new and existing techniques or to determine the effectiveness of different control and mitigation techniques designed to reduce risks; (3) to select sites for potentially hazardous operations or facilities; and, (4) to set management priorities, such as which of several activities should be considered first for regulatory or corrective action.[5,8]

By definition, risk is the possibility of suffering harm from a hazard and is created by a hazard. A hazard is therefore, a source of risk; and is a substance or action that can cause harm. A complete technical analysis of risk describes the hazard, the event or events that create the possibility of harm, and, a statistical estimation of the likelihood that harm will occur. A chemical that is considered to be toxic and a hazard to human health is not a risk unless people are exposed to that chemical. The chemical must be present, interact with the human organism and ultimately the target organ, and, have the potential to cause some alteration to the health of the human to be classified a source of risk.[11]

The "toxicity" of a material is its inherent ability to cause damage to living organisms or portions of living organisms.[9,11] The "hazard" of a material takes into account the probability of biological organisms being exposed to the toxic material. Terms such as highly toxic, moderately toxic, and non-toxic are of little value to workers unless a point of reference, familiar to the worker, can be applied. Table 24.1 presents a common scheme for classification of materials as related to their oral toxicity in humans.

Table 24.1 — Relative Ranking of Toxic Materials Based on Oral Toxicity in Humans[12]

Toxicity Class	Dose	For Average Adults
Practically non-toxic	>15,000 mg/kg	More than 1 quart
Slightly Toxic	5,000–15,000 mg/kg	Between 1 pint and 1 quart
Moderately toxic	500–5,000 mg/kg	Between 1 ounce and 1 pint
Very toxic	50–500 mg/kg	Between 1 teaspoon and 1 ounce
Extremely toxic	5–50 mg/kg	Between 7 drops and 1 teaspoon
Supertoxic	<5 mg/kg	Less than 7 drops

Caution must be exercised in the interpretation of data such as those presented in Table 24.1. Though a compound may be "highly toxic", it may not present a significant hazard if the probability of exposure is remote. In contrast, material of "low toxicity" may present a significant hazard under the proper exposure conditions. For example, a small amount of water in the human lung can cause severe pulmonary problems.

When evaluating the four components of the risk assessment process, the definitions for each reveal distinct delineations. Risk assessment is the process of using factual bases to delineate the probabilities of health effects of exposure to humans, and, effects to individuals, populations and communities of organisms in the environment, to hazardous materials. There are four steps to the risk assessment process: (1) hazard identification; (2) dose-response assessment; (3) exposure assessment; and, (4) risk characterization.[3,4,13,14] Further discussion of this aspect of risk analysis will be provided later in the chapter.

The second leg of the risk analysis process is risk evaluation and is basically the determination of which risks are acceptable to whom and why.[15] The evaluative process is usually determined by the evaluator and is based on their background in science and management. Some evaluators determine the risk of a hazard based entirely on the likelihood of that hazard yielding adverse effects to the biologic entity; while other evaluators are concerned with the hazard's effect on the biologic entity itself.

Risk management, the third part of the risk analysis process, is controlling risks through personal, business, and/or government decision-making processes. More precisely, it is the process of weighing policy alternatives and then selecting the most appropriate regulatory action, integrating the results of risk assessments with engineering data and with social, economic, and political concerns to reach a decision. Risk managers use information from hazard identification and characterization to determine what necessary action to take to reduce or eliminate a risk.[16]

Finally, risk communication, the fourth step in the overall risk analysis, is a purposeful exchange of information about risks and the entire analytical process. It is the process of conveying information about the levels of risk to human health or the environment, the significance of these risks to human health or the environment, and the decisions, actions, or policies aimed at managing or controlling these human health or environmental risks.[15] Communication must include the assumptions and uncertainties included in the risk assessment process (see Chapter 30, "Industrial Chemical Hazard Communication"). The ability to communicate the results of a complete risk assessment to lay individuals is paramount to a successful industrial hygiene program; the conduct of the science portion of risk assessment is the easy part that all industrial hygienists are trained to accomplish. However, the aspect of risk communication is not covered strongly enough in the academic environment and must be learned on the job in most cases.

Risk Assessment Process

The risk assessment process for chemicals, including mixtures[17], involves four primary steps[3,4,9,13]: hazard identification, dose-response assessment, exposure assessment, and risk characterization. All four steps are necessary for a fully successful risk assessment.

Hazard Identification

This step of the process involves gathering and evaluating data on the types of health effects that may be produced by a chemical. Inclusive in this step are the conditions under which the material may produce injury or disease. Hazard identification incorporates the identity of the contaminant suspected of posing health hazards, a quantification of the concentrations at which the contaminants are present in the environment, a description of the specific forms of toxicity that can be caused by the contaminants of concern (see Chapter 9, "Neurotoxicology"; Chapter 10, "Hepatic Toxicology"; and Chapter 14, "Carcinogenesis".) and an evaluation of the conditions under which these forms of toxicity might be expressed in exposed humans.[8,9,13,18] These data are gathered from three primary sources: environmental monitoring, epidemiological studies, and animal studies conducted under controlled conditions. Hazard identification is not risk assessment; it is simply determining whether it is scientifically correct to infer that toxic effects observed in one setting will occur in other settings. For example, if a chemical is found to be carcinogenic in laboratory animal studies this chemical will likely have the same result in humans. Of the four steps to the risk assessment process, hazard identification is the most easily recognized in the actions of regulatory agencies such as the Environmental Protection Agency (EPA).[11,19–21]

Dose-Response Assessment

Dose-response assessment involves describing the quantitative relationship between the amount of exposure to a chemical and the extent of toxic injury.[9,22,23,24] It is the evaluation of the conditions under which the toxic properties of a chemical might be manifested in exposed people. Particular emphasis is placed on the quantitative relationship between the dose and the toxic response. This step may include an assessment of variations of response, for example the differences in susceptibility between infants and adults. Simplistically stated, the dose-response assessment is the process of characterizing the inherent toxicity of a chemical and involves determining the adverse effects and how much of the chemical is required to produce the adverse effect in the target population. The observed adverse effect is usually termed the toxic endpoint, i.e., a biological effect used as an index of the effect of a chemical/substance on an organism and is used to select which data sets are appropriate for use in the risk assessment. The route of entry into the body and the disposition of the chemical in the body are of paramount importance to the dose-response step of the process. The usual routes of entry for humans are inhalation, ingestion and skin absorption (see Chapter 2, "Principles of Toxicology" and Chapter 4, "Disposition of Toxicants"). People are exposed to chemicals in the environment because of the chemical presence in the air, water, or food. Further, laboratory animal experiments for studying the toxicity of a particular chemical usually involve the intentional administration of the chemical under study by way of diet, air to be inhaled or direct application to the skin. Other routes of administration include injection, intravenous, and intraperitoneal. The key routes of chemical absorption, distribution, and excretion are covered in detail in the chapter on disposition. These routes of entry to the body and the ultimate excretion avenues are the major areas of concern and identification for the determination of exposure to hazardous materials. These three areas of concern, absorption, distribution, and excretion, are the major variables influencing the potential toxicity of chemicals.[25,26]

Dose is either absorbed or effective. Absorbed dose is the amount of agent that is absorbed by the lungs, gastrointestinal tract, or skin; effective dose, also called internal dose, is the amount of agent reaching a tissue or an organ where it can inflict damage. In toto, dose-response describes the relationship that exists between the degree of exposure to a chemical (i.e., the dose) and the magnitude of the effect (response) in the exposed organism. No chemical present, yields no response. Once in the body, the general mechanism of chemical toxicity is interference with some important cellular reaction, the details of which will vary with the individual chemical. The chemical may react with key cellular molecules, changing their properties causing damage or rendering them ineffective; or, the chemical may substitute for a normal body chemical and lead to formation of unusual new by-products which may be more or less toxic than the parent chemical and prevent formation of normal products.

Exposure Assessment

The third step in the risk assessment process is exposure assessment. This step specifies the population that might be exposed to the agent of concern, identifies the routes through which exposure can occur, and estimates the magnitude, duration, and timing of the doses that workers may receive as a result of their exposure to the chemical of concern. The first determinant of exposure assessment is to identify the concentration of chemical to which workers are exposed. This may be accomplished by direct measurements, use of models, or by analogy. Analogy is often used by collecting exposure measurements on a small group of workers and then applying those values to other segments of the worker population. Particular attention is given to various grouping of workers in a given area and exposed to a specific chemical. Some groups in an exposed population may be especially susceptible to adverse health effects. For example, pregnant women, very young and very old people, and health impaired individuals may be particularly important in evaluating the exposure assessment. This step in risk assessment is covered in detail in Chapter 23, "Exposure Assessment."

Risk Characterization

This, the final step in the risk assessment process, is the complete integration of information from the preceding three steps, i.e., hazard identification, dose-response assessment and exposure assessment. During this phase the collected information is used to develop a qualitative or quantitative estimate of the likelihood that any of the hazards associated with the chemical of concern will be realized in exposed workers. If exposure data are not available, hypothetical risk can be characterized by the integration of hazard identification and dose-response data. Risk is generally characterized based upon the two very general categories of chemicals: non-carcinogens and carcinogens. Definitive procedures are used for determining risk of each category, but will not be covered in this chapter. Ultimately risk characterization is the process of estimating the incidence of a health effect under various conditions of exposure. It is during this phase that any resultant uncertainties encountered during the preceding steps are taken into account and described.

The existing relationships among the four steps of risk assessment and between risk assessment and risk management and the types of research needed are illustrated in Figure 1. Note that each categorical relationship in the figure is interactive. The process of risk assessment identifies research needs and specific research programs enhance the understanding of the individual risk assessment steps.

Industrial hygiene, as discussed in the Chapter 1, is the science devoted to the anticipation, recognition, evaluation and control of health hazards encountered in an occupational setting. A concomitant tenet of the practice of Industrial Hygiene is to provide worker training in the recognition, evaluation, and control of hazards which the worker might encounter, either directly or indirectly. As such, Industrial Hygienists are trained in the ability to recognize hazards and anticipate risks encountered in the workplace. The health effects of toxic hazards are summarized in an organizing paradigm illustrated in Figure 24.2. A comparison of these two human health assessment paradigms, Industrial Hygiene and Risk Assessment, is detailed in Table 24.2.

Table 24.2 — Human Health Assessment Paradigms; a comparison between Industrial Hygiene and Risk Assessment/Risk Analysis.

Categorical Question	Industrial Hygiene	Risk Assessment/Analysis
Is there a Problem?	Anticipation/ Recognition	Hazard Identification
Nature and Magnitude of the Problem	Evaluation	Assessment: Dose Response Exposure Risk Characterization
What to do:	Control	Risk Management
Will workers cooperate?	Training	Risk Communication

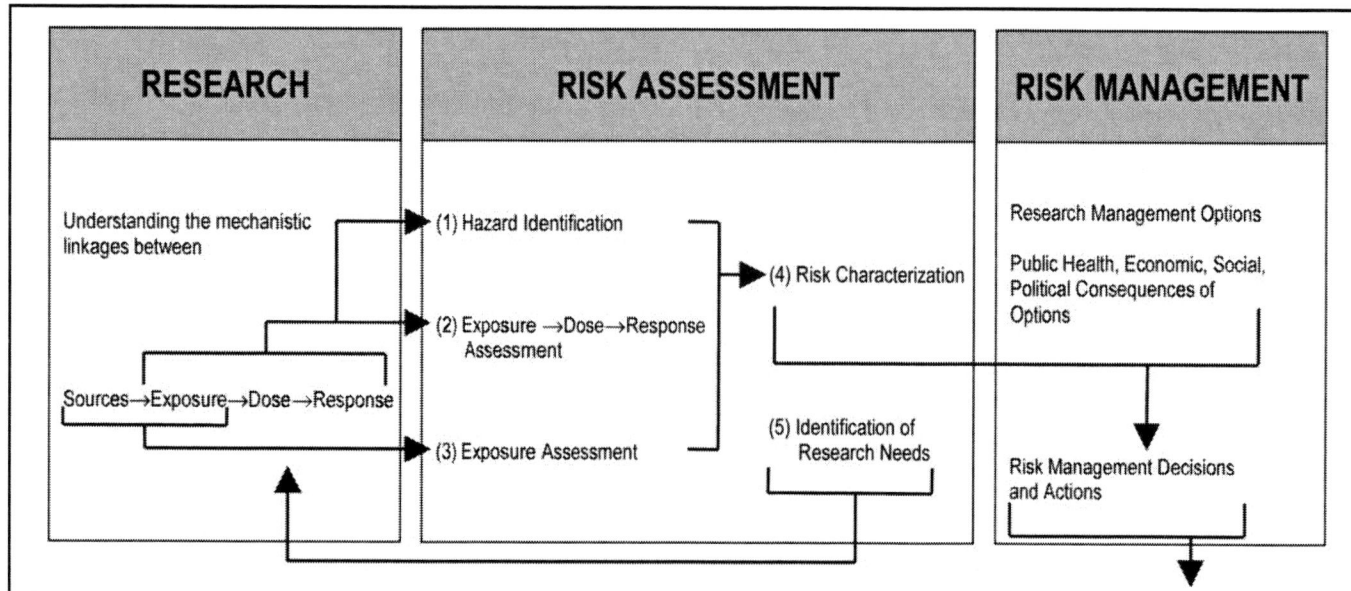

Figure 24.1 — NAS/NRC risk assessment/management paradigm.
Source: Adapted from NRC, 1983a. From: Science and Judgment in Risk Assessment.

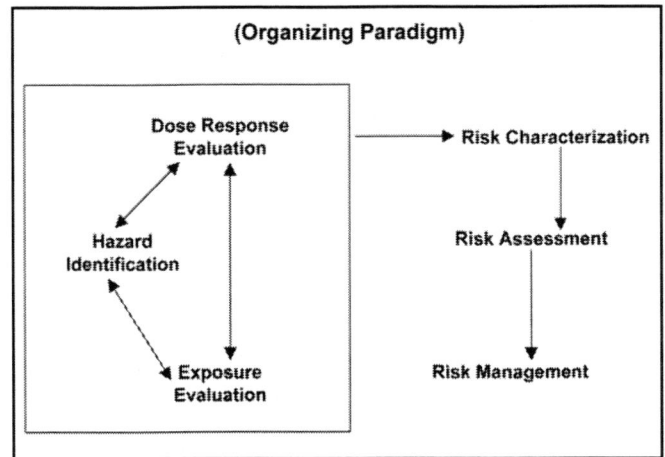

Figure 24.2 — Health Effects of Toxic Hazards
Source: Principles of Risk Assessment: A Non-Technical Review, EPA Office of Policy Analysis, 1987.

As indicated in Table 24.2, positive comparisons between the practice of Industrial Hygiene and the practice of Risk Assessment/Risk Analysis exist and both serve to work toward the preservation of worker health. The tenets of Industrial Hygiene serve the field of risk analysis and risk assessment well and provide the necessary methodology for collecting risk assessment data and integrating all data into the science side of the house and the policy side of the house.

Application of Toxicology Data

Though a comprehensive review of the development and application of mathematical paradigms to human health and environmental risk assessments is beyond the scope of this chapter, a review of the principles and illustration of some of the formulae will demonstrate the criticality (and limitations) of the use of toxicological data in this process.

Whether calculating the life-time risk associated with an environmental toxicant or the risk associated with an occupational exposure, the principles are the same.

Equation 1 presents a generic approach to calculating the Reference Dose (RfD) as described by the U.S. Environmental Protection Agency. The RfD is defined as "An estimate (with uncertainty spanning perhaps an order of magnitude) of a daily oral exposure to the human population (including sensitive subgroups) that is likely to be without an appreciable risk of deleterious effects during a lifetime. It can be derived from a No Observed Adverse Effect Level (NOAEL), Lowest Observed Adverse Effect Level (LOAEL), or benchmark dose, with uncertainty factors generally applied to reflect limitations of the data used. These equations are generally used in EPA's non-cancer health assessments."[25] Note that the calculations in Equation 1, and many EPA assessment models, are based on a "lifetime" exposure assessment, which is generally considered to be 70 years for humans. By comparison, the Occupational "lifetime" is generally defined as 40 years, which is the length of time people are in the workforce.[26] The difference in the exposure period for the general population and workers provides an initial explanation for why occupational exposure limits [Occupational Safety and Health Administration Permissible Exposure Limits (PELs) and the American Conference of Governmental Industrial Hygienists (ACGIH) Threshold Limit Values (TLV®s)] are not directly applicable in non-occupational exposure scenarios and the exposure factors used to calculate them are different.[27]

Equation 1 is presented to illustrate the kind of reasoning used to derive a reference dose (RfD) that could be used as one element of an assessment. When using Equation 1 and EPA assessment models a number of factors need to be considered: (1) intraspecies variation, (2) interspecies variation, (3) use of RfD based on a different time period than the salient animal research model, or (4) use of LOAEL rather than the NOAEL. RfDs for many industrial chemicals may be found in the Integrated Risk Information System (IRIS) database of the U.S. EPA. When specific data are missing with regard to exposure parameters, defaults have been established[21] and should be used. Some examples of the default values are given in Table 24.3 and 24.4. Table 24.3 presents the default values used for inhalation exposures and 24.4 presents some default values for humans for an area intended to be used for building residents.

Table 24.3 — EPA Default Respiratory Values

	Man	Woman	Child
Respiration			
Resting Rate	7.3 L/min	6 L/min	4.8 L/min
Light Activity	20 L/min	19 L/min	13 L/min
Volume Breathed	23 m³/day	21 m³/day	15 m³/day
Fluid Consumption	2 L/day	1.4 L/day	1.4 L/day
Food Consumption (all)	1,500 gm/day		

Table 24.4 — Selected EPA Human Default Exposure Values

Exposure Pathway	Daily Intake Rate	Exposure Frequency	Exposure Duration	Body Weight
Ingestion of Potable Water	2 liters	350 days/year	30 years	70 kg
Ingestion of soil and dust	200 mg (child) 100 mg (adult)	350 days/year	6 years	15 kg (child) 70 kg (adult)
Inhalation of contaminants	20 m³ (total) 15 m³ (indoor)	350 days/year	30 years	70 kg

Equation 1: Reference Dose (RfD):

$$\mathbf{RfD = NOAEL \text{ or } LOAEL/(UF \times MF)}$$

RfD = Reference dose (mg/kg/day)
NOAEL = No-Observed-Adverse Effect Level (mg/kg/day)
LOAEL = Lowest-Observed-Adverse Effect Level (mg/kg/day)
UF = Uncertainty Factor (unitless) — used to adjust toxicity data to account for unknown variations. Where toxicity is measured on only one test species, other species may exhibit more sensitivity to that effluent. An uncertainty factor would adjust measured toxicity upward and downward to cover the sensitivity range of other, potentially more or less sensitive species.
MF = Modifying Factor (unitless) — used to convert NOAELs/LOAELs to RfDs, range from greater than zero to ten and reflect professional judgment of uncertainties not addressed by uncertainty factors; the default value for the MF is one.

Equations (2 & 3) illustrate the general form of calculations used for environmental applications.

Equation 2. General Equation for Potential Average Daily Dose:

ADD = Total Potential Dose/(BW x AT)

ADD = average daily dose (mg/kg-day)
BW = bodyweight (kg)
AT = averaging time (days), for non-carcinogenic effects AT = ED, for carcinogenic or chronic effects AT = 70 years or 25,550 days (lifetime)

Equation 3. Total Potential Dose (TPD):

TPD = C x IR x ED

C = contaminant concentration
IR = intake rate
ED = exposure duration

Before using default values, the reader is cautioned to ascertain familiarity with the underlying data and review its applicability to the situation they are evaluating. For example, exposure values for military members or first responders in emergency situations will not be adequately covered.

CASE STUDY[28]
RfD Example: Acrylamide (CASRN 79-06-1)
Chemical: Acrylamide
RfD = NOAEL or LOAEL/(UF x MF)
    = 0.2 mg/kg/day/(1000 x 1)
Study: Rat Subchronic Drinking Water
Doses: NOAEL = 0.2 mg/kg/day LOAEL = 1 mg/kg/day
<u>UF and MF</u>: (10 X 10 X 10) X 1
<u>Critical Effect</u>: Nerve Damage

(UF = 1000. The UF of 1000 allows for uncertainty in the extrapolation of dose levels from animals to humans (10), uncertainty in the threshold of sensitive humans (10) and uncertainty in the effect of subchronic to chronic exposure (10). The chronic study did not adequately address the latter uncertainty because of the lack of sensitive measurement of the critical effect).

MF = 1
(MF =1 due to the quality of the study used.)

In this case the critical effect of interest was nerve damage in rats. That does not mean that other toxicologic effects were not seen. This illustrates that the criteria for the data selected for the risk assessment must clearly identified. In many instances, multiple studies are available and may present conflicting values from multiple species. The risk assessor must include in the documentation the rationale for the data set used. As can be seen, even when good data are available the resulting risk description requires the application of assumptions and professional knowledge. The process is not an exact science and is designed to be conservative.

References

1. **Office of Management and Budget, Office of Info. & Regulatory Affairs:** Proposed Risk Assessment Bulletin (Jan. 2006) [Online] Available at www.whitehouse.gov/omb/inforeg/proposed_risk_assessment_bulletin_010906.pdf . [Accessed September 25, 2007].
2. National Academies. Review of the OMB Risk Assessment Bulletin. BEST-K-06-02-A (E. Mantus) [Online] Available at: www8.nationalacademies.org/cp/projectview.aspx?key=34282. (Accessed: 25 September 2007)
3. **National Research Council:** *Risk Assessment in the Federal Government: Managing the Process.* Washington D.C.: National Academy Press, 1983.
4. **National Research Council:** *Science and Judgment in Risk Assessment.* Washington D.C.: National Academy Press, 1994.
5. **Cohrssen, J.J. and V.T. Covello:** *Risk Analysis: A Guide to Principles and Methods for Analyzing Health and Environmental Risks.* Council on Environmental Quality, PB89-137772. 1989
6. **National Research Council:** *Issues in Risk Assessment.* Washington D.C.: National Academy Press, 1993.

7. **Molak, V. (ed.):** *Fundamentals of Risk Analysis and Risk Management.* Boca Raton, FL: CRC Lewis Publications, 1997.
8. **Tardiff, R.G.:** Risk Analysis for the Workplace (Chapter 46). In *Patty's Industrial Hygiene*, 5th edition, Volume 3. Harris, R.L. (ed.). New York: John Wiley and Sons, 2000.
9. **Klaassen, C.D. (ed.):** *Casarett and Doull's Toxicology: The Basic Science of Poisons*, 6th edition. New York: McGraw-Hill, Inc., 2001.
10. **Covello, V.T. and J. Mumpower:** Risk Analysis and Risk Management: An Historical Perspective. *Risk Anal. 5(2)*:103–120 (1985).
11. **U.S. Environmental Protection Agency (EPA):** Risk Assessment Guidance for Superfund, Vol. 1, Human Health Evaluation Manual, Part A, Interim Final. EPA/540/1-90/002, Office of Emergency and Remedial Response. 1989.
12. **Williams, P.L. and J.L. Burson:** *Industrial Toxicology, Safety and Health Application in the Workplace.* New York: Van Nostrand Reinhold, 1985.
13. **Fan, A., R. Howd, and B. Davis:** Risk Assessment of Environmental Chemicals. *Ann. Rev. Pharmacol. Tox. 35*: 341–368 (1995).
14. **Fan, A.M. and L.W. Chang (eds.):** *Toxicology and Risk Assessment, Principles, Methods, and Applications.* New York: Marcel Dekker, Inc., 1996.
15. **Fischhoff, B., A. Bostrom, and M.J. Quandrel:** Risk perception and communication. *Ann. Rev. Pub. Health 14*: 183–203 (1993).
16. **Salem, H. and E.J. Olajos (eds.):** *Toxicology in Risk Assessment.* Abingdon, Oxford, UK: Taylor and Francis, 2000.
17. **U.S. Environmental Protection Agency (EPA):** Guidelines for the Health Risk Assessment of Chemical Mixtures. Federal Register 51 (185):34014-34025 (1986).
18. **Hallenbeck, W.H.:** *Quantitative Risk Assessment for Environmental and Occupational Health.* Boca Raton, FL: Lewis Publishers, 1986.
19. **U.S. Environmental Protection Agency (EPA):** Guidelines for Exposure Assessment. Federal Register 57: 22888-22938, 1992.
20. **U.S. Environmental Protection Agency (EPA):** *Exposure Factors Handbook*, Final Report. Washington, D.C.: Exposure Assessment Group, Office of Health and Environmental Assessment. 1989.
21. **U.S. Environmental Protection Agency (EPA):** Exposure Factors Handbook, Washington D.C.: National Center for Environmental Assessment, Office of Research and Development, 1997.
22. **Jayjock, M.A., J.R. Lynch and D.I. Nelson:** *Risk Assessment Principles for the Industrial Hygienist.* Fairfax, VA: AIHA Press, 2000.
23. **Hallenbeck, W.H.:** *Quantitative Risk Assessment for Environmental and Occupational Health*, 2nd edition. Lewis Publishers, 1993.
24. **Nelson, D.I., F. Mirer, G. Bratt, and D.O. Anderson:** Risk Assessment in the Workplace. In *The Occupational Environment: Its Evaluation, Control and Management*, 2nd Edition, DiNardi, S.R. (ed.). Fairfax, VA: AIHA Press, 2003. pp 143–171.
25. **U.S. Environmental Protection Agency (EPA):** A Review of the Reference Dose and Reference Concentration Processes, EPA/630/P-02/002F, Risk Assessment Forum. Washington D.C.: U.S. EPA, 2002.
26. **U.S. Environmental Protection Agency (EPA):** A Review of the Reference Dose and Reference Concentration Processes, EPA/630/P-02/002F, Risk Assessment Forum. Washington D.C.: U.S. EPA, 2002.
27. Threshold Limit Values for Chemical Substances and Physical Agents & Biological Exposure Indices: ACGIH, Cincinnati, OH, 2007.
28. Integrated Risk Information System (IRIS) [Online] Available on the web at: www.epa.gov/iris/subst/0286.htm. [Accessed August 9, 2007].

Additional Reading:

Kolluru, R.V.: Health Risk Assessment: Principles and Practices. In *Risk Assessment and Management Handbook for Environmental, Health, and Safety Professionals.* Kolluru, R.V., S. Bartell, R. Pitblado, and S. Stricoff (eds.). New York: McGraw-Hill, Inc., 1996. pp. 4.3–4.68.

Harvard School of Public Health: *A Historical Perspective on Risk Assessment in the Federal Government*, Center for Risk Analysis. Boston, MA: Harvard School of Public Health, 1994.

Boa, E., J. Lynch, D.R. Lillquist: Risk Assessment Resources. February 4, 2000; Revised by M.L. Herr, December 2, 2002. [Online] Available at: www.aiha.org/1documents/Committees/RA-Resources.pdf. [Accessed September 25, 2007)

Chapter 25

Military Toxicology for Industrial Hygienists in an Operational Context

Outcome Competencies
This chapter primarily discusses aspects of chemical toxicology relevant to the practice of industrial hygiene in military settings. It does not address heat stress or vibration and only lightly touches on biological (e.g., anthrax) and radiation hazards. A broad goal of the chapter is to illustrate how fundamental industrial hygiene principles and skills can be applied to unfamiliar circumstances. Upon completion of this chapter, the reader should be able to:

- Understand the general nature of chemical, biological, and radiological hazards and the contexts in which a military unit may face such potential exposures.
- Recognize within the military context those situations that parallel typical civilian environmental and occupational safety and health concerns.
- Recognize special environmental and occupational safety and health challenges that may arise in an operational situation.
- Modify and apply fundamentals of environmental and occupational safety and health principles to non-traditional situations and environments.
- Contrast toxicological threats and risks that arise from the use of toxic substances as weapons with those which arise inadvertently.
- Integrate the potential role of industrial hygiene practices and capabilities, as adapted to an operational situation, and their role in supporting operational risk assessment and decision making.
- Defend the need to define and assess environmental and occupational safety and health risks in an operational environment in which casualties from enemy action is a reality.
- Understand the relationship between the practice of industrial hygiene in the field and the delivery of effective occupational and environmental medical care to the individual member.

Prerequisite Knowledge
No specific knowledge is required for the reader to understand this chapter. Many of the subjects discussed are treated in greater detail throughout other chapters in this text. However, since the vignettes provided concern a wide range of topics, the reader who is naive to these subjects may feel inadequately prepared. It was, in fact, the authors' intention in selecting these topics to demonstrate that general principles and common sense can serve one pretty well even under such circumstances.

Key Terms
anesthetics, ATSDR, asphyxiation, bacteria, CBRNE, CDC, Comprehensive Military Health Surveillance, composite materials, conceptual site model, contaminants, dermal absorption, exposure, health surveillance, ingestion, IDLH, inhalation, intoxication, medical surveillance, Mortality and Morbidity Weekly Report (MMWR), NIOSH, occupational and environmental health surveillance, OSHA, PEL, REL, risk assessment, TIC, TIM, TLV®, spore, U.S. EPA, virus

Key Topics
1. Venues of Toxic Exposures
2. Media and Routes of Toxic Exposures
3. Toxins
4. Radioactivity
5. Area Reconnaissance and Survey
6. Medical and Legal Issues
7. Practical Approaches for the Military Leader
8. Looking Forward to Prospects for the Future

Chapter 25

Military Toxicology for Industrial Hygienists in an Operational Context

*By Michael E. Ottlinger, PhD, DABT,
John Cardarelli, PhD, CHP, CIH, and
Dino Mattorano, MS, CIH*

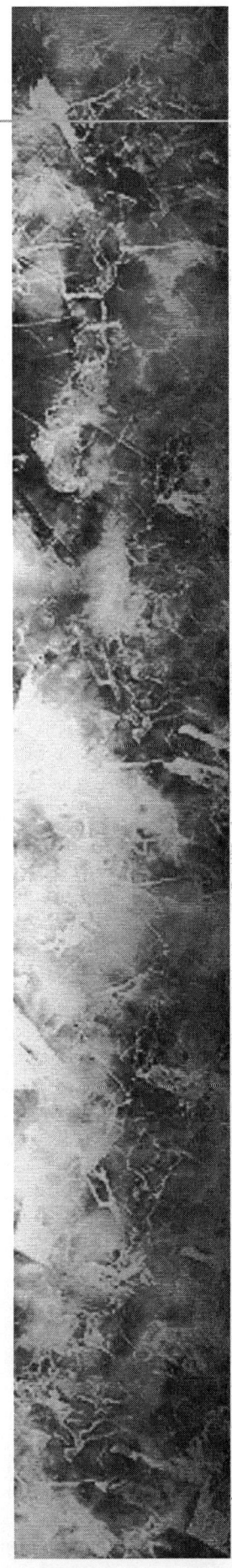

Introduction

Military commanders face challenges in identifying and assessing risks to personnel stemming from exposures to chemical, biological, and physical agents. On bases, aboard ships or aircraft, and, in the field, personnel are often in proximity to toxic substances in the course of their normal workday, paralleling typical civilian environmental and occupational safety and health concerns (see Chapter 1, "The Role of Toxicology in Industrial Hygiene), and in the course of some uniquely military circumstances. While the risk of fire and explosion is universally recognized, the risks associated with exposures to toxic materials are generally less so.

In the field, many potentially hazardous chemicals exist in surprising proximity and abundance. Service members in an operational status may be exposed to the chemicals in a conventional form, such as carbon monoxide containing vehicle or diesel generator exhaust or vapors arising from spilled fuel. As we experienced during the Gulf War, they may also be exposed to contaminants stemming from unusual or unconventional events, such as the wide-spread intentional burning of oil wells.[1] Burning vehicles, buildings, and their contents, may pose similar risks, especially since it is impossible to know what might have been contained in them.

Furthermore, as a result of the national disruption that usually accompanies events requiring military intervention, manufacturing facilities or industrial chemical stocks may not be maintained to the same rigorous and health protective standards that most Americans have come to take so much for granted. These conditions can include the interruption of normal regulatory oversight; sloppy or spotty maintenance; uncontrolled dumping of industrial wastes or sewage; and the presence of deteriorating or damaged facilities. Maintaining large numbers of personnel in, or moving them through such, typically unfamiliar, areas can make addressing such factors extremely difficult if not impossible. Indeed, the total risk management equation for service members in combat or near combat situations may not be able to cope with considerations of this kind.

After the 1990–1991 Gulf War, the Department of Defense (DoD) moved aggressively to institute many far reaching and progressive programs designed to improve force health protection for deployed personnel. Some of the key areas, and some initial planning steps, were noted in a seminal Government Accounting Office (GAO) Report[2] and were already being implemented during other interim deployments. Throughout the period, a large body of other relevant DoD INSTRUCTIONS and DIRECTIVES have been developed stating the aims and describing the detailed implementation of "Comprehensive Health Surveillance"[3] and "Deployment Health"[4] and other related programs. Pre-deployment preparations may include the geographical mapping and assessment of potentially dangerous locations and screening for any pollutants of concern in the air, soil, or water. Early recognition of hazards provides the greatest window of time for forward planning.[2]

Expertise in the recognition of chemical hazards in the environment, and an appreciation of the possible consequences of their release, can be useful across the entire spectrum of operations. Toxic chemicals released into the environment not only present a potential threat to personnel operating in an area, but, their release onto the battlefield could provide a possible means of area denial, either through a real or a perceived danger. The presence of persistent chemicals also complicates long term recovery planning and operations, whether or civilian or military[5] (see Chapter 27, "Toxicology in Emergency Response Planning"). In target selection and planning, collateral damage estimates involve consideration of the toxicity of chemicals present either at the prospective target site or nearby. Toxic chemicals stored in the operational area present a risk under various circumstances to both friendly forces and civilians. It is therefore an advantage to the commander to know in sufficient detail what these chemicals are, where they are located, and what risks they represent. Needless to say, toxic chemicals, whether warfare agents, industrial, agricultural, pharmaceutical, or other stocks of chemicals may be exploited as a means of conducting asymmetric warfare or civilian terrorist attacks.[5]

Since there are such a huge range of chemical substances to deal with, it is essential to find some helpful means of stratifying the risk and impact that they might potentially exert. There are several excellent textbooks providing detailed scientifically[6] or medically oriented discussions.[7-10] Among the resources written specifically for occupational safety and health professionals (see Chapters 34–36), military personnel can find concise and conveniently accessible guidance in the National Institute for Occupational Safety and Health (NIOSH), an institute of the Centers for Disease Control and Prevention, document *NIOSH Pocket Guide to Chemical Hazards*[11] which is available in hard copy, compact disc, or convenient internet format. This document lists OSHA permissible exposure levels, NIOSH recommended exposure levels, immediately available to life and health (IDLH) values, short term exposure levels, personal protective equipment recommendations, and a wealth of other useful and conveniently formatted information. Other web sites, including those belonging to the Agency for Toxic Substances and Diseases Registry (ATSDR), the U.S. Environmental Protection Agency (EPA), and the National Library of Medicine (NLM) also offer an extensive and growing list of chemical, biological, and radiological information (see Chapter 36, "Websites and Electronic Databases"). Specialized technical and medical information on biological and chemical warfare agents is also available.[10,12]

Although military personnel may be compelled at times to endure greater risks from chemical or other hazardous substance exposures, it is not reasonable for them to go without the benefit of greater protection when it can be provided. However difficult the total risk management equation, it remains the obligation of commanders to provide for the safety and health of their personnel under all circumstances and to ensure, to the maximum extent possible, that such exposures are anticipated, recognized, assessed, promptly responded to, both from an industrial hygiene and a medical perspective, and documented in the individuals' medical record.[2] Those tasked with supporting the commander, including medical personnel and deployed industrial hygienists, will be required to develop strategies and priorities to accomplish their part of the force protection mission.

Venues of Toxic Exposures

The wide spread presence of chemicals in businesses and factories is a recognized fact of life in modern industrial societies. Chemicals are used in the manufacture of clothing, plastics, electronic components, paints, pharmaceuticals, agricultural products, vehicles, aircraft, healthcare, research, petroleum purification, and as a wide variety of cleaning, lawn care, and other assorted products in the home. People who live in urban environments may not appreciate the abundance of chemicals also present on farms, mines, ore processing, and other unfamiliar settings. Pesticides, rodenticides, and fungicides, for instance, may often be found in large quantities, or elevated concentrations, in farm storage buildings, grain silos, agricultural supply businesses, etc.

Toxic chemicals are commonly found in pure form or as waste products in containers, pipelines, small shops, large industrial facilities, occupied or abandoned, homes, restaurants, hospitals, aircraft, vehicles, or abandoned sites. They may be labeled correctly or not. They may be labeled in the English language or not. They may also be present as contaminants not readily visible in the air, soil, water, wildlife, or food. They may emanate from the smokestacks or be contained in the effluents or waste pits of industrial facilities. Substances well known to be toxic, such as lead, mercury, arsenic, or asbestos, may be present as contaminants in soil, water, or air, at levels that would be considered unacceptable in the United States, but, which may be tolerated as a matter of course in other parts of the world. Even in western societies in which governments exert control and regulatory authority, it is impossible to track and account for all of those present in an area.

Case Study

A mechanic awoke during the night with excruciating pain in his right hand and arm and left fingers. Later at the base clinic he was noted to have reddened and blistering skin. Mustard gas was immediately suspected (owing to the forward deployed location of the base), however, survey teams using M-8 paper and instruments could find no evidence of it and there were no further casualties. The base safety officer was tasked to survey his work spaces and look for other possible causes.

Questions: How should you approach an entry into these work spaces? Should you wear PPE? What types of information are you looking for?

Mustard gas is an unlikely, but a highly threatening possibility. An experienced IH will certainly be familiar with many other commonly used potentially-injurious chemicals. A reasonable place to start is to ask the individual what sort of tasks he was engaged in and what types of chemicals, cleaning products, or other substances he may have used. (Refer to chapter entitled: Chemical Warfare Agents). Using PPE that ensures skin protection, such as a disposable Tyvek garment and gloves, along with a full face respirator, such as an N95, may be sufficient for this investigation. If symptoms of a possible inhalational exposure, such as headaches, dizziness, irritation, or, if fumes are noted, use of a powered, air-purifying respirator (PAPR) or self-contained breathing apparatus (SCBA) may be indicated. Examining and cataloging chemicals in the workplace is a good place to start, but it is also worth exploring the chance that this chemical contact occurred at another location, including at home.

Among the items the safety officer observed were, solvents, paints, cutting fluid, automobile anti-freeze, various commercial cleaning products, drain cleaner, hydrofluoric acid, and gasoline.

Questions: Which of the items might be related to the symptoms noted? If you had this list of chemicals, where might you go to find useful information as to their potential toxicity? Whom might you call for advice and assistance?

Solvents, caustic drain clearing compounds, and hydrofluoric acid can all cause injuries to the skin. Hydrofluoric acid, however, sometimes used to etch surfaces, is a very dangerous material known to cause severe pain, injury to the skin, and other serious systemic effects. In this instance, the chemical hazards inventory for the operation should be available. Also, maintenance cards often list the hazardous materials required. Materials Safety Data Sheets (MSDS) should be available and the local supporting preventive medicine specialist should be consulted.

The demand for chemicals in both industrial and agricultural settings often requires that they be produced, transported, and stored in large quantities. Ships, large trucks, specialized train cars, and pipelines, are vehicles to transport chemicals across countries, through populous cities, and through or near critical infrastructure (bridges, tunnels). Therefore, even among unmarked vehicles on busy roadways or parked on roadsides or on railway, there is always a risk of one or more chemicals being present. The quantity may be large or small. Risks may be difficult to predict.

Physical agents, and ionizing radiation, are a natural component in our environment from cosmic, terrestrial, and man-made sources. Man-made sources can be present at toxic levels resulting from industrial applications (i.e. weapons manufacturing, commercial and defense nuclear power applications). Non-ionizing radiation (i.e. microwave, lasers, telecommunications sources) is man-made and can be present at toxic levels near the transmitting sources. Lasers present additional hazards depending on the class ratings. Heat and Cold-stress are physical hazards commonly encountered in field applications (i.e., hot and cold weather environments, hot machinery operations).

Media and Routes of Toxic Exposures

Chemical, biological and physical hazards exist in the environment in many different media (air, water, soil, and surface contaminants). For example, fuels and organic solvents may be present in liquid or gas, as well as, aerosol, mist or vapor forms. Such chemicals can pool on hard surfaces, permeate cloth, furniture, or drywall, soak the soil, leach into groundwater, sewers or drainage systems, or collect in underground or above ground closed spaces of any kind. Trapped there they may present a risk of asphyxiation, due to displacement of the air, as well as possibly constituting fire and explosion hazards. Odors and appearances may be a valuable tip off to the presence of such potentially dangerous chemicals. However, it is important to understand that the threshold concentration of a chemical that produces a sensation of an odor may be well below the concentration required to do harm. All of these hazards are intensified when troops are forced to enter a confined space, such as an unoccupied building or the cargo holds of ships during security boarding operations.

Exposures to chemical, biological, and physical substances may occur via inhalation, ingestion, absorption, or injection (see Chapters 5 and 6, "Respiratory Toxicology" and "Dermal Toxicology"). Many chemicals may be inhaled as true gases, vapors, mists, aerosols of liquids, or particulates (dry fine powders, contaminated dust). Some of these substances will remain in trapped in the lungs, while others will rapidly enter the bloodstream and spread systemically throughout the body. Inhaled particles partition differentially within the respiratory tract based on their size, aqueous solubility, and other factors. High concentrations of dust and debris, as experienced by many responders following the collapse of the World Trade Center in New York City, may potentially cause both short and long term consequences[13] (see Chapter 19, "Toxicology of Particulate Matter"). Asbestos fibers may be inhaled without producing any immediate symptoms, but may pose a serious long term risk due to the possibility of cancer.[6]

Aircraft manufacturing is continuing to expand its use of a family of new materials described as carbon fiber-containing advanced composite materials.[14] These fiber reinforced polymeric composite materials are engineered to provide strong and lightweight substitutes for metals. Typically carbon or boron fibers are embedded in a matrix of various epoxy polymer resins. When these materials are consumed by fire, the composite materials degrade and release toxic gases, especially carbon monoxide; particulates, including soot; along with small fiber fragments. All of these combustion products heighten safety and health concerns for emergency responders while fighting the fire and performing rescue operations. Similar precautions must be observed by disposal crews whose work may reaerosolize these materials. Fire fighting foam or other fixant materials may be applied to the debris to impede this reaerosolization. While the health risks due to small carbon fiber exposures are not yet definitively known, the operative approach is to exert caution and prevent unnecessary exposure. Decontamination of personnel using a high efficiency particulate absorbing or high efficiency particulate arrestance (HEPA)-filtered vacuum has been recommended (see the U.S. Navy and U.S. Air Force Aviation Safety websites for more details on aviation-related hazards). Personnel in the field may also be exposed to these combustion products when in the area of burning aircraft and should be advised of the risks.

Compounds, such as hydrogen cyanide, or hydrogen sulfide (see Chapter 20, "Toxicology of Gases"), so severely interfere with the basic cellular processes of energy generation and as such interfere with multiple organ systems of the body as to present a severe and rapid risk of injury or death, even after relatively brief exposures.(6–10) Carbon monoxide, a common combustion product, binds tightly to hemoglobin blocking oxygen transport and again impeding cellular energy metabolism.(6–10) Inhaled organic solvents, or even some alkanes which exist in the gaseous state, may induce narcosis or anesthetic-like effects causing drowsiness, impairment of mental performance, perception, judgment, and possibly even a loss of consciousness(6–10) (see Chapter 16, "Toxicology of Organic Solvents"). Of course, any gas present at a concentration high enough to displace oxygen sufficiently could produce similar results.

While inhalation is one means by which chemicals may enter the body, dermal contact is another (see Chapter 6, "Dermal Toxicology"). Some chemicals may pass relatively easily through clothing and into the skin. Most common gloves, shoes, boots, and other items of clothing, military or civilian, are not designed to resist chemical penetration. Special clothing may be needed to ensure that this does not happen.(2) Such contact could occur during ground combat or other activities that may involve kneeling, sitting or lying on the ground. It may not be immediately obvious that such contact is taking place. One should therefore exercise caution as to where one sits or sleeps. Dermal absorption of chemicals may or may not produce noticeable effects, such as numbness, a rash, redness, or other physical signs. Some may produce appearances or sensations that the victim does not recognize as a possible sign of a chemical exposure. Any such symptom should be evaluated medically as soon as possible. Similar indications in more than one person may result from a group exposure.

Case Study

Three members of a vehicle maintenance platoon got sick with gradually worsening flu-like symptoms and were hospitalized in rapid succession. Others soon began feeling weak and vaguely unwell. All shared the same general messing, berthing and working spaces. A medical officer took charge of the men while an industrial hygienist was directed to investigate for possible occupational or environmental factors. In examining their working spaces the IH noted that the exhaust hood to an engine parts degreaser was not functioning properly and that a chemical odor pervaded the spaces.

Questions: What actions might you take to identify the odor? Where might you look to find information on this chemical?

Again, common sense and some observation are likely to pay dividends. Chemicals that are obviously present in any kind of quantity or that are in use are immediate candidates. In this case, solvents are a potential cause. Air sampling, using the MultiRAE, Drager tubes, or similar devices can be helpful. Removing the personnel from the source of exposure, limiting the source of vapors or fumes, wearing the proper PPE, and repairing any defective engineering controls, such as a chemical hood, are indicated approaches. Risk awareness education is also an important part of the corrective action. Reference to maintenance documents and procedures may reveal the potentially toxic materials used. The supporting Safety Office or supporting preventive medicine unit may have a list of materials and exposure data. The MSDS should be locally available for quick reference by medical personnel.

Ingestion of chemical, biological, or radiological toxins is usually associated with eating contaminated foods or drinking contaminated water. These are two avenues of intoxication that modern military forces usually avoid through self reliance and an abundant use of our own logistical capabilities. However, it must be borne in mind that personnel may still have opportunities to eat and drink from local sources. Local providers of food are most likely to use the resources conveniently and cheaply available to them in the immediate area. These include, water, domesticated or free range animals, processed foods, canned, bottled, or dried, and stored locally. In these instances it is impossible to know what chemicals or pathogens may have entered the food our troops may be consuming, or how the food has been stored or handled.

Case Study

Four soldiers reported chronic headaches and malaise. After clinical examination and several laboratory tests, a heavy metal screen identified elevated blood lead levels in three of the individuals. No occupational or environmental causes were identified and no complaints were noted in others working or living in the same general environment. The soldiers reported that they ate all their meals on base. Further questioning only noted that all four had been visiting a local emporium and tea shop in town.

Questions: How might tea drinking result in lead poisoning? Is lead likely to be found in tea?

Lead or other heavy metals can be a contaminant in food items, herbal medicines, teas, etc. The metals may be derived from the containers these items were stored in or from other causes. Some cooking ware, such as teapots, may even be made by using lead solder or coated using lead glazes. This practice is particularly present in several geographic areas of the world.

These days, the threat of asymmetrical warfare and terrorism makes any and all such possibilities open for exploitation, either by an organized military force or by terrorist entities. It behooves the first responders, environmental specialists, general contractors, recovery workers, as well as military commanders, to understand the nature of these risks and to exercise prudent concern for their impact on operations, be they recovery and restoration or military in nature. Deployed military personnel should only consume water and food from sources approved by military industrial hygiene and preventative medicine personnel.

Chemical warfare agents have been used for a long time, certainly most people are aware of their use in World Wars I and II as well as their use by Saddam Hussein against the Kurdish people in Iraq.(10) Nerve agents, such as Sarin, have been used by states and terrorists. These compounds block neuromuscular transmission and paralyze the respiratory muscles quickly causing unconscious collapse and death. It is worth mentioning that many agricultural pesticides and insecticides cause similar reactions and are much more readily available.(5,7) While not as toxic as Sarin and its congeners, these chemicals may also present serious health risks (see Chapter 18, "Toxicology of Pesticides").

Other chemical warfare agents include mustards and related agents[10,12] produce blisters on the skin and have been traditionally categorized in that way (see Chapter 26, "Toxicology of Chemical Warfare Agents"). These agents readily penetrate ordinary clothing and the unprotected skin. Mustard agents can exist in liquid form, as aerosols, and as vapors. Therefore, they may also be inhaled into the lungs or possibly ingested. Cyanide, cyanogens, and various cyanide compounds, act directly at the molecular level to poison and block the cellular biochemical machinery of metabolism.[6–10] Cyanide can be released as a gas, ingested in food or drink, or, as a liquid, absorbed through the skin. Cyanide is a factor in many smoke inhalation cases since it is often produced as a by-product of the combustion process.[6] Cyanide is also occasionally used in suicide attempts, especially cyanide salts, since they are available and only a small quantity is required when the poison is ingested. It was also used in Nazi gas chambers and in criminal executions.[10] Modern toxicology has compiled an enormous list of potentially toxic chemicals, of many chemical forms and physical characteristics, and acting through many different toxic mechanisms.

Toxins

Toxins, which are produced by bacteria, fungi, plants, and other living organisms, must also enter the host, but, do not replicate themselves. Toxins of this type are molecular in structure, not cellular or viral, and in this sense are more like chemical agents. The concept of a "dose" does not apply to infectious agents, although the terms "minimally infectious dose" or "minimally infectious innoculum" are used in a somewhat analogous fashion. This concept of "dose" is very relevant to the effects of a toxin as it would be to a chemical agent. Toxins typically must be designed and released in a manner that facilitates their internalization into the body via the routes of exposure discussed earlier.

Radioactivity

Radioactivity exists both in the form of long lived naturally occurring elements as well as less stable isotopes that are produced in reactors or accelerators. Without spending much time here on the technical issues involved, radioactive elements should be included in the list of potentially toxic substances. There are various types of radioactivity, and the classification of them is traditionally based on the type of matter that is ejected from the nucleus of the "parent" radioactive element. The three categories of emitters are typically listed as: 1) alpha particles, 2) beta particles, and 3) gamma-rays or x-rays. Without discussing the mechanisms by which these radiations are produced, their physical characteristics, or the manner in which they damage cells or tissues of the body, one can recognize that, like chemicals, they also exert a toxic effect according to a "dose" of radiation to which the body is exposed. The concept of dose from radiation exposures is similar to that for chemicals in that it is the amount of radioactive energy absorbed per unit mass of tissue. Also, the potency of alpha, beta, or gamma exposures depends on whether or not they have been internalized. Inhalation or ingestion of radioactive isotopes is of particular concern for alpha and beta particles. If internalized, the dose from these particles can deliver a dose to sensitive internal tissues leading to local or systemic injury that otherwise would not be possible outside the body. In contrast to chemicals, radiation in the form of gamma-rays (or x-rays) can produce injuries at a distance from the source since these emissions can travel through space and substantial barriers. Owing to the different properties of these elements and their emissions, there is a spectrum of possible risks that come into play for radiation exposures. It is advisable to seek expert assistance (e.g., health physicist, nuclear physicists or engineers, medical physicists, radiopharamacists) once radioactivity has been detected. It is also important for industrial hygienists to have some basic knowledge of radioactivity and to be familiar with detection devices available to them (see Chapter 21, "Toxicology of Radioactive Materials").

From 1946 to 2000, over 120 fatalities have been documented due to radiation accidents. Most occurred due to external exposures, at least one from misadministration of gold-198 (internal exposure), and several from combined external and internal exposures.[15] For example, on September 13, 1987, in the city of Goiâna, Brazil, two individuals pulled the radiation source (Cesium-137) from an abandoned medical teletherapy unit. They brought the source to one of their homes and ruptured the source canister. Astonished with the blue glow from the material, they shared it with friends and relatives and some even rubbed the material on their skin. The spread and distribution continued for 16 days before authorities discovered the problem and initiated an emergency response lasting nearly 6 months. Radiation surveys in the environment identified contamination in houses, vehicles, and public places. A total of 112,800 people from the general public were registered and monitored for potential contamination. Only 249 showed signs of contamination and 4 died of bleeding disorders and sepsis within 4 weeks after entering the hospital. Their deaths were caused by external and internal exposures to the radioactive source.

Depleted uranium (DU) is another radioactive element likely to be encountered by military forces in the form of dusts, contact with DU munitions or armored tanks, or ingesting DU in food or through the water supply. It is not a weapon of mass destruction and is defined as uranium metal in which the concentration of uranium-235 has been reduced from the 0.7% that occurs naturally to a value less than 0.2%. Unlike the example above, exposure to DU does not result in acute radiation sickness. If high level exposure to DU is suspected, the general approach is to conduct a clinical evaluation which includes an assessment (e.g., time and date of exposure, evidence of wounds, environmental data indicates DU contamination) and a routine examination (e.g., blood and urine analyses). In the short term, the kidneys are the most susceptible organ if large amounts of DU are inhaled or ingested and absorbed into the bloodstream. Confirmed high-level exposures should be handled as any heavy metal incorporation (see Chapter 17, "Toxicology of Metals"), including an assessment of any possible nephrotoxicity. Even with confirmed exposures, the likelihood that any health effects will develop is low[16] (see Chapter 21, "Toxicology of Radioactive Materials").

Case Study

An escorted truck convoy en route to its destination unexpectedly detected the presence of radioactivity. The convoy immediately stopped and a quick survey indicated that the dominant radioactive species seemed to be cesium and that it was present over an extended area of the road. After pulling the vehicles fifty yards off the road and establishing perimeter security, the unit commander wrestled with the tactical and medical threats posed to her personnel.

Questions: Is immediate medical attention necessary? Is decontamination needed? What PPE might you recommend? How would you estimate the potential radiation dose from the shine of the roadway exposure? How do you weigh the mission needs against the risks to health and safety?

Generally, a source of radiation that is spread over a large area will present a lower radiation exposure hazard than a source of equal concentration confined to a small area (i.e., dilution reduces the health hazard). Any activity in a potentially contaminated, but unsurveilled area, requires the use of MOPP (mission-oriented protective posture) gear, which can degrade unit performance. In this case, having identified the potential contaminate as cesium provides critical information to the unit commander. This information can be conveyed to a technical specialist or communicated to the appropriate authorities for additional assistance. Quickly establishing the security perimeter outside the contaminated area was consistent with the three basic principles of radiation protection: Time, Distance, and Shielding. Reducing the time spent in the contaminated area reduces the dose to the unit. Increasing distance from the source reduces the exposure and creates a shield (air) that reduces the intensity of the source. Provided no symptoms (e.g. nausea) are presented, immediate medical attention is not necessary. However, details about the unit movements, distance from the contaminated area, and position-specific exposure rate measurements will be needed to conduct a dose assessment if dosimetry is not available. Decontamination of vehicles and any personnel is recommended, especially if the contamination level is high, but can be delayed depending on mission urgency and objectives. Weighing the mission needs against the potential radiological hazard is a challenge, especially for those not familiar with radiation, because the fear of any level of radiation exposure tends to limit mission objectives in favor of health and safety. The unit commander needs to know if the radiation levels present an immediate danger to the unit [potential doses above 125 rem (1.25 Gy)], if not, then mission objectives can take precedence provided the mission objectives justify the unit dose. The dose limits and health and safety practices are different for civilian environments.

Area Reconnaissance and Survey

Area reconnaissance consists of several possibilities. Some of these functions fall within the scope of dedicated units with specific medical responsibilities, such as the U.S. Army, Air Force or Marine Corps Preventative Medicine Units and Preventative Medicine Support Units; the U.S. Army Special Medical Augmentation Response (SMART) Teams; and the U.S. Air Force Medical Global Reach Laydown Team (FFGRL); but many of these functions will be carried out by industrial hygienists in the field assigned in a variety of support roles. In some instances it may be possible to identify chemical, biological or radiological hazards beforehand. Public information, particularly where businesses are concerned, aerial photography and human intelligence can provide such information. Certainly, these issues should be considered for key locations, such as berthing, messing, and hospital areas. Such information may be used in considering routes of advance and communications, etc. Identification of such sites, followed by an estimate of the likely volume of materials, would enable a risk characterization and at least a qualitative risk assessment. More detailed information could be obtained as required.

In the field there are a variety of hand held devices that can be used to detect and identify chemical or radiological hazards, such as: the MultiRAE Plus multi-gas monitor for toxic gases, combustibles, and oxygen; the AP2Ce and APD 2000 Chemical Warfare Agent Detectors; or for radioactive materials, the Surveillance and Measurements (SAM) System as well as the very familiar Ludlum Radiation Meters. Biological agent detection is more difficult since we exist in a world full of naturally occurring biological substances. Detection of a toxic biological substance usually may follow the recognition of casualties, the investigation of so-called "white powder" incidents, or the use of immunoassay or polymerase chain reaction methods on samples collected by a variety of methods. It is also possible to methodically sample a larger area and send the specimens to an off-site laboratory for analysis. From such a site or area analysis, along with a careful consideration of the activities and exposure of personnel, it might be possible to construct a "conceptual site model." This is the development of an abstract model that includes environmental risk factors and potential exposures in the context of their activities and length of time within the area.

Medical and Legal Issues

Given the full range of hazardous chemical, biological, or radiological exposures that may confront our personnel, it is important for us to understand, not only, the unique nature of the threats involved and how to respond to them, but, also to understand and address the unique medical and legal issues that arise in these situations (see chapter entitled: Regulations, Standards, and Guidelines). With military roles spanning the continuum from civil support to less than combat, and combat, the needs, resources, and expectations will vary. However, in all contexts, we accept the need to provide the best possible care and the obligation to keep our troops fully informed of any and all health risks to which they are either known or suspected to have been exposed. Documentation is obviously a crucial aspect of providing care, both immediately, as well as continuing care throughout and following the period of active military service.

A safety and health plan should be designed and briefed, if possible, prior to deployment and throughout the duration of the mission. It will be crucial to involve the medical department. Exposure assessment (see Chapters 23 and 24, "Exposure Assessment" and "Risk Assessment Process for Industrial Hygienists"), clinical evaluation, specimen collection (see Chapter 29, "Biomarker-Based Monitoring"), follow-up, and documentation are all important aspects of the plan that should be included. While exposure assessment focuses on the identification and measurement of chemicals in the environment, generally presumed to be in the vicinity of personnel, the uptake and accumulation of toxins in body tissues or fluids is an important factor to understand for medical evaluation and treatment. For example, medical monitoring for heavy metal exposures, such as lead, arsenic, or mercury, should be given careful consideration if they are present in soil or water, especially if water is directly consumed or used for cooking, if personnel remain in that environment for a significant period of time. (Off duty activities, such as eating in local restaurants, or from street vendors, should be taken into consideration.) When implemented, these data, along with any records of exposure, and with a record of the nature and location of each individuals employment, should be made part of the permanent occupational and medical history of all those exposed.

It seems reasonable to expect that the more normal the working environment, the higher the expectations will be that the personnel potentially exposed receive a degree of medical attention more closely commensurate with that accorded to military or civilian personnel within the U.S. or when attached to well equipped ships or bases. In addition, there will be a more natural expectation that traditional norms of occupational safety and health, such as Occupational Safety and Health Administration (OSHA) standards, be observed. These include specific exposure standards, guidelines for the appropriate use of engineering or administrative controls and personal protective equipment. As military occupational medicine focuses more comprehensively on the long range health and safety of the individual, the expectations for limiting or mitigating any hazardous exposures will only increase. The industrial hygienist may find himself or herself filling a vital niche through detecting, evaluating, and taking steps to mitigate any such risks at the unit level. They may also play a key role in initiating medical care and providing essential documentation, including details of work tasks and measurements of exposure, when required.

Practical Approaches for the Military Leader

Awareness and common sense go a long way towards minimizing risk. Information is available on-line, by reach-back, or through specially trained personnel in the field. Industrial hygienists have skills that are adaptable to the field and that can help ensure the health and safety of personnel first and foremost by anticipating, recognizing, evaluating, and controlling potential exposures. This is the objective of the industrial hygienist in the field. Safety and health training will have to evolve to include more emphasis on these occupational health and safety issues as applied in non-traditional settings. Ideally, personnel should be exposed to this sort of training from the day of their induction into the military throughout their entire career as part of a structured and cumulative program of safety and health training. This practice would be consistent with the global health, safety, and fitness standards currently adopted by US military forces. Leadership at all levels must be more aware, and better trained, to meet these responsibilities. The rewards achieved will be a healthier, fitter, more capable force.

Looking Forward to Prospects for the Future

Industrial hygienists may find themselves shouldering increased responsibility for providing advice to operational commanders. In forward deployed settings their training and experience will be crucial as they may be on their own to deal with this broad range of issues. They may be key advisors with respect to increasing the individual and the unit's awareness of such exposures, as well as the selection and use various approaches to mitigating those threats, including work practices, engineering controls, personal protective equipment, etc.

Specialization may inevitably be the career approach best suited to industrial hygienists working in many civilian contexts, such as: various industries, medical facilities, universities, etc. Within the varied and demanding paradigms of military life and operations, however, broad training and varied experiences will always prove to be an essential element of successful career development. With this in mind, one must look at the types of training, formal and otherwise, that may provide the best foundations for such a challenging, and sometimes unpredictable, future. Industrial hygienists, most of whom possess at least a four year college degree with some specialized training in the physical sciences, biology, epidemiology, toxicology, etc., ongoing professional development may be best served by a more comprehensive training across all these disciplines with an overt public health leaning. Industrial hygienists have been responsible for many aspects of environmental and occupational safety and health, including: detailed work studies, environmental monitoring, taking measurements of environmental exposure, biological monitoring, record keeping, administrative and engineering controls, and personal protective equipment selection. It is not hard not to envision industrial hygienists expanding their traditional health and safety roles to include assuming more responsibilities in the areas of environmental and occupational medicine, especially while serving independent duty assignments. Innovation and adaptation to the needs of the situation will continue to demand the utmost technical skill, initiative and leadership from this relatively small and dedicated community.

References

1. **Dalia, M., A. Spektor:** Review of the Scientific Literature as it Pertains to Gulf War Illnesses; Volume 6: Oil Well Fires. National Defense Research Institute RAND, (1988).
2. **GAO Defense Health Care:** Medical Surveillance Improved Since Gulf War, but Mixed Results in Bosnia, GAO/NSIAD-97-1363. 1997.
3. DoD DIRECTIVE 6490.2, "Comprehensive Health Surveillance," October 21, 2004, (1997).
4. DoD INSTRUCTION 6490.3 "Deployment Health," August 11, 2006.
5. **Karasik, T.:** Toxic Warfare, National Defense Research Institute RAND, (2002).
6. **Klaasen, C. (ed.):** *Casarett and Doull's Toxicology, The Basic Science of Poisons*, 6th edition. New York: McGraw Hill, (2001).
7. **Dart, R.C. (ed.):** *Medical Toxicology* 3rd edition. Philadelphia, PA: Lippincott, Williams & Wilkins, 2004.
8. **Bronstein, A. and P. Currance:** *Emergency Care for Hazardous Materials Exposure,* 2nd edition. Hanover, MD: Mosby Lifeline, 1994.
9. **Olson, K. (ed.):** *Poisoning and Drug Overdose*, 4th edition. New York: Lange Medical Books, McGraw-Hill, 2004.
10. **Sidell, F.R., E.T. Takafuji, and D.R. Franz:** *Textbook of Military Medicine Series: Military Aspects of Chemical and Biological Warfare.* Washington D.C.: Borden Institute, 1997.
11. **National Institute for Occupational Safety & Health (NIOSH):** *NIOSH Pocket Guide to Chemical Hazards,* DHHS (NIOSH) Publication No. 2005-149. Washington D.C.: NIOSH, 2006.
12. **Marrs, T., R. Maynard, F. Sidell:** *Chemical Warfare Agents: Toxicology and Treatment.* New York: John Wiley and Sons, 1996.
13. **Centers for Disease Control and Prevention (CDC):** Mortality and Morbidity Weekly Report (MMWR): Physical Health Status of World Trade Center Rescue and Recovery Workers and Volunteers — New York City, July 2002 – August 2004. *MMWR 53(35)*:807–812 (2004).
14. **Gandhi, S. and R.E. Lyon:** Health Hazards of Combustion Products from Aircraft Composite Materials, U.S. Department of Transportation, Federal Aviation Administration document DOT/FAA/AR-98/34, (1998).
15. **Gusev, I., A. Guskova, and F.A. Mettler:** *Medical Management of Radiation Accidents,* 2nd edition. New York: CRC Press, 2001.
16. **World Health Organization (WHO):** Depleted Uranium: sources, exposure, and health effects. Geneva, Switzerland: WHO, 2001.

Chapter 26

Toxicology of Chemical Warfare Agents

*By Warren W. Jederberg, MS, CIH, RPIH
and Kenneth R. Still, PhD, FATS, CIH, CSP, CHMM*

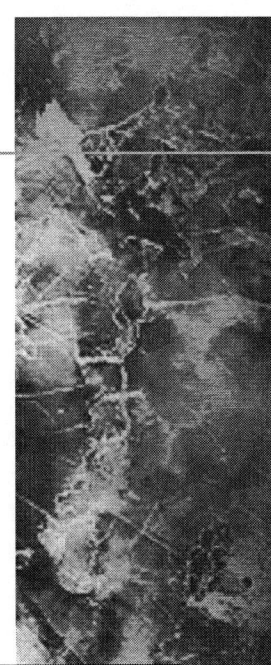

Introduction

The intent of this chapter is to provide the reader with a basic knowledge of the history, toxicological effects and treatment for the classic chemical warfare agents (Nerve, Blister, Choking, Blood, and Incapacitants). Though not considered "Warfare Agents", riot control agents will also be discussed because they are part of the history of chemical warfare agents and still have the potential to be used by both legitimate agencies and terrorists. The detection of these agents uses the same technologies that are used for other industrial chemicals and is an ongoing area of research and development. Therefore a discussion of detectors will not be provided in this chapter. The reader is referred to current literature on hazardous materials detection. This topic has become particularly timely with the increased availability and use of deadly agents by terrorist groups. In 2005 the public disclosure that the allies dumped surplus chemical munitions in the ocean at the end of World War II and that the U.S. Army continued this practice until 1975 has renewed concerns about accidental exposure to fishermen, divers, etc.[1-6] The potential impact on the environment has yet to be fully addressed.

The use of noxious chemicals to influence the outcome of conflict has been noted since ancient times. An extensive review of the history of chemical warfare is beyond the scope of this chapter but the interested reader is referred to the recent text by Tucker.[7] The principles that are used to recognize, evaluate, and control Toxic Industrial Materials (TIMs) and Toxic Industrial Chemicals (TICs), are equally applicable to the classic chemical warfare agents. By examining the toxicology of the classic agents, principles can be learned that are valuable in considering the potential use of industrial chemicals as weapons of mass destruction. Indeed as can be seen from the history of chemical warfare, many of these agents are simply industrial chemicals used for inflicting large numbers of casualties.[7-9]

Outcome Competencies

After completion of this chapter, the reader should be able to:

- Describe the mechanisms of action of the classic classes of chemical warfare agents.
- Describe the signs and symptoms of exposure to the classic classes of chemical warfare agents.
- Describe the treatment for exposure to the classic classes of chemical warfare agents.
- Describe how the basic tools of Industrial Hygiene can be applied in preparing for and responding to chemical warfare agents.
- Apply the principles of recognition, evaluation and control in dealing with chemical warfare agent exposure scenarios.

Prerequisite Knowledge

- College level chemistry.
- Industrial Hygiene exposure assessment methods.
- Basic biology.

Key Terms

nerve agent, blister agent, pulmonary agent, cyanide, soman, sarin, tabun, mustard "gas", incapacitant, riot control agent, vesicant, nerve agent aging

Key Topics

1. Chemical Warfare
2. Toxic Industrial Materials
3. Toxic Industrial Chemicals.

Nerve Agents

The first agents to be discussed are the Nerve Agents. A listing would include: Tabun (GA: Ethyl N-dimethylphosphoramidocyanidate), Sarin (GB: Isopropyl methylphosphonofluoridate), Soman (GD: Pinacolyl methylphosphonofluoridate) and V agents typified by VX (O-Ethyl-S-[2(diisopropylamino)ethyl] methylphosphonothioate). These agents were discovered and refined subsequent to development of organophosphate pesticides.[10–13] The first nerve agent identified was Tabun. It is designated GA because it was the first German agent identified by the Allied Forces during World War II. Other agents were developed and deployed but not used during the war. Nerve agents were alleged to have been used by Suddam Hussein to suppress the uprising of the Kurds before Operation Desert Shield/Desert Storm in the early 1990s.[14–15]

Table 26.1 details the main characteristics of the Nerve Agents. Their toxicity is based on their ability to disrupt the normal function of the nervous system through interference with acetylcholine function. During normal of nerve cell depolarization, acetylcholine is released, crosses the neuromuscular junction, is absorbed at the receptor endplate and is then inactivated by acetylcholine esterase. The nerve agents block the acetylcholine esterase resulting in a continual stimulation of the nerve cells by the excess acetylcholine. The resulting over stimulation of the involved neurologic systems results in the classic symptoms of organophosphate poisoning.[10–13,16–18]

Two mnemonics have been developed to describe the symptoms of Nerve Agent poisoning. For mild vapor exposures: Diarrhea and diaphoresis, Urination, Miosis, Breathing Difficulty, Lacrimation, and Emesis (DUMBLE). For severe vapor exposures: Salivation, Lacrimation, Urination, Dyspnea, Gastrointestinal distress, and Emesis (SLUDGE).[19,20] Moderate exposure to liquid on the skin results in muscle "twitching" at the exposure sight, localized sweating, nausea and vomiting, with generalized weakness. A severe dermal dose results in the same symptoms as a mild exposure plus convulsions and loss of bladder and bowel control. It is important to note that miosis may not attend dermal exposure until a significant dose has already been absorbed and distributed by the circulatory system.[11,21]

Treatment of nerve agent poisoning consists of the administration of atropine and anticonvulsants. Atropine blocks the acetylcholine at the post-synaptic junction thus alleviating some of the effects of the excess acetylcholine. An oxime, 2-pralidoxime chloride (2-PAMCL), is administered to remove the agent from the cholinesterase.[12,16,18,19,22]

After interacting with the acetylcholine esterase molecule for a period of time (so called "aging"), the nerve agent can no longer be removed from the enzyme by an oxime. This reaction consists of monodealkylation of the dialkyl enzyme, creating a more stable monoalkylphosphonyl enzyme.[10,12,16] The "aging" half-lifes for the classic agents are: GA >14 hours, GB 5 hours, GD – 2–6 minutes, VX – 48 hours.[23] However, the fact that the

Table 26.1 — Characteristics of Nerve Agents*

Properties:	Tabun (GA)	Sarin (GB)	Soman (GD)	VX
Molecular Weight:	162.3	140.1	182.18	267.36
Specific Gravity at 25°C:	1.073	1.0087	1.022	1.0083
Boiling Point:	230°C	158°C	198°C	298°C
Vapor Pressure	0.037 mm Hg at 20°C	2.1 mm Hg at 20°C	0.40 mm Hg at 25°C	0.0007 mm Hg at 20°C
Vapor Density: (Air = 1.0)	5.6	4.86	6.3	9.2
Liquid Density:	1.08 g/mL at 25°C	1.10 g/mL at 20°C	1.02 g/mL at 25°C	1.008 g/mL at 20°C
Volatility:	610 mg/m^3 at 25°C	22,000 mg/m^3 at 25°C	3,900 mg/m^3 at 25°C	10.5 mg/m^3 at 20°C
Water Solubility:	9.8 g / 100 g at 25°C	Miscible	2.1 g/100 g at 20°C	Miscible < 9.4°C
LCt50 (Vapor):	400 mg•min/m^3	100 mg•min/m^3	50 mg•min/m^3	10 mg•min/m^3
LD50 (liquid, skin):	1.0 g/70-Kg man	1.7 g/70-Kg man	350 mg g/70-Kg man	10 mg g/70-Kg man
IDLH	0.1 mg/m^3 (CDC Airborne Limit)	0.1 mg/m^3 (CDC/NIOSH)	0.05 mg/m^3 (CDC/Army)	0.003 mg/m^3 (CDC/Army)
STEL	1 X 10^{-4} mg/m^3 (Army)	1 X 10^{-4} mg/m^3 (Army)	5 X 10^{-5} mg/m^3 (Army)	1 x 10^{-5} mg/m^3 (Army)
TLV®, PEL**	1 X 10^{-4} mg/m^3 (Military, not ACGIH)	N/A	3 X 10^{-5} mg/m^3 (Military, not ACGIH)	1 x 10^{-5} mg/m^3 (Military not ACGIH)

* These agents are designated the "G" agents by the allies as they were first developed by the Germans. "GC" was not used as this designation was already in use for the causative microbe for Gonorrhea.
**Value from Emergency Response Cards, CDC at www.bt.cdc.gov/agent

other agents do not age as quickly as Soman can not be used as a rational for delay in treatment.[10]

Pyridostigmine, a carbamate, also inhibits acetylcholine esterase. However, it is easily reversible. Because the active site is blocked, the carbamoylated esterase is protected from nerve agent attack. Therefore, oral dosage with pyridostigmine before nerve agent exposure provides a pool of esterase that will become available following agent exposure. The administration of atropine and 2-PAMCL are still necessary after an exposure. Pyridostigmine has been used for years in therapy of myasthemia gravis (a disease of neuromuscular transmission).[12,23,24]

All occupational/safety and health personnel should be aware of the potential for becoming involved in incidents resulting from the intentional or accidental release of these materials. With these agents in particular, there is likely to be a high index of suspicion that they are present in the area or being sought/used by specific groups. The standard practice of working with emergency response personnel in planning and exercising for response to these materials is a requirement. The standard approaches used for other highly toxic materials would be used in these incidents. Particular attention must be paid to decontamination and control of potentially exposed personnel. As was seen in the Aum Shinrikyo attack in Japan, many potentially exposed personnel may leave the scene and "self report" to a medical facility. Therefore, communication of the event throughout an area will be essential. The ability to rapidly differentiate between the "worried well" and those that have actually been exposed is critical. Evaluation and control of personal protective equipment, potential sheltering facilities, and medical facilities must be part of the planning and require the expertise of the Industrial Hygienist.

Nerve Agent Case Study

June 27, 1994. At 11:30 p.m. the police station at Matsumoto in Nagano, Japan received an urgent report from the City Fire Defense Bureau ambulance team. They reported some patients had been transported to the hospital. Typical symptoms of the 274 people who were treated included darkened vision, ocular pain, nausea, miosis, and a decreased serum cholinesterase activity. Five dead residents were found in their apartments and two victims died immediately after admission to the hospital. Autopsies showed post-mortem lividity (paleness, pallor), miosis, pulmonary edema, increased bronchial secretions, and congestion. Nearly all of the casualties occurred in a sector-shaped residential area within a radius of 150 meters from the center, near a pond. Dead fish and crayfish were found in the pond near the scene the next day. Also, carcasses of dogs, sparrows, a dove, and a large number of caterpillars were found under trees in the area. Trees and grass on the scene were withering, and the color of leaves had changed. A routine analysis of on-site samples failed to find any toxic substances. Three days later Nagano Public Health and the Forensic Science Laboratory detected Sarin in pond water samples.[25] This was a prelude to the attack on March 20, 1995 in the Tokyo subway system by the Aum Shinrikyo cult which resulted in 12 people being killed and some 5,500 seeking medical aid. The impacts on occupational exposed personnel during this incident have been well documented.[26–28]

Vesicant Agents

Commonly known as "Blister agents," the list of vesicants includes Sulphur Mustard (H: Bis(2-chloroethyl) sulphide), Distilled Mustard (HD), the Nitrogen Mustards (HN-1: N-ethyl-2,2'-di(chloroethyl)amine, HN-3: 2,2',2"-tri(chloroethyl)-amine), Mustargen (HN-2: N-methyl-2,2'di(chloroethyl)amine) and Lewisite (L:Chlorovinyl dichloroarsine). Phosgene Oxime (CX: dichloroformoxime), though an urticant, is included because its main action is on skin and has been stockpiled by some nations. Table 26.2 details the characteristics of the classic vesicating agents. The characteristics of the nitrogen mustards are similar to the sulphur mustards. They have been used in the treatment of some cancers and have been stockpiled by some nations. The Nitrogen Mustards are not discussed in detail, as their use in warfare has not been documented.

The term "mustard gas" is a misnomer. This agent is dispersed as an aerosol. Sulphur mustard was used for the first time on July 12, 1917 at Ypres, France. It accounted for the greatest number of chemical casualties during World War I, but resulted in low numbers of deaths.[30–32] The mustard agents were not used in the World War II. However, one of the worst naval catastrophies of World War II occurred when allied vessels were attacked in Bari Harbor, Italy. Some of the vessels (the USS John Harvey in particular) carried mustard containing munitions. During a German aerial attack, 17 ships were sunk (the USS John Harvey, exploded) and personnel were exposed to mustard mixed with seawater and many were exposed to the by-products of burning mustard and other materials. Of 628 mustard casualties among military and merchant marines diagnosed with mustard exposure, 69 died within two weeks. An unknown number of civilians in the port were killed. Medical personnel were not made aware of the presence of mustard agent until well after they had received and were treating large numbers of casualties.[9,30–32] Italy used sulphur mustard against unprotected Ethiopian troops in 1935–1936.[29,30,33] Sulphur mustard was also used during the Iran-Iraq conflict in the 1980s and much of our recent knowledge about the pathology comes from casualties from this conflict treated in European countries.[31,32] Occasionally dredging, fishing or other operations uncover munitions discarded at the end of the world wars.[31] The agent is still active and casualties have resulted. In 2005, many articles appeared in the popular press and investigations were undertaken to identify and clean up sites where allied forces dumped surplus chemical weapons (a large portion of which were mustard munitions).[1–6]

Two mechanisms have been developed to describe the effects of mustard agents. One hypothesis involves the alkylation of DNA with cellular events leading to blister formation. A second hypothesis describes the interaction of mustard with glutathione, the depletion of glutathione and the consequent loss of protection against oxygen-derived free radicals causing lipid peroxidation. According to this hypothesis, these oxidizing compounds

Table 26.2 — Characteristics of Vesicant Agents*

Properties:	Impure Sulphur Mustard (H)	Distilled Sulphur Mustard (HD)	Phosgene Oxime (CX)	Lewisite (L)
Molecular Weight:	159.08+/-	159.08	113.94	207.35
Boiling Point:	Varies	227°C	128°C	190°C
Vapor Pressure:	Varies	0.072 mm Hg at 20°C	11.2 mm Hg at 25°C (solid) 13 mm Hg at 40°C (Solid)	0.39 mm Hg at 20°C
Vapor Density: (Air = 1.0)	Approx. 5.5	5.4	<3.97	7.1
Liquid Density:	Approx. 1.24 g/mL at 25°C	1.27 g/mL at 20°C	Not Determined	1.89 g/mL at 20°C
Solid Density:	Not Applicable	Crystal: 1.37 g/ml at 20°C	Not Applicable	Not Applicable
Volatility:	Approx. 920 mg/m^3 at 25°C	610 mg/m^3 at 20°C	1,800 mg/m^3 at 20°C	4,480 mg/m^3 at 20°C
Water Solubility:	0.092 g/ 100 g at 22°C	0.092 g/ 100 g at 22°C	70%	Slight
LCt$_{50}$ (Vapor):	1,500 mg•min/m^3	1,500 mg•min/m^3 (Inhaled) 10,000 mg•min/m^3 (masked)	3,200 mg•min/m^3 (estimated)	1,200-1,500 mg•min/m^3 (Inhaled) 100,000 mg•min/m^3 (masked)
LD$_{50}$ (liquid, skin):	Approx. 7000 mg/- 70 Kg man	7000 mg/- 70 Kg man	N/A	2800–3500 mg/- 70 Kg man
IDLH	N/A	0.7 mg/m^3 (CDC/Army)	N/A	N/A
TLV®, PEL**	3 X 10^{-6} mg/m^3 (Military not ACGIH)	3 X 10^{-6} mg/m^3 (Military not ACGIH)	N/A	3 X 10^{-3} mg/m^3 (Ceiling value)

* The first of these agents was designated "HS" during WWI for "Hun Stoffe." The "H" continues to be used for the mustard agents.
**Value from Emergency Response Cards, CDC at www.bt.cdc.gov/agent

lead to membrane alterations, changes in membrane fluidity, and eventual cellular membrane breakdown.[31,34]

In the field, the characteristics that make sulphur mustard useful are its low volatility and the latency of the symptoms. Personnel exposed may not be aware of it until hours afterward. In the meantime, they may have contaminated other individuals, material and facilities. Onset of erythema is seen 4–8 hours after exposure with vesication 2–18 hours later and may take several days to become complete. Commonly, small vesicles will develop within or on the periphery of the erythematus area and coalesce to form larger blisters. The fluid from these blisters does not contain agent. After the agent penetrates the skin (within 2 minutes) it "fixes" to tissue components and cannot be removed. Thus decontamination is to prevent further exposure and protect other material and personnel from contamination. Exposed individuals are likely to develop photophobia. Temporary blindness resulting from blepharospasm is common, but very few victims will have any permanent sight problems unless the eye has been directly exposed to a high concentration of mustard agent. The majority of deaths resulting from mustard exposure in World War I were due to pneumonias and other infections. Some immunosuppression is seen and sulphur mustard is considered to be radiomimetic. Therefore, antibiotics should not be administered unless a specific microorganism has been identified. A pseudomembrane may form in the bronchus and must be managed to prevent airway blockage.[31,34]

Incidents of cancers among munitions workers have been documented.[35–37] Though the association between cancer and exposure on the battlefield is not clear, a review of the evidence by the National Academy of Sciences resulted in the US Veterans Association recognizing several type of cancer as "service related injuries" among veterans exposed to sulphur mustard during manufacture of weapons and as a result of military operations.[35]

Lewisite was developed by the allies near the end of World War I. It was not used on the battlefield but is in the chemical weapons inventories of several nations. The toxicological effects cannot be solely attributed to the arsenic in lewisite. The underlying mechanisms of damage are still under investigation. When mixed with sulphur mustard, it could be used to change the persistence of the material. It differs from sulphur mustard in several ways. There is immediate pain upon exposure to lewisite. Within minutes after exposure the tissue show signs of damage and death. Lewisite does not cause damage to the bone marrow. Exposure can cause leakage of fluid from the systemic capillaries and result in hypovolemic shock.[31,39]

British Anti-Lewisite (BAL: dimercaprol) was developed to treat exposure to lewisite and other arsenicals. Other drugs (DMSA – *meso-2,3*-dimercaptosuccinnic acid and DMPS – 2,3-dimercapto-1-propanesulfonic acid) have been found to be equally effective and less toxic than BAL.[9,31,38,39]

Though not a vesicant, phosgene oxime is usually covered in discussions of "blister agents." It is an urticant and its effects are like stinging nettle. Its characteristics are similar to Lewisite: immediate pain, visible damage to tissue within a few minutes, no effect on bone marrow. It is also in the inventories of several nations.[21,31,39]

Vesicant Agent Case Study

June 12, 1998. Three individuals complaining of blister formation presented to an outpatient medical clinic. All 3 had been involved in routine chemical collection from an allegedly uncontaminated chemical storage site. All wore personal protective equipment which consisted of chemical protective masks and butyl rubber boots, glove and aprons. None noted any unusual odor during the operation. All underwent standard decontamination with soap and water at the work site. The evening before reporting to the clinic, 2 or the 3 began to notice mild symptoms of burning and puritus. One patient presented with three 5-mm vesicles on his lower abdomen and back. Each vesicle was surrounded by an erthematous base and contained straw-colored fluid. Later smaller vesicles appeared on this patient's back and left knee. The second patient presented with a circumferential lesion on the right side of the abdomen. It consisted of multiple small vesicles around the periphery which eventually coalesced into a single large bulla. The third patient had a single 5-mm blister on the left thigh.

All three patients had normal vital signs and denied symptoms of dyspnea, nausea, vomiting or diarrhea. All clinical tests were negative. A diagnosis of mild chemical burns resulting from sulphur mustard exposure was made based on the clinical findings and the analysis of chemical samples taken. The pattern of burns suggested that secondary areas on the patients were either not covered by the protective equipment or areas were superficially decontaminated because the risk was perceived to be low.

The burns were treated with silver sulfadiazine cream with daily sterile dressing changes. All patients had good results with this treatment. Their burns healed with minimal scarring. Two patients did develop hypopigmentation at the burn sites.[40]

Pulmonary Agents

The classic pulmonary "Lung" or "Choking" agents are Chlorine (Cl) and Phosgene (CG: Carbonyl Chloride). Table 26.3 details some of the characteristics of the pulmonary agents. The first large-scale use of an industrial chemical in warfare was the use of Chlorine by the Germans in World War I. The first attack on April 22, 1915, resulted in 15,000 wounded and 5000 dead among Allied troops.[7–9] Chlorine was later replaced by Phosgene. Chlorine and Phosgene were used by both sides in World War I. Phosgene was responsible for 85% of all deaths attributed to chemical weapons in World War I.[9,13,41] Chlorine is widely used in industry and in many household products. It is still used as a primary disinfectant for water supplies but is being replaced by other methods. Chlorine gas combines with the moisture in the atmosphere and in the lungs to form hydrochloric acid. Therefore low-level exposure results in irritation of the eyes and upper respiratory tract. Higher exposure leads to edema in the larynx and pharynx as well as pulmonary edema. As a consequence of pulmonary edema, untreated victims of high-level exposure to chlorine or phosgene, succumb to "dry land drowning".

Phosgene is another common industrial chemical. It is used as an intermediate in the production of organic compounds such as acid chlorides and isocyanates. It can also be generated when ultraviolet light interacts with chlorinated hydrocarbon solvents.[42,43] Phosgene causes damage only at the alveolar-capillary membrane and therefore must be inhaled to produce casualties. It has the odor of "fresh mown hay", but the odor threshold is close to the level that will cause damage and should not be relied upon for warning.[42–44]

Treatment for either agent consists of immediate removal from exposure, decontamination and supportive care. Chest X-rays and spirometry may be used to evaluate the extent of damage. Because the pulmonary edema may not develop immediately, victims must be observed and refrain from any exertion. Long-term consequences may include air-way hypersensitivity.[22,44,45]

Awareness of the presence of sources of these chemicals must be an element of any emergency response/anti-terrorism efforts at each governmental level and industrial cite. The industrial hygienist can play a significant role in designing controls to limit the potential for release or access and providing guidance for personal protective equipment and mitigation strategies in the case of release.

Table 26.3 — Characteristics of Pulmonary Agents

Properties:	Chlorine (Cl)	Phosgene (CG)
Molecular Weight:	70.9	98.9
Boiling Point:	-34°C	48°C
Vapor Pressure:	4,800 mm Hg at 20°C	1,215 mm Hg at 20°C
Vapor Density: (Air = 1.0)	2.5	3.48
Liquid Density:	1.41 at 20°C	1.37 at 20°C
Solid Density:	NA	NA
Volatility:	NA	4,3000,000 at 7.6°C
Water Solubility:	0.72 g/ 100 g at 20°C	Slight
LCt_{50} (Vapor):	3000 mg•min/m^3	3200 mg•min/m^3
LD_{50} (liquid, skin):	Not Established	25 mg/Kg
IDLH	29 mg/m^3	8.1 mg/m^3
TLV®, PEL	1.45 mg/m^3	0.4 mg/m^3

Pulmonary Agent Case Study

A patient had worked as a drycleaner for three months. Studies indicated that the average concentration of trichloroethylene in the room was 488 ppm. This level was exceeded when clothing was removed from the cleaning machine. The patient was known to smoke 40 cigarettes/day. He frequently smoked in the cleaning room. He left work and 90 minutes later he collapsed and died. An autopsy showed pulmonary edema. Phosgene was believed to have been generated by the decomposition of trichloroethylene in contact with the hot tip of a burning cigarette.[46]

Cyanide Agents

The Cyanide Agents, commonly called "Blood Agents", include Hydrogen Cyanide (AC: HCN), Cyanogen Chloride (CK: ClCN) and Arsine (SA: AsH_3). Table 26.4 details the characteristics of AC and CK. Though commonly referred to as "Blood Agents", these materials act by interfering with cellular respiration. The cell dies from the lack of oxygen utilization. Cyanide is present in many industrial processes (electroplating, ore extraction, tanning, and chemical syntheses) and significant amounts are found in some common foods (peach pits, apple seeds, lima beans). Cyanide may be a by-product of burning materials or industrial accidents.[47–50]

While not successfully employed on the battlefield, HCN was the agent used for mass extermination in WWII. The Zyklon B briquettes used were calcium sulfate impregnated with HCN and were 40% HCN by weight.[7,41,44] Cyanide is a common agent in suicides and has been used for assassinations.

Table 26.4 — Characteristics of Cyanide Agents

Properties:	Hydrogen Cyanide (AC)	Cyanogen Chloride (CK)
Molecular Weight:	27.03	61.48
Boiling Point:	25.7°C	12.9°C
Vapor Pressure:	740 mm Hg	1,000 mm Hg
Vapor Density: (Air = 1.0)	0.99 at 20°C	2.1
Liquid Density:	0.68 g/mL at 25°C	1.18 g/mL at 20°C
Solid Density:		Crystal: 0.93 g/mL at 12.9°C
Volatility:	1.1X106 mg/m³ at 25°C	2.6X106 mg/
Water Solubility:	100% at 25°C	6.9 g/100 ml at 20°C
LCt_{50} (Vapor):	2,500-500 mg•min/m³ (time-dependent)	11,000 mg•min/m³
LD_{50} (liquid, skin):	7000 mg/-70 Kg man	N/A
IDLH	55 mg/m³ (NIOSH)	N/A
TLV®, PEL	PEL – 11 mg/m³ TLV® – 5 mg/m³ (Ceiling value)	0.3 mg/³ (Ceiling value)

The signs and symptoms of exposure to HCN are rapid in onset. Since cyanide is rapidly distributed, hyperventilation consequent to inhalation leads to increased dose. Death occurs from respiratory and/or cardiac arrest. Long term effects, particularly from near fatal doses, include mental confusion, intellectual deterioration, and parkinsonism.[49–53]

Immediate irritation to the eyes, nose and airways are seen on exposure to cyanogen chloride. Similar symptoms are seen upon exposure to riot control agents.

The cyanide agents are reported to have the odor of "bitter almonds", but this is an unreliable characteristic for identification as many people are unable to smell cyanide.

Due to the circulation of well-oxygenated blood, the skin and organs may appear "cherry-red". However, this is inconsistent and may not be obvious. This is in contrast to the "cyanosis" seen in carbon monoxide (CO) poisoning. In the case of CO poisoning the term "cyanotic" refers to the "bluish" color of the patient not the causative agent.

Immediate removal from exposure to a well-ventilated area is essential. In cases of low exposure, no further action may be required. Treatment regimes are based on any of three basic principles: enzymatic detoxication (e.g. sodium thiosulfate), direct binding (cobalt compounds), or indirect binding (methemoglobin generation).[49–53]

In the United States the Cyanide Antidote Package consists of amyl nitrate and sodium thiosulfate. Oxygen has been advocated as a necessary adjunct to managing cyanide toxicity.[48,52–54]

Cyanide Agent Case Studies

The most well known incident involving exposure to cyanide occurred as a result of the industrial release in Bhopal, India in 1984. The release resulted in over 2,500 deaths within a week and 3,598 after five years. Ocular problems evidenced in the victims included an increased risk of eye infection, hyperresponsive phenomena, excess cataracts, and corneal erosions. Respiratory effects included necrotizing lesions in the upper and lower respiratory tree, pulmonary edema, hemorrhage, bronchopneumonia, and acute bronchiolitis. Significant increases in chromosomal aberrations were seen in a study of lymphocytes from person exposed after 2.5 and 3 years.[55]

On a smaller scale, fatal accident occurred aboard a trawler of the coast of the Mauritania in West Africa. The vessel was near the end of a 30 day fishing spell and the crew was engaged in sorting the last hauls. Immediately after opening the side door of a refrigerated salt water tank, a crewman collapsed. Unaware of the danger, several other crewmen went to their fallen shipmates' aid. By the time the situation was recognized, three crewmen were dead and six other injured. The three who died did so in 45–60 seconds after exposure. The survivors suffered a variety of symptoms including blackouts, seizures, chest pain, vomiting, and difficulty breathing. Investigations lead to the conclusion that death had resulted from cyanide and methane generated by bacteria on the stored fish.[56]

Incapacitating Agents

According to the dictionary, "incapacitate" means to make incapable or unfit; to deprive of capacity.[57] In the military sense this means any agent that produces temporary physiological and/or mental effects that make individuals incapapble of concerted effort in the performance of assigned duties. In a more general context, the term is used to mean "disable" as used in occupational medicine. Any of the agents discussed thus far, of course are incapacitating, however the materials in this section were specifically selected because they are not normally considered lethal, and their effects are temporary when used as intended.[58-61]

Incapacitating agents include: BZ (Agent 15: 3-quinuclidinyl benzilate), and Adamsite (DM: Diphenylaminechloroarsine). They affect different systems. BZ acts on the nervous system by competitive inhibition of acetylcholine at postsynaptic and postjunctional receptor sited in exocrine glands, smooth muscle, autonomic ganglia, and the brain. It causes peripheral nervous system effects that are generally opposite of those seen with the organophosphate agents. The ICt_{50} (the dose which would incapacitate 50% of those exposed) is 112 mg-min/m^3. The LCt_{50} (the dose which would kill 50% of those exposed) is 200,000 mg-min/m^3. So it can be seen that BZ has a large "margin of safety". The hall mark symptoms have been described as: "Hot as a hare, dry as a bone, mad as a hatter, red as beet, blind as a bat". Effects from exposure to BZ are not seen until 30 minutes to 24 hours afterward. Victims may experience illusions and hallucinations. These hallucinations may be shared with other victims and can present a hazard to those trying to aid the victims. These effects typically last 72 to 96 hours. In the period from 4–24 hours, exposed individuals generally enter a stupor and become hyperthermic. Between 20 to 96 hours there is full-blown delirium. During the last phase, there is deep sleep, paranoia, crawling or climbing automatisms, and eventually reorientation. Specific treatment is with the carbamate anticholinesterase physostigmine. Physostigmine temporarily raises acetylcholine concentrations by reversibly binding the anticholinesterase. Such therapy is minimally effective during the first four hours after exposure but is very effective if given later.[58,60,62,63]

BZ patients are at greatest risk from injuries from his or her own erratic behavior (or from behavior from similarly intoxicated victims) and hypothermia.

There are no field detectors for BZ. Awareness of the signs and symptoms and the knowledge of a probable exposure to aerosols are clues that would lead to the diagnosis. A HEPA filter canister in a protective mask will protect the face and respiratory tract to aerosolized agent, and should be worn in environments potentially contaminated with BZ. Inhalation of aerosolized BZ is the greatest risk, but terrorists could easily choose to disseminate it in forms that could be ingested or absorbed through the skin.

DM has anti-cholinergic effects. Exposure can be through inhalation, ingestion, dermal or eye contact. Ingestion is an uncommon route of exposure. It is commonly known as a vomiting agent. The LCt_{50} for DM is 11,000–15,000 mg-min/m^3 and the ICt_{50} (vomiting) is 22–150; nausea, vomiting: approximately 370 mg-min/m^3. After 5–10 minute latency, there is irritation of the eyes, lungs and mucous membranes followed by nausea, headache and persistent vomiting. DM has never been deployed on the battlefield, but would be used to force victims to remove their protective mask and make them more vulnerable to more lethal agents.[59-65]

There is no specific antidote for DM exposure. Antiemetics and analgesics may be used for symptomatic relief. Usually no medical treatment beyond removal from exposure and decontamination are necessary. Long-term consequences of exposure are unknown.[59,63]

Riot Control Agents

The materials commonly listed in this category include: Tear Gas (CS: 2-Chlorobenzilidene malononitrile), Mace™ (CN: 2-Chloroacetophenone), and Oleoresin capsicum (OC - Pepper spray). The LD_{50} for CS and CN are estimated to between 25,000–100,000 mg-min/m^3 and 7,000 mg-min/m^3 respectively.[59,60,64]

As indicated by the name of this category, these agents are specifically selected to do no permanent harm but to in some way degrade the performance of the individual. Some are also called "Riot Control Agents" as that has historically been their main use.

While the U.S. does not consider these materials to be "warfare" agents, much of the rest of the world does. Some have been used in warfare and are still considered potential threats.[59,60]

These agents are not "gases," but are dispersed as crystalline aerosols. They all result in immediate pain and discomfort. All cause a burning of the eyes, skin and mucous membranes.

Immediate removal from exposure and thorough washing is required. Long-term or frequent exposures have resulted in hypersensitivity responses. Though these agents are meant to have only temporary effects, the risk associated with exposure and underlying medical conditions is not well characterized.[22,66] CS and CN are considered to be not classifiable as human carcinogens though they do give a positive result with some bacterial strains in the Ames mutagenesis assay.[64,59,67]

Though these agents are selected for their low toxicity, their use by law enforcement agencies is still highly controversial.[68-70] Many law enforcement agencies are replacing the use of CS with Pepper Spray. Pepper Spray is available from commercial sources and the regulations for its use vary widely. It causes immediate pain and irritation to the skin, eyes and respiratory tract. Treatment for CS, CN and Pepper Spray includes removal from exposure and thorough washing.

Physical injuries have occurred when the delivery device has been handled or the individual was too close to an explosive delivery device.

Incapacitating/Riot Control Agent Case Study

A store owner tightened a screw on the door of an old safe that had a chemical theft-deterrent device. The metal housing on the device contained a glass vial of liquid, which cracked as the screw tightened. About 4 ounces of CS were released. The store owner sustained eye and skin irritation and was treated at a hospital and released.[71]

Occupational and Emergency Exposure Guidelines

Occupational and emergency exposure guidelines have been established for most of the agents discussed.[72–77] The derivation of these values is not in the scope of this chapter, but other chapters in this book address the principles and methodologies used. A good discussion of the approach used for the derivation of Acute Exposure Guideline Levels (AEGLs) can be found in reference cited and in the "Standard Operating Procedures for Developing Acute Exposure Guideline Levels for Hazardous Chemicals".[78] A review of that methodology will familiarize the reader with some of the constraints required when developing standards based on limited data.

Conclusions

Chemical Warfare Agents demonstrate a large spectrum of toxic mechanisms similar to those that would be seen in numerous industrial chemicals throughout commerce. Understanding these mechanisms helps to prepare for response to mass exposure from intentional or accidental release. Industrial Hygiene and preventive medicine professionals are becoming more involved with planning for and responding to incidents involving exposure to these materials. Such compounds in industry represent a large pool of "weapons of opportunity" for terrorists.

References

1. **Bull, J.:** "Vast Chemical Dumping Found At Sea." *Los Angeles Times* (October 30, 2005).
2. **Bull, J.:** "Unsafe Dumping." *Newport News Daily Press* (November 2, 2005).
3. **TenBruggencate, J.:** "Dumped Toxic Weapons Still Lurk In Sea Off Oahu." *Honolulu Advertiser* (November 3, 2005).
4. **Bull, J.:** "House To Probe Chemical Dumping." *Newport News Daily Press* (November 13, 2005).
5. **TenBruggencate, J.:** "Army Data Conflicting Over Toxic Dump Sites." *Honolulu Advertiser* (November 17, 2005).
6. **Bull, J.:** "Army Starts to Monitor Dump Zone." *Newport News Daily Press* (November 21, 2005).
7. **Tucker, J.B.:** *War of Nerves: Chemical Warfare from World War 1 to Al-Qaeda.* New York, NY: Pantheon Books, 2006.
8. **Langford, R.E.:** Introduction to chemical agents. In *Introduction to Weapons of Mass Destruction — Radiological, Chemical and Biological.* New Jersey: John Wiley & Sons, Inc., 2004. pp. 211–224.
9. **Joy, R.J.T.:** Historical aspects of medical defense against chemical warfare. In *Textbook of Military Medicine — Medical Aspects of Chemical and Biological Warfare*, Sidell, F.R, E.T. Takafuji, and D.R. Franz (eds.). Washington DC: The Borden Institute, 1997. pp. 87–109.
10. **Marrs, T.C., R.L. Maynard, and F.R. Sidell:** Organophosphate Nerve Agents. In *Chemical Warfare Agents – Toxicology and Treatment.* New York: John Wiley & Sons Ltd, 1996. pp.83–100.
11. **Sidell, F.R.:** Nerve Agents. In *Textbook of Military Medicine — Medical Aspects of Chemical and Biological Warfare,* Sidell, F.R, Takafuji, E.T. and D.R. Franz (eds.). Washington DC: The Borden Institute, 1997. pp.129–179.
12. **Taylor, P.:** Anticholinesterase Agents. In *Goodman & Gilman's The Pharmacological Basis of Therapeutics*, 9th edition. Molinoff, P.G. and R.W. Ruddon (eds.). New York: The McGraw-Hill Companies, Inc., 1996. pp. 161–176.
13. **Langford, R.E.:** Effects of chemical weapons and medical treatments. In *Introduction to Weapons of Mass Destruction — Radiological, Chemical and Biological.* Hoboken, NJ: John Wiley & Sons, Inc., 2004. pp. 225–280.
14. **Nezan, K.:** "When our 'friend' Saddam was gassing the Kurds." *Le Monde diplomatique(Eng)* (March 1998).
15. **Kucera, J.:** "1988 gassing still killing Iraqi Kurds — Chemical attack causing cancers, multitude of other illnesses." *San Francisco Chronicle* (July 1, 2002)
16. **Echobichon, D.J.:** Toxic Effects of Pesticides. In *Casarett & Doull's Toxicology: The Basic Science of Poisons*, 6th edition. Klaassen, C.D. (ed.). New York: McGraw-Hill Health Professions Division, 2001. pp. 763–810.
17. **Rotenberg, J.S. and Newmark, J.:** Nerve Agent Attacks on Children: Diagnosis and Management. *Pediatrics 112(3)*:648–658: 2003.
18. **Nishijima, D.K., and S.W. Weimer:** Toxicity, Organophosphate and Carbamate. [Online] http://www.emedicine.com/emerg/topic346.htm [Accessed December 13, 2005].
19. **Folton, G., et al.:** Pediatric Nerve Agent Poisoning: Medical and Operational Considerations for Emergency Medical Services in a Large American City. *Pediatric Emergency Care. 22(4)*:239–244 (2006).
20. **Noeller, T.P.:** "Chemical Weapons — The Cleveland Clinic Disease Management Project." [Online] Available at http://www.clevelandclinicmeded.com/diseasemanagement/infectiousdisease/chemical/chemical.htm [Accessed August 26, 2006].
21. **Sidell, F.R., W.C. Patrick, T.R. Dashiell, K. Alibek, and S. Layne:** Chapter 3: Chemical Agents. In *Jane's Chem-Bio Handbook*, 2nd edition. Alexandria, VA: Jane's Information Group, 2003.
22. **Sidell, F.R., W.C. Patrick, T.R. Dashiell, K. Alibek, and S. Layne:** Chapter 4. Chemical Agents. In *Jane's Chem-Bio Handbook*, 2nd edition. Alexandria, VA: Jane's Information Group, 2003.

23. **Dunn, M.A., B.R. Hackley, and F.R. Sidell:** Pretreatment for nerve agent exposure. In *Textbook of Military Medicine — Medical Aspects of Chemical and Biological Warfare*, Sidell, F.R., E.T. Takafuji, and D.R. Franz (eds.). Washington DC: The Borden Institute, 1997. pp.181–196.
24. **Marrs, T.C., R.L. Maynard, and F.R. Sidell:** Treatment and prophylaxis of organophosphate nerve agent poisoning. In *Chemical Warfare Agents — Toxicology and Treatment.* New York: John Wiley & Sons Ltd, 1996. pp.101–113.
25. **Nozakai, H., et al.:** Secondary exposure of medical staff to sarin vapor in the emergency room. *Intensive Care Med. 21*:1032–1035 (1995).
26. **Nishiwaki, Y., K. Maekawa, Y. Ogawa, N. Asukai, M. Minami, and K. Omae:** Effects of Sarin on the Nervous System in Rescue Team Staff Members and Police Officers 3 Years after the Tokyo Subway Sarin Attack. *Environmental Health Perspectives 109(11)*:1169–1173 (2001).
27. **Miyaki, K., et al.:** Effects of Sarin on the Nervous System of Subway Workers Seven Years after the Tokyo Subway Sarin Attack. *J. Occup. Health 47*:299–304 (2005).
28. **Seto, Y.:** "The sarin gas attack in Japan and the related forensic investigation." [Online] Available at http://www.opcw.org/synthesis/html/s6/p14prt.html [Accessed December 7, 2005].
29. **Marrs, T.C., R.L. Maynard, and F.R. Sidell:** Mustard Gas. In *Chemical Warfare Agents — Toxicology and Treatment.* New York: John Wiley & Sons Ltd, 1996. pp.139–173.
30. **Sidell, F.R., and D.R. Franz:** Overview: Defense against the effects of chemical and biological warfare agents. In *Textbook of Military Medicine — Medical Aspects of Chemical and Biological Warfare*, Sidell, F.R, Takafuji, E.T. and D.R. Franz (eds.). Washington DC: The Borden Institute, 1997. pp.1–7.
31. **Sidell, F.R., J.S. Urbanetti, W.J. Smith, and C.G. Hurst:** Vesicants. In *Textbook of Military Medicine — Medical Aspects of Chemical and Biological Warfare*, Sidell, F.R, Takafuji, E.T. and D.R. Franz (eds.). Washington DC: The Borden Institute, 1997. pp.197–228.
32. **Reminick, G.:** *Nightmare in Bari: The World War II Liberty Ship Poison Gas Disaster and Cover-up.* Palo Alto, CA: The Glencannon Press, 2001.
33. **Bridel G.:** "Ethiopia 1935-36: mustard gas and attacks on the Red Cross." [Online] Available at www.icrc.org/Web/eng/siteeng0.nsf/iwpList96/DEB07F09BE30F4B8C1256DB000479398 [Accessed September 2, 2006].
34. **Dacre, J.C., and M. Goldman:** Toxicology and pharmacology of the chemical warfare agent sulfur mustard. *Pharm. Reviews 48(2)*:289–326 (1996).
35. **Pechura, C.M. and D. Rall:** *Veterans at Risk: The Health Effects of Mustard Gas and Lewisite.* Washington DC: National Academy Press, 1993.
36. "Chemical Emergencies: CDC Fact Sheet — Facts About Sulfur Mustard." [Online] Available at http://www.bt.cdc.gov/agent/sulfurmustard/basics/pdf/sulfur-mustard-facts.pdf#search=%22CDC%20Fact%20Sheet%20-%20Facts%20about%20sulfur%20mustard%22. [Accessed September 2, 2006].
37. "VA Fact Sheet: Mustard Gas Exposure and Long-Term Health Effects." [Online] Available at http://www.va.gov/pressrel/99mustd.htm. [Accessed September 2, 2006]
38. **Marrs, T.C., R.L. Maynard, and F.R. Sidell:** Organic arsenicals. In *Chemical Warfare Agents — Toxicology and Treatment.* New York: John Wiley & Sons Ltd, 1996. pp.175–184.
39. **Klaasen, C.D.:** Heavy metals and heavy-antagonists. In *Goodman & Gilman's The Pharmacological Basis of Therapeutics,* 9th edition. Molinoff, P.G. and R.W. Ruddon (eds.). New York: The McGraw-Hill Companies, Inc., 1996. pp. 1649–1671.
40. **Kurt, G.D., and G. Aspera:** Exposure to liquid mustard. *Ann. Emerg. Med. 37(6)*:653–656 (2001).
41. **Marrs, T.C., R.L. Maynard, and F.R. Sidell:** Phosgene. In *Chemical Warfare Agents — Toxicology and Treatment.* New York: John Wiley & Sons Ltd, 1996. pp.185–202.
42. **Burgess, W.A.:** Welding. In *Recognition of Health Hazards in Industry: A Review of Materials and Processes.* New York: John Wiley & Sons, Inc., 1995. pp. 191–193.
43. **Lipsett, M.J., D.J. Shusterman, and R.R. Beard:** Inorganic Compounds of Carbon, Nitrogen, and Oxygen. In *Patty's Industrial Hygiene and Toxicology,* 4th edition. Clayton, G.D. and F.E. Clayton (eds.). New York: John Wiley & Sons, Inc., 1994. p.4557.
44. **Urbanetti, J.S.:** Toxic inhalation injury. In *Textbook of Military Medicine — Medical Aspects of Chemical and Biological Warfare.* Sidell, F.R, E.T. Takafuji, and D.R. Franz (eds.). Washington DC: The Borden Institute, 1997. pp.247–270.
45. "Pulmonary Agents CG." [Online] Available at http://vnh.org/CHEMCAS/02Pulmonaryagents.html [Accessed December 15, 2005].
46. "Phosgene" [Online] Available at http://www.headlice.org/lindane/chemicals/phosgene.htm. [Accessed September 4, 2006].
47. **Norton, S.:** Toxic Effects of Plants. In *Casarett & Doull's Toxicology: The Basic Science of Poisons*, 5th edition. Klaassen, C.D. (ed.). New York: McGraw-Hill Health Professions Division, 1996. p. 849.
48. **Baskin, S.I. and T.G. Brewer:** Cyanide Poisoning. In *Textbook of Military Medicine — Medical Aspects of Chemical and Biological Warfare*, Sidell, F.R, E.T. Takafuji, and D.R. Franz (eds.). Washington DC: The Borden Institute, 1997. pp. 271–277.
49. **Bryson, P.D.:** Cyanide. In *Comprehensive Review in Toxicology for Emergency Clinicians,* 3rd edition. Washington DC. Taylor & Francis, 1996. pp. 352–256.
50. **Gossel, T.A. and J.D. Bricker:** Plants. In *Principles of Clinical Toxicology*, 3rd edition. New York: Raven Press, 1994. p. 254.

51. **Hartung, R.:** Cyanides and Nitriles. In *Patty's Industrial Hygiene and Toxicology*, 4th edition. Clayton, G.D. and F.E. Clayton (eds.). New York: John Wiley & Sons, Inc., 1994. p.3124.
52. **Marrs, T.C., R.L. Maynard, and F.R. Sidell:** Cyanides. In *Chemical Warfare Agents — Toxicology and Treatment*. New York: John Wiley & Sons Ltd, 1996. pp. 203–219.
53. **Gossel, T.A. and J.D. Bricker:** Carbon Monoxide, Cyanide, and Sulfide. In *Principles of Clinical Toxicology*, 3rd edition. New York: Raven Press, 1994. pp. 109–134.
54. **Bryson, P.D.:** Cyanide. In *Comprehensive Review in Toxicology for Emergency Clinicians*, 3rd edition. Washington DC: Taylor & Francis, 1996. pp. 360–364.
55. **Dhara, R.:** Health Effects of Bhopal Gas Leak: A Review. *New Solutions 4(3)*:35–48 (1994).
56. **Cherian, J.A., and I. Richmond:** Fatal methane and cyanide poisoning as a result of handling industrial fish: a case report and review of the literature. *J. Clin. Pathol. 53*:794–795 (2000).
57. **Stein, J. (ed.):** *The Random House College Dictionary*, Revised Edition. New York: Random House Inc., 1982.
58. **Ketchum, J.S., and F.R. Sidell:** Incapacitating Agents. In *Textbook of Military Medicine — Medical Aspects of Chemical and Biological Warfare*, Sidell, F.R., E.T. Takafuji, and D.R. Franz (eds.). Washington DC: The Borden Institute, 1997. pp. 294–296.
59. **Sidell, F.R.:** Riot Control Agents. In *Textbook of Military Medicine — Medical Aspects of Chemical and Biological Warfare*, Sidell, F.R., E.T. Takafuji, and D.R. Franz (eds.). Washington DC: The Borden Institute, 1997. pp. 307–324.
60. FM 3-11.9/MCRP 3.37.1B/NTRP 3-11.32/AFTTP(I), II. Chemical Warfare Agents and their properties. In: *Potential Military Chemical/Biological Agents and Compounds*, January 2005 (Available at www.us.army.mil).
61. "Incapacitating agent: [Online] Available at http://en.wikipedia.org/wiki/Incapacitating_agent. [Accessed September 8, 2006].
62. CBRNE – Incapacitating Agents, 3-Quinuclidinyl Benzilate" [Online] Available at www.emedicine.com/emerg/topic912.htm. [Accessed September 2, 2006].
63. "Emergency Response Card: ADAMSITE" [Online] Available at http://ershdb.consolidatedsafety.com/printableERC.asp?AgentID=29750017 [Accessed September 2, 2006].
64. **Marrs, T.C., R.L. Maynard, and F.R. Sidell:** Riot-Control Agents. In *Chemical Warfare Agents — Toxicology and Treatment*. New York: John Wiley & Sons Ltd, 1996. pp. 221–229.
65. "Adamsite" [Online] Available at http://en.wikipedia.org/wiki/Adamsite [Accessed September 2, 2006].
66. "CS Gas" [Online] Available at http://en.wikipedia.org/wiki/CS_Gas [Accessed September 9, 2006].
67. Tear Gases — An overview of some riot control agents. In: *A FOA Briefing Book on Chemical Weapons*, S-172 90, Swedish National Defense Research Agency, 1992 [Online] Available at http://www.lsic.ucla.edu/classes/mimg/robinson/micro12/Webste_Active/chemicalweapons/tear.htm. [Accessed September 9, 2006].
68. "Montreal medical team exposes documents on tear gas danger." [Online] Available at http://www.afn.org/~iguana/archives/2001_05/20010512.html [Accessed September 2, 2006].
69. **Smith, C.G, and W. Stopford:** Health Hazards of Pepper Spray. *North Carolina Medical Journal 60*:268–274 (1999).
70. **Fraunfelder, F.T.:** Is CS gas dangerous? *Brit. Med. J. 320*:458–459 (2000).
71. "Brief Report: Exposure to Tear Gas from a Theft-Deterrent Device on a Safe Wisconsin, December 2003," *MWR Weekly 53*(08) 2004.
72. **National Institute for Occupational Safety and Health (NIOSH):** NIOSH Pocket Guide to Chemical Hazards. NIOSH Publication No. 2005-151, 2005.
73. OSHA/NIOSH Interim Guidance — (February 2006) — Chemical — Biological — Radiological — Nuclear (DBRN) Personal Protective Equipment Selection Matrix for Emergency Preparedness: Nerve Agents. [Online] Available at: http://www.osha.gov/SLTC/emergencypreparedness/cbrnmatrix/nerve.html [Accessed September 9, 2006].
74. OSHA/NIOSH Interim Guidance — (February 2006) — Chemical — Biological — Radiological — Nuclear (DBRN) Personal Protective Equipment Selection Matrix for Emergency Preparedness: Blister Agents. [Online] Available at: http://www.osha.gov/SLTC/emergencypreparedness/cbrnmatrix/blister.html [Accessed September 9, 2006].
75. **National Research Council:** Acute Exposure Guideline Levels for Selected Airborne Chemicals (Vol. 3). Washington D.C.: NAC Press, 2003.
76. **National Advisory Committee for Acute Exposure Guideline Levels (AEGLs) for Hazardous Substances:** Proposed AEGL Values. EPA [OPPTS-00312; FRL-6776-3] Federal Register 66(85), 21940. May 2, 2001.
77. Chemical Warfare Agent Criteria/Summary Information March 2006. [Online] Available at: http://chppm-www.apgea.army.mil/chemicalagent/PDFFiles/ChemicalWarfareAgentCriteria_SummaryMar2006.pdf [Accessed September 9, 2006].
78. **National Research Council:** *Standing Operating Procedures for Developing Acute Exposure Guideline Levels for Hazardous Chemicals*. Washington D.C.: National Academy Press, 2001.

Additional Reading

1. **Alibek, K.:** *Biohazard*. New York: Random House, 1999.
2. **Benjamin, D. and S. Simon:** *The Next Attack*. New York: Times Books, 2005.
3. **Butler, R.:** *The Greatest Threat*. New York: Perseus Books Group, 2000.

4. **Carroll, M.C.:** *Lab 257.* New York: HarperCollins Publishers Inc., 2004.
5. **Falkenrath, R.A., R.D. Newman, and B.A. Thayer:** *America's Achilles' Heel.* Cambridge, MA: The MIT Press, 2001.
6. **Greenberg, M.I., R.J. Hamilton, and S.D. Phillips (eds).:** *Occupational, Industrial, and Environmental Toxicology.* St. Louis, MO: Mosby-Year Book Inc., 1997.
7. **Karasik, T.:** *Toxic Warfare.* Santa Monica, CA: RAND Corporation, 2002.
8. **Sidell, F.R., W.C. Patrick, and T.R. Dashiell:** *Jane's Chem-Bio Handbook.* Alexandria, VA: Jane's Information Group, 2000.
9. **Tucker, J.B.:** *War of Nerves: Chemical Warfare from World War 1 to Al-Qaeda.* New York, NY: Pantheon Books, 2006.

Chapter 27

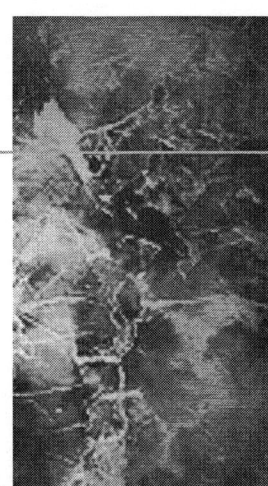

Toxicology in Emergency Response Planning

By Warren W. Jederberg, MS, CIH, RPIH

Outcome Competencies
After completing this chapter, the reader should be able to:

- Define underlying terms used in this chapter.
- Describe three main sources for toxicological data used in response planning and describe the use of each source.
- Describe the use of toxicology data in preparing for local incidents.
- Explain the constraints on the use of main sources of toxicological data in incident response planning.
- Discuss the potential roles that industrial hygienists may play in planning for and responding to an incident involving toxic materials.

Prerequisite Knowledge
1. General industrial hygiene background.
2. General knowledge of how to access toxicology data.

Key Terms
AEGL, ERPG, stressor, TLV® – C, TLV® – STEL, TLV® – TWA

Key Topics
1. Concept of "All Hazards"
2. Common Sources of information
   - Material Safety Data Sheets
   - Threshold Limit Values
   - Emergency Response Planning Guides
   - Acute Exposure Guideline Levels
   - 2004 Emergency Response Guide
   - Interaction between chemical and physical stressors
   - Risk communication
   - Integration of information
   - Potential roles of the industrial hygienist in planning for and responding to an incident involving toxic materials.

Introduction

The popular notion of "toxicology" includes the disciplines of clinical and forensic toxicology wherein the principles of toxicology are applied after exposure has occurred. It is the intent of this chapter to review some of the issues and sources of toxicological information available to those tasked with planning for and responding to emergency situations involving multiple hazards. The information is used in all five phases of incident management system to be discussed in detail at the end of this chapter.

The interpretation and use of technical data (toxicologic) has always presented problems for professionals and lay persons not involved in its development and distribution. This difficulty has been somewhat addressed through the requirement to have Material Safety Data Sheets (MSDS) and other risk communication devices in the workplace. This is an area of ongoing effort.[1] The problem is compounded when the data is needed to make rapid decisions in a dynamic emergency response environment. Complications arise as multiple stressors (hazards) are considered. The tools of "risk communication" are available, but are generally applied to a specific singular hazard in restricted exposure conditions.[2] As seen consequent to the events of 9/11, all personnel in the area of an incident may be affected and standard practices for prevention of even routine exposures may be ignored.[3,4]

Concept of "All Hazards"

The universe of potential incidents includes man-made and natural disasters. In the post 9/11 environment, it is understood that separating incidents fails to fully integrate response planning. Most "disaster" planning has been conducted for natural disasters (tornadoes and earthquakes), but was separate from technical/man-made disasters (spills, fires, civil disobedience, etc.). In the past, environmental disasters have been considered as "natural." The new climate of terrorism requires consideration of intentional environmental disaster along with other technical/man-made incidents.[5–7] Previously, health care providers and emergency medical personnel were trained in universal precautions and the workplace was regulated by the Occupational Safety and Health Administration (OSHA) requirements for a "blood borne pathogen" program.[8] Every workplace that handles hazardous chemicals is required to have a "hazardous materials awareness" and "hazardous materials spill response plan."[9,10] However, these plans are not adequate for an intentionally dispersed agent or combination of stressors (i.e. multiples chemicals, adverse physical environments) or the "biological incident" (i.e. anthrax, ricin), where there is an intentional "release" of dangerous material.

The "all hazards" approach is based on the concept that few events present a single stressor. The definition of "stressor" for purposes of this chapter: a stressor may be physical (i.e., noise, vibration, heat, radiation), chemical (acid, base, asphyxiant), or biological (i.e., bacteria, virus, mold, pollen, toxin) in nature that results in a response in the human system. An extension of this concept is "Full Spectrum Emergency Preparedness" or "All Hazards" (Figure 27.1). The overlap between the "Biological" and "Natural Disaster" circles indicates there are background rates for some biological events (endemic and seasonal disease outbreaks) that can confound or mask intentional incidents. Therefore, response planning requires consideration of all potential elements of the event. It is, however, impossible to plan and resource for response to all possible combinations of events and stressors. Response planning should begin with the risks associated with the most likely natural incident based on geography and history.[10–12] In the case of man-made or intentional incidents, including the release of chemicals, the probability and consequent impact vary based on the specific type of event (Figure 27.2). While most toxicity data is based on inhalation exposures, multiple routes of exposure (inhalation, dermal, gastrointestinal, injection) can be expected in disaster incidents as a direct consequence of the incident and as by-products of remediation efforts.[6] Current threat information would suggest that the likelihood of a chemical or biological incident is greater than a radiological (radiation dispersal device) event. The physical, economic and social impact of each type of event must be considered and appropriate resources to deal with them identified. For example, the real hazard associated with a release of a small amount of radioactive material may be minor, but the psychological impact should not be trivialized. Planners must be linked with threat assessors for current information. This will narrow the spectrum of technical information needed by the responders at the site of the incident.

Emergency response planning has addressed two phases: crisis response, and consequence management. Figure 27.3 shows the requirements for resources in each phase. The 24 hour point is arbitrarily drawn by the author to illustrate that there is a transition point. It may be before or after 24 hours, depending on the situation. Crisis response requires the resources of first responders (Fire Fighters, Security, Emergency Medical, Hazardous Materials Response Teams, etc.). The consequence management stage requires the support functions delineated in the National Response Plan (NRP) and the Department of Homeland Security (DHS).[10] The traditional sources of threat/risk information must be combined with knowledge of technical evaluation of the potential for use of industrial resources as "weapons of opportunity."[5,7] There are clear overlaps between the two kinds of events and both must be considered in any response plan. When this approach is taken, the spectrum of technical information that must be available and interpretable for response planning is narrowed.

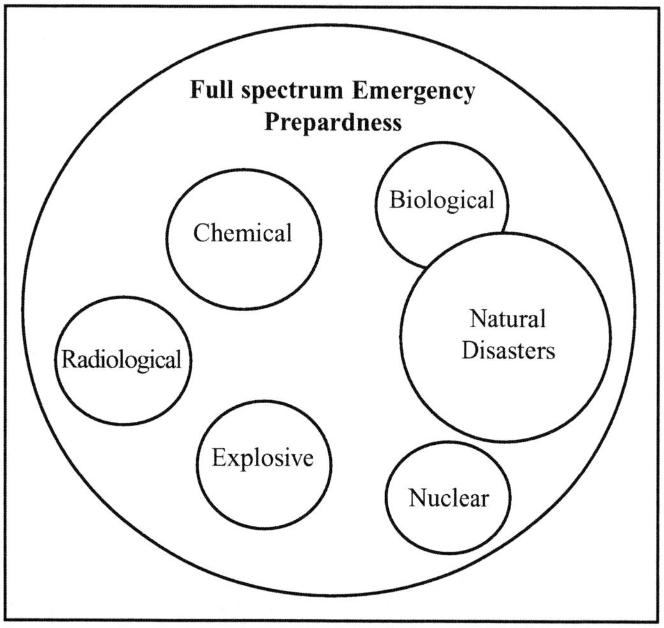

Figure 27.1 — This figure graphically represents the concept of "Full Spectrum" or "All Hazards."

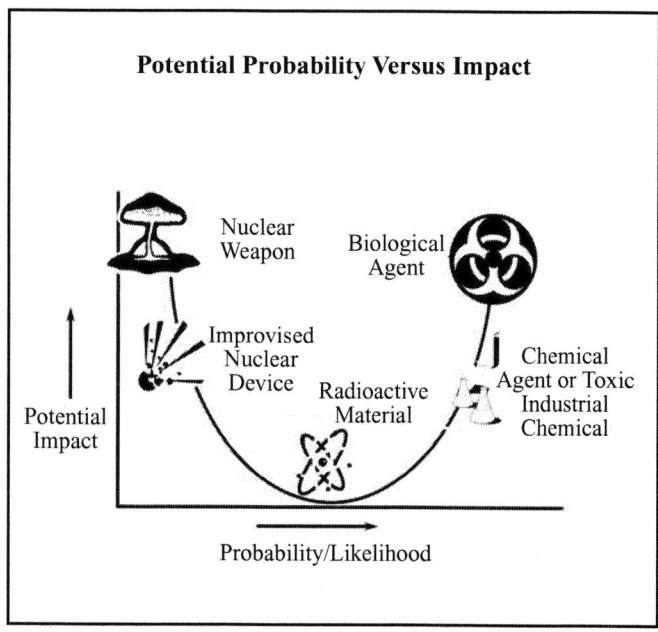

Figure 27.2 — Conceptual presentation of the probability versus impact of various kinds of man made incidents.

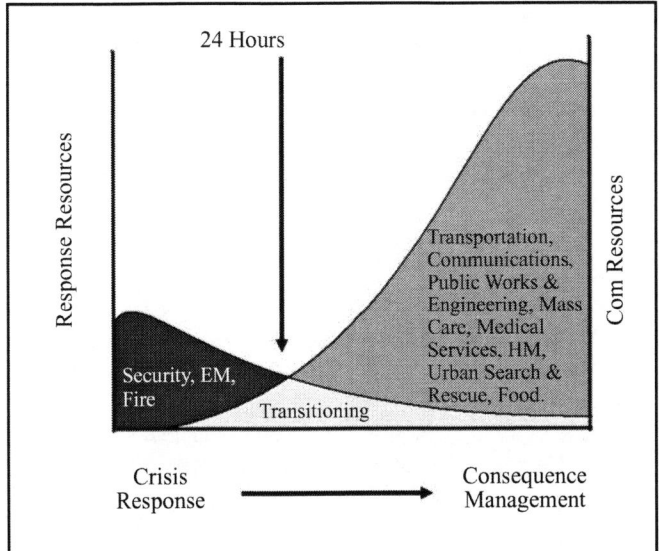

Figure 27.3 — Resources required for crisis response and consequence management (CoM).

Common Sources of Information

Among the most common sources of information available to response planners and responders are Material Safety Data Sheets (MSDS), Threshold Limit Values (TLVs®)[13], Emergency Response Planning Guidelines (ERPG)[14], Acute Exposure Guideline Levels (AEGL)[15], and the 2004 Emergency Response Guidebook (ERG2004).[16] This list is not meant to be comprehensive. Other strategies have been developed, such as the Department of Energies Temporary Emergency Exposure Limits (TEEL), but are based on the same approach used by the four systems discussed and are used when ERPGs or AEGLs are not available.[17]

Material Safety Data Sheets (MSDS)

MSDSs are part of the requirements of the Federal Hazard Communications Standard (HCS) for the control of occupational exposures to industrial chemicals.[18,19] While the contents of MSDSs are specified, the format is not. The intent of the information is to provide workers with knowledge of the hazards associated with the specific chemical or product that they deal with in daily work. The technical information presented in MSDS is limited and includes: chemical and common names, physical and chemical characteristics, health hazards, primary route(s) of entry, exposure limits, carcinogenicity, precautions for safe handling and use, control measures, emergency and first aid procedures, the date of preparation of the MSDS, and contact information for emergencies. In the case of mixtures, if the material has been tested for toxicity as a whole, then the information shall be used for hazard communications. When the composite material has not been tested, the hazard is considered to be the same as the individual components. If a chemical component is present in concentrations of 1% or greater, this mixture is presumed to produce the same hazard. No consideration is given for the compounding effects of physical and chemical hazards. MSDSs are required for most of the chemicals in commerce. The information is not intended for use in response to large scale spills or incidents.[17,19,20]

Threshold Limit Values (TLV®)

The American Conference of Governmental Industrial Hygienists (ACGIH®) annually publishes guidance exposure values for the workplace. These values are not regulatory, but are intended to be used only as guidelines or recommendations for use in the evaluation and control of potential hazards in the workplace. They are presented here because they are generally used as references by industrial hygienists, but are of limited value in emergency response planning. In standard workplace scenarios, the Threshold Limit Value-Time Weighted Average (TLV®-TWA) represents a value to which most workers can be exposed for 8 hours a day (40 hours per week) for a working life time without adverse effect. In most instances the primary toxicological effect upon which the limit is based is provided. A complete discussion of the derivation of these values is beyond the scope of this chapter, but is available in the documentation available from ACGIH. The Threshold Limit Value-Short Term Exposure Limit (TLV®-STEL) is defined as the level to which workers can be exposed for short periods without suffering irritation, chronic or irreversible tissue damage, dose rate dependent toxic effects, or disability that would hinder the ability to self-rescue or impair work. It is intended to supplement and not replace the TLV®-TWA. Exposure to the TLV®-STEL should be less than 15 minutes and occur not more than four times per day with a minimum of 60 minutes between exposures. A more complete discussion of the development and use of Occupation Exposure Levels (OELs) can be found in the chapter entitle "Derivation of Occupational Exposure Limits:. These values would therefore be of limited use in a major incident involving chemical, physical or other agents. The Threshold Limit Value – Ceiling (**TLV®-C**) is a value that should not be exceeded during any part of a working exposure. Whenever there is sufficient toxicological data for the substance under consideration to establish a TLV®-STEL or TLV®-C, these values take precedence over excursion limits. ACGIH provides a rationale and discussion for the use of TLV®-TWAs, TLV®-STELs, and TLV®-Cs when mixtures are involved. For a discussion of the difficulty in evaluating the potential toxicology of complex chemical mixtures, see Chapter 22, "Toxicology of Complex Chemical Mixtures." The approach does not address the issue of combined chemical and physical stressors and the fact that all TLV® values are based on assumptions about the potentially exposed population that are not valid for the general population.

Emergency Response Planning Guidelines (ERPG)

ERPGs are permissible exposure limits that have been developed by the American Industrial Hygiene Association. ERPGs are "designed as a tool to assist … in the development of emergency response strategies for protecting workers and the general public against the harmful effects of specific chemicals and substances."[14] The number of chemicals covered is limited. ERPGs are based on the probable health hazards associated with exposures up to one hour. ERPGs are developed based on a comprehensive review of the data available in published literature resulting in a weight of the evidence recommendation. Human data are used when available, but are generally not available. The reader is referred to the ERPG/Workplace Environmental Exposure Level Guides (WEEL) handbook for a complete discussion.[14] There is no prescribed formula for determining ERPG limits and no fixed ratio or relationship between the three ERPG values for a given chemical.

They are defined as follows:

- ERPG-1 is the maximum airborne concentration below which it is believed nearly all individuals could be exposed for up to 1 hour without experiencing more than mild, transient adverse health effects or without perceiving a clearly defined objectionable odor.
- ERPG-2 is the maximum airborne concentration below which it is believed nearly all individuals could be exposed for up to 1 hour without experiencing or developing irreversible or other serious health effects or symptoms that could impair an individual's ability to take protective action.
- ERPG-3 is the maximum airborne concentration below which it is believed nearly all individuals could be exposed for up to 1 hour without experiencing or developing life-threatening health effects.[14,15,18,21,22]

Acute Exposure Guideline Levels (AEGL)

Under the authority of the Federal Advisory Committee Act of 1972, (FACA)[23], the National Advisory Committee for Acute Exposure Guideline Levels (NAC/AEGL) has been established to develop AEGLs for high priority, acutely toxic chemicals. AEGLs represent exposure limits for the general public for emergency situations (e.g. spills and catastrophic technical failures) and are applicable to exposure periods ranging from ten minutes to eight hours. There are three levels developed for each of five exposure periods (10 minute, 30 minute, 1 hour, 4 hours, and 8 hours).[22] The three levels are defined as:

- "AEGL-1 is the airborne concentration [expressed as ppm (parts per million) or mg/m^3 (milligrams per cubic meter)] of a substance above which it is predicted that the general population, including susceptible individuals, could experience notable discomfort, irritation, or certain asymptomatic effects. However, the effects are not disabling and are transient and reversible upon cessation of exposure.
- AEGL-2 is the airborne concentration (expressed as ppm or mg/m^3) of a substance above which it is predicted that the general population, including susceptible individuals, could experience irreversible or other serious, long-lasting adverse health effects or an impaired ability to escape.
- AEGL-3 is the airborne concentration (expressed as ppm or mg/m^3) of a substance above which it is predicted that the general population, including susceptible individuals, could experience life-threatening health effects or death."[24]

The process by which AEGLs are established involves a comprehensive review of available literature and the application of standard calculation methodologies by a panel of experts. Recommendations are reviewed by the National Academy of Sciences Committee on Toxicology before public release.[24,25] Like the ERPGs, AEGLs cover a limited number of chemicals.

2004 Emergency Response Guidebook (ERG2004)

The 2004 Emergency Response Guidebook was developed jointly by the U.S. Department of Transportation (DOT), the Secretariat of Transport and Communications of Mexico (STC), and Transport Canada (TC), for use by police, firefighters, and other emergency response personnel who may be the first to arrive on the scene of an incident involving dangerous goods. It is primarily a guide to aid first responders in quickly identifying the specific or generic classification of the materials involved and to protect themselves and the general public. The guide provides initial isolation and protective action distances based on likely transportation accidents involving hazardous materials. The guidebook itself states: "It is not intended to provide information on the physical or chemical properties of dangerous goods."[26] Toxicological and chemical characteristics are considered in determining evacuation areas, personal protective equipment and medical support requirements. First aid information is provided for each class and category of substance, but the guidance is again based on general principles. Responders must get details on the specific compounds involved in order to develop the most effective response. It is the intention of the DOT to place a copy of this guide in each emergency service vehicle, nationwide through state and local public safety authorities.[27] An electronic copy and a personal computer software version are available through Transport Canada at www.tc.gc.ca/canutec. ERG2004 also contains lists of points of contact for further information. The guide is in the process of being updated.[28] It is an excellent reference and any occupational health specialist involved in planning for or responding to an incident should be familiar with its use.

A recommended hierarchy of emergency planning guidelines is presented in Table 27.1. Included are alternate guides that represent consensus standards. Table 27.2 is presented to illustrate the potential confusion among different sources and their authority. Planners should decide before an incident which guidelines will be used and formulate responses consistent with them, including exposure sampling strategies.

It must be remembered that none of the sources discussed above cover all potential chemicals. Also, the assumptions going into the final recommended value may or may not include consideration for potential sensitive subpopulations. For example, when performing community response planning, the potential special needs of personnel in convalescent homes, day care centers, schools, and other facilities must be addressed. Those involved in planning for and responding to incidents involving hazardous materials/mixtures should establish standard data bases and other reference materials that they fully understand. Documentation for such a data base should include a clear delineation of the limits of its use.

Table 27.1 — Recommended Hierarchy of Emergency Planning Guidelines*

Primary Guideline	Hierarchy of Alternative Guidelines	Sources of Exposure Limit Concentration
ERPG-3 or AEGL-3	TEEL-3 EEGL (30 minutes) IDLH (≤10 minutes)	AIHA or EPA DOE (SCAPA) NAS (COT) NIOSH
ERPG-2 or AEGL-2	TEEL-2 EEGL (60 minutes) PEL$_{ceiling}$ TLV$_{ceiling}$ TLV$_{TWA}$ X 5	DOE (SCAPA) NAS (COT) EPA; FEMA, DOT OSHA ACGIH ACGIH
ERPG-1 or AEGL-1	TEEL-1 PEL$_{STEL}$ TLV$_{STEL}$ TLV$_{TWA}$ X 3	DOE (SCAPA) OSHA ACGIH ACGIH

Note:
ACGIH = American Conference of Governmental Industrial Hygienists; AEGL = Acute Exposure Guideline Level; AIHA = American Industrial Hygiene Association; DOE (SCAPA) = Department of Energy (Subcommittee on Consequence on Consequence Assessment on Protective Actions); DOT = U.S. Department of Transportation; EEGL = Emergency Escape Guidelines; EPA = Environmental Protection Agency; ERPG = Emergency Response Planning Guidelines; FEMA = Federal Emergency Management Agency; IDLH = Immediately Dangerous to Life and Health; NAS (COT) = National Academy of Science Committee on Toxicology; NIOSH = National Institute for Occupational Safety and Health; OSHA = Occupational Safety and Health Administration; PEL = permissible exposure limit; STEL = Short-Term Exposure Limit; TEEL = Temporary Emergency Exposure Limits; TLV® = Threshold limit value

*After Ripple 2003[12].

In emergency/disaster situations, the general public will rely on newspapers, radio, and television stations for information. Much of the information provided is incorrect or misleading. The Incident Command System (ICS) is the tool for command, control and coordination of response to emergency situations and provides a means to coordinate efforts among agencies and individuals. It is required for all responses to hazardous materials incidents and is used nationally for response to all hazards events.[10] It has been endorsed by the American Public Works Association and the International Association of Chiefs of Police. ICS has been adopted by the National Fire Protection Association (NFPA) and is included it its "Recommended Practices for Disaster Management."[29] A critical part of the ICS structure provides for dissemination of information to the public and across responding agencies through the information officer. Consequently, the information that is immediately available to the information officer must not only be technically sound but interpretable to the wide audience of inquiry.

Interaction Between Chemical and Physical Stressors

The toxicology of chemical mixtures presents unique research and communications challenges (see Chapter 22, "Toxicology of Complex Chemical Mixtures").[30,31] Multiple chemical sensitivities (MCS) and the surrounding controversies provide evidence of the difficulties in identifying and documenting the real and potential results from exposures to chemicals in occupational and non-occupational settings.[32–38] The biological consequences of simultaneous exposure to chemical and physical stressors are an area of ongoing research. There is reliable evidence that there are toxic consequences to the simultaneous exposure to some organic solvents and sound.[39] Other interactions between physical and chemical stressors have been studied.[40–42] The immunosuppressive effects of radiation are well known and are considered in the consequence management stage of most anticipated crises.[43,44] The impact of exposure to vesicants on the immune system is well known.[45,46] While some guidance is given for the calculation of allowable exposure levels in multiple chemical scenarios[13,15,30], a satisfactory and solid toxicological data base to validate such approaches has not been established. Further studies are needed to identify strategies and develop tools that will provide easily understandable and usable data to plan for and respond to any combination of physical, chemical and biological agents.

Risk Communication

Risk communication has been a topic of concern for some time. Most publications have addressed the issue with regard to its importance as a subset of concerns for EPA type risk assessments, community preparedness and occupational exposures.[47] These efforts have focused on long-term risks and communications technologies. Recently, "crisis communication" has come to the forefront.[48–50] Indeed a simple search of the internet results in numerous sources of crisis communication planning and training. Most of these sources emphasize technique rather than content. The technical content of such communications must be at the level of the recipient and convey the limitations on the certainty of application of the data in the given scenario. As previously described, an example of the kinds of information that can be very useful, but requires an understanding of the assumptions, underlying the recommendations is the Department of Transportation Emergency Response Guidebook.[16] In the U.S., training in the use of this document is required for first responders by the Occupational Safety and Health Administration (OSHA, 29 CFR 1910.120) and the U.S. Environmental Protection Agency (EPA, 40 CFR Part 311). Consideration must also be given to the possible delayed effects on exposed personnel. Understanding concepts of toxicology is necessary when confronted with unforeseen exposures, decontamination requirements, personal protective equipment selection, and emergency medical intervention.[51]

Table 27.2 — Competing Agency "Standards"

Reference Value	Organization	Legal Standing	Type Value	TWA (Yes/No)	Exposure Duration
PEL (Permissible Exposure Level)	OSHA	Standard	Occupational	Yes	8 hours
Ceiling	OSHA	Standard	Occupational	No	≤ 10 minutes
REL (Recommended Exposure Limit)	NIOSH	Guideline	Occupational	Yes	8 hours
IDLH (Immediately Dangerous to Life and Health)	NIOSH	Guideline	Occupational	No	≤ 10 minutes
STEL (Short Term Exposure Limit)	NIOSH	Guideline	Occupational	Yes	15 minutes
TLV (Threshold Limit Value)	ACGIH	Guideline	Occupational	Yes	8 hours
TLV-STEL (TLV Short Term Exposure Limit)	ACGIH	Guideline	Occupational	Yes	15 minutes
AEGL (Acute Exposure Guideline Level)	NAC/AEGL NAS/AEGL	Guideline	Emergency Response	Yes	10, 30 minutes and 1, 4, 8 hours
ERPG (Emergency Response Planning Guideline)	AIHA	Guideline	Emergency Response	Yes	1 hour
TEEL (Temporary Emergency Exposure Level)	DOE	Guideline	Emergency Response	Yes	1 hour
ERG (Emergency Response Guidebook)	DOT	Guideline	Emergency Response	Yes	Specialized application to determine evacuation
MRL (Minimal Risk Level)	ATSDR	Guideline	Public Health	Yes	1 – 14 days (acute) 15–364 days (intermediate) >365 days (chronic)
REL (Reference Exposure Level)	OEHHA	Guideline	Public Health	Yes	1-8 hours

Organizations: ACGIH – American Conference of Governmental Industrial Hygienists, AIHA – American Industrial Hygiene Association, ATSDR – Agency for Toxic Substances and Disease Registry, DOE – Department of Energy, DOT – Department of Transportation, NAC – National Advisory Council, NAS – National Academy of Sciences, NIOSH – National Institute for Occupational Safety and Health, OEHHA – Office of Environmental Health Hazard Assessment (California EPA), OSHA – Occupational Safety and Health Administration.

Integration of Information

Information pertaining to the potential threats should be acquired and used in training exercises before an actual event. Interpretation of the data and its application in a variety of scenarios will help ensure that in a real incident the strengths and weaknesses of available data can be understood and incorporated in decision making. As mentioned above, the focus of the information accumulation and interpretation should be on the most likely scenarios. This does not preclude anticipating extreme events. As exercises are conducted, they should include broader ranges of individuals and organizations both municipal (neighborhood, city, county, state) and private sector (business division, plant, company) with interlaced and overlapping jurisdictions and responsibilities. At each level the sophistication of the data and the application of that data may become more complex. This will require well conceived communication plans and experts to respond to the dynamics of the emergency response and application of standards in the consequence management phase.

During the incident, concise and accurate information must be communicated effectively. Misinterpretation can result in unnecessary exposures and inefficient utilization of resources.

It is incumbent on those that generate toxicological data to understand how the data will be used and articulate the potential weaknesses of the data. Efforts must be made to more clearly understand the impact of multiple stressors (mixed chemicals, chemicals and physical stressors, chemicals and radiation, etc). Additionally, the standard methodologies used for routine occupational exposures must be modified to accommodate nonstandard exposure times and varying populations.

Potential Roles of the Industrial Hygienist in Planning for and Responding to an Incident Involving Toxic Materials

As the organizing paradigm for this discussion, the five phases of incident management, as described in the National Response Plan (NRP)[10,52] will be used. The potential roles for industrial hygienists will be discussed. The American Industrial Hygiene Association (AIHA) Emergency Planning and Response Task Force has addressed this issue and made recommendations that are still being explored and discussed.[53–57]

Prevention

This phase is described as actions taken to avoid an incident or to intervene to stop an incident from occurring. This function is a normal part of the responsibility of an industrial hygienist to anticipate potential hazards. In industry and communities these professionals can evaluate the risks and potentials of those materials and processes which could, either through mishap or intentional release, cause harm to the community.

Preparedness

In the preparedness phase, emergency managers develop plans of action for when the disaster strikes. Common preparedness measures include:

- Communication plans with easily understood terminology and chain of command
- Development and practice of multi-agency coordination and incident command
- Proper maintenance and training of emergency services
- Development and exercise of emergency population warning methods combined with emergency shelters and evacuation plans
- Stockpiling, inventory, and maintenance of supplies and equipment

The industrial hygienist should be involved in reviewing plans and participating in exercises to provide technical information to other team members. Suggested roles include: Safety Officer, Safety Coordinator, Technical Specialist (Industrial Hygienist, Air Monitoring Group Supervisor/Member, Field Observer, Health and Safety Trainer, Respiratory Protection Program Manager, and Risk Assessor/Hazard Analyst).

Response

This phase includes those activities to build, sustain, and improve the operational capability to prevent, protect against, respond to, and recover from domestic incidents. Industrial hygienists can participate in the development and implementation of exposure assessment methods to identify and prioritize hazards during the incident response and consequence management phases. Subsequentially, the industrial hygienist could be expect to be called upon to interpret sampling data and make recommendations for limiting exposures through the application of technology, administrative actions, or personal protective equipment.

Recovery

This phase includes post-disaster activities that help return property/conditions to normal. Long after the incident has passed, there will be hazards at the site that must be managed. This is an ideal opportunity for the practicing industrial hygienist to apply all the tools of the profession in assuring that further unnecessary risk is not taken. All of the technical and social skills will be necessary to help communicate and control the ongoing risk, though many workers may feel, since the crisis is over, they can relax vigilance.

Mitigation

Mitigation activities are designed to reduce or eliminate risks to people or property or to lessen the actual or potential effects of an incident. Throughout the incident and recovery, lessons learned and communicated by the industrial hygienist will prove useful in further identifying risk, best practices and methodologies to prevent or lesson the probability and impact of future similar events.

Summary

As can be seen from the discussion is this chapter, the potential for the use of toxicological data by industrial hygienists in preparing for and responding to incidents involving hazardous materials and other stressors is increasing. The interpretation and application of the data are dependent upon the specific characteristics and the dynamics of the incident. General guidance documents and exposure levels are available but each has its limits. The occupational health professional involved must be thoroughly familiar which ever data set is intended for use. Familiarization can be accomplished through training and exercises. Application of the standard principles of anticipation, evaluation, and control can be applied in a wide variety of endeavors supporting efforts to be prepared for those incidents which are most likely to occur. Full engagement with other professionals in such preparations and responses will assure full utilization of the variety of skills available of industrial hygienists.

Case Study[58]

A pilot study was undertaken to evaluate the potential health risks associated with a significant earthquake in the Los Angeles, CA area. The focus was on the potential impact of releases of anhydrous ammonia and chlorine into the atmosphere. An inventory of facilities was obtained and twenty two facilities were identified for inclusion in the study. These represented storage capacities from 4 to 1000 tons of chlorine and 206 tons of ammonia. The selected health criteria were the ERPG-3s. This exposure level would represent 20 ppm for chorine and 1000 ppm for ammonia. Instantaneous (catastrophic storage vessel failure), continuous release (piping failure), and a finite duration release (failed pipe) scenarios were modeled. A zone of vulnerability or hazard footprint was projected. Plum maps were projected and a probabilistic model used to determine the likelihood that a given population center would be within a hazardous material plum. The following results were estimated:

- In a magnitude 7 earthquake on the Newport-Inglewood fault, as many as 133,000 people would be exposed.
- In a magnitude 8+ earthquake on the southern San Andreas fault, over 20,000 people would be exposed.
- In a simulation of the magnitude 5.9 Whittier Narrows earthquake, approximately 7,000 people were estimated to suffer hazardous materials exposure. (A chlorine tank ruptured and released 240 gallons of chlorine in the city of Santa Fe during the 1987 Whittier Narrows earthquake).

This study highlights the potential hazards posed by storage of large quantities of chlorine and ammonia in areas expected to suffer strong ground shaking. The identification of these materials as a threat, and modeling the potential consequences enables responsible jurisdictions to address the risk and prepare for an event. The industrial hygienist might ask questions similar to these:

- What personal protective equipment (PPE) will be provided to first responders?
- Who purchases and maintains it?
- Who qualifies the wearers of any respiratory protection equipment?
- Will any PPE be provided for potential evacuees?
- If designated shelters exist in the response plan, who evaluates their ventilation systems for use in exposure scenarios?
- If personnel in shelters must be moved, what equipment (to include personal protective equipment) will they need?
- If there is a policy for "sheltering in place", what measures are planned?
- What PPE will be needed for the remediation effort?
- Who will provide monitoring?
- What are the legal implications of involvement in the response?

References

1. **American National Standards Institute (ANSI):** *American National Standard for Hazardous industrial Chemicals – Material Safety Data Sheets – Preparation* (ANSI Z400.1-1998). New York: ANSI, 1998.
2. **Garrick, B.J., and W.C. Gekler (eds.):** *The Analysis, Communication, and Perception of Risk.* New York: Plenum Press, 1991.
3. **Banauch, G., et al.:** Injuries and illnesses among New York city fire department rescue workers after responding to the World Trade Center Attacks. *MMWR 51*:1–5 (2002).
4. **Service, R.F.:** Chemical studies of 9/11 disaster tell complex take of 'Bad Stuff'. *Sci., 301*:649 (2003).
5. **Karasik, T.:** *Toxic Warfare.* Santa Monica, CA: Rand, 2002.
6. **Landrigan, P.J., et al.:** Health and environmental consequences of the World Trade Center disaster. *Environ. Health Pers. 112*:731–739 (2004).
7. Potential Military Chemical/Biological Agents and Compounds (FM 3-11.9), January 2005 [Online] Available at: https://atiam.train.army.mil/soldierPortal/atia/adlsc/view/public/9655-1/FM/3-11.9/toc.htm. [Accessed March 11, 2007].
8. **U.S. Labor Department (USLD):** Occupational Safety & Health Administration (OSHA) *Bloodborne Pathogens.* Regulations (Standards - 29 CFR), 29 CFR 1910.1030, 1992 [Online] Available at: http://www.osha.gov/SLTC/bloodbornepathogens/index.html [Accessed February 26, 2007].
9. **U.S. Labor Department (USLD):** Occupational Safety & Health Administration (OSHA) *Hazardous waste operations and emergency response. Regulations* (Standards - 29 CFR), 29 CFR 1910.120, 2003. [Online] Available at: http://www.osha.gov/SLTC/emergencypreparedness/index.html [Accessed February 26, 2007].
10. **U.S. Department of Homeland Security:** National Response Plan. December 2004. [Online] Available at: http://www.au.af.mil/au/awc/awcgate/nrp/nrp.pdf [Accessed February 26, 2007].
11. **Drabek, T.E. and G.J. Hoetmer (eds.):** *Emergency Management Principles and Practice for Local Government.* Washington D.C.: ICMA, 2000.
12. **Ripple, S.D.:** Emergency Planning in Crisis Management in the Workplace (Chapter 38). In *The Occupational Environment: Its Evaluation, Control and Management*, 2nd edition. DiNardi, S.R. (ed.). Fairfax, VA: AIHA Press, 2003. pp. 984–995.
13. **American Conference of Governmental Industrial Hygienists (ACGIH):** *TLVs® and BEIs® — Threshold Limit Values for Chemical Substances and Physical Agents — Biological Exposure Indices.* Cincinnati, OH: ACGIH, 2006.
14. **American Industrial Hygiene Association (AIHA):** *2004 Emergency Response Planning Guidelines and Workplace Environmental Exposure Level Handbook.* Fairfax, VA: AIHA Press, 2004.
15. **National Research Council:** *Acute Exposure Guideline Levels for Selected Airborne Chemicals.* Washington D.C.: National Academy Press, 2000.
16. **U.S. Department of Transportation (DOT):** Research & Special Programs Administration. *2004 Emergency Response Guidebook*, [Online] Available at: http://hazmat.dot.gov/gydebook.htm. [Accessed February 26, 2007].
17. **Silk, J.:** Hazard Communication (Chapter 40). (In: *The Occupational Environment: Its Evaluation, Control and Management*, 2nd edition. DiNardi, S.R. (ed.). Fairfax, VA: AIHA Press, 2003. pp. 1018–1039.
18. **Craig, D.K., et al.:** Alternative Guideline Limits for Chemicals Without Environmental Response Planning Guidelines. *Am. Ind. Hyg. Assoc. J. 56*:919–925 (1995).
19. **Kaplan, S.A.:** Development of Material Safety Data Sheets. *SAFETY LINKS: MSDS History*, [Online] 2004. Available at: www.phys.ksu.edu/Safety/kaplan.html. [Accessed February 26, 2007].

20. **Fishel, F. and P. Andres:** Understanding the Material Safety Data Sheet — *Agricultural publication G1913.* University of Missouri — Columbi, 1999. [Online] Available at: http://muextension.missouri.edu/explorepdf/agguides/agengin/g01913.pdf [Accessed February 28, 2007].
21. **American Industrial Hygiene Association (AIHA):** Procedures and Responsibilities, AIHA ERP Committee, November 1, 2006 [Online] Available at: www.aiha.org/1documents/committees/ERP-SOPs2006.pdf. [Accessed March 11, 2007].
22. **Cavender, F.:** Protecting the Community, One Guideline at a Time. *The Synergist 13(9):*29–30, 2002.
23. Federal Advisory Committee Act (FACA) *1972. P.L. 92-463* Approved October 6, 1972 (86 Stat. 770).
24. **National Research Council:** *Acute Guideline Levels for Selected Airborne Chemicals.* Washington D.C.: National Academy Press, 2000.
25. **Bruckner, J.V., D.A. Keys, and J.W. Fisher:** The Acute Exposure Guideline Level (AEGL) Program: Applications of Physiologically Based Pharmacokinetic Modeling. *J. Toxicol. Environ. Health, Part A 67:*621–634 (2004).
26. **U.S. Department of Transportation, Transport Canada, Secretariat of Transport and Communications of Mexico:** 2004 Emergency Response Guidebook. Neenah, WI: J.J. Keller & Associates, 2004. p 2.
27. **Pipeline and Hazardous Materials Safety Administration:** [Online] Available at: www.hazmat.dot.gov/pubs/erg/gydebook.htm. [Accessed February 23, 2007].
28. **Federal Register:** July 19, 2006 (Vol. 71, Number 138) Pages: 41071-41073. [Online] Available at: www.edocket.access.gpo.gov/2006/E6-11395.htm [Accessed February 23, 2007].
29. **National Fire Protection Association (NFPA):** NFPA 1600: Standard on Disaster/Emergency Management and Business Continuity Programs, 2004 edition. Quincy, MA: NFPA, 2004.
30. **Craig, D.K., et al.:** Recommended Default Methodology for Analysis of Airborne Exposures to Mixtures of Chemicals in Emergencies. *Appl. Occup. Envir. Hyg. 14(9):* 609–617 (1999).
31. **Yang, R.S.H. (ed.):** *Toxicology of Chemical Mixtures.* New York: Academic Press, 1994.
32. **Davidoff, A.L., and L. Fogarty:** Psychogenic origins of Multiple Chemical Sensitivities Syndrome: A critical review of the research literature. *Arch. Environ. Health 49:* 316–325 (1994).
33. **Bronstein, A.C.:** Multiple chemical sensitivities — new paradigm needed. *Clin. Tox. 33:*93–94 (1995).
34. **Spyker D.A.:** Multiple Chemical Sensitivities — Syndrome and solution. *Clin. Tox. 33:*95–99 (1995).
35. **Dehart, R.L.:** Multiple Chemical Sensitivity. *Am. Family Physician,* 58(3) Sept. 1998 [Online] Available at: www.aafp.org/afp/980901ap/edit.html [Accessed February 11, 2007].
36. **Magill, M.K. and A. Suruda:** Multiple Chemical Sensitivity Syndrome. *Am. Family Physician,* 58(3) Sept. 1998. [Online] Available at: http://www.aafp.org/afp/980901ap/magill.html [Accessed September 6, 2007].
37. **Bronstein, A.C.:** Multiple chemical sensitivities — new paradigm needed. *Clin. Tox. 33:*93–94 (1995).
38. **Cullen, M.R.:** The worker with multiple chemical hypersensitivities: An overview. *Occup. Med. 2:*655–661 (1987).
39. **Morata, T.C., et al.:** Audiometric findings in workers exposed to low levels of styrene and noise. *J. Occup. Environ. Med. 44:*806–814 (2002).
40. **Nelson, B.K., and D.L. Conover:** Experimental interactions of Glycol Ethers and physical agents: Developmental toxicology. *Occ. Hyg. 2:*303–310 (1996).
41. **Nelson, B.K.:** Exposure interactions in occupational and environmental toxicology. *Appl. Occ. Environ. Hyg. 12:* 356–361 (1997).
42. **Fechter, L.D.:** Promotion of noise-induced hearing loss by chemical contaminants. *J. Tox. Environ. Health. Part A, 67:*727–740, 2004.
43. **Walker, R.I.:** Infectious Complications of Radiation Injury. In *Textbook of Military Medicine Part I — Warfare, Weaponry, and the Casualty: Medical Consequences of Nuclear Warfare.* Zajtchuk, R., D.P. Jenkins, R.F. Bellamy, and V.M. Ingram (eds.). Bethesda, MD: Armed Forces Radiobiology Research Institute, 1989. pp. 67–83.
44. **Brook, I., et al.:** Management of post irradiation infection: lessons learned from animal models. *Mil. Med. 169(3):* 194–197 (2004).
45. **Sidell, F.S.:** Triage of Chemical Casualties (In *Textbook of Military Medicine, Part I — Medical Aspects of Chemical and Biological Warfare,* Sidell, R.R., Takafuji, E.T. and D.R. Franz (eds.). Washington D.C.: Borden Institute, 1997. pp 337–349.
46. **Sidell, F.R., W.C. Patrick, and T.R. Dashiell:** Jane's Chem-Bio Handbook. Alexandria, VA: Jane's Information Group, 2000.
47. **Sandman, P.M.:** *Responding to Community Outrage: Strategies for Effective Risk Communication.* Fairfax, VA: AIHA, 1993.
48. **Gillooly, P.B., et al.:** Risk Communication in the Workplace (Chapter 39). In *The Occupational Environment: Its Evaluation, Control and Management,* 2nd edition. DiNardi, S.R. (ed.). Fairfax, VA: AIHA Press, 2003. pp. 998–1016.
49. **Sandman, P.M.:** Crisis communication: a very quick introduction. *The Synergist,* 15:26–28, 2004.
50. **Wallace, H.:** Crisis communications: Lead with the future. *The Synergist,* 18:26–27, 2007.
51. **Varel, J. (ed.):** *Hazardous Materials Handbook for Emergency Responders.* New York: Van Norstrand Reinhold, 1996.
52. Department of Homeland Security, National Response Plan Update. [Online] Available at: http://www.dhs.gov/xlibrary/assets/NRP_Notice_of_Change_5-22-06.pdf [Accessed: February 27, 2007].

53. **American Industrial Hygiene Association (AIHA):** White Paper — Industrial Hygienist's Role and Responsibilities In Emergency Preparedness and Response [Online] Available at: www.aiha.org/1documents/Government Affairs/EPRWhitePaper_Final.pdf. [Accessed March 11, 2007].
54. **Umbrell, C.:** Emergency Response: Lessons Learned From September 11. *The Synergist 13(9)*: 23–26, 2002.
55. **Tranchell. P.:** Industrial Hygienists: Partners in Homeland Defense. *The Synergist 15(4)*:82, 2004.
56. **Ignacio, J.S.:** Health and Safety In Emergency Response: Who Is In Charge Anyway? *The Synergist 16(1)*:28–30, 2005.
57. **Renshaw, F.:** We're on Our Way: AIHA Addresses Emergency Preparedness and Response. *The Synergist 16(9)*: 10–12, 2005
58. **Seligson, H.A., R.T. Eguchi, and K.J. Tierney:** A Methodology for Estimating the Risk of Post-Earthquake Hazardous Materials Release: Pilot Application to County of Los Angeles. *NCEER Bulletin, 10(3)*:6–8: 1996 [Online] Available at: mceer.buffalo.edu/publications/bulletin/96/10-04/oct96n2.html. [Accessed March 2, 2007].

Suggested Further Reading

- **Drabek, T. E. and G.J. Hoetmer (eds.):** *Emergency Management Principles and Practice for Local Government*; ICMA, Washington, DC. 2000
- **Maniscalco, P.M., and H.T. Christen:** *Understanding Terrorism and Managing the Consequences*. Pearson Education, Inc., Upper Saddle River, NY 2001
- **Schaper, M., and M. Bisesi:** Environmental and Occupational Toxicology. (In: *The Occupational Environment: Its Evaluation, Control, and Management*, 2nd edition. DiNardi S.R. (ed.) American Industrial Hygiene Press, Fairfax, VA, 2003. Pp. 21–49.
- **Steinberg, L.J., et al.:** Risk Management Practices at Industrial Facilities during the Turkey Earthquake of August 17, 1999: Case Study Report. *Nat. Haz. Rev. 5(3)*:121–130, 2004
- **Stringfield, W.H.:** *Emergency Planning and Management: Ensuring Your Company's Survival in the Event of a Disaster.* Government Institutes, Inc., Rockville, MD 1995
- **American Industrial Hygiene Association (AIHA):** Compendium of Emergency Response References for Industrial Hygiene Professionals, AIHA Emergency Planning and Response Task Force. [Online] Available at: www.aiha.org/1documents/EPRTaskforce/EPR21HReference/Sept2005.doc [Accessed March 11, 2007].

Chapter 28

Derivation of Occupational Exposure Limits

*By Kenneth R. Still, PhD, FATS, CIH, CSP, CHMM,
Warren W. Jederberg, MS, CIH, RPIH, and William E. Luttrell, PhD, CIH*

Background

Occupational exposure standards are established primarily by three different types of organizations: regulatory, consensus and private industry. Regulatory organizations are governmental agencies, either federal, state, county, or city that may use the standards developed by the consensus establishing organizations as the starting point for legal limits. These consensus organizations are private groups that use knowledge of a specific industry and their injury records or results from scientific studies to establish standards that are protective of worker health. In many cases the consensus standards are more restrictive than the legal standards. Regulatory agencies develop exposure limits based on risk and exposure assessments using the consensus level as the beginning but then expand these consensus levels into limits that carry the weight of law. Regulatory limits are designed to protect a much wider population than the consensus standards and include older and younger individuals, pregnant women, hypersensitive/hyposensitive individuals, immuno-compromised individuals, and other individuals not considered in the general working population. Private industry groups may have unique chemicals that are used in their processes and consequently develop occupational exposure limits for their personnel. In many cases these private industries will adopt existing consensus standards or will develop limits that are more restrictive than regulatory standards. However, if there are no existing standards then the industry may opt to develop their own set of standards.

Consensus Organizations

There are numerous consensus organizations which produce and publish standards for their respective organizations. Many of these have had their consensus standards enacted directly into law, either in toto or partially. Examples of the more common occupational exposure limit consensus standard setting organizations include the American Conference of Governmental Industrial Hygienists (ACGIH), the American National Standards

Outcome Competencies

Upon completion of this chapter, the reader should be able to:

- Familiarize themselves with the overall process used to develop occupational exposure limit (OEL) values.
- Suggest specific components necessary to derive an OEL.

Prerequisite Knowledge

Basic understanding of industrial hygiene, toxicology, biochemistry, chemistry, risk and exposure assessment principles is necessary.

Key Terms

Consensus Standard, occupational exposure limit, risk, uncertainty factor

Key Topics

1. History of Standards
2. Consensus Organizations
3. Regulatory Setting Organizations
4. Private Industry Exposure Level Setting
5. Specific Components for Derivation of OELs
6. Corporate Risk Model
7. Decision Logic for OEL Development
8. Examples of Derivations of OELs

Institute (ANSI), American Industrial Hygiene Association (AIHA), National Academy of Sciences/National Research Council (NAS/NRC), The National Council on Radiological Protection and Measurements (NCRP), National Institute of Occupational Safety and Health (NIOSH), and many others. Regulatory agencies that establish exposure limits that are supported by legal enforcement include the Occupational Safety and Health Administration (OSHA), the Environmental Protection Agency (EPA), the Nuclear Regulatory Commission (NRC), the Department of Transportation (DOT), and others. International organizations, both governmental and private, also develop and publish exposure standards which are mostly recommended values and have no legal support in the United States. Organizations such as Germany's MAK, the International Commission on Radiological Protection (ICRP), the International Organization for Standardization (ISO), the World Health Organization (WHO), and many others recommend exposure levels for their respective areas. Most of these international standards are simply recommended values although some carry the force of law within signatory nations.

Many of the consensus organizations publish their values under specific names and the names often are trademarked for that organization. ACGIH publishes the Threshold Limit Values (TLVs®) and the Biological Exposure Indices (BEIs®) for occupational exposure to common industrial chemicals.[1] TLVs® and BEIs are not consensus standards, by definition of the consensus process, because TLV® and BEI values are based on a review of existing peer-reviewed scientific literature by committees with experts in the respective fields.[1] This organization annually publishes TLV® and BEI® values and has for many years. AIHA annually produces Workplace Environmental Exposure Levels (WEELs®) which are also health based chemical exposure limits for which there is no published guidance for health professionals.[2] WEELs are developed by committee using scientifically sound state-of-the-art risk assessment procedures.[2] The WEEL committee coordinates the development of WEEL values with the TLV® committee to avoid duplication of effort in occupational exposure level development.

Another important organization which releases exposure values based upon scientific review by committee is the NAS/NRC. This organization functions through sub-committees for the review and development of position recommendations and is an advisory body to the U.S. government for a wide area of research, including chemical toxicology and radiological protection. The National Academy of Sciences has provided overall guidance for chemical risk assessment as further developed and applied by U.S. regulatory agencies.[3–5] The National Research Council of the National Academies has published numerous reports addressing the development of OELs for confined and non-confined workplaces and for various activities and groups.[6–30] In the area of chemical toxicology, the NAS/NRC has evaluated the science behind the Emergency and Continuous Exposure Limits for Selected Airborne Contaminants, which established Emergency Exposure Guidance Levels (EEGLs), Short Term Public Emergency Guidance Levels (SPEGLs), and Continuous Exposure Guidance Level (CEGLs) for a small number of chemicals of concern. Specific definitions for these exposure levels can be found in the respective references. The Department of Defense (DOD) and the National Aviation and Space Administration (NASA) were the original requesters of the services of the NAS/NRC in this regard. Best known in radiation are the volumes entitled Biological Effects of Ionizing Radiation (BEIR), which have carefully evaluated the status and quality of the science on setting radiation standards, especially considering low-level exposures.[31] The U.S. EPA requires New Chemicals Exposure Limits (NCELs or "Nickels") for certain chemicals under TSCA 8(e) and 5(e) consent orders. They are generally developed in conjunction with specified work practices, engineering controls, and PPE requirements. There are approximately 100 limits to date.[32]

Regulatory Setting Organizations

Regulatory standard setting organizations produce and distribute standards that have the support of law behind them. Many of the standards from these organizations are derived from those values developed by consensus organizations. The two primary standard-setting organizations that enforce occupational and/or public community exposure level values are the Occupational Safety and Health Administration (OSHA) and the Environmental Protection Agency (EPA). OSHA was established in 1970 as a part of the Department of Labor as set forth in the OSHAct. Simultaneously, the National Institute of Occupational Safety and Health (NIOSH) was established as part of the Department of Health, Education, and Welfare (DHEW). DHEW subsequently became the Department of Health and Human Services (DHHS). NIOSH has many functions but the primary tasking set forth by the 1970 law was with being the scientific, research, and training arm of the occupational safety and health program at the Federal level. The Williams Steiger Occupational Safety and Health Act, Public Law 91 596, which created both OSHA and NIOSH, required the establishment of workplace occupational standards "as soon as possible." Many consensus organization standards were adopted in their entirety by OSHA for expediency.[33–35] The extremely rapid establishment of these standards has been the source of much OSHA criticism regarding legal standards. OSHA's limits were established with the Occupational Safety and Health Act of 1970. The limits OSHA initially adopted were ACGIH's 1968 TLVs® and ANSI's 1966, 1967, and 1968 limits.[36] The existing 1968 ACGIH TLVs® for chemicals were adopted in their entirety and constitute a chief criticism of many of the current OSHA limits for chemicals. Since the term "Threshold Limit Value®" and abbreviation "TLV®" were copyrighted by the ACGIH, OSHA consequently chose to use the term Permissible Exposure Limits (PELs) to represent these values. The use of the term "permissible" has been the source of some confusion since it appears to imply an allowed exposure.

NIOSH, functioning under its research mission, evaluated the OSHA standards, and made suggestions which were called Recommended Exposure Limits (RELs), many of which were based on a ten hour occupational exposure period rather than the eight hours used in the TLVs® and PELs.[37,38] NIOSH recommendations are still referenced and used today.[39] Most values of the TLVs®, PELs, and RELs are similar or the same, although there are differences both in philosophy and value for many chemicals. Subsequent to the 1970 OSHAct, the TLV® and PEL values have begun to differ somewhat, especially for chemicals of great public concern such as asbestos, benzene, and ethylene oxide. In some cases the OSHA PEL is lower than the ACGIH TLV®. In 1989, OSHA released a large number of new PELs, many lower in value than existing PELs. Industry questioned these new values and went to Federal court to stay the setting of these new standards. The court decreed that there were problems in the setting of the new standards; consequently the new PELs were set aside. The new values are still under consideration by OSHA. OSHA standards are found in Title 29, Code of Federal Regulations (CFR), Part 1910 for general industry, Part 1915 for shipyards, Part 1917 for marine terminals, Part 1918 for longshoring, Part 1926 for construction industry, Part 1928 for agriculture, and Part 1960 for Federal employees.

The U.S. EPA establishes standards for air contaminants, water contaminants, hazardous wastes, and toxic chemicals. This government agency is charged with protecting community public health including the most susceptible individuals, and the environment in general. When the U.S. EPA was created, there were fewer standards for environmental protection than for worker protection. Consequently, the EPA had to develop standards or use those set by the National Institute for Environmental Health and Safety (NIEHS). U.S. EPA regulations are found in Title 40, Code of Federal Regulations (CFR).

The EPA has the broadest scope of standard setting of all U.S. government agencies because they are responsible for all aspects of hazardous waste, the manufacture of toxic chemicals, air pollution, water and groundwater protection, and radiation from naturally occurring radionuclides. It has established standards for water quality and treatment under the Clean Water Act (CWA); hazardous waste operations under the Resource, Conservation, and Recovery Act (RCRA); past hazardous waste practices under the Comprehensive Environmental Response, Compensation, and Liability Act (CERCLA or "Superfund"); air releases under the Air Pollution Control Act (APCA) and the Superfund Amendments and Reauthorization Act (SARA); and, environmental radiation. Historically, EPA is less involved in environmental radiation except for recommended public exposure levels to radon.

The U.S. EPA conducts much of the necessary research itself, unlike the relationship that exists between OSHA and NIOSH. EPA standards have been promulgated by the agency although inputs from the National Institute for Environmental Health Sciences (NIEHS) have been used in setting standards. The EPA must consider the public at large, not just occupationally exposed workers. Workers are generally healthier, young adults, and aware of potential exposures. The public consists of people with greater susceptibility to injury from chemical and physical exposures; infants, children, the elderly, and the ill especially.

These individuals need to be protected by EPA standards more so than workers who are protected by the OSHA standards. Furthermore, unlike workers, these individuals are not in control of their exposures. Numerous questions regarding exposure limit development have been raised: how protective should exposure standards be; should individuals who are genetically predisposed to harm or with compromised immune systems be protected; should only a statistical portion of the entire population be protected, for example the lower 5% to upper 95%. These questions have yet to be answered.

How can the general public or workers in general be assured that promulgated standards are protective of their health? Currently, a cost-benefit ratio philosophy is used to help make this decision. Based on this philosophy there will always be a few individuals who fall outside the parameters that are set, regardless of the limits. However, it is believed that health based standards are protective of the large majority of the population. When regulatory and consensus organizations develop standards, the uppermost concern is protecting the most individuals.

Private Industry Exposure Level Setting

Private industry also establishes standards for their specific companies or groups of similar industries. These standards do not have the effect of law, may not be based upon scientific consensus, and are usually developed by company health and management professionals. The foundation for establishing any occupational exposure limit (OEL) is based on historical or current risk assessments. Paracelsus stated that "all substances are poisons; there is none without a poison. The right dose differentiates a poison from a remedy." This then is the foundation for establishing any OEL. Commonly, the OEL is regarded as a level of exposure to any airborne contaminant that is considered safe to nearly all workers. Individual susceptibility plays a role in response to the OEL levels; there may be adverse health effects at or below the established OEL. OELs are developed by various organizations and companies, and are primarily based upon the risk model discussed in the NRC red book.[4] This model incorporates risk assessment, risk characterization and risk management as graphically shown in Figure 28.1; additional discussion regarding risk and exposure assessment can be found in other chapters of this book. The concepts of the time-weighted average (TWA), short-term exposure limit (STEL) and Ceiling (C) limits as discussed in the exposure assessment chapter are also pertinent when developing an OEL. Duration of exposure is of considerable concern when developing OELs which can be based on these concepts. As defined in the ERPG/WEEL Handbook[2], the eight-hour TWA is the most frequently used exposure guideline used in the OSHA PELs and the ACGIH TLVs®. The STEL represents a time weighted average exposure that should not be exceeded for any 15-minute period; the STEL is referenced in the OSHA PEL-STEL and the ACGIH's TLV®-STEL. Finally, the ceiling limit is the maximum allowable human exposure limit for an airborne substance which is not to be exceeded even momentarily; again these ceiling limits are used in the OSHA PELs and the ACGIH TLVs®. Frequently, ceiling OELs are used for fast acting substances such as hydrogen fluoride or ozone; STELs are used with irritants such as formaldehyde or SO_2; and, TWAs are associated with slow acting irritants and chronic disease agents such as benzene, vinyl chloride or silica.

The ACGIH TLVs® also may contain notations for skin and sensitizer. The skin designation refers to "the potential significant contribution to the overall exposure by the cutaneous route, including mucous membranes and the eyes, by contact with vapors, liquids, and solids."[1] The notation for sensitization refers to "the potential for an agent to produce sensitization, as confirmed by human or animal data."[1] These two aspects are not covered in a numerical OEL but need to be considered in the management of occupational health risk. In general, OELs are not reduced to account for these two aspects, but must be considered by the industrial hygienist when developing protective measures.

Specialized OELs developed by NIOSH are the Immediately Dangerous to Life and Health (IDLH) limits.[38] These IDLH limits were established to determine the airborne concentration from which a worker could escape without injury or irreversible health effects in the event of a respirator failure. Some transient effects, which could prevent escape, were also considered, such as disorientation, incoordination, severe eye or respiratory irritation. These IDLH values are based on effects that might occur from a 30-minute exposure period. However, NIOSH emphasizes that workers should not remain in the exposure for 30-minutes, but rather they should exit immediately upon exposure. As defined by NIOSH[38], IDLH exposure conditions are "conditions that pose an immediate threat to life or health, or conditions that pose an immediate threat of severe exposure to contaminants, such as radioactive materials, which are likely to have adverse cumulative or delayed effects on health."

Companies set occupational exposure limits (OELs) for numerous reasons: (1) No OELs exist from any governmental or consensus-setting organizations, i.e., PELs, TLVs®, RELs, WEELs; (2) novel compounds are produced by the company; (3) under the OSHAct general duty clause, employers are responsible for providing a safe workplace; (4) company professionals do not trust an existing limit; (5) EPA under TSCA Sections 5 and 8, New Chemical Use, requires the development of New Chemical Exposure Limits (NCELs). The currently established PELs only address a few hundred chemicals and the TLVs® only slightly more. More and more companies are developing company specific OELs to protect the health of their workers and to hopefully protect against future potential litigation.

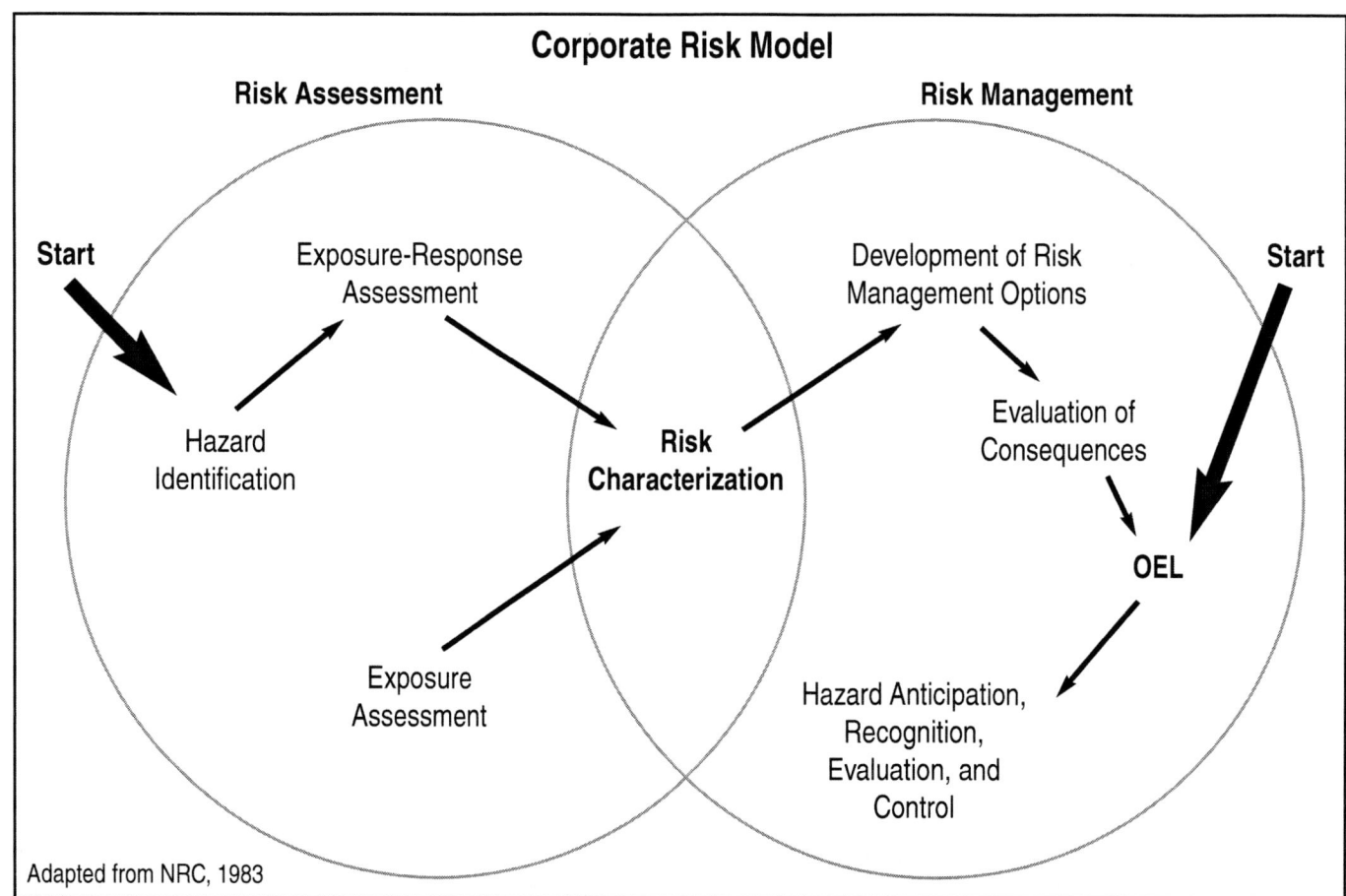

Figure 28.1 — From: Paul Hewett presentation in PDC 410, AIHce 2006, titled: "Establishing, Interpreting and Applying Occupational Exposure Limits: Current Practices and Future Directions."

OEL Development Process

Initially a candidate chemical must be selected. This candidate substance will have no existing TLV® or PEL, be produced in significant quantity, be handled by a significant number of employees, and be suspected of possibly causing adverse health effects or harm to workers upon exposure. The overall OEL setting process requires: (1) collecting a complete data set on the chemical substance of interest; (2) evaluating published peer-reviewed human and animal studies relevant to the chemical of interest; and, (3) identifying the critical endpoint(s). The primary critical endpoint is considered to be the most sensitive adverse effect relevant to humans. Documentation is critical for the entire process and must include: nomenclature; physiochemical properties; animal data; human use and experience; and, the rationale used to derive the OEL.

The complete data set for the suspect chemical would include physiochemical properties, toxicological properties which address both animal data and human use/experience, and toxicokinetics/pharmacokinetics. Physiochemical properties to be considered are the potential exposure, mode of entry, and the ability to cross biological membranes. The rationale used to establish the OEL must be clearly documented and should include: (1) key studies used in the derivation; (2) selection of the critical endpoint(s) and why they were selected; (3) selection of safety factors if used in the derivation; (4) uncertainties associated with the derivation; and, (5) any other factor that a user would need to be aware of for the derivation. Such consideration would include the different hazards present when the compound of interest might be present in different formulations.[40] Also, every mixture containing the chemical has the potential to present unique physical and chemical properties that may exacerbate, mask or otherwise modify the toxic manifestation of that chemical.[40,41] (See Chapter 22, "Toxicology of Complex Chemical Mixtures" and Chapter 30 "Industrial Chemical Hazard Communications.")

The following outline presents components that should be considered when developing an OEL. This outlined process considers potential aspects for an OEL derivation, but may not be all-inconclusive. Modifications to this process are usually found in the published literature dependent upon the study. A good example of the overall process can be found in the Haber and Maier, 2002 publication.[42]

Development of OELs—specific components for a derivation scenario:

I. Chemical Identification
   A. IUPAC name
   B. Synonyms
   C. CAS number
   D. Molecular formula
   E. Structural formula

II. Physical and Chemical Properties of Material
   A. Physical state and appearance [Standard temperature and pressure (STP) and normal temperature and pressure (NTP)]
   B. Odor description
   C. Odor threshold
   D. Molecular weight
     1. Conversion factors: ppm to mg/m^3 and reverse
   E. Melting point: degrees C and F
   F. Boiling point: degrees C and F at 760 mm Hg
   G. Vapor pressure: mm Hg at C and F with 25° C preferred
   H. Saturated vapor concentration: at 25° C preferred
   I. Flammability limits: Lower Explosive Limit (LEL) and Upper Explosive Limit (UEL) as percent
   J. Flash point: closed cup preferred
   K. Autoignition temperature: degrees C
   L. Specific gravity: degrees C
   M. Solubility in water: percent by weight and degrees C
   N. Stability
   O. Reactivity and incompatibilities
   P. Partition coefficient: (Ko/w)
   Q. Measure of strength of acidity

III. Animal Toxicity Data Required
   A. Acute toxicity and irritancy studies (less than 5 days)
     1. oral LD_{50} in rats/mice
     2. dermal LD_{50} in rabbits
     3. LC_{50} in rats/mice
     4. eye irritation in rabbits
     5. dermal irritation in rabbits
     6. dermal sensitization in guinea pigs
     7. neurotoxicity in chickens
     8. Other—subcutaneous, intraperitoneal, intravenous, etc.
   B. Subacute toxicity studies
     1. 5–14 days—dosing periods lying between the acute dose and 10% of the lifespan.
     2. not included in standard test guidelines
     3. OECD can provide information if needed [OECD, Organization for Economic Cooperation and Development (1981). Guidelines for the testing of chemicals. Section 4: Health Effects, 1981 and subsequent addenda (1984, 1987, 1993). Environmental Health and Safety Division, Paris, France.]
   C. Subchronic toxicity studies (less than 6 months)
     1. 90-day rodent/non-rodent feeding studies
     2. 21-day repeated dose dermal studies
     3. 90-day dermal study
     4. 90-day inhalation study in rats
     5. 90-day neurotoxicity test in chicken and mammals
   D. Chronic and long-term studies (greater than 6 months)
     1. chronic feeding studies in rodent and non-rodent
     2. oncogenicity studies in rats and mice
   E. Teratogenicity, developmental and reproductive studies
   F. Mutagenicity/genotoxicity studies
     1. bacteriological screening tests

2. *in vitro* tests
3. *in vivo* tests
G. Metabolism studies
H. Dermal studies
I. Other testing, as indicated. For example, neurotoxicity batteries.
IV. Human Use and Experience Data
A. Industrial hygiene
B. Epidemiological
C. Medical case studies
D. Other exposure levels, subjective response data or medical observations
V. Non-carcinogen Derivation
A. Administered and systemic dose levels
B. Exposure route
C. Exposure duration
D. Exposure frequency
E. Interspecies differences in chemical tolerance
F. Intraspecies variability in chemical tolerance
G. Differences in exposure regimes
H. Differences in exposure routes
VI. Carcinogen Derivation
A. Dose-response models
1. linear one-hit
2. multi-stage
3. multihit
4. logistics
5. log-probit
6. Benchmark Dose
B. Extrapolation from animal to human exposure
VII. Rationale
A. Describe data, critical endpoints and judgments used in deriving the OEL value
B. Only use data that are presented in the above sections—no new data can be introduced
C. Do not cite references in this section
D. If non-traditional work shifts are anticipated, so indicate and indicate significance to the developed OEL
VIII. Recommended OEL
A. Usually based on physicochemical characteristics and expressed in both ppm and mg/m^3 with time unit
B. Express as 8-hour TWA
C. State a short-term exposure limit if adverse effects are reasonably expected
D. State a ceiling limit if effects are immediate upon exposure
E. If skin is a possible route of entry, indicate if material can be absorbed in toxicologically significant amounts
IX. References
A. Include databases searched
B. Preference is to cite primary references
C. Secondary references must not be the critical study used to establish the OEL

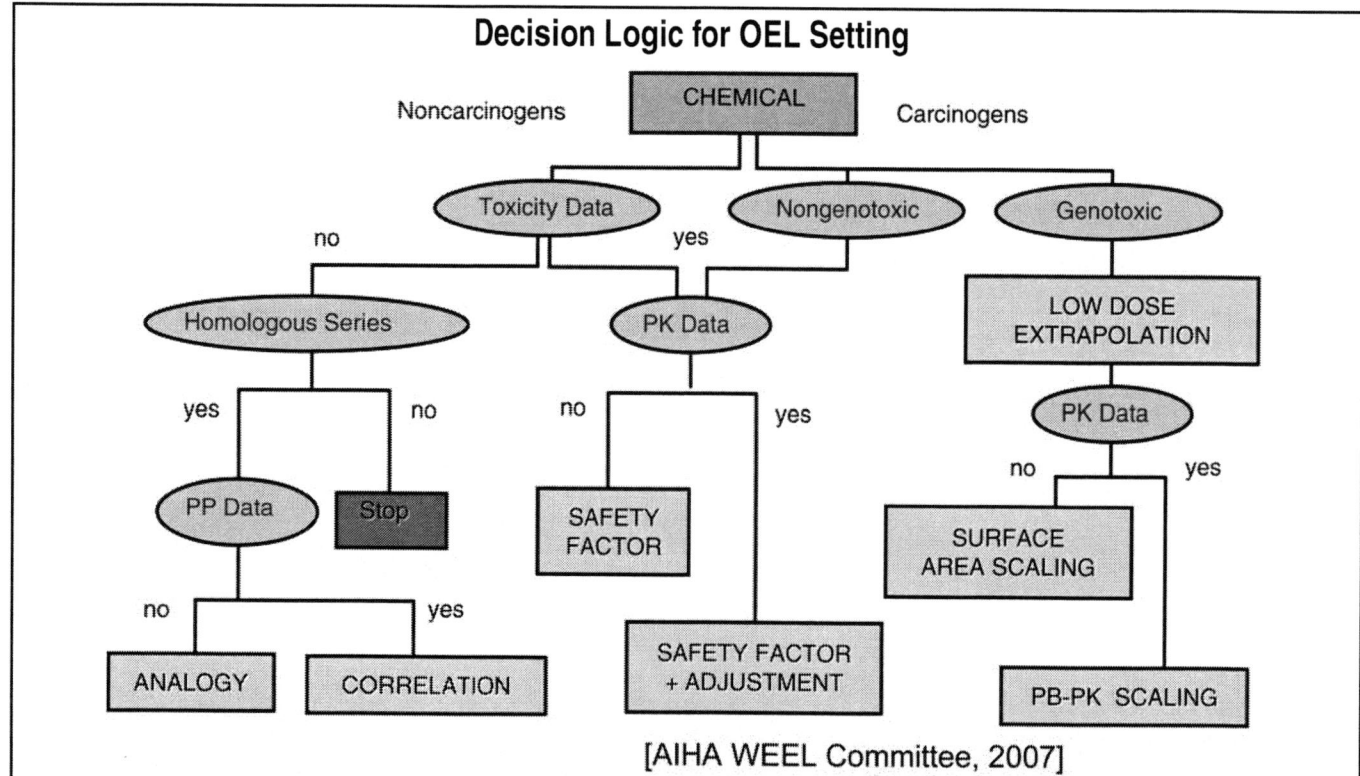

Figure 28.2 — Adapted from Andrew Soiefer Presentation, AIHce 1998 PDC titled: "Establishing, Interpreting and Applying Occupational Exposure Limits: Current Practices and Future Directions."

All of the components in the above suggested scenario do not have to be completed for the derivation. However, as many components as applicable or as many that can be found in the published literature should be included. The more aspects that are incorporated, the better supported will be the derivation. When addressing references, only primary references should be used to help establish the OEL. However, professional judgment will always play a role in developing OELs. Figure 28.2 is one example of a decision logic tree that can be used to develop an OEL.

When developing company specific OELs, rationale and documentation are extremely important. The more complete the documentation the better supported will be the derived OEL value. Rationale for the derived OEL must include the key studies used in the derivation and human data are preferred to animal data. However, if no human data are available, the use of animal data is indicated.[43] The more studies available with more than one animal species used, the better the resulting rationale. For the protection of worker health and to help reduce the cost of the protection for management sound rationale and good documentation are paramount.

Examples of Derivations of OELs

The final section of this chapter presents examples of derivations of OELs, providing the details of the rationale for establishing specific OELs for workplace contaminants, including benzaldehyde, acrolein, beryllium, butyraldehyde, ethyl acetate, 1,1,1,3,3,3-hexafluoropropane, methyl ethyl ketone, naphthalene, pharmaceutical agents, propylene glycol, and 2,3,7,8-tetrachlorodibenzo-p-dioxin. In each case, when available, the following pertinent information will be summarized: the key studies used in the derivation; the selection of the critical endpoint(s) and why they were selected; selection of safety factors, if used in the derivation; uncertainties associated with the derivation; and any other factors important to the derivation. The purpose of this final section is to illustrate the diversity of the OEL development process and how decisions are made in arriving at OEL recommendations for a variety of workplace chemicals. OEL development processes used by the ACGIH, the European Union, the Netherlands, the pharmaceutical industry, and others are included.

Benzaldehyde OEL Recommendations

Being an aldehyde, this compound causes irritation to the upper respiratory tract and the eyes. Air sampling in the workplace has found that 2.1 ppm benzaldehyde is associated with a strong penetrating odor but little irritation. Most toxicological data has shown that adverse acute and chronic effects occur at high doses and overall toxicity is moderate. The airborne concentration of benzaldehyde that will cause a 50% reduction in respiratory rate (RD_{50}) was found to be 333 ppm in Swiss-Webster mice and 394 ppm in B6C3F1 mice. Using the RD_{50} value and multiplying by a factor of 0.03, a WEEL of approximately 10 ppm would be derived. However, because there have been reports of human exposures to lower concentrations causing irritation, a lower WEEL has been indicated. In order to prevent respiratory and eye irritation from chronic and short-term exposures to benzaldehyde, the following WEEL values have been recommended: 8-hr time-weighted average (TWA) of 2 ppm (8.7 mg/m^3); short-term exposure level (STEL) of 4 ppm (17.4 mg/m^3).[44]

Acrolein OEL Recommendations

Inhalation of acrolein as low as 10 ppm was reported to cause human fatalities. Although monkeys, dogs, and guinea pigs repeatedly exposed to 0.22 ppm acrolein for 90 days did not show signs of acute toxicity, they developed emphysema and nonspecific pulmonary inflammation. It was found that acrolein is a more potent respiratory irritant than crotonaldehyde or formaldehyde. The rodent irritation data suggested that acrolein airborne concentrations would need to be controlled to 0.03 ppm to prevent irritation complaints in workers. Providing a margin of safety and minimizing the potential for irritation and pulmonary edema, a TLV®-Ceiling of 0.1 ppm (0.23 mg/m^3) was recommended for this compound. This value was based upon the following information: (1) the 90-day subchronic animal inhalation lowest-observed-adverse-effect level (LOAEL) of 0.22 ppm; (2) human mucous membrane irritation occurs at concentrations as low as 0.25 ppm; and (3) ceiling values are always assigned to rapidly acting irritants. A TLV®-Ceiling of 0.1 ppm was intended to minimize the potential for intense irritation of the eyes, mucous membranes, and the respiratory tract and the development of pulmonary edema.[45]

Beryllium OEL Recommendations

Rats exposed to beryllium fluoride at 9 ug/m^3 for 65 weeks caused pulmonary inflammation. A study found that acute beryllium disease occurred in humans following exposure to more than 100 ug/m^3 of beryllium. Cases of chronic beryllium disease in humans was found to be a sequel to brief, high exposures and possibly bouts with acute beryllium disease, rather than exposure to accumulated doses acquired over a long period of time. A study demonstrated a statistically significant increase in lung cancer mortality in persons who worked at specific plants during the 1940s while exposed to extremely high concentrations of beryllium. This justified an A1, confirmed human carcinogen, designation for beryllium metal and its compounds. Because of deaths and cases of severe respiratory disease in beryllium workers in the 1940s, an OEL of 2 ug/m^3 was established in 1949. This was based upon an analogy between beryllium and the toxic metals mercury, thallium, and cadmium which had TLVs® of 100 ug/m^3. If beryllium were equally toxic on a molar basis, its TLV® should be about 4 ug/m^3. Being conservative, a TLV® of 2 ug/m^3 was recommended. This OEL dramatically reduced the incidence of acute and chronic beryllium disease and probably lung cancer among beryllium workers in future years. Due to the success of this OEL, it has been the recommended TLV® since that time. However, it has been under review in recent years. Since acute beryllium disease did not appear in workers exposed below 15 ug/m^3, it appeared that a TLV®-STEL of 10 ug/m^3 (0.01 mg/m^3) would be appropriate. Since both chronic beryllium disease and lung cancer appeared to be associated with short, high exposures, it has been recommended that airborne beryllium concentrations not be permitted to exceed 10 ug/m^3 during any 15-minute period in the working day. It is not known if the TLV®-TWA of 2 ug/m^3, or the TLV®-STEL of 10 ug/m^3 or any non-zero OEL will eliminate the risk of lung cancer in workers exposed to beryllium. However, these TLV® values have been intended to minimize the likelihood of developing acute and chronic beryllium disease and potential lung cancer.[46]

In spite of the success of the beryllium OEL of 2 ug/m^3 to reduce beryllium related diseases in exposed workers, a new 8-hr OEL for beryllium has been recommended. Unfortunately, a number of reports have appeared that suggest that 2 ug/m^3 may not protect the worker population from chronic beryllium disease (CBD). Cases of CBD and beryllium sensitization have appeared in administrative personnel associated with workplaces handling beryllium where the potential exposure was expected to be low, intermittent, and so unlikely that air monitoring was not indicated. One situation that has linked health effects of low-level beryllium exposures to measured air concentrations has come from a late 1940s study of the Lorain, Ohio, population living around a beryllium plant. It was estimated that the beryllium concentration which had existed at the 0.75 mile boundary, representing the lowest concentration that could have caused beryllium disease, was greater than 0.01 ug/m^3 long-term average. This average ambient concentration was extrapolated to a workplace level by the following method: It was assumed that the worker received all beryllium exposure at work and that any exposure off-work was negligible. Going from a 24-hour-a-day, 7-day-per-week exposed general population to an 8-hour-per-day, 5-day-per-week exposed working population, the following calculation was performed to estimate the average exposure of the worker (u_x):

$$u_x = 0.01 \text{ ug/m}^3 \times (24 \text{ hr/day} \times 7 \text{ days})/(8 \text{ hr/day} \times 5 \text{ days}) = 0.042 \text{ ug/m}^3.$$

Assuming that workplace exposures are lognormally distributed and there is 95 percent compliance with the OEL, the value of the recommended OEL should be 0.1033 ug/m^3 as an 8-hour TWA. This OEL should provide worker protection comparable to the Lorain population which did not develop CBD. It was concluded that an 8-hr TWA exposure limit of 0.1 ug/m^3 along with exposure monitoring to assure a high rate of day-to-day compliance would provide better control of both long-term and short-term average exposure levels than would the current OEL.[47]

Butyraldehyde OEL Recommendations

The odor threshold for this compound was found to be about 10 ppm. It is not expected to accumulate in the tissues of the body because it is metabolized quickly. Butyraldehyde caused ocular and upper respiratory tract irritation in rats and dogs following a subchronic inhalation study involving exposure to 117 ppm. 50 ppm was found to be the no-observable effect level in a subchronic inhalation study in rats. Positive genotoxicity results were seen *in vitro* only and spermatogenic abnormalities in mice were not confirmed in another 90-day study using mice and rats. The potential for low acute lethality and the lack of systemic effects in subchronic inhalation studies indicated that a WEEL for this compound should be based on its ocular and upper respiratory tract irritation. A structure-activity study of sensory irritation of aldehydes indicated that an exposure limit of 10–100 ppm butyraldehyde should prevent sensory irritation. The current toxicological literature supports a WEEL of 25 ppm (75 mg/m^3) as an 8-hr TWA. This level is considered satisfactory for preventing irritation and minor histopathologic changes in the upper respiratory tract.[48]

Ethyl Acetate OEL Recommendations

A TLV®-TWA of 400 ppm (1440 mg/m^3) has been recommended for this compound to minimize the likelihood of irritation of the eyes, nose, and upper respiratory tract. Data from animal studies and worker exposure experiences have shown that ethyl acetate is a substance with low toxicity. This OEL provides a significant safety factor from adverse health effects, although at this concentration it may be irritating to some workers who are exposed for the first time. There has been insufficient data available to recommend skin, sensitization, or carcinogenicity notations or a TLV®-STEL.[49]

Ethyl acetate was originally evaluated in the European Union in 1990–1992. Even though very little data was available, it was clear that sensory irritation was the primary health effect from this compound. The Scientific Committee on Occupational Exposure Limits (SCOEL) considered data obtained from a study involving human volunteers who were exposed to estimated concentrations of 200 and 400 ppm for 3–5 minutes. Several volunteers complained of an odor at 200 ppm, and at 400 ppm responses were consistent with "slightly irritating." However, there was no definition of "irritating" given. Using the results of this human study, the SCOEL recommended a provisional 8-hour TWA OEL of 200 ppm at which residual irritant effects should be minimal. They also recommended a 15-minute STEL of 400 ppm. Subsequent to recommending these provisional OELs, additional data has become available. Another human volunteer study was conducted in which participants were exposed to 400 ppm ethyl acetate for 4 hours. Compared to air-only controls, the volunteers reported increased "irritancy." Also, volunteers were exposed to 200 and 400 ppm for 4 hours and to 600, 800, and 1000 ppm for 15 minutes. Irritation to the eyes, nose, mouth, and throat were measured, as well as odor perception and general health symptoms. Irritant effects were not found at 200 ppm, with odor rated as pleasant to neutral. At 400 ppm there were increases in reporting of sensations in the eye. 15-minute exposures to 600–1000 ppm resulted in increases in the reporting of subjective sensations in the mild to moderate categories. In regards to general health, increases in mild symptoms were reported with the 4-hour exposure to 400 ppm. The SCOEL concluded that these studies, which have become available in recent years, have been supportive of the provisional OELs. Therefore, the SCOEL has now recommended that the provisional OELs become their final recommendations.[50]

Methyl Ethyl Ketone OEL Recommendations

Methyl ethyl ketone (MEK) is present in the workplace as a vapor. It is absorbed easily through the respiratory tract and skin. MEK is eliminated unchanged in exhaled air and in urine of exposed workers. Urinary excretion of its metabolites, 3-hydroxy-2-butanone and 2,3-butenediol, is fast. MEK is not a product of endogenous metabolism and so is not present in the urine of unexposed people. However, exposure to 2-butanol, which is metabolized to MEK, may result in MEK being present in the urine. MEK appears in the urine shortly after exposure begins. Since it is excreted in the urine by simple diffusion, measurements should not be affected by renal disease. Studies have shown a linear relationship between degree of exposure and MEK excretion in urine collected at the end of a working shift. In one study, volunteers exposed to the TLV-TWA of 200 ppm (590 mg/m^3) MEK resulted in a urinary MEK concentration of 4.9 umol/L, which is equivalent to 3.5 mg/L. Two other field studies showed that a concentration of 2 mg/L resulted from an exposure at 200 ppm. The difference between these studies may have been caused by individual variability in metabolism, ethnic differences of the studied groups, workload, and dermal exposure. To include a margin of safety, the value of 2 mg/L has been recommended as the BEI for MEK. Therefore, it has been recommended that MEK be monitored in urine, be collected at the end of the shift, as an indicator of TWA daily exposure to MEK.[51]

1,1,1,3,3,3-Hexafluoropropane (HFC-236fa) OEL Recommendations

HFC-236fa has been developed to be a chlorofluorocarbon replacement as a refrigerant and a fire extinguishing agent. Toxicology studies have shown it to have low toxicity. In rats its LC_{50} (lethal inhalation concentration in 50%) was greater than 450,000 ppm. Cardiac sensitization was detected in dogs following exposure to 150,000 ppm. In a two week inhalation study with rats, the NOAEL was 5,000 ppm based on reduced alerting response. In a 90-day inhalation study with rats, reduced alerting response was detected during exposure at 50,000 ppm. But, a normal alerting response was observed immediately after exposure. Based upon these findings, the NOAEL for this study was 20,000 ppm. At exposures as high as 50,000 ppm there were no reports of developmental toxicity in rats or rabbits. This compound was also not found to be genotoxic in vitro or in vivo. Therefore, it was concluded that HFC-236fa has very low potential for acute or subchronic toxicity in humans. Based upon this conclusion, an analogy with other low toxicity hydrofluorocarbons, such as HFC-134a, an OEL of 1000 ppm was considered appropriate for this compound and should provide a sufficient margin of safety.[52]

Naphthalene OEL Recommendations

Naphthalene is a well known ocular irritant. Inhaled naphthalene has caused acute hemolysis. It has induced blood dyscrasias in humans characterized by erythrocytic anisocytosis and poikilocytosis, jaundice, anemia, decreased hemoglobin, and reduced hematocrit. Severe poisoning in humans has resulted in hemoglobinuria, methemoglobinemia, the production of Heinz bodies, and death with kernicterus. Those who survived the acute hematotoxicity have suffered from life-threatening acute renal failure. Napthalene exposure has also caused cataracts in humans and animals. In one study workers reported ocular irritation at 15 ppm with continued exposure causing more severe ocular toxicity. As a result of this study, a TLV®-TWA of 10 ppm and a TLV®-STEL of 15 ppm have been recommended. It is believed that these values should minimize the potential for eye and respiratory tract irritation and ocular toxicities that can include cataract formation, optical neuritis, lens opacities, and retinal degeneration. However, the margin of safety provided by the TLV® for hypersusceptible workers with glucose-6-phosphate dehydrogenase defective erythrocytes to naphthalene-induced blood dyscrasias is not known. Due to systemic poisoning seen in humans following skin contact with naphthalene, the Skin notation with the TLV® has been considered appropriate. Although there has been some evidence of carcinogenicity in female mice, there was no evidence of carcinogenicity in male mice or in rats of both sexes. Therefore, an A4, Not Classifiable as a Human Carcinogen, notation has been given to naphthalene.[53]

Pharmaceutical Agents OEL Recommendations

Pharmaceutical corporations have long recognized the risk of the active components of their products causing pharmacological effects in employees whose exposures have not been adequately controlled. Any clinically significant pharmacological effect occurring after exposure in workers has been considered unacceptable. When sufficient scientific data has been available, the pharmaceutical industry has established numerical OELs. Formal OELs are usually established and approved by a panel of professionals from the fields of occupational toxicology, occupational medicine, and industrial hygiene. Panels also have members from product discovery and development, including medicinal and process chemists, pharmacologists, toxicologists and chemical engineers.[54]

As discussed in detail in Chapter 24, "Risk Assessment Process for Industrial Hygienists", the traditional "safety factor" approach has been typically used by the pharmaceutical industry to derive OELs. The general equation that has been used is as follows:

$$OEL = (NOAEL\ (mg/kg) \times BW\ (kg)) / (UF \times MF \times V\ (m^3) \times \alpha \times S)$$

If available, the NOAEL is adjusted by the body weight (BW) and then divided by an uncertainty factor (UF) to account for different sources of uncertainty, a modifying factor (MF) that allows professional judgment to be used in the calculation, and then the volume (V) of air breathed by a worker over an eight hour period (10 m^3). Adjustment factors for bioavailability (α) differences that may exist between the inhalation route and the clinical route for which the NOAEL was derived, and for steady state (S) plasma concentrations if they are higher due to accumulation from repeated exposures when compared to single exposures. Typically, the uncertainty factor and modifying factor together range from 1 for compounds with a clear no effect level in humans for a non-serious endpoint (like irritation) to above 1000 for compounds, such as antineoplastic agents, that can produce serious toxicities at very low dosages in animals or human populations. OELs are usually established on an 8-hour time-weighted average basis. OELs can also be derived for alternative work schedules. Short-term 15 minute exposure limits may be needed to protect against reversible, pharmacologic effects with rapid onset.[54]

The trend in the pharmaceutical industry has been to identify and develop more selective compounds with increasing potency. There has also been increasing difficulty in identifying no effect levels for these compounds. In order to address these two troubling issues, a new performance-based approach for setting OELs was developed. This approach involved assigning materials into one of five hazard categories according to the toxicological and pharmacological properties of the material. Compounds were assigned into performance-based exposure control limit (PB-ECL) categories based upon the degree to which exposure would impact human health. Each hazard category dictated the level of containment required to protect employee safety by the use of engineering controls and safe handling procedures. Typical handling practices were required for low potency (PB-ECL Category 1) materials; systems that result in no open handling were required for potent or toxic (PB-ECL Category 3) materials; and closed facilities with the use of robotics were required for extremely potent (PB-ECL Category 5) materials. Assigning compounds into PB-ECL categories reflected an overall assessment of all available data with emphasis on potential immediate, life-threatening effects and delayed or chronic, irreversible effects. PB-ECL assignments have been used alone and with numerical ECLs to identify strategies known to protect employees and the environment.[55]

Propylene Glycol OEL Recommendations

Studies have shown propylene glycol to be minimally irritating to the eyes and skin of rabbits. This compound is also irritating to a small percentage of humans. After 60 second exposures to aerosols of 175–850 mg/m^3, humans have increased eye and respiratory tract irritation. Studies have shown that it is not a dermal sensitizer in the mouse ear sensitization assay or local lymph node assay. There was no evidence of sensitization in humans tested using the Draize or repeat insult patch test methodologies under semi-occlusive or occlusive application conditions. However, a few hypersensitive individuals developed skin reactions upon challenge with propylene glycol. Taken together, all of this evidence shows that propylene glycol is not a dermal sensitizer. The possibility of allergic skin conditions following dermal contact with propylene glycol in an occupational setting appears to be of low concern. Following acute or chronic ingestion or inhalation of this compound, it is expected that systemic effects will be very low. Evidence has shown that propylene glycol does not affect fertility or fetal development; it is not carcinogenic; and it is not genotoxic.[56]

Based upon an overall low toxicity profile for this compound, the primary endpoint used in deriving an OEL value is to minimize any risk of possible nose and eye irritation following exposure to airborne propylene glycol. A study has shown that 160 mg/m^3 is a probable threshold for slight eye irritation and a NOAEL for nasal irritation in the rat with a six hour exposure period. Another study has shown no ocular or nasal discharge in rats or Rhesus monkeys exposed continuously to super-saturated propylene glycol vapor (in excess of 330–414 mg/m^3) for twelve to eighteen months. This also suggested that propylene glycol has little potential to cause mucosal irritation. Even though a higher WEEL value could be assigned based upon the low toxicology, the recommended OEL should not exceed 10 mg/m^3 as an 8 hour TWA. This concentration is known to maintain good industrial hygiene procedures for nuisance liquid and particulate aerosols.[56]

2,3,7,8-Tetrachlorodibenzo-p-dioxin (TCDD) OEL Recommendations

This final example of the derivation of an OEL uses methods that were consistent with those used by the Ontario Ministry of Environment, West Germany, the Netherlands, the National Academy of Sciences, the U.S. Food and Drug Administration, and the ACGIH.[57]

Due to concerns about worker exposure to TCDD-contaminated soil (dust) during remediation of hazardous waste sites, an OEL for TCDD was needed. As a result, a proposed OEL based upon all available animal toxicology and human exposure experience on dioxin was developed. Studies have shown TCDD to be inactive in mutagenicity tests, showing little evidence of genotoxicity. Due to this, the safety-factor approach to establishing an OEL was considered appropriate. In a reproduction study in rats, a NOEL of 0.001 ug/kg/day was determined. In rodents two lifetime cancer bioassays also suggested the NOEL was 0.001 ug/kg/day. Available evidence from epidemiologic studies and industrial experience suggested that TCDD was not a human carcinogen. However, since it was found to be carcinogenic in rats, TCDD was assigned the A2 designation, a chemical suspected of carcinogenic potential in man. As a result, safety factors from two to ten have been applied to the NOEL to establish the OEL value. In the case of TCDD, a safety factor of 100 was suggested since there were other likely sources of exposure because of its ubiquitous nature. Therefore, a time-weighted average OEL for TCDD was estimated by applying the 100-fold safety factor to the animal NOEL of 0.001 ug/kg/day to obtain an acceptable intake of 0.01 ng/kg/day, and assuming 40 years of work, equating a 70 year human lifetime to a rodent's 2 year lifespan, and assuming 220 workdays per year during which an average worker inhales 10 m^3 of air in an 8 hour workday:

OEL = (acceptable intake) (70/40) (365/220) (body weight) / (air breathed)
OEL = (0.01 ng/kg) (1.75) (1.66) (70 kg) / (10 m^3)
OEL = 0.2 ng/m^3

Therefore, based upon available human and animal data at the time of this proposal, a time-weighted average OEL of 0.2 ng/m^3 was considered satisfactory to protect against any adverse effects of TCDD exposure for time periods up to 8 hours/day, 5 days/week, for a 40 year working lifetime. This proposal recommended that this proposed OEL be reevaluated when additional epidemiology, toxicity and bioavailability data became available.[57]

Summary

Although this chapter addresses primarily the development of OELs for chemical agents, the underlying principles can also be used to develop OELs for physical and biological agents. While OELs are developed and efficiently used, there is a movement today to develop and utilize alternative methods of containing or restricting worker exposure. One alternative to numerical OELs is "Control Banding" or "Performance-Based OELs (PB-OELs)", as seen in the pharmaceutical industry. A concern regarding these PB-OELs is determining the safe handling procedures for the chemicals of concern. The preliminary process is to assign chemicals to categories based on their inherent properties; list operations in the facility; and, pre-assign safe handling procedures for each operation. These pre-assigned safe handling procedures are based on each operations potential to result in exposure. PB-OELs can be divided into five categories: low, moderate, moderate-high, high, and extreme. AIHA recently published guidance regarding control banding analyses.[58]

References

1. **American Conference of Governmental Industrial Hygienists (ACGIH):** *2007 TLVs® and BEIs®: Threshold Limit Values® for Chemical Substances and Physical Agents.* Cincinnati, OH: ACGIH, 2007.
2. **American Industrial Hygiene Association (AIHA):** *2007 Emergency Response Planning Guidelines and Workplace Environmental Exposure Levels Handbook.* Fairfax, VA: AIHA, 2007.
3. **National Academy of Sciences (NAS):** *Risk Assessment in the Federal Government: Managing the Process.* Washington, D.C.: National Academy Press, 1983.
4. **National Academy of Sciences (NAS):** *Science and Judgment in Risk Assessment.* Washington, D.C.: National Academy Press, 1994.
5. **General Accounting Office (GAO):** *Chemical Risk Assessment, Selected Federal Agencies Procedures, Assumptions and Policies.* GAO-01-810. Washington, D.C., 2001.
6. **National Research Council of the National Academies:** *Emergency and Continuous Exposure Limits for Selected Airborne Contaminants.* Vol. 1. Washington, D.C.: National Academy Press, 1984.
7. **National Research Council of the National Academies:** *Emergency and Continuous Exposure Limits for Selected Airborne Contaminants.* Vol. 2. Washington, D.C.: National Academy Press, 1984.
8. **National Research Council of the National Academies:** *Emergency and Continuous Exposure Limits for Selected Airborne Contaminants.* Vol. 3. Washington, D.C.: National Academy Press, 1984.
9. **National Research Council of the National Academies:** *Toxicity Testing: Strategies to Determine Needs and Priorities.* Washington, D.C.: National Academy Press, 1984.
10. **National Research Council of the National Academies:** *Emergency and Continuous Exposure Limits for Selected Airborne Contaminants.* Vol. 4. Washington, D.C.: National Academy Press, 1985.
11. **National Research Council of the National Academies:** *Emergency and Continuous Exposure Limits for Selected Airborne Contaminants.* Vol. 5. Washington, D.C.: National Academy Press, 1985.
12. **National Research Council of the National Academies:** *Emergency and Continuous Exposure Limits for Selected Airborne Contaminants.* Vol. 6. Washington, D.C.: National Academy Press, 1986.
13. **National Research Council of the National Academies:** *Criteria and Methods for Preparing Emergency Exposure Guidance Level (EEGL), Short-Term Public Emergency Guidance Level (SPEGL), and Continuous Exposure Guidance Level (CEGL) Documents.* Washington, D.C.: National Academy Press, 1986.
14. **National Research Council of the National Academies:** *Emergency and Continuous Exposure Limits for Selected Airborne Contaminants.* Vol. 7. Washington, D.C.: National Academy Press, 1987.
15. **National Research Council of the National Academies:** 1988. Emergency and Continuous Exposure Limits for Selected Airborne Contaminants. Vol. 8. Washington, D.C.: National Academy Press, 1988.
16. **National Research Council of the National Academies:** *Guidelines for Developing Spacecraft Maximum Allowable Concentrations for Space Station Contaminants.* Washington, D.C.: National Academy Press, 1992.
17. **National Research Council of the National Academies:** *Guidelines for Developing Community Emergency Exposure Levels for Hazardous Substances.* Washington, D.C.: National Academy Press, 1993.
18. **National Research Council of the National Academies:** *Spacecraft Maximum Allowable Concentrations for Selected Airborne Contaminants.* Volume 1. Washington, D.C.: National Academy Press, 1994.
19. **National Research Council of the National Academies:** *Spacecraft Maximum Allowable Concentrations for Selected Airborne Contaminants.* Volume 2. Washington, D.C.: National Academy Press, 1996.
20. **National Research Council of the National Academies:** *Spacecraft Maximum Allowable Concentrations for Selected Airborne Contaminants.* Volume 3. Washington, D.C.: National Academy Press, 1996.

21. **National Research Council of the National Academies:** *Spacecraft Maximum Allowable Concentrations for Selected Airborne Contaminants.* Volume 4. Washington, D.C.: National Academy Press, 2000.
22. **National Research Council of the National Academies:** *Methods for Developing Spacecraft Water Exposure Guidelines.* Washington, D.C.: National Academy Press, 2000.
23. **National Research Council of the National Academies:** *Standing Operating Procedures for Developing Acute Exposure Guideline Levels for Hazardous Chemicals.* Washington, D.C.: National Academy Press, 2001.
24. **National Research Council of the National Academies:** *Acute Exposure Guideline Levels for Selected Airborne Chemicals.* Washington, D.C.: National Academy Press, 2001.
25. **National Research Council of the National Academies:** *Acute Exposure Guideline Levels for Selected Airborne Chemicals,* Volume 2. Washington, D.C.: National Academy Press, 2002.
26. **National Research Council of the National Academies:** *Acute Exposure Guideline Levels for Selected Airborne Chemicals.* Volume 3. Washington, D.C.: National Academy Press, 2003.
27. **National Research Council of the National Academies:** *Acute Exposure Guideline Levels for Selected Airborne Chemicals.* Volume 4. Washington, D.C.: National Academy Press, 2004
28. **National Research Council of the National Academies:** *Spacecraft Water Exposure Guidelines for Selected Contaminants.* Volume 1. Washington, D.C.: National Academy Press, 2004.
29. **National Research Council of the National Academies:** *Acute Exposure Guideline Levels for Selected Airborne Chemicals.* Volume 5. Washington, D.C.: National Academy Press, 2006.
30. **National Research Council of the National Academies:** *Spacecraft Water Exposure Guidelines for Selected Contaminants.* Volume 2. Washington, D.C.: National Academy Press, 2006.
31. **BIER Reference:** Health Risk from Exposure to Low Levels of Ionizing Radiation (BEIR Phase 2), Committee to assess Health Risks from Exposure to Low Levels of Radiation. Washington, D.C.: National Research Council, The National Academies Press, 2006.
32. 40 CFR 700 Subchapter R—Toxic Substances Control Act, Section 5 and 5(e) and Section 8 and 8(e)
33. **Nims, D.:** *Basics of Industrial Hygiene.* New York NY: John Wiley & Sons Inc., 1999. p. 51.
34. **Markiewicz, D.S.:** Occupational Safety. In *The Occupational Environment: Its Evaluation, Control and Management*, 2nd edition. DiNardi, S.R. (ed.). Fairfax, VA: AIHA Press, 2003. pp. 120–1210.
35. **Mintz, B.J.:** History of the Federal Occupational Safety and Health Administration. In *Fundamentals of Industrial Hygiene*, 4th edition. Plog, B.A., J. Niland, and P.J. Quinlan (eds.). Itasca IL: National Safety Council, 1996. pp. 787–841.
36. **Occupational Safety and Health Administration (OSHA):** OSHA Act of 1970. 50-204.50, Gases, Vapors, fumes, dusts, and Mists. Washington, D.C.: U.S. Government Printing Office, 1970.
37. **National Institute for Occupational Safety and Health (NIOSH):** Registry of Toxic Effects of Chemical Substances. Christensen, H.E. and E.J. Fairchild (eds.).. Entry: MP03500. Washington, D.C.: NIOSH, 1976.
38. **National Institute for Occupational Safety and Health** (NIOSH): Recommendations for Occupational Safety and Health, Compendium of Policy Documents and Statements. NIOSH Pub No. 92-100. Washington, D.C.: U.S. Government Printing Office, 1992.
39. **National Institute for Occupational Safety and Health (NIOSH):** NIOSH Pocket Guide to Chemical Hazards. DHHS (NIOSH) Publication No. 2005-149. Washington, D.C.: U.S. Government Printing Office, 2005.
40. **Klonne, D.R.:** Occupational Exposure Limits. In *The Occupational Environment: Its Evaluation, Control and Management*, 2nd edition. DiNardi, S.R. (ed.). Fairfax, VA: AIHA Press, 2003. pp. 51–65.
41. **Musch, A.:** Toxicity of Mixtures. In *Toxicology: Principles and Applications.* Niesink R.J.M., J. deVries, and J.A. Hollinger (eds.). New York, NY: CRC Press, 1996. pp. 271–287.
42. **Haber, L.T. and A. Maier:** Scientific Criteria for the Development of Occupational Exposure Limits for Metals and Other Mining-Related Chemicals. *Reg. Toxicol. Pharmacol. 36:*262–279 (2002).
43. **American Conference of Governmental Industrial Hygienists (ACGIH):** *ACGIH Operations Manual. Threshold Limit Values For Chemical Substance Committee.* Cincinnati, OH: ACGIH, 2005. http://www.acgih.org/TLV/Ops-Manual.pdf.
44. **American Industrial Hygiene Association (AIHA):** Benzaldehyde. Workplace Environmental Exposure Level. AIHA, Fairfax, VA, 1998.
45. **American Conference of Governmental Industrial Hygienists (ACGIH):** Acrolein. Documentation of the Threshold Limit Values (TLV®) and Biological Exposure Indices (BEI®) for Chemical Substances, 7th edition. Cincinnati, OH: ACGIH, 2001.
46. **American Conference of Governmental Industrial Hygienists (ACGIH):** Beryllium and Compounds. Documentation of the Threshold Limit Values (TLV®) and Biological Exposure Indices (BEI®) for Chemical Substances, 7th edition Cincinnati, OH: ACGIH, 2001.
47. **Wambach, P.F. and R.M. Tuggle:** Development of an eight-hour occupational exposure limit for beryllium. *Appl. Occup. Environ. Hyg.15(7):*581–587 (2000).
48. **American Industrial Hygiene Association (AIHA):** Butyraldehyde. Workplace Environmental Exposure Level. Fairfax, VA: AIHA, 2004.

49. **American Conference of Governmental Industrial Hygienists (ACGIH):** Ethyl Acetate. Documentation of the Threshold Limit Values (TLV®) and Biological Exposure Indices (BEI®) for Chemical Substances, 7th edition. Cincinnati, OH: ACGIH, 2001.
50. **Meldrum, M.:** Setting occupational exposure limits for sensory irritants: The approach in the European Union. *Am. Ind. Hyg. Assoc. J. 62*:730–732 (2001).
51. **American Conference of Governmental Industrial Hygienists (ACGIH):** Methyl Ethyl Ketone. Documentation of the Threshold Limit Values (TLV®) and Biological Exposure Indices (BEI®) for Chemical Substances, 7th edition. Cincinnati, OH: ACGIH, 2001.
52. **American Industrial Hygiene Association (AIHA):** 1,1,1,3,3-Hexafluoropropane. Workplace Environmental Exposure Level. Fairfax, VA: AIHA, 1998.
53. **American Conference of Governmental Industrial Hygienists (ACGIH):** Naphthalene. Documentation of the Threshold Limit Values (TLV®) and Biological Exposure Indices (BEI®) for Chemical Substances, 7th edition. Cincinnati, OH: ACGIH, 2001.
54. **Naumann, B.D. and E.V. Sargent:** Setting occupational exposure limits for pharmaceuticals. *Occup. Med.: State of the Art Reviews 12(1)*:67–80 (1997).
55. **Naumann, B.D., E.V. Sargent, B.S. Starkman, W.J. Fraser, G.T. Becker, and G.D. Kirk:** Performance-based exposure control limits for pharmaceutical active ingredients. *Am. Ind. Hyg.e Assoc. J. 57*:33–42 (1996).
56. **American Industrial Hygiene Association (AIHA):** Propylene Glycol. Workplace Environmental Exposure Level. Fairfax, VA: AIHA, 2004.
57. **Leung, H.-W., F.J. Murray, and D.J. Paustenbach:** A proposed occupational exposure limit for 2,3,7,8-tetrachlorodibenzo-p-dioxin. *Am. Ind. Hyg. Assoc. J. 49(9)*:466–474 (1988).
58. **Nelson, D.I., S. Chiusano, A. Bracker, L. Erickson, C.Geraci, M. Harper, C. Harvey, A. Havics, M. Hoover, T. Lentz, R. Niemeier, S. Ripple, E. Stewart, E. Sullivan, and D. Zalk:** *Guidance for Conducting Control Banding Analyses.* Fairfax, VA: AIHA, 2007.

Chapter 29

Biomonitoring

Outcome Competencies

Upon completion of this chapter, the reader should be able to:

Knowledge
- Realize the purpose of biomonitoring.

Comprehension
- Explain what biomarkers are and how they may be produced.

Application
- Define and discuss the categories of biomarkers.

Analysis
- Identify and discuss where the categories of biomarkers can be applied in the continuum between exposure and clinical disease.

Synthesis
- Analyze and categorize potential biomarkers.

Evaluation
- Develop a methodology for identifying potential biomarkers and where they may be identified along the exposure/ disease gradient pathway.

Key Terms

adduct, allele, angiosarcoma of the liver (ASL), at-risk population, bioavailable, biological effective dose, biological exposure index (BEI), biomarker, biomarkers of effect, biomarkers of exposure, biomarkers of susceptibility, biomonitoring, biotransformation, DNA microarray, erythrocyte, etiology, external dose, fast acetylator, half-life, hemoglobin (Hb), internal dose / internal absorbed dose, mesothelioma, missense point mutation, N- acetyltransferase, oncogene, paraoxonase, polymorphism, sister chromosome exchange (SCE), slow acetylator, Threshold limit value (TLV®), xenobiotic

Key Topics

1. Biomarkers of Exposure
2. Biomarkers of Effect
3. Biomarkers of Susceptibility

Chapter 29

Biomonitoring

By Ayodele O. Olabisi, PhD, Dean J. Wagner, PhD, Gail D. Chapman, PhD, Michael Stockelman, PhD, Timothy Naylor, MS, Erin Wilfong, PhD, Nancy Loy, AS, and Bradley B. Phillips, MS

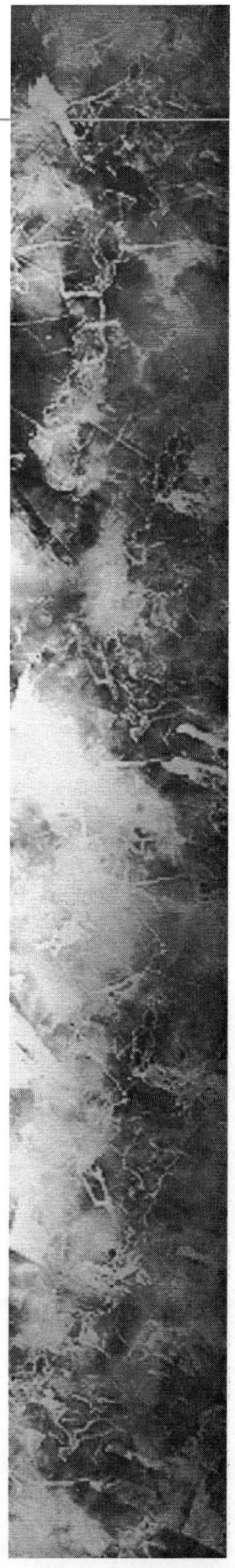

Introduction

Humans are routinely exposed to many chemicals that are potential health hazards. These exposures present a formidable public health challenge. According to the U.S. National Institute for Occupational Safety and Health (NIOSH), millions of workers are exposed to potentially harmful agents in United States every year; and up to approximately 40,000 of those lead to some sort of cancer. The ability to detect the potential toxic effects of exposure prior to the onset of clinical symptoms could provide an enormous benefit, in terms of both human and monetary costs.[1]

The identification of the causes of outbreaks of illness or disease, whether in a small, concentrated group of individuals or a large population, has been principally the role of epidemiologists. However, it is likely that most individuals are exposed to hazardous materials in the work place, and it is the role of the industrial hygienist to promote and advance occupational health. Finally, it is the toxicologist who assesses the effects of specific compounds on health. While distinct, the duties of these specialties do sometimes overlap.

Traditionally, epidemiologists have approached public health from a "top-down" perspective. This approach looks at environmental factors experienced by a population, including the various social structures and networks, and attempts to determine what factors influence the population's overall health. After these influences have been identified, it may be possible to implement measures to reduce or eliminate exposure to those factors that are harmful. These measures may include monitoring, such as tracking air pollution levels and warning at-risk populations at appropriate times; intervention, such as improving drinking water sanitation or health management; and informing the public of individual behaviors that may be unsafe, such as smoking or physical inactivity.[2-4]

In the occupational setting, industrial hygienists follow a similar tack to relate the exposure to a suspected hazard with clinical symptoms or disease; for example, direct contact with contaminated body fluids as related to hepatitis, or the exposure to asbestos fibers as related to malignant mesothelioma. Once these connections are made, various measures can be taken to modify the work environment in order to limit or prevent exposure to the hazard. These measures can include changes in work practices, the development and use of specialized safety equipment, or finding an alternative to the hazard.[5]

While these approaches have been effective in the past, and continue to be so today, they are essentially a "structural model of causation," which correlates underlying events, such as risk factors, and disease. Unfortunately, this model relies on the onset of clinical symptoms and disease before management strategies can be developed. Also, they may be ineffective in more subtle situations, such as when there is a mix of exposure hazards, low levels of exposure, aggregate exposure (exposure through various routes and pathways), or intermittent exposure. Correlations may also be missed if there is a long latency period before the onset of symptoms or disease. In some cases, these deficiencies can lead to misdiagnosis or missed diagnosis. An example is a case where a worker had been exposed to an organic solvent mixture and was initially misdiagnosed with early stage Alzheimer's Disease, when in fact the individual was suffering from the neurotoxic effects of the solvent.[2-4,6-8]

A recent emergence in the field of epidemiology is a "bottom-up" approach, or "biomedical model." With this approach, biological systems are examined using molecular-based analytical methods to evaluate the causes of symptoms and disease. This allows for the assessment of risk factors at what has been termed the "micro-level." By taking a molecular approach, epidemiologists can go beyond simply cause and effect to gain clues into the etiology of disease. When the underlying mechanism between exposure and disease can be determined, the biological plausibility of the observed association is enhanced and the relative risk association is improved.[3,4,9,10]

By taking a "bottom up" approach, and rather than simply waiting for the onset of disease, the public health community can look more closely at the natural progression of disease and may identify preclinical or sub-clinical biological events. Such events might be indicative of the early stages of disease. When these events can be identified and quantified in terms of changes in the biological system as a result of exposure to a hazard, or collection of hazards, they are collectively referred to as 'biological markers' or 'biomarkers.'[11–13]

Biomarkers can be used to complement more traditional practices of public health practitioners in the assessment and prevention of health risks. For biomarkers to be effective, there must be epidemiologic validation of the association of marker and biological outcome. It also must be determined whether the biomarker varies between populations or within different subgroups of a given population, such as by age, race or gender, etc.[7,14]

Different structural levels of organization can be used to measure biomarkers. They are used to evaluate entire ecosystems or populations, monitor the health of an individual organism, or assess the physiological state of a specific cell type at the molecular and biochemical level. This allows for an almost infinite number of markers that can be used, as techniques and probes are developed.[13–15]

The public health specialties have already benefited from biomarker-based technologies. This is especially true with regard to specificity and detection limits in instrumentation. Instruments that are now commonly used include high resolution mass spectrometers, magnetic resonance imaging (MRI), nuclear magnetic resonance (NMR), positron emission tomography (PET) and computer-aided tomography (CAT or CT). New and emerging technologies such as DNA microarrays may eventually play a role. The wide range of instrumentation being applied has expanded the spectrum of biomarkers that are available. Biomarkers have been derived from the metabolic byproducts of xenobiotics (chemical substances or entities not normally produced by an organism), alterations of DNA or protein structure called adducts (complexes that form when a compound binds to a biological molecule), and changes to physiological structures that have been correlated with exposure. Samples for assay can come from a variety of sources, including blood, urine, saliva and spinal fluid, depending on the target biomarker and the technique being employed.[5,13,16–21]

Three classes of biomarkers will be discussed here: *biomarkers of exposure, biomarkers of effects of exposure* and *biomarkers of susceptibility*. The three classes can overlap in their conceptual usage in relating exposure to potential health effects and disease. However, they collectively provide biological measurements that improve the accuracy, reliability, and scientific basis for quantitative risk assessment and environmental health management.[5,12,13,16–18,20,21]

Finally, biomarkers may be valuable not only for establishing etiological pathways and in developing measures to reduce or eliminate exposure to toxins, but also in assessing exposure levels and individual susceptibility. In this capacity, they may serve as a warning so that effective intervention measures can be taken before the onset of clinical symptoms and the establishment of disease.[5,13,20]

Biomarkers of Exposure

Biomarkers of exposure can indicate exposure to toxicants or other health hazards and can be identified either as the agent itself, or as metabolic byproducts or adducts. This class of biomarker can be useful in estimating or determining the amount of toxicant absorbed into a biological system, also known as the 'internal absorbed dose.' They can also be useful in determining the amount of toxicant that is required to interact with macromolecules and other biological targets, also known as the biological *effective dose*.[12,13]

Biological specimens, such as blood, urine, saliva, and even exhaled air, can routinely be assessed for biomarkers of exposure. Reference guidelines of known biomarkers are established by the American Conference of Governmental Industrial Hygienists through the *threshold limit value* (TLV®) and the *biological exposure index* (BEI®). The TLV® is a reference of the upper concentration limit of a substance to which an individual can be subjected during a normal 40-hour work week without anticipated adverse health effects. The BEI® lists what is likely to be observed in biological specimens following inhalation exposure to a toxicant at the level listed in the TLV®. Table 29.1 shows some common toxicants and their BEI. Information on TLV® and BEI® reference values can be obtained through the American Conference of Governmental and Industrial Hygienists (http://acgih.org).[5,12,13,17,18,20,22,23]

In the reconstruction of dose exposure, the examination of biomarkers of exposure can be more useful and accurate than conventional environmental monitoring and questionnaire data. This is due to the fact that exposure to an agent does not always result in adverse health effects in an individual or population; or, if it does, the effects are not always immediate. A significant reason for this is that an agent, or its metabolites, must be able to move within the body to its target site in a high enough concentration and for enough time to manifest an adverse health effect. Conventional environmental monitoring techniques generally provide information on the *external dose* of an individual or population. The external dose refers to the amount of agent that is actually found in the environment, such as in the air, water, soil or even food, in an occupational or residential setting. However, what is important in examining the health effects of a toxicant is the *internal dose*. The internal dose reflects the amount of toxicant that has successfully crossed physical and physiological barriers, such as the skin or lung epithelia, to enter the body, and the subsequent gradient distribution of the toxicant across all biological structure levels (organ, cell, etc.) to the ultimate target site. The ability of an agent to cross barriers is dependent an a number of parameters, including the toxicokinetics, which refers to how quickly and to what extent the molecule reaches the target organ, and toxicodynamics, which refers to actions and interactions of the molecule within the organism. The internal dose is generally a fraction of the external dose.[5,8,12,13,16,20,21]

The gradient distribution is a measure of the bioavailability of the toxicant and its metabolites. It illustrates the decreasing concentration of the agent from the external dose to the target site. While it is desirable to measure the gradient of distribution throughout, it is the biological effective dose at the end of the distribution that is generally of greatest interest. This is a measurement of the fraction of the internal dose that actually interacts with the target sites, whether organelle, cell, tissue, or organ. This measurement can often be directly related to the mechanism of the induced health effect.[8,12,13,20]

The ability to measure biomarkers of exposure has been driven by a substantial effort in discovery and identification. Protein and DNA adducts are commonly used and are being developed as molecular markers, using radio- and fluorescence labeling and immunoassays and several spectroscopic and spectrometric techniques for analysis. Biomarkers of exposure have been

Table 29.1 — Toxicants and Corresponding BEI® Values

Exposure (Chemical Agent)	Biomarkers of Exposure	BEI® Value
Acetone	Urinary acetone	50 mg/L
Aniline	Urinary Total p-aminophenol	50 mg/L
	Methemoglobin in blood	1.5% of hemoglobin
Arsenic & Arsine	Urinary inorganic arsenic metabolites	35 µg As/L
Benzene	Urinary S-Phenylmercapturic acid	25 µg /g creatinine
	Urinary t,t-Muconic acid	500 µg /g creatinine
Cadmium	Blood cadmium	5 µg/L
	Urinary cadmium	5 µg/g creatinine
Chromium (VI)	Urinary chromium	25 µg/g creatinine
	Water soluble fume	10 micro g/g creatinine
Chlorobenzene	Urinary 4-chlorocatechol	150 mg/g creatinine
	Urinary p-chlorophenol	25 mg/g creatinine
Carbon Monoxide	Carbon monoxide in end-exhaled air	~ 20 ppm
	Blood carboxyhemaglobin	~ 3.5% of hemoglobin
N,N-Dimethylformamide (DMF)	Urinary N-methylformamide	15 mg/L
Fluorides	Urinary fluorides	10 mg/g creatinine
Furfural	Urinary furoic acid	200 mg/g creatinine
Lead	Blood lead	30 µg/100 mL
Methanol	Urinary methanol	15 mg/L
Mercury	Urinary inorganic mercury	35 µg/g creatinine
	Blood inorganic mercury	15 µg/L
Methyl ethyl ketone	Urinary methyl ethyl ketone	2.0 mg/L
Nitrobenzene	Urinary p-nitrophenol	5 mg/g creatinine
	Urinary methemoglobin	1.5% of hemoglobin
Parathion	Urinary p-nitrophenol	0.5 mg/g creatinine
Phenol	Urinary phenol	250 mg/g creatinine
Styrene	Venous blood styrene	0.2 mg/L
	Urinary mandelic acid plus phenylglyoxylic acid	400 mg/g creatinine
Toluene	Urinary o-cresol	0.5 mg/g creatinine
	Venous blood toluene	0.05 mg/L
	Urinary hippuric acid	1.6 g/g creatinine
Xylenes	Urinary methylhippuric acid	1.5 g/g creatinine

(Adapted from The American Conference of Governmental Industrial Hygienists, 2006).

developed for, and detected in, a variety of cell types, including lymphocytes, specific tissues and organs, and bodily fluids such as urine.[5,12,13,17,18,20]

Adducts of the hemoglobin (Hb) molecule from erythrocytes (red blood cells) have been developed as important molecular markers. Hb has been useful in monitoring the cumulative dose of a variety of agents, including hydrocarbons, such as those found in fuels, and epoxides, such as those found in industrial solvents, under chronic exposure conditions. An advantage of using Hb as a molecular marker is its relatively long physiological life in red blood cells, since erythrocytes circulate, on average, for 120 days. The abundance of Hb in red blood cells and its relative ease of access also make it an attractive marker. Therefore, using an Hb-adduct, exposure to a toxicant or its metabolite can be tracked and quantified for relatively long periods of time. Other proteins, including albumin, collagen and histones, are being developed as informative carriers of adducts.[5,12,13,17,18,20]

Biomarkers of exposure can be useful in identifying the type and the magnitude response a biological system may undergo upon exposure. They can also be helpful in distinguishing among the external dose, internal dose, the biological effective dose of an agent, and the susceptibility of an individual to that agent. Other parameters can be investigated as well, such as the time and frequency of exposure to a toxicant that is required to produce an effect. These are important parameters in determining the toxicity of an agent. This is because the agent and its resulting metabolites may have very different half-life, an index of the amount of time it takes for a molecule to be metabolized or removed from the system. Some molecules, especially protein- and DNA-adducts, while being only a small fraction of the total internal exposure, may have a very long half-life as compared to the toxicant. This may allow them to accumulate to high levels with repeated exposure.[5,12,13,17,18,20]

Essentially, a recent exposure to a toxicant will produce many biomarkers of exposure, some with short half lives, such as the toxicant itself, and some with long half-lives, such as adducts.

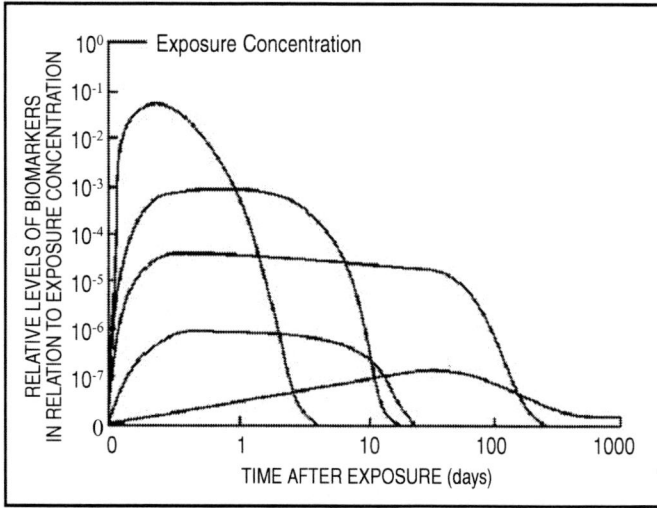

Figure 29.1 — Example of biomarkers of exposure half-life (Adapted from Henderson et al., 1989).

Some of the biomarkers may reach levels that are detectable, while others may not, depending on the degree and intervals of exposure. With repeated exposure, those with longer half-lives will continue to accumulate. If they were not detectable early on, they may eventually reach the point where they are measurable. Figure 29.1 is a hypothetical example of half-lives of biomarkers of effect following an exposure.[17,24]

The examination of several biomarkers of exposure provides a clearer picture of the nature of the exposure and its effects than the tracking of a single marker. Many markers can provide information on health effects under different conditions, as well as quantitative and kinetic relationships between markers at different times following exposure.

Epidemiological Case Study on Biomarkers of Exposure

The ability to accurately measure a biomarker depends on an understanding of the chemistry and toxicological effects of the agent being studied. The toxic effects of many hydrocarbon solvents, especially those produced and used in petroleum industries, have been extensively studied. One common solvent, n-hexane, has been shown to produce neurotoxic effects that include numbness in the extremities with eventual muscle weakness upon exposure. If exposure is continued, a progressive loss of sensory and motor function may develop.

Toxic metabolites have been shown to be produced as a result of exposure to n-hexane. One of the metabolites, 2,5 hexanedione, has been shown to interact with lysine residues in proteins to form a chemical adduct. Exposure to n-hexane in workers can be monitored by the appearance of this metabolite in urine after a few hours and for as long as a few days. Dose response studies in animals and humans have shown that these chemical adducts can provide an accurate measurement of cumulative exposure to n-hexane and a quantitative assessment of its toxic effects.[25–29]

Other biomarkers of exposure include trans, trans-muconic acid (t, t-MA) and S-phenylmercapturic acid (S-PMA) produced following benzene exposure. These markers can also be measured in the urine, and show a dose response relationship with inhaled benzene.[25,29]

Biomarkers of Effect

Biomarkers of effect are often biological changes that are linked to, or predictive of, pathogenesis or disease. This class of biomarkers can be either metabolic byproducts or a part of biological processes that reflect functional or structural changes, at both the cellular and biochemical levels. These processes may be reversible and found in both target and non-target tissues. Biomarkers of effect may include altered gene expression, enzyme inhibition, or cellular changes. They may also involve immunologic responses, behavioral changes or other clinical symptoms that suggest the presence of a disease or illness.[8,11,13]

The measurements of biomarkers of effect generally reflect events that take place at the latter end of the continuum between exposure and disease manifestation. Therefore, they are usually less specific identifying a single causative agent, but they can be more predictive of ultimate toxicity. This is partially due to individual variation in response to toxicant exposure.[11,13]

Specific biomarkers of effect are used to assess exposure to a variety of environmental toxicants. Exposure to lead causes inhibition of ferrochelatase and levulinate dehydratase, enzymes involved in heme synthesis. The degree of levulinate dehydratase inhibition can be used to determine the extent of lead exposure in an individual. Erythrocyte, lymphocyte and thrombocyte blood cell counts, can be used to monitor benzene-exposed workers. And cell counts of lymphocyte subsets, such as suppressor and T-cells, can be used in situations involving heavy exposure to asbestos. Cadmium exposure can be evaluated through the appearance of proteins, such as albumin and enzymes like N-acetylglucosaminidase, in the urine. Also seen may be eicosanoids and tubular antigens, both of which are involved in immune responses. Finally, elevated levels of cytokines, such as tumor necrosis factor (TNF), secreted by pulmonary macrophages, have been observed in individuals exposed to coal dust.[13,17,18,20,30–33]

Epidemiological Case Studies Using Biomarkers of Effect

Ethylene oxide is a soluble and flammable gas with a sweet odor. It is produced in large volumes and has a range of applications. It is used industrially in the production of other chemicals, particularly ethylene glycol, which in turn is used to make other products, such as antifreeze and polyester. In the healthcare industry, it is used to sterilize medical equipment and supplies; agriculturally, it is used on produce as a fumigant against insects.

When ethylene oxide is produced or used, some of the gas is released to the atmosphere. Its solubility in water makes it particularly bioavailable. There are a variety of biomarkers of effects from ethylene oxide exposure. These include a dose-related increase in hemoglobin adducts, chromosomal aberrations, and sister chromosome exchanges (SCEs) in peripheral blood lymphocytes, as well as micronuclei in bone marrow cells of exposed workers.[34]

Organophosphate insecticides or pesticides were developed in the 1940s and are used primarily in agriculture. However, they are also used in residential settings for pest control, and as a measure against vector-borne diseases. Organophosphate compounds can remain stable for extended periods of time, for months or even years, and, therefore, can remain potentially available for repeated exposure to individuals. High levels of exposure to organophosphates have been shown to affect the central nervous system and can cause a variety of neurological dysfunctions. The biological effects of exposure are well documented and understood, in part because all organophosphates share common chemical properties. This means that they also have similar mechanisms of toxicity, generally through inhibitory effects on enzymes found in nervous tissue, red blood cells, and circulating in blood plasma.[35,36]

Biomarkers of effect produced after exposure to organophosphate include the inhibition or suppression of activity of cholinesterase enzymes, which are involved in metabolizing neurotransmitters. Erythrocyte acetyl-cholinesterase measurement has been found to correlate with changes occurring in target tissues, such as the central nervous system and muscle tissue. However, for low level or acute exposure to organophosphates, only about 1% cholinesterase activity may be suppressed, which is below the detection limits when using standard cholinesterase assays. Recently a more sensitive analytical technique has been developed to accurately measure the amount of cholinesterase enzyme bound to organophosphate nerve agents. This technique involves monitoring and quantifying the relative amount of organophosphate-enzyme complex to free enzyme population.[35,36]

Biomarkers of Susceptibility

Biomarkers of susceptibility are used to identify whether a person or groups of people are susceptible to damage caused by a certain chemical or other toxicant. This class of biomarkers serves to describe individual variations in the relationship of biomarkers of exposure and biomarkers of effect. These variations may help explain why different individuals with similar experiences of environmental exposure sometimes produce markedly different levels of biomarkers of exposure and/or biomarkers of effect, which in turn may correlate with different severities of clinical symptoms.

These differences may arise from genetic or non-genetic factors. Genetic factors include polymorphisms (sequence-level variations of genes among individuals) that may affect expression and function of activation and detoxification enzymes, DNA repair mechanisms, or other processes. These differences may result in changes in target biological molecules for toxic chemicals, changes in the biologically effective dose from an exposure, or resistance to toxicity; and ultimately they may affect the pathogenic state or disease of the exposed individual. Examples of observable differences due to genetic polymorphisms and their corresponding suspected biomarkers of susceptibility are given in Table 29.2.[37–39]

Non-genetic factors that may have similar effects on biological responses or susceptibility may include age, diet, sex, lifestyle, culture, health status, medication, or exposure to other environmental chemical agents. These factors are independent of exposure but they identify those individuals in a population who may be more susceptible or resistant to the effects of a chemical exposure.[5,12,13,16–18,20,21]

Epidemiological Case Study on Biomarkers of Susceptibility

The most pronounced biomarkers of susceptibility are genetically-based and can be separated into three types: 1) differences in alteration of a xenobiotic by innate enzymes, 2) genetic

Table 29.2 — List of Some Known and Assumed Biomarkers of Susceptibility.

Exposure	Acquired/Genetic Biomarkers of Susceptibility
Nitro, aromatic, carbon monoxide, Cyanide and amino compounds	Sickle cell phenotype
Benzene and lead	Thalassemia phenotype
Lead, hexachlorobenzene and variety of drugs such as Chloroquine, barbituates, sulfonamides, etc.	Erythrocyte porphyria
Aromatic amines, oxidants, and nitro-aromatic compounds	Glucose-6P-dehydrogenase deficiency phenotype
Respiratory irritants	IgA deficiency
Sulfite, bisulfite and sulfur dioxide	Sulfite oxidase deficiency heterozygotes
Cross-linking agents	Franconi's anemia phenotype
Polycyclic aromatic hydrocarbons	Glutathione S-transferase M1 (GSTM1)
Aromatic amines and aflatoxin	Acetylator phenotype
Epoxides and bleomycin	Ataxia telangiectasia phenotype
Cigarette smoke	Alpha-1-antitrypsin
Cigarette smoke	GSTµ phenotype
Cigarette smoke	Debrisoquine hydroxylation phenotype
Alcohol consumption	Induced P-450 IIE1
Chemicals and Dusts	Antigen-specific antibodies

(Adapted from Calabrese E.J., 1986.)

differences to DNA damage repair function, and 3) pre-existing inherited genetic abnormalities that tend to increase the risk of cancer. In the case of differences in xenobiotic alteration, most chemicals that enter the body can be acted on by enzymes to cause structural changes to the chemical, called biotransformation. These changes may increase or decrease the ability of a chemical to interact with macromolecules such as proteins, RNA, or DNA. The balance between enzymes that detoxify and activate chemicals differs among individuals and ethnic groups. For example, the metabolism of organophosphates by enzymes with varying activity may make a person more or less susceptible to the effects of exposure.

One such enzyme that is being studied as a biomarker of susceptibility is *paraoxonase*. This enzyme is responsible for the hydrolysis and deactivation of paraoxon, an organophosphate compound. A polymorphism in the human paraoxonase gene has one form with an arginine at position 192 and a second with glutamine at 192. The version of the enzyme that has arginine at that position hydrolyzes paraoxon with a higher rate than the version with glutamine. This is an example of how polymorphisms may affect the efficiency with which an individual will metabolize a toxin or its byproducts. Such biomarkers of genetic susceptibility may prove to be important in assessing an individual's risk of adverse effects from exposure.[40,41]

The second type of biomarker of susceptibility is based on genetic differences in the ability of cells to repair DNA damage. Cells deficient in DNA repair genes may suffer DNA damage that can be manifested in a variety of ways. There may be increased levels of DNA adducts, or alterations in the structure or copy number of chromosomes. Or, oncogenes or their protein products may be activated. The consequences of these manifestations are often seen in higher incidences of cancer. For example, mutations in the p53 tumor suppressor gene are the most common genetic alteration in human cancers. These changes are typically missense point mutations, meaning that there is a mutation, but the gene still codes for a full length protein, with altered amino acid sequence. There is growing evidence that many of these mutations generate mutant p53 proteins that have acquired new biochemical and biological properties, and through this gain of function activity, mutant p53 is believed to contribute to tumor malignancy.

Studies have shown a significant dose-response relationship between vinyl chloride (VC) exposure and mutations in p53, as observed in workers exposed to the chemical. Vinyl chloride is commonly used in plastic products and it is a known animal and human carcinogen associated with angiosarcoma of the liver (ASL), which is a very rare form of cancer. The biomarker of susceptibility in this case is a change in a DNA repair gene, caused by a change in the level of the mutated form of p53, resulting in higher incidences of cancer.[40,42,43]

A third type of biomarker of susceptibility is based on preexisting, inherited genetic abnormalities that increase the risk of cancer. If an individual inherited one or more genetic changes that contribute to cancer development, fewer steps may be required for a chemical to cause cancer and put the individual at an increased risk. For example, the association between lung cancer and smoking is long-established, and now there is evidence of a link between smoking and bladder cancer. In a study of bladder cancer patients and control subjects, researchers found that roughly half of all subjects inherit an allele of the gene that encodes for the enzyme glutathione S-transferase M1 (GSTM1), which makes them more susceptible to bladder cancer. GSTM1 metabolizes and detoxifies a large number xenobiotics, including carcinogens such as the polycyclic aromatic hydrocarbons (PAHs) found in tobacco smoke.

The most common sources of occupational PAH exposure are coal tars and their derived products. The International Agency for Research on Cancer (IARC) reported that workers from industrial settings where airborne PAH levels are high, such as coke workers, gas workers, and those involved in primary aluminum production, show excess rates of cancers. Because the DNA nucleotide sequence of the GSTM1 gene is known, it was possible to use a common molecular technique known as polymerase chain reaction (PCR) to rapidly screen patient blood samples and determine whether a subject had two copies, one copy, or no copy of the gene. Persons who had at least one functional copy of the GSTM1 gene were less likely to develop bladder cancer than persons without the gene. Persons who have two copies of the gene probably have an even greater level of protection. Here, the epidemiological findings show that genetic predisposition combined with environmental exposure is an important factor in the development of disease associated with PAHs; and the biomarker of susceptibility in this case is GSTM1 gene variation.[44–46]

A particularly complex example of a biomarker of susceptibility is the enzyme N-acetyltransferase (NAT). This enzyme catalyzes a major pathway for biotransformation of xenobiotics. Genetic variation at this gene in the human population results in what are described as "fast acetylator" and "slow acetylator" individuals, depending on the behavior of their NAT enzymes. There is a strong correlation between ethnicity and prevalence of fast and slow acetylator phenotypes: the slow acetylator phenotype is predominant in Middle Eastern populations, intermediate in European populations, and infrequent in Asian populations. This variation has implications on how these groups tend to respond to xenobiotics, due to the importance of NAT in biotransformation. Determination of acetylator phenol type is an informative biomarker of susceptibility.

NAT is involved in metabolism of certain therapeutic drugs. Slow acetylators respond poorly to some of those drugs, and experience increased side effects, because their NAT fails to metabolize the drug to an active form as quickly, and instead allows the drug to accumulate in its original form to higher levels in circulation.

NAT also acts in the body's metabolism of many carcinogens. Smokers who are slow acetylators experience a higher incidence of bladder cancer, compared to those with at least one copy of the fast acetylator version. On the other hand, people with fast acetylator phenotype are more susceptible colorectal cancer. Thus the implications of a particular biomarker status are not categorically good or bad, but instead need to be interpreted in the context of lifestyle and occupational risk.[44,45]

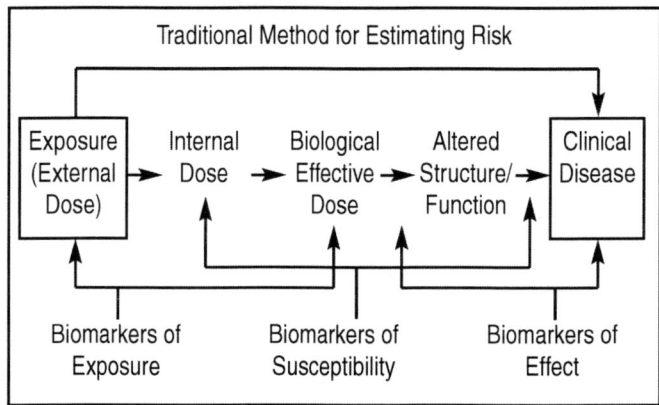

Figure 29.2 — The exposure/ disease gradient pathway (adapted from the Committee of Biomarkers, 1987).

Conclusions

Biomarkers can be considered in three categories, biomarkers of exposure, of effect, and of susceptibility. While there may not always be a clear distinction between the markers of each category, Figure 29.2 models the place of each type of biomarker in the exposure-disease continuum.

The discovery and use of biomarkers is an important and developing aspect of today's epidemiological approach in reducing the burden of diseases. The development and validation of potential biomarkers is a long-term effort that begins with basic research, leading to human studies and on to full-scale epidemiological investigations. The effort to date has provided knowledge and understanding of the sequence and relevance of molecular events that take place between environmental agents and human exposure.

A successful interpretation and validation of biomarker discovery must be followed by the incorporation of that mechanistic information into the next phases of disease prevention, including risk assessment and management. However, these processes are still in their early stages of development. The selection, validation and subsequent application of any biomarker is a complex process, and the complexity of this process will vary for different biomarkers. Also, research and use of biomarkers involves a mixture of social, legal and ethical issues, which may vary across nations and cultures, and requires careful consideration prior to any application.[9,14]

If biomarker technology becomes fully developed and used in public health, medical and industrial hygiene practices, it will ultimately impact the day-to-day work of epidemiologists and hygienists involved in regulatory and public health activities. We have seen the use of biomarker technology as an emerging trend, reflecting the need for an improved scientific basis for risk assessment, risk management and incorporating mechanistic data into the exposure-disease correlation discussion.

Dean J. Wagner would like to thank
Maura Tyrrell of Stonehill College for her helpful insights.

References

1. "National Institute for Occupational Safety and Health (NIOSH) Safety and Health Topic: Occupational Cancer." [Online] Available at http://www.cdc.gov/niosh/topics/cancer/ [Accessed January 23, 2007].
2. **Armstrong, D.:** An outline of Sociology as Applied to Medicine. Bristol, England. Wright. 1980.
3. **Pearce, N.:** Traditional Epidemiology and Public Health. *Am. J. Public Health. 86(5)*:678–682 (1996).
4. **Pekkanen, J. and N. Pearce:** Environmental Epidemiology: Challenges and Opportunities. *Environ. Health Persp. 108(1)*:1–5 (2001).
5. **Gillette, M.A., D.R. Mani, and S.A. Carr:** Place of Pattern in Proteomic Marker Discovery. *J. Proteome Res. 4*: 1143–1154 (2005).
6. **McCunny, R.J.:** Clinical Applications of Biomarkers in Occupational Medicine. In *Biomarkers and Occupational Health: Progress and Perspectives*, M. L. Mendelsohn, J. P. Peeters, and M. J. Normandy (eds.). Washington D. C.: National Academy Press, 1995. pp. 148–162.
7. **Schulte, P.A.:** Introduction: The Role of Biomarkers in the Prevention of Occupational Disease. In *Biomarkers and Occupational Health: Progress and Perspectives*, M. L. Mendelsohn, J. P. Peeters, and M. J. Normandy (eds.). Washington D. C.: National Academy Press, 1995. pp. 1–6.
8. **Schulte, P.A. and N. Rothman:** Epidemiological Validation of Biomarkers of Early Biological Effect and Susceptibility. In *The Biomarkers: Medical and Workplace Applications*. Mohr, L.C., J.P. Peeters and M. L. Mendelsohn (eds.). Washington D. C.: Joseph Henry Press, 1998. pp. 23–32.
9. **Hunter, D. J.:** The Future of Molecular Epidemiology. *Int. J. Epidemiol. 28(5)*:S1012–S1015 (1993).
10. **Susser, M.:** Does Risk Factor Epidemiology Put Epidemiology at Risk? Peering into the Future. *J. Epidemiol. Comm. Health. 52*:608–611 (1998).
11. **Hatch, M. C. and G. Friedman-Jimenez:** Using Reproductive Effect Markers to Observe Subclinical Events, Reduce Misclassification, and Explore Mechanism. *Environ. Health Persp. 90*:255–259 (1991).
12. **Grandjean P., S.S. Brown, P. Reavey, and D.S. Young:** Biomarkers of Chemical Exposure: State of the Art. *Clin. Chem. 40(7)*:1360–1352 (1994).
13. **DeCaprio, A.P.:** Biomarkers: Coming of Age for Environmental Health and Risk Assessment. *Environ. Sci. Tech. 31(7)*:1837–1848 (1997).
14. **Schulte, P.A.:** Use of Biological Markers in Occupational Health Research and Practice. *J. Tox. Environ. Health. 40*: 359–366 (1993).
15. **Theodorakis, C. W. and L. R. Shugart:** Genetic Ecotoxicology II: Population Genetic Structure in Mosquitofish Exposed in situ to Radionucleotides. *Ecotoxicology. 6*: 335–354 (1997).
16. **Gao, J., L.-A. Garulacan, S.M. Storm, G.J. Opiteck, Y. Dubaquie, S.A. Hefta, D.M. Dambach, and A.R. Dongre:** Biomarker Discovery in Biological Fluids. *Methods. 35*:291–302 (2005).
17. **World Health Organization (WHO):** *Principles and Methods for the Assessment of Nephrotoxicity Associated with Exposure to Chemicals. Environmental Health Criteria 119.* [Standard] Geneva: 1991.
18. **World Health Organization (WHO):** *Biomarkers and Risk Assessment: Concepts and Principles. Environmental Health Criteria 155.* [Standard] Geneva: 1993.
19. **Mendelsohn, M.L., L.C. Mohr, and J.P. Peeters:** Preface. In *The Biomarkers: Medical and Workplace Applications*. Mohr, L.C., J.P. Peeters and M.L. Mendelsohn (eds.). Washington D.C.: Joseph Henry Press, 1998. pp. iii–iv.
20. **Draper, W.M.:** Biological Monitoring: Exquisite Research Probes, Risk Assessment and Routine Exposure Measurement. *Anal. Chem. 73*:2745–2760 (2001).
21. **Kennedy, S.:** Proteomic Profiling from Human Samples: The Body Fluid Alternative. *Tox. Lett. 120*:379–384 (2001).
22. **International Union of Pure and Applied Chemistry (IUPAC):** "Compendium of Chemical Terminology." [Online] Available at http://www.iupac.org/goldbook [Accessed January 2007].
23. **American Conference of Governmental Industrial Hygenists (ACGIH):** [Online] Available at http://www.acgih.org/home.htm [Accessed January 2007].
24. **Henderson, R. F., W. E. Bechtold, J. A. Bond, and J. D. Sun:** The use of biological markers in toxicology. *Crit. Rev. Toxicol. 20(2)*:65–82 (1989).
25. **Costa, L.G.:** Biomarker Research in Neurotoxicology: The Role of Mechanistic Studies to Bridge the Gap Between the Laboratory and Epidemiological Investigations. *Environ. Health Persp. 104(1)*:55–67 (1996).
26. **Mayan, O., J.P. Teixeira, S. Alves, and C. Azevedo:** Urinary 2, 5 Hexanedione as a Biomarker of n-Hexane Exposure. *Biomarkers 7(4)*:299–305 (2002).
27. **Harrison, R., L. Isreal, P. Larabee:** n-Hexane Related Peripheral Neuropathy Among Automotive Technicians, California, 1999-2000. *Centers for Disease Control and Prevention, Morbidity and Mortality Weekly Report. 50(45)*:1011–1013 (2001).
28. **Jin, T., Q. Kong, T. Ye, X. Wu, G.F. and Nordberg:** Renal Dysfunction of Cadmium Exposed Workers Residing in a Cadmium-Polluted Environment. *Biometals. 17*:513–518 (2004).
29. **Garte, S., T. Popov, T. Georgieva, C. Bolognesi, E. Taioli, P. Bertazzi, P. Farmer, and D.F. Merlo:** Biomarkers of Exposure and Effect in Bulgarian Petrochemical Workers Exposed to Benzene. *Chem. Biol. Interact. 153–154*:247–251 (2005).
30. **Committee on Biological Markers of the National Research Council:** Biological Markers of Health Research. *Environ. Health Persp. 74*:23–29 (1987).

31. **Schins, R. P. F. and P. J. A. Borm:** Plasma Levels of Soluble Tumor Necrosis Factor Receptors are Increased in Coal Miners with Pneumoconiosis. *Eur. Respir. J.* 8:1658–1663 (1995).
32. **Roels, H. A., P. Hoet, and D. Lison:** Usefulness of Biomarkers of Exposure to Inorganic Mercery, Lead or Cadmium in Controlling Occupational and Environmental Risks of Neurotoxicity. *Renal Failure. 21(3&4)*:251–262 (1999).
33. **Kelada, S.N., E. Shelton, R.B. Kaufmann, and M.J. Khoury:** Delta-Aminolevulinic Acid Dehydratase Genotype and Lead Toxicity: A HuGE Review. *Am. J. Epidemiol. 154(1)*:1–13 (2001).
34. **Rothman, N., W. F. Stewart, and P. A. Schulte:** Incorporating biomarkers into cancer epidemiology: a matrix of biomarker and study design categories. *Cancer Epidemiol. Biomarkers Prev. 4(4)*:301–311 (1995).
35. **Fidder, A., A.G. Hulst, D. Noort, R. de Ruiter, M.J. van der Schans, H.P. Benschop, and J.P. Langenberg:** Retrospective detection of exposure to organophosphorus anticholinesterases: mass spectrometric analysis of phosphylated human butyrylcholinesterase. *Chem. Res. Toxicol. 15(4)*:282–290 (2002).
36. **Wessels, D., D.B. Barr, and P. Mendola:** Use of biomarkers to indicate exposure of children to organophosphate pesticides: implications for a longitudinal study of children's environmental health. *Env. Health Pers. 111(16)*:1939–1946 (2003).
37. **Calabrese, E.J.:** Ecogenetics: Historical Foundation and Current Status. *J. Occup. Med. 28(10)*:1096–1102 (1986).
38. **Guengerich, F.P.:** Individual Variation in Biotransformation and Carcinogens: Basis and Relevance. In *The Molecular Dosimetery and Human Cancer — Analytical, Epidemiological and Social Considerations.* Groopman, J.D. and P.L. Skipper (eds.). Boca Raton: CRC Press, 1991. pp.27–52.
39. **Kadlubar, F.F., R. Butler, H.-S. Kaderlick, N.P. Lang:** Polymorphisms for Aromatic Amine Metabolism in Humans: Relevance for Human Carcinogenesis. *Environ. Health Perspect. 98*:69–74 (1992).
40. **Conforti-Froes, N., R. El-Zein, and W. Au:** Genetic Polymorphism and their Contribution to Cancer Susceptibility. *Cad. Saúde Pública. 14(3)*:7–13 (1998).
41. **Costa, L.G., T.B. Cole, and C.E. Furlong:** Polymorphisms of Paraoxonase (PON1) and their Significance in Clinical Toxicology of Organophosphates. *J. Tox. Clin. Tox. 41(1)*: 37–45 (2003).
42. **Todd, G.D., O.M. Faroon, D.E. Jones, M.H. Lumpkin, J. Stickney, and M.J. Citra:** Toxicological Profile for Vinyl Chloride. US Department for Health and Human Services, Agency for Toxic Substances and Disease Registry (ATSDR). pp. 1–86. Atlanta, 2006.
43. **Pugacheva, E. N., A. V. Ivanov, J. E. Kravchenki, B. P. Kopnin, A. J. Levine, and P. M. Chumakov:** Novel Gain of Function Activity of p53 Mutants: Activation of the dUTPase Gene Expression Leading to Resistance to 5-Fluorouracil. *Oncogene. 21*:4595–4600 (2002).
44. **Zeiger, M.:** Biomarkers: The Clues to Genetic Susceptibility. *Environ. Health Persp. 102(1)*:50–57 (1994).
45. **Godschalk, R. W., J.W., Dallinga, H. Wikman, A. Risch, J.C. Kleinjans, H. Bartsch, and F.J. Van Schooten:** Modulation of DNA and Protein Adducts in Smokers by Genetic Polymorphisms in GTM1, GSTT1, NAT1 and NAT2. *Parmacogenetics. 11(5)*:389–398 (2001).
46. **Jongeneelen, F. J.:** Benchmark Guidline for Urinary 1-Hydroxypyrene as Biomarker of Occupational Exposure to Polycyclic Aromatic Hydrocarbons. *Ann. Occup. Hyg. 45(1)*:3–13 (2001).

Chapter 30

Industrial Chemical Hazard Communications

By Warren W. Jederberg, MS, CIH, RPIH

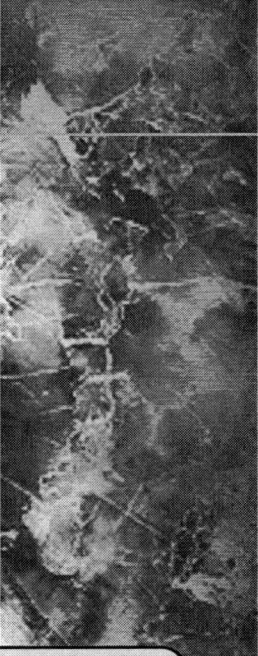

Introduction

In 1983, OSHA published the Hazard Communications Standard as 29 CFR 1910, 1200. The standard has also become known as the "worker's right to know" and is intended to assure that workers are fully informed on the toxicology and other safety risks associated with materials they use is available and understandable.[1,2] The intent of this chapter is to review the standard. There are three components to the standard: Labeling, Material Safety Data Sheets (MSDS) and training.[2,3]

Labeling

Any container of hazardous material must be labeled with the following minimal information (only the first two are required for "ready use" containers):

- Identity of the Chemical — Although the OSHA regulation does not mandate how the chemical will be identified, the Chemical Abstract Service (CAS) number and common name are widely used. CAS registry numbers are unique identifiers assigned by the American Chemical Society. Most chemical databases allow for searching by CAS numbers. By the end of March of 2006, there were over 27,000 substances in the CAS registry.
- Appropriate Hazard Warning — what is deemed "appropriate" is the subject of much discussion.[4] The hazard warnings can be indicated by words, pictures, symbols or a combination of these. Consideration must be given to the cultural background and general education level of the intended users. Name and address of the chemical manufacturer, importer, or other responsible party are required.
- Labels or other forms of warning must be prominently displayed on the container, be in English, and be legible. Where there are a large portion of non-English speaking employees, information in their language may be added to the label.[1]

Outcome Competencies

Upon completion of this chapter, the reader should be able to:

- Describe the three elements of the Federal Hazard Communication Standard.
- Describe the minimal elements of a Hazard Communications Standard training program.
- Describe the information elements required on a Material Safety Data Sheet.

Prerequisite Knowledge

None

Key Terms

MSDS, Hazard Communication, Global Harmonization

Key Topics

Labeling, MSDS content, training, responsibilities, record keeping, international harmonization, hazard communications in crisis situations.

MSDS

Though a specific format is not required by the standard, the following sixteen elements have been recommended for the MSDS by the Chemical Manufacturers Association (CMA)[1,5,6]: Chemical Product and Company Identification: This would include trade name, common name and a detailed address for the manufacturer/distributor of material to include phone number.

- **Composition:** If the chemical mixture as a whole has been tested to characterize its hazards, the chemical and common name(s) of the components which contribute to the hazards must be identified. For mixtures which have not been characterized as a whole, the chemical and common name(s) of all ingredients which constitute 1% or greater and for which the hazards have been individually identified must be listed. Chemical components that have been identified as carcinogens must be listed if they constitute 0.1% or greater of the mixture. Also, all ingredients determined to be health hazards, which comprise <1% (0.1% for carcinogens), if there is evidence that they could be released in concentration which would exceed OSHA permissible exposure limits (PELs) or American Conference of Governmental Industrial Hygienists (ACGIH) Threshold Limit Values®, or could present a health risk to employees.
- **Hazard Identification:** A description of the physical hazards associated with the ingredients including potential for fire, explosion and reactivity as well as a description of environmental hazards that may be of concern for personnel responding to release of the material should be provided.
- **First Aid Measures:** These include emergency first aid procedures that could be followed by fellow workers. It should be in layman's terms and therefore easy to understand. A description of first aid procedures for each route of exposure should be included. If detailed information that would be useful to an attending physician is available, it should be included in a special "Notes to Physicians" section.
- **Fire Fighting Measures:** Fire and explosive properties of the material, including media to be used should be described in this section.
- **Accidental Release Measures:** This section is intended for emergency response personnel and includes information on preventing or minimizing adverse exposures to employees, neighbors, property, waterways and the environment in general.
- **Handling and Storage:** This section should include information in regards to storage temperature, any requirements for inert atmosphere, specific storage conditions to avoid, etc.
- **Exposure Controls, Personal Protection:** Exposure guidelines, such an ACGIH TLV®s and OSHA PELS should be included in this section. Information on any engineering controls, and personnel protective equipment required should be provided.
- **Physical and Chemical Properties:** Those characteristics which would assist in determining proper handling and storage should be included. Physical state (gas, liquid, solid), pH, vapor pressure, density, melting and freezing points, solubility, flash point, odor, and specific gravity should be included. Other unique characteristics should be provided.
- **Stability and Reactivity:** A description of conditions that my result in a potentially hazardous reaction, such as the generation/release of a hazardous gas, production of heat, or other hazards should be contained in this section.
- **Toxicological Information:** Any known toxicity information resulting from animal testing or human exposures to the material should be included in this section. Any information on its potential for causing cancer and any acute, subchronic or chronic exposure data should also be addressed. Caution must be exercised in interpreting such data as many MSDSs have no data or provide inaccurate data.[7–9]
- **Ecological Information:** Impacts to the environment that may occur if the material is released and information on the impact of the material in waste treatment management should be found in this section.
- **Disposal Considerations:** Information necessary to provide guidance for environmental and other technical professionals who are responsible for management of the waste stream from this material is provided.
- **Transport Information:** This section provides information on the classification for shipping the material and should include U.S. Department of Transportation (DOT) classifications or an indication that the material is not regulated.[10,11]
- **Regulatory Information:** This section should contain information on the regulatory status of the material, including specific OSHA and EPA regulations should be cited. The requirements of other regulatory agencies may be included, if appropriate.
- **Other Information:** The preparer of the MSDS may include further information that is pertinent, but is not included in the other sections. Such information may include further label information, hazard ratings, revision dates, and references to other related information.

Training

The Hazard Communications Standard requires that each employee be given the following minimal training:

- Methods and observations that may detect the presence or release of a hazardous chemical in the work area,
- The physical and health hazards of the chemicals in the work area,
- Measures employees can take to protect themselves from these hazards.

Responsibilities of the Chemical Manufacturer/Importer

Under the Hazard Communications Standard, the manufacturer/importer of hazardous materials must provide information on the MSDS that accurately reflects the scientific evidence used in making the hazard determination. Any new information that comes to the attention of the manufacturer/importer must be incorporated in the MSDS within three months.

Responsibilities of the Distributor

Distributors are obligated to provide MSDSs with shipped containers, or send them to employer or other distributors before shipment. Wholesale distributors of hazardous materials that provide them over-the-counter may provide an MSDS as requested or provide information as to the availability of an MSDS. If the material is provided by a retail distributor that does not normally use the material, or does not have commercial accounts, they may provide the name, address, and telephone number of the chemical manufacturer, importer, or distributor where an MSDS may be obtained.

Responsibilities of the Workers' Supervisor/ Manager

MSDSs are to be readily available in the workplace. MSDSs for each hazardous material may be maintained in printed or electronic form, as long as they are easily accessible during each work shift. They may also be part of the operating procedures for an area. Every employee working with hazardous materials must be informed of the hazards associated with that material the first time that they use it. The worker must also be given the location and availability of the written hazard communication program and the required lists of hazardous chemicals used in his work place.

The worker must also be informed as to the measure that they must take to protect themselves. This information will include descriptions of what efforts the employer is taking such as appropriate work practices, emergency procedures, and personal protective equipment to be used.

Record Keeping

There are no long-term record keeping requirements under the HCS. Written programs must be kept current and MSDSs in the workplace must be kept for those materials that are in current use. Under the "Access to Employee Exposure and Medical Records" requirements of 29 CFR 1910.20, MSDSs must be kept for 30 years, if no exposure records have been kept. If monitoring has been recorded, which includes the names of chemicals, locations, and other information, then an MSDS need not be kept.

International Harmonization

With the increasing international commerce involving hazardous materials, efforts have been undertaken to "harmonize" regulations.[1,3,12] In December of 2002, the Globally Harmonized System for the Classification and Labeling of Chemicals (GHS) was formally adopted by the United Nations. The goal is to have it adopted by as many nations as possible by 2008. The mandates of the Sub-Committee of Experts on Globally Harmonized System for the Classification and Labeling of Chemicals (SCEGHS) are to act as custodians of the harmonization efforts, keep the system up to date, promote understanding and encourage feedback, make the system available worldwide, make guidance available on the application of the system, and to prepare work programs and submit recommendations to other committees concerned with the transport of hazardous materials.[13]

Hazard Communications in Crisis Situations

In view of recent events and the continuing potential for intentional release of hazardous materials, a new emphasis has been placed on providing useful chemical hazard information. The reader must be aware that the barriers to communicating accurate information in a crisis situation and to an audience that will contain individuals who have not received training are amplified. The tools used for risk communication in the workplace[14] provide some tools, but other considerations are required.[15–17] A good series discussing the principles of hazard communications in crisis situations has been published by the American Industrial Hygiene Association (AIHA).[18–22]

Case Study

A review of a random sample of 61 MSDSs for toluene diisocyanate (TDI) products by 30 manufacturers was conducted. Two physicians independently recorded data on to standardized forms. Asthma was listed as a potential health effect by only 15 (50%) of the manufacturers. Sensitizing or allergic reactions were list by 21 (70%) of the manufacturers. Many of the MSDSs had not been updated since 1990 .The authors concluded that many MSDSs for TDI do not clearly communicate that exposure can cause or exacerbate asthma.[23]

Conclusion

In summary, the Hazard Communications Standard provides an integrated framework to assure that information is provided so that workers are able to make decisions with regards to the potential health hazards (toxicological and safety) they face in the workplace. While the amount of information available is extensive, the specificity and quality still vary greatly. Efforts continue within the United States and across the world to make the information more uniform and useful.

Though not discussed in detail in this chapter, it must be recognized that the HCS is but a part of the necessary tools used to inform the workers, industry, and the public concerning potential risks/hazards associated with the intentional or accidental release of toxic chemical. It is intended to seamlessly integrate the concepts of hazard communications with other environmental and emergency response guides, regulations and information.

Suggested Further Reading

1. **Kaplan, S.A.:** "Development of Material Safety Data Sheets." Presented at American Chemical Society meeting, April 1986. [Online] Available at jrm.phys.ksu.edu/Safety/kaplan.html. [Accessed March 4, 2006].
2. **Wright, M.J.:** Statement before the Subcommittee on Employment, Safety and Training Committee on Health Education, Labor and Pensions, U.S. Senate Hearing on Hazard Communication in the Workplace, March 2004. [Online] Available at www.senate.gov/~enzi/wright2.htm. [Accessed March 4, 2006].

References

1. **Henshaw, J.L.:** Statement before the Subcommittee on Employment, Safety and Training Committee on Health Education, Labor and Pensions, U.S. Senate, March 2004. [Online] Available at www.senate.gov/~enzi/hensha2.htm. [Accessed April 22, 2006].
2. "Hazard Communication Standard." *Code of Federal Register Title 29 Section 1910.1200.*
3. **Silk, J.C.:** Hazard Communication. In *The Occupational Environment, Its Evaluation, Control, and Management*, 2nd edition. DiNardi, S.R. (ed.). Fairfax, VA: AIHA Press, 2003. pp 1017–1039.
4. **Sattler, B., B. Lippy, and T.G. Jordan:** "Hazard Communication: A Review of the Science Underpinning the Art of Communication for Health and Safety." 23 May 1997. [Online] Available at www.osha.gov/SLTC/hazardcommunications/hc2inf2.html. [Accessed March 5, 2006].
5. **Gullickson, R:** "Reference Data Sheet on Material Safety Data Sheets", May 1996. [Online] Available at meridianeng.com/msds.html. [Accessed March 4, 2006].
6. American National Standard for Hazardous Industrial Chemicals — Material Safety Date Sheets — Preparation, ANSI400.1-1993. New York: American National Standards Institute, 1993.
7. **Kolp, P.W., P.L. Williams, and R.C. Burton:** Assessment of the accuracy of Material Safety Data Sheets. *Am. Ind. Hyg. Assoc. J. 56(2)*:178–183 (1995).
8. **Jederberg, W.W., and K.R. Still:** Definition of the Toxicity of Materials. *The Layman's Guide to Toxicology.* Still, K.R. and C.L. Wilson (eds.). CPIA Publication 686. Columbia, MD, 1999. pp. 7–11.
9. **Jederberg W.W.:** Issues with the Integration of Technical Information in Planning for and Responding to Non-Traditional Incidents. *J. Toxicol. Environ. Health 68(11–12)*: 877–888 (2005).
10. "Hazardous Materials Regulations." *Code of Federal Regulations Title 49 Sections 100-199.* "Transportation."
11. "Hazardous Materials Transportation Guides" [Online] Available at ntl.bts.gov/DOCS/hmtg.html. [Accessed April 22, 2006].
12. "Hazard Communication in the 21st Century Workplace," March 2004. [Online] Available at www.osha.gov/dsg/hazcom/finalmsdsreport.html. [Accessed January 1, 2006].
13. "Mandate of the Sub-Committee of Experts on GHS" [Online] Available at www.unece.org/trans/danger/publi/ghs/mandate_e.html. [Accessed April 23, 2006].
14. **Gillooly, P.B., T. Flynn, H.E. Maupin, M.A. Simmons, and S.M. Forrest:** Risk Communication in the Workplace. In *The Occupational Environment, Its Evaluation, Control, and Management*, 2nd edition. DiNardi, S.R. (ed.). Fairfax, VA: AIHA Press, 2003. pp 998–1016.
15. **Sandman, P.M.:** *Responding to Community Outrage: Strategies for Effective Risk Communications.* Fairfax, VA: American Industrial Hygiene Association, 1993.
16. **Agency for Toxic Substances and Disease Registry (ATSDR):** ATSDR Report on Chemical Terrorism: "Industrial Chemicals and Terrorism: Human Health Threat Analysis, Mitigation and Prevention" [Online] Available at www.mapcruzin.com/scruztri/docs/cep1118992.htm. [Accessed January 4, 2006].
17. **Agency for Toxic Substances and Disease Registry (ATSDR):** "A Primer on Health Risk Communication Principles and Practices" [Online] Available at www.atsdr.cdc.gov/HEC/primer.html. [Accessed January 11, 2006].
18. **Sandman, P.E.:** Risk Communication: When People Are "Overreacting" to Risk. *The Synergist, 15(2)*: 22–24, 2004.
19. **Sandman, P.E.:** Risk Communication: Crisis Communication: A Very Quick Introduction. *The Synergist, 15(4)*: 26–28, 2004.
20. **Sandman, P.E.:** Risk Communication: When People are "Underreacting" to Risk. *The Synergist, 15(7)*: 24–25, 2004.
21. **Sandman, P.E.:** Risk Assessment: Acknowledging Uncertainty. *The Synergist, 15(11)*: 21–22,24, 2004.
22. **Behar, J.:** Communicating Risk – An Art More than a Science. *The Synergist 16(11)*: 32–35, 2005.
23. **Frazier, L.M., B.W. Beasley, G.K. Sharma, and A.A. Mohyuddin:** Health Information on Material Safety Data Sheets for a Chemical that Causes Asthma. *J. Gen Intern Med 16*:89–93, 2001.

Chapter 31

Evaluation of Industrial/Commercial Materials

By J. Thomas Pierce, MBBS, PhD, Lutz W.D. Weber, PhD, DABT, and Jerry A. Formisano, Jr., PhD, CIH, CSP

Introduction and Purpose

This chapter addresses an underserved area of toxicology, that of decision-making relative to material toxicity. Industrial hygiene and toxicology collaborative panels are faced with a high level task when it comes to permitting materials. Beyond the prerequisite skill sets, there is an important body of information concerning decision making that can improve the substance of toxicological decisions. Materials toxicology often involves decision making that spans from science to policy and its public perception. This chapter will reinforce the assurance of safety in the context of definable risk estimates. While this chapter will introduce students and young professionals to critical topics, considered judgment of these topics will likely be left to seasoned industrial hygiene and toxicology professionals in the workplace.

Making Good Decisions Based on Toxicological Knowledge

The study of thought is sometimes termed **meta-cognition**. Flavell[1] defined meta-cognition as 'the ability to stand apart from one's own thought processes, to observe (processes) and to apply interventional thinking strategies to gain improvements in outcomes." Scientists may be reluctant at first to admit there is anything more than 'data' or 'facts' but the extension of knowledge past so-called facts is the case in point for the toxicological sciences.

Disciplines as diverse as emergency medicine and even piloting (aeronautics) have become advocates for 'thought within or about thought.' Christopher[2] posits that decision theory or "the logic of consequence enables a sound and logical decision that considers expectations, alternatives, consequences and preferences."

Ultimately, decisions are dependent upon the level of evidence assembled through the scientific literature and on account of additional ordered tests. The strength of recommendation is limited by the level of evidence assembled. To be able to successfully defend a product as appropriately 'safe within a stated qualification' derives from the level of evidence assembled. Uruquart posits levels of data for biological or pharmacological or

Outcome Competencies

Upon completion of this chapter the reader should be able to:

- Determine the complexity of the assessment of a new material;
- Describe the steps leading up to a comprehensive evaluation of its toxicity;
- Differentiate between relatively non-toxic main components and high-risk contaminants;
- Propose an action plan for the safe introduction of a new material;
- Justify decisions concerning the risks associated with major and minor components of a mixture.

Prerequisite Knowledge

A solid knowledge of the principles of biology, physiology, toxicology, chemistry, and an in-depth understanding of industrial hygiene.

Key Terms

Anchoring, ascertainment, bias, decomposition, editing, framing, heuristics, meta-cognition, momentum, order effects, premature closure, recency

Key Topics

1. Making Good Decisions Based on Toxicological Knowledge
2. Scientific and Regulatory History
3. The Scope of Materials Toxicology
4. Connecting Toxicological Risk and Safety
5. The Span (or Extent) of Toxicological Features
6. Criteria for Accepting or Rejecting Projects

toxicologic inquiry[3] (Table 31.1). When there is no particular consonance between or among these levels, it is reasonable to conclude that the level of evidence is weak, lessening the strength of recommendation.

Table 31.1 — Levels of Toxicologic Inquiry

Level	Constituents
1	Populations
2	Closely intercommunicating groups of organisms (special needs groups, neighborhoods)
3	Mothers and fetuses
4	Whole organisms (mature or immature)
5	Organ systems (CNS, PNS, heart, lungs, kidneys, adrenals, muscles in exercise)
6	Organs (brain, heart, muscles, liver, kidneys, endocrine glands)
7	Groups of directly intercommunicating cells (neurons, glia, Schwann cells)
8	Cells
9	Subcellular structures (microsomes, mitochondria, nucleus)
10	Groups of interacting molecules (genome, enzyme systems, drug receptors, internal signaling mechanism)
11	Molecules (genes, enzymes, receptors)

Source: Uruquart[3]

It may also be useful to review toxicity as defined by an adverse event that has an attribution of **possible, probable or definite** significance. Thus, the level of evidence feeds the strength of recommendation to constitute a dynamic area for further inquiry. Decision making should be periodically revisited to determine its accuracy and relevance. Theorists such as Christopher[2] warn of five fundamental simplifications: (1) editing, (2) heuristics, (3) framing, (4) decomposition, and (5) bias.

Editing represents the thought process of simplification, in which the thinker may discard or ignore relevant information or prematurely terminate thought. Arbitrarily restricting references to those appearing past a given date when, in fact, key studies were previously completed constitutes a good example of editing. Minimalist approaches to designation of significant figures in calculations constitute another example.

The term **heuristics** refers to the recognition of patterns in certain situations and application of scripted behaviors or responses (sometimes called rule-of-thumb or **ball-parking**). Heuristics have been defined with four signatures by the engineering theorist Koen[4]: (1) they do not guarantee a solution; (2) they may contradict other heuristics; (3) they reduce search time for solving problems; and (4) acceptance depends on the immediate context of problem solving rather than any absolute standard. As such the process of engineering design, testing and verification must embrace a toxicologic perspective.[5]

Framing refers to decision processes set within beliefs that attempt to define the problem to be addressed, the information that must be collected and the dimensions that should be evaluated. When previous toxicologic evaluations have been performed according to a series of government guidelines, for instance, these same guidelines may be invoked even though a new set of compounds are significantly different.

Decomposition is sometimes explained in terms of algorithm development. While assembling an algorithm, its developer may find a sub-optimal solution which could be improved by refining what is termed an underlying decomposition. Thus, decomposition refers to a temporary error in an emerging algorithm (or thought process). The decomposition problem occurs when its developer forces the algorithm past the underlying decomposition without acknowledging a temporary error.

Bias exists when a thinker responds to a given set of information in a predictable, set manner, aware or unaware of this bias. **Omission bias** is the tendency toward inaction or reluctance to further investigate. While any of the five simplifications is important, a phenomenon termed the 'bias of the failed heuristic' has been singled out as critical to improving decision making. The bias of the failed heuristic is further defined by its own five serious errors: (1) anchoring, (2) ascertainment, (3) momentum, (4) order effects, and (5) premature closure.

Anchoring is the tendency to fixate on specific features early in the evaluation process. Finding a major error in toxicological data may cause the evaluator to discount other valid information that is present. **Ascertainment** refers to processes that are driven by expectations or by what one hopes to find, e.g., stereotyping. If industrial hygienists have evaluated a similar series of compounds, they may be inclined to reach a similar conclusion beyond the merits of the present materials. **Momentum** refers to establishing a position without adequate supporting data. A good example would be undue adherence to the position of a major toxicologic figure who never actually shared detailed supporting arguments.

Order effects refers to information transfer at the beginning and at the end (also called **recency**); the extremes of recollection becoming more important than what has been termed the 'middle bit.' Studies have indicated that the first and the last read documents are better remembered, if not acted upon, than those in the middle.[2] **Premature closure** defines acceptance without verification through independent means. Meta-cognition has certain parallels in hypothesis testing in terms of a type I error (null hypothesis is really true) and a type II error (a true difference exists).

To summarize, meta-cognitive approaches are most useful in terms of including a critical analysis of the process of assignment along with the product of review, e.g., the assignment of risk. The goal is always one of making good decisions based upon toxicological knowledge.

Scientific and Regulatory History

As derived from the ancients (Papyrus Ebers, Egypt, 1552 BC, Charaka Samhita, India, 600 BC and writings of Pliny the Elder, Rome 23–79 AD), the term toxicity refers to the study of poisons. The conceptual architecture of toxicology owes much to Philippus Aureolus Theophrastus Bombast von Hohenheim, also known as Paracelsus (1493–1541). A contemporary of Paracelsus, Georg Bauer, better known by his Latinized name, Georgius Agricola (1494–1555), penned chapters and sketches depicting protective equipment, workplace safety, ventilation devices, and the diseases of miners. The study of the scientific history surrounding these and other greater thinkers permits the modern health professional to strengthen his or her own understanding, even in light of contemporary scientific developments.

A review of American legislation is one way of recounting progress in materials toxicology (Table 31.2). In particular the Toxic Substances Control Act (1976) provides 'pre-manufacturing notification' relative to pre-selected panels of chemicals. REACH (Registration, Evaluation and Authorization of Chemicals) is a new policy adopted by the European Union (December 2006 – 27 countries).[6] REACH's central tenet has been tersely described as 'no data–no market.' The next chapter section focuses on assembling and analyzing key data of a toxicologic nature. Realizing that the legislative process cannot mirror each scientific development much of the onus for responsibility continues to rest upon health and safety professionals.

The Scope of Materials Toxicology

One must know the composition of a material to estimate the extent of its toxic action. A certificate of analysis corresponding to the commercial product helps to answer the first question. Liaison with the purchasing department is critical to ensuring that materials' suppliers acknowledge that buying decisions are dependent upon their ability to supply a certificate of authenticity that will withstand toxicological scrutiny.

The authenticity issue questions whether materials being supplied are, in fact, the same as those originally specified. Manufacturer's data on lot variability becomes part of a (statistical) power analysis that estimates the minimum number of samples for chemical analysis.[7] Toxicity can occur in response to all chemicals that are present in physiologically significant concentrations, not just those of manufacturing significance. The viewpoint of toxicology is that possessing material safety data sheets is essential but that their contents may not always be reliable. Omission bias can occur when material safety data sheets are substituted for an authentic chemical analysis.

By convention, contaminants are agreed to be largely physiologically unimportant when their concentrations are kept below 50 parts per million (ppm, weight basis).[8] However, (high) toxicity ingredients such as heavy metals and fused ring compounds may merit further consideration even at concentrations below 50 ppm. The classic paper of Courtney and co-workers[9] noted serious developmental effects for 2,3,7,8-tetrachlorodibenzo-p-dioxin (TCDD) at about 27 ppm (weight basis) in a defoliant preparation. This example illustrates the potential risks of the 'bias of the failed heuristic' inherent in blanket adoption of a 50 ppm exclusion rule. Typically, commercial products fall outside of the true extremes of toxicity, e.g., they are rarely benign, but they possess toxicities less than recognized poisons such as strychnine or cyanide. While no one rule can satisfy all conditions or scenarios, it is universally true that the earlier this discussion takes place, the greater the likelihood that all interested parties will be satisfied.

Toxicity testing and analytical characterization of a product can be considered as complementary to one another. The approach of focusing materials characterization on priority groups of chemicals allows analyses to be uniformly conducted. Groups may involve defined subsets, e.g., metals, metalloids, complex anions or various organic groupings devised in order to direct analysis at a manageable number of compounds. There can be a **momentum** effect to uniformly analyze products without really understanding the significance of particular subsets of them or perhaps in neglecting other toxicologically important substances.

While additives must be specified in commercial products, the presence of impurities is more subtle. Spectral and analytical grades represent the cleanest grades, e.g., most pure, but technical or even industrial grades are more commonly used and sometimes substituted. A certificate of analysis represents a

Table 31.2 — Protecting Health: Important U.S. Regulatory Acts Addressing Materials Toxicology since 1927

Year	Act	Features
1927	Federal Caustic Poison Act	Labeling of concentrated caustics
1930	Food and Drug Administration	Established as successor to the Bureau of Chemistry
1948	Federal Insecticide, Fungicide and Rodenticide Act	Federal control for pesticide sale, distribution and use
1960	Federal Hazardous Substances Labeling Act	Mandated prominent labeling warnings on hazardous household chemical products
1963	Clean Air Act	Regulated air emissions by setting maximum pollutant standards
1970	Poison Prevention Packaging Act	Mandated child-resistant safety caps on selected pharmaceuticals
1976	Toxic Substances Control Act	Authorized U.S. EPA to track more than 75,000 industrial chemicals
1980	Comprehensive Environmental Response, Compensation, and Liability Act (CERCLA)	Authorized tax on chemical and petroleum industries to defray cleanup costs (Superfund)
2002	Public Health Security and Bioterrorism Preparedness and Response Act	Tightened control on biological agents and toxins

time-fixed snapshot. For substances of uncertain composition or for those stored well past expected lifetimes, special analyses can be required. Knowledge of reaction chemistry, particularly that involving oxidation-reduction chemistry, is helpful to understanding changes associated with storage of materials.[10]

An initial step in dealing with a new material is a search at the National Library of Medicine's Hazardous Substances Data Bank, the WHO-sponsored International Programme on Chemical Safety, or any other easily accessible database (see Table 31.3).

Accurate chemical and even trade nomenclature is critical to understand what is tested and what is actually going to be used. While many schemes can be devised to assign chemicals to various categories, the radico-functional is perhaps most helpful in estimating toxicological reactivity. A radico-functional name is that formed from the name of a functional group (radical) and the name of the chemical class. Such a system has the advantage of focusing attention on the radical portion of the molecule that often signifies its toxicity. Table 31.4 highlights the importance of a radico-functional approach in predicting toxicity. This table gives the reader an idea of functionality than can be important in devising a strategy for categorizing materials.

Historically the radico-functional group has been more concerned with the functional groups in the xenobiotic than with those in the cell or tissue. Elegant new methods now calculate the extent of interaction for xenobiotic groups with those in proteins of skin (such as thiols). This is one example of new means of in silico toxicology, employing critical structure-activity characteristics.[5] While it is tempting to term this computerized toxicology, its underlying assumptions still require meticulous bench work of a chemical or biological basis.

Connecting Toxicological Risk and Safety

Toxicity has been defined as an adverse event that has an attribution of possible, probable or definite significance. In contrast, an adverse event can be considered to be an unfavorable **symptom, sign,** or **disease**, including an abnormal laboratory finding temporally associated with the use of a chemical that may or may not be considered related to the exposure.

While many references define the toxicity or risk associated with the use of a material, fewer connect safety with risk along a common axis. While the term assessment is appropriate for risk, the term assurance is more appropriate for safety. The conceptualization of toxicological safety in the context of risk has proven to be a continuing challenge, although vital to understanding and communication of results.

Toxicological risk and safety are like the terms acidity and alkalinity in that they are complementary and also span extremely broad scales. Thus, Sorensen's experience in devising a

Table 31.3 — Sources of Toxicological Data

Source	Website (URL)
U.S. Environmental Protection Agency, Integrated Risk Information System (IRIS)	http://www.EPA.gov/IRIS
Centers for Disease Control (CDC) Agency for Toxic Substances and Disease Registry (ATSDR)	http://www.ATSDR.CDC.gov/
CDC National Institute of Occupational Safety and Health (NIOSH)	http://www.CDC.gov/NIOSH/database.html
CDC NIOSH Registry of Toxic Effects of Chemical Substances (RTECS)	http://www.CDC.gov/NIOSH/rtecs/RTECSaccess.html
National Institute of Health (NIH) National Library of Medicine (NLM) Hazardous Substances Data Bank (HSDB)	http://toxnet.NLM.NIH.gov/cgi-bin/sis/htmlgen?HSDB
NIH NLM Toxicology Data Network (TOXNET)	http://toxnet.NLM.NIH.gov
NIH NLM National Center for Biotechnology Information (NCBI) PubMed	http://www.NCBI.NLM.NIH.gov/sites/entrez
National Institutes of Environmental Health and Safety (NIEHS) National Toxicology Program (NTP) Reports on Carcinogens (RoCs)	http://NTP.NIEHS.NIH.gov/index.cfm?objectid=72016262-BDB7-CEBA-FA60E922B18C2540
U.S. Department of Labor Occupational Safety and Health Administration (OSHA)	http://www.OSHA.gov/
U.S. Food and Drug Administration (FDA)	http://www.fda.gov/cder/cancer/toxicityframe.htm
American Conference of Governmental Industrial Hygienists (ACGIH)	http://www.ACGIH.org/
International Agency for Research on Cancer (IARC)	http://www.IARC.fr/eng/Databases/index.php
World Health Organization (WHO) International Programme on Chemical Safety (IPCS)	http://www.inchem.org/
Manufacturer's data, including material safety data sheets	Various

Table 31.4 — A brief overview of common chemical groups and their toxicological significance

Chemical Name	Suffix	Description	Reaction
Alkane	-an(e), yl,	>C–C<	With low molecular weight, smell (gasoline), flammability, CNS depressant. Paraffin: Higher molecular weight alkane, no scent, less flammable, low toxicity.
Alkene, olefin(e)	-en(e)	–C=C–	Properties similar to alkane, but due to the double bond increased chemical and biological reactivity. Can form epoxides.
Alkyne	-ene, in(e)	–C≡C–	Highly flammable (acetylene), but biologically rather inert.
Alcohol	-ol	>C–OH	Properties similar to alkanes, but with higher biological reactivity and toxicity (especially CNS depressant). Can form more toxic metabolites (aldehydes, ketones, acids)
Aldehyde	-al	–C(H)=O	Frequently used as chemical intermediate. Pungent odor, prone to causing eye and respiratory tract irritation. Chemically and biologically very reactive, high toxicity potential (carcinogen).
Acid	carboxy(l)	–C(OH)=O	Can be toxic due to acidity (corrosiveness), or, with two or more carboxyl groups, because they can chelate di- and trivalent cations
Ketone	-on(e)	>C=O	Chemical intermediates, solvents. Pungent odor. Chemically and biologically less reactive than aldehydes. May react with amino groups in proteins. 2,5-Diketones, such as 2,5-hexanedione, a metabolite of n-hexane, cause a heinous neuropathy by crosslinking amino groups of proteins in the axons of nerves.
Ester	n/a	–C(=O)–O–C– –C(=O)–S–C– others	May also consist of an alcohol with sulfuric, phosphoric, or other acids (also sulfhydryl ester). Lower molecular weight esters are used as flavoring agents. Because the carboxyl group cannot dissociate, they are generally taken up easily and are also easily cleaved in the organism where they yield alcohol and acid, each with its own toxicity.
Ether	n/a	>C–O–C<	At lower molecular weights very volatile, flammable, characteristic scent, CNS depressant. Forms highly explosive peroxides. Chemically and biologically not very reactive, but may be metabolized to alcohols by the organism.
Glycol	-diol	Varies	Contains two alcohol groups on adjacent or closely distanced carbons. Common solvents or process intermediates. Because they can form dicarboxylic acids such as oxalic acid, which precipitates cellular calcium, they may be toxic (antifreeze).
Epoxide	-oxide	O / \\ –C—C–	Common reaction and metabolism intermediates. Because of their high chemical and biological reactivity they are among the most dangerous agents (DNA damage, cancer).
Peroxide	n/a	–C–O–O–C–	Used to introduce oxygen into chemicals. In biological systems tends to form radicals and start chain reactions (lipid peroxidation), giving rise to DNA damage: highly toxic.
Amine	amino	–C(=O)–NH$_2$	Frequently ammonia-like smell. Prone to causing sensitization and irritation. Tends to react with carbonyl groups (see ketone, aldehyde). Can be severely toxic and/or carcinogenic (aniline).
Amide	amido	>N–H	Chemical intermediate, biologically rather inactive.
Imine	imino, imido	H–N=C<	Biologically generally quite inactive.
Nitrate	nitro	>C–NO$_3$	Chemical intermediates or end-products (explosives: trinitrotoluene, trinitroglycerin). During metabolism they release the potent biological signaling molecule, nitric oxide, which is vasoactive (use of (tri)nitroglycerin to prevent heart attacks). Aromatic nitrates, such as nitrobenzene, are toxic because they cause methemoglobin formation.
Nitroso compound	nitroso	>C–N=O	Chemical intermediate. Quite reactive, generally a cause of toxicological concern.
Nitrosamine	n/a	>N–N=O	Chemically highly reactive intermediates. Biologically very dangerous because of the ability of this group to damage cellular DNA by oxidation or alkylation (DNA adduct formation, mutation, carcinogenesis).

(continued on next page.)

Table 31.4 — A brief overview of common chemical groups and their toxicological significance (continued)

Chemical Name	Suffix	Description	Reaction
Azo compound	azo, diimide	–N=N–	Mostly with aromatics on either side of the nitrogens. Tend to be colored because of conjugated double bonds. May explode with heating. Can split at the N=N double bond with radical formation: highly active (mutagen, carcinogen: p dimethylaminoazobenzene = butter yellow).
Azide	n/a	–N3	Tend to form insoluble salts with heavy metals, therefore rather toxic. Some salts are highly explosive (firearm priming compound).
Sulfhydryl compound, mercaptan	thio, mercapto-	>C–S–H	Nauseating odor. Chemically and biologically reactive. Toxic because they precipitate heavy metal, but also react with essential –S–S– (disulfide) groups in proteins, which may render them inactive. However, one of the most important detoxication compounds in the organism is glutathione, a sulfhydryl compound. N Acetylcysteine (Mucomyst), also a sulfhydryl compound, has very low toxicity; it is used pharmacologically as a mucolytic, but also as the antidote for paracetamol poisoning.
Sulfone	n/a	C–(O=)S(=O)–C	Typical intermediate that may become toxic when it is prone to release an alkyl group (see alkylating agent).
Sulfoxide	n/a	C–(O=)S–C	Can act as an alkylating agent. The quite non-toxic dimethyl sulfoxide (DMSO; garlic odor) is used as a penetration helper in topical drugs.
Hydrocarbon	Varies	Varies	General term for compounds that contain only hydrogen atoms on a carbon backbone without further distinction as to linear, ring-shaped, double bonds, etc. Because numerous compounds fall into this category, it is biologically and toxicologically non-descript, but by no means trifling.
Polycyclic aromatic hydrocarbon	Varies	Varies	Made up of two to multiple rings with carbon backbone that has conjugated double bonds, i.e., repeat sequence of single and double bonds. Rings may have 3 or more carbon atoms (5 and 6 carbons are most frequent). Aromatic smell with two rings. Despite the multiple double bonds chemically rather stable, but can be metabolized to highly toxic (carcinogenic) intermediates.
Heterocyclic compound	Varies	Varies	A chemical consisting of one or more rings that are built from carbons plus one ore more other atoms, mostly nitrogen, sulfur, or oxygen. Frequently used as solvents. Volatile, flammable, pungent odor, may be very toxic (pyridine).
Alkylating agent	Varies	Varies	General term for chemicals that are prone to releasing alkyl groups (methyl, ethyl, etc.). Commonly used as chemical reaction intermediates. Because they can, in the organism, introduce an alkyl group into DNA bases, they are a matter of high concern.
Halogenated or halo-compound	fluoro- chloro- bromo- iodo-	C–F C–Cl C–Br C–I	Very common solvents or intermediates. Generally more stable than the corresponding hydrocarbon. Strong odor. Can form highly reactive metabolites: always a matter of concern.

common scale proves illustrative of a promising strategy. Working with physiologic preparations, Sorenson noted there should be some way to compare acidity and alkalinity, and, hence, proposed the logarithm-based pH scale. His work is noted here not so much because of the importance that pH has in toxicology but rather because of the general approach Sorensen employed.[11] Uruquart[12] was the first to recognize a logarithmic relationship applicable to both risk and safety, although not specifically adapted to toxicity determinations. One of us, JTP, found the concept of complementary scales useful and adapted them to broad questions of toxicity relevant to a new class of largely uncharacterized nanomaterials. The logarithmic transformations noted herein generally do not require an extensive reference list but may be reviewed using any algebra text.

Toxicological consideration of a commercial material should be guided by assessment of both risk and safety factors, e.g., the concept of risk should be defined through an understanding of safety. As originally developed, a simple system of toxicological risk units (TRU) and toxicological safety units (TSU) is applied.[13] For such a system, the sum of

$$TRU + TSU = 10 \quad (1)$$

The two numbers always add to 10. Thus, if chemical safety were arbitrarily defined as low, say a value of 2, the corresponding risk measure would be 8, rather high. The TRU (risk) is related to the probability of an event in the following manner.

$$TRU = 10 + \log 10\,[(E)] \quad (2)$$

Thus, for circumstances where the probability of a toxic insult is estimated the TRU/TSU system becomes more than an arbitrary rating scale. As an example, for an event with a relatively high probability, say 1 in 100, the TRU equals 8, a high risk, whereas for a relatively low probability event, say 1 in 10 million, the TRU would equal 3.

Like pH, the decibel, or even the Richter scale, the inherent advantage of this system is that the logarithmic transformation permits enormous differences to be easily compressed along a 1–10 scale. TRU and TSU also sum to yield an easily remembered number (10). Thus, estimates of risk spanning actual differences of 100 billion are logarithmically transformed to yield a TRU spanning 1–10.

Using primarily linear, no threshold models, regulatory agencies have developed risk scales (probabilities) corresponding to concentrations of interest. Furthermore, a series of probabilistic risk estimates can be correlated to target concentrations. For instance, the U.S. Environmental Protection Agency (EPA) assigns a formaldehyde cancer risk of 1:10,000 to an air concentration of 8 micrograms per cubic meter. A probability of 1:10,000 yields a TRU equal to 6 (from Equation 2), making the TSU 4 (Equation 1). The point is that it is possible with this (or some other) technique to begin to connect the toxicological risk-safety axis.

The cusp of decision making for many environmentally based risks often lies in probabilities of 1:10,000 to 1:1,000,000. From the viewpoint of the euphemistic and unfortunate 'one,' even these low probabilities are unacceptable. Ultimately, it is a public policy decision to limit toxicologically based risks to those with frequencies less than 1:10,000 or even 1:100,000. Table 31.5 provides an adaptation of the original Food and Drug Administration definitions within a TRU/TSU context for the reader's inspection.

Comparable ten-point scales resonate within several public health-defined fields, including the designation of pain as the fifth vital sign and various stakeholder questionnaires where individuals are asked to rate their perception of risk. TRU/TSU 'couples' present a single context within which toxicological risk and safety can be discussed and, hopefully, communicated among broader audiences. The discussion of benefits derived from the introduction of a new material is often omitted from this dialogue.

The Span (or Extent) of Toxicological Features

The thought process involved in evaluating new materials inevitably derives from the previous successes and even failures of evaluation. While probabilistic issues in terms of risk and safety provide an important link, consideration of these issues still does not embrace the character of toxic injury. A topic termed the span of toxicological features stems from an understanding of physiologic, pathophysiologic and pathologic processes.

Clinical Likert scales (0–4) spanning multiple organ, tissue and symptom domains serve to highlight areas of toxicological interest. Such note taking is not intended to over-interpret data but rather to estimate the range of important effects. Once the range of effects is agreed upon it is then possible to try to quantify significant elements of interest. The Food and Drug Administration (FDA), through its Combined Toxicity Criteria provides definitions applicable to practical toxicity scenarios associated with chemotherapy.[14] A simple example is shown within the neural suite of toxic effects for ataxia. It serves to illustrate the place-holding effect of a particular description. Consistent with the use of hypothesis testing in other settings, it is critical to identify and estimate the significance of an effect before dealing with a particular data set.

Table 31.5 — Adapted FDA Toxicity Categories in a TRU/TSU Context

FDA classification	Description	TRU/TSU classification
Super toxic or extremely toxic (prohibited substances)	Prohibitive risk / inadequate safety features	Probability ≤ 1:100 (TRU ≥ 8; TSU ≤ 2)
Very toxic or higher (significant risk acknowledged)	High risk / inadequate safety, although process improvements could move to a lower toxicity category	Probability 1:1000-1:10,000 (TRU = 6-7; TSU = 4-3)
Moderately toxic (limited risk acknowledged)	Moderate risk suggests strict control measures are appropriate	Probability 1:10,000-1:100,000 (TRU = 5-6; TSU = 5-4)
Slightly toxic (slight risk acknowledged)	Limited risk – suggests control measures are adequate	Probability ≤ 1:100,000 (TRU ≤ 5; TSU ≥ 5)
Lacks a described toxicity (only trivial risk exists)	Control measures appropriate as a precautionary measure	Risks ≤ 1:1,000,000 (TRU ≤ 3; TSU ≥ 7)

Adapted from Chan, P.K., and A.W. Hayes: Principles and methods for acute toxicity and eye irritancy. In: *Principles and Methods of Toxicology*, 2nd edition. Hayes, A.W. (ed.). New York: Raven Press, 1989. pp. 169–183.

Toxicity	Grade 0	Grade 1	Grade 2	Grade 3	Grade 4
Ataxia (incoordination)	Normal	Asymptomatic but abnormal on physical examination, and not interfering with function	Mild symptoms interfering with function, but not interfering with activities of daily living	Moderate symptoms interfering with activities of daily living	Bedridden or disabling

Toxicity	Grade 0	Grade 1	Grade 2	Grade 3	Grade 4
Hemoglobin (Hgb)	WNL	< LLN – 10.0 g/dL or < LLN – 100 g/L or < LLN – 6.2 mmol/L	8.0 – < 10.0 g/dL or 80 – < 100 g/L or 4.9 – < 6.2 mmol/L	6.5 – < 8.0 g/dL or 65 – 80 g/L or 4.0 – < 4.9 mmol/L	< 6.5 g/dL or < 65 g/L or < 4.0 mmol/L

WNL = within normal limits; LLN = lower limit of normal.

The low end of the change scale is always important because it indicates where changes begin to take place. Any demonstrable change should be interpreted in light of the dose-response relationship while the absence of any change takes on its own significance. A more quantitative example is illustrated for an anemic agent that interferes with the production of hemoglobin.

For this case the expression is quantitative in nature, although it is often necessary to revisit these tables to see whether the grades are appropriate for a particular setting. Thus, it is possible to organize suites of concern along the lines of important organs or tissues of concern. Whether adapted from FDA or from the World Health Organization, a concise system of definitions and gradations of effect become critical to estimating major versus minor effects.[15] It becomes important as well from the standpoint of coding and in other applications. The issue becomes one of making entries in a consistent manner. These kinds of notes should be archived for later reference as they are critical to writing justifications. The character of anticipated effects will become crucial to designing industrial hygiene and medical surveillance steps that serve to confirm or verify the accuracy of preliminary assessments.

Professional judgment is necessary to try to integrate the breadth and range of effects. An example is in order here. The seemingly unrelated chemical classes of bromates and aminoglycosides have both been found to affect the cochlea (ear) and renal tubules (kidney) in seemingly remote anatomical locations. A unifying explanation is that specialized cells in both organs maintain electrochemical gradients in a similar fashion.[16] The effects of bromates and aminoglycosides are, in fact, similar in that they both disturb these gradients. Again, this simple example illustrates the need to 'think while thinking' about the broader implications of toxicologic findings. Conversely, the phenomenon of ascertainment or rush to judgment is not desirable. One must appropriately use certain knowledge subsets while remaining open to new findings.

Adapting hypothesis testing is a key to successful materials evaluations. One of the tenets of hypothesis testing is an *a priori* determination of significance. Because a particular commercial chemical may possess dozens of effects as described by various toxicity test panels, it is important to know where emphasis should belong.[17] Although the significance of particular kinds of effects, say cardiovascular or neural, is fairly obvious, it is helpful to define descriptors such as mild, moderate, severe or life-threatening ahead of data analysis. Care should be exercised in the use of descriptors, lest one arrive at nonsensical impressions of 'life-threatening dandruff' or 'mild lethality.'

To sum up, a pathophysiologic approach is always intermediate, resting between physiology and a truly disordered state, that of frank pathology. The pathophysiologic approach allows the reviewer to assess underlying physiology in light of pathologies attributable to toxic agents or even the processes of inflammation, infection or tumorigenesis. Important clues are revealed that are helpful to explain the breadth of effects noted. The next stage of evaluation is to either review pertinent toxicity studies or perhaps order additional panels. The latter task often requires consultation across a broader panel of experts. Most of this discussion has presumed that considerable data are available for a new commercial material.

When data are not so plentiful an often-tried approach to materials evaluation has been termed the list-based method. Its premise is that an individual with appropriate training can search a series of toxicology-pertinent lists (Table 31.3). List-basing implies specialized knowledge of the technology of commercial materials. A good place to start is with handbook-type references (polymers, paints, coatings, adhesives).

Newly ordered toxicity testing can complement existing data. Toxicity tests use biological systems to detect the presence of toxic chemicals in materials. It is not synonymous with toxicology research which is generally focused on a better understanding of the underlying biology as opposed to the specifics of product. Toxicity testing consists of pre-determined batteries or assays. Today, toxicity testing batteries are as often based on human as on animal cells. A team of individuals with training in industrial hygiene and toxicology, along with those with training in occupational medicine, nursing, and safety engineering may suggest other assays and tests that may be helpful regarding acute and chronic toxicity, as well as fire and explosion characteristics. The credo of REACH, that being 'no data-no market,' denotes the importance of pertinent data en route to a basic decision.

One of the dilemmas evaluators face is that of integrating a 'cacophony of studies,' e.g., those ranging from the molecular or receptor scale to those reflective of global epidemiology. Uruquart[3] posits a taxonomy for them (Table 31.1). His levels echo particular academic disciplines, e.g., biochemistry is defined mostly at levels 11 and 10, virology is defined at level 10, cell biology at levels 9 and 8, physiology and toxicology range from 7 to 3. Epidemiology is largely defined at levels 1 and 2. An **editing error** can occur when the characteristics of a panel are inadequate to properly estimate data derived at different levels. Consistently referring to biology, using multiple ranges, ranging from molecular and genetic scales, to those of cells and tissues, to those that are organismic and beyond, helps to strengthen any finding. What is meant by cacophony here is the unfortunate situation when there is a consistent theme or finding that embraces the totality of biology.

Two principal means of interpreting studies at various levels exist: 1) a weight-of-evidence approach, suggesting dampening at the extremes of interpretation; and 2) a precautionary approach, meaning a toxicity warning of sort would be most broadly applied. The reality of contemporary industrial hygiene is that conflicting and often overlapping results are the rule.

An understanding of pathophysiologic principles enables an evaluator to review existing studies and to decide when it is necessary to order additional data. Key developments such as TSCA (1976) or REACH (2006) have the potential to improve data quality and to encourage additional toxicological interpretation based upon a broader range of available studies. Knowledge of the span of toxicological features enables an evaluator to begin the next phase of activity, that of developing criteria for accepting and rejecting products.

Criteria for Accepting or Rejecting Products

Toxicity has been defined as an adverse event that has an attribution of possible, probable or definite significance. Findings connecting toxicological risk with safety, and across the span of toxicological findings, drive the decision to accept or reject products. Ultimately, a responsible party must make a decision concerning the scope of use. Scope of use could range from 'no use permitted' to increasingly permissive conditions of use. At least four outcome categories apply:

(1) Safe in the practices of use and in described concentrations;
(2) Safe with qualifications that should be heeded;
(3) Insufficient data to support safety; or
(4) Unsafe for use.

Indiscriminate assignment to category (3), while conservative, is not particularly helpful. Category (2) reflects a condition that has supported decades of industrial hygiene activity. For 'never previously used' materials, their actual use can generate additional industrial hygiene and biological monitoring (medical surveillance) data. It is important to revisit categories (1)–(4) on a definable schedule in light of emerging data.

The summary statement should be conceptualized early on in the process. The fact that a conclusion will be necessary can encourage refinement of thought. This doesn't mean that a conclusion is prematurely published. Early attempts to articulate a conclusion serve to highlight data shortfalls. As materials are undergoing review, it is thoughtful to select a standard form of language that can be applied:

> Based on available data contained in this report, the panel (their names and affiliations listed here or separately) has concluded that (list of individual chemicals) as used in (name of product) should be regarded as (condition 1, 2, 3 or 4). This statement is made in the context of the practices of use and for the concentrations described in the accompanying toxicologic risk and safety assessment.

Extensive air and surface monitoring steps are rarely conducted prior to the acceptance of a material. During product acceptance, large and small environmental chamber measurements can be supported by modeled concentrations derived from simple vapor pressure calculations or more involved models.[18–20] Not only industrial hygiene, but fields as disparate as community air pollution and health physics, provide important ancillary insights into materials' evaluation. Air pollution engineering's distinction among micro- (breathing zone), meso- (small interior environments) and macro- environments (air shed) provides critical insights into the scope of possible contamination. Historically, the discipline of health physics has provided comparative risk estimates and continues to provide insights into exposure-dose linkages.

In writing an opinion it may be necessary to denote areas that are not discussed in an encyclopedic sense. A good example of a possible exception is that of reproductive risk. By convention, reproductive risk in pregnancy is handled differently than any other rating scheme. A unique feature of pregnancy is that there are always two (or more) lives involved. According to the FDA, guidelines for drug substance categories (A)–(D), include categories (X) and (N). A simple outline of the guidelines is shown in Table 31.6. These categories were originally developed for drug substances although they have occasionally been adapted to non-drug chemicals. The situation is a bit different in that drug substances may have appreciable benefit to patients in addition to the risks they impose while the risk:benefit ratio is less applicable to non-drug chemicals.

Table 31.6 — Rating of Drugs in Pregnancy

A. Controlled studies showing no risk;
B. No evidence of risk in humans
C. Risk cannot be ruled out
D. Positive evidence of risk; use only when no safer alternative exists (as a drug)
X. Contraindicated (in pregnancy), and
N. Effect not rated.

Note: While pregnancy is itself not a disease or classifiable in that manner, there are obvious concerns regarding reproductive outcomes. An A-D type system is used to provide a measure of comparative risk. Ratings are not specific to type of effect but rather to its presumed extent.

Source: U.S. Food and Drug Administration[14]

Summary

Knowing why and how material evaluations should be performed often turns out to be as important as noting the actual results of the toxicity evaluations. This chapter begins with a review of the history of materials toxicology and progresses through a practical means of doing this work, relying upon an examination of chemical and biological principles. Means of conceptually connecting toxicological risk and safety prove useful to materials acceptance decisions. The span of toxicologic features in a pathophysiologic sense implies the adaptation of hypothesis testing or the scientific method in the sense of defining toxicologic significance in advance of interpreting findings. The process of toxicologic interpretation is by its nature an evolving heuristic that must recognize and eliminate bias.

In recent times, segments of the food and toy markets were brought to the edge of collapse when imported products or ingredients fell far short of U.S. health standards for the respective product categories. This brings to the foreground the issue of how globalization may affect the materials sector. When manufacturers from low labor cost countries bring their products into far-away markets, or when manufacturers of one high-tech country want to sell their specialty products in other high-tech countries, the question becomes imminent: whose standards apply to these products? One example is the prominent discussion of the European Union's REACH program in this chapter targeting U.S. industrial hygienists. The "no data-no market" approach of this legislation shows how the European Union intends to make sure that their standards apply to all products marketed in their jurisdiction. Manufactures from other countries will have to heed such regulations if they want to stay competitive. The farther globalization proceeds, the more necessary it will become for nations who want to partake in the global system to harmonize their regulations in an effort to reduce trade barriers for their own economies. The ultimate question, at least initially, may not be: How high do we set our standards?, but much more likely: What do we do to raise the standards of our trade partners from developing countries to our own lowest level of concern?

Case Study

The case study presented here is intended not so much to better acquaint the reader with the specific properties of the chemicals involved as to illustrate the inter-disciplinary, often times confusing, nature of evaluating certain commercial products. Meta-cognitive terms such as editing, framing and anchoring have striking meaning as applied to this case.

In May 2000, the Missouri Department of Health and Senior Services was approached by an occupational medicine physician who had observed eight cases of fixed obstructive lung disease in former workers who had worked at the same popcorn factory at some time between 1992 and 2000. All eight patients' illness resembled bronchiolitis obliterans, a rare, severe lung disease, and four of them were already on lung transplant lists. The symptoms of this illness are cough and dyspnea on exertion and airway obstruction not responsive to bronchodilators. Spirometric test results in the workers were lower than normal for both FEV_1 (forced expiratory volume in 1 second) and the FEV_1/FVC (forced vital capacity) ratio. The workers had been employed at the factory between 8 months and 9 years. Missouri authorities requested assistance from CDC/NIOSH in evaluating the popcorn factory for respiratory hazards to workers. An epidemiologic investigation was initiated that indicated that workers exposed to flavorings at microwave popcorn factories are at risk for developing fixed obstructive lung disease.[21,22]

The Missouri Department of Health and Senior Services identified 425 former workers of the factory and classified them according to job categories, as determined by their work in proximity to a large heated mixing tank in which soybean oil, salt, and flavorings were combined. The process produces dust, aerosols, and volatile organic compounds (VOC's) with a strong buttery odor. Job categories were: (1) workers who mixed oil, salt, and flavorings and who had direct contact with the tank; (2) microwave-packaging workers who worked 5 to 30 meters from the tank; (3) workers in other areas of the factory who were >30 meters from the tank. Of the eight patients with bronchiolitis obliterans, four were mixers and four were microwave-packaging workers. All were part of the 425 former workers group, of which 13 (3%) had been mixers, 276 (65%) had worked in microwave packaging, and 136 (32%) had worked in more remote areas (i.e., >30 meters away) of the factory. This allowed an initial conclusion that proximity to the flavoring tank was a major determinant for developing the illness. As a matter of fact, the chi-square trend analysis for proximity to the tank and incidence of the illness was highly significant ($p < 0.0001$): group (1), 4 ill workers out of 13 (30.8%); group (2), 4/276 (1.4%); group (3), 0/136 (0%).[21,22]

An investigation of the worksite for possible exposures to known airborne respiratory toxins that could explain the illnesses came up negative. Therefore the investigation was widened to new substances. Of note, NIOSH recommended that workers in proximity to the tank should wear respiratory protection gear until the cause of the disease had been identified. Because no underlying disease could be identified among the eight patients, a cross-sectional survey of 117 current plant workers was launched. It showed that obstructive lung disease in this cohort was elevated, with a relative risk of 3.3 for all participants of the cohort that became as high as 10.8 for never-smokers. Next, the workplace air was analyzed. The concentrations of total and respirable dust were below permissible exposure limits. There were approximately 100 VOCs in the plant air; among them was diacetyl (2,3-butanedione), a ketone with butter-flavor characteristics, which was measured as a marker for exposure to flavoring agent vapors. Mean air concentration of diacetyl was 18 ppm in the room where the mixing tank was located, 1.3 ppm in the microwave-packaging area, and 0.02 ppm in other areas of the plant. There was a strong relation between the quartile of estimated cumulative exposure to diacetyl and the frequency and extent of airway obstruction.[21] Diacetyl was recognized as the likely cause of bronchiolitis obliterans in the workers at the popcorn manufacturing plant, and also at plants where diacetyl is being produced. In 2006, United Food and Commercial Workers International Union and the International Brotherhood of Teamsters petitioned the U.S. Secretary of Labor to issue an OSHA Emergency Temporary Standard (ETS) for diacetyl.[23] As of the writing of this chapter, a decision is still pending.

References

1. **Flavell, J.H.:** Metacognition and cognitive monitoring: A new area of cognitive-developmental inquiry. *Am. Psychol. 34:*906–911 (1979).
2. **Christopher, N.:** (Abs.) Cognitive thought: How decisions are made and how errors happen. 10th annual Forrest White Lecturer. Norfolk, VA: 7th Annual Pediatric Emergency Medicine Update, April 2005.
3. **Uruquart, J.:** Valedictory Lecture — University of Maastricht (2003).
4. **Koen, B.V.:** *Discussion of the Method: Conducting the Engineer's Approach to Problem Solving.* Oxford, UK: Oxford University Press, 2003.
5. **Casey, R.J., and M.J. Frazer:** *Problem Solving in the Chemical Industry.* London, UK: Pitman, 1984.
6. **European Union:** Regulation (EC) No 1907/2006 of The European Parliament and of The Council of 18 December 2006 concerning the Registration, Evaluation, Authorisation and Restriction of Chemicals (REACH), establishing a European Chemicals Agency, amending Directive 1999/45/EC and repealing Council Regulation (EEC) No 793/93 and Commission Regulation (EC) No 1488/94 as well as Council Directive 76/769/EEC and Commission Directives 91/155/EEC, 93/67/EEC, 93/105/EC and 2000/21/EC. Available online at http://eur-lex.europa.eu/LexUriServ/site/en/oj/2006/l_396/l_39620061230en00010849.pdf. [Accessed on October 30, 2007].
7. **Skoog D.A., and J.J. Leary:** *Principles of Instrumental Analysis*, 4th edition. Philadelphia, PA: Saunders Publishing, 1992.
8. **Anonymous:** Cosmetics Ingredients Review Panel - CIR. *Int. J. Toxicol. 26:* Suppl. 1 (2007).
9. **Courtney K.D., D.W. Gaylor, M.D. Hogan, H.L. Falk, R.R. Bates, and I. Mitchell:** Teratogenic evaluation of 2,4,5-T. Science 168:864-866 (1970).
10. **Dimitrov, S.D., L.K. Low, G.Y. Patlewicz, et al.:** Skin Sensitization: Modeling based on skin metabolism simulation and formation of protein conjugates. *Intl. J. Toxicol. 24:*189–204 (2005).
11. **Sørensen, S. P. L.:** Enzymstudien. II: Mitteilung. Über die Messung und die Bedeutung der Wasserstoffionenkoncentration bei enzymatischen Prozessen (in German). *Biochem. Zeitschr. 21:*131–304 (1909).
12. **Uruquart, J., and K. Heilman:** *Risk Watch: The Odds of Life.* Munich, Germany: Kindler Verlag Gmbh, 1984.
13. **Pierce, J.T.:** U.S. Copyright Office - January 2006.
14. **Food and Drug Administration (FDA):** Combined Toxicity Criteria. http://www.fda.gov/cder/cancer/toxicityframe.htm. [Accessed on October 30, 2007].
15. **Hoffman, R.S., L.S. Nelson, M.A. Howland, and N.A. Lewin:** *Goldfrank's Toxicologic Emergencies.* New York, NY: McGraw-Hill Professional (2007).
16. **Mumtaz, M.M., C.T. DeRosa, and P.R. Durkin:** Approaches and challenges in risk assessments of chemical mixtures. In: *Toxicology of Chemical Mixtures.* Yang, R.S.H. (ed.). San Diego, CA: Academic Press (1994). pp. 565–598.
17. **Farland, W.H., W.P. Wood, and K.L. Dearfield:** Cancer Risk Assessment of Environmental Agents: Approaches to the incorporation and analysis of new scientific information. In *Toxicological Testing Handbook*, 2nd edition. Jacobson-Kram, D. and K.A. Keller (eds.). New York: Informa Healthcare, 2006.
18. **Jayjock, M.A. and N.C. Hawkins:** A Proposal for Improving the Role of Exposure Modeling in Risk Assessment. *Am. Ind. Hyg Assoc. J. 54(12):*733–741 (1993).
19. **Franke, J.E., and R.A. Wadden:** Indoor contamination emission rates characterized by source activity factors. *Environ. Sci. Technol. 12:*45–51 (1987).
20. **Gmehling, J., U. Weidlich, E. Lehmann, and N. Frölich:** Method for calculating airborne concentrations of substances when emitted from liquid product mixtures. *Staub Reinh. Luft 49:*227–230 (1989).
21. **Kreiss, K., A. Gomaa, G. Kullman, et al.:** Clinical bronchiolitis obliterans in workers at a microwave-popcorn plant. *New Engl. J. Med. 347:*330–338 (2002).
22. **Centers for Disease Control and Prevention (CDC):** Fixed obstructive lung disease in workers at a microwave popcorn factory — Missouri, 2000–2002. MMWR 51:345-347 (2002). Available online at http://www.cdc.gov/mmwr/preview/mmwrhtml/mm5116a2.htm. [Accessed on October 30, 2007].
23. **Hansen, J.T., and J.P. Hoffa:** Petition for an OSHA Emergency Temporary Standard for Diacetyl. April 2006. Available online at http://www.worksafe.org/images/contentEdit/docs/2006-07-26_UFCW-IBT_diacetly_Petition%5B4pps%5D.pdf. [Accessed on October 30, 2007].

Section 5

Sources of Toxicological Information

Chapter 32

Toxicology Test Data

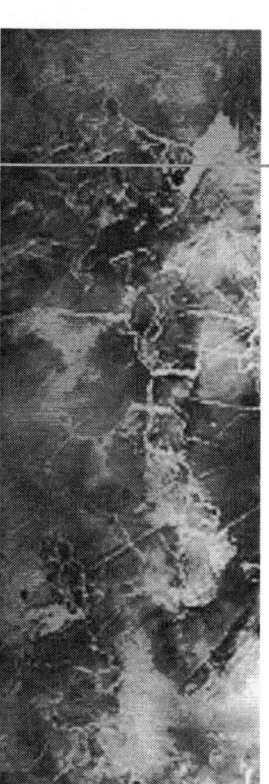

Outcome Competencies

Upon learning the information presented in this chapter the reader will be able to:

- Define the key terms listed for this chapter.
- Discuss the common tests used to determine the toxicological properties of a substance.
- Describe how doses are reported in toxicological studies.
- Discuss alternatives to animal testing.

Prerequisite Knowledge

Prior to studying this chapter, the reader should be familiar with the concepts presented in parts I and II of this book. The reader should also have a working knowledge of the basic concepts and principles of physiology and chemistry.

Key Terms

acute toxicity, chronic toxicity, LD_{50}, LCt_{50}, *in vivo*, *in vitro*, Draize tests, sensitization, intravenous, intraperitoneal, subcutaneous, intramuscular, good laboratory practice (GLP), cell culture, SAR, mechanistic, routes of entry, ataxia, absorption rate, mutagenicity, teratogenicity

Key Topics

1. Objectives of Toxicology Tests
2. Dose-Response Relationships
3. Duration of Tests
4. Choice of Animal Species for Testing
5. Dose Levels and Routes of Administration
6. *In Vitro* and *In Vivo* Testing
7. Structure Activity Relationships (SAR)
8. Good Laboratory Practice (GLP)
9. Types of Tests
    - Functional versus histological tests
    - Clinical observations
    - Clinical chemistry
    - Hematology
10. Tests for Damage to Specific Organs or Organ Systems
    - Skin Irritation and Corrosion
    - Eye Irritation
    - Hepatotoxicity
    - Nephrotoxicity
    - Neurotoxicity
    - Cardiovascular toxicity
    - Respiratory system toxicity
11. Additional Types of Testing
    - LCt_{50}
    - Carcinogenesis
    - Reproductive system tests
    - Mechanistic studies
    - Toxicokinetics
12. National Toxicology Program (NTP)

Chapter 32

Toxicology Test Data

By Brad T. Garber, PhD, CIH, DABT, CSP and William Luttrell, PhD, CIH

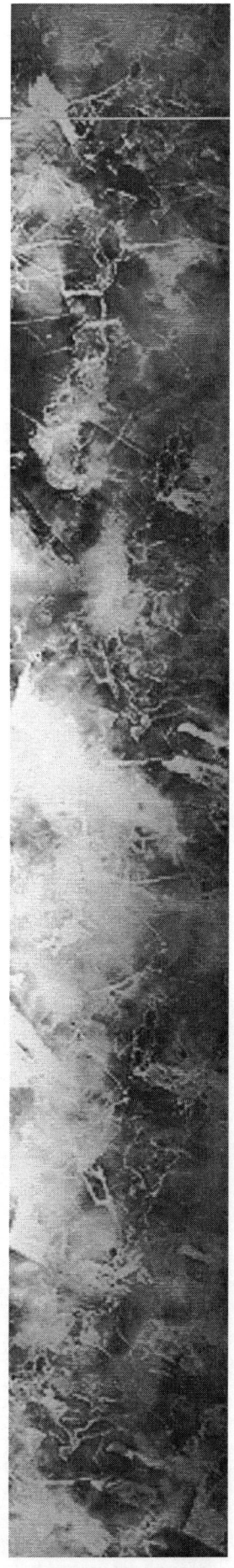

Objectives of Toxicology Tests

The results of toxicological testing are critical to industrial hygienists evaluating the potential for adverse effects arising from exposure to chemical agents. The amount of information available varies widely from substance to substance. The degree to which a specific compound is tested depends on a variety of factors such as how it is used, how much is being produced, the results of initial toxicity screening tests, and regulatory requirements. Generally tests are categorized according to the duration of exposure and the specific effects that are being studied. In order to properly interpret results, it is necessary to understand the nature of the tests and the limitations of applying the results in predicting the effects in actual human exposures.

Dose-Response Relationships

One of the primary purposes of toxicity testing is to determine the dose required to cause adverse effects. An underlying principle of toxicology is that any chemical can cause harm if the dose is high enough, but there is almost always a dose below which the likelihood of harm is negligible. For example, if one ingests excessive amounts of water, one of the safest of all chemicals, a sometimes life-threatening condition called hyponatremia can result. Conversely, botulinum toxin, which is among the most deadly of known substances (it is considered to be a potential weapon of mass destruction), can be diluted to the point that it is safe to inject it into the skin for the treatment of wrinkles (Botox® treatment).[1]

Dose-response relationships are often plotted using the response in probit units as the y-axis and the log of the dose as the x-axis. The use of the probit and log scales allows dose-response relationships to be plotted as a straight line. It should be noted that the slope of dose-response curves can vary considerably from chemical to chemical. A steeply sloping curve indicates that there is little difference between the dose that causes virtually no effect and the dose that causes a dramatic effect. One of the most commonly reported measures of toxicity is the LD_{50}. It represents the dose that is lethal to 50% of the exposed animals (median lethal dose). Although two substances may have LD_{50}s that are close in value, it is quite possible for the LD_1 or LD_{99} to be vastly different. Thus when studying lethality as a toxicological endpoint, it is valuable to examine the entire dose response curve rather than just the median lethal dose.[2]

In toxicological testing, doses are usually reported in mg/kg. This represents the amount administered per kilogram of body weight. One reason for using this convention is to facilitate comparisons between species. Another is the ease with which body weight determinations can be made. As a first approximation, a dose of 20 mg/kg would be expected to produce about the same level of response in a 20 gram mouse as in a 70 kg human, even though the actual amount administered in the human is 1.4 g and the amount for the mouse is 0.4 mg. This system of reporting doses is a simple way of adjusting for differences in body size. Although other methods of reporting doses, such as mg per square centimeter of body surface area, tend to produce superior results for purposes of interspecies comparisons, they are much more difficult to measure and thus used less frequently.[3] The EPA provides guidance for examining dose-response relationships using Benchmark Doses (BMD).[4]

Duration of Tests

Toxicological tests are often categorized according the length of exposure. Studies involving a single dose or exposure over a period of a few hours or less are referred to as acute tests. Tests that are described as sub-acute or sub-chronic can last for several months or even years in long-lived species. Testing is referred to as chronic if dosing occurs over most of the life span of the animal under study. Because normal life spans differ dramatically, the length of exposure that constitutes sub-acute, sub-chronic, and chronic varies significantly according to which animal species is being studied. Standard protocols for testing often define these terms in the context of the type of study being performed.[5] The results of acute toxicity testing are most useful for evaluating the potential effects of a single high level exposure that could occur in a workplace accident, while chronic testing results would be better for predicting the effects of repeated exposures to the low levels that are typically encountered under routine workplace conditions.

Choice of Animal Species for Testing

Most toxicological tests are performed to predict adverse effects in humans. Results of studies using animal species that closely resemble humans in their physiological and biochemical characteristics usually provide the most useful information for predicting human response. Nevertheless, because of considerations such as the cost of obtaining, housing and caring for animals, rodent species (mice and rats) are most often used for testing purposes. For certain types of testing, however, other species are preferentially used. Eye and skin irritation tests are usually performed using rabbits. It should be noted that significant physiological and metabolic differences between species can exist and they must be considered when designing toxicology tests. For example, the inability of rats to vomit makes them a poor choice for predicting human response to orally administered, emesis-inducing substances.

In some limited circumstances, human subjects are used in toxicity testing. Typically this involves the testing of consumer products. The human repeat insult patch test (HRIPT), which involves applying test substances to the skin, has been employed to test laundry detergents.[6]

Dose Levels and Routes of Administration

Most comprehensive toxicological tests involve observing the effects of different dose levels. They also examine the effects of route of entry on toxicity. Animals are divided into groups and each individual in a particular group receives the same dose using the same route of administration. Group sizes vary depending on the nature of a study but 10 per group is common. Good practice requires the use of control groups which do not receive the substance under study but are otherwise handled as identically as practical to the treated groups. If a carrier is used to administer a substance to the treated animals, the control group also receives the carrier. The specifics of how many animals are used and what dose levels are administered is determined by the intended purpose of the study.

Historically, LD_{50} determinations were performed using about 50 animals evenly divided into approximately 5 dose groups. Newer methods of estimating the median lethal dose have reduced the number of animals required.

Ideally, an animal study will use the route of entry that is likely to be encountered in human exposure situations. Typically the inhalation, ingestion, and dermal routes are most relevant from a human safety standpoint. In the occupational setting, inhalation exposure tends to be the greatest concern, whereas ingestion is the most important route of entry for most consumer products (due to the possibility that a child will accidentally eat or drink a product). A difficulty that arises in using the inhalation, ingestion, or dermal routes of administration in animal studies, however, is that absorption rates can vary greatly from individual to individual. Furthermore, for a particular individual the absorption rate can vary significantly from one administration to another. As a result, injection is sometimes used in toxicology studies so that the amount of substance that actually enters the body is more carefully controlled. Intraperitoneal (through the membrane that lines the wall of the abdomen), intravenous, subcutaneous (beneath the skin), and intramuscular are common routes of injection in animal studies.

In Vitro and *In Vivo* Testing

Testing involving live animals are categorized as *in vivo* tests, while testing involving artificial environments created outside of live animals are called *in vitro* tests. Due to an increasing concern with animal welfare and rights, there has been a significant movement to develop *in vitro* methods to replace traditional *in vivo* tests. For example, it is sometimes possible to successfully predict human toxicity by exposing cells grown in culture, thus avoiding harming living animals. New genomic and metabonomic techniques that make use of databases containing information regarding genetic makeup and normal metabolic products are also being utilized to predict toxicity. The desirability of replacing animal testing with *in vitro* methods is a subject of ongoing debate.

Structure Activity Relationships (SAR)

Another approach to predicting the toxicity of chemicals is to use information about their molecular structure and chemical and physical properties to determine the expected physiological effects. As with *in vivo* tests, structure activity relationship (SAR) studies can reduce the need to use animal testing.[7]

Sophisticated computer models that incorporate large numbers of properties have proven to be valuable in toxicological evaluations. It should be noted that although there have been many successes in using SAR studies to predict toxicity, in some cases the results differ from experimental data.[8]

Good Laboratory Practice

Good laboratory practice (GLP) is a set of practices and procedures used to ensure that toxicology testing is performed in a high quality manner. The specifics of what constitutes GLP can be found in the publications of organizations and agencies concerned with toxicity testing. One such organization, the Organization for Economic Cooperation and Development (OECD), has developed a widely used set of GLP specifications.[9]

GLP procedures tend to include requirements such as the designation of a project director, preparation of written standard operating procedures (SOPs) and protocols, scheduled inspections of facilities, training of personnel, proper labeling of chemicals, documentation of compliance with required practices, maintenance and inspection of equipment, proper handling and treatment of animals and signed final reports of results.

GLP protocols are typically used by organizations that conduct toxicology testing, such as governmental agencies, private testing labs, and manufacturers. Results that come from laboratories not using recognized GLP procedures have diminished credibility and in many cases would not be acceptable for purposes such as complying with governmental testing requirements. It should be noted that the fact GLP is used does not guarantee a test is the best or most appropriate for a particular study.

Types of Tests

Functional Versus Histological Tests

Because most organ systems have significant reserve functional capacity, it is possible for substantial damage to occur before they can no longer carry out normal physiological functions. Sometimes, functional tests such as detecting abnormal levels of marker substances in the blood or urine do not detect damage until it is extensive. As a result, examination of tissue samples using microscopy is also employed in toxicological testing. The science of examining microscopic changes in tissues and cells is called histology. Histological procedures involve preparing thin slices of tissues for microscopic examination that includes the identification of tissue damage, cellular damage, or infiltration of inflammatory cells.

Clinical Observations

Clinical observations are widely used in toxicological testing as indicators of adverse effects. The results of these observations are often used to determine what types of additional tests should be performed to fully evaluate the substance under study. Animals are examined for effects such as behavioral and motor abnormalities, respiratory distress, cardiovascular disturbances, gastrointestinal upset, skin and fur changes, and damage to the eyes. In addition, body weight and food and water consumption levels are frequently monitored.

Clinical Chemistry

Results of clinical chemistry studies can be used to assist in identifying which organ systems are being adversely affected as the result of an exposure to a toxic substance. For example, elevated levels of BUN (blood urea nitrogen), blood creatinine, and urinary protein levels are indicative of damage to the kidney. Increased serum levels of alanine aminotransferase (ALT) are used as an indicator of liver damage.

Hematology

Many toxic substances affect the blood and blood forming system. Hematological examination is used to detect changes in the blood resulting from exposure to these substances. Measurements include mean corpuscular volume, hemoglobin levels, packed cell volumes and counts of the different types of blood cells. The results of these measurements are used in determining the nature of the damage that a particular toxic substance causes.

Tests for Damage to Specific Organs or Organ Systems

Skin Irritation and Corrosion

In evaluating the toxicity of both industrial chemicals and consumer products, it is important to determine what happens when they come into direct contact with the skin. Standardized methods based on work performed by John Draize have been extensively used to evaluate the potential for skin damage. The tests, often referred to as Draize tests, involve applying a test chemical to the shaven skin of rabbits and holding it into place using a patch.[3] Injury to the skin after 24 and 72 hours of exposure is determined visually using a technique that involves comparing the observed effects to those shown on a chart that contains pictures of skin exhibiting different degrees of damage and their corresponding skin irritation scores. There is considerable ongoing research to develop effective alternative *in vitro* approaches to determining skin irritancy.[10] See Chapter 6 — Dermal Toxicology for additional information about skin irritation.

In addition to testing for skin irritation and corrosion, chemicals are frequently tested for sensitization potential. Sensitization involves an immunological reaction. It usually requires more than one exposure for a reaction to occur because sensitization does not occur immediately after initial contact with a chemical, but instead requires a period of time to develop. Guinea pigs are often used as test subjects for dermal sensitization studies. See Chapter 12 — Immunotoxicology for additional information about sensitization.

Eye Irritation

Systems for testing chemicals to determine eye irritation potential are similar to those used for evaluating the skin. Scoring systems and test procedures, based on the methods originally developed by Draize[11,12] and modified over the years, are in common use. Rabbits are usually used for eye irritancy testing. There is a movement to develop non-animal tests for eye irritation in order to address animal welfare concerns. See Chapter 8, "Toxicology of Sensory Organs" for additional information on eye damage.

Hepatotoxicity

Hepatotoxins, substances that damage the liver, are found in many workplaces. Carbon tetrachloride, ethanol, and vinyl chloride are three well known examples. The effects that can occur as a result of exposure include increased levels of fat in the liver (fatty liver), cell death (necrosis), stoppage or decrease in the flow of bile (cholestasis), hepatitis, cirrhosis, and carcinogenesis. Damage to the liver can be detected by visual examination and histology. Functional tests, such as changes in the activity levels of certain serum enzymes or changes in the levels of substances that normally occur in the blood can also be performed.[13] Liver cells can be grown in culture to perform *in vitro* tests.[14] One of the most commonly used indicators of damage is changes in liver weight. See Chapter 10 — Hepatic Toxicology for additional information about damage to the liver.

Nephrotoxicity

Substances that damage the kidneys are referred to as nephrotoxins. Analysis of the urine for abnormally high levels of protein and glucose can be used to evaluate kidney function. Blood levels of urea nitrogen (BUN) and creatinine are also used as indicators of toxicity. Urine output levels are a critical indicator of renal damage. It is important to perform histological examinations because functional tests will not always detect early or mild damage due to the significant reserve functional capacity of the kidneys. Kidney weight changes are a common and easily obtained measure of impairment in laboratory animals. See Chapter 7 — Systemic Toxicology for additional information on kidney damage.

Neurotoxicity

Many of the tests employed to detect adverse effects on the central nervous system (CNS) involve observation of test animals for abnormalities such as changes in behavior, ataxia (staggering gait), tremors, convulsions, and sensory and motor function difficulties. It is also common to examine tissues for cellular level damage.[15] See Chapter 9 — Neurotoxicology for additional information about damage to the nervous system.

Cardiovascular Toxicity

Measurement of changes in blood pressure and heart rate are employed to detect adverse effects on the cardiovascular system. In addition, electrocardiography can be used to detect damage to the heart. Examination of the hearts removed from euthanized animals is performed in some studies. See Chapter 7 — Systemic Toxicology for additional information about damage to the cardiovascular system.

Respiratory System Toxicity

Most agents that damage the respiratory system do so as the result of inhalation exposure. Therefore, inhalation toxicology studies are commonly employed to evaluate respiratory system toxicants. These tests are hard to perform due to the technical challenges of designing and operating exposure chambers that maintain a known and consistent concentration of the substance under study. Tests involving particulate materials are particularly difficult, because of the tendency of particles to settle and the possibility that an animal will be also exposed by ingestion as a result of licking their fur. Settled particles may also result in skin absorption.

Measurements of breathing rate are often used to detect respiratory distress. Microscopic examination of lung tissue is employed to determine the precise nature of lung damage if it occurs. Damage usually takes the form of one or more of the following: cell necrosis, edema, irritation of airway passage linings, and fibrosis. See Chapter 5 — Respiratory Toxicology for additional information about damage to the respiratory system.

Additional Types of Toxicity Testing

LCt_{50}

In inhalation studies, exposure levels are a function of concentration and time. It is therefore important to report both when describing the tests. Median lethal exposures are reported as LCt_{50}s in which the C stands for concentration and the t for time.

Carcinogenesis

In evaluating the toxicological properties of chemical substances, one of the most important determinations is whether it potentially causes cancer in humans. Animal models are frequently used for this purpose. Because the latency period for many types of cancer can be quite long, animal studies are performed over a time period that constitutes most of the normal life span of the species being used for the study. Mice and rats are most commonly employed in carcinogenicity testing. Because of the relatively short life span of these species, testing can be completed in a period of about 2 years.

Due to the expense of performing long-term animal tests and concerns relating to animal rights, *in vitro* tests are often used for initial carcinogenicity screening. Some of these tests involve determining if the substance under study is a mutagen, with the presumption that mutagenic substances are very likely to also be carcinogens. *In vitro* test methods include detecting mutations in bacteria, observing cell transformations in cultures, measuring unscheduled DNA synthesis and looking for changes in chromosome morphology. The best known of these is the Ames test which makes use of the detection of mutations in bacteria.[16] Because some carcinogens require metabolic activation, test procedures in which liver homogenate is added, are sometimes employed. The reasoning behind this modification is that the liver is rich in enzymes involved in the metabolism (biotransformation) of many toxic substances. One of the problems with *in vitro* tests is that there is a significant potential for false positives and false negatives. As a result, substances are frequently subjected to a battery of procedures, and the findings are interpreted in the context of the strengths and weaknesses of each individual test. See Chapter 14 — Carcinogenesis for additional information.

Reproductive System Tests

Reproductive toxicity tests are used to detect adverse effects on sexual function, fertility, or development of offspring. Tests are designed to detect adverse effects such as libido or sexual behavior changes, hormone level alterations, sperm or egg abnormalities, and fertility level shifts. Multi-generational studies detect inheritable and non-inheritable changes in offspring.

Substances that cause abnormalities in an embryo or fetus are called teratogens. Testing for teratogenesis involves dosing a pregnant female animal with the test substance during the period of organogenesis (this is when susceptibility tends to be greatest) and subsequently examining the offspring for abnormalities. It is important to use several carefully selected animal species for testing, as some species may produce false negatives for some substances. A well known example of this phenomenon occurs when testing the drug thalidomide in mice and rats. They are resistant to the teratogenic effects that occur readily in humans. Because the teratogenic effects were unknown when it was first used in humans, a number of cases of severe birth defects involving limb abnormalities occurred in the children of women who took the drug during pregnancy.[17] See Chapter 11 — Reproductive and Developmental Toxicology for additional information.

Mechanistic Studies

Whereas most toxicity testing focuses on determining what types of damage a toxic substance causes, it is also often of interest to study the mechanism of action. For example, it may be known that exposure to a toxicant causes anemia, but the underlying reasons might not be clear. There may be alternate plausible explanations, such as increased red blood cell fragility or interference with the heme synthesis biochemical pathway. It would be the task of a mechanistic toxicology study to determine the actual underlying cause. By their nature, mechanistic studies frequently use techniques not employed in routine toxicological testing and are therefore often performed by researchers whose expertise is highly specialized. See Chapter 3 — Mechanisms of Toxicity for additional information in this area.

Toxicokinetics

One of the goals of toxicity testing is to establish safe exposure levels. In order to achieve this goal, it is important to determine the rate at which the body absorbs, excretes, and metabolizes (biotransforms) substances. It is also critical to ascertain where a substance is localized in the body and the rate at which it moves from one site to another. The field of study that focuses on these issues is often referred to as toxicokinetics. Many of the techniques employed are taken from the science of pharmacokinetics which studies the same questions as they apply to drugs.[19]

The results of toxicokinetic studies are especially useful in determining the relationship between exposure levels and tissue concentrations. This information is critical in setting occupational exposure limits for those toxicants for which tissue levels that result in adverse effects have been established. See Chapter 4 — Disposition of Toxicants for additional information about toxicokinetics.

National Toxicology Program (NTP)

There are many substances that are used in workplaces for which there is little or no published toxicology data. For example, chemicals that are produced for research proposes or are produced in limited quantities are not likely to be thoroughly tested. Chemical intermediates also tend to be studied less than final products. In order to address this deficiency, various organizations throughout the world, both governmental and non-governmental, have devised programs for improving the state of knowledge. One of the most successful initiatives is the National Toxicology Program, which is housed in the U.S. National Institute of Environmental Health Sciences (NIEHS). Much of the information made available to the public can be obtained through the website: http://ntp-server.niehs.nih.gov/ (accessed September 14, 2007). The accessible publications include full text study reports for many of the substances that have been examined.

References

1. **Flynn, T. C.:** Update on Botulinum Toxin: *Semin. Cutan. Med. Surg.* 25 :115–121, 2006.
2. **Lu, F.C. and S. Kacew:** *Lu's Basic Toxicology,* 4th ed. New York: Taylor and Francis, 2002. Chapter 6.
3. **Eaton, D.L. and C.D. Klaassen:** Principles of Toxicology in *Casarett and Doull's Toxicology.* 6th ed. Klaassen, C.D. (ed.). New York: McGraw-Hill, 2001, Chapter 2.
4. **EPA:** Benchmark Dose Methodology. http://www.epa.gov/ncea/bmds_training/methodology/intro.htm Accessed May 29, 2007.
5. **Gad, S.C. and C. P. Chengelis:** *Acute Toxicology Testing*, 2nd ed. San Diego, California: Academic Press, 1998.
6. **P&G:** P&G Laundry Detergents: Testing for skin allergies. http://www.scienceinthebox.com/en_UK/safety/skinallergies_en.html Accessed May 29, 2007.
7. **Hall, L. H. and L.M. Hall:** QSAR Modeling Based on Structure-Information for Properties of Interest in Human Health. SAR and QSAR in *Environ. Res.* Feb.–Apr., 2005, 16(1-2) 13-41.
8. **Chun, J., V. Nabholz and M.J. Wilson:** Comparison of Measured Aquatic Toxicity Data with EPA, OPPT SAR Predictions. 1999-2000. www.epa.gov/oppt/newchems/pubs/sustainable/ppg-sar-study-1999-2000.pdf Accessed March 21, 2007.

9. **Organization of Economic Cooperation and Development (OECD):** OECD Series on Principles of Good Laboratory Practice and Compliance Monitoring. http://www.oecd.org/document/63/0,3343,en_2649_34381_2346175_1_1_1_1,00.html Accessed July 5, 2007
10. **Tornier, C., M. Rosdy and H. I. Maibach:** *In vitro* skin irritation testing on reconstituted human epidermis: Reproducibility for 50 chemicals tested with two protocols. *Toxicol. In Vitro 20(4)*:401–416, 2006.
11. **Griffith, J. F., G. A. Nixon, R. D. Bruce, P. J. Reer and E. A. Bannan:** Dose-Response Studies with Chemical Irritants in the Albino Rabbit Eye as a Basis for Selecting Optimum Testing Conditions for Predicting Hazard to the Human Eye. *Toxicol. Appl. Pharmacol. 55*:501–513, 1980.
12. **Doucet, O., M. Lanvin, C. Thillou, C. Linossier, C. Pupat, B. Merlin and L. Zastrow:** Reconstituted human corneal epithelium: A new alternative to the Draize eye test for the assessment of the eye irritation potential of chemicals and cosmetic products. *Toxicol. In Vitro 20(4)*:499–512, 2005.
13. **Plaa, G. L., and M. Charbonneau:** Detection and Evaluation of Chemically Induced Liver Injury in *Principles and Methods of Toxicology,* 3rd ed. Hayes, A.W. (ed.). New York: Raven Press, 1994, pp. 839–870.
14. **Klaassen, C. D., and N. H. Stacey:** Use of Isolated Hepatocytes in Toxicity Assessment in *Toxicology of the Liver* Plaa, G.L. and W. R. Hewitt (eds.). New York: Raven Press, 1982, pp. 147–179.
15. **Anthony, D.C., T.J. Montine, W.M. Valentine and D.G. Graham:** Toxic Responses of the Nervous System in *Casarett and Doull's Toxicology,* 6th ed. Klaassen, C.D. (ed.). New York: McGraw-Hill, 2001, Chapter 16.
16. **McCann, J., E. Choi, E. Yamasaki, and B. N. Ames:** Detection of carcinogens as mutagens in the Salmonella/microsome test: Assay of 300 chemicals. *Proc. Natl. Acad. Sci. USA 72(12)*:5135–5139, 1975.
17. **Dally, A.:** Thalidomide: Was The Tragedy Preventable? *Lancet 351(9110)*:1197,1998.
18. **Andersen, M. E., M. G. MacNaughton, H. J. Clewell III and D. J. Paustenbach:** Adjusting Exposure Limits for Long and Short Exposure Periods Using a Physiological Pharmacokinetic Model. *Am. Ind. Hyg. Assoc. J. 48(4)*: 335–343, 1987.
19. **Buxton, I.L.O.:** Pharmacokinetics and Pharmacodynamics in *Goodman and Gilman's The Pharmacological Basis of Therapeutics*, 11th ed. Brunton, L.L., Lazo, J.S. and Parker. K.L. (eds.). New York: McGraw-Hill, 2006, Chapter 1.

Additional Reading

Ecobichon, D. J.: *The Basis of Toxicity Testing*, Boca Raton, Florida: CRC, 1992.

Fan, A. and Chang, L. (Editors): *Toxicology and Risk Assessment: Principles, Methods, and Application*, New York: Marcel Dekker, Inc., 1996.

Frazier, J. M., Gad, S. C., Goldberg, A. M., and McCulley, J. P.: *A Critical Evaluation of Alternatives to Acute Irritation Testing*, New York: Mary Ann Liebert, 1987.

Turnheim, D.: Benefits of good laboratory practice as a tool to improve testing. *Hum. Exp. Toxicol. 12(6)*:528–532, 1993.

Wexler, P., Hakkinen, P. J., Kennedy, G. L., and Stoss, F. W. (Editors): *Information Resources in Toxicology*, 3rd Edition, New York: Academic Press, 2000.

Chapter 33

Regulations, Standards, and Guidelines

By Jeffrey A. Church, CIH

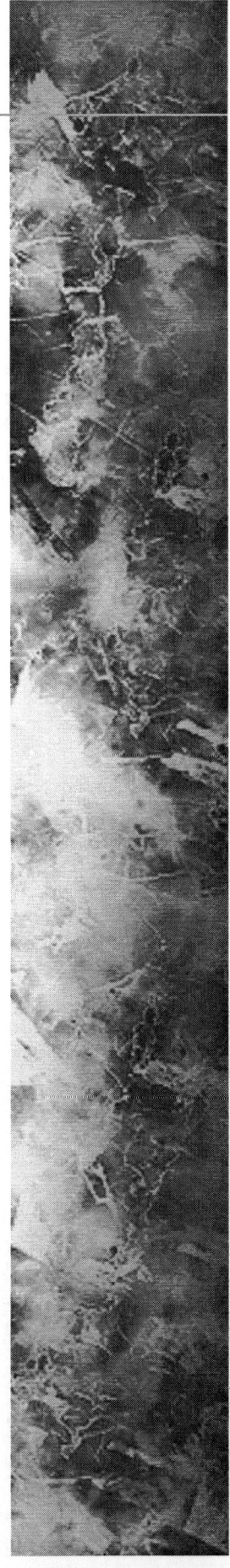

Introduction

This chapter covers many of the occupational and environmental regulations that have toxicological application to the work of a practicing industrial hygienist. Both government and private organizations have contributed widely to the profession through the development of various tools, data systems, and guidelines. Some of those organizations and their notable contributions are described briefly in the guidelines section of this chapter. Contact information and applicable web links are provided as an aid to obtaining further information or utilizing those resources.

Regulations

The occupationally-related health and safety regulations in the United States are developed and promulgated by the Occupational Safety and Health Administration (OSHA) under the U.S. Department of Labor as enacted by Congress in the Occupational Safety and Health Act. Those regulations are codified in Title 29 of the Code of Federal Regulations (CFR) and cover Parts 1900 through 1999. The principal occupations covered by Federal regulations include those employed in general industry (Part 1910), shipyards (Part 1915), marine terminals (Part 1917), longshoring (Part 1918), construction (Part 1926), and agriculture (Part 1928). Within each Part separate standards may be found regulating exposure to individual chemical stressors. OSHA standards which primarily address potential toxic exposures are found in 29CFR1910 Subpart Z — Toxic and Hazardous Materials. The standards in Subpart Z may apply to all occupations or be exempted from certain occupations, in part or in whole. Provided below are a listing and brief summary of the OSHA general industry standards for chemical stressors.

- **Air Contaminants** (29CFR1910.1000) — Air contaminants listed in the three tables of this standard are regulated by 8-hour, time-weighted average (TWA) permissible exposure limits (PELs) and ceiling limits based on personal breathing-zone sampling.
- **Asbestos** (29CFR1910.1001) — Specified in this standard are requirements for air sampling and methods by which it is to be accomplished, the establishment of an 8-hour TWA PEL and 30-minute excursion limit, and medical surveillance requirements for workers exposed at or above the TWA or excursion limit.
- **13 Carcinogens** (29CFR1910.1003) — This standard focuses on the control of exposures to the following listed 13 carcinogens that are manufactured, processed, repackaged, released, handled, or stored. Specific occupational exposure limits are not cited, but engineering and administrative controls are prescribed along with personal protection and medical surveillance.

4-Nitrobiphenyl
alpha-Naphthylamine
Methyl chloromethyl ether
3,3'-Dichlorobenzidine
Bis-chloromethyl ether
beta-Naphthylamine
Benzidine
4-Aminodiphenyl
Ethyleneimine
beta-Propiolactone
2-Acetylaminofluorene
4-Dimethylaminoazobenzene
N-Nitrosodimethylamine

- **Vinyl chloride** (29CFR1910.1017) — This standard establishes an 8-hour TWA action level and PEL and a ceiling limit based on a ≤ 15-minute average for airborne concentrations and requires prevention of direct contact with its liquid form. Initial air monitoring is specified. Periodic and continuous air monitoring and medical surveillance are indicated, based on actual and potential exposure concentrations.
- **Inorganic Arsenic** (29CFR1910.1018) — This standard requires initial personal air sampling and sets conditions for further sampling. An 8-hour TWA action level and PEL and an exposure limit which necessitates a daily change of clean protective clothing are identified for airborne concentrations of inorganic arsenic. Medical surveillance is required for personnel exposed above the action level for ≥ 30 days/year.
- **Lead** (29CFR1910.1025) — An initial determination of potential airborne lead exposures is called for to ascertain initial personal air sampling requirements. The 8-hour TWA action level and PEL and an exposure limit which necessitates a daily change of clean protective clothing are identified for airborne concentrations of lead. The action level and PEL are also used to determine exposure controls, hygiene practices, and medical surveillance requirements.
- **Cadmium** (29CFR1910.1027) — An 8-hour TWA action level and PEL and Separate Engineering Control Airborne Limits (SECALs) for processes in selected industries are specified in this standard. Unless objective data indicates personnel exposures will not exceed the action level, initial personal air sampling is directed and conditions requiring further sampling are described. The action level, PEL, and SECALs are also used to determine exposure controls, hygiene practices, and medical surveillance requirements.
- **Chromium (VI)** (29CFR1910.1026) – This standard establishes an 8-hour TWA action level and PEL, exempting exposures related to portland cement, application of regulated pesticides, and chromium-related occupations that demonstrate with objective data that airborne exposure concentrations will not exceed 0.5 µg/m3 as an 8-hour TWA under any expected conditions of use. Approaches and conditions related to conducting exposure determinations for affected employees are described. The action level and PEL are also used to determine requirements for regulated areas, engineering and work practice controls, personal protective equipment, and medical surveillance.
- **Benzene** (29CFR1910.1028) — Initial personal air sampling is indicated along with provisions for further sampling. The standard establishes an 8-hour TWA action limit and PEL, and a short-term exposure limit (STEL) based on a 15-minute average. Those values and an 8-hour TWA concentration of 10 parts per million (ppm) are used to specify exposure controls and medical surveillance.
- **Coke oven emissions** (29CFR1910.1029) — Specified in this standard are requirements for personal air sampling, establishment of an 8-hour TWA PEL, and medical surveillance for personnel who work in a regulated area, as defined in the standard by work area, ≥ 30 days/year.
- **Cotton dust** (29CFR1910.1043) — The standard prescribes personal air sampling and regulates equipment to be used. Different 8-hour TWA action levels and PELs are assigned based on the industry operation. Medical surveillance consisting of initial examinations is required for all employees exposed to cotton dust, with further periodic examinations instructed for workers exposed above the action level or based on certain medical outcomes.
- **1,2-Dibromo-3-chloropropane** (29CFR1910.1044) — Initial air sampling is required and conditions for further sampling are addressed. The standard requires prevention of dermal or eye contact with liquid or solid 1,2-dibromo-3-chloropropane, establishes an 8-hour TWA PEL for airborne exposures, and directs medical surveillance.
- **Acrylonitrile** (29CFR1910.1045) — Initial air sampling is required and conditions for further sampling are addressed. The standard requires prevention of dermal or eye contact with liquid or solid acrylonitrile; establishes an 8-hour TWA action level and PEL, and ceiling limit based on a 15-minute average, for airborne exposures; and directs medical surveillance for workers exposed at or above the action limit.
- **Ethylene oxide** (29CFR1910.1047) — Initial air sampling is required and conditions for further sampling are addressed. A 15-minute excursion limit and an 8-hour TWA action level and PEL are developed for airborne concentrations of ethylene oxide. Medical surveillance is required for personnel exposed above the action level for ≥ 30 days/year.
- **Formaldehyde** (29CFR1910.1048) — Unless objective data documents that exposures above the action level or STEL will not occur, initial air sampling is required and conditions for further sampling are specified. A 15-minute STEL and an 8-hour TWA action level and PEL are indicated for airborne concentrations of formaldehyde. The standard requires prevention of dermal and eye contact with liquid products containing ≥ 1% formaldehyde and full body protection for entry into areas where air concentrations exceed 100 ppm or are unknown. Medical surveillance is required for personnel exposed at or above the action level or STEL.
- **Methylenedianiline** (29CFR1910.1050) — Initial air sampling is required and conditions for further sampling are addressed. A 15-minute STEL and an 8-hour TWA action level and PEL are developed for airborne concentrations of methylenedianiline. The standard requires prevention of direct contact with methylenedianiline and includes medical surveillance for personnel subject to dermal exposure ≥ 15 days/year and those exposed above the action level for ≥ 30 days/year.
- **1,3-Butadiene** (29CFR1910.1051) — Unless objective data document that exposures above the action level or STEL will not occur, initial air sampling is required and conditions for further sampling are specified. A 15-minute STEL and an 8-hour TWA action level and PEL are established for airborne concentrations of 1,3-butadiene. For operations where airborne concentrations are below the PEL but

exceed the action level, the employer must develop an exposure goal program to limit exposures to concentrations below the action limit. The standard also requires prevention of dermal and eye contact with 1,3-butadiene. Medical screening and surveillance is directed for employees with current exposures at or above the action level for ≥ 30 days/year or PEL for ≥ 10 days/year, with previous exposures at prescribed levels and durations, and those exposed during a significant release.

- **Methylene chloride** (29CFR1910.1052) — An initial determination of potential airborne methylene chloride exposures is called for to ascertain initial personal air sampling requirements. Conditions requiring further sampling are also addressed. The standard requires prevention of dermal or eye contact with liquid methylene chloride, establishes a 15-minute STEL, and specifies an 8-hour TWA action level and PEL. Medical surveillance must be made available to workers exposed at or above the action level for ≥ 30 days/year; above the PEL or STEL for ≥ 10 days/year; above the PEL or STEL at any time, who have a qualifying medical condition and request surveillance; and during an uncontrolled release.

In addition to the regulatory standards themselves, OSHA publishes a preamble to the final rule of newly-established standards in the *Federal Register*. The preamble describes information used in the decision-making process to develop new regulations, which may include toxicological data. Although not formally published, OSHA provides standards interpretations in response letters to questions from the public and compliance directives through internal instruction documents on their website at www.osha.gov. Those documents can be another resource providing amplifying information on standards related to toxic and hazardous materials.

OSHA may approve State Safety and Health Plans that allow states to adopt and enforce federal standards or establish their own standards which are at least as effective. Some state governments have promulgated occupational regulations that are more stringent than OSHA's and include regulations for chemical stressors not addressed by OSHA. State regulations will not be individually discussed in this chapter, but states operating their own plans are listed below, and contact information can be found at the OSHA website.

Alaska	Michigan	South Carolina
Arizona	Minnesota	Tennessee
California	Nevada	Utah
Connecticut	New Jersey	Vermont
Hawaii	New Mexico	Virgin Islands
Indiana	New York	Virginia
Iowa	North Carolina	Washington
Kentucky	Oregon	Wyoming
Maryland	Puerto Rico	

The Federal Mine Safety and Health Act gives authority to the Mine Safety and Health Administration (MSHA) to produce occupational health and safety regulations for the mining industry. MSHA regulations are recorded in 30CFR1-199, and summarized below are those addressing chemical stressors.

- **Safety and Health Standards for Surface Metal and Nonmetal Mines, Exposure Limits for Airborne Contaminants** (30CFR56.5001); **and Safety and Health Standards for Underground Metal and Nonmetal Mines, Exposure Limits for Airborne Contaminants** (30CFR57.5001) — These regulations establish occupational exposure limits for asbestos and incorporate exposure limits with reference to those found in the American Conference of Governmental Industrial Hygienists (ACGIH) publication, *TLV's Threshold Limit Values for Chemical Substances in Workroom Air Adopted by ACGIH for 1973*.

- **Safety and Health Standards for Underground Metal and Nonmetal Mines, Limit on Concentration of Diesel Particulate Matter** (30CFR56.5060) — The regulation cites the current and future occupational exposure limits for total carbon and describes procedures to apply for a special extension if the exposure limit cannot be met due to technological constraints.

- **Mandatory Health Standards for Underground Coal Mines, Respirable Dust Standards** (30CFR70.100); **Mandatory Health Standards for Underground Coal Mines, Respirable Dust Standard When Quartz is Present** (30CFR70.101); **Mandatory Health Standards for Surface Coal Mines and Surface Work Areas of Underground Coal Mines, Respirable Dust Standards** (30CFR71.100); and **Mandatory Health Standards for Surface Coal Mines and Surface Work Areas of Underground Coal Mines, Respirable Dust Standard When Quartz is Present** (30CFR71.101) — Occupational exposure limits are cited for respirable dust, with and without >5% quartz, and limits are established for fugitive respirable dust around the intake airways of underground coal mines.

- **Mandatory Health Standards for Underground Coal Mines, Exhaust Gas Monitoring** (30CFR70.1900) — Establishes an action level for carbon monoxide and nitrogen dioxide of 50% of the 1972 ACGIH publication, *TLV's Threshold Limit Values for Substance in Workroom Air*, based on shift air monitoring during operations.

- **Mandatory Health Standards for Surface Coal Mines and Surface Work Areas of Underground Coal Mines, Inhalation Hazards: Threshold Limit Values for Gases, Dusts, Fumes, Mists, and Vapors** (30CFR71.700); and **Mandatory Health Standards for Surface Coal Mines and Surface Work Areas of Underground Coal Mines, Asbestos Dust Standard: Measurement** (30CFR71.702) — These regulations establish occupational exposure limits for asbestos and incorporate exposure limits by referencing those found in the 1972 ACGIH publication, *Threshold Limit Values of Airborne Contaminants*.

- **Mandatory Safety Standards for Underground Coal Mines, Air Quality** (30CFR75.321); and **Mandatory Safety Standards for Underground Coal Mines, Harmful Quantities of Noxious Gases** (30CFR75.322) — Establishes occupational exposure limits for carbon dioxide and limits other gases, by reference to the 1972 ACGIH publication, *TLV's® Threshold Limit Values for Substance in Workroom Air*.
- **Mandatory Health Standards for Coal Miners Who Have Evidence of the Development of Pneumoconiosis, Respirable Dust Standard** (30CFR90.100); and **Mandatory Health Standards for Coal Miners Who Have Evidence of the Development of Pneumoconiosis, Respirable Dust Standard When Quartz is Present** (30CFR90.101) — This regulation cites occupational exposure limits for respirable dust with and without >5% quartz, for areas where miners diagnosed with pneumoconiosis work.

The Department of Energy (DOE) regulates beryllium exposures for DOE personnel and contractor employees under their Chronic Beryllium Disease Prevention Program (10CFR850). That regulation requires a baseline beryllium inventory to identify potential exposures, hazard assessment to evaluate exposures, and initial monitoring to determine personnel exposures to airborne beryllium. Specified worker protection provisions, including periodic monitoring and medical surveillance, are directed when personal air sampling exceeds an action level of 0.2 micrograms per cubic meter ($\mu g/m^3$).

The Clean Air Act mandates the U.S. Environmental Protection Agency (EPA) to develop regulations to control pollution and improve air quality. Highlighted below are regulations that set forth air quality controls and standards.

- **National Ambient Air Quality Standards** (40CFR50) — Minimum national air quality standards for six criteria air pollutants have been developed. The regulation establishes primary air standards for carbon monoxide and primary and secondary standards for lead, nitrogen dioxide, particulate matter, ozone, and sulfur oxides. Primary standards are health-based limits to protect the public and are created to protect to the most-sensitive sub-populations. Secondary standards address aesthetics and protect property.
- **National Emission Standards for Hazardous Air Pollutants** (40CFR61-63) — This regulation focuses on control of 188 toxic air pollutants to protect public health and the environment. The developed standards address various sources of release identified for each specific chemical stressor and set forth control technologies.

The Clean Water Act requires EPA to promulgate and enforce regulations to control the discharge of pollutants into United States waters. EPA approves state-established water quality standards for bodies of water, requires effluent standards, and addresses spill controls. Specific regulations are found in 40CFR100-140, 230-233, 404-471, and 501-503.

Through the Safe Drinking Water Act, EPA is charged with the responsibility to protect public drinking water and its sources. EPA regulations include the creation of national health-based standards for drinking water, as well as those that govern public water systems and control contamination of ground water. Those regulations can be found in 40CFR141-149.

- **National Primary Drinking Water Regulations** (40CFR141) — These regulations establish maximum contaminant levels (MCLs) and maximum contaminant level goals (MCLGs) for 90 chemical, biological, and radiological contaminants in drinking water. The MCLs take into consideration treatment technology, whereas MCLGs are strictly based on toxicological science.

The Federal Insecticide, Fungicide, and Rodenticide Act authorizes EPA to regulate pesticide use in the United States to protect human health and the environment. EPA requires registration and review of all pesticides, registration of manufacturing facilities, and certification of applicators and establishes laboratory practice and worker protection standards. Pesticide-related regulations are contained in 40CFR150-189.

Through the Marine Protection, Research, and Sanctuaries Act, EPA governs the dumping of materials into the marine environment to protect human health and the environment. Regulations covered in 40CFR220-233 establish procedures and criteria for the issuance of permits for, and requirements for reporting of, emergency dumping to safeguard life at sea.

Under the Resource Conservation and Recovery Act, EPA regulates the generation, storage, transportation, and treatment of hazardous wastes. Specific hazardous waste regulations are in 40CFR261-299.

The Comprehensive Environmental Response, Compensation and Liability Act set up a tax on chemical and petroleum industries to fund cleanup at hazardous waste sites. EPA was given authority to develop a national priority list of hazardous waste sites and to clean up or conduct remedial actions at uncontrolled or abandoned waste sites to protect public health. Regulations were also established by EPA to direct the formation of a National Contingency Plan for spill response, indicate reporting requirements, identify hazardous wastes and their reportable quantities, and list cleanup criteria. Those regulations are covered under 40CFR300, 302.

Under the Emergency Planning and Community Right-to-Know Act, EPA has created regulations that require disclosure of chemicals manufactured, used, or emitted by businesses in order to protect public health. Facilities meeting the reporting requirements must develop emergency response plans, report chemical inventories, release information, and make important chemical information available to health professionals. Those regulations are found in 40CFR350, 355, 370, 372.

The Toxic Substances and Control Act is aimed at controlling chemical hazards that pose an unreasonable risk to health and the environment through their production, processing, distribution, use, and disposal. In fulfilling that mandate, EPA regulations require reporting and record keeping for specific chemicals, health and safety studies, and reporting of chemicals that cause significant adverse health reactions; import and export notifications; pre-manufacture and new chemical use notifications; creation of a chemical inventory; warning and labeling requirements for certain metal working fluids and water treatment chemicals; prohibitions for polychlorinated biphenyls (PCBs); and testing requirements for dibenzo-para-dioxins and dibenzofurans. Through amendments, the Act was expanded to cover asbestos hazards in schools and in commercial and public buildings, indoor radon abatement, and lead-based paint poisoning prevention in certain residential structures. Regulations developed by EPA under this Act are promulgated in 40CFR700-789. EPA also regulates potential worker exposures through Consent Orders and Significant New Use Rules for new chemical substances that are proposed for commercial manufacture or import. Those directives may contain various requirements for worker protection, including New Chemical Exposure Limits (NCELs), which are risk-based, 8-hour TWA airborne exposure limits.

Guidelines

Agency for Toxic Substances and Disease Registry (ATSDR)
Centers for Disease Control and Prevention
1600 Clifton Road, NE
Atlanta, GA 30333
888-422-8737 or 404-498-0110
www.atsdr.cdc.gov

ATSDR produces toxicological profiles for those chemical stressors that are most frequently found at National Priority List sites and those that pose the greatest threat to human health. Included in their toxicological profiles are Minimal Risk Levels that are used by the Agency and which estimate the lowest daily doses for acute, sub-acute, and chronic exposures likely to occur without detectable risk of adverse non-cancer health effects. In addition, ATSDR maintains acute and chronic exposure data and develops interaction profiles for some chemical mixtures, Case Studies in Environmental Medicine, Public Health Assessments and Health Consultations on hazardous waste sites, and chemical-specific toxicological frequently asked questions (ToxFAQs).

American Conference of Governmental Industrial Hygienists (ACGIH®)
1330 Kemper Meadow Drive
Cincinnati, OH 45240-1634
513-742-2020
www.acgih.org

ACGIH® is a non-profit organization of occupational health and safety professionals dedicated to advancing worker health and safety. Among the various industrial hygiene-related scientific publications produced by ACGIH® are *Threshold Limit Values for Chemical Substances and Physical Agents and Biological Exposure Indices*, which is updated yearly, and *Documentation of Threshold Limit Values and Biological Exposure Indices*, 7th edition. Those documents contain health-based exposure assessment guidelines and the scientific information from which they were derived.

American Industrial Hygiene Association (AIHA)
2700 Prosperity Avenue, Suite 250
Fairfax, VA 22031
703-849-8888
www.aiha.org

AIHA is a non-profit organization of occupational and environmental health and safety professionals who promote the protection of worker and public health through published scientific works, education and information exchange, and laboratory accreditation programs. Chemical exposure guidelines produced by AIHA include Workplace Environmental Exposure Levels (WEELs) for assessing repetitive occupational exposures to airborne concentrations at various durations and Emergency Response Planning Guidelines (ERPGs) for determining airborne concentrations below which specified health conditions are not expected to occur for most members of the general public within a 1-hour exposure period. WEELs and ERPGs are updated yearly.

National Center for Environmental Health (NCEH)
Centers for Disease Control and Prevention
1600 Clifton Road, NE
Atlanta, GA 30333
888-422-8737 or 404-498-0110
www.cdc.gov/nceh

NCEH promotes health and quality of life through prevention and control of injury, illness, and death resulting from interactions between people and their environment. The Center conducts public health surveillance, applied research, and education programs and develops standards, guidelines, and recommendations.

National Institute for Occupational Safety and Health (NIOSH)
Centers for Disease Control and Prevention
200 Independence Avenue, SW
Washington, DC 20201
800-356-4674
www.cdc.gov/niosh

NIOSH carries out research and education programs, conducts field investigations, maintains databases, develops chemical and safety information resources, and makes formal recommendations to prevent occupational illnesses, injuries, and deaths. Recommended Exposure Limits (RELs) and Immediately Dangerous to Life and Health (IDLH) concentrations are non-regulatory occupational exposure limits developed by NIOSH. Chemical-specific occupational hazard information is found in various NIOSH publications which include alerts, current intelligence bulletins, criteria documents, chemical safety cards, *Pocket Guide to Chemical Hazards*, and occupational safety and health guidelines for chemical hazards. NIOSH sustains numerous databases where information related to occupational chemical exposures can be obtained. Those databases include NIOSH Technical Information Center-2 (NIOSHTIC2), National Occupational Exposure Survey (NOES), National Occupational Respiratory Mortality System (NORMS), Work-Related Injury Statistics Query System (Work-RISQS), National Agriculture Safety Database (NASD), and Electronic Library of Construction Safety and Health (ELCOSH).

U.S. Coast Guard (USCG)
2100 Second Street, SW
Washington, DC 20593
202-267-0031
www.uscg.mil
www.chrismanual.com

The USCG is a multimission maritime service that is one of the five branches of the US Armed Forces and has responsibility for hazardous material discharges that may impact navigable waterways. The Chemical Hazards Response Information System (CHRIS) manual is an emergency response reference maintained by the USCG. The manual contains chemical, physical, toxicological, thermodynamic, health hazard, and response information for hazardous chemical cargoes.

Office of Environment, Safety and Health
U.S. Department of Energy
1000 Independence Avenue, SW
Washington, D.C.
202-586-6151
www.eh.doe.gov

The Office of Environment, Safety and Health serves to protect workers at their facilities, the public, and the environment while performing DOE operations. Temporary Emergency Exposure Limits (TEELs) are guidelines to help protect the public in the event of a chemical release. TEELs are air concentration action values for emergency response and planning. Each chemical for which a TEEL has been derived has four different limits: one that represents a threshold concentration for no effects and three limits below which specified health conditions are not expected to occur for most members of the general public.

Office of Hazardous Materials Safety (OHM)
U.S. Department of Transportation
400 7th Street, SW
Washington, DC 20590
800-467-4922 or 202-366-4488
http://hazmat.dot.gov/index.html

The mission of OHM is to reduce risks to life and property associated with hazardous material transport through a national safety program. OHM publishes and distributes the *Emergency Response Guidebook* free to public emergency responders with the goal of protecting first responders and the public during hazardous material releases. The guidebook provides hazard and initial response information by material classification.

Office of Research and Development (ORD)
U.S. Environmental Protection Agency
1200 Pennsylvania Avenue, NW
Washington, DC 20460
202-272-0167
www.epa.gov/ord

EPA conducts and supports expansive research on chemical exposure and risk assessment and manages various chemical data systems. EPA's Envirofacts website (www.epa.gov/enviro) allows users to search EPA databases for chemical sampling or release information or search for a complete listing of all EPA chemical references. ORD is the primary scientific research arm facilitating EPA's mission to prevent pollution, protect human health, and reduce risk. It produces numerous toxicology-based research publications, risk assessments, and assessment tools, which include various guidelines, models, and databases. ORD's Integrated Risk Information System (IRIS) is a database of human health assessment information based on chronic toxicity data. Data include reference doses and reference concentrations for non-carcinogenic endpoints and carcinogenic quantitative risk estimates based on lifetime exposure.

Office of Prevention, Pesticides, and Toxic Substances (OPPTS)
U.S. Environmental Protection Agency
1200 Pennsylvania Avenue, NW
Washington, DC 20460
202-272-0167
www.epa.gov/oppts

Through regulatory and voluntary programs, OPPTS protects human health and the environment, including worker safety with regard to pesticide and new chemical exposures. OPPTS develops risk assessments for pesticides and other toxins, fact sheets containing toxicity information and health and safety precautions, various models and databases, and Acute Exposure Guideline Levels (AEGLs). AEGLs are a collaborative effort to identify guidelines for emergency planning and response. Those guidelines represent values below which most individuals of the general population would be unharmed after a once-in-a-lifetime airborne exposure of less than 8 hours.

Office of Water (OW)
U.S. Environmental Protection Agency
1200 Pennsylvania Avenue, NW
Washington, DC 20460
202-272-0167
www.epa.gov/water

OW develops and enforces regulations, funds research, provides education and training, and maintains databases and software centered on protecting human health and water quality. OW establishes health guidelines for water, fish, and shellfish. National fish advisories and safe consumption guidelines produced through risk assessments and associated references are available on-line. Non-regulatory drinking water health advisories generated by OW are toxicologically-derived water contaminant concentrations for 1-day, 10-day, and lifetime exposures not expected to produce adverse health effects apart from cancer. OW also develops drinking water health advisories based on cancer risk estimates.

The National Academies
500 Fifth Street, NW
Washington, DC 20055
888-624- 8373 or 202-334-3313
www.nas.edu
www.nap.edu

The National Academies is comprised of the National Academy of Sciences, National Academy of Engineering, National Research Council, and the Institute of Medicine. They are private, non-profit organizations whose membership is made up of national experts elected by their peers. The National Academies provides advice to the federal government through its research and scientific reports. AEGLs, Continuous Exposure Guidance Levels (CEGLs), Emergency Exposure Guidance Levels (EEGLs), and Short-Term Public Emergency Guidance Levels (SPEGLs) are among the various exposure guidelines developed or reviewed by the National Research Council. Published and electronic reports on a variety of occupational and public health topics are available through the National Academies Press.

National Institute of Environmental Health Sciences (NIEHS)
National Institutes of Health
111 Alexander Drive
Research Triangle Park, NC 27709
919-541-3345
www.niehs.nih.gov

NIEHS has a mission to reduce human illness and dysfunction from environmental causes by studying the interaction between environmental factors, individual susceptibility, and age. NIEHS conducts and funds research, publishes a journal and other educational resources, and administers the National Toxicology Program (NTP). Through NIEHS, the NTP releases a biennial report to Congress on carcinogens, maintains a database collection of toxicology and carcinogenesis studies, and partners with other federal agencies to investigate the effects of exposures that impact both occupational and public health.

National Library of Medicine (NLM)
National Institutes of Health
8600 Rockville Pike
Bethesda, MD 20894
888-346-3656
www.nlm.nih.gov

The NLM is the world's largest medical library. It provides extensive access to toxicology and environmental health information that can be searched electronically for references, resources, articles, publications, databases, and databanks.

Summary

While this chapter has highlighted many of the existing toxicology-based regulations and guidelines, it is essential that the industrial hygienist stay abreast of the latest developments in the field. The broad base of information and research is continually updated and revised, especially for internet resources. All official United States government notices and regulations, including those proposed for comment as well as the final rules, are published each business day in the *Federal Register* and are available at www.gpoaccess.gov/fr/index.html and www.regulations.gov. Professional association and trade newspapers, reports, journals, and websites are also valuable aids to staying up-to-date with the current regulations and guidelines.

Chapter 34

Sources of Chemical Hazard Information

By Warren W. Jederberg, MS, CIH, RPIH

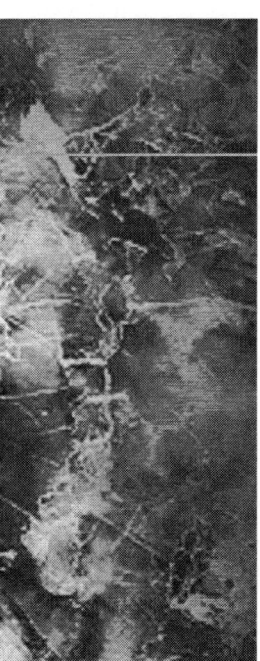

Introduction

The intention of this chapter is to provide the practicing Industrial/Occupational Hygienist and other Occupational Medicine specialists with a short review of readily available sources of toxicologic information. It has been estimated that the United States imports or produces close 4.4 to 7.1 trillion pounds of some 3,000 chemicals at over 1 million pounds each per year. This is from some 70,000 in commerce. Of these, 43% have no toxicity testing data and only seven percent have a full set of basic data.[1–3] Thus, the ability of the practicing Industrial/Occupational Hygienist to find sufficient data to assess potential health hazards in the workplace can be daunting.

Sources fall into three broad categories: Material Safety Data Sheets (MSDS), Books, and websites. Though required to be available for every material in the workspace, their usefulness in assessing the health risk of the worker can be very limited and requires some expertise to interpret and may not include essential toxicologic information.[4–7] Because the data contained on MSDSs vary in quantity and quality, efforts are being made to standardize the information and format for MSDSs.[8] There are many commercially available MSDS databases. Some books that are useful and commonly available include (NOTE: These texts are frequently updated).

1. **Klaasen, C.D. (ed.):** *Casarett & Doull's Toxicology — The Basic Science of Poisons,* 6th edition. New York: McGraw-Hill, 2001.
2. **Bingham, E., Cohrssen, B. and C.H. Powell (eds.):** *Patty's Toxicology,* 5th edition, New York: John Wiley & Sons, 2001.
3. **Lewis, R.J. (ed.):** *Sax's Dangerous Properties of Industrial Materials,* 11th edition. New York: John Wiley & Sons, 2004.

Also readily available are publications from professional organizations and governmental agencies. Good examples are the *Threshold Limit Values (TLV®) for Chemical and Physical Agents and Biological Exposure Indices (BEIs®)* of the Ameri-

Outcome Competencies

Upon completion of this chapter, the reader should be able to:

- Be able to find relevant toxicological data through references and internet searching.

Prerequisite Knowledge

Basic Internet search capability.

Key Terms

Material Safety Data Sheet, web search.

Key Topics

1. Internet Information
2. Hazardous Chemical Information

Table 34.1 — Internet Search Examples

Search Phrase	MSN Search® Hits	Google® Hits	Yahoo® Hits
Toxicology of Cobalt	20,294	118,000	96,800
Toxicology of Benzene	50,687	285,000	225,000
Toxicology of Formaldehyde	37,867	202,000	167,000
Toxicology of Hydrogen Sulfide	3,380	74,100	67,800

can Conference of Governmental Industrial Hygienists (published annually), and the National Institute for Occupational Safety and Health (NIOSH) Pocket Guide to Chemical Hazards (NIOSH Publication No. 2005-151). These are also updated regularly. However, the information provided by them is for very specific uses and does not provide detailed toxicology.

With the proliferation of the Internet and the growing social awareness of the impact of chemicals in the workplace and the environment as a whole, the ability to obtain toxicologic information by "web surfing" continues to increase. However, as can be seen from the following examples (Table 34.1, all searches were performed on January 17, 2006) from some of the most common search engines, the data can be overwhelming. If the searcher is unfamiliar with the logic used to optimize such efforts, they may find the Internet an inefficient way to find data, particularly if they need it in a very timely manner. Many of the sites that are found by such searches are sponsored by organizations that have a vested interest in how the data are perceived and caution must be used in relying solely on the data from any one site. The following Internet sources are provided to help the reader narrow their effort to authoritative and readily available sources.

Internet Websites (U.S. Government)

- Agency for Toxic Substances and Disease Registry (ATSDR) — www.atsdr.cdc.gov.
- Environmental Protection Agency (EPA) Ecological Toxicity (ECOTOX) — www.epa.gov/ecotox/.
- National Institute of Occupational Safety and Health (NIOSH) — www2.cdc.gov/nioshtic-2/nioshtic2.htm (this is a publication search website).
- National Library of Medicine — www.toxnet.nlm.nih.gov.
- National Toxicology Program (Department of Health and Human Services) — www.ntp-server.niehs.nih.gov/
- Registry of Toxic Effects of Chemical Substances (RTECS) — www.cdc.gov/niosh/srchpage.html
- U.S. Coast Guard — www.chrismanual.com

Internet Websites (Non U.S. governments)

- Australian Government Department of Health and Aging (NICNAS) — www.nicnas.gov.au/publications/car/default.asp
- European Chemical Substances Information System (EU ESIS) — www.ecb.jrc.it/esis
- Global Information Network on Chemicals (Ministry of Health, Labor and Safety, Japan) — www.db.mhlw.go.jp/ginc/index.html
- International Programme on Chemical Safety (IPCS INCHEM) — www.inchem.org
- International Programme on Chemical Safety (IPCS Intox) — www.intox.org/databank/index.htm
- Substances in Preparation in Nordic Countries (Norway, Sweden, Denmark, and Finland) — http://195.215.251.229/DotNetNuke/default.aspx

A comprehensive list of sources has been compiled and is available to members of the American Industrial Hygiene Association at www.aiha.org/webapps/taxonomy/portal.htm titled "Essential Resources for Industrial Hygiene – Chapter 4 Occupational Toxicology" written by W.E. Luttrell.

Conclusion

Regardless of the source, without some familiarity with basic principles of toxicology, interpretation of data as it applies to any given exposure scenario can be difficult. Part of the purpose of this publication is to introduce the practicing Industrial/Occupational Hygienist or other Occupational/Preventive Medicine specialist with enough information to know when they need to consult with someone with more expertise in the area of applied toxicology.

References

1. **U.S. Environmental Protection Agency (EPA):** *Chemical Hazard Data Availability Study: What Do We Really Know About the Safety of High Production Volume Chemical?* U.S. EPA Office of Pollution Prevention and Toxics, April 1998. [Online] Available at www.environmental defense.org/documents/657_HPV%20Chemical%20Challenge%20Initiative.htm. [Accessed July 9, 2007].
2. *Chemical Profiles: High Production (HPV) Chemicals.* [Online] www.scorecard.org/chemical-profiles/def/hpv.html. [Accessed July 9, 2001].
3. **U.S. Environmental Protection Agency (EPA):** *Chemical Hazard Data Availability Study: High Production Volume (HPV) Chemicals and SIDS Testing.* Office of Pollution Prevention and Toxics, EPA, Washington, DC. 1998.

4. *Position Statement: Material Safety Data Sheet.* American Industrial Hygiene Association. [Online] Available at www.aiha.org/1documents/GovernmentAffairs/P-MSDS-09-02-2005.pdf. [Accessed July 9, 2007].

5. **Jederberg, W.W.:** Issues with the Integration of Technical Information in Planning for and Responding to Non-Traditional Incidents. *J. Toxicol. Environ. Health 68(11–12)*: 877–888 (2005).

6. **Silk, J.C.:** Hazard Communication. In *The Occupational Environment, Its Evaluation, Control, and Management (2nd Edition).* DiNardi, S.R. (ed.). Fairfax VA: AIHA Press, 2003.

7. **Kopstein, M.:** Potential Uses of Petrochemical Products Can Result in Significant Benzene Exposures: MSDSs Must List Benzene as an Ingredient. *J. Occ. Environ. Hyg. 3*:1–8 (2006).

8. **Grumbles, T.G.:** Hearing on Material Safety Data Sheets and Hazard Communication. U.S. Senate Committee on Health, Education, Labor and Pensions Subcommittee on Employment, Safety and Training held March 25, 2005 [Online] www.enzi.senate.gov/grumble2.htm. [Accessed July 9, 2007].

Chapter 35

Professional Organizations and Publications

By Glenn J. Leach, PhD

Introduction

This chapter first provides an overview of the major scientific societies with a focus on some aspect of toxicology relevant to industrial hygienists. In all cases, the overview includes a description of the society, the goals and function of the group, and their web site link. Any unique information or data the web site may provide is also pointed out.

This chapter then provides a listing of some key toxicology textbooks and other reference materials which may be of interest to individuals studying for the American Board of Industrial Hygiene certification exam. The chapter ends with a listing of some of the most useful toxicological journals that include studies involving toxic materials originating in the workplace.

Associations and Organizations

In 2001, over 40 professional toxicology organizations with web sites were identified.[1] Some of the most well known organizations are listed below in alphabetical order, along with a brief description of services available from the web site. In most cases, the web sites provide useful member information and services such as resources available and conference registration. A number of the web sites provide member access to on-line journals sponsored by the organization; in most cases non-members can read abstracts of current issues and in some cases the back issues.

American College of Toxicology (ACT)
9650 Rockville Pike
Bethesda, Maryland 20814
Tel: (301) 634-7840
http://www.actox.org/

The mission of the ACT is to educate and lead professionals in industry, government and related areas of toxicology. They focus on new developments in safety assessment and the application of new developments in toxicology. Their web site has primarily membership and meeting information. The ACT sponsors the *International Journal of Toxicology* which publishes peer reviewed articles in general toxicology, mechanisms of toxicity, risk assessments safety testing and alternatives to animals in toxicology testing. Archived abstracts are available to non-members through Medline.

American Conference of Governmental Industrial Hygienists (ACGIH®)
1330 Kemper Meadow Drive
Cincinnati, OH 45240
Tel: (513) 742-2020
http://www.acgih.org/home.htm

The Independent National Conference of Governmental Industrial Hygienists first met in 1938. The conference originally limited membership to individuals from the government. The name was changed to the American Conference of Governmental Industrial Hygienists (ACGIH®) in 1946 and membership was opened to all industrial hygienists. While primarily of interest to industrial hygienists, the publications put out by the ACGIH contain information on occupational exposures and recommendations for safe exposure levels that are useful to toxicologists working in occupational health areas. The ACGIH co sponsors (with the American Industrial Hygiene Association) the *Journal of Occupational and Environmental Hygiene (JOEH)*. This journal publishes peer reviewed papers in industrial hygiene, occupational medicine, toxicology and ergonomics. The ACGIH also publishes the Threshold Limit Values for Chemical Substances and Physical Agents & Biological Exposure Indices. This is a pocket sized booklet that provides recommendations for workplace exposure levels for over 700 chemicals and biological exposure indices for approximately 80 compounds. This information is particularly useful to individuals working in industrial toxicology.

American Industrial Hygiene Association (AIHA)
2700 Prosperity Ave., Suite 250
Fairfax, VA 22031
Tel: (703) 849-8888.
http://www.aiha.org

The AIHA was founded in 1939 as a non profit organization and today has over 12,000 members. Their goal is to improve the knowledge and practice of industrial hygiene and worker safety. The AIHA web site has current news and issues related to industrial hygiene and occupational health. The site also provides access to the *JOEH* as well as publications. *The Journal of Occupational and Industrial Hygiene (JOEH)* is a joint publication of the AIHA and the American Conference of Governmental Industrial Hygienists (ACGIH®). The journal is available on line for members. AIHA also publishes *The Synergist*, a monthly magazine intended to provide AIHA members with general news and information about industrial hygiene with a focus on industry trends, regulatory issues and other association news and activities. These journals are also of interest to toxicologists working in industrial settings and perhaps regulatory toxicologists as well.

International Society for Regulatory Toxicology and Pharmacology (ISRTP)
6546 Belleview Drive
Columbia, MD 21046-1054
Tel: (410) 992-9083
http://www.isrtp.org/

The mission of the ISRTP is to promote sound science in developing regulations affecting human health and the environment. The ISRTP website has meeting announcements, recent council actions and links of interest. The society sponsors the *Journal of Regulatory Toxicology and Pharmacology*. This journal publishes peer reviewed articles from government agencies, academia and industry on any aspect of regulatory toxicology including risk assessments and safety evaluations. Non-members can access abstracts through the Science Direct web site.

International Union of Toxicology (IUTOX)
1821 Michael Faraday Drive, Suite 300
Reston, VA, 20190
Tel: (703) 438-3103
http://www.iutox.org/

IUTOX serves as a world wide organization for toxicologists to address global issues in the field of toxicology. It was founded in 1980 and now has 47 national or regional members representing toxicologists worldwide. The IUTOX does not sponsor any journals but they do hold meetings every 3 years. Their web site offers links to member societies, meeting announcements and educational opportunities.

Society of Environmental Toxicology and Chemistry (SETAC)
SETAC North America
1010 North 12th Avenue
Pensacola, FL 32501-3370
Tel: (850) 469-1500
http://www.setac.org/

The SETAC is a non-profit worldwide organization founded in 1979. Its focus is not occupational health, but the website has useful information related to environmental problems. The society sponsors *Environmental Toxicology and Chemistry*. This journal has three sections: Environmental Chemistry, Environmental Toxicology and Hazard/Risk Assessment. SETAC also produces Integrated Environmental Assessment and Management (IEM), a quarterly publication which, in addition to research papers in environmental assessment and management, includes case studies, editorials and legal policy issues. Non-members can access abstracts of current and archived papers.

Society of Toxicology (SOT)
1821 Michael Faraday Drive, Suite 300
Reston, VA 20190
Tel: (703) 438-3115
http://www.toxicology.org/

The SOT was established in 1961 as a non-profit scientific society and currently has over 5000 members from 44 countries. The members are from academia, government and private industry and the society goal is the promotion of all aspects of toxicology. The SOT web site has fact sheets and public out reach educational material available to non members. The official SOT journal *Toxicological Sciences* is available on line to members. Non-members can access abstracts from the current issues and complete papers from archived issues. The journal publishes peer reviewed papers in all aspects of toxicology including descriptive toxicology, mechanistic studies, safety testing, and risk assessment The SOT web site has fact sheets and public outreach educational material available to non members.

Basic Reference Textbooks

In addition to association resources and journals, there are a number of textbooks containing toxicological information which an industrial hygienist would find useful. This listing of textbooks is not complete, but rather provides some key sources of basic toxicity information.

- **National Research Council:** *Acute Exposure Guideline Levels for Selected Airborne Chemicals,* Vol. 1–4. Subcommittee on Acute Exposure Guideline Levels, Committee on Toxicology. Washington D.C.: National Academies Press, 2000. ISBN: 0-309-08511-X

This series of publications provides recommendations for short term exposure levels for the general population. Three hazard severity levels are describes and exposure durations from 10 minutes to 8 hours are covered. These guideline levels are useful for emergency planning and first responders to chemical incidents. Each volume contains information on 4–5 selected chemicals and volumes are published about once a year as the guidelines are developed.

- **Klassen, C.D. (ed.):** *Casarett and Doull's Toxicology, The Basic Science of Poisons*, 6th edition. New York: McGraw Hill. 2001. ISBN: 0-07-134721-6

Although this is primarily a text for graduate courses in toxicology it provides an excellent reference for all aspects of toxicology. The book is divided into seven sections: general principals, disposition of toxicants, sections on the major types of toxic endpoints, target organ toxicity, toxic agents and sections on environmental toxicology and applications of toxicology.

- **Rom, W.N. (ed.):** *Environmental and Occupational Medicine*, 3rd edition. Philadelphia, PA: Lippincott-Raven Publishers, 1998.

This textbook provides a comprehensive review of occupational and environmental diseases. It is intended for medical students and residents in occupational medicine as well as professionals in public health. There are sections dealing with the mechanisms of occupational disease, organ system toxicity and exposure to environmental and occupational chemicals. In addition to these traditional toxicology topics there are sections dealing with radiation, physical agents and the control of occupational diseases and exposures.

- **National Institute for Occupational Safety and Health (NIOSH):** *NIOSH Pocket Guide to Chemical Hazards*. NIOSH Publication No. 97-140. Springfield, VA: National Technical Information Service, 2004.

This guide is a source of general industrial hygiene information on several hundred chemicals. It includes the chemical name, synonyms, CAS, RTECS and DOT numbers, NIOSH recommended exposure limits (RELs), NIOSH Immediately Dangerous to Life and Health Values (IDLH) and OSHA permissible exposure limits (PELs). The guide also contains information on personal protection and respriator selection.

- **Bingham, E., B. Cohrssen, and C. Powell (eds.):** *Patty's Toxicology*, 5th edition, Vol. 1–9. New York: John Wiley & Sons, Inc. 2001. ISBN: 0-471-31943-0

This nine volume set is probably the most comprehensive source of toxicological information for industrial chemicals. Volume 1 covers Toxicology issues, inorganic particulates, dusts and pathogens. Volumes 2 and 3 look at metal and metallic compounds as well as radiation and neurotoxicity. Volumes 4 and 5 address hydrocarbons, organic halogenated hydrocarbons, ethers and aldehydes. Volumes 6 and 7 continue with various organic compounds and in volume 8, physical agents, interactions and mixtures are discussed. Volume 9 is a complete index for the entire 8 volume set of books.

- **Hays, A.W.:** *Principles and Methods of Toxicology*, 3rd edition. New York: Raven Press. 1994. ISBN: 0-7817-0131-7

This book was intended to be used in courses in dealing with toxicological data and with methodologies used in toxicology. This book is an excellent reference on current testing procedures and data interpretation. It is organized into three sections. The first section describes basic principles in toxicology. The second section covers basic testing methods and especially the procedures required by regulatory agencies. The final section covers specific organ systems, kinetics and target organs.

- **Pohanish, R.:** *Rapid Guide to Chemical Incompatibilities*. New York: Van Nostrand Reinhold. 1997. ISBN 0-44202-394-4.

This reference contains information on over 8500 compounds and potentially hazardous interactions. The chemicals are listed alphabetically and include incompatibility data for thousands of common commercial chemicals. The chemical data also includes information on generating toxic gases, rupture containers detonation and the formation of more toxic compounds.

- **Lewis, R.J.:** *Rapid Guide to Hazardous Chemicals in the Workplace*, 4th edition. New York: John Wiley and Sons, Inc., 2000. ISBN: 0-471-35542-9.

This book is a pocket guide to the most frequently found hazardous chemicals in the workplace. It includes the latest OSHA regulations and other guidance, updated Threshold Limit Values, DOT labeling requirements as well as cross references for CAS numbers, common names and synonyms.

- **Lewis, R.J. (ed.):** *Sax's Dangerous Properties of Industrial Materials,* 10th edition, Vol. 1–3. New York: John Wiley & Sons, Inc., 2000. ISBN: 0-471-37858-5.

This is a key reference for professionals who evaluate the hazards of chemicals in the workplace or in commerce. Volume I contains an index of CAS numbers and common names and synonyms. Volumes II and III contain a comprehensive listing of over 20,000 materials with toxicological properties, fire, reactivity, explosive potential and regulatory information.

- **O'Neil, M.J., A. Smith, and P.E. Heckelman, (eds.):** *The Merck Index*, 13th edition. Whitehouse Station, NJ: Merck & Co., 2001.

The Merck index is a one volume encyclopedia of chemicals, drugs and biologicals. It contains over 10,000 monographs describing the compound. These entries include the chemical name, CAS number, synonyms, molecular formula and structure, physical data, limited toxicity data and the therapeutic category which includes pharmacological information.

- **Hardman, J.G., L.E. Limbird, and A.G. Gilman, (eds.):** *The Pharmacological Basis of Therapeutics*, 10th edition. New York: McGraw Hill, 2001. ISBN 0-0701354697

This text has been the primary reference in pharmacology for 60 years. It includes information on the mechanisms of drug effects on the various body systems, chemical properties, drug interactions and toxic effects

- **Derelanko, M.J.:** *Toxicologist's Pocket Handbook*. Boca Raton, FL: CRC Press, 2000.

This handbook is a condensed version of the CRC Handbook of Toxicology. It provides many useful tables of biological and toxicological information. It also has basic information on toxicology studies and test protocols and risk assessment information. This is extremely handy source of toxicology information when attending meetings and conferences.

Toxicological Journals

In addition to professional organizations and textbooks, there are several toxicological journals that publish articles dealing with chemical substances in and around the workplace. The following journals are peer-reviewed and excellent sources of additional information for the industrial hygienist with particular interests.

- The Journal of Occupational and Environmental Hygiene (joint AIHA & ACGIH journal)
- American Industrial Hygiene Association Journal (AIHAJ)
- Applied Occupational and Environmental Hygiene
- The Annals of Occupational Hygiene
- International Archives of Occupational and Environmental Health
- Journal of Occupational and Environmental Medicine
- Occupational and Environmental Medicine
- The Occupational and Environmental Medicine Report (The OEM Report)
- Scandinavian Journal of Work, Environment & Health
- Toxicology and Industrial Health
- Archives of Environmental Contamination and Toxicology
- Bulletin of Environmental Contamination and Toxicology
- Chemical Research in Toxicology
- Ecotoxicology and Environmental Safety
- Environmental Health Perspectives
- Fundamental and Applied Toxicology
- Journal of Environmental Pathology and Toxicology
- Journal of Environmental Pathology, Toxicology, and Oncology
- Regulatory Toxicology and Pharmacology
- Toxicological and Environmental Chemistry
- Toxicological and Environmental Chemistry Reviews
- Toxicological Sciences
- Toxicology
- Toxicology and Applied Pharmacology
- Toxicology Letters
- CIS Abstracts
- Job Safety & Health Quarterly
- Occupational Health & Safety
- Safety and Health at Work: ILO-CIS Bulletin

References

1. **Kehrer, J.P., and J. Mirsalis:** Professional Toxicology Societies: Web-based Resources. *Toxicol. 157(1-2)*:67–76 (2001).

Chapter 36

Websites and Electronic Databases

By Amy C. Moscatelli, MS

Introduction

It is hard to believe that in just over a decade from its introduction, the Internet has changed from a mysterious and misunderstood resource to something we rely upon every single day for nearly everything relating to information and communication. Research gathering and information searches have been all but streamlined with its invention, and for industrial hygienists, it has become an integral part of every day work. From searching for anything from ventilation standards and machinery requirements to Permissible Exposure Limits (PELs), people can save countless time getting the information we need in seconds, rather than taking minutes to look it up in a reference book.

Toxicological databases are abounding on the Internet and are readily available. Most of them are free, offering information such as peer reviewed papers, chemical interactions, toxic properties, physical properties, and personal protective equipment (PPE) recommendations, all with a click of a mouse.[1]

When the World Wide Web was invented by CERN, the European Laboratory for Particle Physics, it was meant to assist scientists with sharing research documents and other information. Unfortunately, since it was released to the world with the same intent in 1992, it has been bogged down with many uncredited and unsubstantiated information resources. While the databases and informational resources described in this chapter are considered legitimate and are recognized by many toxicologists and agencies, it is highly likely that while doing a toxicological related search on the Internet one will happen upon a website not listed below. The credibility and accuracy of information gathered is crucial to investigating occupational exposures, emergency situations or developing sampling strategies. There are endless websites providing guidance on credibility of online sources, but they all have the same basic tips. The first step is to assess the type of site being visited and the information it is providing. Certainly, PDF or HTML versions of peer reviewed scientific journals with verifiable authors working in the profession give the website immediate credibility. Sites with .gov and .edu websites are credible as well. Use a little more

Outcome Competencies

Upon completion of this chapter, the reader should be able to:

- Identify credible websites for toxicological information.
- Utilize credible databases to obtain relevant chemical and toxicological information.
- Locate search engines for peer-reviewed toxicology related abstracts, articles and professional papers.

Prerequisite Knowledge

- Basic internet navigation.
- General terminology concerning internet/worldwide web usage.

Key Topics

1. Government websites and databases
2. University websites and databases
3. Organizational websites and databases
4. Free websites and databases
5. Fee for service websites and databases
6. Useful search engines

caution when accessing .org, .com or .net domain websites as anyone can apply for and use these domain categorizations for their website. Additionally, people should be cautious of biased information or inflated statistics used to persuade the reader. Make note of the last update to the website as well as when the information was last added to the website. Out-of-date websites could not only contain old standards or information, but could also contain false information.[2,3]

This chapter will focus on the wide range of types of toxicologically focused databases and websites and electronic resources for any industrial hygienist.[4] Primarily, free access to toxicological information is found on government and university sponsored websites.[5] Search engines and privately sponsored websites are excellent resources for finding full text articles. These websites are explained in detail in this chapter. Other excellent toxicological databases can be found on fee for service websites and are often helpful in filling in the gaps on some toxicological information sought after by industrial hygienists.

Government Sponsored Websites
OSHA — Occupational Safety and Health Administration

http://www.osha.gov — Main web page for OSHA providing up-to-date OSHA news, links to state OSHA offices, federal regulations and commentary links to proposed rules concerning industrial toxicants.

http://www.osha.gov/SLTC/healthguidelines — Provides recognition, evaluation and control recommendations on nearly 200 industrial chemicals.

http://www.osha.gov/html/a-z-index.html — a searchable index of industrial related chemicals and other topics available on the website. Searches on specific chemicals return information including applicable standards, specific industries the chemical is used in, evaluating workplace exposures to the chemical as well as recommendations for controlling exposures. Additional links provide information to hazards, precautions and toxicity studies. It also includes many links to eTools, which are interactive on-line training modules concerning a particular toxicant.

http://www.osha.gov/pls/oshaweb/owadisp.show_document?p_table=STANDARDS&p_id=9992 — 29 CFR 1910.1000 Table Z-1, Limits for Air Contaminants

http://www.osha.gov/pls/oshaweb/owadisp.show_document?p_table=STANDARDS&p_id=9993 — 29 CFR 1910.1000 Table Z-2 Toxic and Hazardous Substances

http://www.osha.gov/pls/oshaweb/owadisp.show_document?p_table=STANDARDS&p_id=9994 — 29 CFR 1910.1000 Table Z-3 Mineral Dusts

EPA — U.S. Environmental Protection Agency

http://www.epa.gov — Main web page for the Environmental Protection Agency.

http://www.epa.gov/natlibra/ols.htm — The EPA's Online Library System (OLS). Designed to search various databases using keywords, title, author, report number etc. to retrieve reports, books and audiovisual media.

http://www.epa.gov/iris/index.html — Integrated Risk Information System (IRIS) a searchable database of nearly 500 chemicals. Provides a summary of exposures to a particular chemical via several routs such as ingestion and inhalation. Some chemical searches provide toxicity papers as well as carcinogenicity data.

http://www.epa.gov/srs — The Substance Registry System (SRS) provides regulatory information on chemicals regulated by the EPA.

http://www.epa.gov/pesticides/science/models_db.htm — Models and Databases. Provides links to EPA databases pertaining primarily to pesticides, environmental fate, ground and surface water effects, regulatory information as well as symptoms of exposure. Provides direct links to IRIS, TOXNET and EXTOXNET and other pesticide management databases. Information on specific pesticides, reporting and labeling requirements, toxicological profiles and exposure modeling can also be accessed through additional links on this website.

http://www.epa.gov/hpv/ — High Production Volume (HPV) Challenge Program. Provides links to EPA and external databases concerning chemicals in the United States that are manufactured or imported at over one million pounds per year. It is not necessary to know whether or not the toxicant being researched is considered HPV since many of the nearly 30 links provided are to databases containing information on several chemicals, rather than only HPV chemicals.

National Institute for Occupational Safety and Health (NIOSH)

http://www.cdc.gov/niosh/rtecs/default.html — Registry of Toxic Effects of Chemical Substances (RTECS). Toxicological reference providing primary irritation, mutagenic effects, reproductive effects, tumorigenic effects, acute toxicity, and other multiple dose toxicity based upon information gathered from scientific literature. The document can be downloaded in part or in its entirety from the website, or can be ordered through points of contact given on the website.

http://www.cdc.gov/niosh/homepage.html — Workplace Safety and Health Topics. Provides visitors with a drop down menu of safety and health topics ranging from aerosols to organic solvents to a section titled "Take Home Toxins." Topic information varies, but most contain research on the particular toxin, downloadable informational brochures, NIOSH Publication documents and links to NIOSHTIC-2 database results for the chemical or class of chemicals.

http://www.cdc.gov/niosh/chem-inx.html — Index of Occupational Health Guidelines for Chemical Hazards. Information on over 300 chemicals including chemical and physical properties, exposure limits, heath hazard information, medical surveillance recommendations, and controlling exposures in the workplace. Each information sheet contains a full bibliography.

http://www.cdc.gov/niosh/npg/npg.html — NIOSH Pocket Guide to Chemical Hazards. A resource for information on 677 chemicals that presents key information and data in abbreviated or tabular form. The following information is listed for each chemical: Chemical Names, synonyms, trade names, conversion factors, CAS, RTECS, and DOT Numbers, NIOSH Recommended Exposure Limits (NIOSH RELs), Occupational Safety and Health Administration Permissible Exposure Limits (OSHA PELs), NIOSH Immediately Dangerous to Life and Health values (NIOSH IDLHs), a physical description of the agent with chemical and physical properties, measurement methods, and personal protection as well as information on health hazards including route, symptoms, first aid and target organ information. The Pocket Guide can be searched directly from the website, downloaded to the computer or ordered in CD-rom format.

http://www.cdc.gov/niosh/idlh/intridl4.html — Immediately Dangerous to Life and Health (IDLH) Concentrations for 387 chemicals. Information provided includes CAS number, PEL, REL, TLV, LEL, IDLH, acute toxicity data and a bibliographical list for each chemical.

http://www.cdc.gov/niosh/ipcs/nicstart.html — International Chemical Safety Cards (ICSCs). A listing of over 1400 chemicals and their synonyms, molecular weight, hazards of exposure, storage and disposal precautions, physical properties, exposure limits, routes of exposure, and identifying numbers such as ICSC number, CAS number and RTECS number.

http://www.cdc.gov/niosh/nmam — NIOSH Manual of Analytical Methods (NMAM). A database of methods for sampling and analysis of contaminants in workplace air, and in the blood and urine of workers who are occupationally exposed. Also included are chapters on quality assurance, sampling, portable instrumentation, etc.

http://www.cdc.gov/niosh/topics/emres/chemagent.html — A listing of resources for primary first responders during disaster incidences.

http://www2a.cdc.gov/nioshtic-2/default.html — NIOSHTIC-2, a bibliographic database of occupational safety and health publications and documents supported by NIOSH. Contains over 35,000 citations easily searched by CAS numbers, author, title, keywords, or any other identifying chemical or report information.

Centers for Disease Control & Prevention (CDC)

http://www.atsdr.cdc.gov — Agency for Toxic Substances and Disease Registry (ATSDR). Provides links toxicological profiles, public health statements and fact sheets on over 162 chemicals through the HazDat database. Also provides information on minimum risk levels, interaction profiles and information concerning hazardous waste sites.

National Library of Medicine/National Institutes of Health

http://www.nlm.nih.gov/databases — A listing of databases and electronic resources offered by the National Library of Medicine. Some databases are also accessible on the TOXLINE home page, but others are not. Of particular relevance to industrial hygienists includes Haz-Map, a quick industrial reference with keyword searches, job categories or symptoms being experienced. Depending on the type of search performed, information including potential exposures to any of 1200+ chemicals causing symptoms, additional symptoms often experienced, as well as exposure limits, diseases caused and most common processes where symptoms and chemicals are found. PubMed/MEDLINE access is also available providing references including abstracts from thousands of biomedical journals.

http://toxnet.nlm.nih.gov/index.html — TOXNET, a group of databases on toxicology, hazardous chemicals, and related areas that can be searched individually or combined for toxic and exposure information. The databases are broken down as follows.

- Hazardous Substances Data Bank (HSDB) — HSDB is a toxicology database focused on the toxicology of potentially hazardous chemicals. It provides information on human exposure, industrial hygiene, emergency handling procedures, environmental fate, regulatory requirements, and related areas. HSDB is peer-reviewed by the Scientific Review Panel (SRP). HSDB is organized into individual chemical records, and contains over 4,700 such records that can be easily searched by chemical or other name, chemical name fragment, CAS number and/or subject terms.

- IRIS database provided by the EPA. (previously mentioned above).

- International Toxicity Estimates for Risk (ITER) contains over 600 chemical records with key data from the Agency for Toxic Substances & Disease Registry (ATSDR), Health Canada, National Institute of Public Health & the Environment (RIVM) — The Netherlands, U.S. Environmental Protection Agency (EPA), and independent parties whose risk values have undergone peer review. ITER provides a comparison of international risk assessment information in a side-by-side format and explains differences in risk values derived by different organizations. ITER data, focusing on hazard identification and dose-response assessment, is extracted from each agency's assessment and contains links to the source documentation. Among the key data provided in ITER are ATSDR's minimal risk levels; Health Canada's tolerable intakes/concentrations and tumorigenic doses/concentrations; EPA's carcinogen classifications, unit risks, slope factors, oral reference doses, and inhalation reference concentrations; RIVM's maximum permissible risk levels; and non-cancer and/or cancer risk values (that have undergone peer review) derived by independent parties.

- Genetic Toxicology (GENE-TOX). Created by the EPA, the database contains genetic toxicology (mutagenicity) information gathered from peer review of the scientific literature available on over 3,000 chemicals.

- Chemical Carcinogenesis Research Information System (CCRIS). A database developed and maintained by the National Cancer Institute (NCI) that contains over 8,000 chemical records with carcinogenicity, mutagenicity, tumor promotion, and tumor inhibition test results. Information is derived from studies cited in primary journals, current awareness tools, NCI reports, and other special sources.
- Toxicology Bibliographic Info. (TOXLINE). Scientific literature and references on biochemical, pharmacological, physiological, and toxicological effects of drugs and other chemicals.
- Developmental and Reproductive Toxicology and Environmental Teratology Information Center (DART/ETIC) — Scientific literature on developmental and reproductive toxicology associated with drugs and other chemicals.
- Toxic Release Inventory (TRI) — the EPA's annual estimated releases of toxic chemicals to the environment for reporting years 1995–2000.
- CHEMID Plus — Database that contains chemical synonyms, structures, regulatory list information, and links to other databases containing information concerning over 300,000 chemicals.

http://sis.nlm.nih.gov/enviro.html — Environmental Health and Toxicology home page. Provides information and links to list-servers, current toxicological news, toxicological tutorials as well as interactive software called Tox Town, which is an introduction to toxic chemicals and environmental health risks you might encounter in everyday life, as well as a household products database link that provides MSDS information on anything from brake fluid and laundry detergent to pet shampoo and paint thinner.

http://gateway.nlm.nih.gov/gw/Cmd — National Library of Medicine Gateway. Provides an informational retrieval system of bibliographic resources, consumer health resources and other informational resources that can be searched simultaneously using a single search interface.

National Toxicology Program

http://ntp-apps.niehs.nih.gov/ntp_tox/index.cfm — Database provides abstract and basic study results and information on toxicology and carcinogenesis studies, reproductive studies, developmental studies, immunology studies, and genetic toxicity from animal studies.

New Jersey Department of Health and Senior Services

http://web.doh.state.nj.us/rtkhsfs/indexfs.aspx?lan=english — Right to Know Hazardous Substance Fact Sheets. Thousands of chemical fact sheets containing hazard information and exposure limits, health effects, handling, storage and disposal, as well as frequently asked questions.

University Websites

http://potency.berkeley.edu — The Carcinogenic Potency Database (CPDB) provided by the University of California at Berkeley. Provides tabular summary of results for (carcinogenicity), target organ, carcinogenic potency in rats, mice, hamsters, dogs and nonhuman primates for 1,485 chemicals.

http://extoxnet.orst.edu — The EXTension TOXicology NETwork (EXTOXNET) is a collaborative effort between the University of California–Davis, Oregon State University, Michigan State University, Cornell University, and the University of Idaho. The database provides pesticide information, current toxicological issues of concern, fact sheets and other toxicological information.

http://ull.chemistry.uakron.edu/erd — The Chemical Database provided by the University of Akron containing chemical structure and formula information, physical properties, handling and storage procedures, health effects and transportation guidelines for over 23,000 chemicals.

Organizational Websites

http://www.inchem.org — International Programme on Chemical Safety Homepage. Provides a searchable database of over 7,000 documents including International Chemical Assessment documents, Health and Safety Guides, International Chemical Safety Cards, Pesticide documents etc.

http://solvdb.ncms.org/solvdb.htm — SOLV-DB is a solvent database that provides health and safety information as well as physical characteristics, regulatory data and environmental fate information on over 200 industrially available solvents.

http://dels.nas.edu/best/mission.shtml — National Academy of Science's Board on Environmental Studies and Toxicology (BEST). Provides current and ongoing reports and projects on toxicological issues.

http://www.toxicology.org — Society of Toxicology home page providing resources for student and toxicology professionals dedicated to fostering, sharing, and utilization of toxicology information including newsletters and other publications, spotlight articles, career development, as well as links to other online toxicology related websites and resources.

http://www.nssn.org — National Resource for Global Standards. Provides a searchable database for standards developed by over 800 organizations including ANSI, ACGIH, ASTM, DOE, DOT, ISO, NIOSH and US DOD for an annual fee.

http://www.cas.org — Chemical Abstracts Service (CAS) home page providing links and information to 9,500 journals, 50 patent-issuing authorities, scientific search engines as well as links to searching in the CAS Registry.

http://reprotox.org — REPROTOX, a pay for service searchable database by Reproductive Toxicology Center. The database can be used directly from the website, ordered in CD-rom form or downloaded to PDAs.

http://www.iutox.org — International Union of Toxicology website providing global information sharing on toxicology and toxicological issues. Provides links to a small number of toxicological resources as well as self guided tutorials on toxicology.

Free Websites

http://www.msdssearch.com/DBLinksN.htm — MSDS Search database page. Provides databases from Cornell University, Oxford University, National Library of Medicine and many others that provide MSDS information. Searches can be done by NINN (Department of Defense data), product name, ingredients, manufacturer etc.

http://www.oshweb.com/ — Oshweb is a group of industrial hygienists and information technology specialists providing links to hundreds of international databases and websites. This site provides direct links to 30 toxicological websites and databases. Additionally, provides information and links to dangerous substances websites and MSDS websites.

Fee for Service Websites

http://www.rmis.com/db/dbchemicals.htm — Risk Management Information Systems Library's Chemical Database. Conduct online searches of numerous chemical databases to obtain information such as: Material Safety Data Sheets (MSDS), toxicology profiles, chemical health hazards, chemical labeling requirements, Threshold Limit Values (TLVs), government lists of hazardous substances, pesticide information, storage compatibility, chemical safety guides and related materials. Examples of databases: CCRIS, DART, EMIC, EMCI, ETICBACK, GENE-TOX, IRIS, HESIS, HSDB, ISSDS, OPPT, RTECS, SAGE, SOLV-DB, SSDS, TOXNET, TRI. Subscription required.

http://www.thesafetylibrary.com/db/dbchemicals.php — Managerial Technologies Corporation Resource Libraries. Provides access to over 200 international databases providing chemical safety information, exposure limits, toxicity profiles and NFPA handling instructions. Monthly or annual subscription required.

Useful Search Engines

http://scholar.google.com — A Beta website powered by Google. Searches for articles, journals, books and organizations providing the most recent research on any topic imagined.

http://www.scirus.com/srsapp — Scirus is a comprehensive search engine dedicated to locating scientific and technical information by filtering out non scientific websites. Provides access to peer reviewed articles, journal databases, digital archives found on over 200 million scientific websites.

http://highwire.stanford.edu/lists/freeart.dtl — High Wire Press, a division of Stanford University, boast access to over one million free online full-text journal articles. Journals published by high wire are free access while other journals require an annual subscription. Subscriptions are based on individual and institutional memberships.

Conclusion

Continuing reliance on technology such as the internet and the need for instantaneous information is inevitable as industrial hygienists. Now more than ever the internet and its boundless resources are becoming tools to make jobs not only easier, but more efficient for customers. From scholarly papers, to informational websites to endless databases, the Internet and its resources are ready and waiting to answer the most daunting chemical and toxicological questions — all with a simple keystroke.

References

1. **Guerbet, M. and G. Guyodo:** Efficiency of 22 online database in the search for physiochemical, toxicological and ecotoxicological information on chemicals. *Ann. Occup. Hyg. 46(2)*:261–268 (2002).
2. **Grassian, E.:** UCLA College Library: Thinking Critically About WWW Resources. (1995). Accessed from www.library.ucla.edu/libraries/college/help/critical/ on February 16, 2007.
3. **Grassian, E.:** UCLA College Library: Thinking Critically About Discipline-Based World Wide Web Resources. (1997). Accessed from www.llibrary.ucla.eduu/libraries/college/help/critical/discipline.htm on February 16, 2007.
4. **Harris, M.K.:** *Essential Resources for Industrial Hygiene: A Compendium of Current Practice Standards and Guidelines.* Fairfax, VA: AIHA Press, 2000.
5. **Wright, L.:** Searching fee and non-fee toxicology information resources: an overview of selected databases. *Tox. 257(1–2)*:89–110 (2001).

Glossary

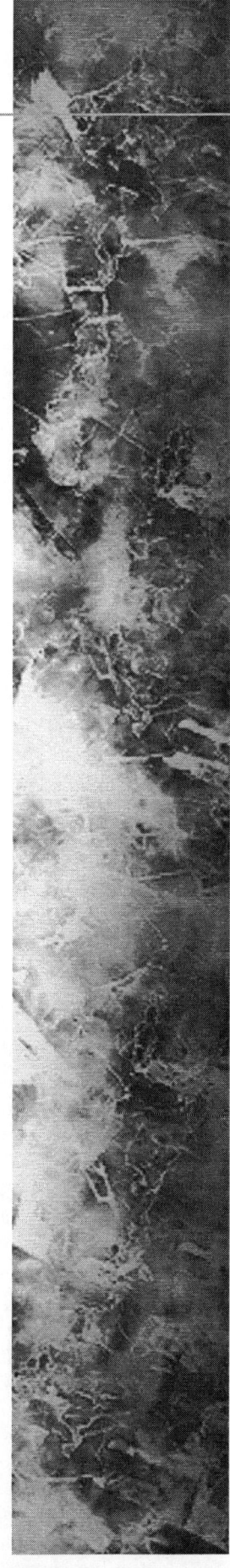

2-PAMCL: (2-pralidoxime chloride) re-activates the poisoned enzyme (acetyl cholinesterase) by "scavenging" the phosphoryl from the enzyme.

Absorbed dose: Describe the amount of a toxicant that actually enters the bloodstream and is bioavailable; the amount of a substance penetrating the exchange boundaries of an organism. It is usually expressed as mg/kg/day. In terms of ionizing radiation, the absorbed dose is (also known as Total Ionizing Dose, TID) is a measure of the energy deposited in a medium and is equal to the energy deposited per unit mass of medium (J/kg, which is given the special name Gray).

Absorption: The process by which a toxicant moves from the site of exposure, such as skin, lungs, or gastrointestinal tract, to the systemic circulation.

Absorption half-life: The time for one-half of a chemical to be absorbed into the body.

Acaricide: A substance or preparation for killing acarids (mites and ticks).

Acetylcholine: A chemical transmitter in both the peripheral nervous system (PNS) and central nervous system (CNS), Acetylcholine is the neurotransmitter in all autonomic ganglia.

Acetylcholinesterase: A natural enzyme, which inactivates the neurotransmitter acetylcholine. Organophosphate nerve agents and insecticides inhibit acetylcholine esterase.

Acne: Is an inflammatory disease of the skin, caused by changes in the pilosebaceous units (skin structures consisting of a hair follicle and its associated sebaceous gland).

Actin/myosin: The two structural proteins that together ascertain the contraction of muscle cells.

Action potential: An electrical discharge that occurs across the membrane of an excitable cell.

Active metabolite: Metabolites of a toxicant that possess toxicological activity.

Acute Exposure Guideline Level (AEGL): Guidelines developed by the U.S. EPA based on extensive peer review of available data and regularly published in the Federal Register.

Acute toxicity: Toxic effects seen after a single dose or single exposure to a substance. Usually refers to effects seen within a short time after exposure (24 hours).

Adamsite: (DM: Diphenylaminechloroarsine), a chemical warfare agent used to induce vomiting.

Adaption: A change in the threshold of a receptor to respond to a stimulus, towards higher or lower levels.

Adaptive immunity: Acquired or specific immunity, which reacts to specific antigens, and memory, plays an important role, since foreign antigens are recognized from prior exposures, leading to a more vigorous immune response.

Additive interaction: The combined effect is equal to the sum of the effect of each chemical given alone.

Adduct: A chemical abnormally bonded to a macromolecule such as DNA or protein.

Adenosine triphosphatase (ATPase): The enzyme that cleaves adenosine triphosphate (ATP), freeing energy required to drive "uphill" processes, such as the establishment of a membrane potential.

Adrenergic receptor antagonist: Substance that binds to adrenergic receptors, blocking the binding of adrenergic compounds.

Aerodynamic diameter: The diameter of a sphere of unit density (1 g/cc) that has the same gravitational settling velocity as the particle in question.

Afebrile: Without fever.

Afferent nerves: Nerves of the peripheral nervous system that transmit sensory information to the central nervous system.

Agent aging: The process by which the temporary phosphorylated bond between the organophosphate and acetylcholinesterase undergoes hydrolysis of the alkyl group, resulting in a permanent covalent bond. The different organophosphate agents have different rates of "aging" and this must be taken into consideration in a treatment regimen.

Airway remodeling: Any structural change in airway wall of lungs or the nose that is long-lived and that may affect airway function. Specific examples are the replacement of normal tissue with fibrotic tissue (fibrosis), loss of airways (emphysema) chronic inflammatory cell infiltration (e.g., asthma and COPD), smooth muscle proliferation.

Aldosterone: A steroid hormone that regulates mineral homeostasis.

Algicide: A substance or preparation for killing algae.

Aliphatics: Pertaining to open carbon chains; there are three groups of aliphatics: alkanes, alkenes, and alkynes.

Aliquots: (small portions) are taken for testing to represent larger volume of identical or similar ingredients.

Alkylating agent: A compound capable of reacting with another molecule through the substitution of an alkyl group for an active hydrogen. According to the number of reactive groups they contain, alkylating agents are classified as mono-, bi-, or polyfunctional; chemotherapeutic anticancer drug class that adds an alkyl group to proteins and DNA, thereby killing the cells.

Allele: A version of a gene. If more than one form of a gene occurs in a population, the different possible forms are called alleles.

Alopecia: Hair loss in an area where it is usually found. It can be caused by disease, trauma, exposure to chemicals, or to ionizing radiation.

Alpha particle: A charged particle emitted from the nucleus of an atom having a mass and charge equal in magnitude of a helium nucleus, i.e., two protons and two neutrons and a mass of 4 atomic mass units (amu).

Ames test: A test in which bacteria (Salmonella typhimurium) that require histidine are exposed to a test material and mutants that have been changed back to normal (histidine independence) are counted as a measure of mutagenic potential.

Amino acids: The basic building block of a protein. Each amino acid is characterized by an amino group (-NH2) at one end of the molecule and a carboxylic acid group (-COOH) at the other, as well as one of 20 unique side chains. Important properties of amino acids include their various shapes, sizes, and charges.

Anesthetics: A category of drugs, most often used in a medical setting, to reduce sensation or consciousness.

Aneugen/Aneuploidy: A compound causing aneuploidy. Aneuploidy results in a change in chromosome number that is not an exact multiple of the typical haploid set of chromosomes.

Angiogenesis: The process of vascularization of a tissue involving the development of new capillary blood vessels.

Angiosarcoma of the liver (ASL): A rare, rapidly growing, highly invasive variety of cancer, commonly associated with toxic exposure to thorium dioxide (Thorotrast), vinyl chloride, and arsenic.

Anorexia: Lack or loss of the appetite for food.

Anosmia: Inability to perceive smell. Anosmia can be caused by genetic factors or exposure to chemicals.

Antagonism: The combined effect of two chemicals is less than the sum of the effect of each chemical given alone.

Antibody: Immunoglobulin proteins produced and secreted by immune cells that specifically recognize foreign antigens and assist in the removal of pathogen. Antibody antigen interactions induce the activation host defense cells to either kill.

Anticholinesterase: Characteristic of a substance that binds directly to acetylcholinesterase, and inhibits it from breaking down.

Antidote: A drug or other remedy for counteracting the effects of a poison.

Antiemetics: Compounds used to prevent or alleviate nausea and vomiting.

Antigen: Protein molecules, usually those on microorganism cell surfaces, or viral components, which are recognized by the immune system as being foreign, against which immune responses are directed, such as developing antibodies, or engulfed by cells.

Antineoplastic drugs: Drugs directed at cancer cells to treat the disease, also commonly referred to as chemotherapeutic drugs.

Antioxidants: Molecules or chemicals that interact and neutralize oxidant molecules such as oxygen-derived free radicals. Antioxidants can also repair cell macromolecules that are damaged by interaction with oxidants.

Apnea: Cessation of breathing.

Apoptosis: Programmed cell death that results from the body's normal method of destroying damaged, unwanted, or unneeded cells characterized by fragmentation of nuclear DNA.

Area Under the Curve (AUC): (from zero to infinity) represents the total amount of a chemical absorbed by the body, irrespective of the rate of absorption.

Arthalgias: Pain in the joints.

Asphyxiant: A chemical causing suffocation either through pathologic interaction (Chemical Asphyxiant) with the living organism or displacement of oxygen (Simple Asphyxiant).

Asthenia: A feeling of weakness without, loss of strength.

Asthma: A chronic disease of the respiratory system in which the airway occasionally constricts, becomes inflamed, and is lined with excessive amounts of mucous, often in response to one or more triggers. Episodes may be triggered by such things as exposure to an environmental stimulant (or allergen), cold air, warm, moist air, exercise or exertion, or emotional stress.

Astrocyte: Star shaped cell; processes of this cell form a portion of the blood-brain barrier.

Ataxia: Staggering gait.

Atropine: Atropine a naturally occurring alkaloid of "atropa belladonna", is a competitive antagonist of muscarinic cholinergic receptors. It is used as an antidote for nerve agent poisoning.

Autocrine: Relating to stimulation of a specific receptor by a factor produced within the same cell.

Autosomal: Referring to all chromosomes other than the sex chromosomes X and Y.

Axon: Long and single process from the neuron cell body; carries impulses away from the cell body of the neuron; axons of sensory nerves carry information to the central nervous system; axons of motor nerves carry information to muscles and glands.

Axonopathy: Damage to axons; most often in the peripheral nervous system with resulting sensory and motor dysfunction.

Azoospermia: No sperm are measurable for an individual.

Bactericide: Any substance capable of killing bacteria.

Baroreceptor: Sensory nerve cell or sense organ that respond to changes in blood pressure.

Base excision repair: A cellular DNA repair mechanism that involves removing a single damaged nucleotide base and replacing it with the correct nucleotide base.

Basepair substitution: A type of mutation that involves the replacement of the correct nucleotide base with an incorrect nucleotide base. There are two subtypes of basepair substitutions: Transitions, an incorrect purine is substituted for the correct purine or an incorrect pyrimidine is substituted for the correct pyrimidine; transversion, a purine is substituted for a pyrimidine or vice versa.

Basophils: Type of white blood cell that releases inflammatory mediators that amplify the inflammatory response, especially histamine in allergic reactions.

Benign: Not malignant or recurrent. Often used to describe tumors that might grow in size but do not spread throughout the body.

Beta particle: A charged particle emitted from the nucleus of an atom, with a mass and charge equal to that of the electron, 0.000549 amu (atomic mass units). Beta particles are high-energy, high-speed electrons or positrons emitted by certain types of radioactive nuclei such as potassium-40.

Bioaccumulation: The accumulation or concentration of material in the body over a period of time usually from sources other than ingestion.

Bioactivation: When a parent compound is transformed into a toxic metabolite by biotransformation.

Bioamplification/Bio-magnification: The result of bioaccumulation in the organism by itself or in conjunction with continuous presence in the environment. The concentration may be substantially increased as higher organisms ingest lower forms.

Bioavailability: Refers to the ability of a substance to enter into the matrix of biologically directed absorption, distribution, metabolism, and excretion; the percentage of a toxicant that is absorbed into the systemic circulation.

Biocide: Refers to chemicals intentionally added to coating that retard or prevent the growth of various biological species.

Biogenic amine: Group of neurotransmitters in the central and autonomic nervous systems, including norepinephrine, epinephrine, dopamine, serotonin, and histamine.

Biological Exposure Index® (BEI®): Guidance values, developed and published by the American Conference of Governmental Industrial Hygienists (ACGIH), of biological monitoring results likely to be observed in specimens collected from healthy workers who have been exposed to chemicals to the same extent as workers with inhalation exposure at the Threshold Limit Value.

Biological factors: The Absorption, Distribution, Metabolism, and Elimination (ADME) processes, pre-existing conditions, and other variables that can be associated with differences in the exposure/dose relationship and adverse health outcomes between individuals.

Biological monitoring: Measurement and assessment of agents or their metabolites either in tissues, secreta, excreta, expired air or any combination of these to evaluate exposure.

Biomarker: Measurable properties of a biological system that are assayed to provide information about exposure to, biological effects of, or susceptibility to a toxicant.

Biomonitoring: A technique using analysis of biological specimens to assess human exposure to natural and synthetic chemicals.

Bio-persistence: Usually refers to a type of half-time in lung for respirable pollutants.

Biotransformation: The chemical modification of a chemical by biological processes by which a chemical is made more water-soluble, and (usually) more readily excretable.

Blastocyst: An embryo that is approximately five days old and consists of some 100 cells that form an outer layer surrounding a fluid core. The outer cells develop into the placenta, which protects the fetus and is created from the inner cells.

Blepharospasm: Tonic spasm of the eyelid muscle, producing more or less completes closure.

Blood-Brain barrier: An effective barrier that decreases the rate of absorption of many substances into brain tissue; consists of the cell processes of astrocytes that form close association with capillary endothelial cells.

B-lymphocytes: (Bursal-equivalent in man; develop in Bursa of Fabricius in birds) are responsible for humoral immunity via secretion of immunoglobulins.

Bradycardia: Slowness of the heart.

Bradykinesia: Abnormal slowness or sluggishness of physical and mental processes or movement.

Breathing zone (BZ): The volume surrounding a worker's nose and mouth from which he or she draws breathing air over the course of a work period. This zone can be pictured by inscribing a sphere with a radius of about 10 inches centered at the worker's nose.

British Anti-Lewisite (BAL: dimercaprol): A metal complexing (chelating) agent used in the treatment of lewisite, arsenic, gold, mercury and other metal exposures.

Bronchoconstriction: Acute response of narrowing of conducting airway caliber caused by constriction of smooth muscles in the airway walls. Bronchocontriction is controlled by both the central nervous system and by tissue inflammatory cells in airway walls that produce inflammatory proteins.

BZ: See quinuclidinyl benzilate.

Calcium homeostasis: The maintenance of calcium concentration at constant levels in the cell and extracellularly.

Carboxyhemoglobin: Formed by carbon monoxide binding to hemoglobin.

Carcinogen: A substance or agent capable of causing or producing cancer in mammals, including humans. A chemical is considered to be a carcinogen if: a) it has been evaluated by IARC and found to be a carcinogen or potential carcinogen; b) it is listed as a carcinogen or potential carcinogen in the Annual Report on Carcinogens published by the National Toxicology Program (NTP); or c) it is regulated by OSHA as a carcinogen.

Carcinogenesis: The development of malignant tumors or neoplasms composed of abnormal cells exhibiting uncontrolled growth, invasiveness, and metastasis.

Cell-mediated hypersensitivity: Also known as delayed-type hypersensitivity (DTH) or Type IV Hypersensitivity is an immune response that does not involve antibodies but rather involves the activation of macrophages, natural killer cells (NK), antigen-specific cytotoxic T-lymphocytes, and the release of various cytokines in response to an antigen.

Central nervous system (CNS): The brain and spinal cord.

Centromere: A region of a chromosome to which spindle traction fibers attach during mitosis and meiosis.

Chelating agents: Are chemical structures that bind to metals to make the metal more soluble in water.

Chemicals Abstract Service (CAS): An organization under the American Chemical Society. CAS abstracts and indexes chemical literature from throughout the world in "Chemical Abstracts." "CAS Numbers" are used to identify specific chemicals or mixtures.

Chemokines: A family of small cytokines, or proteins secreted by cells. Proteins are classified as chemokines according to shared structural characteristics such as small size (they are all approximately 8–10 kilodaltons in size), and the presence of four cysteine residues in conserved locations that are key to forming their 3 dimensional shape.

Chemoreceptor: A receptor responding to and mediating chemical stimuli (taste and smell).

Cholinergic syndrome: Symptoms resulting from the overstimulation of the cholinergic system at central and peripheral sites. May includes miosis, increased tracheobranchial secretions, laryngospasm, bronchial constriction, sweating, tremor, convulsions, urinary and fecal incontinence, muscle fasciculations, convulsions and seizures depending on exposure.

Chromosomal nondisjunction: The failure of the chromosomes to properly segregate during meiotic or mitotic anaphase, resulting in daughter cells with abnormal numbers of chromosomes.

Chromosomal translocation: A chromosome abnormality in which segments of chromosomes are rearranged to different chromosomal locations.

Chronic toxicity: Adverse health effects that can occur from prolonged, repeated exposure to relatively low levels of a substance; might have a chronic effect from an acute exposure.

Citric acid cycle: Also called the Krebs cycle or tricarboxylic acid cycle. It is the final metabolic process for the oxidation of acetyl groups from the major organic fuel molecules of the cell (carbohydrates, fatty acids, and amino acids) during catabolism.

Classic compartmental pharmacokinetics: Mathematical models of the movement of chemicals throughout the body based on compartments that do not necessarily represent organs or tissues in the body. See also physiologically-based pharmacokinetics.

Clastogen: An agent that causes breaks in chromosomes.

Clinical toxicologist: A medical toxicologist trained in emergency care capable of medically managing a poisoned patient.

Chloracne: A severe and sometimes persistent form of acne resulting from exposure to chlorine compounds, such as dioxin.

Choreoathetosis: The occurrence of involuntary movements in a combination of chorea (a kind of dance) and athetosis (writhing movements of the hands and feet).

Cochlea: The auditory part of the inner ear that contains the nerve cells that when damaged results in hearing impairment.

Codon: A group of three nucleotide bases that code for a specific amino acid in a protein. Genes are comprised of an ordered series of 3-base codons.

Cohort Study: The method of epidemiologic study in which subsets of a defined population can be identified who are, have been, or in the future might be exposed or not exposed — or exposed in different degrees — to a factor or factors hypothesized to influence the probability of occurrence of a given disease or other outcome.

Colony-stimulating factor (CSF): Cytokine which stimulates the committed stem cells to proliferate and mature into producing various white blood cells.

Complement: Soluble serum proteins that complement the action of antibodies in immune responses.

Composite materials: Strong and lightweight fiber reinforced polymeric composite materials used as structural alternatives to metals and other materials in aircraft and buildings.

Consensus standard: a standard generally accepted by a profession or group and established through input from one or more professional groups knowledgeable in the subject area of the standard. Such standards may or may not be adopted by regulatory agencies.

Concentration: The amount of a given substance in a stated unit of measure. Common methods of stating concentration are percent by weight or by volume; weight per unit volume; normality; etc.

Conducting airways: Serve to deliver air to the deep lung and the respiratory airways. Anatomically the conducting airways begin at the tip of the nose and end at the terminal bronchioles.

Congenital: Describes a condition acquired during in utero development and not through heredity.

Contact dermatitis: An acute or chronic inflammation of the skin resulting from irritation by or sensitizing to some substance coming in contact with the skin.

Contaminants: Non-endogenous materials, typically chemicals, found in soil, air or water.

Cross-sensitization: A condition in which sensitization to a chemically related molecule is acquired after sensitization to the

Curie: The special unit of radioactivity. One Curie equals 3.7×10^{10} nuclear transformations per second (1 transformation per second equals 1 Becquerel), equivalent to the activity of 1 gram of radium. A curie does not measure the energy or the type of radiation being released.

Cutaneous: Pertaining to the skin.

Cytochrome oxidase: An electron transport system located within the mitochondria of the cell.

Cytochrome P450 enzymes: A large group of cellular proteins that use both exogenous and endogenous compounds as substrates in enzymatic reactions; usually forms part of the electron transport chain; most common reaction catalyzed by cytochrome P450 is a monooxygenase reaction; usually associated with microsomal membranes.

Cytokine: A heterogeneous group of proteins and peptides that regulate crucial processes within a cell or between cells at the molecular level. Different from hormones, cytokines are not produced in specific glands or tissues, but basically in all cells. Cytokines are produced by T-lymphocytes and monocytes, which serve as local and distant cellular messengers and attractants. They are involved in both innate and adaptive immune responses.

Cytotoxic: Referring to toxic action directed at a cell rather than a tissue or organism.

Cytotoxicity: A fast, rather inexpensive test that provides good baseline information regarding cell-mediated effects. Both human and other mammalian cell lines are frequently used.

Defoliant: A preparation for removing leaves from plants.

De minimis risk: A risk that is so low as to be negligible (i.e., one case of disease per million persons exposed).

Delayed neuropathy: Describes the appearance of symptoms of weakness and even paralysis of the lower limbs one to two weeks after acute exposure to some neurotoxins.

Deletion mutation: The loss of a segment of genetic material from a chromosome. The size of the deletion can vary from a single nucleotide base to a section containing a number of genes.

Demyelination: Loss of myelin.

Dendrite: Relatively short and branching process from the cell body of the neuron; carries impulses toward the cell body of the neuron; receive stimuli from touch, pain, smell, and other neurons.

Depolarization: In electrophysiology, reversal of the resting potential in excitable cell membranes when stimulated.

Depurination: Hydrolysis of a purine base from the deoxyribose-phosphate backbone of DNA.

Depyrimidination: Hydrolysis of a pyrimidine base from the deoxyribose-phosphate backbone of DNA.

Dermal absorption: The transfer of contaminant across the skin and subsequent incorporation into the body.

Dermatitis: Is a blanket term literally meaning "inflammation of the skin." It is usually used to refer to eczema, which is also known as Dermatitis eczema. There are two general types: primary irritation dermatitis and sensitization dermatitis.

Descriptive toxicologist: An individual involved with assessing the safety of chemicals with protocols developed by regulatory agencies. A descriptive toxicologist is the individual responsible for overseeing toxicology studies and ensuring that the toxicity testing is properly performed.

Developmental toxicology: Is a subset of reproductive toxicology that focuses on agents that could cause abnormal development of the fertilized egg through the embryo, fetus, and the offspring all the way to maturity.

Dicumarol: A synthetic coumarin derivative, used chiefly to prevent blood coagulation and in the treatment of arterial thrombosis.

Diastole: The relaxation of a heart chamber during which it fills with blood.

Distal axonopathy: Damage to distal portion of the axon; often includes degeneration of myelin; often appears first in the axon terminal.

Distribution: The process by which a chemical is delivered to the organs and tissues of the body by the bloodstream.

Dioxin: A general name for a family of chlorinated hydrocarbons, typically used to refer to one isomer, TCDD, a by-product of pesticide manufacture: a toxic compound that is carcinogenic and teratogenic in certain animals.

DMPS: (2,3-dimercapto-1-propanesulfonic acid) a chelating agent that forms complexes with various heavy metals, used in the treatment of Lewisite poisoning.

DMSA: (meso-2,3-dimercaptosuccinnic acid) is an FDA approved chelating agent for lead toxicity, but has been shown clinically to detoxify other heavy metals as well. DMSA is also used in treatment for Lewisite exposure.

DNA adduct: A chemical covalently bound to a DNA nucleotide.

Dose: A term used interchangeably with dosage to express the amount of energy or substance absorbed in a unit volume of an organ or individual.

Dose adjustment: Modification of doses used in animal experimentation to equivalent levels for human beings. The usual method is to calculate the ratio of body weights raised to some power, which is roughly equivalent to the ratio of surface areas; a simple ratio of body weights has also been used.

Dose-response relationship: With increasing dose, greater biological effects (i.e., responses) will be elicited; that is to say a dose-response relationship can be demonstrated.

Draize test: Tests to assess skin or eye damage potential. A standardized scoring system originally developed by John Draize is used.

Efferent nerves: Nerves of the peripheral nervous system that carry information from the central nervous system to glands or muscles.

Electrophilic: The electron-attracting atom or agent in an organic reaction.

Elimination: The removal of a chemical from the body, either by metabolism or excretion via the kidneys, feces, lungs, breast milk or sweat.

Elimination half-life: The time it takes for one-half of a chemical in the body to be eliminated by metabolism or excretion.

Embryonic state: A period of intensive differentiation, mobilization, organization, and a majority of organogenesis and ranges from Gestation Days 8–56 in the human.

Emergency Response Planning Guide (ERPG): Values intended to provide estimates of concentration ranges above which one could reasonably anticipate observing adverse health effects. The documentation is contained in a series of guides produced by the Emergency Response Planning Committee of the American Industrial Hygiene Association.

Endocytotic: A process of cellular ingestion by which the plasma membrane folds inward to bring substances into the cell.

Endothelin: A vasoconstrictive peptide produced in the kidney.

Endotoxin: A lipopolysaccharide (LPS) located in the cell wall of gram-negative bacteria, which is released during cellular destruction.

Environmental persistence: The tendency to remain unchanged in the environment in original form.

Environmental toxicologist: A toxicologist trained to examine a wide range of adverse effects that chemicals have on organisms within an ecosystem.

Enzyme induction: A process by which an increase in the synthesis of a large protein molecule occurs, resulting in more of that protein being present in the cell.

Eosinophils: Type of white blood cell that releases inflammatory mediators that amplify the inflammatory response (particularly important in parasitic diseases).

Epidemiology: The science that deals with the incidence distribution and control of disease in a population.

Epidermis: In vertebrates, the outermost layer of the skin.

Epigenetic: Relating to, being, or involving a modification in gene expression that is independent of the DNA sequence of a gene.

Erethism: An abnormal irritability or responsiveness to stimulation, applied frequently to an irritable condition of the brain and nervous system.

Erythrocytes: Red blood cells (RBCs).

Erythropoietin (EPO): Cytokine produced to stimulate RBC production.

Etiology: The study or knowledge of the causes of disease.

Excretion: The removal of a chemical from the body via urine, feces, breast milk, sweat or expired air.

Exfoliation: The falling off in scales or layers of the skin.

Exon: A segment of DNA that is transcribed into the nuclear RNA (pre-mRNA) and that remains in mRNA after the removal of intron nucleotides.

Exposure: Contact of an organism with a chemical or physical agent, quantified as the amount of chemical available at the exchange boundaries of the organism and available for absorption. It is usually calculated as the mean exposure and some measure of maximum exposure. Also, the amount of an environmental agent that has reached the individual (external dose) or has been absorbed into the individual (internal dose or absorbed dose).

Exposure assessment: Determination or estimation (qualitative or quantitative) of the magnitude, frequency, duration, and route of exposure.

Fast acetylator: One of two main N-acetyltransferase phenotypes in humans.

Fetal programming: A concept relating fetal adjustments made in response to adverse changes in the biological environment during development. Such adjustments may have been advantageous in fetal life, but also have permanent consequences that may confer disease or dysfunction after birth.

Fetal stage: A major period of growth and functional maturation in development and ranges from Gestation Days 56–267 in the human.

Fibrosis: The development in an organ of excess fibrous connective tissue usually as a reparative or reactive process.

Fick's laws of diffusion: This law describes diffusion and can be used to solve for the diffusion coefficient, which is a proportionality constant between the mass flux due to diffusion and the gradient in the concentration of the species undergoing diffusion.

Follicicle stimulating hormone (FSH): Promotes development of egg and follicle in ovary of females and sperm production in males.

Folliculitis: The inflammation of one or more hair follicles. The condition may occur anywhere on the skin.

Forensic toxicologist: Individuals trained in the medical and legal aspects of toxicology that work with medical examiners in establishing cause of death in situations involving poisonings.

Frameshift mutation: A mutation caused by inserting or deleting one or a small number of nucleotides from the protein-coding region of DNA. Frameshifts result in a change in reading frame when mRNA is made from DNA, thus causing an incorrect sequence of amino acids in the protein product.

Free radicals: Atoms or molecules with an unpaired electron; highly reactive chemicals.

Fungicide: A substance or preparation, as a spray or dust, used for destroying fungi.

Gamma ray: Short wavelength electromagnetic radiation of nuclear origin (range of energy from 10 KeV to 9 MeV) emitted from the nucleus.

Gamma-aminobutyric Acid (GABA): An amino acid that serves as a neurotransmitter throughout the nervous system; it is inhibitory in nature.

Ganglion: A group of nerve cells that allows communication between the central nervous system and muscle and gland cells through preganglionic and postganglionic neurons.

Gastrulation: The process whereby the cells of the blastocyst are translocated to establish three germ layers. Also, it is sometimes used as the mark of the end of the blastocyst stage and the beginning of the next stage of embryonic development.

Gene amplification: The process, which specific DNA replicates, sequences causing the inclusion of one or more repeated segments in DNA.

Genotoxicity: The process of causing alteration or damage to the DNA or chromosomes.

Glomerulus: The structure within in the nephron where primary urine is filtered from blood plasma through special permeable capillaries.

Glutathione: A key cellular antioxidant tripeptide containing cysteine, glutamine and glycine. The sulfhydryl group on cysteine (-SH) interacts with reactive, electrophilic sites on oxidants and damaged macromolecules.

Good Laboratory Practice (GLP): A set of standardized practices and procedures designed to ensure that testing is performed in a high quality manner. Defined in 21 CFR 58.

Granulocytes: White blood cells so-named due to their prominent cytoplasmic granules seen microscopically.

Gray: The newer SI unit for a Rad is a Gray, abbreviated Gy, where one Gy = 100 Rad.

Haber's Law: The Haber relationship expresses the constancy of the product of exposure concentration and exposure duration (Ct = K, where C represents exposure concentration, t is time, and K is constant). The Haber relationship does not hold over more than small differences in exposure time.

Habituation: The process of getting used to a stimulus over time, increasing the threshold to strong stimuli, decreasing it to the weaker ones.

Haemangiosarcoma: A rare malignant neoplasm characterized by rapidly proliferating, extensively infiltrating, anaplastic cells derived from blood vessels and the lining of irregular blood-filled or lumpy spaces.

Half-life: Description of an agent's persistence in a biological system; the time required for its concentration to drop by 50%.

Hatch-Choate equation: In 1929, Hatch and Choate developed mathematical tools to derive higher moments (mass, surface area, volume) based on the count median diameter (weighted distributions). The premise of the equations is that the distribution is perfectly lognormal. Any deviation from lognormal will induce error. Derivation of the Hatch-Choate equations can be found in many aerosol textbooks.

Hazard: The capability of a substance to cause an adverse effect.

Hazard Communications Standard (HCS): 29 CFR 1910.1200., Sometimes referred to as the Worker Right-to-Know Legislation, or more often just as the Right-to-Know law. Although the original HCS applied only to the manufacturing industry, subsequent court challenges have modified the scope of the law so that today the HCS applies to nearly all sectors or the work force.

Hazard identification: Determining whether a chemical can cause adverse health effects in humans and what those effects might be.

Hematopoietic stem cell (HSC): Pleuripotent cell in the bone marrow, which can develop into any of the blood cell types. It occurs by first differentiating into a progenitor cell.

Hepatoma: A tumor of the liver.

Hemoglobin (Hb): An abundant metalloprotein for transporting oxygen in red blood cells.

Hepatomegaly: Enlargement of the liver.

Herbicide: A substance or preparation for killing plants, especially weeds.

Hippocampus: Part of the brain involved in acquiring memories; part of the limbic system, which has a role in emotions.

Homocysteine: An amino acid used normally by the body in cellular metabolism. Elevated concentrations in the blood are thought to increase the risk for heart disease by damaging the lining of blood vessels and enhancing blood clotting.

Homologous recombination repair: An event in which the two chromosomes of a chromosome pair exchange identical or nearly identical stretches of chromosomal material.

Hprt gene: A gene coding for hypoxanthine-guanine phosphoribosyltransferase (HPRT), which primarily functions in the nucleoside salvage pathway whereby purines are made from degraded DNA.

Hypovolemic shock: Is a particular form of shock in which the heart is unable to supply enough blood to the body. It may be a consequence of exposure to a large dose of Lewisite.

Hypoxemia: Inadequate oxygenation of the blood.

ICt$_{50}$: Incapacitating Concentration 50 — the concentration of a substance that will incapacitate 50% of the group exposed.

Immediately dangerous to life and Health (IDLH): Defined by NIOSH as exposure to airborne contaminants that is "likely to cause death or immediate or delayed permanent adverse health effects or prevent escape from such an environment."

Immunoglobulin: Protein produced by B-lymphocytes, which recognizes and binds to foreign antigens. Also known as an antibody.

in vitro: Literally means "in glass;" experimental work done on cell cultures.

in vivo: Literally means "in life;" an experiment that was conducted in the living organism.

Incident Response System (ICS): A management system used to organize emergency response. ICS offers a scalable response to an emergency (incident) of any magnitude, and provides a common framework within which people can work together

Initiation: The first stage of tumor induction by a carcinogen; subtle alteration of cells by exposure to a carcinogenic agent so that they are likely to form a tumor upon subsequent exposure to a promoting agent (promotion).

Innate immunity: The part of the immune system that is present at birth, and requires no prior exposure to foreign proteins or microorganisms to function.

Insecticide: A substance or preparation for killing insects.

Insertion mutation: A mutation caused by the addition of one or more nucleotide bases into the DNA.

Integrate Risk Information System (IRIS): U.S. EPA database containing verified reference doses (RfDs), slope factors, and current health and regulatory information. It is the EPA's preferred source of toxicity information for Superfund.

Interstitial cell stimulating hormone (ICSH): Interstitial cell stimulating hormone acts on the testes to produce and control testosterone, the primary male sex hormone. Testosterone is also required for sperm production.

Intron: A segment of DNA within a gene that is transcribed into nuclear RNA (pre-mRNA), but is subsequently removed from the nascent mRNA molecule and rapidly degraded.

Inulin: A high molecular weight polysaccharide that is filtered in the glomerulus, but not reabsorbed in the nephron. Inulin is used to determine glomerular filtration rate.

Inversion mutation: A mutation caused by a section of DNA that has reversed direction.

Irritant: A chemical, which is not corrosive, that causes a reversible inflammatory effect on living tissue by chemical action at the site of contact.

Irritant dermatitis: A non-immune related response caused by the direct action of a substance on the skin.

Irritants (respiratory): Any material that elicits irritant responses in the nose (sensory irritant) or lung (pulmonary irritant). All irritants initiate inflammatory and adverse physiological responses, and may also cause cytotoxicity. Sensory and pulmonary irritants differ in their site of action and types of neural pathways that are activated.

Isotope: 1. Two or more nuclides with the same atomic number but different atomic mass. 2. Atoms of the same element that differ in atomic weight.

Juxtaglomerular apparatus: A group of specialized cells positioned on the afferent arteriole next to Bowman's capsule. These cells produce renin.

Keratinocytes: The major cell type of the epidermis, making up about 90% of epidermal cells.

Kinetochore: The protein structure in eukaryotes, which assembles on the centromere and links the chromosome to microtubule polymers from the mitotic spindle during mitosis and meiosis.

Knudsen number: A dimensionless number, which represents the ratio between the mean free path and the particle radius. Knudsen numbers divide motion into four flow regimes, which are: continuum, slip, transition, and free-molecular.

Langerhan's cell: Are dendritic cells abundant in epidermis containing large granules called Birbeck granules, can be found in other organs in the condition Histiocytosis. Named after German anatomist and physician Paul Langerhans (1847–1888) who described it in skin.

Larvicide: An agent for killing larvae.

Latency Period: Time between exposure to a toxic chemical and onset of the symptoms of poisoning.

Lesch-Hyhan syndrome: A rare, inherited neurodegenerative disease caused by a mutation in the HPRT gene which results in a deficiency of the enzyme, hypoxanthine-guanine phosphoribosyltransferase.

Lethal concentration "X" (LC_X): The concentration that was lethal to X percent of test animals. It may be expressed, for example, as LC_{50}, LC_{10}, etc.; these would represent the concentrations producing deaths in 50%, 10%, etc., of the exposed animals, respectively.

Lethal dose "X" (LD_X): The dose that was lethal to X percent of test animals. It is the amount of a chemical, per unit of body weight that will cause death in X percent of test animals. Most commonly used as LD_{50}, the dose producing deaths in 50% of the exposed animals.

Leukotriene: Inflammatory soluble protein mediator formerly known as slow reacting substance of anaphylaxis, released by inflammatory cells as part of immune response.

Lipid peroxidation: When free radicals and other xenobiotics attack the fatty acids, removing hydrogen atoms and converting the fatty acids into free radicals themselves; these free radicals then react with oxygen to form more free radicals and unstable peroxides.

Lowest Observed Adverse Exposure Level (LOAEL): Lowest exposure level at which there are statistically or biologically significant increases in frequency or severity of adverse effects between the exposed population and its appropriate control group.

Lowest Observed Effect Level (LOEL): Lowest dose observed that caused an effect on the organism exposed.

Loop of Henle: Part of the nephron consisting of a descending tubule (extending away from the glomerulus) and an ascending part (returning towards the glomerulus and ending in a collecting duct).

Loss of heterozygosity: The loss of one of two different alleles from the chromosome.

Luteinizing hormone (LH): Hormone acts on cells of the developing follicle to produce estrogen, the primary female sex hormone and is involved in ovulation.

Lymphocytes: Type of white blood cells involved in the immune response.

Lymphoid progenitor cell: Develops into the various types of lymphocytes (B, T, NK).

Macrophage: Type of white blood cell that is involved in phagocytizing (engulfing) foreign proteins and microorganisms. Macrophages respond to infection or toxic stimuli by signaling the recruitment of inflammatory cells from circulating blood.

Major histocompatibility complex (MHC): Protein antigens on the surface of most cells of the human body, which is unique to the individual, and is the primary way the body distinguishes self from non-self. Close matching of these antigens is what allows a "match" for organ transplantation.

Malignant: Tending to become progressively worse and to lead to death; often used to describe tumors that grow in size and also spread throughout the body.

Malodorant: Materials that activate specific olfactory receptors and can induce nausea and vomiting. The difference between malodorants and sensory irritants in the specific neural pathways they activate.

Mast cells: Tissue-based immune cell, which releases inflammatory mediators that amplify the inflammatory response, especially important in allergic responses.

Material Safety Data Sheet (MSDS): A document containing information on a specific chemical substance's hazardous ingredients, their properties, and precautions for use.

Mechanistic toxicologist: A research toxicologist who examines the various pathways or mechanisms involved in chemical toxicities.

Mechanoreceptor: Sensory nerve cell or sense organ that responds to mechanical stimuli, such as sound or light waves, pressure, stretching, etc.

Medical surveillance: The systematic collection, analysis, and evaluation of health data in the workplace to identify cases, patterns, or trends suggesting an adverse effect on workers' health. Medical surveillance can be used to evaluate the effectiveness of control activities.

Membrane potential: The electric voltage (generally in the order of magnitude of 0.1 volt) that exists across the outer membrane of living cells, established by an asymmetrical distribution of ions between the inside and outside.

Mesothelioma: A form of cancer that is almost always caused by previous exposure to asbestos.

Metabolism: Biotransformation; the process by which a chemical is made more water-soluble, and (usually) more readily excretable.

Metal toxicity: Metal toxicity is an excessive build-up of metals in the body. Oftentimes, the vague symptoms produced by heavy metal toxicity are mistakenly misdiagnosed as incurable chronic conditions.

Metastasis: The transfer of disease from one organ or part to another not directly connected with it. It may be due either to the transfer of pathogenic microorganisms (for example, tubercle bacilli) or to transfer of cells, as in malignant tumors. The capacity to metastasize is a characteristic of all malignant tumors.

Methemoglobin: Produced when iron in hemoglobin is oxidized to the ferric state; has no oxygen binding ability.

Micronucleus: A second small nucleus that results when either a section of chromosome or a whole chromosome fails to be incorporated into the nucleus during cell division.

Miosis: Contraction of the pupil.

Missense mutation: A single-base mutation in DNA resulting in a single amino acid change in the encoded protein, generally altering the function of the resulting protein.

Miticide: A substance or preparation for killing mites.

Modifying factor: Used in converting NOAELs/LOAELs to reference doses (RfDs). Range from >0 to 10, reflects professional judgment of uncertainties not addressed by uncertainty factors.

Molluscide: A substance or preparation for killing mollusks (snails).

Monosomy: The loss of one chromosome from a pair of chromosomes.

Morbidity and Mortality Weekly Report (MMWR): A publication of the Centers for Disease Control and Prevention (CDC). The data in the weekly MMWR are provisional, based on weekly reports to CDC by state health departments.

Mucous: Viscous secretion that consists of water, mucin glycoproteins and a variety of anti-inflammatory and antiseptic proteins. The mucus layer in airways consists of two layers, an a aqueous, or sol phase which surrounds the cilia of epithelial cells, and viscous gel phase, which contains mucin glycoproteins and rides atop the sol phase.

Muscarinic blocker: Substance that binds to muscarinic receptors, blocking the binding of acetylcholine.

Muscarinic sites: Muscarinic receptors are found in all effector cells stimulated by the postganglionic neurons of the parasympathetic nervous system as well as in those stimulated by postganglionic cholinergic neurons of the sympathetic system.

Mutagen: A substance or agent capable of altering the genetic material in a living cell.

Mutagenesis: The process involved in producing mutations, the occurrence or induction of mutations.

Mutation: A genetic alteration that is heritable to daughter and granddaughter cells.

Mycotoxin: A toxin produced from a fungus. Mycotoxins may be produced when foodstuffs (e.g. hay, grain), or other materials (e.g. wood, drywall) become moldy. Satratoxins are an example of mycotoxins produced by stachybotrys.

Myelin: Electrically non-conducting fatty substance surrounding nerve fibers.

Myelin sheath: Concentric layers of cell membrane around the nerve cell axon; serves as a good insulator, allowing easy movement of ions into and out of the axon, facilitating the propagation of the action potential.

Myelinopathy: Damage to the myelin.

Myloid progenitor cell: Gives rise to monocytes, neutrophils, eosinophils and basophils, erythrocytes and platelets.

N-acetyltranferase: A type of enzyme that helps metabolize drugs and other chemicals through the addition of an acetyl group. In humans, there are fast and slow acetylator phenotypes.

Narcosis: State of stupor or unconsciousness produced by the influence of narcotics or other chemicals.

National Response Plan (NRP): A unified and standardized approach for protecting citizens and managing homeland security incidents within the United States. The NRP is being replaced by the National Response Framework (NRF), which serves the same function.

Natural Killer (NK) cells: "Natural Killer cells" are a type of lymphocyte that can kill tumor cells, microorganisms, and virally infected cells.

Neoplasia: The process of tumor formation.

Nephron: The functional unit of the kidney consisting of the glomerulus within Bowman's capsule, the proximal and distal convoluted tubules, the loop of Henle with the descending and ascending tubules, and the collecting duct.

Neuron: Component of the autonomic nervous system; when stimulated, it causes many of the opposite effects of stimulation of the sympathetic nervous system, such as decrease in heart rate, constriction of bronchioles, constriction of the pupil, increase in activity of digestive smooth muscle, and an increase in secretions from glands.

Neurasthenic: Relating to toxicity of the central nervous system that results in impaired functioning in interpersonal relationships; includes fatigue, depression, and headaches.

Neuroglia: Supporting cells of the nervous system; includes oligodendrocytes, Schwann cells, and astrocytes.

Neuronopathy: Degeneration of the entire nerve cell, including dendrites and axons; can be caused by toxic substances.

Neuropathy: Functional disturbance or pathology of the nervous system; may be central (affecting the brain or spinal cord) or peripheral (affecting nerves outside the brain and spinal cord).

Neuropathy target esterase (NTE): Esterase present in peripheral lymphocytes and the nervous system that is used to predict the development of OPIDP. Neuropathy target esterase (NTE) is an integral membrane protein present in all neurons and in some non-neural-cell types of vertebrates.

Neuropeptide: Acts as a neurotransmitter, but at much lower concentration and its actions last much longer than other neurotransmitters; affects membrane potential or is released along with another neurotransmitter, altering its release or binding; includes opioid peptides.

Neurotoxic esterase: The esterase enzyme that is inhibited during delayed neuropathy caused by some organophosphate compounds; different from acetylcholinesterase.

Neurotransmitter: A chemical messenger (such as norepinephrine or acetylcholine) released at the end of an axon by the stimulation of an action potential.

Neutron: Elementary nuclear particle with the mass about the same as a proton, but that is electrically neutral and a mass of 1.008 amu.

Neutrophil: Type of white blood cell (WBC) that engulfs foreign proteins and microorganisms. They are the most common granular leukocyte and an early responder to infection or an inflammatory stimulus. Neutrophils rapidly move from the circulation and into tissues where they can produce inflammatory mediators including reactive oxidants.

Nicotinic receptor: Receptor that normally binds acetylcholine, but it binds to and is stimulated by nicotine; found in the central nervous system and in the neuromuscular junction.

Nicotinic sites: Denoting the effect of nicotine and other drugs in initially stimulating and subsequently, in high doses, inhibiting neural impulses at autonomic ganglia and neuromuscular junction.

No Observed Adverse Effect Level (NOAEL): Exposure level at which there are no statistically or biologically significant increases in frequency or severity, or any adverse effects when the exposed population is compared to its appropriate control group.

Nociception: Perception of harmful or hurtful, i.e., noxious stimuli.

No Observed Effect Level (NOEL): That quantity of a chemical to which laboratory animals are chronically exposed (expressed in parts per million [ppm] in their diets or mg/kg of body weight) that produces no effect when compared with control animals.

Nonhomologous end-joining repair: A pathway used to repair double-strand breaks in DNA by directly joining the broken ends of DNA without the need for a homologous template.

Nonsense mutation: A basepair substitution mutation in the protein-coding region of DNA that results in a premature stop to the synthesis of the protein product. Generally nonsense mutation results in a truncated non-functional protein.

Nucleotide excision repair: A DNA repair mechanism that recognizes bulky distortions in the shape of the DNA double helix, remove a short single-stranded DNA segment including the lesion to create a single-strand gap in the DNA, and subsequently fills in the gap using DNA polymerase and the undamaged strand as a template.

Nystagmus: Involuntary rhythmic movements of the eye(s).

Occupational Asthma: A response characterized by hyper-responsiveness and/or airflow limitation resulting from exposure to substances primarily found in the workplace. Examples of these substances would include isocyanates, wood dusts and latex.

Occupational Exposure Limits (OELs): Exposure limits designed to protect healthy workers from overexposure to chemicals and physical agents in the workplace. Two examples of published OELs are the OSHA Permissible Exposure Limits (PELs) and the Threshold Limit Values (TLV®s) developed by the American Conference of Governmental Industrial Hygienists (ACGIH). Many corporations also develop their own internal standards, which are more stringent than the existing regulatory

Olfactory: Relating to the sense of smell.

Oligodendrocyte: Sends out processes that surround nerve cell axons in the central nervous system, forming the myelin sheath.

Oligospermia: The sperm count is lower than normal.

Oncogene: A gene that can contribute to development of cancer when mutated.

Opsonization: A means to enhance the susceptibility of bacterial cells to phagocytosis.

Organogenesis: The time period during embryonic development in which all major organs and organ systems are formed. During this period, the embryo is most susceptible to factors interfering with development and begins with formation of the neural plate, around human Gestation Days 21–56.

Organophosphate-induced delayed polyneuropathy (OPIDP): Caused by some organophosphorus compounds and characterized by flaccid paralysis of the lower limbs with involvement of the upper limbs in severe cases. The sensory peripheral nervous system is also affected, but to a smaller degree. Other symptoms may include the lack of coordination, ataxia, and spasticity.

Oxidative phosphorylation: The process of metabolic degradation of simple metabolic entities (particularly acetate) into carbon dioxide associated with the production of metabolic energy (adenosine triphosphate).

Oxime: A compound having the following general structure: $R_2C=NOH$ (R = alkyl group); formed by action of hydroxylamine on aldehydes or ketones; used as antidotes for nerve agents, such as pralidoxime; reactivates acetylcholinesterase by attaching to the phosphorus atom and forming an oxime-phosphonate which then splits away from the acetylcholinesterase molecule.

Oxon: An organic compound derived from another chemical in which a phosphorus-sulfur bond in the parent chemical has been replaced by a phosphorus-oxygen bond in the derivative. The oxons then inhibit an enzyme that breaks down acetylcholine.

Oxygen radical: An oxygen molecule with an unpaired electron, which makes it very reactive with other molecules and proteins. Interaction of oxygen radicals with cellular proteins, lipids or DNA can compromise their function and cause toxicity.

Paracrine: Relating to stimulation of a specific receptor by a factor produced not within the same cell, but in a spatially close-by cell.

Paraoxonase: Enzyme that hydrolyzes organophosphates such as in some insecticides.

Parasympathetic nervous system: Component of the autonomic nervous system; when stimulated, it causes many of the opposite effects of stimulation of the sympathetic nervous system, such as decrease in heart rate, constriction of bronchioles, constriction of the pupil, increase in activity of digestive smooth muscle, and an increase in secretions from glands.

Paresthesia: Sensation of pricking, tingling, or creeping on the skin; due to spontaneous action potentials arising in demyelinated neurons.

Pediculicide: A substance or preparation for killing lice.

Peripheral nervous system: All the nerves outside the central nervous system.

Peripheral neuropathy: Damage to the peripheral nervous system; occurs often through demyelination.

Peristalsis: Successive waves of involuntary contraction passing along the walls of the intestine.

Permissible Exposure Limit (PEL): Established by OSHA (see 29 CFR 1910.1000, Subpart Z). The permissible concentration in air of a substance to which nearly all workers may be repeatedly exposed 8 hours a day, 40 hours a week, for 30 years without adverse effects.

Personal sampling: The collection of airborne chemicals in the worker's breathing zone by having the worker wear sampling equipment throughout the workday.

Pesticide: A chemical preparation for destroying plant, fungal, or animal pests; a biocide.

Phagocytosis: Ability of certain cells to surround and engulf foreign material or organisms, and then secrete chemicals to destroy these foreign invaders.

Pharmacodynamic(s): The study of the biochemical and physiological effects of drugs, their mechanisms of action, and the relationships between drug concentration and effect ("what a drug does to the organism").

Pharmacokinetics: The study of the uptake, distribution, metabolism, and excretion of substances in an organism or system ("what the body does to a drug"). Also, mathematical descriptions of the movement of a drug or chemical throughout the body over time; includes the processes of absorption, distribution, metabolism, and excretion; often used interchangeably with the word toxicokinetics.

Phase I and II detoxification enzymes: Two different groups of enzymes involved in detoxifying waste products and foreign materials; phase I enzymes add single nitrogen or oxygen molecules preparing the structure for reaction with phase II enzymes; phase II enzymes bind the altered chemical to another substance, such as glutathione, forming conjugates that are more polar, and therefore more water soluble, and more readily excreted in the urine.

Pheromone: Any chemical substance released by an animal that serves to influence the physiology or behavior of other members of the same species; an attractant.

Photosensitization: Reaction to light that causes the skin to become sensitive. Photosensitivity includes two types of reactions: phototoxicity and photoallergy. Phototoxicity is more common and affects all individuals if the UV dose or the dose of the photosensitizer is high enough. Photoallergy is an acquired altered reactivity in the exposed skin resulting from an immunologic response.

Physical-chemical models: Equations based upon first principles incorporating the physical and chemical properties of agents that predict airborne concentrations.

Physiologically-based pharmacokinetics (PBPK): Mathematical models (pharmacokinetic models) of the movement of chemicals through body organs or tissues using known or estimated physiological parameters such as organ blood flow.

Physostigmine: A reversible anticholinesterase derived from Calabar (*Physositgma venenosum*) beans. Used in the treatment of quinuclidinyl benzilate (BZ or QNB) exposure. Carbamate insecticides are chemical analogues of physostigmine.

Pneumonconiosis (pneumoconiosis): A chronic disease of the lungs resulting from the inhalation of various kinds of dusts. The pneumoconioses that include siderosis (iron oxide), silicosis (free silica), asbestosis (asbestos), etc., generally require a period of years for development.

Polydisperse: Particles of more than one diametric size are contained within the aerosol.

Polymorphism: Having multiple alleles of a gene within a population, usually expressing different phenotypes.

Polypeptide: The formation of a chain of amino acids which are connected through peptide bonds. A peptide bond is formed between the carboxyl group of one amino acid and the amino group of another amino acid.

Polypoidy: The presence of more than two homologous sets of chromosomes in a cell.

Postsynaptic membrane: The cell membrane of the stimulated neuron or tissue cell.

Potentiation: When the toxicity of a substance on a particular tissue is significantly increased by another substance that alone has no toxic effect on that tissue.

Precautionary principle: Principle in which one is cautioned to err on the side of safety; the burden of proof is in demonstrating safety rather than an adverse income before taking action. Accordingly, conservatism is traded for data.

Presbycusis: The hearing loss normally occurring due to age because of the degeneration of the nerve cells due to the ordinary wear and tear of the aging process.

Presynaptic terminal: The end of the axon in the synapse.

Progenitor cell: A stem cell committed to developing into any of the various types of blood cell lines.

Progesterone: Is produced by the corpus luteum of the ovary after ovulation and is the hormone necessary for the maintenance of pregnancy.

Progression: A series of discrete changes in the evolution of a tumor characterized by karyotypic instability and generally results in increasing malignancy.

Promotion: Stimulation of tumor induction, following initiation, by a promoting agent, which may of itself be non-carcinogenic.

Proprioception: The perception of self, including the organism's and its extremities' positions.

Proteomics: The study of proteins, proteomics is the next step after genomics in discovering protein pathway and sequencing.. The term proteomics is derived from "genomics" and "protein."

Prothrombin: A plasma protein involved in blood coagulation that on activation by factors in the plasma is converted to thrombin.

Proton: Elementary nuclear particle with a positive electric charge equal numerically to the charge of the electron and a mass of 1.007277 mass units.

Proximal axonopathy: Damage to portion of axon closer to the neuronal cell body; results in giant axonal swelling because the transport of proteins from the cell body to the rest of the axon is blocked.

Psoralen: (Also called psoralene) is the parent compound in a family of natural products known as furocoumarins. It is structurally related to coumarin by the addition of a fused furan ring, and may be considered as a derivative of umbelliferone. It is widely used in PUVA (=Psoralen +UVA) treatment for psoriasis, eczema and vitiligo.

Pulmonary edema: Extravascular accumulation of fluid in pulmonary tissues and air spaces.

Pyridostigmine bromide: A reversible cholinesterase inhibitor used in the treatment of myasthemia gravis and as a "pretreatment" of organophosphate poisoning.

Quality factor: A multiplying factor used with absorbed dose to convert to dose equivalent and therefore to express the radiation's effectiveness in causing biological effects.

Quinuclidinyl benzilate (BZ or QNB): A chemical warfare agent that affects the cholinergic activity in both the peripheral and central nervous systems. It is considered to be a hallucinogenic.

Radiation: The emission and propagation of energy through space. Ionizing radiation is any radiation capable of producing ion pairs, directly or indirectly, in its passage through matter.

Radiation absorbed dose (RAD): The unit of absorbed dose. One rad equals 100 ergs per gram, or 0.01 Joule per kilogram.

Radioactive half-life: Time required for a radioactive substance to lose 50 percent of its activity by decay. Each radionuclide has a distinctive half-life.

Radioactivity: The property of certain nuclides of spontaneously emitting particles or gamma radiation or of emitting x irradiation following orbital electron capture or of undergoing spontaneous fission. Each nuclide has a unique emission spectrum.

Radionuclide: A species of atom characterized by instability, and the emission of radiation to achieve a more stable state.

Reactive oxygen species: Inorganic or organic oxidizing agents including oxygen ions, free radicals and peroxides. They are molecules that contain oxygen that has an unstable electron configuration, which makes them highly reactive with cellular molecules and proteins.

Recommended Exposure Limit (REL): An occupational exposure limit recommended by NIOSH as being protective of worker health and safety over a working lifetime. The REL is used in combination with engineering and work practice controls, exposure and medical monitoring, labeling, posting, worker training, and personal protective equipment.

Redistribution: The process by which a chemical moves from an organ or tissue of the body back into the bloodstream, making it available for excretion or delivery to other organs or tissues.

Regulatory toxicologist: A toxicologist generally employed by the state or federal government. They use the risk assessment process to establish exposure levels for various chemicals, such as the establishment of standards for the amount of chemicals permitted in ambient air, in drinking water or in occupational environments.

Renin/angiotensin: A substantive part of the kidney's blood pressure self-regulation. Renin is a proteolytic enzyme that activates angiotensinogen to the biologically active angiotensin.

Repolarization: Restitution of the membrane potential to its resting value following a depolarization event. Repolarization results from the movement of ions across the cell membrane against a concentration gradient at the expense of metabolic energy.

Resting membrane potential (RMP): The RMP is the charge difference that exists across the nerve cell membrane during the resting phase.

Reynold's number: A dimensionless number proportional to pipe or duct diameter, velocity, and density of fluid, and inversely proportional to the viscosity of the fluid. A Reynolds number greater than 2500 indicates turbulent flow; less than 2500, it indicates streamlined flow.

Risk: Probability and magnitude of harm. For exposures to chemicals, risk is a function of both exposure and toxicity.

Risk assessment: The process of determining, either quantitatively or qualitatively, the probability and magnitude of an undesired event and estimating the cost to human society or the environment in terms of morbidity, mortality, or economic impact.

Rodenticide: A substance or preparation for killing rodents.

Roentgen equivalent man (REM): Common measurement for internal dose that includes the quality factor for various forms of the same energy levels. The dose equivalent in rems is numerically equal to the absorbed dose in rads multiplied by the quality factor and any other necessary modifying factors. This unit allows doses of different forms of radiation to be directly comparable.

Sarin: (GB: Isopropyl methylphosphonofluoridate), an organophosphate nerve agent.

Scabicide: A substance or preparation destructive to the organisms causing scabies.

Schiff base: A functional group consisting of a carbon-nitrogen double bond with the nitrogen atom connected to an aryl or alkyl group-but not to a hydrogen atom.

Schwann cell: Surrounds nerve cell axons in the peripheral nervous system, forming the myelin sheath.

Selectivity: Preference of a drug for one mechanism of action over others that cause side effects; targeting of a pesticide for one species and having few side effects in other species.

Senescense: The phenomenon whereby normal diploid differentiated cells lose the ability to divide.

Sensitization: Induction of the ability of the body to produce an immunological response to a substance. More substances are known to elicit dermal sensitization than those exhibiting pulmonary counterparts.

Sequestration: When toxic substances are deposited or stored in certain tissues for long periods of time.

Sievert: The SI unit of any of the quantities expressed as dose equivalent. The dose equivalent in sieverts is equal to the absorbed dose in gray multiplied by the quality factor (1 Sv = 100 rem).

Signal transduction: The cascade of processes by which an extracellular signal (typically a hormone or neurotransmitter) interacts with a receptor at the cell surface, causing a change in the level of a second messenger and ultimately effects a change in the cells functioning.

Silent mutation: A mutation that has no effect on the functioning of the cell.

Sister chromatid exchange (SCE): The exchange of genetic material between the two copies of a chromosome in a cell.

Slimicide: A substance or preparation for killing slime molds, fungus-like organisms.

Slope factor: Plausible upper-bound estimate of the probability of a response per unit intake of a chemical over a lifetime. The slope factor is used to estimate an upper-bound probability of an individual developing cancer as a result of a lifetime of exposure to a particular level of a potential carcinogen.

Slow acetylator: One of two main N-acetyl transferase phenotypes in humans.

Solvent Neurotoxic Syndrome: Describes the major symptoms of the central nervous system when affected by exposure to a mixture of volatile organic solvents; also called painters' syndrome, chronic toxic encephalopathy, or psycho-organic syndrome.

Soman: (GD: Pinacolyl methylphosphonofluoridate), an organophosphate nerve agent.

Specificity: The selective attachment or influence of one substance on another, as an antibiotic and its target organism or an antibody and its specific antigen.

Spermatogenesis: The formation of spermatozoa, including spermatocytogenesis and spermiogenesis.

Splenomegaly: Enlargement of the spleen.

Spore: A nonvegetative form assumed by some bacteria and fungi, typically under conditions that do not support growth that is resistant to heat, drying, or chemicals.

Standard: The maximum concentration of a chemical to which human exposure is considered safe; expressed in ppm, ppb, mg/m^3, or comparable units.

Stochastic effects: Radiation effects, generally occurring without a threshold level of dose, whose probability is proportional to the dose and whose severity is independent of the dose. Typically, cancer is the effect of concern.

Stokes' law: This law predicts the settling velocity of small spheres in fluid, either air or water.

Stratum corneum: ("The horny layer") is the outermost layer of the epidermis (the outermost layer of the skin). It is composed mainly of dead cells that lack nuclei. As these dead cells slough off, they are continuously replaced by new cells from the stratum germinativum (basale). In the human forearm, for example, about 1300 $cells/cm^2/hr$ are shed and commonly accumulate as house dust.

Structure activity relationship (SAR): The relationship between the chemical structure of a substance and its toxicological effects. In radiation, SAR is "specific absorption rate."

Sub-chronic toxicity: Exposure to a toxicant for an intermediate period of time (5–90 days).

Subcutaneous injection: Injection beneath the skin.

Subfertility: Pregnancy is achieved but more than 1 year of unprotected intercourse was required to attain the pregnancy.

Sulfhemoglobin: Produced when sulfur binds to the heme moiety in hemoglobin; has no oxygen carrying capacity.

Sympathetic nervous system: Component of the autonomic nervous system; when stimulated, it causes the "fight or flight" response, which includes increase in heart rate, dilatation of bronchioles, dilation of the pupil, constriction of peripheral blood vessels, and a decrease in digestive system activity.

Synapse: Special sub-cellular structure that allows transmission of nerve impulses from one nerve cell to another.

Synergistic interaction: Cooperative action of substances whose total effects is greater than the sum of their separate effects.

Systemic toxicity: Adverse effects which affect the body in general rather than solely at the site of exposure (local toxicity).

Systole: The contraction of a heart chamber during which blood is expelled.

Tabun: (GA: Ethyl N-dimethylphosphoramidocyanidate), an organophosphate nerve agent.

Tachycardia: An abnormally rapid beating of the heart, defined as a resting heart rate of 100 or more beats per minute in an average adult.

Target organ toxicity: A method of toxicant classification based upon the organ of the body most affected by exposure to the toxicant.

Temporary Emergency Exposure Limits (TEEL): Are developed by Department of Energy (DOE) Subcommittee on Consequence Assessment and Protective Actions (SCAPA) for use by DOE and DOE contractors. Recognizing that ERPGs exist for a limited number of chemicals, DOE SCAPA developed TEELs so that DOE facilities could do complete hazard analyses and consequence assessments, even for chemicals lacking ERPGs.. The four levels of TEEL values are based on a 15-minute time-weighted average (similar to a short-term exposure limit) for a total of four values.

Teratogen: A substance that causes birth defects in the offspring.

Th cells: Type of helper T-lymphocytes (also known as CD4+ cells).

Thalidomide: (2-(2,6-dioxo-3-piperidenyl)-1H-isoindole-1,3(2H)-dione), A sedative hypnotic used in Europe in the late 1950's and early 1960's. It was shown to cause congenital anomalies in the fetus when taken in early pregnancy.

Thermoreceptor: Receptor responding to temperatures deviating from the range perceived as indifferent.

Threshold: The minimum concentration of toxicant sufficient to elicit a measurable effect. Also, characterizes a dose-response curve that does not pass through the origin of the graph, indicating there is an exposure level that will not result in an increase in the probability of occurrence of an adverse health effect. Used by the U.S. EPA for noncarcinogens and developmental toxins.

Threshold Limit Value (TLV®): Promulgated by ACGIH and refers to the airborne concentration of a chemical substance to which nearly all workers may be repeatedly exposed for 8 hours a day over a working lifetime without adverse health effects.

Thyroxine: The thyroid gland hormone that regulates the metabolic rate of the body.

T-lymphocytes: (Thymus-derived) are responsible for the cell-mediated immunity.

Toxicity: A relative property of a chemical agent; refers to a harmful effect on some biologic mechanism and the condition under which this effect occurs.

Toxicokinetics: Mathematical descriptions of the movement of a toxicant throughout the body over time; includes the processes of absorption, distribution, metabolism, and excretion. Often used interchangeably with the work pharmacokinetics. See also pharmacokinetics.

Toxicologist: An individual trained to assess the adverse effects of chemical, physical or biological agents on living organisms and the ecosystem, including the prevention and amelioration of such adverse effects.

Toxicology: The study of the adverse effects of chemical, physical or biological agents on living organisms and the ecosystem, including the prevention and amelioration of such adverse effects.

Trisomy: The addition of one chromosome to the normal pair of chromosomes.

Tumor: An abnormal mass of tissue that results from excessive cell division that is uncontrolled and progressive, also called a neoplasm. Tumors perform no useful body function. They may be either benign (not cancerous) or malignant.

Tumor suppressor gene: Any of a class of genes (e.g., TP53) that act in normal cells to inhibit unrestrained cell division and that when inactivated (as by mutation) place the cell at increased risk for malignant proliferation.

Ultrafine particles: Particles with a diameter less then 100 nanometers.

Uncertainty factor: Sometimes called the "safety factor." A mathematical adjustment for reasons of safety when knowledge is incomplete. For example, factors used in the calculation of doses that are not harmful (adverse) to people. These factors are applied to the lowest-observed-adverse-effect-level (LOAEL) or the no-observed-adverse-effect-level (NOAEL) to derive a minimal risk level (MRL).

Uncoupling of biochemical reactions: Disruption of specific cellular functions by the inhibition of an enzyme or protein.

Urticant: A material that causes itching/burning of the skin. Phosgene Oxime (CX: dichloroformoxime) is an urticant chemical warfare agent.

Urticaria: Or hives is a relatively common form of allergic reaction that causes raised red skin welts. Urticaria is also known as nettle rash or uredo. These welts can be 5 mm (0.2 inches) in diameter or more, itch severely, and often have a pale border. Urticaria is generally caused by direct contact with an allergenic substance, or an immune response to food or some other allergen.

V(D)J recombination: The process by which cells undergo extensive rearrangement of genetic material to assemble the wide variety of immunoglobin and T-cell receptor genes that is necessary to mount a normal immunological response.

Vanilloid Receptor: Neural receptor that mediate sensations of pain and burning. Activation of vanilloid receptors by the binding of capsaicin or endogenous neurotransmitters will induce a reversible loss of receptor function.

Vasoconstriction: The (physiological or harmful) process of narrowing blood vessels to restrict blood flow.

Vasomotor: Nerve-mediated effects relating to the tension of blood vessel walls and hence to the resistance of blood flow.

Vertigo: A specific type of dizziness ("spinning").

Vesicant: A material that causes blisters, the list of chemical warfare vesicants includes Sulphur Mustard (H: Bis(2-chloroethyl) sulphide), Distilled Mustard (HD), the Nitrogen Mustards (HN-1: N-ethyl-2,2'-di(chloroethyl)amine, HN-3: 2,2',2"-tri(chloroethyl)amine, Mustargen (HN-2: N-methyl-2,2'di(chloroethyl)amine) and Lewisite (L:Chlorovinyl dichloroarsine).

Vestibular: Referring to the inner ear organ.

Virus: A small, subcellular, organism containing genetic material that can infect cells and produce illness in humans, animals, or plants. Viruses differ from bacterial in that they cannot replicate independently of their host cells.

Volume of distribution: The theoretical volume that a chemical occupies in the body.

VX: (O-Ethyl-S-[2(diisopropylamino)ethyl] methylphosphonothioate), a nerve agent.

Weapons of Mass Destruction (WMD): Weapons which can kill large numbers of humans, animals, and plants, and/or cause great damage to man-made or natural structures; term includes nuclear, biological, chemical, and radiological weapons.

Weapons of opportunity: Any chemical, material or equipment that would normally be expected to be found in the industrial environment that could be used by a terrorist as a weapon of mass destruction (WMD).

Workplace Environmental Exposure Limit (WEEL): Exposure guidelines developed by AIHA intended to protect the health and safety of workers exposed to hazardous substances or conditions.

Xenobiotic: A substance not normally found in a living organism.

X-rays: Penetrating electromagnetic radiations whose wavelengths are shorter than those of visible light. They are usually produced by bombarding a metallic target with fast electrons in a high vacuum.

Zygote: The single cell formed when a sperm fertilizes an egg.

Index

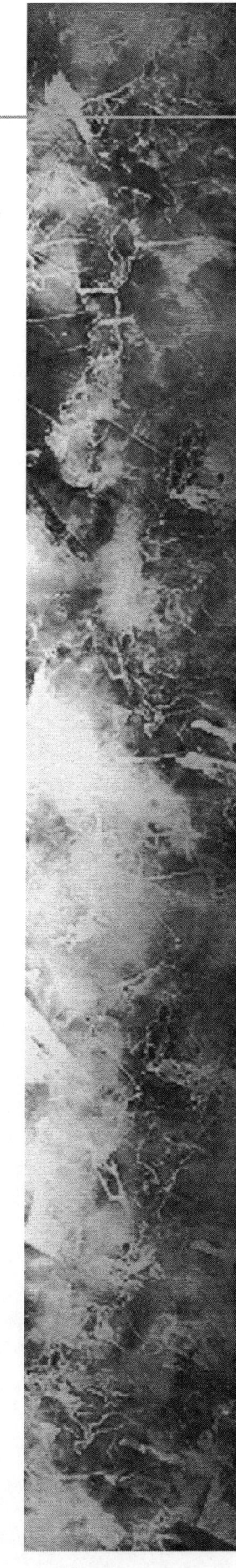

Note: figures, tables and sidebars are indicated by *f, t* or *s* following the page number.

A

Absorption
    biomonitoring and, 354
    chemical warfare agents and, 323
    disposition of toxicants and, 24–25
    exposure assessments and, 292
    extent/rate of, 24
    gas toxicology and, 255–56, 258, 259, 261
    half-life, 30
    metal toxicity and, 210–15
    military toxicology and, 311
    organic solvent toxicity and, 194–96
    pesticide toxicology and, 224, 228
    risk assessments and, 303
    toxicity testing and, 382, 385
    See also ADME (absorption, distribution, metabolism and excretion)
Accumulation of chemicals, 33, 33*f,* 34*f,* 194, 195*f*
    See also Bioaccumulation
Acetaminophen, 103
    See also Analgesics
Acetone, 202, 278
Acetylator phenol type, 359
Acetylcholine, 85, 90–91, 92, 318, 323
Acetylcholinesterase (AChE), 227–30
ACGIH. *See* American Conference of Governmental Industrial Hygienists (ACGIH)
Acid-base balance, 64, 370, 372
Acinus, 98, 99*f*
Acne, 53
Acquired Immune Deficiency Syndrome (AIDS), 129
Acrolein, 345
Acrylamide, 88
Acrylonitrile, 388

Action potential, 60, 72, 84–85, 89, 91
Active metabolites, 26
Acute beryllium disease, 211, 345–46
Acute Exposure Guideline Levels (AEGLs), 324, 332
Acute Exposure Guideline Levels for Selected Airborne Chemicals (NRC), 400–401
Acute myelogenous leukemia, 193, 200–201
Acute myeloid leukemia, 131
Acute radiation syndrome (ARS), 269, 272
Acute respiratory distress syndrome (ARDS), 258
Acute *versus* chronic toxicity
    carcinogenesis and, 158
    gas toxicology and, 259, 261
    neurotoxicology and, 92
    OEL derivation and, 345–46
    of organic solvents, 189, 192–93
    pesticide toxicology and, 224
    principles of toxicity and, 9–10
    radioactive material toxicology and, 269
    toxicity testing and, 382
Adamsite, 323
Adaptation, 72, 79
Adaptive immunity, 128–29
ADBE (absorption, distribution, biotransformation, and excretion). *See* ADME (absorption, distribution, metabolism and excretion)
Additive interactions, 15, 277–78
Additive Mixture Formula, 280
Adducts
    biomonitoring and, 354–55, 357
    carcinogenesis and, 162
    genetic toxicology and, 141, 142, 144
Adenine, 144

425

ADME (absorption, distribution, metabolism and excretion)
  absorption, 24–25
  cellular membrane permeability and, 23–24
  chemical exposures and, 2, 2f
  chemical mixture toxicology and, 279
  disposition of toxicants and, 23–34
  distribution, 25
  elimination, 25–26
  mathematical descriptions of, 27–34
  particulate matter toxicology and, 242
  risk assessments and, 303
  toxicity testing and, 385
  urine *versus* blood samples and, 34
  See also Absorption; Distribution; Excretion; Metabolism
Adrenergic receptor antagonists, 91
Adverse events, 370
AEGLs (Acute Exposure Guideline Levels), 324, 332
Aerodynamic Equivalent Sphere, 246
Aerodynamic particle sizing instruments, 246–47
Aerodynamics, 243, 246–47, 289
Aerosols, 190, 241–51, 289, 323
Afferent nerves, 83
Aflatoxin B_1, 158, 164
Agency for Toxic Substances & Disease Registry (ATSDR)
  description of, 391
  on exposure limit derivation, 8
  on metal toxicity, 216
  on military toxicology, 310
  on radioactive material toxicology, 270
  Website for, 396, 405
Agent Orange, 232
Aging, 77, 162, 357
Agriculture, 223, 258
  See also Herbicides; Insecticides
AIDS (Acquired Immune Deficiency Syndrome), 129
AIHA. *See* American Industrial Hygiene Association (AIHA)
Air, 213, 272, 310
Air Force Medical Global Reach Laydown Team, 314
Air Force Preventative Medicine Units, 314
Air pollution, 93, 248, 341, 390
Air Pollution Control Act, 341
Air sampling, 78, 288–89, 291, 376
Air Sampling Instruments (ACGIH), 291
Airborne concentrations
  exposure assessments and, 291, 294, 296
  materials toxicology and, 373
  OEL derivation and, 345–49
  of organic solvents, 196
  of pesticides, 236–37
Airborne contaminants
  exposure assessments and, 290
  OEL derivation and, 9, 341
  organic solvent toxicity and, 196–97
  physical classes of, 190
  regulations on, 387
  respiratory toxicology and, 39–46
Airway myocyte, 247
Airway structure and function, 39–40, 40f
Albumin, 101–2
Alcohol, 61, 92, 103, 104, 182
  See also Ethanol
Aliphatic alcohols, 61
Aliphatic hydrocarbons, 61, 65–66, 116, 197, 197f, 202
Alkalinity and acidity, 64, 370, 372
Alkylating agents, 142
All Hazards concept, 329–30, 330f
Allergic contact dermatitis, 19, 52, 54
Allergic reactions
  to chemical exposures, 10
  immunotoxicology and, 128, 129
  metal toxicity and, 211, 212, 215
  sensitization and, 18–19
Allyl amine, 62
Alpha particles, 267, 313
Alpha-naphtylthiourea (ANTU), 234
Aluminum, 87
American Board of Industrial Hygiene certification exam, 399
American Chemical Society, 363
American College of Toxicology, 399
American Conference of Governmental Industrial Hygienists (ACGIH)
  on arsenic, 34
  on benzene, 131
  on biomonitoring, 354
  on cadmium, 211
  on carcinogens, 3, 108
  on chemical hazard communications, 364
  on chemical mixture toxicology, 275, 276, 280, 280s
  on dermal toxicology, 53, 292
  description of, 391, 399–400
  on emergency response planning, 331
  on exposure assessments, 291, 292
  on genotoxicity data, 149
  guidelines of, 396 (*See also* Biological Exposure Indices (BEIs®); Short-term exposure limits (STELs); Threshold Limit Values® (TLVs®))
  on hepatic toxicants, 103, 104–5, 107, 108–9
  on mercury, 33
  OEL derivation by, 8, 339–40, 348
  on organic solvents, 189
  on pesticide toxicology, 225, 228
  regulations and, 389–90
  on reproductive and developmental toxicity testing, 121
  risk assessments and, 305
  on toluene, 182
American Industrial Hygiene Association (AIHA)
  on chemical hazard communications, 365
  description of, 391, 400
  on emergency response planning, 331, 335
  on exposure assessments, 286

OEL derivation by, 8, 340
Website for, 396
American Industrial Hygiene Association Journal, 402
American National Standards Institute (ANSI), 339–40
American Public Works Association, 333
Ames Test, 146, 384
Amino acids, 86, 101
Ammonia, 101, 144
Ammonium perchlorate, 279
Analgesics, 65, 103, 278
Analytical characterization, 369
Analytical observation studies, 163–64
Anaphylactic shock, 18
Anchoring, 368
Andersen sampler, 290
Anemia, aplastic, 131, 200, 201
Aneuploidy, 140, 145
Angiosarcomas, 107–9
Animal models
    carcinogenesis and, 165–67, 170*t*
    gas toxicology and, 261–62
    in genotoxicity assays, 145–49
    hepatic toxicology and, 104–5, 107
    OEL derivation and, 343–49
    organic solvent toxicity and, 192, 203–4, 203*f*
    particulate matter toxicology and, 247–50
    pesticide toxicology and, 234–35
    radioactive material toxicology and, 271
    reproductive and developmental toxicology and, 115–23
    risk assessments and, 303, 305–6
    teratogenesis and, 180, 182
    toxicity testing and, 1–2, 382–85
Annals of Occupational Hygiene, The, 402
Anosmia, 75–76
ANSI (American National Standards Institute), 339–40
Antagonism, 15–16, 91, 279–80
Antibiotics, 64–65, 278, 320
Antibodies, 42–43, 45, 105, 127–30
Anticholinesterase agents, 92–93, 227–29
Anticoagulant rodenticides, 234
Antidotes
    chemical warfare agents and, 318–19, 321, 322, 323
    pesticide toxicology and, 229, 234
Antigen-presenting cells, 129
Antigens, 42–43, 45, 105, 128–29
Anti-neoplastic drugs, 132–34
Antioxidants, 40–41
ANTU (alpha-naphtylthiourea), 234
Aplastic anemia, 131, 200, 201
Apoptosis, 103, 142, 158, 181
Applied Occupational and Environmental Hygiene, 402
ARDS (acute respiratory distress syndrome), 258
Area reconnaissance surveys, 314
Area under the curve (AUC), 33
Army Medical Command, 271

Army Preventative Medicine Units, 314
Army Special Medical Augmentation Response (SMART) Teams, 314
Aromatic hydrocarbons, 93, 130–32, 193, 198–99, 198*f*, 359
Aromatic solvents, 61, 65–66, 92, 104
Aromaticity, 198–99
ARS (acute radiation syndrome), 269, 272
Arsenic, 34, 74, 121, 210, 388
Arsenical herbicides, 232–33
Arsine gas, 210, 322
Artificial flavorings, 45, 376
Asbestos, 165–66, 290, 357, 387, 389
Ascertainment, 368
Aspartate, 86
Aspirin. *See* Analgesics
Assays, 145–49, 145*t*
    See also Toxicity testing
Association, 163–64, 358
Associations. *See* Professional organizations
Asthma
    gas toxicology and, 261
    hygiene theory of, 129
    immunotoxicology and, 128, 129
    metal toxicity and, 212, 215
    occupational, 44, 215, 261
    pesticide toxicology and, 231
    respiratory toxicology and, 41, 42–44
Astrocytes, 84
Ataxia, 86
Atherosclerosis, 193
Atmospheric pressure, 295
Atropine, 90–91
ATSDR. *See* Agency for Toxic Substances & Disease Registry (ATSDR)
AUC (area under the curve), 33
Auditory system, 73–74
    See also Mechanoreceptors
Aum Shinrikyo attack, 319
Australian Governmental Department of Health and Aging, 396
Authentic chemical analysis, 369
Automobile exhaust, 142
Autonomic nervous system, 83
Avoidance, 71
Axon, 84
Axonal neuropathies, 193, 202
Axonopathy, 88–89

B

B_{12} vitamins, 258–59
Bacteria, 45–46, 146, 250, 290, 313
Balance. *See* Vestibular system
Baritosis, 43
Barrier cream, 106, 106*f*
Base excision repair (BER), 143

Basepairs, 139–40, 144, 146
Bauer, Georg (Georgius Agricola), 369
Behavior, 71, 177
    See also Lifestyle
Behavior-environment interactions, 41
BEIs®. See Biological Exposure Indices (BEIs®)
Benchmark doses, 305
Benzaldehyde, 345
Benzene
    acute versus chronic exposure to, 10
    biomonitoring and, 357
    chemical mixture toxicology and, 279
    chlorinated, 225
    immunotoxicology and, 130–32
    metabolites, 201f
    organic solvent toxicity and, 196, 196f
    properties of, 198f
    regulations on, 388
    solvent-unique effects of, 198–201
    structure of, 199f
BER (base excision repair), 143
Beryllium, 43, 211, 345, 390
Beta particles, 267, 313
Beta-chloroprene, 121
Bias, 368, 404
Biliary system (bile), 100, 102, 107, 194, 224
Bilirubin, 100, 102, 107
Binding
    benzene and, 199
    chemical mixture toxicology and, 276
    covalent versus non-covalent, 16
    gas toxicology and, 256, 258
    genetic toxicology and, 141–42
    hepatic toxicology and, 105, 108
    neurotoxicology and, 85–86, 90–91
    pesticide toxicology and, 227
    preferential, 17
    toxicants effects on, 16–19
Bingham, E., 395, 401
Bioaccumulation, 224
    See also Accumulation of chemicals
Bioactivation
    carcinogenesis and, 157, 162
    chemical mixture toxicology and, 276
    hepatic toxicology and, 99–100, 104–9
    metabolism and, 17
    organic solvent toxicity and, 193–94
    respiratory toxicology and, 41
Bioavailability, 33, 355
Biochemical reactions, 16
Biogenic amines, 85
Biological disasters, 330
Biological effects, 268–69
Biological environment, 179
Biological Exposure Indices (BEIs®)
    biomonitoring and, 354, 355t
    on carcinogens, 3
    exposure assessments and, 288–89, 292, 293
    OEL derivation and, 340
    on pesticides, 228
    as resource, 395
Biological factors, 164–65, 242
Biological hazards, 311–13
Biological membranes. See Cell, membrane permeability
Biological particles, 290
Biological stressors, 330, 333
Biomarkers
    biomonitoring and, 354–59, 359f
    of effect, 356–57
    of exposure, 354–56, 355t, 356f
    exposure assessments and, 293
    genetic toxicology and, 149–50
    of susceptibility, 357–59, 358t
Biomonitoring, 149–50, 194–96, 293, 352–59
Biotransformation. See Metabolism
Bipyridyl compounds, 232
Bladder cancer, 358–59
Blister agents, 318, 319–21, 320t
Blocking agents, 90
Blood
    cell development, 129–30
    chemical warfare agents and, 322
    clotting factors, 101–2, 234
    concentrations, 25, 27–34
    gas toxicology and, 255–63
    pressure, 60, 62, 384
    red blood cells, 130, 200, 356
    samples, 34, 195–96, 354, 359, 383–84
    vessels, 60, 62, 98–100, 99f
    white blood cells, 129–30
    See also hematology-related entries
Blood concentration time curves, 29–33, 29f, 30f, 31f
Blood-brain barrier, 84, 86, 91, 250
Blood-to-gas partition coefficient, 256
B-lymphocytes, 128–29
Body weight, 381
Bond angles, 199
Bone marrow, 129–34, 147, 357
Bone softening, 211
Brain cancer, 213
Breast cancer, 145, 158, 164, 165, 224
British anti-lewisite, 321
Brominated compounds, 122
Bronchiolitis obliterans, 45, 376
Bronchogenic carcinoma, 166–67
Butyraldehyde, 346
BZ, 323

C

Cadmium, 62, 65, 211, 357, 388
Caffeine, 62, 91
Calcium homeostasis, 16
Calculations, 31–32
    See also Mathematical descriptions
Canalicular cholestasis, 107
Cancer
    biomonitoring and, 353, 358–59
    chemical warfare agents and, 320
    genetic toxicology and, 140–42, 145–50
    hepatic toxicology and, 107–9
    immunotoxicology and, 132–33
    metal toxicity and, 213
    OEL derivation and, 345–46
    particulate matter toxicology and, 248
    pesticide toxicology and, 224
    radioactive material toxicology and, 269, 270, 272, 273
    risk factors for, 163–67
    toxicants and (*See* Carcinogens)
    See also Carcinogenesis; Leukemia; *other types of cancer (i.e., breast cancer, bladder cancer, etc.)*
Cancer Risk Assessment Guidelines (EPA), 145–46
Carbamate insecticides, 92–93, 122, 229–30
Carbohydrates, 101
Carbon, 389
Carbon dioxide, 255, 390
Carbon disulfide, 62, 88, 196, 196f, 204
Carbon fiber-containing advanced composite materials, 311
Carbon monoxide
    carboxyhemoglobin levels and, 32 (*See also* Carboxyhemoglobin)
    cardiotoxicity and, 62
    gas toxicology and, 256–57
    neurotoxicology and, 88, 93
    regulations on, 389, 390
Carbon tetrachloride (CCl_4), 103–4, 194, 197, 278–79
Carboxyhemoglobin, 17, 32–33, 93
Carcinogenesis, 154–71
    benzene and, 200–201
    classification of carcinogens and, 167–70, 168t, 169t, 170t
    embryogenesis and, 181
    history of, 155–56
    mechanisms of, 156–61, 159f
    pesticide toxicology and, 232
    risk factors for, 163–67
    stages of, 161–63, 161t
    toxicity testing and, 384–85
    tumor nomenclature and, 156, 156t
    See also Cancer; Carcinogens; Tumor
Carcinogenic Potency Database, 406
Carcinogens
    benzene as, 131
    classification of, 167–70, 168t, 169t, 170t
    definition of, 2
    genetic toxicology and, 145–49
    key targets of, 160–61
    proximate to ultimate, 156–57
    ratings of, 3
    regulations on, 387
Cardiovascular system, 59–66, 257, 384
Cardiovascular toxicity, 59–62, 65–66
Carrier-mediated transport, 24, 25
Cartesian (non-log) scales, 29f, 30f
CAS (Chemical Abstract Service), 363, 406
Casarett & Doull's Toxicology - The Basic Science of Poisons (Klaasen), 395, 401
Case-control studies, 163–64
Cataracts, 269
Causative agents, 77
C-benzene, 199
CCl_4. *See* Carbon tetrachloride (CCl_4)
Ceiling limits, 331, 341–42, 345–49
Cell
    antigen-presenting, 129
    cycle control, 158
    death, 103–9
    endothelial, 99
    functions, 16, 17–18, 139–43, 261
    germ, 145, 148–49, 158, 160
    growth and differentiation, 158, 160, 161, 161f
    hair, 72, 73–76
    hematopoietic stem, 130
    Ito, 100
    Kupffer, 99–100, 101
    membrane permeability, 18, 23–24, 60, 84–85, 91, 249–50
    parenchymal, 98
    red blood, 130, 200, 356
    replication, 157–58
    Schwann, 84, 89–90, 225
    structure, 19
    white blood, 129–30
Cellular oncogenes, 160
Cellular oxidative stress, 158
Cellular toxicity, direct, 19
Centers for Disease Control and Prevention (CDC). *See* Agency for Toxic Substances & Disease Registry (ATSDR)
Central nervous system (CNS)
    gas toxicology and, 257, 258, 261
    metal toxicity and, 214
    neurotoxicology and, 84, 89–90
    organs in, 83
    pesticide toxicology and, 224, 225, 231
    toxicity testing and, 384
    See also Nervous system; Peripheral nervous system (PNS)
CERN (European Laboratory for Particle Physics), 403
Certificates of analysis, 369
Cervical cancer, 164–65
Cesium, 272, 314
CFR (Code of Federal Regulations), 387–91

Chelators, 17, 215–16
Chemical Abstract Service (CAS), 363, 406
Chemical carcinogenesis. *See* Carcinogenesis
Chemical Carcinogenesis Research Information System, 406
Chemical Database, 406
Chemical exposures. *See* Exposure(s)
Chemical groups, 371–72*t*
Chemical interactions
    chemical mixture toxicology and, 276–80
    chemical warfare agents and, 320
    emergency response planning and, 333
    mechanisms of toxicity and, 15–16
    metal toxicity and, 210
    neurotoxicology and, 89, 92
    particulate matter toxicology and, 249
    reproductive and developmental toxicity testing and, 122–23
    respiratory toxicology and, 45
    sensory toxicology and, 74
    systemic effects of, 59–66
Chemical irritations, 19
    See also Irritations
Chemical Manufacturers Association, 364
Chemical mixture toxicology, 275–81, 331–33, 364
Chemical neurotransmitters, 85–86
Chemical properties
    chemical hazard communications and, 364
    of herbicides, 233*t*
    of insecticides, 224, 226*t*, 227, 229–31
    OEL derivation and, 343
    particulate matter toxicology and, 242, 247–50, 289
    of rodenticides, fumigants and fungicides, 235*t*
    toxicity testing and, 382–83
Chemical stressors, 330, 333
Chemical Warfare Agent Detectors, 314
Chemical warfare agents, 312–13, 317–24
Chemicals
    accumulation of, 33, 33*f*, 34*f*, 194, 195*f*
    analysis of, 369
    carcinogenesis and, 167, 168*t*, 169*t*
    chemical hazard communications and, 363–65
    electrophilic, 279
    emergency response planning and, 331–33
    genetic toxicology and, 145–49
    identification of, 189–90, 303, 343
    industrial, 61, 363–65, 367–77
    military toxicology and, 309–15
    sensory toxicology and, 73–76
    teratogenesis and, 177, 181–82, 181*t*
    See also specific chemicals; Toxicants
CHEMID Plus, 406
Chemoreceptors, 71–72
Chemotherapy, 132–33, 142, 373
Chernobyl accident, 269, 271–73
Chloracne, 232

Chlordecone, 225
Chlorinated benzenes, 225
Chlorinated disinfectant products, 42
Chlorinated insecticides, 224–27
Chlorinated solvents, 104, 193
Chlorine, 321
Chlorophenoxy compounds, 232
Choate-Hatch equations, 243
CHO/*Hprt* mutation assay, 147
Cholestasis, 107
Cholesterol, 101
Cholinergic syndrome, 228
Cholinesterase, 357
Chromatogram, 190
Chromium, 211–12, 388
Chromosome aberration assay, 147, 150
Chromosomes
    aberrations of, 150, 157, 163, 322, 357
    genetic toxicology and, 140, 144, 148
    mutations of, 18, 140
    radioactive material toxicology and, 269
    translocations of, 144–45, 148
Chronic beryllium disease, 43, 211, 345–46
Chronic fatigue, 229
Chronic infections, 164–65
Chronic toxic encephalopathy, 92
Chronic *versus* acute toxicity
    carcinogenesis and, 158
    gas toxicology and, 259, 261
    neurotoxicology and, 92
    OEL derivation and, 345–46
    of organic solvents, 189, 192–93
    pesticide toxicology and, 224
    principles of toxicity and, 9–10
    radioactive material toxicology and, 269
    toxicity testing and, 382
Cigarette smoke
    biomonitoring and, 358–59
    carcinogenesis and, 164, 165
    genetic toxicology and, 142
    immunotoxicology and, 129, 132
    neurotoxicology and, 93
    respiratory toxicology and, 41
    See also Nicotine
Circulatory system, 60
    See also Blood; Hematoxicants
Cirrhosis, 104, 105–7
Clara cells, 41
Classic compartmental pharmacokinetics, 29–30
Clean Air Act, 390
Clean Water Act, 341, 390
Cleaning solutions, 42, 276
Clearance, 40, 64–65, 102, 244
Clinical chemistry, 383
Clinical observations, 383

Clinical toxicologist, 8
Clouds, 289
Clusters of Differentiation, 128–29
CNS. *See* Central nervous system (CNS)
Coal workers' pneumoconiosis, 43
Coarse particles, 248–49
Coast Guard, 392, 396
Cobalt, 62, 212
Cocaine, 91
Code of Federal Regulations (CFR), 387–91
Cohort studies, 163–64
Cohrssen, B., 395, 401
Coke oven emissions, 388
Cold, 311
   See also Hypothermia
Color perception, 73, 77–78
Combined Toxicity Criteria, 373
Combustion products, 311–12, 313
Commercial materials toxicology, 367–77
   See also Chemicals
Communication
   crisis, 333, 365
   hazard, 331, 363–65
   plans, 333–35
   risk, 303, 329, 333
Complement proteins, 128
Complex mixtures, 275–81
Components, 44, 275–81, 364
   See also Chemicals; Toxicants
Comprehensive Environmental Response, Compensation, and Liability Act, 341, 390
"Comprehensive Health Surveillance" (DoD), 309
Computational models, 294–97, 375
   See also Mathematical descriptions
Computer-aided tomography, 354
Concentration
   airborne (*See* Airborne concentrations)
   exposure assessments and, 288, 295
   gas toxicology and, 260, 261–62, 261t
   gradients, 24, 25
   materials toxicology and, 369
   of organic solvents, 191
   particulate matter toxicology and, 242, 248, 290
   risk assessments and, 303
   toxicity testing and, 384
Conducting airways, 39, 40f, 41, 255
Confidence, degree of, 296
Congenital malformations, 177–82
   See also Developmental toxicology
Connective tissue, 156
Consensus organizations, 334t, 339–40
   See also Professional organizations
Consequence management, 330, 331f, 335
Contact dermatitis
   allergic *versus* irritant, 19

   dermal toxicology and, 52, 54
   metal toxicity and, 211
   pesticide toxicology and, 231, 232
Contact photosensitization, 52
Contaminants, 303
   See also Chemicals; Components; Toxicants
Contraceptives, oral steroid, 62, 165
Control banding analysis, 348
Control groups, 163–64, 382
Coronary heart disease, 204
Corrosion, 383
Cotton dust, 388
Covalent binding, 16
C-reactive protein, 128
Creatinine, 34, 64
Crisis communication, 333, 365
Crisis response, 330, 331f, 335
Crohn's disease, 129
Crosslinking, 142, 144, 205f
Cross-sectional studies, 163–64
Cross-sensitization, 18
Culture, 357
   See also Ethnicity; Lifestyle
Cunningham Slip Correction Factor, 243
Curvilinear motion, 243
Cutaneous *versus* visceral sensations, 74
Cyanide, 313
   See also Hydrogen cyanide
Cyanide agents, 322, 322t
Cyanogen chloride, 322
Cyclic aromatic hydrocarbons, 198–99, 198f
Cyclodienes, 225
Cyclohexane, 199, 199f, 225, 227
Cytochrome oxidase, 17
Cytokines, 61, 128–29, 248, 250, 357
Cytosine, 144
Cytotoxicity, 158, 234–36

D

Dairy products, 273
Damp building syndrome, 45–46
Databases, 403–7
DBCP (1,2-Dibromo-3-chloropropane), 118, 234–35, 388
DBP (di-n-butyl phthalate), 117
DDT (dichlorodiphenyl trichloroethane), 91, 164, 224–25
Decision logic tree, 344f, 345
Decision-making, 367–77
   meta-cognition and, 367–68
   product acceptance or rejection and, 375–76
   risk-safety connections and, 370, 372–75
   scientific and regulatory history and, 368–70
Decomposition, 368
Default values, 305–6, 305t
Defense mechanisms, 40, 40f
Delayed neuropathies, 89, 228

Demyelination, 89–90
Dendrites, 84
Density of particulates, 243
Department of Defense (DoD), 3, 309, 340
Department of Energy, 390, 392
Department of Health, Education, and Welfare, 340
Department of Health and Human Services (HHS), 270, 340
Department of Homeland Security, 330
Department of Labor, 340, 387
Department of Transportation (DOT), 3, 332–33, 340, 364, 392
Depleted uranium, 270–71, 313
"Deployment Health" (DoD), 309
Deployment toxicology, 2
    See also Chemical warfare agents; Military toxicology
Depolarizing agents, 91
Deposition mechanisms, 243, 244, 289–90
Depressants, 91–92
Derelanko, M. J., 402
Dermal exposure
    benzene and, 131
    chemical mixture toxicology and, 276
    chemical warfare agents and, 320–21, 323
    emergency response planning and, 330
    exposure assessments and, 288–89, 291–93
    gas toxicology and, 262
    to hepatic toxicants, 103–9
    immunotoxicology and, 133
    inhalation and, 53–54
    to isocyanates, 43
    metal toxicity and, 210–15
    military toxicology and, 312
    OEL derivation and, 347–48
    to organic solvents, 190, 193, 194
    to pesticides, 225, 228, 232, 234, 236
    as route of entry, 9, 24–25, 51
    toxicity testing and, 382, 383
Dermal Exposure Assessments: Principles and Applications (EPA), 293
Dermal toxicology, 51–54, 52*f*, 53*t*
Dermatitis, 19, 190, 193
    See also Contact dermatitis
Dermatoxicants, 2
Descriptive toxicologist, 7
Descriptive toxicology, 2
Desensitization, 72, 76, 79
Deterministic effects, 269
Detoxication, 17, 279
Developmental and Reproductive Toxicology and Environmental Teratology Information Center, 406
Developmental susceptibility, 179–80, 179*t*
Developmental toxicology, 114–23
    animal studies on, 120–23
    definition of, 115
    fertility effects of, 117–20
    occupational exposures and, 116–17
    principles of, 115
    toxicity testing and, 385
    See also Teratogenesis
Diabetes, 77
Diacetyl, 45, 376–77
Diameter of particulates, 243–47, 248, 289–90
Dichlorodiphenyl trichloroethane (DDT), 91, 164, 224–25
Diet, 164, 177, 179, 357
    See also Food contaminants
Diffusion, 243, 255–56, 289, 295–96
    See also Passive diffusion
Dimethylmercury, 86
Di-n-butyl phthalate (DBP), 117
Dinitrophenols, 233
Dioxins, 93–94
Dip tanks, 188*f*, 190
Diquat, 232
Direct-reading instruments, 247, 291
Disasters, 329–30, 330*f*
Disease-exposure gradients, 359*f*
Diseases, 140, 223, 293, 353–54
    See also specific diseases (i.e., cancer, diabetes, etc.)
Dispersion models, 295–96
Disposal considerations, 364
Disposition of toxicants, 23–34
    absorption and, 24–25
    cellular membrane permeability and, 23–24
    definition of, 23
    distribution and, 25
    elimination and, 25–26
    mathematical descriptions of, 27–34
    risk assessments and, 303
    urine *versus* blood samples and, 34
Dispositional antagonism, 279
Distal axonopathies, 88–89
Distance, 314
Distilled mustard, 319
Distribution
    biomonitoring and, 355
    disposition of toxicants and, 25
    of organic solvents, 191–92
    particulate matter toxicology and, 241–42, 245–46, 245*f*, 246*f*
    risk assessments and, 303
    volume of, 25
    See also ADME (absorption, distribution, metabolism and excretion)
Distributors, 365
Dithiocarbamates, 236
Diuretics, 65
DMEs (drug metabolizing enzymes), 157, 162
DNA
    adducts (*See* Adducts)
    biomarkers and (*See* Biomarkers)

carcinogenesis and, 157
damage to, 141–42, 141*t*, 157, 358
genotoxicity assays on, 145–49, 145*t*
mechanisms of mutation induction and, 143–45
methylation, 159
microarrays, 354
mutations and, 139–41, 140*f*
radioactive material toxicology and, 268
repair of, 141*t*, 142–43, 157–58, 162
tumor viruses, 165
Documentation, 343–45, 365, 374, 390–91
 See also Material Safety Data Sheets (MSDS)
DoD (Department of Defense), 3, 309, 340
Dominant lethal assay in male mice, 148–49
Dopamine, 85
Dose
 additivity, 277
 benchmark, 305
 definition of, 285
 effective, 354–55
 exposure assessments and, 288
 external *versus* internal, 354–55
 military toxicology and, 313
 of organic solvents, 191
 particulate matter toxicology and, 242, 243, 244
 potential average daily, 306
 radioactive material toxicology and, 268–73
 reference, 305–6
 total potential, 306
 toxicity testing and, 382
Dose response relationships
 chemical mixture toxicology and, 278
 dose response curves depicting, 3–4, 10–11, 10*f*
 immunotoxicology and, 131
 materials toxicology and, 374
 organic solvents and, 192–93
 risk assessments and, 303, 305*f*
 teratogenesis and, 180
 toxicity testing and, 381–82
Dosimeters, 268
DOT (Department of Transportation), 3, 332–33, 340, 364, 392
Down syndrome, 145
Drag, 244
Draize tests (John Draize), 383–84
Drinking water, 121, 390
Drug metabolizing enzymes (DMEs), 157, 162
Drugs. *See* Analgesics; Antibiotics; Pharmaceuticals
Duration of exposure, 291, 314, 341, 382, 384
Dusts
 exposure assessments and, 289–90
 metals in, 209, 210
 particulate matter toxicology and, 249
 regulations on, 388, 389, 390
 sensory toxicology and, 75

Dye clearance tests, 102
Dynamic shape factor, 243
Dysesthesia, 74
Dysrhythmias, 61

E

E. coli test, 146, 148
Ears. *See* Auditory system; Vestibular system
Earthquakes, 335–36
Eddy diffusivity, 296
Editing, 368
Effective dose, 354–55
Effects
 biological, 268–69
 biomarkers of, 356–57
 deterministic, 269
 fertility, 117–20
 inotropic, 61–62
 irreversible (*See* Irreversible effects)
 local, 10, 19, 191–93, 269
 magnitude of (*See* Dose response relationships)
 order, 368
 range of, 373–75
 reversible (*See* Reversible effects)
 significance of, 4
 solvent-unique, 197–204
 systemic, 10, 59–66, 98–102, 98*f*, 191–93
 toxicant classifications by, 8
 See also Response
Efferent nerves, 83
EGE (ethylene glycol ethers), 118
Electrocardiography, 384
Electroencephalograph, 90
Electron impact gas chromatography with mass spectrometry detection, 190
Electronic databases, 403–7
Electronic particle counters, 290
Electrophilic chemicals, 279
Electrostatic attraction, 243
Electrostatic precipitators, 247
Elemental mercury, 87, 214
Elimination
 disposition of toxicants and, 25–26
 gas toxicology and, 256
 half-life, 30–31, 31*t*
 hepatic toxicology and, 100–101
 organic solvent toxicity and, 193–94, 195*f*
 routes of, 25, 194
 See also Excretion; Renal system
Embryogenesis, 179, 179*t*, 181
Emergency exposures, 324
Emergency Planning and Community Right-to-Know Act, 390
Emergency planning guidelines, 333*t*
Emergency Response Guidebook (ERG2004), 332–33
Emergency response planning, 329–36, 365, 390

Emergency Response Planning Guidelines (ERPG), 331–32
Emergency Temporary Standard, 377
Employee health data
    carcinogenesis and, 164
    cardiovascular and renal toxicity and, 66
    immunotoxicology and, 131–32
    reproductive and developmental toxicology and, 118
    respiratory toxicology and, 43
    sensory toxicology and, 75–78
Employers, 44, 365
Endorphins, 86
Endothelial cells, 99
Endotoxins, 250
Enkephalines, 86
Enterohepatic circulation, 100
Environment
    behavior interactions with, 41
    biological, 179
    carcinogenesis and, 163
    gene interactions with, 41
    sensory system and, 71–72
    teratogenesis and, 177
Environmental and Occupational Medicine (Rom), 401
Environmental contamination
    chemical hazard communications and, 364
    chemical warfare agents and, 317
    pesticide toxicology and, 224–25
    radioactive material toxicology and, 270, 272
    regulations on, 390
Environmental disasters, 329–30
Environmental Health Criteria document, 148
Environmental Protection Agency (EPA)
    on cadmium, 211
    on carcinogens, 145–46, 168, 170t
    on chemical hazard communications, 364
    on default values, 305t
    on dermal exposure assessments, 293
    on dermal toxicology, 53
    description of offices of, 392–93
    on emergency response planning, 333
    on hazard identification, 303
    on military toxicology, 310
    OEL derivation by, 340–41
    on perchlorate, 132
    on pesticides, 223, 224–25, 232
    radioactive material toxicology and, 270
    on Reference Doses, 305
    regulatory standards of, 390
    on reproductive and developmental toxicology, 116, 120–21
    on safety assessments, 7
    on toxicological testing, 4, 120–21
    Websites for, 396, 404
Environmental toxicologist, 8, 189
Enzymes
    biomonitoring and, 358–59
    carcinogenesis and, 157, 162
    cardiotoxicity and, 62
    chemical mixture toxicology and, 276, 278–79
    elimination and, 25–26
    gas toxicology and, 258
    genetic toxicology and, 146
    hepatic toxicology and, 98–99, 100, 102, 102t, 104
    induction of, 16
    inhibition of, 16
    insecticides and, 227, 228, 230
    neurotoxicology and, 85, 92–93
    nucleotide damage and, 18
    organic solvent toxicity and, 193, 194
    renal system and, 64
    respiratory toxicology and, 40–41
    sensory toxicology and, 75
    See also Metabolism
EPA. *See* Environmental Protection Agency (EPA)
Epidemiology, 163–64, 286, 353–54, 359
Epigenetic mechanisms, 158–60, 159f, 179, 181
Epinephrine, 85
Epithelial tissue, 156, 247–48
Epstein-Barr virus, 164
Equations, 31–32, 243
    See also Mathematical descriptions
Equivalent diameters, 243
ERG2004 (2004 Emergency Response Guidebook), 332–33
ERPG (Emergency Response Planning Guidelines), 331–32
Erythropoeisis, 147
Ethanol
    acute *versus* chronic exposure to, 10
    chemical mixture toxicology and, 278, 279
    metabolism and, 27f
    neurotoxicology and, 92
    organic solvent toxicity and, 194
    reproductive and developmental toxicology and, 116–17
    See also Alcohol
Ethnicity, 359
Ethyl acetate, 346
Ethylene glycol ethers (EGE), 118
Ethylene oxide, 134, 261–63, 357, 388
Etiology of disease, 353–54
European Chemical Substances Information System, 396
Excretion
    carcinogenesis and, 157
    gas toxicology and, 258, 259
    hepatic toxicology and, 100–101
    of insecticides, 224, 228, 230, 231
    of metals, 209–15
    risk assessments and, 303
    as route of elimination, 25
    toxicity testing and, 385
    See also ADME (absorption, distribution, metabolism and excretion); Elimination; Renal system; Urine
Exhalation, 194, 195–96, 256, 258, 259

Exhaust ventilation
   gas toxicology and, 257
   hepatic toxicology and, 106
   immunotoxicology and, 133
   organic solvents and, 190
   respiratory toxicology and, 42, 44
   sensory toxicants and, 78
Explosions, 309, 364
Exponential decay curve, 194, 195*f*
Exposure assessments, 285–97
   Biological Exposures Indices (BEIs®) and, 293
   computational models and, 294–97
   dermal exposure assessment and, 291–93
   exposure monitoring and, 288–91
   goals of, 285–86
   in industrial hygiene, 287*f*
   military toxicology and, 315
   process of, 286–88, 287*f*
   risk assessments and, 303–4, 305
   sample duration and toxicology, 291
Exposure-disease gradients, 359*f*
Exposure-dose models, 242
Exposure(s)
   ADME and, 2
   biomarkers of, 354–56, 355*t*, 356*f*
   considerations, 4
   definition of, 285
   duration of, 291, 314, 341, 382, 384
   emergency, 324
   genetic toxicology and, 142
   guidelines on, 291
   hepatic toxicology and, 97–98, 102–9
   immunotoxicology and, 130–34
   levels of, 262*t*, 269*t*, 302, 331–33, 385
   likelihood of, 4, 9
   limit derivation, 8 (*See also* Occupational exposure limits (OELs))
   magnitude of (*See* Dose response relationships)
   monitoring of, 288–91
   multiple (*See* Multiple exposures)
   radioactive material toxicology and, 271–72, 272*t*
   routes of (*See* Routes of exposure)
   timing of, 179–80, 179*t*
   undesired effects of, 10
   See also Occupational exposures
Exposure-toxicity interactions, 286
   See also Dose response relationships
EXTension TOXicology NETwork (EXTOXNET), 406
External dose, 354–55
Eye irritation, 383–84
Eyes. *See* Vision

F

Farmer's lung, 45–46
Fat solubility. *See* Lipid solubility
Fatty liver, 103–9, 103*f*
FDA. *See* Food and Drug Administration (FDA)
Feces, 194
Federal Advisory Committee Act of 1972, 332
Federal Hazard Communications Standard, 331, 363–65
Federal Insecticide, Fungicide, and Rodenticide Act, 390
Federal Mine Safety and Health Act, 389–90
Federal Register, 389, 393
Feret's Diameter, 243
Fertility, 117–20
Fetal period, 179
   See also Prenatal development
Fibers, 166–67, 290, 311
Fibrosis, 43, 104–9, 167, 212
Fick's Law of Diffusion, 243
"Fight or flight" response, 85
Filaments, 166
Fine particles, 248–49
Fire extinguishers, 103–4, 103*f*
Fire retardants, 122
Fires, 309, 311–12, 313, 364
First aid measures, 364
First responders, 330, 332, 333, 364, 405
First-order elimination curve, 194, 195*f*
First-order pharmacokinetics, 27–28
Flavorings, 45, 376
Fluorescent tracers, 293
Fluoroacetic acid, 234
Fluorocarbons, 61
Fog, 289
Food and Drug Administration (FDA)
   on genotoxicity assays, 147
   on materials toxicology, 373, 375
   OEL derivation by, 348
   on safety assessments, 7
   toxicity categories, 373*t*
Food contaminants, 164, 273, 310, 312
Foreign substances. *See* Xenobiotics
Forensic toxicologist, 8
Formaldehyde, 388
Fractal dimension, 243
Frameshifts, 144
Framing, 368
Free radicals
   binding and, 16
   cellular membranes and, 18
   gas toxicology and, 260
   genetic toxicology and, 142
   hepatic toxicology and, 104, 105
   organic solvent toxicity and, 194
   pesticide toxicology and, 232
   radioactive material toxicology and, 268

Fruits, 164, 273
Fuels, 116, 120
  See also Gasoline
Fugacity, 191
Full Spectrum Emergency Preparedness, 330, 330f
Fumes, 289
Fumigants, 234–35, 235t
Functional antagonism, 279
Functional tests, 383, 384
Fungi, 45–46, 290, 313
Fungicides, 235–36, 235t

G

Gall bladder, 100
Gamma-aminobutyric (GABA), 86
Gamma-rays, 267, 313
Ganglions, 83
Gap junction intercellular communication (GJIC), 158–59
Gas chromatography, 189–90, 204, 291
Gas solubility, 256
Gas toxicology, 254–63, 256f
Gases, 190, 234, 290–91
Gasoline, 121, 131, 198, 276, 276t
Gastric cancer, 164
Gastrulation, 178–79
Gender differences, 117, 357
Gene expression
  carcinogenesis and, 159, 160, 162, 165
  chemical mixture toxicology and, 277
  teratogenesis and, 179
Gene-environment interaction, 41
General ventilation model, 295
"Generic Exposure Assessment Standards" (AIHA), 286
Genes
  carcinogenesis and, 157–58, 165
  immunotoxicology and, 128
  mutations to, 18, 139–40
  teratogenesis and, 177, 179
  See also DNA; Heredity; *other gene/genetics-related entries*
Genetic diseases, 177
Genetic polymorphisms, 41, 357–58
Genetic toxicology, 138–50
  biomarkers and, 149–50
  carcinogenesis and, 155, 158–60, 159f
  definition of, 139
  DNA damage and, 141–42, 141t
  DNA repair and, 142–43
  genotoxicity assays and, 145–49, 145t
  mechanisms of mutation induction and, 143–45
  mutations and, 139–41, 140f
  teratogenesis and, 180–81
  See also DNA
Genetic Toxicology (GENE-TOX) database, 405–6
Genotoxicity assays, 145–49, 145t

Geometric standard deviation (GSD), 246
Germ cell mutagenicity, 145, 148–49, 158, 160
Germline mutations, 140
GFR (glomerular filtration rate), 64–65
Gilman, A. G., 401
"Ginger Jake" paralysis, 89
GJIC (gap junction intercellular communication), 158–59
Global Information Network on Chemicals, 396
Globalization, 376
Globally Harmonized System for the Classification and Labeling of Chemicals, 365
Glomerular filtration rate (GFR), 64–65
Glucose, 64, 101
Glutamate, 86
Glutathione, 194, 279
Glutathione S-transferase M1 (GSTM1), 359
Glycine, 86
Glycol ethers, 118
Good Laboratory Practice, 383
Google, 407
Gradient distribution, 355
Grain products, 273
Gram negative bacteria, 250
GSD (geometric standard deviation), 246
GSTM1 (glutathione S-transferase M1), 359
Guidelines
  Acute Exposure Guideline Levels (AEGLs), 324, 332
  Cancer Risk Assessment Guidelines (EPA), 145–46
  emergency planning, 333t
  Emergency Response Planning Guidelines (ERPG), 331–32
  exposure, 291
  Guidelines for Carcinogen Risk Assessment, 168–69
  Guidelines for Reproductive Toxicity Risk Assessment (EPA), 116
  Health Effects Test Guidelines, 7
  by professional organizations, 391–93
  See also specific guidelines (i.e., Threshold Limit Values®)
Gustatory system, 76
  See also Chemoreceptors

H

H. pylori infections, 164
Haber's Law (Haber's Rule), 61, 78–79
Habituation, 72, 76, 79
Hair cells, 72, 73–76
Half-life
  biomonitoring and, 356, 356f
  chemical warfare agents and, 318
  disposition of toxicants and, 30–31, 31t, 32
  exposure assessments and, 293
  organic solvent toxicity and, 194, 195f
Hallucinations, 323
Halogenated aliphatic hydrocarbons, 61, 65–66
Halogenated alkanes, 61
Halogenated aromatic hydrocarbons, 93

Halogenated hydrocarbons, 122
Halothane, 105
Handling and storage, 364
Hard metal lung disease, 43, 212
Hardman, J. G., 401
Hatch-Choate equations, 243
Hays, A. W., 401
Hazard Communications Standard, 331, 363–65
Hazard Index approach, 277
Hazard warnings, 363
Hazardous chemicals, 3
    See also Chemicals; Toxicants
Hazardous materials, 3
Hazardous materials awareness, 330
Hazardous Materials Information System (HMIS), 3
Hazardous materials spill response plan, 330
Hazardous Substances Data Bank, 370, 405
Hazardous wastes, 341, 390
Hazards
    biomonitoring and, 353–54
    definition of, 2, 302
    emergency response planning and, 329–30, 335
    exposure assessments and, 285
    identification of, 303, 364
    military toxicology and, 309–15
    physical, 311–13
    See also Chemicals; Toxicants
HBV (Hepatitis B virus), 164–65
Health and safety professionals, 44, 167, 329–36, 369
    See also Industrial hygiene
Health Effects Test Guidelines, 7
Health Physics Society, 268, 269
Health status, 357
    See also Employee health data
Hearing. *See* Auditory system
Heart. *See* Cardiovascular system; Cardiovascular toxicity
Heart rate, 384
Heat, 119, 120, 311
    See also Hyperthermia
Heavy metals, 17, 61, 65–66, 74–75, 209
    See also Metals; *specific heavy metals (i.e., lead)*
Heckelman, P. E., 401
Hematology, 383
    See also Blood
Hematopoietic stem cells, 130
Hematoxicants, 2
Hematoxicity, 200, 213
Hemoglobin, 17, 256, 258, 356, 357
    See also Carboxyhemoglobin
Hemolysis, 17
Henry's law constant, 295
Hepatic toxicology, 97–109
    chemical mixture toxicology and, 278–79
    increased chemical exposure and, 97–98
    liver injuries from workplace chemicals and, 102–9

    liver structure and function and, 98–102, 98*f*
    organic solvent toxicity and, 194
    toxicity testing and, 384
    See also Liver
Hepatitis, 103
Hepatitis B virus (HBV), 164–65
Hepatitis C, 129
Hepatocellular carcinoma, 164, 165
Hepatocytes
    hepatic toxicology and, 100–101, 103–9
    liver functions and, 98–100, 102
Hepatotoxicants, 2
Herbicides, 210, 232–34, 233*t*
Heredity
    biomonitoring and, 358
    carcinogenesis and, 157–58, 160
    genetic toxicology and, 139–40, 144–45, 148–50
    sensory toxicology and, 76–77
    teratogenesis and, 179, 180–81
    toxicity testing and, 385
    vision and, 73
    See also gene-related entries; Predisposition
Heterozygosity, loss of, 144–47
Heuristics, 368
Hexachlorobenzene, 225
Hexachlorocyclohexane, 225, 227
Hexachlorophene, 89–90
Hexane isomers, 197, 197*f*
HFC-236fa (1,1,1,3,3,3-Hexafluoropropane), 347
HHS (Department of Health and Human Services), 270, 340
High Production Volume Challenge Program, 404
High resolution mass spectrometers, 354
High Wire Press, 407
Highly toxic, definition of, 3
Histamine, 85
Histogram, 245, 245*f*, 246*f*
Histological tests, 383, 384
Histone deacetylation, 159
HIV (Human Immunodeficiency Virus), 129
Homeostasis, 101
Homocysteine, 62
Homologous recombination repair, 143
Hormones, 62, 158, 162, 163, 164–65
HPV (Human Papilloma Virus), 164–65
Human development. *See* Developmental toxicology; Prenatal development
Human Health Risk Assessments, 53
Human Immunodeficiency Virus (HIV), 129
Human Papilloma Virus (HPV), 164–65
Hydrocarbons
    aliphatic, 61, 65–66, 116, 197, 197*f*, 202
    aromatic, 93, 130–32, 193, 198–99, 198*f*, 359
    halogenated, 61, 65–66, 93, 122
    volatile aromatic, 130–32
Hydrogen cyanide, 88, 235, 322

Hydrophilic molecules. *See* Water solubility
Hygiene theory of asthma, 129
Hypermethylation, 159
Hyperplasia, 161, 162
Hypersensitization
    cardiotoxicity and, 62
    chemical warfare agents and, 321, 323
    chemicals causing, 18–19
    dermal toxicology and, 52–53
    metal toxicity and, 211, 212
    respiratory toxicology and, 41, 42–43, 45–46
Hyperthermia, 177
Hyperthyroidism, 132
Hypoesthesia, 74
Hypomethylation, 159
Hypothermia, 61, 323
Hypotheses, 294, 374
Hypoxemia, 229
Hypoxia, 61, 256

I

IARC. *See* International Agency for Research on Cancer (IARC)
Ibuprofen. *See* Analgesics
Immediately Dangerous to Life and Health limits, 342, 405
Immune system, 105, 127–30, 261
Immune-mediated damage, 105
Immunity, 127–29
Immunizations, 128
Immunoglobulins, 128
Immunosuppression, 18–19
Immunotoxicants, 2
Immunotoxicology, 127–34
    chemical exposures and, 10
    particulate matter toxicology and, 249
    structure and functions of immune system and, 127–30
    toxic exposures and, 130–34
Impaction, 243, 289
Importers, 364–65
In vitro chromosome aberration assay, 147
In vitro genotoxicity assays, 146
In vitro testing, 146, 147, 382–85
In vivo genotoxicity assays, 146
In vivo testing, 146, 382–85
Inactive metabolites, 26
Incapacitating agents, 323–24
Incident Command System, 333
Incident management, 335
Index of Occupational Health Guidelines for Chemical Hazards, 404–5
Individual dose response relationships, 10
Indoor air quality, 45–46, 93
Industrial chemicals, 61, 363–65, 367–77
    See also Chemicals
Industrial hygiene
    biomonitoring and, 353, 359
    chemical warfare agents and, 319, 321
    emergency response planning and, 335
    exposure assessments and, 285–97, 287f
    genetic toxicology assay data in, 149
    military toxicology and, 308–15
    organic solvents and, 189
    resources on, 395–96, 399–402, 403–7
    risk assessments in, 301–6, 304f, 304t
    toxicology and, 1, 5, 191–92, 204, 206
    See also Health and safety professionals
Industries, 167t
Industry groups, 339, 341–42, 342f
Inertial separators, 246–47
Infections, 164–65
Infertility, 117–20
Inflammation
    carcinogenesis and, 162, 165, 167
    hepatic toxicology and, 103
    immunotoxicology and, 128–29
    particulate matter toxicology and, 248, 249–50
Infrared spectrometry, 189
Ingestion
    chemical warfare agents and, 323
    emergency response planning and, 330
    exposure assessments and, 289
    metal toxicity and, 210–15
    military toxicology and, 311, 312
    OEL derivation and, 348
    of organic solvents, 191
    of pesticides, 224, 228, 232
    radioactive material toxicology and, 270, 273
    as route of entry, 9
    toxicity testing and, 382
Inhalation
    benzene and, 131
    chemical mixture toxicology and, 276
    chemical warfare agents and, 323
    dermal exposure and, 53–54
    emergency response planning and, 330
    exposure assessments and, 288–91, 293
    gas toxicology and, 255–63
    of hepatic toxicants, 103–9
    immunotoxicology and, 133
    metal toxicity and, 210–15
    military toxicology and, 311–12
    OEL derivation and, 345–49
    organic solvent toxicity and, 190, 195, 196–97
    of particulate matter, 241–51
    of pesticides, 224, 225, 228, 232, 234
    radioactive material toxicology and, 270
    as route of entry, 9
    toxicity testing and, 382, 384
    See also Respiratory system; Respiratory toxicology
Initiation, 161–62, 161t, 162f

Injection, 31, 33, 311, 330, 382
Innate immunity, 127–28
Inorganic arsenic, 121, 210, 388
Inorganic lead, 213
Inorganic mercury, 87, 214
Inorganic tin, 215
Inotropic effects, 61–62
Insecticides
    carbamates as, 92–93, 122, 229–30
    chemical structures of, 224, 226t, 227, 229–31
    neurotoxicology and, 89, 91, 92–93
    organochlorines as, 224–27, 277
    organophosphates as, 89, 92–93, 227–29, 318, 357
    pyrethroids as, 230–32
Institute of Medicine, 393
Integrated Risk Information System (IRIS), 305, 404
Interactions
    additive, 15, 277–78
    behavior-environment, 41
    chemical (*See* Chemical interactions)
    exposure-toxicity, 286
    gene-environment, 41
    noise-chemical, 74
    synergistic, 15, 278
    See also Bioactivation; Dose response relationships
Interception, 243
Interdisciplinary coordination, 335, 375–77
Interferon, 129
Internal dose, 354–55
International Agency for Research on Cancer (IARC)
    on asbestos, 166
    on chemical carcinogens, 167, 168t, 169t
    on metals, 210–13, 215
    on vinyl chloride, 141
International Archives of Occupational and Environmental Health, 402
International Association of Chiefs of Police, 333
International Brotherhood of Teamsters, 377
International Chemical Safety Cards, 405
International Commission on Radiological Protection, 340
International Labor Office, 271
International Organization for Standardization (ISO), 340
International Programme on Chemical Safety, 148, 370, 396, 406
International regulatory organizations
    on chemical hazard communications, 365
    classification of carcinogens by, 167–70
    on exposure assessments, 296–97
    on military toxicology, 310
    on mutagen classification schemes, 149, 149t
    OEL derivation by, 340, 348
    Websites for, 396
International Society for Regulatory Toxicology and Pharmacology, 400
International Toxicity Estimates for Risk, 405
International Union of Toxicology, 400, 407

Internet, as resource, 396, 396t, 403–7
Interstitial lung disease, 43
Intervention measures, 354
Intestinal tract, 100
Intravenous injections, 31, 33
Invasion, 163
Iodine, 279
Iodine, radioactive, 273
Ionizing radiation
    carcinogenesis and, 165–66
    definition of, 267
    genetic toxicology and, 142, 145
    immunotoxicology and, 133–34
    military toxicology and, 311
    radioactive material toxicology and, 269t, 272
    teratogenesis and, 177, 179, 180
IRIS (Integrated Risk Information System), 305, 404
Iron, 101, 200
Irreversible effects
    of binding, 16
    carcinogenesis and, 162–63
    chemical exposures and, 10, 19
    chemical warfare agents and, 323
    gas toxicology and, 259, 261
    genetic toxicology and, 142
    hepatic toxicology and, 103, 105
    neurotoxicology and, 89–90, 92–93
    reproductive and developmental toxicology and, 117
    sensory toxicology and, 74
Irritant contact dermatitis, 19, 52
Irritations, 19, 41–42, 76, 193, 383–84
ISO (International Organization for Standardization), 340
Isocyanates, 42–43, 44
Ito cells, 100

J

Jaundice, 106–7
Journal of Occupational and Environmental Hygiene, The, 402
Journal of Occupational and Environmental Medicine, 402
Journals, toxicological, 402

K

Karyotypic instability, 163
Kepone, 225
Ketones, 202, 202f, 347–48
    See also Methyl *n*-butyl ketone (2-hexane)
Kidneys, 211, 270, 384
    See also Nephrotoxicants; Renal toxicity
Kinetics, 23
    See also Pharmacokinetics; Toxicokinetics
Klaasen, C. D., 395, 401
Knudsen Number, 244
Kupffer cells, 99–100, 101

L

Labeling, 363
Latency period
   biomonitoring and, 353, 354
   carcinogenesis and, 155, 165, 166
   chemical warfare agents and, 320, 321, 322, 323
   hepatic toxicology and, 106
   metal toxicity and, 211
   neurotoxicology and, 86
   radioactive material toxicology and, 269, 273
   toxicity testing and, 384
LCt_{50}, 384
LD_{50}, 2, 11, 381
Lead
   biomonitoring and, 195, 357
   cardiovascular and renal toxicity and, 62
   metal toxicity and, 212–13
   neurotoxicology and, 90
   radioactive material toxicology and, 269
   regulations on, 388, 390
   renal toxicity and, 65
   reproductive and developmental toxicology and, 119–20
Learning, 71
Legal issues, 314–15
Legge, T. M., 106
Leptophos, 89
Lesions, 155, 156
Lethal concentration, 11
   See also LCt_{50}
Lethal dose, 11
   See also LD_{50}
Leukemia
   benzene and, 131, 200–201
   genetic toxicology and, 145
   immunotoxicology and, 133–34
   organic solvent toxicity and, 193
   radiation and, 165
   radioactive material toxicology and, 269, 273
Lewis, R. J., 395, 401
Lewisite, 320–21
LFTs (liver function tests), 102, 102t
Lifestyle, 164, 177, 179, 357
Lifetime exposure assessments, 305, 384
Li-Fraumeni syndrome, 158, 160
Light sensitivity, 73
Limbird, L. E., 401
Lindane, 225, 227
Lipid peroxidation, 18, 104, 194, 248–49
Lipid solubility
   carcinogenesis and, 164
   cellular membranes and, 18
   dermal exposure and, 292
   disposition of toxicants and, 24, 25
   neurotoxicology and, 94
   of organic solvents, 191–92
   pesticide toxicology and, 224–25
Lipophilic molecules. See Lipid solubility
Lipophilic solvents, 193
Lipopolysaccharides (LPS), 250
Lipoproteins, 101, 260
Liquids, 234, 276, 276t
List-based methods, 374
Liver
   cancer, 164, 224
   injuries to, 102–9
   structure and function of, 25, 98–102, 98f, 99f
   toxicity testing and, 384
   See also Hepatic toxicology; Hepatotoxicants
Liver function tests (LFTs), 102, 102t
LOAEL (lowest observed adverse effect level), 305–6
Lobules, 98–99, 99f
Local effects, 10, 19, 191–93, 269
LOEL (lowest observed effect level), 104–5
Log scales, 29f, 30f
Logarithmic transformations, 372–73
Lognormal distribution, 245–46, 246f
Loss of heterozygosity (LOH), 144–47
Lowest observed adverse effect level (LOAEL), 305–6
Lowest observed effect level (LOEL), 104–5
LPS (lipopolysaccharides), 250
Ludlum Radiation Meters, 314
Lung cancer, 165, 211–13, 270, 345–46
Lungs, 25, 39, 255–56
   See also Inhalation; *pulmonary-related entries*; Respiratory system; Respiratory toxicology
Lymphocytes, 128–29, 130, 134, 357
Lymphomas, 164, 200

M

Mace, 323
Macromolecules, 101
Macrophages, 247–48
Magnetic resonance imaging (MRI), 354
Major Histocompatibility Complex (MHC), 129
MAK (Maximum Concentration at the Workplace) Commission, 149, 150t, 340
Malignancy. See Carcinogenesis; Tumor
Malignant mesothelioma, 166–67
Managerial Technologies Corporation Resource Libraries, 407
Manganese, 87, 213–14
Man-made disasters, 329–30, 330f
Man-made vitreous fibers (MMVFs), 166, 166t
Manual of Analytical Methods, 291, 405
Manufacturers, 364–65, 376
Marine Corps Preventative Medicine Units, 314
Marine Protection, Research, and Sanctuaries Act, 390
Martin's Diameter, 243
Mass of particulates, 243, 244, 248, 290
Material Safety Data Sheets (MSDS)
   chemical hazard communications and, 364–65

database for, 407
　emergency response planning and, 329, 331
　materials toxicology and, 369
　toxicity information on, 3, 395
Materials toxicology, 367–77
　acts addressing, 369t
　meta-cognition and, 367–68
　product acceptance or rejection, 375–76
　risk-safety connections and, 370, 372–75
　scientific and regulatory history and, 368–70
Maternal conditions, 177
Mathematical descriptions
　disposition of toxicants and, 27–34
　exposure assessments and, 288, 294–97
　materials toxicology and, 372–73
　organic solvent toxicity and, 194
　particulate matter toxicology and, 242–47
　risk assessments and, 305–6
Maximum Concentration at the Workplace (MAK) Commission, 149, 150t, 340
MDS (myelodysplastic syndrome), 131, 133–34
Mean free path, 244
Meat, 273
Mechanisms of action
　for carcinogenesis, 156–61, 159f
　for chemical mixtures, 277, 279
　classification of toxicants by, 9
　deposition, 243, 244, 289–90
　epigenetic, 158–60, 159f, 179, 181
　for hepatic toxicity, 104–5, 106–7, 108
　for insecticides, 224, 227–28, 230, 231
　for mustard agents, 319–20
　for mutation induction, 143–45
　for neurotoxic effects, 86–90
　for particles, 247–49
　for radioactive damage, 268–70
　for teratogenesis, 180–81
　for toxicity, 15–19, 20t
　toxicity testing and, 385
Mechanistic studies, 385
Mechanistic toxicologist, 7–8
Mechanistic toxicology, 2
Mechanoreceptors, 71–72, 73, 74, 76
Media, 311–13
　See also Air; Soil; Surface contaminants; Water
Medical monitoring programs, 131–32, 133, 314–15
Medication. See Analgesics; Antibiotics; Pharmaceuticals
Men. See Gender differences
Merck Index, The (O'Neil, Smith and Heckelman), 401
Mercury
　accumulation of, 33
　cardiovascular and renal toxicity and, 62
　metal toxicity and, 214
　neurotoxicology and, 86–87
　renal toxicity and, 65

sensory toxicology and, 74
Metabolic transformation reactions, 26t, 27t
Metabolism
　benzene and, 131, 200–201
　biomonitoring and, 358–59
　carcinogenesis and, 156–57, 162
　chemical mixture toxicology and, 276, 278–79
　definition of, 17
　disposition of toxicants and, 27f
　gas toxicology and, 257–61
　genetic toxicology and, 146–47
　insecticides and, 228, 230, 231
　liver functions and, 25, 98–102
　organic solvent toxicity and, 193–94, 203
　as route of elimination, 25–26
　toxicity testing and, 384, 385
　See also ADME (absorption, distribution, metabolism and excretion)
Metabolites
　active versus inactive, 26
　benzene and, 200–201, 201f
　biomonitoring and, 354, 356
　gas toxicology and, 259
　organic solvent toxicity and, 193
　reactive, 105, 107
　toxic, 17
Meta-cognition, 367–68
Metal-induced fibrosis, 43
Metallic co-factors, 17
Metals
　carcinogenesis and, 158–59
　definition of, 209
　particulate matter toxicology and, 250
　radioactive material toxicology and, 270–71
　reproductive and developmental toxicology and, 119
　toxicology of, 209–16, 216t
　See also Heavy metals
Metastasis, 156, 163
Methanol, 27f, 87–88, 92, 193, 279
Methemoglobin, 17
Methyl ethyl ketone, 347
Methyl n-butyl ketone (2-hexane), 88–89, 193, 201–4, 203f
Methylated aromatic compounds, 199f
Methylation, 159
Methylene chloride, 193, 389
Methylene dianiline, 107, 388
Methylmercury, 86
MHC (Major Histocompatibility Complex), 129
Microscopy, 245–46
Military exposures
　carcinogenesis and, 165
　hepatic toxicology and, 97–98, 104, 105–7
　metal toxicity and, 210, 215
　pesticide toxicology and, 227, 231, 232
　radioactive material toxicology and, 267, 270, 271

reproductive and developmental toxicology and, 116, 120
Military toxicology, 308–15
Milk, 273
Mine Safety and Health Administration, 389–90
Minerals, 101, 213
Ministry of Health, Labor and Safety, Japan, 396
Mismatch repair, 143
Mission objectives, 314
Missouri Department of Health and Senior Services, 376
Mist, 289
Mitigation, 335
Mixtures. *See* Chemical mixture toxicology
MMVFs (man-made vitreous fibers), 166, 166*t*
Mobility, 244
Modeling, 294–97, 375
Mode-of-action (MOA), 145–49, 169, 276, 279
Molds, 45–46
Momentum, 368
Monitoring
    biological, 149–50, 194–96, 293, 352–59
    exposure, 288–91
    medical, 131–32, 133, 314–15
    multi-gas, 314
Monocytes, 130
Monodisperse, 244
Moore, Benjamin, 106
Morphology, 244, 261
Motion, 243, 244–45
Mouse lymphoma assay, 147
Mouse specific locus test, 148
MRI (magnetic resonance imaging), 354
MSDS. *See* Material Safety Data Sheets (MSDS)
MSDS Search database, 407
Multi-agency coordination, 335, 375–77
Multi-gas monitoring, 314
Multiple chemical sensitivity, 79, 333
Multiple exposures
    biomonitoring and, 356
    disposition of toxicants and, 33, 33*f*, 34*f*
    gas toxicology and, 258–59
    hepatic toxicology and, 105
    respiratory toxicology and, 42
    toxicity testing and, 382
Multiple organ systems. *See* Systemic effects
Multiple stressors, 329–30, 333–34
MultiRAE Plus, 314
Muscarinic blocker, 90–91
Muscular tissue, 156
Mustard agents, 313, 319–21
Mustargen, 319
Mutagenesis
    carcinogenesis and, 157
    gas toxicology and, 262
    genetic toxicology and, 139, 146, 150
    teratogenesis and, 180–81

Mutagenicity, 145, 148–49, 158, 160, 232
Mutagens, 18, 139, 144, 145–49, 149*t*
Mutations
    carcinogenesis and, 155, 157–58, 162
    genetic toxicology and, 139–41, 140*f*, 141*t*, 148–49
    genotoxicity assays measuring, 145–49
    mechanisms of induction, 143–45
Myelin, 89
Myelinopathy, 89–90
Myelodysplastic syndrome (MDS), 131, 133–34
Myeloid metaplasia, 200

N

N-acetyltransferase (NAT), 359
Nanoparticles, 249–50, 290
Nanotechnologies, 249
Naphthalene, 347
NASA (National Aviation and Space Administration), 340
Nasal passages, 255
NAT (N-acetyltransferase), 359
National Academy of Engineering, 393
National Academy of Sciences
    on chemical warfare agents, 320
    description of, 393
    on emergency response planning, 332
    OEL derivation by, 340, 348
    on radioactive material toxicology, 270
    on risk assessments, 301
    Website for, 406
National Advisory Committee for Acute Exposure Guideline Levels, 332
National Ambient Air Quality Standards, 390
National Aviation and Space Administration (NASA), 340
National Center for Environmental Health, 391
National Council on Radiological Protection and Measurements, 340
National Emission Standards for Hazardous Air Pollutants, 390
National Fire Protection Association (NFPA), 333
National Institute for Occupational Safety and Health (NIOSH)
    on anti-neoplastic drugs, 133
    description of, 391–92
    on exposure assessments, 296
    Manual of Analytical Methods, 291, 405
    Method 7400, 290
    on nickel, 215
    OEL derivation by, 8, 340–41, 342
    on pesticide toxicology, 229
    Pocket Guide to Chemical Hazards, 310, 396, 401, 405
    as resource, 396, 401
    on respiratory toxicology, 45
    on tin, 215
    on toluene, 182
    Websites for, 396, 404–5

National Institute of Environmental Health and Safety, 341, 385
National Institute of Environmental Health Sciences, 41, 168, 393
National Institutes of Health (NIH), 41, 405–6
National Library of Medicine (NLM), 310, 370, 393, 396, 405–6
National Primary Drinking Water Regulations, 390
National Research Council (NRC), 301, 340, 341, 393, 400–401
National Resource for Global Standards, 406
National Response Plan (NRP), 330, 335
National Toxicology Program (NTP)
    classification of carcinogens by, 168, 170
    on ethylene oxide, 262
    toxicity testing and, 385
    Website for, 396, 406
Natural disasters, 329–30
Naturally occurring toxins, 1–2
NCELs (New Chemicals Exposure Limits), 340, 342
Necrosis, 103–9
    See also Tumor, necrosis factors
Neoplasia, 156, 160, 161
Neoplastic transformation, 160
Nephrons, 63–66
Nephrotoxicants, 2, 64–66, 384
    See also Kidneys; Renal toxicity
NER (nucleotide excision repair), 143
Nerve agents, 312, 318–19, 318t
Nervous system
    anatomy and physiology of, 83–86, 84f
    chemical warfare agents and, 318, 323
    See also Central nervous system (CNS); Neurotoxicology; Peripheral nervous system (PNS); Sensory system
Nervous tissue, 156
Neuroactive peptides, 86
Neuroglia, 84
Neurologic disorders, 93–94
Neuronopathy, 86–88
Neurons, 83–84, 85, 86
Neuropathies
    axonal, 193, 202
    delayed, 89, 228
    hereditary, 77
    organic solvent toxicity and, 202, 204
    peripheral, 77, 90, 203f, 204, 278
Neurotoxicants, 2
Neurotoxicology, 82–94
    axonopathy and, 88–89
    metal toxicity and, 213–14
    myelinopathy and, 89–90
    nervous system structure and, 83–86, 84f
    neurologic disorders and, 93–94
    neuronopathy and, 86–88
    neurotransmitters and, 84–86, 90–93

    organic solvent toxicity and, 203, 203f
    pesticide toxicology and, 231
    sensory toxicology versus, 71
    toxicity testing and, 384
Neurotransmitters, 17–18, 84–86, 90–93
Neutral free radicals, 16
Neutrons, 267
New Chemicals Exposure Limits (NCELs), 340, 342
New Jersey Department of Health and Senior Services, 406
Newton's Law, 244
NFPA (National Fire Protection Association), 333
n-hexane
    biomonitoring and, 356
    chemical mixture toxicology and, 278
    metabolism of, 203f
    neurotoxicology and, 88–89
    organic solvent toxicity and, 193, 196, 196f
    sensory toxicology and, 77–78
    solvent-unique effects of, 201–4
Nickel, 214–15
Nicotine, 91
    See also Cigarette smoke
Night blindness, 73
NIH (National Institutes of Health), 41, 405–6
NIOSH. See National Institute for Occupational Safety and Health (NIOSH)
Nitrogen, reactive, 158
Nitrogen dioxide, 42, 257–59, 389, 390
Nitrogen mustards, 319
Nitrogen oxides, 257–59
    See also Nitrogen dioxide
NLM (National Library of Medicine), 310, 370, 393, 396, 405–6
NOAEL (no observable adverse effect level), 11, 305–6
Nociceptors, 71–72, 76
NOEL (no observable effect level), 11
Noise, 74
Nomenclature
    materials toxicology and, 370, 371–72t
    tumor, 156, 156t
Non-covalent binding, 16
Non-fibrous particles, 289
Non-homologous end-joining, 143
Norepinephrine, 85
Nose. See Olfactory system
n-pentane, 197
NRC (National Research Council), 301, 340, 341, 393, 400–401
NRP (National Response Plan), 330, 335
NTP. See National Toxicology Program (NTP)
Nuclear magnetic resonance, 189, 354
Nuclear power industry, 134, 165, 267–68, 271–73
Nuclear Regulatory Commission, 340
Nucleotide excision repair (NER), 143
Nucleotides, 18, 139, 143, 157–58

Nutrient homeostasis, 101
Nutrition. *See* Diet; Food contaminants
Nystagmus, 73

O

Obesity, 164, 165
Occlusions, 24
Occupational acne, 53
Occupational and Environmental Medicine, 402
Occupational asthma, 44, 215, 261
Occupational exposure assessments, 286
Occupational exposure limits (OELs)
    chemical mixture toxicology and, 280s
    consensus organizations and, 339–40
    derivation of, 339–49
    development process, 343–45, 344f
    dose response relationship and, 11
    organic solvent toxicity and, 191, 196–97
    private industry on, 341–42
    risk assessments and, 305
Occupational exposures
    carcinogenesis and, 165–67, 167t, 168t, 169t
    chemical warfare agents and, 324
    definition of, 286
    emergency response planning and, 331–33
    gas toxicology and, 256–63
    metal toxicity and, 210–15
    to organic solvents, 187–89, 188f
    pesticide toxicology and, 224, 225
    See also Exposure(s)
Occupational lifetime, 305
Occupational medicine, 192, 195
    See also Medical monitoring programs
Occupational respiratory toxicants, 41–43, 45–46
Occupational Safety and Health Administration (OSHA)
    on anti-neoplastic drugs, 133
    on benzene levels, 131–32
    on dermal exposure assessments, 292
    on emergency response planning, 330, 333
    on ethylene oxide, 261
    Hazard Communications Standards, 331, 363–65
    on hazardous chemicals, 3
    on materials toxicology, 377
    military toxicology and, 315
    OEL derivation by, 8, 305, 340–43
    on radiation, 134
    regulatory standards of, 387–89
    on silica, 290
    on toluene, 182
    Websites for, 404
Occupational skin disorders, 52–53
Odors, 311, 312, 321–22, 346
    See also Olfactory system
OECD (Organization for Economic Cooperation and Development), 121, 147–48, 383

OELs. *See* Occupational exposure limits (OELs)
Office of Environment, Safety and Health, 392
Office of Environmental Health Hazard Assessment, 121
Office of Hazardous Materials Safety, 392
Office of Prevention, Pesticides and Toxic Substances (OPPTS), 120, 392
Office of Research and Development, 392
Office of Water, 392–93
Oleoresin capsicum, 323
Olfactory system, 75–76
    See also Chemoreceptors; Odors
Oligodendrocytes, 84
Omission bias, 368
Oncogenes, 160–61, 160t
One compartment pharmacokinetic models, 29, 29f
O'Neil, M.J., 401
1,1,1,3,3,3-Hexafluoropropane (HFC-236fa), 347
1,1,2,2-Tetrachloroethane, 98, 104, 109
1,3-Butadiene, 388–89
1,2-Dibromo-3-chloropropane (DBCP), 118, 234–35, 388
Ontario Ministry of Environment, 348
Opioid peptides, 86
OPPTS (Office of Prevention, Pesticides and Toxic Substances), 120, 392
Opsonization, 244
Oral steroid contraceptives, 62, 165
Order effects, 368
Organ damage, 383–84
    See also specific organs (i.e., liver, kidney, etc.)
Organic arsenic, 210
Organic lead, 213
Organic mercury, 214
Organic solvent toxicity, 186–206
    biological monitoring and, 194–96
    biotransformation, elimination and, 193–94
    distribution and, 191–92
    dose response relationships in, 192–93
    identification of xenobiotic and exposure route, 189–91
    local *versus* systemic toxicity of, 191–92
    solvent-unique effects of, 197–204
    vapor hazard ratio and, 196–97
Organic solvents
    chlorinated, 193
    neurotoxicology and, 92
    physical properties of, 188t
    teratogenesis and, 182
    uses of, 187–89, 188f
    volatile, 91–92
    See also Solvents
Organic tin, 215
Organization for Economic Cooperation and Development (OECD), 121, 147–48, 383
Organochlorines, 224–27, 277
Organogenesis, 179
Organomercurials, 65, 236

Organophosphate insecticides, 89, 92–93, 227–29, 318, 357
Organophosphate-induced delayed polyneuropathy, 228
Organophosphorus compounds, 122
Organotin Antifouling Paints Control Act, 215
Orphan source accidents, 272
OSHA. *See* Occupational Safety and Health Administration (OSHA)
OSHAct, 301, 340–41, 387
Oshweb, 407
Ototoxicity, 73–74
Oxidative damage, 159
Oxidative stress, 158, 249
Oxygen, 17, 99, 255–56, 260
    See also Reactive oxygen
o-xylene, 199*f*
Ozone, 260–61, 261*t*, 390

P

Pain. *See* Nociceptors; Somatosensory system
Painters' syndrome, 92, 193, 198
Paracelsus (Philippus Aureolus Theophrastus Bombast von Hohenheim), quotations by, 1, 7, 57, 61, 69, 81, 113, 137, 175, 191, 221, 253, 265, 341, 369
Paraoxonase, 358
Paraquat, 232
Parasympathetic nervous system, 83, 85
Parenchymal cells, 98
Paresthesia, 74–75, 89
Particle counters, 290
Particle sizing instruments, 246–47
Particles
    alpha, 267, 313
    beta, 267, 313
    biological, 290
    coarse, 248–49
    definition of, 244
    exposure assessments and, 289–90
    fine, 248–49
    ultrafine, 245, 248–50
Particulate matter
    aerodynamics of, 243, 246–47, 289
    cardiotoxicity and, 61
    chemical classification of, 242, 247–50, 289
    diameter of, 243–47, 248, 289–90
    mass of, 243, 244, 248, 290
    regulations on, 390
    shapes of, 242–44
    size of, 241–51, 245*f*, 246*f*, 289–90
Particulate matter toxicology, 240–51
    aerosol characterization and, 245–47
    chemical classification of particulates and, 247–50
    exposure assessments and, 289–90
    history of, 241–42
    key concepts of, 242–45
Part-washer, 190

Passive diffusion, 18, 23–24, 25
Patch sampling, 292
Pathological approach, 373, 374
Pathophysiologic approach, 373, 374
Patty's Toxicology (Bingham, Cohrssen, and Powell), 395, 401
PB-OEL (performance-based occupational exposure limits), 348
PELs. *See* Permissible Exposure Limits (PELs)
Pentachlorophenol, 236
Pepper spray, 323
Perception of self, 75, 76
Perchlorate, 132, 279
Perfluoroalkyl acids, 121–22
Performance-based occupational exposure limit (PB-OEL), 348
Peripheral nervous system (PNS), 83, 84, 90, 231, 323
Peripheral neuropathies, 77, 90, 203*f*, 204, 278
Peripheral polyneuropathies, 278
Permissible Exposure Limits (PELs)
    for benzene, 131
    chemical hazard communications and, 364
    for ethylene oxide, 261
    OEL derivation and, 8, 340–43
    risk assessments and, 305
    for toluene, 182
Peroxisome proliferator action, 159
Persistence, 224–25
Personal protective equipment. *See* Protective equipment
Pesticide toxicology, 222–37
    fumigants and, 234–35
    fungicides and, 235–36
    herbicides, 232–34
    insecticides and, 224–32
    rodenticides and, 234
    use of pesticides and, 223–24
Pesticides
    carcinogenesis and, 164
    chemical mixture toxicology and, 276
    classification of, 236*t*
    definition of, 223
    history of, 223
    metal toxicity and, 210
    regulations on, 390
    value of, 223–24
Phagocytosis, 167
Pharmaceuticals
    anti-neoplastic, 132–34
    biomonitoring and, 357
    cardiotoxicity and, 61
    chemical mixture toxicology and, 278
    drug metabolizing enzymes and, 157, 162
    hepatic toxicology and, 102–3
    OEL recommendations on, 347–48
    pregnancy and, 375*t*
    teratogenesis and, 177

See also Analgesics; Antibiotics
Pharmacodynamics, 15, 23, 276, 278
Pharmacokinetics
   chemical mixture toxicology and, 276, 278
   classic compartmental, 29–30
   definition of, 23
   first-order *versus* zero-order, 27–28
   physiologically-based, 34, 34*f*
   teratogenesis and, 179–80, 180*t*
Pharmacological Basis of Therapeutics, The (Hardman, Limbird and Gilman), 401–2
Pharmacology, 7
Phosgene, 321–22
Phosgene oxime, 319, 321
Photoallergy, 52
Photons, 267
Photoreceptors, 71, 73
Photosensitization, 52
Physical conditions, 61
Physical diameter of particulates, 243
Physical hazards, 311–13
   See also Physical stressors
Physical properties
   chemical hazard communications and, 364
   of insecticides, 224, 227, 229–31
   OEL derivation and, 343
   of organic solvents, 188*t*
   particulate matter toxicology and, 244–45, 247, 289
   toxicity testing and, 382–83
Physical states
   chemical mixture toxicology and, 276, 276*t*
   exposure assessments and, 289
   of metals, 210
   military toxicology and, 311–13
   pesticide toxicology and, 234
   toxicant classifications by, 8–9
Physical stressors, 330, 333
Physical-chemical models, 294–96
Physiological approach, 373, 374
Physiologically-based pharmacokinetic models, 34, 34*f*
Placenta, 180
Plants
   dermal toxicology and, 52
   metals in, 209, 211
   military toxicology and, 313
   as naturally occurring toxins, 1–2
   pesticide toxicology and, 232–34
   radioactive material toxicology and, 273
   See also Vegetables
Plutonium, 271, 272
Pneumoconiosis, 19, 43, 215
Pneumonia, 212
PNS (peripheral nervous system), 83, 84, 90, 231, 323
Pocket Guide to Chemical Hazards (NIOSH), 310, 396, 401, 405

Pohanish, R., 401
Poisoning potential
   insecticides and, 224, 228, 230, 231
   pesticide toxicology and, 224
   rodenticides and, 234
   toxicant classifications by, 9, 9*t*
Polar molecules, 157, 199
Polycyclic aromatic hydrocarbons, 193, 198, 198*f*, 359
Polydisperse, 245
Polymorphisms, 41, 157, 182, 357–58
Polymorphonuclear white cells, 130
Polyneuropathies, 228, 278
Polyol components, 44
Polyploidy, 140, 145
Polyvinyl chloride (PVC), 107–9
Population dose response relationships, 11
Portable survey meters, 268
Positron emission tomography, 354
Potency, 277, 348
Potential average daily dose, 306
Potentiation, 15, 278–79
Pott, Percival, 155, 192–93
Powell, C. H., 395, 401
Precautionary approach, 375
Predictions, 294–96, 334
Predisposition, 157–58, 357–59
   See also Heredity
Preferential binding, 17
Pregnancy, 375*t*
   See also Prenatal development
Premature closing, 368
Prenatal development, 177–79, 178*f*, 178*t*
   See also Developmental toxicology
Preparedness, emergency, 335
Pressure treated lumber, 210, 212
Prevention, 335
Primary irritants, 41
Principles and Methods of Toxicology (Hays), 401
Private industry groups, 339, 341–42, 342*f*
Probabilities, 373
Professional organizations, 334*t*, 339–40, 391–93, 399–400, 406–7
   See also specific organizations
Progression, 161, 161*t*, 163
Projected Area Diameter, 243
Promotion, 161–62, 161*t*
Proportions, 275–81
Proprioception, 75, 76
Propylene glycol, 348
Prostate cancer, 164
Protective equipment
   chemical hazard communications and, 364
   chemical warfare agents and, 321, 323
   exposure assessments and, 292
   hepatic toxicology and, 106, 106*f*

immunotoxicology and, 133
military toxicology and, 310–11, 312
pesticide toxicology and, 229
radioactive material toxicology and, 268–69, 271
Proteins
biomonitoring and, 355, 357
carcinogenesis and, 157, 160, 165
hepatic toxicology and, 98, 101, 102, 108
immunotoxicology and, 128
respiratory toxicology and, 41
sensory toxicology and, 72, 75, 76
See also Lipoproteins
Proto-oncogenes, 160
Proximal axonopathies, 88
Proximate carcinogens, 156–57
Psychological disturbances, 213–14, 323
Psycho-organic syndrome, 92
Psychophysics, 79
Psychosis, 204
Public health, 353–54
Publications, 395, 400–402
Pulmonary agents, 321–22, 321*t*
See also Lungs; *respiratory-related entries*
Pulmonary edema, 211, 321–22
Pulmonary exposure. *See* Inhalation
Pulmonary fibrosis, 43
Pulmonary irritants, 42
Pulmonotoxicants, 2
Pupillary responses, 73
PVC (polyvinyl chloride), 107–9
Pyrene fire extinguishers, 103–4, 103*f*
Pyrethroids, 230–32

Q

Quantum dot toxicity, 250

R

Radiation
biological effects of, 268–69
definition of, 267
ionizing (*See* Ionizing radiation)
therapy, 267
ultraviolet, 119, 165, 260
Radico-functional approach, 370, 371–72*t*
Radioactive material toxicology, 266–73, 330
Radioactivity, 267, 313–14
Radiological accidents, 269, 271–73, 272*t*
Radiologists, 165
Radionuclide, 267, 268
Radium, 270
Radon, 270
RADS (reactive airway dysfunction syndrome), 259
RAND Corporation, 270
Range of effects, 373–75

Raoult's law, 295
Rapid Guide to Chemical Incompatibilities (Pohanish), 401
Rapid Guide to Hazardous Chemicals in the Workplace (Lewis), 401
Rationale, 344–49
Rb allele, 160
REACH (Registration, Evaluation, and Authorization of Chemicals), 369, 374–75
Reactive airway dysfunction syndrome (RADS), 259
Reactive intermediate, 157
Reactive metabolite, 105, 107
Reactive nitrogen, 158
Reactive oxygen, 158, 248–49
Reactivity, 364, 370, 371–72*t*
Receptive field, 74
Receptor antagonism, 279
Receptors, 71–72
Recommended Exposure Limits (RELs), 8, 182, 340–41
"Recommended Practices for Disaster Management" (NFPA), 333
Reconnaissance surveys, 314
Record keeping, 365, 390–91
See also Material Safety Data Sheets (MSDS)
Recovery, 335
Red blood cells, 130, 200, 356
Red Book (NRC), 301, 341
Redbook (FDA), 7
Redistribution, 25
Reference Dose, 305–6
Reference textbooks, 395, 400–402
Registry of Toxic Effects of Chemical Substances, 396, 404
Regulatory applications, 145–49
Regulatory history, 368–70
Regulatory organizations
acts on materials toxicology by, 369*t*
on chemical hazard communications, 364
classification of carcinogens by, 167–70
on emergency response planning, 334*t*
on exposure assessments, 296–97
on military toxicology, 310
OEL derivation by, 339
regulatory standards of, 387–91
on risk management, 302
Websites of, 396
See also specific organizations (i.e., OSHA, EPA)
Regulatory toxicologist, 8
Regulatory toxicology, 2
Relative potency factor approach, 277
Relative toxicity, 9*t*, 302*t*
RELs (Recommended Exposure Limits), 8, 182, 340–41
Renal system, 59–66, 64*f*
Renal toxicity, 59, 63–66, 64*f*, 214, 384
Repeated exposures. *See* Multiple exposures
Report on Carcinogens (RoC), 168, 170
Reproductive toxicology, 114–23

animal studies on, 120–23
definition of, 115
fertility effects of, 117–20
materials toxicology and, 375, 375t
metal toxicity and, 213
occupational exposures and, 116–17
reproductive disorders and, 115
toxicity testing and, 385
See also Teratogenesis
REPROTOX (Reproductive Toxicology Center), 406
Research, 5, 296, 304, 304f, 374
See also Toxicity testing
Resistance, 244
Resource, Conservation and Recovery Act, 341, 390
Resources, informational, 395–96, 399–402, 403–7
Respirators, 229, 310–11
Respiratory system
airway structure and function in, 39–40, 40f
chemical warfare agents and, 320–22
exposure assessments and, 288–91
gas toxicology and, 255–56, 256f
OEL derivation and, 345–49
particulate matter toxicology and, 241–51
as route of exposure, 39
toxic irritation to, 19
toxicity testing and, 384
See also Inhalation; Lungs; *pulmonary-related entries*
Respiratory toxicology, 39–46
airway structure and function in, 39–40, 40f
defense mechanisms and, 40, 40f
metal toxicity and, 210–15
occupational respiratory toxicants and, 41–43, 45–46
susceptibility and, 40–41
toxicity testing and, 384
See also Gas toxicology
Response. *See* Dose response relationships; Effects; Emergency response planning
Response additivity, 277–78
Resting membrane potential, 85, 91
Retinoblastoma, 160
Retroviruses, 164
Reversible effects
of binding, 16
carcinogenesis and, 162–63
chemical exposures and, 10, 19
chemical warfare agents and, 323
gas toxicology and, 259, 261
genetic toxicology and, 142
hepatic toxicology and, 103, 105
neurotoxicology and, 89–90, 92–93
reproductive and developmental toxicology and, 117
sensory toxicology and, 74
Reynolds Number, 245
Rheumatoid arthritis, 129
Riot control agents, 322, 323–24

Risk, definition of, 302
Risk analysis, 301–3, 310, 341, 342f
Risk assessments
biomonitoring and, 359f
definition of, 302
emergency response planning and, 335
exposure assessments and, 286, 296, 305
in industrial hygiene, 301–6, 304f, 304t
military toxicology and, 314
organic solvent toxicity and, 192
Risk characterization, 304–5
Risk communication, 303, 329, 333
See also Hazard communications
Risk evaluation, 302
Risk factors
for carcinogenesis, 163–67
radioactive material toxicology and, 268, 271
safety factor connections with, 370, 372–75
Risk management, 302, 304f, 335
Risk Management Information Systems Library's Chemical Database, 407
RNA, 157
RoC (Report on Carcinogens), 168, 170
Rocks, 213
Rodent micronucleus assay, 147–48
Rodenticides, 234, 235t
Roentgen, Wilhem Conrad, 267, 268
Rom, W. N., 401
Routes of elimination, 25, 194
See also Excretion
Routes of entry, 2, 2f, 9, 303, 382
Routes of exposure
disposition of toxicants and, 33
emergency response planning and, 330
exposure assessments and, 288–89, 293
to hepatic toxicants, 103–9
military toxicology and, 311–13
to organic solvents, 189–91
in reproductive and developmental toxicity testing, 120
respiratory system as, 39
See also Dermal exposure; Ingestion; Inhalation; Injection

S

S9 exogenous metabolic activation, 146–47
Safe Drinking Water Act, 390
Safe Drinking Water and Toxic Enforcement Act, 121
Safety and health plans, 315
Safety assessments, 7
Safety factors, 11, 345–49, 370, 372–75
Saliva samples, 354
Salmonella test, 146
Samples
air, 78, 288–89, 291, 376
blood, 34, 195–96, 354, 359, 383–84
duration of, 291

Index

patch, 292
saliva, 354
size-selective, 290
skin, 53
spinal fluid, 354
surface, 53, 288–89, 292
tissue, 53, 383
urine (*See* Urine samples)
wipe, 292
Sarin, 312, 318–19
Saturation models, 294–95
Sax's Dangerous Properties of Industrial Materials (Lewis), 395, 401
Schwann cells, 84, 89–90, 225
Science and Judgment in Risk Assessment, 301
Scientific and regulatory history, 368–70
Scientific Committee on Occupational Exposure Limits, 346
Scirus, 407
Screening Information Data Set (SIDS), 1214
Scrotal cancer, 155
Search engines, 396, 404, 407
Secondary irritants, 41
Secretariat of Transport and Communications of Mexico, 332
Secretion, 100
Sedimentation, 243, 289
Self, perception of, 75, 76
Sellafield accident, 272
Semi-log scale, 31*f*
Senescence, 142, 158
Sensitization, 18, 42–43, 52, 383
    See also Desensitization; Hypersensitization; Multiple chemical sensitivity
Sensory amplitudes, 90
Sensory irritants, 41–42
Sensory system
    hereditary diseases affecting, 76–77
    structure and functions of, 71–76
    toxicology of, 71–79
    See also Nervous system
Sensory toxicology, 71–79
    auditory and vestibular systems and, 73–74
    gustatory system and, 76
    hereditary diseases and, 76–77
    irritations and, 41–42, 76
    neurotoxicology *versus*, 71
    nociceptors and, 76
    olfactory system and, 75–76
    proprioception and, 76
    receptors and, 72
    sensory system functions and, 71–72
    somatosensory system and, 74–75
    stimuli and, 72
    vision and, 72–73
Septicemia, 134
Sequestration, 19

Serotonin, 85
Serum liver enzyme tests, 102*t*
Service personnel. *See* Military exposures; Military toxicology
Sex. *See* Gender differences
Shapes of particulates, 242–44
Shielding, 314
    See also Protective equipment
Shock, 18, 62
Short-term exposure limits (STELs), 291, 331, 341–42, 345–49
Sick building syndrome, 45
Siderosis, 43
SIDS (Screening Information Data Set), 121
Sight. *See* Vision
Silica, 290
Silico toxicology, 370
Silicosis, 43
Silo filler's disease, 258
Simple mixtures, 276–80, 280*s*
Simplification, 368
Sinusoids, 99–100, 99*f*
Size of particulates, 241–51, 245*f,* 246*f,* 289–90
Size-selective sampling, 290
Skin
    cancer, 165
    notation issues, 53–54, 53*t,* 292
    as route of entry (*See* Dermal exposure)
    sampling for exposure, 53
    sensory toxicology and, 74–75
    structure and function of, 51–52, 52*f*
    toxicants in, 2
    toxicity testing and, 383
SMART (Army Special Medical Augmentation Response Teams), 314
Smell. *See* Odors; Olfactory system
Smith, A., 401
Smog, 289
Smoke, 289
Smoking. *See* Cigarette smoke; Nicotine
Society of Environmental Toxicology and Chemistry, 400
Society of Toxicology, 400, 406
Soil
    metals in, 209, 210, 213
    military toxicology and, 310
    radioactive material toxicology and, 270, 272
Solids, 234
Solubility. *See* Gas solubility; Lipid solubility; Water solubility
SOLV-DB, 406
Solvent neurotoxic syndrome, 92
Solvents
    aromatic, 61, 65–66, 92, 104
    cardiotoxicity and, 61
    chemical mixture toxicology and, 276
    definition of, 187

lipophilic, 193
renal toxicity and, 66
reproductive and developmental toxicology and, 116, 120
sensory toxicology and, 74, 75, 77–78
toxicological testing and, 5
See also Organic solvents; *specific solvents*
Solvent-unique effects, 197–204
Soman, 318–19
Somatic mutations, 140, 158
Somatosensory system, 74–75
See also Mechanoreceptors; Thermoreceptors
Sources of information, 395–96, 399–402, 403–7
Span of toxicological features, 373–75
Specific locus test, 148
Spinal fluid samples, 354
Spray painting, 188*f*
Stability, 364
Stachybotrys, 46
"Standard Operating Procedures for Developing Acute Exposure Guideline Levels for Hazardous Chemicals," 324
Stannosis, 43, 215
State government occupational regulations, 389
Steady state, 33, 33*f*, 194, 243, 295–96
Steatosis, 103–9, 103*f*
STELs (short-term exposure limits), 291, 331, 341–42, 345–49
Stem cells, 130
Steroid hormones, 62, 158, 162
Stimulants, 91, 224
Stimuli, 72, 84–85, 91
Stokes Equivalent Sphere, 246
Stokes Law, 243, 245
Storage, 101, 364, 370
Straight chain aliphatic hydrocarbon compounds, 197, 197*f*
Straight chain saturated alkane, 197, 201
Stressors, 329–30, 333–34
Strontium, 272
Structure-activity relationships, 370, 382–83
Study design, 296
Styrene, 119
Substance Registry System, 404
Substances in Preparation in Nordic Countries, 396
Suites of concern, 374
Sulfhemoglobin, 17
Sulfur dioxide, 259–60, 260*t*
Sulfur oxides, 259–60, 260*t*, 390
Sulphur mustard, 319–21
Superfund, 341, 390
Superfund Amendments and Reauthorization Act, 341
Suppliers, 369
See also Manufacturers
Surface area, 248–50, 255, 381–82
Surface contaminants, 311–13
Surface sampling, 53, 288–89, 292
Surveillance and Measurements System, 314

Susceptibility
biomarkers of, 357–59, 358*t*
OEL derivation and, 341
respiratory toxicology and, 40–41
to sensory toxicants, 79
teratogenesis and, 179–80, 179*t*
Sympathetic nervous system, 83, 85
Synapse, 85, 85*f*
Synergistic interactions, 15, 278
Synthesis, 100, 101, 102, 143
Systemic effects, 10, 59–66, 98–102, 98*f*, 191–93

T

T helper lymphocytes, 129
Tabun, 318
Target molecules, 16
Target organ toxicity, 8
Taste. *See* Gustatory system
TCDD (2,3,7,8-tetrachlorobenzo-p-dioxin), 117, 232, 348–49
Tear gas, 323
Tears, 72
Technical disasters, 329–30, 330*f*
Temperature. *See* Cold; Heat; Somatosensory system
Teratogenesis, 175–82
chemicals and, 181–82, 181*t*
exposure timing and susceptibility to, 179–80, 179*t*
mechanisms of, 180–81
metal toxicity and, 213
pesticide toxicology and, 232
prenatal development and, 177–79, 178*f*, 178*t*
principles of, 179
toxicity testing and, 385
See also Developmental toxicology
Terrorism, 329–30
Texas Department of Health, 229
Textbooks, 395, 400–402
Thalidomide, 115–16, 179, 180, 385
Thermal precipitators, 247
Thermoreceptors, 71, 75
Three Mile Island accident, 273
Threshold levels, 11, 72, 131, 180
Threshold Limit Values® (TLVs®)
on benzene, 131
biomonitoring and, 354
on carcinogens, 3
chemical hazard communications and, 364
chemical mixture toxicology and, 280, 280*s*
on crystalline silica, 290
dermal toxicology and, 9, 53
emergency response planning and, 331
exposure assessments and, 292
gas toxicology and, 258
on genotoxicity data, 149
on hepatic toxicants, 103, 104–5, 107, 108–9
on neurotoxicants, 92

OEL derivation and, 8, 340–43, 345–49
  on organic solvents, 189, 196
  pesticide toxicology and, 225
  regulations and, 389–90
  on reproductive and developmental toxicity testing, 121
  as resource, 395
  risk assessments and, 305
  on sensory toxicants, 78
  on toluene, 182
  toxicant classification and, 8
Thymine, 144
Thyroid, 132, 273, 279
Time. *See* Duration of exposure
Time curves, blood concentration, 29–33, 29*f,* 30*f,* 31*f*
Tin, 215
Tissue
  concentrations, 27, 29–30, 34, 194–96, 385
  epithelial, 156, 247–48
  of origin, 156
  samples, 53, 383
TLVs®. *See* Threshold Limit Values® (TLVs®)
T-lymphocytes, 128–29
TMT (trimethyltin), 87, 121
TNT (trinitrotoluene), 105–7, 106*f*
Tobacco. *See* Cigarette smoke; Nicotine
TOCP (tri-o-cresyl phosphate), 89
Toluene, 182, 199*f,* 200, 227, 279
Total bilirubin, 102
Total potential dose, 306
Touch. *See* Somatosensory system
ToxFAQs™ (ATSDR), 216
Toxic actions, 16–19
Toxic agents. *See* Toxicants
Toxic endpoints, 303
Toxic equivalency approach, 277
Toxic jaundice, 106–7
Toxic metabolites, 17
Toxic Release Inventory, 406
Toxic Substances Control Act (TSCA), 4, 369, 390–91
Toxicants
  biomonitoring and, 354, 355*t,* 356
  classifications of, 2, 8–9, 8*t*
  detoxication of, 17
  disposition of (*See* Disposition of toxicants)
  military toxicology and, 313
  sequestration of, 19
  See also Chemicals; Components
Toxicity
  acute *versus* chronic (*See* Acute *versus* chronic toxicity)
  definition of, 2–3, 368, 370
  mechanisms of, 15–19, 20*t* (*See also* Mechanisms of action)
  ratings, 3*f,* 302*t,* 373*t*
  relative, 9*t,* 302*t*
Toxicity testing

animal models and, 1–2, 382–85 (*See also* Animal models)
  carcinogenesis and, 163–70, 170*t*
  chemical mixture toxicology and, 276
  disposition of toxicants and, 34
  dose levels and routes of entry in, 382
  dose response relationships and, 381–82
  duration of exposure and, 382
  exposure assessments and, 288–97
  genotoxicity assays as, 145–49, 145*t*
  Good Laboratory Practice and, 383
  materials toxicology and, 369, 373–75
  objectives of, 381
  OEL derivation and, 343–49
  for organ damage, 383–84
  organic solvent toxicity and, 192, 197–98, 202–3
  particulate matter toxicology and, 247–50
  pesticide toxicology and, 225, 228–29, 233–35
  reproductive and developmental toxicology and, 115–23
  sensory toxicants and, 78
  structure-activity relationships in, 382–83
  teratogenesis and, 180, 182
  types of, 4, 383, 384–85
  uses and interpretation of, 4–5
  in vitro versus in vivo, 146, 147, 382–85
  See also Research; Samples
Toxicodynamics, 23
Toxicokinetics, 23, 256, 258–61, 385
Toxicological data
  chemical hazard communications and, 364
  emergency response planning and, 329–35
  materials toxicology and, 374–76
  OEL derivation and, 343–49
  resources on, 395–96, 399–402, 403–7
  risk assessments and, 305–6
  sources of, 370*t*
  from toxicity testing, 380–85
  uses and interpretation of, 4–5
Toxicological databases, 403–7
Toxicological inquiries, 368, 368*t*
Toxicological journals, 402
Toxicological Profiles, 8
Toxicological Profiles for Uranium (HHS), 270
Toxicological risk units (TRU), 372–73, 373*t*
Toxicological safety units (TSU), 372–73, 373*t*
Toxicologist, 7
Toxicologist's Pocket Handbook (Derelanko), 402
Toxicology
  definition of, 2, 7, 189
  history of, 1–2
  principles of, 3–4, 9–11, 277–80, 281
Toxicology Bibliographic Info. (TOXLINE), 406
Toxins. *See* Chemicals; Toxicants
TOXNET, 405
TP53 mutant allele, 158, 160
Training programs, 304, 315, 334, 335, 364

Transforming growth factors, 41
Transgenic rodent mutation assay, 148
Translesion synthesis, 143
Translocations, 144–45, 148, 244, 249
Transport Canada, 332
Transport information, 364
Transporters, 24, 25, 64
Triazines, 232
Triethyltin, 89
Trimethyltin (TMT), 87, 121
Trinitrotoluene (TNT), 105–7, 106f
Tri-o-cresyl phosphate (TOCP), 89
TRU (toxicological risk units), 372–73, 373t
TSCA (Toxic Substances Control Act), 4, 369, 390–91
TSU (toxicological safety units), 372–73, 373t
Tumor
    acute *versus* chronic exposures and, 158
    benign *versus* malignant, 156, 156t
    DNA tumor viruses, 165
    initiation, 161–62, 162f, 167
    necrosis factors, 41, 247, 357
    nomenclature, 156, 156t
    progression, 163, 163f
    promotion, 162, 163f
    radioactive material toxicology and, 270, 272
    suppressor genes, 160–61, 160t
Two compartment pharmacokinetic models, 29–30, 30f
2004 Emergency Response Guidebook (ERG2004), 332–33
2-bromopropane, 116
2,5-hexanedione, 203–4, 205f

U

U.S. Coast Guard, 392, 396
U.S. government departments. *See Department and Offices entries*
Ultimate carcinogens, 156–57
Ultrafine particles, 245, 248–50
Ultraviolet radiation, 119, 165, 260
Uncertainty, 296, 305–6, 347–48
Uniform motion, 245
United Food and Commercial Workers International Union, 377
United Nations, 365
University Websites, 406
Uranium, 270–71
Urea synthesis, 101
Urine, 78, 194
    See also Renal system
Urine samples
    biomonitoring and, 354
    blood samples *versus*, 34
    organic solvent toxicity and, 195–96, 196f
    toxicity testing and, 383, 384
Urticarial reactions, 52–53
Use, classification by, 8

V

Vaccinations, 128
Valence states, 209–10, 211
Vanishing bile duct syndrome, 107
Vapor hazard ratio, 196–97, 197f, 197t, 199
Vapor pressure, 295
Vapors, 190, 234, 276, 276t, 290–91
Vascular system. *See* Cardiovascular system; Circulatory system
Vegetables, 164, 273
Velocity, 243
Ventilation. *See* Exhaust ventilation
Vesicant agents (V agents), 318, 319–21, 320t
Vestibular system, 73–74
    See also Mechanoreceptors
Veterans Association, 320
Veterinary Medicines Directorate, 229
Vibration thresholds, 90
Vinyl chloride, 107–9, 121, 141, 388
Viruses, 160, 164–65
Visceral *versus* cutaneous sensations, 74
Viscose rayon industry, 204
Vision, 72–73, 269, 320, 322, 347
    See also Photoreceptors
Vitamins, 101, 258–59
Volatile aromatic hydrocarbons, 130–32
Volatile organic compounds (VOC), 45–46, 250
Volatile organic solvents, 91–92
Volume
    of distribution, 25
    of particulates, 242, 243

W

Warfarin, 234
Wartime casualties
    carcinogenesis and, 165
    hepatic toxicology and, 97–98, 104, 105–7
    metal toxicity and, 210, 215
    military toxicology and, 309–15
    pesticide toxicology and, 227, 231, 232
    radioactive material toxicology and, 267, 270, 271
Water
    drinking, 121, 390
    metals in, 209, 210, 211, 213
    military toxicology and, 310, 312
    pollution, 390
    radioactive material toxicology and, 272
Water solubility
    of benzene, 199
    cellular membranes and, 18
    disposition of toxicants and, 25
    gas toxicology and, 258, 259, 260
    hepatic toxicology and, 100–101
    metal toxicity and, 215

of organic solvents, 193, 195, 196f
   of solvents, 187
Websites, 396, 403–7
WEEL (Workplace Environmental Exposure Levels), 8, 340
Weight-of-evidence approach, 375
Welding exposures, 119
Wheezing, 212
White blood cells, 129–30
WHO. *See* World Health Organization (WHO)
Williams Steiger Occupational Safety and Health Act, 340
Windscale accident, 272
Wipe sampling, 292
Women. *See* Gender differences
Wools, 166
Worker training, 304, 315, 334, 335, 364
Workplace Environmental Exposure Levels (WEEL), 8, 340
World Health Organization (WHO)
   Expert Committee on Insecticides, 236, 236t
   International Programme on Chemical Safety, 148, 370, 396, 406
   OEL derivation by, 340

X

Xenobiotics
   cardiovascular system functions and, 60
   cellular membranes and, 18
   identification of, 189–91
   immunotoxicology and, 127–34
   liver metabolism and, 98–102
   mechanisms of toxicity and, 15
   organic solvents as, 187–206
   reproductive and developmental toxicology and, 116–23
   teratogenesis and, 179–80
   See also Chemicals
Xeroderma pigmentosum, 157–58
X-rays, 267, 268, 313
Xylene, 227

Z

Zero ventilation models, 294–95
Zero-order elimination curve, 194
Zero-order pharmacokinetics, 27–28, 28t